THEORIES OF

Personality

Third Edition

CHAPTER 5

Carl Jung

In part, people are motivated by archetypes that are inherited from ancient ancestors and that form a collective unconscious. The most inclusive archetype is the notion of self-realization, achieved by a balance between two attitudes (introversion and extraversion) and among four functions (thinking, feeling, sensing, and intuiting).

CHAPTER 6

Harry Stack Sullivan

Anxiety interferes with interpersonal relations; both shape personality at each pre-adult stage of development (infancy, childhood, juvenile era, preadolescence, early adolescence, late adolescence). Intimacy should develop in preadolescence, lust in early adolescence. In late adolescence, intimacy and lust should be directed toward the same person.

CHAPTER 7

Karen Horney

Social and cultural — not biological — influences shape personality. When affection needs are not satisfied during childhood, people suffer basic anxiety, which prevents them from spontaneously moving toward, against, or away from others. Neurotics are driven compulsively by neurotic trends to move toward, against, or away from people.

CHAPTER 8

Otto Kernberg

Children who experience a healthy relationship with their mother develop an integrated ego, a punitive superego, a stable self-concept, and satisfying interpersonal relations. In contrast, children who have poor relations with their mother will have difficulty integrating their ego and may suffer from some form of psychopathology during adulthood.

CHAPTER 8

Heinz Kohut

A sense of self develops during early infancy when adults, in caring for their children's physical and psychological needs, treat them as if they had a sense of self. As a result, the parents' behaviors and attitudes help the children form a sense of self that gives unity and consistency to their experiences.

CHAPTER 8

John Dollard
Neal Miller

Personality, is largely learned, and all learning involves drives (which impel action), cues (which guide action), responses, and reinforcement. People use higher mental processes, such as reasoning and foresight, to solve conflicts and other problems. Three important conflicts are approach-avoidance, avoidance-avoidance, and double approach-avoidance.

Jess Feist

McNeese State University

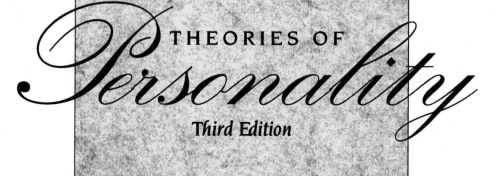

THEORIES OF

Personality

Third Edition

Brown & Benchmark

PUBLISHERS

Madison   Dubuque, IA   Guilford, CT   Chicago   Toronto   London
Caracas   Mexico City   Buenos Aires   Madrid   Bogota   Sydney

Times Mirror
Higher Education Group

Acknowledgments and photo credits appear at the back of the book.

Copyright © 1994, 1990, 1985 by Holt, Rinehart and Winston, Inc.

All rights reserved. No part of this publication may be reproduced or transmitted in any form or by any means, electronic or mechanical, including photocopy, recording, or any information storage and retrieval system, without permission in writing from the publisher.

ISBN 0–697–27661–9
ISBN 0–697–27392–X

Library of Congress Catalog Card Number: 92–75765

Printed in the United States of America

4 5 6 7 8 9 0 1 2   039   9 8 7 6 5 4 3

Preface

What makes people behave as they do? Are people ordinarily aware of the underlying reasons for their behavior? Are some people naturally good and others basically evil, or do we all have potential to be either good or bad? Is human conduct principally a product of nature or of nurture? Are people best described by their similarities or by their differences? What causes some people to develop disordered personalities? Can people change and grow toward psychological health?

These questions have been asked and debated by philosophers, scholars, and religious thinkers for several thousand years, but most such discussions were based on personal opinions and colored by political, economic, religious, and social considerations. Then, near the end of the nineteenth century, the emergence of psychology as the scientific study of human behavior marked the beginning of a more systematic approach to the study of human personality.

Early personality theorists, such as Freud, Adler, Jung, Horney, Erikson, and Fromm, relied mostly on clinical observations to construct models of human behavior. Although their data were more systematic and reliable than those of earlier observers, they continued to introject their own individualized way of looking at things and thus arrived at different conceptions of the nature of humanity.

Later personality theorists tended to use more empirical studies to learn about human behavior. They developed tentative models, tested hypotheses, and then reformulated their models. In other words, they applied the tools of scientific inquiry and scientific theory to the area of human personality. Science, of course, is not divorced from speculation, imagination, and creativity, all of which are needed to formulate theories. Each of the personality theorists discussed in this book has evolved a theory based both on scientific evidence and on imaginative speculation, and each theory is a reflection of the personality of its creator.

It follows, therefore, that within the science of psychology there would be many different and even contrasting theories, each reflecting to some extent the unique cultural background, family experiences, and professional training of its original theorist. Divergent theories, however, may still be useful. The usefulness of a theory depends, not on its agreement with some established theory, but on its ability to (1) generate research, (2) integrate existing empirical knowledge, and (3) suggest practical answers to everyday problems. Therefore, I evaluate each theory discussed in this book on the basis of these three criteria, as well as on (4) its internal consistency and (5) its simplicity.

THE THIRD EDITION

Theories of Personality, third edition, provides comprehensive coverage of 24 of the most influential theorists of personality. It emphasizes normal personality, although it also includes brief discussions on the attendant systems of abnormality and the appropriate theory and method of psychotherapy. Because each theory is an expression of its builder's unique view of the world and of humanity, I have included more biographical information than is usual in survey books on personality theory. As a reader, therefore, you will have an opportunity to develop an acquaintance not only with theories but with the theorists' lives as well.

New Features

I have introduced several new features into the third edition of *Theories of Personality*. First, the coverage has been expanded to include two additional theories— the object relations theory of Melanie Klein, Margaret Mahler, Otto Kernberg, and Heinz Kohut in Chapter 8, and the cognitive social learning theory of Walter Mischel in Chapter 11. Second, I have added a boxed discussion of Sigmund Freud's ambivalent attitude toward women, and a critique of Freud as a scientist. Third, I have included more biographical information on Harry Stack Sullivan, Erich Fromm, and Hans Eysenck, which may shed more light on their own personalities. Fourth, I have reorganized the Alfred Adler chapter to facilitate a smoother presentation of the components of his Individual Psychology. Fifth, I have included more of Carl Jung's own dreams to demonstrate his rationale for the collective unconscious. Sixth, I have added more material on Erik Erikson's book on Gandhi. Seventh, I have included material from the more recent writings of Albert Bandura, Raymond Cattell, Hans Eysenck, and Rollo May.

However, the major change in the third edition is the discussion of significantly more contemporary research. Personality theories are more than interesting templates through which we search for explanations of human nature. They are also dynamic entities that spawn much of the current psychology research. Thus, I have included in each chapter a Related Research section devoted to a sampling of the contemporary research and applications generated by each theory. Readers will be able to see that the older theories of Freud, Adler, Jung, and others are not merely historical curiosities; they continue to spark important research. Like the newer theories of Bandura, Mischel, and others, they have a symbiotic relationship with research in that they generate hypotheses, which then alter and expand the original theory.

Familiar Features

The third edition of *Theories of Personality* continues to emphasize the strong and unique features of the second edition; namely, the chapter introductions, chapter summaries, structured evaluations of each theory, concepts of humanity as seen by each theorist, annotated suggested readings, and real-life case studies. As with earlier editions, the third edition is based on original sources and the most recent formulation of the theory. Early concepts and models are included only if they retained their importance in the later theory or if they provided vital groundwork for understanding the final theory.

COVERAGE

I have divided the third edition of *Theories of Personality* into six broad areas, beginning with the *introductory remarks* found in Chapter 1. The so-called *psychodynamic theorists* are discussed in Chapters 2–8. Freud, the original personality theorist, heads this list. The others—Erikson, Adler, Jung, Sullivan, Horney, Fromm, Klein, Mahler, Kernberg, Kohut, and Dollard and Miller—all tended to emphasize unconscious determinants of behavior and all, in one way or another, were influenced by Freud.

Part Three presents the *behavioral and cognitive learning theories*. Included in this group are Skinner's radical behavioral approach, Bandura's cognitive learning theory, Rotter's social learning theory, and Mischel's cognitive social learning theory.

Next, I discuss the *dispositional theories*, including the trait and factor theories of Cattell and Eysenck, as well as the personal disposition theory of Allport. However, Allport's emphasis on the uniqueness of personality gives his theory a strong humanistic complexion.

The fifth section presents the *humanistic/existential theories* of Kelly, Maslow, Rogers, and May. Kelly's unique theory, however, almost defies classification.

Finally, in the concluding remarks, I invite readers to take a final look at the various theories and to speculate about future directions in personality theory.

WRITING STYLE

Although *Theories of Personality*, third edition, explores difficult and complex theories, I use concise, comprehensible language and an informal writing style. The book is designed for undergraduate students and should be understood by those with a minimal background in psychology. However, I have tried not to oversimplify or violate the theorist's original meaning. I have made ample comparisons between and among theorists, where appropriate, and have included many examples to illustrate how the different theories apply to day-to-day situations. A glossary defines technical terms; the same terms appear in **boldface** and are defined within the text.

INSTRUCTIONAL AIDS

Besides an end-of-book glossary, several other features aid both the student and the instructor. These include:

Case Studies

Every chapter begins with a case study, a brief story of some one person, chosen to help the student relate the subsequent theory to the real world. After introducing the case study, I present additional information on the person throughout the chapter to help readers better comprehend certain theoretical concepts.

Outlines, Overviews, and Summaries

Chapter outlines orient the reader to each chapter by previewing major topics to be discussed. Chapter overviews follow each case study and introduce readers to the general tone of the subsequent theory. At the end of each chapter, a summary reviews key topics.

Annotated Suggested Readings

At the end of each chapter are several suggested readings, with a short description of each. These readings have been carefully chosen for their readability, content, and interest level. They direct readers in further study.

INSTRUCTOR'S MANUAL

Accompanying this text is an instructor's manual that contains lecture outlines and a test bank of multiple-choice questions. The *lecture outlines* are intended to help busy instructors organize lecture notes and grasp quickly the major concepts of each chapter. With some general familiarity with a particular theory, instructors should be able to lecture directly from the lecture outline.

The *test bank* contains more than 1500 multiple-choice items designed to reduce an instructor's work in preparing tests. Each item is marked with the correct answer. Further, for many items I have determined both a difficulty level and a discrimination index. The *difficulty level* of an item is the percentage of students who answered that question correctly, and the *discrimination index* is an item's ability to discriminate top students from bottom ones. Computerized versions of the test bank are also available.

STUDY GUIDE

A study guide is also available to students who wish to organize their study methods and to enhance their chances of achieving their best scores on class quizzes. This study guide includes learning objectives and chapter summaries. In addition, it contains a variety of test items, including fill-in-the-blank, true/false, multiple-choice, and short-answer questions.

ACKNOWLEDGMENTS

I wish to acknowledge my gratitude to the many people who have contributed to the completion of this book. Again, I wish to thank librarian Joanne Durand for her assistance in supplying materials and Patrick Moreno for his helpful suggestions for improving the manuscript. I also wish to thank Linda Brannon for her help in solving myriad computer problems. The people at Harcourt Brace College Publishers have provided much professional help as well as personal encouragement. Eve Howard, psychology acquisitions editor, has made many helpful suggestions during the initial phase of the manuscript. Karl Yambert, developmental editor, has demonstrated a high level of knowledge of personality theory, which has greatly enhanced this book. Jane Ponceti, production manager, Burl Sloan, art director, Greg Meadors, picture development editor, and Mike Hinshaw, project editor, have expertly guided the book in its final production phases. Karen Anderson, ancillary project editor, Tom Urquhart, ancillary production coordinator, and Mike Beaupre, electronic publishing supervisor, shepherded the ancillary program with great skill and understanding.

The third edition has benefited from the insightful suggestions of a number of reviewers, whose contributions I gratefully acknowledge: Clinton E. Browne (Liberty University), Richard E. Dowell, Jr. (Lycoming College), David A. F. Haaga (American University), Ralph W. Hood, Jr. (University of Tennessee-Chattanooga), and Robert H. Williams (Maple Woods Community College). With special appreciation for their detailed comments, I thank Lenore E. DeFonso (Indiana University-Purdue University at Fort Wayne) and Terence J. Tracey (University of Illinois-Champaign).

I remain indebted and grateful also to the reviewers of the previous editions: William Arndt (University of Missouri, Kansas City), James Barger (Missouri Western State College), John Brockway (Davidson College), Ana Mari Cauce (University of Washington), Calvin Claus (National College of Education), W. Grant Dahlstrom (University of North Carolina), Boyce Daughtery (East Carolina University), Cooper Holmes (Emporia State University), Deborah Huntley (Wichita State University), Gary King (Rose State College), Alfred Kornfeld (Eastern Connecticut), Phil Lau (DeAnza College), Paul Lewan (Green River Community College), Mariam London (Northern Arizona), John McBrearty (Temple University), Joseph McCormack (Washburn University), Kathleen McCormick (Ocean County College), Eugene McCown (Northwest Missouri State College), Lesly Morey (Vanderbilt University), Richard Pasework (University of Wyoming), Joseph Philbrick (California State Polytechnic,

Pomona), James Pullen (Central Missouri State University), Kathryn Ryan (Lycoming College), Keith Thrasher (Rose State College), Brian Yates (American University), and Edward Yellinek (Wilson College).

I am also indebted to the following personality theorists for their kindness in taking time to discuss appropriate sections of the manuscript: Albert Bandura, Raymond B. Cattell, Hans J. Eysenck, Carl R. Rogers (deceased), Julian B. Rotter, and B. F. Skinner (deceased).

Finally, I wish to thank my wife, Mary Jo, for her patience and understanding during the course of this project and also during the course of our relationship.

Brief Contents

PART ONE

INTRODUCTION

1 Introduction   2

PART TWO

PSYCHODYNAMIC THEORIES

2 Freud: Psychoanalysis   22
3 Erikson: Post-Freudian Theory   76
4 Adler: Individual Psychology   118
5 Jung: Analytical Psychology   156
6 Sullivan: Interpersonal Theory   200
7 Horney and Fromm: Psychoanalytic Social Theory   238
8 Klein, and Dollard and Miller: Extensions of Psychoanalytic Theory   290

PART THREE

LEARNING THEORIES

9 Skinner: A Behavioral Analysis   346
10 Bandura: Social-Cognitive Theory   390
11 Rotter and Mischel: Cognitive Social Learning Theory   430

PART FOUR

DISPOSITIONAL THEORIES

12 *Cattell and Eysenck: Trait and Factor Theories*   474

13 *Allport: Psychology of the Individual*   522

PART FIVE

HUMANISTIC/EXISTENTIAL THEORIES

14 *Kelly: Psychology of Personal Constructs*   558

15 *Maslow: Holistic-Dynamic Theory*   590

16 *Rogers: Person-Centered Theory*   632

17 *May: Existential Psychology*   674

PART SIX

CONCLUSIONS

18 *A Final Word*   710

GLOSSARY   721

REFERENCES   741

NAME INDEX   765

SUBJECT INDEX   771

Contents

PART ONE
Introduction

1 INTRODUCTION 2
Overview 4
Personality 5
    Popular Definition 5
    Psychological Definition 6
Theory 7
    What a Theory Is Not 7
        Not a Philosophy 8
        Not Idle Speculation 8
        Not a Hypothesis 9
        Not a Taxonomy 9
    Theory Defined 9
    Theory and Observation 10
    What Makes a Theory Useful? 10
        A Theory Generates Research 11
        A Theory Organizes Known Data 12
        A Theory Guides Action 13
        A Theory Is Internally Consistent 13
        A Theory Is Parsimonious 14
    Why Different Theories? 14
Dimensions for a Concept of Humanity 15
Research in Personality Theory 16
Chapter Summary 17
Suggested Readings 18

PART TWO
Psychodynamic Theories

2 FREUD: PSYCHOANALYSIS 22
Overview 25

Biography of Sigmund Freud   26
Levels of Mental Life   31
    The Unconscious   32
BOX: Why Freud Abandoned the Seduction Theory   32
    The Preconscious   35
    The Conscious   35
Provinces of the Mind   37
    Id   37
    Ego   39
    Superego   40
Dynamics of Personality   42
    Instincts   42
        The Sexual Instinct   42
            Narcissism   43
            Love   43
            Sadism and Masochism   43
        The Destructive Instinct   44
    Anxiety   44
Defense Mechanisms   46
    Repression   46
    Reaction Formation   47
    Fixation   47
    Regression   48
    Undoing and Isolation   48
    Projection   49
    Sublimation   50
Stages of Development   51
    Infantile Period   51
        Oral Phase   51
        Anal Phase   53
        Phallic Phase   54
            Male Oedipus Complex   54
            Female Oedipus Complex   56
BOX: What Does the Woman Want?   58
    Latency Period   60
    Genital Period   60
    Maturity   61
Applications of Psychoanalytic Theory   61
    Dream Analysis   62
    Freudian Slips   65
    Psychotherapy   65
Concept of Humanity   67
Related Research   69
Critique of Freud   71
Chapter Summary   73
Suggested Readings   74

3   ERIKSON: POST-FREUDIAN THEORY   76

Overview   79
Biography of Erik Erikson   79
Importance of the Ego   82
    Description of Ego Psychology   82
    Society's Influence   83
    Epigenetic Principle   84
Stages of Psychosocial Development   85
    Infancy   87
        Oral-Sensory Mode   88
        Basic Trust vs. Basic Mistrust   88
        Hope: The Basic Strength of Infancy   89
    Early Childhood   89
        Anal-Urethral-Muscular Mode   90
        Autonomy vs. Shame and Doubt   90
        Will: The Basic Strength of Childhood   90
    Play Age   91
        Genital-Locomotor Mode   91
        Initiative vs. Guilt   92
        Purpose: The Basic Strength of the Play Age   92
    School Age   93
        Latency   93
        Industry vs. Inferiority   94
        Competence: The Basic Strength of the School Age   94
    Adolescence   95
        Puberty   95
        Identity vs. Identity Confusion   96
        Fidelity: The Basic Strength of Adolescence   97
    Young Adulthood   98
        Genitality   98
        Intimacy vs. Isolation   98
        Love: The Basic Strength of Young Adulthood   99
    Adulthood   100
        Procreativity   100
        Generativity vs. Stagnation   100
        Care: The Basic Strength of Adulthood   101
    Old Age   101
        Generalized Sensuality   102
        Integrity vs. Despair   102
        Wisdom: The Basic Strength of Old Age   103
    Summary   104
Erikson's Methods of Investigation   105
    Anthropological Studies   105
    Psychohistory   106
    Play Construction   108
Concept of Humanity   109

Related Research   111
Critique of Erikson   113
Chapter Summary   114
Suggested Readings   116

4   ADLER: INDIVIDUAL PSYCHOLOGY   118

Overview   121
Biography of Alfred Adler   121
Introduction to Adlerian Theory   124
Unity of Personality   125
    Organ Dialect   126
    Conscious and Unconscious   126
Subjective Perceptions   127
    Fictionalism   127
    Organ Inferiorities   128
Social Interest   129
    Development in a Social Environment   129
    Necessity of Social Interest   131
    Criterion of Human Values   131
Striving for Success or Superiority   132
    The Final Goal   132
    The Striving Force as Compensation   133
    Striving for Personal Superiority   134
    Striving for Success   134
    Summary of the Striving Force   135
Style of Life   136
BOX: Understanding Life Style through Early Recollections   136
Creative Power   138
Abnormal Development   139
    General Description   139
    External Factors in Maladjustment   140
        Exaggerated Physical Deficiencies   140
        Pampered Style of Life   140
        Neglected Style of Life   141
    Safeguarding Tendencies   141
        Excuses   142
        Aggression   142
        Withdrawal   143
    Masculine Protest   144
Applications of Individual Psychology   145
    Birth Order   145
    Early Recollections   147
    Dreams   147
    Psychotherapy   148

Concept of Humanity   149
Related Research   150
Critique of Adlerian Theory   152
Chapter Summary   153
Suggested Readings   155

5   JUNG: ANALYTICAL PSYCHOLOGY   156

Overview   159
Biography of Carl Jung   159
Levels of the Psyche   162
    The Conscious   163
    The Unconscious   163
        The Personal Unconscious   163
        The Collective Unconscious   164
        Archetypes   165
            The Persona   167
            The Shadow   167
            The Anima   168
            The Animus   169
            The Great Mother   169
            The Old Wise Man   170
            The Hero   170
            The Self   171
Dynamics of the Psyche   174
    Principles of Equivalence and Entropy   174
    Causality and Teleology   175
    Progression and Regression   175
Typology of the Psyche   176
    Attitudes   176
        Introversion   177
        Extraversion   177
    Functions   177
        Thinking   178
        Feeling   178
        Sensation   179
        Intuition   179
Development of Personality   182
    Stages of Development   182
        Childhood   182
        Youth   183
        Middle Life   183
        Old Age   184
    Self-Realization   185

Jung's Methods of Investigation   186
    Word Association Test   186
    Dream Analysis   187
    Active Imagination   189
    Psychotherapy   190
Concept of Humanity   193
Related Research   194
Critique of Jung   196
Chapter Summary   198
Suggested Readings   199

6   SULLIVAN: INTERPERSONAL THEORY   200
Overview   203
Biography of Harry Stack Sullivan   203
Introduction to Interpersonal Theory   207
Tensions   208
    Needs   208
    Anxiety   209
    Energy Transformations   210
Dynamisms   210
    Malevolence   211
    Intimacy   211
    Lust   212
    Self-System   212
Personifications   214
    Bad Mother, Good Mother   214
    "Me" Personifications   214
    Eidetic Personifications   215
Levels of Cognition   215
    Prototaxic Level   216
    Parataxic Level   216
    Syntaxic Level   217
Stages of Development   218
    Infancy   218
    Childhood   219
    Juvenile Era   221
    Preadolescence   223
    Early Adolescence   224
    Late Adolescence   226
    Adulthood   227
Mental Disorders   227
Psychotherapy   228
    Parataxic Perceptions in Therapy   229
    Sleep, Dreams, and Myths   230
    Summary   230

Concept of Humanity   230
Related Research   232
Critique of Sullivan   233
Chapter Summary   235
Suggested Readings   236

**7   HORNEY AND FROMM: PSYCHOANALYTIC
SOCIAL THEORY   238**
Overview   241
Biography of Karen Horney   242
Horney's Psychoanalytic Social Theory   244
   Horney and Freud Compared   244
   The Impact of Culture   245
   The Importance of Childhood Experiences   245
Basic Anxiety   246
Compulsive Drives   248
   Neurotic Needs   248
   Neurotic Trends   249
      Moving toward People   250
      Moving against People   251
      Moving Away from People   251
Intrapsychic Conflicts   253
   The Idealized Self-Image   253
      The Neurotic Search for Glory   254
      Neurotic Claims   255
      Neurotic Pride   255
   Self-Hatred   256
Feminine Psychology   258
Psychotherapy   259
Introduction to Fromm's Humanistic Psychoanalysis   260
Biography of Erich Fromm   260
Basic Assumptions   263
Human Needs   264
   Relatedness   264
   Transcendence   266
   Rootedness   266
   Sense of Identity   267
   Frame of Orientation   268
   Summary   268
The Burden of Freedom   269
   Mechanisms of Escape   269
      Authoritarianism   270
      Destructiveness   270
      Conformity   270
   Positive Freedom   271

Character Orientations   271
   Nonproductive Orientations   272
      Receptive   272
      Exploitative   272
      Hoarding   272
      Marketing   273
   The Productive Orientation   273
Personality Disorders   274
   Necrophilia   274
   Malignant Narcissism   275
   Incestuous Symbiosis   275
Psychotherapy   277
Fromm's Methods of Investigation   277
   Social Character in a Mexican Village   278
   A Psychohistorical Study of Hitler   279
Concept of Humanity   281
Related Research   282
Critique of Psychoanalytic Social Theory   284
Chapter Summary   285
Suggested Readings   287

**8   KLEIN, AND DOLLARD AND MILLER: EXTENSIONS OF
     PSYCHOANALYTIC THEORY   290**
Overview   293
Biography of Melanie Klein   294
Introduction to Object Relations Theory   296
Psychic Life of the Infant   297
   Fantasies   297
   Objects   298
Positions   298
   Paranoid-Schizoid Position   299
   Depressive Position   300
Psychic Defense Mechanisms   300
   Introjection   301
   Projection   301
   Splitting   301
   Projective Identification   302
Internalizations   302
   Ego   303
   Superego   303
   Oedipus Complex   304
      Male Oedipal Development   305
      Female Oedipal Development   305
Later Views of Object Relations   306
   Margaret Mahler's View   306

Otto Kernberg's View   309
Heinz Kohut's View   310
Psychotherapy   311
Concept of Humanity   312
Related Research   313
Critique of Object Relations Theory   315
Biographies of John Dollard and Neal E. Miller   316
Introduction to Dollard and Miller's Learning Theory   318
Four Fundamentals of Learning   319
Drive   319
Innate Drives   319
Learned Drives   320
Cue   321
Response   321
Reinforcement   322
Gradient of Reinforcement   322
Drives and Reinforcement   323
Higher Mental Processes   323
Foresight   324
Reasoning   325
Social Training   325
Conflict   327
Basic Assumptions   327
Types of Conflict   328
Approach-Avoidance   329
Avoidance-Avoidance   331
Double Approach-Avoidance   331
Repression and the Unconscious   333
Abnormal Development   334
Psychotherapy   336
Concept of Humanity   336
Related Research   337
Critique of Dollard and Miller   339
Chapter Summary   340
Suggested Readings   342

PART THREE
Learning Theories

9   SKINNER: A BEHAVIORAL ANALYSIS   346
Overview   349
Biography of B. F. Skinner   349
Scientific Behaviorism   353
Philosophy of Science   354

Operant Conditioning   354
Shaping   355
Reinforcement   358
Positive Reinforcement   358
Negative Reinforcement   358
BOX: Kamikaze Pigeons   359
Punishment   360
Effects of Punishment   360
Punishment and Reinforcement Compared   361
Conditioned and Generalized Reinforcers   361
Schedules of Reinforcement   362
Fixed-Ratio   362
Variable-Ratio   363
Fixed-Interval   363
Variable-Interval   364
Extinction   364
The Human Organism   365
Natural Selection   365
Cultural Evolution   366
Inner States   367
Self-Awareness   367
Drives   368
Emotions   368
Purpose and Intention   369
Complex Behavior   369
Higher Mental Processes   370
Creativity   371
Unconscious Behavior   371
Dreams   372
Social Behavior   372
Control of Human Behavior   373
Social Control   373
Operant Conditioning   373
Describing Contingencies   374
Deprivation and Satiation   374
Physical Restraint   374
Self-Control   375
The Unhealthy Personality   377
Counteracting Strategies   377
Inappropriate Behaviors   377
BOX: Walden Two—Utopia or Tedium?   378
Psychotherapy   380
Concept of Humanity   381
Related Research   383
Critique of Skinner   385

Chapter Summary   387
Suggested Readings   388

10   BANDURA: SOCIAL-COGNITIVE THEORY   390
Overview   393
Biography of Albert Bandura   393
Introduction to Social-Cognitive Theory   395
Reciprocal Determinism   395
    Differential Contributions   397
    Meaning of Determinism   398
BOX: Can Chance Change Your Life?   398
    Chance Encounters and Fortuitous Events   399
Self System   400
    Self-Regulation   401
        Self-Observation   401
        Judgmental Process   401
        Self-Reaction   402
    External Factors in Self-Regulation   403
        Standards of Evaluation   403
        External Reinforcement   403
        Selective Activation   403
        Disengagement of Internal Standards   404
            Redefinition of Behavior   404
            Displacement or Diffusion of Responsibility   405
            Disregard or Distortion of the Consequences
              of Behavior   405
            Blame the Victims   406
            Disengagement and Defense Mechanisms   406
    Self-Efficacy   406
        Self-Efficacy Defined   407
        Sources of Self-Efficacy   407
        Self-Efficacy as a Predictor of Behavior   411
Learning   411
    Observational Learning   412
        Modeling   412
        Processes Governing Observational Learning   413
            Attention   413
            Representation   413
            Behavioral Production   414
            Motivation   414
    Enactive Learning   414
        Imparting Information   415
        Motivating Future Behavior   415
        Reinforcing Present Behavior   415

Dysfunctional Behavior   416
    Depressive Reactions   416
    Phobias   417
    Aggressive Behaviors   417
Therapy   418
Concept of Humanity   420
Related Research   423
Critique of Bandura   426
Chapter Summary   427
Suggested Readings   428

11   ROTTER AND MISCHEL: COGNITIVE SOCIAL LEARNING THEORY
    430
Overview   433
Biography of Julian Rotter   433
Introduction to Rotter's Social Learning Theory   434
Four Variables of Prediction   435
    Behavior Potential   435
    Expectancy   436
    Reinforcement Value   437
    Psychological Situation   438
Basic Prediction Formula   439
Generalized Expectancies   440
    Needs   441
    Categories of Needs   441
      Recognition–Status   441
      Dominance   441
      Independence   442
      Protection–Dependency   442
      Love and Affection   442
      Physical Comfort   442
    Need Components   442
      Need Potential   442
      Freedom of Movement   443
      Need Value   443
General Prediction Formula   444
    Internal vs. External Control of Reinforcement   445
    Interpersonal Trust Scale   446
Maladaptive Behavior   448
Psychotherapy   449
    Changing Goals   449
    Eliminating Low Expectancies   450
Introduction to Mischel's Cognitive Social Theory   452
Biography of Walter Mischel   453

Consistency Paradox   455
    Person Variables   456
        Competencies   456
        Encoding Strategies   457
        Expectancies   457
        Subjective Values   458
        Self-Regulatory Systems   458
    Interaction of Person and Situation Variables   460
    A Conditional View of Personal Dispositions   461
Concept of Humanity   461
Related Research   463
Critique of Cognitive Social Learning Theory   467
Chapter Summary   468
Suggested Readings   469

PART FOUR
Dispositional Theories

12   CATTELL AND EYSENCK: TRAIT AND FACTOR THEORIES   474
Overview   476
Biography of Raymond B. Cattell   477
Basics of Factor Analysis   479
Cattell's Trait Theory   480
    P Technique   481
    Media of Observation   482
Source Traits   483
    Temperament Traits   483
        Normal Traits   484
        Abnormal Traits   485
        Second-Stratum Traits   489
        Measurement of Traits   491
    Dynamic Traits   491
        Attitudes   491
        Ergs   493
        Sems   493
        The Dynamic Lattice   496
The Dynamic Calculus   496
The Heritability of Traits   497
Eysenck's Factor Theory   499
Biography of Hans J. Eysenck   499
Measurement of Personality   502
    Criteria for Identifying Factors   503
    Hierarchy of Measures   503

BOX: What Dimensions Underlie Personality?   504
Types   505
    Extraversion   506
    Neuroticism   508
    Psychoticism   510
Concept of Humanity   512
Related Research   513
Critique of Trait and Factor Theories   517
Chapter Summary   519
Suggested Readings   520

13   ALLPORT: PSYCHOLOGY OF THE INDIVIDUAL   522
Overview   525
Biography of Gordon Allport   526
Allport's Approach   527
    Open System   528
    Eclecticism   529
Personality Defined   530
Structure of Personality   531
    Personal Dispositions   531
        Levels of Personal Dispositions   532
            Cardinal Traits   532
            Central traits   532
            Secondary Traits   533
            Motivational and Stylistic Traits   533
    Proprium   534
BOX: Mr. Clean Meets Dr. Freud   534
Growth of Personality   535
    The Developing Person   536
    Cultural Influences   538
    Motivation   538
        Functional Autonomy   538
            Perseverative Functional Autonomy   540
            Propriate Functional Autonomy   541
            Criterion for Functional Autonomy   541
            Limitations of Functional Autonomy   541
        Conscious and Unconscious Motivation   542
    The Healthy Personality   543
The Study of the Individual   545
    Morphogenic Science   545
    Letters from Jenny   546
Concept of Humanity   548
Related Research   549
Critique of Allport   551
Chapter Summary   553
Suggested Readings   554

PART FIVE
Humanistic/Existential Theories

14   KELLY: PSYCHOLOGY OF PERSONAL CONSTRUCTS   558

Overview   561
Biography of George Kelly   561
Kelly's Philosophical Position   564
    Person as Scientist   564
    Scientist as Person   564
    Constructive Alternativism   565
Personal Constructs   566
    Basic Postulate   567
    Supporting Corollaries   568
        Similarities among Events   568
        Differences among People   568
        Relationships among Constructs   569
        Dichotomy of Constructs   570
        Choice between Dichotomies   570
        Range of Convenience   571
        Experience and Learning   572
        Adaptation to Experience   572
        Incompatible Constructs   573
        Similarities among People   574
        Social Processes   574
Applications of Personal Construct Theory   576
    Abnormal Development   576
        Threat   577
        Fear   577
        Anxiety   577
        Guilt   578
    Psychotherapy   578
    The Rep Test   579
Concept of Humanity   581
Related Research   583
Critique of Kelly   585
Chapter Summary   587
Suggested Readings   588

15   MASLOW: HOLISTIC-DYNAMIC THEORY   590

Overview   593
Biography of Abraham H. Maslow   593
Motivation   597
    Hierarchy of Needs   598
        Physiological Needs   598
        Safety Needs   599

Love and Belongingness Needs   600
Esteem Needs   601
Self-Actualization Needs   602
Aesthetic Needs   602
Cognitive Needs   603
Neurotic Needs   603
General Discussion of Needs   604
Reversed Order of Needs   604
Unconscious Motivation   605
Unmotivated Behavior   605
Expressive and Coping Behavior   605
Deprivation of Needs   606
Instinctoid Nature of Needs   606
Comparison of Higher and Lower Needs   607
Self-Actualization   607
Values of Self-Actualizers   608
Definition and Description   609
Characteristics of Self-Actualizing People   610
More Efficient Perception of Reality   611
Acceptance of Self, Others, and Nature   611
Spontaneity, Simplicity, and Naturalness   611
Problem-Centered   612
The Need for Privacy   612
Autonomy   613
Continued Freshness of Appreciation   613
The Peak Experience   613
Gemeinschaftsgefühl   614
Profound Interpersonal Relations   614
The Democratic Character Structure   615
Discrimination between Means and Ends   615
Philosophical Sense of Humor   615
Creativeness   616
Resistance to Enculturation   616
Love, Sex, and Self-Actualization   617
BOX: Can You Fake Self-Actualization?   618
Applications of Maslow's Theory   618
Abnormal Development   618
Psychotherapy   620
Philosophy of Science   620
Research Methods   621
Concept of Humanity   622
Related Research   624
Research on Hierarchy of Needs   624
Research on the Peak Experience   625
Critique of Maslow   627

Chapter Summary   628
Suggested Readings   629

16   ROGERS: PERSON-CENTERED THEORY   632
Overview   634
Biography of Carl Rogers   635
Person-Centered Theory   639
    Basic Assumptions   639
        Formative Tendency   639
        Actualizing Tendency   640
    The Self   640
        The Self-Concept   641
        The Ideal Self   642
    Awareness   642
        Levels of Awareness   642
        Denial of Positive Experiences   643
    Needs   643
        Maintenance   644
        Enhancement   644
        Positive Regard   644
        Self-Regard   644
    Conditions of Worth   645
    Psychological Stagnation   646
        Incongruence   646
        Anxiety and Threat   647
        Defensiveness   647
        Disorganization   648
Psychotherapy   649
    Conditions   649
        Counselor Congruence   650
        Unconditional Positive Regard   651
        Empathic Listening   652
    Process   653
    Outcomes   655
The Person of Tomorrow   656
    Characteristics   657
    Implications   658
BOX: The Rogers/Skinner Debate   658
Philosophy of Science   660
Concept of Humanity   661
Related Research   662
    Chicago Studies   663
        Hypotheses   663
        Selection of Instruments   663
        Subjects and Procedure   664

Findings   665
Summary of Results   666
Later Research on the Growth-Facilitative Conditions   667
The Case of Mrs. Oak   669
Critique of Rogers   671
Chapter Summary   671
Suggested Readings   672

17   MAY: EXISTENTIAL PSYCHOLOGY   674
Overview   677
Biography of Rollo May   677
Background of Existentialism   681
What Is Existentialism?   681
Basic Concepts   682
Being-in-the World   682
Nonbeing   684
Anxiety   686
Normal Anxiety   686
Neurotic Anxiety   687
Guilt   687
Intentionality   688
Care, Love, and Will   689
Union of Love and Will   690
Forms of Love   690
Sex   691
Eros   691
Philia   691
Agape   692
Freedom and Destiny   693
Freedom Defined   693
Forms of Freedom   693
Existential Freedom   693
Essential Freedom   694
Destiny Defined   694
Philip's Destiny   695
The Power of Myth   696
Psychopathology   698
Psychotherapy   698
Concept of Humanity   700
Related Research   702
Critique of May   703
Chapter Summary   704
Suggested Readings   706

PART SIX
Conclusions

18   A FINAL WORD   710
     Concepts of Humanity Summarized   712
     Evaluation of Personality Theories   716
     Theories of Personality   719
     Future Directions   719

GLOSSARY   721

REFERENCES   741

NAME INDEX   765

SUBJECT INDEX   771

PART ONE

Introduction

Introduction

OVERVIEW
PERSONALITY
    Popular Definition
    Psychological Definition
THEORY
    What a Theory Is Not
    Theory Defined
    Theory and Observation
    What Makes a Theory Useful?
    Why Different Theories?
DIMENSIONS FOR A CONCEPT OF HUMANITY
RESEARCH IN PERSONALITY THEORY
CHAPTER SUMMARY
SUGGESTED READINGS

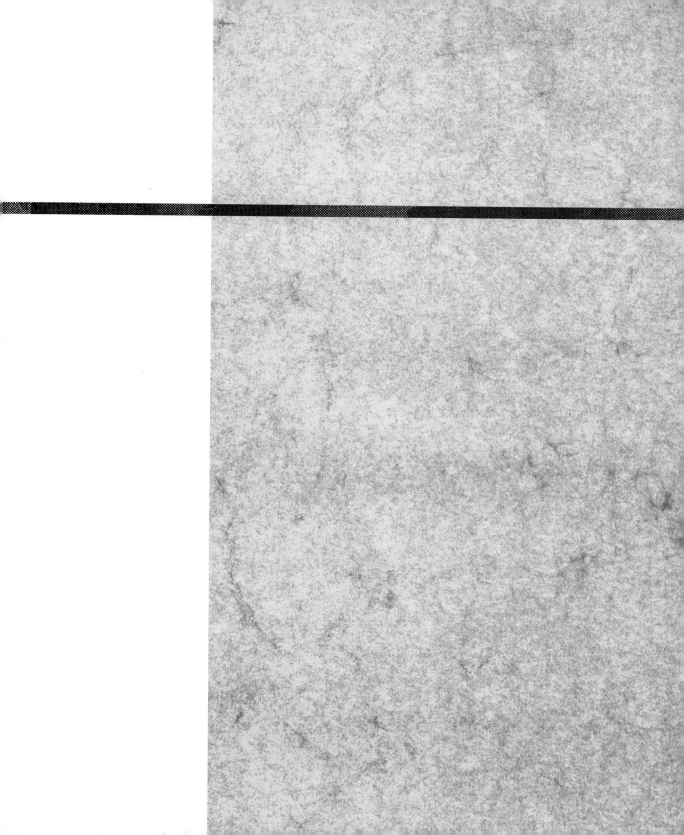

ne hundred years ago a gifted young Viennese neurologist named Sigmund Freud was curious about the nature of humanity. His questions differed little from those asked for centuries by philosophers and theologians. What motivates people? Is there some goal or end toward which people strive? What accounts for similarities among people? For differences? What makes people act in predictable ways? Why are they unpredictable? Do dreams have meaning? Are there hidden or unconscious forces that control people's behavior? What causes mental disturbances? Are people shaped more by heredity or by environment? By society or biology? What is the nature of human nature?

Unlike many who preceded him, Freud was not content to merely speculate about such questions. He transformed his thoughts into tentative concepts and then searched for evidence that would either confirm his notions or offer insight into how they could be changed. Where could such evidence be found?

As a neurologist, Freud was treating neurotic patients, many of whom suffered from a then-common disorder called **hysteria.** He listened to these people, trying to find out what hidden conflicts lay behind their odd assortment of symptoms. "Listening became, for Freud, more than an art; it became a method, a privileged road to knowledge that his patients mapped out for him" (Gay, 1988, p. 70).

Freud's method gradually became more scientific as he formulated hypotheses and checked their plausibility against his clinical experiences. Whether or not Freud was truly scientific is not an issue at this point. What is important is the fact that his early formulations eventually led to a highly structured concept or *theory of personality.*

OVERVIEW

Since Freud's original formulations, many other men and women have developed a theory of personality. Some are based largely on philosophical speculation, others mainly on empirical evidence. In this chapter we will see that a useful theory should be founded on *both.*

Many of the advances that have been made in the understanding of human behavior have come from personality theorists who have done two things: (1) They have made controlled observations of behavior, and (2) they have imaginatively speculated on the meaning of those observations. There have been many such men and women, but the ones who are widely recognized as having made significant contributions to our present understanding of personality are Sigmund Freud, Erik Erikson, Alfred Adler, Carl Jung, Harry Stack Sullivan, Karen Horney, Erich Fromm, Melanie Klein, Margaret Mahler, Otto Kernberg, Heinz Kohut, John Dollard, Neal E. Miller, B. F. Skinner, Albert Bandura, Julian Rotter, Walter Mischel, Raymond B. Cattell, Hans J. Eysenck, Gordon Allport, George Kelly, Abraham H. Maslow, Carl Rogers, and Rollo May. The theories of personality formulated by these people are the topic of this book.

Personality theories differ, not merely in terminology, but on basic issues concerning the nature of humanity. Each personality theory reflects its author's concept of humanity, and this chapter presents a structure for organizing the various issues dealing with the nature of human nature.

PERSONALITY

Personality is a topic of universal interest, yet it remains a subject clouded with mystery and misunderstanding. Most of us have heard such comments as "Jim has a wonderful personality"; "Kathy has an outgoing personality" or "Jan has no personality at all." Most psychologists, however, believe that personality cannot be adequately described by such simple statements. Before looking at the psychological definition, it might help to define personality according to popular usage.

Popular Definition

For many people, the term *personality* refers to one's social value. People have personality to the extent that they behave in likable ways, are charming, generous, and popular, get along well with others, and generally manifest socially desirable qualities. Personality means being a good conversationalist, witty, socially outgoing, sincere, well-groomed, and inoffensive to others. According to this popular definition, people have "personality" if they are friendly, extraverted, smile frequently, and have a soft, pleasant voice.

This lay person's conception of personality seems to imply that not everyone has a personality, that some people are either so nasty or so inconspicuous that they are completely devoid of personality.

Politicians are frequently described in terms of this popular definition and are said to have "personality" if they have charisma and charm, are able to project a folksy, relaxed appearance on television, or have an exciting, scandalous, or tragic private life. Again, the implication is that some politicians possess personality and others do not.

Psychological Definition

The popular definition of personality resembles the original meaning of the term, namely, a façade or mask that one shows to other people. However, psychologists use the term to refer to what one really is, not to mere surface appearance. Psychologists differ among themselves as to the meaning of personality, with no single definition being acceptable to all of them. Nor would such unanimity be desirable at the present stage of psychological science. The study of personality, including the development of differing theories, is best served by an incomplete, tentative definition. Personality theorists evolve unique and vital theories because they lack agreement as to the nature of humanity, and because each sees personality from an individual reference point. The personality theorists discussed in this book have had a variety of backgrounds. Some were born in Europe and lived their entire lives there; others were born in Europe, but migrated to other parts of the world, especially the United States; still others were born in North America (the U.S. and Canada) and have remained there. Many have been influenced by early religious experiences; others have not. Most, but not all, have been trained in either psychiatry or psychology. Many have been clinicians, drawing on their psychotherapist experiences; others have relied more on empirical research to gather data on human personality. Although they have all dealt in some way with what we call personality, each has approached this global concept from a different perspective. Some have tried to construct a comprehensive theory; others have been less ambitious and have dealt with only a few aspects of personality. Although few formally defined "personality," all have had their own view of it.

The person who probably did more than anyone to shed light on the many meanings of personality was Gordon Allport (1937; 1961). In his now-classic 1937 book, *Personality: A Psychological Interpretation*, he traced the history of the term and then listed 50 definitions of it, the final being his own.

Allport pointed out that philologists are in some disagreement as to the exact origin of the word, but that they generally concur that the Latin **persona** (from which personality is derived) referred to a theatrical mask worn in Greek drama by Greek actors before the birth of Christ. The persona was used to project a false appearance to others; that is, the role one plays in life. It is similar to the lay person's definition of the term personality; both indicate a surface appearance, not what one really is.

After an exhaustive discourse in which he approached personality from a variety of angles, Allport (1961, p. 38) offered his definition: "Personality is the dynamic organization within the individual of those psychophysical systems that determine his characteristic behavior and thought."

Allport's definition is acceptable for Allport's theory of personality, but for no other. No single definition can be acceptable to all personality theorists. Of necessity, each must have a unique definition, just as each has a unique concept of humanity and an individual manner of looking at human personality. In general, however, we can say that personality refers to a pattern of relatively permanent traits, dispositions, or characteristics within the individual that give some measure

No two people, not even identical twins, have exactly the same personality.

of consistency to that person's behavior. These traits may be unique, common to some group, or shared by the entire species, but their pattern is different for each individual. Thus everyone, although like others in some ways, has a unique personality.

THEORY

The word **theory** is a frequently used term, but in everyday language it is seldom employed with the kind of precision necessary to science. Before defining the term, let's look at some common misconceptions about theory.

What a Theory Is Not

People sometimes confuse theory with philosophy, or idle speculation, or hypothesis, or taxonomy. Although theory is related to each of these concepts, it is not the same as any of them.

Not a Philosophy

First of all, a theory is not a **philosophy**, which is a much broader term. Philosophy means love of wisdom, and philosophers are people who pursue wisdom through thinking and reasoning. Philosophers are not scientists; they do not ordinarily conduct controlled studies in their pursuit of wisdom. Philosophy encompasses at least five branches, one of which is **epistemology**, or the nature of knowledge. Theory relates most closely to this branch of philosophy, because it is a tool used by scientists in their pursuit of knowledge. Other branches of philosophy include **metaphysics**, or the nature of reality; **axiology**, or the nature of values; **ontology**, or the nature of being; and **cosmology**, or the nature of causation. A theory is none of these.

Theories do not deal with "oughts" and "shoulds." Therefore, a set of principles about how to live one's life cannot be a theory. Such principles involve values and are the proper concern of axiology. Although theories are not free of values, they are built on scientific evidence that has been obtained in a relatively unbiased fashion. Thus, there are no theories on why society should help homeless people or on what constitutes great art.

Philosophy deals with what ought to be or what should be; theory does not. Theory deals with broad sets of if-then statements, but the goodness or badness of the outcomes of these statements is beyond the realm of theory. For example, a theory might tell us that if children are brought up in isolation, completely separated from human contact, then they will not develop human language, exhibit parenting behavior, and so on. This statement says nothing, however, concerning the morality of such a method of child rearing.

Not Idle Speculation

Second, a theory is not mere armchair speculation. Although theories involve speculation, they must never be totally separated from empirical observation. They are closely tied to science and are based on scientifically gathered data.

What is the relationship between theory and science? **Science** is the branch of study concerned with observation and classification of data and with the verification of general laws through the testing of hypotheses. Theories are useful tools employed by scientists to give meaning and organization to observations. In addition, theories provide fertile ground for the production of testable hypotheses. Without some kind of theory to tie observations together and to point to directions of possible research, science would be greatly handicapped.

Theories are not useless fantasies fabricated by impractical scholars fearful of soiling their hands in the machinery of scientific investigation. In fact, theories themselves are quite practical and are essential to the advancement of any science. Speculation and empirical observation are the two essential cornerstones of theory building, but speculation must not run rampantly in advance of controlled observation. The reader will notice that the later theorists in this book, especially Skinner,

Cattell, Bandura, Mischel, and Rogers, have speculated cautiously and have kept theoretical statements only a small step ahead of laboratory or clinical observation.

Not a Hypothesis

Although theory is a narrower concept than philosophy, it is a broader term than hypothesis. A good theory is capable of generating many hypotheses. A **hypothesis** is an educated guess or prediction specific enough for its validity to be tested through the use of the scientific method. A theory is too general to lend itself to direct verification. One comprehensive theory, such as Freud's theory of psychoanalysis, may generate thousands of hypotheses. Hypotheses, then, are more specific than the theories that give them birth. The offspring, however, should not be confused with the parent.

Of course, a close relationship exists between a theory and a hypothesis. Using *deductive reasoning*, a scientific investigator can derive testable hypotheses from a useful theory. After these hypotheses are tested, the results—whether they support or contradict the hypotheses—feed back into the theory. Using *inductive reasoning*, the investigator then alters the theory to reflect these results. As the theory grows and changes, other hypotheses can be drawn from it and, when tested, they, in turn, reshape the theory.

Not a Taxonomy

A **taxonomy** is a classification of things according to their natural relationships. Taxonomies are essential to the development of a science, because without classification of data science could not grow. One must not confuse a taxonomy with a theory, however. Mere classification of people into groupings—such as introverts and extraverts, or endomorphs, mesomorphs, and ectomorphs—does not constitute a theory. Even the combining of several taxonomies, each having several complex subsystems, does not produce a theory. Unlike theories, taxonomies are not generative. They are dynamic only in the sense that new systems can be added to them, but they ordinarily lead nowhere as far as the production of testable hypotheses is concerned.

Theory Defined

If a theory is not a philosophy, not idle speculation, not a hypothesis, and not a taxonomy, what is it? A scientific theory can be defined as *a set of related assumptions from which, by logical deductive reasoning, testable hypotheses can be drawn.*

This definition needs further explanation. First, a theory is *a set* of assumptions. A single assumption can never fill all the requirements of an adequate theory. A single assumption, for example, could not serve to integrate known facts, something a useful theory should do.

Second, a theory is a set of *related* assumptions. Isolated assumptions could not generate meaningful hypotheses. Neither would they be internally consistent—a criterion for a useful theory.

A third key word in the definition is *assumptions*. The components of a theory are not proven facts in the sense that their validity has been absolutely established. They are, however, accepted *as if* they were true. This is a practical step, taken so that useful research can be conducted and further theory building can proceed.

Fourth, *logical deductive reasoning* is used by the researcher to formulate hypotheses. The tenets of a theory must be stated with sufficient precision and logical consistency to permit scientists to deduce clearly stated hypotheses. The hypotheses are not components of the theory, but flow from it. It is the job of the imaginative scientist to begin with the general theory and, through deductive reasoning, arrive at a particular hypothesis that can be tested. If the general theoretical propositions are illogical, they remain sterile and incapable of generating hypotheses. Moreover, if the researcher uses faulty logic in deducing hypotheses, the resulting research will be meaningless and will make no contribution to the ongoing process of theory construction.

The final part of the definition includes the qualifier *testable*. Unless a hypothesis can be tested in some way, it is worthless. The hypothesis need not be tested immediately, but it must suggest the possibility that scientists in the future might develop the necessary means to test it.

Theory and Observation

What is the relationship between theory and observation? If a theory is a useful one, then the interaction between it and observation is both mutual and dynamic. The relationship generally proceeds as follows:

Theories generate a number of *hypotheses* that can be experimentally investigated. The results from the subsequent experimental research, called *observations*, then flow back into the theory and restructure it so that, in the future, additional hypotheses can be generated. This cyclic relationship is shown in Figure 1.1. As the theory changes and grows, it extends its utility to a wider range of possible perceptions. More hypotheses can be tested and additional observations made, which, in turn, reshape and enlarge the theory even more. This cyclic effect continues for as long as the theory proves useful. When a theory is no longer able to explain related observations, it is set aside in favor of a better one, not because it has been disproven, but because it has ceased to be useful.

What Makes a Theory Useful?

The value of any theory rests on its usefulness, not on its truthfulness. What makes one theory useful and another not? Scientists use several standards to establish the value of a theory, and each of the theories presented in this book will be evaluated on the basis of the following five criteria.

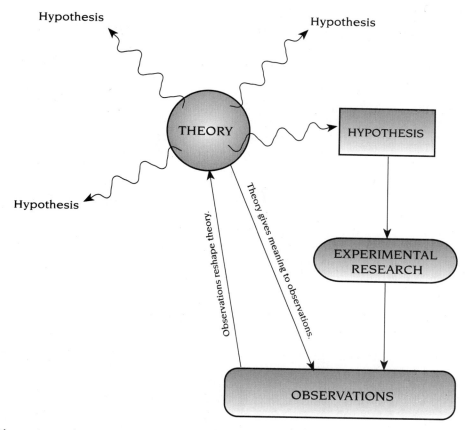

Figure 1.1   *The Interaction among Theory, Hypothesis, Experimental Research, and Observation*

A Theory Generates Research

Perhaps the most important criterion of a useful theory is its ability to guide further research. Without an adequate theory to point the way, many of our present empirical findings would have remained undiscovered. In astronomy, for example, the planet Neptune was discovered because the theory of motion generated the hypothesis that the irregularity in the path of Uranus must be caused by the presence of another planet. Useful theory provided astronomers with a roadmap that guided their search for and discovery of the new planet.

In order for a theory to generate meaningful research, it must be **verifiable;** that is, it must be sufficiently precise to suggest research that may either *confirm or disconfirm* its major tenets. Theories that rely heavily on unobservable transformations in the unconscious are exceedingly difficult to verify. In Freud's theory, for example, many of our emotions and behaviors are said to be motivated by unconscious tendencies that are directly opposite the ones we express. For instance, unconscious hate might be expressed as conscious love, and so forth. Transformations of this sort hamper verification of the theory, because alternative explanations can too readily be given to the same set of observations. If the results of a study reveal a particular finding, then that finding can be interpreted as support for Freud's theory. But if the study reveals the opposite findings, then this too can be seen as support for the same theory. Later, we will see that Freud's theory is not the only one that has problems with verification. All theories must be evaluated on their ability to be confirmed or disconfirmed.

A useful theory will generate two different kinds of research: *descriptive* and *hypothesis testing*. Descriptive research is that which is carried out in order to expand an existing theory. It is concerned with the measurement, labeling, and categorization of the units employed in theory building. Descriptive research has a symbiotic relationship with theory. On one hand, it provides the building blocks for the theory, and, on the other, it receives its impetus from the ever-expanding theory. The more useful the theory, the more research generated by it; the greater the amount of descriptive research, the more complete the theory.

The second kind of research generated by a useful theory, hypothesis testing, leads to an indirect verification of the usefulness of the theory. A useful personality theory will generate many hypotheses that, when tested, add significantly to our understanding of human personality.

A Theory Organizes Known Data

A useful theory should also be able to organize observations. Without some organization or classification, observations made from research would remain isolated and meaningless. Unless observations are organized into some intelligible framework, a scientist is left with no clear direction to follow in the pursuit of further knowledge. Intelligent questions cannot be asked unless observations have some order. Without intelligent questions, further research is severely curtailed.

A useful theory of personality must be capable of integrating what is currently known about human behavior and personality development. It must be able to shape as many bits of information as possible into a meaningful arrangement. If a personality theory does not offer a reasonable explanation of at least some kinds of behavior, its usefulness is extremely questionable. On the other hand, personality theorists should not force every observation of behavior into their theory, nor should they rationalize every negative research finding. When theorists become compelled to offer their theory as an explanation for all personality, they risk mistaking theory for truth. The theory then ceases to be viable and rigor mortis sets in.

Messer and Warren (1990) suggested that a useful personality theory should be able to explain how people change. It must recognize that personality develops over a lifetime, and that assumptions regarding one stage of development may not be valid for another stage. A personality theory should not only explain these developmental changes, but it must also be able to explain short-term changes, such as those that take place during psychotherapy. Later, we will see that most of the theorists discussed in this book developed their theory out of their therapeutic practice, and, therefore, they were intimately concerned with the issue of personality change through psychotherapy. However, many of their theories do not adequately explain life-span development. The theories that did not spring from psychotherapy—namely the behavioral and cognitive theories—take a more empirical approach to personality change, but they too generally explain short-term change better than life-span development.

A Theory Guides Action

A third criterion of a useful theory is its ability to guide the practitioner over the rough course of day-to-day problems. For example, psychotherapists are confronted continually with an avalanche of questions for which they try to find workable answers. Good theory provides a structure for finding many of those answers.

For therapists concerned with such questions as "What are the causes of this patient's neurosis?" or "How can I best treat my client?" a theoretical framework provides a needed shortcut to decision making. Without theory, practitioners would stumble in the darkness of trial-and-error techniques, but, with sound theoretical orientation, they can discern a suitable course of action.

For the Freudian analyst and Rogerian counselor, answers to the same question would be very different. To the question "How can I best treat this patient?" the psychoanalytic therapist might answer along these lines: "If psychoneuroses are caused by childhood sexual conflicts that have become unconscious, then I can help this patient best by delving into these repressions and allowing the patient to relive the experiences in the absence of conflict." To the same question, the Rogerian therapist might answer: If people need empathy, unconditional positive regard, and congruence to grow psychologically, then I can best help this client by providing an accepting, nonthreatening atmosphere. Notice that both therapists constructed their answers in an *if-then* framework, even though the two answers call for very different courses of action.

A Theory Is Internally Consistent

A theory can be useful only if its components are logically compatible. For example, the language of a theory must be consistent; that is, the same term must not have two separate meanings nor be applied in more than one way. Also, one tenet of the theory cannot be opposed to another tenet.

A good theory will include a taxonomy that is logical and that has been systematically constructed. It will use concepts and terms that have been clearly and operationally defined and used only in consonance with those definitions. An **operational definition** is one that defines units in terms of specific operations to be carried out by the observer.

An internally consistent theory cannot offer opposing answers to the same question. Also, it does not force incompatible observations into a framework where they do not fit. Its limitations of scope are carefully defined and it does not offer explanations that lie beyond that scope.

A Theory Is Parsimonious

When two theories are equal in their ability to generate testable hypotheses, to give meaning to observations, and to guide the practitioner, the simpler one is preferred. This is the law of parsimony. In fact, of course, two theories are never exactly equal in these abilities, but, in general, simple, straightforward theories are more useful than ones that bog down under the weight of complicated concepts and esoteric language.

In building a theory of personality, it is usually more desirable to begin on a limited scale and avoid sweeping generalizations that attempt to explain all of human behavior. That was the course of action followed by most of the theorists discussed in this book. For example, Freud began with a theory based largely on hysterical neuroses and, over a period of years, gradually expanded it to include more and more of the total personality.

Why Different Theories?

If theories of personality are truly scientific, why do we have so many different ones? The very nature of a theory allows the theory builder to make speculations from a particular point of view, and each of the theorists discussed in this book has had his or her unique perspective. Theorists must be as objective as possible when gathering data, but their decisions as to what data are collected and how these data are interpreted are personal ones. Theories are not immutable laws; they are built, not on proven facts, but on assumptions that are subject to individual interpretation.

All theories are a reflection of their authors' personal backgrounds. One's childhood experiences, unconscious motivation, philosophy of life, and interpersonal relationships all influence one's view of humanity. Because observations are colored by the individual observer's frame of reference, it follows that there may be many diverse theories. Nevertheless, divergent theories can be useful. The usefulness of a theory depends on its ability to integrate known observations and to generate research, not on its agreement with some other established theory.

There is room for several theories of personality because there are several ways of looking at human personality—several philosophical orientations that allow for different approaches to the scientific study of personality. Scientific investigation cannot exist apart from one's basic assumptions concerning the nature of humanity. A scientist does not operate within a vacuum but gathers data and makes speculations within some preexisting frame of reference, some preestablished *concept of humanity*.

DIMENSIONS FOR A CONCEPT OF HUMANITY

The basic assumptions concerning human nature rest on several broad dimensions that separate the various personality theorists. We can use six of these dimensions as a framework for viewing each theory's concept of humanity.

The first dimension is *determinism vs. free choice*. Are people's behavior and personality determined by forces over which they have no control? Can we choose to be what we wish to be? Is our behavior partially free and partially determined? Although the dimension of determinism vs. free will is more philosophical than scientific, the position theorists take on this issue shapes their way of looking at people and colors their concept of humanity.

A second, perhaps related issue is one of *pessimism vs. optimism*. Are people doomed to live miserable, conflicted, and troubled lives, or can they change and grow into psychologically healthy, happy, fully functioning human beings? In general, personality theorists who believe in determinism tend to be pessimistic (Skinner was a notable exception), whereas those who believe in free choice are usually optimistic.

A third dimension for viewing a theorist's concept of humanity is *causality vs. teleology*. Briefly, **causality** holds that behavior is a function of past experiences, whereas **teleology** is an explanation of behavior in terms of future goals or purposes. Do people act as they do because of what has happened to them in the past, or do they act because they have certain expectations of what will happen in the future?

A fourth consideration that divides personality theorists is their attitude toward *conscious vs. unconscious determinants of behavior*. Are people ordinarily aware of what they are doing and why they are doing it, or do unconscious forces impinge upon them and drive them to act without awareness of these underlying forces?

The fifth question is one of *biological vs. social influences on personality*. Are people mostly creatures of biology, or are their personalities shaped mostly by their social relationships? A more specific element of this issue is heredity vs. environment; that is, are personal characteristics more the result of heredity, or are they environmentally determined?

A sixth issue is *uniqueness vs. similarities*. Is the salient feature of people their individuality, or is it their common characteristics? Should the study of personality concentrate on those traits that make people alike, or should it look at those that make people different?

These and other basic issues that separate personality theorists have resulted in truly different personality theories, not just differences in terminology. We could not erase the differences among personality theories by adopting a common language. The differences are philosophical and deep-seated. Each personality theory reflects the individual personality of its creator, and each creator has a unique philosophical orientation, shaped in part by early childhood experiences, birth order, gender, training, education, and pattern of interpersonal relationships. These differences help determine whether a theorist will be deterministic or a believer in free choice, pessimistic or optimistic, and adopt a causal explanation or a teleo-logical one. They also help determine whether the theorist emphasizes conscious-ness or unconsciousness, biological or social factors, and the uniqueness or simi-larities of people. These differences do not, however, negate the possibility that two theorists with opposing views of humanity can be equally scientific in their data gathering and theory building.

RESEARCH IN PERSONALITY THEORY

Earlier we saw that theories and observations have a cyclic relationship: Theory gives meaning to observations, and observations result from experimental research designed to test hypotheses generated by the theory. Not all observations, however, flow from experimental research. Each of us makes many observations everyday. To observe simply means to notice something, to pay attention.

You have been observing human personalities for nearly as long as you have been alive. You notice that some people are talkative and "outgoing"; others are quiet and reserved. You may have even labeled such people as extraverts and intro-verts. Are these labels accurate? Is one extraverted person like another? Does an extravert always act in a talkative, outgoing manner? Can all people be classified as either introverts or extraverts?

In making observations and asking questions, you are doing some of the same things psychologists do; that is, observing human behaviors and trying to make sense out of these observations. However, psychologists, like other scientists, try to be *systematic* so that their *predictions* will be consistent and accurate.

To improve their ability to predict, personality psychologists have developed a number of assessment techniques, including personality inventories. Much of the research reported in the remaining chapters of this book includes various assess-ment procedures, which purport to measure different dimensions of personality. For these instruments to be useful they must be both reliable and valid. The **reli-ability** of a measuring instrument is the extent to which it yields consistent results. It can be determined by several methods: (1) comparing scores on two or more administrations of the same instrument; (2) comparing scores yielded by parallel (equivalent) forms of the same instrument; (3) comparing half the test items with the other half (split-half reliability); or (4) comparing ratings made by two or more judges observing the same phenomenon (interrater reliability).

Reliability is most frequently expressed in terms of **correlation coefficients**, which result from a mathematical procedure that expresses the degree of corre-spondence between two sets of scores. High positive reliability coefficients (for example, 0.80 to 0.90) indicate that subjects obtained nearly the same scores on two administrations of the test. Low scores (near .00) indicate a lack of correspon-dence, and high negative scores indicate a strong tendency for high scores on one administration of the test to be associated with low scores on a second administration.

Personality inventories may be reliable and yet lack validity or accuracy. **Validity** is the extent to which an instrument measures what it is supposed to measure. In determining validity, test scores are compared to an independent or outside criterion. For example, a personality inventory designed to measure extraversion and introversion must first be able to differentiate people into an extraverted category and an introverted category. Next, people scoring high in the extraverted direction must be the ones judged by some other criterion to be extraverted, and those scoring in an introverted direction must be independently identified as introverts.

Most of the early personality theorists did not use standardized assessment inventories. Although Freud, Adler, and Jung all developed some form of projective tool, none of them used the technique with sufficient precision to establish its reliability and validity. However, the theories of Freud, Adler, and Jung have spawned a number of standardized personality inventories as researchers and clinicians have sought to measure units of personality proposed by those theorists. Later personality theorists, especially Rotter, Cattell, and Eysenck, have developed and used a number of personality measures and have relied heavily on them in constructing their theoretical models.

Chapter Summary

Personality is one of the most fascinating topics in psychology. Nearly everyone is interested in personality, although fewer people might be attracted to the concept of theory. The term personality comes from the Latin *persona*, or the mask that people present to the outside world. This original meaning is similar to the popular definition of personality, which is associated with charm and charisma.

The psychological definition of personality, however, is more likely to include everything that one is. It views personality as comprising all those relatively permanent traits or characteristics that render some consistency to a person's behavior.

A *theory* is defined as a set of related assumptions from which testable hypotheses can be drawn. Theory should not be confused with

philosophy, idle speculation, hypothesis, or taxonomy, although it is related to each of these terms.

Five criteria determine the usefulness of a scientific theory: (1) Does the theory generate research? (2) Does it organize knowledge? (3) Does it suggest practical solutions to everyday problems? (4) Is it internally consistent? and (5) Is it simple or parsimonious?

Each personality theorist has had either an implicit or explicit *concept of humanity*, and each theorist's view of human nature can be discussed from six perspectives: (1) determinism vs. free choice, (2) pessimism vs. optimism, (3) causality vs. teleology, (4) conscious vs. unconscious determinants, (5) biological vs. social factors, and (6) uniqueness vs. similarities in people.

Suggested Readings _____

McCain, G., & Segal, E. M. (1988). *The game of science* (5th ed.). Pacific Grove, CA: Brooks/
Cole.
This consistently popular book presents a very readable and interesting account of
some of the new developments in science, including a look at the role of scientific
theory.

Stanovich, K. E. (1986). *How to think straight about psychology.* Glenview, IL: Scott, Foresman.
Misconceptions about psychology in general and theory in particular are cleared up in
this small volume. Basic methods used in psychological research are also included.

PART TWO

Psychodynamic
Theories

2 **Freud**
Psychoanalysis

3 **Erikson**
Post-Freudian Theory

4 **Adler**
Individual Psychology

5 **Jung**
Analytical Psychology

6 **Sullivan**
Interpersonal Theory

7 **Horney and Fromm**
Psychoanalytic Social Theory

8 **Klein, and Dollard and Miller**
Extensions of Psychoanalytic Theory

Psychoanalysis

OVERVIEW
BIOGRAPHY OF SIGMUND FREUD
BOX: WHY FREUD ABANDONED THE SEDUCTION
   THEORY
LEVELS OF MENTAL LIFE
   The Unconscious
   The Preconscious
   The Conscious
PROVINCES OF THE MIND
   Id
   Ego
   Superego
DYNAMICS OF PERSONALITY
   Instincts
   Anxiety
DEFENSE MECHANISMS
   Repression
   Reaction Formation
   Fixation
   Regression
   Undoing and Isolation
   Projection
   Sublimation
STAGES OF DEVELOPMENT
   Infantile Period
BOX: WHAT DOES THE WOMAN WANT?
   Latency Period
   Genital Period
   Maturity
APPLICATIONS OF PSYCHOANALYTIC THEORY
   Dream Analysis
   Freudian Slips
   Psychotherapy
CONCEPT OF HUMANITY
RELATED RESEARCH
CRITIQUE OF FREUD
CHAPTER SUMMARY
SUGGESTED READINGS

Chapter Two

FREUD

When visitors first see George's home they are immediately impressed by the neatness and orderliness of his yard and house. The lawn is carefully manicured, with each blade of grass seemingly the same height, the sidewalks and curbs are precisely edged, and the flower garden is perfectly groomed. The 15-year-old car parked in the driveway is in showcase condition—not a nick has ever marred the waxed exterior, the whitewall tires are snow-white, and the interior is immaculate. The house, though 20 years old, shows no signs of age or deterioration. Because most houses in this suburban neighborhood are attractive and well kept, the exterior of George's house is not altogether remarkable. A look at the interior, however, reveals an unusually clean and orderly appearance. The 20-year-old carpets seem brand-new. The plastic runners that lead from one room to the next protect the carpets from unsightly footprints. The formal living room looks little used, with plastic covering all the chairs and sofas. The family room appears more informal—rather than plastic covers, bed sheets are used to protect the furniture.

Although he neither cooks nor washes dishes (leaving these chores to his wife), George spends much of his time in the kitchen. Here, while entertaining guests, he habitually and somewhat automatically dusts the furniture, woodwork, and countertop with his white handkerchief. A visitor would be hard-pressed to find any dust above the door frame.

George's bedroom and closet are also extremely tidy. Suits and slacks are hung with equal spacings and according to color, shade, and season. Shoes are all neatly placed in a rack, again by color. His bathroom gleams and sparkles. George showers three times a day—once before work, again after work, and finally before retiring. He patiently towels off all the tile after each shower and cleans the faucets until they shine.

George works as a supervisor in an exclusive clothing store. In spite of his modest income, his frugality allows him to afford his luxurious house, located in a neighborhood where the incomes of most of the residents are two or three times that of George. At work, George dresses very neatly, although many of his suits are ten years old or more. On weekends, George relaxes around the house, seldom going out to eat or to a movie. While doing chores around the house and yard, he wears blue jeans and a plain white T-shirt. Both, however, are starched and neatly pressed.

George's neatness and orderliness extends to all aspects of his life—his car, house, yard, workshop, personal appearance, and the attire of his wife and children.

Most readers know someone like George, someone who is uncomfortable amid clutter and who apparently must keep his or her personal possessions in meticulous order. What accounts for such rigid behavior? What theories would Sigmund Freud offer to explain the compulsively neat personality? Later we will address these questions, but, first, we will present a brief overview of Freud's personality theory, and then look at the life of the man who created a complex and fascinating approach for reviewing human personality.

OVERVIEW

Sigmund Freud's contributions to personality theory have been both substantial and controversial. Freud's theory, **psychoanalysis**, is not only the most comprehensive of all personality theories—it has generated the greatest amount of critical interest, both positive and negative.

What makes Freud's theory so interesting? First, the twin cornerstones of psychoanalysis, sex and aggression, are two subjects of continuing popularity. Second, the theory was spread beyond its Viennese origin by an ardent and dedicated group of followers, many of whom romanticized Freud as a nearly mythological and lonely hero. Third, Freud's heavy emphasis on unconscious motivation allows several opposing explanations for the same observed behaviors.

Freud's contributions to our understanding of humanity provide a logical starting point in any discussion of personality theories. Besides originating a comprehensive theory of personality, Freud founded a theory of mental disorders as well as a theory and technique of psychotherapy. These three concerns—normal personality, abnormal development, and psychotherapy—cannot be separated. Each complements and supplements the other two. The present discussion focuses on the first. Abnormal personality and psychotherapy are partially explored to elucidate Freud's theory of personality.

Freud's experiences with patients in psychotherapy provided the basic data for the evolution of his theories. To him, theory followed observation, and his concept of personality underwent constant revisions based on his experiences as a practicing psychotherapist. Evolutionary though it was, Freud insisted that psychoanalysis could not be subjected to eclecticism, and disciples who deviated from his basic ideas soon found themselves personally and professionally ostracized by Freud.

Although Freud regarded himself primarily as a scientist, his definition of science would be somewhat different from that held by most psychologists today. He relied more on deductive reasoning than on rigorous research methods, and he made observations subjectively and on a relatively small sample of patients, most of whom were from the upper-middle and upper classes. He did not quantify his data, nor did he make observations under controlled conditions. He utilized the case study approach almost exclusively, typically formulating hypotheses after the facts of the case were known.

BIOGRAPHY OF SIGMUND FREUD

Freud was born either on March 6 or May 6, 1856, in Freiberg, Moravia, which is now part of the Czech Republic. (Scholars disagree on his birth date—the first date was but eight months after the marriage of his parents.) Sigmund was the firstborn child of Jacob and Amalie Nathanson Freud, although his father had two grown sons, Emanuel and Philipp, from a previous marriage. Jacob and Amalie Freud had seven other children within 10 years, but Sigmund remained the favorite of his young, indulgent mother, a fact that may have partially contributed to his lifelong optimism and self-confidence (Jones, 1953, Vol. 1). A scholarly, serious-minded youth, Freud did not have a close friendship with any of his younger siblings. He did, however, enjoy a warm, indulgent relationship with his mother, a fact that led in later years to his observation that the mother/son relationship was the most perfect, the most free from ambivalence of all human relationships (Freud, 1933/1964).

Freud's earliest playmates were his half-nephew John and his half-niece Pauline. John was about a year older and Pauline a little younger than Sigmund. One of Freud's earliest memories was of him and John taking away a bouquet of flowers from Pauline and causing the young girl to run away in tears (Vitz, 1988).

When Sigmund was three, the two Freud families left Freiberg. Emanuel's family and Philipp moved to London, while the Jacob Freud family moved first to Leipzig and then the following year to Vienna. The Austrian capital remained Sigmund Freud's home for nearly 80 years, until 1938 when the Nazi invasion forced him to emigrate to London, where he lived until his death on September 23, 1939.

When Freud was about a year old, his mother gave birth to a second son, an event that was to have a significant impact on Freud's psychic development. Sigmund was filled with hostility toward his brother and harbored an unconscious wish for his death. When the boy died at eight months of age, Sigmund was left with feelings of guilt at having caused his brother's death. Only in later years was Freud able to understand that the death wish for a sibling was not only common in young children, but also that his wish did not actually cause his brother's death. This discovery during middle age purged Freud of the guilt he had carried into adulthood and, by his own analysis, contributed to his later psychic development (Freud, 1900/1953).

Freud was drawn into medicine, not so much out of love for medical practice but out of an intense curiosity concerning human nature (Ellenberger, 1970). He entered the University of Vienna Medical School in 1873, but when he graduated in 1881 he had no intention of practicing medicine. He preferred instead to do research in physiology. To pursue his career, however, he was dependent on his father and friends for financial support. After his graduation, he remained at the university's Physiological Institute, having primary duties in research as well as some teaching responsibilities.

Freud might have continued his work indefinitely had it not been for two factors. First, he believed (probably without justification) that, as a Jew, his opportunities for academic advancement would be limited. Second, his father became less able to provide financial aid. Reluctantly, Freud turned from his laboratory to the practice of medicine. He worked for three years in the General Hospital of Vienna, becoming familiar with the practice of various branches of medicine, including psychiatry and nervous diseases (Freud, 1925/1959).

In 1885 he received a traveling grant from the University of Vienna and decided to study in Paris with the famous French neurologist Jean-Martin Charcot. He spent four months with Charcot, from whom he learned the hypnotic technique for treating hysteria, a disorder typically characterized by paralysis or the improper functioning of certain parts of the body. It was through hypnosis that Freud became convinced of the psychogenic origin of hysterical symptoms.

While still a medical student, Freud developed a close professional association and a personal friendship with Joseph Breuer, a well-known Viennese physician 14 years older than Freud and a man of considerable scientific reputation. Breuer taught Freud about *catharsis*, a method of removing hysterical symptoms through "talking them out." While using catharsis, Freud gradually and laboriously discovered the *free association* technique, which soon

replaced hypnosis as his principal therapeutic technique.

From his early years as a physician, Freud was strongly driven by the idea of making some monumental discovery and also of achieving fame (Ellenberger, 1970). His first opportunity to gain recognition came in 1884–1885 and involved his experiments with cocaine. Freud believed he had achieved an important breakthrough with his work with cocaine and was led to proclaim the wonderful virtues of that drug. After taking cocaine himself without any harmful effects, Freud praised it as a near panacea as well as an effective anesthetic (Byck, 1974). However, he was doomed to disappointment when his associate, Carl Koller, received credit for the discovery of the drug's anesthetic properties while Freud was away from Vienna visiting his fiancée Martha Bernays. Further trouble followed when he used cocaine in treating a friend for morphine addiction and succeeded in causing that friend to become a cocaine addict (Ellenberger, 1970).

While working with Charcot in Paris, Freud had learned about male hysteria, and he believed that this knowledge would gain him respect and recognition from the Imperial Society of Physicians of Vienna. Hysteria was originally thought to be a female disorder because early physicians believed that it was the result of a "wandering womb." However, in 1886, when Freud presented a paper on male hysteria to the Society, most of the physicians present were already familiar with the illness and, because originality was expected, Freud's paper was not well

Sigmund Freud with his daughter, Anna, who was a psychoanalyst in her own right.

received. Also, Freud's constant praise of Charcot, a Frenchman, cooled the Viennese physicians to his talk. Unfortunately, in his autobiographical study, Freud (1925/1959) told a very different story, claiming that his lecture was not well received because members of the learned society could not fathom the concept of male hysteria. Freud's account of this incident, now known to be in error, was nevertheless perpetuated for years and, as Sulloway (1979) argued, is but one of many denials created by Freud and his followers to mythologize psychoanalysis and to make a lonely hero of its founder.

Disappointed in his attempts to gain fame, and afflicted with feelings (both justified and otherwise) of professional opposition due to his defense of cocaine and his belief in the sexual factors in neuroses, Freud felt the need to join with a more respected colleague. He turned to Breuer with whom he had worked while still a medical student, and with whom he enjoyed a continuing personal and professional relationship. Breuer had discussed in detail with Freud the case of Anna O, a young woman he had spent many hours treating for hysteria several years earlier. After his rebuff by the Imperial Society of Physicians, and desirous of establishing a reputation for himself, Freud urged Breuer to collaborate with him in publishing an account of Anna O and several other cases of hysteria, along with theoretical and therapeutic considerations of the illness. Breuer, however, was not as eager as the younger and more revolutionary Freud to publish a full treatise on hysteria built on only a few case studies. Finally, and with some reluctance, he agreed to publish with Freud *Studies on Hysteria* (Breuer & Freud, 1895/1955). The beginning of psychoanalysis is sometimes traced to the original date of this publication, but the embryonic period of Freudian theory lay just ahead.

At about the time *Studies on Hysteria* was published, Freud and Breuer had a professional disagreement and became estranged personally. Freud then turned to his friend Wilhelm Fliess (a Berlin ear, nose, and throat physician), who served as a sounding-board for Freud's newly developing ideas. Freud's letters to Fliess constitute perhaps the most accurate account of the beginnings of psychoanalysis (Freud, 1985).

Freud and Fliess had become friends in 1887, but their relationship became more intimate following Freud's break with Breuer. During the latter part of 1895 and the first few months of 1896, Freud was laboring feverishly on what was called the *Project for a Scientific Psychology* (Freud, 1950/1966). The manuscript was sent to Fliess for criticism, but Freud soon abandoned the "Project," and its existence was not discovered until after World War II. Although the significance of the "Project" is still controversial among Freud scholars, the work does contain many concepts and terms later associated with Freud and psychoanalysis.

The late 1890s were for Freud a time of personal crises and professional isolation. His friendship with Fliess was beginning to cool, eventually to rupture in 1903. He had begun to analyze his own dreams and, after the death of his father in 1896, he initiated the practice of analyzing himself daily. Although his self-analysis was a lifetime labor, it was especially difficult for him during the late 1890s. During this period, Freud regarded himself as his own best patient (Ellenberger, 1970). A final contributing factor to his personal crisis was his realization that he was now middle-aged and had yet to achieve the fame he so passionately desired.

During this time he had suffered yet another disappointment in his attempt to make a major scientific contribution. He once again believed himself to be on the verge of an important breakthrough with his "discovery" that neuroses have their etiology in a child's seduction by a parent. Freud likened this finding to the discovery of the source of the Nile. However, by 1897 he came to believe that his seduction theory was not tenable because so many fathers, including his own, would be guilty of seducing their children. Disappointed, he abandoned the seduction theory (see box—"Why Freud Abandoned the Seduction Theory").

Freud's biographer, Ernest Jones (1953, 1955, 1957), believed that Freud suffered from a severe psychoneurosis during the late 1890s, although Max Schur (1972), Freud's personal physician during the final decade of his life, contended that his illness was due to a cardiac lesion, aggravated by addiction to nicotine. Peter Gay (1988, p.141) suggested that during this time immediately after his father's death, Freud "relived his oedipal conflicts with peculiar ferocity." But Henri

Ellenberger (1970) described this period in Freud's life as a time of "creative illness," a condition characterized by depression, neurosis, psychosomatic ailments, and an intense preoccupation with some form of creative activity. In any event, it is safe to assert that at midlife Freud suffered from self-doubts, depression, and an obsession with his own death.

Despite these difficulties, Freud completed his greatest work, *The Interpretation of Dreams* (1900/1953), during this period. This book, finished in 1899 as an outgrowth of Freud's self-analysis, contained many of his own dreams, some disguised behind fictitious names. Although *The Interpretation of Dreams* did not create an international stir for several years, it eventually gained for Freud the fame and recognition he had sought.

In the five-year period following the publication of *The Interpretation of Dreams*, Freud, now filled with self-confidence, wrote several important works that helped solidify the foundation of psychoanalysis (Freud, 1901/1953, 1901/1960, 1905/1953a, 1905/1953b, 1905/1953c, 1905/1960). These publications gave Freud some local prominence in scientific and medical circles, and a group of followers was soon attracted to him. In 1902 the Wednesday Psychological Society was formed with Freud, Alfred Adler, Wilhelm Stekel, Max Kahane, and Rudolf Reitler as participants. In 1908 the name of the organization was changed to the Vienna Psychoanalytic Society.

In 1910 the International Psychoanalytic Association was founded with Carl Jung of Zürich as president. Freud was attracted to Jung because of his keen intellect and also because he was neither Jewish nor Viennese. Between 1902 and 1906, all 17 of Freud's disciples had been Jewish (Kurzweil, 1989), and Freud was interested in giving psychoanalysis a more cosmopolitan flavor. Although Jung was a welcome addition to the Freudian circle and had been designated as the "Crown Prince" and "the man of the future," like Adler and Stekel before him, he eventually quarreled bitterly with Freud and left the psychoanalytic movement. The seeds of disagreement probably were sown when Freud and Jung, along with Sandor Ferenczi, traveled to the United States in 1909 to deliver a series of lectures. To pass the time while traveling, Freud and Jung interpreted one another's dreams, a potentially explosive practice that eventually led to the end of their relationship in 1913 (McGuire, 1974).

The years of World War I were difficult for Freud. He was cut off from communication with his faithful followers, his psychoanalytic practice dwindled, his home was sometimes without heat, and he and his family had little food. After the war, despite advancing years and pain suffered from 33 operations for cancer of the mouth, he made important revisions in his theory. The most significant of these were the elevation of the death instinct to a level with the life instinct; the inclusion of repression as one of the defenses of the ego; and the clarification of the female Oedipus complex.

Freud's personal life had many highlights: his marriage to Martha Bernays in 1886 after a long engagement; the birth of their six children between 1887 and 1895; the beginning of his self-analysis in 1897 as a reaction to the death of his father; his trip with Jung to the United States in 1909 to speak at Clark University; his gaining worldwide recognition; his winning the Goethe prize for literature in 1930; and finally, at age 82, his emigration to England after the Nazis had marched into Austria.

What personal qualities did Freud possess? For a more complete insight into his personality the reader is directed to Clark (1980); Ellenberger (1970); Gay (1988); Isbister (1985); Jones (1953, 1955, 1957); Sulloway (1979); and Vitz (1988). Above all, Freud was a sensitive, passionate person. He had the capacity for intimate, almost secretive relationships. While still a young student, he and a close friend, Edward Silberstein, formed a Spanish society with the purpose of learning that language, but also with the effect of solidifying a close union—one that distrusted others and viewed the world with suspicion. Similar relationships were repeated throughout Freud's life. He had the capacity for revealing intimate aspects of his personality to those who were close to him while, at the same time, feeling persecuted by others. He seemed to have needed these intense relationships, which were both exclusive and somewhat distrustful in attitude toward the outside world. His passionate nature is revealed in his correspondence with his intimates (Freud, 1960, 1985; McGuire, 1974).

Freud was also an exceptionally gifted writer. He knew several foreign languages fluently, but he was a master of the German tongue. He was an excellent translator, having translated the English philosopher John Stuart Mill, and the French psychiatrist Jean-Martin Charcot, among many others. Among other qualities, Freud possessed an intense intellectual curiosity; unusual moral courage, demonstrated by his daily self-analysis; extremely ambivalent feelings toward his father and other father figures; the tendency to hold grudges disproportionate to the alleged offense; a burning ambition, especially during his earlier years; strong feelings of isolation even while surrounded by many followers; and an intense and somewhat irrational dislike of the United States and its people, a feeling that became more intense after his trip to that country in 1909.

Freud's greatest contribution to personality theory is his exploration of the unconscious and his insistence that people are motivated primarily by instinctual forces of which they have little or no awareness. Therefore, we begin the discussion of Freudian theory by looking at the different levels of mental life.

LEVELS OF MENTAL LIFE

The fundamental assumption of psychoanalysis is that mental life is divided into two levels, the **unconscious** and the **conscious**. The unconscious, in turn, has two different levels, the unconscious proper and the **preconscious**. (In Freudian psychology the three levels of mental life are used to designate both a process and a location. The existence as a specific location, of course, is merely hypothetical and has no real existence within the body. Yet, Freud spoke of *the* unconscious as well as unconscious processes.)

The Unconscious

The unconscious contains all those drives, urges, or instincts that are beyond our awareness, but that nevertheless motivate most of our words, feelings, and actions. Although we may be conscious of our overt behaviors, we often are not

Why Freud Abandoned the Seduction Theory

Most readers are familiar with Freud's idea of the *Oedipus complex*, a condition in which a young child desires a sexual relationship with one parent, while experiencing feelings of hostility toward the other parent. Freud believed that all children have these unconscious sexual and aggressive fantasies toward their parents, a belief that has been perpetuated through the years by psychoanalytically oriented therapists and that has cast doubt on many reports of child sexual abuse.

As we have seen, prior to his belief that young children possess incestuous wishes toward their parents, Freud had held the opposite view; that is, he believed that neurotic symptoms resulted from the seduction of children by adults. This "seduction theory" was summarized by Freud (1896/1962, p. 203) in these words.

I therefore put forward the thesis that at the bottom of every case of hysteria there are *one or more occurrences of premature sexual experience*, occurrences which belong to the earliest years of childhood but which can be reproduced through the work of psychoanalysis in spite of intervening decades. I believe that this is an important finding, the discovery of a *caput* Nili [source of the Nile] in neuropathology.

However, in 1897 Freud repudiated his seduction theory and soon afterward replaced it with his concept of the Oedipus complex. The Oedipus complex was in direct contradiction to the seduction theory, in as much as it placed the origin of most parental seductions within the mind of the child and not in reality.

Actually, Freud never completely abandoned his seduction theory; he always retained some belief in real sexual trauma as a source of neurosis. In his autobiography, Freud (1925/1959) stated that childhood seductions account for some neuroses, but the seducer usually turns out to be other children rather than the father. Because Freud had considered his seduction theory to be equivalent to the discovery of the source of the Nile, why would he deemphasize his treasured theory?

Freud himself offered four reasons in his famous letter of September 21, 1897, to Wilhelm Fliess. First, Freud said, the seduction theory had not enabled him to successfully aware of the mental processes that lie behind them. For example, George (in the case study introduced at the beginning of this chapter) is aware of his desire to maintain a neat and orderly environment, but he has no insight into the origins or causes of his compulsive behavior.

Because the unconscious is not available to the conscious mind, how can one know if it really exists? Freud felt that its existence could be proved only indirectly. To him the unconscious is the only explanation for the meaning behind dreams, slips of the tongue, neurotic symptoms, and certain kinds of forgetting, called *repressions*. Dreams serve as a particularly rich source of unconscious material. For example, Freud believed that childhood experiences sometimes reappear in adult dreams even though the dreamer has no conscious recollection of them.

Unconscious processes often enter into consciousness but only after being disguised or distorted enough to elude censorship. Freud (1917/1963) used the

treat even a single patient. Second, a great number of fathers, including his own, would have to be accused of sexual perversion because hysteria was quite common even among Freud's siblings. Third, Freud believed that the unconscious mind could probably not distinguish reality from fiction, a belief that later evolved into the Oedipus complex. And fourth, he found that the unconscious memories of advanced psychotic patients almost never reveal early childhood sexual experiences (Freud, 1985).

In time, Freud became more and more strongly convinced that neurotic symptoms were related to childhood *fantasies* rather than to material reality. In his autobiography, he expressed relief that he had corrected the "error" that would have had fatal consequences for psychoanalysis, and wondered how anyone could have believed that childhood seductions were so common (Freud, 1925/1959).

Many observers now believe that the seduction theory was not an error, and that Freud went astray when he attributed the fault of seduction to the child rather than to the parent. Balmary (1979/1982) stated that psychoanalysis got off the right track when Freud repudiated the seduction theory and thus set psychological reality above physical reality. Lerman (1986) took a more standard Freudian view of the Oedipus complex and rejected it as inferior to the original theory as an explanation for neurotic symptoms. She cited evidence from Kinsey that 25 percent of women had some sexual encounter with an adult by the time they were 13 years old, and that 80 percent of the time the adult was a relative or family friend.

Masson (1984) claimed that psychoanalysis took a wrong turn when Freud abandoned the seduction theory. By shifting the emphasis from actual child sexual abuse to the inner world of childhood fantasies, Masson (p. 144) contended, "Freud began a trend away from the real world that . . . is at the root of the present-day sterility of psychoanalysis and psychiatry throughout the world."

The history of psychoanalysis would have been quite different if Freud had not reversed himself and shifted emphasis away from his belief that neuroses spring from actual childhood seductions. In fact, Anna Freud, in a 1981 letter to Jeffrey Masson, stated that if her father had retained the seduction theory "there would have been no psychoanalysis afterwards" (Masson, 1984, p. 113).

analogy of a guardian or censor blocking the passage between the unconscious and preconscious and preventing undesirable anxiety-producing memories from entering awareness. To enter the conscious level of the mind, these unconscious images first must be sufficiently disguised to slip past the primary censor, and then they must elude a final censor that watches the passageway between the preconscious and the conscious. By the time these memories enter our conscious mind, we no longer recognize them for what they are; instead, we see them as relatively pleasant, nonthreatening experiences. In most cases, these images have strong sexual or aggressive motifs, because sexual and aggressive behaviors are the ones that our parents quite likely punished or suppressed when we were children. Punishment and suppression then created feelings of anxiety, and the anxiety, in turn, stimulated *repression* of sexual and aggressive fantasies. **Repression** is the forcing of unwanted, anxiety-ridden experiences into the unconscious in order to defend us against the pain of that anxiety.

Not all unconscious processes, however, spring from repression of childhood events. Freud believed that a portion of our unconscious originates from the experiences of our early ancestors that have been passed on to us through hundreds of generations of repetition. He called these inherited unconscious images our **phylogenetic endowment** (Freud, 1917/1963, 1933/1964). Freud's notion of phylogenetic endowment is quite similar to Carl Jung's idea of a collective unconscious (see Chapter 5). However, one important difference exists between the two concepts. Whereas Jung placed primary emphasis on the collective unconscious, Freud relied on the notion of inherited dispositions only as a last resort. That is, when explanations built on individual experiences were not adequate, Freud would turn to the idea of collectively inherited experiences to fill in the gaps left by individual experiences. Later we will see that Freud used the concept of phylogenetic endowment to explain several important concepts such as guilt and castration anxiety.

Unconscious drives may appear in consciousness, but only after undergoing certain transformations. A person may express either erotic or hostile urges, for example, by teasing or joking with another. The original instinct (sex or aggression) is thus disguised and hidden from the conscious minds of both persons. The unconscious of the first person, however, has directly influenced the unconscious of the second. Both people gain some satisfaction of either sexual or aggressive urges, but neither is conscious of the underlying motive behind the teasing or joking. Thus the unconscious mind of one person can communicate with the unconscious of another without either person being aware of the process.

Unconscious, of course, does not mean inactive or dormant. Instincts in the unconscious constantly strive to become conscious, and many of them succeed, although they may no longer appear in their original form. Unconscious ideas can and do motivate the individual. For example, a son's hostility toward his father may masquerade itself in the form of ostentatious affection. In an undisguised form, the hostility would create too much anxiety for the son. His unconscious mind, therefore, motivates him to express hostility indirectly through an exaggerated show of love and flattery. Because the disguise must successfully deceive the person, it often takes an opposite form from the original feelings, but it is almost always overblown and ostentatious. (This mechanism, called a *reaction formation*, is discussed later under "Defense Mechanisms.")

Besides being active, unconscious ideas can also be intense enough to motivate neurotic and psychotic symptoms. For example, Freud (1922/1955) believed that the persecution complex of the paranoid patient is a defense against unconscious homosexual urges. Paranoia is thus seen as an expression of unconscious sexual impulses toward the persecutor, who is always a former friend of the same sex. The unconscious impulse becomes quite intense and, at times, dominates the life of the paranoid person even though that person remains completely unaware of any true feelings toward the persecutor (Freud, 1917/1963).

The Preconscious

The preconscious level of the mind contains all those elements that are not conscious but can become so quite readily (Freud, 1933/1964). The contents of the preconscious come from two sources, the first of which is conscious perception. What a person perceives is conscious for only a transitory period; it quickly passes into the preconscious when the focus of attention shifts to another idea. These ideas that alternate easily between being conscious and preconscious are largely free from anxiety and, in reality, are much more similar to the conscious images than to unconscious urges.

The second source of preconscious content is the unconscious. According to Freud, ideas can slip past the vigilant censor and find their way into the preconscious, albeit in a disguised form. Some of these ideas never become conscious because, if we recognized them as derivatives of the unconscious, we would experience increased levels of anxiety. Therefore, our final censor represses these anxiety-laden ideas and pushes them back into the unconscious. Other ideas from the unconscious do gain admission to consciousness, but only because their true nature is cleverly disguised through the dream process, a slip of the tongue, or an elaborate defensive measure.

The Conscious

Consciousness, which plays a relatively minor role in psychoanalytic theory, can be defined as those mental elements in awareness at any given point in time. It is the only level of mental life directly available to us. Ideas can reach consciousness from two different directions. The first is from the **perceptual conscious** system, which is turned toward the outer world and acts as a medium for the perception of external stimuli. In other words, what we perceive through our sense organs, if not too threatening, enters into consciousness (Freud, 1933/1964).

The second source of conscious elements is from within the mental structure and includes nonthreatening ideas from the preconscious as well as menacing but disguised images from the unconscious. As we have seen, these latter elements escaped into the preconscious by disguising themselves as harmless images and evading the primary censor. Once in the preconscious, they are capable of coming under the eye of consciousness by avoiding a final censor. By the time they reach the conscious system, these ideas are greatly distorted and camouflaged, often taking the form of neurotic symptoms or dream images.

In varying degrees, all of us are guided and controlled by our unconscious instincts. Psychologically mature people are generally relatively conscious of their actions and feelings, and they may even have some awareness of the motivations behind their behavior. However, psychologically unhealthy individuals are frequently out of touch with their feelings, and they usually have very little or no awareness of the motives that underlie their actions.

In summary, Freud's concept of the unconscious can be compared to a large anteroom in which many diverse, energetic, and disreputable people are milling

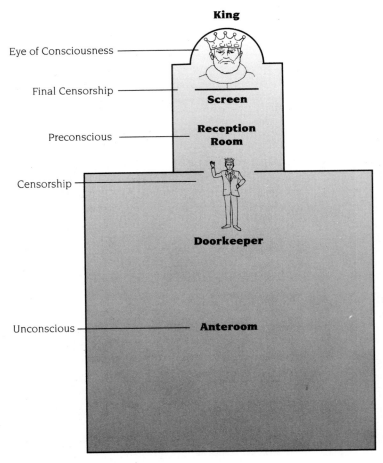

Figure 2.1 *Levels of Mental Life*

about, crowding one another, and striving incessantly to escape to a smaller adjoining room. However, a watchful guardian protects the threshold between the large anteroom and the small reception room. This doorkeeper has two methods of preventing undesirables from escaping from the anteroom. One way is to turn them back at the door, or to throw out those people who earlier had clandestinely slipped into the reception room. The effect in either case is the same; the menacing, disorderly people are prevented from coming into view of a king who is seated at the far end of the reception room behind a screen. The meaning of the analogy is obvious. The people in the anteroom represent unconscious mental excitations. The small reception room is the preconscious and its inhabitants represent preconscious ideas. People in the reception room (preconscious) may or may not come into view of the king who, of course, represents the eye of consciousness. The doorkeeper who guards the threshold between the two rooms is the primary censor that prevents unconscious ideas from becoming preconscious and renders preconscious ideas unconscious by throwing them back. The screen that guards the king is the final censor, and it prevents many, but not all, preconscious elements from reaching consciousness. The analogy is presented graphically in Figure 2.1.

PROVINCES OF THE MIND

For nearly two decades, Freud's only model of the mind was the topographic one we have just outlined, and his only portrayal of psychic strife was the conflict between conscious and unconscious forces. Then, during the 1920s, Freud (1923/1961a) introduced a three-part structural model. This division of the mind into three provinces did not supplant the topographic model, but it helped him explain mental images according to their functions or purposes (Westen, 1990a).

To Freud, the most primitive part of the mind was *das Es*, or the "it," which is almost always translated into English as **id**; a second division was *das Ich*, or the "I," translated as **ego**; and a final province was *das Über-Ich*, or the "above-I," which is rendered into English as **superego**. These provinces or regions have no territorial existence, of course, but are merely hypothetical constructs. They interact with the three levels of mental life so that the ego cuts across the various topographic levels and has conscious, preconscious, and unconscious components, while the superego is both preconscious and unconscious. Figure 2.2 shows the relationship between the provinces of the mind and the levels of mental life.

Id

At the core of personality and completely unconscious to the individual is the psychical region called the **id,** a term derived from the impersonal pronoun meaning "the it," or the not-yet-owned component of personality. The id has no contact with reality, yet it strives constantly to reduce tension by satisfying instinctual desires. Because its sole function is to seek pleasure, we say that the id serves the **pleasure principle.**

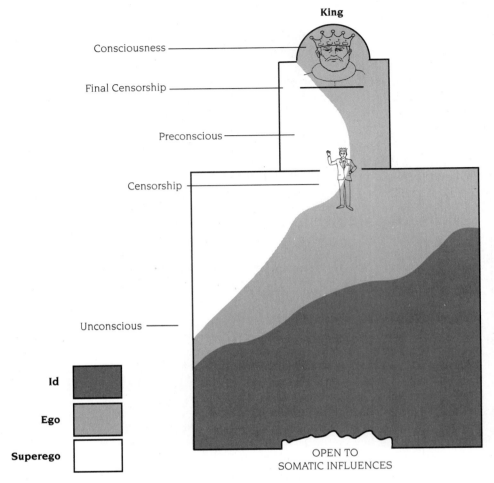

King

Consciousness

Final Censorship

Preconscious

Censorship

Unconscious

Id

Ego

Superego

OPEN TO
SOMATIC INFLUENCES

Figure 2.2   *Levels of Mental Life and Provinces of the Mind*

The newborn baby may be seen as a personification of an id unencumbered by restrictions of ego and superego. The baby seeks gratification of needs without regard for what is possible or what is proper, sucking when the nipple is either present or absent. Gaining pleasure in either case, the infant receives nutrition only in the former. The extranutritional sucking continues because the id-dominated infant is not in contact with reality. It fails to realize that thumb sucking behavior cannot sustain life. Because the id has no direct contact with reality, it is not altered by the passage of time or by the experiences of the person. Childhood wish impulses remain unchanged in the id for decades (Freud, 1933/1964).

Besides being unrealistic and pleasure-seeking, the id is illogical and can simultaneously entertain incompatible ideas. For example, a man may have an unconscious wish for the death of his wife, while at the same time desiring sex with her. Or he may consciously love his father, while unconsciously wishing to destroy him.

Another characteristic of the id is lack of morality. Because it cannot make value judgments or distinguish between good and evil, the id is not immoral, merely amoral. All of the id's energy is spent for one purpose—to seek pleasure without regard for what is proper or just (Freud, 1923/1961a, 1933/1964).

In review, the id is primitive, chaotic, inaccessible to consciousness, unchangeable, amoral, illogical, unorganized, and filled with energy received from the instincts and discharged for the satisfaction of the pleasure principle.

As the region that houses the instincts (primary motivators), the id is said to operate through the **primary process.** Because it blindly seeks to satisfy the pleasure principle, its survival is dependent upon the development of a **secondary process** to bring it into contact with the external world. This secondary process functions through the ego.

Ego

The **ego,** or I, is the region of the mind in contact with reality. It grows out of the id during infancy and becomes a person's only source of communication with the external world. It is governed by the **reality principle**, which it tries to substitute for the pleasure principle of the id. As the sole region of the mind in contact with the external world, the ego becomes the decision-making or executive branch of personality. However, because it is partly conscious, partly preconscious, and partly unconscious, the ego can make decisions on each of these three levels. For instance, George's need to be excessively neat and orderly is probably not a conscious decision, but one based on some hidden or unconscious desire.

When performing its cognitive and intellectual functions, the ego must take into consideration the incompatible, but equally unrealistic, demands of the id and the superego. In addition to these two tyrants, the ego must serve a third master—the external world. Thus, the ego constantly tries to reconcile the blind claims of the id and superego with the realistic demands of the external world. Finding itself surrounded on three sides by divergent and hostile forces, the ego reacts in a predictable manner—it becomes anxious. It then uses repression and the other *defense mechanisms* to defend itself against anxiety by preventing threatening elements from reaching consciousness (Freud, 1926/1959a).

According to Freud (1933/1964), the ego becomes differentiated from the id when the baby learns to distinguish itself from the outer world. While the id remains unchanged, the ego continues to develop; while the id insists on unrealistic and unrelenting demands for pleasure, the ego must be realistic; while the id provides the person with energy, the ego must furnish the control. In comparing the ego to the id, Freud used the analogy of a person on horseback. The rider checks and inhibits the greater strength of the horse but is at times ultimately at the mercy of the animal. Sometimes the rider permits the horse free rein in order to avoid falling off. Similarly, the ego checks and inhibits id impulses, but it is more or less constantly at the mercy of the stronger but more poorly organized id. The ego has no strength of its own but borrows energy from the id. In spite of this dependence on the id, the ego sometimes comes close to gaining complete control, for instance, during the prime of life of a psychologically mature person.

As children begin to experience parental rewards and punishments, they learn what to do in order to gain pleasure and avoid pain. This is an ego function, inasmuch as very young children are still exclusively concerned with self. As they reach five or six years of age, they identify with their parents and begin to learn what they should and should not do. This is the origin of the superego.

Superego

In Freudian psychology, the **superego,** or above-I, is the moral or ethical province of personality. It is guided by the **idealistic principle** as opposed to the pleasure principle of the id and the realistic principle of the ego. The superego grows out of the ego, and, like the ego, it has no energy of its own. However, the superego differs from the ego in one important respect; it has no contact with the outside world and is therefore unrealistic in its demands for perfection (Freud, 1923/1961a).

The superego has two subsystems, the **conscience** and the **ego-ideal.** Freud did not clearly distinguish between these two functions, but, in general, the conscience results from experiences with punishments for improper behavior, whereas the ego-ideal develops when a child is rewarded for proper behavior. A primitive conscience comes into existence when the child conforms to parental standards out of fear of loss of love or approval. Later, during the Oedipal phase of development, these ideals are internalized through identification with the mother and father. (The Oedipus complex will be discussed in a later section.)

The well-developed superego acts to control sexual and aggressive impulses through the process of repression. It cannot produce repressions by itself, but it can order the ego to do so. The superego watches closely over the ego, judging its actions and intentions. Guilt is the result when the ego acts, or even intends to act, contrary to the moral standards of the superego. Feelings of inferiority will arise if the ego is unable to meet the superego's standards of perfection. Guilt, then, is a function of the conscience; inferiority feelings stem from the ego-ideal (Freud, 1933/1964).

The superego is not concerned with the happiness of the ego. It strives blindly and unrealistically toward perfection. It is unrealistic in the sense that it does not take into consideration the difficulties or impossibilities faced by the ego in carrying out its orders. Not all its demands, of course, are impossible to fulfill, just as not all demands of parents and other authority figures are impossible to fulfill. The superego, however, is like the id in that it is completely ignorant of, and unconcerned with, the practicability of its requirements. One might guess, for example, that George's ego-ideal has higher standards for order than even George is able to obtain. This demand for perfection keeps George's ego working hard, but never completely successfully.

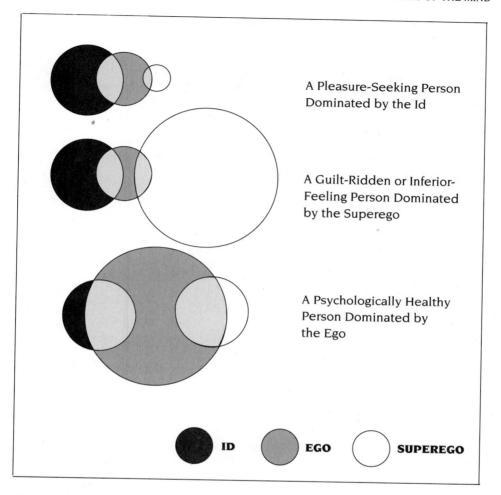

A Pleasure-Seeking Person
Dominated by the Id

A Guilt-Ridden or Inferior-
Feeling Person Dominated
by the Superego

A Psychologically Healthy
Person Dominated by
the Ego

ID   EGO   SUPEREGO

Figure 2.3   *The Relationship among Id, Ego, and Superego in Three Hypothetical Persons*

Freud (1933/1964) pointed out that the divisions between the different regions of the mind are not sharp and well-defined. The development of the three divisions varies widely in different individuals. For some, the superego does not grow after childhood; for others, the superego may dominate the personality at the cost of guilt and inferiority feelings. For yet others, the ego and superego may take turns controlling personality, which results in extreme fluctuations of mood and alternating cycles of self-confidence and self-deprecation. In the healthy individual, the id, ego, and superego are well integrated and operate in harmony and with a minimum of conflict. Figure 2.3 shows the relationships among id, ego, and superego in three hypothetical persons. The first person, with a dominating id and a weak ego, has a superego so feeble that it is not capable of counterbalancing the incessant demands of the id. The second person, with strong feelings of either guilt or inferiority and a weak ego, will experience many conflicts because the ego cannot arbitrate the strong but opposing demands of the superego and the id. The third person, with an ego that has incorporated many of the demands of the id and nearly all those of the superego, is a psychologically healthy individual, one who is in control of both the pleasure principle and the moralistic principle.

DYNAMICS OF PERSONALITY

Levels of mental life and provinces of the mind refer to the *structure* or composition of personality. But personalities also *do* something, so Freud postulated a *dynamic* or motivational principle to explain the driving forces behind people's actions. To Freud, people are motivated to seek pleasure and to reduce tension and anxiety. This motivation is derived from psychical and physical energy that springs from the instincts.

Instincts

Freud used the German word "Trieb" to refer to a drive or a stimulus within the person. This term is usually translated as **instinct,** but it might more properly be called "drive" or "impulse." An instinct, then, is an internal drive or impulse that operates as a constant motivational force. As an internal stimulus it differs from external stimuli in that it cannot be avoided through flight.

According to Freud (1933/1964), the many individual instincts can all be grouped under two major drives: the **life instinct,** generally called Eros or sex, and the **death instinct**, sometimes known as destruction or aggression. Instincts originate in the id, but they come under the control of the ego. Each instinct has its own form of psychic energy. The force by which the life or sexual instinct works is called **libido**; the psychic energy of the death instinct was never named.

The Sexual Instinct

The aim of the sexual instinct is to bring about pleasure within the organism by removing the state of sexual excitation. This pleasure, however, is not limited to genital pleasure. The entire body is invested with libido. Besides the genitals, the mouth and anus are especially capable of producing sexual pleasure and are called **erogenous** or erotogenic zones. The ultimate aim of the sexual instinct (reduction of sexual tension) cannot be changed, but the path by which the aim is reached can be varied. It can take either an active or a passive form, or it can be temporarily or permanently inhibited (Freud, 1915/1957a). Because the path is flexible and because sexual pleasure stems from organs other than the genitals, much behavior originally motivated by Eros is difficult to recognize as sexual behavior. To Freud, however, all pleasurable activity is traceable to the sexual instinct.

The flexibility of the sexual *object* or person can bring about a further disguise of Eros. The erotic object can easily be transformed or displaced. Libido can be withdrawn from one person and placed in a state of free-floating tension, or it can be reinvested in another person, including the self. For example, an infant prematurely forced to give up the nipple as a sexual object may substitute the thumb as an object of oral pleasure.

Freud called the sexual instinct conservative because the power of its drive is essential to perpetuate the species. Eros can also be called conservative because it protects individual life. For example, the infant, dominated by the pleasure principle, sucks from the nipple in order to gain sexual pleasure, but, at the same time, it acquires the nourishment essential to life.

Eros manifests itself in many ways, including narcissism, love, sadism, and masochism. The last two also possess generous components of the death instinct.

NARCISSISM.   During early infancy a child is primarily self-centered, with its libido invested almost exclusively in its own ego. This condition, which is universal, is known as **primary narcissism.** As the ego develops, the child usually gives up much of its primary narcissism and develops a greater interest in others. In Freud's language, narcissistic libido is then transformed into object libido. During puberty, however, adolescents often redirect the libido back to the ego and become preoccupied with personal appearance and other self interests. This pronounced **secondary narcissism** is not universal, but a moderate degree of self-love is common to nearly everyone (Freud, 1914/1957).

LOVE.   A second manifestation of Eros is love, which develops when the libido is invested in an object or person other than self. The child's first sexual interest is the person who cares for it, generally the mother. During infancy the child of either sex experiences sensual love for the mother, but overt sexual love for members of one's family ordinarily is repressed, and a second type of love comes into existence. This is called aim-inhibited love because the original aim of reducing sexual tension is inhibited or repressed. Aim-inhibited love continues throughout a lifetime, with the person loving parents, brothers, and sisters in a nonsexual way.

Obviously, love and narcissism are closely interrelated. Narcissism, of course, involves the love of self, whereas love is often accompanied by narcissistic tendencies, as when a person loves another who serves as an ideal or model of what one would like to be.

SADISM AND MASOCHISM.   Two other instincts that are also intertwined are sadism and masochism. Not only are they inseparable, one from another, but they are interwoven with the life instincts—narcissism and love—as well as being strongly endowed with psychic energy from the death instinct (Freud, 1933/1964).

Sadism is the instinct manifested when sexual pleasure is attained from inflicting pain or humiliation on another. Carried to an extreme, it is considered a sexual perversion, but in moderation sadism is a common need and exists to some extent in all sexual relationships. It is perverted when the sexual aim of erotic pleasure becomes secondary to the destructive aim (Freud, 1905/1953c).

Masochism, like sadism, is a common need, but it becomes a perversion when Eros becomes subservient to the destructive instinct. Masochists experience sexual pleasure from suffering pain and humiliation inflicted either by themselves or by others. Because masochists can provide self-inflicted pain, they do not depend on another person for the satisfaction of masochistic needs. Sadists, on the other hand, must seek and find another person on whom to inflict pain or humiliation. In this respect, they are more dependent than masochists on other people.

Sadism and masochism serve as cornerstones to the two-instinct theory. They demonstrate the workings of the sexual instinct and the destructive instinct in combination.

The Destructive Instinct

When Freud first elevated the death instinct to the level of Eros in *Beyond the Pleasure Principle* (1920/1955a), he did so tentatively and with some caution. With time, however, the destructive instinct became more and more a dogma despite the fact that it was not generally accepted by Freud's close followers.

The aim of the destructive instinct, according to Freud, is to return the organism to an inorganic state. Because the ultimate inorganic condition is death, the final aim of the death instinct is self-destruction. As with the life instinct, the death instinct is flexible and the object of destruction is generally transformed from self to others. It then goes under a pseudonym—**aggression**.

The aggressive tendency is present in everyone and is the explanation for wars, atrocities, religious persecution, and murder, as well as malicious gossip, sarcasm, and humiliation. The death instinct also explains the need for the barriers people have erected to check aggression. For example, commandments like "Love thy neighbor as thyself" are necessary, Freud believed, to inhibit the strong, though usually unconscious, drive to inflict injury upon others. These precepts are actually *reaction formations*. They involve the repression of strong hostile impulses and the overt and obvious expression of the opposite tendency.

Throughout our lifetime, life and death instincts constantly struggle against one another for ascendancy, but at the same time, both must bow to the reality principle, which represents the claims of the outer world. These demands of the real world prevent a direct, unopposed fulfillment of either sex or aggression, create conflict and anxiety, and relegate many sexual and aggressive desires to the realm of the unconscious.

Anxiety

As important as they are, instincts must share the center of Freudian dynamic theory with the concept of **anxiety**. In defining anxiety, Freud (1933/1964) emphasized that it is a felt, affective, unpleasant state, accompanied by a physical sensation that warns the person against impending danger. The unpleasantness is often vague and hard to pinpoint, but the anxiety itself is always felt.

Only the ego can produce or feel anxiety, but the id, superego, and the external world each are involved in one of the three kinds of anxiety that Freud identified. The ego's dependence on the id results in neurotic anxiety; its dependence on the superego produces moral anxiety; and its dependence on the outer world leads to realistic anxiety.

Neurotic anxiety is defined as apprehension about an unknown danger. The feeling itself exists in the ego, but it originates from id impulses. People may experience neurotic anxiety in the presence of a teacher, employer, or some other authority figure, because they earlier felt unconscious feelings of destructiveness against one or both of their parents. During childhood these feelings of hostility were often accompanied by fear of punishment, and this fear became generalized into unconscious neurotic anxiety.

A second type of anxiety, **moral anxiety**, stems from the conflict between the ego and the superego. After we establish our superego, usually by the age of five or six, we may experience anxiety as an outgrowth of the conflict between our realistic needs and the dictates of our superego. Moral anxiety, for example, would result from sexual temptations if we believe that yielding to the temptation would be morally wrong. It may also result from the failure to behave consistently with what we regard as morally right, for example, failing to care for our aging parents or to adequately support our children.

Realistic anxiety, also known as objective anxiety, bears a close resemblance to fear. This third type of anxiety is defined as an unpleasant, nonspecific feeling involving a possible danger. For example we may experience realistic anxiety while driving in heavy, fast-moving traffic in an unfamiliar city, a situation fraught with real, objective danger. However, realistic anxiety is different from fear in that it does not involve a specific fearful object. We would experience fear, for example, if our car suddenly began sliding out of control on an icy highway.

These three types of anxiety are seldom clear-cut or easily separated. They often exist in combination as when fear of water, a real danger, becomes disproportionate to the situation and hence precipitates neurotic anxiety as well as realistic anxiety. This situation indicates that an unknown instinctual danger is connected with the external one.

Anxiety serves as an ego-preserving mechanism because it signals us that some danger is at hand (Freud, 1933/1964). For example, an anxiety dream signals our censor of an impending danger from the instincts, which allows us either to awaken and stop dreaming or to better disguise the manifest level of the dream. The ego, constantly vigilant for signs of threat and unpleasantness, is alerted to potential danger by the experience of anxiety. This signal then stimulates us to mobilize for either flight of defense.

Anxiety is also self-regulating because it precipitates repression, which, in turn, reduces the pain of anxiety (Freud, 1933/1964). If the ego had no recourse to defensive behavior, the anxiety would become intolerable. For example, when people suffering from claustrophobia are prevented from enjoying the defensive behavior of avoiding enclosed spaces, they frequently become overwhelmed with anxiety and paralyzed with fear. Individual differences among people are, in part, explained by the unique ways in which they build defenses against anxiety.

DEFENSE MECHANISMS

Defensive behaviors, therefore, serve a useful function by protecting the ego against the pain of anxiety. Freud first elaborated on the idea of **defense mechanisms** in 1926 (Freud, 1926/1959a), but his daughter Anna (A. Freud, 1946) refined the concept and listed the various mechanisms in a single book. Although defense mechanisms are normal and universally used, when carried to an extreme they lead to compulsive, repetitive, and even neurotic behavior. Because we must expend psychic energy to establish and maintain defense mechanisms, the more defensive we are the less psychic energy we have left to satisfy id impulses. This, of course, is precisely the ego's purpose in establishing defense mechanisms—to avoid dealing directly with instinctual demands and to defend itself against the anxiety that accompanies them (Freud, 1926/1959a).

The principal defense mechanisms identified by Freud include repression, reaction formation, fixation, regression, undoing and isolation, projection, and sublimation.

Repression

The most basic defense mechanism, because it is involved in each of the others, is *repression*. Whenever impulses from the id become too threatening, anxiety is intensified to the point where the ego can no longer tolerate it. To protect itself, the ego represses the instinct; that is, it forces the unwanted feeling into the unconscious (Freud, 1926/1959a). In many cases the repression is then perpetuated for a lifetime. For example, a young boy may repress his sexual feelings for his mother because this impulse causes too much anxiety. The boy may later marry someone who reminds him of his mother, or, if this would cause too much anxiety, he may marry a woman who is quite opposite from his mother. In either case, his incestuous impulses remain unconscious through the process of repression.

No society permits a complete and uninhibited expression of sexual and aggressive instincts. When children have their sexual and aggressive behaviors punished or otherwise suppressed, they learn to be anxious whenever they experience these impulses. This anxiety then leads to a partial repression of their sexual and aggressive drives.

What happens to these impulses after they have become unconscious? Freud (1933/1964) believed that several possibilities exist. First, the impulses may remain unchanged in the unconscious. Second, they could force their way into consciousness in an unaltered form, in which case they would create more anxiety than the person could handle, and the person would be overwhelmed with anxiety. A third and much more common fate of repressed instincts is that they find expression in a displaced or disguised form. The disguise, of course, must be good enough to deceive the ego. Repressed drives may disguise themselves as physical symptoms, for example, sexual impotency in a man troubled by sexual guilt. The impotency prevents the man from having to deal with the guilt and anxiety that would result from normal enjoyable sexual activity. Repressed drives may also find an outlet in dreams, slips of the tongue, or one of the other defense mechanisms.

Reaction Formation

One of the ways in which a repressed impulse may show itself is through adopting a disguise that is directly opposite from its original form. This defense mechanism is called a **reaction formation**. Reactive behavior can be identified by its exaggerated character and by its obsessive and compulsive form (Freud, 1926/1959a). An example of a reaction formation would be a girl who deeply resents and hates her mother, but because society demands affection toward parents, such conscious hatred for her mother would produce too much anxiety. To avoid painful anxiety, the girl concentrates on the opposite impulse—love. Her "love" for her mother, however, is not genuine. It is showy, exaggerated, and overdone. Other people may easily see the true nature of this love, but the girl must deceive herself and cling to her reaction formation, which helps conceal the anxiety-arousing truth that she unconsciously hates her mother.

Fixation

Psychical growth normally proceeds in a somewhat continuous fashion through the various stages of development. The process of psychologically growing up, however, is not without stressful and anxious moments. When the prospect of taking the next step becomes too anxiety-provoking, the ego may resort to the strategy of remaining at the present, more comfortable psychological stage. Such a defense is called **fixation.** Technically, fixation is the permanent attachment of the libido onto an earlier, more primitive stage of development (Freud, 1917/1963). Like other defense mechanisms, fixations are universal. Everyone who continues to derive pleasure from the oral function can be said to have a degree of oral fixation. Anal fixations, too, are not uncommon. George, the middle-aged man we introduced at the beginning of this chapter, has an anal fixation. His entire life has been characterized by excessive compulsiveness and reluctance to change. His fixation serves to avoid the anxiety that would accompany the novelty and flexibility of situations encountered in normal development. Fixations result in rigid, conforming, and compulsive behavior and make psychological growth or change difficult.

Regression

Once the libido has passed a developmental stage, it may, during times of stress and anxiety, revert back to that earlier stage. Such a reversion is known in psychoanalytic theory as **regression** (Freud, 1917/1963). Regressions are quite common and can be seen readily in children. A completely weaned three-year-old child, for example, may regress to demanding a bottle when a baby brother or sister is born. The attention given to the new baby poses a threat to the older child. Regressions are also frequent in older children and in adults. A common way for adults to react to anxiety-producing situations is to revert to earlier, safer, more secure patterns of behavior and to invest their libido on more primitive and more familiar objects. Under extreme stress one adult may adopt the fetal position, another may return home to her mother, and still another may react by remaining all day in bed, well covered from the cold and threatening world. Regressive behavior is similar to fixated behavior in that it is rigid and infantile. Regressions, however, are usually temporary, whereas fixations demand a more or less permanent expenditure of psychic energy.

Undoing and Isolation

Two defense mechanisms that are closely related to one another and can be discussed under a single heading are **undoing** and **isolation**. Freud (1926/1959a) felt that undoing and isolation are important variations of repression and deserve to be considered separately from it.

Undoing and isolation each serve in an auxiliary position to the basic defense mechanism of repression, but they are distinguished from repression by their close association with repetitive and ceremonial acts and with persistent and recurrent thoughts. Freud believed that undoing and isolation emerge when true repression would block out too much reality. The symptoms of undoing and isolation—*compulsions* and *obsessions*—do not remove the ego as far from the real world; that is, they do not block out as much of the earlier, painful experience as do hysteria and amnesia, both symptoms of repression.

Undoing is a type of repression in which the ego attempts to do away with unpleasant experiences and their consequences. It is like negative magic in that ideas or events are made to disappear, erased through a compulsive ceremonial act performed for that purpose. The ceremonial act cancels out the earlier event, so that the ego is convinced that it did not happen. A classical example of undoing is found in Shakespeare's account of Lady Macbeth as she ceremonially rubs her hands in an effort to wash away the guilt of Duncan's murder. By cleansing her hands she hopes to undo the part she played in the king's death. Her attempts at repressing guilt, however, do not meet with complete success. When undoing is complete, no conscious memory of the guilt-producing event remains.

According to Freud (1926/1959a), undoing is the salient feature in compulsion neuroses. (A **compulsion** involves the irresistible repetition of an act.) Undoing can be either severe or mild. An example of severe undoing would be an extremely compulsive man who repeats in a desirable manner an event that happened in an undesirable way, thus preventing his ego from having to deal with the unwanted event. His behavior then becomes exceedingly rigid and inflexible, inasmuch as he must expend psychic energy to maintain the compulsions and to repress the unwanted experience.

Undoing shades into normal behavior, where it may consist of repeatedly making the same mistakes, habitually and ritualistically wasting time, or compulsively looking in the same place for a "lost" possession. In normal undoing the person looks away from an unpleasant experience as if it had never happened. Repression is not complete in normal undoing, but operates with enough strength to keep the repressed experience from regularly intruding on the conscious mind. This differs from severe undoing where the attempt is to make the past completely nonexistent.

A closely related defense mechanism is isolation, a maneuver that keeps an unpleasant experience isolated in the unconscious by establishing a period of blacked-out affect immediately following the experience. With isolation the person simply does nothing and feels nothing following the painful event. This lack of affect severs the associations between the event and all subsequent experiences. The undesirable event is thus isolated and cannot be reproduced through ordinary thought processes. Although Freud (1926/1959a) did not clearly differentiate between undoing and isolation, some general distinctions exist. Undoing most often produces compulsions, whereas isolation leads to obsessive symptoms (an **obsession** is a persistent or recurrent idea, usually involving an urge toward some action). Also, undoing wipes out or at least partially erases an event, whereas isolation leaves the event intact but emotionally isolates it from other events in one's experience.

Severe isolation is characterized by persistent and debilitating obsessions, which often have their source in the taboo of touching. Because touching is the immediate aim of both sex and aggression, the obsessive person builds up a prohibition against physical contact. The prohibition becomes abnormal when the obsessive person avoids all physical contact with others, and is plagued incessantly by thoughts of touching. The person refuses to shake hands or kiss another and recoils in horror when inadvertently touched.

Freud (1926/1959a) believed that a degree of isolation is common in normal behavior where the ego functions to keep certain thoughts separate. This breaks the chain of associations between those ideas and protects the ego from having to recall an anxiety-arousing experience.

Projection

When an internal, instinctual impulse becomes too anxiety-provoking, the ego may get rid of it by attributing the unwanted impulse to an external object, usually another person. This is the defense mechanism of **projection**, which can be defined as seeing in others unacceptable feelings or tendencies that actually reside in one's own unconscious (Freud, 1915/1957b). For example, a young woman may consistently interpret the actions of older men as attempted seductions. Consciously, the thought of sexual intercourse with older men may be intensely repugnant to her, but buried in her unconscious is a strong erotic attraction to these men. In general, the more strongly she protests, the more likely it is that she is projecting her own sexual feelings onto others. In this example, the young woman deludes herself into believing that she has no sexual feelings for older men. Although this projection erases most of her anxiety and guilt, it permits her to maintain a sexual interest in men who remind her of her father.

An extreme type of projection is **paranoia**, a mental disorder characterized by powerful delusions of jealousy and persecution. Paranoia is not an inevitable outcome of projection but simply a severe variety of it. According to Freud (1922/1955), a crucial distinction between projection and paranoia is that paranoia is always characterized by repressed homosexual feelings toward the persecutor. Freud believed that the persecutor is inevitably a former friend of the same sex, although sometimes the person may transfer his or her delusions onto a person of the opposite sex. When homosexual impulses become too powerful, the persecuted paranoiac defends himself by *reversing* these feelings and then projecting them onto their original object. The transformation proceeds as follows. Instead of saying, "I love him," the paranoid person says, "I hate him." Because this also produces too much anxiety, he says, "He hates me." At this point, he has disclaimed all responsibility and can say, "I like him fine, but he's got it in for me." The central mechanism in all paranoia is projection with accompanying delusions of jealousy and persecution.

Sublimation

Each of the above defense mechanisms serves the individual by protecting the ego from anxiety, but each is of dubious value from society's viewpoint. According to Freud (1917/1963), one mechanism helps both the individual and the social group. This is **sublimation**, defined as the repression of the genital aim of Eros by substituting a cultural or social aim. The sublimated aim is expressed most obviously in creative cultural accomplishments such as art, music, and literature, but more subtly, it can be manifested in all human relationships and all social pursuits. A prominent example of sublimation, Freud (1914/1953) believed, is the art of Michelangelo, who found an indirect outlet for his libido in painting and sculpting. In most people sublimations combine with direct expression of Eros and result in a kind of balance between social interests and personal pleasure. Most of us are capable of sublimating a part of our libido in the service of higher cultural values, while at the same time retaining sufficient amounts of the sexual instinct to pursue individual erotic pleasure.

In summary, all defense mechanisms protect the ego against anxiety. They are universal in that everyone engages in defensive behavior to some degree. Each defense mechanism combines with repression, and each can be carried to the point of **psychopathology.** Normally, however, defense mechanisms are beneficial to the individual and harmless to society and, in the case of sublimations, they can even be beneficial to society.

STAGES OF DEVELOPMENT

Psychosexual development was seen by Freud as proceeding from birth to maturity in ordered, but overlapping, stages. The first four or five years of life, or the **infantile stage**, is the most crucial for personality formation. It is followed by a six- or seven-year period of **latency** during which time little or no sexual growth takes place. At puberty there is a renaissance of sexual life, and the **genital stage** is ushered in. Psychosexual development eventually culminates in **maturity**.

Infantile Period

One of Freud's (1905/1953c, 1923b/1961b) most important assumptions is that infants possess a sexual life and go through a period of pregenital sexual development during the first four or five years after birth. At the time Freud originally postulated the existence of infantile sexuality, the concept, though not new, was met with some resistance, but today nearly all close observers accept the idea that children delight in pleasure gained through the erogenous zones, show an interest in the genitals, and even manifest sexual excitement. Childhood sexuality differs from adult sexuality in that it is not capable of reproduction and is exclusively autoerotic. With both children and adults, however, the sexual instinct can be satisfied through organs other than the genitals. The mouth and anus are particularly sensitive to erogenous stimulation (Freud, 1933/1964).

Freud (1917/1963) divided the infantile stage into three phases according to which of the three primary erogenous zones is undergoing the most salient development. The oral phase begins first and is followed by the anal phase and the phallic phase in that order. The three infantile stages overlap, with earlier phases continuing after the onset of later ones.

Oral Phase

Because the mouth is the first organ to provide the infant with pleasure, Freud's first infantile stage of development is the **oral phase**. The infant obtains life-sustaining nourishment through the oral cavity, but, beyond that, it also gains pleasure through the act of sucking.

Infants satisfy oral needs one way or another.

The sexual aim of *early oral* activity is to incorporate or receive into one's own body the instinctual object-choice—the nipple. During this *oral-receptive* phase the infant feels no ambivalence toward the pleasurable object, and its needs are usually satisfied with a minimum of frustration and anxiety. As the baby grows older, however, feelings of frustration and anxiety are more likely to be experienced as a result of scheduled feedings, increased time lapses between feedings, and eventual *weaning.* These anxieties are generally accompanied by feelings of ambivalence toward the love object (mother), and by the increased ability of the budding ego to defend itself against the environment and against anxiety (Freud, 1933/1964).

The infant's defense against the environment is greatly aided by the emergence of teeth. At this point the baby passes into a second oral phase, which Freud (1933/1964) called the *oral-sadistic* period. During this phase the baby responds to others through such diverse means as biting, cooing, closing the mouth, smiling, and crying. The child's first autoerotic experience is thumb sucking, which it uses as a defense against anxiety. Thumb sucking satisfies the sexual, but not the nutritional, needs of the infant.

As the child grows older, the mouth continues to be an erogenous zone, but by the time a person becomes an adult, oral needs can be gratified in a variety of ways, including sucking candy, chewing gum, biting pencils, overeating, smoking cigarettes, "chewing out" other people, and making biting, sarcastic remarks.

Anal Phase

The aggressive instinct, which during the first year of life takes the form of oral sadism, reaches a fuller development during the second year when the anus emerges as a sexually pleasurable zone. Because this period is characterized by satisfaction gained through aggressive behavior and through the excretory function, Freud (1933/1964) called it the *sadistic-anal phase* of development, but more recently it has simply been called the **anal phase**. The anal phase is divided into two subphases, early and late.

During the *early anal period*, children receive satisfaction by destroying or losing objects. At this time the destructive nature of the sadistic instinct is stronger than the erotic one, and children often behave aggressively toward their parents for frustrating them with *toilet training*.

Then when children enter the *late anal period*, they sometimes take a friendly interest toward their feces, an interest that stems from the erotic pleasure of defecating. Frequently, children will present their feces to the parents as a valued prize (Freud, 1933/1964). If their behavior is accepted and praised by their parents, then they are likely to grow into generous and magnanimous adults. On the other hand, if their "gift" is rejected in a punitive fashion, they may adopt another method of obtaining anal pleasure—withholding the feces until the pressure becomes both painful and erotically stimulating. This mode of narcissistic and masochistic pleasure lays the foundation for the **anal character**—people like our case study George, who continue to receive erotic satisfaction by keeping and possessing objects and by arranging them in an excessively neat and orderly fashion. Freud (1933/1964) hypothesized that people who grow into anal characters were, as children, overly resistant to toilet training, often holding back their feces and prolonging the time of training beyond that usually required. This anal eroticism becomes transformed into the **anal triad** of *orderliness*, *stinginess*, and *obstinacy*, which typifies the adult anal character.

Although compulsive neatness is George's most outstanding trait, he also has a high degree of stinginess and obstinacy. His stinginess might better be termed parsimoniousness because George is exceedingly careful in spending his money, rather than petty or ungenerous. He lives in an expensive house, dresses well, and is a gracious host, always offering guests coffee, tea, or a soft drink. Nevertheless, saving money (as well as childhood toys and possessions) is extremely important to George, and he has accumulated a savings account far in excess of what might be expected from his modest income.

Similarly, George's obstinacy or stubbornness is well hidden from the casual observer. He is not argumentative or aggressive, but he persists in his beliefs and opinions long after others would have discarded them as childish or immature. George, then, is characterized by the anal triad of compulsive neatness, miserliness, and stubbornness, with neatness being his most visible trait.

Not all anal erotic impulses are transformed into these three adult character traits. Some are more completely repressed and emerge in the form of neurotic symptoms, and others find expression during the phallic and genital periods of development. Freud (1933/1964) believed that, for girls, anal eroticism is carried over into penis envy during the phallic stage and can eventually be expressed by giving birth to a baby. He also believed that in the unconscious the concepts of penis and baby—because both are referred to as a "little one"—mean the same thing. Also, feces, because of its elongated shape and because it has been removed from the body, is indistinguishable from baby, and all three concepts—penis, baby, and feces are represented by the same symbols in dreams (Freud, 1917/1955b).

No basic distinction exists between male and female psychosexual growth during either the oral stage or the sadistic-anal phase. Children of either gender can develop an active or a passive orientation. The active attitude often is characterized by what Freud (1933/1964) considered the masculine qualities of dominance and sadism, whereas the passive orientation is usually marked by the feminine qualities of voyeurism and masochism. However, either orientation, or any combination of the two, can develop in both girls and boys.

Phallic Phase

At approximately age three or four, the child enters into a third stage of infantile development—the **phallic phase**, a time when the genital area becomes the leading erogenous zone. This stage is marked for the first time by a dichotomy between male and female development, a distinction that Freud (1925/1961) believed to be due to the anatomical differences between the sexes. Freud (1924/1961, p. 178) took Napoleon's remark, "History is destiny" and changed it to "Anatomy is destiny." This dictum underlies Freud's belief that physical differences between males and females account for many important psychological differences.

Masturbation, which originated during the oral stage, now enters a second, more crucial phase. During the phallic stage, masturbation is nearly universal, but because parents generally suppress these activities, children usually repress their conscious desire to masturbate by the time their phallic period comes to an end. Just as earlier experiences with weaning and toilet training help shape the foundation of psychosexual development, so, too, do children's experiences with the *suppression of masturbation* (Freud, 1933/1964). Children's experience with the Oedipus complex, the prominent feature of the phallic phase, however, plays an even more important role in personality development.

MALE OEDIPUS COMPLEX.   Preceding the phallic stage, Freud (1925/1961) said, the infant boy forms an *identification* with his father; that is, he wants to *be* his father. Later the boy develops a sexual desire for his mother; that is, he wants to *have* his mother. These two wishes do not appear mutually contradictory to the underdeveloped ego, so they are able to exist side by side for a time. When the boy finally recognizes their inconsistency, he gives up his identification with the father and retains the stronger feeling—the desire to have his mother. The boy now sees his father as a rival for the mother's love. He desires to do away with his father and to possess his mother in a sexual relationship. This condition of rivalry toward the father and incestuous feelings toward the mother is known as the simple **male Oedipus complex.** The term is taken from the Greek tragedy by Sophocles in which Oedipus, King of Thebes, is destined by fate to kill his father and marry his mother.

Freud (1923/1961a) believed that the bisexual nature of the child (of either sex) complicates the picture. Before he enters the Oedipus stage, the young boy develops, to some degree, a feminine disposition. During the Oedipal period, therefore, his feminine nature may lead him to display *affection toward his father* and express *hostility toward his mother*, while, at the same time, his masculine tendency disposes him toward hostility for father and lust for mother. During this ambivalent condition, known as the *complete Oedipus complex*, affection and hostility co-exist because one or both feelings may be unconscious. Freud believed that these feelings of ambivalence in the boy play a role in the evolution of the **castration complex**, which in boys takes the form of **castration anxiety** or the fear of losing the penis.

To Freud (1905/1953c, 1917/1963, 1923/1961b), the castration complex begins after the young boy (who has assumed that all other people, including girls, have genitals like his own) becomes aware of the absence of a penis on girls. This awareness becomes the greatest emotional shock of his life. After a period of mental struggle and attempts at denial, he is forced into the conclusion that the girl has had her penis cut off. This conclusion may be reinforced by parental threats to castrate or otherwise punish him for his sexual behaviors. Thus, the boy is forced to conclude that the little girl has been punished for masturbation or for seduction of her mother by having her penis removed. The threat of castration now becomes a dreaded possibility. This castration anxiety cannot long be tolerated. The boy represses his impulses toward sexual activity, including his fantasies of carrying out a seduction of his mother.

Prior to the sudden experience of castration anxiety, little boys may have "seen" the genital area of little girls or their mother, but this sight does not automatically instigate the castration complex. Castration anxiety bursts forth only when the boy's ego is mature enough to comprehend the connection between sexual desires and the removal of the penis.

Freud believed that castration anxiety was present in all boys, even those not personally threatened by their fathers or others with the removal of the penis or the stunting of its growth. According to Freud (1933/1964), a boy does not need to receive a clear threat of castration. Any mention of injury or shrinkage in connection with the penis is sufficient to activate the child's phylogenetic endowment. As we have seen, *phylogenetic endowment* is capable of filling the gaps of our individual experiences with the inherited experiences of our ancestors. Ancient man's fear of castration supports the individual child's experiences and results in universal castration anxiety. Freud (1933/1964, p.86) stated: "It is not a question of whether castration is really carried out; what is decisive is that the danger threatens from the outside and that the child believes in it." He went on to say that "hints at . . . punishment must regularly find a phylogenetic reinforcement in him."

Ideally, the Oedipus complex should be dissolved and replaced by a mature superego. If, however, the Oedipus complex is merely repressed, it later expresses itself in some neurotic form (Freud, 1924/1961).

Once the Oedipus complex is dissolved or repressed, the boy surrenders his incestuous desires and develops feelings of tender love for his parent. He may identify with either the father or the mother, depending on the strength of his feminine disposition. Normally identification is with the father, but it is not the same as pre-Oedipal identification. The boy no longer wants to be his father; instead, he uses the father as a model for determining right and wrong behavior. He introjects or incorporates the father's authority into his own ego, thereby sowing the seeds of a mature superego. The budding superego takes over the father's prohibitions against incest and ensures the continued repression of the Oedipus complex (Freud, 1933/1964).

FEMALE OEDIPUS COMPLEX.   The female phallic phase takes a different and more complicated path for girls than the one it follows for boys. To understand it we must realize that for girls the castration complex, which takes the form of penis envy, *precedes* the Oedipus complex. The opposite is true with the boy, for whom the castration complex (castration anxiety) follows and breaks up the Oedipus complex.

Differences between boys' and girls' Oedipus complexes are due to anatomical differences between the sexes (Freud, 1925/1961). Like the boy, the pre-Oedipal girl assumes that all other children have genitals similar to her own. Soon she discovers that boys not only possess different genital equipment, but apparently something extra. She becomes envious of this appendage, feels cheated, and desires to have a penis. This experience of **penis envy** is a powerful force in the formation of the girl's personality. Unlike castration anxiety in boys, which is quickly repressed, penis envy may last for years in one form or another. Freud (1933/1964) believed that penis envy is often expressed as a wish to be a boy or a desire to have a man. Almost universally, it is carried over into a wish to have a baby, and eventually it may find expression in the act of giving birth to a baby, especially a boy.

Preceding the castration complex, the girl has established an identification with her mother similar to that developed by the boy, in that she fantasizes being seduced by her mother. These incestuous feelings, according to Freud (1933/1964), are later turned into hostility when the girl holds her mother responsible for bringing her into the world without a penis. Her libido is then turned toward her father who can satisfy her wish for a penis by giving her a baby, an object that to her has become a substitute for the phallus. The desire for sexual intercourse with the father and accompanying feelings of hostility for the mother are known as the **female Oedipus complex**. Incidentally, Freud (1920/1955b, 1931/1961) objected to the term *Electra Complex*, sometimes used by others when referring to the female Oedipus complex, because it suggests a direct parallel between male and female development during the phallic stage. Freud believed that no such parallel exists from the phallic stage onward and that differences in anatomy determine different courses in male and female sexual development.

Not all girls, however, transfer their sexual interest onto their fathers and develop hostility toward their mothers. Freud (1931/1961, 1933/1964) suggested that when pre-Oedipal girls acknowledge their castration and recognize their inferiority to boys, they will rebel in one of three ways. First, they may give up their sexuality—

both the feminine and the masculine dispositions—and develop an intense hostility toward their mothers; second, they may cling defiantly to their masculinity, hoping for a penis and fantasizing being a man; and third, they may develop normally, that is, they may take their fathers as a sexual choice and undergo the simple Oedipus complex that we have been discussing. A girl's choice is influenced in part by her inherent bisexuality and the degree of masculinity she developed during the pre-Oedipal period.

The simple female Oedipus complex is resolved when the girl gives up masturbatory activity, surrenders her sexual desire for her father, and identifies once again with her mother. However, the female Oedipus complex is usually broken up more slowly and less completely than the male's. Because the superego is built from the relics of the shattered Oedipus complex, Freud (1924/1961, 1933/1964) believed that the girl's superego is usually weaker, more flexible, and less severe than the boy's. The reason the girl's superego is not as strict as the boy's is traceable to the difference between the sexes during their Oedipal histories. For boys, castration anxiety follows the Oedipus complex, breaks it up nearly completely, and renders unnecessary the continued expenditure of psychic energy on its remnants. Once the Oedipus complex is shattered, energy used to maintain it is then free to establish a superego. For girls, however, the Oedipus complex *follows* the castration complex (penis envy) and, because girls do not experience a threat of castration, they experience no traumatic sudden shock. The female Oedipus complex is only incompletely resolved by the girl's gradual realization that she may lose the love of her mother and that sexual intercourse with her father is not forthcoming. Her libido thus remains partially expended to maintain the castration complex and its relics, thereby blocking some psychic energy that might otherwise be used to build a strong superego (Freud, 1931/1961). The simple male and female Oedipus complexes are summarized in Figure 2.4.

Freud presented his views on the female Oedipus complex more tentatively than he did his ideas regarding the male phallic stage. Nevertheless, his views on

Male Phallic Phase

1. **Oedipus complex** (Sexual desires for the mother; hostility for the father)

2. **Castration complex** in the form of **castration anxiety** shatters the Oedipus complex

3. **Identification** with father

4. Strong **superego** replaces the nearly completely dissolved Oedipus complex

Female Phallic Phase

1. **Castration complex** in the form of **penis envy**

2. **Oedipus complex** develops as an attempt to obtain a penis (Sexual desires for the father; hostility for the mother)

3. Gradual realization that the Oedipal desires are self-defeating

4. **Identification** with the mother

5. Weak **superego** replaces the partially dissolved Oedipus complex

Figure 2.4   *Separate Paths of the Simple Male and Female Phallic Phases*

feminine development have been attacked as being sexist and uncomplimentary to women (Balmary, 1979/1982; Chodorow, 1989; Gallop, 1982; Irigaray, 1986). Throughout his career he often proposed theories without much clinical or experimental evidence to support them. With most of these theories, he would later come

What Does the Woman Want?

In a letter to his friend Marie Bonaparte, written near the end of his life, Freud asked the question, "What does the woman want?" Such a question, posed after 50 years of theorizing, suggests that Freud regarded women not only as quite different from men but as enigmas, not comprehensible to the male gender.

Although several women, such as Bonaparte, Helene Deutsch, Melanie Klein, Joan Riviere, Lou Andreas-Salomé, and Anna Freud, exerted some influence on Freud, they were not able to convince him that similarities between the genders outweigh differences. However, these women also were products of the first half of the 20th century, and their views, though generally quite liberal for that time, would now be considered by some observers to relegate women to second-class status.

Freud himself was a proper bourgeois Viennese gentleman whose sexual attitudes were formed during a time when women were expected to nurture their husbands, manage the household, care for the children, and stay out of their husbands' business or profession. Martha Freud was no exception to this rule. She showed no interest in Sigmund's professional life, ran the household, provided meals, accepted primary responsibility in rearing their six children, and generally tried to make her husband's life as easy as possible (Gay, 1988).

Freud seemed to have known that many women wanted more from life than what his wife and his mother had, but he seemed to have had a dichotomous view of women. On

the one hand, he saw them as less fit than men to be scientists and philosophers, while on the other, he regarded women as emotionally and physiologically stronger than men (Gay, 1988).

Freud continually grappled with trying to understand women, and his views on femininity changed several times during his lifetime. As a young student, he exclaimed to a friend, "How wise our educators that they pester the beautiful sex so little with scientific knowledge" (quoted in Gay, 1988, p. 522). During the first half of his psychoanalytic career, he viewed male and female psychosexual growth as mirror images of each other, with different but parallel lines of development. From about 1923 onward, however, he proposed the notion that the little girl is a failed boy and the adult woman is a kind of castrated man (Gay, 1988).

Although Freud framed these views in a tentative and provisional manner, he defended them stubbornly and uncompromisingly. When some of his followers objected to his harsh view of women, Freud became even more rigid in his position and insisted that psychological differences between men and women could not be erased by culture because they were the inevitable consequences of anatomical differences between the sexes (Freud, 1925/1961).

Despite his steadfast public position, Freud privately was uncertain that his views on women represented a final answer. One year after his pronouncement that "anatomy is destiny," he expressed some doubts, admitting that his understanding of girls and to see them as established facts, even though he possessed no intervening substantiating evidence. With his theories on women, however, he remained doubtful of their absolute validity for as long as he lived (see box—"What Does the Woman Want?").

women was incomplete. "We know less about the sexual life of little girls than of boys. But we need not feel ashamed of this distinction; after all, the sexual life of adult women is a 'dark continent' for psychology" (Freud, 1926/1959b, p. 212). Then in 1933 he concluded his final essay on femininity with these words.

> That is all I had to say to you about femininity. It is certainly incomplete and fragmentary and does not always sound friendly. But do not forget that I have only been describing women in so far as their nature is determined by their sexual function. It is true that that influence extends very far; but we do not overlook the fact that an individual woman may be a human being in other respects as well. If you want to know more about femininity, enquire from your own experiences of life, or turn to the poets, or wait until science can give you deeper and more coherent information (Freud, 1933/1964, p. 135).

Certainly, Freud meant these words (which today sound quite sexist) to be complimentary to women.

Although some of Freud's close associates inhabited the "dark continent" of womanhood, his most intimate friends were men. Moreover, women such as Marie Bonaparte, Joan Riviere, Lou Andreas-Salomé, and Minna Bernays (his sister-in-law), who did exert some influence on Freud, were mostly cut from a similar pattern. Ernest Jones (1955, p. 421) referred to them as intellectual women with a "masculine cast." These women were quite apart from Freud's mother and his wife, both of whom were proper Viennese wives and mothers whose primary concerns were for their husband and children. Freud's female colleagues and disciples were selected for their intelligence, emotional strength, and loyalty—the same qualities Freud found attractive in men. But none of these women could substitute for a intimate male friend. In August of 1901, Freud wrote to his friend Wilhelm Fliess, "In my life, as you know, woman has never replaced the comrade, the friend" (Masson, 1985, p. 447).

Freud's preference was for male comrades, such as Fliess, Carl Jung, and the six members of his "Palace Guard," a clandestine committee composed of Otto Rank, Karl Abraham, Max Eitingon, Ernest Jones, Sandor Ferenczi, and Hanns Sachs. With these men he could reveal his private thoughts and feelings. Toward women, however, his attitude was more ambivalent. He admired and respected those who projected "masculine" qualities, but he reserved a special passion for his mother and wife, whose "feminine" traits were so attractive to him. What did Freud want from women? Peter Gay expressed the answer well. "Freud wanted only everything from women: strength, tenderness, wildness—and intelligence" (1988, p. 512).

These were qualities that Freud wanted from women, yet he remained in doubt about what women themselves really wanted. Toward the end of his life, he still had to ask, "What does the woman want?" The question itself reveals Freud's sexual bias because it assumes that women all want the same things and that their wants are somehow different from those of men.

Latency Period

Freud believed that, from the fifth or sixth year until puberty, both boys and girls go through a period when psychosexual development is at a standstill. This period in the child's life, the **latency stage**, is brought about partly by the suppression of the sexual instinct and partly by organic factors that owe their existence to prehistoric people. Freud (1913/1953) suggested that the Oedipus complex and the subsequent period of sexual latency could possibly be explained by the following hypothesis. Early in human development a group of brothers, denied the rights to have sexual relations with their mother or sisters, joined together and killed the father. Because they felt affection as well as hostility toward the father, they were left with strong feelings of guilt, which subsequently caused them to develop strong negative attitudes about sexual relations with members of the family and to repress their hostility toward the father. Later, when they became fathers, they suppressed sexual activity in their own children whenever it became noticeable, probably around age three or four. This suppression became complete and a period of sexual latency resulted. After this experience was repeated in different families, clans, or totems over a period of many generations, it became an active, though unconscious force in the individual's psychosexual development. This prohibition of sexual activity, then, is part of our phylogenetic endowment and is one possible explanation for the latency period.

Continued latency is reinforced through constant suppression by parents and teachers and by internal feelings of shame, guilt, and morality. The sexual instinct, of course, still exists during this period, but its aim has been inhibited. The now-sublimated libido now shows itself in social and cultural accomplishments, such as schoolwork and the development of friendships. During this time children form groups or cliques, an impossibility during the infantile period, when the sexual drive was completely autoerotic.

Genital Period

Puberty signals a reawakening of the sexual aim and the beginning of the **genital period**. During puberty the diphasic sexual life of the person enters a second stage, which has certain basic differences from the infantile period (Freud, 1923/1961b). First, adolescents give up autoeroticism and direct their sexual energy toward another person instead of toward themselves. Second, reproduction for the first time is a possibility. Third, although penis envy may continue to linger, the vagina finally obtains the same status for girls that the male organ had for them during infancy, so that boys now see the female organ as a sought-after object rather than a traumatic threat. Fourth, the entire sexual instinct takes on a more complete organization, and the component instincts that had operated somewhat independently during the early infantile period gain a kind of synthesis during adolescence; thus the mouth, anus, and other pleasure-producing areas take an auxiliary position to the genitals, which now attain supremacy as an erogenous zone.

This synthesis of Eros, the elevated status of the female genital organ, the reproductive capacity of the life instinct, and its direction outward rather than onto the self, represent the major distinctions between infantile and adult sexuality. In several other ways, however, Eros remains more or less unchanged. It may continue to manifest itself in sublimated forms; it may be repressed; or it may be expressed in masturbation or other sexual acts. The subordinated erogenous zones also continue as vehicles of erotic pleasure. The mouth, for example, retains many of its infantile activities, perhaps dropping thumb sucking but possibly adding smoking or prolonged kissing.

Maturity

The genital period begins at puberty and continues throughout the individual's lifetime. It is a stage attained by everyone who reaches physical maturity. In addition, Freud alluded to but never fully conceptualized a period of *psychological maturity*, a stage attained after a person has passed through the earlier developmental periods in an ideal manner. Unfortunately, this seldom happens because we have too many opportunities to develop pathological disorders or neurotic predispositions.

Although Freud never fully conceptualized the notion of psychological maturity, we can draw a sketch of psychoanalytically mature individuals. Such people would have a balance among the structures of the mind, with the ego controlling the id and superego but, at the same time, allowing for reasonable desires and demands (see Figure 2.3). Therefore, the id impulses would be expressed honestly and consciously, with no traces of shame or guilt, and the superego would move beyond parental identification and control, with no remnants of antagonism or incest. The ego-ideal would be realistic and congruent with the ego, and, in fact, the boundary between the superego and the ego would become nearly imperceptible.

Consciousness would play a more important role in the behavior of mature people, who would have only minimal need to repress sexual and aggressive urges. Indeed, most of the repressions of psychologically healthy individuals would emerge in the form of sublimations rather than neurotic symptoms. Because the Oedipus complex is completely or nearly completely dissolved, mature people have few if any traces of sexual and aggressive desires remaining in the unconscious. Therefore, the libido, which was formerly directed toward their parents, would be released to search for both tender and sensual love. In short, psychologically mature people would come through the experiences of childhood and adolescence in control of the psychic energy and with the ego functioning in the center of an ever-expanding world of consciousness.

APPLICATIONS OF PSYCHOANALYTIC THEORY

Freud was an innovative speculator, probably more concerned with theory building than with treating sick people. He spent much of his time conducting therapy, not only to help patients, but to gain the insight into human personality necessary to expound psychoanalytic theory. A circular relationship existed between his theory and practice, with his theoretical framework growing out of his experiences as a practitioner, and his applied psychoanalysis being shaped by his theoretical orientation.

The three practical pillars upon which psychoanalytic theory rests are dream analysis, unconscious slips, and psychotherapy.

Dream Analysis

Throughout his professional career, Freud was continually concerned with the problem of dreams and their meanings, but unlike most other aspects of his theory, he made no major revisions of his ideas on dreams from *The Interpretation of Dreams* (1900/1953) until his death in 1939.

In interpreting dreams Freud felt that the **latent content** must be given priority over the **manifest content**. The latent content refers to the unconscious material, whereas the manifest content is the surface meaning or the conscious description given by the dreamer.

The basic assumption of Freud's dream analysis is that nearly all dreams are *wish-fulfillments*. Some wishes are obvious and are expressed through the manifest content, as when a person goes to sleep hungry and dreams of eating large quantities of delicious food. Most wish-fulfillments, however, are expressed in the latent content and can be known only through interpretation of the dream. The exception to the rule that dreams are wish-fulfillments is found in patients suffering from traumatic neuroses, whose dreams are often composed of repetitions of traumatic experiences. These dreams, which obey the principle of **repetition compulsion** rather than wish-fulfillment, occur frequently with battle-weary soldiers who repeatedly dream of frightening or traumatic experiences (Freud, 1920/1955a, 1933/1964).

Before discussing Freud's method of dream interpretation, we should look at his ideas concerning the construction of dreams. Freud believed that the formation of a dream was not the result of physiological stimuli such as hunger or pain, although at times the manifest content of dreams may come from these sources. Dreams are formed in the unconscious and originate as attempts of our unconscious wishes to become conscious. To do this, the wishes must slip past both the primary and the final censors (refer again to Figure 2.1). Even during sleep, these guardians maintain their vigil, forcing unconscious psychic material to adopt a disguised form. The disguise can operate in two basic ways.

First, the dream content can be distorted through either condensation or displacement. *Condensation* refers to the fact that the manifest dream content is not as extensive as the latent level, indicating that the unconscious material has been abbreviated or condensed before appearing on the manifest level. *Displacement* means that the dream image is replaced by some other idea only remotely related to it (Freud, 1900/1953). Condensation and displacement of content both take place through the use of symbols. Certain images are almost universally represented by seemingly innocuous figures. For example, the phallus may be symbolized by any elongated objects such as sticks, snakes, or knives; the female organ often appears as any small box, chest, or oven; parents appear in the form of a king, queen, governor, or president; the dreamer may take the form of a prince or princess; and a woman may be represented by a room, with an open room standing for a sexually promiscuous woman and a closed room an unobtainable one. Sexual intercourse can be disguised as ascending or descending steep inclines like ladders or stairs, and castration anxiety expresses itself in dreams of growing bald, losing teeth, or any act of cutting (Freud, 1900/1953, 1901/1953, 1917/1963).

Second, dreams can deceive the dreamer through the inhibition and reversal of affect. Strong negative emotions, which ordinarily would result in feelings of unpleasantness if allowed to become conscious, might be completely inhibited. The dreamer, though faced with a fearful or anxiety-provoking situation, feels nothing during the dream. The deceptive nature of the manifest content is also illustrated by the reversal of the affect into its opposite. Deeply felt unconscious hostility can be transformed into love by the workings of the dream. The dreamer is fooled into believing that hate is love or that joy is sorrow, as when one mourns the death of a parent whose extinction would be welcomed by the primitive unconscious (Freud, 1900/1953, 1915/1957a, 1917/1963).

After the dream content has been distorted and the affect has been inhibited or reversed, it appears in its manifest form and may be recalled by the dreamer. The manifest content nearly always relates to conscious or preconscious experience of the previous day (Freud, 1900/1953). Only the latent content, however, has any psychoanalytic importance.

The unconscious wishes that make up the dream usually originate during our early years of life because our childhood wishes are more intense than those we experience as adults (Freud, 1917/1963). This intensity results from the suppression or punishment of infantile sexual and destructive behavior, but the original desires are not erased and may remain for years in the unconscious, finding expression in a disguised form during dreams. Not all dreams, however, originate in childhood repressions—some are expressions of adult wishes. The only requisite is that the wish be psychologically intense enough to force its way out of the unconscious.

In interpreting dreams Freud (1917/1963) ordinarily followed one of two methods. The first was to ask patients to relate the dream and all the associations to it, no matter how unrelated or illogical these associations seemed. Freud believed that such associations revealed the unconscious wish behind the dream. If the dreamer was unable to relate association material, Freud used a second method— dream symbols—to discover the unconscious elements underlying the manifest content. The purpose of both methods (associations and symbols) was to trace the dream formation backward until the latent content was reached. Freud (1900/1953, p. 608) believed that dream interpretation was the most reliable approach to the study of unconscious processes, and he referred to it as the "royal road" to the unconscious.

Anxiety dreams offer no contradiction to the rule that dreams are wish-fulfillments. The explanation is that anxiety belongs to the preconscious system, while the wish belongs to the unconscious. Freud (1900/1953) reported three typical anxiety dreams: the embarrassment dream of nakedness, dreams of the death of a beloved person, and dreams of failing an examination

In the embarrassment dream of nakedness, the dreamer feels shame or embarrassment at being naked or improperly dressed in the presence of strangers. The spectators usually appear quite indifferent, although the dreamer is very much embarrassed. The origin of this dream is the early childhood experience of being undressed in the presence of adults. In the original experience the child feels no embarrassment, but the adults often register disapproval. The pleasure of nakedness, therefore, is repressed and replaced by shame and embarrassment. Freud (1900/1953) believed that wish-fulfillment is served in two ways by this dream. First, the indifference of the spectators fulfills the infantile wish that the witnessing adults refrain from scolding. Second, the fact of nakedness fulfills the wish to exhibit oneself, a desire usually repressed in adults but present in young children.

Dreams of the death of a beloved person also originate in childhood and are wish-fulfillments. If a person dreams of the death of a younger person, the unconscious mind is expressing the wish for the destruction of a younger brother or sister who was a hated rival during the infantile period. When the dead person is older than the dreamer, for example, a parent, the dreamer is fulfilling the Oedipal wish for the death of a parent. If the dreamer feels anxiety and sorrow during the dream, it is because the affect has been reversed. Dreams of the death of a parent are typical in adults, but they do not mean that the dreamer has a present wish for the death of that parent. These dreams were interpreted by Freud (1900/1953) as meaning that, as a child, the dreamer longed for the death of the parent, but the wish was too threatening to find its way into consciousness. Even during adulthood the death wish ordinarily does not appear in dreams unless the affect has been changed to sorrow.

A third typical anxiety dream is of failing an examination in school. According to Freud (1900/1953), the person always dreams of failing an examination that has already been successfully passed, never one that was failed. These dreams usually occur when the dreamer is anticipating a difficult task. By dreaming of failing an examination already passed, the ego can reason, "I passed the earlier test that I was worried about. Now I'm worried about another task, but I'll pass it too. Therefore, I need not be anxious over tomorrow's task." The wish to be free from worry over a difficult job is thus fulfilled.

In summary, Freud believed that dreams are motivated by wish-fulfillments. Their latent content is formed in the unconscious and usually, but not always, has its origin in childhood experiences. The manifest content often stems from experiences of the previous day. The interpretation of dreams serves as the "royal road" to the unconscious, but dreams should never be interpreted without the dreamer's associations to them. Latent material is transformed into manifest content through the dream work. The dream work achieves its goal by the processes of condensation, displacement, and inhibition of affect. The manifest dream may have little resemblance to the latent material, but accurate interpretation reveals the hidden connection by tracing the dream work backward until the unconscious images are revealed.

Freudian Slips

Freud believed that many everyday slips of the tongue or pen, misreadings, incorrect hearings, as well as the misplacing of objects and the temporary forgetting of names or intentions are not chance accidents but reveal the person's unconscious intentions. In writing of these faulty acts, Freud (1901/1960) used the German *Fehlleistung*, or "faulty function," but James Strachey, one of Freud's translators, invented the term **parapraxes** to refer to what many people now simply call "Freudian slips."

Parapraxes or unconscious slips are so common that we usually pay little attention to them and deny that they have any underlying significance. Freud, however, insisted that these faulty acts have meaning; they reveal the real, that is, the unconscious intention or purpose of the person: "They are not chance events but serious mental acts; they have a sense; they arise from the concurrent actions—or perhaps rather, the mutually opposing action—of two different intentions" (Freud, 1917/1963, p. 44). One opposing action emanates from the unconscious, the other from the preconscious. Unconscious slips, therefore, are similar to dreams in that they are a product of both the unconscious and the preconscious, with the unconscious intention being dominant and interfering with and replacing the preconscious one.

The fact that most people strongly deny any meaning behind their parapraxes was seen by Freud as evidence that the slip, indeed, had relevance to unconscious images that must remain hidden from consciousness. A young man once walked into a convenience store, became immediately attracted to the young woman clerk, and ordered a "sex-pack of beer." When the clerk accused him of improper behavior, the young man vehemently protested his innocence. Another man, a hospital patient who had been heavily sedated, bumped into a pretty nurse and exclaimed, "Pardon me, ma'am. I've been heavily seduced." Examples such as this can be extended almost indefinitely. Freud provided many in his book *Psychopathology of Everyday Life* (1901/1960). In all parapraxes the intentions of the unconscious supplant the weaker intentions of the preconscious, thereby revealing the true purpose of the ego.

Psychotherapy

The primary goal of psychoanalytic therapy is to uncover repressed memories. "Our therapy works by transforming what is unconscious into what is conscious, and it works only in so far as it is in a position to effect that transformation" (Freud, 1917/1963, p. 280). More specifically, the purpose of psychoanalysis is "to strengthen the ego, to make it more independent of the superego, to widen its field

Freud's *consulting room*, Vienna.

of perception and enlarge its organization, so that it can appropriate fresh portions of the id. Where id was, there ego shall be" (Freud, 1933/1964, p. 80).

To bring unconscious images to consciousness, Freud (1900/1953, 1905/1953b) utilized two techniques—free association and dream analysis. With **free association**, patients are required to verbalize every thought that comes to their mind, no matter how irrelevant or repugnant it may appear. The purpose of free association is to arrive at the unconscious by starting with a present conscious idea and following it through a train of associations to wherever it leads. The process is not easy and some patients never master it.

For this reason, dream analysis remained a favorite therapeutic technique with Freud. In interpreting dreams, the analyst asks patients to reveal a dream and all thoughts associated with it. In addition to asking for the dreamer's associations, Freud used symbolism to interpret dreams. Although he would suggest possible meanings of symbols, patients had to accept the interpretation and to make additional associations to the dream images. Whether associations and symbols were used individually or in combination, the resulting interpretation usually (but not always) revealed latent content that was sexual in nature.

In order for analytic treatment to be successful, libido previously expended on the neurotic symptom must be freed to work in the service of the ego. This takes place in a two-phase procedure. "In the first, all the libido is forced from the symptoms into the transference and concentrated there; in the second, the struggle is waged around this new object and the libido is liberated from it" (Freud, 1917/1963, p. 455). The transference situation is vital to psychoanalysis. **Transference** refers to the strong sexual or aggressive feelings, positive or negative, that patients develop toward the analyst during the course of treatment. Transference feelings are unearned by the therapist and are merely transferred to her or him from patients' earlier experiences, usually with their parents. In other words, patients feel toward the analyst the same way they previously felt toward one or both parents. As long as these feelings manifest themselves as interest or love, transference does not interfere with the process of treatment but is a powerful ally to the therapeutic progress. Positive transference permits patients to more or less relive childhood experiences within the nonthreatening climate of the analytic treatment. However, negative transference in the form of hostility must be recognized by the therapist and explained to patients so that they can overcome any **resistance** to treatment (Freud, 1905/1953a, 1917/1963). Resistance, which refers to a variety of unconscious responses used by patients to block their own progress in therapy, can be seen as a positive sign because it indicates that therapy has advanced beyond superficial material.

Several limitations of psychoanalysis were noted by Freud (1933/1964). First, not all old memories can or should be brought into consciousness. Second, treatment is not as effective with **psychoses** or with constitutional illnesses as it is with the various transference neuroses such as phobias, hysterias, and obsessions. A third limitation, by no means peculiar to psychoanalysis, is that a patient, once cured, may later develop another neurosis. Recognizing these limitations, Freud felt that psychoanalysis could be used in conjunction with other therapies. However, he repeatedly insisted that it could not be shortened or modified in any essential way.

When analytic treatment is successful, patients no longer suffer from debilitating symptoms; they use psychic energy to perform ego functions; and they have an expanded ego that includes previously repressed experiences. They do not experience a major personality change, but they do become what they might have been under the most favorable conditions.

 ## CONCEPT OF HUMANITY

Chapter 1 outlined several dimensions for a concept of humanity. Where does Freud's theory fall on these various dimensions?

The first of these is *determinism vs. free choice*. On this dimension Freud's views on the nature of human nature would fall easily toward determinism. Freud believed that most of our behavior is determined by past events rather than molded by present goals, and that we have little control over our present actions because many of our behaviors are rooted in unconscious strivings that lie beyond our present awareness. Although we usually believe that we are in control of our own lives, Freud believed that, in reality, we have little control over the forces that shape our personality.

Adult personality is largely determined by childhood experiences—especially the Oedipus complex—that have left their residue in the unconscious mind. Freud

(1917/1955a) held that humanity in its history has suffered three great blows to its narcissistic ego. The first was the rediscovery by Copernicus that the earth is not the center of the universe; the second was Darwin's discovery that humans are no different from the other animals; the third, and most damaging blow of all, was Freud's own discovery that we are not in control of our own actions or, as he stated it, "the ego is not master in its own house" (Freud, 1917/1955a, p. 143).

A second and related issue is *pessimism vs. optimism*. Again, psychoanalytic theory must be regarded as essentially pessimistic. According to Freud, we come into the world in a basic state of conflict, with life and death forces operating on us from opposing sides. The innate death wish drives us incessantly toward self-destruction or aggression, while the life instinct causes us to seek blindly after pleasure. The ego experiences a more or less permanent state of conflict, attempting to balance the contradictory demands of the id and superego, while at the same time making concessions to the external world.

Underneath a thin veneer of civilization, we are savage beasts with a natural tendency to exploit others for sexual and destructive satisfaction. Antisocial behavior lies just underneath the surface of even the most peaceful person, Freud believed. Worse yet, we are not ordinarily aware of the reasons for our behavior, nor are we conscious of the hatred we feel for our friends, family, and lovers.

A third approach for viewing humanity is the dimension of *causality vs. teleology*. Basically, Freud believed that our present behavior is mostly shaped by past causes rather than by our goals for the future. We do not move toward a self-determined goal but, instead, are helplessly caught in the struggle between Eros and the death instinct. The two conservative instincts force us to compulsively repeat primitive patterns of behavior. Our behavior as adults is one long series of reactions. We constantly attempt to reduce tension; to relieve anxieties; to repress unpleasant experiences; to regress to earlier, more secure stages of development; and to compulsively repeat behavior that is familiar and safe.

On the dimension of *conscious vs. unconscious*, psychoanalytic theory obviously leans heavily in the direction of unconscious motivation. Freud believed that everything from slips of the tongue to religious experiences is the result of a deep-rooted desire to satisfy sexual or aggressive instincts. These motives make us slaves to our unconscious. Although we are aware of our actions, Freud believed that the motivations underlying those actions are deeply embedded in our unconscious and are frequently quite different from what we believe them to be.

A fifth dimension is *biology vs. culture*. As a physician, Freud's medical training disposed him to see human personality from a biological viewpoint. True, Freud (1913/1953, 1985) frequently speculated about the consequences of prehistorical social units, but the core of his argument was that customs in these early societies have, through evolution, affected our present biological development. Much of our unconscious and many of our infantile fantasies and anxieties have a biological rather than a social origin.

Sixth is the issue of *uniqueness vs. similarities*. On this dimension, psychoanalytic theory takes a middle position. Our evolutionary past gives rise to a great many similarities among people. Nevertheless, our individual experiences, especially those of early childhood, shape each of us in a unique manner and account for many of the differences among personalities.

Related Research

The first criterion of a useful theory is its ability to *generate both descriptive research and testable hypotheses*. By this standard, Freudian theory rates very high because its basic assumptions are so comprehensive that nearly any aspect of human behavior can be tested from a Freudian viewpoint. However, the theory rates low on *verifiability* because little empirical research truly confirms or disconfirms the major tenets of psychoanalytic theory. Thus, the results of most psychological research during the past 40 years can be explained without reference to Freudian principles. Verifiability of psychoanalysis is problematical because the theory relies heavily on an unconscious mind, which lies beyond the scope of direct observation. The unconscious, along with such concepts as the id, ego, and superego, are merely assumptions, and are not capable of being directly tested. The most formidable problem presented by psychoanalysis is the assumption that instincts in the unconscious can be altered, displaced, sublimated, or otherwise transformed. Therefore, *any* finding can be rationalized as fitting into Freudian theory, but such findings do not verify or confirm the theory.

One such example of research that is consistent with Freudian theory but yet does not confirm it is the work conducted by Jonathan Winson. Viewing psychoanalysis from the field of neuroscience, Winson (1985) has found biological evidence consistent with some of Freud's views on the nature of unconscious processes. He has studied rapid eye movement (REM) sleep in a variety of mammals and has suggested that such studies build a bridge between neurobiology and psychoanalysis, and that they provide a biological basis for Freud's concept of the unconscious. Winson hypothesized that the link between brain and psyche began some 140 million years ago when the brains of mammals were undergoing an evolutionary change. As mammals evolved from reptiles, they became less dependent on reflexive action and more dependent on organizing and integrating sensory perceptions. This organization and integration was not instantaneous, but took place over a long period of time. In order to survive, mammals, including humans, must be able to integrate new experiences with past memories without necessarily being conscious of such a process. For humans this is done largely during dreams (REM sleep), when they incorporate early childhood memories into present problem-solving situations.

REM sleep is not found in reptiles but is present in nearly all mammals. One exception is the echidna, a small egg-laying mammal found in the forest of Australia. The echidna possesses a large prefrontal cortex, greater in size relative to the rest of its brain than any other mammal, including humans. Winson's experiments with the echidna have led him to believe that the huge prefrontal cortex of these mammals enables them to correlate new impressions with past experiences, which is necessary for any mammal to survive. Other mammals, however, with their relatively smaller prefrontal cortex, need not accomplish this task while awake, but they use REM sleep (dreams) as a means of associating recent experience with the old.

Winson (1985, p. 209) suggested that REM sleep is fundamental to mammals and that "in man, dreams are a window on the neural process whereby, from early childhood on, strategies for behavior are being set down, modified, or consulted," and that "when Freud dissected and analyzed dreams and from them constructed his concept of the unconscious, he was looking at this process."

Although Winson believed that his neurobiological work supported Freud's idea that most unconscious impulses have a childhood origin, his studies neither confirm nor repudiate psychoanalytic theory.

Another example of research related to psychoanalytic theory is the work on subliminal perception conducted by Lloyd Silverman and his associates (Silverman, 1983, 1985; Silverman & Weinberger, 1985; Weinberger & Silverman, 1990). Findings from their work on subliminal perception are not only consistent with psychoanalytic theory but can be taken as evidence that verifies or supports some Freudian assumptions.

Research in Silverman's laboratory generally uses a design in which subjects are exposed for 4 milliseconds to stimuli intended to activate symbiotic-like fantasies. The most effective of such stimuli, especially with men, has been the message, "Mommy and I are one," accompanied by a picture of a man and woman merged at the shoulders. Silverman & Weinberger (1985) reviewed research that showed consistent effects for this subliminal message in a variety of situations. Male schizophrenic patients exposed repeatedly to the "Mommy and I are one" message showed greater improvement than those exposed to no subliminal message or to different messages. Female schizophrenic patients, however, showed no improvement to this message, but they did show decreased pathology after being exposed to a "Daddy and I are one" message.

Silverman and Weinberger (1985) also reviewed studies that found that the "Mommy and I are one" message was effective in helping people to stop smoking, quit drinking, increase assertiveness, reduce personality disorders, decrease phobic reactions, and develop better eating habits. In addition, a later study (Thorton, Igleheart, & Silverman, 1987) found that male heroin addicts who received this message reported greater reduction in heroin and other drug use, more effectiveness at work, and an increased number of pleasant dreams involving women than did a control group that received the message "People are walking." Weinberger and Silverman (1990) argued that such research demonstrates that psychoanalysis is scientifically testable and that the results of their studies show that activated unconscious symbiotic-like fantasies produce a therapeutic effect in a wide variety of circumstances. They further suggested that the "Mommy and I are one" message may be effective because it reduces anxiety, gratifies dependency needs, or helps patients see the therapist as warm, accepting, and empathic—characteristics that Carl Rogers (see Chapter 16) regarded as necessary to therapeutic change.

CRITIQUE OF FREUD

In criticizing Freud, we must first ask, "Was Freud a scientist?" Although he repeatedly insisted that he was primarily a scientist and that psychoanalysis was a science, Freud's definition of science needs some explanation. When he called psychoanalysis a science, he was attempting to separate it from a philosophy or an ideology; he was not claiming that it was a natural science. The German language and culture of Freud's day made a distinction between a natural science (*Naturwissenschaften*) and a human science (*Geisteswissenschaften*). Unfortunately, James Strachey's translations in the *Standard Edition* make Freud seem to be a natural scientist. However, other scholars (Federn, 1988; Holder, 1988) believe that Freud clearly saw himself as a human scientist, that is, a humanist or scholar, and not a natural scientist.

Bruno Bettelheim (1982, 1983) was also critical of Strachey's translations. He contended that the *Standard Edition* and other English translations used precise medical concepts and misleading Greek and Latin terms instead of the ordinary, often ambiguous German words that Freud had chosen. Such precision tended to render Freud more scientific and less humanistic than he appears to the German reader. To Bettelheim, for instance, psychoanalytic therapy should be seen as a spiritual journey into the depths of the soul (translated by Strachey as "mind") and not a mechanistic analysis of the mental apparatus.

As a result of Freud's 19th-century German view of science, many contemporary psychologists regard his theory-building methods as untenable and rather unscientific. His theories were not based on experimental investigation but rather on subjective observations that Freud made of himself and his clinical patients. These patients were not representative of people in general but came mostly from the middle and upper classes.

Despite these limitations, Freud developed the most comprehensive and most widely known of all personality theories. This widespread reputation of psychoanalysis is due largely to Freud's gifts as a writer, the comprehensiveness of his psychoanalytic theory, his acceptance of unconscious motivation, and finally his heavy emphasis on sex and aggression. For nearly a century his theory has been honored and condemned, glorified and vilified, praised and disparaged.

Apart from this widespread popular and professional interest, the question remains: Was Freud scientific? Present opinions differ on this issue. Paul Kline (1984) argued that Freud used free association as the scientific data base for exploring the unconscious and that his methods were consistent with proper scientific practice. However, even Robert Holt (1989), a strong supporter of Freud, cautioned that Freud's ideas should not be taken as absolute truth, but as beginning points in our understanding of human personality.

Other writers, such as Marie Balmary (1979/1982), Hannah Lerman (1986), Jeffrey Masson (1984), and Paul Vitz (1988), have criticized Freud for adopting a male-oriented theory and for allowing many of his personal biases to influence his theories. These writers generally found Freud to have been unscientific and to have been greatly influenced by his own unconscious needs, especially those springing from the early periods of his life. They agreed with Karl Popper (1963), who regarded psychoanalysis as a pseudo-science and with Hans Eysenck (1990b), who claimed that it was not a science at all but simply a way of interpreting events. Freud's own description of science permits much room for subjective interpretations and indefinite definitions:

> We have often heard it maintained that sciences should be built up on clear and sharply defined basic concepts. In actual fact no science, not even the most exact, begins with such definitions. The true beginning of scientific activity consists rather in describing phenomena and then in proceeding to group, classify and correlate them. Even at the stage of description it is not possible to avoid applying certain abstract ideas to the material in hand, ideas derived from somewhere or other but certainly not from the new observations alone (Freud, 1915/1957a, p. 117).

Perhaps Freud himself left us with the best description of how he built his theories. In 1900, shortly after the publication of *The Interpretation of Dreams*, he wrote to his friend Wilhelm Fliess confessing that "I am actually not at all a man of science, not an observer, not an experimenter, not a thinker. I am by temperament nothing but a conquistador—an adventurer . . . with all the curiosity, daring, and tenacity characteristic of a man of this sort" (Freud, 1985, p. 398).

Although Freud at times may have seen himself as a conquistador, he also believed that he was constructing a scientific theory. How well does that theory meet the criteria for a useful theory that we enumerated in Chapter 1?

We have seen that, despite serious difficulties in testing Freud's assumptions, researchers have conducted studies that relate either directly or indirectly to psychoanalytical theory. Westen (1990) has presented an extensive review of much of this research. Because of this current activity, we have rated Freudian theory very high in its ability to generate research. However, because much of this research can be explained by non-Freudian models, it fails to verify or confirm psychoanalytic theory.

A second criterion of any useful theory is its ability to *organize knowledge* into a meaningful framework. Unfortunately, the framework of Freud's personality theory, with its emphasis on the unconscious, is so loose and flexible that seemingly inconsistent data can coexist within its boundaries. Thus, psychoanalysis appears to have the power to organize nearly everything we know about personality and to explain almost all causes of human behavior. Compared with other theories of personality, it ventures more answers to questions concerning why people behave as they do. But only some of these answers come from scientific investigations—most are simply logical extensions of Freud's basic assumptions. Because many psychologists no longer accept most of these assumptions, psychoanalysis can receive only a moderate rating on its ability to organize knowledge.

Third, a useful theory should serve as *a guide for the solution of practical problems.* Because Freudian theory is unusually comprehensive, many psychoanalytically trained practitioners rely on it to find solutions to practical day-to-day problems. However, psychoanalysis no longer dominates the field of psychotherapy, and most present-day therapists use other theoretical orientations in their practice. Nevertheless, those who do believe in basic Freudian theory rely on psychoanalytic principles in their work with patients, as well as their dealings with people outside of therapy. Overall, psychoanalysis receives a low-to-moderate rating as a guide to practice.

The fourth criterion of a useful theory deals with *internal consistency*, including operationally defined terms. Psychoanalysis is an internally consistent theory, if one remembers that Freud wrote over a period of more than 40 years and gradually altered the meaning of some concepts during that time. However, at any single point in time the theory generally possessed internal consistency, although some specific terms were used with less than scientific rigor.

Does psychoanalysis possess a set of operationally defined terms? Here the theory definitely falls short. Such terms as id, ego, superego, conscious, preconscious, unconscious, oral stage, sadistic-anal stage, phallic stage, Oedipus complex, latent level of dreams, and many others are not operationally defined; that is, they are not spelled out in terms of specific operations or behaviors. Investigators must originate their own particular definition of most psychoanalytic terms. This, of course, can lead to chaos, with different researchers defining the same term in different ways.

Fifth, psychoanalysis is not a simple or *parsimonious* theory, but considering its comprehensiveness and the complexity of human personality, it is not needlessly cumbersome.

Chapter Summary

The personal traits and experiences of Sigmund Freud permeate and color nearly all aspects of psychoanalytic theory. Freud's character is clearly stamped on the concepts that comprise his personality theory. First among these concepts are the three *levels of mental life*—the *unconscious, preconscious,* and *conscious.* Freud's exploration of the unconscious mind, including his own, ranks as one of his greatest contributions to our understanding of human personality. Many years after his original investigation of these three levels of mental life, Freud postulated three *provinces of the mind*—the *id, ego,* and *superego.* These three regions of personality overlap with, but are not the same as, the three levels of the mind. The id is a completely unconscious, chaotic "cauldron full of seething excitations" (Freud, 1933/1964, p. 73), serving the *pleasure principle* and completely out of contact with reality. The ego is the executive branch of personality, and, as the only province of the mind in contact with the real world, it serves the *reality principle*. The superego, which serves the *moral and idealistic principles*, begins to evolve after the resolution of the Oedipus complex, around ages four to six.

The two great *instincts* or drives in Freudian psychology are *sex* and *aggression*. These urges are often punished during childhood and, as a result, become repressed. Nevertheless, a sufficient number of these threatening impulses remain to produce anxiety within the ego. To protect itself against the pain of anxiety, the ego initiates a number of *defense mechanisms*, the most basic of which is *repression*.

Freud suggested three major *stages of development—infancy, latency,* and a *genital period*. The infantile stage lasts from birth to about ages four to six and is characterized by the child's first psychosexual experiences. It is the most crucial of the stages in the sense that the foundation for future personality structure is formed then. Infancy is divided into three subphases—*oral, anal,* and *phallic,* the last of which is accompanied by the *Oedipus complex.* Following the infantile stage is a period of psychosexual latency that lasts until puberty, at which time the genital stage begins. The genital stage signals the onset of a second, or mature, stage of

sexuality. This is the final stage conceptualized by Freud, although psychoanalytic concepts suggest a hypothetical period of psychological maturity.

Both *dreams* and "*Freudian slips*" are disguised means of expressing unconscious impulses. Also, both ordinarily express some hidden wish. Freud used dreams along with *free association* in psychotherapy for the purpose of uncovering portions of the patient's unconscious, thus alleviating neurotic conflicts and symptoms.

The Freudian view of humanity is essentially pessimistic and deterministic. According to Freud, people must perpetually struggle to balance the sexual and aggressive instincts of the id with the realistic demands of the ego and the restrictive prohibitions of the superego. People are seldom aware of the forces underlying their behavior and, for the most part, have little control over their lives.

Psychoanalytic theory, with its heavy emphasis on such nebulous concepts as the unconscious, presents many difficulties for scientific research. Some present-day researchers and psychotherapists use psychoanalytic concepts to organize knowledge and to treat patients, but most practitioners now view Freud's theory as having very limited practical value. Moreover, psychoanalysis is only moderately parsimonious and is deficient in its use of operationally defined terms.

Suggested Readings

BETTELHEIM, B. (1983). *Freud and man's soul.* New York: Knopf.
In this small book Bettelheim suggests that Americans have been misled by existing

translations of Freud from German to English. Born in Vienna in 1903, Bettelheim, as a young man, read Freud's books as they appeared in his native German. After emigrating to the United States, he began to hear and read English translations that rendered Freud more scientific and less humanistic than he appears to the German reader. Here, Bettelheim attempts to tell us what Freud really said.

FREUD, S. (1952). *An autobiographical study.* (J. Strachey, Trans.). New York: Norton. (Original work published 1925).

Freud's own story of his life and work up to 1925. For a more objective account, the reader may wish to supplement this brief autobiography with the writings of such modern "revisionists" as Ellenberger (1970), Isbister (1985), or Sulloway (1979).

FREUD, S. (1966). *The complete introductory lectures on psychoanalysis.* (J. Strachey, Trans.). New York: Norton. (Original works published 1917, 1933).

The best single-volume introduction to the central ideas of psychoanalysis by Freud himself, this book contains Freud's *Introductory Lectures*, first delivered at the University of Vienna from 1915 to 1917, and his *New Introductory Lectures*, which were never delivered, but which contain all the major changes that Freud made in his theory after World War I.

GAY, P. (1988). *Freud: A life for our time.* New York: Norton.

Although not an easy book to read, Gay's comprehensive, scholarly work is "must" reading for the serious Freud student.

JACOBS, M. (1992). *Sigmund Freud.* London: Sage.

A readable and brief overview of Freud's life, theory, and therapy, this book also includes a critique of psychoanalysis as a science.

MALCOLM, J. (1983). *In the Freud archives.* New York: Knopf.

An intriguing account of the story of Kurt Eissler, guardian of the Freud archives in the Library of Congress and his relationship with two important young Freudian scholars. The first was Jeffrey Masson, who, as provisional Projects Director of the Archives, gained access to early documents that led him to conclude that Freud's abandonment of the seduction theory was a grave mistake that greatly weakened psychoanalysis. The second young scholar was Peter Swales, a self-taught authority on Freud, who finds the father of psychoanalysis to have been much less courageous and virtuous than the image perpetuated by his followers.

Post-Freudian Theory

OVERVIEW
BIOGRAPHY OF ERIK ERIKSON
IMPORTANCE OF THE EGO
    Description of Ego Psychology
    Society's Influence
    Epigenetic Principle
STAGES OF PSYCHOSOCIAL DEVELOPMENT
    Infancy
    Early Childhood
    Play Age
    School Age
    Adolescence
    Young Adulthood
    Adulthood
    Old Age
    Summary
ERIKSON'S METHODS OF INVESTIGATION
    Anthropological Studies
    Psychohistory
    Play Construction
CONCEPT OF HUMANITY
RELATED RESEARCH
CRITIQUE OF ERIKSON
CHAPTER SUMMARY
SUGGESTED READINGS

Chapter Three

ERIKSON

When she died in 1962, Eleanor Roosevelt was one of the most loved and respected women in the world. Moreover, psychologist Abraham H. Maslow (1970) had regarded her as a self-actualizing person, meaning that she would have had confidence in her ability to love and be loved and would have had a high degree of self-esteem. In addition, she would have enjoyed a level of psychological health attained by only a very few people. If she truly met Maslow's criteria for self-actualization, then she would have achieved a remarkable transformation, inasmuch as her early life was filled with rejection, misery, and self-doubt.

Anna Eleanor Roosevelt was born in 1884, the oldest of three children and the only daughter of wealthy and socially prominent parents. She idolized her father and enjoyed a warm but brief relationship with him. Unfortunately, Eleanor did not share a close relationship with her mother, who was outspoken in her resentment of her daughter. When Eleanor was eight, her mother died of diphtheria at the age of 29. Eleanor's mother had named her own mother as guardian of her three children and specifically excluded Eleanor's father from overseeing their upbringing. Eleanor and her two brothers went to live with Grandmother Hall, but her life continued to be one of rejection and sadness. Her father visited occasionally, and these visits were the highlights of Eleanor's life. A few months after her mother died, her four-year-old brother died, also of diphtheria. Her father was a heavy drinker who had been in and out of sanitariums for a number of years. His health quickly deteriorated after a fall from a horse, and he died in 1894 when Eleanor was only 10. His death devastated Eleanor, who felt she had lost the only person who truly cared for her.

When Eleanor was 15, her grandmother, who was having trouble with her own children, decided to send Eleanor to a boarding school in England. There Eleanor developed a warm friendship with Marie Souvestre, the headmistress, and the three years under her tutelage were happy and productive ones. Eleanor came to value service to less fortunate people, developed an interest in world affairs, stopped wearing the unattractive dresses that had been her custom, and began to see herself as possessing an inner attractiveness.

When Eleanor returned to New York she wanted to go to college, but her grandmother, who did not believe in formal education for women, refused to allow it. After a year of exhausting and boring debutante parties, Eleanor directed her attention toward more socially useful activities—improving conditions of the underprivileged. At about the same time she met her distant cousin, Franklin Roosevelt, and the two young socialites gradually developed a romantic relationship. In 1905, at age 21, Eleanor married Franklin. She was given in marriage by her Uncle Theodore, who was then President of the United States.

Franklin's mother had always dominated her son, and she continued to exercise close control over both him and Eleanor long after they were married. In 1908 she built a joint house for herself and her son and his growing family. Many years would pass before Eleanor was able to stand up to her mother-in-law and lead an independent life. After Franklin developed polio in 1921, his mother felt that his political and social life was over, and she wanted to treat him as an invalid. Eleanor was able to oppose her mother-in-law on this point and refused to allow her husband to be coddled. Finally, in midlife, Eleanor was beginning to exert her independence.

OVERVIEW

According to Erik Erikson, the life of Eleanor Roosevelt, like that of any other person who has lived to old age, proceeded in a series of eight stages. In this chapter we examine in some detail Erikson's psychosocial stages of development and illustrate them with excerpts from the life of Eleanor Roosevelt. But before doing so, we compare Erikson's work with that of Freud, a man who had considerable direct and indirect influence on Erikson. In general, Erikson differs from Freud in placing more emphasis on the ego, on social and historical influences, and on his extension of developmental stages into adulthood and old age.

Unlike Freud, Erikson is not a physician. In fact, he has no college degree of any kind. Yet, he is one of the world's foremost psychoanalysts, having been analyzed by Freud's daughter, Anna. In contrast to Adler (Chapter 4) and Jung (Chapter 5), Erikson has never repudiated Freud's ideas. Instead, he has constructed a personality theory on the foundation laid by Freud. Thus, his way of looking at personality can rightly be called post-Freudian theory.

Erikson's theory, like those of others, is a reflection of his background, a background heavily steeped in art.

BIOGRAPHY OF ERIK ERIKSON

The life of Erik Homburger Erikson, like that of Eleanor Roosevelt, has been marked by several "identity crises," a term Erikson began to popularize 50 years ago.

Erikson's early identity crises were in part due to his own clouded origins. He was born June 15, 1902, near Frankfurt, Germany, the son of Karla Abrahamsen and a father of unknown identity. During his first three years, he lived alone with his mother, who then married Dr. Theodor Homburger, Erik's pediatrician (Coles, 1970). Erikson grew up in Karlsruhe, a town in southern Germany, believing he was Homburger's son. In his autobiography, Erikson (1975, p. 27) claimed that his parents "kept from me the fact that my mother had been married previously, and that I was the son of a Dane who had abandoned her before my birth." However, Paul Roazen (1976) cited a speech Erikson had given 20 years earlier in which he reported that his father had died around the time of his birth. Roazen further suggested that Erikson may have been born out of wedlock, and that his unknown paternal lineage has contributed to an image of himself as a perpetual stepson. This image is seen in Erikson's persistent loyalty to Freud who, in many ways, became Erikson's mythical stepfather.

Erikson's real stepfather Theodor Homburger was from a small Jewish bourgeois family. He was a kindly man who expected his stepson to become a doctor like himself. Erikson's mother, a native of Copenhagen, Denmark, was from a Jewish family, but her own religious affiliation, like that of her son, is not clear. We do know that Erik attended temple, where his blond hair and blue eyes made him appear to be an outsider. At school, on the other hand, his classmates referred to him as a Jew, so Erik felt out of place in both arenas.

At 18 Erikson completed school at the Gymnasium—the last academic graduation of his life. Feeling "alienated from everything my bourgeois family stood for," he set out in quest of a different style of life (Erikson, 1975, p. 28). Gifted at sketching, he divided his time between art school and wandering throughout southern Germany and northern Italy, hiking and carrying a knapsack with books of his favorite authors. His identity as an artist meant a kind of rebellious way of life rather than a specific occupation, and that way of life was antiestablishment. These were "years of discontent, rebellion, and confusion" (Erikson, 1975).

At 25 he returned to Karlsruhe to teach art. However, a letter from his friend, Peter Blos, was to have a permanent effect on the direction of his life. Erikson had known Blos from their youth in Karlsruhe, and the two were friends in Italy. Both were artists and both later became well-known psychoanalysts. Erikson (1975) considers Blos's letter to have rescued him from the life of a wandering artist. The letter asked Erikson to join with Blos in teaching in a newly established school for children in Vienna. The school was run by a friend of Anna Freud, and many of the students were daughters and sons of future psychoanalysts. During the six years he spent in Vienna, Erikson studied psychoanalysis and Montessori education. In addition, he completed a personal analysis with Anna Freud, Sigmund Freud's youngest daughter. Anna, seven years older than Erikson, shared a waiting room with her father, then in his 70s. Erikson rarely addressed the older Freud, not only out of shyness and deference, but also because speech was quite painful for Freud, who wore a prosthetic device in his jaw due to the oral cancer from which he was suffering. Even though Erikson's personal relationship with Freud was minimal, he has remained a life-long ardent admirer of the father of psychoanalysis.

While in Vienna, Erikson met and married Joan Serson, a Canadian-born,

American-trained dancer and teacher who had also undergone psychoanalysis. With her psychoanalytic background and her facility with the English language, she has proven to be a capable editor and occasional co-author of Erikson's books. The Eriksons have three children, a daughter and two sons. The older son, Kai Erikson, is a professor of sociology and has occasionally collaborated with his father on professional writings.

In 1933, Erikson (still known as Homburger) graduated from the Vienna Psychoanalytic Institute. Then, with fascism on the rise, the Eriksons left Vienna for Denmark, the land of Erik's biological parents. After one summer in Copenhagen they immigrated to the United States, settling first in the Boston area.

With neither medical credentials nor an academic degree of any kind, Erikson was offered a position at the Harvard Medical School. While there, he enrolled in the Ph.D. program in psychology but soon dropped out. While at Harvard, he met Margaret Mead, Ruth Benedict, Henry Murray, Kurt Lewin, and others who had also influenced Harry Stack Sullivan (Chapter 6) and Karen Horney (Chapter 7).

In 1936 Erikson went to Yale, where he was associated with the famous Institute of Human Relations and where he also taught at the Medical School. Three years later he moved to the University of California at Berkeley, but not before living among and studying the Sioux Indians in South Dakota. (He later lived with the Yurok Indians in northern California, and these experiences in cultural anthropology have added much to the richness and completeness of his theory of personality.)

At about the same time Erikson moved to the West Coast, he became a United States citizen and changed his name. Erikson was not his biological father's name, and his choice of that name is not adequately explained in his autobiography (Erikson, 1975). Perhaps his newly acquired American identity allowed him to identify with Leif Ericsson, the first European explorer to land in North America. Or perhaps Erik's sons wanted to be known as Erikson.

During his California period Erikson gradually evolved a theory of personality, separate from but not incompatible with Freud's. In 1950 he published *Childhood and Society*, a book that has now become a classic, and that made for Erikson an international reputation as an imaginative thinker.

Erikson remained at Berkeley until 1950, when faculty members were being asked to sign a loyalty oath. As a matter of principle, Erikson refused to sign and left California for Stockbridge, Massachusetts, where he worked at Austen Riggs, a treatment center for psychoanalytic training and research. He returned to Harvard in 1960 and remained there until his retirement in 1970. After retirement he continued an active career—writing, lecturing, seeing a few patients, and doing research with his wife Joan on aging (see J. M. Erikson, 1988; Erikson, Erikson, & Kivnick, 1986).

Erikson's best-known works include *Childhood and Society* (1950, 1963); *Young Man Luther* (1958); *Identity, Youth and Crisis* (1968); *Gandhi's Truth*

(1969), a book that won both the Pulitzer Prize and the National Book Award; *Dimensions of a New Identity* (1974); *Life History and the Historical Moment* (1975); *Identity and the Life Cycle* (1980); and *The Life Cycle Completed* (1982). Many of his papers have been compiled in A *Way of Looking at Things* (Schlein, 1987).

Erikson has lived through the eight stages of development and is thus able to see each with a personal perspective. He has traveled extensively and has lived in many geographically and culturally diverse localities. Wherever he lived, Erikson has taken his acceptance for granted. Yet, he has not always felt completely at home. In his autobiography (Erikson, 1975, p. 29), he explained his adoption by the Freudian circle with these words:

> I can only surmise . . . that it was a kind of positive stepson identity that made me take for granted that I should be accepted where I did not belong. By the same token, however, I had to cultivate not-belonging and keep contact with the artist in me.

Erikson has kept track, not only of his artist identity, but with his identity as a cultural anthropologist and a clinical psychoanalyst as well.

IMPORTANCE OF THE EGO

Erikson's identity as a clinical psychoanalyst can be traced to his early acceptance into the Freudian circle and his training with Anna Freud. He takes psychoanalysis for granted, and Freudian theory provides the foundation for his life-cycle approach to personality theory. Erikson's theoretical model, however, is more than merely a refinement of psychoanalysis; it is an extension—something Freud might have done in time. For this reason Erikson prefers the term *post-Freudian* rather than *revisionist* or *neo-Freudian*.

Erikson has made three important additions to Freudian theory. First, to Freud's early psychosexual stages (oral, anal, phallic, and latency), he has added four later stages, thus extending the life cycle throughout adulthood and into old age. Second, he has moved beyond the consulting room and has gathered data from historical and cultural sources, thereby elevating social factors above biological explanations. Third, he has emphasized the ego over the id as the key to personality development.

Description of Ego Psychology

In Chapter 2 we saw that Freud used the analogy of a rider on horseback to describe the relationship between the ego and the id. The rider (ego) is ultimately at the mercy of the stronger horse (id). The ego has no strength of its own, but must borrow its energy from the id. Moreover, the ego is constantly attempting to balance blind demands of the superego against the relentless forces of the id and the realistic opportunities of the external world. Freud believed that, for mature people, the ego may be sufficiently developed to rein in the id, even though its control is still tenuous, and id impulses might erupt and overwhelm the ego at any time.

In contrast, Erikson holds that the ego is more than a mediator between the irrational forces of the id and the unrelenting demands of the superego. To him the ego is a positive force, one that establishes self-identity and also adapts to the various conflicts and crises of life. The adaptation is not always constructive. At times the ego struggles to defend itself and, on occasion, it may even succumb to the forces of society. In any event it is the ego (the sense of "I" or self-identity) that is the center of personality.

The ego is not synonymous with the individual, but it is indispensable to a person's individuality (Erikson, 1963). The ego is weak, pliable, and fragile during childhood, but by adolescence it should begin to take form and gain strength. Throughout life, it unifies personality and guards indivisibility. Erikson (1963, p. 16) defines the ego as a person's "capacity to unify his experiences and his actions in an adaptive manner."

In formulating his ideas on ego psychology, Erikson (1982) acknowledges his debt to three earlier formulations: Freud's (1923/1961a) conception of the ego as restraint on the biological forces of the id; Anna Freud's (1946) view of a defensive ego; and Heinz Hartmann's (1939/1958) notion of an adaptive ego.

Erikson (1968) sees the ego as a partially unconscious organizing agency that synthesizes present experiences with past selves and also with anticipated selves. He also identified three interrelated aspects of ego: (1) the *body ego*, which refers to experiences with one's body; (2) the *ego ideal*, which represents the image we have of ourselves in comparison with an established ideal; and (3) *ego identity*, the image we have of ourselves in a variety of social roles. Although adolescence is ordinarily the time when these three components are changing most rapidly, alterations in body ego, ego ideal, and ego identity can and do take place at any stage of life.

In summary, the ego has both a defensive and an adaptive function. Its principal task is to turn the demands of the id and the superego into allies in the pursuit of ego identity. The ego operates actively to unify experiences and to guard one's sense of identity.

Society's Influence

Although inborn capacities are important in personality development, the ego emerges from and is largely shaped by society. Erikson's emphasis on social and historical factors is in contrast with Freud's mostly biological viewpoint. Whereas Freudian theory emphasizes the power of the genetically based id, Erikson sees the ego as developing within a social structure. In an interview with Richard Evans, Erikson said, "The ego can only remain strong in interaction with cultural institutions and can only remain strong when the child's inborn capacities and potentials are developed" (Evans, 1967, p. 26). In other words, the ego exists as potential at birth, but it must emerge from within a cultural environment.

Different societies, with their variations in child-rearing practices, tend to shape personalities that fit the needs and values of their culture. For example, Erikson (1963) found that prolonged and permissive nursing of Sioux Indian infants (sometimes for as long as four or five years) resulted in what Freud would call "oral" personalities. The Sioux place great value on generosity, and Erikson believes that the reassurance resulting from unlimited breast feeding lays the foundation for the virtue of generosity. However, biting is quickly suppressed in infants, and this practice may contribute to the child's fortitude and to the "hunter's ferocity" needed by Sioux society. On the other hand, the Yurok Indians have strict regulations concerning elimination of urine and feces, practices that tend to develop "anality." In Euro-American societies orality and anality are often considered undesirable traits or neurotic symptoms. Erikson (1963), however, argues that orality among the Sioux hunters and anality among the Yurok fishermen are adaptive characteristics that help both the individual and the culture within which the individual resides. The fact that Euro-American culture views orality and anality as deviant traits merely displays its own ethnocentric view of other societies. Erikson (1968, 1974) argues that historically all tribes or nations, including our own, have developed what he calls a **pseudospecies,** or the illusion perpetrated and perpetuated by a particular society that it is somehow chosen to be *the* human species. In past centuries this belief has aided the survival of the tribe, but with modern means of world annihilation, such a prejudiced perception (as demonstrated by Nazi Germany) threatens the survival of every nation.

As noted earlier, one of Erikson's principal contributions to personality theory is his extension of the Freudian early stages of development to include school age, youth, adulthood, and old age. Before looking more closely at Erikson's theory of ego development, we must discuss his view of how personality develops from one stage to the next.

Epigenetic Principle

According to Erikson, the ego develops throughout the various stages of life according to an **epigenetic principle**. This term, borrowed from embryology, needs some explanation. In embryology, epigenetic development implies a step-by-step growth of fetal organs. The embryo does not begin as a completely formed little person, waiting to merely expand its structure and form. Rather, it develops, or should develop, according to a predetermined rate and in a fixed sequence. If the eyes, liver, or other organs do not develop during that critical period when normal development takes place, then they will never attain proper maturity. In similar fashion, the ego follows the path of epigenetic development, with each stage developing at its proper time. One stage emerges from and is built upon a previous stage, but it does not replace that earlier stage. This is analogous to the physical development of children who crawl before they walk, walk before they run, and run before they jump. When children are still crawling, they are developing the potential to walk, run and jump, and after they are mature enough to jump, they still retain their ability to run, walk and crawl. Erikson (1968, p. 92) described the epigenetic principle, saying that "anything that grows has a ground plan, and that out of this ground plan the parts arise, each part having its time of special ascendancy, until all parts have arisen to form a functioning whole." More succinctly, "epigenesis means that one characteristic develops on top of another in space and time" (Evans, 1967, pp. 21–22).

The epigenetic principle is illustrated in Figure 3.1, which depicts the first three Eriksonian stages. The sequence of stages (1, 2, 3) and the development of their component parts (A, B, C) are shown in the heavily lined boxes along the diagonal. Figure 3.1 shows that each part exists before its critical time (at least as biological potential), then emerges at its proper time, and finally continues to develop during subsequent stages. For example, component Part B of Stage 2 (early childhood) exists during Stage 1 (infancy) as shown in Box 1_B. Part B reaches its full ascendance during Stage 2 (Box 2_B), but continues into Stage 3 (Box 3_B). Similarly, all components of Stage 3 exist during Stages 1 and 2, reach full development during Stage 3, and continue throughout all later stages (Erikson, 1982).

STAGES OF PSYCHOSOCIAL DEVELOPMENT

To appreciate Erikson's eight stages of psychosocial development several points must be understood.

1. As explained above, growth takes place according to the *epigenetic principle.* That is, one component part arises out of another, has its own time of ascendancy, but it does not entirely replace earlier components.

2. In every stage of life there is an *interaction of opposites*, that is, a conflict between a **syntonic** (harmonious) element and a **dystonic** (disruptive) element. For example, during infancy *basic trust* (a syntonic tendency) is opposed to *basic mistrust* (a dystonic tendency). Both trust and mistrust, however, are necessary for proper adaptation. An infant who learns only to trust becomes gullible and is ill-prepared for the realities encountered in later development. Of course, an infant who learns only to mistrust becomes overly suspicious and cynical. Similarly, during each of the other seven stages, people must have both harmonious (syntonic) and disruptive (dystonic) experiences.

3. At each stage the conflict between the dystonic and syntonic elements produces an ego quality or **basic strength**. For instance, from the antithesis between trust and mistrust emerges "hope," an ego quality that allows the infant to move into the next stage. Likewise, each of the other stages is marked by a basic strength that emerges from the clash between the harmonious and the disruptive elements of that stage.

4. Although Erikson refers to these periods as *psychosocial stages*, he never loses sight of the *somatic* (biological) aspect of human development.

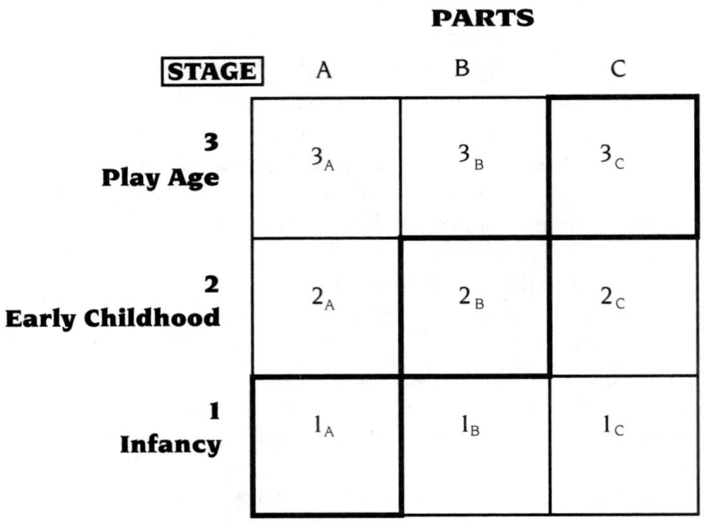

PARTS

STAGE	A	B	C
3 **Play Age**	3_A	3_B	3_C
2 **Early Childhood**	2_A	2_B	2_C
1 **Infancy**	1_A	1_B	1_C

Figure 3.1   *Three Eriksonian Stages, Depicting the Epigenetic Principle*

5. Events in earlier stages do not "cause" later personality development. Ego identity is shaped by a *multiplicity of conflicts and events*—past, present, and anticipated.

6. During each stage, but especially from adolescence forward, personality development is characterized by an **identity crisis**, which Erikson (1968, p. 96) calls "a turning point, a crucial period of increased vulnerability and heightened potential." Thus, during each crisis, a person is especially susceptible to major modifications in identity, either positive or negative. Contrary to popular usage, an identity crisis is not a catastrophic event, but rather an opportunity for either adaptive or maladaptive adjustment.

Erikson's eight stages of psychosocial development are shown in Figure 3.2. The boldfaced, capitalized words are the ego qualities or basic strengths that emerge from the conflicts or psychosocial crises that typify each period. The "vs." separating syntonic and dystonic elements signifies not only an antithetical relationship but also a complementary one. Only the boxes along the diagonal are filled in; that is, Figure 3.2 highlights only the basic strengths and psychosocial crises that are *most* characteristic of each stage of development. However, the epigenetic principle suggests that all other boxes would also be filled (as in Figure 3.1), though with items less characteristic of their stage of psychosocial development. Each item in the ensemble is vital to personality development, and each is related to all the others. Although one may wish to start at old age and work backward (as Erikson does in *The Life Cycle Completed*), we begin our discussion of the developmental stages with infancy.

PARTS

STAGE	A	B	C	D	E	F	G	H
Old Age 8								**WISDOM** Integrity vs. Despair, Disgust
Adulthood 7							**CARE** Generativity vs. Stagnation	
Young Adulthood 6						**LOVE** Intimacy vs. Isolation		
Adolescence 5					**FIDELITY** Identity vs. Identity Confusion			
School Age 4				**COMPETENCE** Industry vs. Inferiority				
Play Age 3			**PURPOSE** Initiative vs. Guilt					
Early Childhood 2		**WILL** Autonomy vs. Shame, Doubt						
Infancy 1	**HOPE** Basic Trust vs. Basic Mistrust							

Figure 3.2   Erikson's Eight Stages of Development with Their Appropriate Basic Strengths and Psychosocial Crises

Infancy

The first psychosocial stage is **infancy**, a period encompassing approximately the first year of life and paralleling Freud's oral phase of development. However, Erikson's model adopts a broader focus than Freud's, whose description of the oral stage was concerned almost exclusively with the mouth. To Erikson (1963, 1989), infancy is a time of *incorporation*, with the infant "taking in" not only through the mouth but through the various sense organs as well. As the infant takes in food and sensory information, it learns to either trust or mistrust the outside world, a situation that gives it realistic hope. Infancy, then, is marked by the *oral-sensory* psychosexual mode, the psychosocial crisis or *basic trust vs. basic mistrust*, and the basic strength of *hope*.

Oral-Sensory Mode

Erikson's expanded view of infancy is expressed in the term **oral-sensory**, a phrase he uses to describe the infant's principal *psychosexual* mode of adapting.

The oral-sensory stage is characterized by two modes of incorporation—receiving and accepting what is given. An infant can receive even in the absence of other people, that is, it can take in air through the lungs and can receive sensory data without having to manipulate others. The second mode of incorporation, however, implies a social context. The infant not only must *get*, but it also must get someone else to *give*. This early training in interpersonal relations helps the infant learn to eventually become a giver. In getting other people to give, the infant learns to trust or mistrust other people, thus setting up the basic *psychosocial crisis* of infancy, namely, basic trust vs. basic mistrust.

Basic Trust vs. Basic Mistrust

The infant's most significant interpersonal relations are with the maternal person or primary care giver, ordinarily its mother. If the infant realizes that the mother will provide food regularly, then it begins to learn *basic trust*; if it consistently hears the pleasant, rhythmic voice of its mother, then more basic trust is developed; if it can rely on an exciting visual environment, then basic trust is solidified even more. In other words, if an infant's pattern of accepting things corresponds with the culture's way of giving them, then that infant will learn basic trust. On the other hand, if an infant finds no correspondence between its oral-sensory needs and its environment, then it learns *basic mistrust*.

Basic trust is ordinarily syntonic and basic mistrust dystonic. Nevertheless, the infant must develop both attitudes. As noted earlier, too much trust makes one gullible and vulnerable to the vagaries of the world, whereas too little trust leads to frustration, anger, hostility, cynicism, or depression.

Both trust and mistrust are inevitable experiences of the infant. All babies who have survived have been fed and otherwise cared for, and thus have some reason to trust. In addition, all have been frustrated by pain, hunger, or discomfort, and therefore have a reason to mistrust. Erikson believes that some ratio of trust and mistrust is critical to our ability to adapt. He says that "when we enter a situation, we must be able to differentiate how much we can trust and how much we must mistrust, and I use mistrust in the sense of a readiness for danger and an anticipation of discomfort" (Evans, 1967, p. 15).

The inevitable conflict between basic trust and basic mistrust results in the person's first psychosocial crisis, which in turn leads to the first basic strength—*hope*.

Hope: The Basic Strength of Infancy

Hope emerges from the conflict between basic trust and basic mistrust, and thus becomes the person's first basic strength. In his earlier writings, Erikson referred to basic strengths as "virtues," but he abandoned this term because the origin of the word implied manly strength and was thus not appropriate for women (Hall, 1983).

Without the antithetical relationship between trust and mistrust, people cannot develop hope. Infants must experience hunger, pain, and discomfort as well as the alleviation of these unpleasant conditions. By having both painful and pleasurable experiences, infants learn to expect that future distresses will meet with satisfactory outcomes. This "enduring predisposition to believe in the attainability of primal wishes in spite of anarchic urges and rages of dependency" is called hope (Erikson, 1968, p. 106). To Erikson, "hope is a very basic human strength without which we couldn't stay alive" (Evans, 1967, p. 17).

The antithesis of hope is *withdrawal*, which Erikson calls the **core pathology** of infancy. With little to hope for, the infant retreats from the outside world and begins the journey toward serious psychological disturbance.

According to the epigenetic principle discussed earlier, hope is an element of each of the other basic strengths; that is, hope is a component of will, purpose, competence, fidelity, love, care, and wisdom (see Figure 3.2). For example, in the lower right corner (Box 1_H), basic trust and basic mistrust meet with wisdom (Erikson, 1979). The seeds of wisdom, then, are planted during infancy as the baby learns to trust and mistrust its mother and the world.

Early Childhood

The second psychosocial stage is **early childhood**, a period paralleling Freud's anal stage and encompassing approximately the second and third years of life. Again, there are differences between the views of Freud and Erikson. As you recall from Chapter 2, Freud regarded the anus as the primary erogenous zone during this period. During the early sadistic-anal phase, children receive pleasure in destroying or losing objects, while later they take satisfaction in defecating. Once again, Erikson takes a broad view. To him, young children receive pleasure not only from mastering the sphincter muscle but also from mastering other body functions such as urinating, walking, throwing, holding, and so on. In addition, children develop a sense of control over their interpersonal environment, as well as a measure of self-control. However, this is also a time of experiencing doubt and shame as children learn that many of their attempts at autonomy are unsuccessful. From the conflict between autonomy and shame and doubt emerges a basic strength called will.

In summary, early childhood is characterized by the *anal-urethral-muscular psychosexual mode*; the psychosocial crisis of *autonomy vs. shame and doubt*; and the emergence of *will* as a basic strength.

Anal-Urethral-Muscular Mode

During the second year, children's primary psychosexual adjustment is the **anal-urethral-muscular** mode. At this time children learn to control their body, especially in relation to cleanliness and mobility. Early childhood is more than a time of toilet training; it is also a time of learning to walk, run, hug parents, and hold on to toys and other objects. With each of these activities, young children are likely to display some stubborn tendencies. They may retain their feces or eliminate them at will; snuggle up to their mothers or suddenly push them away; delight in hoarding objects or ruthlessly discard them.

Early childhood is a time of contradiction, a time of stubborn rebellion and meek compliance, a time of *impulsive* self-expression and *compulsive* deviance, a time of loving cooperation and hateful resistance (Erikson, 1968). This obstinate insistence on conflicting impulses triggers the major psychosocial crisis of childhood: autonomy vs. shame and doubt.

Autonomy vs. Shame and Doubt

If early childhood is a time for self-expression and *autonomy*, then it is also a time for *shame and doubt*. As children stubbornly express their anal-urethral-muscular mode, they are likely to find a culture that attempts to inhibit some of their self-expression. Parents may shame their children for soiling their pants or for making a mess with their food. They may also instill doubt by questioning their children's ability to meet their standards. The conflict between autonomy and shame and doubt becomes the major psychosocial crisis of childhood.

Ideally, children should develop a proper ratio between autonomy and shame and doubt, and, of course, the ratio should be in favor of autonomy, the syntonic quality. If children develop too little autonomy, then they will have difficulties in subsequent stages. They will lack the initiative required during the play age and will continue to be handicapped in their later development. According to Erikson's epigenetic diagrams (see Figures 3.1 and 3.2), autonomy grows out of basic trust, and if basic trust has been established in infancy, then children learn to have faith in themselves, and their world remains intact while they experience the psychosocial crisis of childhood. Conversely, if children do not develop basic trust during infancy, then their attempts to gain control of their anal, urethral, and muscular organs during childhood will be met with shame and doubt. *Shame* is a feeling of self-consciousness, of being looked at and exposed. *Doubt*, on the other hand, is the feeling of not being certain, the feeling that something remains hidden and cannot be seen. Both shame and doubt are dystonic qualities, and both grow out of the basic mistrust that was established in infancy.

Will: The Basic Strength of Childhood

The basic strength of *will* or willfulness evolves from the resolution of the crisis of autonomy vs. shame and doubt. This is the beginning of free will and will power—

but only a beginning. Mature will power and a significant measure of free will are reserved for later stages of development, but they have their origins in the rudimentary will that emerges during early childhood. Anyone who has spent much time around two-year-olds knows how willful they can be. Toilet training often epitomizes the conflict of wills between adult and child, but willful expression is not limited to this area. The basic conflict during this stage is between the child's striving for autonomy and the parent's attempts to control the child through the use of shame and doubt.

Rudimentary will can emerge only if children are permitted some self-expression in the control of their sphincters and other muscles. If culture instills too much shame and doubt and inhibits autonomy, children will not adequately develop this second important basic strength. Inadequate will is expressed as *compulsion*, the core pathology of early childhood. Too little will and too much compulsivity carry forward into the play age as lack of purpose and into the school age as lack of confidence.

Play Age

Erikson's third stage of development is the **play age**, a period covering the same time as Freud's phallic phase—roughly ages three to five. Again, we find differences between the views of Freud and Erikson. Freud paid little attention to the child's social development. Instead, he found great significance in the Oedipus complex, that is, the child's sexual feelings for one parent and hostile feelings for the other. After the Oedipus complex is resolved, the child ordinarily identifies with the parent of the same sex and gives up his sexual feelings for the parent of the opposite sex. Whereas the Oedipus complex is a central theme in Freudian theory, it is but one of several important developments during Erikson's play age. Erikson (1968) says that, in addition to identifying with their parents, preschool-age children are developing the ability to move around more freely (locomotion), language skills, curiosity, imagination, and the ability to set goals. During this psychosexual period of *genital and locomotor* development, young children undergo the crisis of *initiative vs. guilt* and develop a realistic sense of *purpose*.

Genital-Locomotor Mode

The primary psychosexual mode during the play age is **genital-locomotor.** Erikson (1982, p. 77) sees the Oedipal situation as a prototype "of the lifelong power of human playfulness." In other words, the Oedipus complex is a drama played out in the child's imagination and includes the budding understanding of such basic concepts as reproduction, growth, future, and death. The Oedipus and castration complexes, therefore, are not always to be taken literally. A child may play at being a mother, a father, a wife, or a husband, but such play is an expression, not only of the genital mode, but also of the child's rapidly developing locomotor abilities. A little girl may envy boys, but this is not due to boys' possession of a penis but rather to the prerogatives most societies grant to children with a penis. A little boy may have anxiety about losing something, but this refers not only to the penis but to other body parts as well. The Oedipus complex, then, is both more than and less than what Freud believed, and infantile sexuality is "a mere promise of things to come" (Erikson, 1963, p. 86). Unless sexual interest is provoked by cultural sex play or by adult sexual abuse, the Oedipus complex produces no harmful effects on later personality development.

Play-age children's interest in genital activity is accompanied by their increasing facility at locomotion. They can now move with ease, running, jumping, and climbing with no conscious effort, and their play shows both initiative and imagination. The rudimentary will developed during the preceding stage is evolving into activity with a *purpose*. Their cognitive abilities enable them to manufacture elaborate fantasies including, perhaps, Oedipal fantasies, but also including imagining what it is like to be grown-up, to be omnipotent, or to be a ferocious animal. These fantasies, however, also produce guilt and thus contribute to the psychosocial crisis of the play age, namely, initiative vs. guilt.

Initiative vs. Guilt

As children begin to move around more easily and vigorously and as their genital interest awakens, they adopt an intrusive head-on mode of approaching the world. Although they begin to adopt *initiative* in their selection and pursuit of goals, many goals, such as marrying the mother or father or leaving home, must either be repressed or delayed. The consequence of these taboo and inhibited goals is *guilt*. The conflict between initiative and guilt becomes the dominant psychosocial crisis of the play age.

Again, the ratio between these two should favor the syntonic quality, initiative. Unbridled initiative, however, may lead to chaos and a lack of moral principles. On the other hand, if guilt is the dominant element, children may become compulsively moralistic or overly inhibited. *Inhibition*, which is the antithesis of purpose, constitutes the core pathology of the play age.

Purpose: The Basic Strength of the Play Age

The conflict of initiative vs. guilt produces the basic strength of *purpose*. Children now play with a purpose, competing at games in order to win or to be on top. Their genital interests have a direction, with Mother or Father being the object of their sexual desires. They set goals and pursue them with purpose.

Play age is also the stage in which children are developing a conscience and beginning to attach labels such as right and wrong to their behavior. Erikson (1968, p. 119) refers to this youthful conscience as the "cornerstone of morality." However, if children evolve a conscience that is too strict and uncompromising, their initiative becomes stifled, they lose their sense of purpose, and they develop a vindictive attitude toward others. Later in life they may show unrelenting initiative, overaggressiveness, and strain, all of which may lead to various psychosomatic illnesses. Erikson (1968, p. 121) summed up the play age with these words:

> We may now see what induced Freud to place the Oedipus complex at the core of man's conflicted existence, and this not only according to psychiatric evidence but also to the testimony of great fiction, drama, and history. For the fact that man began as a playing child leaves a residue of play-acting and role playing even in what he considers his highest purposes.

We began this chapter with a brief biography of Eleanor Roosevelt and will use her life story to illustrate her psychological development during each of the five subsequent stages of Erikson's theory. Unfortunately, little is known of Roosevelt's early life with regard to psychosexual development or psychosocial crises. We do know that she remembered her mother telling her during early childhood that she looked like an old woman, without any semblance of spontaneous fun (Steinberg, 1958). Her play age must have been stilted and serious as she strove to acquire the manners and demeanor of adulthood far before her time.

School Age

School age covers the period from about 6 to 12 or 13 and matches the stage Freud called "latency." As you recall from Chapter 2, Freud called this period latency because he believed that *psychosexual* growth was at a standstill. Only in a general way did he write of the social and academic development taking place during this time. Erikson looks more at the whole child, emphasizing the growth of the ego within a cultural setting. For the first time, a child's social world expands beyond family members to include peers as well as teachers and other adult models. For school-age children, the wish to know becomes strong and is tied to their basic striving for competence. In normal development children strive industriously to read and write, to hunt and fish, or to learn the skills required by their culture.

School age does not necessarily mean formalized schools. In contemporary literate cultures, schools and professional teachers play a major part in children's education, whereas in preliterate societies, adults use less formalized but equally effective methods to instruct children in the ways of society.

In summary, school age is marked by the psychosexual stage of *latency*, the psychosocial crisis of *industry vs. inferiority*, and the emergence of the basic strength of *competence*.

Latency

During school age, children undergo a period of psychosexual **latency**, a time after their infantile sexuality has become mostly dormant and before they have achieved full genital maturity. Sexual latency is important because it allows children to divert their energies to learning the technology of their culture and the strategies of meaningful social relations. As children work and play hard to acquire these essentials, they begin to form a picture of themselves as competent or incompetent. These self images are the origin of *ego identity*—that feeling of "I" or "me-ness" that evolves more fully during adolescence.

Industry vs. Inferiority

If school age is a period of little psycho*sexual* development, then it is a time of tremendous psycho*social* growth. The psychosocial crisis of this stage is industry vs. inferiority. *Industry*, of course, is a syntonic quality and means industriousness, a willingness to remain busy with something and to finish a job. School-age children learn to work and play at activities directed both toward acquiring job skills and toward learning the rules of cooperation. Erikson (1982) contended that at no other time are children so eager and ready to learn.

As children learn to make and do things well, they develop a sense of industry, but if their work is insufficient to accomplish their goals, they acquire a sense of *inferiority*, the dystonic quality of the school age. Earlier inadequacies can also contribute to children's feelings of inferiority. For example, if children acquire too much guilt and too little purpose during the play age, they will likely feel inferior and incompetent during the school age. However, failure is not inevitable. Erikson is optimistic in suggesting that people can successfully handle the crisis of any given stage even though they were not completely successful in previous stages.

The ratio between industry and inferiority should, of course, favor industry, but inferiority, like the other dystonic qualities, should not be avoided. As Alfred Adler (Chapter 4) pointed out, inferiority can serve as an impetus to do one's best. Conversely, an oversupply of inferiority can block productive activity, and stunt one's feelings of competence.

Competence: The Basic Strength of the School Age

From the conflict of industry vs. inferiority, school-age children develop the basic strength of *competence*. Erikson (1968, p. 126) defines competence as "the free exercise of dexterity and intelligence in the completion of serious tasks unimpaired by an infantile sense of inferiority." Competence lays the foundation for "cooperative participation in productive adult life" (Erikson, 1968, p. 126).

If the struggle between industry and inferiority favors either inferiority or an overabundance of industry, children are likely to give up and regress to an earlier stage of development. They may become preoccupied with infantile genital and Oedipal fantasies and spend most of their time in nonproductive play. This regression is called *inertia*, which is the antipathy of competence and represents the core pathology of the school age.

For Eleanor Roosevelt school age was a time of doubt, self-pity, deep feelings of inferiority, and sadness. When she was eight, her mother, who had been constantly critical of her, died. This death left no great impression on Eleanor, but when her beloved father died 18 months later, she was grief-stricken. She regressed into a fantasy life, day-dreaming of many imaginary adventures involving her and her father. Her reaction to her father's death is quite consistent with Erikson's hypothesis that children of school age with overriding feelings of inferiority are likely to regress to Oedipal fantasies. At this time Eleanor had little of the basic strength of competence, being neither successful at making intimate friends of her peers nor at achieving adequate grades in school. Recall that, although Erikson believes that basic strengths build on earlier ones, he optimistically suggests that people can grow toward maturity in spite of some childhood pathologies. Such was the case with Eleanor Roosevelt.

Adolescence

Adolescence, the period from puberty to young adulthood, is one of the most crucial developmental stages because by the end of this period the person must gain a firm sense of *ego identity*. In the epigenetic configuration, ego identity neither begins nor ends with adolescence, but it is during this time that the crisis between *identity* and *identity confusion* reaches its ascendance. From this crisis emerges *fidelity*, the basic strength of adolescence.

Erikson (1982) sees adolescence as a period of psycho*social* latency, just as school age is a time of psycho*sexual* latency. Although adolescents are developing sexually and cognitively, they are allowed to postpone lasting commitment to an occupation, a sex partner, or an adaptive philosophy of life. They are permitted to experiment in a variety of ways and to try out new roles and beliefs while seeking to establish a sense of ego identity. Adolescence, then, is an adaptive phase of personality development, a period of trial and error.

Puberty

The principal psychosexual mode of the adolescent stage is *puberty*, defined by Erikson (1968) as genital maturation. Actually, puberty itself plays a relatively minor role in Erikson's concept of adolescence. For most young people, genital maturation presents no major sexual crisis (Erikson, 1967). Nevertheless, puberty is important psychologically because it triggers expectations of adult roles yet ahead—roles that are essentially social and, can be filled only through a struggle to attain a clear sense of ego identity.

In Freudian theory puberty ushers in the genital period, but Freud was not specific in describing the psychosocial conflicts of this, the final stage of his developmental theory. Erikson, on the other hand, devotes much attention to youth's quest for identity and establishment of a stable system of beliefs.

Identity vs. Identity Confusion

The search for ego *identity* reaches its climax during adolescence as young people strive to find out who they are and who they are not. With the advent of puberty, adolescents search for new roles to help them discover their sexual, ideological, and occupational identities.

In this search, young people draw from a variety of earlier self-images that have been accepted or rejected. Identity, then, begins during infancy and develops through childhood, play age, and school age. During adolescence, identity evolves into a crisis as the person copes with the psychosocial conflict of identity vs. identity confusion. The word *crisis* should not suggest a threat or catastrophe but rather "a turning point, a crucial period of increased vulnerability and heightened potential" (Erikson, 1968, p. 96). An identity crisis may last for many years and can result in either greater or lesser ego strength.

Erikson (1982) holds that identity emerges from two sources: The first is the affirmation or repudiation of childhood identifications; the second is the historical and social context that dictates conformity to certain standards. Young people frequently reject the standards of their elders, preferring instead the values of a peer group or gang. In any event, the society in which they live plays a substantial role in shaping their identity. Identity is defined both positively and negatively, as adolescents are deciding what they want to become and what they believe. They are also finding out, however, what they *do not* wish to be and what they *do not* believe. Often they must either repudiate the values of parents or reject those of the peer group, a dilemma that may intensify their *identity confusion*.

Identity confusion is a syndrome of problems that includes a divided self-image, an inability to establish intimacy, a sense of time urgency, a lack of concentration on required tasks, and a rejection of family or community standards (Erikson, 1968, 1980). As with the other dystonic tendencies, some amount of identity confusion is both normal and necessary. Young people must experience some doubt and confusion about who they are before they can evolve a stable identity. This may involve leaving home (as Erikson did) to wander alone in search of self; experimenting with drugs and sex; identifying with a street gang; joining a religious order; or railing against the existing society, with no alternative answers. Or it may simply involve a quiet consideration of where one fits into the world and what values one holds dear.

Although identity confusion is a necessary part of one's search for identity, too much confusion can lead to pathological adjustment in the form of regression to earlier stages of development. The responsibilities of adulthood are thus postponed for years as a young man or woman drifts aimlessly from one job to another, from one sex partner to another, or from one ideology to another. Conversely, the proper ratio of identity to identity confusion results in (1) the establishment of *faith* in some sort of ideological principle; (2) the ability to freely decide how one should behave; (3) trust in peers and adults who give advice regarding goals and aspirations; and (4) an eventual choice of occupation.

The late adolescent's search for identity includes a discovery of sexual identity.

Fidelity: The Basic Strength of Adolescence

The basic strength emerging from the identity crises of adolescence is *fidelity*, that is, faith in some ideological view or vision of the future (Erikson, 1975). With the establishment of internal standards of conduct, adolescents are no longer in need of parental guidance, and they can now have confidence that their religious, political, and social ideologies will provide a consistent standard of conduct.

The trust learned in infancy is basic for fidelity in adolescence. Young people must learn to trust others before they can have faith in their own view of the future. They must have developed hope during infancy, and they must follow hope with the other basic strengths—will, purpose, and competence. Each is a prerequisite for fidelity, just as fidelity is required for the acquisition of subsequent strengths.

The pathological counterpart of fidelity is **role repudiation**, or the inability to synthesize various self-images and values into a workable identity. Role repudiation can take the form of either diffidence or defiance (Erikson, 1982). *Diffidence* is an extreme lack of self-trust or self-confidence and is expressed as shyness or hesitancy to express oneself. *Defiance*, on the other hand, is the open act of rebelling against authority. Defiant adolescents stubbornly hold to socially unacceptable beliefs and practices simply because these beliefs and practices are unacceptable. Some amount of role repudiation, Erikson believes, is necessary, not only for the formation of personal identity, but also for the injection of new ideas and new vitality into the social structure.

As an adolescent, Eleanor Roosevelt had little self-confidence, few friends her age, and no basic ideology. She was still living in a fantasy world, refusing to believe that her late father had been a heavy drinker and had brought shame and disgrace to the family. In searching for her own identity, Eleanor did what many adolescents do—she developed a hero-worship attitude toward a person whom she greatly respected, Marie Souvestre, the headmistress at Eleanor's boarding school. Souvestre became instrumental in forming many of Eleanor's opinions and in shaping her philosophy of life. Eleanor, like all people, was a product of her time and culture. As a woman in the early-20th-century United States, her identity was incomplete until she could find a man, and even after marriage it was closely tied to that of her husband. For many women, identity is threatened when they change their names with marriage. With Eleanor's marriage to Franklin Roosevelt, no name change was required because Eleanor had been born a Roosevelt.

Young Adulthood

Adolescence and the search for identity are indispensable to the next stage—**young adulthood**, a time from about 19 to 30 for most people. During adolescence people must acquire a solid sense of who they are in order to be able to fuse their identity with the identity of another person, a necessary condition for young adulthood.

The period of young adulthood is circumscribed not so much by time as by the acquisition of *intimacy* at the beginning of the stage and the development of *generativity* at the end. For some people this is a relatively short time, lasting perhaps only a few years. For others, young adulthood may continue for several decades. During young adulthood mature *genitality* develops, the person experiences the conflict between *intimacy* and *isolation*, and the basic strength of *love* emerges.

Genitality

Much of the sexual activity during adolescence is an expression of one's search for identity and is basically self-serving. True **genitality** can develop only during young adulthood when it is characterized by mutual trust and a more or less permanent sharing of sexual satisfactions with a loved person. It represents the chief psychosexual accomplishment of young adulthood and can be found only in an intimate relationship in which the two partners neither compulsively obey nor sadistically dominate one another (Erikson, 1963).

Intimacy vs. Isolation

Young adulthood is marked by the psychosocial crisis of intimacy vs. isolation. **Intimacy** is the ability to fuse one's identity with that of another without fear of losing it. Because intimacy can only be achieved after people have formed a stable ego, the infatuations that often characterize young-adolescent life are not true intimacy. People who are unsure of their identity may either shy away from psychosocial intimacy or desperately seek intimacy through meaningless sexual encounters.

In contrast, mature intimacy means an ability and willingness to share a mutual trust. It involves sacrifice, compromise, and commitment within a relationship of two equals. It should be a requirement for marriage, but many marriages lack intimacy because young people frequently get married as part of their search for the identity they failed to establish during adolescence.

The psychosocial counterpart to intimacy is **isolation**, which Erikson (1968, p. 137) defined as "the incapacity to take chances with one's identity by sharing true intimacy." Some people become financially or socially successful, yet retain a deep sense of isolation because they are unable to accept the adult responsibilities of productive work, procreation, and mature love.

Again, some degree of isolation is essential to the acquisition of mature love. Too much togetherness can diminish one's sense of ego identity, which leads the person to a psychosocial regression and an inability to face the next developmental stage. The greater danger, of course, is too much isolation, too little intimacy, and a deficiency in the basic strength of love.

Love: The Basic Strength of Young Adulthood

Love, the basic strength of young adulthood, emerges from the crisis of intimacy vs. isolation. Erikson (1968, 1982) defined love as mature devotion that overcomes basic differences between males and females. Although love includes intimacy, it also contains some degree of isolation because each partner is permitted to retain a separate identity. Mature love means commitment, sexual passion, cooperation, competition, and friendship. It is the basic strength of young adulthood, enabling a person to cope productively with the final two stages of development.

The antithesis of love is *exclusivity*, the core pathology of young adulthood. Some exclusivity, however, is necessary for intimacy because a person must be able to exclude certain people, activities, and ideas in order to develop a strong sense of identity. Exclusivity becomes pathological when it blocks one's ability to cooperate, compete, or compromise, all prerequisite ingredients for intimacy and love.

As a young woman, Eleanor Roosevelt was much confused in her identity. She had a strong desire to help others, yet little appreciation of human weaknesses. She was shy, awkward, and still lacking in self-confidence (Black, 1940). Despite these traits and before her 21st birthday, she met and married a handsome distant cousin named Franklin Delano Roosevelt. The young couple were much alike in many respects. Both had come from the same aristocratic social class, both had an interest in history, literature, and travel, and both were profoundly immature. Although Eleanor was "in love" with her young debonair husband, she had not yet achieved true intimacy or love.

Adulthood

The seventh stage of development is **adulthood**, that time when people begin to take their place in society and assume responsibility for whatever that society produces. For most people this is perhaps the longest stage of development, spanning the years from about 31 to 60. Adulthood is characterized by the psychosexual mode of *procreativity*, the psychosocial crisis of *generativity vs. stagnation*, and the basic strength of *care*.

Procreativity

Erikson's psychosexual theory assumes an instinctual drive to perpetuate the species. This drive is the counterpart of an adult animal's instinct toward procreation and is an extension of the genitality that marks young adulthood (Erikson, 1982). However, **procreativity** refers to more than genital contact with an intimate partner. It includes assuming responsibility for the care of offspring that result from that sexual contact. Ideally, procreation should follow from the mature intimacy and love established during the preceding stage. Obviously, people are physically capable of producing offspring before they are psychologically ready to care for the welfare of these children. Intimacy alone is not sufficient for mature adulthood. Two people can be intimate yet, as a pair, remain isolated from society at large.

Mature adulthood demands more than the procreation of offspring; it includes the care of one's children as well as other people's children. In addition, it encompasses productive work and the perpetuation of society. It requires a willingness and readiness to be a part of society and to transmit culture from one generation to the next.

Generativity vs. Stagnation

The syntonic quality of adulthood is *generativity*, defined as "the generation of new beings as well as new products and new ideas" (Erikson, 1982, p. 67). Generativity, which is concerned with establishing and guiding the next generation, includes the procreation of children, the production of work, and the creation of new things and ideas that contribute to the building of a better world.

People have a need not only to learn but also to teach and to instruct. This need extends beyond one's own children to an altruistic concern for other young people. Generativity grows out of earlier syntonic qualities, such as intimacy and identity. As we have seen, intimacy calls for the ability to fuse one's ego to that of another without fear of losing it. This meeting of ego identities leads to a gradual expansion of interests. One-to-one intimacy is no longer enough. Other people, especially children, become part of one's concern. Instructing others in the ways of culture is a drive found in all societies. For the mature adult, this is not merely an obligation or a selfish need, but an evolutionary drive to make a contribution to succeeding generations and to ensure the continuity of human society as well.

The antithesis of generativity is *self-absorption and stagnation*. The generational cycle of productivity and creativity is crippled when people become too absorbed in themselves and too self-indulgent. Such an attitude fosters a pervading sense of stagnation.

However, some elements of stagnation and self-absorption are necessary. Creative people must, at times, remain in a dormant stage and be absorbed with themselves in order to eventually generate new growth. The interaction of generativity and stagnation produces care, the basic strength of adulthood.

Care: The Basic Strength of Adulthood

Erikson (1982, p. 67) defines **care** as "a widening commitment to *take care of* the persons, the products, and the ideas one has learned to *care for.*" As the basic strength of adulthood, care arises from each earlier basic strength. One must have hope, will, purpose, competence, fidelity, and love in order to take care of that which one cares for. Care is not a duty or obligation but a natural desire emerging from the conflict between generativity and stagnation or self-absorption.

The antithesis of care is *rejectivity*, the core pathology of adulthood. Rejectivity is the unwillingness to take care of certain persons or groups (Erikson, 1982). It manifests itself as self-centeredness, provincialism, or *pseudospeciation*; that is, the belief that other groups of people are, by nature, a different species from our own. It is responsible for much of human hatred, destruction, atrocity, and war. According to Erikson (1982, p. 70), rejectivity "has far-reaching implications for the survival of the species as well as for every individual's psychosocial development."

The long period of adulthood brought many changes in Eleanor's life. She began this stage as a dependent, young wife living under the domination of a possessive mother-in-law, and she ended it as a respected, admired, and self-confident woman.

This was a period of procreativity for Eleanor as she gave birth to six children from 1906 to 1916. After the birth of her youngest child, she suspended sexual relations with her husband because she found evidence that he had been having an affair. Her first impulse was to divorce Franklin, but, again, her mother-in-law intervened and threatened to cut off her son's flow of money. Although Eleanor stayed with Franklin until he died, she became more emotionally detached from him and began to lead a more independent life style.

Eleanor now entered the generativity stage, nurturing her own children and helping the less fortunate of the world. When Franklin was elected to the presidency in 1932, she knew that all hopes of an intimate life with him were gone and that her mission in life was to care for others.

Old Age

The eighth and final stage of development is **old age**, that period from about 60 to the end of life. Old age need not mean that people are no longer generative.

Procreation, in the narrow sense of producing children, is absent, yet old people can remain productive and creative in other ways. They can be good grandparents, not only to their own grandchildren, but also to other younger members of society. Erikson, in an interview with Elizabeth Hall, said, "I'm convinced that old people and children need one another and that there's an affinity between old age and childhood that, in fact, rounds out the life cycle" (Hall, 1983, p. 24). Old age can be a time of playfulness, joy, and wonder, but it also can be a time of senility, depression, and despair. The psychosexual mode of old age is *generalized sensuality;* the psychosocial crisis is *integrity vs. despair;* and the basic strength is *wisdom.*

Generalized Sensuality

The final psychosexual stage is *generalized sensuality.* Erikson has little to say about this mode of psychosexual life, but one may infer that it means to take pleasure in a variety of different physical sensations—sights, sounds, tastes, odors, embraces, and perhaps genital stimulation. Generalized sensuality may also include a greater appreciation for the traditional life style of the opposite sex. Men become more nurturant and more acceptant of the pleasures of nonsexual relationships, including those with their grandchildren and great-grandchildren. Women become more interested and involved in politics, finance, and world affairs (Erikson, Erikson, & Kivnick, 1986). A generalized sensual attitude, however, is dependent on one's ability to hold things together, that is, to maintain integrity in the face of despair.

Integrity vs. Despair

A person's final identity crisis is *integrity vs. despair.* At the end of life, the dystonic quality of despair may prevail, but for people with a strong ego identity, who have learned intimacy, and who have taken care of both people and things, the syntonic quality of integrity will predominate. Integrity means a feeling of wholeness and coherence, an ability to hold together one's sense of "I-ness" despite diminishing physical and intellectual powers.

Ego integrity is sometimes difficult to maintain when people see that they are losing familiar aspects of their existence—spouse, friends, body strength, mental alertness, independence, and social usefulness. Under such pressure, people often feel a pervading sense of despair, which they may express as disgust, depression, contempt for others, or any other attitude that reveals a nonacceptance of the finite boundaries of life.

Despair literally means to be without hope. A reexamination of Figure 3.2 reveals that despair, the last dystonic quality of the life cycle, is in the opposite corner from hope, the person's first basic strength. From infancy to old age, there is always hope. Once hope is lost, despair follows and life ceases to have meaning.

Erikson's stages of development extend into old age.

Wisdom: The Basic Strength of Old Age

Some amount of despair is natural and necessary for psychological maturity. The inevitable struggle between integrity and despair produces *wisdom*, the basic strength of old age. Erikson (1982, p. 61) defined wisdom as "informed and detached concern with life itself in the face of death itself." A detached concern does not mean a lack of concern; rather it implies an active but dispassionate interest. Mature wisdom maintains the integrity of a lifetime of experience in spite of declining physical and mental abilities. It draws from and contributes to the traditional knowledge passed from generation to generation. In old age, it is concerned with ultimate issues, including nonexistence (Erikson, Erikson, & Kivnick, 1986).

The antithesis of wisdom and the core pathology of old age is *disdain*, which Erikson (1982, p. 61) defined as "a reaction to feeling (and seeing others) in an increasing state of being finished, confused, helpless." Disdain is a continuation of rejectivity, the core pathology of adulthood. It means to reject with aloof contempt. It is a natural reaction to human depravity, deceit, and weakness.

When her husband died in 1945, Eleanor Roosevelt was not yet 62 years old and still in the adulthood stage of her life. Her remaining 17 years were productive ones as she passed easily and gracefully into old age. She emerged from Franklin's shadow and achieved greatness on her own. She consulted with world leaders, lectured, wrote, and worked diligently for her political party. She identified with all humankind in a comfortable and confident manner and displayed the integrity and wisdom that would have been consistent with Erikson's views of old age.

Stages	A Psychosexual Stages and Modes	B Psychosocial Crises	C Radius of Significant Relations	D Basic Strengths	E Core-pathology Basic Antipathies	F Related Principles of Social Order	G Binding Ritualizations	H Ritualism
I Infancy	Oral-Respiratory, Sensory-Kinesthetic (Incorporative Modes)	Basic Trust vs. Basic Mistrust	Maternal Person	Hope	Withdrawal	Cosmic Order	Numinous	Idolism
II Early Childhood	Anal-Urethral, Muscular (Retentive-Eliminative)	Autonomy vs. Shame, Doubt	Parental Persons	Will	Compulsion	"Law and Order"	Judicious	Legalism
III Play Age	Infantile-Genital, Locomotor (Intrusive, Inclusive)	Initiative vs. Guilt	Basic Family	Purpose	Inhibition	Ideal Prototypes	Dramatic	Moralism
IV School Age	"Latency"	Industry vs. Inferiority	"Neighborhood", School	Competence	Inertia	Technological Order	Formal (Technical)	Formalism
V Adolescence	Puberty	Identity vs. Identity Confusion	Peer Groups and Outgroups: Models of Leadership	Fidelity	Repudiation	Ideological Worldview	Ideological	Totalism
VI Young Adulthood	Genitality	Intimacy vs. Isolation	Partners in friendship, sex, competition, and cooperation	Love	Exclusivity	Patterns of Cooperation and Competition	Affiliative	Elitism
VII Adulthood	(Procreativity)	Generativity vs. Stagnation	Divided Labor and shared household	Care	Rejectivity	Currents of Education and Tradition	Generational	Authoritism
VIII Old Age	(Generalization of Sensual Modes)	Integrity vs. Despair	"Mankind" "My Kind"	Wisdom	Disdain	Wisdom	Philosophical	Dogmatism

Figure 3.3   *Erikson's Eight Stages of the Life Cycle*

Summary

Erikson's cycle of life is summarized in Figure 3.3. Each of the eight stages is characterized by a psychosexual mode as well as a psychosocial crisis. The psychosocial crisis is stimulated by a conflict between the predominating syntonic element and its antithetical dystonic element. From this conflict emerges a basic strength or ego quality. Each basic strength has a basic antithesis that becomes the core pathology of that stage. The person has an ever-increasing radius of significant relations, beginning with the maternal person in infancy and ending with an identification with humanity during old age.

Personality always develops during a particular historical period and within a given society. Nevertheless, the eight developmental stages transcend chronology and geography and are appropriate to nearly all cultures, past or present.

ERIKSON'S METHODS OF INVESTIGATION

Most personality theorists have based their models on their experiences with relatively homogeneous populations. For example, Freud, although widely read, limited his investigations largely to upper-middle- and upper-class adults who visited his clinic at Berggasse 19 in Vienna. Erikson, on the other hand, insisted that personality is a product of history, culture, and biology, and this approach is reflected in the breadth of his methods of investigation. No other theorist has studied personality development in such a variety of settings. He has employed anthropological, historical, sociological, and clinical methods to learn about children, adolescents, mature adults, and elderly people. He has studied middle-class Americans, European children, Sioux and Yurok Indian tribes, and even sailors on a submarine. He has written biographical portraits of Adolf Hitler, Maxim Gorky, Martin Luther, and Mohandas K. Gandhi among others. In this section we look at three approaches Erikson has used to explain and describe human personality—anthropological studies, psychohistory, and play construction.

Anthropological Studies

In 1937 Erikson made a field trip to the Pine Ridge Indian Reservation in South Dakota to investigate the causes of apathy among Sioux children. During this excursion Erikson relied on his clinical training as a psychoanalyst and his experience working with John Dollard and other anthropologists at the Yale Institute of Human Relations. Erikson (1963, Chapter 3) reported on early Sioux training in terms of his newly evolving theories of psychosexual and psychosocial development. He found that apathy was an expression of an extreme dependency the Indians had developed by relying on various federal programs. At one time they had been courageous buffalo hunters, but by 1937 the Sioux had lost their group identity as hunters and were trying half-heartedly to scrape out a living as farmers. Child-rearing practices, which in the past had trained young boys to be hunters and young girls to be helpers and mothers of future hunters, were no longer appropriate for an agrarian society. As a consequence, the Sioux children of 1937 had great difficulty achieving a sense of ego identity, especially after they reached adolescence.

Two years later Erikson made a similar field trip to northern California to study the Yurok Indians, a tribe that lived mostly on salmon fishing. Although the Sioux and Yurok had vastly divergent cultures, each tribe had a tradition of training its youth in the virtues of its society. The Yuroks, trained to catch fish, had little taste for war, and did not possess a strong national feeling or rigid organizational hierarchy. Obtaining and retaining provisions and possessions were highly valued among the Yuroks. Erikson (1963, Chapter 4) was able to show that early childhood training was consistent with this strong cultural value and that, once again, history and society helped shape personality.

Psychohistory

During this century a relatively new discipline called psychohistory has evolved that combines psychoanalytic concepts with historical methods. Freud (1910/1957) originated psychohistory with an investigation of Leonardo Da Vinci, and later collaborated with American Ambassador William Bullitt to write a book-length psychological study of President Woodrow Wilson (Freud & Bullitt, 1967). Although Erikson (1975) deplored this latter work, he took up the methods of psychohistory and refined them, especially in his study of Martin Luther (Erikson, 1958, 1975) and Mohandas Gandhi (Erikson, 1969, 1975).

Erikson (1974, p. 13) defined psychohistory as "the study of individual and collective life with the combined methods of psychoanalysis and history." He used psychohistory to demonstrate his fundamental belief that each person is a product of his or her historical time. Psychohistory differs from a case history in that it is more likely to deal with a person who is able to maintain ego identity and integrity in the face of neurotic conflict. In contrast, case histories usually depict neurotic individuals who are unable to maintain integrity.

As an author of psychohistory, Erikson believed that he should be emotionally involved in his subject. This involvement is similar to the concept of **countertransference**, first recognized by Freud and extensively elucidated by others. Countertransference is the counterpart of **transference**, and refers to a therapist's irrational emotional attachment or attraction to a patient. Erikson, for example, developed a strong emotional attachment to Gandhi, which he attributed to his own lifelong search for the father he had never seen (Erikson, 1975).

In *Gandhi's Truth* Erikson (1969) revealed his strong positive feelings for Gandhi as he attempted to answer the question of how healthy individuals such as Gandhi work through conflict and crisis when other people are debilitated by lesser strife. In searching for an answer, Erikson examined Gandhi's entire life cycle but concentrated on one particular crisis, which climaxed when a middle-aged Gandhi first used self-imposed fasting as a political weapon.

As a child, Gandhi was close to his mother but experienced conflict with his father. Rather than viewing this situation as an Oedipal conflict, Erikson saw it as Gandhi's opportunity to work out conflict with authority figures—an opportunity Gandhi was to have many times during his life.

Gandhi was born October 2, 1869, in Porbandar, India. As a young man, he studied law in London, and was inconspicuous in manner and appearance. Then, dressed like a proper British subject, he returned to India to practice law. After two

According to Erikson, Mahatma Gandhi developed basic strengths from his several identity crises.

years of unsuccessful practice, he went to South Africa, another British colony. He intended to remain for a year, but his first serious identity crisis kept him there for more than 20 years.

A week after a judge excluded him from a courtroom, he was thrown off a train when he refused to give up his seat to a "white" man. These two experiences with racial prejudice changed Gandhi's life. By the time he resolved this identity crisis, his appearance had changed dramatically. No longer attired in silk hat and black coat, he dressed in the cotton loincloth and shawl that were to become familiar to millions of people throughout the world. During those years in South Africa, he evolved the technique of passive resistance known as *Satyagraha* and used it to solve his conflicts with authorities.

After returning to India, he experienced another identity crisis when, in 1918, at age 49, he became the central figure in a workers' strike against the mill owners at Ahmedabad. Erikson referred to the events surrounding the strike as "The Event," and it is this crisis that dominates *Gandhi's Truth*. Although this strike was only a minor event in the history of India and received only scant attention in Gandhi's autobiography, Erikson (1969) saw it as having a great impact on Gandhi's identity as a practitioner of militant nonviolence.

The mill workers had pledged to strike if their demands for a 35% pay increase were not met. But the owners, who had agreed among themselves to offer no more than a 20% increase, locked out the workers and tried to break their solidarity by offering the 20% increase to those who would come back to work. Gandhi, the workers' spokesman, agonized over this impasse. Then, somewhat impetuously, he pledged to eat no more food until the workers' demands were met. This, the first of his 17 "fasts to the death," was not undertaken as a threat to the mill owners, but to demonstrate to the workers that a pledge must be kept. In fact, Gandhi feared that the mill owners might surrender out of sympathy for him rather than from recognition of the worker's desperate plight. Indeed, on the third day a compromise was reached whereby both the workers and the owners could save face—the workers would work one day for a 35% increase, one day for a 20% increase, and then for whatever amount an arbitrator decided. The next day Gandhi ended his hunger strike, but his passive resistance had helped shape his identity and had given him a new tool for peaceful political and social change.

Unlike neurotic individuals whose identity crises result in core pathologies, Gandhi had developed basic strength from this and other crises.

Erikson (1969, p. 363) described the difference between conflicts in great people, such as Gandhi, and psychologically disturbed people: "This, then, is the difference between a case history and a life-history: patients, great or small, are increasingly debilitated by their inner conflicts, but in historical actuality inner conflict only adds an indispensable momentum to all superhuman effort."

Play Construction

From his clinical experiences with children, Erikson developed a projective technique called **play construction**. Although he employed this approach with play-age children (see Erikson, 1977), his most famous and controversial use of play construction involved somewhat older children.

Three times over a two-year period, Erikson asked ten-to-twelve-year-old boys and girls to imagine that they were movie directors and then to construct an exciting scene from a movie, using a random selection of available toys. The toys included people, animals, furniture, cars, blocks, and other assorted objects. Interestingly, very few subjects actually re-created an existing movie scene or named their dolls after real movie stars. Erikson (1963) believed that the stories the children told about the scenes, as well as the scenes themselves, were an unconscious expression of their life history.

Erikson looked for both common and unique elements in play construction. To test for reliability and objectivity, he asked two independent observers to make judgments based on photographs of the completed scenes. The most significant and controversial common element noted was a difference between girls and boys in the way they arranged their scenes. The two sexes used space differently, with girls tending to construct interior scenes and boys exterior ones. Girls used more furniture, people, and domesticated animals to construct peaceful scenes, whereas boys more often selected blocks, cars, and wild animals to build scenes dominated by height, downfall, and motion. The arrangements of girls were simple, static, and low; those of boys were complex, action-oriented, and tall or elongated. Girls frequently constructed circular enclosures with low doors and gates that might be either open or closed. In contrast, boys usually built tall towers and included action themes such as rising and falling.

Erikson (1963, 1968) suggested that these differences were at least partially due to anatomical differences between the sexes. He pointed out that play constructions "closely parallel the morphology of the sex organs; in the male, *external* organs, *erectable* and *intrusive* in character, *conducting* highly *mobile* sperm cells; *internal* organs in the female, with a vestibular *access* leading to *statically expectant* ova" (Erikson, 1963, p. 106).

Such an interpretation has not gone uncriticized. Some critics (see Janeway, 1971) have accused Erikson of sexism, pointing out that socialization practices might easily explain these differences. Erikson (1975) accepted the argument that social influences might account for some of the differences, but he insisted that anatomy is the principal source of gender differences in play constructions. Does this mean that Erikson agreed with Freud that anatomy is destiny? Erikson's answer was yes, anatomy is destiny, but he quickly qualified that dictum to read: "Anatomy, history, and personality are our combined destiny" (Erikson, 1968, p. 285). In other words, anatomy alone does not determine destiny, but it combines with past events, including socialization practices and various personality dimensions such as temperament and intelligence, to determine who a person will become. "Destiny, for both men and women, depends on what you can make of the fact that you have a specific kind of body in a particular historical setting " (Erikson, 1974, p. 116).

In addition to sex differences (which, incidentally, were not expected at the beginning of the study), Erikson investigated unique elements in play constructions and found that children consciously or unconsciously arranged scenes and built dramatic plots that were consistent with their life histories. Each of these children was part of a larger study and each had been intensively investigated almost since birth. With this vast information on the child's life history, Erikson was able to see ways in which play constructions were an expression of hidden needs and motives.

Erikson's investigation of play construction is unique among personality theorists. He used this method as a kind of projective technique in much the same way that Freud used free association and dream interpretation as a means of uncovering unconscious aspects of personality. In Chapter 2 we saw that Freud believed that dreams were the "royal road" to the unconscious. Similarly, Erikson saw children's play as the royal road to understanding personal history. To Erikson (1975, p. 39), play construction is the *"via regia* [royal road] to an understanding of growing man's conflicts and triumphs, his repetitive working through of the past, and his creative self-renewal in truly playful moments."

CONCEPT OF HUMANITY

How does Erikson conceptualize humanity in terms of the six dimensions we introduced in Chapter 1? First, is the life cycle determined by *external forces* or do people have some *choice* in molding their personalities and shaping their lives? Erikson is not as strongly deterministic as Freud, but neither does he believe strongly in free choice. His position is somewhere in the middle. Although our destiny lies with anatomy, history, and personality, we retain some limited control over both history and personality, giving us some measure of choice. We can search for our own identities and are not completely constrained by history or society. Individuals, in fact, can change history and alter their environment. The two subjects of Erikson's most extensive psychohistories, Luther and Gandhi, each had a profound effect on world history and on his own immediate surroundings. Similarly, each of us has the power to determine our own life cycles, even though our global impact may be on a lesser scale.

On the dimension of *pessimism vs. optimism* Erikson tends to be somewhat optimistic. If core pathologies predominate in our early stages of development, we are not inevitably doomed to continue a pathological existence in later stages. Although weaknesses in early life make it more difficult for us to acquire basic strengths later on, we remain capable of changing at any stage of life. Each psychosocial conflict consists of a syntonic and a dystonic quality. Each crisis can be resolved in favor of the harmonious element, regardless of past resolutions.

Erikson does not specifically address the issue of *causality vs. teleology*, but his view of humanity suggests that we are influenced more by biological and social forces than by our view of the future. We are a product of a particular historical moment and a specific social setting. Although we can set goals and actively strive to achieve these goals, we cannot completely escape the powerful causal forces of anatomy, history, and sociology. For this reason, Erikson rates high on causality.

On the fourth dimension, *conscious vs. unconscious determinants*, Erikson's position is mixed. Prior to adolescence, our personality is largely shaped by unconscious motivation. Psychosexual and psychosocial conflicts during the first four developmental stages occur before we have firmly established our identity. We seldom are clearly aware of these crises and the ways in which they mold our personalities. From adolescence forward, however, we ordinarily are aware of our actions and most of the reasons underlying them.

Erikson's theory, of course, is more *social* than *biological*. However, it does not overlook anatomy and other physiological factors in personality development. Each psychosexual mode has a clear biological component. However, as we advance through the eight stages, social influences become increasingly more powerful. Also, the radius of social relations expands from the single maternal person to a global identification with all humanity. Erikson's emphasis on social forces is in sharp contrast to Freud's biological theory. Indeed, Erikson's model is sometimes identified as a social psychoanalytic theory.

The sixth dimension for a concept of humanity is *uniqueness vs. similarities*. Erikson tends to place somewhat more emphasis on individual differences than on universal characteristics. Although people in different cultures advance through the eight developmental stages in the same order, myriad differences are found in the pace of that journey. Each of us resolves our psychosocial crises in a unique manner, and each uses the basic strengths in a way that is peculiarly ours.

Related Research

The popularity of Erikson's work has sparked numerous studies, both descriptive and experimental. James E. Marcia has been at the forefront of researchers investigating components of Eriksonian stages of development. He and his associates have assessed intimacy and isolation during young adulthood (Orlofsky, Marcia, & Lesser, 1973), industry during school age (Kowaz & Marcia, 1991), and identity during adolescence (Marcia, 1966).

Most of Marcia's research has been conducted with people in late adolescence, a period that Erikson regards as a time of *commitment* to personal ideologies and occupational goals. Young people are, or should be, deciding who they are, what they believe, and what kind of work they wish to pursue. Central to Erikson's developmental theory is the notion that late adolescents experience an identity crisis, a period of both increased vulnerability and heightened potential.

To study ego identity during adolescence, Marcia (1966) developed an identity status interview that measures both commitment and crisis in the areas of (1) occupation, (2) religion, and (3) politics. The interview classifies people into one of four identity status categories. *Identity achievement*, the highest level of development, involves the formation of secure ego-identity and takes place after questions of identity have been asked and successfully resolved. *Psychosocial moratorium* takes place when adolescents are involved in an ongoing crisis of indecision, exploring their identity but not yet making a commitment to it. *Identity foreclosure* suggests a time when adolescents have not yet begun to question their identity but instead take on the values and expectations of their parents. *Identity diffusion* is characterized by a lack of commitment and the absence of concern or struggle with problems of identity. Progress toward identity proceeds from diffusion to foreclosure to moratorium to achievement.

Because identity achievement is the most developmentally mature state, it follows that older, more experienced college students will more likely have reached this stage than younger, less experienced students (Marcia, 1980). To investigate this hypothesis, Prager (1986) used an identity status interview to assess the presence or absence of crisis and commitment in four areas for 86 women from a large American university. The four areas of identity were occupational goals, religious ideology, political ideology, and sexual values. Prager classified each subject into one of Marcia's four identity status categories for each of these four areas and then assigned them an overall rating on identity. As expected, older subjects (23–24 years old) and those with three or four years of college were mostly classified in the identity achievement stage, whereas younger women and those with fewer years of college were predominantly classified in the identity foreclosure status. Contrary to prediction, however, Prager found that identity diffusion was equally distributed among all subject groups. In general, Prager's study supported Erikson's hypothesis that the most developmentally mature outcome of late adolescent identity crisis is identity achievement.

In an earlier study of college men, Marcia (1976) examined the relationship between identity status and intimacy. He found that subjects classified six years earlier as having identity achievement, as well as those currently so classified, were more likely to have established intimate relationships. Subjects who had changed to a foreclosed or diffused status had either stereotyped relationships or were experiencing interpersonal isolation. This study indicates that the identity status interview can predict a person's ability to become involved in intimate and satisfying interpersonal relationships.

Bilsker, Schiedel, and Marcia (1988) found gender differences in the identity status of college students. They administered the identity status interview to 75 women and 76 men and found that the religious and political ideology domains were most predictive of identity for men, whereas the sexual-interpersonal domains were most predictive of identity for women. Interestingly, these researchers found that women are now equal to men in their ability to achieve identity through occupational status. These results suggest that issues of interpersonal functioning are more relevant to women than to men in achieving identity.

In a later study, Bilsker and Marcia (1991) focused on the moratorium stage of identity formation and the psychological processes related to it. They reasoned that because adolescents in the moratorium status are actively involved in questioning their parents' beliefs as a means of forming their own commitments, they should show greater tendencies toward "regressive experience" than adolescents in the other three categories. Regressive experience refers to such states as distorted perceptions, belief in the supernatural, ecstatic emotions, daydreaming, and taking pleasure in childish behavior. Bilsker and Marcia (1991) found that 17-to-24-year-old college students in the moratorium status were more likely to report regressive experiences than those in any of the other status categories. This finding suggests that adaptive regression is specific to the moratorium status, a time when late adolescents are involved in exploring who they are without yet having established a firm commitment to personal identity.

In addition to the work of Marcia and his colleagues, McAdams and de St. Aubin (1992) have recently developed the Loyola Generativity Scale (LGS) designed to tap into different aspects of generativity, the syntonic element of adulthood. The LGS includes such items as "I have important skills that I try to teach others" and "I do not volunteer to work for a charity." In the first part of their study, McAdams and de St. Aubin determined that the LGS has acceptable reliability and that it accurately measures one of seven interrelated aspects of generativity, namely, *concern* for the next generation. Next, the researchers investigated how well *concern* related to two additional qualities of generativity: (1) generative *action* in creating, maintaining, and offering up, and (2) personal *narration*, or the subjective story or theme that an adult creates about providing for the next generation. They assessed action by objective reports of real-life behavior and narration by open-ended descriptions of personally meaningful autobiographical events. This second part of the study, which used adults ranging in age from 15 to 74, found that *concern* was related to both *action* and *narration*, suggesting that people who are concerned for the next generation tend to transform that concern into action and to have a dominant and recurrent theme of generativity that runs throughout their lives. Somewhat surprisingly, McAdams and de St. Aubin (1992) also found that generativity scores were unrelated to age, indicating that as people grow older they do not necessarily become more interested in the next generation.

CRITIQUE OF ERIKSON

Erikson's work is widely recognized in both professional and popular circles, and the eight stages of human development are frequently cited in the scientific literature as well as in the popular press. His popularity, in part, is due to his decision to extend Freud's theories rather than to attack them. Many observers have seen Erikson's work as a continuation of what Freud might have done had he lived another 50 years. Erikson has never repudiated Freud, and thus has avoided much condemnation by orthodox psychoanalysts. More important, he has emphasized the ego and normal functioning and thus has gained the favor of many anti-Freudians.

Erikson has built his theory largely on ethical principles and not necessarily on scientific data. He came to psychology from art and acknowledges that he sees the world more through the eyes of an artist than through those of a scientist. In *Childhood and Society* (1950) he wrote that he had nothing to offer except "a way of looking at things." His books are admittedly subjective and personal, which undoubtedly adds to their appeal. Nevertheless, Erikson's theory must be judged by the standards of science, not ethics or art.

The first criterion of a useful theory is its ability to *generate research*, and by this standard Erikson's theory is rated somewhat higher than average. In addition to the work of Marcia and his colleagues, Hamachek (1988) has developed a series of behavioral expressions designed to help researchers know the specific behavioral characteristics of people who have (1) a high or low sense of basic trust, (2) a sense of autonomy vs. a sense of shame and doubt, (3) a sense of initiative or of guilt, (4) a sense of industry or of inferiority, and (5) a sense of identity or of identity confusion. Such an instrument should help future researchers assess levels of development among children and adolescents.

In its ability to *organize knowledge*, Erikson's theory is limited mostly to developmental stages. It does not adequately address such issues as personal traits or motivation, a limitation that subtracts from the theory's ability to shed meaning on much of what is currently known about human personality. The eight stages of development remain an eloquent statement of what the life cycle should be, and research findings in these areas usually can be fit into an Eriksonian framework. However, the theory lacks sufficient scope to be rated high on this criterion.

As a *guide to action*, Erikson's theory provides many general guidelines, but offers little specific advice. Compared to other theories discussed in this book, it ranks near the top in suggesting approaches to dealing with middle-aged and older adults. Erikson's views on aging have been helpful to people in the field of gerontology, and his ideas on ego identity are nearly always cited in adolescent psychology textbooks. In addition, his concepts of intimacy vs. isolation and generativity vs. stagnation have much to offer to marriage counselors and others concerned with intimate relationships among young adults.

Erikson's theory is rated high on *internal consistency*, mostly because the terms used to label the different psychosocial crises, basic strengths, and core pathologies are very carefully chosen. English is not Erikson's first language, and his extensive use of a dictionary while writing has increased the precision of his terminology. Yet concepts like hope, will, purpose, love, care, and so on are not operationally defined. They have little scientific usefulness, although they rank high in both literary and emotional value. On the other hand, Erikson's epigenetic principle and the eloquence of his description of the eight stages of development mark his theory with conspicuous internal consistency.

On the criterion of simplicity or *parsimony*, the theory has only a moderate rating. The precision of its terms is a strength, but the descriptions of psychosexual stages and psychosocial crises, especially in the later stages, are not always clearly differentiated. In addition, Erikson uses different terms and even different concepts to fill out the 64 boxes (see Figure 3.2) that constitute his developmental theory. Such inconsistency subtracts from the theory's simplicity.

Chapter Summary

The work of Erik Erikson provides a logical extension of Freud's psychoanalysis. An artist by early training, Erikson has offered a "way of looking at things" rather than a theory based on scientifically gathered data. Although he takes for granted most of Freud's work, he has (1) placed more emphasis on the ego and less on the id, (2) extended the stages of development into adulthood and old age, and (3) elevated social influences over the biologically based instincts.

The eight stages of development rest on an *epigenetic principle*, meaning that each component proceeds in a step-by-step fashion with later growth building on earlier development. In every stage people face an interaction of opposing attitudes, which leads to

a conflict or *psychosocial crisis*. Resolution of the crisis produces an appropriate *basic strength* and enables the person to move on to the next stage. In addition, *biological components* lay a ground plan for each individual, but a multiplicity of historical, social, and physiological events shape ego identity.

The first stage of development is *infancy*, characterized by the oral-sensory mode of incorporation, the psychosocial crisis of basic trust vs. mistrust, the basic strength of hope, and the core pathology of withdrawal. Infancy covers the first year of life, a time equivalent to Freud's oral stage.

The second stage is called *early childhood* and parallels Freud's anal stage. During early childhood the anal, urethral, and muscular psychosexual modes are in ascendance, and the psychosocial conflict of autonomy vs. shame and doubt produces the basic strength called will or its antithesis, called compulsion.

From about ages three to five, the child goes through the *play age*, a time corresponding to the phallic or Oedipal period. A play-age child experiences genital-locomotor psychosexual development and undergoes a psychosocial crisis of initiative vs. guilt. Either the basic strength of purpose or the core pathology of inhibition may emerge from the play age.

Erikson's fourth stage, *school age*, covers the period from about six to eleven, and corresponds to Freud's latency stage. The school-age child experiences the psychosocial crisis of industry vs. inferiority, from which arises the basic strength of competence or the core pathology of inertia. The school-age child's radius of significant relations expands beyond the family to include peers and teachers who serve as models.

Adolescence is a crucial stage in Erikson's theory because one's clear and consistent image of self—ego identity—should emerge from this period. However, identity confusion may dominate the psychosocial crisis, thereby postponing identity. Fidelity is the basic strength of adolescence; role repudiation its core pathology.

Young adulthood, the time from about 19 to 30, is characterized by genitality, a psychosexual mode that can exist in the absence of intimacy. Ideally, however, intimacy should win out in its conflict with isolation and produce the basic strength of love. If the psychosocial crisis is not completely resolved, the core pathology of exclusivity results.

The seventh and often longest stage is *adulthood*, a time not only of procreation but also of productive work and social commitment. The dominant psychosocial crisis is generativity vs. stagnation, while care is the basic strength, and rejectivity a possible core pathology.

The final stage, *old age*, is marked by a generalized sensuality and the crisis of integrity vs. despair. Wisdom, the basic strength, is opposed by disdain, the core pathology.

Erikson's *concept of humanity* is generally optimistic and idealistic. People can overcome early pathologies, but crisis, anxiety, and conflict are a normal and necessary part of living. People cannot be abstracted from society or from the historical period in which they live. Although we are one species, history, culture, and biology lead to individual differences among us.

Erikson's theory has been well received both popularly and professionally. Although not built on an abundance of scientific data, it has sparked a great deal of research and discussion. The theory has an eloquent logic and consistency, but it is only moderately successful in organizing knowledge and providing guidelines to practitioners.

Suggested Readings

ERIKSON, E. H. (1950, 1963). *Childhood and society.* New York: Norton.
> This is Erikson's first important work, the one that laid the foundation to his post-Freudian theory. It is one of the most popular and frequently recommended psychology books in the United States. Erikson added some afterthoughts in 1985, the 35th-anniversary edition.

ERIKSON, E. H. (1989). Elements of a psychoanalytic theory of psychosocial development. In S. I. Greenspan & G. H. Pollock (Eds.), *The course of life: Vol.1. Infancy* (pp. 15–83). Madison, CT: International Universities Press.
> In this chapter Erikson presents a summary of his theory of psychosocial development.

ERIKSON, J. M. (1988). *Wisdom and the senses: The way of creativity.* New York: Norton.
> In this book, Erikson's wife, Joan gives a unique perspective on the life cycle, including color charts of how the various basic strengths might be woven into one's life pattern.

HALL, E. (1983, June). A conversation with Erik Erikson. *Psychology Today,* pp. 20–30.
> In this article, Elizabeth Hall, former managing editor of *Psychology Today,* interviews Erikson at age 81. Erikson talks of the human life cycle, with emphasis on old age. Included is an interesting "box" of Kenneth Keniston's memories of Erikson at Harvard.

ROAZEN, P. (1976). *Erik H. Erikson: The power and limits of a vision.* New York: Free Press.
> Roazen's account of Erikson is more critical than that of Robert Coles (1970), whose biography borders on hero-worship. Throughout, Roazen compares Erikson to Freud and finds him too preachy, utopian, and philosophical. However, he believes that Erikson's hopeful view of humanity may be more helpful in individual therapy than Freud's skeptical attitude toward the human condition.

Individual Psychology

Chapter Four

OVERVIEW
BIOGRAPHY OF ALFRED ADLER
INTRODUCTION TO ADLERIAN THEORY
UNITY OF PERSONALITY
    Organ Dialect
    Conscious and Unconscious
SUBJECTIVE PERCEPTIONS
    Fictionalism
    Organ Inferiorities
SOCIAL INTEREST
    Development in a Social Environment
    Necessity of Social Interest
    Criterion of Human Values
STRIVING FOR SUCCESS OR SUPERIORITY
    The Final Goal
    The Striving Force As Compensation
    Striving for Personal Superiority
    Striving for Success
    Summary of the Striving Force
STYLE OF LIFE
BOX: UNDERSTANDING LIFE STYLE THROUGH EARLY
    RECOLLECTIONS
CREATIVE POWER
ABNORMAL DEVELOPMENT
    General Description
    External Factors in Maladjustment
    Safeguarding Tendencies
    Masculine Protest
APPLICATIONS OF INDIVIDUAL PSYCHOLOGY
    Birth Order
    Early Recollections
    Dreams
    Psychotherapy
CONCEPT OF HUMANITY
RELATED RESEARCH
CRITIQUE OF ADLERIAN THEORY
CHAPTER SUMMARY
SUGGESTED READINGS

ADLER

Christine is a 42-year-old English teacher deeply concerned with her students. She encourages them to talk to her about their personal problems and is always willing to take time to listen and to help. She never seems to object to late-night and weekend telephone calls. She apparently is quite willing to sacrifice her own needs to those of others. To many students she seems to be a model of maternal love and concern.

To other people, however, she appears to be weak, petty, insincere, and hypo-critical. Most students have little to do with her, avoiding personal conversation at almost any cost. Her principal sees her as mostly a nuisance, constantly asking for favors and adopting the manner of a weak, helpless little girl. Her female colleagues usually find her annoying, overly cheerful, and too self-deprecating. Some of the male faculty members view her as strangely coquettish, a peculiar attitude in light of the fact that Christine is a somewhat large, unattractive woman and not overtly flirtatious.

Christine is completely oblivious to the negative opinions many of her students and colleagues have toward her. How could anyone not like her! She is dedicated, caring, nonaggressive, and willing to do almost anything for anyone.

A gifted student in school, Christine was headed toward a medical career when she met Joe and dropped out of college to get married and start a family. Although her parents and friends encouraged her to remain in school, the decision to leave was an easy one for Christine. People were surprised that she so easily changed her plans, but Christine has had a history of surprising others. Although her behavior toward Joe is usually like that of a passive and compliant daughter, sometimes, for reasons Joe cannot fathom, she will become quite assertive and demanding. For instance, on her fortieth birthday she announced to Joe that she was leaving him for another man—a young teacher with whom she was "in love." However, the young teacher did not share Christine's feelings. Christine never left Joe and, in fact, continued to behave toward him as if nothing had happened.

Christine has two adolescent children, a daughter and a son. Diane and Rusty have always been encouraged to bring their friends home, and Christine's house is often filled with young people. Christine takes a personal interest in all of them and is delighted that many see her as a second mother.

OVERVIEW

Christine's concern for others and her self-sacrificing behavior might appear to be a noble expression of maturity and love, but Alfred Adler would see it as a neurotic attempt to strive for personal superiority. Adler, in fact, viewed all motivation as springing from our attempts to gain superiority or success. An original member of the Vienna Psychoanalytic Society, Adler was the first to break from Freud and establish an important and opposing theory. Unlike Erikson, who extended Freud's theory without repudiating it, Adler accepted little of psychoanalysis. In contrast to Freud, Adler was optimistic and idealistic. He emphasized social rather than biological factors; final goals rather than past causes; individual choice and responsibility rather than determinism; and the unity of personality rather than separate and somewhat antagonistic regions of the mind.

Adler's differences from Freud cannot be explained in terms of religion or geography. Each came from a middle-class Jewish family, and each lived most of his life in Vienna. Adler himself might explain these differences in terms of birth order, social interest, style of life, and subjective perceptions, all important concepts in Individual Psychology.

BIOGRAPHY OF ALFRED ADLER

Alfred Adler was born on February 7, 1870, in Rudolfsheim, a suburb of Vienna, the second son of a middle-class Jewish grain merchant. In contrast to his older brother Sigmund, who was strong and healthy, Alfred was weak and sickly. His earliest memories were concerned with the unhappy comparison between his brother's good health and his own illness. Sigmund Adler, the childhood rival that Adler attempted to surpass, remained a worthy opponent, and in later years he was a very successful businessman (Bottome, 1939).

The lives of Freud and Adler have several interesting parallels. Although both men came from middle- or lower-middle-class Viennese Jewish parents, neither was devoutly religious. However, Freud was much more conscious of his Jewishness than Adler and often believed himself to be persecuted because of his religion. On the other hand, Adler never claimed to have been mistreated and in later years converted to Protestantism. Despite this conversion, he held no deep religious convictions, and, in fact, one of his biographers (Rattner, 1983) regarded him as an agnostic.

Like Freud, Adler had a younger brother who died in infancy. In both men this early experience had a profound effect but in vastly different ways. Freud, by his own accounting, had wished unconsciously for the death of his rival, and when the boy, in fact, died, he was filled with guilt and self-reproach, conditions that continued into his adulthood. For Adler, on the other hand, the death of his younger brother, along with his own sickly constitution, brought home to him the reality of death. He saw this experience as a challenge and determined then that his goal in life would be to conquer death. Because medicine offered some chance to forestall death, Adler decided at that time to become a physician (Ellenberger, 1970).

Whereas Freud was the oldest and favorite child of his mother, Adler was second-born and enjoyed a warm relationship with his mother for only a short time. He lost that pampered position at age 20 months when his younger sister was born. He then became the favorite of his father and remained so throughout his childhood. Although Freud was surrounded by a large family, including seven younger brothers and sisters, two grown half-brothers, and a nephew and niece about his age, he was more oriented toward his parents than to these other family members. Intellectual analysis and personal courage were more valued by Freud than were intuition and social relationships. For Adler, the reverse was true—intuition and social relationships were more important than scientific analysis. Although his family was slightly smaller than Freud's, relationships with siblings and peers played a more pivotal role in Adler's development. He spent much time with friends and schoolmates, and throughout his life he was comfortable in group situations. In contrast, Freud developed several intense one-to-one relationships during his lifetime and did not enjoy group activities. Freud's professional organizations, the Vienna Psychoanalytic Society and the International Psychoanalytic Association, were highly structured in

pyramid fashion, with an inner circle of Freud's trusted friends forming a kind of oligarchy at the top. Adler, by comparison, was more democratic. He often met with his group, which included patients as well as colleagues and friends, in Vienna coffee houses. The Individual Psychology Society, in fact, suffered from a loose organization, and Adler had a relaxed attitude toward business details that did not enhance his movement (Ellenberger, 1970).

Adler attended elementary and secondary school with neither problem nor distinction (Furtmuller, 1964). He then entered the Vienna Medical School and again completed work with no special honors. When he received his medical degree near the end of 1895, he realized his childhood goal of becoming a physician. Following a tour of military duty in the Hungarian army (he was a citizen of Hungary until 1911, when he became an Austrian citizen), Adler returned to Vienna for postgraduate study. He began private practice as an eye specialist, but his interest in the whole person led him to give up specialization and to turn to general medicine. During these early years as a general practitioner he demonstrated an intense interest in the complete person, regarding illness as a reflection of the total personality and recognizing the essential unity between the physical and mental aspects of a disease. His concern for the whole person led him to the study of psychiatry, which, of course, did not diminish his interest in general medicine. It did, however, attract the attention of Sigmund Freud.

In 1902, Freud invited Adler to join him in forming the organization that later became the Vienna Psychoanalytic Society. Adler was not a disciple of Freud and did not consider himself a psychoanalyst. He never underwent psychoanalysis and could not accept the heavy sexual emphasis Freud placed on neuroses. Despite the fact that Adler was one of the original members of Freud's inner circle, the two men never shared a warm personal relationship. Theoretical as well as personal differences grew, especially after publication in 1907 of Adler's *Study of Organ Inferiority and Its Psychical Compensation* (1907/1917).

In 1911, Adler, who was then president of the Vienna Psychoanalytic Society, was asked to present his views before the group. In a series of three papers, he expressed his opposition to the strong sexual proclivities of psychoanalysis. Both Freud and Adler then saw that their differences were irreconcilable. Adler resigned his presidency and, along with six other men, left the Freudian circle and formed the Society for Free Psychoanalysis, a term that irritated Freud with its implication that his organization was opposed to a free expression of ideas. The following year Adler changed the name of his group to the Society for Individual Psychology (Ellenberger, 1970).

In retrospect, we can easily see that personality differences between Freud and Adler would have made a lasting harmonious relationship extremely unlikely. Freud was personally very ambitious, and he jealously guarded the sacrosanct doctrines of psychoanalysis. Adler,

however, was combative and less than respectful to Freud and his fixed ideas. He had developed a fierce boyhood rivalry with his older brother, Sigmund, that carried over in his dealings with the older Freud, also named Sigmund. Adler was a very vocal member of the Vienna Psychoanalytic Society and often questioned some of the orthodox psychoanalytic views. His quarrelsome attitude was not designed to please Freud, who was quite sensitive to criticism. Adler's competitive nature, it seems, made it necessary for him to become independent of Freud and to establish a psychology that would oppose psychoanalysis.

During his early years of independence, Adler spent much of his time lecturing before audiences of both physicians and lay persons. Then, during World War I, he served as a physician in the Austrian army and, like Freud, his theoretical views were modified by his experiences with war. Whereas Freud erected aggression as the final pillar in his theory, Adler went in a different direction and evolved the concept of social interest.

After the war Adler returned to his lectures in Vienna, established several child guidance clinics, and helped train teachers for the city of Vienna. In his role as an educator of teachers, he was ahead of his time, advocating experimental methods and antiauthoritarian attitudes.

From 1926 until his death, he frequently visited the United States, holding the position of Visiting Professor for Medical Psychology at Long Island College of Medicine, now Downstate Medical Center, State University of New York. During the last five years of his life he made his home in the United States, although he returned to Europe regularly. Unlike Freud, he was impressed by Americans and admired their open-mindedness (Rattner, 1983).

Adler married Raissa Epstein, a Russian, and they had four children. His daughter Alexandra and his only son Kurt became psychiatrists, and both continued Adler's work in Individual Psychology.

Adler's favorite relaxation was music, but he also maintained an active interest in art and literature. In his work he often borrowed examples from fairy tales, the Bible, Shakespeare, Goethe, and numerous other literary works. He identified himself closely with the common

person, and his manner and appearance were consistent with that identification. His patients included a high percentage of people from the lower and middle classes, a rarity among psychiatrists of his time.

On May 28, 1937, Adler died of a heart attack in Aberdeen, Scotland, while on one of his many lecture tours. Freud, who was 14 years older than Adler, had outlived his long-time adversary. On hearing of Adler's death, Freud (as quoted in Jones, 1957, p. 208) sarcastically remarked, "For a Jew boy out of a Viennese suburb, a death in Aberdeen is an unheard-of career in itself and a proof of how far he had got on. The world really rewarded him richly for his service in having contradicted psychoanalysis."

INTRODUCTION TO ADLERIAN THEORY

After his death, Adler's popularity and prestige waned for a time, but in more recent years his views have come to acquire greater acceptance in both academic and clinical circles. His ideas on the importance of interpersonal relationships have been further developed by Harry Stack Sullivan, Karen Horney, Julian Rotter, Abraham H. Maslow, Carl Rogers, and others. His emphasis on subjective perception is the basis for Albert Ellis's rational-emotive therapy, and he has also influenced Rollo May and other existentialists.

Yet Adler remains today less well known than either Freud or Carl Jung. Several reasons account for this. First, he did not establish a tightly run organization to perpetuate his theories. Second, he was not a particularly gifted writer, and most of his books are compiled from scattered lectures. Third, many of his views were incorporated into the works of later theorists and thus became dissociated from his name. Fourth, Adler lacked Freud's drive to gain recognition and fame. He was more content to help individuals and small groups through his clinical work and lectures.

Although his writings revealed great insight into the depth and complexities of human personality, Adler evolved a basically simple and parsimonious theory of personality. The main tenets of his theory can be stated in outline form. The following is adapted from a list that represents the final statement of Adler's theory (Adler, 1964, pp. 24–25).

1. All psychological phenomena are *unified* within the individual in a self-consistent manner.
2. The *subjective perceptions* of the individual shape behavior and personality.
3. The usefulness of all human activity must be seen from the viewpoint of *social interest*.
4. The one dynamic force behind the person's activity is the *striving for success or superiority*.
5. All human potentialities develop in accordance with the individual's self-consistent *style of life*.
6. The style of life is developed by the individual's *creative power*. The creative power, then, is responsible for unity, subjective opinions, the level of social interest, the manner of striving, and, of course, one's unique style of life.

Each of these six tenets is discussed in the following subsections, beginning with unity of personality.

UNITY OF PERSONALITY

All psychological phenomena are unified within the individual in a self-consistent manner.

In choosing the term "individual," Adler wished to stress his belief that each person is unique and indivisible. Thus, **Individual Psychology** insists on the fundamental unity of personality. A person's thoughts, feelings, and actions are all directed toward a single goal and serve a single purpose. Inconsistent behavior does not exist. If seen in relation to the final goal of superiority or success, all of a person's actions are consistent and meaningful (Adler, 1930).

When people such as Christine (our case study) behave erratically or unpredictably, they do so for a single purpose. Such behavior forces other people to be on the defensive, to be watchful so as not to be confused by such capricious actions. When Christine suddenly announced to her husband that she was leaving him for another man, she did so in an emotionless, matter-of-fact way that left Joe bewildered and baffled. Then, just as unexpectedly, she told him that she had changed her mind. Her relationship toward her husband continued as if nothing had happened. She proceeded to alternate between being warm and cold to Joe. This inconsistent behavior left him puzzled and uncertain about how to react to her. Her behavior, however, merely appears inconsistent. Close examination reveals that her alternating warm and cold attitudes are each consistent with a single goal—the goal of personal superiority over her husband. By consistently baffling and puzzling Joe, Christine subordinates him to her own superiority strivings. Joe then becomes inferior because he is incapable of comprehending her. This situation provides Christine with the upper hand in the marital relationship. The fact that she is successful in her attempts to gain superiority over her husband does not necessitate conscious intent. She probably does not fully understand her goal; that is, she is not aware of her true motive and, undoubtedly, she would never admit that she wants to gain superiority at the expense of Joe.

Adler (1956) recognized several ways in which the entire personality operates with unity and self-consistency. The first of these he called organ dialect.

Organ Dialect

According to Adler (1956), the whole person strives in a self-consistent fashion toward a single goal, and all separate actions and functions can be understood only as parts of that goal. The disturbance of one part of the body cannot be viewed in isolation; it affects the entire person. In fact, the diseased organ expresses the direction of the individual's goal, a condition known as **organ dialect.**

One example of organ dialect, or organ jargon, might be a man suffering from rheumatoid arthritis in his hands. His stiff and deformed joints voice his whole style of life. It is as if they cry out, "See my deformity. See my handicap. You can't expect me to do manual work." Without an audible sound, his hands speak of his desire for sympathy from others.

Another example of organ dialect is Christine, who suffers from tachycardia, or abnormally rapid heartbeat. The symptoms, although quite real and often frightening, nevertheless are not ordinarily life threatening. Once, when her husband was planning to attend an out-of-state conference alone, Christine developed tachycardia just hours before he was to depart. She bravely insisted that he go anyway, that she could survive his absence. Joe, of course, could not leave his sick wife, so he cancelled his travel plans. Christine did not fake her illness, but her physical symptoms speak a dialect of their own. It is as if they say "I am seriously ill and must be attended to." At the same time Christine is verbalizing the opposite attitude: "Please go on your trip. I don't need any special attention." Thus, her exaggerated strivings for personal superiority are served in two ways. First, she is able to control Joe's actions and, second, she appears courageous and magnanimous.

Conscious and Unconscious

A second example of a unified personality is the harmony between conscious and unconscious actions. The unconscious is defined by Adler (1956) as that part of the goal that is neither clearly formulated nor completely understood by the individual. With this definition Adler avoids a dichotomy between the unconscious and the conscious, which he sees as cooperating parts of the same unified system. Conscious thoughts are those that are understood and regarded by the individual as helpful in striving for success. Whatever a person cannot justify as being helpful is pushed into the unconscious.

We cannot oppose "consciousness" to "unconsciousness" as if they were antagonistic halves of an individual's existence. The conscious life becomes unconscious as soon as we fail to understand it—and as soon as we understand an unconscious tendency it has already become conscious (Adler, 1929/1964, p. 163).

Consciousness and unconsciousness, rather than being opposing factions, are complementary entities operating under the dominance of a unifying style of life. Whether a thought is conscious or unconscious, it has but one purpose—to realize the goal of superiority or success.

SUBJECTIVE PERCEPTIONS

The subjective perceptions of the individual shape behavior and personality.

Personality is shaped, not by external causes such as organ inferiorities or basic drives, but by the individual's subjective perception of reality. Adler believed that people are motivated more by **fictions**, or expectations of the future, than by experiences of the past. Behavior is consistent with one's perception of the fictional final goal. This goal does not exist in the future but in the person's present perception of the future. It molds contemporary behavior because it is subjectively perceived in the here and now (Adler, 1956).

Fictionalism

Adler's ideas on fictionalism originated with Hans Vaihinger's book, *The Philosophy of "As If"* (1911/1925). Vaihinger believed that fictions are ideas that have no real existence, yet they influence people *as if* they really existed. An example of a fiction might be, "Men are superior to women." Although this notion is a fiction, many people, both men and women, act as if it were a reality. People are motivated not by what is true, but by their subjective perceptions of what is true

Christine acts as if other people are helpless and in need of her care and concern. When her neighbor's mother died, Christine insisted on driving her to the funeral home and helping make arrangements. After all, a grieving person should not have to drive a car or worry about funeral details. Such "thoughtful consideration" is characteristic of Christine's style of life, but it is also consistent with her final goal of gaining superiority over others by being kinder and gentler than anyone else.

Adler's emphasis on fictions is consistent with his strongly held teleological view of motivation. **Teleology,** an explanation of behavior in terms of its final purpose or aim, is opposed to **causality,** which considers behavior as springing from a specific cause. Teleology is usually concerned with future goals or ends, whereas causality ordinarily deals with past experiences that produce some present effect. Freud's view of motivation was basically causal because he believed that people are driven by past events that activate present behavior. Adler, on the other hand, adopted a teleological view, one in which people are motivated by present perceptions of the future. As fictions, these perceptions need not be true and, in fact, they do not have to be conscious or understood. Nevertheless, they bestow a purpose on all of one's actions and are responsible for a consistent pattern than runs throughout a person's life.

Personality is molded, not by reality, but by subjective beliefs concerning the future. The most important fiction is the goal of superiority or success, a goal created early in life, but one that may remain largely unknown. This subjective, fictional final goal guides our style of life, gives unity to our personality, and, when understood, it confers purpose on all our behavior. Whether that behavior leads to neurotic style of life or to a psychologically healthy one depends on the degree of social interest that we develop during the early years of our life.

Organ Inferiorities

Because we all begin life small, weak, and inferior, we develop a belief system about how to overcome these physical deficiencies and become big, strong, and superior. But even after we attain size, strength, and superiority, we may act *as if* we are still small, weak, and inferior.

Adler (1930, 1964) insisted that the whole human race is "blessed" with organ inferiorities. These physical handicaps have little or no importance by themselves but take on meaning when they stimulate subjective feelings of inferiority (Adler, 1929/1969), which serve as an impetus toward perfection or completion. Some people compensate for these feelings of inferiority by moving toward psychological health and a useful style of life, whereas others overcompensate and are motivated to subdue or retreat from other people and to live an essentially useless style of life. History provides many examples of people like Demosthenes or Beethoven overcoming a handicap and making significant contributions to society. Adler himself was weak and sickly as a child, and his illness moved him to become a physician and to conquer death. Other people, however, overcompensate for feelings of inferiority by becoming criminals or deeply neurotic. As a young girl, Christine made unfavorable comparisons between her own plain features and the unusual beauty of her mother. In addition, she saw herself as being inferior and quite fragile compared to boys, and she learned to compensate for this inferiority by using verbal and social skills to manipulate boys and men.

Adler (1929/1969) emphasized that physical deficiencies alone do not *cause* a particular style of life; they simply provide present motivation for reaching future goals.

SOCIAL INTEREST

The usefulness of all human activity must be seen from the viewpoint of social interest.

Social interest is a somewhat inaccurate translation of the German word, ***Gemeinschaftsgefühl***. A better translation might be "social feeling" or "community feeling," but *Gemeinschaftsgefühl* actually has a meaning that is not fully expressed by any English word or phrase. Roughly, it means a feeling with all of humanity; it implies membership in the social community of all people. A person with well-developed *Gemeinschaftsgefühl* strives not for personal superiority but for perfection for all people in an ideal community. Social interest can be defined as an attitude of relatedness with humanity in general, as well as an empathy for each member of the human race. It manifests itself as cooperation with others for social advancement rather than for personal gain (Adler, 1964).

Adler (1964) believed that social interest is part of human nature and that some amount of it exists in everyone—the criminal, the psychotic, and the mentally healthy. Social interest is rooted as potentiality in everyone, but it must be developed before it can contribute to a useful style of life.

Development in a Social Environment

According to Adler (1956), other people, especially one's mother, contribute to the development of social interest. Before birth a fetus experiences a oneness with its mother, and then after birth the infant strives to reunite with her through the sucking movement of the lips. Young children depend heavily on their mothers to satisfy both their physiological and their psychological needs.

Because social interest arises from the mother–child relationship, every person who has survived infancy has some amount of it. The mother's task, according to Adler, is to encourage mature social interest in her child. She must develop a bond with her child, thus fostering a sense of cooperation. Ideally, she should have a genuine and deep-rooted love for her child—a love that is centered on the child's well-being, not on her own needs or wants. This healthy love relationship develops from a true caring about people. If the mother has learned to give and receive love from others, she will have little difficulty broadening her child's social interest. On the other hand, if she concentrates affection solely on her child, she will not be able to teach it to transfer social interest to other people. The mother's love for her husband, for her other children, and for society provides a model for the child. By observing the mother's widespread social interest, a child learns that there are important people other than one's mother and oneself.

Adler (1956) believed that the mother must give equal attention to her three ties—children, husband, and society—if her children are to develop social interest. When a mother favors her children, to the neglect of husband and society, the children become pampered and spoiled. Conversely, if she directs her attention exclusively to her husband or to society, her children become neglected and

Both mother and father can contribute powerfully to the developing social interest of their children.

unloved. Either mistake hampers the children's independence and ability to cooperate.

The father is the second important person in a child's social environment. He has a difficult function, one that few fathers are able to successfully fulfill. He must have a good attitude toward his wife, his occupation, and society. In addition, his broad social interest must manifest itself in his relationship with his child. The ideal father cooperates on an equal footing with his wife in caring for the child and treating it as a human being. According to Adler's (1956) standards, a successful father avoids the dual errors of emotional detachment and paternal authoritarianism. These errors may represent two attitudes, but they are often found in the same father. Both prevent the growth and spread of social interest in a child. A father's emotional detachment may influence the child to develop a warped sense of social interest, a feeling of neglect, and possibly a neurotic attachment to the mother. A child who experiences paternal detachment creates a goal of personal superiority rather than one based on social interest. The second error, paternal authoritarianism, may also lead to a neurotic style of life. A child who sees the father as tyrannical learns to strive for power and personal superiority.

Adler (1956) believed that the effects of the early social environment are extremely important. The relationship a child has with the mother and father is so powerful that it smothers the effects of heredity. Adler believed that after age five, the effects of heredity become blurred by the powerful influence of one's social environment. By that time learning has modified or shaped nearly every aspect of a child's personality.

Necessity of Social Interest

Adler (1927) believed that social life is the natural condition of the human species and that social interest is the cement that binds society together. The natural inferiority of individuals necessitates their joining together to form a society. Without protection and nourishment from the father and mother, a baby would perish. Without protection from the clan, the individual would be destroyed by animals that are stronger, more ferocious, or endowed with keener senses. Social interest, therefore, is a necessity. It is even responsible for our existence because if a man and woman did not cooperate in the procreation and subsequent protection of a child, the human race could not survive.

Adler believed that the child naturally looks toward others for love and affection. An infant's inadequacy predisposes it toward a mothering person. People therefore develop an early interest in other people, and most continue to be socially oriented. Adler objected to Freud's belief that people are basically narcissistic. People who appear self-centered simply lack a relationship with their mother that fostered social interest. Narcissism is a form of neurosis, not an inherent characteristic of people. It grows from a neurotic mother–child relationship because an overly indulgent or overly negligent mother teaches her child to be concerned primarily with self-interest (Ansbacher, 1985).

Criterion of Human Values

Social interest was Adler's yardstick for measuring psychological health and is thus "the sole criterion of human values" (Adler, 1927, p. 167). To the degree that people possess social interest, they are psychologically mature. Immature people lack *Gemeinschaftsgefühl*, are self-centered, and strive for personal power and superiority over others. Healthy individuals are genuinely concerned about people and have a goal of success that encompasses the well-being of all people. Life has no value unless a person contributes to the life of other people and even to the life of future generations. Social interest is the only gauge to be used in judging the worth of a person. Adler (1956) referred to it as the *barometer of normality*, that is, the standard to be used in determining the usefulness of a life.

Social interest is not synonymous with charity and unselfishness. Acts of philanthropy and kindness may or may not be motivated by *Gemeinschaftsgefühl*. A wealthy man may regularly give large sums of money to the poor and needy, not because he feels a oneness with them, but, quite to the contrary, because he wishes to maintain a separateness from them. The gift implies, "You are inferior, I am superior, and this charity is proof of my superiority." Adler believed that the worth of all such acts can only be judged against the criterion of social interest.

Christine consistently gives the appearance of a devoted mother and teacher—a person motivated by an abundance of social interest. However, her need to be the best, most self-sacrificing mother and teacher in the world suggests that she is motivated by personal superiority rather than social interest. She seems intent on convincing her children and her students that she is extra special, a selfless martyr willing to endure personal pain and suffering in order to help others. This self-image supports the grandiose fiction that she is the greatest mother and teacher in the world. In reality, she is not striving for a better community of humans but for self-aggrandizement and personal superiority.

STRIVING FOR SUCCESS OR SUPERIORITY

The one dynamic force behind the person's activity is the striving for success or superiority.

The concept of a single governing force behind motivation underwent a metamorphosis in Adler's thinking. As early as 1908 he believed aggression to be the dynamic power behind all motivation. Soon after, he changed the name to "masculine protest," which implied will to power or a domination of others. By 1912, Adler found that masculine protest had become an unsatisfactory term for explaining the motivation of normal people. It retained a subsidiary position in his final theory and is discussed below under his theory of abnormal development. As the central dynamic power, masculine protest was replaced by "striving for superiority." This, in turn, was followed in his later writings by "striving for success" or "perfection," terms more in tune with his final concept of social interest (Adler, 1956).

The Final Goal

According to Adler (1956), we all strive toward a final goal of superiority or success, a fictional goal that has no objective existence. As a subjective ideal, however, this final goal has great significance because it unifies personality and renders all behavior comprehensible.

Each individual has the power to create a personalized fictional goal, one constructed out of the raw materials provided by heredity and environment. However, the goal is neither genetically nor environmentally determined; it is the product of a free *creative power.* By the time children are four or five years of age, their creative minds have reached the stage of development that enables them to set their final goals. But even infants have an innate drive toward growth, completion, or success. As noted earlier, because they are small, incomplete, and weak, they feel inferior and powerless. To compensate for this deficiency, they eventually set fictional goals—to overcome, to be above, to be big and strong, to be superior or successful. The goal reduces the pain of inferiority feelings and points young children in the direction of superiority wishes and fantasies.

If children are neglected or pampered, their goal remains largely unconscious. Adler hypothesized that children will compensate for feelings of inferiority in devious ways that have no apparent relationship to their fictional goal. The goal of superiority for a pampered girl, for example, may be to make permanent her parasitic relationship with her mother. As an adult, she may appear dependent and self-deprecating. Such behavior may seem to be inconsistent with a goal of superiority, but it is quite consistent with the goal of being a parasite that she set at age four or five, a time when her mother appeared large and powerful, and attachment to her became a natural means of attaining superiority. The fact that the adult behavior of the neglected or pampered person seems inconsistent with a goal of superiority is indicative of an unconscious goal.

Conversely, if children experience love and security, they set goals that are largely conscious and understood. Psychologically secure children strive toward superiority defined in terms of success and social interest. Although their goal never becomes completely conscious, psychologically mature individuals understand and pursue it with a high level of awareness.

In striving for the final goal, many preliminary goals must be created. These subgoals are often conscious, but the connection between them and the final goal usually remains unknown. Furthermore, the relationship among preliminary goals is seldom realized. From the point of view of the final goal, however, they fit together in a self-consistent pattern. Adler (1956) used the analogy of the playwright who builds the characteristics and the subplots according to the final goal of the drama. When the final scene is known, all dialogue and every subplot acquire new meaning. When an individual's final goal is known, all actions make sense and each subgoal takes on new significance.

The Striving Force as Compensation

Every person, whether normal or neurotic, is pulled in the direction of success or superiority. We are all born with the tendency toward completion or perfection. "The striving for perfection is innate in the sense that it is a part of life, a striving, an urge, a something without which life would be unthinkable" (Adler, 1956, p. 104).

Although the striving for success is innate, it must be developed. At birth it exists as potentiality, not actuality, and it remains for each of us to actualize this potential in our own manner. We begin this process when we are about four or five—old enough to set a direction to the striving force by establishing a goal of superiority. The goal provides guidelines for motivation, shaping our psychological development and giving it an aim.

People strive for superiority or success as a means of compensation for feelings of inferiority or weakness. As noted earlier, all humans are "blessed" at birth with small, weak, and inferior bodies. These physical deficiencies ignite feelings of inferiority only because people, by their nature, possess an innate tendency toward completion or wholeness. People are continually pushed by the need to overcome inferiority feelings and pulled by the desire for completion. The minus and plus situations exist simultaneously and cannot be separated because they are two dimensions of a single force. The force itself is innate, but its nature and direction are due both to feelings of inferiority and to the goal of superiority. Without the innate movement toward perfection, children would never feel inferior; but without feelings of inferiority, they would never set a goal of superiority or success. The goal, then, is set as compensation for the deficit feeling, but the deficit feeling would not exist unless a child first possessed a basic tendency toward completion (Adler, 1956).

The goal is not set as a blind reaction to the deficit feeling, nor does it need be set in the exact opposite direction. As a creation of the individual, it may take any form. The goal is not necessarily the mirror image of the deficiency, even though it is a compensation for it. For example, a person with a weak body will not necessarily become a robust athlete but, instead, may become an artist, an actor, or a writer. Success is an individualized concept and all of us formulate our own definition of it. Our creative power is ultimately responsible for that definition, but it is swayed by the forces of heredity and environment. Heredity establishes the potentiality, while environment contributes to the development of social interest and courage. The forces of nature and nurture can never deprive us of the power to set a unique goal or to choose a unique style of reaching for the goal (Adler, 1956).

Although each of us strives for completion in a unique manner, there are two general avenues of striving. The first is the socially nonproductive attempt to gain personal superiority; the second involves social interest and is aimed at success or perfection for everyone.

Striving for Personal Superiority

Some people strive for superiority with little or no concern for others. Their goals are personal ones, and their strivings are motivated largely by exaggerated feelings of personal inferiority. Murderers, thieves, and con artists are obvious examples of people who strive only for personal gain. However, on a more subtle level, many other people cover their strivings for personal gain behind the cloak of social concern.

Christine, for example, appears to the casual observer to be a deeply caring person, taking a much greater interest in her students than any other teacher in her school. She encourages them to talk to her concerning their personal problems, and she reinforces their revelations of private and painful experiences with conspicuous displays of sympathy and concern. She receives perverted pleasure from her belief that she is the most accessible and dedicated teacher in her school. Christine never criticizes her colleagues directly because she is far too "professional" to engage in petty bickering. However, she has become an expert at nonverbally communicating her displeasure whenever another teacher expresses a lack of concern for a student. She will sigh, gasp, or frown to show her superior standards of professional conduct. When talking to her husband Joe, she is overtly and relentlessly critical of her colleagues. If Joe is not yet convinced that his wife is the greatest teacher in the world, it's not because she hasn't told him often enough!

Striving for Success

Psychologically healthy people do not strive for personal gain but for the success of all humankind. They are motivated by social interest and are concerned with

Figure 4.1   *Two Basic Methods of Striving Toward the Final Goal*

goals beyond themselves. Unlike Christine, they are capable of helping others without demanding or expecting a personal payoff. They see others not as opponents but as people with whom they can cooperate for social benefit. Their own success is not gained at the expense of others, but is a natural tendency to move toward completion or perfection.

People who strive for success rather than personal superiority maintain a sense of self, of course, but they see daily problems from the view of society's development rather than from a strictly personal vantage point. Their sense of personal worth is tied closely to their contributions to human society. Social progress is more important to them than personal credit (Adler, 1956).

Summary of the Striving Force

In summary, each individual begins life with an innate striving force that is activated by ever-present physical deficiencies. These organic weaknesses lead inevitably to feelings of inferiority. Thus all people, neurotic as well as healthy, possess feelings of inferiority, and all set a final goal at around age four or five. However, neurotics develop exaggerated feelings of inferiority and attempt to compensate by setting a goal of personal superiority. They are motivated by personal gain rather than by social interest. On the other hand, healthy people are motivated by normal feelings of incompleteness and high levels of social interest. They strive toward the goal of success, defined in terms of perfection and completion for everyone. Figure 4.1 illustrates how the innate striving force can lead to either a neurotic or a healthy style of life. Notice also that neither physical deficiencies nor their consequent feelings of inferiority lead inexorably to neurotic development. Whether we form a useless style of life or a socially useful one depends on how we view these inevitable feelings of inferiority.

STYLE OF LIFE

All *human potentialities develop in accordance with the individual's self-consistent style of life.* **Style of life** is the term Adler used to refer to the flavor of a person's life. It

Understanding Life Style Through Early Recollections

The key to understanding people's style of life comes from asking them to relate their earliest recollections (ERs). Adler believed that early recollections offer the most productive and reliable approach to understanding style of life. The objective validity of the recollection is of no importance, and many ERs are probably more fictional than real. What is important is people's interpretation of these early childhood events.

Adler (1929/1969, 1931) insisted that our earliest memory is always consistent with our present style of life. Our subjective account of this experience yields a clue to understanding both our final goal and our style of life. On the surface, many of our early recollections may seem mundane and meaningless, but Adler believed that proper interpretation will reveal our underlying style of life.

To illustrate this point, Adler used the following example. A seemingly successful man who distrusted everyone, but especially women, reported the following memory: "I was going with my mother and little brother to market. Suddenly it began to rain, and my mother took me in her arms, and then, remembering that I was the older, she put me down and took up my younger brother" (Adler, 1929/1964, p. 123). What can we make of this early recollection? The older brother, left to fend for himself, was both confused and hurt and felt that another had gained a favorite position with his mother. This memory relates directly to his adult style of life and gives it meaning. The pattern or theme running throughout this man's life had been one of distrust and suspicion. Although people may claim to love him and although they give him initial recognition, in the end these people will surely withdraw their affection and attention.

People with unpleasant earliest recollections usually have a life style marked by the negative attitude, "Everything bad happens to me." On the other hand, people with a pleasant first recollection often have a style of life that is optimistic and positive. But in either case, the early experiences did not *cause* or determine the style of life. Quite the opposite. People's recollection of early experiences are simply shaped by their present style of life.

If style of life shapes early recollections, then, as style of life changes, we should expect to find that one's early recollections also change. This belief, widely held by Adlerians, has been succinctly stated by Croake (1975, p. 517): "Early recollections change when therapy has been effective.

includes not only the person's goal but also self-concept, feelings for others, and attitude toward the world. It is the product of the interaction of heredity, environment, goal of success, social interest, and creative power.

Style of life is similar to Freud's concept of ego in that it is the governing force of personality. Adler's concept of style of life, however, includes no id or superego waging war against the self; rather it is the whole organism plus the person's unique manner of self-expression. Adler (1956) used a musical analogy to elucidate style of life. The separate notes of a composition are meaningless without the entire melody, but the melody takes on added significance when we recognize the composer's style or unique manner of expression.

Either the recollections are new or the old ones are remembered in a different light." Similarly, Mosak (1958) suggested that patients may reflect progress in therapy by (1) producing new early recollections, (2) forgetting some of the pretherapy recollections, (3) changing the emotional tone of the original early recollections, or (4) altering the pretherapy early recollections with additions and omissions so that they provide a different theme.

What evidence exists to suggest that early recollections actually change during the course of therapy? Savill and Eckstein (1987) obtained early recollections and mental status of psychiatric patients both before and after therapy and compared them to ERs and mental status of a matched group of control subjects. They found significant changes in both mental status and early recollections for the therapy group but not for the controls, indicating that when therapy is successful, patients, indeed, change their early recollections.

Similarly, Statton and Wilborn (1991) looked at the three earliest recollections of 5-to-12-year-old children after each of 10 weekly counseling sessions, and compared them to the early recollections of a control group of elementary-school children who did not receive counseling. Compared to the control group, the counseling group showed greater changes in the theme, the character, the setting, the amount of detail, and the affect of their early recollections. Among other changes, children in the treatment group reported more activity in posttreatment early recollections than in their precounseling memories. For example, before counseling one child recalled an event that indicated passivity.

"My uncle and dad took me fishing. They were fishing and my uncle got his line hung on a tree stump in the water. He yanked on the pole and the hook came back and hooked me in the head. . . . I waited for them to pull it out of my head" (Statton & Wilborn, p. 344).

After counseling, the child recast the early recollection in a more active light.

I went fishing when I was about 5 [years old] . . . I caught a fish . . . and my uncle threw his line out and he got it hung on a tree stump and he yanked it back and the hook came back and got me in the head. . . . I pulled it out. . . . (Statton & Wilborn, p. 344).

Although both recollections are of the same objective experience, they reveal two different subjective life style attitudes—one passive, the other active.

Our style of life is fairly well established by age four or five. After that time all of our actions revolve around our unified style of life. This self-consistent style of life is formed by the creative power in response to our final goal, which we have set by that time.

Although the final goal is singular, style of life need not be narrow or rigid. Psychologically unhealthy individuals often lead rather inflexible lives that are marked by an inability to choose new ways of reacting to their environment. But healthy people behave in diverse and flexible ways with styles of life that are complex, enriched, and, to some extent, subject to change. These mature individuals see many ways of striving for success and continually seek to create new options for themselves. Even though their final goal remains constant, the way in which they perceive it continually changes. Thus, they can choose new options at any point in life.

CREATIVE POWER

The style of life is developed by the individual's creative power.

Adler believed that each of us is empowered with the freedom to create our own style of life. Ultimately, we are responsible for who we are and how we behave. Our **creative power** places us in control of our own lives, is responsible for our final goal, determines our method of striving for the goal, and contributes to the development of our social interest. In short, our creative power makes each of us a free individual (Adler, 1964).

Adler acknowledged the importance of heredity and environment in forming personality. Every child is born with a unique genetic makeup and soon comes to have social experiences different from those of any other human. People, however, are much more than a product of heredity and environment. They are creative beings who not only react to their environment but also act on it and cause it to react to them.

Adler (1956) believed that each of us uses heredity and environment as the brick and mortar to build personality, but the architectural design reflects our own style. Of primary importance is not what we have been given, but how we put those materials to use. The building materials of personality are secondary. We are our own architects and can build either a useful or a useless life, choose to remain psychologically healthy or become neurotic, construct a gaudy façade or expose the essence of the structure. We are not compelled to grow in the direction of social interest, inasmuch as we have no inner nature that forces us to be good. Conversely, we have no inherently evil nature from which we must escape. We are who we are because of the use we have made of our brick and mortar.

Creative power is a dynamic concept implying *movement*, and this movement is the most salient characteristic of life. All psychic life involves movement toward a goal, movement with a direction.

Adler (1929) used an interesting analogy, which he called "the law of the low doorway," to illustrate the free powers of both the neurotic and the healthy individual. If we are trying to walk through a doorway four feet high, we have two basic choices. First, we can use our creative power to bend down as we approach the doorway, thereby successfully solving the problem. This is the manner in which the psychologically healthy individual solves most of life's problems. On the other hand, if we bump our head and fall back, we must still solve the problem correctly or continue bumping our head. Neurotics often choose to bump their heads on the realities of life. When approaching the low doorway, we are neither compelled to stoop nor forced to bump our heads. We have a creative power that permits us to follow either course.

ABNORMAL DEVELOPMENT

Adler believed that people are what they make of themselves. The creative power endows humans, within certain limits, with the freedom to be either psychologically healthy or unhealthy and to follow either a useful or useless style of life.

Early in his career, Adler's writings were almost exclusively centered around the inadequate personality. Later he gave more emphasis to the healthy individual and placed abnormal psychology in a secondary position. Nevertheless, some knowledge of his ideas on maladjustment helps complete an understanding of Individual Psychology.

General Description

According to Adler (1956), the one factor underlying all types of maladjustment is an *underdeveloped social interest*. Besides lacking social interest, neurotics tend to (1) set their goals too high, (2) have a rigid and dogmatic style of life, and (3) live in their own private world. These three characteristics are inevitable concomitants to lack of social interest. In short, people become failures in life because they are overconcerned with themselves and care little about others.

Maladjusted people set their goals too high as an overcompensation for exaggerated feelings of inferiority. Extravagant goals lead to dogmatic behavior, and the higher the goal the more rigid the striving. To compensate for deeply rooted feelings of inadequacy and basic insecurity, these individuals narrow their perspective and strive compulsively and rigidly for unrealistic goals.

The exaggerated and unrealistic nature of neurotics' goals set them apart from the community of other people. They live in a private world and endow their goals with private meaning. They approach the problems of friendship, sex, and occupation from a personal angle that precludes successful solutions. Their view of the world is not in focus with that of other individuals, and they possess what Adler (1956) called "private intelligence."

External Factors in Maladjustment

Why do some people create maladjustments? Adler (1964) recognized the following three contributing factors, any one of which is sufficient to contribute to abnormality: (1) exaggerated physical deficiencies; (2) a pampered style of life; and (3) a neglected style of life.

Exaggerated Physical Deficiencies

Exaggerated physical deficiencies, whether congenital or the result of injury or disease, are not sufficient to lead to maladjustments. They must be accompanied by accentuated feelings of inferiority. These subjective feelings may be greatly encouraged by a defective body, but they are the progeny of the creative power.

Anyone can develop exaggerated feelings of inferiority, but children born with physical disabilities have an even greater burden and a higher probability of maladjustment than physically healthy children. Physical deficiencies drive children to compensate and often to overcompensate for their inadequacy. As adults, these people tend to be overly concerned with themselves and to develop exaggerated inferiority feelings, which are manifested as an absence of self-confidence, little courage, and no consideration for others. They feel as if they are living in enemy country, fear defeat more than they desire success, and are convinced that life's major problems can only be solved in a selfish manner (Adler, 1927).

Pampered Style of Life

Adler believed that the pampered style of life lies at the heart of most neuroses. Children who are pampered have little social interest and low activity level. They possess strong wishes to be pampered, regardless of whether or not they seem to be. Their primary desire is to make permanent the parasitic relationship they originally had with their mothers. They expect others to look after them, overprotect them, and satisfy all their selfish needs. They are characterized by extreme discouragement, indecisiveness, oversensitivity, impatience, and exaggerated emotion, especially anxiety. They believe that other people exist for them, and they expect others to pamper them as their mothers once did. They see the world with private vision and believe that they are entitled to be first in everything.

Pampered children have not received too much love; rather, they are unloved. They have been overprotected, hovered over, smothered, and shielded from responsibilities. Their parents have demonstrated their lack of love by doing too much for them and by treating them as if they were incapable of solving their own problems. At least this is their interpretation of the situation, and it is the children's view that matters. If children feel pampered and spoiled, then they are pampered and spoiled (Adler, 1964).

Pampered children also feel neglected. Having been protected by a doting mother, they are fearful in her absence. Whenever they must fend for themselves, they feel left out, mistreated, and neglected. These experiences add to the pampered child's stockpile of inferiority feelings (Adler, 1927).

Neglected Style of Life

The third external factor contributing to maladjustments is neglect. Adler (1927) believed that children who feel unloved and unwanted are likely to borrow heavily from these feelings in creating a neglected style of life. Neglect is a relative concept. No one feels totally neglected or completely unwanted. The fact that a child survived infancy is proof that someone cared for that child and that the seed of social interest has been planted.

Abused and mistreated children develop little social interest and tend to create a neglected style of life. They have little confidence in themselves and tend to overestimate difficulties connected with life's major problems. They expect society to be cold because people have generally treated them coldly. They are spiteful toward others, distrustful of themselves, and unable to cooperate for the common welfare. They see society as enemy country, feel alienated from all other people, and experience a strong sense of envy toward the success of others. Neglected children have many of the characteristics of pampered ones, but generally they are more suspicious and more likely to be dangerous to others (Adler, 1927).

Safeguarding Tendencies

According to Adler, all neurotic symptoms are created to safeguard the individual's self-esteem. The symptoms themselves serve as **safeguarding tendencies**, protecting an inflated self-image and maintaining a neurotic style of life.

Adler's concept of safeguarding tendencies is similar to Freud's concept of defense mechanisms. Basic to both is the idea that symptoms are formed as a protection of the self or ego. However, there are several differences between the two. First, Freud's defense mechanisms protect the ego against anxiety from instinctual sources, whereas Adlerian safeguarding tendencies protect the person from outside demands. Also, Freudian defense mechanisms are common to everyone, but Adler (1956) discussed safeguarding tendencies only with reference to the construction of neurotic symptoms. Nevertheless, probably everyone, the normal as well as the abnormal, relies occasionally on safeguarding tendencies to protect tenuous feelings of self-esteem. Another difference is that whereas defense mechanisms operate solely on an unconscious level, safeguarding tendencies may be either conscious or unconscious.

Individual Psychology holds that neurotics fear that their goal of personal superiority will be revealed as erroneous and that they will suffer public disgrace. To compensate for this fiction, they construct safeguarding tendencies that protect them against the embarrassing emergence of exaggerated inferiority feelings.

Excuses, aggression, and withdrawal are three commonly used safeguarding tendencies. They are generally unconscious—but occasionally conscious—devices for protecting the neurotic's style of life and for maintaining a fictional, elevated feeling of self-importance (Adler, 1964).

Excuses

The most common safeguarding tendency is **excuses**. The neurotic, as well as the normal individual, typically makes use of the "Yes, but" and the "If only" excuses. In the "Yes, but" excuse, people first state what they claim they would like to do—something that sounds good to others—then they follow with an excuse. A housewife might say, "I would like to go to college, *but* my children demand too much of my attention." An executive explains, "I agree with your proposal, *but* company policy will not allow it."

The "If only" statement is the same excuse phrased in a different way. "*If only* my wife were more supportive, I would have advanced faster in my profession." "*If only* I did not have this physical handicap, I could compete successfully for a job." These excuses protect a weak sense of self-worth and deceive people into believing that they are more superior than they really are (Adler, 1956).

Aggression

Another common safeguarding tendency is **aggression**. Adler (1956) held that neurotics use aggression to safeguard their exaggerated superiority complex, that is, to protect their fragile self-esteem. Safeguarding through aggression may take the form of depreciation, accusation, or self-accusation.

Depreciation is the tendency to undervalue another's achievement and to overvalue one's own. This safeguarding tendency is evident in such aggressive behaviors as sadism, gossip, envy, and intolerance. The intention behind each act of depreciation is to belittle another so that the neurotic, by comparison, will be placed in a favorable light.

Accusation, the second form of neurotic aggression, is the tendency to blame others for one's failures and to seek revenge, thereby safeguarding one's own tenuous self-esteem. Adler (1956) believed that there is an element of aggressive accusation in all neuroses. Neurotics invariably act to cause people around them to suffer more than they do.

Christine combines the "If only" excuse with aggressive accusation against her husband. She had wanted to attend medical school, but when she married Joe, she willingly gave up those plans in favor of having a family. After her children were in school, she went back to college to finish a degree in education, but she constantly reminds Joe that she would have been a successful doctor, *if only* he had not wanted her to have children. Her accusations against him protect her feelings of self-esteem and keep her from facing the possibility that, even under favorable circumstances, she may not have become a successful physician.

The third form of neurotic aggression, **self-accusation**, is characterized by self-torture and guilt. Self-torture is evident in masochism, depression, and suicide, and it is a means of safeguarding neurotics' power to hurt those people who are close to them. Adler (1956) believed that guilt is often aggressive, self-accusatory behavior.

Self-accusation is the converse of depreciation, although both are aimed toward personal superiority. In depreciation, neurotics devalue other people to make themselves look good by comparison. In self-accusation, neurotics devalue themselves, with the ultimate purpose of inflicting suffering on others, again, to protect their magnified feelings of self-esteem.

Withdrawal

Personality development is sometimes arrested due to neurotics' tendency to run away from difficulties. Adler referred to this tendency as **withdrawal**, or safeguarding through distance. Neurotics unconsciously escape life's problems by setting up a distance between themselves and those problems.

Adler (1956) recognized four modes of safeguarding through withdrawal: moving backward, standing still, hesitating, and constructing obstacles. People are well served by each mode. By making a show of their deficiencies, such as a physical illness, they gain power over others, are relieved from normal obligations, and generally get their own way.

Adler used the term **moving backward** to refer to any tendency to safeguard the fictional goal of superiority by psychologically reverting to a more secure period of life. Moving backward is similar to Freud's concept of regression in that both involve attempts to return to earlier, less anxiety-ridden phases of life. Whereas regression takes place unconsciously and includes the repression of painful experiences, moving backward may sometimes be conscious and is directed at protecting an inflated goal of superiority. It includes suicide, attempts at suicide, most phobias, hysterical disorders, amnesia, and severe anxiety. People sometimes seek attention from others in order to gain some control over them. For example, attempted suicide usually attracts attention and thus forces other people to worry and fret over the person's well-being. Moving backward is designed to elicit sympathy, the deleterious attitude offered so generously to pampered children.

Psychological distance can also be created by **standing still**. This withdrawal tendency is similar to moving backward but, in general, is not as severe. It is comparable to Freud's concept of fixation in that it blocks normal psychological development. However, it differs from fixation in that it may be partly conscious and that, rather than protecting the ego against anxiety, it safeguards the person's inflated feelings of superiority. People who stand still simply do not move in any direction; thus, they avoid all responsibility by ensuring themselves against any threat of failure. They safeguard their fictional aspirations because they never do anything to prove that they cannot accomplish their goals. Christine never applied to any medical school and therefore was never denied entrance. By doing nothing she was able to safeguard her self-esteem and protect herself against failure.

Closely related to standing still is **hesitating.** Some people hesitate or vacillate when faced with difficult problems. Their procrastinations eventually give them the excuse, "It's too late now." Most compulsions, Adler believed, are attempts to waste time. Compulsive washing, retracing one's steps, excessive orderliness, destroying work already begun, and leaving work unfinished are examples of hesitation. From a social viewpoint, the hesitating tendency is self-defeating because a person wastes time until it becomes too late to accomplish a task. The tendency, however, is useful from the individual's point of view because it protects the neurotic's inflated sense of self-esteem.

The least severe of the withdrawal safeguarding tendencies is **constructing obstacles**. Some people build a straw house to show that they can knock it down. By overcoming the obstacle, they protect their self-esteem and their prestige. If they fail to hurdle the barrier, they can always resort to an excuse.

Safeguarding tendencies are found in nearly everyone, but when they reach a level of rigidity, they become the essential traits of neuroses. Overly sensitive people create safeguarding tendencies to buffer their fear of disgrace, to eliminate their exaggerated inferiority feelings, and to attain self-esteem. However, safeguarding tendencies are self-defeating because their built-in goals of self-interest and personal superiority actually block people from securing authentic feelings of self-esteem. Adler believed that neurotics seldom realize that their self-esteem would be better safeguarded if they gave up their self-interest and developed genuine interest in others.

Masculine Protest

Due to cultural influences, many men and women overemphasize the importance of being "manly". This condition was Adler's definition of **masculine protest**. In most societies, both men and women place an inferior value on being a woman, an unfortunate and unnatural state of affairs that is the cause of much marital discord and many individual problems of superiority and inferiority complexes. In Western societies, boys are taught early that being masculine means being courageous, strong, and dominant. The epitome of success for boys is to win, to be powerful, to be on top. Failure is associated with being a "sissy." Girls, on the other hand, often learn to be passive and to accept an inferior position in society.

In contrast to Freud, Adler (1930, 1956) believed that the psychic life of women is essentially the same as that of men, and that the nearly universal phenomenon of a male-dominated culture is not a natural state of affairs. Rather, it is the product of our historical development. In contemporary Western societies, women are believed to be weak, inferior, and defenseless, an alleged inferiority that causes many women to fight against their feminine roles. Some revolt by developing a masculine orientation and becoming assertive and competitive, whereas others revolt by adopting a passive "feminine" role, becoming exceedingly helpless, humble, and obedient. Still others become resigned to the belief that they are inferior human beings. They approve of men's privileged position and, in revenge, shift all responsibilities to their husbands or to other men. Each of these modes of adjustment results from cultural influences, not from inherent psychic difference between the sexes.

Christine possesses many traits associated with the masculine protest. To her husband, she adopts a helpless and defenseless posture. In her eyes she is completely unable to perform any "masculine" task. She has never fixed a faucet, started a lawn mower, or repaired a light switch. Although she loves to plant flowers, Joe always performs the spade work. Her helplessness in such simple jobs is not due to physical frailty, but is a clever, though unconscious, ploy to seek revenge on men in general and Joe in particular. To her high-school students, Christine appears to be an aggressive champion of women's rights. Her support for women's causes, however, is shallow and one-sided. She advocates superiority, not equality, for women. She has given no reflective thought to the views that she professes. Her deeply feminine biases are simply a reflection of a basic belief that women are inferior to men, that is, a masculine protest.

APPLICATIONS OF INDIVIDUAL PSYCHOLOGY

The practical applications of Individual Psychology can be divided into four areas: birth order, early recollections, dreams, and psychotherapy.

Birth Order

In therapy, Adler almost always asked patients about their family constellation, that is, their birth order, the sex of their siblings, and the age spread between them. Although people's perception of the situation into which they were born is more important than numerical rank, Adler did form some general hypotheses about birth order.

Firstborn children, according to Adler (1931), are likely to have intensified feelings of power and superiority, high anxiety, and overprotective tendencies. They occupy a unique position, being an only child for a time and then experiencing a traumatic dethronement when a younger sibling is born. This event dramatically changes the situation and the child's view of the world. If firstborn children are three or older when a baby brother or sister is born, they incorporate this dethronement into a previously established style of life. They likely will feel hostility and resentment toward the new baby, but, if they have already developed a cooperating style, they will eventually adopt this same attitude toward the new sibling. If the firstborn is less than three, hostility and resentment will be largely unconscious, which makes these attitudes more resistant to change in later life.

Secondborn children begin life in a better situation for developing cooperation and social interest, Adler claimed. To some extent the personalities of secondborn children are shaped by their perception of the older child's attitude toward them. If this attitude is one of extreme hostility and vengeance, the second child may become highly competitive or overly discouraged. The typical second child, however, does not develop in either of these two directions, but matures toward moderate competitiveness, having a healthy desire to overtake the older rival. If some success is achieved, the child is likely to develop a revolutionary attitude and feel

Siblings may feel superior or inferior, and adopt different attitudes toward the world, depending in part on their order of birth.

that any authority can be challenged. Again, children's interpretations are more important than their chronological position.

Youngest children are often the most pampered and, consequently, run a high risk of being problem children. They are likely to have strong feelings of inferiority and to lack a sense of independence. Nevertheless, they possess many advantages. They are often highly motivated to exceed older siblings and to become the fastest runner, the best musician, the most skilled athlete, or the most ambitious student.

Only children are in a unique position of competing, not against brothers and sisters, but against father and mother. They often develop an exaggerated sense of superiority, an inflated self-concept, and a feeling that the world is a dangerous place, especially if their parents were overly concerned with their health. Adler (1931) stated that only children may lack well-developed feelings of cooperation and social interest, possess a parasitic attitude, and expect other people to pamper and protect them.

Christine is a middle child; that is, she is the third of four children, all born about a year apart. The oldest sibling is a sister, followed by a brother, then Christine, then another brother. Interestingly, Adler has little to say about a middle child (other than the secondborn). However, Christine may have some of the characteristics of a second child, competing against a sister only two years older. The sister was strong, active, and very much a "tomboy." Christine adopted quite the opposite style of life; that is, she saw herself as weak, passive, cute, and overly "feminine."

Early Recollections

To gain an understanding of patients' personalities, Adler would ask them to reveal their **earliest recollections (ERs).** Although he believed that the recalled memories yield clues for understanding patients' styles of life, he did not consider them to have a causal effect. Whether the recalled experiences correspond with objective reality or are complete fantasies is of no importance. People reconstruct the events so they are consistent with a theme or pattern that runs throughout their lives.

Along with Freud's technique of free association (Chapter 2) and Jung's method of the word association test (Chapter 5), Adler's use of early recollections was one of the first projective techniques employed in psychotherapy. Early recollections, however, offer one distinct advantage over free association and word association methods. The technique is not threatening to the patient, arouses little anxiety and resistance, and most patients are usually quite willing to relate their earliest memories (Adler, 1931).

Highly anxious patients will often project their current life style onto their memory of childhood experiences by recalling fearful and anxiety-producing events, such as auto accidents, temporary or permanent loss of parents, or that they were bullied by other children. For example, two of Christine's early memories reveal frightening experiences. In her earliest recollection, she recalled that when she was about three or four her father had gone away on a business trip, and she and her mother were visiting some of his relatives. Several of the older male cousins and uncles began teasing Christine's mother by making reference to her beautiful eyes and pretty long hair. This frightened Christine and she perceived that her mother was also frightened. She and her mother quickly fled from the house, but Christine remained afraid for days afterward.

In the second recollection, Christine was a little older—about five—but the memory is remarkably similar. She was attending a family reunion when she and a girl cousin about her age were confronted by a boy (apparently another cousin) also about her age. Although she could not recall any of the boy's specific actions, she felt threatened and frightened. She avoided danger by maneuvering the other little girl between herself and the boy. Then she ran sobbing to her mother.

In both memories males are seen as menacing and threatening, and females are unsafe in their presence. The threat can be avoided by running away, but the fear lingers.

Dreams

An individual's style of life is also expressed in dreams. Adler rejected Freud's notion that dreams are expressions of infantile wishes, and instead viewed them as forward-looking and as providing clues for solving future problems. Dreams, however, are not prophetic. Although they represent the dreamer's attempt to solve a problem that cannot be solved by common sense alone, dreams are disguised in a manner to deceive the dreamer. The more an individual's goal is inconsistent with reality, the more likely that dreams will be used for self-deception. For example, a man may have the goal of reaching the top, being above, or becoming President. If he also possesses a dependent style of life, his ambitious goal may be expressed in dreams of being lifted onto another's shoulders or being shot from a cannon. A more courageous and independent man with similar ambition may dream of unaided flying. The dream unveils the style of life, but it fools the dreamer by presenting him with an unrealistic, exaggerated sense of power and accomplishment.

Because dreams are essentially self-deceptions, they are not easily understood by the dreamer, and thus must be interpreted by a trained person. In interpreting dreams, Adler began with the assumption that every dream creates a mood or emotion that effectively screens the unconscious style of life from conscious understanding. If dreams were logical and reasonable, they would not serve their purpose of deceiving the dreamer. The interpreter's task is to help the dreamer make sense out of the illusive feeling tone of the dream (Adler, 1929/1969, 1931).

Psychotherapy

Because maladjustment results from lack of courage, exaggerated feelings of inferiority, and underdeveloped social interest, Adler tried to help patients eliminate these negative characteristics. Courage, self-esteem, and social interest are nurtured by the human relationship between patient and doctor. The therapist's warm maternal attitude encourages a patient to expand social interest. In addition, the therapist, in a more paternal role, helps the patient overcome a faulty style of life and find solutions to the three problems of life: sexual love, social interest, and occupation.

Although Adler was quite active in setting the goal and direction of psychotherapy, he maintained a warm and permissive attitude toward the patient. He established himself as a friendly coworker, refrained from moralistic preachings, and placed great value on the human relationship. By cooperating with their therapists, patients establish contact with another person. The therapeutic relationship awakens their social interest in the same manner that children gain social interest from their mother. With neurotic patients, in fact, therapists must assume the dual functions of motherhood: First, they strive to establish a relationship of human fellowship; and second, they attempt to strengthen patients' independence and courage and to spread social interest to people outside the therapeutic relationship (Adler, 1956).

In understanding the life style of his patients, Adler utilized five possible avenues: early childhood recollections, dreams, birth order, childhood difficulties, and external factors involved in their disorder. All five methods rely on patient's subjective descriptions, and each should complement the other four in revealing an understanding of the whole person (Adler, 1946).

Adler innovated a unique method of therapy with problem children by treating them in front of a large group of people in mental health clinics. When children receive therapy in public, they learn to appreciate that their difficulty is a community problem. Adler was careful not to blame the parents for a child's misbehavior, but, instead, he tried to persuade them to change their attitudes toward the child. With children, as well as adults, he often used the motto, "Everybody can accomplish everything." Except for certain limitations set by heredity, he strongly believed this maxim and repeatedly emphasized that what children do with what they have is more important than what they have (Adler, 1925/1968, 1956).

CONCEPT OF HUMANITY

Adler believed that people are basically self-determined and that they shape their personalities from the meaning they give to experiences. The building material of personality is provided by heredity and environment, but the creative power shapes this material and puts it to use. Adler frequently emphasized that the use that people make of their abilities and perceptions is the most crucial factor in determining the value of their style of life. In discussing an individual's relationship to the outside world, Adler (1956, p. 206) wrote:

> It is neither heredity nor environment which determines his relationship to the outside. Heredity only endows him with certain abilities. Environment only gives him certain impressions. These abilities and impressions, and the manner in which he "experiences" them—that is to say, the interpretation he makes of these experiences—are the bricks which he uses in his own "creative" way in building up his attitude toward life. It is his individual way of using these bricks, or in other words his attitude toward life, which determines this relationship to the outside world.

Adler believed that people's interpretations of experiences are more important than the experiences themselves. Neither the past nor the future determines present behavior. Instead, people are motivated by their present perceptions of the past and their present expectations of the future. These perceptions do not necessarily correspond with reality but are a reflection of people's individual psychological needs. Adler (1956, p. 208) stated that "meanings are not determined by situations, but we determine ourselves by the meanings we give to situations."

People are forward-moving, motivated by future goals rather than innate instincts or causal forces. These future goals are often rigid and unrealistic, but our internal freedom allows us to reshape them and thereby change our lives. We create our personalities and are capable of altering them by learning new attitudes. These attitudes encompass an understanding that change can occur, that no other person or circumstance is responsible for what we are, and that personal goals must be subordinated to social interest.

Although the final goal is fixed during early childhood, people remain free to change their style of life. Because the goal is fictional and unconscious, we can set and pursue temporary goals. These momentary goals are not rigidly circumscribed by the final goal but are created by us merely as partial solutions. Adler (1927, p. 24) expressed this ideas as follows: "We must understand that the reactions of the human soul are not final and absolute: Every response is but a partial response, valid temporarily, but in no way to be considered a final solution of a problem." In other words, even though our final goal is set during childhood, we are capable of change at any point in life. However, Adler maintained that not all our choices are conscious and that style of life is created through both conscious and unconscious choices.

Adler believed that ultimately we are responsible for our own personalities. Our creative power is capable of transforming feelings of inadequacy into either social interest or into the self-centered goal of personal superiority. This means that we remain free to choose between psychological health and neuroticism. Adler regarded self-centeredness as pathological and established social interest as the standard of psychological maturity. Healthy people have a high level of social interest, but throughout their lives they remain free to accept or reject normality and to become what they will.

On the six dimensions of a concept of humanity listed in Chapter 1, Adler could be rated as follows: high on *free-choice*; very high on *optimism*; very low on *causality*; moderate on *unconscious influences*; high on *social factors* underlying personality; and high on *uniqueness* of individuals. In summary, Adler held that we are self-determining social creatures, forward-moving, and motivated by present fictions to strive toward perfection for ourselves and society.

Related Research

During the last several years many researchers have become interested in studying Adler's concept of early recollections not only as a projective technique but as predictors of a wide range of personal variables. Prompting much of this research has been the development of several instruments that assess early recollections. Guy Manaster and Thomas Perryman have constructed the *Manaster-Perryman Manifest Content Early Recollection Scoring Manual* (Manaster & Perryman, 1974, 1979), which allows judges to score early recollections in seven broad categories: (1) *Characters*, or people involved in the memory, (2) *Themes*, or topics of the ER, (3) *Concern with Detail*, visual, auditory, and motor, (4) *Setting*, or location of the ER, (5) *Active-Passive*, that is, the degree to which the subject initiated action or was acted upon, (6) *Internal-External Control*, or subject's acceptance of responsibility for what happened in the early recollection, and (7) *Affect*, or overall feeling tone of the ER. Interrater reliability of the Manaster-Perryman is generally quite high (Buchanan, Kern, & Bell-Dumas, 1991).

Also, A. Rahn Bruhn and his former graduate student Jeffrey Last have developed instruments for scoring early recollections. The Comprehensive Early Memory Scoring System (CEMSS) is a multidimensional scoring system that assesses pathological and adaptive early recollection characteristics in eight separate categories: (1) Characters, (2) Settings, (3) Sensory-motor aspect, (4) Relation to reality, (5) Object relations, (6) Themes, (7) Affect, and (8) Damage aspect (Last, 1983; Last & Bruhn, 1983). In addition, Bruhn (1989, 1990) has designed an Early Memories Procedure (EMP) that asks for six spontaneous ERs, as well as 15 directed memories, such as first school memory, clearest memory of mother, most traumatic memory, and happiest memory. The EMP has not yet generated much research beyond that conducted by Bruhn and his associates, partly because it requires up to four hours to complete.

However, investigators have used the Manaster-Perryman scoring system to relate early recollections to a number of variables, including birth order (Fakouri & Hafner, 1984), depression (Allers, White, & Hornbuckle, 1990; Fakouri, Hartung, & Hafner, 1985), college major (Coram & Shields, 1987), alcoholism in women (Hafner, Fakouri, & Chesney, 1988), alcoholism in men (Chaplin & Orlofsky, 1991), and success in counseling (Statton & Wilborn, 1991).

Evidence that early recollections change through the course of psychotherapy (Savill & Eckstein, 1987; Statton & Wilborn, 1991) suggests that ERs are subjective reconstructions of childhood events rather than accurate renderings of those events. If ERs are fictional reconstructions amenable to present shifts in a person's style of life, then we might also expect that created early recollections will also accurately predict general themes in that person's life. Buchanan, Kern, and Bell-Dumas (1991) compared the thematic content of created early recollections with those of actual ERs and found that asking people to make up an early recollection yielded nearly the same manifest content as did actual ERs. These researchers first conducted a pilot study with university students that used only the theme dimension of the *Manaster-Perryman Manifest Content Early Recollection Scoring Manual* (1974). After asking subjects for their first three early recollections, Buchanan et al. (1991, p. 350) then requested them to "create ERs which could have happened in someone's life but did not happen in your own." Interestingly, the researchers found that created ERs produced themes that were consistent with those of actual ERs.

In the second phase of the study, Buchanan et al. (1991) included two additional variables from the *Manaster-Perryman Manifest Content Early Recollection Scoring Manual*—affect and activity. Subjects, who included psychiatric inpatients, alcohol and drug outpatients, and graduate students, were again asked for both actual ERs and created ERs. The researchers found no consistency in either the affect or the activity variables, but, once again, they found consistency between themes produced by actual ERs and those yielded by created ERs. The authors suggested that when people are asked to make up early recollections, "to some degree, their life style may be projected in the created recollections" (Buchanan et al., 1991, p. 352). Results from this and other studies are generally consistent with Adler's belief that early recollections reflect present style of life and will thus change as a person's style of life changes.

CRITIQUE OF ADLERIAN THEORY

Even though Individual Psychology is philosophically at the opposite pole from psychoanalysis, as a scientific theory of personality it is faced with many of the same problems encountered by Freudian theory.

A serious limitation of Adlerian psychology is that some of its tenets do not readily lend themselves to *verification* through scientific investigation. For example, the results previously cited studies on early recollections do not prove that present style of life shapes one's early recollections. An alternative, causal explanation is also possible; that is, one could counter that early experiences determine present style of life. Thus, one of Adler's most important concepts—the notion that present style of life determines early memories rather than vice versa—is not verifiable, an important component of a theory's ability to generate meaningful research.

On a more positive note, Adler's theory has encouraged researchers to construct several scales that attempt to measure such concepts as style of life and social interest. For example, Thorne (1975) devised a 200-item questionnaire called The Life-Style Analysis, which purports to measure various Adlerian life styles. More recently, Wheeler, Kern, and Curlett (1982, 1986, 1991) constructed the Life Style Personality Inventory, an instrument that uses present perceptions of childhood experiences and that also has a Social Interest Index. In addition, other research has been reported on the construction, validation, and use of scales for measuring social interest (Crandall, 1975, 1981, 1984; Crandall & Lehman, 1977; Crandall & Putnam, 1980; Greever, Tseng, & Friedland, 1973, 1974; Mozdzierz & Semyck, 1980; Zarski, Sweeney, & Barcikowski, 1977; Zarski, West, & Bubenzer, 1982). Although more research is needed on all these scales before their usefulness in clinical settings is established, the work currently being conducted on early recollections, life style types, and social interest is indicative of Adlerian theory's ability to generate substantial amounts of research.

In addition to its ability to generate research, a theory's usefulness rests on how comprehensive it is in organizing knowledge and how well it guides the practitioner. Of lesser importance is the theory's internal consistency and its simplicity. First, how well does Adlerian theory *organize knowledge* into a meaningful framework? Although not as global as Freudian theory, Adlerian theory nevertheless is sufficiently broad to encompass possible explanations for much of what is known about human behavior and development. Even seemingly self-defeating and inconsistent behaviors, such as those displayed by our case study Christine, can be fit into the framework of striving for superiority. Therefore, we rate Individual Psychology high on its ability to make sense out of what we know about human behavior.

As a *guide to action*, Adlerian theory serves the psychotherapist, the teacher, and the parent with guidelines for the solution to practical problems in a variety of settings. Adlerian practitioners gather information through reports on birth order, dreams, early memories, childhood difficulties, and organ deficiencies. They then use this information to understand a person's style of life and to apply those specific techniques that will both increase that person's individual responsibility and broaden his or her freedom of choice.

Is Individual Psychology *internally consistent*, with a set of operationally defined terms? A serious weakness of Adlerian theory, and one that also applies to Freudian and Jungian theory, is the lack of *precise operational definitions*. Terms like "goal of superiority" and "creative power" have no scientific definition. Nowhere in Adler's works are they operationally defined, and the potential researcher will look in vain for precise definitions that lend themselves to rigorous study.

The term "creative power" is an especially illusory one. Just what is this magical force that takes the raw materials of heredity and environment and molds a unique personality? How does the creative power transform itself into specific actions or operations needed by the scientist to carry out an investigation? Unfortunately, Individual Psychology is somewhat philosophical—even moralistic—and does not provide answers to these questions.

The concept of creative power, of course, is a very appealing one. Probably most of us prefer to believe that we are composed of something more than the interactions of heredity and environment. Intuitively, we feel that we have some agent (soul, ego, self, creative power) within us that allows us to make choices, to be free, and to create our own personality or style of life. As appealing as it is, however, the concept of creative power simply cannot be scientifically studied. Due to lack of operational definitions, therefore, Individual Psychology is rated low on internal consistency.

The final criterion of a useful theory is simplicity or *parsimony*, and on this standard Individual Psychology can be rated about average. The theory itself is quite unified and relatively simple, especially as extracted and edited by Ansbacher and Ansbacher (Adler, 1956, 1964). However, Adler's complete writings are more awkward and unorganized and, therefore, detract from the theory's rating on parsimony.

Chapter Summary

The Individual Psychology of Alfred Adler stands in sharp contrast to Freud's pessimistic view of personality. It suggests that people are self-determined, forward-moving, motivated by present perceptions, and capable of putting aside personal needs and of striving for the betterment of all humanity.

Adler believed that each of us begins life with an innate striving force, which receives additional impetus from our inevitable physical deficiencies. These organic weaknesses contribute to our feelings of inferiority, and these feelings in turn contribute to our final goal, which we set at around age four or five. Some people develop exaggerated feelings of inferiority and overcompensate by setting a goal of personal superiority. Other people are motivated by normal feelings of incompleteness and high levels of social interest, which they define as perfection and completion for all humankind.

This chapter looked at six major tenets of Adlerian theory: (1) unity of personality, (2) the subjectivity of perceptions, (3) social interest, (4) striving for superiority or success, (5) style of life, and (6) creative power. In addition, it discussed both abnormal development and the applications of Individual Psychology.

Adler held that all aspects of personality are *unified* and that all actions are consistent with one's *final goal* or purpose in life. Seemingly inconsistent behaviors all serve a single purpose.

Behavior is shaped neither by past events nor by objective reality, but rather by our *subjective perception* of a situation. Objective realities such as organ deficiencies, order of birth, and early childhood experiences are not as important as our view of them, ourselves, and our environment.

Social interest, or a deep concern for the welfare of others, is the sole criterion by which human actions should be judged. The three major problems of life—neighborly love, work, and sexual love—can only be solved through social interest. Criminals and neurotics lack social interest and try to solve problems with an eye toward personal gain.

The essential nature of humans dictates that they will *strive for completion* or improvement. Although all people have this innate tendency, not all strive for the welfare of others. Some are motivated more toward personal superiority. However, those with a high level of social interest strive for success, defined as improvement or upward development

for everyone.

All of our human potentialities develop in accordance with our self-consistent *style of life*, which includes our final goal, self-concept, feelings toward others, and attitudes toward the world.

The style of life is developed by our *creative power*, that is, our free will. Although we forge our personality from the building materials provided by heredity and environment, our creative power is ultimately responsible for what we make of ourselves.

Adler insisted that neurotics are different from normal individuals to the extent that they lack social interest. People who perceive themselves to have had exaggerated *physical deficiencies*, a *pampered style of life*, or a *neglected style of life* are most likely to become neurotic. All people, but especially neurotics, make use of various *safeguarding tendencies*, such as excuses, aggression, and withdrawal. Each of these represents conscious or unconscious attempts to protect inflated feelings of superiority against public disgrace.

The *masculine protest*, or the belief that men are superior to women, lies at the root of many neuroses, both for men and for women.

Adler used *birth order*, *early recollections*, and *dreams* in his practice of *psychotherapy*. The goal of Adlerian therapy is to foster courage, self-esteem, and social interest through a healthy relationship between the patient and therapist.

Adler's *concept of humanity* is basically optimistic and purposive. People strive toward a final goal of their own creation and have the potential to bring about significant personality change at any time of life. Although social influences are important, ultimately we are all responsible for who we are and what we do with what we have.

As a scientific theory, Individual Psychology is limited by a lack of operationally defined terms, and many of its major tenets elude rigorous empirical investigation. Nevertheless, it provides a useful explanation for much of what is known about human personality and is a helpful model for the practitioner.

Suggested Readings

ADLER, A. (1956). *The Individual Psychology of Alfred Adler: A systematic presentation in selections from his writings.* H. L. Ansbacher & R. R. Ansbacher (Eds.). New York: Basic Books.
A systematic presentation of Adler's theory and practice, edited by two advocates of Individual Psychology.

ADLER, A. (1979). *Superiority and social interest: A collection of later writings* (3rd ed.). H. L. Ansbacher & R. R. Ansbacher (Eds.). New York: Norton.
A compilation of Adler's later writings designed to supplement the 1956 volume.

ELLENBERGER, H. F. (1970). *The discovery of the unconscious* (Chap. 8). New York: Basic Books.
An unbiased, scholarly chapter on Adler's life and work.

ORGLER, H. (1963). *Alfred Adler: The man and his work: Triumph over the inferiority complex.* New York: Capricorn Books.
A readable account of Adler's life and his personality in light of his psychological theories.

RATTNER, J. (1983). *Alfred Adler.* (H. Zohn, Trans.). New York: Frederick Ungar. (Original work published 1983.)
A pro-Adlerian introduction to Individual Psychology intended for both the lay person and the professional.

SICHER, L. (1991). *The collected works of Lydia Sicher: An Adlerian perspective.* A. K. Davidson (Ed.). Ft. Bragg, CA: QED Press.
The collected works of one of Adler's associates, this book gives a unique perspective of Adlerian concepts such as individual responsibility, style of life, final goals, family constellation, early recollections, and the masculine protest.

Analytical Psychology

Chapter Five

OVERVIEW
BIOGRAPHY OF CARL JUNG
LEVELS OF THE PSYCHE
    The Conscious
    The Unconscious
DYNAMICS OF THE PSYCHE
    Principles of Equivalence and Entropy
    Causality and Teleology
    Progression and Regression
TYPOLOGY OF THE PSYCHE
    Attitudes
    Functions
DEVELOPMENT OF PERSONALITY
    Stages of Development
    Self-Realization
JUNG'S METHODS OF INVESTIGATION
    Word Association Test
    Dream Analysis
    Active Imagination
    Psychotherapy
CONCEPT OF HUMANITY
RELATED RESEARCH
CRITIQUE OF JUNG
CHAPTER SUMMARY
SUGGESTED READINGS

JUNG

The middle-aged doctor sat at his desk in deep contemplation and concern. A six-year relationship with an older friend and mentor had recently ended on bitter terms, and the doctor felt isolated and uncertain of his future. He no longer had confidence in his manner of treating patients and had begun to simply allow them to talk, not offering any specific advice or treatment. For some months he had been having bizarre, inexplicable dreams and seeing strange, mysterious visions. None of this seemed to make sense to him. He felt lost and disoriented—unsure whether or not the work he had been trained to do was indeed science.

A moderately gifted artist, he had begun to illustrate his dreams and visions with little or no comprehension of what the finished product might mean. He had also been writing down his fantasies without really trying to understand them. On this particular day he began to ponder, "What am I really doing?" He doubted if his work was science, but was uncertain as to what it was. Suddenly, to his astonishment, he heard a clear, distinct feminine voice from within him say, "It is art." He recognized the voice as that of a gifted female patient who had strong positive feelings for him. He protested to the voice that his work was not art, but no answer was immediately forthcoming. Then, returning to his writing, he again heard the voice say, "That is art." When he tried to argue with the voice, no answer came. He reasoned that the "woman within" had no speech center so he suggested that she use his. This she did, and a lengthy conversation followed.

The middle-aged doctor who talked to the "woman within" was Carl Gustav Jung, and the time was the winter of 1913–1914. Jung had been an early admirer and friend of Sigmund Freud, but when theoretical differences arose, their personal relationship broke up, leaving Jung with bitter feelings and a deep sense of loss. He then spent more than three years undergoing what Erikson might call a midlife crisis.

The above story is but one of many strange and bizarre occurrences experienced by Jung during his midlife "confrontation with the unconscious." An interesting account of his unusual journey into the deep recesses of his psyche is found in his autobiography *Memories, Dreams, Reflections* (Jung, 1961). I have chosen Jung himself for the case study to open this chapter because his life history seems to closely parallel and vividly illuminate his theory of personality.

OVERVIEW

Jung firmly believed that occult phenomena can and do influence the lives of all of us. At the same time, however, he believed himself to be a tough-minded empirical scientist. His theory is a compendium of polarities. He viewed people as being both introverted and extraverted; rational and irrational; male and female; conscious and unconscious; and pushed by past events while being pulled by future expectations.

This chapter looks with some detail into the long and colorful life of Carl Jung and uses fragments from his life history to illustrate his concepts and theories. Jung believed that each of us is motivated not only by repressed experiences but also by certain emotionally toned experiences we have inherited from our ancestors. These inherited images form what Jung called the "collective unconscious," which includes those elements that we have never experienced individually, but which have come down to us from our ancestors. The "woman within," with whom Jung had a prolonged conversation, represents one element of the collective unconscious. Jung's complex theory is one of the most intriguing of all conceptions of personality.

BIOGRAPHY OF CARL JUNG

Carl Gustav Jung was born on June 26, 1875, in Kesswil, a town on Lake Constance in Switzerland. His paternal grandfather, the elder Carl Gustav Jung, was a prominent physician in Basel and one of the best-known men of that city. A local rumor suggested that he was the illegitimate son of the great German poet, Goethe. Although the elder Jung never acknowledged the rumor, the younger Jung, at least sometimes, believed himself to be the great-grandson of Goethe and possibly even his reincarnation. In any event, Jung, who had many mystical experiences, believed that he had lived an earlier life during the 18th century (Ellenberger, 1970).

Jung's parents were Paul Jung, a minister, and Emilie Preiswerk Jung, the daughter of a theologian. His mother's family had a tradition of spiritualism and mysticism, and his maternal grandfather, Samuel Preiswerk, was a believer in the occult and often talked to the dead. He kept an empty chair for the ghost of his first wife and had regular and intimate conversations with her. Quite understandably, these practices greatly annoyed his second wife. His granddaughter, Helene Preiswerk (Carl Jung's first cousin) was also a medium and the subject of Jung's medical dissertation on the occult phenomenon. Thus, Jung's interest in spiritualism and the occult was acquired as part of a family tradition (Ellenberger, 1970).

Jung's parents had three children, an older son who lived only three days, and a daughter nine years younger than Carl. The girl was never an important rival of Carl's and did not play a prominent role in his life.

Thus Carl's early life was that of an only child.

Jung's father was a sentimental idealist, with strong doubts about his religious faith. His mother was more realistic, possessed an animal warmth, and had a strong attachment to Carl. At age three, Carl was separated from his mother, who had to be hospitalized for several months. This separation deeply troubled young Carl and for a long time after he felt distrustful whenever the words "love" or "mother" were mentioned.

Jung was an emotional and sensitive child. He felt deeply attached to both parents but seemed to fear a close relationship with either. His parents' frequent disagreements greatly troubled young Carl because he disliked having to take sides. His mother compounded this confusion by treating him as an adult. She confided in him by telling him things she could not reveal to her husband. Despite her attempts to drive a wedge between the boy and his father, Carl retained a deep affection for both parents.

Before Carl's fourth birthday his family moved to a suburb of Basel. It is from this period that his earliest dream stems. This dream, which was to have a profound effect on his later life and on his concept of a collective unconscious, will be recounted later (Jung, 1961).

Jung's first career choice was archeology, but he was also interested in philology, history, philosophy, and the natural sciences. Limited financial resources forced him to attend a school near home, so he enrolled in Basel University, which, however, did not have an archeology teacher.

Forced to choose another field, he decided to study natural science after twice dreaming of making important discoveries in the natural world (Jung, 1961). His choice eventually narrowed to medicine.

While Jung was still in medical school his father died. Carl then became the head of the family, which, at the time, included his mother and sister. After completing his medical degree from Basel University in 1900, he became a psychiatric assistant to Eugene Bleuler at Burghöltzli Mental Hospital in Zürich. During 1902–1903 he studied for six months in Paris with Pierre Janet, successor to Charcot. When he returned to Switzerland in 1903, he married Emma Rauschenbach, a young woman from a wealthy Swiss family. Two years later he began teaching at the University of Zürich, but continued his duties at the hospital.

The first decade of the 20th century was a period of outward growth and activity in Jung's life. Among other activities at this time, he was busily involved with the International Psychoanalytic Association, developed the word association test, established a family, and conducted a private psychiatric practice, all in addition to his work at Burghöltzli. In Jung's own terminology, this was a period of extraverted activity and progression. He had not yet reached the turning point of his life, a time marked by introverted activity and regression.

In 1909 he gave up his position at Burghöltzli, probably because of a difference of opinion with Bleuler. Four years later he surrendered his instructorship at the University of Zürich to give more time to his private practice in psychiatry and especially to devote his energy to his personal rebirth, a critical undertaking that took the form of a long, arduous journey into the unconscious. Jung (1961) felt that it would be unfair to continue teaching young students when his own intellectual life was still a mass of doubt and confusion.

Early in his professional career, Jung became acquainted with Freud's ideas by reading The Interpretation of Dreams (Freud, 1900/1953). Deeply taken with Freud's writings, he became an early defender of psychoanalysis, and the two men began a steady correspondence. (See McGuire, 1974, for the Freud/Jung letters.) In 1907 Freud invited Jung to Vienna and a warm friendship quickly developed. Freud's respect for the younger man led him to groom Jung as his successor and to select him as first president of the International Psychoanalytic Association. In 1909 the two men journeyed to America to deliver a series of lectures at Clark University. En route, they took great interest in interpreting one another's dreams, a pastime likely to strain any relationship.

In Memories, Dreams, Reflections Jung (1961) claimed that Freud was both unable to interpret Jung's dreams and unwilling to give Jung the details of his personal life, which Jung needed in order to interpret one of Freud's dreams. According to Jung's account, when asked for intimate details, Freud protested, "But I cannot risk my authority!" (Jung, 1961, p. 158). This comment triggered the end of Jung's

filial respect for Freud and probably marked the beginning of the end of their friendship.

Back in Europe personal as well as theoretical differences slowly emerged, and the friendship between Freud and Jung gradually cooled. In 1913 the two men terminated their personal correspondence, and the following year Jung resigned his presidency and shortly afterward withdrew his membership in the International Psychoanalytic Association (Brome, 1978).

The years immediately following the break with Freud were filled with loneliness and self-analysis for Jung. From December of 1913 until 1917 he underwent the most profound and dangerous experience of his life—a trip through the underground of his own unconscious psyche. This experience bears some similarity to Freud's self-analysis. Both men began their search for self while in their late 30s or early 40s: Freud as a reaction to the death of his father, Jung as a result of his split with his spiritual father, Freud. Both underwent a period of loneliness and isolation and both were deeply changed by the experience. However, differences also existed. Freud's self-analysis, though not as intense as Jung's, nevertheless lasted longer and became part of his daily routine for the remainder of his life. Freud was filled with outward activity and published his first great book, The Interpretation of Dreams (Freud, 1900/1953) during the early phase of his self-analysis. In contrast, Jung published little during the time of his self-analysis and, instead, turned his energies inward and became acquainted with what he termed his collective unconscious mind. During the period of his self-analysis, Jung suspended the formulation of new theoretical concepts, and treated his patients by simply listening to and learning from them.

Jung used the techniques of dream interpretation and active imagination to force himself through his underground journey. (These two techniques will be discussed under the heading "Jung's Methods of Investigation.") By writing down his dreams, drawing pictures of them, telling himself stories, and then following these stories wherever they moved, he came to an acquaintance with his personal unconscious. (See Jung, 1974, for a collection of many of his paintings during this period.) Prolonging the method and going more deeply, he came upon the contents of the collective unconscious—the archetypes. He heard his anima speak to him in a clear feminine voice; he uncovered his shadow, the evil side of his personality; he spoke with the old wise man and the great mother archetypes; and finally, near the end of his journey, he achieved a kind of psychological rebirth called individuation (Jung, 1961).

Even before his association with Freud, Jung had sown the seeds of his own personality theory. His approach to theory and therapy, known as

Analytical Psychology, was originally influenced by Freud, but his mature theory is uniquely Jungian.

Although he traveled widely in his study of personality, Jung remained a citizen of Switzerland, residing in Küsnacht, near Zürich. He and his wife, who was also an analyst, had five children, four girls and a boy. Jung was a Christian, but not a church-goer. He held honorary degrees from several famous universities, including Harvard, Oxford, and the University of Calcutta. Throughout his career he divided his time among conducting research, lecturing, writing, and seeing patients. His hobbies included wood carving, stone cutting, and sailing his boat on Lake Constance. He also maintained an active interest in alchemy, archeology, gnosticism, Eastern philosophies, history, religion, mythology, and ethnology.

In 1944 he became professor of medical psychology at the University of Basel, but poor health forced him to resign his position the following year. After his wife died in 1955 he was mostly alone, the "old wise man of Küsnacht." He died on June 6, 1961, in Zürich, three weeks short of his 86th birthday. At the time of his death his reputation was world-wide, extending beyond psychology. Jung is popularly regarded as one of the great thinkers of the 20th century (Brome, 1978).

LEVELS OF THE PSYCHE

Jung, like Freud, based his personality theory on the primary assumption that the mind, or psyche, has both a conscious and an unconscious level. Unlike Freud, however, he strongly asserted that the most important portion of the unconscious springs, not from personal experiences of the individual, but from the distant past of human existence. The psyche, therefore, can be divided into the *conscious* and the *unconscious*, the latter being subdivided into the *personal unconscious* and the *collective unconscious*.

The Conscious

Conscious images are those that are sensed by the ego, whereas unconscious elements have no relationship with the ego. The **ego**, in Jung's view, is more restrictive than it is in Freudian theory. Jung saw the ego as the center of consciousness, but not the core of personality. It is not the whole personality, but must be completed by the more comprehensive *self*, which is the center of personality. The ego develops as a child becomes aware of itself and evolves a sense of "I" or "me," but it should not grow to the point where it dominates the unconscious self (Jung, 1951/1959a).

Consciousness plays a relatively minor role in Analytical Psychology, and an overemphasis on expanding one's conscious psyche can lead to psychological imbalance. Healthy individuals are in contact with themselves and the outer world, of course, but they also allow themselves to experience the unconscious self and thus to achieve *individuation*, a concept that will be discussed later.

The Unconscious

The **unconscious**, that part of the psyche that adds depth and completeness to personality, refers to all psychic processes that are not related to the ego. Unconsciousness includes all previously conscious images that have been repressed or have merely fallen below the threshold of consciousness. In addition, it comprises those psychic elements that have never been conscious. Many of these elements form the seeds of future consciousness, but some images are not capable of becoming conscious.

The Personal Unconscious

The top layer of the unconscious, which embraces all repressed, forgotten, or subliminally perceived experiences of the individual, is known as the **personal unconscious**. Jung used the term personal because it pertains exclusively to one particular person. One's personal unconscious is formed by that individual's experiences and, for this reason, the personal unconscious of each human being is unique. The personal unconscious contains repressed infantile memories and impulses, forgotten events, and experiences originally perceived below the threshold of consciousness. Many of these images can be recalled easily, some remembered with difficulty, and still others are beyond the reach of consciousness. This concept of the personal unconscious differs little from Freud's view of the unconscious and preconscious combined (Jung, 1931/1960b).

Contents of the personal unconscious are called **complexes**. A complex is an emotionally toned conglomeration of associated ideas. For example, a person's experiences with "Mother" become grouped around a core, which is loaded with affect. The person's mother, or even the word "mother," sparks an emotional response that may block the smooth flow of thought. Complexes are largely personal, but they may also be partly derived from humanity's collective experience. In the above example, the mother complex comes not only from one's personal relationship with Mother but also from the entire species' experiences with Mother. In addition, the mother complex is partly formed by a person's conscious image of Mother. Thus complexes may be partly conscious and may stem from both the personal and the collective unconscious (Jung, 1928/1960).

The Collective Unconscious

In contrast to the personal unconscious, which results from individual experiences, the **collective unconscious** has roots in the ancestral past of the entire species. It represents Jung's most controversial, and perhaps his most distinctive, concept. The physical contents of the collective unconscious are inherited and pass from one generation to the next as psychic potential. Our distant ancestors' experiences with universal concepts such as God, Mother, water, earth, and so forth have been transmitted through the generations so that people in every clime and time have been influenced by the primitive human's primordial experiences (Jung, 1937/1959).

The contents of the collective unconscious do not lie dormant but are active and influence a person's thoughts, emotions, and actions. They are revealed through their activity. The collective unconscious is responsible for people's many myths, legends, and religious beliefs. It also produces universal or "big dreams," that is, dreams that have meaning beyond the individual dreamer and are laden with significance for all people (Jung, 1948/1960b).

The collective unconscious does not refer to inherited ideas, but rather to our innate tendency to react in a particular way whenever our experiences stimulate a biologically inherited response tendency. For example, a young mother may unexpectedly react with love and tenderness to her newborn infant, even though she previously had negative or neutral feelings toward the fetus. The tendency to respond was part of the woman's innate potential or inherited blueprint, but such innate potential needs an individual experience before it will become activated. Humans, like other animals, come into the world with inherited predispositions to act or react in certain ways if their present experiences touch upon these biologically based predispositions. For example, a man who falls in love at first sight may be greatly surprised and perplexed by his own reactions. His beloved may not resemble his conscious ideal of a woman, yet something within him moves him to be attracted to her. Jung might suggest that the man's collective unconscious contained biologically based impressions of Woman and that these impressions were activated when the man first saw his beloved.

How many biologically based predispositions do humans have? Jung said that we have as many of these inherited tendencies as we have typical situations in life. Countless repetitions of these typical situations have made them part of our biological constitution. At first, they are *"forms without content,* representing only the possibility of a certain type of perception or action" (Jung, 1954/1959b, p. 48). With more repetition these forms begin to develop some content and to emerge as *archetypes.*

Archetypes

Archetypes are ancient or archaic images that derive from the collective unconscious. They are similar to complexes in that they are emotionally toned collections of associated images. Whereas complexes are individualized and make up the contents of the personal unconscious, archetypes are generalized and compose the contents of the collective unconscious.

Archetypes should also be distinguished from *instincts.* Jung (1948/1960a) defined an instinct as an unconscious physical impulse toward action and saw the archetype as the psychic counterpart of an instinct. Both archetypes and instincts impel a person to action and in both cases the person remains unconscious of the true motives behind the action. Simply, then, instincts are unconsciously determined physiological drives, whereas archetypes are unconsciously determined psychological drives.

Jung believed that archetypes originated through the repeated experiences of our early ancestors. The potential for countless numbers of archetypes exists within each person, and when a personal experience corresponds to the latent primordial image, the archetype becomes activated, affecting one's personal life.

The archetype itself cannot be directly represented, but, when activated, it expresses itself through several modes, primarily dreams, fantasies, and delusions. During his midlife encounter with his unconscious, Jung had many archetypal dreams and fantasies. He frequently initiated fantasies by imagining that he was descending into a deep cosmic abyss. He could make little sense of his visions and dreams at that time, but later, when he began to understand that dream images and fantasy figures were actually archetypes, these experiences took on a completely new meaning (Jung, 1961).

Dreams are the main source of archetypal material, and certain dreams offer what Jung considered proof for the existence of the archetype. These dreams produce motifs that could not have been known to the dreamer through personal experience. The motifs often coincide with those known to ancient people or to natives of contemporary aboriginal tribes. Jung presented a vivid illustration in one of his earliest dreams, which took place before his fourth birthday. He dreamed he was in a meadow when suddenly he saw a dark rectangular hole in the ground. Fearfully he descended a flight of stairs and at the bottom encountered a doorway with a round arch covered by a heavy green curtain. Behind the curtain was a dimly lit room with a red carpet running from the entrance to a low platform. On the platform was a throne and on the throne was an elongated object that appeared to Jung to be a large tree trunk.

> It was a huge thing, reaching almost to the ceiling. But it was of a curious com-position: it was made of skin and naked flesh, and on top there was something like a rounded head with no face and no hair. On the very top of the head was a single eye, gazing motionlessly upward. (Jung, 1961, p. 12)

Filled with terror, the young boy heard his mother say, "Yes, just look at him. That is the man-eater!" This frightened him even more and jolted him awake.

Jung thought often about the dream, but 30 years would pass before the obvi-ous phallus became apparent to him. An additional number of years were required before he could accept the dream as an expression of his collective unconscious rather than the product of a personal memory-trace. In his own interpretation of the dream, the rectangular hole represents death; the green curtain symbolizes the mystery of Earth with her green vegetation; the red carpet signifies blood; and the tree, resting majestically on a throne, is the erect penis, anatomically accurate in every detail. After interpreting the dream, Jung was forced to conclude that no three-and-one-half-year-old boy could produce such universally symbolic material solely from his own experiences. A collective unconscious, common to the species, was the only explanation (Jung, 1961).

Hallucinations of psychotic patients also offer evidence for universal arche-types. In 1906, while working as a psychiatric assistant at Burghöltzli, Jung observed a paranoid schizophrenic patient looking through a window at the sun. The patient begged the young psychiatrist to observe, too.

> He said I must look at the sun with eyes half shut, and then I could see the sun's phallus. If I moved my head from side to side the sun-phallus would move too, and that was the origin of the wind. (Jung, 1931/1960b, p. 150)

Four years later Jung came across a book by the German philologist Albrecht Die-terich that had been edited in 1910 but was originally published in 1903, still some years after the patient was committed. The book, written in Greek, dealt with a liturgy derived from the so-called Paris magic papyrus, which described an ancient rite of the worshippers of Mithras, the Persian god of light. In this liturgy, the initiate was asked to look at the sun until he could see a tube hanging from it. The tube, swinging toward the east and west, was the origin of the wind. Dieterich's account of the sun-phallus of the Mithraic cult was nearly identical to the hallucination of the mental patient who, almost certainly, had no personal knowledge of the ancient initiation rite. Jung offers many similar examples as proof of the existence of arche-types and the collective unconscious (Jung, 1931/1960b).

As noted in Chapter 2, Freud also believed that people collectively inherit pre-dispositions to action His concept of "phylogenetic endowment," however, differs somewhat from Jung's formulation. The first difference is a matter of emphasis. Freud looked first to the personal unconscious, and only when individual explanations failed did he resort to the collective. Jung, on the other hand, placed primary emphasis on the collective unconscious and used personal experiences to round out the total personality. The major distinction between the two, though, was Jung's differentiation of the collective unconscious into autonomous forces called *archetypes*, each with a life and a personality of its own.

Although a great number of archetypes exist as vague images, only a few have evolved to the point where they can be conceptualized. The most notable of these include the persona, shadow, anima, animus, great mother, old wise man, the hero, and the self.

THE PERSONA.   That side of personality one shows to the world is designated as the **persona**. The term is well-chosen because it refers to the mask worn by actors in the early theater. Society dictates a particular role for each of us. The physician must adopt a characteristic "bedside manner," the truck driver must look and act like a truck driver, and the actress must exhibit the style of life demanded by her public (Jung, 1916/1953).

Although the persona is a necessary side of our personality, we should not confuse our public face with our complete self. If we identify too closely with our persona, we remain unconscious of our individuality and are blocked from attaining *self-realization*. True, we must acknowledge society, but if we over-identify with our persona we lose touch with our inner self and remain dependent on society's expectations of us. To become psychologically healthy, Jung believed, we must strike a balance between the demands of society and what we truly are. To be unaware of one's persona is to underestimate the importance of society, but to be unaware of one's deep individuality is to be nothing (Jung, 1950/1959).

During Jung's near break with reality from 1913 to 1917, he struggled hard to remain in touch with his persona. He knew that he must maintain a normal life, and his work and family provided that contact. He was frequently forced to tell himself, "I have a medical diploma from a Swiss university, I must help my patients, I have a wife and five children, I live at 228 Seestrasse in Küsnacht" (Jung, 1961, p. 189). Such self-talk kept Jung's feet rooted to the ground and reassured him that he really existed.

THE SHADOW.   The **shadow**, the archetype of darkness and repression, represents those qualities we do not wish to acknowledge but attempt to hide from ourselves and others. The shadow consists of morally objectionable tendencies as well as a number of constructive creative qualities, such as instincts and other archetypes that we, nevertheless, are reluctant to face (Jung, 1951/1959a).

Jung contended that to be whole we must continually strive to know our shadow, and that this quest is our *first test of courage*. It is easier to project the dark side of our personality onto others, to see in them the ugliness and evil that we refuse to see in ourselves. To come to grips with the darkness within ourselves is to achieve the "realization of the shadow." Unfortunately, most of us never realize our shadow, for to do so we would need to have enough courage to undertake a deep self-analysis, comparable to the one experienced by Jung during his middle years. Instead, most of us choose to identify only with the bright side of our personality. People who never realize their shadow may, nevertheless, come under its power and lead tragic lives, constantly running into "bad luck" and reaping harvests of defeat and discouragement for themselves (Jung, 1954/1959a).

In *Memories, Dreams, Reflections* Jung (1961) reported a dream in which his shadow, a brown-skinned savage, killed the hero, a man named Siegfried who represented the German people. Because he was beginning the process of independence, Jung no longer needed Sigmund Freud (Siegfried), so his shadow had the task of eradicating Jung's former hero.

THE ANIMA.   Like Freud, Jung believed that all humans are psychologically bisexual and possess both a masculine and a feminine side. The feminine side of men, the **anima**, originates in the collective unconscious as an archetype and remains extremely resistant to consciousness. Few men become well-acquainted with their anima because this task requires great courage. Most men find it far easier to become acquainted with their shadow, which merely demands that they overcome moral obstacles such as vanity and conceit and admit the inferior side of their nature. To overcome the projections of the anima, however, men must, in addition, overcome intellectual barriers, delve into the far recesses of their unconscious, and realize the feminine side of their personality. In Jungian psychology, a man's *second test of courage* is to recognize his anima, a task that can only be achieved after he has realized his shadow (Jung, 1954/1959a, 1954/1959b).

The anima originated from early men's experiences with women—mothers, sisters, and lovers—that combined to form a generalized picture of Woman. In time, this global concept became embedded in the collective unconscious of all men as the anima archetype. Since prehistoric days, every man has come into the world with a predetermined concept of womanhood that shapes and molds all his relationships with individual women. A man is especially inclined to project his anima onto his wife and to see her not as she really is, but as his personal and collective unconscious have determined her. This is the cause of much misunderstanding in marriage, but it is also responsible for the alluring mystique woman has in the minds of men.

The anima is the source of much of man's attitudes and personality. She is responsible for the superhuman qualities that men attribute to their mothers, and helps explain why one man might choose to insult another by making disparaging references to his mother. The anima also influences the feeling side in man and is the explanation for certain irrational moods and feelings. During these moods a man almost never admits that his feminine side is casting her spell, but, instead, he either ignores the irrationality of the feelings or tries to explain them in a very rational, masculine manner. In either event he denies that an autonomous archetype, the anima, is responsible for his mood.

At the beginning of this chapter we saw that the cunning, seductive anima was trying to convince Jung that his work was art, not science. Jung (1961, p. 187) interpreted this experience further.

What the anima said seemed to me full of a deep cunning. If I had taken these fantasies of the unconscious as art, they would have carried no more conviction than visual perceptions, as if I were watching a movie. I would have felt no moral obligation toward them. The anima might then have easily seduced me into believing that I was a misunderstood artist, and that my so-called artistic nature gave me the right to neglect reality. If I had followed her voice, she would in all probability have said to me one day, "Do you imagine the nonsense you're engaged in is really art? Not a bit." Thus the insinuations of the anima, the mouthpiece of the unconscious, can utterly destroy a man.

THE ANIMUS.   The masculine archetype in women is called the **animus**. Whereas the anima represents irrational moods and feelings, the animus is symbolic of thinking and reasoning. It is capable of influencing the thinking of a woman, yet it does not actually belong to her. It belongs to the collective unconscious and originates from the encounters of prehistoric women with men. In every relationship a woman has with a man she runs the risk of projecting her distant ancestors' experiences with fathers, brothers, lovers, and sons onto the unsuspecting male. In addition, of course, her personal experiences with men, buried in her personal unconscious, enter into her relationships with men. Couple this with projections from the man's anima and with images from his personal unconscious, and one has the basic ingredients of any male–female relationship. How much room remains for genuine opinions and feelings based on the individuality of the other person? Is it any wonder that men and women may sometimes find one another perplexing and have trouble in relating to one another?

Jung believed that the animus is responsible for thinking and opinion in women just as the anima produces feelings and moods in men. The animus is also the explanation for the irrational thinking and illogical opinions often attributed to women. Many opinions held by women are objectively valid, but, according to Jung, close analysis reveals that they were not thought out, but existed ready-made. If a woman is dominated by her animus, no logical or emotional appeal can shake her from her prefabricated beliefs (Jung, 1951/1959a).

Both anima and animus appear in dreams, visions, and fantasies in a personified form. A man may dream about a woman with no definite image and no particular identity. The woman represents no one from his personal experience, but enters his dream from the depths of his collective unconscious. The anima need not appear in dreams as a woman, but can be represented by a feeling or mood (Jung, 1945/1953).

THE GREAT MOTHER.   Two other archetypes, the great mother and the old wise man, are derivatives of the anima and animus. Everyone, male or female, possesses a **great mother** archetype. This preexisting concept of Mother is always associated with both positive and negative feelings. Jung (1954/1959c), for example, spoke of the "loving and terrible mother." The great mother, therefore, represents two opposing forces—fertility and nourishment on the one hand and power and destruction on the other. She is capable of producing and sustaining life, but she may also devour or destroy her offspring.

A man dominated by the great mother archetype cannot separate the concepts of Woman and Mother, has a stunted view of women, possesses an incapacitating *mother complex*, and fails to achieve the autonomy necessary to gain psychological maturity.

The fertility and nourishment dimension of the great mother archetype is symbolized by a tree, garden, plowed field, the sea, heaven, home, country, church, and hollow objects such as ovens and cooking utensils. Because the great mother also represents power and destruction, she is sometimes symbolized as a *grand*mother, the Mother of God, Mother Nature, Mother Earth, mother-in-law, or a witch.

Fertility and power combine to form the concept of *rebirth*, which may be a separate archetype, but its relation to the great mother is obvious. Rebirth is represented by such processes as reincarnation, baptism, resurrection, and individuation. This concept always remains somewhat unconscious because it derives from an inherited archetypal image (Jung, 1952/1956, 1954/1959c).

The strong fascination Mother has for both men and women, often in the absence of a close personal relationship, was taken by Jung as evidence for the great mother archetype. Legends, myths, religious beliefs, art, and literature of all kinds are filled with symbols of the great mother, a person who is both nurturing and destructive.

THE OLD WISE MAN.   The archetype of wisdom and meaning, the **old wise man,** symbolizes our preexisting knowledge of the mysteries of life. This archetypal meaning, however, is unconscious and cannot be directly or individually experienced. Politicians and others who speak authoritatively (but not authentically) often sound sensible and wise to others who are all too willing to be misled by their own old wise man archetypes. A man (or woman) dominated by his old wise man archetype may gather a large following of disciples with his profound verbiage, but his words make little sense because the collective unconscious cannot directly impart its wisdom to an individual. Political, religious, and social prophets who appeal to reason as well as emotion (archetypes are always emotionally tinged) are guided by this unconscious archetype. The danger to society comes when the prophet attains power and his or her pseudoknowledge is mistaken for real wisdom.

The old wise man archetype is personified in dreams as father, grandfather, teacher, philosopher, guru, doctor, or priest. He appears in fairy tales as the king, the sage, or the magician who comes to the aid of the troubled hero and, through superior wisdom, helps him escape from his current misadventures. The old wise man is also symbolized by life itself. Literature is replete with stories of young people leaving home, venturing out into the world, experiencing the trials and sorrows of life, and in the end acquiring a measure of wisdom (Jung, 1954/1959a).

THE HERO.   The hero archetype is represented in mythology and legends as a powerful man, sometimes part god, who fights against great odds to conquer or vanquish evil in the form of dragons, monsters, serpents, or demons. In the end, however, the hero often is undone by some seemingly insignificant person or event

(Jung, 1951/1959b). For example, Achilles, the courageous hero of the Trojan War,was killed by an arrow in his only vulnerable spot—his heel. Similarly, Macbeth was a heroic figure with a single tragic flaw—ambition. This was also the source of his greatness, but it contributed to his fate and his downfall.

The image of the hero touches an archetype within us, as demonstrated by our fascination with the heros of movies, novels, plays, and television programs. When the hero conquers the villain, he frees us from feelings of impotence and misery; at the same time, he serves as our model for the ideal personality (Jung, 1934/ 1954a).

The origin of the hero motif goes back to earliest human history—to the dawn of consciousness. In conquering the villain, the hero is symbolically overcoming the darkness of prehuman unconsciousness. The achievement of consciousness was one of our ancestors' greatest accomplishments, and the image of the archetypal, conquering hero represents victory over the forces of darkness (Jung, 1951/1959b).

THE SELF. Jung believed that each of us possesses an inherited tendency to move toward growth, perfection, and completion, and he called this innate disposition the **self.** The most comprehensive of all archetypes, the self can be seen as the *archetype of archetypes* because it pulls together the other archetypes and unites them in the process of **self-realization**. Like the other archetypes, it possesses conscious and personal unconscious components, but it is mostly formed by collective unconscious images.

As an archetype, the self is symbolized by our ideas of perfection, completion, and wholeness, but its ultimate symbol is the **mandala,** which is depicted as a circle within a square, a square within a circle, or any other concentric figure. It represents the strivings of the collective unconscious for unity, balance, and wholeness.

The self includes both personal and collective unconscious images and thus should not be confused with the ego, which represents consciousness only. In Figure 5.1, consciousness (the ego) is represented by the outer circle and is only a small part of total personality; the personal unconscious is depicted by the middle circle; the collective unconscious is represented by the inner circle; and totality of all three circles symbolizes the self. Only four archetypes—persona, shadow, animus, and anima—have been drawn in this mandala, and each has been idealistically depicted as being the same size. For most people the persona is more conscious than the shadow, and the shadow may be more accessible to consciousness than either the anima or the animus. As shown in Figure 5.1, each archetype is partly conscious, partly personal unconscious, and partly collective unconscious.

The balance shown in Figure 5.1 between consciousness and the total self is also somewhat idealistic. Many people have an overabundance of consciousness and thus lack the "soul spark" of personality; that is, they fail to realize the richness and vitality of their personal unconscious and, especially, of their collective unconscious. On the other hand, people who are overpowered by their unconscious are often pathological, with one-sided personalities. (Jung, 1951/1959a).

Although the self is almost never perfectly balanced, each person has in the collective unconscious a concept of the perfect, unified self. The mandala represents

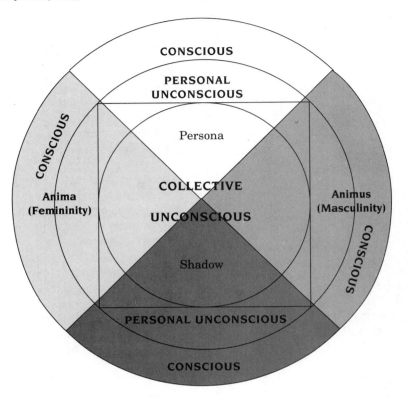

Figure 5.1   *Jung's Conception of Personality*

the perfect self, the archetype of order, unity, and totality. Because self-realization involves completeness and wholeness, it is represented by the same symbol of perfection (the mandala) that sometimes signifies divinity. In the collective unconscious, the self appears as an ideal personality, sometimes taking the form of Jesus Christ, Buddha, or other deified figures.

Jung found evidence for the self archetype in the mandala symbols that appear in dreams and fantasies of contemporary people who have never been conscious of their meaning. Historically, people produced countless mandalas without appearing to have understood their full significance. Jung (1951/1959a) believed that the increasing number of mandala motifs in the dreams of psychotic patients at the exact time that they are undergoing a period of serious psychic disorder is further evidence that people strive for order and balance. It is as if the unconscious symbol of order counterbalances the conscious manifestation of disorder.

In summary, the self includes both the conscious and unconscious mind, and it unites the opposing elements of psyche—male and female, good and evil, light and dark forces. These opposing elements are often represented by the Yang and Yin (see Figure 5.2), whereas the self is usually symbolized by the mandala. This latter motif stands for unity, totality, and order; in a word, self-realization. Complete

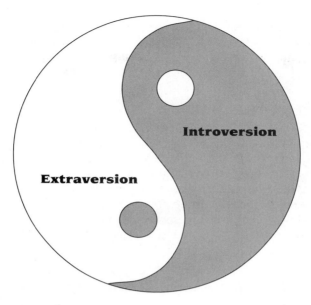

Figure 5.2 *The* Yang *and* Yin

self-realization is seldom if ever achieved, but as an ideal it exists within the collective unconscious of everyone. To actualize or fully experience the self, we must overcome our fear of the unconscious; prevent our persona from dominating our personality; recognize the shadow as our own, that is, come to grips with the dark side of ourselves; and then muster even greater courage to face our anima or animus.

On one occasion during Jung's midlife crisis, he had a vision in which he confronted a bearded old man who was living with a beautiful, blind, young girl and a large, black snake. The old man explained that he was Elijah and that the young girl was Salome, both biblical figures. Elijah had a certain, sharp intelligence, although Jung did not clearly understand him. Salome gave Jung a feeling of distinct suspiciousness, while the serpent showed a remarkable fondness for Jung. At the time he experienced this vision, Jung was unable to comprehend its meaning, but many years later he came to see the three figures as archetypes. Elijah represented the old wise man, seemingly intelligent, but not making a good deal of sense; the blind Salome was an anima figure, beautiful and seductive, but unable to see the meaning of things; and the snake was the counterpart of the hero, showing an affinity for Jung, the hero of the vision (Jung, 1961). Jung believed that he had to identify these unconscious images in order to maintain his own identity and not lose himself to the powerful forces of the collective unconscious. He later wrote:

The essential thing is to differentiate oneself from these unconscious contents by personifying them, and at the same time to bring them into relationship with consciousness. That is the technique for stripping them of their power. It is not too difficult to personify them, as they always possess a certain degree of autonomy, a separate identity of their own. Their autonomy is a most uncomfortable thing to reconcile oneself to, and yet the very fact that the unconscious presents itself in that way gives us the best means of handling it. (Jung, 1961, p. 187)

DYNAMICS OF THE PSYCHE

We have seen that Jung divided the psyche into a conscious and an unconscious layer, with the latter being further divided into the personal unconscious, and the collective consciousness. Now we turn to a consideration of the *dynamics* of the psyche, that is, the nature of the energy that moves us.

Jung made no distinction between physical and psychic energy. The same laws or principles apply to both. In this section we look at the principles of *equivalence* and *entropy*, the concepts of *causality* and *teleology*, and Jung's ideas on *progression* and *regression*.

Principles of Equivalence and Entropy

From physics, Jung borrowed the principles of equivalence and entropy to explain human motivation. The first law of thermodynamics, the **principle of equivalence**, states that when a given quantity of energy is expended in the performance of an activity, an equal amount of energy will appear elsewhere (Jung, 1928/1960). In other words, energy cannot be destroyed but is merely displaced. Transferred to psychology, this principle holds that for each psychic system a given quantity of energy is available, either actually or potentially. When one psychic function no longer demands a constant expenditure of energy, that same amount of energy is available to perform a second function. The total amount of energy, however, remains the same. For example, we expend some psychic energy whenever we repress an anxiety-provoking image. If the repressed material continually and forcefully threatens to emerge into our consciousness, we must use more energy from other sources to maintain the repression. As a result, we are handicapped in our intellectual functioning, interpersonal relationships, and other activities that demand the free use of psychic energy. Most repressions, fortunately, drain only small amounts of psychic energy, thus freeing the remainder to perform other psychic functions.

An example of the principle of equivalence is an adolescent boy deeply infatuated with an older girl. The large level of energy he expends maintaining his infatuation is diverted from the amount he previously used to concentrate on academic and athletic activities. After the infatuation wears off, he may show a noticeable improvement in both schoolwork and sports.

The second law of thermodynamics, the **principle of entropy**, states that when objects of different temperatures meet, heat flows from the hotter one into the colder one, bringing about an equalization of temperature. In Jungian psychology the principle of entropy holds that the greater the differences between two poles, the greater the tension generated by them, and the longer lasting and more satisfying the resulting attitude.

The principle of entropy can also be stated this way: The stronger the conflict within a person, the greater the measure of psychic energy flowing from the conflict. Once resolved, strong conflict situations lead to an equalization of tension, a relatively permanent attitude, and the pleasant experience of overcoming a troublesome obstacle. Thus, we experience more satisfaction in conquering a formidable opponent than in defeating an easy one.

The principle of entropy is responsible for the stability (sometimes called tranquility or rigidity depending on point of view) of values in older people. After the stormy tensions unleashed in youth by the confrontation of opposites, psychic energy gradually achieves a leveling process that solidifies attitudes, opinions, and prejudices. Older people do not necessarily possess less psychic energy than younger ones; they merely transform the oscillating activity of youth into the balanced stability of old age (Jung, 1928/1960).

Causality and Teleology

Does motivation spring from past causes or from teleological goals? Jung insisted that it comes from both. **Causality** holds that present events have their origin in previous experiences. Freud, for example, relied heavily on a causal viewpoint in his explanations of adult behavior in terms of early childhood experiences. Jung criticized Freud for being one-sided in his emphasis on causality and insisted that a causal view could not explain all motivation. Conversely, **teleology** holds that present events are motivated by goals and aspirations for the future that direct our destiny. Adler, for example, held this position, insisting that people are motivated by unconscious perceptions of fictional final goals. Jung is less critical of Adler, but he insisted that human behavior is shaped by *both* causal and teleological forces, and that causal explanations must be balanced with teleological ones.

Jung's insistence on balance is seen in his conception of dreams. He agreed with Freud that many dreams have their origins in past events; that is, they are caused by earlier experiences. On the other hand, Jung claimed that some dreams can help a person make decisions about the future, just as his dreams of making important discoveries in the natural sciences eventually led to his choice of a career.

Progression and Regression

To achieve self-realization people must adapt not only to their outside environment but to their inner world as well. Adaptation to the outside world involves the forward flow of psychic energy and is called **progression**, whereas adaptation to the inner world relies on a backward flow of psychic energy and is called **regression**. Both progression and regression are essential if we are to achieve individual growth or self-realization.

Progression attempts to achieve adaptation to the outer world through an attitude that inclines a person to react consistently to a given set of environmental conditions. Conversely, regression is a necessary backward step in the successful attainment of a goal (Jung, 1928/1960). Regression activates the unconscious psyche, an essential aid in the solution of most problems. Solutions often come only after the conscious mind stops concentrating and allows the unconscious to take over. Many of us have had the experience of trying to remember someone's name, but the name did not come to us until after our conscious psyche had given up and turned the problem over to the unconscious. The value of regression is also seen in dreams that provide us with clues for solving problems that could not have solved by conscious thought. Unconscious material, distasteful and repugnant though it sometimes is, provides a valuable and necessary resource to the process of individual growth.

Regression is exemplified in the life of Jung, who underwent a prolonged regressive experience from 1913 until about 1917. During that time his psychic life was turned inward toward the unconscious and away from any significant outward accomplishments. He spent most of his energy becoming acquainted with his unconscious psyche and did little in the way of writing or lecturing. Regression dominated his life, while progression nearly ceased. Subsequently, he emerged from this period with a greater balance of the psyche, and once again he became interested in the extraverted world. However, his regressive experiences with the introverted world had left him permanently and profoundly changed. Jung believed that the regressive step is necessary to create a balanced personality and to grow toward self-realization.

Alone, neither progression nor regression leads to development. Either can bring about too much one-sidedness and failure in adaptation; but the two, working together, can activate the process of healthy personality development (Jung, 1928/1960).

TYPOLOGY OF THE PSYCHE

Besides the levels and the dynamics of the psyche, Jung recognized various psychological types, which grow out of a union of two basic *attitudes*—introversion and extraversion—and four separate *functions*—thinking, feeling, sensing, and intuiting.

Attitudes

An **attitude** is an inclination to act or react in a characteristic direction. Jung insisted that each person has both an *introverted* and an *extraverted* attitude. If introversion is conscious, then extraversion is unconscious; if extraversion is conscious, then introversion is unconscious. Like other opposing forces in Analytical Psychology, introversion and extraversion serve in a compensatory relationship to one another and can be illustrated by the Yang and Yin motif (see Figure 5.2).

Introversion

According to Jungian psychology, **introversion** is the turning inward of psychic energy with an orientation toward the subjective. Introverts are tuned in to their inner world with all its biases, fantasies, dreams, and individualized perceptions. These people perceive the external world, of course, but they do so selectively and with their own subjective view (Jung, 1921/1971).

The introverted personality is clearly illustrated by Jung himself during his mid-life confrontation with his unconscious. His conversations with his anima, his bizarre dreams, and his self-induced visions were the "stuff of psychosis" (Jung, 1961, p. 188). His fantasy life was individualized and subjective. Other people, including even Jung's wife, could not accurately comprehend what he was experiencing. During this time he suspended or discontinued much of his extraverted or objective attitude. He no longer actively treated his patients, he resigned his position as lecturer at the University of Zürich, he stopped his theoretical writing, and for three years, he found himself "utterly incapable of reading a scientific book" (Jung, 1961, p. 193). He was in the process of discovering the introverted pole of his existence.

Jung's voyage of discovery, however, was not totally introverted. He knew that unless he retained some objective hold on the outer world he would risk becoming absolutely possessed by his inner world. Afraid that he might become completely psychotic, he forced himself to continue as much of a normal life as possible with his family and his profession. By this technique, Jung eventually emerged from his inner journey and established a balance between introversion and extraversion.

Extraversion

In contrast to introversion, **extraversion** is the attitude characterized by the turning outward of psychic energy so that a person is oriented toward the objective and away from the subjective. Extraverts are more influenced by their surroundings than by their inner world. They tend to focus on the objective attitude while suppressing the subjective. They are somewhat pragmatic and well-rooted in the realities of everyday life. At the same time, they are overly suspicious of the subjective attitude, whether their own or that of someone else.

No designation of worth should be placed on introversion or extraversion. Each tendency has strengths as well as weaknesses but, unfortunately, introverts and extraverts frequently undervalue one another.

Few people are either completely introverted or completely extraverted. Most have some elements of both attitudes; that is, they are influenced by both the subjective and the objective world.

Functions

Both introversion and extraversion can combine with any one or more of four functions, forming eight possible orientations or **types**. The four functions—sensation, thinking, feeling, and intuition—can be briefly defined as follows.

Sensation tells us what something is; thinking enables us to recognize its meaning; feeling tells us its value; and intuition allows us to "see around corners" and gain knowledge of it without knowing how we know.

Thinking

Logical intellectual activity that produces a chain of ideas is called **thinking.** The thinking type can be either extraverted or introverted, depending on a person's basic attitude.

Extraverted thinking flows primarily from objective phenomena and is essentially a conscious process. Extraverted-thinking persons rely heavily on concrete thoughts, but may also use abstract ideas if these ideas have been transmitted to them from without, for example, from parents or teachers. Mathematicians and engineers make frequent use of extraverted thinking in their work. Accountants, too, are extraverted-thinking types because they must be objective and not subjective in their approach to numbers. Not all objective thinking, however, is productive. If too little individual interpretation is brought to objective data, the resulting process is merely the presentation of previously known facts, with no originality or creativity (Jung, 1921/1971).

Thinking involves a subject (the thinker) and an object (the ideas thought about). In this sense, it is both subjective and objective, but when the subjective is dominant it is called *introverted thinking*. Introverted-thinking people react to external stimuli, but their interpretation of an event is colored more by the internal meaning they bring with them than by the objective facts themselves. Inventors and philosophers are often introverted-thinking types because they react to the objective world in a highly subjective and creative manner, interpreting old data in new ways. When carried to an extreme, introverted thinking results in unproductive, mystical thoughts that are so individualized that they are useless to any other person (Jung, 1921/1971).

Feeling

The process of valuing an idea or event is called **feeling**. In Analytical Psychology, the term feeling is limited to affective *value* responses, such as "I feel sorry for him," or "That is a funny story." It excludes the processes of sensing and intuiting, which are sometimes confused with the feeling function. When a person says, "This surface feels smooth," she is using her sensing function, and when she says, "I have a feeling that this will be my lucky day," she is intuiting, not feeling.

The feeling function is distinguished from emotion. Feeling is the valuation of every conscious activity, even those valued as indifferent. Most of these valuations have no emotional content, but are capable of becoming emotions if their intensity increases to the point of stimulating physiological changes within the person. Emotions, however, are not limited to feelings; any of the four functions can lead to emotion when their strength is increased.

Like the other functions, feeling can be either extraverted or introverted. *Extraverted-feeling types* use objective data to make valuations. They are not guided so much by their subjective opinion, but by external values and widely accepted standards of judgment. They are likely to be at ease in social situations, knowing on the spur of the moment what to say and how to say it. They are usually well liked because of their sociability, but in their quest to conform to social standards they may appear artificial, cold, and unreliable. Their value judgments will have an easily detectable false ring. Extraverted feeling people often become businesspeople or politicians because these professions demand and reward the making of value judgments based on objective information (Jung, 1921/1971).

The *introverted-feeling attitude* is found in people who base their value judgments primarily on subjective perceptions rather than objective facts. Critics of the various art forms make much use of this attitude because their judgments are based heavily on subjective individualized data. When one's entire attitude is colored by subjective valuations, the person is known as an introverted-feeling type. These people have an individualized conscience, a taciturn demeanor, and an unfathomable psyche. They ignore traditional opinions and beliefs, and their nearly complete indifference to the objective world (including people) often causes persons around them to feel uncomfortable and to cool their attitude toward them (Jung, 1921/1971).

Sensation

The psychic function that receives physical stimuli and transmits them to perceptual consciousness is called **sensation**. Sensation is not identical to the physical stimulus, but is simply the individual's perception of sensory impulses. These perceptions are not dependent on logical thinking or feeling, but exist as absolute, elementary facts within each person.

Sensations may be perceived with either an extraverted or an introverted attitude. People with an *extraverted-sensing attitude* perceive external stimuli objectively, in much the same way that they exist in reality. Their sensations are not greatly influenced by their subjective attitudes. This facility is essential in such occupations as proofreader, house painter, wine taster, or any other job demanding sensory discriminations congruent with those of most people (Jung, 1921/1971).

A person in tune with subjective sensations is said to have an *introverted-sensing attitude*. This attitude can be illustrated by asking several people to describe or reproduce accurately a picture exposed to them for a short length of time. Extraverted-sensing people will vary little in their reproductions, whereas introverted-sensing people will have widely different interpretations. Portrait artists, especially those whose paintings are extremely personalized, rely on an introverted-sensing attitude. They give a subjective interpretation to objective phenomena, yet are able to communicate meaning to others. When the subjective-sensing attitude is carried to its extreme, however, it may result in hallucinations or esoteric ramblings that lie beyond the comprehension of other people (Jung, 1921/1971).

Intuition

The most difficult function to understand or describe is **intuition**, inasmuch as it involves perception beyond the workings of consciousness. Intuition, like sensation, is based on the perception of absolute, elementary facts, ones that provide the raw material for the thinking and feeling functions. It differs from sensation in that it is more creative, often adding or subtracting elements from conscious sensation.

Intuition, too, can be extraverted or introverted. *Extraverted intuitive people* are oriented toward facts in the external world. Rather than fully sensing them, however, they merely perceive them subliminally. Because strong sensory stimuli interfere with intuition, intuitive people suppress many of their sensations and are guided by hunches and guesses contrary to sensory data. An example of an extraverted intuitive type might be the inventor who must inhibit distracting sensory data and concentrate on unconscious solutions to objective problems. This person may create things that fill a need few other people realized existed. Often inventors also remain unaware of the inner workings of their inventive process (Jung, 1921/1971).

Introverted intuition is unconscious perception of facts that are basically subjective. These internal facts usually have little or no resemblance to external reality but exist in the unconscious as psychological reality. Subjective intuitive perceptions are often remarkably strong and capable of motivating decisions of monumental magnitude. Introverted intuitive people, such as mystics, prophets, surrealistic artists, or religious fanatics, often appear peculiar to people of other types who have little comprehension of their motives. Actually, Jung (1921/1971) believed that intuitive introverted people may not clearly understand their own motivations, yet they are deeply moved by them.

The eight Jungian types with some possible examples are seen in Figure 5.3.

The functions usually appear in a hierarchy, with one occupying a *superior* position, another a *secondary position*, and the other two *inferior* positions. Jung regarded

ATTITUDES

Functions	Introversion	Extraversion
Thinking	Philosophers, Theoretical Scientists, Certain Inventors	Research Scientists, Accountants, Mathematicians
Feeling	Subjective Movie Critics, Editorial Writers	Real Estate Appraisers, Objective Movie Critics, Politicians
Sensation	Artists, Classical Musicians	Wine Tasters, Proofreaders, House Painters, Popular Musicians
Intuition	Prophets, Mystics, Religious Fanatics	Certain Inventors, Religious Reformers

Figure 5.3   *Examples of the Eight Jungian Types*

thinking and feeling as **rational functions** because they require reason and judgment. Both functions rely on raw data gathered through analyzing and synthesizing sensation and intuition, making deductions, and drawing conclusions. In other words, both are involved in the reasoning process; thinking is required in intellectual decisions, feeling in value judgments. The processes of thinking and feeling are always rational, but the decisions and judgments are not necessarily valid or "reasonable."

Sensation and *intuition*, on the other hand, are **irrational functions**. They are not subject to the laws of reason because both involve the immediate perception of data, with no judgment or reasoning required. Facts gathered through sensation and intuition have an absolute existence independent of the rational functions.

Most people cultivate only one function so that they characteristically approach a situation relying on the one dominant or superior function. Some people develop two functions, and a few very mature individuals have cultivated three. A person who has theoretically achieved self-realization or individuation would have all four functions highly developed.

In his later years, long after his journey into his unconscious, Jung came close to developing all four functions. He relied on thinking to construct his theoretical models; on feeling to judge the value of his and other works; on sensation to paint pictures and carve wooden figures; and on intuition to interpret his dreams and fantasies.

The four functions are like the points on a compass, with the self in the center facing a given direction, but using all four points as guides (Jung, 1921/1971) (see Figure 5.4).

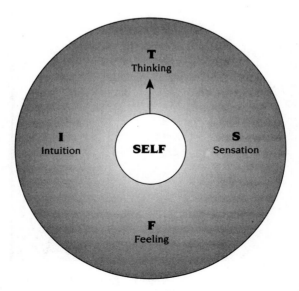

Figure 5.4   *The four functions are like points on a compass, with the self facing one direction but using all four points as guides.*

DEVELOPMENT OF PERSONALITY

Jung believed that personality develops through a series of stages that culminate in individuation. In contrast to Freud, he emphasized the second half of life, the period after 35 or 40, when a person has the opportunity to bring together the various aspects of personality and to attain self-realization. However, the opportunity for degeneration and neurotic reactions is also present at that time. The direction people travel depends on their ability to achieve balance between the poles of the various opposing processes. This ability is proportional to the success achieved in journeying through the previous stages of life.

Stages of Development

The stages of life can be grouped into four general periods—*childhood, youth, middle life,* and *old age.* Jung compared the trip through life with the journey of the sun through the sky, with the brightness of the sun representing consciousness. The early morning sun is childhood, full of potential, but still lacking in brilliance (consciousness); the morning sun is youth, climbing toward the zenith, but unaware of the impending decline; the early afternoon sun is middle life, brilliant like the late morning sun, but obviously headed for the sunset; the evening sun is old age, its once bright consciousness now markedly dimmed (see Figure 5.5). Jung (1931/1960a) argued that values, ideals, and modes of behavior suitable for the morning of life are inappropriate for the second half, and that people must learn to find new meaning in their declining years of life.

Childhood

Jung divided childhood into three substages: (1) the anarchic, (2) the monarchic, and (3) the dualistic. The *anarchic phase* is characterized by chaotic and sporadic consciousness. "Islands of consciousness" may exist, but there is little or no

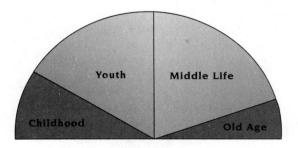

Figure 5.5 *Jung compares the stages of life to the sun's journey through the sky, with the brilliance of the sun representing consciousness.*

connection between these islands. Experiences of this phase are either completely undifferentiated from one another, or they occur on a low level of differentiation that makes later recall impossible. Experiences of the anarchic phase sometimes enter consciousness as primitive images, incapable of being accurately verbalized.

The *monarchic phase* of childhood is characterized by the development of the ego and by the beginning of logical and verbal thinking. During this time children see themselves objectively and often refer to themselves in the third person. The islands of consciousness become larger, more numerous, and inhabited by a primitive ego. Although the ego is perceived as an object, it is not yet aware of itself as perceiver.

The ego as perceiver arises during the *dualistic phase* of childhood when the ego is divided into the objective and subjective. Children now refer to themselves in the first person and are aware of their existence as separate individuals. During the dualistic periods the islands of consciousness become continuous land, inhabited by an ego-complex that recognizes itself as both object and subject (Jung, 1931/1960a).

Youth

The period from puberty until middle life is called youth. Young people strive to gain psychic and physical independence from their parents, find a mate, raise a family, and make a place in the world. According to Jung (1931/1960a), it is, or should be, a period of increased activity, maturing sexuality, growing consciousness, and recognition that the problem-free era of childhood is gone forever. The major difficulty facing youth is to overcome the natural tendency (found also in middle and later years) to cling to the narrow consciousness of childhood, thus avoiding problems pertinent to the present time of life. This desire to live in the past is called the *conservative principle*.

People of Western civilization, especially Americans, often place great value on youth, an age of sexual attractiveness, athletic prowess, and career achievement. However, youth is also a stage of limited consciousness, with the inner workings of the psyche being almost completely ignored during that time. When Jung was young he had the extraverted attitudes of many of his peers. As a student, he joined a fraternity, enjoyed pranks, loved to dance, courted several women, and fell in love. After graduation he was married, pursued a medical career, became a father, and generally was not involved with his inner psyche. By his own standards, his values and behaviors were appropriate for a youthful person.

A person who attempts to hold on to youthful values with advancing age, however, faces a crippled second half of life, handicapped in the capacity to achieve self-realization and impaired in the ability to establish new goals and seek new meaning to life (Jung, 1931/1960a).

Middle Life

Jung believed that middle life begins at approximately age 35 for women and 40 for men. By this time the sun has passed its zenith and begins its downward descent, presenting the middle-aged person with increasing anxieties. However, middle life is also a period of tremendous potentiality.

If middle-age people retain the social and moral values of their early life, they become rigid and fanatical in trying to hold on to their physical attractiveness and agility. Finding their ideals shifting, they may fight desperately to maintain their youthful appearance and life style. Most of us, said Jung (1931/1960a, p. 399), are unprepared to "take the step into the afternoon of life; worse still, we take this step with the false assumption that our truths and ideals will serve us as hitherto. . . . we cannot live in the afternoon of life according to the programme of life's morning; for what was great in the morning will be little at evening, and what in the morning was true will at evening have become a lie."

How can middle life be lived to its fullest? People who have lived youth by neither childish nor middle-age values are well prepared to advance to middle life and to live fully during that stage. They are capable of giving up the extraverted goals of youth and moving in the introverted direction of expanded consciousness. Their psychological health is not enhanced by success in business, prestige in society, or satisfaction with family life. They must look forward to the future with hope and anticipation, surrender the life style of youth, and discover new meaning in middle life. This often, but not always, involves a mature religious orientation, especially a belief in some sort of life after death (Jung, 1931/1960a).

Old Age

As the evening of life approaches, people experience a diminution of consciousness, just as the light and warmth of the sun diminish at dusk. If people fear life during the early years, then they will almost certainly fear death during the later ones. Fear of death is often taken as normal, but Jung believed that death is the goal of life, and that life can only be fulfilling when death is seen in this light. In 1934, during his 60th year, Jung wrote:

> Ordinarily we cling to our past and remain stuck in the illusion of youthfulness. Being old is highly unpopular. Nobody seems to consider that not being able to grow old is just as absurd as not being able to outgrow child's-size shoes. A still infantile man of thirty is surely to be deplored, but a youthful septuagenarian— isn't that delightful? And yet both are perverse, lacking in style, psychological monstrosities. A young man who does not fight and conquer has missed the best part of his youth, and an old man who does not know how to listen to the secrets of the brooks, as they tumble down from the peaks to the valleys, makes no sense; he is a spiritual mummy who is nothing but a rigid relic of the past. (Jung, 1934/1960, p. 407)

Most of Jung's patients were middle-aged or older, and many of them suffered from a backward orientation, clinging desperately to goals and life styles of the past and going through the motions of life aimlessly. In treating these people, Jung attempted to help them establish new goals and to find meaning in living by first finding meaning in death. He accomplished this through dream interpretation, because the dreams of elderly people are often filled with symbols of rebirth, such as baptism, long journeys, or changes in location. Jung used these and other symbols to determine patients' unconscious attitudes toward death and to help them discover a meaningful philosophy of life (Jung, 1934/1960).

Self-Realization

Psychological rebirth, also called **self-realization** or **individuation,** was defined by Jung (1939/1959; 1945/1953) as the process of becoming an individual or whole person. Analytical Psychology is essentially a psychology of opposites. Consciousness is opposed to unconsciousness, the personal unconscious to the collective unconscious, persona to individual, ego to self, anima to animus, introversion to extraversion, thinking to feeling, sensing to intuiting, rational functions to irrational functions, and progression to regression.

Self-realization is the process of integrating the various poles into a single, homogeneous individual. This process of "coming to selfhood" means that a person has all psychological components functioning in unity, with no psychic process atrophying. A person who has gone through this process has achieved realization of the self; has minimized the persona while actualizing the individual; has become conscious of the anima or animus; has acquired a workable balance between introversion and extraversion; and, perhaps most difficult of all, has elevated all four functions to a superior position.

Self-realization is relatively rare, being achieved only by people who are able to assimilate their unconscious into their total personality. To come to terms with the unconscious is a difficult process because it demands courage to face the evil nature of one's shadow and even greater fortitude to accept one's feminine or masculine side. This process is almost never achieved before middle life and then only by men and women who are able to remove the ego as the dominant concern of personality and replace it with the self. One must allow the unconscious self to become the core of personality. To merely expand consciousness is to inflate the ego and to produce a one-sided person who lacks the soul spark of personality. The self-realized person is dominated neither by unconscious processes nor by the conscious ego, but achieves a balance between all aspects of personality.

Both progression and regression are necessary for self-realization. Progression, the process of adaptation to the demands of the outer world, must be secured before people can make a satisfactory adjustment to the inner world. People must be in contact with reality before they can grow psychologically; that is, they must make allowances for body functions and for the existence of other people prior to achieving inner development. To continue either progression or regression singly for a long period of time leads to one-sided development. For example, if progression is pursued to the neglect of the inner world, people become overly concerned with external values, such as achievement, social status, or material wealth; if regression goes unchecked, they retreat to their private world and become unable to cope with the problems of the external world.

Self-realized people are able to contend with both the external and the internal. Unlike psychotic individuals, they live in the real world and make necessary concessions to it. However, unlike average people, they are neither ignorant nor distrustful of the regressive process. Seeing unconscious images as potential material for new psychic life, self-realized people welcome unconscious images and find satisfaction in coming to terms with them in both dreams and introspective reflections (Jung 1939/1959, 1945/1953).

JUNG'S METHODS OF INVESTIGATION

Jung looked beyond psychology in his search for data to build his conception of humanity. He made no apologies for his ventures into the fields of sociology, history, anthropology, biology, physics, philology, religion, mythology, and philosophy. He strongly believed that the study of personality was not the prerogative of any single discipline, and that the whole person could be understood only by pursuing knowledge wherever it existed. However, Jung did not consider himself to be a philosopher, theologian, or anything other than a medical psychologist. He simply used knowledge obtained through these various approaches to build a scientific psychological theory.

Like Freud, Jung persistently defended himself as a scientific investigator, eschewing the labels of mystic and philosopher. At the same time, however, he asserted that the psyche could not be understood by the intellect alone, but must be grasped by the total person. Along the same lines, he once said, "Not everything I bring forth is written out of my head, but much of it comes from the heart also" (Jung, 1943/1953, p. 116).

Jung gathered data for his theories from extensive reading in many disciplines, but, primarily, his basic facts came from a systematic observation of people, including himself. Most of these observations were made on patients through the *word association test, dream analysis, active imagination,* and *psychotherapy.* This information was then combined with readings on medieval alchemy, the other occult sciences, or any other subject in an effort either to confirm or reject the hypotheses of Analytical Psychology.

Word Association Test

Jung was not the first to use the word association technique, but he can be credited with helping to develop and refine the test. He originally used the technique as early as 1903 when he was a young psychiatric assistant at Burghöltzli, but he seldom employed it in his later career. In spite of this inattention, the test continues to be closely linked with Jung's name.

His original purpose in using the word association test was to demonstrate the validity of Freud's hypothesis that the unconscious operates as an autonomous process. However, the basic purpose of the test in Jungian psychology today is to uncover feeling-toned complexes. As noted earlier, a complex is an individualized, emotionally toned conglomeration of images grouped around a central core. The test is based on the principle that complexes create emotional responses in the subject, and that these responses can then be measured through the use of such devices as a stop watch, a pneumograph, and a galvanometer.

In administering the test, Jung typically used a list of about 100 stimulus words chosen and arranged to elicit an emotional reaction. He instructed the subject to respond to each stimulus word with the first word that came to mind. Jung recorded each verbal response, time taken to make a response, rate of breathing, and galvanic skin response. Usually, he would then repeat the experiment, instructing the subject to duplicate the original verbal responses. Certain types of reactions would indicate that the stimulus word had touched a complex.

Critical responses included restricted breathing, as measured by the pneumograph; changes in the electrical conductivity of the skin, detected by the galvanometer; and delayed reactions, or any response time markedly longer than the subject's mean reaction time. Other revealing reactions included multiple responses, that is, those that contained many words; disregard of instructions; inability to reproduce a word, for example; errors in pronunciation not usually made; unusual facial expressions, including blushing; nonverbal sounds such as stammering, laughing, coughing, sighing, clearing the throat, or crying; excessive body movement, especially of the hands or feet; repetition of the stimulus word; silence or failure to give a verbal response; and inconsistency on test–retest. Any one, or combination, of these types of responses might indicate that a complex had been reached (Jung, 1935/1968; Jung & Riklin, 1904/1973).

Dream Analysis

Jung agreed with Freud that dreams have meaning and that they must be taken seriously. He also agreed with Freud that dreams spring from the depths of the unconscious and that their latent meaning is expressed in symbolic form. However, he objected to Freud's notion that nearly all dreams are wish fulfillments and that most dream symbols represent sexual urges. He also believed that Freud was too one-sided in his insistence that dreams are rooted in past experiences. Some dreams, Jung agreed, spring from early childhood experiences, but he insisted that many others are aimed toward the future. Thus he balanced Freud's *causal* view of dreams against Adler's *teleological* view; that is, he theorized that dreams may reveal the past as well as provide guidelines for making future decisions. As with other psychic events, dreams have both a cause and a purpose. Jung said that some dreams could be interpreted as infantile wish-fulfillments and others as exaggerated strivings for superiority. However, any attempt to explain dreams solely from either position is too narrow and does an injustice to the full nature of dreams.

The purpose of Jungian dream interpretation is to uncover elements from the personal and collective unconscious and to integrate them into the conscious in order to facilitate the process of self-realization. The Jungian therapist must realize that dreams are often compensatory, that is, feelings and attitudes not expressed during waking life will find an outlet through the dream process. Jung held that the natural condition of humans is to move toward completion or self-realization. Thus, if our conscious life is incomplete in a certain area, our unconscious self will strive to complete that condition through the dream process. For example, if the anima in a man receives no conscious development, she will express herself through dreams filled with self-realization motifs so that the man's masculine side will be balanced by his feminine disposition (Jung, 1916/1960).

To correctly interpret dreams, one needs to know the dreamer's conscious attitude because the dream is made up of the unconscious opposite. However, we cannot interpret our dreams by dwelling only on their conscious content; the unconscious meaning must eventually be discovered. Jung (1934/1954b, p. 154) provided an example of how the conscious and unconscious work together in constructing and interpreting dreams. A young man reported the following dream:

> My father is driving away from the house in his new car. He drives very clumsily, and I get very annoyed over his apparent stupidity. He goes this way and that, forward and backwards, and manoeuvres the car into a dangerous position. Finally he runs into a wall and damages the car badly. I shout at him in perfect fury that he ought to behave himself. My father only laughs, and then I see that he is dead drunk.

To interpret this dream, Jung needed to know something about the young man's conscious life and about his relationship with his father. In reality, the young man's father was a very well respected man in his community and would never get drunk, much less drive a car while intoxicated. Also, Jung's patient had an excellent relationship with his father, perhaps too good. He greatly admired his father, who was still providing for his welfare, a condition that was blocking the young man's growth toward self-realization. Jung noted that one would make a grave error to interpret this dream to mean that the young man wished to discredit his father. Such an interpretation would take into account only the unconscious wish of the young man. In Jung's interpretation, the purpose of the dream was to contrast the dreamer with the father so that the young man could gain more confidence in himself and to develop a personality uniquely different from that of his father. Such an analysis relied on information about the dreamer's conscious situation and seemed to have hit the mark because the young man immediately saw that the interpretation was correct.

Recall that Jung felt certain dreams offered proof for the existence of the collective unconscious. At least three kinds of dreams are considered as archetypal dreams.

Under the first heading are *"big dreams,"* those that seem to have special meaning and inexplicable attraction for all people. Jung had such a dream while traveling to the United States with Freud. It was one of several dreams that Jung claimed Freud was unable to accurately interpret, an inability that led Jung to lose some respect for his older mentor. It was also the dream that first led Jung to the idea of a collective unconscious. In this dream Jung was living in the upper floor of a two-story house. This floor had an inhabited atmosphere, although its furnishings were somewhat old. In the dream Jung realized that he did not know what the ground floor was like, so he decided to explore it. After descending the stairs, he noticed that all the furnishings were medieval and dated to the 15th or 16th centuries. While exploring this floor he discovered a stone stairway that led down into a cellar. "Descending again, I found myself in a beautifully vaulted room which looked exceedingly ancient. . . . As soon as I saw this I knew that the walls dated from Roman times" (Jung, 1961, p. 159). As he looked at the floor of this cellar, Jung noticed a ring on one of the stone slabs. When he lifted it, he saw another narrow stairway leading to an ancient cave. There, he discovered broken pottery, scattered animal bones, and two human skulls, half disintegrated and very old.

When Jung finished telling the dream, Freud insisted that he reveal his associations to the two human skulls. Whom did Jung wish were dead? To placate Freud, Jung said his wife and his sister-in-law, two people for whom he had no death wish. Jung's interpretation, of course, was quite different. To him the house and its cellars represented the different levels of the psyche. The top floor was consciousness, while the ground level symbolized the first layer of the unconscious. The cellar was a deeper level of the personal unconscious, and the cave represented the collective unconscious, "the world of the primitive man within myself—a world which can scarcely be reached or illuminated by consciousness" (Jung, 1961, p. 160).

The second kind of collective dreams are the *typical dreams*, those that are common to most people. These include archetypal figures, like Mother, Father, God, devil, or old wise man; archetypal events, such as birth, death, separation from parents, baptism, marriage, flying, or exploring a cave; and archetypal objects, for example, sun, water, fish, snakes, or predatory animals.

The third category includes *earliest dreams* remembered. These can be traced back to about age three or four and contain mythological and symbolic images and motifs that could not have reasonably been experienced by the individual child. These early childhood dreams often contain archetypal motifs and symbols such as the hero, the old wise man, the tree, the fish, and the mandala. Jung (1948/1960b, p. 291) wrote of these images and motifs: "Their frequent appearance in individual case material, as well as their universal distribution, prove that the human psyche is unique and subjective or personal only in part, and for the rest is collective and objective." Earlier, we described a dream Jung had at age three and a half where he entered a dark rectangular hole in the ground and encountered several archetypal images beyond the personal experience of a young child. Such a dream, Jung said, suggests the existence of a collective unconscious.

Active Imagination

A technique Jung used during his own self-analysis as well as with many of his patients was active imagination. This method requires the subject to begin with any impression—a dream image, vision, picture, or fantasy—and to concentrate until the impression begins to "move." These images are then followed to wherever they lead, and the subject must have the courage to face these autonomous images and to freely communicate with them.

The purpose of active imagination is to reveal archetypal images emerging from the unconscious. It can be an aid to an artist or writer in generating creative material, but it can be even more helpful to the thinking person because it enables that person to develop the other functions, especially feeling and sensing. Active imagination is a useful technique for anyone who wants to become better acquainted with the collective and personal unconscious and who is willing to overcome the resistance that ordinarily blocks open communication with the unconscious.

Jung believed that active imagination has an advantage over dream analysis in that its images are produced during a conscious state of mind, thus making them more clear and reproducible. The feeling tone is also quite specific, and ordinarily the subject has little difficulty reproducing the vision or remembering the mood (Jung, 1937/1959).

As a variation to active imagination, Jung sometimes asked patients who were so inclined to draw, paint, or express in some other nonverbal manner the progression of their fantasies. Jung relied on this technique during his own self-analysis, and many of these reproductions, rich in universal symbolism and often exhibiting the mandala and the quaternity symbols, are scattered throughout his books. *Man and His Symbols* (1964), *Word and Image* (1979), and *Psychology and Alchemy* (1952/1968) are especially prolific sources for these drawings and photographs.

Jung (1961, p. 192) wrote the following about his experiences with active imagination during his midlife confrontation with the unconscious:

> When I look back upon it all today and consider what happened to me during the period of my work on the fantasies, it seems as though a message had come to me with overwhelming force. There were things in the images which concerned not only myself but many others also. It was then that I ceased to belong to myself alone, ceased to have the right to do so. From then on, my life belonged to the generality. . . . It was then that I dedicated myself to service of the psyche: I loved it and hated it, but it was my greatest wealth. My delivering myself over to it, as it were, was the only way by which I could endure my existence and live it as fully as possible.

Psychotherapy

The hypotheses of Analytical Psychology rest on data gathered from widely scattered sources, but the backbone of Jung's investigations was his observations of patients during psychotherapy.

Jung (1931/1954b) identified four basic approaches to therapy, representing four developmental stages in the history of psychotherapy. The first is confession of a pathogenic secret. This is the cathartic method practiced by Joseph Breuer and earlier psychiatrists. For patients who merely have a need to share their secrets, catharsis is effective. The second stage involves interpretation, explanation, and elucidation. This approach, used by Freud, gives the patients insight into the causes of their neuroses, but may still leave them incapable of solving social problems. At this point Adlerian therapy may be indicated. This third stage involves the education of patients as social beings. Unfortunately, says Jung, this development of social interest often leaves patients merely socially well-adjusted. To go beyond adjustment to the outer world, Jung suggested a fourth stage, **transformation**, by which he meant that the doctor must first be transformed into a healthy human being, preferably by undergoing psychotherapy. Only after being free from neuroses (but not necessarily complexes) and having established a philosophy of life is the therapist able to help patients move toward individuation, wholeness, or self-realization. This fourth stage is especially employed with patients who are in the second half of life and who are concerned with realization of the inner self, with moral and religious problems, and with finding a unifying philosophy of life.

Jung was quite eclectic in his theory and practice of psychotherapy. His treatment varied according to the age, the stage of development, and the particular neurosis of the individual patient. He used both Freudian and Adlerian techniques when appropriate, but these, he felt, were useful primarily for patients with sexual neuroses or power conflicts, problems that are crucial mostly during the first half of life. About two-thirds of Jung's patients, however, were in the second half, and a great many of them suffered from a loss of meaning, general aimlessness, and a fear of death. Jung attempted to help these patients find their own philosophical orientation. He was careful not to prescribe a ready-made philosophy but to encourage them to discover their own individual meaning to life.

The ultimate purpose of Jungian therapy is to help neurotic patients become healthy and to encourage healthy people to work independently toward self-realization. Jung sought to achieve this purpose by using such techniques as dream analysis and active imagination to aid patients in discovering unconscious material and to bring this in line with their conscious attitude.

Jung usually began therapy with four consultations a week, but as soon as possible he would reduce the number of therapeutic hours to one or two a week. This was to encourage patients to try to interpret some of their own dreams and to independently strive toward a unity of ego and self, that is, conscious and unconscious. Ideally, this process should continue after therapy is terminated. "My aim is to bring about a psychic state in which my patient begins to experiment with his own nature—a state of fluidity, change, and growth where nothing is externally fixed and hopelessly petrified " (Jung, 1931/1954a, p. 46). This is essentially what Jung himself accomplished with his journey into his unconscious during the three-year period following his break with Freud.

Although Jung encouraged patients to be independent, he admitted the importance of **transference**, particularly during the first three stages of therapy. He regarded both positive and negative transference as a natural concomitant to patients' revelation of highly personal information. He thought it quite alright that a number of male patients referred to him as "Mother Jung" and quite

Carl Jung, the old wise man of Küsnacht

understandable that others saw him as God or savior. Jung also recognized the process of **countertransference**, a term used to describe a therapist's feelings toward the patient. Like transference, countertransference can be either a help or a hindrance to treatment depending on whether or not it leads to a better relationship between doctor and patient, something that Jung felt was indispensable to successful psychotherapy.

Jung also emphasized the importance of the unique personality of both therapist and patient and was one of the first to stress the concept that therapy should be a growth-producing experience for the doctor as well as the patient. In 1931 he wrote:

> For two personalities to meet is like mixing two different chemical substances; if there is any combination at all, both are transformed. . . . You can exert no influence if you are not susceptible to influence. It is futile for the doctor to shield himself from the influence of the patient and to surround himself with a smokescreen of fatherly and professional authority. (Jung,1931/1954b, p. 71)

Because Jungian psychotherapy has many goals and an equal number of techniques, no universal description of a person who has successfully completed analytical treatment is possible. For the mature person, the goal may be to find meaning in life and strive toward achieving balance and wholeness. The self-realized person is able to assimilate much of the unconscious self into consciousness but, at the same time, remains fully aware of the potential dangers hidden in the far recess of the unconscious psyche. Jung once warned against digging too deeply in land not properly surveyed, comparing this practice to a person digging for an artesian well and running the risk of activating a volcano.

CONCEPT OF HUMANITY

Jung's view of humanity can be described as neither *pessimistic* nor *optimistic*, neither *deterministic* nor *purposive*. Humans are complex organisms composed of many opposing factors. People are motivated partly by *conscious* thoughts, partly by images from their personal *unconscious*, and partly by latent memory traces inherited from their ancestral past. Their motivation comes both from *causal* and *teleological* factors.

The complex makeup of humans invalidates any simple or one-sided description. According to Jung, no one is totally good or completely bad; each person is a composition of opposing forces. No one is completely introverted or totally extraverted; all male or all female; solely a thinking, feeling, sensing, or intuitive person; and no one proceeds invariably in the direction of either progression or regression.

The persona is but a fraction of an individual. What one wishes to show others is usually only the socially acceptable side of personality. Every person has a dark side, a shadow, and most try to conceal it from both society and themselves. In addition, each man possesses an anima and every woman an animus, which are even more likely to be hidden. The stronger and more dominant a man appears, the more frantically he is trying to repress his anima. The more helpless a woman seems, the more she is attempting to hide her animus.

The various complexes and archetypes cast their spell over us and are responsible for many of our words and actions and most of our dreams and fantasies. Although we are not masters in our own houses, neither are we completely dominated by forces beyond our control. We have some limited capacity to determine our lives. Through our will, and with great courage, we can explore the hidden recesses of our psyches. We can recognize our shadows as our own, become partially conscious of our feminine or masculine sides, and cultivate more than a single function. This process, which Jung called individuation or self-realization, is not easy and demands more fortitude than most of us can muster. Ordinarily, it means we have reached middle life and have lived successfully through the stages of childhood and youth. During middle age, we must be willing to set aside the goals and behaviors of youth and adopt a new style appropriate to our stage of psychic development.

Even when we have achieved individuation, made an acquaintance with our inner world, and brought the various opposing forces into balance, we still are not in complete control of our self. Our impersonal collective unconscious remains the source of many of our creations, new ideas, prejudices, interests, fears, and even our dreams.

On the dimension of *biological vs. social* aspects of personality, Jung's theory is decidedly in the direction of biology. The collective unconscious, responsible for so many of our actions, is part of our biological inheritance. Except for the therapeutic potential of the doctor–patient relationship, Jung had little to say about differential effects of specific social practices. In fact, in his studies of various cultures, he found the differences to be superficial, the similarities profound. For this same reason Analytical Psychology can also be rated high on *similarities* among people and low on *individual differences*.

Related Research

No area of Jungian psychology has been researched as extensively as the concept of types. The Myers-Briggs Type Indicator (MBTI) (Myers, 1962) and, to a lesser extent, the Jungian Type Survey (JTS) (Wheelwright, Wheelwright, & Buehler, 1964) have stimulated most of these investigations. Of these two type indicators, the JTS is shorter, simpler, and easier to score, but there is some evidence that the JTS has only limited validity due primarily to its brevity (Woehlke & Piper, 1980).

The Myers-Briggs Type Indicator employs terminology slightly different from Jung's. It is based on four bipolar personality dimensions that oppose extraversion (E) to introversion (I); sensing (S) to intuition (N); thinking (T) to feelings (F); and judgment (J) to perception (P). This last dimension (J vs. P), does not reflect basic Jungian typology, but was added by Myers. Although some investigators (McCrae & Costa, 1989) have questioned whether the MBTI adequately measures Jungian typology, others have reported that it is a reliable and valid measure of Jung's basic concept. For example, Carlson (1980) found the MBTI generally supported Jungian type theory, and McCaulley (1990) cited evidence that the inventory is an accurate representation of Jung's ideas on typology. Also, a study by Steele and Kelley (1976) obtained a very high relationship between the extraversion–introversion scale of the MBTI and the extraversion–introversion scale of the factor-analytically developed Eysenck Personality Questionnaire (see Chapter 12 for Eysenck's concept of extraversion/ introversion). This relationship is especially impressive because the two instruments are based on quite different theoretical approaches. Myers and McCaulley (1985) reported substantial reliability and validity for the MBTI as a measure of Jungian personality types. In addition, a study by Levy and Ridley (1987) found that, over a 10-year period, college women changed their scores very little, thus suggesting that the Myers-Briggs Type Indicator measures relatively stable personality traits.

Many investigators have administered the MBTI to college students to determine the relationship between personality types and a number of other variables and experiences. Robert Apostal at the University of North Dakota has conducted several studies that have tied the Myers-Briggs to vocational interest patterns. In one study Apostal (1991) administered the Strong-Campbell Interest Inventory and the MBTI to 130 female and 89 male undergraduate students. Both sexes reported similar vocational interests, but, when personality types were added to the mixture, some interesting differences emerged. Apostal found that conventional vocational interests were significantly related to the Sensing personality in women but not in men. On the other hand, Artistic and Investigative interests were significantly related to the Intuitive personality type in both women and men. These findings are consistent with Jung's notion that intuitive people would be inclined toward creative interests, whereas sensing people would be rooted in conventional interests.

Nolan and Patterson (1990) compared MBTI scores with television-viewing preferences for college students. They found that Sensing students had a preference for action/adventure programs, sports, situation comedies, and game shows; Intuiting subjects had no preference for any programs; Thinking subjects preferred action/adventure programs; and Feeling students preferred daytime interview shows. In another study Kean, Mehlhoff, and Sorensen (1988) found that students majoring in textile, clothing, and design were predominantly Intuitive–Feeling types, whereas those majoring in agronomy were mostly Sensing–Thinking types. Also, Jacka (1991) studied teacher-education students and found that Intuitive subjects, with their orientation toward internal, unconscious experiences, reported dreams that were more emotionally intense and disturbing than those reported by Sensing subjects. Again, these findings are consistent with Jung's concept of typology. For a more complete review of the literature on the Myers-Briggs Type Indicator, the reader may wish to consult Murray (1990) or McCaulley (1990).

In addition to the very active research on the MBTI, some researchers have recently attempted to investigate the validity of Jung's more inaccessible notion of the collective unconscious. To test the relationship between archetypal symbols and the meanings attributed to them, Rosen, Smith, Huston, & Gonzalez (1991) developed the Archetypal Symbol Inventory (ASI), which consists of 40 pictures depicting archetypal symbols, and 40 associated words that indicate the symbol's meaning. For example, the numeral 6 should be associated with "harmony," a window with "possibility," an apple with "knowledge," and so forth. Rosen et al. (1991) first administered the ASI to a sample of college students to determine if they had conscious knowledge of the symbols' meanings. Subjects were briefly exposed to the 40 symbols and asked to write down the one word that best described the figure's symbolic meaning. Because only 1% of the responses were correct, the authors concluded that the students had little or no conscious knowledge of what the symbols meant. Next, the experimenters showed the 40 symbols and 80 descriptive words (40 correct and 40 incorrect) to a second group of college students to see if they could correctly match the correct word with a symbol. Again, the students showed very little conscious knowledge of the symbols' meanings. Finally, Rosen et al. (1991) selected a third sample of students, divided them into two groups, and gave each group 20 matched and 20 mismatched symbol/word pairs. The order of presentation was reversed for the two groups. Both groups viewed each of the 40 symbol/word pairs for five seconds and were later asked to recall the word that had previously been paired with the symbol. Subjects in both groups recalled more matched words that were archetypically correct than those that were not, suggesting that they had some unconscious knowledge of the symbols' meanings. Although the differences were quite small, they were highly statistically significant. Whereas, the two groups correctly recalled only 43% and 49% of the mismatched words, both groups recalled about 54% of the correct matches. Rosen et al. (1991, p. 223) stated that these differences indicate that the ASI "is truly an inventory of archetypal (universal) symbols related to the collective unconscious." Even though more cautious conclusions are clearly called for, the Archetypal Symbol Inventory or some modification of it may open the door to research into some of Jung's more difficult concepts.

CRITIQUE OF JUNG

Although Jung considered himself to be a medical psychologist and a scientific observer of human behavior, many readers may regard him as a fantasy writer, a philosopher, or an introspective mystic. He is sometimes criticized as being a creator of interesting stories who neglected the rigors of science in his approach to theory building.

Analytical Psychology, like any other theory, can be evaluated in reference to the five criteria of a useful theory established in Chapter 1. To be useful, a theory (or any major component such as the collective unconscious) need not be absolutely proven. It must only meet those criteria.

For a theory to be useful, it must *generate testable hypotheses and descriptive research*, which have the capacity to verify that theory. The part of Jung's theory concerned with classification and typology, that is, the functions and attitudes, can be studied and tested and, in fact, has yielded large amounts of research, most of it involving the Myers-Briggs Type Indicator. However, the crux of his theory, the collective unconscious, remains a difficult concept to test empirically.

Much of the evidence for the concepts of archetype and the collective unconscious has come from Jung's own inner experiences, which he admittedly found difficult to communicate to others, so that acceptance of these concepts rests more on faith than on empirical evidence. Jung (1943/1953, p. 116) wrote that "not everything I bring forth is written out of my head, but much of it comes from the heart also." In a similar vein, he stated: "Archetypal statements are based upon instinctive preconditions and have nothing to do with reason; they are neither rationally grounded nor can they be banished by rational argument" (Jung, 1961, p. 353). Such a statement may be acceptable to the artist or the theologian, but it is not likely to win adherents from among scientific researchers faced with the problems of designing studies and formulating hypotheses. Perhaps the most serious limitation of Analytical Psychology is that its most important concepts—the archetypes and the collective unconscious—simply cannot be verified.

Second, a useful theory should *organize observations* into a meaningful framework. Analytical Psychology is unique because it adds a new dimension to personality theory, namely, the collective unconscious. Those aspects of human personality dealing with the occult, the mysterious, and the parapsychological are not touched upon by most other personality theories. Even though the collective unconscious is not the only possible explanation for these phenomena, and other concepts could be postulated to account for them, Jung is the only modern personality theorist to make a serious attempt to include such a broad scope of human activity within a single theoretical framework.

A third criterion of a useful theory is its *practicality*. Does the theory aid therapists, teachers, parents, or others in solving everyday problems? The theory of psychological types or attitudes and the Myers-Briggs Type Indicator are used by many clinicians, but the usefulness of most of Analytical Psychology is limited to those therapists who subscribe to basic Jungian tenets. The concept of a collective unconscious does not easily lend itself to empirical research, but it may have some usefulness in helping people adjust to life's trauma. Busick (1989), for example, developed an 8-week course for cancer patients, their family, and friends that relied on Jungian therapy. By getting in touch with their collective unconscious, these people are better able to cope with the fear and anger that frequently follow a diagnosis of cancer.

Is Jung's theory of personality *internally consistent*? Does it possess a set of operationally defined terms? The first question receives a qualified affirmative answer; the second a definite negative one. Jung generally used the same terms consistently, but he often employed several terms to describe the same concept. The words "regression" and "introverted" are so closely related that they can be said to describe the same process. This is also true of "progressive" and "extraverted," and the list could be expanded to include several other terms such as "individuation" and "self-realization," which are not clearly differentiated either. Jung's language is often arcane and many of his terms are not adequately defined. As for operational definitions, they are totally absent from his writings, but, in fairness to Jung, he did not construct his theory with this criterion in mind.

The final criterion of a useful theory is *parsimony*. Jung's psychology is not simple, but neither is human personality. However, his theory is the most complex of all theories and probably more cumbersome than it need be. Jung's proclivity for searching for data from a variety of disciplines and his willingness to explore his own unconscious even beneath the personal level contribute to the great complexities and the broad scope of his theory. The law of parsimony states, "When two theories are equally useful, the simpler one is preferred." In fact, of course, no two are ever equal, and Jung's theory adds a dimension to human personality not greatly dealt with by others.

Chapter Summary

The life of Carl Jung provides an appropriate illustration of the basic concepts of Jungian theory. Jung's midlife journey into the deep recesses of his psyche provided the data for his theories concerning a *collective unconscious*. This notion that important segments of our unconscious are inherited from our ancient ancestors is Jung's most distinctive and controversial concept. Repeated experiences of past generations are passed down through inheritance and form the bases of our collective unconscious.

Some of the contents of the collective unconscious become highly developed and are identified as *archetypes*. Jung became acquainted with several of these ancient images during his midlife self-analysis. They included the *anima*, or feminine side of men; the *animus*, or masculine disposition in women; the *shadow*, the dark side of our personality; the *old wise man*, the intelligent but deceptive voice of accumulated experience; the *great mother*, the archetype of nourishment and destruction; the *persona*, or mask we show to the outside world; the *hero*, our unconscious image of a person who conquers or vanquishes an evil foe; and the *self*, the archetype of completeness and wholeness.

The layer of the psyche above the collective unconscious is the *personal unconscious*, comprised of complexes or emotionally toned images revolving around a core concept. Above the personal unconscious is the *conscious*, or those images perceived by the *ego*.

In discussing the dynamics of personality Jung relied on the principles of equivalence, entropy, progression, and regression. The *principle of equivalence* states that energy is never lost or destroyed but merely transformed to another function. The *principle of entropy* provides the foundation for Jung's psychology of opposites. It states that energy flows from the tension produced by opposing poles such as introversion and extraversion. The concepts of *progression* and *regression* are similar to those of extraversion and introversion and refer to the forward and backward flow of energy necessary to attain eventual balance.

Jung postulated two basic attitudes—*introversion* and *extraversion*. Introversion is a tendency to see the world subjectively, whereas extraverts tend to take an objective view. When these two attitudes combine with the four functions—*thinking, feeling, sensation*, and *intuition*—eight basic types are produced.

Jung emphasized the last half of life, although he suggested that a healthy *middle life* and *old age* depend on proper solutions to the problems of *childhood* and *youth*.

Early in his career Jung developed the *word association test*, which was designed to uncover *complexes*. Later, during his midlife crisis, he used *dream analysis* and *active imagination* to discover the contents of his own collective unconscious. Subsequently, he made use of these techniques in his practice of *psychotherapy*.

Finally, Jung saw humans as exceedingly complex organisms comprising several opposing forces. He was neither optimistic nor pessimistic, although he believed that people can attain *individuation* or *self-realization* during the second half of life. Analytical Psychology is the most complex of all personality theories, but it falls short of meeting the standards for a scientific theory, especially in its inability to verify several of its key concepts and its lack of operationally defined terms.

Suggested Readings

JACOBI, J. (1973). *The psychology of C. G. Jung: An introduction with illustrations.* New Haven, CT: Yale University Press.
    This brief paperback by one of Jung's former associates is an excellent introduction to Jungian psychology. It includes a lengthy section on the practical application of Analytical Psychology.
JUNG, C. G. (1961). *Memories, dreams, reflections.* (A. Jaffe, Ed.). New York: Random House.
    Of all of Jung's works, this is possibly the easiest to read and the most interesting. Written by Jung as he entered his ninth decade, this book contains an exciting firsthand account of his midlife confrontation with the unconscious.
JUNG, C. G. (1979). *Word and image.* (A. Jaffe, Ed.). Princeton, NJ: Princeton University Press.
    Mostly biographical and pictorial, this large book includes a chronology and a glossary of technical terms. Anyone interested in Jung will enjoy a leisurely perusal of these pages.
SHELBURNE, W. A. (1988). *Mythos and logos in the thought of Carl Jung: The theory of the collective unconscious in scientific perspective.* Albany: State University of New York Press.
    Shelburne argues that the idea of the collective unconscious can be reconciled with scientific evidence. He also includes a discussion of Jung's attitude toward science.
STEVENS, A. (1990). *On Jung.* London: Routledge.
    Stevens relates Jung's personal and professional development to his theories, especially his ideas on stages of development, dream symbolism, and the collective unconscious. He agrees with Shelburne that the collective unconscious is a respectable scientific hypothesis, and he also provides a physiological explanation for its existence.

Interpersonal Theory

Chapter Six

OVERVIEW
BIOGRAPHY OF HARRY STACK SULLIVAN
INTRODUCTION TO SULLIVAN'S
    INTERPERSONAL THEORY
TENSIONS
    Needs
    Anxiety
    Energy Transformations
DYNAMISMS
    Malevolence
    Intimacy
    Lust
    Self-System
PERSONIFICATIONS
    Bad Mother, Good Mother
    "Me" Personifications
    Eidetic Personifications
LEVELS OF COGNITION
    Prototaxic Level
    Parataxic Level
    Syntaxic Level
STAGES OF DEVELOPMENT
    Infancy
    Childhood
    Juvenile Era
    Preadolescence
    Early Adolescence
    Late Adolescence
    Adulthood
MENTAL DISORDERS
PSYCHOTHERAPY
    Parataxic Perceptions in Therapy
    Sleep, Dreams, and Myths
    Summary
CONCEPT OF HUMANITY
RELATED RESEARCH
CRITIQUE OF SULLIVAN
CHAPTER SUMMARY
SUGGESTED READINGS

SULLIVAN

$\mathcal{S}$heila is a popular 20-year-old college student preparing for a secondary-school teaching career. Her popularity, however, is limited almost exclusively to men. She has no close women friends even though she lives in a dorm suite with three other women. Her suite mates view Sheila as a pleasant, socially outgoing person who is not very serious about her schoolwork. Despite Sheila's somewhat effervescent personality, none of her suite mates like her. Indeed, she spends little time with them, preferring instead the company of men. She has "gone steady" dozens of times since she was 13 and has been engaged twice. Nearly all these relationships became sexual, some almost immediately.

The younger of two children by four years, Sheila and her brother have never enjoyed a close relationship. Neither has she ever been close to her father, a drug salesman, who spends little time at home and almost none with his daughter. Sheila's mother, a cook in a school cafeteria, tries to make up for her husband's absence by pampering her children and showering them with gifts and attention. As a consequence, Sheila had few responsibilities as a young girl. Her mother kept her room clean, gave her a generous allowance, inevitably took her side in her frequent disputes and fights with playmates, and often completed her homework after Sheila complained that she didn't understand how to do it.

In early elementary school, Sheila played with both boys and girls, but her insistence on always having things her way made her somewhat unpopular among her peers. She frequently quarreled with playmates, and occasionally these confrontations culminated in angry brawls. By the time Sheila was in the fourth grade, she began to feel more isolated from her classmates. The boys showed little interest in any of the girls, and the other girls had their own cliques and small groups from which Sheila was excluded. Although Sheila felt left out, neither her mother nor her teachers at this time would have described her as a social isolate. She was frequently seen talking with other children, but these conversations were seldom initiated or welcomed by others. Her classmates tolerated her, and she even seemed to have had a few girlfriends a year or two younger than herself.

When Sheila reached puberty, her life began to change. First, her physical appearance underwent a dramatic metamorphosis. From a rather plain-looking young girl, she became a physically attractive adolescent. By the time she was 13, she was drawing the attention of older boys. Sheila relished this attention and began to learn how to attain it. She dressed in an attractive though somewhat alluring manner, kept her hair neat and stylish, and wore makeup in a judicious fashion. In addition, she became quite skillful at inane, meaningless conversation and enjoyed shocking others with graphic sexual and scatological language.

At college, and away from home for the first time, Sheila began to use alcohol and other drugs with some regularity. She relied on them especially to buffer hurt feelings after each of her many love affairs came to an unsatisfactory end. However, she was seldom long without a "boyfriend" but also seldom long with one. She seemed to turn men off almost as quickly as she turned them on.

OVERVIEW

In this chapter we look at the interpersonal theory of Harry Stack Sullivan and attempt to use some of its major concepts to explain the problems Sheila faced in her personal relationships. Like Sheila, Sullivan led a lonely and unsatisfying life as a youngster. Nevertheless, he went on to develop the first comprehensive personality theory by an American.

The outstanding feature of Sullivan's theory of personality is its strong emphasis on interpersonal relationships. Sullivan insisted that personality—healthy or unhealthy—is shaped largely by our relations with other people. He contended that scientific psychiatry deals neither with the mind nor the brain, and that knowledge of human personality can be gained only through the scientific study of interpersonal relations.

BIOGRAPHY OF HARRY STACK SULLIVAN

Ironically, the personality theorist who so emphatically stressed the importance of interpersonal relationships was himself the product of isolation and loneliness. Harry Stack Sullivan was born in the small farming town of Norwich, New York, on February 21, 1892, the sole surviving child of poor, Irish-Catholic parents. His mother, Ella Stack Sullivan, was 32 when she married Timothy Sullivan, and 39 when Harry was born. She had given birth to two other sons, neither of whom lived past the first year. As a consequence, she pampered and protected her only child, whose survival she knew was her last chance for motherhood. Harry's father, Timothy Sullivan, was a shy, withdrawn, and taciturn man who never developed a close relationship with his son until after his wife had died and Harry had become a prominent physician. Timothy Sullivan had been a farm laborer and a factory worker who moved to his wife's family farm outside the village of Smyrna, some 10 miles from Norwich, before Harry's third birthday. At about this same time, Ella Stack Sullivan was mysteriously absent from the home, and Harry was cared for by his maternal grandmother, whose Gaelic accent was not easily understood by the young boy. After more than a year's separation, Ella Stack Sullivan— who probably had been in a mental hospital—returned home. In effect, Harry then had two women to mother him—his mother and his grandmother. Even after his grandmother died in 1903, he continued to have two mothers because a maiden aunt then came to share in the childrearing duties.

Although both parents were of Irish-Catholic descent, his mother regarded the Stack family as socially superior to the Sullivans. Harry accepted the social supremacy of the Stacks over the Sullivans until he was a prominent psychiatrist developing an interpersonal theory that emphasized similarities among people rather than differences. He then realized the folly of his mother's claims.

As a preschool child, Harry had neither friends nor acquaintances of his age, although he did invent several imaginary playmates before the age of five. After beginning school he still felt like an outsider, being an Irish-Catholic boy in an Anglo-Saxon Protestant community. His Irish brogue and his sharp mind made him unpopular with his classmates throughout his years of schooling in Smyrna.

When Harry was eight and a half, he formed a close friendship with a 13-year-old boy from a neighboring farm. This chum was Clarence Bellinger, who lived a mile beyond Harry in another school district, but who was now beginning high school in Smyrna. The boys' parents made arrangements for Clarence to pick Harry up and give him a ride to school in a type of vehicle almost unknown in 1900—an automobile. Although the two boys were not peers

chronologically, they had much in common socially and intellectually. Both were retarded socially but advanced intellectually; both later became psychiatrists and neither ever married.

Chapman (1976) believes that this was probably a homosexual relationship, although Perry (1982) doubts that any overt sexual activity ever took place between the two. In either case, the relationship had a transforming effect on Sullivan's life. It awakened in him the power of intimacy, that is, the ability to love another who was more or less like himself. In Sullivan's mature theory of personality, he placed heavy emphasis on the therapeutic, almost magical power of an intimate relationship during the preadolescent years. This belief, along with many other Sullivanian hypotheses, seems to have grown out of of his own childhood experiences.

Sullivan was interested in books and science, not in farming. Although he was an only child growing up on a farm that required much hard work, Harry was able to escape many of the chores by absentmindedly "forgetting" to do them. This ruse was successful because his indulgent mother completed them for him and allowed Harry to receive the credit.

A bright student, Sullivan graduated from high school as valedictorian at age 16. He then entered Cornell University intending to become a physicist, although he and Clarence also shared an interest in psychiatry. His academic performance at Cornell was less than satisfactory, however, and he was suspended after one year. The suspension may not have been solely for academic deficiencies. He got into trouble with the law at Cornell, probably for mail fraud. He was probably a dupe of older, more mature students who used him to pick up some chemicals illegally ordered through the mail. In any event, for the next two years Sullivan mysteriously disappeared from the scene. Perry (1982) thinks he may have suffered a schizophrenic breakdown at this time and was confined to a mental hospital. His later intense interest in schizophrenia may have had its origins in his personal history.

In 1911, with only one year of undergraduate work, he enrolled in the Chicago College of Medicine and Surgery. By Sullivan's claim, this school was little more than a "diploma mill" (Chapman, 1976, p. 27). In reality, however, the Chicago College of Medicine and Surgery was a branch of the respected Valparaiso University. Still a poor-to-mediocre student, Sullivan managed to finish his studies by 1915, but his degree was not granted until 1917.

The period from 1915 until 1921 was again a shadowy and unsettled time in Sullivan's life. He claimed to have worked from 1915 until 1917 to pay off the tuition debts that he said were the reason his degree was delayed two years. During this time he was also undergoing 75 hours of psychotherapy, probably because he was suffering another schizophrenic episode.

During World War I, Sullivan entered the armed forces as a medical officer and, after the war, he continued to serve in that capacity, first for the Federal Board for Vocational Education, and then for the Public Health Service. However, this period in his life was still confusing and unstable, and he showed no promise of the brilliant career that lay just ahead (Perry, 1982).

In 1921, with no formal training in psychiatry, he went to St. Elizabeth's Hospital in Washington, D.C., where he became closely acquainted with William Alanson White, an outstanding neuropsychiatrist. There Sullivan had his first opportunity to work with large numbers of schizophrenic patients. The following year he began an association with the Medical School of the University of Maryland and with the Sheppard and Enoch Pratt Hospital in Towson, Maryland. During this "Baltimore period" of his life, he conducted intensive studies of schizophrenia, which led to his first hunches about the importance of interpersonal relationships. In trying to make sense out of the speech of schizophrenic patients, Sullivan realized that their illness was a means of coping with the anxiety generated from social and interpersonal environments. His experiences as a practicing clinician gradually transformed themselves into the beginnings of an interpersonal theory of psychiatry.

Sullivan spent much of his time and energy at Sheppard selecting and training hospital attendants. Although he did little therapy himself, he developed a system in which nonprofessional but sympathetic attendants treated schizophrenic patients with human respect and care. This innovative program gained him a reputation as a clinical wizard. However, he became disenchanted with the political climate at Sheppard when he was passed over for a position as head of the new reception center that he had advocated. In March of 1930 he resigned from Sheppard.

Later that year he moved to New York City and opened a private practice, hoping to enlarge his understanding of interpersonal relations by investigating nonschizophrenic disorders, especially those of an obsessive nature (Perry, 1982). Times were hard, however, and his expected wealthy clientele did not come in the numbers he needed to maintain his expenses.

On a more positive note, his residence in New York brought him into contact with several psychiatrists and social scientists with a European background. Among these were Karen Horney, Erich Fromm, and Frieda Fromm-Reichmann, who, along with Sullivan, Clara Thompson, and others, formed the Zodiac group, an informal organization that met regularly over drinks to discuss old and new ideas in psychiatry and the related social sciences. Sullivan had met Thompson earlier and the two were close friends. Sullivan had persuaded Thompson to travel to Europe to take a training analysis under Sandor Ferenczi, a disciple of Freud. Sullivan learned from all members of the Zodiac group, and, through Thompson, his therapeutic technique was indirectly influenced by Freud. Sullivan also credited two other outstanding practitioners, Adolf Meyer and William Alanson White, as having had an impact on his practice of therapy. Despite some Freudian influence on his therapeutic technique, Sullivan's theory of interpersonal psychiatry is neither psychoanalytic nor neo-Freudian.

During his residence in New York, Sullivan also came under the influence of several noted social scientists from the University of Chicago, which was the center of American sociological study during the 1920s and 1930s. Included among them were social psychologist George Herbert Mead, sociologists Robert Ezra Park and W. I. Thomas, anthropologist Edward Sapir, and political scientist Harold Lasswell. Sullivan formed a close personal friendship with Sapir and Lasswell, and the three men were primarily responsible for establishing the William Alanson White Psychiatric Foundation in Washington, D.C. This institution, named for the man who had influenced Sullivan's thinking during the previous decade, was founded for the purpose of joining psychiatry to the other social sciences. Sullivan served as president of the foundation from its beginning in 1933 until 1943. He was also co-editor, then editor, of the foundation's journal, *Psychiatry*, from its inception in 1938 until he died in 1949. Under Sullivan's guidance, the foundation also began a training institution known as the Washington School of Psychiatry. Because of these activities, Sullivan gave up his New York practice, which was not very lucrative anyway, and moved back to Washington, D.C., where he remained closely associated with the school and the journal.

In January, 1949, Sullivan attended a meeting of the World Federation for Mental Health in Amsterdam. While on his way home, January 14, 1949, he died of a cerebral hemorrhage in a Paris hotel room, a few weeks short of his 57th birthday. Not uncharacteristically, he was alone at the time.

On the personal side, Sullivan never married and was probably a homosexual. In any case, he was not comfortable with his sexuality and had ambivalent feelings toward marriage (Perry, 1982). As an adult, he "adopted" James Inscoe, a 15-year-old boy, who remained with Sullivan, looking after his financial affairs, typing manuscripts, and generally running the household. Although Jimmie was never officially adopted, Sullivan regarded him as a son and even had his legal named changed to James I. Sullivan.

Sullivan also had ambivalent attitudes toward his religion. Born to Catholic parents who attended church only irregularly, he early abandoned Catholicism. In later life his friends and acquaintances regarded him as nonreligious or even anti-Catholic, but, to their surprise, Sullivan had written into his will a request to receive a Catholic burial. Incidentally, this request was granted despite the fact that Sullivan's body had been cremated in Paris. His ashes were returned to the United States where they were placed inside a coffin and received a full Catholic burial, complete with a requiem mass.

INTRODUCTION TO SULLIVAN'S INTERPERSONAL THEORY

Sullivan believed that we develop our personality within a social context and that, without other people, we would have no personality. He contended that "a personality can never be isolated from the complex of interpersonal relations in which the person lives and has his being" (Sullivan, 1953a, p. 10). He defined personality as *"the relatively enduring pattern of recurrent interpersonal situations which characterized a human life"* (Sullivan, 1953b, pp. 110–111). Interpersonal situations, then, provide the subject matter for Sullivan's study of personality.

Sullivan was constantly concerned with the problem of accurate and coherent communication as the crucial ingredient in the interpersonal situation. Although he adopted a somewhat technical language, he tried to avoid the use of psychiatric neologisms. In *The Interpersonal Theory of Psychiatry* (1953b, p. 7) he wrote, "I think we should try to pick a word in common usage in talking about living and clarifying just what we mean by that word, rather than to set about diligently creating new words by carpentry of Greek and Sanskrit roots." Despite this intention, however, much of Sullivan's writings reveal a unique and colorful style of expression, including some esoteric terms not often found in the writings of other personality theorists.

Sullivan's chief contribution to personality theory is his conception of developmental stages. Unlike Freud, who had little to say about development after the latency stage, Sullivan contributed to our understanding of personality development through late adolescence and up to adulthood. Unlike Erikson, however, he did not continue to conceptualize developmental stages during adulthood and into old age. Before turning to Sullivan's ideas on the stages of development, we need to understand some of his unique terminology.

TENSIONS

Like Freud and Jung, Sullivan saw personality as an energy system. Energy can exist as *tension* (potentiality for action) or as actions themselves (*energy transformations*). Sullivan (1953b) defined **tension** as potentiality for action that may or may not be experienced in awareness. Thus, not all tensions are consciously felt. Many tensions, such as anxiety, premonitions, drowsiness, hunger, and sexual excitement, are felt but not always on a conscious level. In fact, probably all felt tensions are at least partial distortions of reality.

Tensions are divided into those of *needs* and those of *anxiety*. Tensions of needs represent potentiality for productive actions, whereas tensions of anxiety bring about nonproductive or disintegrative behaviors.

Needs

Needs are tensions brought on by a biological imbalance between the person and the physiochemical environment, both inside and outside the organism. Needs are episodic—once we satisfy them they temporarily lose their power, but, after a time, they are likely to recur. Needs differ from tensions of anxiety in that they are integrative or conjunctive, whereas anxiety is disjunctive in nature (Sullivan, 1953b).

Although needs originally have a biological component, many of them stem from the interpersonal situation. The most basic *interpersonal need* is that of **tenderness**. An infant develops a need to receive tenderness from its primary caretaker (called by Sullivan "the mothering one"). Unlike some needs, tenderness requires actions from at least two people. For example, an infant's need *to receive* tenderness may be expressed as a cry, smile, or coo, whereas the mother's need *to give* tenderness may be transformed into touching, fondling, or holding. In this example, the infant uses its *mouth*, while the mother uses her *hands* to satisfy the need for tenderness.

Tenderness is a *general need* because it is concerned with the overall wellbeing of the person. General needs, which also include oxygen, food, and water, are opposed to *zonal needs*, which arise from a particular area of the body. Several areas of the body are instrumental in satisfying both general and zonal needs. For example, the mouth satisfies general needs by taking in food and oxygen, but it also satisfies the zonal need for oral activity. Also, the hands may be used to help satisfy the general need of tenderness, but they can likewise be used to satisfy the zonal need for manual activity. Similarly, other body zones, such as the anus and the genitals, can be used to satisfy both kinds of needs.

Very early in life the various zones of the body gain importance beyond the satisfaction of general needs and begin to play a significant and lasting role in interpersonal relations. While satisfying general needs for food, water, and so forth, an infant expends more energy than necessary, and the excess energy is transformed into consistent or characteristic modes of behavior, which Sullivan called *dynamisms*. One person, for instance, may satisfy her oral needs through extranutritional sucking, smoking, or excessive talking. Another may satisfy manual needs by snapping his fingers, fondling his genitals, or painting pictures. These consistent patterns of behavior help make up our unique personality.

Anxiety

Another important contributor to our basic personality is the way in which we react to **anxiety**, the second type of tension. Anxiety differs from tensions of needs in that it is disjunctive, is more diffuse and vague, and calls forth no consistent actions for its relief. If an infant lacks food (a need), its course of action is clear, but if it is anxious, there is little it can do to escape. Sullivan (1953b, p. 42) said:

> There is in the infant no capacity for action toward the relief of anxiety.... No action of the infant is consistently and frequently associated with the relief of anxiety; and therefore the need for security, or freedom from anxiety, is highly significantly distinguished from all other needs from its very first hypothetical appearance.

How does anxiety originate? Sullivan (1953b) postulated that it is transferred from the parent to the infant through the process of **empathy.** Anxiety in the mothering one inevitably induces anxiety in the infant. Because all mothers have some amount of anxiety while caring for their babies, all infants will become anxious to some degree.

Just as the infant does not have the capacity to reduce anxiety, the parent also is ineffective in dealing with the baby's anxiety. Any signs of anxiety or insecurity by the infant are likely to lead to attempts by the parents to satisfy the infant's *needs*. For example, a mother may feed her baby who is crying because it is anxious, not because it is hungry. If the baby hesitates in accepting the milk, the mother may become more anxious, thereby generating additional anxiety within the infant. Finally, the baby's anxiety reaches a level at which it interferes with sucking and swallowing. Anxiety, then, operates in opposition to tensions of needs and prevents them from being satisfied.

Anxiety has a deleterious effect on adults, too. It interferes with our foresight, prevents us from recalling solutions to past problems, prevents us from satisfying needs, and is the chief disruptive force blocking our development of good interpersonal relations. Sullivan (1953b) likened severe anxiety to a blow on the head. It makes us incapable of learning, impairs memory, narrows perception, and may result in complete amnesia. It is unique among the tensions in that it maintains the status quo even to our overall detriment. Whereas other tensions result in actions directed specifically toward their relief, anxiety produces behaviors that (1) prevent us from learning from our mistakes; (2) keep us pursuing the childish wish for security; and (3) generally ensure that we will not learn from our experiences.

Sullivan held that anxiety and loneliness are unique among all experiences in that they are totally unwanted and undesirable. Because anxiety is painful, we have a natural tendency to avoid it, inherently preferring the state of **euphoria,** or complete lack of tension. Sullivan (1954, p. 100) summarized this concept by stating simply that *"the presence of anxiety is much worse than its absence."*

Sullivan distinguished anxiety from fear in several important ways. First, anxiety usually stems from complex interpersonal situations and is only vaguely represented in awareness; fear is more clearly discerned and its origins more easily pinpointed. Second, anxiety has no positive value. Only when transformed into another tension, for example anger or fear, can it lead to profitable actions. Third, anxiety blocks the satisfaction of needs, whereas fear sometimes helps us satisfy certain needs. This opposition to the satisfactions is expressed in words that can be considered to be Sullivan's definition of anxiety. "Anxiety is a tension in opposition to the tensions of needs and to action appropriate to their relief" (Sullivan, 1953b, p. 44).

Energy Transformations

Tensions that are transformed into actions, either overt or covert, are called **energy transformations.** This somewhat awkward term simply refers to our behaviors that are aimed at satisfying needs and reducing anxiety, the two great tensions. Not all energy transformations are obvious, overt actions; many take the form of emotions, thoughts, or covert behaviors that can be hidden from other people.

In summary, Sullivan identified two kinds of experience—tensions and energy transformations. Tensions, or potentialities for action, include tensions of needs and tensions of anxiety. Needs arise due to an imbalance between a person and the environment and are helpful or conjunctive when satisfied. Anxiety, on the other hand, arises from the interpersonal situation and is always disjunctive. Energy transformations literally involve the transformation of potential energy into actual energy or behavior for the purpose of satisfying needs or reducing anxiety.

DYNAMISMS

Energy transformations become organized as typical behavior patterns that characterize a person throughout a lifetime. Sullivan (1953b) called these behavior patterns **dynamisms,** a term that means about the same as traits or habit patterns. Dynamisms are of two major classes: first, those related to specific zones of the body, including the mouth, anus, and genitals; and second, those related to tensions. This second class is composed of three categories—the disjunctive, the isolating, and the conjunctive. Disjunctive dynamisms include all those destructive patterns of behavior that are related to the concept of *malevolence;* the isolating dynamisms include those such as *lust,* which are unrelated to interpersonal relations; and the conjunctive dynamisms are beneficial behavior patterns, such as *intimacy* and the *self-system*.

Malevolence

Malevolence is the disjunctive dynamism of evil and hatred, which is characterized by the feeling that one is living among one's enemies (Sullivan, 1953b). It originates around age two or three when children's actions, which earlier had brought about maternal tenderness, are rebuffed, ignored, or met with anxiety and pain. Many parents attempt to control their children's behavior by inflicting punishments, usually in the form of physical pain or reproving remarks. Consequently, some children learn to withhold any expression of the need for tenderness and to protect themselves by adopting the malevolent attitude. Parents and peers then find it more and more difficult to react with tenderness, and this, in turn, solidifies the child's negative attitude toward the world. Malevolent actions often take the form of timidity, mischievousness, cruelty, or other kinds of nonsocial or antisocial behavior. Sullivan (1953b, p. 216) expressed the malevolent attitude with this colorful statement: "Once upon a time everything was lovely, but that was before I had to deal with people."

Intimacy

Intimacy grows out of the earlier need for tenderness but is more specific and involves a close interpersonal relationship between two people who are more or less of equal status. Both tenderness and intimacy are related to the popular term "love." Tenderness refers to an increase in euphoria brought on by anyone—mother, father, siblings, friends, or pet animals. Intimacy, however, is restricted to the tender feelings one person has for an equal.

Intimacy involves a close relationship between two persons who must react to each other in the give-and-take of close collaboration. Each is seen by the other as a person of equal value, not merely as an object of gratification. Intimacy must not be confused with sexual interest. In fact, it develops prior to puberty, ideally during preadolescence, and, at that time, it usually exists between same-sexed pairs. Ordinarily, intimate relationships with a person of the opposite sex do not develop until late adolescence or even later. Because intimacy is a dynamism that requires an equal partnership, it does not usually exist in parent–child relationships. For example, the relationship that Sheila (our case study) has with her mother is one of emotional closeness and dependency, but because the two are not equals, the relationship cannot be called intimate.

Intimacy is an integrating dynamism that tends to draw out loving reactions from the other person, thereby decreasing anxiety and loneliness, two extremely painful experiences. Because intimacy helps us avoid anxiety and loneliness, it is also a rewarding experience that most healthy people desire (Sullivan, 1953b).

Significant intimate relationships prior to puberty are usually boy-boy or girl-girl friendships, according to Sullivan.

Lust

On the other hand, **lust** is an isolating tendency, requiring no other person for its satisfaction. It manifests itself as autoerotic behavior even when another person is the object of one's lust. But lust can combine with intimacy to form consistent homosexual or heterosexual activity. It is an especially powerful dynamism during adolescence, at which time it often leads to a reduction in self-esteem, since attempts at lustful activity are likely to be rebuffed by authority figures, resulting in anxiety and surreptitious behavior. Besides reducing self-esteem and personal worth, lust may also hinder intimacy. For example, the lustful interest that Sheila has in men prevents her from building an intimate relationship with other women—or with men. Her sexual relations with many males may satisfy her lustful needs, but they do not give her what she is seeking—intimacy.

Self-System

The most complex and inclusive of all the dynamisms is the **self-system**, a consistent pattern of behaviors that maintains our interpersonal security by protecting us from anxiety. Like intimacy, the self-system is a conjunctive dynamism that arises out of the interpersonal situation. However, it develops earlier than intimacy, at about 12 to 18 months of age when a child begins to learn which behaviors are related to an increase or decrease in anxiety. Prior to this time, fear and pain were the principal forms of unpleasant experience, and their arrival seemed independent of the infant's behavior. Now, however, the mothering one begins the process of training by rewarding some behaviors and punishing others. The punishments and disapprovals result in a third unpleasant condition—anxiety.

Intelligence and foresight enable people to detect slight increases and decreases in anxiety, and this ability provides the self-system with a built-in warning device. This is a mixed blessing, however. On the one hand, the warning serves as a signal, alerting people to increasing anxiety and giving them an opportunity to protect themselves. On the other hand, this same characteristic makes the self-system resistant to change and prevents people from profiting from anxiety-filled experiences. Because the primary task of the self-system is to protect people against anxiety, it is "the principal stumbling block to favorable changes in personality" (Sullivan, 1953b, p. 169). Personality is not static, however, and is especially subject to change at the beginning of the various stages of development when newly maturing needs begin to emerge (Sullivan, 1964).

As the self-system develops, people begin to form a consistent image of themselves. Thereafter, any interpersonal experiences that they perceive as contrary to their self-regard threatens their *security*. As a consequence, people attempt to defend themselves against interpersonal tensions by means of **security operations**, the purpose of which is to reduce feelings of insecurity or anxiety that result from endangered self-esteem. People tend to deny or distort interpersonal experiences that conflict with their self-regard. For example, when people who think highly of themselves are called incompetent, they may choose to believe that the name-caller is stupid or, perhaps, merely joking. Sullivan (1953b, p. 374) called security operations "a powerful brake on personal and human progress."

Sullivan (1953a) distinguished between the pursuit of security and the pursuit of *satisfactions*. Whereas security operations are connected with interpersonal experiences, satisfactions are end states connected with such physiological conditions as fullness (satiety), sleep, lust, and loneliness. The needs for satisfaction and the needs for security sometimes collide, as when a person on a diet feels hungry but believes that an attractive physique is essential to maintain self-regard.

Two important security operations are *dissociation* and *selective inattention*. **Dissociation** includes those impulses, desires, and needs that a person refuses to allow into awareness. Some infantile experiences become dissociated when a baby is neither rewarded nor punished for its behavior, so those experiences simply do not become part of the self-system. Adult experiences that are too foreign to one's standards of conduct can also become dissociated. These experiences do not cease to exist but continue to influence personality on an unconscious level. Dissociated images manifest themselves in dreams, day-dreams, and other unintentional activities outside of awareness and are directed toward maintaining interpersonal security (Sullivan, 1953b).

Selective inattention is the control of focal awareness and involves a refusal to see those things that we do not wish to see. It differs from dissociation in both degree and origin. Selectively inattended experiences are more accessible to awareness and more limited in scope. They originate after the self-system has come into being and are a reaction to it. Once people develop a self-system, they can block out those experiences that are not consistent with it. For example, people who regard themselves as scrupulously law-abiding drivers may "forget" about the many occasions when they exceeded the speed limit or the times when they failed to stop completely at a stop sign. Like dissociated experiences, selectively inattended perceptions remain active even though they are not fully conscious. They are crucial in determining which elements of an experience will be attended and which will be ignored or denied (Sullivan, 1953b).

PERSONIFICATIONS

Beginning in infancy and continuing throughout the various developmental stages, we acquire certain images of ourselves and others. These images, called **personifications**, may be relatively accurate or, because they are colored by our needs and anxieties, they may be grossly distorted. Sullivan (1953b) described three basic personifications that develop during infancy—the bad-mother, the good-mother, and the me. In addition, some children acquire an eidetic personification (imaginary playmate) during childhood.

Bad-Mother, Good-Mother

The *bad-mother personification* grows out of the infant's experiences with the bad-nipple, that is, the nipple that does not satisfy hunger needs. Whether the nipple belongs to the mother or to a bottle held by the mother, the father, a nurse, or anyone else is not important. The bad-mother personification is almost completely undifferentiated, inasmuch as it includes everyone involved in the nursing situation. It is not an accurate image of the "real" mother but merely the infant's vague representation of not being properly fed.

After the bad-mother personification is formed, an infant will acquire a *good-mother personification* based on the tender and cooperative behaviors of the mothering one. These two personifications, one based on the infant's perception of an anxious, malevolent mother and the other on a calm, tender mother, combine to form a complex personification composed of contrasting qualities projected onto the same person. Until the infant develops language, however, these two opposing images of mother can easily co-exist (Sullivan, 1953b).

"Me" Personifications

During midinfancy a child acquires the three "me" personifications (bad-me, good-me, and not-me), which form the building blocks of the self personification. Each is related to the evolving conception of "me" or "my body."

The *bad-me personification* is fashioned from experiences of punishment and disapproval that an infant receives from the mothering one. The resulting anxiety is strong enough to teach the infant that it is "bad," but it is not so severe as to cause the experience to be dissociated or selectively inattended. Like all personifications, the bad-me is shaped out of the interpersonal situation; an infant can learn that it is bad only from someone else, ordinarily from the "bad-mother."

The *good-me personification* results from an infant's experiences with reward and approval. The infant feels good about itself when it perceives its mother's expressions of tenderness, and such experiences lead to diminishing anxiety.

However, sudden severe anxiety may cause the infant to form the *not-me personification* and to either dissociate or selectively inattend experiences related to that anxiety. The infant denies these experiences to the "me" image so that they become part of the not-me personification. These shadowy not-me personifications are also encountered by adults and are expressed in dreams, schizophrenic episodes, and other dissociated reactions. However, these nightmarish experiences are always preceded by a warning. When adults are struck by sudden severe anxiety, they are overcome by *uncanny emotion*. Although this experience incapacitates people in their interpersonal relationships, it serves as a valuable signal for approaching schizophrenic reactions. Uncanny emotion may be experienced in dreams or may take the form of awe, horror, loathing, or a "chilly crawling" sensation (Sullivan, 1953b).

Eidetic Personifications

Not all interpersonal relations are with real people. Children often have *imaginary playmates*, which are a form of **eidetic personification,** that is, unrealistic traits or people that we invent in order to protect our self-esteem. Sullivan (1964) believed that these imaginary friends may be as significant to a child's development as real playmates.

Eidetic personifications are not limited to children; most adults see fictitious characteristics in other people. Eidetic personifications can create conflict in interpersonal relations when people project onto others imaginary traits that are remnants from previous relationships. They also hinder communication and prevent people from functioning on the same level of cognition.

LEVELS OF COGNITION

Sullivan recognized three levels or modes of cognition: *prototaxic, parataxic,* and *syntaxic*. Levels of cognition refer to ways of perceiving, imagining, and conceiving. Experiences on the prototaxic level are impossible to communicate; parataxic experiences are personal, prelogical, and communicated only in distorted form; and syntaxic cognition is meaningful interpersonal communication.

Prototaxic Level

Prototaxic cognitions are the earliest and most primitive experiences of an infant. Because these experiences cannot be communicated to others, they are difficult to describe or define. We can try to understand the term by attempting to imagine the earliest subjective experiences of a newborn baby. These experiences must, in some way, relate to different zones of the body. A neonate feels hunger and pain, and these prototaxic experiences result in observable action, for example, sucking or crying. The infant does not know the reason for the actions and sees no relationship between its actions and being fed. During early infancy, hunger and pain are prototaxic because they cannot be differentiated from one another or from any other stimuli. As undifferentiated experiences, prototaxic events are beyond conscious recall.

In adults prototaxic experiences take the form of momentary sensations, images, feelings, moods, and impressions. These primitive images of dream and waking life are dimly perceived or completely unconscious. Although they are incapable of being communicated to others, we can sometimes tell another person that we have just had a strange sensation, one that we cannot put into words.

Parataxic Level

Parataxic experiences are prelogical and usually result when a person assumes a cause-and-effect relationship between two events that occur coincidentally. Parataxic cognitions are more clearly differentiated than prototaxic experiences, but their meaning remains private. Therefore, they can be communicated to others only in a distorted fashion.

The parataxic level of cognition begins very early in infancy and continues to be an important mode of experience throughout a person's lifetime. For example, the infant sucking the nipple at first sees no relationship between sucking and receiving nourishment, but very soon it makes a connection between its behavior and that of its mother. Because sucking and feeding occurred coincidentally, the infant believes that its sucking behavior *caused* the mother's feeding behavior. This process of seeing a cause-and-effect relationship between two events in close temporal proximity is called a **parataxic distortion**.

An example of parataxic thinking is the conditioning experiences of humans and animals. If children are conditioned to say "please" in order to receive candy, they may eventually reach the illogical conclusion that their supplications caused the candy's appearance. This is a parataxic distortion because uttering the word "please" does not, by itself, cause the candy to appear. A dispensing person must be present who hears the word and is able and willing to honor the request. When no such person is present, a child may ask God or imaginary people to grant favors. A good bit of adult behavior comes from similar parataxic thinking.

Syntaxic Level

Syntaxic experiences are those that are consensually validated and that can be symbolically communicated. Consensually validated experiences are those upon whose meaning two or more person agree. Words, for example, are consensually validated because different people more or less agree on their meaning. The most common symbols used by one person to communicate with another are those of language, including words and gestures.

Sullivan hypothesized that the first instance of syntaxic thinking appears about 12 to 18 months after birth when a sound or gesture begins to have the same meaning for the mother as it does for the child. The syntaxic level of cognition becomes more prevalent as the child begins to develop formal language, but it never completely supplants prototaxic and parataxic cognition. Adult experience takes place on all three levels.

In summary, Sullivan held that there are two kind of experience: *tensions*, or potential for action; and *energy transformations*, or the actions themselves. Some actions form consistent patterns of behavior called *dynamisms*. Sullivan also recognized two categories of tension: *needs*, which are conjunctive or helpful to development; and *anxiety*, which is the chief disjunctive force in interpersonal relations and which interferes with the satisfaction of needs. In addition, experience takes place on three levels or modes of cognition: *prototaxic*, *parataxic*, and *syntaxic*. Table 6.1 summarizes Sullivan's concept of experience.

TABLE 6.1   *Summary of Sullivan's Concept of Experience and Related Terms*

Experience takes place on three levels: prototaxic, parataxic, and syntaxic. In addition, there are two kinds of experience—tensions and energy transformations
I.   **Tensions** (potential for action)
     A. Needs (conjunctive; help integrate personality)
        1. General needs (facilitate the overall wellbeing of a person)
           a. Interpersonal (tenderness, intimacy, and love)
           b. Physiological (food, oxygen, water, and so forth)
        2. Zonal needs (may also satisfy general needs)
           a. Oral
           b. Genital
           c. Manual
     B. Anxiety (disjunctive; interferes with the satisfaction of needs)
II. **Energy Transformations** (overt or covert actions designed to satisfy needs or to reduce anxiety). Some energy transformations become relatively consistent patterns of behavior called *dynamisms*.
III. **Dynamisms** (traits or behavior patterns)
     A. Malevolence (a feeling of living in enemy country)
     B. Intimacy (an integrating experience marked by a close personal relationship with another person who is more or less of equal status)
     C. Lust (an isolating dynamism characterized by an impersonal sexual interest in another person)

STAGES OF DEVELOPMENT

Sullivan (1953b) postulated seven epochs or stages of development, each crucial to the formation of human personality. The thread of interpersonal relations runs throughout the stages; other people are indispensable to a person's development from infancy to mature adulthood.

Personality change can take place at any time, but it is most likely to occur during the transition from one stage to the next. In fact, these threshold periods are more crucial than the stages themselves. Experiences previously dissociated or selectively inattended may enter into the self-system during one of the transitional periods. Sullivan (1953b, p. 227) hypothesized that, "as one passes over one of these more-or-less determinable thresholds of a developmental era, everything that has gone before becomes reasonably open to influence." His seven stages are infancy, childhood, the juvenile era, preadolescence, early adolescence, late adolescence, and adulthood.

Infancy

The period of infancy begins at birth and continues until a child develops articulate or syntaxic speech, usually at about 18 to 24 months. Sullivan believed that an infant becomes human through tenderness received from the mothering one. The satisfaction of nearly every human need demands the cooperation of another person. Infants cannot survive without a mothering one to provide food, shelter, moderate temperature, physical contact, and the cleansing of waste materials.

The emphatic linkage between mother and infant leads inexorably to the development of anxiety for the baby. Being human, the mother enters the relationship with some degree of previously learned anxiety. Her anxiety may spring from any one of a variety of experiences, but the infant's first anxiety is always associated with the nursing situation and the oral zone. Unlike its mother, the infant's repertory of behaviors is not adequate to handle anxiety. So, whenever it feels anxious (a condition originally transmitted to it by the mother), the infant tries whatever means it has to reduce anxiety. These means will most likely take the form of rejection of the nipple, but this neither reduces anxiety nor satisfies the need for food. The infant's rejection of the nipple, of course, is not responsible for the mother's original anxiety but now adds to it. Eventually the infant discriminates between the good-nipple and the bad-nipple, the former being associated with relative euphoria in the feeding process, the latter with enduring anxiety. This anxiety has all sorts of unwholesome effects, including the obstruction of both memory and foresight (Sullivan, 1953b).

Because the infant uses crying to express both anxiety and hunger, the mothering one may mistake anxiety for hunger and force the nipple onto an anxious (but not hungry) infant. Conversely, the mother may soon learn that the cry does not always signify hunger, and she may neglect to feed the infant even during times of true hunger. The infant's unsatisfied need leads to rage, which increases the mother's anxiety and interferes with her ability to cooperate with her baby. With mounting tension the infant loses its capacity to receive satisfaction, but its need for food, of course, continues to increase. Finally, as tension approaches terror, the infant experiences difficulty with breathing. It may even stop breathing and turn a bluish color, but the built-in protections of **apathy** and **somnolent detachment** keep it from death. Apathy and somnolent detachment allow the infant to fall asleep despite its hunger; they do not completely abolish the need for food but lessen it, thus allowing the infant to return to a relative state of euphoria (Sullivan, 1953b).

During the feeding process the infant not only receives food but also has some of its needs for *tenderness* satisfied. The tenderness received by the infant at this time demands the cooperation of the mothering one and introduces the infant to the various strategies required by the interpersonal situation. The mother/infant relationship, however, is like a two-sided coin. The infant develops a dual personification of mother who is seen as both "good-mother" and "bad-mother;" she is "good" when she satisfies the baby's needs and "bad" when she stimulates anxiety.

Around midinfancy, infants begin to learn how to communicate through language. In the beginning, their language is not consensually validated but takes place on an individualized or parataxic level. This period of infancy is characterized by **autistic language**, defined as "a primary unsocialized, unacculturated state of symbol activity" (Sullivan, 1953a, p. 17). Early communication takes place in the form of facial expressions and the sounding of various phonemes. Both are learned through imitation, and eventually gestures and speech sounds have the same meaning for the infant as they do for other people. This marks the beginning of syntaxic language and the end of infancy.

Sheila, of course, has no memory of her infancy. We know that her mother did not work outside the home during Sheila's early years and was never absent for a prolonged period. However, Sheila's older brother made heavy demands on the mother and had a difficult time adjusting to Sheila's birth. Consequently, the mother felt herself being pulled between the opposing demands of her two children and, at the same time, found herself resenting her husband, who seemed to welcome every opportunity to be away from home.

Childhood

The era of childhood begins with the advent of syntaxic language and continues until the appearance of the need for playmates of an equal status. The age of childhood varies from culture to culture and from individual to individual, but in Western society it covers the period from about 18 to 24 months until about five or six years.

During this stage the mother remains the most significant other person, but her role is different from what it was in infancy. The dual personifications of mother are now fused into one, and the child's perception of the mother is more congruent with the "real" mother. Nevertheless, the good-mother and bad-mother personifications are usually retained on a parataxic level. In addition to combining the mother personifications, the child differentiates the various persons who previously formed the concept of the mothering one, separating mother and father and seeing each as having a distinct role.

At about the same time, children are fusing the me-personifications into a single self-dynamism. Once they establish syntaxic language, they can no longer consciously deal with the bad-me and good-me at the same time; now they label behaviors as "good" or "bad" in imitation of their parents. However, these labels differ from the old personifications of infancy because they are on a syntaxic level and originate from children's behavior rather than from decreases or increases in their anxiety. Also, "good" and "bad" now imply social or moral value and no longer refer to the absence or presence of that painful tension called anxiety.

During childhood, emotions become reciprocal; a child is able to give tenderness as well as receive it. The relationship between mother and child becomes more personal and is less one-sided. Rather than seeing the mother as good or bad based on how she satisfied hunger needs, the child evaluates the mother syntaxically according to whether she is rejecting, shows reciprocal tender feelings, or develops a relationship based on the mutual satisfaction of needs.

Besides their parents, preschool-aged children often have one other significant relationship—an *imaginary playmate*. This eidetic friend enables children to have a safe, secure relationship that produces little anxiety. Parents sometimes observe their preschool-aged children talking to an imaginary friend, calling the friend by name and possibly even insisting that an extra place be set at the table or space be made available in the car or the bed for this playmate. Also, many adults can recall their own childhood experiences with imaginary playmates. Sullivan insisted that having an imaginary playmate is not a sign of instability or pathology but a positive event that helps children become ready for intimacy with real friends during the preadolescence stage. These playmates offer children an opportunity to interact with another "person" who is safe and who will not increase their level of anxiety. This comfortable, nonthreatening relationship with an imaginary playmate permits children to be more independent of parents and to make friends in later years.

Sullivan (1953b) referred to childhood as a period of rapid acculturation. Besides acquiring language, children learn cultural patterns of cleanliness, toilet training, eating habits, and sex-role expectancies. They also learn two other important processes: *dramatizations* and *preoccupations*. Dramatizations are attempts to act like or sound like significant authority figures, especially mother and father. Preoccupations are strategies for avoiding anxiety and fear-provoking situations by remaining occupied with an activity that has earlier proved useful or rewarding.

The malevolent attitude reaches a peak during the preschool years, giving some children an intense feeling of living in hostile or enemy country. At the same time, children learn that society has placed certain restraints on their freedom. From these restrictions and from experiences with approval and disapprobation, children evolve their self-dynamism, which helps them handle anxiety and stabilize their personality. In fact, the self-system introduces so much stability that it makes future changes exceedingly difficult.

Although Sheila's childhood was marked by some feelings of living in enemy country, she probably did not experience fully developed feelings of malevolence. Her earliest memory dates back to about age three when she was frightened by a violent argument between her mother and father. She recalled thinking that her father was going to seriously hurt or even kill her mother. This experience left Sheila with the continuing concern that her once secure world might, at any time, come to an abrupt end.

On a more pleasant note, Sheila remembered having an imaginary playmate during her childhood whom she called Boo. Her mother welcomed those peaceful times when Sheila would remain in her room for long periods playing with and scolding her imaginary playmate. She also indulged Sheila's demands to have an extra place set at the table, and Boo was frequently blamed for broken dishes, messy floors, and other minor disasters. Sheila had few playmates prior to attending school, and her friendship with Boo provided a safe interpersonal relationship in which she could always have her way.

Juvenile Era

The juvenile era begins with the appearance of the need for peers or playmates of equal status and ends when one finds a single chum to satisfy the need for intimacy. In American society the juvenile stage is roughly parallel to the first three

During the juvenile stage, children need to learn competition, cooperation, and compromise.

years of school, beginning around age five or six and ending at about age eight and a half. (It is interesting that Sullivan was so specific with the age at which this period ends and the preadolescent stage begins. Remember that Sullivan was eight and a half when he began an intimate relationship with a 13-year-old boy from a nearby farm.)

During the juvenile stage, Sullivan believed, a child should learn three characteristics: competition, compromise, and cooperation. The degree of *competition* found among children of this age varies with the society, but Sullivan believed that people in the United States have generally overemphasized competition. Parents and teachers conspire to teach youngsters to be competitive and successful, and when success does not come, the child is liable to be ridiculed by authorities and peers alike. *Compromise*, too, can be overdone. A seven-year-old child who learns to continually give in to others is handicapped in the socialization process, and this yielding trait may continue to characterize the person in later life. *Cooperation* involves more than simply combining competition and compromise; it includes all those processes necessary to get along with others. The juvenile must learn to cooperate with others in the real world of interpersonal relationships. This is a critical step in becoming socialized and is the most important task confronting a person during the juvenile era.

During the juvenile stage, children associate with other children who are of equal standing. One-to-one relationships are rare, but, if they exist, they are more likely to be based on convenience than on genuine intimacy. Boys and girls play with one another with little regard for the gender of the other person. Although permanent dyadic (two-person) relationships are still in the future, children of this age are beginning to make discriminations among themselves and to distinguish among adults. They see one teacher as kinder than another, one parent as more indulgent. To them the real world is coming more into focus as they begin to operate increasingly on the syntaxic level and no longer get by with childish expressions of fantasy. They usually surrender their eidetic playmates in favor of real ones. When they confront stories and ideas that they cannot consensually validate, they experience increased anxiety, which consequently diminishes their initiative and enthusiasm.

The world begins to appear more complex and complicated to the primary-school child. If the complexity is too anxiety-provoking, a juvenile may simplify matters by blocking it from awareness. This selective inattention safeguards a person from having to deal with things that make no sense to the self-system, but the process has both fortunate and unfortunate consequences. On the positive side, a person can become free from the burden of meaningless bits of information by tuning out the details of background noises and sights. On the other hand, by ignoring or distorting certain significant experiences that are inconsistent with the self-system, the person loses some ability to communicate syntaxically, which may lead to problems in interpersonal relationships. These interpersonal difficulties are the price one pays for maintaining security.

By the end of the juvenile stage, a child should have developed an orientation toward living that makes it easier to consistently handle anxiety, satisfy zonal and tenderness needs, and set goals based on memory and foresight. This *orientation toward living* readies a person for the deeper interpersonal relationships to follow (Sullivan, 1953b).

The juvenile era was a troubling time for Sheila. Although she had above-average intelligence, she did not perform well in school. She dreaded going to school and missed many days because of "illness." She had problems with competition, compromise, and cooperation and often fought (usually verbally) with her classmates. Her mother recognized that Sheila was frequently unhappy and tried to help by blaming the other children for Sheila's many quarrels.

Preadolescence

The period from the appearance of the need for intimacy until puberty is called preadolescence. This stage, which begins around age eight or nine and ends with adolescence, is a time for interest in one particular person of the same sex. All preceding stages have been egocentric, with friendships being formed on the basis of self-interest. A preadolescent, for the first time, takes a genuine interest in the other person. Sullivan (1953a, p. 41) called this process of becoming a social being the "quiet miracle of preadolescence," a likely reference to the personality transformation he experienced during his own preadolescence.

The outstanding characteristic of preadolescence is the genesis of the capacity to love. Previously, all interpersonal relationships were based on personal need satisfaction, but during preadolescence intimacy and love become the essence of friendships. Intimacy involves a relationship in which the two partners consensually validate one another's personal worth. Love exists "when the satisfaction or the security of another person becomes as significant to one as is one's own satisfaction or security" (Sullivan, 1953a, pp. 42–43).

A preadolescent's intimate relationship ordinarily involves another person of the same sex and of approximately the same age or social status. Infatuations with teachers or movie stars are not intimate relationships because they are not consensually validated. The significant relationships of this age are boy–boy or girl–girl chumships. These pairs are often interlocked so that sociograms with 9-to-12-year old children will usually show chains of friendships. To be liked by one's peers is more important to the preadolescent than to be liked by teachers or parents. Chums are able to freely express opinions and emotions to one another without fear of humiliation or embarrassment. This free exchange of personal thoughts and feelings initiates the preadolescent into the world of intimacy. Each chum becomes more fully human, with an expanded personality and a wider interest in the humanity of all people.

Sullivan believed that in American society preadolescence is the most untroubled and carefree time of life. Parents are still significant, even though they have been reappraised in a more realistic light. Preadolescents can experience unselfish love that has not yet been complicated by lust. The cooperation they acquired during the juvenile era evolves into collaboration or the capacity to work with another, not for self-prestige, but for the wellbeing of that other.

Preadolescence is critical for the future development of personality. If intimate collaboration is not learned at this time, a person is likely to be seriously stunted in later personality growth. During preadolescence a person may show symptoms of maladjustment that can be traced to unsatisfactory interpersonal relationships in earlier stages. Earlier negative influences, however, can be extenuated by the positive effects of an intimate relationship. Even the malevolent attitude can be reversed, and many other juvenile problems, such as loneliness and self-center-edness, are diminished by the achievement of intimacy. The dyadic relationship, however, is not the only therapeutic factor in preadolescence—the peer group itself serves as a microcosm, giving a person experience in various kinds of social situations. This relatively brief and uncomplicated period of life is shattered by the onset of puberty.

Many of Sheila's later problems with interpersonal relations are probably trace-able to an unsatisfactory preadolescence. Even though Sheila had some previous interpersonal difficulties, the ones she experienced during the crucial stage of pre-adolescence were more critical than any others encountered earlier or later. Her self-centered façade and her inability to compete, compromise, or cooperate impeded her ability to establish an intimate interpersonal relationship during this time. While the other girls were developing dyadic and chain relationships, Sheila felt left out and lonely. She wanted desperately to be friends with the most popular girl in class, but her overtures toward this girl were inevitably rebuffed. Sheila then turned to girls one or two years younger, but she always demanded to be the "boss" in these relationships, a situation that eventually led to problems, disagreements, and termination of the relationship. Near the end of preadolescence, Sheila became interested in boys, but her male classmates seemed to be more concerned with sports, science fiction, and silliness.

Early Adolescence

Early adolescence begins with puberty and ends with the need for love with one person of the opposite sex. It is characterized by the eruption of genital interest and the advent of lustful relationships. In the United States early adolescence is generally parallel with the junior high-school years. As with most other stages, however, Sullivan placed no great emphasis on chronological age.

The need for intimacy achieved during the preceding stage continues during early adolescence, now accompanied by a parallel but separate need—lust. In addition, security, or the need to be free from anxiety, remains active during early adolescence. Intimacy, lust, and security often collide with one another, bringing stress and conflict to the young adolescent. Lust interferes with security operations because genital activity in American culture is frequently ingrained with guilt, embarrassment, and anxiety.

During preadolescence, intimacy involves a chum of the same sex, but after puberty a person ordinarily seeks intimate friendships with members of the oppo-

The early adolescent's search for intimacy can increase anxiety and threaten security.

site sex. These attempts are fraught with self-doubt, uncertainty, and ridicule from others, usually leading to loss of self-esteem and an increase in anxiety. Thus, intimacy, or at least a shift in intimacy, also threatens security.

Finally, intimacy and lust frequently collide during early adolescence. For at least four reasons adolescents have difficulty combining lust with intimacy. First, some adolescents sublimate their genital need, thereby preventing a union of lust and intimacy. Second, intimacy is inclined toward other people, whereas lust is isolating. The powerful genital tensions seek outlet without regard for the intimacy need. Because lust can be satisfied autoerotically or in nonintimate relationships, the early adolescent has no compelling reason to combine it with intimacy. Third, society divides sexual objects into "good" and "bad," whereas chums are always seen as "good." Adolescent boys often learn that prostitutes or sexy girls are "bad" and that "good" girls are untouchable, although suitable for marriage. A fourth reason for the chasm between lust and intimacy is also culturally induced. Parents, teachers, and other authority figures actively dissuade early-adolescent boys and girls from becoming intimate. They sanction same-sex friendships, but, from fear of pregnancy and early marriage, they often discourage opposite-sex chumships.

Because the lust dynamism is biological, it bursts forth at puberty regardless of the individual's interpersonal readiness for it. A boy with no previous experience with intimacy may become a Don Juan, sexually conquering girls but with no real interest in them; a girl may become a "teaser," exploiting the lust dynamism but unable to relate to a boy on an intimate level. Such was the case with Sheila.

Sullivan (1953b) believed that early adolescence is a turning point in personality development. The person either emerges from this stage in command of the intimacy and lust dynamisms or faces serious interpersonal difficulties during future stages. Although sexual adjustment is important to personality development, Sullivan felt that the real issue lies in getting along with other people.

During early adolescence, Sheila, perhaps to her ultimate disadvantage, grew into an attractive, sexually sophisticated young woman. Having missed out on intimacy with other girls during preadolescence, she found great difficulty in becoming chums with her boyfriends during early adolescence. Biologically and socially she had less in common with boys than with girls. She shared few common interests—

other than sex—with her male companions and was conspicuously incapable of developing an intimate relationship with any of them. Because she still possessed the same unlikable characteristics that accounted for her previous lack of intimacy, she continued to have difficulty making friends with girls. As she became more sexually aggressive and adventuresome, however, her popularity among boys, especially those a couple of years older, began to increase.

Late Adolescence

Late adolescence begins when young people are able to feel both lust and intimacy toward the same person, and it ends in adulthood when they establish a lasting love relationship. Late adolescence embraces that period of self-discovery when adolescents are determining their preferences in genital behavior, usually during the senior high-school years or about ages 15 to 17 or 18. Like all stages of development, however, its attainment is individual—many reach it several years later; others, like Sheila, never attain it.

The outstanding feature of late adolescence is the fusion of intimacy and lust. The troubled attempts at self-exploration of early adolescence evolve into a stable pattern of sexual activity in which the loved one is also the object of lustful interest. People of the other sex are no longer desired solely as sexual objects but as people who are capable of being loved nonselfishly. Unlike the previous stage that was ushered in by biological changes, late adolescence is completely determined by interpersonal relations.

Successful late adolescence is characterized by growth of the syntaxic mode. At college or in the workplace, late adolescents begin "bumping heads" with others, exchanging ideas, and having their opinions and beliefs validated or repudiated. They learn from others how to live in the adult world, but a successful journey through the earlier stages facilitates this adjustment. When previous periods of development have been lacking, young people come to this age with no intimate interpersonal relations, inconsistent patterns of sexual activity, and a great need to maintain security operations. They rely heavily on the parataxic mode to avoid anxiety and strive to preserve self-esteem through selective inattention, dissociation, and neurotic symptoms. They face serious problems in bridging the gulf between society's expectations and their own inability to form intimate relations with persons of the other sex. Believing that love is a universal condition of young people, they are often pressured into "falling in love." However, only the mature person has the capacity to love; others merely go through the motions of being "in love" in order to maintain security (Sullivan, 1953b).

Sheila is now chronologically a late adolescent, but her interpersonal development has been stunted by her inability to form an intimate relationship during preadolescence. In her search for intimacy she consistently confuses sex with friendship. As a result, each of her sexual relationships has ended in confusion and disappointment. Nevertheless, she continues her quest for that elusive closeness that she has not yet captured.

Adulthood

The successful completion of late adolescence culminates in adulthood, a stage characterized by the establishment of a love relationship with at least one significant other person. Writing of this love relationship, Sullivan (1953b, p. 34) stated that "this really highly developed intimacy with another is not the principal business of life, but is, perhaps, the principal source of satisfaction in life."

Sullivan had little to say about adulthood because he believed that maturity was beyond the scope of interpersonal psychiatry; people who have achieved the capacity to love are not in need of psychiatric counsel. His sketch of the mature person, therefore, was not founded on clinical experience but was an extrapolation from the preceding stages.

Mature adults are perceptive of other people's anxiety and security, sensitive to their needs, and genuinely understanding of their problems. They have a low level of anxiety, operate predominantly on the syntaxic level, find life interesting and exciting, and are no problem to themselves or others (Sullivan, 1953b).

MENTAL DISORDERS

Sullivan believed that all mental disorders have an interpersonal origin and can be understood only with reference to the person's social environment. He also held that the deficiencies found in psychiatric patients are found in every person, but to a lesser degree. There is nothing unique about mental difficulties; they are derived from the same kind of interpersonal troubles faced by all people. Sullivan (1953a, p. 96) insisted that "everyone is much more simply human than unique, and that no matter what ails the patient, he is *mostly* a person like the psychiatrist."

Most of Sullivan's early therapeutic work was with schizophrenic patients, and many of his subsequent lectures and writings dealt with schizophrenia. Sullivan (1962) distinguished two broad classes of schizophrenia. The first includes all those symptoms that originate from organic causes and are, therefore, beyond the study of interpersonal psychiatry. The second class includes all schizophrenic disorders grounded in situational causes. These were the only ones of concern to Sullivan because they are the only ones amenable to change through interpersonal psychiatry.

Dissociated reactions, which often precede schizophrenia, are characterized by loneliness, low self-esteem, the uncanny emotion, unsatisfactory relations with others, and ever-increasing anxiety (Sullivan, 1953b). People with a dissociated personality, in common with normal people, attempt to minimize anxiety by building an elaborate self-system that permits them to block out those experiences that threaten their security. Whereas normal individuals feel relatively secure in their interpersonal relations and do not need to constantly rely on dissociation as a means of protecting self-esteem, mentally disordered individuals dissociate many of their experiences from their self-system. If this strategy becomes persistent, these people will begin to operate more and more in their own private worlds, with increasing parataxic distortions and decreasing consensually validated experiences (Sullivan, 1956).

PSYCHOTHERAPY

Because he believed that mental disorders grow out of interpersonal difficulties, Sullivan based his therapeutic procedures on an effort to improve a patient's relationship with others. To facilitate this process, the therapist serves as a *participant observer*, becoming part of an interpersonal, face-to-face relationship with the patient and providing the patient an opportunity to establish syntaxic communication with another human being.

Although they are participants in the interview, Sullivanian therapists avoid getting personally involved. They do not place themselves on the same level with the patient, but, on the contrary, they try to convince the patient of their expert abilities. In other words, friendship is not a condition of psychotherapy—therapists must be trained as experts in the difficult business of making discerning observations of the patient's interpersonal relations (Sullivan, 1954).

Sullivan was primarily concerned with understanding patients and helping them to improve foresight, discover difficulties in interpersonal relations, and restore their ability to participate in consensually validated experiences. To accomplish these goals, he concentrated his efforts on answering three continuing questions: Precisely what is the patient saying to me? How can I best put into words what I wish to say to the patient? What is the general pattern of communication between us?

Sullivan divided the interview into four stages: formal inception, reconnaissance, detailed inquiry, and termination. The first stage, *formal inception*, involves the therapist's introduction to the patient, including an inquiry into the reason for therapy and the source of referral. The initial contact is extremely important because it is the first instance of communication between therapist and patient. At this time, the therapist promotes confidence in the patient by demonstrating interpersonal skill, permits the patient to express the reasons for seeking therapy, formulates tentative hypotheses, and decides on a possible course of action (Sullivan, 1954).

During the *reconnaissance stage*, the therapist obtains a general personal and social history, makes observations concerning patients' interpersonal identities, and tries to discover why they came to develop their particular personalities. During this period the therapist will ask open-ended questions that allow patients to respond at random until their thought patterns circle around to something relevant. The reconnaissance stage typically lasts from 7 to 15 hours, but it may be as brief as 20 minutes if therapy is to consist of a single interview. At the end of this phase, the therapist summarizes the important data, after which the patient amends or adds any details. This ensures that therapy can proceed on a consensually valid basis (Sullivan, 1954).

The third stage, *detailed inquiry*, varies with the purpose of the interview, but, in general, it is a time for testing hypotheses formulated during the two preceding stages. The therapist tries to improve understanding by asking a series of detailed questions concerning patients' personal histories and their current attitudes toward themselves and significant others. A skillful therapist must listen carefully to all possible meanings behind the answers to these questions. In the search for durable characteristics of patients, the therapist sifts out communication designed to deceive. Patients often unintentionally hide the truth from their therapist, believing that the truth will somehow be seen as a sign of weakness and failure. During this stage the therapist strives to verify impressions formulated during earlier stages without prematurely increasing patients' anxieties. Later, after patients become convinced that help is forthcoming, sudden elevations in anxiety will no longer have disastrous results (Sullivan, 1954).

The fourth and final stage of the interview is *termination* or, in some cases, *interruption*. Termination means that the therapist would not expect to see the patient again; interruption suggests that an interview session is finished, although it may be resumed the following day, week, or some other designated time. After each interruption, the psychiatrist gives the patient "homework," something to do or some memory to recall. With either interruption or termination, the therapist consolidates whatever progress the patient has made by revealing what has been learned about the patient, by prescribing a course of action, by giving the patient a final assessment of prognosis, and, finally, by taking formal leave. The formal leave-taking must proceed smoothly or else therapeutic benefits so carefully accumulated may be destroyed (Sullivan, 1954).

Parataxic Perceptions in Therapy

Sullivan did not recognize the concept of transference in interpersonal psychiatry, but he did place great emphasis on the importance of the therapist–patient relationship, including the parataxic perceptions the patient may have of the therapist. When earlier situations are reviewed during therapy, a patient may develop a distorted view of the therapist so that there are actually three persons present: the imaginary therapist with whom the patient is conversing, the patient who reacts to the imaginary therapist, and the real therapist who is observing and trying to make sense out of the interview. In one example of parataxic perception, Sullivan (1953a) wrote of a patient who, after about 300 hours of therapy with Sullivan, was surprised to see that he was a thin man with dark, thinning hair. She had previously seen him as a fat old man with white hair.

The therapist attempts to point out the patient's inconsistencies and distortions concerning the doctor and to learn more about the earlier significant authority person who is the source of the patient's delusions. Parataxic attitudes toward the therapist are expressed only after the patient begins to feel secure and less anxious with the doctor. Both therapist and patient can then gain a greater understanding of the patient's past relationships and also facilitate present and future interpersonal relations (Sullivan, 1954).

Sleep, Dreams, and Myths

Sullivan placed some emphasis on sleep, dreams, and myths in his interpersonal psychotherapy. Sleep is important because it relieves patients of the need to maintain security operations and to enjoy a period of relaxation. In addition, it permits patients to satisfy unmet needs through dreaming.

The purpose of dreams, according to Sullivan, is to create a barrier between waking life and sleep by putting into parataxic form problems an individual cannot solve while awake. Because the dream itself is parataxic and partially prototaxic, it is unreachable and cannot be accurately or directly communicated to another person. The therapist deals only with patients' recollections of dreams, and these reports are treated in the same way as any other important event—as revealing clues concerning patients' interpersonal relations.

Myths, like dreams, appear on the parataxic level, but, unlike dreams, they transcend the individual and pertain to the culture. Sullivan believed that myths originate as general dreams incorporated into the culture because they deal with unsolvable problems common to many people. He also believed that the psychotherapist should not try to translate dreams or myths into syntaxic language because they make sense only on the parataxic level (Sullivan, 1953b).

Summary

In summary, the Sullivanian therapist is primarily concerned with uncovering patients' difficulties in relating to others and strives to replace disjunctive motivations with conjunctive ones. Conjunctive motivations integrate personality and allow patients to satisfy their needs and to enhance their feelings of security. To accomplish this, patients must give up some security in dealing with other people and realize that they can achieve mental health only through consensually validated personal relations. The therapeutic ingredient in this process is the face-to-face relationship between psychiatrist and patients, which permits patients to reduce anxiety and to communicate with others on the syntaxic level.

 ## CONCEPT OF HUMANITY

Sullivan's basic conception of humanity is summed up in his *one-genus hypothesis*, which states that *"everyone is much more simply human than otherwise"* (1953b, p. 32). This was his way of saying that similarities among people are much more important than differences. People are more like people than anything else.

> In other words, the differences between any two instances of human personality—from the lowest grade imbecile to the highest-grade genius—are much less striking than the difference between the least-gifted human being and a member of the nearest other biological genus. (Sullivan, 1953b, p. 33)

The one influence separating humans from all other creatures is interpersonal relations. We are born biological organisms, animals with no human qualities except the potential for participation in interpersonal relations. Soon after birth we begin to realize this potential when interpersonal experiences transform us into human beings. Sullivan believed that the mind contains nothing except what was put there through interpersonal experiences. Unlike Freud and Jung, he contended that there are no human instincts. We are motivated only by environmental influences—interpersonal relationships.

Sullivan insisted that humans have no existence outside the interpersonal situation. As isolated entities we are nothing, but through our relationships with other humans we develop our personality. Each of us begins life with a somewhat one-sided relationship with a mothering one who both cares for our needs and imparts anxiety to us. Later we are able to reciprocate feelings for our parents, and these relationships serve as a foundation upon which subsequent interpersonal relations are built. At about the time we first go to school, we should learn to compete, cooperate, and compromise with children our own age, and, if we do, we then have the tools necessary for intimacy and love that come later. Through our intimate and love relationships, we become healthy personalities. However, an absence of these relationships leads to stunted psychological growth.

Personal individuality is an illusion; we exist only in relation to other people and have as many personalities as we have interpersonal relations. Thus the concepts of *uniqueness* and *individuality* do not concern interpersonal psychiatry. The subject matter of Sullivan's theory is the interaction between the observer and the observed, with the observer being a participant in the relationship. This interaction is the essence of personality.

Anxiety and interpersonal relations are tied together in a cyclic manner, which makes significant personality changes difficult. Anxiety interferes with interpersonal relations, and unsatisfactory interpersonal relations lead to the use of rigid behaviors that may temporarily buffer anxiety. Because these inflexible behaviors do not solve the basic problem, however, they eventually lead to increases in anxiety, which leads to further deterioration in interpersonal relations. The increasing levels of anxiety must then be held in check by an ever-rigid self-system. For this reason Sullivan would have to be rated as being *neither optimistic nor pessimistic* concerning the potential for growth and change within human beings. Interpersonal relations can transform us into healthy personalities, but they can also be restrictive by creating anxiety and its resultant rigid self-structure.

Because personality is built solely on interpersonal relations, Sullivan is rated *very high on social influence.* Interpersonal relations are responsible for both positive and negative characteristics in people. If an infant has its needs satisfied by the mothering one, is not disturbed by her anxiety, and receives genuine feelings of tenderness, it can avoid being a malevolent personality during childhood and will develop tender feelings toward others. On the other hand, unsatisfactory interpersonal relations may trigger malevolence and leave some children with the feeling that people cannot be trusted, and that they are essentially alone among their enemies.

Related Research

In recent years a number of researchers have conducted studies on interpersonal theory that relates either directly and indirectly to Sullivan's ideas. Much of this research deals with dyadic (two-person) relationships, either between therapist and patient or between people outside the therapeutic process. In one study Henry, Schacht, and Strupp (1990) used the Structural Analysis of Social Behavior (Benjamin, 1974) to see how interpersonal dynamics between patient and therapist relate to the behavior of each person, and also how it affects the success of therapy. Following Sullivan's (1953b) assumption that people learn to treat themselves as they have been treated by others, Henry et al. studied the third session of 14 different therapy dyads to test this basic hypothesis. In general, they found that patients developed relatively stable behaviors that were consistent with the way their therapist treated them. More specifically, these researchers found that therapists' hostile and controlling statements were highly correlated with patients' self-derogatory statements. Also, patients of therapists who belittled, blamed, ignored, or neglected them tended to blame themselves and to show poor therapeutic progress.

In a somewhat similar study, Horowitz et al. (1991) explored ways in which two people reciprocally influence one another as they interact. They began with the assumption that a depressed person's submissive behavior will invite a reciprocal dominating reaction from other people—a reaction that sustains the depression. In the first two parts of their study, Horowitz et al. demonstrated that self-derogations connote submissiveness and are neutral in affiliation; that is, they do not lead others to either like or dislike the person making self-derogatory statements. In the third part of the study, Horowitz et al. had one male and one female confederate interact with same-sex subjects who had also filled out the Beck Depression Inventory (Beck, 1967). Confederates memorized one-minute monologues on preselected topics and then presented one of three different utterances to a subject: (1) self-derogatory statements, (2) other-derogatory statements, and (3) nonderogating self-disclosures dealing with the confederate's attitude toward smoking or places that he or she had been. Horowitz et al. found that self-derogating confederates were judged to be submissive and neutral in affiliation, whereas other-derogating confederates were judged to be nonsubmissive and hostile. They further found that subjects reacted to self-derogating confederates with dominating responses, such as advice giving, and that they reacted to other-derogating confederates with hostility. Horowitz et al. suggested that their results help explain why depressed people eventually arouse hostility in others. Initially, depressed people appear submissive and neutral in affiliation. This leads others to dominate them through such behaviors as exhorting and advising. However, depressed people who do not change appear to have rejected or ignored this advice or encouragement. This noncompliance is interpreted as hostility, which then elicits hostility from the other person. Such interdependence of behaviors is consistent with Sullivan's interpersonal theory of personality.

Another Sullivanian topic that has received some research attention is imaginary playmates. Are people with clearly identifiable imaginary playmates different in any way from those who do not have such a friend? Pines (1978) looked into this question by reviewing the relevant literature and by talking with people who were conducting research on children's imaginary friends. She reported that one study indicated that 65% of three- and four-year-old children had identifiable imaginary playmates. Most of these children were firstborn or only children, and most of the playmates were males. This latter finding is due to the fact that little girls chose either a boy or a girl as an imaginary friend, but boys almost always picked another boy. Children who had imaginary playmates, in comparison with those who did not, tended to watch far less television and to show a more advanced selection of programs. In addition, these children were more socialized; they showed less aggression and more cooperation; they smiled more, concentrated better, and were less likely to become bored. They also displayed more verbal ability and higher levels of intelligence.

More recent studies have found imaginary playmates to be associated with both positive and negative characteristics. Fern (1991) studied gifted-child humorists in grades 3 to 6 and found that they were more verbally aggressive, showed more imaginative thinking, and had higher IQ scores than a comparison group of children. In addition, the child humorists were more likely to have imaginary playmates. Perhaps more negatively, Ross, Heber, Norton, and Anderson (1989) found that people with multiple personalities, compared to those with schizophrenia, panic disorder, or eating disorder, were more likely to have had an imaginary playmate during childhood. Stanford (1987) found that college-age subjects who reported having an out-of-body experience while falling asleep spent more time during childhood playing with an imaginary friend than subjects who did not report an out-of-body experience.

These findings do not indicate a cause-and-effect relationship between having an imaginary playmate and intelligence, maturity, sociability, humor, multiple personality, or having an out-of-body experience. They do suggest, however, that people who invent and spend time playing with an imaginary friend during childhood are different in several ways from those who do not.

CRITIQUE OF SULLIVAN

Although Sullivan's theory of personality is quite comprehensive, it is not as popular among academic psychologists as the theories of Freud, Adler, Jung, and Erikson. Nevertheless, many medically oriented clinicians such as Gerald L. Klerman (Klerman, 1989a, 1989b; Klerman & Weissman, 1991; Klerman, Weissman, Rounsaville, & Chevron, 1984; Moreau, Mufson, Weissman, & Klerman, 1991) base their therapeutic approach on Sullivan's interpersonal theory. However, the ultimate value of any theory does not rest on its popularity but on the five criteria enumerated in Chapter 1.

The first criterion of a useful theory is its ability to *generate research*. Although much research is currently being conducted on interpersonal theory in general, only a few researchers are actively investigating hypotheses specifically drawn from Sullivan's theory. One possible explanation for this deficiency is Sullivan's lack of popularity among those most apt to conduct research—the academicians. This might be accounted for by Sullivan's close association with psychiatry, his isolation from any university setting, and the relative lack of organization in his writings and speeches. A second possible explanation for the paucity of research on Sullivan's stages of development is that such investigations would almost necessitate longitudinal studies and thus would be time consuming. Probably the most important hypotheses that can be drawn from the theory center around Sullivan's notion of the crucial, almost miraculous stage of preadolescence. He suggested that mistakes made prior to this time can be rectified if the preadolescent is able to establish an intimate relationship with a chum. On the other hand, errors made during this period, that is, the inability to find a chum, cannot easily be remedied during subsequent stages. If longitudinal studies were to lend support to these two hypotheses, then society might better prepare preadolescent children for intimate relationships with others of equal status.

Second, how well does Sullivanian theory provide an organization for all that is known about human personality? Despite its many elaborate postulates, the theory can receive only a moderate rating on its ability to *organize knowledge*. Most of the research findings on interpersonal relationships of children and adolescents are consistent with Sullivan's concepts of the various stages of development. Consistency with its concepts is not verification of its basic tenets, however. Moreover, the theory's extreme emphasis on interpersonal relations subtracts from its ability to organize knowledge, because much of what is presently known about human behavior has a biological basis and does not easily fit into a theory restricted to interpersonal relations.

The relative lack of testing of Sullivan's theory diminishes its usefulness as a *practical guide* for parents, teachers, psychotherapists, and others concerned with the care of children and adolescents. However, if one accepts the theory without supporting evidence, then many practical problems can be managed by resorting to Sullivanian theory. As a guide to action, then, the theory receives a fair-to-moderate rating.

Is the theory *internally consistent*? Sullivan's ideas suffer from his inability to write well, but the theory itself is logically conceptualized and holds together as a unified entity. Although Sullivan used some unusual terms, he did so in a consistent fashion throughout his writings and speeches. Overall, his theory is consistent, but it lacks the organization that might have been achieved had he committed more of his ideas to the printed page.

Finally, is the theory *parsimonious* or simple? Here Sullivan must receive a low rating. His penchant for creating his own terms and the awkwardness of his writing add needless bulk to a theory that, if streamlined, would be far more useful. A more tightly written theory might have generated more interest in potential researchers, which in turn would have resulted in a presently more viable theory.

Chapter Summary

Harry Stack Sullivan was the first American to develop a comprehensive theory of personality. Like many other theorists, his ideas on personality were a reflection of his own life experiences, and his early loneliness and isolation led to a theory that emphasized the importance of personal relationships. Although his isolation also led to a rather esoteric language, his insights as a psychotherapist resulted in an eloquent description of anxiety, interpersonal relations, and the stages of psychological development.

Anxiety is the chief descriptive force in interpersonal relations and is the cause of much pain and suffering. *Interpersonal relations* can either create additional anxiety or lead to healthy psychological growth and development, which reduce anxiety.

The first *developmental stage* in Sullivan's theory is *infancy*—a period lasting from birth to the development of language. During this stage an infant's primary interpersonal relationship is with the mothering one, and its principal source of anxiety is the feeding situation.

Childhood begins when a child begins to develop language and continues until about age five or six. The most important interpersonal relationship for children this age is ordinarily with the mother, yet these children often create a relationship with an imaginary playmate that can have positive and lasting effects on later development.

The third Sullivanian stage is the *juvenile era*, a period roughly encompassing the first three years of school in Western culture. At this time children should learn competition, compromise, and cooperation—skills that will enable them to move successfully through later stages of development.

The most crucial stage of development is *preadolescence*, because mistakes made during this phase are exceedingly difficult to overcome later. During preadolescence a child should learn intimacy, ordinarily with a person of the same age and gender. This close interpersonal relationship is free from the complications of a sexual encounter and is the positive force that allows a person to subsequently relate to members of the opposite sex in an intimate rather than strictly sexual manner.

As young people reach *early adolescence*, their sexual interest is stimulated by biological changes. If they learned intimacy during preadolescence, then they will be able to maintain these same-sex intimate relationships and at the same time develop lustful encounters with adolescents of the opposite sex.

People attain *late adolescence* when they are able to direct their intimacy and lust toward one other person. Unfortunately, not everyone achieves this stage, and many people are never able to develop feelings of genuine love toward the person for whom they have the strongest sexual desire. The successful completion of late adolescence culminates in *adulthood*, a stage marked by a stable love relationship.

Suggested Readings

CHAPMAN, A. H. (1976). *Harry Stack Sullivan: His life and his work.* New York: Putnam's.
A very readable account of Sullivan's life combined with a discussion of the principal principles of interpersonal theory.
PERRY, H. S. (1982). *Psychiatrist of America: The life of Harry Stack Sullivan.* Cambridge, MA: Belknap Press.
Written by the former managing editor of Sullivan's journal, *Psychiatry*, this biography is the result of 20 years of careful research. Sullivan's personality emerges more fully than in any other biography.
SULLIVAN, H. S. (1953). *The interpersonal theory of psychiatry.* New York: Norton.
As the first book prepared from Sullivan's unpublished lectures, this work contains the most complete account of interpersonal theory, including the six developmental epochs.
YOUNISS, J. (1980). *Parents and peers in social development: A Sullivan-Piaget perspective.* Chicago: University of Chicago Press.
In this attempt to integrate the writings of Sullivan with those of Jean Piaget, the author argues that children's social development is greatly influenced by their friends and peers.

Psychoanalytic Social Theory

Chapter Seven

OVERVIEW
BIOGRAPHY OF KAREN HORNEY
INTRODUCTION TO HORNEY'S PSYCHOANALYTIC
   SOCIAL THEORY
      Horney and Freud Compared
      The Impact of Culture
      The Importance of Childhood Experiences
BASIC ANXIETY
COMPULSIVE DRIVES
      Neurotic Needs
      Neurotic Trends
INTRAPSYCHIC CONFLICTS
      The Idealized Self-Image
      Self-Hatred
FEMININE PSYCHOLOGY
PSYCHOTHERAPY
FROMM'S HUMANISTIC PSYCHOANALYSIS
BIOGRAPHY OF ERICH FROMM
BASIC ASSUMPTIONS
HUMAN NEEDS
      Relatedness
      Transcendence
      Rootedness
      Sense of Identity
      Frame of Orientation
      Summary
THE BURDEN OF FREEDOM
      Mechanisms of Escape
      Positive Freedom
CHARACTER ORIENTATIONS
      Nonproductive Orientations
      The Productive Orientation
PERSONALITY DISORDERS
      Necrophilia
      Malignant Narcissism
      Incestuous Symbiosis
PSYCHOTHERAPY
FROMM'S METHODS OF INVESTIGATION
      Social Character in a Mexican Village
      A Psychohistorical Study of Hitler
CONCEPT OF HUMANITY
RELATED RESEARCH
CRITIQUE OF PSYCHOANALYTIC SOCIAL THEORY
CHAPTER SUMMARY
SUGGESTED READINGS

HORNEY FROMM

When his first wife left him, Harold was devastated, confused, and depressed. He had noticed that Nancy was becoming more distant, but he had no notion that she had wanted a divorce. After all, he had been a near-perfect husband. He had frequently surprised Nancy with expensive gifts, continually complimented her on her appearance, and routinely praised her cooking. In addition, he tried hard to satisfy her sexually and had remained faithful to her during their five-year marriage. What more could Nancy desire?

For months after the separation Harold struggled in vain to win Nancy back. Then, as he began to accept the permanence of the situation, he started to analyze the reasons for the separation. At first he had blamed himself, but later he shifted the responsibility to Nancy and criticized her for her newly formed feminist views. The more he thought of it, the more he began to see that Nancy had been unreasonably influenced by some of her friends, was reacting in an irrational manner, and was showing signs of mental instability. When he became convinced that Nancy's newly acquired ideas and bizarre behaviors were responsible for the separation, he quickly agreed to a divorce.

At about the time he accepted the inevitability of a divorce, Harold's outlook began to improve and his depression lifted. Soon he was seeing another woman, and almost as quickly he "fell in love" again.

Harold became completely consumed by his relationship with Denise and spent nearly all his available time with her. When they weren't physically together, they were talking to one another on the telephone. At first, Denise seemed to be as enamored with Harold as he was with her.

In time, however, Denise began to feel stifled by the relationship. She wanted to spend more time alone or with other friends. Frequently, she would not be home when Harold called. As Denise became less and less infatuated with Harold, he became more and more demanding of her. He pushed hard for commitment and marriage, but Denise wanted more freedom to see other men. Harold had never dated another woman after he met Denise, and he could not understand why she wanted to date other men.

As time went on and Denise became less available, Harold became suspicious that she was seeing someone else. He frequently parked his car down the street from her apartment and then would follow her as she left. On several of these occasions she, indeed, met another man. Harold never confronted the couple, but when he was alone with Denise he would become enraged and insulting. After

Harold repeated this behavior several times, Denise placed a restraining order on him.

Legally forced to remain away from Denise, Harold soon began dating Carolyn, and within two months of his breakup with Denise, Harold and Carolyn were married.

After less than a year, this second marriage was in trouble. Carolyn was demanding more time for herself and was complaining that Harold was "smothering" her. Harold reluctantly agreed to allow Carolyn more time with her friends, but he was puzzled when she failed to show appreciation for this freedom. In fact, their arguments became more frequent, and once again Harold began to blame his wife for his marital problems.

Nevertheless, he desperately desired to hold on to the marriage. He was convinced that if only Carolyn would return to her earlier compliant behavior, their happiness would be ensured. However, much to Harold's consternation, Carolyn showed no willingness to recapture the rapture of their early relationship.

Harold was unaware that his demands were driving Carolyn farther away. In fact, he was oblivious of any demands whatsoever. He also failed to see any similarities between his previous relationships with Nancy and Denise and the present one with Carolyn.

As he and Carolyn were on the brink of breaking up, Harold once again became devastated, confused, and depressed. Despite his belief that Carolyn was completely responsible for their problems, he tried hard to hold on to the relationship. When he finally realized that a second divorce was inevitable his outlook became less gloomy, and soon, he was once again seeking the companionship of another woman.

As Harold approached his fourth intimate relationship in three years, he had learned little from the previous three.

OVERVIEW

The **psychoanalytic social theories** of Karen Horney (pronounced horn-eye) and Erich Fromm offer some insight into Harold's case as well as other normal and neurotic personalities. Both Horney and Fromm would say that Harold is suffering from *basic anxiety*. Horney believed that cultural conditions, especially childhood experiences, are largely responsible for the development of basic anxiety, whereas Fromm held that basic anxiety, or feelings of loneliness and isolation, results from humanity's separation from the natural world.

Horney theorized that people combat basic anxiety by adopting one of three fundamental styles of relating to others: (1) moving toward people; (2) moving against people; or (3) moving away from people. Normal individuals may use any of these, but neurotics are compelled to rigidly employ only one. Although Horney's writings are concerned mostly with the neurotic personality, many of her ideas can also be applied to normal individuals.

Fromm, who was influenced by Karl Marx's social theories, believed that the rise of capitalism has, on the one hand, contributed to the growth of leisure time and personal freedom, and, on the other, it has resulted in feelings of anxiety, isolation, and powerlessness. The cost of freedom, Fromm maintained, has exceeded its benefits. The isolation wrought by capitalism has been unbearable, leaving people with two alternatives: (1) to escape from freedom into interpersonal dependencies, or (2) to move to self-realization through productive love and work.

Both Horney and Fromm were influenced by Freud, and each influenced the other. This chapter looks at Horney's basic theory of neurosis, compares her ideas to those of Freud, and briefly discusses her views on feminine psychology. It also examines Fromm's humanistically oriented psychoanalytic theory, one that takes a broad historical and anthropological view of human personality.

BIOGRAPHY OF KAREN HORNEY

Karen Danielsen Horney was born in Eilbek, a small town near Hamburg, Germany, September 15, 1885 (Quinn, 1987). (A 1978 biography by Rubins erroneously reported the date as September 16 and the town as Blankenese.) Karen was the only daughter of Berndt Danielsen, a sea captain, and Clothilda van Ronzelen Danielsen, a woman nearly 18 years younger than her husband. The only other child of this marriage was a son, about four years older than Karen. However, the old sea captain had been married earlier and had four other children, most of whom were adults by the time Karen was born. Karen was never close to her stern, devoutly religious father, who was nearly 50 years older, and who was at sea much of the time. Karen enjoyed a much closer relationship with her mother, who both supported and protected her against her father. Nevertheless, Karen was not a happy child. She resented the favored treatment given to her older brother and, in addition, she worried about the bitterness and discord between her parents.

When she was 14, Karen decided to become a physician, but at that time no university in Germany admitted women (Quinn, 1987). By the time she was 16, this situation had changed, and Karen became one of the first girls in Germany to enter the Gymnasium, a school that would lead to a university and to medical school. On her own for the first time, Karen was to remain independent for the rest of her life.

In 1906 she entered the University of Freiburg, becoming one of the first women in Germany to study medicine. There she met Oskar Horney, a political science student. The relationship began as a friendship, but it eventually became a romantic one. After their marriage in 1909, the couple settled in Berlin, where Oskar, now a Ph.D., worked for a coal company and Karen, not yet an M.D., specialized in psychiatry.

By this time, Freudian psychoanalysis was becoming well established, and Karen Horney became familiar with Freud's writings. Early in 1910, she began an analysis with Karl Abraham, one of Freud's close associates. After her analysis was terminated, she attended Abraham's evening seminars, where she became acquainted with other psychoanalysts. By 1917 she had written her first paper on psychoanalysis, "The Technique of Psychoanalytic Therapy" (Horney, 1917/1968), which reflected the orthodox Freudian view and gave little indication of Horney's subsequent independent thinking.

The early years of her marriage were filled with many notable personal experiences for Horney. Her father and mother, who were now separated, died within less than a year of each other; she gave birth to three daughters in five years; she received her M.D. degree in 1915 after five years of psychoanalysis; and, in her quest for the right man, she had several love affairs (Quinn, 1987).

After World War I the Horneys lived a prosperous, suburban life style, with several servants and a chauffeur. Oskar did well financially, while Karen enjoyed a thriving psychiatric practice. This idyllic scene, however, soon ended. The inflation and economic disorder of 1923 cost Oskar his job, and the family was forced to move back to an apartment in Berlin. A year later Karen and Oskar separated. (They did not officially divorce until 1939, 15 years after their separation.)

The six years following her separation from Oskar were the most productive of Horney's life. In addition to seeing patients and caring for her three daughters, she became more involved with writing, teaching, traveling, and lecturing. Her papers now showed important differences with Freudian theory. She believed that culture, not anatomy, was responsible for psychic differences between men and women. When Freud reacted negatively to Horney's' position, she became even more outspoken in her opposition.

In 1932 Horney left Germany for a position as associate director of the newly established Institute for Psychoanalysis in Chicago. Several factors contributed to her decision to immigrate—the anti-Jewish political climate in Germany (although Horney was not Jewish); increasing opposition to her unorthodox views; and an opportunity to extend her influence beyond Berlin. During the two years she spent in Chicago, she met Margaret Mead, Harry Stack Sullivan, and many of the same scholars who had influenced Sullivan (see Chapter 6). In addition, she renewed acquaintances with Erich Fromm and his wife, Frieda Fromm-Reichmann, whom she had known in Berlin. During the next 10 years, Horney and Fromm were close friends, greatly influencing one another and eventually becoming lovers (Quinn, 1987).

In 1934 Horney moved to New York, where she taught at the New School for Social Research and where she met and was influenced by several other scholars from Europe, including Max Wertheimer. She also became a member of the Zodiac group, which included Fromm, Fromm-Reichmann, Sullivan, and others (see Chapter 6).

Although Horney was a member of the New York Psychoanalytic Institute, she seldom agreed with the established members. Moreover, her book, *New Ways in Psychoanalysis* (1939), made her the leader of an opposition group. In this book she called for abandoning the instinct theory and placing more emphasis on ego and social influences. In 1941 she resigned from the institute over issues of dogma and orthodoxy, and helped form a rival organization, the Association for the Advancement of Psychoanalysis (AAP). However, this new group also quickly suffered from internal strife. In 1943 Fromm (whose intimate relationship with Horney had recently ended) and several others resigned from the AAP, leaving that organization without its strongest members. Despite the rift, the association continued, but under a new name—the Karen Horney Psychoanalytic Institute. In 1952 the Karen Horney Clinic was founded, and both organizations have continued to the present time.

In 1950 Horney published her most important work, *Neurosis and Human Growth*, a book that sets forth theories that were no longer merely a reaction to Freud, but rather an expression of her own creative and independent thinking.

After a short illness, Horney died of cancer on December 4, 1952.

INTRODUCTION TO HORNEY'S PSYCHOANALYTIC SOCIAL THEORY

The early writings of Karen Horney, like those of Adler, Jung, and Erikson, have a distinctive Freudian flavor. Like Adler and Jung she eventually became disenchanted with orthodox psychoanalysis and constructed a revisionist theory that reflected her own personal experiences—clinical and otherwise.

Although Horney wrote nearly exclusively about neuroses and neurotic personalities, her works imply much that is appropriate to normal, healthy development. Culture, especially early childhood experiences, plays a leading role in shaping human personality, either neurotic or healthy. Horney, then, agreed with Freud that early childhood traumas are important, but she differed from him in her insistence that social rather than biological forces are paramount in personality development.

Horney and Freud Compared

Horney criticized Freud's theories on several accounts. First, she cautioned that strict adherence to orthodox psychoanalysis would lead to stagnation in both theoretical thought and therapeutic practice (Horney, 1937). Second, Horney (1937, 1939) objected to Freud's ideas on feminine psychology, a subject we will return to later. Third, she stressed the view that psychoanalysis should move beyond instinct theory and emphasize the importance of cultural influences in shaping personality. "Man is ruled not by the pleasure principle alone but by two guiding principles: safety and satisfaction" (Horney, 1939, p. 73). Similarly, she claimed that neuroses are not the result of instincts but rather the person's "attempt to find paths through a wilderness full of unknown dangers" (Horney, 1939, p. 10). This wilderness is created by society and not by instincts or anatomy.

Despite becoming increasingly critical of Freud, Horney continued to recognize his perceptive insights. Her main quarrel with Freud was not so much the accuracy of his observations but the validity of his interpretations. In general terms, she held that Freud's explanations result in a pessimistic concept of humanity based on innate instincts and the stagnation of personality. In contrast, her view of humanity is an optimistic one and is centered on cultural forces that are amenable to change (Horney, 1950).

The Impact of Culture

Although Horney did not overlook the importance of genetic factors, she repeatedly emphasized cultural influences as the primary bases for both neurotic and normal personality development. Modern culture, she contended, is based on *competition* among individuals. "Everyone is a real or potential competitor of everyone else" (Horney, 1937, p. 284). Competitiveness and the *hostility* it spawns result in feelings of *isolation*. These feelings of being alone in a potentially hostile world lead to intensified *needs for affection*, which, in turn, cause people to overvalue love. As a result, many people in our culture see love and affection as the solution for all their problems. Genuine love, of course, can be a healthy, growth-producing experience, but the desperate need for love (such as that shown by Harold, our case study) provides a fertile ground for the development of neuroses. Rather than benefiting from the need for love, neurotics strive in pathological ways to find it. Their self-defeating attempts result in low self-esteem, increased hostility, basic anxiety, more competitiveness, and a continual excessive need for love and affection.

According to Horney, our society contributes to this vicious circle in several respects. First, we are imbued with the cultural teachings of brotherly love and humility. These teachings, however, run contrary to another prevailing attitude, namely aggressiveness and the drive to win or be superior. Second, society's demands for success and achievement are nearly endless, so that even when we achieve our material ambitions, additional goals are continually being placed before us. Third, our society tells us that we are free, that we can accomplish anything through hard work and perseverance. In reality, however, the freedom of most people is greatly restricted by genetics, social position, and the competitiveness of others.

These contradictions—all stemming from cultural influences rather than biological ones—provide intrapsychic conflicts that threaten the psychological health of normal people and provide nearly insurmountable obstructions for neurotics.

The Importance of Childhood Experiences

Horney believed that neurotic conflict can stem from almost any developmental stage, but childhood is the age from which the vast majority of problems arise. A variety of traumatic events, such as sexual abuse, beatings, open rejection, or pervasive neglect, may leave their impressions on future development, but Horney (1937) insisted that these debilitating experiences can almost invariably be traced to lack of genuine warmth and affection. Horney's own lack of love from her father and her close relationship with her mother must have had a powerful effect on her personal development as well as on her theoretical ideas.

On the other hand, Harold, our case study (who on the surface experienced a childhood similar to Horney's), enjoyed a genuinely close relationship with neither his father nor his mother. His father, like Horney's, was absent much of the time because his job as a truck driver kept him away from home for extended periods. When he was home, he had little time for either Harold or his younger brother. Harold recalls his father as a punitive, grouchy man whose primary paternal task was to discipline his children. Harold, like Horney, turned to his mother for emotional support, but, unfortunately, Harold's mother was a deeply troubled woman, herself desperately striving for love and affection. As the firstborn, Harold seems to have been his mother's favorite. She showered him with gifts and attention, possibly in a neurotic attempt to win his love. As a result, Harold developed a deep dependency on his mother and felt isolated and lonely whenever they were separated.

Horney (1939) hypothesized that a difficult childhood, such as Harold's, is primarily responsible for neurotic needs. These needs become powerful because they are the child's only means of gaining feelings of safety. Harold strove to find safety in the relationship with his mother, who, unfortunately, was incapable of expressing genuine love for her children. Nevertheless, Harold attached himself emotionally to his mother, and she to him.

We cannot say, however, that Harold's current difficulties in attaching himself to a loving wife are an ongoing expression of his desire to possess his mother in a loving relationship. Horney (1939, p. 152) cautioned that no single early experience is responsible for later personality but that "the sum total of childhood experiences brings about a certain character structure, or rather, starts its development." In other words, the totality of early relationships molds personality development. "Later attitudes to others, then, are not repetitions of infantile ones but emanate from the character structure, the basis of which is laid in childhood" (Horney, 1939, p. 87).

Although later experiences can have an important effect, especially in normal individuals, childhood experiences are primarily responsible for personality development. People who rigidly repeat patterns of behavior do so because they interpret new experiences in a manner consistent with those established patterns. For example, Harold's early, unsuccessful attempts to win his mother's genuine love have colored his interpretation of his adult experiences with women. His attitude has been "I am determined to use any means, including bribery, to keep from losing this relationship."

BASIC ANXIETY

Horney (1950) believed that each of us begins life with the potential for healthy development, but, like other living organisms, we need favorable conditions for growth. These conditions must include a warm and loving environment, yet one that is not overly permissive. As children, we need to experience both genuine love and healthy discipline. Such conditions provide for feelings of safety and satisfaction and permit us to grow in accordance with our real selves.

Unfortunately, a multitude of adverse influences may interfere with these favorable conditions. Primary among these is the parents' inability or unwillingness to love the child. Because of their own neurotic needs, parents often dominate, neglect, overprotect, reject, or overindulge. As a result, the child fails to achieve feelings of security and belongingness, and instead develops profound insecurity and a vague sense of apprehension. This condition is called **basic anxiety**, which Horney (1950, p. 18) defined as "a feeling of being isolated and helpless in a world conceived as potentially hostile." Earlier, she gave a more graphic description, calling basic anxiety "a feeling of being small, insignificant, helpless, deserted, endangered, in a world that is out to abuse, cheat, attack, humiliate, betray, envy" (Horney, 1937, p. 92).

Basic anxiety itself is not a neurosis, but "it is the nutritive soil out of which a definite neurosis may develop at any time" (Horney, 1937, p. 89). Basic anxiety is constant and unrelenting, needing no particular stimulus such as taking a test in school or giving a speech. It permeates all relationships with others and leads to unhealthy ways of trying to cope with people.

Horney (1937) identified four basic ways that people in our culture protect themselves against basic anxiety. The first is *affection*, the strategy Harold has used with his mother, wives, and girlfriends. All he wants from these women is to be loved. In his eyes, he demands little and is willing to give much. He has no insights into the real nature of his "love" relationships and is always puzzled when they come to an end.

The second protective device is *submissiveness*. Neurotics may submit themselves either to people or to institutions such as an organization or a religion. Neurotics who submit to another person often do so in order to gain affection. In his marriages Harold believed that he was completely unselfish, self-sacrificing, and willing to submit his wishes to those of his partner.

Neurotics may also try to protect themselves by striving for *power, prestige,* or *possession*. Power is a defense against the real or imagined hostility of others and takes the form of a tendency to dominate others; prestige is a protection against humiliation and is expressed as a tendency to humiliate others; possession acts as a buffer against destitution and poverty and manifests itself as a tendency to deprive others.

The fourth protective mechanism is *withdrawal*. Neurotics frequently protect themselves against basic anxiety either by developing an independence from others or by becoming emotionally detached from them. By psychologically withdrawing, neurotics feel that they cannot be hurt by other people.

These protective devices do not necessarily indicate a neurosis, and Horney believed that all people use them to some extent. They become unhealthy when people feel compelled to rely on them and are thus unable to employ a variety of interpersonal strategies. Compulsion, then, is the salient characteristic of all neurotic drives.

COMPULSIVE DRIVES

Neurotic individuals have the same problems that affect normal people, except neurotics experience them to a greater degree. Everyone uses the various protective devices to guard against the rejection, hostility, and competitiveness of others. But, whereas normal individuals are able to use a variety of defensive maneuvers in a somewhat useful way, neurotics compulsively repeat the same strategy in an essentially unproductive manner.

Horney (1942) insisted that neurotics do not enjoy misery and suffering. They cannot change their behavior by free will but must continually and compulsively protect themselves against basic anxiety. This traps them in a vicious circle in which their compulsive needs to reduce basic anxiety lead to behaviors that perpetuate low self-esteem, generalized hostility, inappropriate strivings for power, inflated feelings of superiority, and persistent apprehension, all of which result in more basic anxiety.

Neurotic Needs

In 1942 Horney tentatively identified 10 categories of **neurotic needs** that characterize neurotics in their attempts to combat basic anxiety. These categories are overlapping, and a single person, such as Harold, might employ more than one. Each of the following neurotic needs relates in some way or another to other people.

1. *The neurotic need for affection and approval.* In their quest for affection and approval neurotics attempt indiscriminately to please others. They try to live up to the expectations of others, tend to dread self-assertion, and are quite uncomfortable with the hostility of others as well as the hostile feelings within themselves.

2. *The neurotic need for a partner.* Lacking self-confidence, neurotics try to attach themselves to a powerful partner. This need includes an overvaluation of love and a dread of being alone or deserted. Harold clung to his relationships with his wives because he had imbued these women with great power, beauty, and importance. Such a relationship, of course, made him feel important, and the loss of the powerful partner was devastating to his self-esteem.

3. *The neurotic need to restrict one's life within narrow borders.* Neurotics frequently strive to remain inconspicuous, to take second place, and to be contented with very little. They downgrade their own abilities and dread making demands on others. For Harold, this need seems to be limited to his relationships with wives and girlfriends, to whom he is submissive and deferent. On his job as a supervisor for an insurance company, however, he dominates his colleagues and tyrannizes his subordinates.

4. *The neurotic need for power.* Power and affection are perhaps the two greatest neurotic needs. The need for power is usually combined with the needs

for prestige and possession and manifests itself as the need to control others and to avoid feelings of weakness or stupidity.

5. *The neurotic need to exploit others.* Neurotics frequently evaluate others on the basis of how they can be used or exploited. At the same time, they fear being exploited by others.

6. *The neurotic need for social recognition or prestige.* Harold was proud that his wives and girlfriends were unusually attractive, and he took pleasure in showing them off. He bought them jewelry and stylish clothes, wore fashionable clothes himself, and always drove an expensive car.

7. *The neurotic need for personal admiration.* Neurotics have a need to be admired for what they are rather than for what they possess. Their inflated self-esteem must be continually fed by the admiration and approval of others.

8. *The neurotic need for ambition and personal achievement.* Neurotics often have a strong drive to be the best—the best salesperson, the best bowler, the best lover. They must defeat other people in order to confirm their superiority.

9. *The neurotic need for self-sufficiency and independence.* Many neurotics have a strong need to move away from people, thereby proving that they can get along without others. The "playboy" who cannot be tied down by any woman exemplifies this neurotic need.

10. *The neurotic need for perfection and unassailability.* By striving relentlessly for perfection, neurotics receive "proof" of their self-esteem and personal superiority. They dread making mistakes and having personal flaws and desperately attempt to hide their weaknesses from others.

Neurotic Trends

As her theory evolved, Horney began to see that the list of 10 neurotic needs could be grouped into three general categories, each relating to a person's basic attitude toward self and others. Later she identified the three basic attitudes or **neurotic trends** as (1) *moving toward people*, (2) *moving against people*, and (3) *moving away from people* (Horney, 1945).

Although these neurotic trends constitute Horney's theory of neurosis, they also apply to normal individuals. There are, of course, important differences between normal and neurotic attitudes. Whereas normal people are mostly or completely conscious of their strategy toward people, neurotics are completely unconscious of their basic attitude; although normals are free to choose their actions, neurotics are forced to act; where normals experience mild conflict, neurotics experience severe and insoluble conflict; and whereas normals can choose from a variety of strategies, neurotics are limited to a single trend.

People can use each of the neurotic trends to solve basic conflict, but unfortunately, these solutions are essentially nonproductive or neurotic. Horney (1950) used the term **basic conflict** because very young children are driven in all three directions—toward, against, and away from people. In healthy children these three drives are not necessarily incompatible. But the feelings of isolation and helplessness that Horney described as *basic anxiety* drive some children to act compulsively, thereby limiting their repertoire to a single neurotic trend. Experiencing basically contradictory attitudes toward others, these children attempt to solve this basic conflict by making one of the three neurotic trends consistently dominant. In moving *toward* people, these children behave in a *compliant* manner as a protection against feelings of *helplessness*; in moving *against* people, other children act with *aggression* to circumvent the *hostility* of others; and in moving *away from* people, still others adopt a *detached* manner as a means of alleviating feelings of *isolation* (Horney, 1945).

Moving Toward People

Horney's concept of **moving toward people** does *not* mean moving toward them in the spirit of genuine love. Rather, it refers to a neurotic need to protect oneself against feelings of helplessness.

In their attempts to protect themselves against feelings of *helplessness*, compliant people employ either or both of the first two neurotic needs, that is, they desperately strive for affection and approval of others, or they seek a powerful partner who will take responsibility for their lives. Horney (1937) referred to these needs as "morbid dependency," a concept that anticipated the currently popular term "codependency."

Harold's behavior is quite consistent with the first two neurotic needs. His strategy is to find an attractive woman, attribute unusual powers to her, and then subordinate his desires to hers. He is willing to allow his partner to choose his clothes, his house, his friends, the movies they see, the food they eat, and the hobbies they have. His weakness and helplessness send a message to his partner, "You must constantly love me and protect me because I am weak and helpless." So far, his wives and girlfriends have received that message, but each has found that taking care of helpless Harold does not meet her own needs.

The neurotic trend of moving toward people involves a complex of strategies. It is "a whole way of thinking, feeling, acting—a whole way of life" (Horney, 1945, p. 55). Horney also called it a philosophy of life. Neurotics who adopt this philosophy are likely to see themselves as loving, generous, unselfish, humble, and sensitive to other people's feelings. They are willing to subordinate themselves to others, to see others as more intelligent or attractive, and to rate themselves according to what others think of them.

Most of these characteristics describe Harold, but only in relation to the woman with whom he is currently "in love." The fact that Harold is capable of adopting other strategies with other people indicates that his behavior is not sufficiently compulsive to be termed neurotic. Unlike a true neurotic, Harold makes generous use of more than one neurotic trend. He is also capable of moving against people.

Moving Against People

Just as compliant people assume that everyone is nice, aggressive people take for granted that everyone is *hostile*; as a result, they adopt the strategy of **moving against people**. Neurotically aggressive people are just as compulsive as compliant people, and their behavior is just as much prompted by basic anxiety. Rather than moving toward people in a posture of submissiveness and dependence, these people move against others by appearing tough or ruthless. They are motivated by a strong need to exploit others and to use them for their own benefit. They seldom admit their mistakes and are compulsively driven to appear perfect, powerful, and superior.

Five of the ten neurotic needs are incorporated in the neurotic trend of moving against people. They include the need to be powerful, to exploit others, to receive recognition and prestige, to be admired, and to achieve.

Harold displays many of these tendencies at work. His subordinates regard him as arrogant, self-centered, and an unreasonable taskmaster. His fellow supervisors and his district manager see him as overly ambitious and somewhat threatening.

Aggressive people play to win rather than for the enjoyment of the contest. They may appear to be hard working and resourceful on the job, but they take little pleasure in the work itself. Their basic motivation is for power, prestige, and personal ambition.

In American society the striving for these goals is usually viewed with admiration. Compulsively aggressive people, in fact, frequently come out on top in many endeavors valued by our society. They may acquire desirable sex partners, high-paying jobs, and the personal admiration of many people. Horney (1945) said that it is not to the credit of our civilization that such characteristics are rewarded while love, affection, and the capacity for true friendship—the very qualities that aggressive people lack—are valued less highly.

Moving toward others and moving against others are, in many ways, polar opposites. The compliant person is compelled to like everyone, whereas the aggressive person sees everyone as a potential enemy. For both types, however, "the center of gravity lies outside the person" (Horney, 1945, p. 65). Both need other people. Compliant people need others to satisfy their feelings of helplessness; aggressive people use others as a protection against real or imagined hostility. With the third neurotic trend, in contrast, other people are of lesser importance.

Moving Away From People

In order to solve the basic conflict of *isolation*, some people behave in a detached manner and adopt a neurotic trend of **moving away from people**. This strategy is an expression of needs for privacy, independence, and self-sufficiency. Again, each of these needs can lead to positive behaviors and, indeed, they are often pursued in a healthy fashion. However, they become neurotic when people try to satisfy them by compulsively putting emotional distance between themselves and other people.

Moving away from people is a neurotic trend that many people use in an attempt to solve the basic conflict of isolation.

Many neurotics find associating with others an intolerable strain. As a consequence, they are compulsively driven to move away from people, to attain autonomy and separateness. They frequently build a world of their own and refuse to allow anyone to get close to them. They value freedom and self-sufficiency and often appear to be aloof and unapproachable. If married, they maintain their detachment even from their spouse. They shun social commitments, but their greatest fear is to need other people.

Although all neurotics possess a need to feel superior, detached personalities have an intensified need to be strong and powerful. Their basic feelings of isolation can be tolerated only by the self-deceptive belief that they are perfect and therefore beyond criticism. They dread competition, fearing a blow to their illusory feelings of superiority. Instead, they prefer that their hidden greatness be recognized without any effort on their part (Horney, 1945).

Although Horney did not explicitly group the 10 neurotic needs within the three neurotic trends, most fit easily into one of these categories. Also, each of the three neurotic trends has an analogous set of characteristics that describe normal individuals. Figure 7.1 summarizes the three *neurotic trends*, the *basic conflicts* that give rise to them, the *outstanding characteristics* of each, the 10 *neurotic needs* that compose them, and the three *analogous* traits that characterize normal people.

NEUROTIC TRENDS

	Toward People	Against People	Away from People
Basic Conflict or Source of Neurotic Trend	Feelings of Helplessness	Protection Against Hostility of Others	Feelings of Isolation
Outstanding Characteristic	Compliant	Aggressive	Detached
Neurotic Needs	1. Affection and Approval 2. Powerful Partner 3. Narrow Limits to Life	4. Power 5. Exploitation 6. Recognition and Prestige 7. Personal Admiration 8. Personal Achievement	9. Self-Sufficiency and Independence 10. Perfection and Unassailability
Normal Analogue	Friendly, Loving	Ability to Survive in a Competitive Society	Autonomous, Serene

Figure 7.1 *Summary of Horney's Neurotic Trends*

INTRAPSYCHIC CONFLICTS

The neurotic trends flow from basic anxiety, which, in turn, stems from a child's relationships with other people. To this point, our emphasis has been on culture and interpersonal conflict. However, Horney did not neglect the impact of intrapsychic factors in the development of personality. As her theory evolved, she began to place greater emphasis on the inner conflicts both normal and neurotic individuals experience. Intrapsychic processes originate from interpersonal experiences, but as they become part of our belief system they develop a life of their own—an existence separate from the interpersonal conflicts that gave them life.

This section looks at two important intrapsychic conflicts; *the idealized self-image* and *self-hatred*. Briefly, the idealized self-image is an attempt to solve conflicts by painting a godlike picture of one's self. Self-hatred is an interrelated yet equally irrational and powerful tendency to despise one's real self. As the person builds an idealized image of the self, the real self lags farther and farther behind. This creates a growing alienation between the real self and the idealized self, and leads the neurotic to hate and despise the actual self because it falls so short in matching the glorified self-image (Horney, 1950).

The Idealized Self-Image

Horney believed that human beings, if given an environment of discipline and warmth, will develop feelings of security, self-confidence, and a tendency to move toward *self-realization*. Unfortunately, early negative influences often impede one's natural tendency toward self-realization, a situation that leaves the person with feelings of isolation and inferiority. Added to this failure is a growing sense of alienation from self.

Feeling alienated from self, the person needs desperately to acquire a stable *sense of identity*. This dilemma can only be solved by creating an **idealized self-image**, an extravagantly positive view of self that exists only in the person's mind. The person "endows himself with unlimited powers and exalted faculties; he becomes a hero, a genius, a supreme lover, a saint, a god" (Horney, 1950, p. 22). The idealized self-image is not a global construction. Neurotics glorify and worship themselves in different ways. Compliant people see themselves as good and saintly; aggressive people build an idealized image of themselves as strong, heroic, and omnipotent; and detached neurotics paint their self-portraits as wise, self-sufficient, and independent.

As the idealized self-image becomes solidified, neurotics begin to believe in the reality of that image. They lose touch with the real self and use the idealized self as the standard for self-evaluation. Rather than growing toward self-realization, they move toward actualizing the idealized self.

Horney (1950) recognized three aspects of the idealized image: (1) the neurotic search for glory; (2) neurotic claims; and (3) neurotic pride.

The Neurotic Search for Glory

As neurotics come to believe in the reality of their idealized self, they begin to incorporate it into all aspects of their lives—their goals, their self-concepts, and their relations with others. Horney (1950) referred to this comprehensive drive toward actualizing the ideal self as the **neurotic search for glory**.

In addition to *self-idealization*, the neurotic search for glory includes three other elements: the need for perfection, neurotic ambition, and the drive toward a vindictive triumph.

The *need for perfection* refers to the drive to mold the whole personality into the idealized self. Neurotics are not content to merely make a few alterations; nothing short of complete perfection is acceptable. They try to achieve perfection by erecting a complex set of "shoulds" and "should nots." Horney (1950) referred to this as the **tyranny of the should.** Striving toward an imaginary picture of perfection, a neurotic "unconsciously tells himself: 'Forget about the disgraceful creature you actually *are*; this is how you *should be'* " (Horney, 1950, p. 64).

A second key element in the neurotic search for glory is *neurotic ambition*, that is, the compulsive drive toward superiority. Although neurotics have an exaggerated need to excel in everything, they ordinarily channel their energies into those activities that are most likely to bring success. This drive, therefore, may take several different forms during a person's lifetime (Horney, 1950). For example, while still in school, a girl may direct her neurotic ambition toward being the best student in school. Later, she may be driven to excel in business or to raise the very best show dogs. Neurotic ambition may also take a less materialistic form, such as being the most saintly or most charitable person in the community.

The third aspect of the neurotic search for glory is the *drive toward a vindictive triumph*, the most destructive element of all. The need for a vindictive triumph may be disguised as a drive for achievement or success, but "its chief aim is to put

others to shame or defeat them through one's very success; or to attain the power
. . . to inflict suffering on them—mostly of a humiliating kind" (Horney, 1950, p. 27).
The drive for a vindictive triumph grows out of the childhood desire to take revenge
for real or imagined humiliations. No matter how successful neurotics are in vin-
dictively triumphing over others, they never lose their drive for a vindictive triumph
but increase it with each victory. Every success raises their fear of defeat and
increases their feelings of grandeur, thus solidifying their need for further vindictive
triumphs.

At work, Harold is not content to get ahead through hard work and equitable
competition. He takes great pleasure in winning promotions, not so much because
he desires the new position, but because it is a way of defeating his rivals for the
job. He frequently uses his superior verbal skills to berate and humiliate both his
fellow supervisors and the employees in his department. Although Harold is
unaware of his vindictive tactics, others are quite aware of them and maintain their
distance from him whenever possible.

Neurotic Claims

A second aspect of the idealized image is **neurotic claims**. In their search for
glory, neurotics build a fantasy world—a world, however, that is out of sync with
the real world. Believing that something is wrong with the outside world, they claim
to the world that they are special and therefore entitled to be treated in accordance
with their idealized view of themselves. Because these demands are very much in
accord with the idealized self-image, they fail to see that their claims of special
privilege are unreasonable.

Neurotic claims grow out of normal needs and wishes, but they are quite different. When normal wishes are not fulfilled, people become understandably frustrated, but when neurotic claims are not met, neurotics become indignant, bewildered, and unable to comprehend why others have not granted their claims. The
difference between normal desires and neurotic claims might be illustrated by a
situation in which many people are waiting in line for tickets for a popular movie.
Most people near the end of the line might wish to be up front, and some of them
may even try some ploy to get a better position. Nevertheless, these people know
that they don't really deserve to cut ahead of others. Neurotic people, on the other
hand, truly believe that they are entitled to be near the front of line, and they feel
no guilt or remorse in moving ahead of others.

Neurotic Pride

The third aspect of an idealized image is **neurotic pride**, a false pride based,
not on a realistic view of the true self, but on a spurious image of the idealized self.

Neurotic pride is qualitatively different from healthy pride or realistic self-
esteem. Genuine self-esteem is based on realistic attributes and accomplishments
and is generally expressed with quiet dignity. Neurotic pride, on the other hand, is

based on an idealized image of self and is usually loudly proclaimed in order to protect and support a glorified view of one's self (Horney, 1950).

Neurotics imagine themselves to be glorious, wonderful, and perfect, so when others fail to treat them with special consideration, their neurotic pride is hurt. To prevent the hurt, they avoid people who refuse to yield to their neurotic claims, and, instead, they try to become associated with socially prominent and prestigious institutions and acquisitions. Harold, for example, was a member of a prestigious social club, wore a Rolex watch, and usually drove a Mercedes. Like others who strive to realize an inflated image through neurotic pride, claims, and search for glory, Harold was filled with unconscious self-hatred.

Self-Hatred

People with a neurotic search for glory can never be happy with themselves, because, when they realize that the real self does not match the insatiable demands of the idealized self, they will begin to hate and despise themselves:

> The glorified self becomes not only a *phantom* to be pursued; it also becomes a measuring rod with which to measure his actual being. And this actual being is such an embarrassing sight when viewed from the perspective of a godlike perfection that he cannot but despise it. (Horney, 1950, p. 110).

Horney (1950) recognized six major ways in which people express self-hatred. First, self-hatred may result in *relentless demands on the self*, which are exemplified by the tyranny of the should. Harold, for example, makes demands on himself that never stop. Even when he achieves a measure of success, he continues to push himself toward perfection.

The second mode of expressing self-hatred is *merciless self-accusation*. Neurotics constantly berate themselves: "If people only knew me, they would realize that I'm pretending to be knowledgeable, competent, and sincere. I'm really a fraud, but no one knows it." Self-accusation may take a variety of forms—from obviously grandiose expressions, such as taking responsibility for natural disasters, to scrupulously questioning the virtue of their own motivations.

Third, self-hatred may take the form of *self-contempt*, which might be expressed as belittling, disparaging, doubting, discrediting, and ridiculing oneself. Self-contempt prevents us from striving for improvement or achievement. A young man may say to himself, "You conceited idiot! What makes you think you can get a date with the best-looking woman in town!" A woman may attribute her successful career to "luck." Although these people may be aware of their behavior, they have no perception of the self-hatred that motivates it.

A fourth expression of self-hatred is *self-frustration*. Horney (1950) distinguished between healthy self-discipline and neurotic self-frustration. The former involves

Self-hatred is sometimes expressed through abuse of alcohol.

postponing or forgoing pleasurable activities in order to achieve reasonable goals. Self-frustration stems from self-hatred and is designed to actualize an inflated self-image. Neurotics are frequently shackled by taboos against enjoyment. "I don't deserve a new car." "I must not wear nice clothes because many people around the world are in rags." "I must not strive for a better job because I'm not good enough for it."

Fifth, self-hatred may be manifested as *self-torment* or self-torture. Although self-torment can exist in each of the other forms of self-hatred, it becomes a separate category when people's main intention is to inflict harm or suffering on themselves. Some people attain masochistic satisfaction by anguishing over a decision, exaggerating the pain of a headache, cutting themselves with a knife, starting a fight that they are sure to lose, or inviting physical abuse.

The sixth and final form of self-hatred is *self-destructive actions and impulses*, which may be either physical or psychological, conscious or unconscious, acute or chronic, carried out in action or enacted only in the imagination. Overeating, abusing alcohol and other drugs, working too hard, driving recklessly, and suicide are common expressions of physical self-destruction. Neurotics may also attack themselves psychologically, for example, quitting a job just when it begins to be fulfilling, breaking off a healthy relationship in favor of a neurotic one, or engaging in promiscuous sexual activities.

Horney (1950, p. 154) summarized the neurotic search for glory and its attendant self-hatred with these descriptive words:

Surveying self-hate and its ravaging force, we cannot help but see in it a great tragedy, perhaps the greatest tragedy of the human mind. Man in reaching out for the Infinite and Absolute also starts destroying himself. When he makes a pact with the devil, who promises him glory, he has to go to hell—to the hell within himself.

FEMININE PSYCHOLOGY

As a woman trained in the pro-masculine psychology of Freud, Horney gradually realized that the traditional psychoanalytic view of women was skewed. She then set forth her own theory of feminine psychology, one that rejected several of Freud's basic ideas.

For Horney, psychic differences between men and women are not the result of anatomy, but rather of cultural and social expectations. Men who subdue and rule women and women who degrade or envy men do so because of the neurotic competitiveness that is rampant in many societies. Horney (1937) insisted that basic anxiety is at the core of men's need to subjugate women and women's wish to humiliate men.

Although Horney (1939) recognized the existence of the *Oedipus complex*, she insisted that it was due to certain environmental conditions and not to biology. If it were the result of anatomy, as Freud contended, it would be universal (as Freud indeed believed). However, Horney (1967) saw no evidence for a universal Oedipus complex. Instead, she held that it is found only in some people and is an expression of the neurotic need for love. We have seen that the neurotic need for affection and the neurotic need for aggression usually begin in childhood and are two of the three basic neurotic trends. A child may passionately cling to one parent and express jealousy toward the other, but these behaviors are means of alleviating basic anxiety and not manifestations of an anatomically based Oedipus complex. Even when there is a sexual aspect to these behaviors, the child's main goal is security, not sexual intercourse.

Horney (1939) found the concept of *penis envy* even less tenable. Although the concept rests on a biological basis, Horney contended that it is contradictory to biological thinking. There is no more anatomical reason why girls should be envious of the penis than boys should desire a breast or a womb. In fact, boys sometimes do express a desire to have a baby, but this is not the result of a universal male "womb envy."

Horney agreed with Adler that many women possess a *masculine protest*; that is, a pathological belief that men are superior to women. This perception easily leads to the neurotic desire to be a man. The desire, however, is not an expression of penis envy but rather "a wish for all those qualities or privileges which in our culture are regarded as masculine" (Horney, 1939, p. 108). (This view is nearly identical to that expressed by Erikson and discussed in Chapter 3.)

Neurotic ambition is at the root of a woman's wish to be a man, just as neurotic feelings of helplessness are the bases for her need to submit herself to a man.

Because these neurotic needs are cultural rather than biological, they can be eliminated through environmental interventions, including psychotherapy.

PSYCHOTHERAPY

Horney believed that neuroses grow out of basic conflict that usually begins in childhood. As people attempt to solve this conflict, they are likely to adopt one of the three neurotic trends, namely, moving toward, against, or away from others. Each of these tactics can produce temporary relief, but eventually they drive the person farther and farther from actualizing the real self and deeper and deeper into a neurotic spiral (Horney, 1950).

The general goal of Horneyian therapy is to help patients gradually grow in the direction of self-realization. More specifically, the aim is to have patients give up the idealized self-image, relinquish the neurotic search for glory, and change self-hatred to acceptance of the real self. Unfortunately, patients are usually convinced that their neurotic solutions are correct, so they are reluctant to surrender their neurotic trends. Even though patients have a strong investment in maintaining the status quo, they do not wish to remain ill. They find little pleasure in their sufferings and would like to be free of them. Unfortunately, they tend to resist change and cling to those behaviors that perpetuate their illness. As we have seen, the three neurotic trends can be cast in favorable terms such as "love," "mastery," and "freedom." Because patients usually see their behaviors in these positive terms, their actions appear to them to be healthy, right, and desirable (Horney, 1942, 1950).

The therapist's task is to convince patients that their present solutions are perpetuating rather than alleviating the core neurosis, a task that takes much time and hard work. Patients may look for quick cures or solutions, but only the long, laborious process of self-understanding can effect positive change. Self-understanding must go beyond information; it must be accompanied by an emotional experience. Patients must understand their pride system, their idealized image, their neurotic search for glory, their self-hatred, their shoulds, their alienation from self, and their conflicts. Moreover, they must see how all these are interrelated and how they all operate to preserve their basic neurosis.

Although a therapist can help encourage patients toward self-understanding, ultimately successful therapy is built on self-analysis (Horney, 1942, 1950). Patients must understand the difference between the idealized self-image and the real self. Fortunately, people possess an inherent curative force that allows them to move inevitably in the direction of self-realization once self-understanding and self-analysis are achieved.

As to techniques, Horneyian therapists use many of the same ones employed by Freudian therapists, especially *dream interpretation* and *free association*. Horney saw dreams as attempts to solve conflicts, but the solutions can be either neurotic or healthy. When therapists provide a correct interpretation, patients are helped toward a better understanding of the real self. "From dreams . . . the patient can catch a glimpse, even in the initial phase of analysis, of a world operating within him which is peculiarly his own and which is more true of his feelings than the world of his illusions" (Horney, 1950, p. 349).

In the second major technique, free association, patients are asked to say everything that comes to mind regardless of how trivial or embarrassing it may seem (Horney, 1987). They are also encouraged to express whatever feelings may arise from the associations. As with dream interpretation, free association eventually reveals patients' idealized self-image and persistent but unsuccessful attempts at accomplishing it.

When therapy is successful, patients gradually develop confidence in their ability to assume responsibility for their psychological development. They move toward self-realization and all those processes that accompany it; they have a deeper and clearer understanding of their feelings, beliefs, and wishes; they relate to others with genuine feelings instead of using them to solve basic conflicts; at work, they take a greater interest in the job itself rather than seeing it as a means to perpetuate a neurotic search for glory.

FROMM'S HUMANISTIC PSYCHOANALYSIS

Although Erich Fromm was trained in Freudian psychoanalysis and influenced by both Harry Stack Sullivan and Karen Horney, he developed a theory of personality that was uniquely his own. Compared with Freud, Fromm placed far more emphasis on social influences on personality; compared with Sullivan, he was much more aware of the influence of culture, economics, and class structure; compared with Horney, he was more likely to take an anthropological and historical view of personality.

Fromm was more than a personality theorist. He was a social critic, psychotherapist, philosopher, biblical scholar, cultural anthropologist, and psychobiographer. His **humanistic psychoanalysis** looks at people from a historical and cultural perspective rather than a strictly psychological one. It is less concerned with the individual and more concerned with those characteristics common to a culture.

BIOGRAPHY OF ERICH FROMM

Like all personality theorists, Erich Fromm's view of human nature was shaped by childhood experiences. With Fromm, a Jewish family life, the suicide of a young woman, and the extreme nationalism of the German people contributed to his conception of humanity.

Fromm was born on March 23, 1900, in Frankfurt, Germany, the only child of middle-class, Orthodox Jewish parents. His father, Naphtali, was the son of a rabbi and the grandson of two rabbis. His mother, Rosa, was the niece of Ludwig Krause, a well-known Talmudic scholar. As a boy, Erich studied the Old Testament with several prominent scholars, including Rabbi Krause. All of these men were "humanists of extraordinary tolerance and with a complete absence of authoritarianism" (Landis & Tauber, 1971, p. xi). Fromm was especially moved by the compassionate and redemptive tone of the prophets Isaiah, Hosea, and Amos. His humanistic psychology can be traced to the reading of these prophets, "with their vision of universal peace and harmony, and their teachings that there are ethical aspects to history— that nations can do right and wrong, and that history has its moral laws" (Landis & Tauber, 1971, p. x). Although Fromm later abandoned organized religion, these early experiences with the Bible and with the Talmudic scholars contributed to his humanistic views.

Fromm's early childhood was less than ideal. He recalled that he had "very neurotic parents," and that he was "probably a rather unbearably neurotic child" (Evans, 1977, p. 56). He saw his father as being moody and his mother as prone to depression. Moreover, he grew up in two very distinct worlds, one the traditional, Orthodox Jewish world, the other the modern, capitalist world. This split existence created tensions that were nearly unbearable, but it generated a lifelong tendency to see events from more than one perspective (Fromm, 1986; Hausdorff, 1972).

When Fromm was 12, he was both shocked and puzzled by the suicide of an attractive young woman who had been an acquaintance of the Fromm family. The woman was intelligent, artistic, and beautiful, yet she killed herself so that she could be buried along with her widowed father who had just died. How could such an action be explained? In the eyes of young Erich, the father was quite uninteresting and unattractive, whereas the daughter seemingly had much to live for. "How is it possible that a beautiful young woman should be so in love with her father that she prefer to be buried with him to being alive to the pleasures of life and painting?" (Fromm, 1962, p. 4).

How was it possible? This question haunted Fromm for the next 10 years and eventually led to an interest in Sigmund Freud and psychoanalysis. As Fromm read Freud, he began to learn about the Oedipus complex and to understand how such an event might be possible. Later, Fromm would interpret the young woman's irrational dependence on her father as a nonproductive symbiotic relationship, but in those early years he was content with the Freudian explanation.

Fromm was 14 when World War I began, too young to fight but not too young to be impressed by the irrationality of the German nationalism that he had observed first hand. He was sure that the British and French were equally irrational, and once again he was struck by a troubling question. How could normally rational and peaceful people become so driven by national ideologies, so intent on killing, so ready to die? "When the war ended in 1918, I was a deeply troubled young man who was obsessed by the question of how war was possible, by the wish to understand the irrationality of human mass behavior, by a passionate desire for peace and international understanding" (Fromm, 1962, p. 9).

During adolescence, Fromm was deeply moved by the writings of Freud and Karl Marx, but he was also stimulated by differences between the two. As he studied more, he began to question the validity of both systems. "My main interest was clearly mapped out. I wanted to understand the laws that govern the life of the individual man, and the laws of society" (Fromm, 1962, p. 9).

After the war, Fromm became a socialist, although, at that time, he refused to join the Socialist Party. Instead, he concentrated on his studies in psychology, philosophy, and sociology at the University of Heidelberg, where he received his Ph.D. at the age of 25. Still not confident that his training could answer such troubling questions as the suicide of the young woman or the insanity of war, Fromm turned to the study of psychoanalysis, believing that it promised answers to questions of human motivation not offered in other fields. From 1925 until 1930 he studied psychoanalysis, first in Munich, then in Frankfurt, and finally at the Berlin Psychoanalytic Institute, where he was analyzed by Hanns Sachs, a student of Freud and the same therapist who later analyzed John Dollard (see Chapter 8). Although Fromm never met Freud, most of his teachers during those years were strict adherents of Freudian theory (Knapp, 1989).

In 1926, the same year that he repudiated Orthodox Judaism, Fromm married Frieda Reichmann, a psychoanalyst who was more than 10 years his senior, and who later would obtain an international reputation for her work with schizophrenic patients. Knapp (1989) claimed that Reichmann was clearly a mother figure to Fromm and that she even resembled his mother. The marriage, however, was not a happy one. They separated in 1930 but were not divorced until much later, after both had emigrated to the United States.

In 1930, Fromm and several others founded the South German Institute for Psychoanalysis in Frankfurt, but with the Nazi threat becoming more intense, he soon moved to Switzerland where he joined the newly founded International Institute of Social Research in Geneva. In 1933, he accepted an invitation to deliver a series of lectures at the Chicago Psychoanalytic Institute. The following year he emigrated to the United States and opened a private practice in New York City.

In both Chicago and New York, Fromm renewed his acquaintance with Karen Horney, whom he had known casually at the Berlin Psychoanalytic Institute. Horney, who was 15 years older than Fromm, eventually became a strong mother figure and mentor to him (Knapp, 1989). Fromm joined Horney's newly formed Association for the Advancement of Psychoanalysis (AAP) in 1941. Although he and Horney had been lovers, by 1943 dissension within the association had made them rivals. When students requested that Fromm, who did not hold an M.D. degree, teach a clinical course, the organization split over his qualifications. With Horney siding against him, Fromm, along with Sullivan, Clara Thompson, and several other members, quit the association and immediately made plans to begin an alternative organization (Quinn, 1987). In 1946, this group established the William Alanson White Institute of Psychiatry, Psychoanalysis and Psychology, with Fromm as both Chairman of the Faculty and Chairman of the Training Committee.

In 1944, Fromm married Henny Gurland, a woman whose interest in religion and mystical thought furthered Fromm's own inclinations toward Zen Buddhism. In 1951, the couple moved to Mexico for a more favorable climate for Henny, who, by then, was in poor health. Fromm joined the faculty at the National Autonomous University in Mexico City, where he established a psychoanalytic department at the Medical School. After his wife died in 1952, he continued to live in Mexico and commuted between his home in Cuernavaca and the United States, where he held various academic positions, including professor of psychology at Michigan State from 1957 to 1961 and adjunct professor at New York University from 1962 to 1970. While in Mexico, he met Annis Freeman, whom he married in 1953. In 1968, Fromm suffered a serious heart attack and was forced to slow down his busy schedule. Still ill, he and his

wife moved to Muralto, Switzerland, in 1974. There he died, March 18, 1980, five days short of his 80th birthday.

Fromm began his professional career as a psychotherapist using orthodox psychoanalytic technique, but after 10 years he became "bored" with the Freudian approach and developed his own more active and confrontational methods (Fromm, 1986; Sobel, 1980). Over the years, his cultural, social, economic, and psychological ideas have attained a wide audience. Among his best known books are *Escape from Freedom* (1941), *Man for Himself* (1947), *Psychoanalysis and Religion* (1950), *The Sane Society* (1955), *The Art of Loving* (1956), *Marx's Concept of Man* (1961), *The Heart of Man* (1964), *The Anatomy of Human Destructiveness* (1973), and *To Have or Be* (1976).

Fromm's theory borrows ideas from Freud, Marx, sociology, cultural anthropology, and religion. Landis and Tauber (1971) listed five important influences on Fromm's thinking: (1) the teachings of the humanistic rabbis; (2) the revolutionary spirit of Karl Marx; (3) the equally revolutionary ideas of Sigmund Freud; (4) the rationality of Zen Buddhism as espoused by D. T. Suzuki; and (5) the writings of Johann J. Bachofen (1815–1887) on matriarchal societies.

BASIC ASSUMPTIONS

Fromm's most basic assumption is that individual personality can only be understood in the light of human history. "The discussion of the human situation must precede that of personality,[and] psychology must be based on an anthro-pologico–philosophical concept of human existence" (Fromm, 1947, p. 45).

Fromm (1947) believed that humans, unlike other animals, have been "torn away" from their prehistoric union with nature. They have no powerful instincts to adapt to a changing world but, instead, have acquired the facility to reason, a condition Fromm called the *human dilemma*. We experience this basic dilemma because we have become separate from nature and yet have the capacity to be aware of ourselves as isolated beings. Our ability to reason, however, is both a blessing and a curse. On the one hand, it permits us to survive, but on the other, it forces us to attempt to solve basic insoluble dichotomies. Fromm referred to these as "existential dichotomies" because they are rooted in our very existence. We cannot do away with these existential dichotomies; we can only react to them relative to our culture and our individual personalities.

The first and most fundamental dichotomy is that between life and death. Self-awareness and reason tell us that we will die, but we try to negate this dichotomy by postulating life after death, an attempt that does not alter the fact that our lives end with death.

A second existential dichotomy is that we are capable of conceptualizing complete self-realization, but, because life is short, we can never reach it. "Only if the life span of the individual were identical with that of mankind could he participate in the human development which occurs in the historical process" (Fromm, 1947, p. 42). Some people try to solve this dichotomy by assuming that their own historical period is the crowning achievement of humanity, while others postulate a continuation of development after death.

The third existential dichotomy is that we are ultimately alone, yet we cannot tolerate isolation. We are aware of ourselves as separate individuals and, at the same time, we are aware that our happiness depends on uniting with our fellow human beings. Although we cannot completely solve the problem of aloneness vs. union, we must make an attempt or else run the risk of insanity.

HUMAN NEEDS

As animals, we are motivated by such physiological needs as hunger, sex, and safety, but we can never resolve our human dilemma by satisfying these animal needs. Only the distinctive *human needs* can move us toward a reunification with the natural world. These **existential needs** have emerged during the evolution of human culture, growing out of our attempts to find an answer to our existence and to avoid becoming insane. Indeed, Fromm (1955) contended that one important difference between mentally healthy individuals and neurotic or insane ones is that healthy people find answers to their existence—answers that more completely correspond to their total human needs. In other words, healthy individuals are better able to find ways of reuniting to the world by productively solving the human needs of *relatedness, transcendence, rootedness, a sense of identity*, and *a frame of orientation*.

Relatedness

The first human or existential need is **relatedness**, the drive for union with another person or persons. Fromm postulated three basic ways in which a person

Relatedness can take the form of submission, power, or love.

may relate to the world: (1) submission, (2) power, and (3) love. A person can submit to another, to a group, or to an institution in order to become one with the world. "In this way he transcends the separateness of his individual existence by becoming part of somebody or something bigger than himself and experiences his identity in connection with the power to which he has submitted" (Fromm, 1981, p. 2).

Whereas submissive people search for a relationship with domineering people, power-seekers welcome submissive partners. When a submissive person and a domineering person find each other, they frequently establish a *symbiotic relationship*, one that is satisfying to both partners. Although such symbiosis may be gratifying, it blocks growth toward integrity and psychological health. The two partners "live on each other and from each other, satisfying their craving for closeness, yet suffering from the lack of inner strength and self-reliance which would require freedom and independence" (Fromm, 1981, p. 2).

Harold, our case study, seeks relatedness through dependency and submission. He depends on his wives or girlfriends to satisfy his needs for submission and wants them to be dependent on him for love, attention, and material possessions. He believes that such a relationship would be true love, but, in reality, it would be founded on mutual dependency. People in symbiotic relationships are drawn to one another, not by love, but by a desperate need for relatedness, a need that can never be completely satisfied by such a partnership. Underlying the union are unconscious feelings of hostility. People in symbiotic relationships blame their partners for not being able to completely satisfy their needs. They find themselves seeking additional submission or power, and, as a result, they become more and more dependent on their partners and less and less of an individual.

Fromm believed that **love** is the only route by which a person can become united with the world and, at the same time, achieve individuality and integrity. He defined love as a "union with somebody, or something outside oneself *under the condition of retaining the separateness and integrity of one's own self*" (Fromm, 1981, p. 3).

Love involves sharing and communion with another, yet it results in a freeing of the person to be unique and separate. It enables a person to satisfy the need for relatedness without surrendering integrity and independence. In love, two people become one, yet remain two.

In *The Art of Loving*, Fromm (1956) identified care, responsibility, respect, and knowledge as four basic elements common to all forms of genuine love. To love another we must *care* for that person and be willing to take care of him or her. Love also means *responsibility*, that is, a willingness and ability to respond. When we love, we respond to our beloveds' physical and psychological needs, respecting them for who they are without trying to change them. But we can respect others only if we have *knowledge* of them. To know others means to see them from their own point of view. Care, responsibility, respect, and knowledge are interrelated. One must *know* another person in order to *respect* her or him; *care* and *responsibility* must be guided by *knowledge*; and knowledge would be shallow if it were not motivated by care and concern (Fromm, 1956).

Transcendence

Like other animals, humans are thrown into the world without their consent or will and then removed from it—again without their consent or will. But unlike other animals, human beings are driven by the need for **transcendence**, that is, the urge to rise above their passive and accidental existence and into "the realm of purposefulness and freedom" (Fromm, 1981, p. 4). Just as relatedness can be pursued through either productive or nonproductive methods, transcendence can be sought through either positive or negative approaches. We can transcend our passive nature by either creating life or by destroying it. Although other animals can create life through reproduction, only humans are aware of themselves as creators. Also, humans can be creative in other ways. They can create art, religions, ideas, laws, material production, and love.

To create means to be active and to care about that which we create. We can also transcend life, however, by destroying it and thus rising above our slain victims. In *The Anatomy of Human Destructiveness* Fromm (1973) argued that humans are the only species to use **malignant aggression**, that is, to kill for reasons other than survival. Although malignant aggression is a dominant and powerful passion in some individuals and cultures, it is not common to all humans. It apparently was unknown to many prehistoric societies, as well as some contemporary "primitive" societies.

Rootedness

A third existential need is for **rootedness**; that is, the need to establish roots or to feel at home again in the world. When humans evolved as a separate species, they lost their home in the natural world. At the same time, their capacity for thought enabled them to realize that they were without a home, without roots. The consequent feelings of isolation and helplessness became unbearable.

Rootedness can be sought in either productive or nonproductive strategies. With the productive strategy, people are weaned from the orbit of their mothers and become fully born; that is, they actively and creatively relate to the world and become whole or integrated. This new tie to the natural world confers security and re-establishes a sense of belongingness and rootedness. However, people may also seek rootedness through the nonproductive strategy of **fixation**, that is, a tenacious reluctance to move beyond the protective security provided by one's mother. People who strive for rootedness through fixation are "afraid to take the next step of birth, to be weaned from the mother's breast. [They] . . . have a deep craving to be mothered, nursed, protected by a motherly figure; they are the externally dependent ones, who are frightened and insecure when motherly protection is withdrawn" (Fromm, 1955, p. 40).

Rootedness can also be seen phylogenetically in the evolution of the human species. Fromm agreed with Freud that incestuous desires are universal, but he disagreed with Freud's belief that they are essentially sexual. According to Fromm (1955, pp. 40–41), incestuous feelings are based in "the deep-seated craving to remain in, or to return to the all-enveloping womb, or to the all-nourishing breasts." Fromm was influenced by J. J. Bachofen's (1861/1967) ideas on early matriarchal societies. Unlike Freud, who believed that early societies were patriarchal, Bachofen held that the mother was the central figure in these ancient social groups. It was she who provided roots for her children and motivated them to either develop their individuality and reason or become fixated and incapable of psychological growth.

Sense of Identity

The fourth human need is for a **sense of identity**, that is, our capacity to be aware of ourselves as a separate entity. Because we have been torn away from nature, the we need to form a concept of the self, to be able to say, "I am I," or "I am the subject of my actions." Fromm (1981) believed that primitive people identified more closely with their clan and did not see themselves as individuals existing apart from their group. Even during medieval times people were identified largely by their social role in the feudal hierarchy. In agreement with Marx, Fromm believed that the rise of capitalism has given people more economic and political freedom. However, this freedom has given only a minority of people a true sense of "I." The identity of most people still resides in their attachment to others or to institutions, such as nation, religion, occupation, or social group.

> Instead of the pre-individualistic clan identity, a new herd identity develops in which the sense of identity rests on the sense of an unquestionable belonging to the crowd. That this uniformity and conformity are often not recognized as such, and are covered by the illusion of individuality, does not alter the facts. (Fromm, 1981, p. 9)

Without a sense of identity, we could not retain our sanity, and this threat provides a powerful motivation for us to do almost anything to acquire a sense of identity. Neurotic people try to attach themselves to powerful others or to social or political institutions. Healthy people, however, have less need to conform to the herd, less need to give up their sense of self. They do not have to surrender their freedom and individuality in order to fit into society because they possess an authentic sense of identity.

Frame of Orientation

A final human need is for a **frame of orientation**. Being split off from nature, we need a road map, a frame of orientation, to make our way through the world. Without such a map we would be "confused and unable to act purposefully and consistently" (Fromm, 1973, p. 230). A frame of orientation enables us to organize the various stimuli that impinge on us. "Man finds himself surrounded by many puzzling phenomena and, having reason, he has to make sense of them, has to put them in some context which he can understand" (Fromm, 1955, p. 63).

Every person has a philosophy, a consistent way of looking at things. Many people take this philosophy or frame of reference for granted so that anything at odds with their view is judged as "crazy" or "unreasonable." Anything consistent with it is seen simply as "common sense." People will do nearly anything to acquire and retain a frame of orientation, even to the extreme of following irrational or bizarre philosophies such as those espoused by Hitler or other fanatical leaders.

A road map without a *goal* or destination is worthless. As humans, we have the mental capacity to imagine many alternative paths to follow. To keep from going insane, however, we need a final goal or "object of devotion." According to Fromm (1973), this goal or object of devotion focuses our energies in a single direction, enables us to transcend our isolated existence, and confers meaning on our lives.

Summary

In addition to physiological or animal needs, people are motivated by five distinctively human needs—relatedness, transcendence, rootedness, a sense of identity, and a frame of orientation. These needs have evolved from our existence as a separate species and are aimed at moving us toward a reunification with the natural world. Fromm believed that lack of satisfaction of any of these needs is unbearable and results in insanity. Thus, we are strongly driven to fulfill them in some way or another, either positively or negatively.

Figure 7.2 shows that relatedness can be satisfied through submission, domination, or love, but only love produces authentic fulfillment; transcendence can be satisfied by either destructiveness or creativeness, but only the latter permits joy; rootedness can be satisfied by either fixation on the mother or by moving forward into full birth and wholeness; the sense of identity can be based on adjustment to

	Negative Components	Positive Components
Relatedness	Submission or Domination	Love
Transcendence	Destructiveness	Creativeness
Rootedness	Fixation	Wholeness
Sense of Identity	Adjustment to a Group	Individuality
Frame of Orientation	Irrational Goals	Rational Goals

Figure 7.2 *Summary of Fromm's Human Needs*

the group, or it can be satisfied through creative movement toward individuality; and a frame of orientation may be either irrational or rational, but only a rational philosophy can serve as a basis for the growth of total personality (Fromm, 1981).

THE BURDEN OF FREEDOM

The central thesis of Fromm's writings is that humans have been torn from nature, yet they remain part of the natural world, subject to the same physical limitations as other animals. As the only animal possessing self-awareness, imagination, and reason, humans are "the freak[s] of the universe" (Fromm, 1955, p. 23). Reason is both a curse and a blessing. It is responsible for feelings of isolation and loneliness, but it is also the process that enables humans to become reunited with the world.

Historically, as people gained more and more economic and political freedom, they came to feel increasingly more isolated. For example, during the Middle Ages people had relatively little personal freedom. They were anchored to prescribed roles in society, roles that provided security, dependability, and certainty. Then, as they acquired more *freedom to* move both socially and geographically, they found that they were *free from* the security of a fixed position in the world. They were no longer tied to one geographic region, one social order, or one occupation. They became separated from their roots and isolated from one another.

A parallel experience exists on a personal level. As children become more independent of their mothers, they gain more *freedom to* express their individuality, to move around unsupervised, to choose their friends and clothes, and so on. At the same time, they experience the burden of freedom; that is, they are *free from* the security of being one with the mother. On both a social and an individual level, this burden of freedom results in **basic anxiety**, or a feeling of being alone in the world.

Mechanisms of Escape

Because basic anxiety produces a frightening sense of isolation and aloneness, people attempt to flee from freedom through a variety of escape mechanisms. In

Escape From Freedom, Fromm (1941) identified three primary mechanisms of escape—authoritarianism, destructiveness, and conformity. Unlike Horney's *neurotic trends*, Fromm's mechanisms of escape are the driving forces in normal people, both individually and collectively.

Authoritarianism

Authoritarianism, which is the tendency to give up one's independence and to unite with a powerful partner, takes two forms—masochism and sadism. **Masochism** results from basic feelings of powerlessness, weakness, and inferiority and is aimed at joining the self to a more powerful person or institution. Masochistic strivings often are disguised as love or loyalty, but, unlike love and loyalty, they can never contribute positively to independence and authenticity.

Compared with masochism, **sadism** is more neurotic and more socially harmful. Like masochism, it is aimed at reducing basic anxiety through achieving unity with another person or persons. Fromm (1941) identified three kinds of sadistic tendencies, all more or less clustered together. The first is manifested as the need to make others dependent on oneself and to gain power over those who are weak. The second is the need to exploit others, to take advantage of them, and to use them for one's benefit or pleasure. A third sadistic tendency is the desire to see others suffer, either physically or psychologically.

Destructiveness

Destructiveness is similar to authoritarianism in that it is rooted in the feelings of aloneness, isolation, and powerlessness. However, unlike sadism and masochism, which depend on a continual relationship with another, destructiveness would eliminate the other.

Both individuals and nations can employ destructiveness as a mechanism of escape. By destroying people and objects a person or a nation attempts to restore lost feelings of power. Serial killers are typically lonely people, searching for union with another person. Their contact with their victims, however, is usually short and ends with the destruction of a human who might have provided intimacy and unity. Obviously, destructiveness is self-defeating, for in destroying, one can no longer unite. Destructive people, however, are attracted to a kind of perverted isolation that would be achieved only if they could eliminate the outside world.

Conformity

The most common means of escape in American society, Fromm believed, is **conformity**. People who conform try to escape from a sense of aloneness and isolation by giving up their individuality and becoming whatever other people desire them to be. Thus, they become automatons or robots reacting predictably and mechanically to the whims of others.

Conformists usually give themselves credit for more individuality than they deserve. They say, "I think so and so," or "I believe this or that," but the "I" to whom they refer is often merely an extension of society and represents a generalized belief or attitude. They tend to value the same music or movies that everyone else values, but, by feeling the way they are supposed to feel in a given situation, they lose their identity as unique individuals.

In summary, people in the modern world are free from many external bonds and free to act according to their own wills, but, at the same time, they do not know what they want, think, or feel. They conform like automatons to some anonymous authority and adopt a self that is not authentic. The more they conform, the more powerless they feel; the more powerless they feel, the more they must conform. People can break this cycle of conformity and powerlessness only by achieving self-realization or positive freedom (Fromm, 1941).

Positive Freedom

The emergence of political and economic freedom does not lead inevitably to the bondage of isolation and powerlessness. A person "can be free and not alone, critical and yet not filled with doubts, independent and yet an integral part of mankind" (Fromm, 1941, p. 257). People can attain this kind of freedom, called **positive freedom**, by a spontaneous and full expression of both their rational and their emotional potentialities. Spontaneous activity is frequently seen in small children and artists who have little or no tendency to conform to whatever others want them to be. They act according to their basic natures and not according to conventional rules.

Positive freedom represents a successful solution to the human dilemma of being part of the natural world and yet separate from it. Through positive freedom and spontaneous activity, we overcome the terror of aloneness, achieve a union of the self with the world, and maintain our individuality.

Fromm (1941) held that love and work are the twin components of positive freedom. Through active love and work we unite with others and with the world without sacrificing our integrity. We affirm our uniqueness as individuals and achieve full realization of our potentialities. Love and work comprise the lone *productive character orientation*.

CHARACTER ORIENTATIONS

Fromm (1947, p. 50) defined *personality* as "the totality of inherited and acquired psychic qualities which are characteristic of one individual and which make the individual unique." The most important of the acquired qualities of personality is **character**, defined as *"the relatively permanent system of all noninstinctual strivings through which man relates himself to the human and natural world"* (Fromm, 1973, p. 226).

People relate to the world in two ways—by acquiring and using things (*assimilation*) and by relating to self and others (*socialization*). In general terms, people can relate to things and to people either nonproductively or productively. The *nonproductive orientations* include the *receptive*, the *exploitative*, the *hoarding*, and the *marketing*.

The single *productive orientation* has three dimensions—*working*, *loving*, and *reasoning*. Personality is always a blend or combination of several orientations, although one orientation is usually dominant.

Nonproductive Orientations

Fromm used the term *nonproductive* to suggest strategies that fail to move people closer to positive freedom and self-realization. Nonproductive orientations are, however, not entirely negative; each has both a negative and a positive aspect.

Receptive

Receptive people feel that the source of all good lies outside themselves and that the only way they can relate to the world is to receive things, including love, knowledge, and material possessions. They are more concerned with receiving than with giving, and they want others to shower them with love, ideas, and gifts. Their positive qualities include loyalty, acceptance, and trust; their negative traits include passivity, submissiveness, servility, and lack of self-confidence.

Exploitative

Exploitative characters, like receptive people, believe that the source of all good is outside themselves. However, unlike receptive people, they aggressively take what they desire, rather than passively receive it. In their social relationships they are likely to use cunning or force to take someone else's friend. An exploitative man may "fall in love" with a married woman, not so much because he is truly fond of her, but because he wishes to exploit her husband. In the realm of ideas, exploitative people prefer to steal or plagiarize rather than create. Unlike receptive characters, they are willing to express an opinion, but it is usually an opinion that has been pilfered.

On the negative side, exploitative characters are egocentric, conceited, arrogant, and seducing. Their positive qualities include impulsiveness, pride, and self-confidence. They are active, captivating, and able to take initiative.

Hoarding

Rather than valuing things outside themselves, **hoarding characters** seek to save that which they have already obtained. They hold everything in and do not let go of anything. They keep their money, their feelings, and their thoughts for themselves. In a love relationship, they try to possess the loved one and to preserve the relationship rather than allowing it to change and grow. They tend to live in the past and are repelled by anything new. They are similar to Freud's anal characters in that they are excessively orderly, stubborn, and miserly. However, Fromm (1964) believed that hoarding characters' anal traits are not the result of sexual drives, but rather are part of their general interest in all that is not alive, including the feces.

Harold has many of the traits of the hoarding character. On the negative side, he is obsessive, possessive, and anxious, but he also has one of the hoarding character's positive traits—loyalty. He would never consider being unfaithful to his wives or girlfriends and is willing to submit himself to their wants and whims.

Marketing

The **marketing character** is an outgrowth of modern commerce, where trade is no longer personal but carried out by large, faceless corporations. Consistent with the demands of modern commerce, marketing characters see themselves as commodities, with their personal value dependent on their exchange value, that is, their ability to sell themselves.

Marketing personalities must see themselves as being in constant demand; they must make others believe that they are skillful and salable. Their personal security rests on shaky ground because they must adjust their personality to that which is currently in fashion. They play many roles and are guided by the motto, "'I am as you desire me'" (Fromm, 1947, p. 73).

Marketing characters are aimless, opportunistic, inconsistent, and wasteful. They are without a past or a future and have no permanent principles or values. They have fewer positive traits than the other orientations because they are basically empty, waiting to be filled with whatever characteristic is most marketable. Some of the positive qualities Fromm (1947) used to describe the marketing personality include changeability, open-mindedness, lack of dogmatism, adaptability, and generosity.

The Productive Orientation

Productive people work toward positive freedom and a continuing realization of their potentials, and thus they are the most healthy of all character types. Only through productive activity can people solve the basic human dilemma, that is, to unite with the world and with others, while, at the same time, retaining their uniqueness and individuality. This task can be accomplished only through productive work, love, and thought. The productive orientation, therefore, is a single type with three interrelated dimensions.

Healthy people value *work*, not as an end in itself, but as a means of creative self-expression. They do not work to exploit others, to market themselves, to withdraw from others, or to accumulate needless material possessions. They are neither lazy nor compulsively active, but use work as a means of producing life's necessities.

Productive *love* is characterized by the four qualities of love discussed earlier—care, responsibility, respect, and knowledge. Healthy people have a passionate love of life and all that is alive (**biophilia**). They desire to further all life—the life of people, animals, plants, ideas, and cultures. They are concerned with the growth and development of themselves as well as others. Biophilic individuals want to influence others through love, reason, and example—not by force. Fromm believed that love of others and self-love are inseparable, but that self-love must come first.

Everyone has the capacity for productive love, but few achieve it because they cannot first love themselves.

Productive *thinking*, which cannot be separated from productive work and love, is motivated by a concerned interest in another person or object. Healthy people see others as they are and not as they would wish them to be. Similarly, they know themselves for who they are and have no need for self-delusion.

Fromm (1970) believed that healthy people rely on some combination of all five character orientations. Their survival as healthy individuals depends on their ability to *receive* things from other people, to *take* things when appropriate, to *preserve* things, to *exchange* things, and to *work*, *love*, and *think* productively.

PERSONALITY DISORDERS

If healthy people are able to work, love, and think productively, then unhealthy personalities are characterized by a failure to use their full potentials, especially their power to love. In our previous discussion of the nonproductive orientations— receptive, exploitative, hoarding, and marketing—the emphasis was mostly on modes of *assimilation*, that is, one's method of acquiring and using objects or things. However, serious psychopathology has its roots in modes of *socialization*, that is, one's pattern of relating to other people. Fromm (1981) held that the psychologically disturbed person is one who is incapable of love and has failed to establish union with others.

Fromm recognized three severe personality disorders—*necrophilia, malignant narcissism*, and *incestuous symbiosis*.

Necrophilia

The term **necrophilia** means love of death and usually refers to a sexual perversion in which a person desires sexual contact with a corpse. However, Fromm (1964, 1973) used necrophilia in a more generalized sense to denote any attraction to death. Necrophilia is an alternative character orientation to *biophilia*. People naturally love life, but when social conditions stunt biophilia, they may adopt a necrophilic orientation.

Necrophilic personalities hate humanity; they are the racists, warmongers, and bullies of the world; they love bloodshed, destruction, terror, and torture; and they delight in destroying life. They are strong advocates of law and order; love to talk about sickness, death, and burials; and are fascinated by dirt, decay, corpses, and feces. They prefer night to day and love to operate in darkness and shadow.

Necrophilic people do not simply *behave* in a destructive manner; rather, their destructive behavior is a reflection of their basic *character*. All of us behave aggressively and destructively at times, but the necrophilic person's entire life revolves around death, destruction, disease, and decay.

Malignant Narcissism

If all of us display some necrophilic behavior, so too are all of us narcissistic. In its benign form, **narcissism** is manifested as a greater interest in our own body and concerns than in those of others. In its malignant form, narcissism impedes our perception of reality so that everything belonging to our self is highly valued and everything belonging to another is devalued. Narcissistic people are preoccupied with themselves, but this concern is not limited to admiring themselves in a mirror. Preoccupation with one's body often leads to **hypochondriasis,** or an obsessive attention to one's health. Fromm (1964) also recognized **moral hypochondriasis**, which is a preoccupation with *guilt* about previous transgressions. People who are fixated on themselves are likely to internalize experiences and to dwell on both physical and moral aspects of their being. "The narcissism underlying physical or moral hypochondriasis is the same as the narcissism of the vain person" (Fromm, 1964, p. 69). Each stems from an intense interest in one's self.

Narcissistic people possess what Horney called "neurotic claims." They achieve security by holding onto the distorted belief that their extraordinary personal qualities give them superiority over everyone else. Because what they *have*—looks, physique, wealth—is so wonderful, they believe that they need not *do* anything to prove their value. Their sense of worth depends on their narcissistic self-image and not on their achievements. When their efforts are criticized by others, they react with anger and rage, frequently striking out against their critics, trying to destroy them. If the criticism is overwhelming, they may be unable to destroy it, and so they turn their rage inward. The result is *depression*, a feeling of worthlessness that marks unconscious narcissism. Whereas depression, intense guilt, and hypochondriasis may appear to be anything but self-glorification, Fromm believed that each of these could be symptomatic of deep underlying narcissism.

Incestuous Symbiosis

A third pathological orientation is **incestuous symbiosis**, or an extreme dependence on the mother or mother surrogate. Incestuous symbiosis is an exaggerated form of the more common and more benign *mother fixation*. Men with a mother fixation need a woman to care for them, comfort them, and admire them; they feel somewhat anxious and depressed when their needs are not fulfilled. This condition is relatively normal and does not greatly interfere with one's daily life.

However, with incestuous symbiosis, people are inseparable from the *host* person; their personalities are blended with the other person, and their individual identities are lost. Incestuous symbiosis originates in infancy as a natural attachment to the mothering one. The attachment is more crucial and fundamental than any sexual interest that may develop during the Oedipal period. Fromm agreed more with Sullivan than with Freud in suggesting that attachment to the mother rests on the need for security and not for sex. "Sexual strivings are not the cause of the fixation to mother, but the *result*" (Fromm, 1964, p. 99).

People living in incestuous symbiotic relationships feel extremely anxious and frightened if that relationship is threatened. They believe that they cannot live without their mother substitute. (The host need not be another human—it can be a family, clan, church, or country.) The incestuous orientation distorts reasoning powers, destroys the capacity for authentic love, and prevents people from achieving independence and integrity.

In summary, Fromm (1964, p. 107) wrote:

> The tendency to remain bound to the mothering person and her equivalents—to blood, family, tribe—is inherent in all men and women. It is constantly in conflict with the opposite tendency—to be born, to progress, to grow. In the case of normal development, the tendency for growth wins. In the other case a severe pathology, the regressive tendency for symbiotic union, wins, and it results in the person's more or less total incapacitation.

In some severely pathological personalities, such as Adolf Hitler, necrophilia, malignant narcissism, and incestuous symbiosis are combined into what Fromm (1964) termed the *syndrome of decay*. Such people are attracted to death, take pleasure in destroying those who are regarded as inferiors, and act in the name of the homeland, the clan, or the party. Fromm contrasted the syndrome of decay with the *syndrome of growth*: The former is a convergence of necrophilia, malignant narcissism, and incestuous symbiosis; the syndrome of growth is made up of the opposite qualities—biophilia, love, and positive freedom. As shown in Figure 7.3, both the

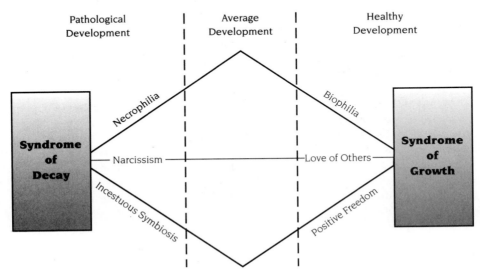

Figure 7.3   *Three pathological orientations converge in the syndrome of decay, and three healthy orientations converge in the syndrome of growth.*

syndrome of decay and the syndrome of growth are extreme forms of development; most people are probably in the average range.

PSYCHOTHERAPY

Fromm was trained as an orthodox Freudian analyst but became bored with standard analytic techniques. "With time I came to see that my boredom stemmed from the fact that I was not in touch with the life of my patients" (Fromm, 1986, p. 106). He then evolved his own system of therapy, which he called *humanistic psychoanalysis*. Compared with Freud, Fromm was much more concerned with the interpersonal aspects of a therapeutic encounter. He agreed with Adler, Sullivan, and Horney that therapy is built on a personal relationship between therapist and patient and that accurate communication is essential to therapeutic growth.

Fromm believed that patients come to therapy seeking satisfaction of their basic human needs—relatedness, transcendence, rootedness, a sense of identity, and a frame of orientation. The task for the therapist, then, is to relate "as one human being to another with utter concentration and utter sincerity" (Fromm, 1963, p. 184). In this spirit of relatedness the patient will once again feel at one with another person. Although *transference* and even *countertransference* may exist within this relationship, the important point is that two real human beings are involved with one another.

As part of his attempt to achieve shared communication, Fromm asked patients to reveal their dreams. He believed that dreams, as well as fairy tales and myths, are expressed in symbolic language—the only universal language humans have developed (Fromm, 1951). Because dreams have meaning beyond the individual dreamer, Fromm would ask for the patient's associations to the dream material. Not all dream symbols, however, are universal; some are accidental and depend on the dreamer's mood before going to sleep; others are regional or national and depend on climate, geography, and dialect. Many symbols have several meanings due to the variety of experiences that are connected with them. For example, fire may symbolize warmth and home to some people, but death and destruction to others. Similarly, the sun may represent a threat to desert people, but growth and life to people in cold climates.

Fromm (1963) believed that the therapist should not try to be too scientific in understanding the patient. Only with the attitude of relatedness can another person be truly understood. The patient should not be viewed as an illness or a thing, but as a person, with all of the same human needs as the therapist.

FROMM'S METHODS OF INVESTIGATION

Fromm gathered data on human personality from many sources, including psychotherapy, cultural anthropology, and psychohistory. In this section we look briefly at his anthropological study of life in a Mexican village and his psychobiographical analysis of Adolf Hitler.

Social Character in a Mexican Village

During the late 1950s and extending into the mid-1960s, Fromm and a group of psychologists, psychoanalysts, anthropologists, physicians, and statisticians studied social character in an unidentified Mexican village about 50 miles south of Mexico City. The team interviewed every adult and half the children in this isolated farming village of 162 households and about 800 inhabitants. The people of the village were mostly farmers, earning a living from small plots of fertile land. As Fromm and Michael Maccoby (1970, p. 37) described them:

> They are selfish, suspicious of each others' motives, pessimistic about the future, and fatalistic. Many appear submissive and self-deprecatory, although they have the potential for rebelliousness and revolution. They feel inferior to city people, more stupid, and less cultured. There is an overwhelming feeling of powerlessness to influence either nature or the industrial machine that bears down on them.

Could one expect to find Fromm's character orientations in such a society? After living among the villagers and gaining their acceptance, the research team employed an assortment of techniques designed to answer this and other questions. Included among the research tools were extensive interviews, dream reports, detailed questionnaires, and two projective techniques—the Rorschach Inkblot Test and the Thematic Apperception Test.

Recall that Fromm believed that the *marketing character* was a product of modern commerce, and that it is most likely to exist in societies where trade is no longer personal and where people regard themselves as commodities. Not surprisingly, the research team found that the marketing orientation did not exist among these peasant villagers.

However, the researchers did find evidence for several other character types, the most common of which was the *nonproductive-receptive type*. People of this orientation tended to look up to others and devoted much energy in trying to please those whom they regarded as superiors. Working men who belonged to this type would, on paydays, accept their pay in servile fashion, as if they had somehow not earned it.

The second most frequently found personality type was the *productive-hoarding character*. People of this type were hard working, productive, and independent. They usually farmed their own plot of land and relied on saving part of each crop for seed and for food in the event of future crop failure. Hoarding, rather than consuming, was essential to their lives.

The *unproductive-exploitative personality* was identified as a third character orientation. Men of this type were most likely to get into knife or pistol fights, whereas the women tended to be malicious gossip mongers (Fromm & Maccoby, 1970). Only about 10 percent of the population were dominantly exploitative, a surprisingly small percentage considering the extreme poverty of the village.

An even smaller number of inhabitants were described as *productive-exploitative*— no more than 15 individuals in the whole village. Among them were the richest and most powerful men in the village—men who had taken advantage of new agricultural technology and the recent increase in tourism to accumulate capital. They had also taken advantage of the nonproductive-receptive villagers by keeping them economically dependent.

In general, Fromm and Maccoby (1970) reported a remarkable similarity between character orientations in this Mexican village and the theoretical orientations that Fromm had suggested some years earlier. This anthropological study, of course, cannot be considered as confirmation of Fromm's theory. As one of the study's principal investigators, Fromm may simply have found what he had expected to find.

A Psychohistorical Study of Hitler

Following Freud (see Chapter 2) and Erikson (see Chapter 3), Fromm examined historical documents in order to sketch a psychological portrait of a prominent

Adolf Hitler personified for Fromm the syndrome of decay.

person, a technique called *psychohistory* or *psychobiography*. The subject of Fromm's most complete psychobiographical study was Freud (Fromm, 1959), but Fromm (1941, 1973, 1986) also wrote at length on the life of Adolf Hitler.

Fromm regarded Hitler as the world's most conspicuous example of a person with the *syndrome of decay*, that is, a combination of necrophilia, malignant narcissism, and incestuous symbiosis. Hitler displayed all three pathological disorders: He was attracted to death and destruction; he was narrowly focused on self-interests, greatly delighting in self-aggrandizement; and he was driven by an incestuous devotion to the Germanic "race," being fanatically dedicated to preventing its blood from being polluted by Jews and other "non-Aryans."

Unlike some psychoanalysts who look only to early childhood for clues to adult personality, Fromm believed that each stage of development is important and that nothing in Hitler's early life bent him inevitably toward the syndrome of decay. As a child, Hitler was perhaps spoiled by his mother, but her indulgence did not cause his later pathology. It did, however, foster narcissistic feelings of self-importance. "Hitler's mother never became to him a person to whom he was lovingly or tenderly attached. She was a symbol of the protecting and admiring goddesses, but also of the goddess of death and chaos" (Fromm, 1973, p. 378).

Hitler was an above-average student in elementary school, but a failure in high school. During adolescence he experienced some conflict with his father, who wanted him to be more responsible and to take a reliable civil service job. Hitler, on the other hand, somewhat unrealistically desired to be an artist. Also during this time he began to lose himself more and more in fantasy. His narcissism ignited a burning passion for greatness as an artist or architect, but reality brought him failure after failure in this area. "Each failure caused a graver wound to his narcissism and a deeper humiliation than the previous one; in the same degree as his failures, grew also his indulgence in fantasy, his resentment, his wish for revenge, and his necrophilia" (Fromm, 1973, p. 395).

The terrible realization of his failure as an artist was blunted by the outbreak of World War I. His fierce ambition could now be channeled into being a great war hero fighting for his homeland. Although he was no great hero, he was a responsible, disciplined, and dutiful soldier. After the war, however, he experienced more failure. Not only had his beloved nation lost, but revolutionaries within Germany had "attacked everything that was sacred to Hitler's reactionary nationalism, and they won. . . . The victory of the revolutionaries gave Hitler's destructiveness its final and ineradicable form" (Fromm, 1973, p. 394).

We saw earlier that *necrophilia* does not simply refer to behavior; it pervades a person's entire character. And so it was with Hitler. After he came to power, he demanded that his enemies not merely surrender, but that they be annihilated as well. His necrophilia was expressed in his mania for destroying buildings and cities, his orders to kill "defective" people, his boredom, and his slaughter of millions of Jews.

Another trait Hitler manifested was *malignant narcissism*. He was interested only in himself, his plans, and his ideology. His conviction that he could build a "Thousand-Year Reich" shows an inflated sense of self-importance. He had no interest in anyone unless that person was of service to him. His relations to women lacked love and tenderness; he seemed to have used them solely for perverted personal pleasure, especially for voyeuristic satisfaction.

According to Fromm's analysis, Hitler also possessed an *incestuous symbiosis*, manifested by his passionate devotion, not to his real mother, but to the Germanic "race." Consistent with this trait, he also was sadomasochistic, withdrawn, and lacking in feelings of genuine love or compassion. All these characteristics, Fromm contended, did not make Hitler psychotic. They did however, make him a sick and dangerous man.

Insisting that Hitler not be seen as inhuman, Fromm (1973, p. 433) concluded his psychohistory with these words: "Any analysis that would distort Hitler's picture by depriving him of his humanity would only intensify the tendency to be blind to the potential Hitlers unless they wear horns."

CONCEPT OF HUMANITY

Whereas Horney's concept of humanity was based almost entirely on her clinical experiences with neurotic patients, Fromm's view came from his understanding of history, anthropology, and economics, as well as his experiences as a therapist. According to Horney, the prime difference between healthy and neurotic individuals is the degree of compulsivity with which they move toward, against, or away from people.

The compulsive nature of neurotic trends suggests that Horney's concept of humanity is deterministic. However, healthy people have a large element of free choice in their lives. Even neurotic individuals, through psychotherapy and hard work, can wrest some control over those intrapsychic conflicts. For this reason Horney's psychoanalytic social theory is rated slightly higher on *free will* than on determinism.

On the same basis, Horney's theory is somewhat more *optimistic* than pessimistic. If basic anxiety (the feeling of being alone and helpless in a potentially hostile world) can be avoided, people will feel safe and secure in their interpersonal relations and consequently will grow toward *self-realization*.

In general, Fromm's social psychoanalytic theory is more pessimistic than Horney's. He believed that human beings are the freaks of nature, the only species to have evolved the unfortunate combination of minimal instinctive powers and maximal brain development.

Fromm believed that most people remain isolated and lost, but he was hopeful enough to believe that some people realize their potentials and become reunited with other people and with nature. He had a rather negative attitude toward modern capitalism, which he insisted results in most people feeling isolated and alone while clinging desperately to the illusion of independence and freedom.

On the dimension of *free choice vs. determinism*, Fromm took a middle position, insisting that this issue cannot be applied to the entire species. Instead, he believed that individuals have degrees of inclinations toward action, even though they are seldom aware of all the possible alternatives. Nevertheless, their ability to reason enables them to take an active part in their own fate (Fromm, 1964).

On the dimension of *causality vs. teleology*, both Horney and Fromm tended to slightly favor teleology. Horney believed that the natural goal for people is self-realization, although childhood experiences can block that movement. Fromm also believed that people constantly strive for a frame of orientation, a roadmap, by which to plan their lives into the future.

Both Horney and Fromm took a middle stance regarding *conscious vs. unconscious motivation*. Horney believed that most people have only limited awareness of their motives. Neurotics, especially, have little understanding of themselves and do not see that their behaviors guarantee the continuation of their neuroses. Fromm placed slightly more emphasis on conscious motivation, contending that one of the uniquely human traits is *self-awareness*. Humans are the only animal who can reason, visualize the future, and consciously strive toward self-erected goals. Fromm insisted, however, that self-awareness is a mixed blessing, and that many people repress their basic character in order to avoid mounting anxiety.

Both Horney and Fromm emphasized *social influences* more than biological ones. For example, Horney believed that psychological differences between men and women are due more to cultural and societal expectations than to anatomy. To her, the Oedipus complex and penis envy are not inevitable consequences of biology but rather are shaped by social forces. Fromm, too, emphasized social influences over biological ones, insisting that human personalities are historically and culturally determined.

Because Horney's theory looks almost exclusively at neuroses, it tends to highlight *similarities among people* more than uniqueness. Not all neurotics are alike, of course, and Horney described three basic types—the helpless, the hostile, and the detached. However, she placed little emphasis on individual differences within each of these categories.

Fromm also tended to emphasize similarities among people, but not to the same extent as did Horney. He believed that, although history and culture impinge heavily on personality, we can retain some degree of uniqueness. We are one species sharing many of the same human needs, but interpersonal experiences throughout our life give us some measure of uniqueness.

Related Research

Although the third issue of Volume 51 of the *American Journal of Psychoanalysis* (1991) was entirely devoted to Horney's theory, psychoanalytic social theory has not produced much research specifically designed to test its major assumptions. Nevertheless, some researchers have investigated issues that relate to the theories of both Horney and Fromm.

In one study of codependency in women with an alcoholic parent, Lyon and Greenberg (1991) relied on Horney's concept of morbid dependency for their definition of codependency. These authors theorized that women learn to receive approval and to build self-esteem by conforming to the demands of an exploitative person, and suggested that women of alcoholic parents will continue to seek opportunities to help people who are exploiting them. Lyon and Greenberg hypothesized that women with an alcoholic parent would offer more help to a person perceived as exploitative than to a person seen as nurturant. In this experiment 24 undergraduate women with one alcoholic parent were compared with 24 women with no alcoholic parent on their willingness to offer assistance. The methodology called for three subjects and one confederate to meet with the male experimenter who was administering a battery of tests. The confederate and the experimenter spoke briefly to each, demonstrating to the subjects that they were acquainted. Then, with the experimenter out of the room, the confederate interrupted the others on the pretense of breaking her pencil. After asking if anyone could lend her a new pencil, she uttered one of two comments regarding the experimenter. In the *nurturant condition*, she said that the experimenter had dated her friend, and she further commented that the experimenter had helped her friend with laundry and other tasks. In the *exploitative condition*, the confederate went through the same routine except that she stated that the experimenter had exploited the friend, getting her to do his laundry and other jobs. Then, when the experimenter came back, he asked the subjects to volunteer their time, anywhere from 0 to 3 hours, to help with a worthwhile project. As expected, women with an alcoholic parent volunteered more than twice as much time to an experimenter perceived as exploitative than to the same person portrayed as nurturant. Moreover, the codependent women liked the exploitative experimenter better than the nurturant one and also saw him as needing to be nurtured. These findings support Horney's concept that people with neurotic needs to move toward others will do nearly anything to win the approval of other people.

Lonky, Kaus, and Roodin (1984) have developed an Existential Coping Interview (ECI) designed to measure Fromm's five existential needs—relatedness, transcendence, rootedness, identity, and frame of orientation. The ECI is a semistructured interview consisting of 35 questions that probe subjects' affirmative (positive) or abortive (negative) modes of coping with personal loss. Responses are ranged on a 4-point scale from "strongly affirmative" to "strongly abortive." For the relatedness need, for example, the interviewer asks subjects whether they sought others or joined groups following a personal loss. Responses indicating that subjects appropriately sought out others were rated as "strongly affirmative," whereas those that reflected an over-reliance on others were seen as "strongly abortive."

From a sample of 70 adult women who had taken the Defining Issues Test (Rest, 1979), Lonky, Kaus, and Roodin (1984) selected 13 principled reasoning subjects and 15 who manifested conventional reasoning. After administering the Existential Coping Interview to these women, they found that conventional moral reasoners dealt with personal loss in an abortive or nonproductive manner, whereas principled reasoners coped with loss by using affirmative or productive strategies. They also found that existential coping was positively related to openness to experience and to problem-focused coping strategies. Although this study suggests that the Existential Coping Interview has both reliability and validity in measuring Fromm's existential needs, little additional research has been generated by ECI.

CRITIQUE OF PSYCHOANALYTIC SOCIAL THEORY

The social psychoanalytic theories of both Horney and Fromm provide interesting perspectives on the nature of humanity. However, both suffer from lack of current research that would support their suppositions.

The strength of Horney's theory is her lucid portrayal of the neurotic personality. No other personality theorist has written so well (or so much) about neuroses. Her comprehensive descriptions of the neurotic, frequently illustrated by interesting case studies, provide an excellent framework for understanding many personalities. However, her nearly exclusive concern with neurotics is a serious limitation to her theory. Her references to the nonneurotic personality are general and not well explicated. She says that people by their very nature will strive toward self-realization, but she paints no clear picture of what self-realization would be.

On its power to *generate research*, Horney's theory falls short. Horney's speculations do not easily yield testable hypotheses, and therefore they lack verifiability. The validity of her objections to Freud's assumptions concerning the Oedipus complex and penis envy could be determined, but this would involve tests of Freud's theory rather than Horney's.

Horney's theory was based largely on clinical practice—experiences that put her in contact mostly with neurotic individuals. To her credit she was reluctant to make specific assumptions about psychologically healthy individuals. Because her theory deals mostly with neurotics, it is rated very high on its ability to *organize knowledge* of neurotics, but very low on its capacity to explain what is known about people in general.

As a *guide to action*, Horney's theory fares somewhat better. Teachers, therapists, and especially parents can use her assumptions concerning the development of neurotic trends to provide a warm, safe, and accepting environment for their students, patients, or children. Beyond this, however, the theory is not specific enough to give the practitioner a clear and detailed course of action. On this criterion the theory receives a moderate rating.

Is Horney's theory *internally consistent*, with clearly defined terms used uniformly? In Horney's book, *Neurosis and Human Growth* (1950), her concepts and formulations are precise, consistent, and unambiguous. However, when all her works are examined, a different picture emerges. Through the years, she used terms such as neurotic needs and neurotic trends sometimes separately and sometimes interchangeably. Also, the terms basic anxiety and basic conflict were not always clearly differentiated. These inconsistencies render her entire work somewhat inconsistent, but, again, her final theory (1950) is a model of lucidity and consistency.

Another criterion of a useful theory is *parsimony*, and Horney's final theory, as expressed in the last chapter of *Neurosis and Human Growth* (Horney, 1950, chap. 15), would receive a high mark on this standard. This chapter, which provides a useful and concise introduction to Horney's theory of neurotic development, is relatively simple, straightforward, and clearly written.

Erich Fromm, perhaps, was the most brilliant essayist of all personality theorists. He wrote beautiful essays on international politics (Fromm, 1961), on the relevance of biblical prophets for people today (Fromm, 1986), on the psychological problems of the aging (Fromm, 1981), on Marx, Hitler, Freud, Christ, and myriad other topics. Regardless of the subject matter, at the core of all Fromm's writings was an unfolding of the essence of human nature.

Like other psychodynamic theorists, Fromm tended to take a global approach to theory construction, erecting a grand, highly abstract model that was, perhaps, more philosophical than scientific. His insights into human nature strike a responsive chord, as evidenced by the popularity of his books; but are they scientific?

How do Fromm's ideas rate on the five criteria of a useful theory? First, Fromm's imprecise and vague terms have rendered his ideas nearly sterile as a *generator of empirical research*. He did not evolve his theory as a consequence of continuing research; rather, his research (for example, his study of the Mexican village) came well after his theory had been established.

Second, the breadth of Fromm's theory enables it to *organize and explain* much of what is known concerning human personality. However, the theory's lack of precision makes prediction and verification difficult.

As a *guide to action*, Fromm's writings have little value, except to stimulate readers to think productively. Unfortunately, neither the researcher nor the therapist receive much practical information from Fromm's essays.

Fromm's views are *internally consistent* in the sense that a single theme runs throughout his writings. However, the theory lacks a structured taxonomy, a set of operationally defined terms, and a clear limitation of scope. Therefore, it rates low on internal consistency.

Finally, are Fromm's writings *parsimonious*? Because he was reluctant to abandon earlier concepts and formulations or to relate them precisely to his later ideas, Fromm's theory lacks simplicity and unity. For example, the three major personality disorders—necrophilia, malignant narcissism, and incestuous symbiosis—are not integrated into the different character orientations. Also, the mechanisms of escape would seem to be related to both the character orientations and the personality disorders, but Fromm did not specify the nature of this relationship.

Chapter Summary

The psychoanalytic social theories of Horney and Fromm go beyond extending psychoanalysis to cultural and sociological issues. Though similar to each other, they are quite different from orthodox Freudian theory. Horney objected to the rigidity of Freud's views, especially those regarding women, and insisted that social and cultural influences were more important than biological ones. To her, people's experiences in childhood with warm and accepting parents or with cold and rejecting ones lay the foundation upon which they erect either a healthy or a neurotic personality. When children lack warmth and affection, their needs for safety and satisfaction are unfilled, and they develop feelings of isolation and helplessness in a potentially hostile world. These feelings of *basic anxiety* prevent them from moving spontaneously toward, against, or away from other people.

The inability to employ different tactics in their relationships with others generates basic conflict, which results in people being compulsively driven to solve their problems by (1) attaching themselves to a powerful partner in a posture of compliance and submissiveness; (2) striking out against people in an effort to exploit, embarrass, or master them; or (3) adopting a detached attitude, manifested by independence and separation from people.

These three *neurotic trends* (moving toward, against, and away from people) are a combination of 10 *neurotic needs* that Horney had earlier identified and are reactions to *interpersonal conflicts*. In her later writings she identified two major *intrapsychic conflicts*—the idealized self-image and self-hatred. The *idealized self-image* represents neurotics' attempts to solve conflicts by constructing a godlike picture of themselves. *Self-hatred* is the tendency for neurotics to hate and despise the real self.

Horney believed that psychological differences between men and women are not due to anatomy but to cultural and social expectations. Many men wish to subjugate women, and many women desire to humiliate men, but these needs are neurotic and result from basic anxiety.

The Horneyian approach to *psychotherapy* is to bring about growth toward actualization of the real self. To accomplish this, the patient must understand that the idealized self-image is a false picture of the true self and he or she must work toward relinquishing the neurotic search for glory and change self-hatred into acceptance of the real self.

Horney's *concept of humanity* is somewhat positive and optimistic. People possess an inherent drive toward self-realization and, in the absence of basic anxiety, will ultimately achieve it. Social influences, especially those of early childhood, sometimes block the road to self-realization, but through therapy and hard work people can overcome those obstacles.

Although Horney's formulation of neurotic development was well-conceived, her general theory of personality rates low on its ability to generate research and to organize knowledge. It is moderately useful as a guide to action and is somewhat parsimonious and internally consistent.

Fromm's basic thesis is that modern-day people have been torn away from their prehistoric union with nature and also with one another, yet they have the power of reasoning, foresight, and imagination. This combination of lack of animal instincts and presence of rational thought makes humans the freaks of the universe. Self-awareness contributes to feelings of loneliness, isolation, and homelessness. To escape from these feelings, people strive to become reunited with others and with nature.

Only the uniquely *human needs* can move people toward reunification. These needs include *relatedness*, the need to unify with another person through submission, power, or love; *transcendence*, the need to rise above a passive existence and create or destroy life; *rootedness*, the need to establish roots; a *sense of identity*, a feeling of "I" or "me;" and a *frame of orientation*, or the need to develop a consistent way of looking at the world.

Fromm believed that during our history as a species, we have gained a degree of economic and political freedom, but this achievement has brought about ever greater feelings of isolation and separation from the world. This *burden of freedom* has produced *basic anxiety*, or a sense of being alone in the world. To relieve basic anxiety, we employ various *mechanisms of escape*, especially authoritarianism, destructiveness, and conformity. Some people succeed in becoming one with the world and acquire *positive freedom*, or the spontaneous activity of a whole, integrated personality.

In his early writings Fromm identified one productive and four nonproductive *character orientations*. The *nonproductive types*, which have both positive and negative traits, include *receiving, exploiting, hoarding*, and *marketing*. The *productive orientation* has three dimensions: loving, working, and thinking. Healthy people are characterized by all three and also by *biophilia*, or a passionate love of life and all that is living.

The opposite of biophilia is *necrophilia*, or the love of death, destruction, and decay. Necrophilia is one of three traits making up the *syndrome of decay*, the other two being *malignant narcissism*, or infatuation with self, and *incestuous symbiosis*, or the tendency to remain bound to the mothering person or her equivalents.

The goal of Fromm's *psychotherapy* is to establish union with patients so that they can become reunited with the world. In his *concept of humanity*, Fromm takes a middle position on free will vs. determinism, optimism vs. pessimism, conscious vs. unconscious forces, and uniqueness vs. similarities. His theory is rated high on teleology and very high on social influences.

As a scientific theory, unfortunately, Fromm's psychoanalytic social theory cannot be rated high. It has above-average ability to organize knowledge, but it has generated very little empirical research. It is also rated low on being a practical guide to action, on internal consistency, and on parsimony.

Suggested Readings

FROMM, E. (1947). *Man for himself: An inquiry into the psychology of ethics*. New York: Holt, Rinehart and Winston.
In this book Fromm discusses the various character orientations and suggests that the productive type is the highest achievement of humanity. He also insists that psychology cannot be separated from philosophical and ethical issues.

FROMM, E. (1981). Values, psychology and human existence. In E. Fromm, *On disobedience and other essays* (pp. 1–15). New York: Seabury Press.

This short chapter is an excellent introduction to Fromm's most recent thinking. Emphasis is on the five human needs—relatedness, transcendence, rootedness, sense of identity, and a frame of orientation.

HORNEY, K. (1950). Theoretical considerations. In K. Horney, *Neurosis and human growth: The struggle toward self-realization* (pp. 366–378). New York: Norton.

A concise summary of Horney's theoretical position, this book is more difficult than *Our Inner Conflicts* (1945), but the two sources together provide a comprehensive view of psychoanalytic social theory.

HORNEY, K. (1967). The flight from womanhood: The masculinity complex in women as viewed by men and women. In H. Kelman (Ed.), *Feminine psychology* (pp. 54–70). New York: Norton.

Originally published in 1926, this article is important because it represents, from a woman's perspective, the first significant opposition to Freud's views on penis envy and the female Oedipus complex.

KNAPP, G. P. (1989). *The art of living: Erich Fromm's life and works.* New York: Peter Lang.

This book presents a critical appraisal of the life and work of Fromm, a man the author calls "one of this century's most influential thinkers." Knapp's book is more accessible than Daniel Burston's (1991) *The Legacy of Erich Fromm.*

O'CONNELL, A. N. (1990). Karen Horney (1885–1952). In A. N. O'Connell & N. F. Russo (Eds.), *Women in psychology: A bio-bibliographic sourcebook* (pp. 185–196). New York: Greenwood Press.

This chapter presents a brief account of Horney's career, her major contributions, and her influence on later personal theorists such as Abraham H. Maslow and Carl Rogers.

QUINN, S. (1987). *A mind of her own: The life of Karen Horney.* New York: Summit Books.

An excellent biography of Horney, more readable, accurate, and better balanced than an earlier one by Rubins (1978).

Extensions of Psychoanalytic Theory

Chapter Eight

OVERVIEW
BIOGRAPHY OF MELANIE KLEIN
INTRODUCTION TO OBJECT RELATIONS THEORY
PSYCHIC LIFE OF THE INFANT
    Fantasies
    Objects
POSITIONS
    Paranoid-Schizoid Position
    Depressive Position
PSYCHIC DEFENSE MECHANISMS
    Introjection
    Projection
    Splitting
    Projective Identification
INTERNALIZATIONS
    Ego
    Superego
    Oedipus Complex
LATER VIEWS OF OBJECT RELATIONS
    Margaret Mahler's View
    Otto Kernberg's View
    Heinz Kohut's View
PSYCHOTHERAPY
CONCEPT OF HUMANITY
RELATED RESEARCH
CRITIQUE OF OBJECT RELATIONS THEORY
BIOGRAPHIES OF JOHN DOLLARD AND NEAL E.
    MILLER
INTRODUCTION TO DOLLARD AND MILLER'S
    LEARNING THEORY
FOUR FUNDAMENTALS OF LEARNING
    Drive
    Cue
    Response
    Reinforcement
HIGHER MENTAL PROCESSES
    Foresight
    Reasoning
    Social Training
CONFLICT
    Basic Assumptions
    Types of Conflict
REPRESSION AND THE UNCONSCIOUS
ABNORMAL DEVELOPMENT
PSYCHOTHERAPY
CONCEPT OF HUMANITY
RELATED RESEARCH
CRITIQUE OF DOLLARD AND MILLER
CHAPTER SUMMARY
SUGGESTED READINGS

KLEIN

DOLLARD MILLER

$\mathcal{O}$ne day while walking in the street near his home, Herbert was suddenly overcome with anxiety. Uncertain of the source of his fear, he nevertheless somehow connected it with being bitten by a horse. Soon, Herbert developed a phobia, a strong irrational fear, of going into the street, and he would only venture away from home when accompanied by his mother or father. Herbert was barely five years old, so a fear of horses might not seem too unusual. However, before his sudden phobic reaction, Herbert had shown no fear of horses and had even displayed some affection and empathy toward them. He had previously been a cheerful, happy, and active child with no signs of psychic distress. Then, on that day in January of 1908, during an era when the street in front of his house in Vienna was usually crowded with horses, young Herbert was overcome with a crippling fear that a horse would bite him.

Herbert's father was Dr. Max Graf, a member of Freud's Wednesday Psychological Society, and his mother was a former patient of Freud. The Grafs, who had agreed to rear their son according to psychoanalytic principles, avoided harsh physical punishment and were relatively open with Herbert in discussions of sexual matters. And Herbert had shown a lively interest in sex, especially penises, feces, and the origin of babies. He had displayed both heterosexual and homosexual behaviors toward each parent as well as toward young boys and girls about his age, whom he would hug and claim to love. He later showed hostility toward each parent by, for example, butting his father in the stomach with his head and by fantasizing about hitting his mother with a carpet-beater. In addition, he associated feces with babies and had fantasies about having babies in his stomach.

These latter fantasies intensified after his younger sister was born, when Herbert was three and a half. He could not yet believe that girls had different genitals from his own, and even while watching his sister being bathed, he reported that she too had a penis—only it was a little one. He was also curious about his mother's penis and assumed that she must have a big one, because horses are big and they have big ones. Herbert had enjoyed playing with his own penis, and even when his mother threatened him with castration for putting his hand to his penis, he felt no anxiety. He calmly replied that if his penis were cut off he would use his bottom to go wee-wee. (Threatened castration was not the Grafs' only violation of Freudian principles—they never told their young son that girls have vaginas.)

After Herbert developed a phobia of being bitten by a horse, his father began to interview him and to report to Freud on the boy's actions, fantasies, and dreams.

On one occasion, Graf took Herbert to see Professor Freud who guessed that horses, with their "eyeglasses" (blinders) and black muzzles reminded Herbert of his father, who wore glasses and supported a large, black moustache. Herbert accepted the professor's hunch, and with great intuition, he also connected his street anxiety with his masturbation.

In the course of an analysis (conducted by the father under Freud's direction), Herbert recalled that some months before his sudden phobia, he had seen a large horse fall down while pulling a heavy cart. He also reported a dream in which a plumber took away his penis and gave him another one. Freud (1909/1955), of course, interpreted Herbert's dream as an expression of castration anxiety, a normal fear for little boys who want to have a baby with their mother and who see their father as an obstacle to this fantasy. In the same vein, Freud saw Herbert's phobia as stemming from an unconscious wish that his father would fall down and die. Because of this wish, Herbert was also afraid that his father would bite him, an unconscious fear that was expressed as severe anxiety about being bitten by a horse. Herbert's phobia began to diminish after his father explained that the horse falling down was the father who he wished dead in order to have his mother to himself. Such an interpretation, of course, is consistent with Freud's ideas on child-hood sexuality and the Oedipus complex.

Herbert Graf grew up to become a well-known stage director and producer of operas in Philadelphia and New York (Holland, 1986). Although he was well known in the world of opera, he is perhaps better known in the world of psychoanalysis. Since 1909 the five-year-old boy whose father analyzed him under Freud's direction has been known as "Little Hans," the pseudonym that Freud gave to one of his most famous case studies.

OVERVIEW

Although Freud's interpretation of Little Hans's (Herbert's) phobia supports his theory (as we described it in Chapter 2), it is not the only explanation possible. In this chapter we look at two other theories for viewing Little Hans's behavior, both of which are extensions rather than rejections of orthodox psychoanalytic theory. The first is *object relations theory* as developed by Melanie Klein and others, and the second is *psychoanalytic learning theory* as proposed by John Dollard and Neal E. Miller.

Klein extended Freud's ideas with her emphasis on very early childhood (the first four to six months after birth) and her insistence that the infant's drives (hunger, sex, and so forth) are directed to an object—a breast, a penis, a vagina, and so on. According to Klein, the child's relation to the breast is fundamental and serves as a prototype for later relations to whole objects, such as mother and father. The very early tendency of infants to relate to partial objects gives their experiences an unrealistic or fantasy-like quality that affects all later interpersonal relations. Thus Klein's ideas tend to shift the focus of psychoanalytic theory from organically based stages of development to the role of early fantasy in the development of interpersonal relationships.

On the other hand, Dollard and Miller's psychoanalytically based learning theory holds that most of personality is learned, and that all learning is acquired on the basis of four fundamental factors. First, people must have a *drive* or motivation; second, they must attend to some *cue* that determines how they are to act; third, they must make some kind of *response*; and fourth, that response must be *reinforced*. Both Dollard and Miller were trained in psychoanalysis, and their theory can be seen as a bridge spanning the gap between Freud and modern learning theory. Using their backgrounds in Freudian psychology and the social sciences, Dollard and Miller were able to apply the fundamental principles of learning to the higher mental processes and to the acquisition of unconsciously motivated behaviors.

BIOGRAPHY OF MELANIE KLEIN

Several parallels can be noted between the lives of Melanie Klein and Karen Horney (see Chapter 7). Each was born during the 1880s, the youngest child of a 50-year-old father and his second wife. Each had older siblings who were favored by their parents, and each felt unwanted and unloved. Also, each had wanted to become a physician, but only Horney fulfilled that ambition.

Melanie Reizes Klein was born March 30, 1882, in Vienna, Austria, to Dr. Moriz Reizes and his second wife Libussa Deutsch Reizes. The youngest of four children, Klein believed that her birth was unplanned and, as a consequence, she felt somewhat rejected by her parents, especially her father, who favored the oldest daughter (Sayers, 1991). By the time Melanie was born, her father had long since rebelled against his early Orthodox Jewish training and had ceased to practice any religion. As a consequence, Melanie grew up in a family that was neither proreligious nor antireligious. Dr. Reizes was a physician who struggled to make a living in medicine, and who, during Melanie's childhood, was relegated to working as a dental assistant. At the same time, Libussa Reizes ran a shop selling plants and reptiles, which caused her considerable humiliation and even fear, since she abhorred snakes (Segal, 1979).

Melanie felt somewhat closer to her mother than to her father, but her true confidant during childhood was her only brother Emanuel, who was nearly five years older. She idolized her brother, and this infatuation may have contributed to her later difficulties in relating to men. Melanie's father died when she was 18, and two years later her beloved brother Emanuel died, leaving Melanie devastated. While still in mourning over Emanuel's death, she married Arthur Klein, an engineer who had been Emanuel's close friend. Her marriage at age 21 prevented Melanie from reaching her goal of becoming a physician, and for the rest of her life she regretted not being a doctor (Grosskurth, 1986).

Like Horney, Klein did not have a happy marriage; she dreaded sex and abhorred pregnancy (Grosskurth, 1986). Nevertheless, her marriage to Arthur produced three children:

Melitta, born in 1904; Hans, born in 1907; and Erich, born in 1914. In 1909, the Kleins moved to Budapest, where Arthur had been transferred. There, Melanie met Sandor Ferenczi, a member of Freud's inner circle and the person who introduced her into the world of psychoanalysis. When her mother died in 1914, Melanie became depressed and entered analysis with Ferenczi, an experience that served as a turning point in her life. The same year she read Freud's *On Dreams* (1901/1953) and also gave birth to her youngest child Erich. Melanie was deeply taken by psychoanalysis and, like Little Hans's parents, she trained her son according to Freudian principles. In addition, she began to psychoanalyze Erich from the time he was very young. She also attempted to analyze Melitta and Hans, both of whom eventually went to other analysts. Melitta, who became a psychoanalyst, was analyzed by Horney, as well as by others (Grosskurth, 1986). Another interesting parallel between Horney and Klein is the fact that Klein later analyzed Horney's two youngest daughters when they were 12 and 9 years old. (The oldest daughter was 14 and refused to be analyzed.) Unlike Melitta's voluntary analysis by Horney, the two Horney children were compelled to attend analytic sessions, not for treatment of any neurotic disorder but as a preventive measure (Quinn, 1987).

Klein separated from her husband in 1919, but, like Horney, she did not obtain a divorce for several years. After the separation, Klein established a psychoanalytic practice in Berlin and made her first contributions to the psychoanalytic literature with a paper dealing with her analysis of Erich (who was not identified as her son). Not completely satisfied with her own analysis by Ferenczi, Klein ended the relationship and began an analysis with Karl Abraham, another member of Freud's inner circle and the person who had earlier analyzed Horney. After only 14 months, however, Abraham died. Then, like Freud before her, Klein began a life-long self-analysis.

Before 1919, psychoanalysts, including Freud, based their theories of child development on their therapeutic work with *adults*. Freud's only case study of a child was Little Hans, a boy whom he saw as a patient only once. Melanie Klein changed that situation by psychoanalyzing children themselves. Her work with very young children, including her own, convinced her that children internalize both positive and negative feelings toward their mothers, and that they develop superegos much earlier than Freud had believed. Her slight divergence from standard psychoanalytic theory brought much criticism from her colleagues in Berlin, causing her to feel increasingly uncomfortable in that city. Then, in 1926, Ernest Jones invited her to London to analyze his children and to deliver a series of lectures on child analysis. These lectures later resulted in her first book, *The Psycho-Analysis of Children* (Klein, 1932). In 1927 she took up permanent residency in England, remaining there until her death on September 22, 1960.

Klein's years in London were marked by division and controversy. Although she continued to regard herself as a Freudian, neither Freud nor his daughter Anna accepted her emphasis on the importance of very early childhood or her analytic technique with children. Her differences with Anna Freud began while the Freuds were still living in Vienna, but they climaxed after Anna moved with her father and mother to London in 1938. Before the arrival of Anna Freud, the English school of psychoanalysis was steadily becoming the "Kleinian School," and Melanie's battles were limited mostly to those with her daughter Melitta. In 1934, Klein's older son, Hans, was killed in a fall. Melitta, who had recently moved to London with her psychoanalyst husband Walter Schmideberg, maintained that her brother had committed suicide, and she blamed her mother for his death. During that same year, Melitta began an analysis with Edward Glover, one of Klein's rivals in the British Society. Klein and her daughter then became even more personally estranged and professionally antagonistic, a situation that persisted with Melitta even after her mother's death.

Although Melitta Schmideberg was not a supporter of Anna Freud, her persistent antagonism toward her mother made Klein's struggle with Anna Freud more difficult (King & Steiner, 1991). The friction between Klein and Freud never abated, with each side claiming to be more "Freudian" than the other (Hughes, 1989). Finally, in 1946 the British Society accepted three training procedures—the traditional one of Melanie Klein, the one advocated by Anna Freud, and a Middle Group that accepted neither training school but was more eclectic in its approach. By such a division, the British Society remained intact, albeit with an uneasy alliance. Although Klein never reconciled with Anna Freud, the three distinct schools that resulted from their bitter personal and professional differences have continued to the present day. As King (1991) pointed out, the diversity of opinion and the freedom of choice are a source of strength of the British Society.

INTRODUCTION TO OBJECT RELATIONS THEORY

Object relations theory is an offspring of Freud's instinct theory, but it differs from its ancestor in at least three general ways. First, object relations theory places less emphasis on biologically based drives and more importance on consistent patterns of interpersonal relationships. Second, as opposed to Freud's rather paternalistic theory that emphasizes the power and control of the father, object relations theory tends to be more maternal, stressing the intimacy and nurturance of the mother. Third, object relations theorists generally see human contact and relatedness—not sexual pleasure—as the prime motivators of human behavior. More specifically, however, the concept of object relations has many meanings, just as there are many object relations theorists. This section concentrates primarily on Melanie Klein's work, but it also briefly discusses the theories of Margaret S. Mahler, Otto

Kernberg, and Heinz Kohut. In general, Mahler's work was concerned with the infant's struggle to gain autonomy and a sense of self; Kernberg's with combining drive theory, ego psychology, and object relations; and Kohut's with the formation of the self.

If Klein is the mother of object relations theory, then Freud himself is the father. Recall from Chapter 2 that Freud (1915/1957a) believed that instincts or drives have an *impetus*, a *source*, an *aim*, and an *object*, with the latter two having the greater psychological significance. Although different drives may seem to have separate aims, their underlying aim is always the same—to reduce tension; that is, to achieve pleasure. In Freudian terms, the **object** of the drive is any person, part of a person, or thing through which the aim is satisfied. Klein and other object relations theorists begin with this basic assumption of Freud and then speculate on how the infant's real or fantasized early relations with the mother or the breast become a model for all later interpersonal relationships. Adult relationships, therefore, are not always what they seem. An important portion of any relationship is the internal psychic representations of early significant objects, such as the mother's breast or the father's penis, that have been *introjected*, or taken into the infant's psychic structure, and then *projected* onto one's partner. These internal pictures are not accurate representations of the other person but are remnants of each person's earlier experiences.

Although Klein continued to regard herself as a Freudian, she extended psychoanalytic theory beyond the boundaries set by Freud. For his part, Freud chose mostly to ignore Klein. When pressed for an opinion on her work, Freud had little to say. For example, in 1925 when Ernest Jones wrote to him concerning Klein's "valuable work" with childhood analysis and play therapy, Freud simply replied that "Melanie Klein's work has aroused considerable doubt and controversy here in Vienna" (Steiner, 1985, p. 30).

PSYCHIC LIFE OF THE INFANT

Whereas Freud emphasized the first five or six years of life, Klein stressed the importance of the first five or six *months*. To her, an infant does not begin life with a blank slate but with an inherited predisposition to reduce the anxiety it experiences as a result of the conflict produced by the forces of the life instinct and the power of the death instinct. The infant's innate readiness to act or react presupposes the existence of phylogenetic endowment, a concept that Freud also accepted.

Fantasies

One of Klein's basic assumptions is that the infant, even at birth, possesses an active fantasy life. These fantasies are psychic representations of unconscious id instincts and must not be confused with conscious fantasies that are possible only in older children. When Klein (1932) wrote of the dynamic fantasy life of infants, she did not suggest that neonates could put thoughts into words. She simply meant that they possess unconscious images of "good" and "bad." For example, a full stomach is "good," an empty one is "bad." Thus, Klein would say that infants who fall asleep while sucking on their fingers are fantasizing about having their mother's "good" breast inside themselves. Similarly, hungry infants who cry and kick their legs are fantasizing that they are kicking or destroying the "bad" breast. This idea of a "good" breast and a "bad" breast is comparable to Sullivan's (Chapter 6) notion of a "good" mother and a "bad" mother.

As the infant matures, unconscious fantasies connected with the breast continue to exert an impact on psychic life, but newer ones emerge as well. These later unconscious fantasies are shaped by both reality and by inherited predispositions. One of these fantasies involves the Oedipus complex, or the child's wish to destroy one parent and sexually possess the other. (The Oedipus complex is discussed more fully later.) Because these fantasies are unconscious, they can be contradictory. For example, Little Hans fantasized both beating his mother and having babies with her. Such fantasies sprang partly from his experiences with his mother and partly from universal predispositions to destroy the "bad" breast and to incorporate the "good" one.

Objects

Klein agreed with Freud that humans have innate drives or instincts, including a *death instinct*. Drives, of course, must have some object. Thus, the hunger drive has the "good" breast as its object, the sex drive has a sexual organ as its object, and so on. Klein (1948) believed that from early infancy children relate to these external objects, both in fantasy and in reality. The earliest object relations are with the mother's breast, but " very soon interest develops in the face and in the hands which attend to his needs and gratify them" (Klein, 1991, p 757). In their active fantasy, infants *introject*, or take into their psychic structure, these external objects, including their father's penis, their mother's hands and face, and other body parts. Introjected objects are more than internal thoughts about external objects; they are fantasies of internalizing the object in concrete and physical terms. For example, children who have introjected their mothers believe that the mother is constantly inside their own bodies. Klein's notion of internal objects suggests that these objects have a power of their own, comparable to Freud's concept of a superego, which assumes that the father's or mother's conscience is carried within the child.

POSITIONS

Klein (1946) saw human infants as constantly engaging in a basic conflict between the life instinct and the death instinct, that is, between good and bad, love and hate, creativity and destruction. Because the ego moves toward integration and away from disintegration, infants naturally prefer gratifying sensations over frustrating ones. In their attempt to deal with this dichotomy of good and bad feelings, infants organize their experiences into **positions**, or ways of dealing with both internal and external objects. Klein chose the term "position" rather than "stage of development" to indicate that positions alternate back and forth; they are not periods of time or phases of development through which a person passes. Although she used psychiatric or pathological labels, Klein intended these positions to represent *normal* social growth and development. The two basic positions are the *paranoid-schizoid position* and the *depressive position*.

Paranoid-Schizoid Position

During the earliest months of life, the infant comes into contact with both the good breast and the bad breast. These alternating experiences of gratification and frustration threaten the very existence of the infant's vulnerable ego. The infant desires to control the breast by devouring and harboring it. At the same time, the infant's innate destructive urges create fantasies of damaging the breast by biting, tearing or annihilating it. In order to tolerate both these feelings toward the same object at the same time, the ego splits itself, retaining parts of its life and death instincts while deflecting parts of both instincts onto the breast. Now, rather than fearing its own death instinct, the infant fears the *persecutory breast*. But the infant also has a relationship with the *ideal breast*, which provides love, comfort, and gratification. The infant desires to keep the ideal breast inside itself as a protection against annihilation by persecutors. To control the good breast and to fight off its persecutors, the infant adopts what Klein (1946) called the **paranoid-schizoid position**, a way of organizing experiences that includes both paranoid feelings of being persecuted and a splitting of internal and external objects into the good and the bad.

According to Klein, infants develop the paranoid-schizoid position during the first three or four months of life, during which time the ego's perception of the external world is subjective and fantastic rather than objective and real. Thus, the persecutory feelings are considered to be paranoid; that is, they are not based on any real or immediate danger from the outside world.

The paranoid-schizoid position is not limited to infants. Little Hans at age five manifested this position with his irrational fear that horses might bite him. He had projected parts of his own destructive instinct onto his father and then, because his father was too good to hate, he changed him into horses. This entire process took place on a primitive, unconscious level. When adults adopt the paranoid-schizoid position, they do so in a primitive, unconscious fashion. As Ogden (1990) pointed out, they experience themselves as passive objects rather than active subjects. They are likely to say "He's dangerous" instead of saying "I am aware that he is dangerous to me." Ogden gave other examples of patients avoiding the use of personal pronouns, such as "Went to school today . . . Teacher's unfair . . . hate him." Fortunately, the paranoid-schizoid position, which is universal in infants, is not the norm for adults.

Depressive Position

Beginning at about the fifth or sixth month, the infant begins to view external objects as whole and to see that good and bad can exist in the same person. At that time the child develops a more realistic picture of the mother and recognizes that she is an independent person who can be both good and bad. Also, the ego is beginning to mature to the point at which it can tolerate some of its own destructive feelings rather than projecting them outward. However, the infant also realizes that the mother might go away and be lost forever. Fearing the possible loss of the mother, the infant desires to protect her and keep her from the dangers of its own destructive forces, those cannibalistic impulses that had previously been projected onto her. But the infant's ego is mature enough to realize that it lacks the capacity to protect the mother, and thus the infant experiences guilt for its previous destructive urges toward the mother. The feelings of anxiety over losing a loved object coupled with a sense of guilt for wanting to destroy that object constitute what Klein called the **depressive position**.

Children in the depressive position recognize that the loved object and the hated object are now one and the same. They reproach themselves for their previous destructive urges toward their mother and desire to make *reparation* for these attacks. Because children see their mothers as whole and also as being endangered, they are able to feel *empathy* for the mother, a quality that will be beneficial in their future interpersonal relations.

The depressive position is resolved when childen fantasize that they have made reparation for their previous transgressions, and when they recognize that their mothers will not go away permanently but will return after each departure. When the depressive position is resolved, children close the split between the good and the bad mother. They are able to not only experience love *from* their mother, but they also display their own love *for* her. However, an incomplete resolution of the depressive position can result in lack of trust, morbid mourning at the loss of a loved one, and a variety of other psychic disorders.

PSYCHIC DEFENSE MECHANISMS

Klein (1955) suggested that from very early infancy, children adopt several psychic defense mechanisms to protect their ego against anxiety aroused by their own destructive fantasies. These intense destructive feelings originate with oral-sadistic anxieties concerning the breast—the dreaded, destructive breast on the one hand and the satisfying, helpful breast on the other. To control these anxieties, infants use several psychic defense mechanisms, including *introjection, projection, splitting,* and *projective identification.*

Introjection

By **introjection**, Klein simply meant that infants fantasize taking into their body those perceptions and experiences that they have had with the external object, originally the mother's breast. Introjection begins with the child's first feeding, when there is an attempt to incorporate the mother's breast into the infant's body. Ordinarily, the infant tries to introject good objects, to take them inside itself as a protection against anxiety. However, sometimes the infant introjects bad objects, such as the bad breast or the bad penis, in order to gain control over them. When dangerous objects are introjected, they become internal persecutors, capable of terrifying the infant and leaving frightening residues that may be expressed in dreams or in an interest in fairy tales, such as "The Big Bad Wolf" or "Snow White and the Seven Dwarfs."

Introjected objects are not accurate representations of the real objects but are colored by children's fantasies. For example, infants will fantasize that their mothers are constantly present; that is, that the mother is always inside their bodies. The real mother, of course, is not perpetually present, but infants nevertheless devour her in fantasy so that she becomes a constant internal object.

Projection

Just as infants use introjection to take in both good and bad objects, they use **projection** to get rid of them. Projection is the fantasy that one's own feelings and impulses actually reside in another person and not within one's body. By projecting unmanageable destructive impulses onto external objects, infants alleviate the unbearable anxiety of being destroyed by dangerous internal forces (Klein, 1935).

Children project both bad and good images onto external objects, especially their parents. An example of projecting a bad impulse is the young boy who desires to castrate his father but projects these castration fantasies onto his father, whom he then believes wishes to castrate him. Similarly, the young girl fantasizes devouring her mother and then projects that fantasy onto her mother, whom she fears will retaliate by persecuting her.

People can also project good impulses. For example, infants who feel good about the mother's nurturing breast will attribute their own feelings of "goodness" onto the breast and imagine that the breast is good. Adults sometimes project their own feelings of love onto another person and become convinced that the other person loves them. Projection thus allows people to believe that their own subjective opinions are true.

Splitting

Infants can only manage the good and bad aspects of themselves and of external objects by **splitting** them, that is, by keeping apart incompatible impulses. In order to separate bad and good objects, the ego must itself be split. Thus, infants develop a picture of both the "good me" and the "bad me" that enables them to deal with both pleasurable and destructive impulses toward external objects.

Splitting can have either a positive or a negative effect on the child. If it is not extreme and rigid, it can be a positive and useful mechanism not only for infants but also for adults. It enables people to see both positive and negative aspects of themselves, to evaluate their behavior as good or bad, and to differentiate between likable and unlikable acquaintances. On the other hand, excessive and inflexible splitting can lead to pathological repression. For instance, if the ego is too rigid to be split into "good me" and "bad me," then bad experiences cannot be introjected into the good ego. When an infant cannot accept its own "bad" behavior, it must then deal with destructive and terrifying impulses in the only way it can—by repressing them.

Projective Identification

A fourth means of reducing anxiety is **projective identification,** a psychic defense mechanism in which infants split off unacceptable parts of themelves, project them onto another object, and finally introject them back into themselves in a changed or distorted form. By taking the object back into themselves, infants feel that they have become like that object, that is, they identifiy with that object. For example, infants typically split off parts of their destructive impulses and project them onto the bad, frustrating breast. But then they identify with breast by introjecting it, a process which permits them to gain control over the dreaded and wonderful breast.

Projective identification exerts a powerful influence in adult interpersonal relations. Unlike simple projection, which can exist wholly in fantasy, projective identification exists only in the world of real interpersonal relationships. For example, a man with strong but unwanted tendencies to dominate others will project those feelings onto his wife, who he then sees as domineering. The man subtly tries to get his wife to *become* domineering. He behaves with excessive submissiveness in an attempt to force his wife to display the very tendencies that he has deposited in her.

INTERNALIZATIONS

When object relations theorists speak of **internalizations**, they mean that the person takes in (introjects) aspects of the external world and then organizes those introjections into a psychologically meaningful framework. In Kleinian theory, three important internalizations are the ego, the superego, and the Oedipus complex.

Ego

Klein (1930, 1946) believed that the ego, or one's sense of self, reaches maturity at a much earlier stage than Freud had assumed. Although Freud hypothesized that the ego exists at birth, he did not attribute complex psychic functions to it until about the third or fourth year. To Freud, the young child was dominated by the id. Klein, however, largely ignored the id and based her theory on the ego's early ability to sense both destructive and loving forces and to manage them through splitting, projection, and introjection.

Klein (1959) believed that although the ego is mostly unorganized at birth, it is still strong enough to feel anxiety, to use defense mechanisms, and to form early object relations in both fantasy and reality. The ego begins to evolve with the infant's first experience with feeding when the good breast fills the infant not only with milk but with love and security. But the infant also experiences the bad breast—the one that is not present or does not give milk, love, or security. The infant introjects both the good breast and the bad breast, and these images provide a focal point for further expansion of the ego. All experiences, even those not connected with feeding, are evaluated by the ego in terms of how they relate to the good breast and the bad breast. For example, when the ego experiences the good breast, it expects similar good experiences with other objects, such as its own fingers, a pacifier, or the father. Thus, the infant's first object relation (the breast) becomes the prototype not only for the ego's future development but for the individual's later interpersonal relations.

However, before a unified ego can emerge, it must first become split. Klein assumed that infants innately strive for integration, but, at the same time, they are forced to deal with the opposing forces of life and death, as reflected in their experiences with the good breast and the bad breast. To avoid disintegration the newly emerging ego must split itself into the "good me" and the "bad me." The "good me" exists when infants are being enriched with milk and love; the "bad me" is experienced when they do not receive milk and love. This dual image of self allows them to manage the good and bad aspects of external objects. As infants mature, their perceptions become more realistic, they no longer see the world in terms of part objects, and their egos become more integrated.

Superego

Klein's picture of the superego differs from Freud's in at least three important respects. First, it emerges much earlier in life; second, it is *not* an outgrowth of the Oedipus complex; and third, it is much more harsh and cruel. Klein arrived at these differences through her analysis of young children, a procedure that Freud never used (except for his single session with Little Hans).

There could be no doubt that a super-ego had been in full operation for some time in my small patients of between two-and-three-quarters and four years of age, whereas according to the accepted [Freudian] view the super-ego would not begin to be activated until the Oedipus complex had died down—i.e. until about the fifth year of life. Furthermore, my data showed that this early super-ego was immeasurably harsher and more cruel than that of the older child or adult, and that it literally crushed down the feeble ego of the small child. (Klein, 1933, p. 267)

Recall that Freud conceptualized the superego as being composed of two subsystems: an ego ideal that produces inferiority feelings and a conscience that results in guilt feelings. Klein would concur that the more mature superego produces feelings of inferiority and guilt, but her analysis of young children led her to believe that the *early superego* produces not guilt but *terror*.

To Klein, young children fear being devoured, cut up, and torn into pieces—fears that are greatly out of proportion to any realistic dangers. Why are the children's superegos so drastically removed from any actual threats by their parents? Klein (1933) suggested that the answer resides with the infants' own destructive instincts, which they experience as anxiety. To manage this anxiety, the child's ego mobilizes libido (life instinct) against the death instinct. However, the life and death instincts cannot be completely separated, so the ego is forced to defend itself against its own actions. This early ego defense lays the foundation for the development of the superego, whose extreme violence is due to the fact that the ego is aggressively defending itself against its own destructive tendencies. Klein (1933) believed that this harsh, cruel superego is responsible for many antisocial and criminal tendencies in adults.

Klein would describe a five-year-old child's superego in much the same way Freud did. By that time the superego arouses little anxiety but a great measure of guilt. It has lost most of its severity, while gradually being transformed into a realistic conscience. However, Klein rejected Freud's notion that the superego is a consequence of the Oedipus complex. Instead, she insisted that it grows along with the Oedipus complex and finally emerges as realistic guilt after the Oedipus complex is resolved.

Oedipus Complex

Although Klein believed that her view of the Oedipus complex was merely an extension and not a refutation of Freud's ideas, her conception departed from the Freudian one in several ways. First, Klein (1946, 1948, 1952) held that the Oedipus complex begins at a much earlier age than Freud had suggested. Recall that Freud believed that the Oedipus complex took place during the phallic stage, when children are about four or five years old and after they have experienced an oral and anal stage. In contrast, Klein held that the Oedipus complex begins during the earliest months of life, overlaps with the oral and anal stages, and reaches its climax during the **genital stage**, at around age three or four. (Klein preferred the term "genital" stage rather than "phallic," because the latter suggests a masculine psychology.) Second, Klein believed that a significant part of the Oedipus complex is children's fear of retaliation from their parents for their fantasies of emptying the parents' bodies. Third, she stressed the importance of children retaining positive feelings toward *both* parents during the Oedipal years. Fourth, she hypothesized that during its early stages the Oedipus complex serves the same need for both sexes, that is, to establish a positive attitude with the good or gratifying object (breast or penis) and to avoid the bad or terrifying object (breast or penis). In this position children of either sex can direct their love either alternately or simultaneously toward each parent. Thus, children are capable of both homosexual or heterosexual relations with both parents. Like Freud, however, Klein assumed that boys and girls eventually come to experience the Oedipus complex differently.

Male Oedipal Development

Klein (1945) believed that during the early months of Oedipal development, the boy shifts some of his oral desires from his mother's breast to his father's penis. At this time the little boy is in his *feminine position*; that is, he adopts a passive homosexual attitude toward his father. Next, he moves to a heterosexual relationship with his mother, but because of his previous homosexual feeling for his father, he has no fear that his father will castrate him. Recall that Little Hans originally had no castration anxiety toward his father. Instead, he adopted a homosexual attitude and believed that his father would give him a baby, just as he had given Hans's mother a baby. Klein (1945) believed that this passive homosexual position is a prerequisite for the boy's development of a healthy heterosexual relationship with his mother. That is, the boy must have a good feeling about his father's penis before he can value his own.

As the boy matures, however, he develops oral-sadistic impulses toward his father and wants to bite off his penis and to murder him. These feelings then arouse castration anxiety and the fear that his father will retaliate against him by biting off his penis. This explanation fits Freud's case study of Little Hans, who feared that a horse (an unconscious symbol for Hans's father) would bite him. This fear convinces the little boy that sexual intercourse with his mother is not only dangerous to him, but to her as well.

The boy's Oedipus complex is resolved only partially by his castration anxiety. A more important factor is his ability to establish positive relationships with both parents at the same time. At that point the boy sees his parents as whole objects, a condition that enables him to work through his depressive position.

Female Oedipal Development

Like the young boy, the little girl first sees the mother's breast as both "good" and "bad." Then around six months of age, she begins to view the breast as more positive than negative. Later, she sees the whole mother as full of good things, and this attitude causes the little girl to imagine how babies are made. She fantasizes that the father's penis feeds the mother with riches, including babies. Because the little girl sees the father's penis as the giver of children, she develops a positive relationship to it and fantasizes that the father will fill her body with babies. If the female Oedipal stage proceeds smoothly, the little girl adopts a "feminine" position and has a positive relationship with both parents.

However, under less ideal circumstances, the little girl will see her mother as a rival and will fantasize robbing her of the father's penis and of her babies. Just as the boy's hostility toward the father leads to fear of retaliation, the little girl's wish to rob her mother produces a paranoid fear that her mother will retaliate against her by injuring her or taking away her babies. The little girl's principal anxiety comes from a fear that the inside of her body has been injured by her mother, an anxiety that can only be alleviated when she later gives birth to a healthy baby. According to Klein (1945), penis envy stems from the little girl's wish to internalize her father's penis and to receive a baby from him. This fantasy precedes any desire for an external penis. Contrary to Freud's view, Klein could find no evidence that the little girl blames her mother for bringing her into the world without a penis. Instead, Klein contended that the girl retains a strong attachment to her mother throughout the Oedipal period.

For both girls and boys, a healthy resolution of the Oedipus complex depends on the ability to allow the mother and father to come together and to have sexual intercourse with each other. No remnant of rivalry remains. Children's positive feelings toward both parents later serve to enhance their adult sexual relations.

LATER VIEWS OF OBJECT RELATIONS

Since Melanie Klein's bold and insightful descriptions, a number of other theorists have expanded object relations theory. Among the more prominent of these later theorists are Margaret Mahler, Otto Kernberg, and Heinz Kohut.

MAHLER

Margaret Mahler's View

Margaret Schoenberger Mahler (1897–1985) was born in Sopron, Hungary, and received a medical degree from the University of Vienna in 1923. In 1938, she moved to New York, where she was a consultant to the Children's Service of the New York State Psychiatric Institute. She later established her own observational studies at the Masters Children's Center in New York. From 1955 to 1974, she was Clinical Professor of Psychiatry at Albert Einstein College of Medicine.

Mahler was primarily concerned with the psychological birth of the individual that takes place during the first three years of life, a time when the child gradually surrenders security for autonomy. Originally, Mahler's ideas came from her observation of the behaviors of disturbed children interacting with their mothers. Later, she observed normal babies as they bonded with their mothers during the first 36 months of life (Mahler, 1952).

To Mahler, an individual's psychological birth begins during the first weeks of postnatal life and continues for the next three years or so. By *psychological birth* Mahler meant that the child becomes an *individual* separate from his or her primary caregiver, an accomplishment that leads ultimately to a *sense of identity*.

To achieve psychological birth and individuation, the child proceeds through a series of three major developmental stages and four substages (Mahler, 1967, 1972; Mahler, Pine, & Bergman, 1975). The first major developmental stage is **normal autism,** which spans the period from birth until about three or four weeks. To describe the normal autism stage, Mahler (1967) borrowed Freud's (1911/1958) analogy that compared psychological birth with an unhatched bird egg. The bird is able to satisfy its nutritional needs autistically (without regard to external reality) because its food supply is enclosed in its shell. Similarly, the newborn infant satisfies various needs within the all-powerful protective orbit of the mother's care. The neonate has a sense of omnipotence because, like the unhatched bird, its needs are cared for automatically and without it having to expend any effort. Unlike Klein, who conceptualized the newborn infant as being terrified, Mahler pointed to the relatively long periods of sleep and general lack of tension in the neonate. She believed that this is a period of absolute primary narcissism in which the infant is unaware of any other person. Thus, she referred to normal autism as an "objectless" stage, a time when the mother's breast is automatically sought through the rooting reflex and not from a desire for the "good breast."

As infants gradually realize that they cannot satisfy their own needs, they begin to recognize their primary caregiver and to seek a symbiotic relationship with her. **Normal symbiosis,** the second developmental stage, begins around the fourth or fifth week but reaches its zenith during the fourth or fifth month. During this time "the infant behaves and functions as though he and his mother were an omnipotent system—a dual unity within one common boundary" (Mahler, 1967, p. 741). In the analogy of the bird egg, the shell is now beginning to crack, but a psychological membrane in the form of a symbiotic relationship still protects the newborn. Mahler (1967) recognized that this is not a true symbiosis because, although the infant's life is dependent on the mother, the mother does not absolutely need the infant. The symbiosis is characterized by a mutual cuing of infant and mother. The infant sends to the mother cues of hunger, pain, pleasure, and so forth, and the mother responds with her own cues, such as feeding, holding, or smiling. By this age the infant can recognize the mother's face and can perceive her pleasure or distress. However, object relations have not yet begun—mother and others are still "preobjects." Older children and even adults sometimes regress to this stage, seeking the strength and safety of their mother's care.

The third major developmental state, **separation-individuation,** spans the period from about the 4th or 5th month until about the 30th or 36th month. During this time children become psychologically separated from their mothers, achieve a sense of individuation, and begin to develop feelings of personal identity. Because children no longer experience a dual unity with their mothers, they must give up their delusions of omnipotence, a surrender that leaves them vulnerable to external threats. Thus, young children in the separation-individuation stage experience the external world as being more dangerous than it was during the first two stages.

Mahler divided the separation-individuation stage into four overlapping sub-stages. The first is *differentiation*, which lasts from about the 5th to the 7th–10th month and is marked by a bodily breaking away from the mother/infant symbiotic orbit. At this age, Mahler observed, infants smile in response to their own mothers, indicating a bond with a specific other person. Psychologically healthy infants who expand their world beyond the mother will be curious about strangers and will inspect them; unhealthy infants will fear strangers and recoil from them.

As infants physically begin to move away from their mothers by crawling and walking, they enter the *practicing* substage of separation-individuation, a period from about the 7th–10th month to about the 15th or 16th month. During this subphase, children easily distinguish their bodies from their mothers', establish a specific bond with their mothers, and begin to develop an autonomous ego. Yet, during the early stages of this period, they do not like to lose sight of the mother; they follow her with their eyes and show distress when she is away. Later, they begin to walk and to take in the outside world, which they experience as fascinating and exciting.

From about 16 to 25 months, children experience a *rapprochement* with their mother; that is, they desire to bring their mother and themselves back together. Mahler noticed that children of this age want their mothers to share with them every new acquisition of skill and every new experience. Now that they can walk with ease, they are more physically separate from the mother, but, paradoxically, they are more likely to show separation anxiety during the rapprochement stage than during the previous period. Their increased cognitive skills make them more aware of their separateness, causing them to try various ploys to regain the dual unity they once had with their mothers. Because these attempts are never com-pletely successful, children of this age often fight dramatically with their mothers, a condition called the *rapprochement crisis*.

The final subphase of the separation-individuation process is *libidinal object con-stancy*, which approximates the third year of life. During this time children must develop a constant inner representation of the mother, so that they can tolerate being physically separate from her. If this libidinal object constancy is not devel-oped, children will continue to depend on the mother's physical presence for their own security. Besides gaining some degree of object constancy, children must con-solidate their individuality; that is, they must learn to function without their moth-ers and to develop other object relationships (Mahler et al., 1975).

The strength of Mahler's theory is its elegant description of psychological birth based on empirical observations that she and her colleagues made on child–mother interactions. Although many of her tenets rely on inferences gleaned from reactions of preverbal infants, her ideas can easily be extended to adults. Any errors made during the first three years—the time of psychological birth—may result in later regressions to a stage when a person had not yet achieved separation from the mother and thus a sense of personal identity.

Otto Kernberg's View

KERNBERG

Otto F. Kernberg (1928–) was born in Vienna, received a medical degree from the University of Chile in 1953, but has lived in the United States since joining the staff at the Menninger Clinic in Topeka in 1957. Besides Menninger's he has held positions at Columbia University and Cornell University, where he is currently Professor of Psychiatry and Medical Director of the Medical Center.

Unlike Klein and Mahler who worked almost exclusively with young children, Kernberg observed mostly older patients. His work with seriously disturbed adults has led him to formulate a model of how the healthy infant develops. Like Klein, he regards his work as an extension of Freudian psychoanalysis rather than an alternate approach.

Kernberg (1975, 1976, 1984, 1986) believes that the key to understanding personality organization—from the extremely disturbed to the normal—is the mother–child relationship. Healthy early object relations result in an integrated ego, a punishing superego, a stable self-concept, and fulfilling interpersonal relations. Inadequate early mother–child relations lead to contradictory ego states and various levels of adult psychopathology.

In all levels of personality organization, Kernberg found the same structural units, or **internalized object relationships**, namely, a self-image, an object-image, and a certain affect that colors the self-image and the object-image. For example, in relating to the mother, an infant might sometimes have the image of a "good me," a "good mother," and a strong positive feeling, while at other times the infant experiences the "bad me," the "bad mother," and strong negative affect. In this example, the infant is able to separate contradictory aspects of self by *splitting* its ego. In an adult, continual splitting would represent a defect in the ego, but in infants and sometimes in adults, splitting is a helpful defense against anxiety.

Kernberg (1986) linked split-off ego states to the defense mechanisms of *introjection* and *identification*. The earliest and most primitive level of internalized object relationships is introjection, or the "swallowing whole" of an object-image, a self-image, and the affect generated by the interaction of the object and the self. At this early stage of development, introjected images are undifferentiated and kept apart by the splitting process, enabling the infant to keep separate images of, for example, the "good mother" *and* the "bad mother." The affective portion of each introjection is important, because it helps the child synthesize images with similar feeling tones. For example, oral gratification, nurturance, and mother–child contact may all fuse to become the "good internal object."

Identification, a higher form of introjection, is the second level of internalized object relations. As infants mature cognitively, they acquire the capacity to see themselves and their mother as having specific social *roles*. "Role implies the presence of a socially recognized function that is being carried out by the object or by both participants in the interaction" (Kernberg, 1976, p. 30). For example, when a mother helps dress a child, she is interacting in a specific way with that child as well as fulfilling the socially acceptable role of a mother. Again, the child has a specific self-image (subject) as a dependent person who needs help getting dressed, an image of the mother (object) as a helper at getting dressed, and a specific affect related to the interaction with mother during the dressing situation. The various roles played by the child eventually lead to consistent patterns of behavior, which in turn facilitate *ego identity*.

Kernberg's concept of ego identity follows closely that of Erikson (Chapter 3). "Ego identity refers to the overall organization of identifications and introjections under the guiding principle of the synthetic function of the ego" (Kernberg, 1976, p. 32). Ego identity gives the person a sense of continuity of the self. An established self-identity organizes other self-images, allows the person to see object-images more consistently, and facilitates stable interpersonal relations. Ego identity is the highest level of organization of the self, and it leads to integrated ego development and a mature, functioning superego. Lack of stable ego identity results in a continuation of the split-off ego, disintegration, and an assortment of psychological disorders.

Kernberg's attempt to synthesize Freudian drive theory, object relations theory, and developmental theory has been accepted more by clinicians—both psychologists and psychiatrists—than by academic psychologists. The theory departs from Freud in that it sees people as being shaped by social experiences rather than by instinctual drives, and it departs from Klein and Mahler in that it is not based on observations of the mother–child interaction and is therefore less specific or detailed.

Heinz Kohut's View

K O H U T

Heinz Kohut (1913–1981) was also born in Vienna, and, like Kernberg, he spent most of his professional life in the United States, where he was a Professional Lecturer in the Department of Psychiatry at the University of Chicago, a member of the faculty at the Chicago Institute for Psychoanalysis, and Visiting Professor of Psychoanalysis at the University of Cincinnati. A neurologist and a psychoanalyst, Kohut upset many psychoanalysts in 1971 with his publication of *The Analysis of the Self*, which replaced the ego with the concept of self. In addition to this book, aspects of his self psychology are found in *The Restoration of the Self* (1977) and *The Kohut Seminars* (1987), the latter of which was edited by Miriam Elson after Kohut's death.

More than the other object relations theorists, Kohut emphasized the process by which the *self* evolves from a vague and undifferentiated image to a clear and precise sense of individual identity. As with the others, he focused on the early mother–child relationship as the key to understanding later development. Human relatedness, not innate instinctual drives, are at the core of our personality.

Infants require adult caregivers not only to gratify physical needs but also to satisfy basic psychological needs. In caring for both physical and psychological needs, adults, or "**selfobjects**," treat infants as if they had a sense of self. For example, parents will act with warmth, coldness, or indifference depending in part on their infant's behavior. Through the process of empathic interaction, the infant takes in the selfobject's responses as pride, guilt, shame, or envy, all attitudes that eventually form the building blocks of the self. Kohut (1977, p. 311) defined the self as "the center of the individual's psychological universe." The self gives unity and consistency to one's experiences, remains relatively stable over time, and is "the center of initiative and a recipient of impressions" (Kohut, 1977, p. 99). The self is also the child's focus of interpersonal relations, shaping how he or she will relate to parents and other selfobjects.

Kohut (1971, 1977) believed that infants are naturally narcissistic. They are self-centered, looking out exclusively for their own welfare and wishing to be admired for who they are and what they do. The early self becomes crystallized around two basic *narcissistic needs*: the need to exhibit the grandiose self and the need to acquire an idealized image of one or both parents. The *grandiose-exhibitionistic self* is established when the infant relates to a "mirroring" selfobject who reflects approval of its behavior. The infant thus forms a rudimentary self-image from messages such as: "If others see me as perfect, then I am perfect." The *idealized parent image* is opposed to the grandiose self because it implies that someone else is perfect. Nevertheless, it too satisfies a narcissistic need because the infant adopts the attitude, "You are perfect, but I am part of you."

Both narcissistic self-images are necessary for healthy personality development. Both, however, must change as the child grows older. If they remain unaltered, they result in a pathologically narcissistic adult personality. Grandiosity must change into a realistic view of self, and the idealized parent image must grow into a realistic picture of the parents. The two self-images should not entirely disappear; the healthy adult continues to have positive attitudes toward self and continues to see good qualities in parents or parent substitutes. However, a narcissistic adult does not transcend these infantile needs and continues to be self-centered and to see the rest of the world as an admiring audience. Freud believed that such a narcissistic person was a poor candidate for psychoanalysis, but Kohut held that psychotherapy could be effective with these patients.

PSYCHOTHERAPY

Klein, Mahler, Kernberg, and Kohut were all psychoanalysts trained in orthodox Freudian practices. However, each modified psychoanalytic treatment to fit her or his own theoretical orientation. Because these theorists varied among themselves on therapeutic procedures, we will limit our discussion of therapy to the approach used by Melanie Klein.

Klein's pioneering use of psychoanalysis with children was not well accepted by other analysts during the 1920s and 1930s. Anna Freud was especially resistive to the notion of childhood psychoanalysis, contending that young children who were still attached to their parents could not develop a transference to the therapist because they have no unconscious fantasies or images. Therefore, she claimed, young children could not profit from psychoanalytic therapy. In contrast, Klein believed that not only could disturbed children benefit from analysis, but that even healthy children could profit from a prophylactic analytic treatment. She therefore insisted that her own children be analyzed. She also insisted that negative transference was an essential step toward successful treatment, a view not shared by Anna Freud and many other psychoanalysts.

To foster negative transference and aggressive fantasies, Klein provided each child with a variety of small toys, pencil and paper, paint, crayons, and so forth. She substituted *play therapy* for Freudian dream analysis and free association, believing that young children express their conscious and unconscious wishes through play. Her young patients often attacked her verbally, which gave her an opportunity to interpret the unconscious motives behind these attacks (Klein, 1943).

The aim of Kleinian therapy is to reduce depressive anxieties and persecutory fears and to mitigate the harshness of internalized objects. To accomplish this, Klein encouraged her patients to re-experience early emotions and fantasies, but this time with the therapist pointing out the differences between reality and fantasy, between conscious and unconscious. She also allowed patients to express both positive and negative transference, a situation that is essential for patients' understanding of how unconscious fantasies connect with present everyday situations. Once this connection is made, patients feel less persecuted by internalized objects, experience reduced depressive anxiety, and are able to project previously frightening internal objects onto the outer world.

CONCEPT OF HUMANITY

Object relations theorists generally see human personality as a product of the early mother–child relationship. The interaction between mother and infant lays the foundation for future personality development because that early interpersonal experience serves as a prototype for subsequent interpersonal relations. For this reason object relations theorists would be rated toward the deterministic end of the *determinism vs. free choice* dimension.

Because early experiences are crucial to later development, object relations theorists could be viewed as either *pessimistic* or *optimistic*, depending of the quality of the early mother–infant relationship. If that relationship is healthy, then the person will grow into a psychologically healthy adult; if it is not, the person will acquire a pathological, self-absorbed personality.

On the dimension of *causality vs. teleology*, object relations theory tends to be more causal. Early experiences are the primary shapers of personality. Expectations of the future play a very minor role in object relations theory.

As an extension of Freudian psychoanalysis, object relations theory is rated rather high on *unconscious determinants of behavior*. Most of the theorists believed that the prime determinants of behavior can be traced back to very early infancy, a time before verbal language. Thus, people acquire many personal traits and attitudes on a preverbal level and remain unaware of the complete nature of these traits and attitudes. In addition, Klein's acceptance of an innately acquired phylogenetic endowment places her theory even farther in the direction of unconscious determinants.

The emphasis that Klein placed on the death instinct and phylogenetic endowment would seem to suggest that she saw biology as more critical than environment in shaping personality. However, as Hughes (1989) suggested, external objects and the intimacy and nurturance that infants receive from the mother are environmental. Also, Klein shifted emphasis from Freud's biologically based infantile stages to an interpersonal one (Cashdan, 1988). Therefore, Klein and object relations theorists are rated moderate to high on *environmental* factors.

On the dimension of *uniqueness vs. similarities*, object relations theorists tend more toward similarities. As clinicians dealing mostly with disturbed patients, Klein, Mahler, Kernberg, and Kohut limited their discussions mostly to the distinction between healthy personalities and pathological ones. Although they wrote about different diagnostic categories, they were little concerned with differences among psychologically healthy personalities.

Related Research

Object relations theory has a long history of generating debate and discussion among clinicians but only a relatively recent history of generating empirical research. Much of that research has been spurred by Drew Westen at the University of Michigan.

In one study Westen, Lohr, Silk, Gold, and Kerber (1990) administered the Thematic Apperception Test (TAT) to three groups: (1) those diagnosed with borderline personalities, (2) those suffering from major depression, and (3) a control group of "normal" personalities. The researchers found that the TAT identified four separate categories of object relations: (1) Complexity of Representations of People, or the extent to which subjects differentiated self and others as stable personalities with complex motives and subjective experiences; (2) Affect-Tone of Relationship Paradigms, or the extent to which subjects expect other people to be malevolent (malicious and hurtful) or benevolent (benign and helpful); (3) Capacity for Emotional Investment in Relationships, or the extent to which subjects see others as ends rather than means to need gratification; and (4) Understanding of Social Causality, or the extent to which subjects make logical attributions of others' actions, thoughts, or feelings. Westen et al. found that people with borderline personality scored lower on all four scales than did normals, prompting them to suggest that object relations is a multidimensional rather than unitary concept. Westen, Ludolph, Misle, Ruffins, and Block (1990) and Westen, Ludolph, Block, Wixom, and Wiss (1990) found very similar results in studies of physically and sexually abused adolescent girls. In addition, this latter study found that the pre-Oedipal experience that these girls had with their mothers contributed to subsequent expectations of malevolent relationships.

Westen (1990b) has argued that these and other recent research findings point to the need to revise the object relations model to include the four dimensions identified by the TAT. Moreover, object relations seem to change over time. Westen, Klepser, Ruffins, Silverman, Lifton, and Boekamp (1991) reported on two studies, one that compared 2nd and 5th graders and another that compared 9th and 12th graders. Both studies found developmental differences on all scales except Affect-Tone. In other words, object relations continue to develop beyond the Oedipal years as children (1) acquire an expanded appreciation of the complexity of others' personalities, (2) increase their capacity for emotional investment, and (3) evolve increased ability to make logical attributions of others' behaviors, thoughts, and feelings.

In addition to Westen and his colleagues, a number of other researchers have recently investigated hypotheses suggested by object relations theory. In one such study, Murray (1991) studied infants periodically from 6–12 weeks to 18 months and found evidence that babies are sensitive to the quality of their interpersonal relationships with their mother. Compared to infants of normal mothers, 18-month-old-infants of mothers who had suffered postpartum depression were more insecurely attached to their mothers and showed more mild behavior problems, such as sleep disturbances, despite the fact that their mothers had manifested no depressive symptoms during the previous 15 months.

Empirical research into object relations theory may have received a boost by the publication of the Bell Object Relations Inventory (BORI) (Bell, Billington, & Becker, 1986). This inventory, which is embedded within a larger questionnaire that also measures reality testing, asks subjects to respond either "true" or "false" to 90 descriptive statements based on their most recent experience. Using a factor analytic approach, Bell et al. identified four main factors that compose object relations. Factor I: Alienation (ALN) is the broadest dimension of object relations. People who score high on ALN lack basic trust, are unable to attain closeness, despair over ever achieving interpersonal intimacy, are suspicious and guarded, and believe that others will fail them. High scorers on the ALN scale almost always receive an independent diagnosis of borderline or pathological personality. The second factor, Insecure Attachment (IA), measures painfulness of interpersonal relations. High scorers on the IA dimension are sensitive to rejection, overconcerned about being liked or accepted, and jealous of other people. They also tend to be involved in intense sadomasochistic relationships, search painfully for security, and fear being abandoned. Factor III, Egocentricity (EGC), indicates self-centeredness and a mistrust of others. People who score high on EGC have a narcissistic view of other people, believing that others exist simply to satisfy their needs and that they may be manipulated for their own self-centered aims. These people are self-protective, exploitive of others, intrusive, coercive, and demanding. They tend to have alternative feelings of omnipotence and powerlessness. Factor IV, Social Incompetence (SI), describes people who have difficulty making friends, especially those of the opposite sex. They are shy, nervous, socially insecure, and find social relations bewildering and unpredictable.

Recently, Heesacker & Neimeyer (1990) used the Bell Object Relations Inventory (BORI) to assess eating disorders. They studied 183 undergraduate women and found that disturbed eating patterns, as measured by the Eating Disorder Inventory of Garner, Olmstead, and Polivy (1983), was linked to disturbances in early object relations. More specifically, college women with a strong "drive for thinness" scored high on the Insecure Attachment (IA) and Social Incompetence (SI) scales of the BORI.

Also, one recent study reported on the use of the BORI to determine whether a person suffering from multiple personality disorder would exhibit different personalities when filling out the inventory while experiencing different identities. Alpher (1991) found that the BORI discriminated four distinct personality profiles for a 27-year-old-woman with multiple personality disorder. This discovery suggests that some people with multiple personality disorder retain an identifiable split ego into adulthood, and that the BORI has some usefulness in measuring that split.

CRITIQUE OF OBJECT RELATIONS THEORY

Currently, object relations theory is more popular in Britain than it is in the United States. The "British School," which included not only Melanie Klein but also W. R. D. Fairbairn and D. W. Winnicott, has exerted a strong influence on psychoanalysts and psychiatrists in England, while in the United States, the influence of object relations theorists has been less direct. Writing about Klein's theory, Robert Caper (1988, p. 129) observed that:

> Despite their opposition to Klein's ideas when presented in direct or undiluted form, many American psychoanalysts have recognized that, in a practical sense, an adequate understanding of their day-to-day clinical experience with patients requires them to employ something like her discoveries. As a consequence, while her ideas as a whole have encountered strong *official* opposition from most American psychoanalysts, many of her fundamental theses are accepted under an alias . . . by those who claim to oppose them.

Object relations theory grew out of orthodox psychoanalytic theory and thus suffers from some of the same limitations that confront Freud's theory. Most of its tenets are based on nonverifiable assumptions about what is happening inside the nescient infant's psyche. The theory does not lend itself to direct verification because it generates very few testable hypotheses.

Perhaps its most useful feature is its ability to *organize information* about the behavior of infants. More than almost any other personality theorists, object relations theorists have speculated on how humans gradually come to acquire a sense of identity. Klein, and especially Mahler, built their theories on careful observations of the mother–child relationship. They watched the interactions between infant and mother and drew inferences based on what they saw. However, beyond the early childhood years, object relations theory lacks usefulness as an organizer of knowledge.

As a *guide to the practitioner*, the theory fares somewhat better. Parents of young infants can learn of the importance of a warm, accepting, and nurturing caregiver. Psychotherapists may find object relations theory useful, not only in understanding the early development of their patients, but also in understanding and working with the transference relationship that patients form with therapists whom they view as substitute parents.

On the criterion of *consistency*, each of the object relations theories discussed in this chapter has a high level of internal *consistency*, but the different theorists disagree among themselves on a number of points. Even though they all place primary importance on human relationships, the differences among them far exceed the similarities.

Object relations theory is not alone as a Freudian extension. The personality theory of John Dollard and Neal E. Miller offers a unique interpretation of how classical psychoanalysis could be integrated into an empirically based learning theory.

BIOGRAPHIES OF JOHN DOLLARD AND NEAL E. MILLER

John Dollard was born on August 29, 1900, in the small community of Menasha, Wisconsin, where his family lived until his father, a railroad engineer, died in a train wreck at about the time John was approaching college age. His mother, a former school teacher, then moved the family to Madison so the children could more easily attend the University of Wisconsin (Miller, 1982).

After a short time in the U.S. Army, Dollard enrolled at the University of Wisconsin, where he studied English and commerce. After he graduated with a bachelor of arts degree in 1922, he remained at the University as a fund-raiser for the Wisconsin Memorial Union. In that

capacity he made friends with Max Mason, who became like a second father to Dollard. When Mason became president of the University of Chicago, Dollard became one of his assistants, a position he held from 1926 until 1929. In 1930 Dollard earned a master of arts degree in sociology from Chicago and the following year was awarded a Ph.D. in sociology. At Chicago he was influenced by the same social scientists who had helped shape the thinking of Harry Stack Sullivan, Karen Horney, and Erich Fromm.

During the year 1931–1932 Dollard went to Germany as a research fellow to study psychoanalysis. As part of his training, he was analyzed by Hanns

Sachs, a close associate of Sigmund Freud, and the same therapist who analyzed Fromm. On returning from Germany, he took a position as assistant professor of anthropology at Yale University, and, then, the following year, he moved to the newly created Institute of Human Relations at Yale as assistant professor of sociology. The institute was established as a multidisciplinary organization and included a number of well-known scholars from the fields of psychology, psychiatry, anthropology, and sociology, including O. Hobart Mower, Robert Sears, and Clark Hull. Neal E. Miller was also at the institute, and he and Dollard soon formed a close working relationship. A man of broad interests and abilities, Dollard held positions in three academic departments at Yale— anthropology, sociology, and psychology. In 1969 he became professor emeritus, a position he held until his death on October 8, 1980.

Dollard's early collaboration with Neal E. Miller produced three volumes, which form the core of the Dollard and Miller theory of personality. The first was a joint project by several members of the Yale group, *Frustration and Aggression* (1939). In 1941 Miller and Dollard published *Social Learning and Imitation* and, in 1950, their most important work, *Personality and Psychotherapy*, appeared. (In this latter book, Dollard was the senior author, but in the 1941 publication, Miller's name appears first. Therefore, the theory has variously been referred to as the Miller and Dollard theory or the Dollard and Miller theory. Either is acceptable.)

Neal E. Miller, also a Wisconsin native, was born in Milwaukee on August 3, 1909. He received a B.S. from the University of Washington in 1931, and a M.S. from Stanford the following year. He then went to Yale to continue his education. While working toward his doctoral degree, he held the position of assistant in psychology at the Institute of Human Relations. After completing his Ph.D. in 1935, he journeyed to Austria to study psychoanalysis at the Vienna Institute of Psychoanalysis, thus paralleling Dollard's training four years earlier. As part of his psychoanalytic training, Miller underwent analysis with Heinz Hartmann, a pupil of Freud.

In 1936, Miller returned to Yale to accept a position as instructor at the Institute of Human Relations, where he worked to integrate the disciplines of economics, sociology, anthropology, psychiatry, psychology, and law. With the outbreak of World War II, he served in the U.S. Army Air Force as an officer in charge of research, and then from 1944 to 1946 he served as director of a psychological research project for the Air Force. After the war he returned to Yale, where he remained for another 20 years.

In 1966 Miller became professor of psychology and head of the Laboratory of Physiological Psychology at Rockefeller University, where he conducted research in a variety of areas, especially biofeedback and brain functioning. An outgrowth of this research led to his involvement in the fields of behavioral medicine, behavioral health, and health psychology (Miller, 1983, 1984a, 1984b). In 1986 Miller moved back to Yale, where he continues his work in health-related areas.

Miller is recognized as a meticulous and productive experimentalist as well as an innovative theorist. His work in experimental psychology led to his selection as President of the American Psychological Association, a position he held during the year 1960–1961. Other honors include serving as James Rowland Angell Professor at Yale from 1952 to 1966; being selected for membership in the National Academy of Science; receiving the Warren Medal from the Society of Experimental Psychologists in 1957, and being elected president of Division 38 (Health Psychology) of the American Psychological Association. In addition, Miller is one of the few behavioral scientists to receive the President's Medal of Science.

INTRODUCTION TO DOLLARD AND MILLER'S LEARNING THEORY

Dollard and Miller believed that, for the most part, human behavior is learned. We learn to be who we are and what we are. Like Little Hans, we learn fears, feelings of guilt, anxiety, and shame. We also learn to set goals, develop aspirations, and to strive toward our goals and aspirations; we learn to adjust to our social environment, to adopt normal and abnormal patterns of adjustment, and to erect a multitude of neurotic symptoms.

No matter how different two learning situations may appear on the surface, the same four fundamental factors apply. From the simplest to the most complex, all learning is based on **drive, cue, response,** and **reinforcement.**

We can illustrate the four principles of learning by considering the case of Little Hans and his phobia of being bitten by a horse while walking in the street. According to Freud (1909/1955), Hans developed his phobia while under a strong Oedipal drive. Dollard and Miller (1950) might suggest that Hans was motivated by several drives at the same time, one of the strongest being affection for his parents who had fed him and cared for many of his other needs. When Hans observed a large horse fall down, he felt saddened because he had learned to like horses. In time, however, he also observed similarities between his father and horses; he saw that they both had "eyeglasses" (blinders) and a large black moustache (muzzle). Later, while walking in the street, he felt anxious at seeing a horse, which in some ways reminded him of his father for whom he had both affectionate and hostile feelings. He was able to partially reduce his anxiety by returning to his house and remaining there. The act of staying at home, therefore, was reinforcing or rewarding because such a behavior avoided additional anxiety. However, when he was forced to go into the street or to look at horses, his anxiety intensified to the point of a debilitating phobia.

FOUR FUNDAMENTALS OF LEARNING

With this explanation in mind, let us turn to a discussion of each of the four fundamentals of learning. A *drive is any stimulus strong enough to impel action.* In the case of Little Hans, at least two previously learned drives were present—affection and hostility for his father. *Cues are stimuli that are distinctive enough to guide responses.* They tell us when, where, and how to respond. In the present example, Little Hans responded by retreating to the safety of his house when he felt uncomfortable at viewing a horse. His internally felt anxiety told him how to respond. Moreover, the sight of the horse and the street became associated with his anxiety so that in the future either or both would serve as cues, telling him to stay near his house. A *response is the behavior that occurs as a reaction to drives and cues.* Before they can be reinforced, responses must first occur. Little Hans had to possess the ability to retreat from an anxiety-laden situation in order to be rewarded by a lessening of anxiety. This escape response had to be within his repertoire of responses—an obvious fact, but one that should not be overlooked. Hans's reinforcement was thus the safety he felt at running into his house. This reinforcement tended to increase the probability that he would make the same response during a future similar situation. *Reinforcement, then, is any event that strengthens the connection between a cue and a response, thereby increasing the tendency for a response to be repeated.*

Before continuing with a more detailed explanation of the four fundamental factors of learning, let us look at a quotation from Dollard and Miller (1950, pp. 29–30) summarizing the relationship among these factors.

> The drive impels responses, which are usually also determined by cues from other stimuli not strong enough to act as drives but more specifically distinctive than the drive. If the first response is not rewarded by an event reducing the drive, this response tends to drop out and others to appear. The extinction of successive nonrewarded responses produces so-called random behavior. If some one response is followed by reward, the connection between the cue and this response is strengthened, so that this response is more likely to occur. This strengthening of the cue-response connection is the essence of learning.

Drive

The term drive can be used interchangeably with motivation. All drives are stimuli, but not every stimulus is a drive. As pointed out earlier, any stimulus can become a drive if it is strong enough to impel action. Dollard and Miller identified two major classes of drives—*innate drives* and *learned drives.*

Innate Drives

Innate, or primary, drives are those that are not weakened by lack of reinforcement. They include pain, hunger, sex, thirst, fatigue, cold, and oxygen deprivation.

That they are not weakened by nonreinforcement is illustrated by the example of a hungry man driven to seek food. If he is reinforced by food he will learn what steps to take in the future to reduce his drive. On the other hand, if his hunger drive goes unreinforced—that is, if he does not get anything to eat—he remains hungry and continues to be motivated by the hunger drive. In fact, the less the reinforcement, the more powerful the drive; ordinarily, the longer the man goes without eating, the stronger his drive becomes. Innate drives are not dependent upon learning. Eating in a certain restaurant involves both a learned drive and an innate drive. A diner finds the food in a particular establishment especially reinforcing and so she learns to eat often in that place. Hunger itself, however, exists in the absence of any prior learning and is not dependent on reinforcement for its continued strength.

Society prevents primary drives from becoming excessively strong by providing opportunities for people to breathe, drink, eat, and regulate body temperature. As for the sex drive, its unrestrained expression is not permitted by most societies; however, all societies allow their members to satisfy this drive under certain conditions, for instance in marriage or through such disguised forms as sublimations and inhibitions.

Because innate drives are usually gratified within the trappings of society, and because they are often disguised, their importance in most learning situations is generally underestimated. Only under unusual conditions, such as war or natural disaster, does it become evident to what extremes people will go in order to satisfy a primary drive. In a smoothly functioning society, however, innate drives are normally satisfied with little cognizance of their primary nature. They are hidden behind the veneer of secondary or learned drives (Dollard & Miller, 1950).

Learned Drives

Learned, or secondary, drives are those that are governed by the principles of learning and extinction and that can be strengthened through reinforcement. Secondary drives are not easily distinguishable from primary drives. For example, fear can be either a primary or a secondary drive depending on whether or not it is learned. In general, however, learned drives are those that, at one time in a person's life, were neutral, but that take on drive value during the course of learning. Money, for example, has neither a positive nor negative value to an infant, but it acquires drive properties as the child learns to attach value to it. Functionally, learned drives have the same value as innate drives; that is, they impel action.

Learned drives differ from primary drives in two important ways. First, learned drives are much more varied. The reason for this is obvious. Innate drives, such as hunger and sex, are the same in all cultures, whereas learned drives differ from culture to culture. In fact, learned drives account for the differences among cultures as well as the differences among individuals within a culture. One person may be driven to achieve various sexual conquests, another to hoard money, a third to acquire social acceptance, and so on. The personality of each individual is characterized by specific learned drives that motivate much of that person's behavior.

A second distinction is that innate drives cannot be extinguished; learned drives can. This difference might well be the criterion for identifying innate drives. If a motivation cannot be extinguished, it is a primary drive. Hunger, of course, is not dependent on reinforcement for its drive value and cannot be extinguished through nonreinforcement or counterconditioning. All secondary drives, because they have been learned, can be unlearned, that is, extinguished. Some learned drives, however, are extremely resistant to extinction. These are the ones Allport (Chapter 13) would term *functionally autonomous*. (In Allport's concept of functional autonomy, the original drive may be replaced by a new motive so that behavior becomes self-sustaining.) Dollard and Miller (1950), however, did not allow for functionally autonomous motivation and insisted that any learned drive is subject to the laws of extinction.

Cue

Cues, like drives, are stimuli, but they differ from drives in that they are not strong enough to impel action but instead are distinctive enough to determine when, where, and how responses will be made. The same stimulus could serve as either a drive or a cue depending on its intensity and its distinctiveness. The five o'clock whistle is a cue for the employees to stop work. They can differentiate its sound from all others and are thus told by it what response they should make. However, for employees working next to the whistle, the intensity of the sound serves as a drive, impelling them to action, that is, to cover their ears.

Internal stimuli like hunger and anxiety may also have cue as well as drive value. A very hungry person is driven to eat—almost anything will do. A moderately or slightly hungry person will differentiate among internal stimuli and recognize a specific hunger, for example, salty foods rather than sweets. This second person will be guided by olfactory and visual cues to select popcorn rather than candy.

Some cues are so weak that they are perceived on an extremely low level of differentiation. Most of us have had the experience of walking into a familiar room and somehow feeling that something is missing or out of place. We do not quite know what it is, yet we perceive that something is wrong. Likewise, Little Hans was able to associate his street anxiety with his masturbatory activity without consciously understanding the connection. Dollard and Miller (1950) believed that much of human personality is *unconscious* because it is learned on the basis of weak cues or cues that have never been verbalized.

Response

Dollard and Miller (1950) suggested that learning depends on an individual making the correct response. One never learns correctly by making an incorrect response. The only thing learned by trial and error is that a particular trial was an error; one must still find and make the right response. Much time is saved if the learner makes the correct response first. Responses, however, need not be overt actions, but can involve the *higher mental processes*, such as thinking and using language. These higher mental processes, especially language, are a major distinction between animal and human learning. Moreover, language greatly facilitates the learning process. Teaching a person to drive an automobile is made easier simply by telling the learner what to do (Dollard & Miller, 1950).

Reinforcement

Reinforcement is any event that strengthens the tendency for a response to be repeated. A paycheck, for example, is one reinforcement that keeps people working. However, if a response is not reinforced, it tends not to be repeated, which then gives other responses a chance to be reinforced. Eventually, some response will be followed by reinforcement and will then tend to occur earlier in subsequent learning trials. If it continues to be strengthened through reinforcement, this response will become a habit. Only reinforcement can strengthen or maintain a habit. Repetition does nothing by itself.

Reduction of a drive serves as a reinforcement so that after a drive has been satiated it loses its power to impel action. Other drives then replace it, which leads to variety in human behavior (Dollard & Miller, 1950).

Dollard and Miller (1950) suggested that reinforcement is often automatic; that is, it is independent of any thought or insight. For example, infants severely punished for soiling their pants may learn to be neat and orderly without having to think about how to avoid future punishment. They need not say to themselves, "I must not be messy or I'll be punished." This belief in automatic and unconscious reinforcement is an important difference between the learning theory of Dollard and Miller and that of Albert Bandura (see Chapter 10). Bandura believes that learning does not take place without cognitive mediation, which means that people are actively involved in evaluating the desirability of their various reinforcements. On the other hand, Dollard and Miller (1950), while recognizing the role of higher mental processes in selecting and evaluating many reinforcement events, insisted that an adequate theory of learning must make room for automatic, unconscious reinforcements.

Dollard and Miller also recognized *secondary reinforcements*, which, like secondary drives, are learned. Money is a good example of a secondary reinforcer. As infants, people attach no value to dollar bills, but later they learn the value of money and may even continue to work for it after they have satisfied all their primary drives. The money itself becomes a reinforcement, and some people hoard it with no intention to spend it for food or shelter.

Gradient of Reinforcement

Dollard and Miller (1950) further speculated that most learning involves a sequence of responses that lead to a final reinforced one. A hungry person may have to plan a meal, go to the grocery store, purchase food, bring it home, prepare it, cook it, and finally eat it. Is only the eating response rewarded? No, because if the preceding behaviors were not reinforced they would not occur. But if they, too, are rewarding, why should the person continue to the final response of eating? In other words, if shopping for groceries is reinforcing (and we know that it is or else it would not occur), why is it not the final response in the sequence? The answer is that eating is more strongly reinforced than cooking, cooking more than preparing food, and so on back to the beginning of the sequence. This progressive strengthening of responses in sequence is called the **gradient of reinforcement** and results in the final response securing a stronger reinforcement value than earlier ones.

The gradient of reinforcement explains why people increase their tendency to approach a goal the closer they are to it. It also explains why, other things being equal, immediate reinforcements are more effective than delayed ones. Students who receive immediate feedback on term papers have their scholarly responses strengthened more than those who must wait three months to receive reinforcement.

Drives and Reinforcement

We have seen that the same object can be either a drive or a reinforcement. Money, for example, can be either a secondary drive or a secondary reinforcement. However, the same event cannot be both a drive and a reward *at the same time*, but it may produce two effects that fluctuate in rapid succession so that they become closely associated. Cooking food, for instance, can be a drive provided it is associated with, or sometimes leads to, the reduction of the hunger drive. Cooking can also be a reward so that, in the aggregate experience of preparing and eating food, the drive and the reward become closely interwoven. Cooking is a reward because cooks know they will eventually eat their preparation. If they did not subsequently eat their own food (for example, a chef in a restaurant), the act of cooking would not be a reward, but instead would be motivated by a drive to acquire a later reward (money), which will enable them to purchase food and other reinforcers.

HIGHER MENTAL PROCESSES

The concepts of drive, cue, response and reinforcement can be applied to animal as well as human learning. In fact, Dollard and Miller relied heavily on animal studies to develop these concepts. Results of animal studies generalize easily to simple human learning. But what about more complex human learning—those higher mental processes that help differentiate humans from other animals? Dollard and Miller (1950) hypothesized that the same four factors that apply to simple learning are equally applicable to higher mental processes, such as thinking and abstract problem solving.

In psychoanalytical terms, higher mental processes are ego functions and are used to solve problems of an emotional or social nature, as well as simple physical problems. They include complex functions like abstract reasoning, intention and planning, language acquisition, and foresight. They are also responsible for such superego functions as shame, guilt, and identification.

In learning theory terms, higher mental processes differ from automatic habits or responses in that they involve no immediate overt response to cues. "The final overt response follows a series of internal responses, commonly called a train of thought" (Dollard & Miller, 1950, p. 98). For example, a man walking on frozen ground slips and falls. He responds automatically by thrusting his hands forward in order to protect his head and body from striking the ground first. This simple response to the immediate cue of falling is done without thinking and involves no higher mental processes. Another person walking on frozen ground thinks, "I must be careful. I have seen others fall so I, too, might slip. Therefore, I must take shorter steps." A final response—slowing down by taking smaller steps—follows a series of internal responses that involved the use of higher mental processes.

We have seen that responses are impelled by drives and elicited by cues. So how can there be a *series* of internal responses? How can one response follow another without an intervening drive or cue? The answer is that one internal response does not follow directly from another response. Instead, Dollard and Miller said, some responses generate cues that, in turn, elicit other responses.

These **cue-producing responses** may be either overt or covert. An example of an overt cue-producing response would be making a list of errands one must run. The response of writing the list evokes a cue that shapes a later response. Covert cue-producing responses function the same way, but the responses and cues take place internally and are not perceptible to others. A hostess planning a party employs many covert cue-producing responses. Her silent thoughts produce cues that mediate further thoughts. She thinks, "I plan to invite Mr. Jones, but if I do I should invite Mr. Brown, his best friend. That reminds me, Mrs. Brown doesn't get along with Mrs. Smith, whom I'd hoped would bring her card table and chairs." In this sequence, one internal response produces a cue that elicits another internal response that, in turn, produces still another cue and so on.

There are two different ways in which cue-producing responses can be used. First, they can serve as cues to other people, as when one person gives a command to another. Second, they can serve as cues to the person producing them, a process that usually but not always involves internal behavior and that is central to higher mental processes (Dollard & Miller, 1950).

Foresight

When words and thoughts serve as stimuli for learning they are called **mediated drives**. Higher mental processes, especially verbal responses, enable us to respond to words and thoughts about the future. People do not live solely in the here and now. Having learned the concept of future, our responses are often mediated by cue patterns consisting of words or thoughts about coming events. An employee works diligently for a whole month in order to obtain a reward at the end of that period. This seems to be contrary to the gradient of reinforcement principle, which hypothesized that immediate reinforcements are more effective than delayed ones. However, foresight and mediated drives generate immediate reinforcement by keeping the worker continuously mindful of a paycheck at the end of the month.

Foresight is largely, but not completely, dependent on language. Verbal ability aids us in thinking about the future. We provide ourselves with nearly continuous reinforcement through thoughts about receiving compliments, reassurances, threats, or disapprovals (Dollard & Miller, 1950).

Reasoning

A second higher mental process, also facilitated by language, is reasoning. The importance of reasoning is shown in the old cliché "Think before you act." Without reasoning, people would be doomed to carry out overt trial-and-error responses in each new learning situation. The hunger drive would impel us to scratch continually for food. Without reasoning, humans would never have planted crops or domesticated animals. Each response designed to make life easier would be trial and error, and no complex inventions could be possible.

Social Training

One of humanity's great advantages over other animals is its capacity to use higher mental processes to preserve culture. Past cultural acquisitions are handed down from one generation to the next so that they do not have to be continually rediscovered. Without social training each generation would be forced to begin culture anew.

Probably our most beneficial cultural heritage is language. Through imitation we quickly learn the language of our parents and our society. As our most highly developed form of cue-producing responses, language is used to think and to give ourselves private verbal cues that greatly facilitate learning. Language, a cultural inheritance, is itself the primary vehicle of cultural transmission and is used to train children to become adult members of a society.

Not all social training is beneficial. Young children are frequently exposed to inescapable conflict, a principal ingredient in neuroses and psychoses. Because children are physically, mentally, and emotionally helpless, they are at the mercy of their environment, particularly their parents who can pick them up, haul them around, punish them, or restrain them. However, the environment can also provide unparalleled comfort, thus trapping children hopelessly in the cycle of "eternal pain" and "endless bliss." Dollard and Miller (1950, p. 130), in fact, called infancy "a period of transitory psychosis."

Dollard and Miller (1950) listed four critical training situations that produce conflict in children: (1) the feeding situation, (2) cleanliness training, (3) sex training, and (4) controlling anger responses. The feeding situation can be distressing to children because they cannot control the time when they are to be fed. But feeding is also an occasion of great pleasure and satisfaction. Children, of course, prefer being held and fed by a comforting parent to being hungry and isolated, but their limited resources prevent them from achieving continual satiation. During childhood people learn many of the personal traits that mark their adult life: apathy, apprehension, and fear of the dark on the one hand, and love, sociability, and confidence on the other.

Cleanliness training, including toilet training, is a second area of potential conflict. Children have no innate aversion to clutter, urine, and feces, but in most cultures they are taught that urine and feces are "dirty," and that dirt and clutter are bad. Cleanliness training is difficult because parents and children have different standards for what is proper and what is pleasurable. Freud (1933/1964) described the conflict between parent and child during the anal stage, or second year of life. At this age children possess somewhat better tools, including early language skills, for coping with conflict, but they are still no match for their prevailing culture. Future personality traits that stem from this age are more likely to be negative than positive. They include stubbornness, excessive conformity, guilt, and a morbid conscience, which Dollard and Miller (1950) likened to cancer in its ability to destroy life.

The conflicts produced by early sex training may also carry over into adult life. As Freud (1905/1953b) pointed out, young children possess a powerful drive for sexual pleasure. When he wrote his essays on infantile sexuality, Western society was, perhaps, more restrictive and punitive toward childhood masturbation than it is today. Nevertheless, even "enlightened" parents often show strong disapproval of their child's sex play. Recall that the parents of Little Hans believed that they were rearing their son according to Freudian principles. Nonetheless, the mother told Hans that if she caught him playing with his penis again, she would take him to a doctor who would cut it off. Actual threats of castration may be uncommon in present society, but parents inhibit sexual behaviors of their children in more subtle ways. Such punishment usually leads to repression of sexual thoughts, guilt, impotency, and frigidity.

The fourth critical training situation is anger control. Children frustrated by weaning, cleanliness training, sexual suppression, or any other event typically react by becoming angry. But anger itself is likely to be punished, and a cycle of anger and punishment may eventually lead to a sense of helplessness, fear of parental figures, extreme compliance and dependence, pervasive anxiety, or displaced aggression.

Each of these early training situations produces conflicts that can only be solved in a nonproductive manner, such as resorting to dysfunctional behaviors. However, some conflicts can be resolved in psychologically healthy ways. One of

Dollard and Miller's ongoing contributions to an understanding of human personality (both normal and dysfunctional) is their analysis of conflict.

CONFLICT

The anatomy of conflict, based on a social learning model, was studied in the laboratory by Miller (1944) and applied to psychotherapy by Dollard and Miller (1950). Conflict exists whenever two equally valued but incompatible responses are desired or required. The two responses are not only incompatible, but they cannot follow one another in sequence. If both responses could be produced, no conflict would exist. People in conflict typically react with tension, anxiety, vacillation, or blocking. They are often unable to make any response, but once they do make an appropriate response, their level of conflict is progressively lessened.

Basic Assumptions

To understand the different kinds of conflict, it is necessary to be familiar with four fundamental principles about approach (positive) and avoidance (negative) gradients.

1. "The tendency to approach a goal is stronger the nearer the subject is to it" (Dollard & Miller, 1950, p. 352). This is called the **gradient of approach** and explains why long-distance runners put forth a progressively greater effort as they come to the finish line.

2. "The tendency to avoid a feared stimulus is stronger the nearer the subject is to it" (Dollard & Miller, 1950, p. 352). This is the **gradient of avoidance** and explains why people show more and more apprehension the closer they get to a fearful stimulus.

3. "The strength of avoidance increases more rapidly with nearness than does that of approach" (Dollard & Miller, 1950, p. 352). This explains why, when a goal has both positive and negative value, a person's tendency to avoid becomes stronger than the tendency to approach as that person nears the goal. When the tendency to approach a stimulus is stronger at a distance than the tendency to avoid, a person will move toward the goal, then stop at the point where the avoidance gradient crosses the approach gradient (see Figure 8.1).

4. "The strength of the tendencies to approach or avoid varies with the strength of the drive upon which they are based" (Dollard & Miller, 1950, p. 353). In other words, the stronger the drive, the greater the tendency to approach a positively valued goal and to avoid a negatively valued one. Strong drives, therefore, increase the height of the gradient at any distance from the goal. Figure 8.2 shows that when the drive is strong enough, the gradient to approach may be higher than the gradient to avoid under weak drive. A person will eat mildly distasteful food when very hungry but not when only moderately hungry.

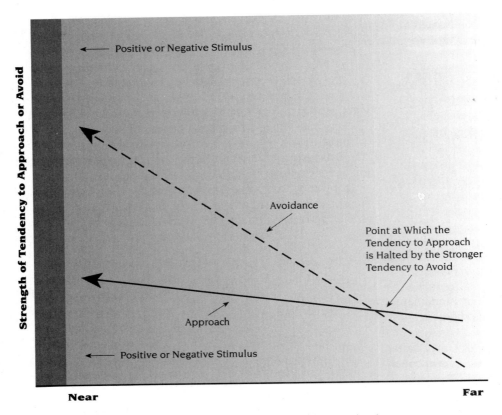

Strength of Tendency to Approach or Avoid

←—— Positive or Negative Stimulus

Avoidance

Point at Which the
Tendency to Approach
is Halted by the Stronger
Tendency to Avoid

Approach

←—— Positive or Negative Stimulus

Near

Far

Figure 8.1   *Gradients of Approach and Avoidance. The gradient approach increases as one nears
a positive stimulus, but the gradient of avoidance increases at an even faster rate as
one approaches a negative stimulus.*

Types of Conflict

Dollard and Miller did not originate the concept of approach-avoidance and avoidance-avoidance conflicts. They did, however, conceptualize conflicts within social
learning theory, and Miller (1959) conducted extensive research that both supported
and enlarged the existing theory.

When people are midway between two equally desirable goals, it is sometimes
said that they experience an approach-approach conflict. Dollard and Miller (1950),
however, do not consider this situation to be a conflict. The donkey halfway between
two haystacks will not starve to death. First of all, it is not likely that a person would
ever be exactly midway between two goals; second, even minor changes in the
perceived value of one or the other goals would pull the person slightly toward one
goal or the other. Because the approach gradient increases the nearer the person
comes to the stimulus, even minor shifts are sufficient to make one goal more

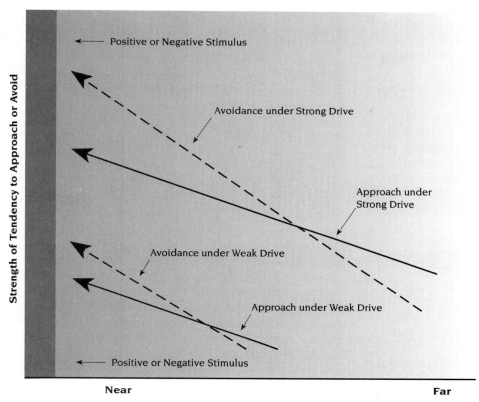

Figure 8.2 *Gradients of Approach and Avoidance under Strong Drive. Strong drive increases the height of both the approach and avoidance gradients. Approach under strong drive may be greater than avoidance under weak drive.*

desirable than the other. No vacillation, tension, or blocking will occur in these situations.

Approach-Avoidance

Dollard and Miller (1950, p. 355) defined an **approach-avoidance conflict** as any "situation in which a person has strong tendencies to approach and avoid the same goal." In an approach-avoidance conflict, a person approaches a negative goal or event until the approach gradient is crossed by the steeper avoidance gradient. At that intersection the tendencies to approach and to avoid are equal, and conflict results. The person remains approximately at this point, unable to move nearer the goal because the tendency to avoid is now stronger than the tendency to approach. If the person is far from the goal and the drive to approach is weak when it meets the avoidance gradient, only mild conflict is experienced. However, as the drive becomes stronger it intersects the avoidance gradient at a point nearer the feared goal. The person then experiences intense conflict because the drive to approach and the tendency to avoid are both quite strong. Figure 8.3 shows that increasing the motivation of the person without reducing the avoidance gradient (fear and anxiety) may result in more severe conflict and still leave the person short of the goal.

Everyone experiences approach-avoidance conflicts, but the lives of troubled and neurotic persons seem to be defined by them. These people are perpetually stuck in neutral gear. They would like to accomplish their goals, but to do so they must surmount "impossible" obstacles. Their fear of the goal is always equal to the tendency to approach it. They remain constantly at the point of conflict, neither able to diminish fear, which in many cases is self-erected, nor able to reduce the drive by accepting the idea that the goal cannot be reached. Either a reduction in

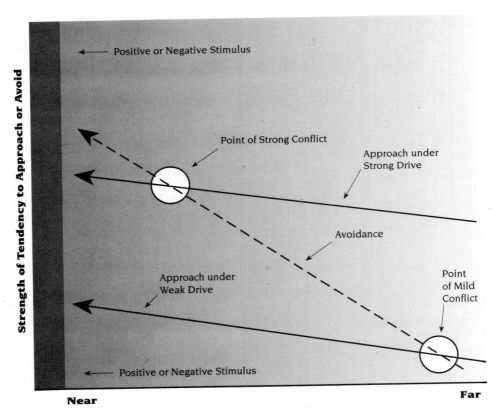

Figure 8.3. Approach-Avoidance Conflict. As a feared goal is approached, avoidance becomes stronger and the person remains where the approach tendency is equal to the avoidance tendency, that is, where the two gradients cross. Increasing the motivation to approach without reducing the fear merely intensifies the conflict.

fear or a reduction in the drive would lessen the conflict. Inability to make a decision becomes a way of life for troubled people. One person complains, "I would like to divorce my husband, but it's too scary." Another worries, "I'd like to quit my job, but my wife would be furious with me."

Approach-avoidance conflicts can be overcome in two ways. First, the motivation to approach can be made stronger than the fear to avoid the goal. Because the avoidance gradient is steeper than the approach gradient, this can be accomplished only if the fear is relatively weak or the original drive is quite strong. If the approach gradient touches the goal before being intersected by the avoidance gradient, the person has reached the goal, but probably at the expense of experiencing ever-increasing anxiety.

A second and usually more successful method of overcoming approach-avoidance conflicts is to reduce the negative value of the goal. Most therapists give priority to this attack, attempting first, by one technique or another, to lessen the patient's anxiety and to alleviate unreasonable fears. The progressive relaxation of Edmond Jacobson (1938) and the meditative relaxation of Herbert Benson (1975) have both been used extensively by psychotherapists.

Avoidance-Avoidance

A person caught between the devil and the deep blue sea is experiencing an **avoidance-avoidance conflict**. This type of conflict is illustrated in Figure 8.4, where two negative stimuli are opposed to each other. As people attempt to escape from one negative situation, they draw nearer the other one. The conflict often results leads people to try to escape by finding some alternate route, such as a psychological breakdown or a denial of the negative aspects of one or both of the opposing stimuli. When people can find no alternate pathway, they are forced to vacillate near the point of conflict until circumstances change the strength of one of the negative stimuli, thereby changing the angle of intersection. This will either alter the point of conflict or eliminate it completely. Take, for example, the would-be watermelon thief who is caught between an angry farmer and a threatening dog. The thief may smile and speak in a friendly manner, thereby reducing the farmer's anger and lowering that negative stimulus, or the thief may notice that the dog is chained to a post, thus restricting its range of movement and allowing for escape in that direction (Dollard & Miller, 1950).

Double Approach-Avoidance

A third type of conflict is the **double approach-avoidance conflict**. Most situations involving human responses are so complex that simple avoidance-avoidance conflicts are rare. In most cases, each of the two situations has both a positive and negative value. If a person has difficulty escaping a single avoidance-avoidance conflict, it is possible that both stimuli also possess some positive value.

In a single approach-avoidance conflict, if the approach gradient is higher at the goal than the avoidance gradient, a person will achieve the goal, but at the

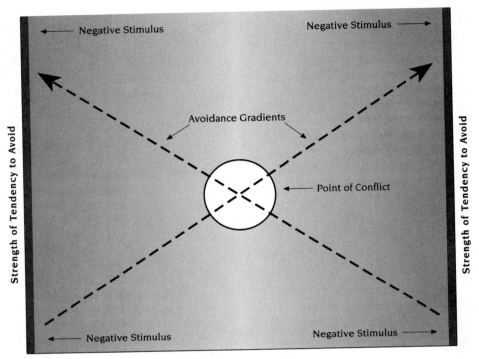

Figure 8.4   *Avoidance-Avoidance Conflict. As one retreats from one negative stimulus, one approaches another negatively valued goal, reaching a point of conflict somewhere beween the two. If one goal is dreaded more than the other, the point of conflict is pushed nearer the less-feared one.*

expense of experiencing increasing amounts of anxiety. The reason for this progressive anxiety is simple. The avoidance gradient is subtracted from the approach gradient to determine the net tendency to approach. Because the avoidance gradient is steeper than the gradient of approach, the net tendency to approach decreases the nearer the person is to the goal.

In double approach-avoidance conflicts, people are caught between two goals that carry both a positive and a negative value. Each goal is both desired and feared. Because people's net tendency to approach an ambivalent stimulus decreases as they get nearer to it, they see distant goals as more desirable than closer ones. With the double approach-avoidance situation (see Figure 8.5), the point of conflict between two equally valued ambivalent situations is midway between the goals, but, because the net tendency to approach becomes progressively weaker as people get nearer the goal, they experience a single approach-avoidance conflict along each gradient. The double conflict arises whenever they near the intersection of the two gradients. The approach-avoidance conflict they feel in nearing their ambivalent

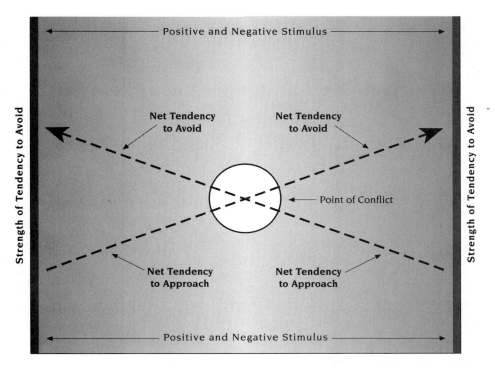

Figure 8.5   *Double Approach-Avoidance Conflict. The net tendency to approach an ambivalent goal decreases as the subject nears the goal. In the double approach-avoidance conflict, the subject remains at a a point of conflict midway between two equally valued ambivalent goals.*

goal is now equaled by the approach-avoidance conflict they experience in pursuing a contradictory ambivalent goal. Prior to reaching the point of conflict, they were progressing toward a feared goal despite feeling ever-increasing levels of anxiety. Eventually, they would reach that ambivalent goal, but when a second ambivalent goal is opposed to the first, their progress stops and they are left vacillating near the point of conflict (Dollard & Miller, 1950).

REPRESSION AND THE UNCONSCIOUS

Dollard and Miller would agree with object relations theorists that experiences that have never been verbalized or that are inadequately labeled become unconscious. These include most experiences prior to the development of fluent language. Unlabeled experiences, however, are not limited to early childhood. Adults, too, repress thoughts, especially those associated with strong unpleasant drives like pain, fear, anxiety, and guilt. In agreement with Freud, Dollard and Miller (1950) believed that sexual and aggressive responses, in particular, are likely to be unlabeled or mislabeled.

Dollard and Miller (1950) defined **repression** as *thoughts not under verbal control,* that is, those for which a person has no adequate label. Repression occurs when people are rewarded by stopping their thoughts about a certain experience. Stopping thinking is a response just as is stopping talking. Like any response, it is impelled by a drive, elicited by cues, and learned through reinforcement. Stopping thinking about painful and fearful experiences is reinforcing because it reduces unpleasant stimuli. For example, Little Hans was threatened with punishment for playing with his genitals, which caused him to stop thinking about sexual play and to repress his sexual feelings toward his parents.

Repression prevents people from labeling thoughts and feelings and makes it difficult for them to think rationally about their problems. This leads to what Dollard and Miller call "stupid" behavior, that is, behavior not mediated by verbal and other cue-producing responses that form the basis of the higher mental processes. Stupid behavior is difficult to unlearn because no language is available to adequately label cues and responses. People may be highly intelligent in some ways, but in the areas of repression they remain stupid (Dollard & Miller, 1950).

ABNORMAL DEVELOPMENT

According to Dollard and Miller (1950), stupidity is one of three chief ingredients in abnormal behavior. The other two are misery and symptoms. Abnormality is learned as the result of conflict, repression, and reinforcement. Conflict produces misery; repression leads to stupidity; and reinforcement is essential for the acquisition of those abnormal symptoms that are learned.

Not all abnormal symptoms, however, are learned. Some are direct physiological effects of strong conflicted drives such as fear, anxiety, guilt, anger, and so on. Abnormal symptoms acquired in this fashion take such forms as muscular tension, agitation, or stomach acidity. They are generally accompanied by other, more numerous symptoms that are learned.

How are abnormal behaviors learned when society does not idealize abnormality? Most are learned in childhood and are taught unintentionally by parents and other socializing agents. Children can learn abnormal behaviors despite parents' attempts to reinforce healthy responses and to withhold reward for unhealthy ones. This is possible for at least three reasons. First, parents are not always present to reinforce behavior, which allows for self-reinforcement and maladaptive responses. Second, the parents' delayed rewards for proper behavior may not be as strong as the immediate reward a child receives for an improper response. The third, and probably most important reason is that many rewards are unconscious and also outweigh the punitive effect of an experience. For some children, for example, a spanking may be more rewarding than it is punishing, but neither the parent nor the child is aware of this fact.

Strong drives, especially fear, are instrumental in learning abnormality. Fear can have a threefold effect on a person's behavior. First, it can lead to *flight* or *escape*, which results in drive reduction. Because fleeing is rewarding, we learn to run away from fear-provoking stimuli. This can be a productive response and is in no way associated with dysfunctional behavior. However, flight may also be maladaptive, as when Little Hans ran away from horses in the street even though he "knew" that his behavior was silly.

The second pathway fear can take in affecting a person's behavior is through *conflict*. Fear is a major component in conflict, and because conflict does not reduce the fear drive, people are left in a more or less permanent state of high drive, which leads to feelings of tension and irritability, that is, *misery*. People suffering from misery have a variety of symptoms including sleeplessness, apathy, phobias and irrational fears, restlessness, and a general lack of zest for living, which prevent them from responding in ways that would ordinarily reduce the strength of their drive (Dollard & Miller, 1950).

Whenever conflict leads to the inhibition of thoughts, *repression* has taken place. This is the third effect that fear can have on behavior. When fear results in repression, no verbal cues are available for the learning of new responses, and without labels people are not able to properly discriminate among the various cues appropriate to a specific learning situation. Repression erases people's ability to think about differences between responses that are followed by punishment and those that are not. Some people are unable to distinguish between intentional and unintentional injury inflicted upon another, so they feel guilty when they accidentally harm someone, and no amount of logical reasoning can change their feelings. In this one area, at least, their thought processes are characterized by *stupidity*. Like miserable people, stupid persons behave in a self-defeating manner. Being unable to think intelligently about their maladaptive behaviors, they are not capable of conscious actions that would either reduce their drive or solve their conflict. At the same time, their stupidity contributes to their misery and to the ever-lengthening list of neurotic symptoms. Because they are unable to resolve their conflicts, they may blame themselves and behave in ways that reflect a self-deprecating attitude. Then again, they may blame others and develop tendencies toward rationalization, projection, hallucination, delusion, or displacement. When conflicts are both strong and unconscious, people do not profit from their experiences and continue to make the same mistakes. This compulsive behavior can itself be reinforcing, since it leads to a reduction of anxiety (Dollard & Miller, 1950).

In summary, the pattern of abnormality consists of a vicious circle of a strong drive, usually fear, which is not reduced but, instead, results in conflict, misery, repression, and stupidity. People are then unable to discriminate among their drives and cues, a situation that leads to a perpetuation of their neurotic symptoms. The symptoms themselves are usually compromises and often represent attempts to escape from an avoidance-avoidance conflict.

PSYCHOTHERAPY

If neuroses and maladaptive responses are learned, then they can be unlearned. In essence, this is the thrust of Dollard and Miller's approach to psychotherapy. They hypothesized that neurotics have learned to be ill and are unable to use higher mental processes to solve personal problems. Therapy, therefore, is a matter of learning new ways to make a better adjustment. Although Dollard and Miller (1950) used many Freudian techniques—including transference, dream interpretation, and free association—they explained the therapeutic process in terms of learning theory.

In using free association, the therapist encourages patients to say everything that comes to mind. This frees them from having to use logic or make sense, thus allowing them to express themselves without threat of cross-examination or non-acceptance. This experience is different from the reaction patients usually receive in social situations. Once repressions and overt inhibitions are removed, the therapist teaches patients to use their higher mental processes to solve personal problems, using their foresight, reasoning, realistic hope, adaptive planning, and insight.

Dollard and Miller (1950) did not accept verbal changes as a goal of therapy. Patients must *do* something different. They must make new responses, which are then rewarded or, at least, no longer punished. For therapy to be effective, the newly learned responses must not be punished by others, as might happen if patients were married to neurotic or punitive spouses. Instead, they must receive positive reinforcement either from others or from themselves.

 ## CONCEPT OF HUMANITY

Dollard and Miller viewed people as complex organisms capable of acquiring enormously intricate and subtle patterns of behavior through the process of learning. To them, people are neither innately good nor inherently evil but endowed with the potential to learn (within the limitations set by society and by one's native abilities) to become healthy or neurotic. Because Dollard and Miller said that personality is determined mostly by learning within a social context, they are rated *high on determinism and low on free choice*.

Dollard and Miller's concept of humanity can be seen as *both pessimistic and optimistic*. We begin life with the possibility of learning maladaptive behavior during early socialization, especially during the feeding situation, cleanliness and sex training, and anger-anxiety conflicts. In addition, we have numerous other possible pitfalls in our path. Nonproductive behaviors can be learned in a wide variety of ways. Behavioral patterns adopted during early childhood may continue to be reinforced throughout a lifetime, resulting in a more or less permanent nonproductive life style. However, potentially troublesome learnings do not predetermine that we will develop in a negative direction. If conflicts are kept to a minimum and if parents are reasonably permissive, we can emerge from this period with healthy habits of coping with our environment. Even when maladaptive responses are learned, there always remains the possibility of relearning them. This process of relearning is facilitated by the acquisition of language and through the higher mental processes.

Dollard and Miller were able to apply their basic principles of learning to the acquisition of higher mental processes such as thinking and reasoning. The ability to think makes us essentially different from other animals, but it does not exempt us or our behavior from the same laws of learning that apply to all animals. Dollard and Miller were willing to generalize from animal studies in developing a theory of human personality, but they never lost sight of the fact that we have a far greater capacity to learn and that our unique social patterns set us apart from all other species.

Not only are humans different from other animals, but each person is unique, different from all others in intelligence and the ability to learn. Dollard and Miller were also cognizant of the role society plays in shaping individual personality. Given these hereditary and environmental factors, no two people will learn exactly the same thing, in precisely the same way, and at the same rate of speed. These differences greatly lessen the possibility that predictions about human behavior will be completely valid. However, enough *similarities exist among people* so that reasonably accurate prognostications can be made and generally valid hypotheses can be stated concerning human behavior.

The Dollard and Miller theory is basically, but not completely, a *causal* one. Behavior, they contended, is shaped by previous experiences with reinforcement, but higher mental processes such as foresight enable us to think about the future and to respond on the basis of these thoughts.

Also contributing to the richness of Dollard and Miller's concept of humanity was their recognition of the role that *unconscious* learnings play in molding personality. Their Freudian training helped them to see people as being motivated by unconscious as well as by conscious forces. Much of what people learn is acquired prior to their ability to verbalize and is therefore beyond their ability to recall. Many thoughts and actions that they learn later are either repressed or overtly inhibited. Although these thoughts and actions are unconscious, they may continue to influence people's behavior and to shape their future learnings.

Related Research

The first criterion of a useful theory is the volume of research it generates, and psychoanalytic learning theory has produced much research and lively discussion, especially concerning the *frustration-aggression hypothesis* and the *drive-reduction hypothesis*.

In 1939, Dollard et al. proposed the idea that frustration always leads to some sort of aggression, and, conversely, that aggression inevitably stems from frustration This frustration-aggression hypothesis immediately generated both controversy and research. Maslow (1941) and Menninger (1942) both criticized the notion, claiming that common sense alone suggests that frustration does not inevitably lead to aggression. Consequently, Miller (1941, p. 338) amended the original hypothesis to read, "Frustration produces instigations to a number of different types of response, one of which is an instigation to aggression." For a number of years, this truncated frustration-aggression hypothesis generated debate and study. Buss (1961) found that aggression has antecedents other than frustration, such as attack and annoyance. In addition, he claimed that "aggression does not necessarily have identifiable antecedents" (Buss, 1961, p. 28).

In addition, Berkowitz (1958) suggested that both attack and insult can lead to aggression. Although he later claimed that aggression can be caused by factors other than frustration, he insisted that the frustration-aggression hypothesis was "the best theoretical framework for the analysis of social aggression" (Berkowitz, 1962, p. xi). Still later Berkowitz (1969) suggested that, although frustration increases the probability of aggression, it does not lead inevitably to it. Then in 1978, Berkowitz restated his belief that aggression is stimulated by conditions other than frustration and suggested that pain is a more frequent cause of aggressive acts.

Miller and Dollard (1941) also proposed the drive-reduction hypothesis that suggests that a reduction in the drive stimulus is a necessary and sufficient condition for reinforcement. As with the frustration-aggression hypothesis, the drive-reduction hypothesis generated a good deal of debate and research. Allport (1961), believing the hypothesis to be too restrictive, pointed out that people are not always motivated to reduce a drive. Sometimes, he claimed, they strive to maintain or even increase tension (see Chapter 13). Olds and Milner (1954) had presented evidence to support Allport's position. They found that reinforcement can be produced by an increase in stimulation, and that it is not exclusively the result of stimulus reduction. Sheffield (1966a, 1966b) suggested an alternative to the drive-reduction hypothesis, which he called the *drive-induction* theory of reinforcement. He presented evidence that tends to support the notion that rats, at least, will learn responses that initiate or arouse motivation, and that a reduction in drive is not an essential of reinforcement. In one study, for example, male rats learned a response that led to copulation without subsequent reduction of the sex drive through ejaculation.

Although research into the frustration-aggression hypothesis and the drive-reduction theory has generally not supported Dollard and Miller's suppositions, both hypotheses have generated an abundance of research, which has yielded useful information about the necessity of drive reduction to learning and about the causes of aggression as well as the consequences of frustration. As we stated in Chapter 1, useful research can be generated from hypotheses that are eventually disproven. This research in turn can suggest better formulas for understanding human behavior.

CRITIQUE OF DOLLARD AND MILLER

Dollard and Miller's psychoanalytically based learning theory provides a unique perspective for viewing Freudian concepts from a learning theory model. Although more recent learning theories have generally ignored or maligned psychoanalysis, Dollard and Miller were able to interpret many of its major tenets from the view of modern learning theory. How does this novel approach to the study of human personality meet the criteria of a useful theory?

Besides generating research, a useful theory should organize knowledge and be practical, consistent, and parsimonious. On its ability to *organize knowledge*, Dollard and Miller's theory receives high marks. It integrates behaviorist principles with psychoanalysis and the social sciences and consequently offers an explanation for a broad base of human personality. It was the first learning theory to emphasize the importance of verbal behavior (covert and overt) as both a cue and a response. The concept of cue-producing responses enables Dollard and Miller to explain thinking in terms of reinforcement theory.

The theory has sometimes been criticized because its basic tenets have been suggested by animal studies, and most of its hypotheses have been tested with animals rather than with humans. Can animal studies tell us anything about humans other than about those characteristics the two species hold in common? Dollard and Miller would say that, first, there are many characteristics that humans have in common with lower-order animals. Fear, hunger, sex, and aggression, for example, are experienced by rats as well as by people. To study the physiological bases for these motivations in humans would present many practical and ethical problems, so it is simply more feasible to use rats. Second, Dollard and Miller believed that most characteristics possessed by rats are also possessed by humans, but that humans have many characteristics that other animals do not. In extrapolating from animals to humans, therefore, they began with animal studies, but then proceeded to check these results against less well-controlled clinical and naturalistic studies of people and also against cross-cultural comparisons of human behavior.

Although Dollard and Miller's learning theory is quite useful in its ability to explain how human behavior is acquired, its heavy emphasis on learning, with only a glancing nod toward biology, is also a limitation of the theory. Hereditary factors and individual constitutional differences are not adequately accounted for by Dollard and Miller.

Another criterion by which a useful theory is judged is its *practicality*. Does it serve as a useful guide to the practitioner? Does it tell the parent, teacher, or therapist what to do in order to shape or control behavior? Learning theory of various kinds is especially useful in guiding action. The practitioner can employ learning theory techniques to help others both to acquire desirable behaviors or to extinguish nonproductive ones. Inappropriate behaviors can be viewed as being acquired in accordance with certain specific principles and as capable of being eliminated by a learning process that is spelled out by Dollard and Miller's theory of personality.

Internal consistency is an additional criterion of any scientific theory. Like most learning theorists, Dollard and Miller were precise in defining their terms and were aware of the importance of internal consistency. When they were forced to make modifications in formulations, they were careful to spell out the new definitions.

Finally, a useful theory is as *parsimonious* or simple as possible. Dollard and Miller attempted to formulate a scientific theory based on observations gleaned from experimentation. To their credit, they did not venture into the realm of story-telling and myth-making, which pervade other theories, notably those of Jung and Freud. However, unlike Skinner (Chapter 9), they postulated the existence of hypothetical internal states such as drives, cues, conflicts, and cue-producing responses. Skinner argued that these hypothetical fictions are not only unnecessary to the scientific analysis of behavior, but they also interfere with an accurate understanding of human personality. The Dollard and Miller personality theory, therefore, receives a moderate rating on parsimony.

Chapter Summary

Several theoretical approaches have extended rather than diverged from Freud's classical psychoanalysis. Two such approaches are the object relations theory of Melanie Klein and others and the psychoanalytic learning theory of John Dollard and Neal E. Miller.

In general, object relations theory extends Freud's theory to the pre-Oedipal years. Whereas Freud believed that the fourth to sixth years are crucial in personality development, Klein and other object relations theorists thought that the first four or five months are the most critical time. Object relations theorists also differ from Freud's paternalistic theory in that they strongly emphasize the mother–child relationship. As a consequence, object relations theory concentrates more on interpersonal relations and less on instinctual drives than does Freudian psychoanalysis.

Klein and other object relations theorists built theories on observation of the mother–child relationship or on speculation concerning the infant's real or fantasized early relations with the mother or the breast. They believed that the quality of adult relationships can be traced back to the very early mother–infant interaction. An important portion of any relationship is the internal psychic representations of early significant objects, such as the mother's breast or the father's penis, that have been introjected, or taken into the infant's psychic structure, and then projected onto an external object, that is, another person. These internal pictures are not accurate representations of the other person but are remnants of earlier interpersonal experiences.

In order to deal with both the nurturing breast and the frustrating breast, infants split these objects into "good" and "bad," and, at the same time, they split their ego so that they have a dual image of self. In older children the ego becomes unified, but separate aspects of the ego may continue to exist. Klein believed that the ego exists at birth and that it can sense both destructive and loving forces. It can experience anxiety and even establish defense mechanisms from the first few weeks. Klein also held that the superego comes into existence much earlier than Freud had speculated and that it grows along with the Oedipus complex rather than being a product of it.

Like Freud, Klein believed that the two sexes experience the Oedipus complex somewhat differently. But unlike Freud whose theory held that the father is the parent responsible for penis envy in girls and castration anxiety in boys, Klein suggested that the child's relationship with the mother plays a central role in the Oedipal process. During the early Oedipal years, the little boy adopts a "feminine" position and has no fear of being castrated as punishment for his sexual feelings for his mother. Later, he projects his destructive drive onto his father, whom he fears will bite or castrate him. The male Oedipus complex is resolved when the boy establishes good relations with both parents and feels comfortable with their having sex with one another. Like the boy, the little girl adopts a "feminine" position toward both parents early in the Oedipal experience. She has a positive feeing both for her mother's breasts and for her father's penis, which she believes

will feed her with babies. Sometimes the little girl develops hostility toward her mother, whom she fears will retaliate against her and rob her of her babies. However, in many cases the female Oedipus complex is resolved without any antagonism and the little girl experiences no jealousy toward her mother.

According to Dollard and Miller, personality is largely learned, and all learning is based on four fundamentals—drive, cue, response, and reinforcement. A *drive* is any stimulus strong enough to instigate action; a *cue* is any stimulus distinctive enough to guide action; a *response* is the behavior that occurs as a result of drives and cues; and *reinforcement* is any event that strengthens the connection between a cue and a response.

Although much of their theory is based on animal studies and simple experiments with humans, Dollard and Miller hypothesized that these same four principles apply to *higher mental processes* such as foresight, reasoning, and language acquisition. The principal difference between higher mental processes and the learning of simple habits is that higher mental processes involve a series of internal or *cue-producing responses*.

Much of human misery and many neurotic symptoms are the result of nearly insoluble *conflict*. The three most difficult of these are the *approach-avoidance conflict*, in which the same stimulus is both desired and feared, the *avoidance-avoidance conflict*, in which the person is stuck between two equally undesirable stimuli, and the *double approach-avoidance conflict*, in which the person is in between two stimuli, each with both a positive and a negative value.

Abnormal development, including fears and anxiety, is learned as the result of conflict, repression, and reinforcement. Because neurotic symptoms are learned, they can also be unlearned through the process of *psychotherapy.*

Dollard and Miller saw humans as complex animals whose personalities are largely determined by social forces outside the individual's personal control. People can use higher mental processes, such as reasoning and

foresight, to solve problems, but, ultimately, even these solutions lie beyond individual choice.

Although few studies are currently being conducted on Dollard and Miller's classical learning theory, their ideas have generated much research, especially on the drive-reduction and frustration-aggression hypotheses. Moreover, the theory still retains its ability to give meaning and organization to observed data. Also, it continues to be a useful guide to the practitioner.

Suggested Readings

DOLLARD, J., & MILLER, N. E. (1950). *Personality and psychotherapy: An analysis in terms of learning, thinking, and culture.* New York: McGraw-Hill.
    An indispensable resource for Dollard and Miller's classical learning theory, this book includes a description of neuroses, conflict, and psychotherapy.
KLEIN, M. (1991). The emotional life and ego-development of the infant with special reference to the depressive position. In P. King & R. Steiner (Eds.), *The Freud-Klein controversies 1941–45* (pp. 752–577). London: Tavistock/Routledge.
    Although all of Klein's writings are difficult, this chapter is perhaps as accessible as any. In it Klein presents a brief summary of her object relations theory.
MILLER, N. E. (1984). Learning: Some facts and needed research relevant to maintaining health. In J. D. Matarazzo, S. M. Weiss, J. A. Herd, N. E. Miller, & S. M. Weiss (Eds.), *Behavioral health: A handbook of health enhancement and disease prevention* (pp.199–208). New York: Wiley.
    In this chapter Miller summarizes his later ideas on reinforcement and motivation and points out the wide range of effects that learning has on maintaining health. Thus, Miller combines his three historical interests—learning theory, biofeedback, and behavioral health.
ST. CLAIR, M. (1986). *Object relations and self psychology: An introduction.* Monterey, CA: Brooks/ Cole.
    St. Clair's introduction to object relations theory and self psychology looks at how the different theorists, including Klein, Mahler, Kernberg, Kohut, and others compare with each other and how they compare to Freudian theory.
SEGAL, J. (1992). *Melanie Klein.* London: Sage.
    This brief paperback is easier to read and less technical than Grosskurth's (1986) book. Segal includes a summary of Klein's life and work, as well as a chapter on criticisms of her theory and rebuttals to those criticisms.

PART THREE

Learning Theories

9 Skinner
A Behavioral Analysis

10 Bandura
Social-Cognitive Theory

11 Rotter and Mischel
Cognitive Social Learning Theories

A Behavioral Analysis

Chapter Nine

OVERVIEW
BIOGRAPHY OF B. F. SKINNER
SCIENTIFIC BEHAVIORISM
    Philosophy of Science
    Operant Conditioning
BOX: KAMIKAZE PIGEONS
THE HUMAN ORGANISM
    Natural Selection
    Cultural Evolution
    Inner States
    Complex Behavior
    Control of Human Behavior
THE UNHEALTHY PERSONALITY
    Counteracting Strategies
    Inappropriate Behaviors
BOX: WALDEN TWO—UTOPIA OR TEDIUM?
PSYCHOTHERAPY
CONCEPT OF HUMANITY
RELATED RESEARCH
CRITIQUE OF SKINNER
CHAPTER SUMMARY
SUGGESTED READINGS

SKINNER

*F*red, an aspiring young writer, was away from home for the first time, attending a small liberal arts college. Although not really homesick, he missed his old friends and family. As a member of the college glee club, Fred was touring with that group during Easter vacation. When the tour ended, he went home to visit his parents and younger brother, Ed.

Fred and his brother were neither rivals nor close friends. They had little in common except mutual respect and affection. Fred was somewhat shy, scholarly, and avidly interested in literature and music; Ed was sociable, athletic, and more emotionally dependent on his parents. In spite of these differences, Fred was pleased to be visiting with his only sibling.

On the Sunday following Easter, Fred and Ed dropped their mother and father at church (Fred had stopped attending several years earlier) and then drove downtown to enjoy an ice cream sundae with one of Ed's friends. After eating their sundaes, they went back to their house, where Ed asked his friend and Fred to wait in the car while he ran in to use the bathroom. After an unusually long time, Ed emerged from the house, complaining of a severe headache. The three young men went into the house where Ed then lay down in his bed in great pain. A doctor was called and after he arrived Fred drove back to the church to get his mother and father. When they got home, they were greeted by their maid, who told them that Ed had died.

Years later when Fred wrote of this incident, he failed to reveal how he *felt* when his brother died. He noted that the death had a devastating effect on the family, and he described in some detail the *behavior* of the various family members. He recalled that his mother threw her arms around her dead son and that his father walked from the room saying "For heaven's sake, for heaven's sake." Fred also described his grandfather's behavior at the funeral and how he looked at the body of his dead grandson and declared his willingness to trade places with him. At no time in his account of his brother's death, however, did Fred report his own emotions or speculate concerning the inner feelings of others.

For a person who aspired to be a poet, how could Fred have been without emotion at such a time? He *wasn't*. By the time Fred described this event more than 50 years later, he had become a writer of a different kind. He was by then a psychologist, a radical behaviorist, a man who, although he believed in inner states such as emotions, insisted that the science of psychology should deal with observable data and not hypothetical events such as feelings. Fred, of course, was Burrhus

Frederic Skinner, probably the most influential and best-known American psychologist of the 20th century.

OVERVIEW

The learning theory of Dollard and Miller can be seen as a bridge spanning the psychodynamic theory of Freud, which relies heavily on speculation gleaned from clinical observations, and the behavioral theory of B. F. Skinner, which minimizes speculation and focuses almost entirely on observable behavior. Dollard and Miller were not reluctant to postulate the existence of internal events such as drives, cues, foresight, reasoning, unconscious processes, and conflict.

Skinner, in contrast, argued that psychology as a natural science must limit itself to the study of observable phenomena. He did not claim, however, that observable behavior is limited to external events. Instead, he included within the scope of observable behavior such private events as thinking, remembering, and anticipating. Skinner's strict adherence to observable behavior earned his approach the label **radical behaviorism**.

Radical behaviorism insists that the scientific study of human behavior must avoid all hypothetical constructs (such as id, ego, superego, style of life, social interest, archetypes, drives, needs, and so forth) often used by other theorists to explain human personality. To Skinner, behaviors, not fictional constructs, are the basic data of psychological science.

In addition to being a radical behaviorist, Skinner can rightfully be regarded as a determinist and an environmentalist. As a *determinist*, he rejected the notion of volition or free will. Human behavior does not stem from an act of the will, but, like any observable phenomenon, it is lawfully determined and can be studied scientifically.

As an *environmentalist*, Skinner held that psychology must not explain behavior on the basis of the physiological or constitutional components of the organism. He recognized that genetic factors are important, but he insisted that, because they are fixed at conception, they are of no help in the control of behavior. The *history* of the individual, rather than anatomy, provides the most useful data for predicting and controlling behavior.

BIOGRAPHY OF B. F. SKINNER

Skinner was born on March 20, 1904, in Susquehanna, Pennsylvania, the first child of William and Grace Madge Burrhus Skinner. His father was a lawyer and an aspiring politician who never quite became successful in politics, but who, nevertheless, earned a comfortable living as an attorney. Both parents had lived in Susquehanna as children and both had attended high school there. All four grandparents lived in the same town, and young Fred (he was almost never called Burrhus or B.F.) often visited with them after school and on weekends. The family's roots were deeply embedded in Susquehanna, and Skinner grew up in a comfortable, happy, upper-middle-class home where his parents practiced the values of temperance, service, honesty, and hard work. The Skinners were Presbyterian, but Fred began to lose his faith during high school and thereafter never practiced any religion.

When Fred was two-and-a-half, a second son, Edward, was born. Fred and Ebbie (as he was known) got along well considering the fact that they did not share many interests and that Fred felt Ebbie was treated more leniently and loved more by both parents. However, Fred did not feel unloved. He was simply more independent and less emotionally attached to his mother and father. But after Ebbie died during Fred's first year at college, the parents became less and less willing to let the older son go. They wanted him to become "the family boy," and indeed succeeded in keeping him financially obligated even after B. F. Skinner became a well-known name in American psychology (Skinner, 1976, 1979).

As a child, Skinner was inclined toward the arts. He learned to play the piano and the saxophone well enough to form a jazz band during his late teenage years. From an early age he was interested in writing, and, by the time he was in high school, he had experimented with writing novels, poems, movie scenes, song lyrics, and plays. His ambition was to be a professional writer, and he made a serious attempt to realize that goal. In addition to an interest in music and literature, he enjoyed painting and liked to invent and build a variety of gadgets. His ability to build things served him well in his career as a behavior psychologist, enabling him to design and construct much of the equipment used in his experiments.

Skinner attended public school in Susquehanna, where all 12 grades were in the same building, and where his favorite teacher moved with him throughout most of his elementary and high-school years. After graduation, Skinner moved with his family to Scranton, Pennsylvania, but immediately thereafter he entered Hamilton College, an all-male, liberal arts school in Clinton, New York.

After taking his bachelor's degree in English, Skinner set about to realize his ambition of being a creative writer. When he wrote his father informing him of his wish to spend a year at home working at nothing except writing, his request was met with lukewarm acceptance. Warning his son of the necessity of making a living, his father reluctantly agreed to support him for the one year on condition that he would get a job if his writing career was not successful. This unenthusiastic reply was quickly followed by a more encouraging letter from Robert Frost, who had read some of Skinner's writings. Skinner returned to Scranton, built a study in the attic and every morning went to work at writing.

But nothing happened. His efforts were unproductive because he had nothing to say and no firm position on any current issue. In his autobiography, Skinner (1976) referred to this period as his "Dark Year."

However, Elms (1981) saw this time as Skinner's first, but not last, major identity crisis.

At the end of this unsuccessful year, Skinner was faced with the task of looking for a new career. Science beckoned. Wanting to understand people better, he turned to psychology. Although he had never taken an undergraduate course in psychology, Harvard accepted him as a graduate student in psychology for the Fall 1928 term. Just prior to entering Harvard, he read about John B. Watson in Bertrand Russell's *Philosophy*. He bought a copy of Watson's *Behaviorism*, read some Pavlov, and determined at that early date to be a behaviorist. He never wavered from that determination.

At Harvard he quickly became a leader of a small group of graduate students dedicated to behaviorism. Upon finishing his Ph.D. in 1931, he was granted a fellowship by the National Research Council to continue his laboratory research at Harvard. His experiments were exclusively with animals, mostly rats, although he also used squirrels and even lobsters. At this same time he drew up a plan for himself, outlining his goals for the years 1930–1960. The plan also reminded him to adhere closely to behavioristic methodology and not to "surrender to the physiology of the central nervous system" (Skinner, 1979, p. 115). By 1960 Skinner had reached the most important phases of the plan, although he fell short in some specifics.

When his fellowship ended in 1933, he was faced for the first time with the chore of hunting for a permanent job. Positions were scarce during this depression year and prospects looked dim. But soon his worries were alleviated. In the spring of 1933 Harvard created the Society of Fellows, a program designed to promote creative thinking among young, intellectually gifted men at the university. Skinner was selected as a Junior Fellow and spent the next three years doing more laboratory research.

At the end of his three-year term as a Junior Fellow he was again in the position of having to look for a job. Curiously, he knew almost nothing of academic psychology and was not interested in learning about it. He had a Ph.D. in psychology, five-and-a-half additional years of laboratory research, but he was ill-prepared to teach within the mainstream of psychology, having "never even read a text in psychology as a whole" (Skinner, 1979, p. 179).

In 1936 Skinner began a teaching and research position at the University of Minnesota, where he remained for nine years. Soon after moving to Minneapolis, he married Yvonne Blue following a short and erratic courtship. Skinner and his wife had two daughters—Julie, born in 1938, and Deborah (Debbie), born in 1944. During his Minnesota years he published his first book, *The Behavior of Organisms* (1938), but, beyond that, he was involved with two of his most interesting ventures—the baby-tender and the pigeon-guided missile.

When the Skinners were expecting their second child (Debbie), they decided to construct a physically and psychologically safe and healthy environment for the baby, one that would also free the parents of unnecessary tedious labor. Thus

Skinner built an enclosed crib with a large sliding window and a heating unit that supplied the baby with fresh warm air. The baby was frequently removed from the crib to play with her parents and older sister, but for most of the day she was alone in her baby-tender.

After *Ladies Home Journal* published an article in October of 1945 on the baby-tender, Skinner was both condemned and praised for his invention. Interest from other parents persuaded him to market the device, but, unfortunately, he experienced many difficulties in securing the necessary patent. Moreover, his association with a business partner who, according to Skinner (1979), was both incompetent and unscrupulous, led him to eventually abandon the commercial venture. When Debbie outgrew the baby-tender at age two-and-a-half, the crib unceremoniously became a home for some of Skinner's pigeons.

Skinner's second unusual adventure at Minnesota took place during World War II when he trained pigeons to pilot missiles into enemy targets. However, that project, too, ended in disappointment. The disappointments and frustrations with the baby-tender and especially the missile project led to what Elms (1981) has referred to as Skinner's midlife crisis. Furthermore, when he left Minnesota in 1945 to become chairman of the psychology department at Indiana University, the move was not without added frustrations. His wife had ambivalent feelings about leaving friends, his administrative duties proved irksome, and he still felt out of the mainstream of scientific psychology. However, his personal crisis was soon to end, and his professional career would take another turn.

In the summer of 1945, while on vacation, Skinner wrote *Walden Two*, a utopian novel that portrayed a society where problems were solved through behavioral engineering. Although not published until 1948, the book provided its author with immediate therapy in the form of an emotional catharsis. At last Skinner had done what he failed to accomplish during his Dark Year nearly 20 years earlier, and according to Elms (1981) his midlife crisis came to an end with the writing of *Walden Two*. The book was also a benchmark in Skinner's professional career. No longer would he be confined to the laboratory study of rats and pigeons, but thereafter would be involved with the application of behavioristic findings to the technology of shaping human behavior. His concern with the human condition was elaborated in *Science and Human Behavior* (1953) and reached philosophical expression in *Beyond Freedom and Dignity* (1971).

In 1948, Skinner returned to Harvard where, he was Professor of Psychology until his retirement in 1974. He remained at Harvard as Professor Emeritus until his death on August 18, 1990. During those years at Harvard, Skinner gained recognition as one of America's best-known psychologists, and his books on human behavior, *About Behaviorism* (1974), *Reflections on Behaviorism and Society* (1978), and *Upon Further Reflection* (1987a) became widely read. In addition, he wrote a three-volume autobiography, *Particulars of My Life*

(1976), *The Shaping of a Behaviorist* (1979), and *A Matter of Consequences* (1983). During his career Skinner received many honors and awards including serving as William James Lecturer at Harvard, being granted the Distinguished Scientific Award of the American Psychological Association (APA), winning the President's Medal of Science, and receiving an unprecedented Citation for Outstanding Lifetime Contribution to Psychology during the 1990 APA convention in Boston, the only person to receive such an award in the 100-year history of APA.

SCIENTIFIC BEHAVIORISM

Skinner assumed that human behavior is subject to the laws of science. Like other natural phenomena, human behavior should be studied scientifically, and no inner motivations should be attributed to it. The wind does not blow because it wants to turn windmills; rocks do not roll downhill because they possess a sense of gravity; birds do not migrate because they like the climate better in other regions; and people do not eat because they feel hungry. Scientists can easily accept the idea that the behavior of the wind, rocks, and even birds can be studied without reference to an internal motive, but most personality theorists assume that people are motivated by internal drives, and that an understanding of these drives is essential.

Skinner disagreed. Why postulate an inner mental function that is outside the scope of scientific analysis? People do not eat because they are hungry. Hunger is an inner condition not directly observable. If psychologists wish to increase the probability that a person will eat, then they must first observe the variables related to eating. If deprivation of food increases the likelihood of eating, then they can deprive a person of food in order to better predict and control subsequent eating behavior. Both deprivation and eating are physical events clearly observable and therefore within the province of science. To say that a person eats due to hunger is to assume an unnecessary and unobservable mental condition between the physical fact of deprivation and the physical fact of eating. This assumption clouds the issue and relegates much of psychology to that realm of philosophy known as **cosmology**, or the concern with causation. To be scientific, Skinner (1953, 1987a) insisted, psychology must avoid internal mental factors and confine itself to observable physical events.

Although Skinner rejected internal states as being outside the domain of science, he did not deny their existence. Such conditions as hunger, paranoia, values, self-confidence, aggressive needs, religious beliefs, and spitefulness exist, but they are not explanations for behavior. To use them as explanations is not only fruitless but also limits the advancement of scientific behaviorism. Other sciences have made greater advances because they have long since abandoned the practice of attributing the motion (behavior) of objects and living things to motives, needs, or will power. Skinner's scientific behaviorism follows their lead (Skinner, 1945).

Philosophy of Science

Scientific behaviorism allows for an *interpretation* of behavior but not an *explanation* of its causes. Interpretation permits generalization from the simple learning condition to the more complex. For example, Skinner generalized from animal studies to children and then to adults. Any science, including that of human behavior, begins with the simple and eventually evolves generalized principles that permit an interpretation of the more complex. Skinner used principles derived from laboratory studies to interpret the behavior of human beings but insisted that interpretation should not be confused with explanation. Events in everyday life take on meaning through knowledge of laboratory studies because the same conditions of learning apply in both cases. However, no explanation should be offered as to why people behave. Explanations are mentalistic fictions and thus lie beyond the scope of physical events that can be observed by science (Skinner, 1978).

The purpose of science, Skinner (1953) wrote, is not only to predict behavior but to control it as well. Science is also concerned with the description of both behavior and the conditions under which it occurs. Prediction, control, and description are possible in scientific behaviorism because behavior is both determined and lawful. Human behavior, like that of physical and biological entities, is neither whimsical nor the outcome of free will. It is determined by certain identifiable variables and follows definite lawful principles, which hypothetically can be known. Behavior that appears to be capricious or individually determined is simply beyond our present capacity to predict or control. But, hypothetically, the conditions under which it occurs can be discovered, thus permitting both prediction and control, as well as description. Skinner devoted much of his time to trying to discover these conditions using a procedure he called operant conditioning.

Operant Conditioning

Skinner (1953) recognized two kinds of conditioning, respondent and operant. In **respondent conditioning**, also called classical or Pavlovian, a response is drawn out of the organism by a specific, identifiable stimulus. The simplest examples include reflexive behavior. Light shined in the eye stimulates the pupil to contract; food placed on the tongue brings about salivation; and pepper in the nostrils results in the sneezing reflex. With reflexive behavior, responses are unlearned, involuntary, and common not only to the species but across species as well. Respondent conditioning, however, is not limited to simple reflexes. It can also be responsible for more complex human learning like phobias, fears, and anxiety. A child bitten by a dog shows a fear response whenever confronted by that dog. A specific stimulus (the dog) now elicits a response (fear) that was not present prior to the time the child was bitten.

A more comprehensive approach to behavior, Skinner believed, is **operant conditioning**. The key to operant conditioning is the immediate reinforcement of a response. The organism first *does* something and then is reinforced by the environment. Reinforcement, in turn, increases the probability that the same behavior will occur again. This is called operant conditioning because the organism operates on the environment to produce a specific effect. Operant conditioning changes the frequency of a response or the probability that a response will occur. The reinforcement does not cause the behavior, but it increases the likelihood that it will be repeated.

One distinction between respondent and operant conditioning is that in respondent conditioning behavior is *elicited* from the organism, whereas in operant conditioning behavior is *emitted*. Skinner made a distinction between elicited and emitted behavior. An elicited response is drawn from the organism, but an emitted response is one that simply appears. Emitted responses do not previously exist inside the organism, and no stimulus or internal cause is responsible for their occurrence. They simply appear because of the organism's individual history of reinforcement or the species' evolutionary history.

Let's look at an example of operant conditioning. A father who wishes to increase the frequency of his daughter's smiles watches the child constantly and gives her candy every time she smiles. In this example, as in all instances of operant conditioning, three conditions are present: the *antecedent* (A), the *behavior* (B), and the *consequence* (C). The antecedent refers to the environment or setting in which the behavior takes place. In our example this would include the home, school, playground, or any other place the child might be.

The second essential in the operant conditioning paradigm is the response or behavior. In our example, the behavior is smiling, a relatively simple response that would undoubtedly occur without any previous training. More complex behavior must be gradually "shaped" through the use of "successive approximations," terms explained below. The response must be within the organism's repertoire and must not be interfered with by competing or antagonistic behaviors.

The third factor in operant conditioning is the consequence. If no consistent consequence follows an operant behavior during the history of the organism, no learning will occur; that is, there will be no change in the frequency of the behavior. But if some consequence does follow the response (and some sort of consequence always does), then the probability of future similar responses will be either increased or decreased, depending on whether the consequence is rewarding or not. In the above example, candy is a reward and it acts to reinforce the behavior of smiling and to increase its frequency. However, if the father gave his daughter candy every time she smiled, the child would eventually reach her fill. To ensure that an organism remained at a certain level of deprivation, Skinner carefully rationed the amount of food given to the animal prior to training, using body weight as a measure of deprivation. He also employed various *intermittent schedules* of reinforcement, so that the organism was not reinforced for every desired response and would thus remain in a state of partial deprivation. This sort of rigorous control is usually not available with the conditioning of humans.

Shaping

In the above experiment, the child was reinforced whenever she smiled. In most cases the desired behavior is more complex than a smile and will be emitted only through the process of **shaping**, a procedure in which the experimenter first rewards gross approximations of the behavior, then closer approximations, and finally the desired behavior itself. Through this process of reinforcing **successive approxi-mations**, the experimenter gradually shapes the final complex set of behaviors (Skinner, 1953).

Shaping can be illustrated by the example of training a severely mentally retarded boy to dress himself. The ultimate behavior is to have the child put on all his own clothes. If the parent withheld reinforcement until this target behavior occurred, the child would never successfully complete the chore. To train the boy, the parent must break down the complex behavior of dressing into simple seg-ments. First, the parent gives the child a reward, say, candy, whenever he approxi-mates the behavior of positioning his left hand near the inside of the left sleeve of his shirt. Once that behavior is sufficiently reinforced, the parent withholds reward until the child places his hand into the proper sleeve. Then the parent rewards the child only for putting his left arm entirely through the sleeve. Following this, the same procedures are used with the right sleeve, the buttons, trousers, socks, and shoes. After the child learns to dress himself completely, reinforcement need not follow every successful trial. By this time, in fact, the ability to put on all his clothes will probably become a reward in itself. Quite apparently, the child can only reach the final target behavior if the parent breaks up the complex behavior into its com-ponent parts and then reinforces successive approximations to each response. Shaping allows conditioning to take place quite quickly. In only two or three minutes Skinner conditioned pigeons to raise their heads to heights never before reached. Chickens have been trained to play a facsimile of baseball, and dogs have been conditioned to jump through hoops in a very short time.

If reinforcement increases the probability that a given response will recur, then how can behavior be shaped from the relatively undifferentiated into the highly complex? In other words, why doesn't the organism simply repeat the old reinforced response? Why does it emit new responses that have never been reinforced, but that gradually move it toward the target behavior? The answer is that behavior is not discrete but continuous, that is, the organism usually moves slightly beyond the previously reinforced response. If behavior were discrete, shaping could not occur because the organism would become locked into simply emitting previously reinforced responses. Because behavior is continuous, the organism moves slightly beyond the previously reinforced response, and this slightly exceptional value can then be used as the new minimum standard for reinforcement. (The organism may also move slightly backward or slightly sideways, but only movements toward the desired target are reinforced.) Skinner (1953) compared shaping behavior to a sculp-tor molding a statue from a large lump of clay. In both cases, the final product seems to be different from the original form, but the history of the transformation reveals continuous behavior and not a set of discrete steps.

Operant behavior always takes place in some environment, and the environ-ment has a selective role in shaping and maintaining behavior. The organism, throughout its history, will have been reinforced by reacting to some elements in the environment but not to others. This history of differential reinforcement results

Even complex behavior, such as learning to work a computer is acquired through shaping and successive approximation.

in **operant discrimination**. Skinner claimed that discrimination does not exist within the person, but is a consequence of that person's reinforcement history. Discrimination, therefore, is not an *ability* that we possess, but a function of environmental variables and our previous experiences with reinforcement. We do not come to the dinner table because we discern that the food is ready; we come because our previous experiences of reacting in a similar way have been mostly reinforced. This distinction may seem to be splitting hairs, but Skinner felt that it had important theoretical and practical implications. The first explanation sees discrimination as a cognitive function, existing within the person; the second accounts for it by environmental differences and by individual history. The first is beyond the scope of empirical observation; the second can be scientifically studied.

A response to a similar environment in the absence of previous reinforcement is called **stimulus generalization**. Buying a ticket to a movie we have never seen because we were reinforced by viewing the director's earlier movies is an example of stimulus generalization. Technically, we do not generalize from one situation to another, but react to the new situation in the same manner that we reacted to the first because the two situations possess identical elements. Skinner (1953, p. 94) put it this way: "The reinforcement of a response increases the probability of all responses containing the same elements."

Reinforcement

We have seen that reinforcement increases the probability that an operant response will be emitted, and we have described the role of reinforcement in shaping behavior. Now let's examine this powerful force more closely.

Reinforcement is anything within the environment that strengthens a behavior. Actually, Skinner (1987a) said that reinforcement has two effects: it *strengthens the behavior* and it *rewards the person*. Reinforcement and reward, therefore, are not synonymous. Not every behavior that is reinforced is rewarding or pleasing to the person. For example, people are reinforced for working, but many find their jobs boring, uninteresting, and unrewarding. Reinforcers exist in the environment and are not something felt by the person. Food is not reinforcing because it tastes good; rather, it tastes good because it is reinforcing (Skinner, 1971).

Any behavior that increases the probability that the species or the individual will survive tends to be strengthened. Because food, sex, and parental care are necessary for the survival of the species, behavior that produces these conditions is reinforced; because injury, disease, and extremes in climate are detrimental to survival, any behavior that tends to reduce or avoid these conditions is likewise reinforced. Reinforcement, therefore, can be divided into that which produces a beneficial environmental condition and that which reduces or avoids a detrimental one. The first is called *positive reinforcement* and the second, *negative reinforcement*.

POSITIVE REINFORCEMENT.   Any stimulus that, when added to a situation, increases the probability that a given behavior will occur is termed a **positive reinforcer** (Skinner, 1953). Food, water, sex, money, social approval, and physical comfort are examples. When made contingent on behavior, each has the capacity to increase the frequency of a response. For example, if clear water appears whenever a person turns on the kitchen faucet, then that behavior is strengthened because a beneficial environmental stimulus has been added. Much human and animal behavior is acquired through positive reinforcement. With humans, reinforcement is often haphazard and therefore learning is inefficient. Under controlled conditions, however, Skinner was able to train animals to perform a multitude of relatively complex tasks (see box—"Kamikaze Pigeons").

NEGATIVE REINFORCEMENT.   The removal of an aversive stimulus from a situation also increases the probability that the preceding behavior will occur. This removal results in **negative reinforcement** (Skinner, 1953). The reduction or avoidance of loud noises, shocks, and hunger pangs would be negatively reinforcing because they strengthen the behavior immediately preceding them. Negative reinforcement differs from positive reinforcement in that it requires the removal of an aversive condition, whereas positive reinforcement involves the presentation of a beneficial stimulus. The effect of negative reinforcement, however, is identical to that of positive reinforcement; both strengthen behavior. Some people eat because they like a particular food; others eat to diminish hunger pangs. For the first group, food is a positive reinforcer; for the second, removal of hunger is a negative reinforcer. In both instances, the behavior of eating is strengthened because the consequences are rewarding.

There is an almost unlimited number of aversive stimuli, the removal of which may be negatively reinforcing. Anxiety, for example, is an aversive stimulus and any behavior that reduces it (repression, making excuses, and so on) is reinforcing. Other examples include guilt, illness, pain, scoldings, threats of imprisonment, and

Kamikaze Pigeons

Are pigeons intelligent enough (or stupid enough) to be trained to fly suicide missions during wartime? The answer, interestingly, is "Yes."

Using the principles of positive reinforcement, B. F. Skinner trained pigeons during World War II to peck at keys that controlled the bomb they were riding. As the enemy ship moved, the pigeons would peck the controls to maintain the missile on track of its target. The Kamikaze pigeons and their guided missiles never saw battle, but simulated tests proved successful.

The history of Project Pigeon is an interesting one, but Skinner was both disappointed and frustrated by the experience. After Germany invaded Norway and Denmark in April of 1940, almost two years before the United States entered the war, Skinner purchased a flock of pigeons for the purpose of training them to guide missiles. At that time the U.S. government showed very little interest. After Pearl Harbor, Skinner resumed Project Pigeon, this time with some help from the University of Minnesota. However, he needed major financial resources, especially after the National Defense Research Committee backed away from granting support.

Undaunted, Skinner obtained an appropriation from General Mills, Inc. to continue the project. He was granted a leave of absence from the university and went to work for General Mills. There, he began anew to work on Project Pigeon, but, unfortunately, he still lacked governmental support.

In an effort to secure the needed funds, he prepared a film of trained pigeons pecking at the control of a missile and guiding it toward a moving target. After viewing the film, government officials rekindled their interest and awarded General Mills $25,000 to develop the project. Nevertheless, frustrations lay ahead. Skinner felt the pigeon-driven weapons could be ready for combat by the summer of 1944, but the government was more cautious.

A final presentation in Washington, D.C., in 1944 was particularly disillusioning. Skinner had demonstrated the feasibility of the project by producing a live pigeon that unerringly tracked a moving target. Despite the spectacular demonstration, some observers laughed and most remained skeptical. Finally, after four years of work, more than two of which were full time, Skinner was notified that the project could no longer be continued. In the final analysis, Project Pigeon was probably scuttled not because of the unconventional proposal to use animals to fly missiles, but because it was in competition with a much more devastating weapon—the atomic bomb (Skinner, 1960, 1979).

fear of damnation. Behavior that reduces or avoids any of these conditions tends to be strengthened. On the other hand, the presence of any of these aversive stimuli is called *punishment*.

Punishment

Negative reinforcement should not be confused with punishment. Negative reinforcers remove, reduce, or avoid aversive stimuli, whereas **punishment** is the presentation of an aversive stimulus, such as an electric shock, or the removal of a positive one, such as disconnecting an adolescent's telephone. A negative reinforcer strengthens a response; punishment does not. Although punishment does not strengthen a response, neither does it inevitably weaken it. The effects of punishment are therefore less predictable than those of reward (Skinner, 1953).

EFFECTS OF PUNISHMENT.   The control of human and animal behavior is better served by positive and negative reinforcement than by punishment. The effects of punishment are not opposite those of reinforcement. When the contingencies of reinforcement are strictly controlled, behavior can be precisely shaped and accurately predicted. With punishment, however, no such exactitude is possible. The reason for this is simple. Punishment is ordinarily imposed to prevent people from acting in a particular way. When it is successful, people will stop behaving in that manner, but they still must do something. What they do cannot be accurately predicted because punishment does tell them what they should do; it merely suppresses the tendency to behave in the undesirable fashion. Consequently, one effect of punishment is to *suppress behavior*. For example, if a boy teases his younger sister, his parents can make him stop by spanking him, but, unfortunately, this punishment will not improve his disposition toward his sister. It merely suppresses teasing temporarily or while in the presence of his parents.

Another effect of punishment is the *conditioning of a negative feeling* by associating a strong aversive stimulus with the behavior being punished. In the above illustration, if the pain of the spanking is strong enough, it will instigate a response (crying, withdrawal, attack) that is incompatible with the behavior of teasing a younger sibling. In the future, when the boy thinks about mistreating his younger sister, that thought may elicit, through classical conditioning, the conditioned response of fear, anxiety, guilt, or shame. This negative emotion then serves to prevent the undesirable behavior from recurring. Lamentably, it offers no positive instruction to the child.

A third outcome of punishment is the *spread of its effects*. Any stimulus associated with the punishment may be suppressed or avoided. In our example, this might include the younger sister, the parent, the paddle, or the place where the spanking occurred. The boy may deny the feelings of hostility toward his parents or he may avoid almost all contact with his sister. As a result, his behavior toward them becomes maladaptive. Yet this inappropriate behavior serves the purpose of preventing future punishment. Skinner recognized the classical *defense mechanisms* as effective means of avoiding pain and its attendant anxiety. The punished person may fantasize, project feelings onto others, rationalize aggressive behaviors, or displace them toward other people or animals.

PUNISHMENT AND REINFORCEMENT COMPARED.   Punishment has several characteristics in common with reinforcement. Just as there are two kinds of reinforcements (positive and negative), there are two types of punishment. The first requires the presentation of an aversive stimulus, the second involves the removal of a positive reinforcer. An example of the former would be pain encountered from falling as the result of walking too fast on an icy sidewalk. An example of the latter is a heavy fine levied against a motorist for driving too fast. This first example (falling) results from a natural condition; the second (being fined) follows from human intervention. This is a second characteristic common to punishment and reinforcement: Both can derive from either natural consequences or from human imposition. A third common ingredient is that both punishment and reinforcement are means of controlling behavior, whether the control is by design or by accident. Skinner obviously favored planned control, and his ideas on the control of human behavior are discussed later.

Conditioned and Generalized Reinforcers

Food is a reinforcement for humans and animals because it removes a condition of deprivation. But how can money, which cannot directly remove a condition of deprivation, be reinforcing? The answer, of course, is that money is a **conditioned reinforcer**. Conditioned reinforcers are those things that are not by nature satisfying, but become so because they are associated with such unlearned or *primary reinforcers* as food, water, sex, or physical comfort. Money is a conditioned reinforcer because it can be exchanged for a great variety of primary reinforcers, and because it is associated with more than one primary reinforcer, it is also considered a **generalized reinforcer**.

Skinner (1953) recognized five important generalized reinforcers that sustain much of our behavior. Attention, approval, affection, submission of others, and tokens (money) are all conditioned generalized reinforcers because they are only indirectly related to primary reinforcers, and because they can each be used as reinforcers in a variety of situations. Attention, for example, is a conditioned generalized reinforcer because it is associated with such primary reinforcers as food and physical contact. When children are being fed or held, they are also receiving attention. After food and attention are paired a number of times, attention itself becomes reinforcing through the process of respondent (classical) conditioning. Children, and adults too, will work for attention with no expectation of receiving food or physical contact. In much the same way, approval, affection, submission of others, and money acquire generalized reinforcement value. Behavior can be shaped and responses learned with generalized conditioned reinforcers supplying the sole reinforcement.

Schedules of Reinforcement

Operant conditioning is based on the fact that any behavior immediately followed by the presentation of a positive reinforcer or the removal of an aversive stimulus tends thereafter to occur more frequently. The frequency of that behavior, however, is subject to the conditions under which training occurred, more specifically, to the various schedules of reinforcement (Ferster & Skinner, 1957).

Reinforcement can follow behavior on either a continuous schedule or an intermittent one. **Continuous schedules** call for reinforcing the organism for every trial, a procedure that leads to an increase in frequency of the response, but which is inefficient in its use of reinforcement. Skinner preferred **intermittent schedules** that make more efficient use of reinforcement because the organism is not reinforced for every response. Intermittent schedules are based either on the behavior of the organism or on elapsed time; they can be set either at a fixed rate or can vary according to a randomized program. Accordingly, Ferster and Skinner (1957) recognized four basic intermittent schedules: *fixed-ratio, variable-ratio, fixed-interval,* and *variable-interval*. In addition, they identified several combinations of schedules, but only the four principal intermittent schedules need to be discussed here.

FIXED-RATIO.   With a **fixed-ratio schedule**, the organism is reinforced intermittently according to the number of responses it makes. Ratio refers to the ratio of responses to reinforcers. An experimenter may decide to reward a pigeon with a pellet of grain for every fifth peck it makes at a disc. The pigeon is then conditioned at a fixed-ratio schedule of 5 to 1, that is, FR 5.

Nearly all intermittent schedules begin by reinforcing the organism for every desired response, that is, on a continuous basis. But soon, continuous reward can be ended and reinforcement can proceed intermittently. In the same way, extremely high fixed-ratio schedules, like 200 to 1, must begin at a low rate of responses and gradually build to a higher one. A pigeon can be conditioned to work long and rapidly in exchange for one food pellet provided it has been previously reinforced at lower rates. Fixed-ratio schedules generate rapid responses in pigeons, some emitting more than 10 pecks per second.

Technically, almost no pay scale follows a fixed-ratio or any other schedule because workers ordinarily do not begin with a continuous schedule of immediate reinforcement. The pay of bricklayers who work by piece-rate approximates a fixed-ratio schedule, but bricklayers are not paid immediately after laying one brick or even 100 bricks. In fact, several individual responses are required to lay a single brick, and these responses have never been rewarded by pay. They were, of course, reinforced by immediate feedback during early training but never on a fixed-ratio basis.

Because slot machines pay off on a variable-ratio schedule, some people become compulsive gamblers.

VARIABLE-RATIO.   With a fixed-ratio schedule. the organism is reinforced after every *n*th response. With the **variable-ratio schedule** it is reinforced after the *n*th response *on the average*. Again, training must start with continuous reinforcement, proceed to a low response number, and then increase to a higher rate of response. A pigeon rewarded every third response on the average can build to a VR 6 schedule, then VR 10, and so on. An organism working on a VR 10 schedule might be reinforced after the second response, the eight, the sixteenth, 2the fourteenth, and so on, but the average is one reinforcement for every 10 responses. The mean number of responses must be increased gradually to prevent extinction. After a high mean is reached, say, VR 500, responses become extremely resistant to extinction. (More on rate of extinction later.)

For humans, playing slot machines is an example of a variable-ratio schedule. The machine is set to pay off at a certain rate, but the ratio must be flexible, that is, variable, to prevent players from predicting payoffs.

FIXED-INTERVAL.   With the **fixed-interval schedule**, the organism is reinforced for the first response following a designated period of time. For example, FI 5 indicates that the organism is rewarded for its first response after every five-minute interval. Employees working for salary or wages approximate a fixed-interval schedule. They are paid every week, every two weeks, or every month, but this is not strictly a fixed-interval schedule. Why do workers distribute their efforts fairly evenly over time rather than loafing most of the time and then showing an end-of-the-period spurt characteristic of the fixed-interval schedule? It is because their rate of work is controlled by many other factors, such as watchful supervisors, threats of dismissal, or promises of promotion.

VARIABLE-INTERVAL.   A **variable-interval schedule** is one in which the organism is reinforced after the lapse of random or varied periods of time. For example, VI 5 means that the organism is reinforced following random-length intervals that average five minutes. Such schedules result in more responses per interval than do fixed-interval schedules. In daily life reinforcement results more often from one's effort rather than the passage of time. For this reason, ratio schedules are more common than interval schedules, and the variable-interval schedule is probably the least common of all. An example of a variable-interval schedule would be television addicts who watch their favorite program every week, hoping it will be enjoyable. Sometimes it is, often it is not.

Extinction

Once learned, responses can be lost for at least four reasons. First, they can simply be forgotten during the passage of time. Second, and more likely, they can be lost because preceding or subsequent learnings interfere. Third, they can disappear due to punishment, repression being included in this category. A fourth cause of lost learnings is **extinction**, defined as the tendency of a previously acquired response to become progressively weakened upon nonreinforcement.

Skinner (1953) recognized two kinds of extinction, respondent and operant. **Respondent extinction** follows respondent conditioning and involves the presentation of the conditioned stimulus in the absence of the unconditioned stimulus. The response elicited by the conditioned stimulus eventually disappears.

Operant extinction is the systematic withholding of reinforcement previously contingent upon a response until the probability of the response diminishes to zero. Rate of operant extinction depends largely on the schedule of reinforcement under which learning occurred. However, the extinction curve may be complicated by emotion, as when anger brings about more violent responses.

Compared to a continuous schedule, behavior trained on an intermittent schedule is much more resistant to extinction. Skinner (1953) has observed as many as 10,000 nonreinforced responses with intermittent schedules. Such behavior appears to be self-perpetuating and is practically indistinguishable from *functionally autonomous* behavior, a concept suggested by Allport and discussed in Chapter 13. In general, the higher the rate of responses per reinforcement, the slower the rate of extinction; the fewer responses an organism must make or the shorter the time between reinforcers, the more quickly extinction will occur. This suggests that praise and other reinforcers should be used sparingly in training children.

Extinction is seldom systematically applied to human behavior outside therapy or behavior modification. Most of us live in relatively uncontrolled environments and almost never experience the methodical withholding of reinforcement. Thus many of our behaviors persist over a long period of time because they are being intermittently reinforced, even though the nature of that reinforcement may be obscure to us.

THE HUMAN ORGANISM

Our discussion of Skinnerian theory to this point has dealt primarily with the technology of behavior, a technology based exclusively on the study of animals. But do the principles of behavior gleaned from rats and pigeons apply to the human organism? Skinner's (1974, 1987a) view was that an understanding of the behavior of laboratory animals can generalize to human behavior, just as physics can be used to interpret what is observed in outer space, and an understanding of basic genetics can help in interpreting complex evolutionary concepts.

Skinner (1953, 1990a) believed that if psychology is to advance as a science, then it must be confined to a scientific study of observable phenomena, namely behavior. Science must begin with the simple and move to the more complex. This sequence might proceed from the behavior of animals to that of psychotics, to that 2of retardates, then to that of children, and finally to the behavior of adults. Skinner (1974, 1987a), therefore, made no apology for beginning with the study of animals.

According to Skinner (1987a, 1990a), human behavior (and human personality) is shaped by three forces. The first is natural selection or the evolutionary history of the species; the second is the evolution of social environments or cultures; and the third is the individual's personal history of reinforcement, which we have discussed.

Natural Selection

The human organism is the product of a long evolutionary history. As individuals, our behavior is determined by genetic composition and especially by our personal histories of reinforcement. As a species, however, we are shaped by the contingencies of survival. Natural selection plays an important part in human behavior (Skinner, 1974, 1987a, 1990a).

Individual behavior that is reinforcing tends to be repeated; that which is not tends to drop out. Similarly, those behaviors that, throughout history, were beneficial to the species tended to survive whereas those that were only idiosyncratically reinforcing tended to drop out. For example, natural selection has favored those individuals whose pupils dilated and contracted with changes in lighting. Their superior ability to see during both daylight and nighttime enabled them to avoid life-threatening dangers and to survive to the age of reproduction. Similarly, infants whose heads turned in the direction of a gentle stroke on the cheek were able to suckle, thereby increasing their chances of survival and the likelihood that this rooting characteristic would be passed on to their offspring. These are but two examples of several reflexes that characterize the human infant today. Some, such as the pupillary reflex, continue to have survival value whereas others, like the rooting reflex, are of diminishing benefit (Skinner, 1969, 1978).

The contingencies of reinforcement and the contingencies of survival interact, and some behaviors that are individually reinforcing also contribute to the survival of the species. For example, sexual behavior is generally reinforcing to the individual, but it also has natural selection value because those individuals who are more strongly aroused by sexual stimulation are also the ones who are most likely to produce offspring capable of similar patterns of behavior.

Not every remnant of natural selection continues to have survival value. In our early history, overeating was adaptive because it allowed people to survive during those times when food was less plentiful. Now, in societies where food is continuously available, obesity has become a health problem to many, and overeating has lost its survival value.

Although natural selection helped shape some human behavior, it is probably responsible for only a small number of our actions. Skinner (1989, p. 18) claimed that the contingencies of reinforcement, especially those that have shaped our culture, account for most of our behavior.

> We can trace a small part of human behavior . . . to natural selection and the evolution of the species, but the greater part of human behavior must be traced to contingencies of reinforcement, especially to the very complex social contingencies we call cultures. Only when we take those histories into account can we explain why people behave as they do.

Cultural Evolution

In his later years, Skinner (1987a, 1989) elaborated more fully on the importance of culture in shaping human behavior. *Selection* is responsible for those cultural practices that have survived, just as selection plays a key role in our evolutionary history and also with the contingencies of reinforcement. "People do not observe particular practices in order that the group will be more likely to survive; they observe them because groups that induced their members to do so survived and transmitted them" (Skinner, 1987a, p. 57). In other words, humans do not possess a group mind nor do they make a corporate decision to do what is best for the society; but those societies whose members behaved in certain ways tended to survive. For example, verbal behavior obviously has had tremendous survival value because it is found in all contemporary societies. Those societies that evolved verbal behavior have had the added advantage of using language as a means of transmitting other cultural practices.

Cultural practices such as tool making and verbal behavior begin when an individual is reinforced for using a tool or uttering a distinctive sound. Eventually, a cultural practice evolves that is reinforcing to the group, although not necessarily to the individual. Both tool making and verbal behavior have survival value for a group, but few of us now make tools, and some people (for example, monks who have taken the vow of silence) do not emit verbal behavior.

The remnants of culture, like those of natural selection, are not all adaptive. For example, the division of labor that evolved from the Industrial Revolution has helped society to produce more goods, but it has led to work that is no longer directly reinforcing. Another example is warfare, which, in the preindustrialized world benefited certain societies, has evolved as a threat to human existence before other cultural practices could be invented to countercontrol it.

In summary, Skinner (1987a, p. 55) writes that

> human behavior is the joint product of (1) the contingencies of survival responsible for the natural selection of the species and (2) the contingencies of reinforcement responsible for the repertoires acquired by its members, including (3) the special contingencies maintained by an evolved social environment. (Ultimately, of course, it is all a matter of natural selection, since operant conditioning is an evolved process, of which cultural practices are special applications.)

Inner States

Although Skinner (1974) rejected explanations of behavior founded on non-observable hypothetical constructs, he did not deny the existence of these internal states. Internal or private events can be studied just as any other behavior, but their observation is, of course, limited. In a personal communication of June 13, 1983, Skinner wrote, "I believe it is possible to talk about private events and, in particular, to establish the limits with which we do so accurately. I think this brings so-called 'nonobservables' within reach."

Radical behaviorism, then, does not ignore various states of the mind, but it holds that explanations of behavior in terms of them is fruitless and retards the advancement of scientific behaviorism. Just as physics and biology began to make strides after abandoning the practice of attributing motion to the willpower of physical things and living organisms, so too will psychology become scientific after it rejects explanations of observable behavior based on fictitious constructs. What, then, is the role of such inner states as self-awareness, drives, emotions, and purpose or intention?

Self-Awareness

Skinner (1974) believed that humans not only have consciousness, but they are also aware of their consciousness; they are not only aware of their environment, but they are also aware of themselves as part of their environment; they not only observe external stimuli, but they are also aware of themselves observing that stimuli.

Behavior is a function of the environment, and part of that environment is within one's skin. This portion of the universe is peculiarly one's own and is therefore private. Each of us is subjectively aware of our own thoughts, feelings, recollections, and intentions. These private events are real; they have physical properties and thus are potentially subject to the same scientific analysis as any other physical phenomena (Skinner, 1974).

Self-awareness and private events can be illustrated by the following example. A worker reports to a friend, "I was so frustrated today that I almost quit my job." What can we make of such a statement? First, the report itself is verbal behavior and, as such, can be studied in the same way as any other behavior. Second, the statement that she was on the verge of quitting her job refers to a nonbehavior. Responses never emitted are not responses and, of course, have no meaning to science. Third, a private event transpired "within the skin" of the worker. This private event, along with her verbal report to the friend, can be scientifically analyzed. At the time the worker felt like quitting, she might have observed the following covert behavior. "I am observing within myself increasing degrees of frustration, which are raising the probability that I will inform my boss that I am quitting." This is more accurate than saying "I almost quit my job," and it refers to behavior that, although private, is within the boundaries of scientific analysis.

Drives

From the viewpoint of radical behaviorism, drives are not causes of behavior but merely explanatory fictions. To Skinner (1953) drives simply refer to the effects of deprivation and satiation and to the corresponding probability that the organism will respond. To deprive a person of food increases the likelihood of eating; to satiate a person decreases that likelihood. However, deprivation and satiation are not the only correlates of eating. Other factors that increase or decrease the probability of eating are internally observed hunger pangs, availability of food, and previous experiences with food reinforcers.

If drives are defined in terms of intervening states between deprivation and response, then they are unnecessary concepts and have no place in a scientific analysis of behavior. If we knew enough about the three essentials of behavior (antecedent, behavior, and consequences), then we would know why a person behaves, that is, what drives are related to specific behaviors. Only then would drives have a legitimate role in the scientific study of human behavior. For the present, however, explanations based on fictionalized constructs like drives or needs are merely untestable hypotheses.

Emotions

Throughout history people have attributed behavior to emotions, but to Skinner, this explanation is unnecessary and impedes the advancement of a scientific analysis of behavior. Psychology must be concerned with observable behavior, and emotions themselves are not directly observable. Physiological concomitants of emotion, obviously, can be measured, but those data are not the subjectively felt emotion.

When Skinner (1976) wrote about the death of his younger brother (as described in the opening of this chapter), he avoided any account of his own behavior in terms of emotions. He didn't tell us if he was sad, frightened, or confused. He simply described his and others' behavior. It wasn't that he had no feelings, but that his feelings, as inner behaviors, were beyond the observation of others.

Skinner, then, did not deny the existence of emotions. He accounted for them by the contingencies of survival and the contingencies of reinforcement. Throughout the millennia individuals most strongly disposed toward fear or anger were those who escaped from or triumphed over danger and thus were able to pass on those characteristics to their offspring. On an individual level, those experiences followed by delight, joy, pleasure, and other pleasant emotions tended to be reinforcing, thereby increasing the probability that they would recur in the life of that person.

Although emotions are subjectively real, Skinner (1974) believed that we must not attribute behavior to them. To say "She slammed the door because she was angry" makes an inference that is unnecessary and misleading. If one wished to know what contingencies accompany door-slamming behavior, then one must observe the environment, not postulate an internal intermediary cause. The probability of door-slamming behavior can be increased by environmental contingencies such as depriving the person of a certain positive reinforcer or by adding certain aversive stimuli. If anger *caused* people to slam doors, there would be many more broken door jambs in the world!

Purpose and Intention

Skinner(1974) recognized the concepts of purpose and intention, but again, he cautioned against attributing behavior to them. Purpose and intention exist within the skin, but they are not subject to direct outside scrutiny.

A felt ongoing purpose may itself be reinforcing. If I believe that my purpose for jogging is to feel better and live longer, then this thought per se acts as a reinforcing stimulus, especially while undergoing the drudgery of jogging or when trying to explain my motivation to a nonrunner.

A person may "intend" to see a movie Friday evening because viewing similar films has been reinforcing. At the time the person intends to go to the movie she feels a physical condition within the body and labels it an "intention." What are called intentions or purposes, therefore, are physically felt stimuli within the organism and not mentalistic events responsible for behavior. "The consequences of operant behavior are not what the behavior is now for; they are merely similar to the consequences that have shaped and maintained it" (Skinner, 1987a, p. 57).

Complex Behavior

Radical behaviorism holds that when a response is followed immediately by either reinforcement or by punishment, the probability of that response recurring

Emotions are subjectively real and may have observable concomitants, but they are not directly observable themselves.

is correspondingly increased or decreased. Human behavior, however, is exceedingly complex, and these complexities need to be understood if behavior is to be predicted or controlled. Skinner did not deny "higher mental processes" such as cognition, reason, and recall; nor did he ignore other complex human endeavors like creativity, unconscious behavior, dreams, and social behavior. He did, however, warn against attributing these behaviors to functions of the mind.

Higher Mental Processes

Skinner (1974) admitted that human thought is the most difficult of all behaviors to analyze; but potentially, at least, it can be understood as long as one does not resort to a hypothetical fiction such as "mind." Thinking, problem solving, and reminiscing are covert behaviors that take place within the skin but not inside the mind. As behavior, they are amenable to the same contingencies of reinforcement as overt behavior. For example, when a man has misplaced his car keys, he searches for them because similar searching behavior has been previously reinforced. Similarly, when he is unable to recall the name of an acquaintance he searches for that name covertly because this type of behavior has earlier been reinforced. However, the acquaintance's name did not exist in his mind any more than did the car keys. Skinner (1974, pp. 109–110) summed up this procedure, saying that "techniques of recall are not concerned with searching a storehouse of memory but with increasing the probability of responses."

Problem solving also involves covert behavior and often requires the person to covertly manipulate the relevant variables until the correct solution is found. Ultimately these variables are environmental and do not spring magically from the person's mind. A chess player seems to be hopelessly trapped, surveys the board, and suddenly makes a move that allows his marker to escape. What brought about this unexpected burst of "insight"? He did not solve the problem in his mind. He manipulated the various markers (not by touching them but in covert fashion), rejected moves not accompanied by reinforcement, and finally selected the one that was followed by internal reinforcement. Although the solution may have been facilitated by his previous experiences of reading a book on chess, listening to expert advice, or playing the game, it was initiated by environmental contingencies and not manufactured by mental machinations.

Creativity

How does the radical behaviorist account for creativity? Logically, if behavior were nothing other than a predictable response to a stimulus, novel or creative behavior could not exist because only previously reinforced behavior would be emitted. Skinner (1974, p. 114) answered this problem by comparing creative behavior with natural selection in evolutionary theory. "As accidental traits, arising from mutations, are selected by their contribution to survival, so accidental variations in behavior are selected by their reinforcing consequences." Just as natural selection explains differentiation among the species without resorting to an omnipotent creative mind, so behaviorism accounts for novel behavior without recourse to a personal creative mind.

The concept of mutation is crucial to both natural selection and creative behavior. In both cases random or accidental conditions are produced that have some possibility of survival. Creative writers change their environment, thus producing responses that have some chance of being reinforced. When their "creativity dries up" they may move to a different location, travel, read, talk to others, put words on paper with little expectancy that they will be the finished product, or try out various words, sentences, and ideas covertly. To Skinner, then, creativity is simply the result of *random* or *accidental* behaviors (overt or covert) that happen to be rewarded. The fact that some people are more creative than others is due both to differences in genetic endowment and to experiences that have shaped their creative behavior.

Unconscious Behavior

As a radical behaviorist, Skinner could not accept the notion of a storehouse of unconscious ideas or emotions. He did, however, accept the idea of unconscious *behavior*. In fact, because we rarely observe the relationship between genetic and environmental variables and our own behavior, nearly all our behavior is unconsciously motivated (Skinner, 1987a). In a more limited sense, behavior is labeled unconscious when we no longer think about it because it has been suppressed through punishment. Behavior that has aversive consequences has a tendency to be ignored or not thought about. A child repeatedly and severely punished for sexual play may both *suppress* the sexual behavior and *repress* any thoughts or memories of such activity. Eventually the child may deny that the sexual activity took place. Such *denial* avoids the aversive aspects connected with thoughts of punishment and is thus a negative reinforcer. In other words, the child is rewarded for *not thinking* about certain sexual behaviors.

Repression also takes place when a person avoids certain thoughts or actions by engaging in opposite or competing forms of behavior. For example, a man troubled by problems at home may enmesh himself in work, thereby not only physically avoiding home life but also blocking out any thoughts of it.

A more severe example of not thinking about aversive stimuli is a child who behaves in hateful ways toward her mother. In doing so, she will also exhibit some less antagonistic behaviors. If the loathsome behavior is punished, it will become suppressed and replaced by the more positive behaviors. Eventually the child will be rewarded for gestures of love, which will then increase in frequency. After a time, her behavior becomes more and more positive, and it may even resemble what Freud (1926/1959) called "reactive love." The child no longer has any thoughts of hatred toward her mother and behaves in an exceedingly loving and subservient manner. Skinner (1953) accounted for this "reaction formation" as an effect of the contingencies of reinforcement. No unconscious feelings of hatred can be observed, only slightly stilted signs of love.

Dreams

Skinner (1953) saw dreams as covert and symbolic forms of behavior that are subject to the same contingencies of reinforcement as any other behavior. He agreed with Freud that dreams may serve a wish-fulfillment purpose. Dream behavior is reinforcing when repressed sexual or aggressive stimuli are allowed expression. To act out sexual fantasies or to actually inflict damage on an enemy are two behaviors likely to be associated with punishment. To even covertly think about these behaviors may have punitive effects, but in dreams these behaviors may be expressed symbolically and without any accompanying punishment.

Social Behavior

Groups do not behave—only individuals can. Individuals establish groups because they have been rewarded for doing so. For example, individuals form clans so that they might be protected against animals, natural disasters, or enemy tribes. Individuals also form governments, establish churches, or become part of lynch mobs because they are reinforced for that behavior.

The social environment, however, is not always reinforcing. People are some-times ridiculed, insulted, or physically abused within the context of a group, yet, for at least three reasons, they continue to remain part of that group. First, because the group consists of several people, the abused person may be receiving positive reinforcement from one or more persons while incurring the punishment from some others. For example, a child abused by the father may be reinforced by family life because his mother shows him loving care. This suggests a second possibility for remaining in a group even while suffering abuse: The person (in this case, a child) may not possess sufficient means of countercontrol and, therefore, he can neither change the behavior of other members nor physically flee from the group. Third, reinforcement may occur on an intermittent schedule so that the abuse suffered by the individual is intermingled with occasional reward. If the positive reinforcement is strong enough and occurs on a variable-ratio or variable-interval schedule, then its effects will be more powerful than those of punishment.

Control of Human Behavior

Ultimately, an individual's behavior is controlled by environmental contingen-cies. Those contingencies may have been erected by society, by another individual, or by oneself, but the environment, not free will, is responsible for behavior.

Social Control

Individuals act to form social groups because such behavior tends to be rein-forcing. Groups, in turn, exercise control over their members by formulating written or unwritten laws, rules, and customs that have physical existence beyond the lives of individuals. The laws of a nation, the rules of an organization, and the customs of a culture transcend any one individual's means of countercontrol and serve as powerful controlling variables in the lives of individual members. In addition, social control includes the influence that one individual exercises over another in a one-to-one relationship (Skinner, 1974).

Social forces control our behavior in a nearly infinite variety of ways, but all these techniques can be grouped under the following headings: (1) operant con-ditioning, (2) describing contingencies, (3) deprivation and satiation, and (4) phys-ical restraint (Skinner, 1953).

OPERANT CONDITIONING.   Society exercises control over its members through the four principal methods of operant conditioning: positive reinforcement, negative reinforcement, and the two techniques of punishment (adding an aversive stimulus and removing a positive one). Each of these methods can be illustrated by observing the controlling techniques available to a fourth-grade teacher.

The teacher shapes the behavior of her students through the use of positive reinforcement when she gives high grades for excellent work, compliments socially desirable behaviors, or awards prizes for perfect attendance. She can also reinforce acceptable behavior through negative reinforcement, such as shortening the time of detention if the punished student remains silent and gives the appearance of hard work, or ceasing to scold a child when he apologizes for unacceptable behavior. On the other hand, she can also rely on two methods of punishment. She can add an aversive, such as extra work for disobedient behavior, or she can remove positive reinforcers, such as moving a very talkative child away from friends.

In all these examples, the teacher makes reward or punishment contingent on the behavior of the child. The effectiveness of each technique depends on the consistency with which it is used, the individual student's genetic makeup and personal history of reinforcement, and the existence of any other conflicting modes of behavioral control.

DESCRIBING CONTINGENCIES.   A second technique of social control is to describe to a person the contingencies of reinforcement. This technique is different from arranging contingencies, a procedure crucial to operant conditioning. Describing contingencies involves language, usually verbal, to inform people of the consequences of their not-yet-emitted behavior.

Many examples of describing contingencies are available. Highway signs warn motorists to watch out for ice on the next bridge; a construction worker yells "Look out below" after dropping a hammer. Threats are also a means of describing contingencies. "If you don't buy me a gift for my birthday, I will divorce you." Advertising in another method of control through describing contingencies. "Invest your money with our bank and receive the highest rate of interest allowed by law." "Use our brand of toothpaste and you will improve your love life." In none of these examples will the attempt at control be perfectly successful, yet each of them increases the likelihood that the desired response will be emitted. Also, none of these attempts is designed to change a person's "mind," but rather to alter the environment.

DEPRIVATION AND SATIATION.   Behavior can also be controlled either by depriving people or by satiating them with reinforcers. Again, even though deprivation and satiation are internal states, the control originates with the environment. Deprived individuals are more likely to respond in ways designed to alleviate deprivation. When children habitually have no appetite at mealtime, parents can increase the chances of them eating dinner by depriving them of snacks between meals.

Satiating a person is also a means of control. A satiated person is less likely to respond with behavior that is undesirable to the controlling person. A parent can diminish, at least temporarily, the likelihood that children will nag by giving them many interesting toys. A government can decrease the chances that its citizens will revolt by establishing generous social welfare programs. In the long run, social control through satiation has the obvious disadvantage of costs to the controller and therefore is likely to be used only by those who can afford those costs.

PHYSICAL RESTRAINT.   Another example of social control involves physically restraining individuals so that they cannot behave in a particular manner. We erect fences to keep others from trespassing on our property; society builds prisons to restrain

Physical restraint is one means of social control.

criminals; and we hold back a child who plays near a deep ravine. Physical restraint acts to counter the effects of conditioning, and it results in behavior contrary to that which would have been emitted had the person not been restrained.

Some people might say that physical restraint is a means of denying an individual's freedom. However, Skinner (1971) held that behavior has nothing to do with personal freedom but is shaped by the contingencies of survival, the effects of reinforcement, and the contingencies of the social environment. Therefore, the act of physically restraining a person does no more to negate freedom than any other technique of control, including self-control.

Self-Control

If personal freedom is a fiction, then how can a person exercise self-control? Skinner would say that, just as we can alter the variables in another person's environment, so we can manipulate the variables within our own environment and thus exercise some measure of self-control. The contingencies of self-control, however, do not reside within the individual and cannot be freely chosen. When we control our own behavior, we do so by manipulating the same variables that we would use in controlling someone else's behavior, and ultimately these variables lie outside ourselves.

How can we exercise self control without resorting to free choice? Skinner (1953) and Skinner and Vaughan (1983) pointed to several techniques, some of which are also used in social control. For example, *physical restraint* is not limited to social control but can also be used for self-control. Although we cannot physically hold ourselves back, we can arrange environmental contingencies so that they will restrict our behavior. An angry person can clench his teeth to prevent himself from speaking inappropriately. A dieting person can ask a friend to hold her money as they walk past a candy store.

Self-control can also be produced through the use of *physical aids* such as tools, machines, and financial resources. A carpenter speeds work by using power equipment; a shopper increases the likelihood of spontaneous purchases by bringing enough money.

Another means of self-control is *changing the stimulus*, thereby increasing the probability of the desired behavior. Students wishing to concentrate on their studies can turn off a distracting television set. A woman desiring to quit smoking can stop carrying cigarettes. A man who wishes to call a friend more frequently can tape the telephone number some place where he will see it more frequently. All these techniques involve the manipulation of environmental variables, thereby increasing the probability that one's own behavior will be changed.

Earlier, we saw that social control could be exercised through depriving or satiating another person. Similarly, self-control can be produced with the same procedures. An example of *self-deprivation* is a person who diets before going on a vacation in order to be able to sample a variety of exotic foods.

Satiation is probably a more effective means of self-control than it is social control because in the latter situation the controller must possess nearly unlimited assets. Self-satiation can utilize smaller quantities of resources. A smoker chews gum to satiate an oral craving and thereby reduce the likelihood of smoking a cigarette. An alcoholic constantly sips on soft drinks to keep from drinking liquor. A worker labors hard so that exhaustion will facilitate sleep. Note again that self-control is not dependent on free will but on altering environmental variables.

Another technique of self-control is to arrange the environment so that one can *escape from aversive stimulation* only by producing the proper response. Skinner (1953) used the illustration of setting an alarm clock so that the aversive sound can be stopped only by getting up to shut off the alarm. Some dieters view their reflection in the mirror to produce an undesirable image that can be avoided only by losing weight.

Skinner (1953) also listed *drugs*, especially alcohol, as a frequent means of self-control. A disgruntled employee takes several drinks, knowing that this behavior will increase his chances of telling off his boss. A drug addict injects heroin to prevent withdrawal discomfort. A person takes tranquilizers to make her behavior more placid. Another smokes nicotine to induce relaxation. Examples of self-control through the use of drugs can be expanded almost endlessly.

The technique of *doing something else* is used solely with self-control and cannot be applied to social control. We do something else in order to avoid behaving undesirably. This procedure is effective only if the substitute behavior is prepotent, that is, more powerful than the unwanted behavior. An obsessive neurotic counts repetitious patterns in wallpaper to avoid thinking about previous experiences that would create guilt. A person tempted to behave sexually goes jogging instead. In these examples counting patterns and jogging attain prepotency over guilt-ridden thoughts and sexual activity because of the aversive stimuli associated with the latter two responses. The substitute behaviors are therefore negatively reinforcing, permitting the person to avoid unpleasant thoughts.

THE UNHEALTHY PERSONALITY

Unfortunately the techniques of social control and self-control sometimes produce detrimental effects, which result in inappropriate behavior and unhealthy personality development.

Counteracting Strategies

When social control is excessive, people can use three basic strategies for counteracting it—they can escape, revolt, or use passive resistance (Skinner, 1953). With the defensive strategy of *escape*, people withdraw from the controlling agent either physically or psychologically. Because the original controlling agent is ordinarily the parents, and very young children have little means of running away from home, a frequent mode of escape is to psychologically withdraw from parents, a strategy that may later lead to seclusion from society. People whose behavior is characterized by escape find it difficult to become involved in intimate personal relationships, tend to be mistrustful of people, and prefer to live lonely lives of noninvolvement.

People who *revolt* against society's controls behave more actively, counterattacking the controlling agent. Children who revolt oppose their parent's control by openly defying their authority, or more indirectly, by writing on the walls and mistreating the furniture. Older people rebel through public vandalism, tormenting teachers, verbally abusing others, pilfering equipment from employers, provoking the police, or overthrowing established organizations such as religions or governments.

People who counteract control through *passive resistance* are more subtle than those who rebel and more irritating to the controllers than those who rely on escape. Skinner (1953) believed that passive resistance is most likely to be used where escape and revolt have failed. The conspicuous feature of this strategy is stubbornness. A child with homework to do finds a dozen excuses why it cannot be finished. The employee slows down progress by undermining the work of others, and the husband allows important chores to pile up by staying busy with trifles.

Inappropriate Behaviors

Inappropriate behaviors follow from self-defeating techniques of counteracting social control or from unsuccessful attempts at self-control, especially when either of these failures is accompanied by strong emotion. Like most behaviors, inappropriate or unhealthy responses are learned. They are shaped by the contingencies of positive and negative reinforcement and especially by the effects of punishment.

Obviously, inappropriate behavior takes many forms, and Skinner (1953) listed several of the more common patterns along with their reinforcement contingencies. The first of these is taking *drugs*. The effects of alcohol and other drugs are reinforcing because they enable the person to avoid aversive stimuli, but their long-term consequences may be detrimental, leading to dependence or to a chronic mode of escape from the problems of everyday life.

Another inappropriate pattern is *excessively vigorous behavior*, which makes no sense in terms of the contemporary situation, but might be reasonable in terms of past history. Excessively vigorous behavior may stem from repression or reaction

Walden Two—*Utopia or Tedium?*

If it is inevitable that human behavior will be shaped by the environment, then why not design a culture that will mold behavior in the most favorable manner possible? This, of course, was Skinner's prime motivation in writing *Walden Two* (1948).

In the summer of 1945, as World War II was coming to a close, Skinner decided to create a society that would give returning soldiers a model for the "good life" after the war. He was at a point in his personal life when he needed self-therapy, and the writing of *Walden Two* filled that need. The book's principal characters, Frazier and Burris, represent Skinner's attempts to reconcile two aspects of his own personality (Skinner, 1967). But the ultimate importance of the book is in its blueprint for a utopian society, based on Skinner's experimental analysis of behavior.

Briefly, the book is an account of a fictional rural community, Walden Two, where about 1000 people are living the "good life" in a deliberately controlled society. The community has been established by the book's protagonist, T. E. Frazier, and none of its inhabitants have to be coerced into living there. In Walden Two the people work only

four hours a day, the children are well cared for, food is plentiful, medical care is excellent, and music, art, and literature flourish. Indeed, this must be the "good life."

Some people, however, have questioned the desirability of residing in Walden Two. Some of the most frequent criticisms of a behaviorally engineered society are (1) the citizens would have no individual freedom; (2) no one would control the controllers; (3) people would have little motivation to achieve, because they would receive no personal credit; and (4) even if such a society were feasible, people would be reluctant to live in such a dull, antiseptic environment. Skinner (1969) has responded to each of these criticisms.

First, he insisted that people are not free anyway, if by freedom one means free from the restraints of environmental contingencies. On the other hand, if one defines freedom as the opportunity to live in a culture that maximizes positive reinforcers and minimizes punishment, then the people of Walden Two would enjoy more freedom than others. According to Skinner (1969), they would also be free to behave in ways that would change the society so that it could formation and is likely to manifest itself as extreme restlessness, preservation, or a compulsive tendency to repeat a response. An opposite pattern is *excessively restrained behavior*, a pattern that develops from a history of punishment. The individual learns responses that avoid the aversive stimuli associated with punishment, and these responses frequently take passive forms like shyness, stubbornness, inhibition, or hysterical paralysis.

Another type of inappropriate behavior is simply *blocking out reality*. This is similar to Sullivan's concept of selective inattention (see Chapter 6) in which a person pays no attention to aversive stimuli like a nagging spouse or the punitive thoughts associated with an earlier guilt-producing experience.

A fifth form of undesirable behavior listed by Skinner reflects *defective self-knowledge* and is manifested in such self-deluding responses as boasting, rationalizing,

meet emergencies and survive into the future.

At present, people act as if freedom exists and they behave as if they are pursuing freedom. Fictional freedom is a powerful incentive for most contemporary people. However, in a well-designed society people could enjoy the "good life," which is, after all, the goal of those now seeking freedom. "The problem, in short, is not to design a way of life which will be liked by men *as they now are*, but a way of life which will be liked by those who live it" (Skinner, 1969, p. 41).

Second, Skinner noted that in our current culture we daily see misuse of power and therefore understandably distrust those who possess it. Skinner obviously was concerned with this problem when he wrote *Walden Two* because he imbued Frazier, the founder, with "negative charisma" and had him abdicate any position of authority as soon as the community was founded. In Walden Two, as in any society, leaders are themselves controlled through the use of countercontrol. The principal difference is that in Walden Two measures of countercontrol are specifically designed into the community so that no one would be rewarded for flagrant abuse of authority.

Third, Skinner believed that the fact that personal credit is a positively valued commodity simply reflects an evolutionary history of haphazard control. Society has now reached the point where it attributes personal credit to individuals in order to assure its own survival. Currently we admire people who apparently behave for the good of society rather than for self-interest. These people are especially commended when they appear to act freely for the good of the whole. In a well-designed society, however, contrived or artificial reinforcers could be minimized and personal credit would no longer have any positive value; people would be reinforced by natural contingencies such as food, sex, art, music, literature, and friendship.

Skinner (1969) responded to the fourth criticism, saying that people who complain that Walden Two is too well designed, with too little spontaneity, are themselves the product of their own culture. Such people, Skinner said, blindly fear anything that might be better than what they are accustomed to. They are compared to children who say "I'm glad I don't like broccoli because if I liked it, I'd eat a lot of it, and I hate it" (Skinner, 1969, p. 42).

or believing oneself to be Jesus Christ or Julius Caesar. This pattern is usually an unsuccessful attempt at self-control and continues to be reinforcing because the person avoids the aversive stimulation associated with thoughts of inadequacy.

A final detrimental effect of control on behavior is *aversive self-stimulation*, exemplified by self-punishment or the arrangement of environmental variables so that one is punished by others. How can this "masochistic" behavior be rewarding? Several possibilities might explain it. First, aversive self-stimulation may permit a person to avoid even more painful stimuli, as when a soldier shoots himself in the foot in order to escape battle. Also, masochistic behavior is negatively reinforcing when it avoids the aversive conditions of guilt or sin by inflicting "deserved" punishment on the person. Finally, self-punishment can be learned through respondent conditioning. For example, when an aversive stimulus (pain) is paired with a strong reward (sex), the pleasure may override the pain so that the entire event (sexual pleasure coupled with pain) becomes reinforcing and, in some cases, the aversive stimulus (pain) may become, by itself, a reward. As a result, a person gains enjoyment from pain inflicted by self or others.

Most of these inappropriate patterns are behavioral descriptions of several Freudian defense mechanisms (repression, regression, reaction formation), Adlerian safeguarding tendencies (excuses, aggression, withdrawal), as well as Sullivan's notion of selective inattention. The psychodynamic theorists viewed these behaviors as totally or partially motivated by unconscious urges within the person, but Skinner saw them simply as overt behaviors shaped by the environmental contingencies of reward and punishment. Whereas the psychodynamic theorists saw these mechanisms as expressing some hidden motive, Skinner attributed no special purpose to them other than the avoidance of aversive stimulation and the attainment of positive reinforcement.

PSYCHOTHERAPY

Skinner (1987b) believed that psychotherapy is one of the chief obstacles blocking psychology's attempt to become scientific. Nevertheless, his ideas on the shaping of behavior (both appropriate and inappropriate) have had a significant impact on the current behavior therapy movement. However, his notions on treatment are not limited to the approach called behavior therapy, but extend to a description of how all therapy works.

The therapist, whether psychoanalytic, client-centered, or behavioral, is a controlling agent. Not all controlling agents, however, are harmful and the patient must learn to discriminate between punitive authority figures (both past and present) and the permissive therapist who dispenses positive reinforcers. Whereas the parent may was been cold and rejecting, the therapist is warm and accepting; although the parent was critical and judgmental, the therapist is supportive and empathic.

The shaping of any behavior takes time, and therapeutic behavior is no exception. The therapist molds desirable behavior by reinforcing slightly improved changes in behavior. The nonbehavioral therapist may do this accidently or unknowingly, whereas the behavioral therapist attends specifically to this technique (Skinner, 1953).

Traditional therapists generally explain behaviors by resorting to a variety of fictional constructs such as the Oedipus complex, striving for superiority, collective unconscious, and self-actualization needs. Skinner, however, believed that psychotherapists should work on the assumption that fantasies, slips of the tongue, defensive mechanisms, safeguarding tendencies, and so on are behaviors that can be accounted for by learning principles. No explanatory fictions or inner causes are needed to explain "neurotic" or inappropriate behavior, and no therapeutic purpose is enhanced by postulating them. Skinner reasons that if behavior is shaped by inner causes, then some force must be responsible for the inner cause. Traditional theories must ultimately account for this cause, but behavior therapy merely skips it and deals directly with the history of the organism; and it is this history that, in the final analysis, is responsible for any hypothetical inner cause.

Behavior therapists have developed a variety of techniques over the years, most based on operant conditioning (Skinner, 1988), although some are built around the principles of respondent conditioning. In general, these therapists play an active role in the treatment process, pointing out the positive consequences of certain behaviors and the aversive effects of others and also suggesting behaviors that, over the long haul, will result in positive reinforcement.

CONCEPT OF HUMANITY

Without doubt, B. F. Skinner held a *deterministic view* of human nature, and concepts like free will and individual choice had no place in his thinking. People are not free but are controlled by environmental forces. They may seem to be motivated by inner causes, but in reality those causes can be traced to sources outside the individual. Self-control depends ultimately on environmental variables and not on some inner strength. When people control their own lives, they do so by manipulating their environment, which in turn, shapes their behavior. This environmental approach negates hypothetical constructs such as will power or responsibility. Human behavior can be perfectly predicted if all genetic and environmental factors are known. At the present stage of the science of human behavior, of course, these factors are not completely known. Human behavior is extremely complex, but people behave under many of the same laws as do machines and animals.

The notion that human behavior is completely determined is an extremely problematic one for many people who believe that they observe daily many examples of free choice in both themselves and others. What accounts for this illusion of freedom? Skinner (1971) held that freedom and dignity are reinforcing concepts because people find satisfaction in the belief that they are free to choose and also in their faith in the basic dignity of human beings. Because these fictional concepts are reinforcing in many modern societies, people tend to behave in ways that increase the probability that these constructs will be perpetuated. Once freedom and dignity lose their reinforcement value, people will stop behaving *as if* they existed.

In the days preceding Louis Pasteur, many people believed that maggots spontaneously generated on the bodies of dead animals. Skinner (1974) used this observation to paint an analogy with human behavior, pointing out that the spontaneous generation of behavior is no more of a reality than the spontaneous generation of maggots. Behavior that is haphazard or random may appear to be freely chosen, but it is actually the product of haphazard or random environmental and genetic conditions. People are not autonomous, but the illusion of autonomy persists because of our ignorance of the individual's history. We attribute free will to humanity simply because we do not take the time to understand behavior. Every action we fail to understand we assign to some internal concept such as beliefs, intentions, values, or motives. Skinner did not deny that people are capable of reflecting upon their own nature, but he insisted that this reflective behavior can be observed and studied just like any other.

Is Skinner's concept of humanity optimistic or pessimistic? At first thought, it may appear that a deterministic stance is necessarily pessimistic. However, Skinner's view of human nature tends, if anything, to be somewhat *optimistic*. Because human behavior is shaped by the principles of reinforcement, the species is quite adaptable. Of all behaviors, the most satisfying ones tend to increase in frequency of occurrence. People, therefore, learn to live quite harmoniously with their environment. The evolution of the species is in the direction of greater control over environmental variables, and this results in an increasing repertoire of behaviors beyond those essential for mere survival. However, Skinner (1987a) was also concerned that modern cultural practices have not yet evolved to the point where nuclear war, overpopulation, and depletion of natural resources can be stopped. In this sense, he was more of a realist than an optimist.

Nevertheless, Skinner (1948) provided a blueprint for a utopian society (see *Walden Two*). If his recommendations were followed, then people could be taught how to arrange the variables in their environments so that the probability of correct or satisfying solutions would be increased. Skinner was interested in improving humanity, and his efforts with the baby-tender and with teaching machines are but two examples of this interest.

Is humanity basically good or evil? Skinner hoped for an idealistic society where people behave in ways that are loving, sensible, democratic, independent, and good, but people are not by nature this way. Neither are they essentially evil, however. Within limits set by heredity, people are flexible in their adaptation to the environment, but no evaluation of good or evil should be placed on an individual's behavior. If a person typically behaves altruistically for the good of others, it is because this behavior, either in the species' evolutionary history or in the individual's personal history, has been previously reinforced. If one behaves cowardly, it is because the rewards for cowardice outweigh the aversive variables (Skinner, 1978).

On the dimension of causality vs. teleology Skinner's theory of personality is very high on *causality*. Behavior is caused by the person's history of reinforcement as well as by the species' contingencies for survival and by the evolution of cultures. Although people behave covertly (within the skin) to think about the future, all those thoughts are determined by past experiences (Skinner, 1990b).

The complex of environmental contingencies responsible for these thoughts, as well as for all other behaviors, are beyond our awareness. We rarely have knowledge of the relationship between all genetic and environmental variables and our own behavior. For this reason Skinner would be placed very high on the *unconscious dimension of personality*.

The history of a person determines behavior, and because each of us has our own history of reinforcement contingencies, behavior and personality are relatively unique. Genetic differences also account for *uniqueness among people*. Biological and historical differences make us unique individuals, and Skinner emphasized those differences more than he does our similarities.

Although he believed that genetics play an important role in personality development, Skinner held that human personality is largely shaped by the environment. Because an important part of that environment is other people, Skinner's concept of humanity inclines more toward social than toward biological determinants of behavior. As a species, humans have developed to their present form because of particular environmental factors with which they have encountered. Climate, geography, and physical strength relative to other animals have all helped shape the human species. But *social environment*, including family structure, early experiences with parents, educational systems, governmental organization, and so forth, has played an even more important role in the development of personality

Skinner hoped that people might be trustworthy, understanding, warm, and empathic, characteristics that his friendly adversary Carl Rogers (see Chapter 16) believed to be at the core of the psychologically healthy personality. In contrast to Rogers, who believed that these positive behaviors are at least partially the result of our capacity to be self-directed, Skinner held that they are completely under the control of environmental variables. We are not by nature good, but we can become so if we are exposed to the proper contingencies of reinforcement. Although his view of the ideal person would be similar to those of Rogers and Abraham H. Maslow (see Chapter 15), Skinner believed that the means of becoming autonomous, loving, and self-actualizing must not be left to chance, but should be specifically designed into the society.

Related Research

Skinner's theory is the most prolific of all theories of personality, having generated thousands of research studies on human subjects. In its early history, operant conditioning was used mostly in studies with animals, then it was applied to simple human responses, but, more recently, it has been used to shape a variety of complex human behaviors. For example, the disciplines of behavioral medicine and health psychology have used Skinnerian techniques to help people change unhealthy life styles, such as overeating and smoking. Incentive programs have also been used to treat addictions and to increase compliance to recommended medical regimens.

In one study with cocaine abusers, Higgins et al. (1991) compared the effectiveness of a contingency management program with a traditional counseling approach. All subjects were outpatients who met criteria for active cocaine dependence, as defined by the DSM-III-R (American Psychiatric Association, 1987). All submitted to regular urine tests, which the experimenters used to detect cocaine use.

Subjects in the contingency management group were awarded voucher points worth 15 cents each for remaining drug free. Although money was not exchanged, the vouchers could be used to purchase retail items such as cameras and bicycles. The first cocaine-free specimen was worth 10 points, or $1.50. The value of each subsequent consecutive drug-free specimen increased by 5 points, so that the second negative report was worth 15 points, the third 20 points, and so forth. In addition, subjects could receive a $10.00 voucher for each four consecutive negative specimens. Submission of a positive specimen or failure to submit a urine specimen would reset the schedule back to $1.50, from which patients could begin again to earn points according to the original schedule. Once earned, points could not be lost. In addition to the vouchers, subjects in the behavioral management group attended counseling sessions that focused on four issues. First, subjects identified a nonabusing spouse, friend, or relative who gave them positive reinforcement whenever they submitted a negative specimen. Second, therapists taught subjects to use drug-refusal skills and to recognize the antecedents and consequences of their cocaine use. Third, unemployed subjects and others who were interested in job information received employment counseling. Fourth, subjects were encouraged to develop new hobbies and recreational activities.

Subjects in the traditional counseling group followed the 12-step program of Narcotics Anonymous, which is patterned after the Alcoholics Anonymous program. Subjects submitted specimens on the same schedule as the contingency management group, except that they were not informed of urinalysis results. Counseling subjects participated in both group and individual therapy sessions, attended lectures on cocaine dependence, AIDS, the disease model of addiction, self-help, and relapse prevention. In addition, they identified a sponsor from a local self-help group who would supply aid and comfort as needed.

Results of the study easily favored the behavioral management approach. More than 80 percent of the patients in the behavioral group remained in treatment for the full 12 weeks, whereas only about 40 percent of the counseling group remained in treatment. Also, compared to subjects in the counseling group, more patients in the behavioral treatment group remained cocaine-free after 4 weeks, 8 weeks, and 12 weeks.

Although these results suggest the superiority of a behavioral treatment approach over traditional drug treatment, at least two weaknesses are apparent. First, the monetary cost was not inconsequential. Patients who remained drug free could receive more than $1,000 over the 12-week program. However, this amount is small compared with the costs of cocaine addiction. The second limitation of this study is lack of follow-up. We do not yet know if patients who received the contingency management treatment have attained long-term abstinence.

Gross, Sanders, Smith, and Samson (1990) have also used a contingency management approach to increase compliance with orthodontic treatment for children ranging in age from 10 to 16. They divided subjects into two groups—an experimental group that received contingency management treatment and a control group that received only attention. An orthodontist instructed both groups on the importance of wearing orthodontic headgear for 12 hours during the day and while sleeping. Also, parents of youngsters in both groups received a small monetary incentive for collecting data on headgear use.

An experimenter helped family members of children in the experimental group to develop a contingency contract to reinforce compliant behaviors. Rewards varied from child to child, and parents were also encouraged to change the incentives regularly. Headgear compliance, for example, might allow a child to stay up later at bedtime or to have a friend spend the night on a weekend. Results indicated that the mean percentage of headgear wear during the duration of the study was 96 percent for patients in the contingency management group and 71 percent for those in the attention control group. A follow-up study two months after the termination of the study revealed slight but insignificant increases for both groups. The authors reported an additional advantage for the experimental group—parents did not have to frequently nag their children about wearing their headgear.

CRITIQUE OF SKINNER

Except for Freud's psychoanalysis, the radical behaviorism of B. F. Skinner is the most maligned, criticized, and condemned personality theory of the 20th century. It has been blamed, by one source or another, for nearly every ill facing society today—the failure of our educational system, the dehumanization of psychology, and even political assassination (Skinner, 1971). A less harsh critique of Skinner's position was presented by Hans J. Eysenck (1988b), who claimed that Skinner ignored such concepts as individual differences, intelligence, genetic factors, and the whole realm of personality. These claims are only partly true, because Skinner did recognize genetic factors, and he did offer a somewhat unenthusiastic definition of personality, saying that it is "at best a repertoire of behavior imparted by an organized set of contingencies" (Skinner, 1974, p. 149).

More positively, Skinner has been recognized as having made, perhaps, the greatest contribution to psychology of any person who has ever lived. A recent survey (Korn, Davis, & Davis, 1991) asked psychology historians and chairpersons to rank the 10 most important psychologists, both contemporary and all-time. The historians, who were APA Fellows, ranked Skinner eighth on the all-time list but first on the contemporary list, and the psychology chairpersons ranked him first on both lists. In fact, both historians and chairpersons believed that Skinner was clearly ahead of anyone else as an important contemporary psychologist.

Nevertheless, neither notoriety nor fame is a criterion for a scientific theory, and Skinner's personality theory must be evaluated by the same criteria used to assess all other theories.

The first criterion of a useful theory is that it should *generate research*. Neither Skinner nor his disciples have conducted much research designed specifically to test hypotheses drawn from his theory of personality. Indeed, Skinner was opposed to hypothetico-deductive systems and the testing of fabricated hypotheses. On the other hand, the quantity of descriptive research generated by Skinner's ideas is unparalleled in the arena of personality theory.

Second, how well does Skinner's theory *organize all that is known about human personality*? On this criterion the theory must receive only a moderate rating. Skinner's approach was to describe behavior and the environmental contingencies under which it takes place. His purpose was to bring together these descriptive facts and to generalize from them. Many personality traits can be accounted for by the principles of operant conditioning, and Skinner even offers explanations for such human characteristics as defense mechanisms, neurotic reactions, altruistic behaviors, and dreams. However, other concepts such as insight, creativity, motivation, inspiration, and self-concept do not fit easily into an operant conditioning framework.

The abundance of descriptive research turned out by Skinner and his followers has made operant conditioning an extremely practical procedure. For example, Skinnerian techniques have been used to train mentally retarded children to speak and dress themselves, condition phobic patients to overcome their fears, enhance compliance to medical recommendations, help people overcome tobacco and drug addictions, improve healthy eating habits, and increase assertiveness. In fact, Skinnerian theory can be applied to almost all areas of training, teaching, and psychotherapy. As a *guide to action*, therefore, the theory must be evaluated very highly.

The fourth criterion of a useful theory is *internal consistency*, and, judged by this standard, Skinnerian theory again would be rated very high. Skinner defined his terms precisely and operationally, a process greatly aided by the avoidance of fictionalized mentalistic concepts.

Is the theory *parsimonious*? On this final criterion Skinner's theory is difficult to rate. On the one hand, the theory is free from cumbersome hypothetical constructs, but, on the other hand, it demands a novel expression of everyday phrases. For example, instead of saying, "I got so mad at my husband, I threw a dish at him, but missed," one would need to say, "The contingencies of reinforcement within my environment were arranged in such a manner that I observed my organism throwing a dish against the kitchen wall."

Chapter Summary

As a radical behaviorist, B. F. Skinner avoided all hypothetical concepts such as "mind" or "personality" and based his concept of humanity solely on observable behavior. Although most of his observations were made on rats and pigeons, Skinner believed that these observations could be generalized to human behavior. Rather than testing hypotheses, he simply observed behavior for the purpose of describing, predicting, and controlling it. His philosophy of science permitted an interpretation of behavior, but not an explanation of its causes.

Although Skinner recognized the existence of inner states such as thinking and feeling, he insisted that these events are beyond the realm of behavioral analysis. Thoughts and feelings can be observed by the individual, but only overt behavior can be studied by the scientist.

Skinner believed that human behavior is shaped by three forces: (1) the individual's personal history of *reinforcement*, (2) *natural selection*, and (3) the *evolution of cultural practices*. His views on natural selection and cultural evolution were based largely on speculation, but his ideas on reinforcement were founded on his laboratory work on *operant conditioning*, a process in which reinforcement (or punishment) is contingent upon the occurrence of a particular behavior.

Skinner recognized two types of reinforcement—positive and negative. A *positive reinforcer* is any event that, when added to a situation, increases the probability that a given behavior will occur. *Negative reinforcement*, which also increases the probability of a given behavior, refers to the removal of an aversive stimulus. Similarly, Skinner identified two types of *punishment*; the first is the presentation of an aversive stimulus and the second involves the removal of a positive stimulus. The effects of reinforcement are more predictable than those of punishment.

Reinforcement can be either *continuous* or *intermittent*, but intermittent schedules are more efficient. The four principal intermittent schedules of reinforcement are the *fixed-ratio*, in which the organism is reinforced after a predetermined number of responses; the *variable-ratio*, where reinforcement occurs after every nth response on the average; the *fixed-interval*, in which reinforcement occurs according to a designated period of time; and the *variable-interval*, where reinforcement occurs after a lapse of random or variable periods of time.

Skinner offered several means by which human behavior is controlled. The first is *social control*, in which another person, a group, a society, or a nation shapes an individual's behavior. This is accomplished through (1) operant conditioning, (2) describing the contingencies of reinforcement, (3) depriving or satiating a person, or (4) physically restraining the individual. People can also control their own behavior through *self-control*, but all control ultimately rests with the environment. Self-control, therefore, is not a function of free will.

Unhealthy *behaviors* are learned in the same way as any other behaviors, that is, mostly through operant conditioning. In order to change unhealthy behaviors many behavior therapists have employed a multitude of techniques based on the principles of operant conditioning.

In his concept of humanity, Skinner was both a *determinist* and an *environmentalist*. As a determinist he rejected the notion of free choice and insisted that all behavior is lawfully determined and, potentially at least, can be perfectly predicted and controlled. As an environmentalist he de-emphasized anatomy and stressed the environment, including natural selection, as the final shaper of human behavior.

Skinner's behavioral analysis has generated volumes of research, most of it descriptive rather than hypothesis testing. The theory receives high marks for being internally consistent and for guiding the practitioner. However, it is only moderately successful in organizing all that we currently know about human behavior.

Suggested Readings

MINDESS, H. (1988). The denial of personality. In H. Mindess, *Makers of psychology: The personal factor* (pp. 84–109). New York: Insight Books.

An interesting and readable chapter on the life of Skinner, a man Mindess calls "the personality that denies personality."

SKINNER, B. F. (1953). *Science and human behavior*. New York: Macmillan.

Skinner's first and most complete work on the science of *human* rather than animal behavior, this book provides a comprehensive foundation for the scientific analysis of behavior.

SKINNER, B. F. (1971). *Beyond freedom and dignity*. New York: Knopf.

In this, his most controversial book, Skinner argued that the concepts of freedom and dignity are detrimental to the building of an effective society. *Beyond Freedom and Dignity* was on nearly every best-seller list in 1971.

SKINNER, B. F. (1974). *About behaviorism*. New York: Knopf.

Skinner defines, analyzes, and defends behaviorism. In his introduction he presents 20 commonly held beliefs about behaviorism, all of which, he believes, are wrong.

SKINNER, B. F. (1987). *Upon further reflection*. Englewood Cliffs, NJ: Prentice-Hall.

A collection of Skinner's later works, this brief book challenges the reader in such areas as survival of the world, the importance of cultural evolution, and cognitive science. Also included is a chapter updating *Walden Two*.

Social-Cognitive Theory

Chapter Ten

OVERVIEW
BIOGRAPHY OF ALBERT BANDURA
INTRODUCTION TO SOCIAL-COGNITIVE THEORY
RECIPROCAL DETERMINISM
    Differential Contributions
    Meaning of Determinism
    Chance Encounters and Fortuitous Events
BOX: CAN CHANCE CHANGE YOUR LIFE?
SELF SYSTEM
    Self-Regulation
    External Factors in Self-Regulation
    Self-Efficacy
LEARNING
    Observational Learning
    Enactive Learning
DYSFUNCTIONAL BEHAVIOR
    Depressive Reactions
    Phobias
    Aggressive Behaviors
THERAPY
CONCEPT OF HUMANITY
RELATED RESEARCH
CRITIQUE OF BANDURA
CHAPTER SUMMARY
SUGGESTED READINGS

BANDURA

One Sunday afternoon Jim received a call from his friend Kevin, who invited him to play tennis. Jim usually enjoyed a good, fast-paced singles match, but on this day Kevin asked him to join Mark and one of Mark's friends in a game of doubles. Jim knew Mark only casually and had never met Mark's friend. Ordinarily, Jim might have declined because he didn't care for doubles—not enough exercise. However, the football game he was watching on television was one-sided and he wasn't much interested in it. Besides, his wife and daughter had gone to visit his mother-in-law, so Jim had little else to do. He accepted the invitation, changed clothes, and drove to the tennis courts.

Although he and Greg—Mark's friend—lost the match, Jim enjoyed the company. When Kevin suggested that the four of them go to his house for a cold drink, Jim went along. At Kevin's, he got to know Greg better. Greg was a young assistant professor of history at the state university and was visiting Mark for the weekend. Because Jim was a high school history teacher, he and Greg quickly began talking about history. Eventually, Greg suggested that Jim might wish to further his studies in history and pursue an advanced degree.

Jim was in his third year of teaching American history at the local high school and had never really considered changing jobs. He enjoyed teaching and was considered a good teacher by his students and colleagues. However, the more Greg talked, the more Jim thought he might be better suited to do research and teach at the college level. Greg encouraged him to apply at his university and Jim replied that he would consider it.

The next day, however, Jim had lost some of his enthusiasm about graduate school. He knew it would be a hardship for his wife Laura and their young daughter Angela. Laura would either have to quit her job as an elementary school teacher and move with him or the two would be separated for three or four years. Neither course of action seemed feasible, and Jim was sure that Laura would object to either.

When Jim told Laura of his encounter with Greg, he was surprised that she encouraged him to go to graduate school. She said that she could probably find another teaching job and that Angela could go to nursery school while he studied history.

With Greg's recommendation and his own superior academic record, Jim not only was accepted into the Ph.D. program but was awarded a teaching fellowship as well. So Jim, Laura, and Angela left friends and relatives in their home town and embarked on a new professional career. From that time on Jim's life would be dramatically changed because of his chance meeting with Greg on the tennis court.

OVERVIEW

Skinner's radical determinism holds that our personality is largely shaped by the reinforcements we receive from our environment. However, Skinner gave little attention to the sometimes unpredictable changes in our environment, such as chance encounters and fortuitous events. The lives of most of us have been substantially changed by chance encounters, such as Jim's meeting with Greg, or fortuitous events, such as a boring football game. The *social-cognitive theory* of Albert Bandura, however, takes fortuity into consideration. Personality is molded by an interaction of behavior, personal factors, and environment, but chance frequently plays a role in determining which environment we live in and even which behaviors we will enact.

Bandura's theory differs from Skinner's views in several fundamental ways. Unlike Skinner, Bandura believes that responses need not occur in order to be learned. According to Bandura, we can learn by observing another person's performance. For example, we might watch a magician do a particular trick, see how it was done, go home, and perform the trick ourselves. Learning obviously occurred prior to our performance. Bandura's theory also differs from Skinner's in that it gives more consideration to the cognitive capacities of the individual and less to environmental factors. Also, Bandura stresses the idea that reinforcement can be vicarious; that is, we can be reinforced by observing another person receive a reward. This indirect reinforcement accounts for a good bit of human learning. Another difference is Bandura's insistence that behavior is not ultimately a function of the environment but of the interaction among the environment, the behavior of the person, and personal factors, especially cognition. Bandura also differs from Skinner on the relationship between reinforcement and cognition. Whereas Skinner held that learning does not occur without reinforcement, Bandura asserts that reinforcement does not occur without prior cognition. In order for an event to be reinforcing, Bandura says, we must be cognizant of the connection between actions and their outcomes. Conditioning is cognitively mediated; it is not an inevitable consequence of the environment alone.

BIOGRAPHY OF ALBERT BANDURA

Albert Bandura is a native of Canada but has spent his professional career in the United States. He was born December 4, 1925, in Mundare, a small town in northern Alberta, where he attended elementary and secondary grades at the only school in town. After graduating from high school, Bandura spent a summer in Alaska working on the Alaska highway, built during World War II to connect the United States with the territory of Alaska. Bandura's experience brought him into contact with a wide variety of fellow workers, many of whom manifested various degrees of psychopathology, and his observations of these workers kindled in him an interest in clinical psychology.

Bandura attended the University of British Columbia in Vancouver, and after only three years, he graduated in 1949 with a major in psychology. In looking for a graduate program, he chose the University of Iowa because of its strong emphasis on learning theory. He completed a master's degree in 1951 and the next year, he was awarded the Ph.D. in clinical psychology.

After leaving Iowa City, Bandura spent a year in Wichita completing a postdoctoral internship at the Wichita Guidance Center. In 1953 he joined the faculty at Stanford University, where, except for one year, he has remained until the present time. In his early years at Stanford, Bandura was influenced by Robert Sears, who had moved there after an active career as a member of the Yale Institute of Human Relations, the same institute where John Dollard and Neal Miller had developed many of their ideas on imitation, aggression, and social learning.

Most of Bandura's early publications were in clinical psychology, dealing primarily with psychotherapy and the Rorschach test. Then, in 1958, he collaborated with the late Richard H. Walters, his first doctoral student, to publish a paper on aggressive delinquents. The following year their book *Adolescent Aggression* (1959) appeared. Since then, Bandura has continued to publish on a wide variety of subjects, often in collaboration with his graduate students. His most monumental work is *Social Foundations of Thought and Action* (1986).

On the personal side, Bandura met his wife, Virginia (Ginny) Varns, when both were at the University of Iowa, but the meeting was quite by chance (see box—"Can Chance Change Your Life?"). Bandura and his wife have two daughters, Mary and Carol. Bandura has received many honors and awards, including the Guggenheim Fellowship in 1972 and the Distinguished Scientific Contribution Award from Division 12 (Clinical) of the American Psychological Association (APA) in the same year. In 1974 he was elected president of APA, and he also was awarded an endowed chair at Stanford, the David Starr Jordan Professor of Social Science in Psychology. In 1977 he received the James McKeen Cattell Award. In 1980 he was elected fellow, American Academy of Arts and Sciences; and the same year he won the Distinguished Contribution Award from the International Society for Research on Aggression, as well as the prestigious Award for Distinguished Scientific Contribution from the American Psychological Association.

INTRODUCTION TO SOCIAL–COGNITIVE THEORY

More than any other personality theorist, Bandura has evolved a model of human functioning based on careful research and cautious speculation. His theorizing is never far ahead of his base of knowledge. To some extent he has built his model on the work of earlier learning theorists such as Clark, Hull, Skinner, and Julian Rotter (see Chapter 11), but the larger portion of his data base results from studies he and his colleagues conducted.

Rather than using animal studies as a model for human behavior, Bandura has keyed his interest on those aspects of humanity that make us different from other animals, namely, our cognitive abilities. Cognition alone, however, does not account for our behavior. Bandura's social-cognitive theory views people as driven neither exclusively by the forces of cognition nor automatically by events within the environment. Instead, human functioning is molded by the reciprocal interaction of behavior; personal factors, including cognition; and environmental events. Bandura calls this triadic model **reciprocal determinism**.

Bandura also holds that people are symbolizing animals. Their ability to use symbols, especially language, enables them to "transform transient experiences into internal models that serve as guides for future action" (Bandura, 1986, p. 18). These transformations give some consistency and structure to the *self system*. Without this capacity people would merely react to sensory experiences and would lack the capacity to anticipate events, create new ideas, or use internal standards to evaluate present experience. People have the capacity for reflective self-consciousness; they not only can think but can think about thinking. "People form beliefs about what they can do, they anticipate the likely consequences of prospective actions, they set goals for themselves, and they otherwise plan courses of action that are likely to produce desired outcomes" (Bandura, 1991b, p. 248).

Finally, although biology plays some role in personality formation, Bandura contends that humans are largely a product of *learning*. We can and do learn through direct experience, but much of our behavior is shaped through the observation of others. Bandura (1986, p. 19) states that "virtually all learning phenomena, resulting from direct experience, can occur vicariously by observing other people's behavior and its consequences for them."

In Bandura's theory of reciprocal determinism, the self system and learning are interrelated, but for convenience we discuss them separately.

RECIPROCAL DETERMINISM

In Chapter 9 we saw that Skinner believed that behavior is a function of the environment; that is, behavior ultimately can be traced to forces outside the person. As environmental contingencies change, behavior changes. But what impetus changes the environment? Several, including human behavior. Thus, Skinner held that, although behavior is determined by the environment, the human organism exercises some measure of countercontrol over the environment. Behavior, then, is a function of the interaction of environment and the organism; but, in the final analysis, it is environmentally determined.

Bandura adopts quite a different stance. In his theory, a reciprocal interaction among three variables—the environment, the behavior, and the person—is responsible for human action. In this scheme, behavior is partially a function of the environment, but, conversely, the environment is partially a function of behavior. However, Bandura also adds a crucial third factor—the person. By "person" he means largely, but not exclusively, internal factors such as cognition. Because people possess cognitive capacities of memory and anticipation, they are able to influence both their environment and their own behavior. Cognition determines, at least partially, which environmental events people will attend, what value they will place on these events, and how they will organize these events for future use. Cognition, however, is not an autonomous entity, independent of behavior and environment. Bandura (1986) criticized those theorists who attribute the source of human behavior to internal forces such as instincts, drives, needs, or intentions. Cognition itself is determined, being formed by both behavior and environment. But behavior and environment are also partially determined by cognition Therefore, Bandura sees personal conduct in terms of *reciprocal determinism*, a term that suggests a triadic interaction of environment, behavior, and person (Bandura, 1977b, 1978b, 1982a, 1986).

Reciprocal determinism is represented schematically in Figure 10.1, where B signifies behavior; E is the external environment; and P represents the person, including physical characteristics such as sex, social position, size, and physical attractiveness, but especially the internal state of cognition, including thought, memory, judgment, foresight, and so on.

Consider this example of reciprocal determinism. A child begging her father for a cookie is, from the father's viewpoint, an environmental event. If the father automatically (without thought) were to give the child a cookie, then the two would be conditioning one another's behavior in the Skinnerian sense. The behavior of the father would be controlled by the environment, but his behavior, in turn, would have a countercontrolling effect on the environment, namely the child. In Bandura's theory, however, the father is capable of thinking about the consequences of rewarding or ignoring the child's behavior. He may think, "If I give her a cookie, she will stop crying temporarily, but in future cases she will be more likely to persist until I give in to her. Therefore, I will not allow her to have a cookie." Hence the father has an effect on both his environment (the child) and his own behavior (rejecting his daughter's request). The child's subsequent behavior (father's environment) helps shape the cognition and the behavior of the father. If the child stops begging, the father may then have other thoughts. For example, he may evaluate his behavior by thinking, "I'm a good father because I did the right thing." The change in environment also allows the father to pursue different behaviors. Thus, his subsequent behavior is partially determined by the reciprocal interaction of his environment, cognition, and behavior.

In this illustration the reciprocal interaction is completed. The child's pleas affected the father's behavior (E → B); they also partially determined the father's

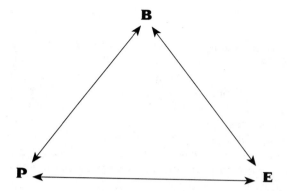

Figure 10.1 *Bandura's Concept of Reciprocal Determinism. Human functioning is a product of the interaction of* (B) *behavior,* (P) *personal variables, and* (E) *environmental events.*

cognition (E → P); the father's behavior helped shape the child's behavior, that is, his own environment (B → E); his behavior also impinged on his own thoughts (B → P); and his cognition partially determined his behavior (P → B). To complete the cycle, P (person) must influence E (environment). How can the father's cognition directly shape the environment, without first being transformed into behavior? It cannot. However, P does not signify cognition alone; it stands for person. Bandura (1978b, p. 346) hypothesized that "People activate different environmental reactions, apart from their behavior, by their physical characteristics (e.g., size, physiognomy, race, sex, attractiveness) and socially conferred attributes, roles, and status." The father then by virtue of his role and status as a father, and perhaps in conjunction with his size and strength, has a decided effect on the child. Thus the final determination is completed (P → E).

Differential Contributions

Bandura uses the term "reciprocal" to indicate a mutual interaction of forces, not a similar or opposite counteraction. The three reciprocal factors need neither to be of equal strength nor to make an equal contribution. The relative potency of the three varies with the individual and with the situation.

At times behavior might be the most powerful, as when a person plays the piano for her own enjoyment. Other times the environment exerts the greatest influence, as when a boat overturns and every survivor begins thinking and behaving in a very similar fashion. At still other times cognition (person) may gain ascendancy, as when a person believes that there are sinister plans being plotted to destroy her.

The relative influence of behavior, environment, and person depends on which of the triadic factors is strongest at a particular moment (Bandura, 1982a).

Meaning of Determinism

Determinism does not mean that behavior is completely determined by forces outside the individual. Bandura (1988a) sees no incompatibility between human agency and determinism. He is not an absolute determinist who believes that all behavior is caused by external events, but neither does he accept the concept of complete free will. Although human personality and behavior are influenced by external events, they are not inevitably determined by them. They are also partly molded by cognition, an internal state that at least partially determines which environmental events will be perceived, evaluated, and acted upon. In other words, the environment itself does not determine our actions, but our perception of the environment is one factor that contributes to our behavior. Within limits, then, people can choose to behave in a manner that increases the probability that the environment will interact with them in a somewhat predictable way. Behavior, therefore,

Can Chance Change Your Life?

We have seen that people have limited choice to act upon and react to their environments. Many situations in life, however, are beyond one's deliberate control. These are *chance encounters* and *fortuitous events*. Bandura (1986, p. 32) defined a chance encounter as "an unintended meeting of persons unfamiliar to each other." A fortuitous event is an environmental experience that is unexpected and unintended.

The everyday lives of people are affected to a greater or lesser extent by the people they chance to meet. One's marital partner, occupation, place of residence, and so on may largely be the result of a fortuitous meeting that was unplanned and unexpected.

Fortuity adds a separate dimension in any scheme used to predict human behavior, and it makes accurate predictions practically impossible. However, chance encounters influence people only by entering the reciprocal determinism paradigm at point E (environment) and adding to the mutual interaction of person, behavior, and environment. In this sense, they influence us in the same manner as do planned events. Once a chance encounter occurs, people behave toward their new acquaintance on the basis of their prior history of reinforcements, their expectations for this new relationship, and the other person's reaction to them. Incidents that have permanently altered an individual's life or even human history are numerous. A number of years ago a young graduate student became bored with his reading assignment, so he and a friend decided to play golf. By chance, this male twosome were playing behind two women golfers. During the course of the round, two twosomes became one foursome, and an acquaintanceship become a romantic interest, which eventually led to a marriage. Thus, by a fortuitous meeting, Albert Bandura met his future wife, Virginia Varns (Bandura, 1982a)

Another young man was passionately in love with his cousin, but he was too bashful to express his love. One day while he was visiting the home of his cousin, the young woman's older sister pushed the man toward his beloved cousin, saying, "For the love of Pete, kiss her, will ya! " (Hoffman, 1988, p.

is not only a dependent variable, but also an independent variable, exerting an influence on both the environment and the person.

Chance Encounters and Fortuitous Events

Bandura believes that people are remarkably flexible and resilient. They "must develop their basic capabilities over an extended period, and they must continue to master new competencies to fulfill changing demands throughout their life span" (Bandura, 1986, p. 20). Resilience is possible because any of the three triadic factors—environment, behavior, or person—may be altered at any time. Two important potential changes are **chance encounters** and **fortuitous events**.

In our introductory case study, we saw that Jim's career as a historian was set in motion by a chance meeting with Greg, the young assistant professor of history.

29). This chance event led to the marriage of Abraham Maslow (see Chapter 15) and Bertha Goodman.

Choice of career is often a matter of chance, and those careers that have made a lasting impression on civilization are no less likely than others to have been fortuitously chosen. Maslow's marriage was the event that turned around his previously aimless life, motivated him to be a serious student of psychology, and eventually changed the course of humanistic psychology in the United States. Also, Hans Eysenck (see Chapter 12), the noted British psychologist, came to psychology completely by chance. He had intended to study physics at the University of London, but first he had to pass an entrance examination. After waiting a year to take the exam, he was told that he had taken the wrong test, and that he would have to wait another year to take the right one. Rather than delaying his education further, he asked whether there might be any scientific subject that he could pursue. When told that he could enroll in a psychology program, Eysenck asked, "What on earth is psychology?" (Eysenck, 1982, p. 290). Eysenck, of course, went on to major in psychology and to become one of the world's most famous psychologists.

Several years ago a college student was commuting to school with pre-med and engineering students who were taking early morning classes. Rather than doing nothing during the early morning hours, this man enrolled in a psychology class. He found it fascinating, especially the clinical aspects. This chance event led him to major in psychology and ultimately to become the leading advocate for cognitive psychology. His name, of course, is Albert Bandura (Evans, 1989).

Similarly, Raymond Dart, the renowned paleoanthropologist, made one of the great discoveries of anthropology quite by accident. He was a physician in need of baboon bones to instruct medical students to distinguish between human and animal skeletons. Then, by chance, one of his students brought in a skull previously used as a paperweight. Dart recognized the skull as the remains of an early human ancestor, which he named *Australopithecus africanus*. This chance event influenced Dart to change careers, and his subsequent work in anthropology has had a significant impact on our understanding of the evolution of the species.

Without this chance encounter, Jim might have spent his professional life as a high school teacher in his home town. By changing careers he changed his environment, behavior, and personal factors, including cognition. Each change has had a reciprocal effect on each of the other triadic factors. However, Jim did not become new person after he switched careers. His previous experiences had provided him with a relatively stable way of interpreting events. For years Jim had seen himself as a person who was academically gifted, intellectually curious, and historically oriented. Even though Jim changed his geographic location, his new environment was self-selected and chosen on the basis of a preexisting interest. In other words, Jim did not become a new person as a result of his chance encounter with Greg, but he did change his life path.

SELF SYSTEM

Bandura deviates from Skinner's radical behaviorism in postulating the existence of a **self system**, which acts upon both the environment and behavior. If behavior were completely a function of the environment, Bandura reasons, then our behavior would be more variable and less consistent because we would constantly be reacting to the great diversity of environmental stimuli. "If actions were determined solely by external rewards and punishments, people would behave like weathervanes, constantly shifting direction to conform to whatever momentary influence happened to impinge upon them" (Bandura, 1986, p. 335). Although personality is largely learned and can be quite complex and variegated within any one person, some consistencies of speech, self-expression, and behavioral traits are difficult to account for on the basis of environmental contingencies alone. Cognitive factors such as memory and foresight bring some unity and consistency to personality (Bandura, 1978b).

However, Bandura does not go to the other extreme and suggest that we have an autonomous agent within us that shapes our behavior to conform to a preexisting self-concept. In fact, Bandura believes that behavior is generally more varied than it appears and that different behaviors should not be attributed to single or dual motives like striving for success (Adler) or sex and aggression (Freud). If behavior were regulated by a single motive, people would be more consistent. For example, a person who is usually moral would never behave immorally, but we know that this frequently happens. In Chapter 13 we will see that Gordon Allport argued that people possess personal dispositions or traits that have the power to render divergent stimuli functionally equivalent. Bandura would not countenance such an argument. An aggressive person, for example, is not always aggressive because the environment does not always reinforce aggressive behavior. Differential experiences with reward and punishment, to a large degree, shape one's behavior.

Bandura uses the term "self system" carefully. Unlike Sullivan's concept of self-system, which evolves mainly as a mechanism to avoid or reduce anxiety, Bandura's term does not refer to an independent agent with such a narrow purpose. It "refers to cognitive structures that provide reference mechanisms and to a set of subfunctions for the perception, evaluation, and regulation of behavior" (Bandura, 1978b,

p. 348). This definition implies that people are capable of observing and symbolizing their own behavior and of evaluating it on the basis of memories of past reinforced or nonreinforced behavior as well as anticipated future consequences. Then, using this cognition as a reference point, they are able to exercise some measure of self-regulation (Bandura, 1982a).

Self-Regulation

Although people have no independent self with the capacity to manipulate the environment at will, they are capable of some degree of self-regulation. By using reflective thought, they can manipulate their environments and produce consequences of their actions. These consequences feed back into the reciprocal determinism paradigm and enable people to partially regulate their own behavior. Three component processes are involved in self-regulatory behavior: self-observation, judgmental processes, and self-reaction (Bandura, 1986, 1991b).

Self-Observation

The first requirement for self-regulation is *self-observation* of performance. We must be able to monitor our own performance, even though the attention we give to it need not be complete or even accurate. We attend selectively to some aspects of our behavior and ignore others altogether. What we observe depends on interests and other preexisting self-conceptions. In achievement situations, such as painting pictures, playing games, or taking examinations, we pay attention to the quality, quantity, speed, or originality of our work; in interpersonal situations, such as meeting new acquaintances or reporting on events, we monitor the sociability or morality of our conduct (Bandura, 1986).

Judgmental Process

Self-observation alone does not provide a sufficient basis for regulating our own behavior. We must also evaluate our performance. This second, or *judgmental process* helps people regulate their behavior through the process of cognitive mediation. We are capable not only of reflective self-awareness but also of judging the worth of our actions on the basis of goals we have set for ourselves. More specifically, the judgmental process depends on personal standards, referential performances, valuation of activity, and performance attribution.

Personal standards allow us to evaluate our performances without comparing them to the conduct of others. To a mentally retarded 10-year-old child, the act of tying his shoelaces may be highly prized. He need not devalue his accomplishment simply because other children can perform this same act at a younger age.

Personal standards, however, are a limited source of evaluation. For most of our activities, we evaluate our performances by comparing them to a standard of reference. Students compare their test scores to those of their classmates, the middle-aged jogger compares times and distances to those compiled by others of the same age, and the bridge player judges personal skill against that of others. In addition, we use our own previous levels of accomplishment as a reference for evaluating present performance. "Are my bowling scores higher than they were last year?" "Has my singing voice improved over the years?" "Is my teaching ability better now than ever?" Also, we may judge our performance by comparing it to that of a single individual, a brother, sister, parent, or even a hated rival; or we can compare it to a standard norm such as par in golf or a perfect score in bowling.

Besides personal and reference standards, the judgmental process is also dependent upon the overall *value* we place on an activity. If we place minor value on our ability to wash dishes or dust furniture, then we will spend little time or effort in trying to improve these abilities. On the other hand, if we place high value on getting ahead in the business world or attaining a professional or graduate degree, then we will spend much effort in order to achieve success in these areas.

Finally, self-regulation also depends on how we judge the causes of our behavior, that is, *performance attribution*. If we believe that our success is due to our own efforts, we will take pride in our accomplishments and tend to work harder to attain our goals. However, if we attribute our performance to external factors, we will not derive as much self-satisfaction and will probably not put forth strenuous effort to attain our goals. Conversely, if we believe that we are responsible for our own failures or inadequate performance, we will work more readily toward self-regulation than if we are convinced that our shortcomings and our fears are due to factors beyond our control (Bandura, 1983, 1986, 1991b).

Self-Reaction

The third and final component of the self-regulatory function is *self-reaction*. We respond positively or negatively to our behavior depending on how it measures up to our personal standards. That is, we create incentives for our own actions through self-reinforcement or self-punishment. For example, a diligent student may reward herself for completing a reading assignment by watching her favorite television program.

Self-reinforcement does not rest on the fact that it immediately follows a response, rather it relies in large part on our use of our cognitive ability to mediate the consequences of our behavior. We set standards for performance that, when met, tend to regulate behavior by such self-produced rewards as pride and self-satisfaction. When we fail to meet our standards, our behavior is followed by self-dissatisfaction or self-criticism.

This concept of self-mediated consequences is a sharp contrast to Skinner's notion that the consequences of behavior are environmentally determined. Bandura hypothesizes that we work to attain rewards and to avoid punishments according to self-erected standards. Even when rewards are tangible, they are often accompanied by self-mediated intangible incentives such as a sense of accomplishment. The Nobel Prize, for example, carries a substantial cash award, but its greater value to most recipients must be the feelings of pride or self-satisfaction in performing the tasks that led to the award.

External Factors in Self-Regulation

Bandura (1989) holds that personal conduct is controlled neither by autonomous internal agencies such as ego or conscience nor by environmental determinants. Rather, behavior is regulated by the reciprocal interaction of person, environment, and prior behavior. People, therefore, have some limited capacity to regulate their own behavior. What processes contribute to this self-regulation?

First, we are capable of monitoring our own behavior and evaluating it in terms of both proximate and distant goals. In addition, self-regulation demands that we possess some capacity to manipulate the external factors that feed into the reciprocal interactive paradigm. Finally, we must be able to perceive the consequences manipulating these external factors. Behavior, then, stems from a reciprocal influence of external factors with personal variables (Bandura, 1977b, 1978b).

Standards of Evaluation

External factors affect self-regulation in at least three ways (Bandura, 1978b). First, they provide us with a standard for evaluating our own behavior. Standards do not stem magically from internal forces. Environmental factors, interacting with personal influences, shape individual standards for evaluation. By precept we learn from parents and teachers the value of honest and friendly behavior; by direct experience, we learn to place more value on being warm and dry than on being cold and wet; and through observing others, we evolve a multitude of standards for evaluating self-performance. In each of these examples personal factors affect which standards we will learn, but environmental forces also play a role.

External Reinforcement

Second, external factors aid self-regulation by providing the means for reinforcement (Bandura, 1977b). Intrinsic rewards are not always sufficient; we also need incentives that emanate from external factors. An artist, for example, may require more reinforcement than self-satisfaction to complete a large mural; environmental support in the form of a monetary retainer, praise and encouragement from others, and especially periodic self-reward may also be necessary.

The incentives to complete a lengthy project usually come from the environment and often take the form of small rewards contingent upon the completion of subgoals. The artist may enjoy a cup of coffee after having completed painting the hand of one of the subjects or break for lunch after finishing another small section of the mural. However, self-reward for inadequate performance is likely to result in environmental sanctions. Friends may criticize or mock the artist's work, patrons may withdraw financial support, or the artist may be self-critical. When performance does not meet self-standards, we tend to withhold rewards from ourselves.

Selective Activation

A third external factor affecting self-regulation is **selective activation**, which refers to Bandura's (1991b) belief that self-regulatory influences are not automatic, but rather operate only if they are activated. How and when one activates the self-regulatory function is influenced both by self-evaluation and by environmental conditions. When we clearly understand that a particular course of action is inconsistent with our self-concept and that it will result in injury to another person, then our self-regulatory process is activated and we will choose a different behavior. However, when the propriety of our action is more ambiguous, then we may disengage evaluative standards from our behavior.

Disengagement of Internal Standards

After we have adopted social and moral standards of conduct, we can regulate our behavior by separating it from the injurious consequences of our actions. Bandura (1991b) refers to this as **disengagement of internal standards**. We can use any one of four techniques to disengage our behavior from self-evaluative consequences. First, we can *redefine the nature of the behavior* itself by such techniques as morally justifying it or euphemistically labeling our actions. Second, we can *displace or diffuse responsibility* for our behavior by obscuring the relationship between our actions and the effects of our actions. Third, we can *distort, minimize, or ignore the detrimental consequences of our behavior*. Fourth, we can *blame or dehumanize the victim* (Bandura, 1986, 1991a). Figure 10.2 illustrates the various points at which the disengagement may occur.

REDEFINITION OF BEHAVIOR.   With *redefinition of behavior* we justify otherwise reprehensible actions by a cognitive restructuring that allows us to minimize or escape responsibility. We can disengage ourselves from responsibility for our behavior by at least three techniques (see upper-left box in Figure 10.2).

The first is moral justification in which otherwise culpable behavior is made to seem defensible or even noble. Bandura (1991a) cited the example of World War I

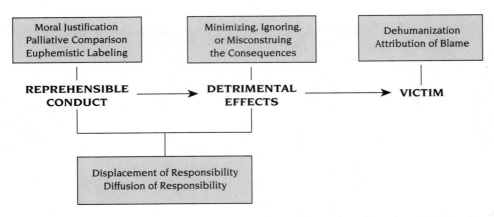

Figure 10.2 *Mechanisms of Internal Control. Internal control is selectively activated or disengaged from reprehensible conduct at different points in the regulatory process.*

hero Sergeant Alvin York who, as a conscientious objector, believed that killing was morally wrong. Then after his battalion commander quoted from the Bible the conditions under which it was morally justified to kill, and after a long prayer vigil, York became convinced that killing enemy soldiers was morally defensible. After redefining killing, York became one of the greatest war heroes in American history, killing or capturing more than 100 German soldiers.

A second method of reducing responsibility through redefining wrongful behavior is to make advantageous or *palliative comparisons* between that behavior and the even greater atrocities committed by others. The incumbent politician claims to be stealing from public funds at a much lower rate than other elected officials. The child who vandalizes a school building uses the excuse that others broke even more windows. Terrorists justify their acts as minor defensive maneuvers against major powers.

A third technique in redefining behavior is the use of *euphemistic labels*. Politicians who have pledged not to raise taxes speak of "revenue enhancement" rather than taxes; some Nazi leaders called the murder of millions of Jews the "purification of Europe" or "the final solution"; thieves sometimes refer to their actions as "liberation," "confiscation," or "redistribution of wealth."

DISPLACEMENT OR DIFFUSION OF RESPONSIBILITY. The second method of disengagement is the *displacement or diffusion of responsibility* (see lower box in Figure 10.2). With *displacement*, we minimize the consequences of our actions by placing responsibility on an outside source. A rapist blames his mother, who, he feels, never showed him physical affection; a civil servant claims that her boss is responsible for her inefficiency; and Nazi prison officers protested that they were carrying out orders from higher officers.

A related procedure is to *diffuse responsibility*—to spread it so thin that no one person is responsible. The civil servant, rather than blaming her boss, may diffuse responsibility throughout the entire bureaucracy with such comments as "That's the way things are done around here," or "That's just policy."

DISREGARD OR DISTORTION OF THE CONSEQUENCES OF BEHAVIOR. A third method of disengagement of internal standards involves *distorting or obscuring the relationship between the behavior and its detrimental consequences* (see center of Figure 10.2). Bandura (1986, 1991b) recognized at least three techniques of disengaging the detrimental consequences of one's actions. First, we can minimize the *consequences of our behavior*. An example of minimizing consequences is seen when a driver runs a red light and strikes a pedestrian. As the injured party lies bleeding and unconscious on the pavement, the driver says, "She's not really hurt badly. She's going to be okay."

Second, we can *disregard or ignore the consequences of our actions*, as when we do not see firsthand the harmful effects of our behavior. In wartime, heads of state and army generals seldom view the total destruction and death resulting from their decisions.

Finally, we can *distort or misconstrue the consequences* of our actions, as when a parent beats a child badly enough to cause serious bruises, but explains that the child needs discipline in order to mature properly.

BLAME THE VICTIMS.   The fourth set of disengagement procedures involves either *dehumanizing the victims or attributing blame to them* (see upper-right box in Figure 10.2). In time of war, people often see the enemy as subhuman, so they need not feel guilty for killing enemy soldiers. At various times, Jews, Blacks, American Indians, orientals, homosexuals, beggars, and the elderly have become *dehumanized victims*. Otherwise kind, considerate, and gentle people have perpetrated acts of violence, insult, or other forms of mistreatment against these groups in order to disengage themselves from an ambiguous situation.

When victims are not dehumanized, they are sometimes *blamed* for the perpetrator's culpable conduct. A rapist may blame his victim for his crime, citing her provocative dress or behavior.

DISENGAGEMENT AND DEFENSE MECHANISMS.   Although Bandura's concept of disengagement may appear similar to Freud's idea of defense mechanisms or Adler's notion of safeguarding tendencies, the similarities are more superficial than substantive. With all three, a person is protected from conditions of discomfort, but aside from this, differences outweigh similarities. Freudian defense mechanisms operate unconsciously and automatically to protect the ego from anxiety. Adlerian safeguarding tendencies are erected for the purpose of protecting a person against external threats to fictionalized feelings of personal superiority. They also operate automatically, can be conscious as well as unconscious, and are directed toward gaining superiority over other people.

On the other hand, disengagement procedures are neither unconscious nor automatic; rather they are cognitively mediated. They protect a person from neither instinctual demands nor external threats, but, instead, they permit us to minimize or avoid responsibility in an ambiguous situation by justifying behavior that ordinarily would be foreign to our self-evaluation. Unlike safeguarding tendencies, they are not specifically directed toward other people, but are used to justify to ourselves behavior that we would otherwise devalue or condemn.

Self-Efficacy

How we will act in a particular situation depends on the reciprocity of environmental and cognitive conditions, especially those cognitive factors that relate to our beliefs that we can or cannot execute the behavior necessary to effect a successful change in that situation. Bandura (1986) calls these expectations **self-efficacy**.

In the triadic reciprocal determinism model, which postulates that the environment, behavior, and person have an interactive influence on one another, self-efficacy refers to the P (person) factor. Although it has a powerful influence on our actions, it is not their sole determinant Rather, self-efficacy combines with environment, prior behavior, and other personal variables to produce behavior.

Self-Efficacy Defined

Bandura (1989, p. 1175) defined self-efficacy as "people's beliefs about their capabilities to exercise control over events that affect their lives." People with high self-efficacy believe that they can do something to alter environmental events; those with low self-efficacy regard themselves as essentially incapable of executing consequential behavior.

Self-efficacy is not the expectation of our action's outcomes or effects. Bandura (1984, 1986) distinguished between efficacy expectations and *outcome expectations*. Efficacy refers to people's confidence that they have the ability to perform certain behaviors, whereas an outcome expectancy refers to one's prediction of the likely *consequences* of that behavior. Outcome should not be confused with successful accomplishment of an act; it refers to the consequences of behavior, not the completion of the act itself. For example, a job applicant may have confidence that she will perform well during an interview, have the ability to answer any possible question, remain relaxed and controlled, and exhibit an appropriate level of friendly behavior. Therefore, she has high self-efficacy in regard to the employment interview. However, despite these high efficacy expectations, she may have low outcome expectations. A low outcome expectancy would exist if she believes that she has little chance of being offered a position. This judgment might be due to unpromising environmental conditions, such as high unemployment, depressed economy, or superior competition. In addition, other personal factors such as age, gender, height, weight, or physical health may negatively affect outcome expectancies.

Besides being different from outcome expectancies, self-efficacy must be distinguished from several other concepts. First, efficacy does not refer to the ability to execute basic motor skills such as walking, reaching, or grasping. Also, personal efficacy does not imply that designated behaviors can be performed without anxiety, stress, or fear; it is merely our judgment, accurate or faulty, as to whether or not we can execute the required actions. Finally, judgments of efficacy are not the same as levels of aspiration. Heroin addicts, for example, often aspire to be drug-free but may have little confidence in their ability to successfully break the habit (Bandura, 1982c).

Sources of Self-Efficacy

Personal efficacy is acquired, enhanced, or decreased through any one or combination of four sources: (1) enactive attainments; (2) vicarious experiences; (3) verbal persuasion; and (4) physiological arousal (Bandura, 1986). With each method, information about oneself and the environment is cognitively processed and, together with recollections of previous experiences, alters perceived self-efficacy. Besides these four sources, efficacy is affected by one's internal standards of conduct.

The most influential source of self-efficacy is performance.

The most influential source of self-efficacy is *enactive attainments*, or performance (Bandura, 1977a, 1986). In general, successful performance raises efficacy expectancies, whereas failure tends to lower them. There are several corollaries to this general statement. First, successful performance raises self-efficacy in proportion to the difficulty of the task. Highly skilled tennis players gain little self-efficacy by defeating clearly inferior opponents, but they gain much by performing well against superior opponents.

Second, tasks successfully accomplished by oneself are more efficacious than those completed with the help of others. In sports, team accomplishments do not increase personal efficacy as much as do individual achievements.

Third, failure is most likely to decrease efficacy when we know that we put forth our best effort. To fail when only half-trying is not as inefficacious as to fall short in spite of our best efforts. Also, failed performance under conditions of high emotional arousal or distress are not as self-debilitating as failure under maximal conditions. "I know I failed that test, but I was worried about my father's health at the time." This, by the way, is not an excuse uttered for public consumption—self-efficacy is contingent on information processed (accurately or not) by the individual, with no aim toward deceiving others.

Another corollary is that *occasional* failure has little effect on efficacy, especially for people with a generally high expectancy of success. However, people with low efficacy seldom give themselves credit even for those occasional successful performances.

A second source of efficacy is **vicarious experiences.** Our self-efficacy is raised when we observe others succeed (Bandura, Adams, Hardy, & Howells, 1980), but it is lowered when we see another person of equal competence fail (Brown & Inouye, 1978). When the model we observe is dissimilar to us, this vicarious experience has little effect on our self-efficacy. An old, sedentary coward watching a young, active, brave circus performer successfully walk a high wire will undoubtedly have little enhancement of efficacy expectations for duplicating the feat.

Vicarious experiences are strongest when people have had little prior experience with the activity. For example, if an experienced golfer and a novice both watch a professional golfer correctly execute the proper golf swing, the beginning golfer will have the greater increase in self efficacy.

In general, the effects of modeling are not as strong as those of personal performance in raising levels of efficacy, but they can have powerful effects where inefficacy is concerned. Watching a swimmer of equal ability fail to negotiate a choppy river will likely dissuade the observer from attempting the same task. The effects of this vicarious experience may even last a lifetime.

Self-efficacy can also be acquired through *verbal persuasion* (Bandura, 1986). The effects of this source are limited, but under proper conditions verbal persuasion can raise or lower self-efficacy (Chambliss & Murray, 1979). First, we must believe the persuader. Exhortations from a credible source have more efficacious power than those from an uncredible person. This may explain why Jim, our case study, became persuaded that he could successfully work toward a Ph.D. in history. Recall that both an assistant professor of history and his wife verbally encouraged him to pursue the degree.

Second, the activity one is being exhorted to attempt must realistically be within one's repertoire of behavior. No amount of verbal persuasion can alter someone's efficacy judgment on the ability to limbo dance under a stick 12 inches from the floor. Jim's past academic record offered evidence that he might successfully attain a Ph.D. Specific knowledge or skills alone do not increase efficacy sufficiently to pursue a particular career. Social skills, the ability to communicate, and the capacity to organize and manage one's time all combine with knowledge and skill to affect Jim's perceived self-efficacy. Bandura (1986) believes that our occupational preferences are determined more by our self-efficacy than by the rewards we expect to receive from the job.

Bandura (1986) hypothesized that the efficacious power of suggestion is directly related to the perceived status and authority of the persuader. Status and authority, of course, are not identical. For example, a psychotherapist's suggestion to phobic patients that they can ride in a crowded elevator is more likely to increase self-efficacy than if a spouse or children made the same suggestion. But if that same psychotherapist tells patients that they have the ability to change a faulty light switch, these patients will probably not enhance their self-efficacy for this activity. Also, verbal persuasion is most effective when combined with successful perfor-

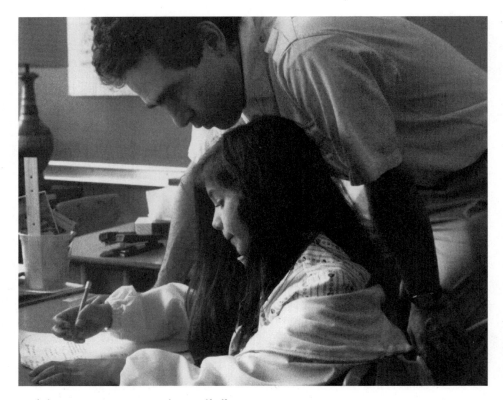

Verbal persuasion can raise or lower self-efficacy.

mance. Persuasion may convince someone to attempt an activity, and, if performance is successful, both the accomplishment and the subsequent verbal rewards will increase future efficacy.

The final source of efficacy is *physiological arousal* (Bandura, 1986). Strong emotion ordinarily lowers performance, so that when people experience intense fear or acute anxiety they are likely to have lower efficacy expectancies. An actor in a school play knows his lines during rehearsal but realizes that the fear he feels on opening night may block his recall. Incidentally, for some situations emotional arousal, if not too intense, is associated with *increased* performance, so that moderate anxiety felt by our actor on opening night may raise his efficacy expectancies. Most of us, when not afraid, have the ability to successfully handle snakes. We merely have to grasp the snake firmly behind the head, but, for most of us, the fear that accompanies snake handling is debilitating and greatly lowers our performance expectancy.

Psychotherapists have long recognized that a reduction in anxiety or an increase in physical relaxation can facilitate performance. Arousal information is related to several variables. First, of course, is the level of arousal—ordinarily, the higher the arousal the lower the self-efficacy. The second variable is the perceived realism of the arousal. If one knows that the fear is realistic, as when driving on an icy mountain road, personal efficacy may be raised. However, when one is cognizant of the absurdity of the phobia, for example, fear of the outdoors, then the emotional arousal tends to lower efficacy. Finally, the nature of the task is an added variable. Emotional arousal may facilitate the successful completion of simple tasks, but it is likely to interfere with performance of complex activities.

Self-Efficacy As a Predictor of Behavior

Self-efficacy is one of several self-influences that affect our behavior. For Bandura, the source of control does not reside in the environment, but in the reciprocation of environmental, behavioral, and personal factors. An important personal variable is self-efficacy, and when combined with specific goals and knowledge of performance, it can serve as an important contributor to future behavior (Bandura, 1988b, 1991b; Bandura & Cervone, 1983).

Bandura (1981) is critical of self-theories, such as the one developed by Carl Rogers (Chapter 16), that center on a composite self-concept rather than many specific self-precepts. Self-efficacy is not a global concept; it varies from situation to situation depending on the competencies required for different activities—the presence or absence of other people; the perceived competence of these others, especially if they are competitors; the person's predisposition to attend to failure of performance rather than to success; and the accompanying physiological states, particularly the presence of anxiety, apathy, or despondency.

High and low efficacy combine with responsive and unresponsive environments to produce four possible predictive variables (Bandura, 1982c). When efficacy is high and the environment is responsive, outcomes are most likely to be successful. When low efficacy is combined with a responsive environment, people may become depressed when they observe that others are successful at tasks that seem too difficult for them. When people with high efficacy encounter unresponsive environmental situations, they usually intensify their efforts to change the environment. They may use protest, social activism, or even force to instigate change, but if all efforts fail, Bandura hypothesized, they will either give up that course and take on a new one or they will seek a more responsive environment. Finally, when low self-efficacy combines with an unresponsive environment, people are likely to feel apathy, resignation, and helplessness. For example, if a junior executive with low self-efficacy realizes the difficulties of becoming company president, she will develop feelings of discouragement, give up, and fail to transfer productive efforts toward a similar but lesser goal.

LEARNING

In the previous section we saw that one source of self-efficacy was vicarious experience. Bandura believes that much of what we learn is acquired through observing others. "If knowledge could be acquired only through the effects of one's own actions, the process of cognitive and social development would be greatly retarded, not to mention exceedingly tedious" (Bandura, 1986, p. 47).

Not all learning, however, comes through observing others. We also learn by experience. We enact or perform behaviors that have consequences and thereby learn from the effects of our actions. Bandura (1986) discusses two major kinds of learning—observational and enactive.

Observational Learning

Bandura believes that *observation* allows us to learn without performing any behavior. We observe natural phenomena, plants, animals, waterfalls, the motion of the moon and stars, and so forth; but especially important to social-cognitive theory is the assumption that we learn through observing the behavior of other people. In this respect, Bandura differs from Skinner, who held that enactive behavior is the basic datum of psychological science. He departs from both Skinner as well as Dollard and Miller in his belief that reinforcement is not essential to learning. True, reinforcement facilitates learning, but it is not a necessary condition for it. We can learn, for example, by observing models being reinforced.

Bandura (1986) believes that observational learning is much more efficient than learning through direct experience. By observing others we are spared countless responses that might be followed by punishment or by no reinforcement. Children observe characters on television, for example, and repeat what they hear or see; they need not enact random behaviors, hoping that some of them will be rewarded.

Modeling

The core of observational learning is **modeling**. Learning through modeling involves adding and subtracting from the observed behavior and generalizing from one observation to another. In other words, modeling involves cognitive processes and is not simply mimicry or imitation. It is more than matching the actions of another and involves symbolically representing information and storing it for use at a future time (Bandura, 1986).

Several factors determine whether or not we will learn from a model in any particular situation. First, the characteristics of the model are important. We are more likely to model high-status people rather than those of low status, competent individuals rather than unskilled or incompetent ones, and powerful people rather than impotent ones.

Second, the characteristics of the observer affect the likelihood of modeling. People who lack status, skill, or power are most likely to model. Children model more than older people and novices are more likely to model than experts.

Third, the consequences of the behavior being modeled may have an effect on the observer. The greater the value the observer places on the behavior, the more likely that behavior will be learned. Also, learning may be facilitated when the observer views a model receiving severe punishment; for example, seeing another

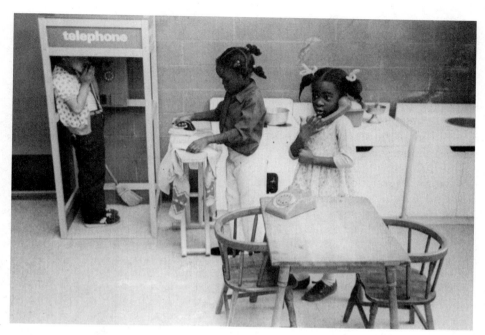

The core of observational learning is modeling.

person receive a severe shock from touching an electric wire teaches us a valuable lesson.

Processes Governing Observational Learning

Bandura (1986, 1988c) recognized four processes that govern observational learning: attention, representation, behavioral production, and motivation.

ATTENTION.   Before we can model another person, we must attend to that person. What factors regulate attention? First, because we have more opportunities to observe individuals with whom we frequently associate, we are most likely to attend to these people. Second, attractive models are more likely to be observed than unattractive ones—popular figures on television, in sports, or in movies are often closely attended. Also, the nature of the behavior being modeled affects our attention—we observe behavior that we think is important to us and from which we believe we can profit.

REPRESENTATION.   In order for observation to lead to new response patterns, those patterns must be symbolically represented in memory. Symbolic representation need not be verbal because some observations are retained in imagery and can be summoned in the absence of the physical model. This process is especially important in infancy when verbal skills are not yet developed.

Verbal coding, however, greatly speeds the process of observational learning. With language we can verbally evaluate those behaviors we are observing and decide which ones we wish to discard and which ones we desire to try. Verbal coding also helps us to rehearse the behavior symbolically, that is, to tell ourselves over and over again how we will perform the behavior once given the chance. Rehearsal can also entail the actual performance of the modeled response, thereby aiding the retention process.

BEHAVIORAL PRODUCTION.   After attending to a model and retaining what we have observed, we then produce the behavior. In converting cognitive representations into appropriate actions, we must ask ourselves several questions about the behavior to be modeled. First we ask, "How can I do this?" After symbolically rehearsing the relevant responses, we try out our new behavior. While performing, we monitor ourselves with the question, "What am I doing?" Finally, we evaluate our performance by asking, "Am I doing this right?" This last question is not always easy to answer, especially if it pertains to a motor skill such as ballet dancing or platform diving in which we cannot actually see ourselves. Carroll and Bandura (1982, 1985), however, found that self-monitoring by use of a video recorder facilitates the learning of some motor skills.

MOTIVATION.   Observational learning is most effective when learners are motivated to perform the modeled behavior. Attention and representation can lead to the acquisition of learning, but performance is facilitated by motivation to enact that particular behavior. Even though observation of others may teach us *how* to do something, we may have no desire to perform the necessary action. One person can watch another use a power saw or run a vacuum cleaner and not be motivated to try either activity. Most sidewalk superintendents have no wish to emulate the observed construction worker.

Observing a model being punished for performance will diminish one's likelihood of enacting the same behavior. For example, if you notice a classmate receiving an embarrassing admonition from a professor after asking a question, you will probably learn not to ask questions in that class. In summary, then, modeling is facilitated by observing appropriate activities, properly coding the events for representation in memory, actually performing the behavior, and being sufficiently motivated.

Enactive Learning

Every response a person makes is followed by some consequence. Some of these consequences are satisfying, some are dissatisfying, and others are simply not cognitively attended and hence have little effect.

Reinforcers can be either positive or negative, but Bandura believes that their effects do not follow automatically from the consequences of a response. Complex human behavior involves the cognitive mediation of the individual in order for the consequences of a response to have an effect. Verbal reinforcement, for example, must be attended and comprehended before it can have meaning. The meaning for the receiver, however, may be different from that intended by the sender. For example, a dance instructor compliments her pupils for performing a particularly difficult maneuver, hoping to encourage them and to improve their skill level. However, her words may have an opposite effect or no effect on the dancers, who may reason that if they really possessed the potential to be great performers, their teacher would not need to compliment them for such a simple move.

The consequences of a response serve at least three functions: to impart information, to motivate future behavior, or to reinforce present behavior (Bandura, 1977b).

Imparting Information

The first function of response consequences is an informative one. We notice the effects of our actions, retain this information, and use it as a guide for future actions. Bakers who have previously been reinforced for faithfully following directions may choose to ignore a recipe item calling for two tablespoons of baking powder. Why? Because in the past they have also been reinforced for noticing the approximate ratio of baking powder to flour and also that printed material sometimes contains typographical errors. Thus, they conclude that the correct amount of baking powder is two teaspoons, not two tablespoons. Information retained from earlier reinforcing situations, therefore, enables people to deviate from their normal procedure of closely following a recipe. Their previous histories of being reinforced for following directions do not dictate that they will respond automatically. The consequences of using the lesser amount of baking powder on this occasion undoubtedly will be noted and probably retained for future reference.

Motivating Future Behavior

A second function of response consequences is to motivate anticipatory behavior. People are capable of symbolically representing future outcomes and acting accordingly. They not only possess insight but are also capable of foresight. We do not have to suffer the discomfort of cold temperatures before deciding to wear a coat when going outside in freezing weather. Instead, we anticipate the effects of cold, wet weather and dress accordingly. The symbolic representation of discomfort serves as a stimulus for our thinking about wearing a coat, and it also increases the likelihood that we will actually wear one and thus be reinforced for that behavior. Receiving reinforcement for wearing warm clothing in cold weather then becomes a motivator in future similar situations.

Reinforcing Present Behavior

The consequences of responses also serve to reinforce behavior, a function that has been firmly documented by Skinner (Chapter 9) and other reinforcement theorists. Bandura (1986), however, contended that, although reinforcement may at times be unconscious and automatic, complex behavioral patterns are greatly facilitated by cognitive intervention. A fledgling basketball player practices free throws with little consistent success. Soon the player realizes that the shots that find their mark are the ones in which he bent his knees and applied backspin to the ball. Without this cognitive intervention, Bandura believes, performance is likely to remain at a low level. Immediate feedback helps shape behavior, but if responses did not impart specific information with which the learner *interacts*, then progress would be slow or nonexistent. Bandura maintains that learning occurs much more efficiently when the learner is cognitively involved in the learning situation and understands what behaviors precede successful responses.

DYSFUNCTIONAL BEHAVIOR

Bandura's concept of reciprocal determinism assumes that behavior is learned as a result of the interaction of person, behavior, and environment. Dysfunctional behavior is no exception, being determined by a mutual interaction of the person, including cognition and neurophysiological processes; the environment, including interpersonal relations and socioeconomic conditions; and behavioral factors, especially previous experiences with reinforcement. Bandura's concept of dysfunctional behavior lends itself most readily to depressive reactions, phobias, and aggressive behaviors.

Depressive Reactions

High personal standards and goals can lead to achievement and self-satisfaction. However, when people set their goals too high, they are likely to fail. Failure frequently leads to depression, and depressed people often undervalue their own accomplishments. The result is chronic misery, feelings of worthlessness, lack of purposefulness, and pervasive depression. Bandura (1986) believes that dysfunctional depression can occur in any of the three self-regulatory subfunctions.

First, during *self-observation* people can misperceive their own performance or distort their memory of past accomplishments. Depressed people are more likely to underestimate their successes and overestimate their failures. More frequently, however, depression relates to distorted recollections. Depressed people tend to exaggerate their past mistakes and minimize their prior accomplishments (Bandura, 1991b).

Second, the *judgmental processes* of depressed people are likely to be faulty. They set their standards unrealistically high so that any performance attainments will be judged as a failure. Even when they achieve success in the eyes of others, they continue to berate their own accomplishments. Depression is especially likely when goals and personal standards are much higher than one's perceived efficacy to attain them. "People who judge themselves unfavorably are not inclined to treat themselves positively.... Compared to nondepressed persons, those who are prone to depression react less self-rewardingly for similar successes but more self-critically for similar failures" (Bandura, 1991b, pp. 274–275).

Finally, the *self-reactions* of depressed individuals are quite different from those of nondepressed persons. Depressed people not only judge themselves harshly, but they are also inclined to treat themselves badly for their shortcomings. Bandura (1986, p. 361) suggested that depressed people "generally evaluate themselves less favorably and reward themselves less than the nondepressed, who are more inclined to savor their successes. The depressed are also inclined to punish themselves more severely for poor performances."

Phobias

Phobias are fears that are strong enough and pervasive enough to have severe debilitating effects on one's daily life. For example, snake phobias (a seemingly favorite topic of Bandura) prevent people from holding a variety of jobs and from enjoying many kinds of recreational activities. Phobias and fears are learned by direct contact, inappropriate generalization, and especially by observational experiences (Bandura, 1986). They are difficult to extinguish because the phobic person simply avoids the threatening object. Unless the fearsome object is somehow encountered, the phobia will endure indefinitely.

Bandura (1986) credited television and other news media for generating many of our fears. Well-publicized rapes, armed robberies, or murders can terrorize a community, causing people to live more confined lives behind locked doors. Most people have never been raped, robbed, or intentionally injured, yet many live in fear of being criminally assaulted. Violent criminal acts that seem random and unpredictable are most likely to instigate phobic reactions.

Once established, phobias are maintained by consequent determinants, that is, the negative reinforcement the phobic person receives for avoiding the fear-producing situation. For example, if people expect to receive aversive experiences (being mugged) while walking through the city park, they will reduce their feeling of threat by not entering the park or even going near it. In this example, dysfunctional (avoidance) behavior is produced by the mutual interaction of people's expectancies (belief that they will be mugged), the external environment (the city park), and behavioral factors (their prior experiences with fear).

Aggressive Behaviors

Aggressive behaviors, when carried to extremes, can also be dysfunctional. Bandura (1986) contends that aggressive behavior is acquired through observation of others, direct experiences with positive and negative reinforcements, training or instruction, and bizarre beliefs.

Once established, people continue to aggress for at least five different reasons: they enjoy inflicting injury on the victim (positive reinforcement); they avoid or counter the aversive consequences of aggression by others (negative reinforcement); they receive injury or harm for not behaving aggressively (punishment); their aggressive behavior enables them to live up to personal standards of conduct (self-reinforcement); and they observe others receiving rewards for aggressive acts or punishment for nonaggressive behavior (Evans, 1976).

Bandura believes that aggressive actions ordinarily lead to further aggression. This belief is based on the now-classic study of Bandura, Ross, and Ross, 1963), which found that children who observe others behaving aggressively displayed more aggression than a control group of children who did not view aggressive acts. In this study, 96 Stanford University nursery-school boys and girls from about three to five-and-a-half years of age were divided into three matched experimental groups and one control group of 24 subjects each.

The first experimental group observed a live model behaving with both verbal and physical aggression toward a number of toys, including a large inflated Bobo doll; the second experimental group observed a film showing the same model behaving in an identical manner; the third experimental group saw a fantasy film in which a model, dressed as a black cat, behaved equally aggressively against the Bobo doll. Children in the control group were matched with those in the experimental groups on previous ratings of aggression, but they were not subjected to an aggressive model.

After subjects in the three experimental groups observed a model scolding, kicking, punching, and hitting the Bobo doll with a mallet, they were brought into another room where they were mildly frustrated. Immediately following this frustration, each child was brought into the experimental room, which contained some toys (such as a smaller version of the Bobo doll) that could be played with aggressively. In addition, some nonaggressive toys such as a tea set and coloring materials were present. The subject's aggressive or nonaggressive response to the toys was observed through a one-way mirror.

As hypothesized, children exposed to an aggressive model displayed more aggressive responses than those who had not been exposed. But contrary to expectations, the researchers found no differences in the amount of total aggression shown by subjects in the three experimental groups. Children who had observed the cartoon character were at least as aggressive as those exposed to a live model or to a filmed model. In general, children in each experimental group exhibited about twice as much aggressive behavior as did those in the control group. In addition, the particular kind of aggressive response was remarkably similar to that displayed by the adult models. Children scolded, kicked, punched, and hit the doll with a mallet in close imitation of the behavior that had been modeled.

THERAPY

According to Bandura, deviant behaviors are not caused by weaknesses of character, a single master motive, or unhappy childhood experiences. They are initiated on the basis of social-cognitive learning principles, and they are maintained because, in some ways, they continue to serve some function. Therapeutic change, therefore, is difficult because it involves eliminating behaviors that are satisfying to the person. Smoking, overeating, and drinking alcoholic beverages, for example, generally have positive effects initially, while their long-range aversive consequences are usually not sufficient to produce avoidance behavior.

The ultimate goal of social-cognitive therapy is self-regulation. To achieve this end, the therapist introduces strategies designed not only to induce behavioral change but to maintain that change. Bandura (1978a) visualized three levels of treatment, the first level being the *induction of change*. If therapy is to be effective, it must at least instigate some change in behavior. For example, if a therapist is able to extinguish fear of height in a previously acrophobic person, then change has been induced and that person is now able to climb a 20-foot ladder.

The second level of treatment accomplishment is *generalization*. The acrophobic person will not only be able to ascend a ladder but also will generalize that behavior to other situations. This is a more effective level than simple induction of change, and it allows the person to ride in airplanes or look out windows of tall buildings.

Some therapies induce change and facilitate generalization, but, in time, the therapeutic effects are lost and the person re-acquires the dysfunctional behavior. This is particularly true with extinguishing maladaptive habits such as smoking and overeating. The most effective therapy reaches the third level of accomplishment, which is *maintenance* of newly acquired functional behaviors.

Because dysfunctional behavior is produced by reciprocal determinism, "the likelihood that a given behavior will be performed can vary markedly in different environmental settings, toward different people, and at different times" (Bandura, 1978a, p. 96). This broad conceptualization of both maladaptive behavior and treatment permits a variety of therapeutic techniques and strategies. The first criterion of any approach is that it bring about behavioral change. Beyond that, generalization and maintenance become important goals.

Bandura suggests several basic treatment approaches, including *overt or vicarious modeling*. People who observe live or filmed models performing threatening activities often feel less fear and anxiety and are then able to perform those same activities (Rosenthal & Bandura, 1978).

In a second treatment mode, *covert or cognitive modeling*, the therapist trains subjects to visualize models performing fearsome behaviors (Bandura et al., 1980). Overt and covert modeling strategies are most effective, however, when combined with performance-oriented approaches (Bandura, 1977b).

A third procedure, called *enactive mastery*, requires subjects to perform those behaviors that previously produced incapacitating fears. Enactment, however, is not ordinarily the first step in treatment. Subjects typically begin by observing models or by having their emotional arousal lessened through **systematic desensitization** (Wolpe, 1973), which involves the extinction of anxiety or fear through self-induced or therapist-induced relaxation. With systematic desensitization, the therapist and client work together to place fearsome situations on a hierarchy from least to most threatening. Clients, while relaxed, enact the least threatening behavior and then gradually move through the hierarchy until they can perform the most threatening activity, all the while remaining at a low state of emotional arousal (Bandura, Blanchard, & Ritter, 1969).

Bandura has demonstrated that each of these strategies can be effective and that they are most powerful when used in combination with one another (Bandura, 1977a; Bandura & Adams, 1977; Bandura et al., 1980). Bandura believes that the reason for their effectiveness can be traced to a common mechanism found in each of these approaches, namely, *cognitive mediation*. When people use cognition to increase self-efficacy, that is, when they become convinced that they can perform difficult tasks, then, in fact, they become able to cope with previously intimidating situations (Bandura, 1989).

Motivation to change dysfunctional behaviors is enhanced when people set realistic goals and then receive feedback on how they are doing relative to achieving those goals. The goals themselves do not provide motivation; rather, people use performance feedback to evaluate their progress toward goals. When self-satisfaction is contingent upon narrowing the gap between performance and adopted goals, then "people give direction to their actions and create self incentives to persist in their efforts until performances match their goals" (Bandura, 1988b, p. 41). Goals should be challenging, yet reasonable. But most of all, people must have knowledge of their performance in relation to their goals.

CONCEPT OF HUMANITY

Bandura sees humans as having the capacity to become many things. "Human nature is characterized by a vast potentiality that can be fashioned by direct and observational experience into a variety of forms within biological limits" (Bandura, 1986, p. 21). Because humans have evolved neurophysiological mechanisms for symbolizing their experiences, their nature is marked by a large degree of plasticity or flexibility. People have the capacity to store past experiences and to use this information to chart future actions.

Our capacity to use symbols provides us with a powerful tool for understanding and controlling our environment. It enables us to solve problems without resorting to inefficient trial-and-error behavior, to imagine the consequences of our actions, and to set goals for ourselves (Bandura, 1988a).

As humans, we are *goal-directed*, purposive animals who can view the future and bestow it with meaning by being aware of the possible consequences of future behavior. We anticipate the future and behave accordingly in the present. The future does not determine behavior, but its cognitive representation can have a powerful effect on present actions. "By representing foreseeable outcomes symbolically, people can convert future consequences into current motivators and regulators of foresightful behavior" (Bandura, 1986, p. 19).

Although we are basically goal-oriented, Bandura believes that we have specific rather than general intentions and purposes. We are not motivated by a single master goal such as striving for superiority or self-actualization, but rather by a multiplicity of goals, some distant and some proximate. These individual intentions, however, are not ordinarily anarchical; they possess some stability and order. Cognition gives us the capacity to evaluate probable consequences and to eliminate behaviors that do not meet our standards of conduct. Personal standards, therefore, tend to give human behavior a degree of consistency, even though that behavior lacks a master motive to guide it.

Bandura's concept of humanity is more *optimistic* than pessimistic, because it holds that people are capable of learning new behaviors throughout their lives. However, dysfunctional behaviors may persist due to low self-efficacy or because they are perceived as being reinforced. Nevertheless, these unhealthy behaviors need not continue, because most people have the capacity to change by imitating the productive behaviors of others and by using their cognitive abilities to solve problems.

Bandura's social-cognitive theory emphasizes *social factors* more than biological ones. However, it recognizes that genetics contribute to the person (P) variable in the reciprocal determinism paradigm. But even within this variable, cognition ordinarily gains ascendance, so that biological factors become less important. Moreover, social factors are clearly more crucial to the other two variables—environment (E) and behavior (B).

Are humans free to control their own actions? Bandura's answer is qualified. Reciprocal determinism postulates a mutual interlocking system in which person, behavior, and environment all influence one another. Thus, neither outside forces nor personal factors are solely responsible for human behavior. People have some capacity to control their behavior. Although they are affected by both the environment and their experiences with reinforcement, they, in turn, have some power to mold these two external conditions. To some extent, people can manage those environmental conditions that will shape their future behavior, and they can choose to ignore or augment their previous experiences. People can "serve as a causal contributor to their own life course by selecting, influencing, and constructing their own circumstances" (Bandura, 1986, p. 38).

This concept of self-regulation goes beyond Skinner's notion of countercontrol. Skinner held that ultimately the environment is the force behind the organism's behavior, whereas Bandura believes that people are *partially free* to create those environments that later impinge upon them. Personal freedom, then, is limited; it is restricted by physical constraints such as laws, prejudices, regulations, and the rights of other people. In addition, personal factors such as perceived inefficacy and lack of confidence restrict individual freedom. Some people, then, have more freedom than others. "Given the same environmental conditions, persons who have the capabilities for exercising many options and are adept at regulating their own behavior will have greater freedom than will those who have limited means of personal agency" (Bandura, 1986, p. 39). Bandura (1986, p. 42) defined freedom as "the number of options available to people and their right to exercise them."

Bandura (1989) believes that neither freedom nor responsibility should be considered antithetical to determinism. To him, outside influences operate deterministically on human behavior, but the person retains some measure of self-influence, which also operates deterministically on behavior. Because a degree of self-regulation is always possible, personal responsibility cannot be abdicated. As people recognize the possibility of alternative actions, they must assume partial responsibility for their actions (Bandura, 1982a, 1986).

Bandura seems to straddle the fence on the issue of *freedom and determinism* because he says that behavior is determined by an interaction of self-regulation and external sources of influence. Philosophically, however, the question of freedom is an either/or issue. Partial freedom *is* freedom. No one seriously holds that behavior is completely free. All personality theorists recognize that outside forces have at least some influence on behavior. They may argue over the degree of restriction, but if they grant even one iota of free human agency, then they must be viewed as believers in personal freedom. If one holds, as does Bandura, that people are partially free, then one must eventually be concerned with the ultimate origin of that freedom. To say that it stems from reciprocal determinism begs the question. Granted, people are influenced by their interaction with their environment and by the contingencies of reinforcement, but the ultimate source of free choice must reside within that part of the reciprocal determinism paradigm labeled "person." Although Bandura is not greatly concerned with the question of ultimate choice, his belief in partial freedom places him within the camp of those who recognize personal freedom.

On the issue of *causality or teleology*, Bandura's position would be described as moderate. Human functioning is a product of environmental factors interacting with behavior and personal variables, especially cognitive activity. We move with a purpose toward goals that we have set, but motivation exists neither in the past nor the future. It is contemporary. Although future events cannot motivate us, our conception of them is "converted into current motivators and regulators of behavior" (Bandura, 1988b, p. 37).

Social-cognitive theory emphasizes *conscious thought* over unconscious determinants of behavior. Self-regulation of actions relies on self-monitoring, judgment, and self-reaction, all of which are ordinarily conscious during the learning situation. "People do not become thoughtless during the learning process. They make conscious judgments about how their actions affect the environment" (Bandura, 1986, p. 116). After learnings are well established, especially motor learning, they may become unconscious. We do not have to be aware of all our actions while walking or driving a car.

Bandura recognizes the limitations that biological forces place on us while, at the same time, he believes that we have a remarkable plasticity. Our social environments allow us a wide range of behaviors, including using other people as models. All of us live in a number of social networks and are thus influenced by a variety of people. Modern technology, in the form of computers and the media, facilitate the spread of social influences (Evans, 1989).

Because we have a remarkable plasticity and capacity for learning, vast individual differences exist among us. Bandura's emphasis on *uniqueness*, however, is moderated by biological and social influences, both of which contribute to some similarities among people.

Related Research

Bandura's approach to theory building has been through empirical research rather than the clinic. From the beginning of his career until the present, he has relied on research findings to speculate on the nature of human personality. His ideas have sparked a tremendous volume of research, much of it carried out by him and his colleagues. A complete review of this research, of course, is beyond our scope, but an examination of three recent studies will give the reader a suggestion of the diversity of Bandura's research in the areas of self-regulation and self-efficacy.

In one study Bandura and Forest J. Jourden (1991) were interested in whether the way people compare themselves with others will affect their ability to make complex managerial decisions. We have discussed Bandura's notion that people regulate their behavior in part by comparing their performance to that of other people. In the Bandura and Jourden study, these social comparisons constituted the cognitive component of the triadic causal structure; the managerial decisions of the subjects comprised the behavioral component; and the properties of a simulated managerial organization made up the environmental component.

Bandura and Jourden hypothesized that different patterns of social comparison would have a differential impact on levels of managerial performance. Subjects were graduate students in business, most of whom were also employed full-time in various corporations and who had previous managerial experience. The experimenters gave each subject a series of very complex managerial tasks that were sufficiently difficult to tax or exceed the subject's ability. First, these business students had to select from a 10-person roster eight fictitious employees who would be working to manufacture furniture items. In addition to matching these employees to appropriate jobs, subjects had to make effective use of incentives, including setting goals, providing feedback, and giving recognition and compliments. They could readjust their managerial strategies when they saw that their workers were not productive.

Next, the subjects were randomly assigned to one of four treatment conditions based on contrived feedback that compared their performance to that of other graduate business students. Subjects in the *similar capabilities* group received information that their comparison group was performing very similarly to them—deviating a few percentage points above and below the subject's performance; subjects in the *superior capabilities* group saw that they outperformed their counterparts and maintained their superiority over the course of the study; subjects in the *progressive mastery* group started slowly but then caught up with and eventually surpassed the performance of their comparison group; and subjects in the *progressive decline* group began the study at about the same level as their managerial counterparts but then saw their performance fall progressively behind.

After subjects had received information on their individual performance relative to that of a comparison group, they made managerial decisions, which they entered into a computer. The computer gave back information on the work of each subject's group, as well as the work performance of the comparison group. Feedback on the comparison group's performance was adjusted according to which of the four treatment conditions the subject had been previously assigned. Subjects performed a series of 18 trials and received feedback after each.

Subjects periodically filled out an efficacy scale that called for them to estimate the strength of their perceived self-efficacy for getting their group to accomplish its work, the efficiency of their managerial strategies, and the level of their dissatisfaction. Bandura and Jourden measured simulated outcome of the furniture workers in terms of the total number of hours needed to complete each weekly order, a figure that could be automatically determined on the basis of each subject's job allocations and selection of motivational factors.

Bandura and Jourden found that social comparisons can have either a detrimental or a beneficial effect. Subjects in the *progressive decline* group experienced a sharp drop in self-efficacy as they learned that their comparison group increasingly outperformed them. They became harshly critical of their own performance, and their managerial strategies remained erratic. In contrast, subjects in the *progressive mastery* group showed increasingly higher self-efficacy, substantially improved managerial strategies, and greater self-satisfaction. Subjects in the *similar capabilities* group showed only slight changes in perceived self-efficacy and a slight drop in organizational performance. Subjects in the *superior capabilities* group began the study with heightened self-efficacy, which dropped slightly over the 18 trials. Interestingly but not unexpectedly, the superior' subjects managerial strategies showed some decline during the course of the study. These subjects set easy goals for themselves and showed self-satisfaction with declining performance because such performance still surpassed that of their comparison group. It seems that "complacent self-assurance creates little incentive to expend the increased effort needed to attain high levels of performance" (Bandura & Jourden, 1991, p. 949).

This study supports Bandura's notion that person factors (self-efficacy) interact with behavior (managerial strategies) and environment (the responsiveness of workers to managerial decisions) in a reciprocal fashion that allows each component to influence the other two.

We have seen that fears are learned largely from vicarious experiences, often from media reports of sensationalized crimes. Such fears frequently leave people with a sense of powerlessness and low self-efficacy to cope with personal attacks. Using a mastery modeling program that incorporated practice with simulated assaults, vicarious coping experiences, verbal persuasion, and feedback of physical capabilities, Elizabeth M. Ozer and Bandura (1990) found that self-defense training could increase women's sense of empowerment. Subjects of this study were 43 women ranging in age from 18 to 55 and who had enrolled in a self-defense program. They participated in a 5-week mastery-modeling program in three groups of about 15 each. The sessions were conducted by a woman instructor assisted by two well-protected men who served as assailants in the simulated assaults. In graduated steps the instructor modeled the skills needed to escape a hold and to disable an assailant. These skills included eye strikes; biting; kicks; elbow, knee, and palm strikes; and foot stomps directed at the assailant's eyes, head, throat, knees, and groin. After observing the model, subjects participated in a simulated attack while the other members of her group were active as observers, shouting the names of the most effective defensive blows. In all, subjects participated in five simulated assaults and were active vicarious participants in 70 other assaults.

Ozer and Bandura used a staggered intragroup control design in which about half the subjects received no intervention for five weeks. At the beginning of the study and five weeks later, they filled out efficacy scales that measured interpersonal self-efficacy, activities self-efficacy, self-defense efficacy, and perceived efficacy to control negative thoughts. The treatment group filled out the same scales, but began the treatment phase immediately. Both groups were retested after a six-month follow-up period.

As expected, subjects exhibited little or no change during the control period. However, subjects receiving the mastery-modeling intervention significantly enhanced their perceived coping self-efficacy, increased their self-efficacy to control intrusive negative thoughts, and decreased their perceived vulnerability to assault. On a behavioral level, the mastery-modeling program resulted in increased recreational and social activities and decreased avoiding behaviors. All these gains were maintained or even increased during the follow-up period. Contrary to a sometimes voiced concern, Ozer and Bandura did not find that increased empowerment and self-confidence led women to behave more recklessly. If anything, their study showed that women who receive self-defense training tend to exhibit realistic caution in potentially dangerous situations.

In recent years Bandura has become interested in the health-related aspect of self-efficacy. In one study, Wiedenfeld, O'Leary, Bandura, Brown, Levine, and Raska (1990) investigated the impact on the immune system of people's perceived self-efficacy to cope with stress. These investigators recruited 20 subjects with severe snake phobia. Ranging in age from 25 to 48, these people, 19 women and 1 man, were so frightened of snakes that they avoided many outdoor activities such as camping, gardening, bicycling, and hiking. "Even a picture or the mere mention of a snake would trigger perturbing ruminative thoughts over which they could exercise little control" (Wiedenfeld et al., 1990, p. 1084). The investigators trained the subjects to gradually overcome their fear of snakes, with the final goal being that they could hold a corn snake on their laps with their hands by their sides.

During the course of this training, subjects filled out a perceived self-efficacy scale that asked them to rate the strength of their capacity to cope with each of the activities leading up to the final goal. Subjects also established baseline readings on several physiological measures, including heart rate, immunological indexes, and endocrine function.

Wiedenfeld et al. found that the stress experienced by subjects as they gained coping mastery enhanced the immune system rather than suppressed it. And these changes in immune system function were not merely transitory. Increased immunological competence tended to persist as self-efficacy continued to strengthen. This study has implications for the rapidly growing field of **psychoneuroimmunology**, which focuses on the interactions among behavior, the nervous system, the endocrine system, and the immune system.

CRITIQUE OF BANDURA

Bandura has evolved his social-cognitive theory by carefully balancing the two principal components of theory building—innovative speculation and accurate observation. Unlike many earlier personality theorists (namely Freud, Adler, Jung, Horney, Fromm, and Sullivan), who based their observations on clinical experiences, and contrary to Skinner's ideas, which were built largely on studies of animals, Bandura's personality theory rests on data carefully obtained from dozens of studies conducted by him and his associates using human subjects. In contrast to Maslow, Allport, and some of the self theorists, Bandura's speculations seldom outdistance his data, but, rather, are carefully advanced only one step in front of observations. This scientifically sound procedure increases the likelihood that hypothesis testing will yield positive results, and that the theory will generate additional testable hypotheses.

As with other theories, the usefulness of Bandura's personality theory rests on its ability to generate research and to organize knowledge. In addition, it must serve as a practical guide to action, be internally consistent, and parsimonious. How does Bandura's theory rate on these five criteria?

Bandura's theory must be given a very high rating on its capacity to *generate research*. This is a theory's heuristic value, that is, its usefulness in stimulating investigation. Bandura and his colleagues have done much of the work, but other researchers, too, have been attracted to the theory. Bandura may be the most meticulous writer of all the personality theorists included in this volume. His carefully constructed formulations lend themselves to the generation of numerous testable hypotheses. Unfortunately, his concepts and phraseology are so precisely stated that they become esoteric. The uninitiated reader, for example, would find *Social Foundations of Thought and Action* (Bandura, 1986) nearly incomprehensible.

On its ability to *organize knowledge*, Bandura's theory receives a very high rating. Much of the important psychological research findings can be organized by social-cognitive theory. Reciprocal determinism is a comprehensive concept that offers a viable explanation for the acquisition of nearly all observable behavior. The inclusion of three variables in this paradigm gives Bandura's theory more flexibility to organize and explain behavior than Skinner's radical behaviorism, which relies nearly exclusively on environmental variables.

How *practical* is Bandura's social-cognitive theory? To the therapist or anyone interested in the acquisition and maintenance of new behaviors, it is an extremely useful guide to action. In addition to possessing the practical value of other learning theories, Bandura's theory presents the useful dimension of observational learning. Therapists, teachers, and trainers can use themselves as models or introduce other forms of observational learning, including such simple procedures as cognitive modeling, which Bandura (1986) has shown to be an effective method of instigating change.

Is the theory *internally consistent*? Bandura chooses words carefully, so that no single term carries more than one definition. The theory itself, because it is not highly speculative, has outstanding internal consistency. Bandura is not afraid to speculate, but he never ventures far beyond the empirical data available to him. The result is a carefully couched, rigorously written, and internally consistent theory.

The final criterion of a useful theory is *parsimony*. Again, Bandura's social-cognitive theory meets high standards. The theory is simple, straightforward, and unencumbered by hypothetical or fanciful explanations.

Chapter Summary

Bandura's social-cognitive theory holds that human functioning is a product of the mutual interaction of environmental events, behavior, and personal factors, especially cognitive activity. This triadic model is called *reciprocal determinism*. The three reciprocal factors do not necessarily make an equal contribution to thought and action. At different times and under different conditions, any one of the three may be the most powerful. However, none of the factors is ever solely responsible for behavior. All three constantly operate in mutual interaction.

Two important environmental factors, often overlooked by other theorists, are *chance encounters* and *fortuitous events*. Bandura believes that many of the crucial influences in our lives originate from these unplanned and unexpected events. Once they occur, however, they enter into the triadic model in the same manner as do planned events.

As cognitive animals, we have the capacity to use symbols, especially language, to transform contemporary experiences into relatively consistent patterns of behavior. This gives the *self system* some stability. The self system refers to cognitive structures that enable us to perceive, evaluate, and regulate our behavior.

Within limits, we have the

capacity for self-regulation. The three component processes of self-regulation are (1) *self-observation*, (2) *judgmental processes*, and (3) *self-reaction*.

External factors are also involved in self-regulation. These include (1) *standards of evaluation*, which stem at least partially from the environment; (2) *external reinforcement* in the form of rewards received from others; (3) *selective activation*, which refers to Bandura's notion that self-regulatory influences operate only if they are activated; and (4) *disengagement of internal standards*, that is, separating ourselves from the injurious consequences of our actions.

Performance is generally enhanced when we have high *self-efficacy*, that is, high expectations that we can perform those behaviors that will produce desired outcomes in a particular situation. Self-efficacy is enhanced by (1) enactive attainment or performance, (2) vicarious experiences, (3) verbal persuasion, and (4) low levels of physiological or emotional arousal.

Bandura believes that people can learn without performing any behavior. He refers to this as *observational learning* and distinguishes it from *enactive learning*. In order to learn through observation, we must attend to our model, organize and retain our observations, try out our new actions, and be motivated to perform the modeled behavior. Enactive learning takes place when our responses produce consequences. Response consequences can impart information, motivate future behavior, or reinforce present behavior.

Like all human behavior, *dysfunctional behavior* is acquired through the reciprocal interaction of environment, personal factors, and behavior. Bandura has most intensely investigated depressive reactions, fears and phobias, and aggressive behaviors.

Social-cognitive theory has influenced a number of behaviorally oriented therapies, but Bandura's chief emphasis is on cognitive mediation, especially perceived self-efficacy.

Bandura conceives humans as having a unique potential to learn a variety of responses through their ability to symbolize experiences. We can recall the past and set goals for the future—but we live in the present. We have some limited capacity for personal freedom, although our behavior is also constricted by social and biological influences.

Overall, Bandura's social-cognitive theory receives the highest marks of any theory discussed in this book. It is rated very high on four of the five criteria for a useful theory—a capacity to generate research, ability to organize knowledge, internal consistency, and parsimony. In addition, it is rated high as a guide to the practitioner.

Suggested Readings

BANDURA, A. (1982b). The psychology of chance encounters and life paths. *American Psychologist, 37,* 747-755.
Chance encounters and fortuitous events cannot be predicted by the science of psychology, yet they frequently exert a major influence on a person's life. Here

Bandura argues that in chance encounters the separate chains of events have their own causal determinants and having once occurred, they enter the reciprocal determinism paradigm and can be analyzed in the same manner as other environmental events.

BANDURA, A. (1986). *Social foundations of thought and action: A social-cognitive theory.* Englewood Cliffs, NJ: Prentice-Hall.

As the most complete expression of social-cognitive theory, this book is "must" reading for any serious student of Bandura. However, the esoteric language and lack of organization make for difficult reading.

BANDURA, A. (1991b). Social-cognitive theory of self-regulation. *Organizational Behavior and Human Decision Processes, 50,* 248-287.

This article presents in brief form the major components of Bandura's latest ideas on social-cognitive theory and self-regulation.

EVANS, R. I. (1989). *Albert Bandura: The man and his ideas—A dialogue.* New York: Praeger.

In April of 1988, Richard Evans interviewed Bandura for several hours. This transcript of the filmed dialogue offers some glimpses into the personal side of Bandura as well as Bandura's views on aggression and violence, moral development, moral disengagement, and self-efficacy.

Cognitive Social Learning Theory

Chapter Eleven

OVERVIEW
BIOGRAPHY OF JULIAN ROTTER
INTRODUCTION TO ROTTER'S SOCIAL LEARNING
   THEORY
FOUR VARIABLES OF PREDICTION
   Behavior Potential Expectancy
   Reinforcement Value
   Psychological Situation
BASIC PREDICTION FORMULA
GENERALIZED EXPECTANCIES
   Internal vs External Control of Reinforcement
   Interpersonal Trust Scale
   Needs
GENERAL PREDICTION FORMULA
MALADAPTIVE BEHAVIOR
PSYCHOTHERAPY
   Changing Goals
   Eliminating Low Expectancies
INTRODUCTION TO MISCHEL'S COGNITIVE
   SOCIAL THEORY
BIOGRAPHY OF WALTER MISCHEL
CONSISTENCY PARADOX
   Person Variables
   Interaction of Person and Situation Variables
   A Conditional View of Personal Dispositions
CONCEPT OF HUMANITY
RELATED RESEARCH
CRITIQUE OF COGNITIVE SOCIAL LEARNING
   THEORY
CHAPTER SUMMARY
SUGGESTED READINGS

ROTTER MISCHEL

As a senior majoring in psychology, Gerry is trying to decide about her future. Since her first year in college she has wanted to receive a Ph.D. in clinical psychology, and throughout her college career she has seen herself as academically capable and has worked hard to maintain a high grade-point average. She has been accepted by several graduate schools but has yet to apply to any of the three prestigious schools that she would really like to attend.

Moreover, her uncle has told her that after she graduates she can have a potentially high-paying position as an advertising salesperson for an independent telephone book publishing company. In addition, her boyfriend, Chuck, wants to marry her, but she is not sure that she loves him.

Gerry is not too worried about her ability to successfully complete graduate-level work at any of the schools that have accepted her. However, she is less confident in her ability to compete in the more prestigious schools. In fact, her reluctance to even apply to these schools reflects not only a fear of being rejected but also of being accepted—and then failing.

In the past Gerry has been able to reach most of her goals, academic as well as nonacademic. In high school she tried out for the tennis team and was successful. In college she joined the staff of the school paper and worked her way up to editor by her junior year.

Although her failures have been few, she usually takes responsibility for them. When she was not chosen for a lucrative and highly prestigious scholarship, she did not blame the selection committee or attribute her loss to luck or fate. She realized that very few students could be accepted and that her scholastic record was not as good as those of the people selected.

Gerry is now at a crucial point in her life, trying to decide whether to apply to the most prestigious graduate schools. Would she be accepted? If accepted, could she succeed? Should she attend one of the regional universities that have already accepted her? How about her uncle's offer? What about marriage to Chuck?

What will Gerry do? Can her behavior be predicted? What factors should be considered in making such a prediction?

OVERVIEW

The cognitive social learning theories of Julian Rotter and Walter Mischel attempt to answer questions such as those raised by Gerry's situation without resorting to the radical determinism of Skinner. Rotter and Mischel believe that *cognitive* factors help shape how people will react to environmental forces. They object to Skinner's explanation that behavior is shaped by immediate reinforcement and suggest that one's *expectations* of future events are prime determinants of performance. Also, Rotter and Mischel differ from Skinner in their insistence that an adequate theory of human personality must be built on the study of humans rather than from extrapolations of animal studies.

BIOGRAPHY OF JULIAN ROTTER

Julian B. Rotter was born in Brooklyn, New York, on October 22, 1916, the third and last son of Jewish immigrant parents. Rotter (1993) recalled that he fit Adler's description of a highly competitive youngest child. As an elementary-school and high-school student, he was an avid reader and by his junior year had read nearly every book of fiction in the local public library. That being the case, he turned one day to the psychology shelves, where he found Adler's *Understanding Human Nature*, Freud's *Psychopathology of Everyday Life*, and Karl Menninger's *The Human Mind*. He was particularly impressed by Adler and Freud and soon returned for more (Rotter, 1982, 1993).

When he entered Brooklyn College, he was already seriously interested in psychology but did not major in it, because the school had no formal psychology department. By his own account, he chose chemistry because it seemed to be a more employable degree during the depression of the 1930s. As a junior at Brooklyn College, he learned that

Adler was, at that time, a professor of medical psychology at Long Island College of Medicine. He attended Adler's medical lectures and several of his clinical demonstrations. Eventually, he came to personally know Adler, who invited him to attend meetings of the Society for Individual Psychology (Rotter, 1993).

When Rotter graduated from Brooklyn College in 1937, he had more credits in psychology than in chemistry. He then entered graduate school in psychology at the University of Iowa, from which he received a master's degree in 1938. He then completed an internship in clinical psychology at Worcester State Hospital in Massachusetts, where he met his future wife Clara Barnes. Next, Rotter entered Indiana University, from which he received a Ph.D. degree in clinical psychology in 1941, the same year he was married.

In 1941, Rotter accepted a position as clinical psychologist at Norwich State Hospital in Connecticut, where his duties included training interns and assistants from the University of Connecticut and

Wesleyan University. In 1942, he was drafted into the army, where he spent more than three years as a psychologist.

After the war, Rotter returned briefly to Norwich, but he soon took a job at Ohio State University, where he attracted a number of outstanding graduate students, including Walter Mischel. Carl Rogers (see Chapter 16) had recently left Ohio State, leaving Rotter and George Kelly (see Chapter 14) as the two most dominant members of the psychology department. However, Rotter was unhappy with the political effects of McCarthyism in Ohio, and, in 1963, he took a position at the University of Connecticut, where he remains.

Among Rotter's most important publications are *Social Learning and Clinical Psychology* (1954); *Clinical Psychology* (1964); *Applications of a Social Learning Theory of Personality*, with J. E. Chance and E. J. Phares (1972); *Personality*, with D. J. Hochreich (1975); *The Development and Application of Social Learning Theory: Selected Papers* (1982); the Rotter Incomplete Sentences Blank (Rotter, 1966); and the Interpersonal Trust Scale (Rotter, 1967). Rotter has been active in professional organizations, serving as president of the Eastern Psychological Association and the divisions of Social and Personality Psychology and Clinical Psychology of the American Psychological Association (APA). He has also served two terms on the APA Education and Training Board. In 1988 he received the prestigious APA Distinguished Scientific Contribution Award. He and his wife, who have a daughter, Jean, and a son, Richard, currently live in Storrs, Connecticut.

INTRODUCTION TO ROTTER'S SOCIAL LEARNING THEORY

Rotter's social learning theory assumes that human behavior rests on an understanding of the *interaction* of people with their meaningful environments (Rotter, 1982). People's reaction to environmental stimuli depends on the meaning or importance that they attach to an event. Rotter contends that our cognitions, past histories, and expectations of the future are keys to predicting behavior.

As an **interactionist**, Rotter holds that neither the environment itself nor the individual is completely responsible for behavior. In this respect he differs from Skinner, who believes that reinforcement ultimately stems from the environment. To Rotter, reinforcements are not solely dependent on external stimuli, but they are given meaning by the individual's cognitive capacity. Likewise, personal characteristics such as needs or traits cannot, by themselves, cause behavior. Rather, Rotter believes that human behavior stems from the interaction of environmental and personal factors. Take, for instance, Gerry, our case study. Her past experience of reinforcement for academic work is not, by itself, sufficient motivation to apply to a prestigious graduate school, but that experience has interacted with her belief or expectation that she would be successful.

A second assumption of Rotter's theory is that human personality is *learned* (Rotter, 1982). Thus, it follows that personality is not set or determined at any particular age of development; instead, it can be changed or modified as long as people are capable of learning. Although our accumulation of earlier experiences gives our personalities some stability, we are always amenable to change through new experiences. We learn from past experiences, but those experiences are not absolutely constant; they are colored by intervening experiences that then affect present perceptions.

Rotter's third assumption is that personality has a *basic unity*, which means that our personalities possess relative stability (Rotter, 1982). As we become more experienced, we learn to evaluate new experiences on the basis of previous reinforcement. This relatively consistent evaluation leads to greater stability and unity of personality.

Rotter's fourth basic assumption is that motivation is *goal directed* (Rotter, 1982). He rejects the notion that people are primarily motivated to reduce tension or seek pleasure, insisting that the best explanation for human behavior lies in people's expectations that their behaviors are advancing them toward goals. For example, Gerry knows that four years of graduate school will be hard work. And rather than reducing tension, the prospect of graduate school promises to increase it.

Other things being equal, people are most strongly reinforced by behaviors that move them in the direction of anticipated goals. This refers to Rotter's **empirical law of effect**, which "defines reinforcement as any action, condition, or event which affects the individual's movement toward a goal" (Rotter & Hochreich, 1975, p. 95). Rotter believes that an adequate theory of personality must take into consideration the assumption that people are capable of anticipating events, and that their criterion for evaluating reinforcers is movement in the direction of the anticipated event.

FOUR VARIABLES OF PREDICTION

Because Rotter's primary concern is the prediction of human behavior, he suggested four variables that must be analyzed in order to make accurate predictions. These are *behavior potential, expectancy, reinforcement value,* and *the psychological situation*. Behavior potential refers to the likelihood that a given behavior will occur in a particular situation; expectancy is a person's expectation of being reinforced; reinforcement value is the person's preference for a particular reinforcement; and the psychological situation refers to a complex pattern of cues that the person perceives during a specific time period.

Behavior Potential

Broadly considered, **behavior potential** (BP) refers to the possibility that a particular response will occur at a given time and place. Rotter and Hochreich (1975,

p. 95) defined it as "the potential for any given behavior to occur in a particular situation or set of situations as calculated in relation to any single reinforcement or set of reinforcements." Several behavior potentials of varying strength exist in any psychological situation. For example, in the case of Gerry, the psychology major, we might be interested in predicting her behavioral potential with reference to her immediate future. Several behaviors are possible. She might apply to one or more highly prestigious graduate programs, attend one that has already accepted her, work toward a master's degree, or not go to graduate school. She might stay in town and marry Chuck or move out of state and take her uncle's job offer. How can we predict which behaviors are most or least likely to occur? *The behavior potential in any situation is a function of both expectancy and reinforcement value.*

If we wish to know the likelihood that Gerry will attend School A rather than School C, for example, we could hold expectancy constant and vary reinforcement value. Assume that each of these behavior potentials carried a 90 percent expectancy of being reinforced, that is, Gerry believes that she has a 90 percent chance of being successful at either School A or School C. Then her choice would be based solely on the reinforcement value of each school. If completing the program at prestigious School A has greater reinforcement value than earning a Ph.D. at mediocre School C, then Gerry is more likely to attend School A.

The second approach to prediction is to hold reinforcement value constant and vary expectancy. If total reinforcements from each possible behavior are of equal value, then the one with the greatest expectation of reinforcement is most likely to occur. More specifically, if graduation from one school has exactly the same reinforcement value as graduation from any other school, then the response with the highest behavior potential is the one that is most likely to produce a reinforcement. In other words, Gerry is most likely to attend the school where she believes she will be successful.

Rotter employs a broad definition of behavior, which refers to any response, implicit or explicit, that can be observed or measured, directly or indirectly. This comprehensive concept allows Rotter to include as behavior such hypothetical constructs as generalizing, problem solving, thinking, analyzing, and so forth.

Expectancy

Rotter and Hochreich (1975, p. 96) defined **expectancy** (E) as "the probability held by the individual that a particular reinforcement will occur as a function of a specific behavior on his part in a specific situation or situations." The probability is not determined by the individual's history of reinforcements, as Skinner contended, but is subjectively held by the person. History, of course, is a contributing factor, but so, too, are unrealistic thinking, expectations based on lack of information, and fantasies, so long as the person sincerely believes that a given reinforcement or group of reinforcements is contingent on a particular response.

Expectancies can be general or specific. Generalized expectancies (GEs) are learned through previous experiences with a particular response or similar responses and are based on the belief that certain behaviors will be followed by positive reinforcement. For example, because Gerry had been previously reinforced by high grades for hard work, she has a generalized expectancy of future reward and will work hard in a variety of academic situations.

Specific expectancies are designated as E' (E *prime*). In any situation the expectancy for a particular reinforcement is determined by a combination of a specific expectancy (E') and the generalized expectancy (GE). For example, Gerry has a general expectancy that a given level of academic work will be rewarded by good grades, and yet she believes that an equal amount of hard work in her French class will go unrewarded. Total expectancy of success is a function of both one's generalized expectancy and one's specific expectancy. This total expectancy partially determines how hard Gerry will work in French class and is, therefore, one of the variables that enables us to predict behavior.

Reinforcement Value

Another variable in the prediction formula is **reinforcement value** (RV), which is defined as "the degree of preference for any reinforcement to occur if the possibilities of their occurring were all equal" (Rotter & Hochreich, 1975, p. 97). Reinforcement value can be illustrated by a vending machine with several possible selections, each costing the same. A woman approaches the machine able and willing to pay 50 cents in order to receive a snack. The vending machine is in perfect working condition so that there is a 100 percent probability that her response will be followed by some sort of reinforcement. Her expectancy of reinforcement, therefore, for the candy bar, corn chips, potato chips, popcorn, tortilla chips, and Danish pastry are all equal. Her response, that is, which button she presses, is determined by the reinforcement value of each snack.

When expectancies and situational variables are held constant, behavior is shaped by one's preference for the possible reinforcements, that is, reinforcement value. In most situations, of course, expectancies are seldom equal, and prediction is difficult because both expectancy and reinforcement value can vary.

In determining reinforcement value, one must consider both positive and negative aspects of reinforcement. Rotter agrees with Skinner that positive reinforcement is any event or condition that increases the probability that a particular behavior will occur again under the same or similar circumstances. However, his definition of negative reinforcement is different. Whereas Skinner defined negative reinforcement as the removal of an aversive stimulus that consequently increases the probability that a particular behavior will occur, Rotter uses the term to refer to any negatively valued event. To Rotter, therefore, negative reinforcement is the same as a punishment, and it decreases the likelihood that a particular behavior will occur again (Rotter, Chance, & Phares, 1972).

Positive and negative reinforcement values can be illustrated by Gerry's situation with regard to graduate school. Gerry has also considered applying to School B, one that is as equally prestigious and positively reinforcing as School A. However,

School B is located in a particularly cold area of the country, and because Gerry hates cold weather a negative value must be subtracted from School B's positive value in predicting which school Gerry is more likely to prefer.

What determines the reinforcement value for any event, condition, or action? First, the individual's perception contributes to the positive or negative value of an event. Rotter calls this **internal reinforcement** and distinguishes it from **external reinforcement**, which refers to events, conditions, or actions that one's society or culture values. Internal and external reinforcements may be either in harmony or at variance with one another. For example, both School A and School B have outstanding reputations, so being accepted to either one would be strongly externally reinforcing. However, Gerry does not regard School B as positively as do other people. In this case internal and external reinforcements are discrepant, but with School A, Gerry's internal and external reinforcements are in harmony.

Another contributor to reinforcement value is one's needs. Generally, a specific reinforcement tends to increase in value as the need it satisfies becomes stronger. A starving child places a higher value on a bowl of soup than does a moderately hungry one. (Needs are more fully discussed below.)

Reinforcements are also valued according to their expected consequences for future reinforcements. Rotter believes that people are capable of using cognition to anticipate a sequence of events leading to some future goal, and that the ultimate goal contributes to the reinforcement value of each event in the sequence. Reinforcements seldom occur independently of future related reinforcements but are likely to appear in **reinforcement-reinforcement sequences,** which Rotter (1982) refers to as clusters of reinforcement.

Humans are goal-oriented; they anticipate achieving a goal if they behave in a particular way. Other things being equal, goals with the highest reinforcement value are most desirable. Desire alone, however, is not sufficient to predict behavior. The potential for any behavior is a function of both expectancy and reinforcement value, as well as the psychological situation.

Psychological Situation

The **psychological situation** (s), the fourth variable in the prediction formula, refers to that part of the external and internal world to which the person is responding. It is not synonymous with external stimuli, although physical events are usually important to the psychological situation.

Behavior is a function neither of environmental events nor of central traits or characteristics within the person, but rather it stems from the interaction of the person with his or her meaningful environment. If physical stimuli alone determined behavior, then two individuals would respond in exactly the same way to identical stimuli. If personal traits were responsible for behavior, then a person would always respond in a consistent and characteristic fashion, even to different events. Because neither of these conditions is valid, something other than the environment or personal traits must shape behavior. Rotter's social learning theory hypothesizes that

People do not behave in a vacuum but respond to cues in their perceived environment.

the *interaction* between person and environment is a crucial factor in shaping behavior.

The psychological situation is "a complex set of interacting cues acting upon an individual for any specific time period" (Rotter, 1982, p. 318). People do not behave in a vacuum, but rather they respond to cues within their perceived environment. These cues serve to determine for them certain expectancies for behavior-reinforcement sequences as well as for reinforcement-reinforcement sequences. The time period for the cues may vary from momentary to lengthy; thus, the psychological situation is not limited by time. One's marital situation, for example, may be relatively constant over a long period of time, whereas the psychological situation faced by a driver during a blowout may be extremely short. The psychological situation must be considered along with expectancies and reinforcement value in determining the probability of a given response.

BASIC PREDICTION FORMULA

As a hypothetical means of predicting behavior, Rotter proposed a basic prediction formula that includes all four variables. The formula represents an idealistic rather than a practical means of prediction, and no precise values can be plugged into it. Consider the case of Gerry in a situation where she is listening to a dull and lengthy lecture by one of her professors. To the internal cues of boredom and the external cues of seeing slumbering classmates, what is the likelihood that she will respond by resting her head on the desk in an attempt to sleep? The psychological situation alone is not responsible for her behavior, but it interacts with her expectancy for reinforcement plus the reinforcement value of sleep in that particular situation. Her behavior potential can be estimated by Rotter's basic formula for the prediction of goal-directed behavior:

$$BP_{x,s1,R_a} = f(E_{x,R_a,s1} \; \& \; RV_{a,s1})$$

This formula is read: The potential for Behavior x to occur in Situation 1 in relation to Reinforcement a is a function of the expectancy that Behavior x will be followed by Reinforcement a in Situation 1 and the value of Reinforcement a in Situation 1 (Rotter & Hochreich, 1975).

Applied to our example, the formula is a means of determining the likelihood (behavior potential or BP) that Gerry will rest her head on her desk (Behavior x) in a dull and boring classroom with other students slumbering (the psychological situation or s_1) with the goal of sleep (Reinforcement or R_a), is a function of her expectation that such behavior (E_x) will be followed by sleep (R_a) in this particular classroom situation (s_1), plus a measure of how highly she desires to sleep (Reinforcement Value or RV_a) in this specific situation (s_1).

Consider a second example. David, who has worked for 18 years in Hoffman's Hardware Store, has just been informed that, due to a business decline, Mr. Hoffman must cut his workforce, and that he may lose his job. How can we predict David's subsequent behavior? Will he beg Mr. Hoffman to let him remain with the company? Will he strike out in violence against the store or Mr. Hoffman? Will he displace his anger and act aggressively toward his wife or children? Will he begin drinking heavily and become apathetic toward searching for a new job? Will he immediately and constructively begin looking for another position?

GENERALIZED EXPECTANCIES

Because most of these possible behaviors are new to David, how can we predict what he will do? At this point the concepts of **generalization** and **generalized expectancy** enter into Rotter's personality theory. If, in the past, David has generally been rewarded for behaviors that have increased his social status, then only a slight probability exists that he will beg Mr. Hoffman for a job, because such actions are contrary to increased social status. On the other hand, if his previous attempts at responsible and independent behaviors have generally been reinforced, and if he has the *freedom of movement*—that is, the opportunity to apply for another job—then, assuming he needs work, a high probability exists that he will apply for another job or otherwise behave independently. This prediction, though not as specific as the one predicting Gerry's likelihood of sleep, is nevertheless, more useful in situations where rigorous control of pertinent variables is not possible. Predicting David's reaction to the probable loss of a job is a matter of knowing how he views the options available to him and also the status of his present *needs*.

Needs

Unlike Skinner, Rotter is willing to hypothesize the existence of inner states such as needs, goals, and expectancies. He assumes that people are goal-oriented, and that needs can be defined as any behavior or set of behaviors that people see as moving them in the direction of that goal. Rotter does not see needs as states of deprivation or arousal but as indicators of the direction of behavior. The difference between needs and goals is semantic only. When focus is on the environment, Rotter (1982) speaks of goals; when it is on the person, he talks of needs.

The concept of needs allows for more generalized predictions than that permitted by the four specific variables that comprise the basic prediction formula. The basic prediction formula permits specific predictions, assuming, of course, that all relevant information is at hand. It is the more appropriate formula for controlled laboratory experiments but is inadequate in predicting everyday behaviors. For this reason, Rotter introduced the concept of needs and their accompanying *general prediction formula*, which will be cited later.

Categories of Needs

Rotter and Hochreich (1975) listed six broad categories of needs, with each category representing a group of functionally related behaviors, that is, behaviors that lead to the same or similar reinforcements. For example, people can have their recognition needs met in a variety of situations and by many different people. Therefore, they can receive reinforcement for a group of functionally related behaviors, all of which satisfy their need for recognition. The following list is not exhaustive, but it represents most of the important human needs.

Recognition-Status

The need to be recognized by others and to achieve status in their eyes is a powerful need for most people. Recognition-status includes the need to excel in those things that a person regards as important, for example, school, sports, occupation, hobbies, and physical appearance. It also includes the need for socioeconomic status and personal prestige. Playing a good game of bridge would be an example of a specific behavior listed under this category.

Dominance

Dominance, or the need to control the behavior of others, includes any set of behaviors directed at gaining power over the lives of friends, family, colleagues, superiors, and subordinates. Talking co-workers into accepting one's ideas is a specific example of dominance.

Independence

Independence is the need to be free of the domination of others. It includes those behaviors aimed at gaining the freedom to make one's own decisions, to rely on oneself, and to attain goals without the help of others. Declining aid in repairing a bicycle is a demonstration of the need for independence.

Protection–Dependency

An opposite set of needs involves protection–dependency. This category includes the needs to have others take care of us, keep us from experiencing frustration and harm, and help us satisfy the other need categories. A specific example of protection–dependency would be asking a spouse to stay home from work and take care of us when we are ill.

Love and Affection

Most of us have a strong need for love and affection, that is, a need for acceptance by others that goes beyond recognition and status to include some indication that other people have warm, positive feelings for us. The need for love and affection includes those behaviors aimed toward securing friendly regard, interest, and devotion from others. An example of this need is seen in a young man who does a favor for his girlfriend, hoping that she will tell him that she loves him.

Physical Comfort

Physical comfort is perhaps the most basic need because other needs are learned in relation to it. This need includes those behaviors aimed at securing food, good health, and physical security. Other needs are learned as an outgrowth of our needs for pleasure, physical contact, and well-being. Behavior resulting in sexual gratification is an example of the need for physical comfort.

Need Components

A need complex has three essential components: *need potential; freedom of movement;* and *need value,* which are analogous to the more specific concepts of behavior potential, expectancy, and reinforcement value (Rotter, Chance, & Phares, 1972).

Need Potential

Need potential (NP) refers to the possible occurrence of a set of functionally related behaviors directed toward the satisfaction of the same or similar goals. Need potential is analogous to the more specific concept of behavior potential. The difference between the two is that need potential refers to a *group* of functionally related behaviors, whereas behavior potential is the likelihood that a *particular* behavior will occur in a given situation in relation to a specific reinforcement.

Need potential cannot be measured solely through observation of behavior because different people behaving in apparently the same manner may be realizing different need potentials. For example, eating in a fancy restaurant may satisfy the need for physical comfort in one person, the need for love and affection in another, and the need for recognition–status in a third person. In fact, probably any of the six broad needs could be satisfied by eating in this restaurant. Whether or not one's need potential is realized, however, depends not only on the value or preference one has for that reinforcement but also on one's freedom of movement in making responses leading to that reinforcement.

Freedom of Movement

We have seen that behavior is partly determined by our expectancies, that is, our best guess that a particular reinforcement will follow a specific response. In the general prediction formula (discussed below), **freedom of movement** (FM) is analogous to expectancy and is defined as the "mean expectancy of obtaining positive satisfactions as a result of a set of related behaviors directed toward obtaining a group of functionally related reinforcements" (Rotter, Chance, & Phares, 1972, p. 34). In other words, freedom of movement is one's overall expectation of being reinforced for performing those behaviors that are directed toward satisfying some general need. To illustrate, a person with a strong need for dominance could behave in a variety of ways to satisfy that need. She might select the clothes her husband will wear, decide what college curriculum her son will pursue, direct actors in a play, organize a professional conference involving dozens of colleagues, or perform any one of hundreds of other behaviors aimed at securing reinforcement for her dominance need. The average or mean level of expectancies that these behaviors will lead to the desired satisfaction is a measure of her freedom of movement in the area of dominance.

Freedom of movement can be determined by holding need value constant and observing one's need potential. For example, if a person places exactly the same value on dominance, independence, love and affection, and each of the other needs, then that person will perform those behaviors judged to have the greatest expectancy of being reinforced. If the person performs behaviors leading to physical comfort, for example, then there will be more freedom of movement in that need complex than any of the other need complexes. Ordinarily, of course, need value is not constant, because most people prefer the satisfaction of one need over others.

Need Value

The degree to which people prefer one set of reinforcements to another is their **need value** (NV). Rotter, Chance, and Phares (1972, p. 33) defined need value as the "mean preference value of a set of functionally related reinforcements." In the general prediction formula, need value is the analogue of reinforcement value. When freedom of movement is held constant, people will perform those behavior sequences that lead to satisfaction of the most preferred need. If people have equal expectancies of obtaining positive reinforcement for behaviors aimed at the satisfaction of any need, then the value they place on a particular need complex will be the principal determinant of their behavior. If they prefer independence to any other need complex, and if they have an equal expectation of being reinforced in the pursuit of any of the needs, then their behavior will be directed toward achieving independence.

GENERAL PREDICTION FORMULA

The basic prediction formula cited above is limited to highly controlled situations where expectancies, reinforcement value, and the psychological situation are all relatively simple and discrete. In most situations, however, prediction of behavior is much more complex because behaviors and reinforcements usually occur in functionally related sequences. Consider again our case study, Gerry. The basic prediction formula gives us some indication of the likelihood that in the specific situation of a boring lecture, she will rest her head on her desk. However, a more generalized prediction formula is needed to predict her need potential for pursuing a Ph.D. degree. To make these more generalized predictions, Rotter introduces the following general prediction formula:

$$NP = f(FM \ \& \ NV)$$

This equation means that need potential (NP) is a function of freedom of movement (FM) and need value (NV). The formula is analogous to the basic prediction formula, and each factor is parallel to the corresponding factors of that basic formula (Rotter & Hochreich, 1975). To illustrate the general prediction formula, we can look at Gerry's situation with regard to her future. To predict her *need potential* for any of the possible alternative behaviors, we would have to measure her *freedom of movement*, that is, her mean expectancy of being reinforced for a series of behaviors necessary to reach her goal, plus *need value* of all those reinforcements, that is, the value she places on recognition–status, independence, or any other need she associates with receiving a Ph.D. in clinical psychology. Gerry's needs for recognition–status, love and affection, and so on, can be satisfied through a set of behaviors. For instance, her need for recognition–status might be satisfied by completing all the steps necessary for receiving a Ph.D. Her need for love and affection might be satisfied by marrying Chuck. The value she places on these various needs (need value), plus her average expectancy of being reinforced for performing the required series of behaviors (freedom of movement), equals her potential for pursuing the

BASIC PREDICTION FORMULA

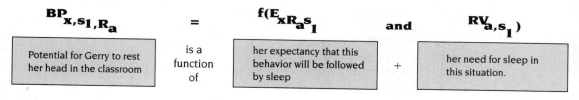

$$BP_{x,s_1,R_a} = f(E_{xR_as_1} \text{ and } RV_{a,s_1})$$

Potential for Gerry to rest her head in the classroom	is a function of	her expectancy that this behavior will be followed by sleep	+	her need for sleep in this situation.

GENERAL PREDICTION FORMULA

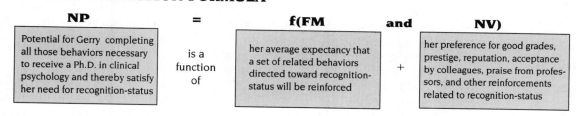

$$NP = f(FM \text{ and } NV)$$

Potential for Gerry completing all those behaviors necessary to receive a Ph.D. in clinical psychology and thereby satisfy her need for recognition-status	is a function of	her average expectancy that a set of related behaviors directed toward recognition-status will be reinforced	+	her preference for good grades, prestige, reputation, acceptance by colleagues, praise from professors, and other reinforcements related to recognition-status

Figure 11.1 *Comparison of the Basic Prediction Formula and the General Prediction Formula*

set of required behaviors (need potential). A comparison of the basic (specific) prediction formula and the generalized prediction formula is shown is Figure 11.1.

Rotter's general prediction formula allows for the fact that people use similar experiences from the past to anticipate present reinforcement. If Gerry fills out an application to School A, she does so not only because that specific type of behavior has a history of reinforcement, but also because she perceives that other similar experiences have been reinforced. In other words, Gerry has a **generalized expectancy** for success in this situation. Her past similar experiences of being accepted when applying for jobs or to other schools have, to some extent, influenced her expectation of being reinforced by applying to School A. Her perceived chances of success may not be the same as they were for other applications, but they have been altered by those similar experiences.

Rotter's two most famous scales for measuring generalized expectancies are the Internal–External Control Scale and the Interpersonal Trust Scale.

Internal vs External Control of Reinforcement

In our introductory case study, we saw that Gerry has generally, but not always, been successful in reaching her goals. When she failed to win an important scholarship, she did not blame the selection committee or luck—she recognized that her scholastic record was not quite good enough. Her behavior was a reflection of a generalized expectancy for *internal* control of reinforcement. Gerry believes that reinforcement is generally contingent on either her actions or her own personal characteristics and not on fate or on other people. Gerry would likely score high on Rotter's (1966) Internal–External (I–E) Control Scale. The Internal–External Control Scale is an attempt to measure the degree to which people perceive a causal relationship between their own efforts and environmental consequences. People will strive to reach their goals, not so much because of the nature of the goals or even because they have a strong internal desire to reach them but because they have a generalized expectancy that such strivings will be successful.

Rotter's Internal–External Control scale assumes that people who believe that they can control their own fate will behave differently in a variety of situations from people who believe that their destiny is controlled by luck, chance, or powerful others. Despite thousands of studies involving the scale, the concepts of internal and external control are not always clearly understood. Although Rotter (1975) pointed out several common misconceptions concerning internal and external control of reinforcement (he seldom refers to it as "locus of control"), people continue to misuse and misinterpret the instrument. One misconception that Rotter mentioned is that scores on the scale are not determinants of behavior. They are indicators of *generalized expectancies* (GEs) and must be considered along with *reinforcement value* (RV) when predicting behavior potential. A second misconception is that locus of control is specific and can predict achievement in a specific situation. Again, the concept refers to *generalized* expectancies of reinforcement and indicates that people ordinarily believe that they are in control of their lives, or that they generally expect that luck or outside forces control what happens to them. A third common misconception is that the scale divides people into two distinct types, with high internal scores signifying socially desirable traits and high external scores indicating socially undesirable characteristics. Actually, extreme scores in either direction would be undesirable. Very high external scores might be related to apathy and despair, with people believing that they have no control over their environments, whereas extremely high internal scores would mean that people accept responsibility for everything that happens to them—accidents, business failure, delinquent children, and so forth. Scores somewhere in between these extremes, but inclined in the direction of internal control, would probably be most healthy or desirable.

Interpersonal Trust Scale

Another example of a generalized expectancy (GE) that has provoked considerable interest and research is the concept of interpersonal trust, defined by Rotter (1980, p. 1) as "a generalized expectancy held by an individual that the word, promise, or oral or written statement of another individual or group can be relied on." Interpersonal trust does not refer to the belief that people are naturally good or that we live in the best of all possible worlds. Neither should it be equated with gullibility. Rotter (1980) saw interpersonal trust as a belief in the communications of others when there is no evidence for disbelieving, whereas gullibility is a belief that most other people would regard as foolish or naive.

Rotter believes that people develop generalized expectancies that the verbal promises and threats of others will be followed by either positive or negative reinforcements. Sometimes these promises and threats are kept; other times they are broken. In this way each of us learns to trust or distrust the words of others.

Because we have differential experiences with the words of others, it follows that there should be individual differences among people with regard to interpersonal trust. To measure these differences Rotter (1967) developed an Interpersonal Trust Scale, which asked people to respond to 25 items such as: "In dealing with strangers one is better off to be cautious until they have provided evidence that they are trustworthy" and "Most elected public officials are really sincere in their campaign promises" (Rotter, 1967, p. 654). Scores for each of the 25 items are added so that high scores indicate the presence of interpersonal trust and low scores mean a generalized expectancy of distrust.

Is it more desirable to score high or low on the scale, to be trustful or distrustful? When trust is defined independently of gullibility, as Rotter (1980) contended, then high trust is not only desirable but essential for the survival of civilization. We trust that the food we buy is not poisoned, that the gasoline in our cars will not explode on ignition, that airline pilots know how to fly the plane in which we travel, and even that the postal service will deliver our mail without tampering with it. Societies can function smoothly only when people have at least a moderate amount of trust in each other.

Rotter (1980) has summarized results of studies that indicate that people who score high in interpersonal trust, as opposed to those who score low, are (1) less likely to lie; (2) probably less likely to cheat or steal; (3) more likely to give others a second chance; (4) more likely to respect the rights of others; (5) less likely to be unhappy, conflicted, or maladjusted; (6) somewhat more likable and popular; (7) more trustworthy; (8) neither more nor less gullible; and (9) neither more nor less intelligent. In other words, high trusters are not gullible or naive and, rather than

Pair skating demands a high level of interpersonal trust.

being harmed by their trustful attitude, they seem to possess many of the characteristics that other people regard as positive and desirable.

MALADAPTIVE BEHAVIOR

Maladaptive behavior in Rotter's social learning theory is any persistent behavior that fails to move a person closer to a desired goal. It frequently, but not inevitably, arises from the combination of high need value and low freedom of movement, that is, from goals that are unrealistically high in relation to one's ability to achieve them (Rotter, 1964).

For example, the need for love and affection is realistic, but some people unrealistically set a goal to be loved by everyone. Hence, their need value will nearly certainly exceed their freedom of movement, resulting in behavior that is likely to be defensive or maladaptive. When people set their goals too high, they cannot learn productive behaviors because their goals are beyond reach. Instead, they learn how to avoid failure or how to defend themselves against the pain that accompanies failure. For example, a woman whose goal is to be loved by everyone inevitably will be ignored or rejected by someone. To obtain love she may become socially aggressive (a nonproductive, self-defeating strategy), or she may withdraw from people, which prevents her from being hurt by them, but which is also nonproductive.

Setting goals too high is only one of several possible contributors to maladaptive behavior. Another frequent cause is low freedom of movement. People may have low expectancies of success because they lack information or the ability to perform those behaviors that will be followed by positive reinforcement. A person who values love, for example, may lack the interpersonal skills necessary to obtain it.

People may also have low freedom of movement because they make a faulty evaluation of the present situation. For example, people sometimes underestimate their intellectual abilities because, in the past, they have been told that they were stupid. Even though their need values are not unrealistically high, they have a low expectation of success because they wrongly believe that they are incapable of performing well in school or competing successfully for a higher level job.

People may also have low freedom of movement because they generalize from one situation in which, perhaps, they are realistically inadequate to other situations in which they could have sufficient ability to be successful. For example, a physically weak adolescent, who lacks the skills to be an accomplished athlete, may erroneously see himself as unable to compete for a role in the school play or to be a leader in a social club. He inappropriately generalizes his inadequacies in sports to lack of ability in unrelated areas.

In summary, maladjusted individuals are characterized by unrealistic goals, inappropriate behaviors, inadequate skills, or unreasonably low expectancies of being able to execute the behaviors necessary for positive reinforcement. Because they have learned inadequate ways of solving problems within a social context, they can unlearn these behaviors and also learn more appropriate ones within the controlled social environment provided by psychotherapy.

PSYCHOTHERAPY

To Rotter (1964, p. 82), "the problems of psychotherapy are problems of how to effect changes in behavior through the interaction of one person with another. That is, they are problems in human learning in a social situation." Although Rotter adopts a problem-solving approach to psychotherapy, he does not limit his concern to quick solutions to immediate problems. His interest is more long range, involving a change in the patient's orientation toward life.

In general, the goal of Rotter's therapy is to bring freedom of movement and need value into harmony, thus reducing defensive and avoidance behaviors. The therapist assumes an active role as a teacher and attempts to accomplish the therapeutic goal in two basic ways: (1) changing the importance of goals and (2) eliminating unrealistically low expectancies for success (Rotter, 1964, 1970, 1978; Rotter & Hochreich, 1975).

Changing Goals

Many patients are unable to solve life's problems because they are pursuing skewed or distorted goals. The role of the therapist is to help these patients understand the faulty nature of their goals and to teach them constructive means of striving toward realistic goals. Rotter and Hochreich (1975) listed three sources of problems that follow from inappropriate goals.

First, two or more important goals may be in conflict. For example, adolescents frequently value both independence and protection–dependency. On the one hand, they wish to be free from their parents' domination and control, but, on the other, they still desire to have a nurturing person care for them and protect them from painful experiences. Their ambivalent behaviors are confusing both to themselves and to their parents. In this situation, the therapist may try to help adolescents see how specific behaviors are related to each of these needs and proceed to work with them in changing the value of one or both needs. By gradually altering need value, patients begin to behave more and more consistently and to experience greater freedom of movement in obtaining their goals.

A second source of problems is a destructive goal. Some patients persistently pursue self-destructive goals that inevitably result in failure and punishment. The job of the therapist is to point out the detrimental nature of this pursuit and the likelihood that it will be followed by negative reinforcement (punishment). One possible technique used by a therapist in these cases is to positively reinforce movements away from destructive goals. Rotter, however, is both pragmatic and eclectic and is not bound to a specific set of techniques for each conceivable problem. To him, the appropriate procedure is the one that works with a given patient.

Many people find themselves in trouble because they set their goals too high and are continually frustrated because they cannot reach or exceed them. This is the third area of inappropriate goals and, perhaps, the most common one. High goals lead to failure and pain, so instead of learning constructive means of obtaining a goal, a person learns nonproductive ways of avoiding pain. Avoidance through flight or repression is the chief symptom and may evolve into an end in itself. Therapy consists of realistically re-evaluating and lowering exaggerated goals by reducing their reinforcement value. Because high reinforcement value is often learned through generalization, the therapist works toward teaching patients to discriminate between past legitimate values and present spurious ones. For example, a patient may have been previously rewarded with food or affection for associating with his mother, who may have praised him for his cleanliness behaviors. As a consequence, the son learned to place an unrealistically high value on compulsive neatness, and, as an adult, he is never quite comfortable amid clutter and disarray. The therapist must teach him that nourishment and love are independent from compulsively neat and orderly behavior. Rotter, however, does not stop with giving patients insight and eliminating their maladjustive behaviors. He also attempts to teach them new behaviors that will lead to the reinforcements they seek.

Eliminating Low Expectancies

Rotter's second general approach is to attack low expectancies of success and its analogue, low freedom of movement. As noted in the section on maladjustment, people may have low freedom of movement for at least three reasons.

First, they may lack the skills or information needed to successfully strive toward their goals (Rotter, 1970). The therapist then becomes a teacher, warmly and empathically instructing patients in more effective techniques for solving problems and satisfying needs. If a patient, for example, has difficulties in interpersonal relationships, the therapist has an arsenal of techniques, including extinguishing inappropriate behaviors by simply ignoring them; using the therapist/patient relationship as a model for an effective interpersonal encounter that may then generalize beyond the therapeutic situation; and advising the patient of specific behaviors to try out in the presence of those other people who are most likely to be receptive.

A second source of low freedom of movement is faulty evaluation of the present situation. For example, an adult may lack assertiveness with her colleagues because, during childhood, she was punished for competing with her siblings. The patient now must learn to differentiate between past and present, as well as between siblings and colleagues. The therapist's task is to help her make these distinctions and, with the present example, teach her assertiveness techniques in a variety of appropriate situations.

Finally, low freedom of movement can spring from inadequate generalization. Patients often use failure in one situation as proof that they cannot be successful in other areas. Earlier we saw the example of the physically feeble adolescent who, because he was unsuccessful in sports, generalized his failure to nonathletic areas. His present problems come from faulty generalization, and the therapist must reinforce even small successes in social relationships, academic achievements, and other situations. The patient will eventually learn to discriminate between realistic shortcomings in one area and successful behaviors in other situations.

Although Rotter recognizes that therapists should be flexible in their techniques and should utilize different approaches with different patients, he does suggest several interesting techniques that he has found to be effective. The first is to teach patients to look for alternative courses of action (Rotter, 1978). Patients frequently complain that a spouse, parent, child, or employer does not understand them, treats them unjustly, and is the source of their problems. In this situation, Rotter would simply teach the patient to change the other person's behavior. This can be accomplished by examining those behaviors of the patient that typically lead to negative reactions by spouse, parent, child, or employer. If the patient can find an alternative method of behaving toward important others, then those others will probably change their behavior toward the patient. Thereafter, the patient will be rewarded for behaving in a more appropriate fashion.

Rotter (1978) suggested a related approach designed to help patients develop a more accurate understanding of other people's motives. Many patients have a suspicious or distrustful attitude toward others. They believe that their spouse, teacher, or boss is intentionally and spitefully trying to harm them. Rotter attempts to teach these patients to look at ways in which they may be contributing to the other person's defensive or negative behavior and to help them realize that these other people are frequently frightened or threatened by the patient and not simply nasty or spiteful.

Rotter (1978) also suggested that the therapist can help a patient look at the long-range consequences of behavior and to understand that many maladaptive behaviors produce secondary gains that outweigh the patient's present frustration. For example, a woman may adopt the role of a helpless child in order to gain control over her husband. She complains to her therapist that she is dissatisfied with her helplessness and would like to become more independent, both for her sake and for the benefit of her husband. What she probably does not realize, however, is that her current helpless behavior is satisfying her basic need for dominance. The more helpless she acts, the more control she exercises over her husband, who must respond to her helplessness. The positive reinforcement she receives from her husband's recognition is stronger than the accompanying negative reinforcement. In addition, she may not clearly see the long-range positive consequences of self-confidence and independence. The task of the therapist is to train the patient to postpone minor present satisfactions for more important future ones.

Another novel technique suggested by Rotter (1978) is to have patients enter into a previously painful social situation, but, rather than speaking as much as usual, they are asked to remain as quiet as possible and largely to observe. By observing others, patients have a better chance of learning their motives They can then use that information in the future to alter their own behavior, thereby changing the reactions of others and reducing the painful effects of future encounters with those other persons.

In summary, Rotter believes that the therapist should be an active participant in a social interaction with the patient. An effective therapist possesses the characteristics of warmth and acceptance, not only because these attitudes encourage the patient to verbalize problems, but also because reinforcement from a warm, accepting therapist is more effective than reinforcement from a cold, rejecting one (Rotter, Chance, & Phares, 1972). The therapist attempts to minimize the discrepancy between need value and freedom of movement by helping patients alter their goals or by teaching effective means of obtaining those goals. Even though the therapist is an active problem solver, Rotter (1978) believes that eventually patients must learn to solve their own problems.

INTRODUCTION TO MISCHEL'S COGNITIVE SOCIAL THEORY

Walter Mischel's cognitive social theory has much in common with Bandura's social–cognitive theory and Rotter's social learning theory. Like Bandura and Rotter, Mischel believes that cognitive factors, such as expectancies, subjective perceptions, values, goals, and personal standards, play important roles in shaping personality. Mischel's unique contributions are his research on **delay of gratification** and his subsequent theory regarding the consistency or inconsistency of personality.

Mischel objects to the trait theory explanation of behavior. Personality theorists from Freud (Chapter 2) to Raymond Cattell (Chapter 12) have seen people as being motivated by a limited number of global traits or dispositions that tend to render a person's behavior somewhat consistent. For example, Freud would say that a person with the anal triad of compulsive neatness, stubbornness, and stinginess is driven to be neat, obstinate, and miserly. Such a person would exhibit these behaviors in a variety of settings or situations. Mischel, however, takes a different position. While recognizing the existence of personal dispositions, he proposes that psychologists should shift their emphasis from global traits inferred from behavior to cognitive activities and to specific situations in which behavior occurs. "The focus shifts from attempting to compare and generalize about what different individuals 'are like' to an assessment of what they *do*—behaviorally and cognitively—in relation to the psychological conditions in which they do it" (Mischel, 1973, p. 265).

Mischel does not suggest that people are empty vessels with no personal traits that endure over time. Rather he holds that many basic dispositions can be stable over a long period, such as the conscientiousness shown by Gerry (our case study) in academic work. His objection to the use of traits as predictors of behaviors rests not with their temporal instability but with their inconsistency from one situation to another. For example, even though Gerry has been conscientious in academic achievement through high school and college, she has not shown the same conscientiousness in sports or maintaining her car in working condition. Gerry's lack of conscientiousness in sports may be due to disinterest, and her neglect of her car may be the result of insufficient knowledge. Thus, the specific situation in interaction with several person variables is the best predictor of behavior. Mischel's cognitive social learning theory holds that the person and the situation are interdependent—people's behavior shapes the situations in their lives, just as situations shape their behavior.

BIOGRAPHY OF WALTER MISCHEL

Walter Mischel, the second son of upper-middle-class parents, was born on February 22, 1930, in Vienna, Austria. He and his brother, Theodore, who later became a philosopher of science, grew up in a pleasant environment only a short distance from Freud's home. The tranquility of childhood, however, was shattered when the Nazis invaded Austria in 1938. That same year, which also marked Freud's departure from Vienna, the Mischel family fled Austria and moved to the United States. After living in various parts of the country, they settled in Brooklyn in 1940, where Walter attended primary and secondary schools. Before he could accept a college scholarship, his father suddenly became ill, and Walter was forced to take a series of odd jobs before eventually attending New York University. Mischel was passionately interested in art (painting and sculpture) and divided his time among art, psychology, and life in Greenwich Village.

In college, Mischel was appalled by the rat-centered introductory psychology classes that seemed to him far removed from the everyday lives of humans. His humanistic inclinations were solidified by reading Freud, the existentialists, and poetry. After graduation he entered the M.A. program in clinical psychology at City College of New York. While working on his degree, he was employed as a social worker in the Lower East Side slums, work that led him to doubt the usefulness of psychoanalytic theory and to see the necessity of using empirical evidence to evaluate all claims of psychology.

Mischel's development as a cognitive social psychologist was further enhanced by his doctoral studies at Ohio State University from 1953 to 1956. At that time the psychology department at Ohio State was informally divided into the supporters of its two most influential faculty members—Julian Rotter and George Kelly. Unlike most students who strongly supported one or the other position, Mischel admired both Rotter and Kelly and learned from each of them. As a consequence, Mischel's cognitive social theory shows the influence of Rotter's social learning theory as well as Kelly's cognitively based theory of personal constructs (see Chapter 14). Rotter taught Mischel the importance of research design for improving assessment techniques and for measuring the effectiveness of therapeutic treatment; Kelly taught him that subjects in psychology experiments are like the psychologists who study them in that they are thinking, feeling human beings.

From 1956 to 1958, Mischel lived much of the time in the Caribbean, studying religious cults that practiced spirit possession and investigating delay of gratification in a cross-cultural setting. He became determined to learn more about why people prefer future, valuable rewards over immediate, less valuable ones. Much of his later research has revolved around this issue.

Next, Mischel taught for two years at the University of Colorado before joining the Department of Social Relations at Harvard. His interest in personality theory and assessment was further stimulated by discussions with Gordon Allport (see Chapter 13), Henry Murray, David McClelland, and others. In 1962, Mischel moved to Stanford, where he was a colleague of Albert Bandura (see Chapter 10). After more than 20 years at Stanford, Mischel returned to New York, joining the faculty at Columbia University, where he remains as an active researcher.

While at Harvard, Mischel met his future wife, Harriet Nerlove, another graduate student in cognitive psychology. The Mischels have three daughters, and have collaborated in producing several scientific projects (H. N. Mischel & W. Mischel, 1973; W. Mischel & H. N. Mischel, 1976, 1983).

Mischel's most important early work was *Personality and Assessment* (1968), an outgrowth of his efforts to identify successful Peace Corps volunteers. His experiences as consultant to the Peace Corps (Mischel, 1965) taught him that under the right conditions people are at least as capable as standardized tests at predicting their own behavior. He argued that traits are weak predictors of performance in a variety of situations and that the situation is more important than traits in influencing behavior. This book upset many clinical psychologists who argued that the inability of personal dispositions to predict behavior across situations was due to the unreliability and imprecision of the instruments that measure traits. Some believed that Mischel was trying to undo the concept of stable personality traits and even of personality. Later, Mischel (1979) answered his critics, saying that he was not opposed to traits as such, but only to generalized traits that negate the individuality and uniqueness of each person.

Much of Mischel's research has been a cooperative effort with a number of his graduate students. His most popular book, *Introduction to Personality* (1971), was revised in 1976, 1981, 1986, and 1993. Mischel has won several awards, including the Distinguished Scientist award from the clinical division of the American Psychological Association (APA) in 1978 and the APA's award for Distinguished Scientific Contribution in 1982.

CONSISTENCY PARADOX

Mischel has long been interested in what he terms the **consistency paradox;** that is, the observation that both laypersons and professional psychologists believe that people's behavior is relatively consistent, yet empirical evidence suggests much variability in behavior. To many people, it seems self-evident that personal dispositions such as aggressiveness, honesty, miserliness, punctuality, and so forth are global traits, and that they account for much of our behavior. We elect people to political office because they have honesty, trustworthiness, decisiveness, and integrity; employers and personnel managers select workers who are punctual, loyal, cooperative, hardworking, organized, and sociable. Many people assume that such traits will be manifested over a period of time and also from one situation to another. Mischel (1990) suggested that, at best, these people are only half right. He contended that some basic traits do persist over time, but he has found little evidence that they generalize from one situation to another.

For many years research has failed to support the consistency of personal traits across situations. Hartshorne and May, in their classic 1928 study, found that school children who were honest in one situation were deceitful in another. For example, some children would cheat on tests but not steal party favors; others would break rules in an athletic contest but not cheat on a test. Some psychologists, such as Seymour Epstein (1979, 1980) have argued that studies such as Hartshorne and May's used behaviors that are too specific. Epstein contended that, rather than relying on single behaviors, researchers must aggregate measures of behavior; that is, they must obtain a sum of many behaviors. In other words, Epstein would say that even though our case study, Gerry, is not *always* conscientious, the sum total of her individual behaviors will reflect a generally conscientious core. However, Mischel (1965) had earlier found that a three-person assessment committee, which used aggregated information from a variety of scores, could not reliably predict performance of Peace Corps teachers. The correlation between the committee's judgment and the performance of the teachers was a nonsignificant 0.20. Moreover, Mischel (1968) contended that correlations of about 0.30 between different measures of the same trait and between trait scores and behaviors represented the outer limits of trait consistency, meaning that this relatively low correlation is not due to the unreliability of the assessment procedures. Even with perfectly reliable measures, Mischel argued, specific behaviors will not accurately predict personal traits.

However, Mischel does not suggest that individuals have no consistent dispositions. Interestingly, one consistency most people have is their judgment of other people's consistency. Although we recognize flexibility in our own behavior, most of us see our friends and acquaintances as possessing a limited number of stable personality traits that relate to their behavior. In addition, Mischel (1973, 1990) suggests that certain abilities, such as intelligence, are relatively stable not only over time but from one situation to a similar one. To predict behavior, Mischel believes, one must consider the *person*, the *situation*, and the *interaction* between person and situation.

Person Variables

Mischel (1973) proposed a set of five overlapping person variables that interact with the situation to determine behavior. These variables shift the emphasis from what a person *has* to what a person *does* in a particular situation. What a person does includes more than actions; it includes cognitive and affective qualities such as thinking, planning, feeling, and evaluating. For example, our case study Gerry is applying to graduate school not because she possesses ambition and intelligence, but because she has construed her abilities as being sufficient to cope with working toward a Ph.D., at least at some universities.

Mischel suggested that person variables have both a structural component and a functional aspect. Structural components refer to the *product* of the individual's physical, cognitive, and social development. Functional components refer to the psychological *processes*, such as reasoning and valuing, that shape an individual's subjective meanings. For example, Gerry's scholastic aptitude is partly a product of her innate intelligence, her past history of reinforcement for academic performance, and so forth. But at the same time, her scholastic aptitude is also shaped by the processes called forth in viewing herself as a competent student.

The five interrelated person variables proposed by Mischel are *competencies, encoding strategies, expectancies, subjective values,* and the *self-regulatory system.*

Competencies

Mischel (1973, 1990) uses the term **competencies** to refer to that vast array of information we acquire about the world and our relationship to it. By observing our own behaviors and those of others, we learn what we can do in a particular situation, as well as what we cannot do. Mischel agrees with Bandura that we do not attend to all stimuli in our environment; rather, we selectively *construct* or generate our own version of the real world. Thus, we acquire a set of beliefs about our performance capabilities, often in the absence of actual performance. For example, Gerry believes that she has the competence to achieve a sufficiently high score on the Graduate Record Exam (GRE), even though she has never taken that test.

Cognitive competencies, such as doing well on the GRE, are generally more stable temporally and cross-situationally than other personality traits. That is, people's scores on mental ability tests do not ordinarily show large fluctuations from one time to the next or from one situation to another. In fact, Mischel (1990) argued that one of the reasons for the apparent consistency of traits is the relative stability of "intelligence," a basic trait that underlies many personal dispositions. He contended that cognitive competencies, as measured by traditional mental ability tests, have proven to be some of the best predictors of social and interpersonal adjustment and thus give social and interpersonal traits some appearance of stability. Moreover, Mischel (1990) suggested that when intelligence is assessed by nontraditional measures that include a person's potential for seeing alternate solutions to problems, then it accounts for even larger portions of the consistency found in other traits.

Encoding Strategies

Person variables also include personal constructs and **encoding strategies**; that is, people's ways of categorizing information received from external stimuli. People use cognitive processes to transform these stimuli into personal constructs, including their self-concept, their view of other people, and their way of looking at the world. Different people encode the same events in different ways, which accounts for individual differences in personal constructs. For example, Gerry views her relationship with her friend Chuck very differently from the way he has constructed it. Gerry has always seen the relationship as a comfortable encounter between two good friends, but Chuck has come to categorize it as a prelude to commitment and marriage.

Again, stimulus inputs are substantially altered by what people selectively attend, how they interpret their experience, and the way in which they categorize those inputs. Mischel and a former Ph.D. student, Bert Moore (1973), found that subjects can transform environmental events by focusing on selected aspects of stimulus inputs. In this delay-of-gratification study, children exposed to pictures of rewards (snacks or pennies) were able to wait longer for the rewards than children who were encouraged to cognitively construct (imagine) real rewards while viewing the pictures. A previous study (Mischel, Ebbesen, & Zeiss, 1972) had demonstrated that children exposed to real rewards during a wait period had more difficulty waiting than those exposed to no reward. These two studies, therefore, suggest that, in at least some situations, cognitive transformations of stimuli can have about the same effect as actual stimuli.

Expectancies

In any situation there are an enormous number of behavioral potentials, but how people behave depends on their specific *expectancies* about the consequences of each of the different behavioral possibilities. From previous experience and by observing others, people learn to enact those behaviors that they expect will result in the most subjectively valuable outcome. If people have no information about what they can expect from a behavior, then they will enact those behaviors that received the greatest reinforcement in past similar situations. For example, Gerry has never taken the Graduate Record Exam, but she has had experience preparing for other tests. What Gerry does in getting ready for the GRE is partially influenced by what previous test-preparation behaviors resulted in the most valuable outcome. Because she has previously been rewarded for using self-relaxation techniques to prepare for tests, Gerry expects that the same techniques will help her do well on the GRE. Mischel (1973, 1990) referred to this type of expectancy as a *behavior-outcome expectancy*; that is, if Gerry behaves in a particular way, then she can anticipate a particular outcome.

Mischel also identified a second type of expectancy—*stimulus-outcome expectancies*, which refers to the "multitude of stimulus conditions that moderate the probable consequences of any pattern of behavior" (Mischel, 1973, p. 271). Stimulus-outcome expectancies help us predict what other events are likely to occur. For example, Gerry believes that if she applies to a prestigious graduate school (one stimulus) she might receive an acceptance (another stimulus), but she does not necessarily regard such an acceptance as a valuable outcome. In fact, being accepted into such a program will probably increase her anxiety and discomfort.

Mischel (1990) believes that one reason for the inconsistency of our behavior is our inability to predict other people's behavior. We have little hesitancy in attributing personal traits to others, but then when we notice that their behavior is inconsistent with those traits, we become less certain about how to react to them. Our behavior will be cross-situationally consistent to the extent that our expectancies are unchanging. But our expectancies are not constant; they change because we can discriminate and evaluate the multitude of potential reinforcers in any given situation.

Subjective Values

Our subjective values, preferences, and goals, therefore, represent a fourth person variable. "Even if individuals have similar expectancies, they may select to perform different behaviors because of differences in the *subjective values* of the outcomes which they expect" (Mischel, 1973, p. 272). For example, Gerry places more value on going to graduate school than on working for her uncle. One of her friends of equal ability has different values and chose to enter the job market after graduation. Gerry and her friend have had many similar experiences during college, but, because they have different goals, they have made very different decisions.

Values, goals, and interests, along with competencies, are among the most stable person variables. One reason for this consistency is the emotion-eliciting properties of these variables. For instance, a person may place a negative value to a certain food because he associates it with the nausea he once experienced while eating that food. Without counterconditioning, this aversion is likely to persist due to the strong negative emotion elicited by the food. Similarly, patriotic values may last a lifetime because they are associated with positive emotions, such as security, attachment to one's home, and love of one's mother.

Self-Regulatory Systems

In Chapter 10 we discussed Bandura's concept of self-regulation, by which people control their own behavior through self-observation, self-evaluation, and such self-reactions as self-reinforcement and self-punishment. Similarly, Mischel believes that people use their **self-regulatory system** to control their own behavior through self-imposed goals and self-produced consequences. Thus, we do not require external rewards and punishments to shape our behavior; we can set goals for ourselves and then reward or criticize ourselves contingent upon whether or not our behavior moves us in the direction of those goals.

Our self-regulatory system enables us to plan, initiate, and maintain behaviors even when environmental support is weak or nonexistent. People such as Abraham

Lincoln and Mahatma Gandhi were able to regulate their own behavior in the face of a nonsupportive and hostile environment, but each of us can persist without environmental encouragement if we have powerful self-produced goals and values. However, inappropriate goals and ineffective strategies increase anxiety and lead to failure. For example, people with inflexible, exaggerated goals may persist in trying to realize those goals, but lack of competence and a nonsupportive environment preclude a positive outcome.

Our self-regulatory system includes (1) contingency rules that specify the goals, standards, and behaviors appropriate in a given situation, (2) the consequences of achieving or failing to achieve our goals, (3) self-instructions to achieve the self-control needed to reach our goals, and (4) plans for achieving our goals in the absence of external support.

In summary, interrelated person variables contribute to behavior as they interact with a receptive environment. The most important of these variables include (1) *competencies*, or what a person can do; (2) *encoding strategies*, or how a person construes or categorizes an event; (3) behavior-outcome and stimulus-outcome *expectancies* in a particular situation; (4) subjective stimulus *values, goals, and preferences* that partially determine selective attention to events; and (5) *self-regulating systems* and plans that a person brings to the situation.

One reason for the inconsistency of our own behavior is our inability to predict the behavior of others.

Interaction of Person and Situation Variables

Person variables *interact* with situation variables to produce behavior. Situation variables include all those stimulus inputs that people attend to in a particular situation. Mischel (1973, p. 276) believes that situations "affect behavior insofar as they influence such person variables as the individual's encoding, his expectancies, the subjective value of stimuli, or the ability to generate response patterns."

We can determine the relative influence of person and situation variables by observing the uniformity or diversity of people's responses in a given situation. When people are behaving in a very similar manner—for example, while watching an emotional scene in an engrossing movie—we know that situation variables are more powerful than personal variables. On the other hand, events that appear the same may produce widely different reactions because personal variables override situational ones. For example, several workers may all be laid off from their jobs, but individual differences will lead to diverse behaviors, depending on the workers' perceived need to work, confidence in their level of skill, and perceived ability to find another job.

Mischel and Staub (1965) looked at conditions that influence the interaction of person and situation variables. First, they asked 8th-grade boys to rate their expectancies for success on verbal reasoning and general information tasks. Three weeks later the subjects worked on a series of problems. Some of the students were told that they had succeeded on those problems; some were informed that they had failed; and the third group received no information. Next, the subjects were asked to choose between an immediate, less valuable, noncontingent reward and a delayed, more valuable, contingent reward. Consistent with Mischel's interaction theory, subjects informed that they had succeeded on the earlier similar task were

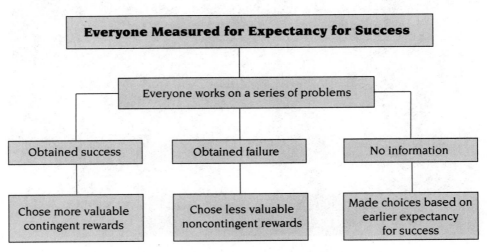

Figure 11.2   *Model Used by Mischel and Staub (1965)*

more likely to wait for the more valued reward that was contingent on their performance; those informed that they had previously failed tended to choose an immediate, less valuable reward; and those who had received no earlier feedback made choices based on their original expectancies for success; that is, subjects in the no-information group who originally had high expectancies for success made choices similar to those who believed that they were successful, whereas those who originally had low expectancies for success made choices similar to those who believed that they had failed. Figure 11.2 shows how situational feedback interacts with the person variable of expectancy for success to influence choice of rewards.

A Conditional View of Personal Dispositions

Wright and Mischel (1987) have proposed a *conditional model* for understanding the influence of traits or personal dispositions. This view suggests that behavior is not caused by global personal traits but by people's perception of themselves in a particular situation. For example, a person who typically is socially shy may, under certain conditions, behave in an outgoing, extraverted manner.

The conditional view of traits emphasizes the importance of *goals* in predicting behavior. Whereas trait theory would suggest that global dispositions predict behavior, the conditional theory holds that behavior is shaped more by a person's specific goals. For example, traditional trait theory suggests that Gerry's conscientiousness will unify much of her behavior around this trait, causing Gerry to generally behave in a conscientious manner. However, goal-based conditional theory holds that Gerry will act to accomplish a specific outcome; that is, to achieve a goal such as admission to graduate school.

In an exploratory study to test this model, Wright and Mischel (1988) interviewed 8-year-old and 12-year-old children as well as adults, and asked them to report everything they knew about "target" groups of children. Both adults and children recognized the variability of other people's behavior, but adults were more certain about the conditions under which particular behaviors would occur. Whereas children would hedge their descriptions in such terms as "Joe sometimes hits other kids," adults would be more specific, for example, "Joe hits when provoked." These findings suggest that people readily recognize the interrelationship between situations and behavior and that they intuitively follow a conditional view of dispositions.

CONCEPT OF HUMANITY

Rotter and Mischel both see people as cognitive animals whose perceptions of events are more important than the events themselves. People are capable of construing events in a variety of ways, and these cognitive perceptions are more influential than the environment in determining the value of the reinforcer. Cognition enables different people to see the same situation differently and to place different values on reinforcement that follows their behavior.

Both Rotter and Mischel see humans as goal-directed animals who do not merely react to their environments, but who interact with their psychologically meaningful environments. Hence, cognitive social learning theory is more *teleological* or future-oriented than it is causal. People place positive value on those events that they perceive as moving them closer to their goals, and they place negative value on those that prevent them from reaching their goals. Goals, then, serve as criteria for evaluating events. People are motivated less by past experiences with reinforcement than by their expectations of future events.

Cognitive social learning theory holds that people move in the direction of goals they have established for themselves. These goals, however, change as people's expectancies for reinforcement and their preferences for one reinforcement over another change. Because people are continually in the process of setting goals, they have some choice in directing their lives. *Free choice* is not unlimited, however, because past experiences and limits to personal competencies partially determine behavior.

Because both Rotter and Mischel are realistic and pragmatic, they are difficult to rate on the *optimism vs. pessimism* dimension. They believe that people can be taught constructive strategies for problem solving and that they are capable of learning new behaviors at any point in life. However, they do not hold that people have within themselves an inherent force that moves them inevitably in the direction of psychological growth.

On the issue of *conscious vs. unconscious motives*, cognitive social learning theory generally leans in the direction of conscious forces. People can consciously set goals for themselves and consciously strive to solve old and new problems. However, people are not always conscious of the underlying motivations for much of their present behavior.

On the issue of personality being shaped by social or biological influences, cognitive social learning theory, of course, clearly emphasizes *social factors*. It does not deny the effects of genetics, but rather insists that the most significant aspects of personality are learned within a social context.

As for stressing *uniqueness or similarities*, Rotter can probably be placed most accurately in a middle position. People have individual histories and unique experiences that allow them to set personalized goals, but there are also enough similarities among people to allow for the construction of mathematical formulas which, if sufficient information were available, would permit reliable and accurate prediction of behavior. On the other hand, Mischel clearly places more emphasis on uniqueness than on similarities. Individual differences among people are due to differences in person variables and to the specific interactions between situations and behavior. In summary, cognitive social learning theory views people as forward-looking, purposive, unified, cognitive, social animals who are capable of evaluating present experiences and anticipated future events on the basis of goals they have chosen for themselves.

Related Research

The cognitive social learning theories of both Rotter and Mischel have generated much research. For example, Rotter's concept of locus of control has stimulated several thousand studies, and Mischel's notion of delay of gratification is a widely researched topic.

One interesting variation of Rotter's *locus of control* model has been the development of several instruments that attempt to measure people's belief that they can control their own health. A research group headed by Kenneth and Barbara Wallston (Wallston, Wallston, Kaplan, & Maides, 1976) originally developed a scale that tried to measure locus of control as it applied to health. Their Health Locus of Control Scale, however, soon proved unsatisfactory, so they constructed the Multidimensional Health Locus of Control Scales (Wallston, Wallston, & Devellis, 1978). The assumption underlying these and other health locus of control scales is that people who believe that they have considerable control over their own health (internals) will tend to have fewer illnesses than people who believe that luck or fate is the primary cause of illness (externals).

Later research by Marshall (1991) supported Wallston and Wallston's notion that health locus of control is multidimensional. In this study Marshall obtained responses to 15 locus-of-control items from 181 men who were receiving care at a Veterans Administration outpatient clinic. His analysis revealed four identifiable factors, which he termed self-blame, self-mastery, illness management, and illness prevention. Marshall hypothesized that, of these four dimensions, only self-mastery would predict health status. His reasoning was influenced by Bandura's concept of self-efficacy (see Chapter 10), which suggests that the perceived capacity to actually achieve desired outcomes is an important predictor of performance.

Just as Marshall had hypothesized, the only dimension of health locus of control that predicted health status was self-mastery. These results suggest that merely recognizing that one's behavior is related to illness is not sufficient to affect subsequent health; one must also be confident that he or she can perform the behaviors necessary to bring about change.

However, single-dimensional scales have also shown some promise in assessing people's beliefs about their personal control over health-related behaviors. Mills (1991) administered Rotter's locus-of-control scale to 18 alcoholic men from 18 to 59 years of age and to 13 obese men, age 19 to 63. All subjects were in treatment for their disorder. Because both obesity and alcoholism are related to "lack of control," one might assume that subjects in both groups would score low on internal control. However, Mills found that obese men were significantly higher on internal locus of control and lower in external control than alcoholic men. The reason for this difference seems to be that obese subjects, although they had little control over food, reported that they could control behaviors not related to food or weight. In contrast, alcoholics lacked control not only over drinking but also over other aspects of their lives.

A second topic that has stimulated a good deal of research is Rotter's concept of *interpersonal trust*. In one recent study, Gurtman (1992) investigated the interpersonal difficulties and complaints of high trusters and low trusters from the perspective of the interpersonal circumplex, developed by Jerry Wiggins (1982) and others. Gurtman assessed interpersonal difficulties with a variety of instruments, including the Inventory of Interpersonal Problems (Horowitz, Rosenberg, Baer, Ureño, & Villaseñor, 1988), which measures self-reported interpersonal problems with assertiveness, control, dependency, intimacy, submissiveness, and sociability.

Gurtman found that college students who scored low in trust reported a variety of interpersonal problems that extended beyond those due simply to lack of trust. Their difficulties tended to cluster around the hostile–dominant intersection of the interpersonal circumplex, indicating that they were more competitive, resentful, and vindictive than students who were high in interpersonal trust. Consistent with Rotter (1980), Gurtman found that high trusters reported few interpersonal difficulties, and that they are neither gullible nor exploitable.

For more than 35 years, Walter Mischel and his colleagues have conducted research on *delay of gratification*. Beginning when he was still at the University of Colorado and continuing when he went to Harvard, Mischel (1958, 1961a, 1961b) reported on a series of experiments he had conducted when he lived in the Caribbean. He found that the citizens of Trinidad who preferred larger delayed rewards over smaller immediate ones had higher needs for achievement and showed more social responsibility. Later, at Stanford University, Mischel teamed with his colleague, Albert Bandura (Bandura & Mischel, 1965), as well as a number of graduate students, to more fully pursue issues related to delay of gratification.

The delay-of-gratification concept avoids such global terms as willpower and ego strength, which do not explain why people who can exhibit self-control in one situation are not able to in others. Mischel has found that delay of gratification or self-control is specific, and that cognitive factors influence how long people will be able to wait for a reward.

Mischel and his colleagues investigated the correlates of delay of gratification in four- and five-year-old children attending the Bing Nursery School at Stanford (Mischel & Ebbesen, 1970; Mischel, Ebbesen, & Zeiss, 1972). The design of their studies generally called for an experimenter to show a child some interesting toys that the child could play with later. Then the experimenter would show the child a pair of treats with slightly different values, for example, two cookies vs. five pretzels or one marshmallow vs. two marshmallows. Next, the experimenter indicated that she must leave the room, but gave the child a choice between eating the less preferred treat at any time or waiting until the experimenter returned and then eating the preferred treat. The child could bring the experimenter back prematurely by ringing a bell, but this impatience, of course, would result in the child receiving the lesser of the two treats. Thus, the experimenter returned to the room when the child rang the bell, began eating a treat, or was able to wait for the entire predetermined length of time, usually 15 to 30 minutes.

In an early study, Mischel and Metzner (1962) found, as expected, that ability to delay gratification increases with age, intelligence, and shorter time intervals that the child is required to wait. Later, Mischel and Ebbesen (1970) were surprised to find that children were able to wait longer when the treat was out of sight. They had theorized that if children could see the reward, they would more likely trust that the experimenter would deliver it. However, their findings were directly opposite those that they had hypothesized; that is, when the children could see a reward, they were more likely to think about it, and thinking about a reinforcement decreased the delay time. Children who were able to wait the longest used a variety of self-distractions to avoid thinking about the reward. They looked away from the treat, closed their eyes, or sang songs in order to change the aversive waiting situation into a more pleasant one. This finding led Mischel and Moore (1973) to use symbolic representations of rewards to see what effect they would have on waiting time. They taught children to imagine that the real rewards were pictures and that the pictures of treats were real. They found that cognitive representations (that is, what children imagine in their heads) are more important than actual rewards in determining how long children can delay gratification. Children who faced real rewards but imagined that they were pictures were able to wait for a long time, whereas children who faced pictures but imagined that they were real were not able to wait as long.

In a review of these studies, Mischel (1978, p. 446) concluded that:

> The data from these experiments seem to contradict the notion that "will power" requires one to bear up and force oneself to maintain directed attention to things that are aversive, difficult, or boring. Rather than trying to maintain aversive activities such as delay of reward through "acts of will" and focused attention, effective self-control may hinge on *transforming* the difficult into the easy, the aversive into the pleasant, the boring into the interesting, while still maintaining the task-required (reward-contingent) activity.

Mischel and Baker (1975) studied *arousal* as a condition in children's ability to delay reinforcement. Using the typical delay-of-gratification design, these researchers gave half the children a choice between one marshmallow or two marshmallows, while the other half chose between one pretzel and two pretzels. All children waited with the relevant rewards facing them, either one or two marshmallows or one or two pretzels. The experimenters instructed children waiting for pretzels to focus their thoughts on the arousing qualities of the pretzels, such as their crunchy, salty taste, and they instructed children waiting for marshmallows to think about the sweet, soft, and chewy taste of the marshmallows. These children comprised the *consume-relevant* group. In this arousal situation, the focus was on the motivating or "hot" qualities of the snack.

The experiment also called for a *consume-irrelevant* condition in which children were given the same instructions, except that those waiting for marshmallows were told to think about the crunchy, salty taste of pretzels, whereas those waiting for pretzels were instructed to think about the soft, sweet, chewy taste of marshmallows.

Mischel and Baker also introduced two transformation conditions. In the *transform-relevant* condition, they gave children instructions designed to distract attention from the consummatory aspects of the snacks. For example, they instructed children waiting for pretzels to think of pretzels as long, thin, brown logs and children waiting for marshmallows to think of them as white, puffy clouds or cotton balls. In the *transform-irrelevant* condition, children were given the same set of instructions, except they were switched, so that children facing pretzels were told to think of marshmallows as white puffy clouds or cotton balls and vice versa. Mischel and Baker also used a control group that received no instructions.

Results showed that children waiting for one snack while thinking about the "cool" or nonconsummatory aspects of the other were able to delay gratification the longest, almost 17 minutes. The second longest mean delay time (about 13 minutes) was achieved by the transform-relevant subjects; that is, those who could cognitively transform pretzels into logs or marshmallows into clouds. However, those who had the same type of thoughts directed at the snack that was not their reward could wait less than five minutes. Children in the consume-relevant group (those focusing on the salty aspect of the pretzels or the sweet taste of the marshmallows) waited only about five-and-a-half minutes. The control group that received no information had a mean delay time of about nine minutes, or somewhat less than that of students who cognitively transformed the snacks, but somewhat more than those who focused on the arousing qualities of the reward object. These results suggest that attention to the rewards may either facilitate or interfere with delay of gratification, depending on whether the focus is arousing or abstract.

Mischel, Shoda, and Rodriguez (1989) summarized much of this earlier research as well as later follow-up studies that investigated characteristics of adolescents who had been subjects in the nursery school experiments. Mischel, Shoda, and Peake (1988) and Shoda, Mischel, and Peake (1990) found that subjects who waited longer at age four were described by their parents 10 years later as being more academically and socially competent than their peers. They were also better able to cope with frustration and stress, more capable of resisting temptation, more verbally fluent, more able to express ideas, more self-assured, and better able to concentrate, plan, and think ahead than their classmates. Moreover, seconds of delay time at age four predicted Scholastic Aptitude Test (SAT) scores when applying for college; that is, the longer children could wait for a reward at age four, the higher they generally scored on the SAT more than 10 years later.

Mischel's research on delay of gratification suggests that self-control is not dependent on willpower, but on people's ability to distract themselves from an unpleasant task. It also demonstrates that one's ability to delay gratification is positively related to later social and academic competence and to the ability to cope with frustration and stress.

CRITIQUE OF COGNITIVE SOCIAL LEARNING THEORY

Cognitive social learning theory is attractive to those who value the rigors of learning theory and the speculative assumption that people are forward-looking, cognitive beings. Rotter and Mischel have evolved learning theories for thinking, valuing, goal-directed humans rather than for laboratory animals. Like other theories, cognitive social learning theory's value rests on how it rates on the five criteria for a useful theory.

The first criterion of a useful theory is its ability to *generate significant research*. We have seen that the theories of Rotter and Mischel have both generated large amounts of research. For example, Rotter's concept of locus of control has been, and continues to be, one of the most widely researched topics in psychological literature (Rotter, 1982; Strickland, 1989). Locus of control, however, is not the core of Rotter's personality theory, and the theory itself has not generated a comparable level of research. On the other hand, Mischel's theory has generated somewhat less research, but that research is more relevant to his core ideas, namely the consistency paradox and delay of gratification.

Second, how well does cognitive social learning theory *organize knowledge*? Here, Rotter's theory fares somewhat better than Mischel's. Most observable behaviors can be made meaningful by Rotter's general prediction formula and its components of need potential, freedom of movement, and need value. When behavior is seen as a function of these variables, it takes on a different hue. Even bizarre or "self-destructive" behaviors can be viewed in terms of freedom of movement and need value. In Rotter's framework, for example, self-destructive behaviors indicate that the person generally expects to be reinforced for those actions (freedom of movement). In addition, that person generally places positive value (need value) on the type of anticipated reinforcements. This schema renders comprehensible much seemingly unintelligible and inappropriate behavior. By comparison, Mischel's theory is narrower and thus does not lend itself to global explanations of behavior. Nevertheless, Mischel provides an excellent explanation for the long-observed but inadequately understood phenomenon of trait inconsistency.

Does cognitive social learning theory serve as a useful *guide to action*? On this criterion the theory would be rated only moderately high. Rotter's ideas on psychotherapy are quite explicit and are a helpful guide to the therapist, but his theory of personality is not as practical. The mathematical formulas serve as a useful framework for organizing knowledge, but they do not suggest any specific course of action for the practitioner because the value of each factor within the formula cannot be known with mathematical certainty. Likewise, Mischel's theory is only moderately useful to the therapist, teacher, or parent. It suggests to practitioners that they should expect people to behave differently in different situations and even from one time to another, but it provides them with few specific guidelines for action.

Are the theories of Rotter and Mischel *internally consistent*? Rotter is careful in defining terms so that the same term does not have two or more meanings. In addition, separate components of the theory are logically compatible. The basic prediction formula, with its four specific factors, is logically consistent with the three broader variables of the general prediction formula. Mischel, like Bandura (see Chapter 10) has evolved a theory from a solid empirical research foundation, a procedure that greatly facilitates consistency.

Is cognitive social learning theory *parsimonious*? In general, it is relatively simple and does not purport to offer explanations for all of human personality. Again, the emphasis on research rather than philosophical speculation has contributed to the parsimony of the cognitive social learning theories of both Rotter and Mischel.

Chapter Summary

The cognitive social learning theories of both Rotter and Mischel attempt to synthesize the strengths of reinforcement theory with those of cognitive theory. According to Rotter, people's behavior in a specific situation is a function of their expectations of reinforcements and the strength of the needs satisfied by those reinforcements. The cognitive processes of thinking and memory allow people to anticipate possible reinforcements in situations that are unique and unfamiliar.

In specific situations behavior is estimated by the *basic prediction formula*, which suggests that the potential for a given behavior to occur—in a particular situation in relation to a specific reinforcement—is a function of the person's expectancy that a specific reinforcement will follow the given behavior, plus the value of the reinforcement in that particular situation.

Because the basic prediction formula is limited to specific situations, Rotter proposed an analogous formula that predicts functionally related behaviors in different situations. This *general prediction formula* states that need potential is a function of freedom of movement and need value.

Need potential refers to the possible occurrence of a set of functionally related behaviors directed toward the satisfaction of a goal or a similar set of goals. *Freedom of movement* is the average expectancy that a set of related behaviors will be reinforced. *Need value* is the degree to which a person prefers one set of reinforcements to another.

In many situations people develop *generalized expectancies* for success because a similar set of experiences has been previously reinforced. Two such generalized expectancies are *internal or external locus of control* and *interpersonal trust*. Locus of control refers to people's belief that they can or cannot control their lives, and interpersonal trust is a generalized expectancy that the word of another can be relied on.

Rotter defined *maladaptive behavior* as those actions that fail to move a person closer to a desired goal. Because maladaptive behavior usually arises from a combination of distorted goals and low expectancies for success, Rotter's method of *psychotherapy* aims toward changing goals and eliminating low expectancies.

Mischel began his research career investigating *delay of reinforcement*, and from this work he developed the notion that people react differently in different situations and that the previously supposed consistency of personal traits is a myth. Mischel does not deny the existence of traits but suggests that we should not rely on them as a major explanation of behavior.

Mischel believes, instead, that behavior is shaped by the *interaction* of person variables with situation variables. Some important person variables include *competencies*, or what one can do; *encoding strategies*, or a person's way of construing and categorizing information; *expectancies*, or one's beliefs about the perceived consequences of one's actions; *values, preferences, and goals*; and the *self-regulatory system*, or one's self-imposed standards.

Mischel has also adopted a *conditional approach* to understanding behavior, which suggests that people's behavior is largely shaped by their perception of themselves in certain conditions.

Cognitive social learning theory adopts a *concept of humanity* that holds that people are motivated by goals, and that they use their cognitive abilities to evaluate movement toward those goals.

The theory is relatively useful in its ability to organize our current knowledge about human behavior. In addition, Rotter's concept of locus of control has been one of the most widely researched topics in psychology during the past 35 years, and Mischel's notions of trait inconsistency and delay of gratification have stimulated much related research.

Suggested Readings

MISCHEL, W. (1990). Personality dispositions revisited and revised: A view after three decades. In L. A. Pervin (Ed.), *Handbook of personality: Theory and research* (pp. 111–134). New York: Guilford Press.

In this chapter Mischel discusses the consistency paradox, explains the person variables for understanding human behavior, reviews some of the research on delay of reinforcement, and suggests a conditional view of personal dispositions.

MISCHEL, W., SHODA, Y., & RODRIGUEZ, M. L. (1989). Delay of gratification in children. *Science, 244*, 933–938.

In this article Mischel et al. review 20 years of research on delay of gratification, including follow-up studies showing that children who are able to wait for a reward grow up to display many positive qualities as adolescents.

PHARES, E. J. (1988). Perceived control. In E. J. Phares, *Introduction to personality* (2d ed.) (pp. 463–493). Glenview, IL: Scott, Foresman.

In this chapter Phares, a student of Rotter who helped develop the Internal–External Control Scale during the late 1950s, discusses the research on perceived control, learned helplessness, and internal–external control of reinforcement.

ROTTER, J. B. (1975). Some problems and misconceptions related to the construct of internal vs. external control of reinforcement. *Journal of Consulting and Clinical Psychology, 43*, 56–67.

Although locus of control is a popular topic in psychology, people have had misconceptions about it almost from the beginning. With this article Rotter hoped to clear up some of the problems and misconceptions related to internal and external control of reinforcement.

ROTTER, J. B. (1982). Introduction. In J. B. Rotter, *The development and applications of social learning theory: Selected papers* (pp. 1–12). New York: Praeger.

In this brief introduction, Rotter discusses seven postulates that underlie his theory of personality.

ROTTER, J. B. (1993). Expectancies. In C.E. Walker (Ed.), *The history of clinical psychology in autobiography*: Vol. 2 (pp. 273–284). Pacific Grove, CA: Brooks/Cole.

This recent autobiography of Rotter provides insights into his personal life and his work.

PART FOUR

Dispositional Theories

12 Cattell and Eysenck
Trait and Factor Theories

13 Allport
Psychology of the Individual

Trait and Factor Theories

Chapter Twelve

OVERVIEW
BIOGRAPHY OF RAYMOND B. CATTELL
BASICS OF FACTOR ANALYSIS
CATTELL'S TRAIT THEORY
    P Technique
    Media of Observation
SOURCE TRAITS
    Temperament Traits
    Dynamic Traits
THE DYNAMIC CALCULUS
THE HERITABILITY OF TRAITS
EYSENCK'S FACTOR THEORY
BIOGRAPHY OF HANS J. EYSENCK
MEASUREMENT OF PERSONALITY
    Criteria for Identifying Factors
    Hierarchy of Measures
TYPES
    Extraversion
    Neuroticism
    Psychoticism
BOX: WHAT DIMENSIONS UNDERLIE PERSONALITY?
CONCEPT OF HUMANITY
RELATED RESEARCH
CRITIQUE OF TRAIT AND FACTOR THEORIES
CHAPTER SUMMARY
SUGGESTED READINGS

CATTELL   EYSENCK

*H*olly, a 24-year-old nurse, is dissatisfied with her job. She has few opportunities to make important decisions and resents the preferential treatment demanded by and given to doctors. A first-born child with a sister 10 years younger, Holly has always been independent. Lack of autonomy at work, however, is creating an almost unbearable situation for her.

Holly has lived with her boyfriend, Tom, for two years, and his tolerant and nonpossessive attitudes toward her are a large measure of her attraction to him. Tom is quite accepting of Holly, even those risk-taking behaviors that he personally finds frightening. Holly smokes, drinks heavily at times, drives her sports car at a high rate of speed, and uses marijuana regularly. In addition, she likes to climb small mountains and sky dive, even though both activities arouse fear in her.

While in high school and college, most of Holly's friends were gay men. She enjoyed their company partly because they had artistic interests but mostly because they were "different." She frequently went to gay bars with several of these men and was sometimes propositioned by gay women. Although she occasionally fantasized about having sex with some of these women, she never did. However, she has had a number of sexual affairs with men, both before and after she began living with Tom.

Holly takes personal pride in her acceptance of those people who are not always understood or accepted by others. She continues to have many friends who are homosexual, African-American, poor, or artistic. Many of her colleagues at work see her as a "radical" with ultraliberal ideas. She antagonizes some of the other hospital staff members with her honest, forthright manner of speaking, and many of the male physicians are irritated by her assertiveness, self-sufficiency, and lack of deference. However, Holly is not a troublemaker. She is sensitive and nurturant to her patients, and they generally respond positively to her. Unfortunately, patient care is becoming an increasingly smaller part of her job and Holly is seriously considering quitting.

OVERVIEW

In this brief description of Holly, we have used several adjectives to describe her characteristic behavior. These descriptive and distinguishing qualities of Holly can be called *traits*. A trait is a relatively permanent disposition of an individual, which is inferred from that person's behavior.

In Chapter 13 we will see that Gordon Allport developed a personality theory that utilized the concept of traits or dispositions. Allport, however, relied more on intuition and deductive reasoning than on mathematical procedures. Raymond B. Cattell and Hans J. Eysenck, on the other hand, have each applied a more systematic method to the problems of identifying traits. The approach they use is **factor analysis,** a technique that will be briefly described later. Because they employed different factor analytic procedures, Cattell and Eysenck arrived at different traits. Cattell identified a comparatively large number of traits, whereas Eysenck remains convinced that only a few basic factors underlie human personality.

Cattell has spent his professional life mapping the entire sphere of human personality. He found a number of both normal and abnormal temperament or structural traits, and then turned his attention to measuring the dynamics of personality. To that end he discovered a variety of motivational traits. Cattell believes that if we know both the structure and the dynamics of personality, we can predict human behavior.

On the other hand, Eysenck has used factor analysis to extract only three general factors or types—extraversion/introversion, neuroticism/stability, and psychoticism/superego.

BIOGRAPHY OF RAYMOND B. CATTELL

Raymond Bernard Cattell was born in Staffordshire, England, on March 20, 1905, of proper Victorian middle-class parents. The second of three sons, he was protected by his mother from a domineering father who centered his scrutiny on the oldest child. This relative freedom allowed young Raymond to roam the beach of Devonshire, where his family had moved when he was six, and to explore the coast in boats he had learned to sail at an early age (Cattell, 1974a). Although three years younger, he nearly caught up to his older brother in school, but the rivalry between the two was lessened when the older boy was moved to a different school.

His relatively carefree childhood was dampened by World War I. Cattell was too young to be a soldier, but he had viewed the devastation of war and had watched the trainloads of bloodstained wounded. Suddenly the tranquility of childhood had vanished: "Silently there came an abiding sense of seriousness into my life, compounded of a feeling that one could not be less dedicated than these [wounded soldiers], and of a new sense, for a boy, of the brevity of life and the need to accomplish while one might" (Cattell, 1974a, p. 63).

At 16 he entered King's College of the University of London and at 19 graduated with highest honors with a degree in chemistry and physics. As an undergraduate, his interests were wide-ranging and included a concern for social problems. By his final year he had realized that his life would be devoted to psychology, so, against the advice of his physical science classmates, he pursued an advanced degree and a career in psychology. In 1929 he received a Ph.D. from the

University of London, and in 1937 was awarded an honorary D.Sc. from the same school. As a graduate student, he worked in the laboratory of Charles Spearman, the noted British quantitative psychologist, who was then at work on his monumental studies of human abilities. After finishing his degree, Cattell found that his friends from undergraduate days were right—there were no jobs available in academic psychology (Cattell, 1974a, 1993).

Consequently, he took a position as an "educationist" at Exeter University, where he remained until 1932, when he moved to Leicester, a city that was beginning a child guidance clinic. His five years as director of the Child Guidance Clinic at Leicester were spent mostly in administration and clinical work, but he was able to conduct some research on intelligence testing and to publish several articles and a book during this time. By 1937, Cattell realized that his research plans could only be realized in a university setting. However, only six psychology professorships existed in all of England, and the same "hale and hearty" professors who had occupied those positions 10 years earlier were still entrenched (Cattell, 1974a).

As a consequence, he decided to accept E. L. Thorndike's offer to journey to the United States and become a research assistant at Columbia University in New York. Thus Cattell followed in the steps of Abraham H. Maslow (Chapter 15), who had been Thorndike's assistant two years earlier. Cattell was reluctant to leave his beloved England and intended to remain in the United

States for only one year. After leaving Columbia, however, he accepted what later became the G. Stanley Hall professorship at Clark University in Worcester, Massachusetts. That position, unfortunately, did not allow him a relaxed atmosphere for psychological research and he soon moved to neighboring Harvard as a lecturer.

During World War II he worked with the Adjutant General's office developing personality tests to use in the selection of officers. His work there taught him the advantages of the team approach, which was generally lacking in most universities. After the war he finally found the academic position that allowed him the opportunity to conduct research in the manner he had long desired. This position was with the University of Illinois, where he was to spend 30 years as director of the Laboratory of Personality and Group Analysis. Most of Cattell's productive years were spent at Illinois, where he was eventually honored as Distinguished Research Professor. In 1949, he helped found the Institute for Personality and Ability Testing (IPAT), an organization that has served as an outlet for the many tests developed by Cattell and his colleagues.

In 1973, Cattell retired from the University of Illinois and moved to Boulder, Colorado, where he established the Institute for Research on Morality and Adjustment. After a short time in Colorado, Cattell joined the Department of Psychology at the University of Hawaii. Currently, he is with the Forest Institute of Professional Psychology in Honolulu, Hawaii. Cattell has remained active, both professionally and physically. Johnson (1980, p. 300) reported that "he swims in the ocean daily, works at least as hard as an assistant professor up for tenure and not sure that it will be granted."

Early in his career, while still in England and even before he completed his Ph.D., Cattell set a plan for his life's work, much as Skinner (Chapter 9) had outlined his goals for the years 1930–1960. Cattell's strategy, which took only a year to design but a lifetime to execute, was to measure and describe personality structure objectively from three media of observation—ratings of life behavior, questionnaires, and objective test data (Cattell, 1974b). These concepts are more fully discussed later.

Cattell's early professional life was not always easy. His long hours of work, poor pay, and residence in a damp basement flat had adverse effects on both his health and his marriage (Cattell, 1974a). He developed, as a result of his work schedule and eating habits, a functional stomach disorder, from which he never completely recovered. Also, his wife of two years, Monica Rogers, not being accustomed to such a Spartan life, left him. Cattell had one son by his first marriage and three daughters and another son by his second marriage to Alberta Schuettler, a mathematician he married in 1946.

Cattell has been a prolific writer, having published some three dozen books and 400 articles. He has also won many awards, including the Darwin Fellowship, the Wenner Gren Prize of the New York Academy of Sciences, presidency of the Society of Multivariate Experimental Psychology, a distinguished foreign honorary membership in the British Psychological Society, and the American Psychological Association Award for Distinguished Service to Measurement. Now in the ninth decade of his life, Cattell continues a diminished, yet active and productive work schedule. He admits that his personality theory still has gaps, but he adds that "filling them is a matter of whether psychologists are ready by training to attack the complex problems involved. But I have no doubts about the firmness of the theory so far built up by the pursuit of measurement of structures and processes" (Cattell, 1993, p. 110).

BASICS OF FACTOR ANALYSIS

Both Cattell and Eysenck use factor analysis to identify traits. A comprehensive knowledge of the mathematical operations involved in factor analysis is not essential to our understanding of trait and factor theories of personality. Nevertheless, a general description of factor analysis should be helpful. To use factor analysis we first begin by making specific observations on many individuals. These observations are then quantified in some manner; for example, height is measured in inches;

weight in pounds; aptitude in test scores; job performance by rating scales; and so on. Let us assume that we have 1000 such measures on 5000 people. Our next step is to determine which of these variables (scores) are related to which other variables and to what extent. To do this, we would calculate the *correlation coefficient* between each variable and each of the other 999 scores. As we saw in Chapter 1, a correlation coefficient is a mathematical procedure for expressing the degree of correspondence between two sets of scores. To correlate 1000 variables with the other 999 scores would involve 499,500 individual correlations (1000 multiplied by 999 divided by 2). Results of these calculations would require a table of intercorrelations or a *matrix* with 1000 rows and 1000 columns. Some of these correlations would be high and positive, some near zero, and some would be negative. For example, we might observe a high positive correlation between leg length and height, because one is partially a measure of the other. We may also find a positive correlation between a measure of leadership ability and ratings on social poise. This relationship might be due to the fact that they are each part of a more basic underlying trait—self-confidence.

With 1000 separate variables, our table of intercorrelations would be too cumbersome. At this point we would turn to *factor analysis*, which can account for a large number of variables with a smaller number of more basic dimensions. For our purposes, these more basic dimensions can be called *traits*; that is, factors that represent a cluster of closely related variables. For example, we may find high positive intercorrelations among test scores in algebra, geometry, trigonometry, and calculus. We have now identified a cluster of scores, which we might call Factor M, which represents mathematical ability. In similar fashion we can identify a number of other **factors**, but that number, of course, will be smaller than the original number of observations.

Our next step is to determine the extent to which each individual score contributes to the various factors. Correlations of scores with factors are called **factor loadings**. For example, if scores for algebra, geometry, trigonometry, and calculus contribute highly to Factor M, but not to other factors, they will have high factor loadings on M. Factor loadings give us an indication of the purity of the various factors and enable us to interpret their meanings.

Traits generated through factor analysis may be either unipolar or bipolar. **Unipolar traits** are scaled from zero to some large amount. Height, weight, and general intelligence are examples of unipolar traits. **Bipolar traits**, on the other hand, extend from one pole to an opposite pole, with zero representing a midpoint. Introversion vs. extraversion, liberalism vs. conservatism, and social ascendancy vs. timidity are examples of bipolar traits.

CATTELL'S TRAIT THEORY

Cattell has opposed the clinical methods of earlier personality theorists as being unscientific and based more on unsupported speculation than on hard data.

In his scientific analysis of personality, he uses an *inductive method* as opposed to a *hypothetical-deductive method*. In the latter approach the investigator has some hypothesis or theory in mind *before* gathering data. In other words, the nature of the scores that enter the correlation matrix is determined by some previous ideas as to what traits are to be measured. With Cattell's inductive approach, the investigator, with no preexisting hypotheses, collects a large body of data, runs a factor analysis on these data, and, only after these results are available, draws hypotheses that can be tested later.

An understanding of Cattell's scientific analysis of personality is enhanced by an acquaintance with his methods of investigation and with the rationale underlying them. Therefore, we must briefly discuss P technique and the three media of observation.

P Technique

When Cattell was a lecturer at Harvard during the early 1940s, he often lunched with Gordon Allport (Chapter 13), and the relationship between the two proved to be productive. Allport was a strong advocate of individual or *unique traits*, and he chided factor analysts in general and Cattell in particular for limiting investigations to *common traits*, that is, traits extracted from the study of many people. At that time the correlational method typically used was the so-called R technique, which involves many persons taking two or more tests on essentially one occasion. Results of factor analytical studies using the R technique can only identify traits that are common to a large number of people. Allport's criticisms stimulated Cattell to begin thinking of ways by which the single case could be extensively and objectively studied. The result was the **P technique**, a correlational method that involves one person taking two or more tests on many occasions. Actually, as used by Cattell, the P technique employs 30 or more variables obtained from one person on more than 100 occasions. In the beginning, that one person was Cattell's second wife, who understandably grew tired after nine weeks of daily testing with "electric shocks and other indignities of the experiment" (Cattell, 1974b, p. 106). Cattell, of course, has since found other volunteers and has continued to use the P technique.

As a companion to the P technique, Cattell devised the dR (differential R) technique, which correlates the scores of a large number of people on many variables obtained on two different occasions. The P and dR techniques should complement one another in determining common state or mood patterns. The P technique alone is susceptible to sampling errors with regard to subjects, whereas the dR technique is open to error in the sampling of occasions. In other words, although the P technique satisfies Allport's call for methods of studying the single case, factors derived from it cannot be generalized to other people. On the other hand, although the dR technique allows for generalization to other people, it samples only two points in time, either one of which might be affected by some unusual event. By combining the P technique with the dR technique, one is able to obtain information about moods or states that are shared by many people.

Cattell distinguishes between mood states and traits. The concept of **state** refers to temporary changes in behavior as the result of immediate environmental changes. Examples of psychological mood states include anxiety, stress, anger, fear, and arousal. Physiological states include heart rate, body temperature, and blood pressure. Fluctuations in these behavioral and physiological states are most reliably calculated by the P and dR techniques. A **trait**, on the other hand, is a relatively permanent property or disposition, defined by Cattell (1979–1980, Vol. 1, p. 14) as "that which defines what a person will do when faced with a defined situation." Traits are revealed by the traditional R technique, a correlational procedure Cattell has continued to use.

Media of Observation

From the beginning of his professional career Cattell has concentrated his psychometric procedures on three different media of observation, that is, three sources of data that enter the correlation matrix (Cattell, 1983). The first is one's life record, or **L data**, which comes from observations made by other people. It includes both objective information—called L(T) data—and more subjective information based on ratings, or L(R) data. An example of L(T) data might be number of residences in a 20-year period, and an example of L(R) data would be an evaluation of a worker by a supervisor.

The second source of information is the person's self-reports, or **Q data**, which are based on questionnaires that call for a person to respond to questions or statements on the basis of self-observation and introspection. Most personality inventories, for example, yield Q data. Because Q data rely on self-observations, they are subject to deliberate faking and self-delusion. Therefore, they should be corroborated by correlations with behavioral data. Unverified self-reports are regarded as Q' data, whereas only those that have been corroborated by objective behavioral scales can truly be called Q data (Cattell & Kline, 1977).

The third medium of observation is **T data**, or information obtained from objective tests, that is, tests for which the true purpose is hidden from the subject or for which answers cannot be faked. Cattell and Warburton (1967) have identified over 200 objective tests, including both behavioral and physiological measures. Ability tests that require subjects to do as well as they can yield T data, but so, too, do personality inventories such as the Rorschach and other "projective" instruments where the subject is unaware of the purpose of the test. These latter tests, however, are not favored by Cattell because a measure of subjectivity enters into their scoring (Cattell & Kline, 1977). Cattell's use of L, Q, and T data gives his investigations a false appearance of being unrelated, but viewed from the perspective of his entire career, one can see that all his studies have been attempts to measure the global concept of personality.

SOURCE TRAITS

Cattell (1950, p. 2) defined personality as "that which permits a prediction of what a person will do in a given situation." How can these predictions most accurately be made? Cattell's answer is to measure and describe the *source traits* that underlie behavior. Source traits must be distinguished from *surface traits*. In Cattell's system surface traits are not very important except as starting points and as indicators of source traits. Allport and Odbert (1936) identified nearly 18,000 trait-names in an unabridged dictionary, then reduced the list to more than 4500, most of which could be considered as surface traits. Cattell used this list as a starting point for factor analyzing personality traits. Many of these 4500 traits are interrelated; that is, they tend to cluster together. If several surface traits are highly interrelated, then some underlying source must be holding the traits together.

The underlying factor responsible for the intercorrelation among surface traits is called a *source trait*. Source traits are smaller in number than surface traits, but they are better predictors of behavior. Figure 12.1 shows a hypothetical example of three surface traits—humor, gregariousness, and unselfishness—that cluster together with considerable overlap or intercorrelation among them. What holds these surface traits together? That is, what do these three traits have in common? If surface traits consistently cluster together, then some common trait, represented by the shaded area in Figure 12.1, must be the unifying source. In this case, that source trait might be called *friendliness*.

Source traits can be identified through each of the three media of observation. Ideally, if measurement techniques in L, Q, and T data were perfectly reliable and valid, then information from any one of the three would yield exactly the same factors or source traits as data from the other two. Practically, of course, this state of infallibility has not yet been reached, but Cattell (1957, 1979–1980) has discovered some significant overlap among the various media of observation, with especially good matches in factors obtained from L and Q data.

Temperament Traits

We have seen that traits can be divided into *common* (shared by many) and *unique* (peculiar to one individual). Also, *source traits* can be distinguished from trait indicators called *surface traits*. A third dimension for dividing traits is by classifying them into *temperament*, *motivation* (dynamic), and *ability*. Traits of temperament are concerned with *how* a person behaves, motivation deals with *why* one behaves, and ability refers to *how far* or *how fast* one can perform. (A discussion of abilities need not detain us here, but the interested reader is referred to Cattell [1971] for a lengthy discussion on the structure of abilities.)

Over the years Cattell and his associates have identified some 35 primary, or first-order, traits measuring personality. Twenty-three of these factors characterize the normal population and 12 measure the pathological dimension. Temperament

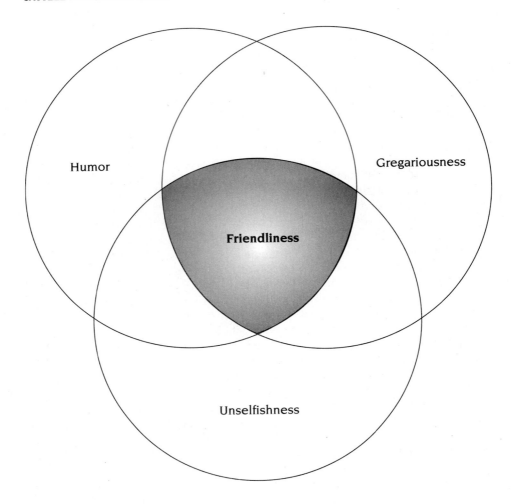

Figure 12.1   *Three Surface Traits Held Together by the Source Trait of Friendliness*

traits have been isolated using L and Q data obtained from both adult and child samples (Cattell, 1983).

Normal Traits

The largest and most frequently studied of the normal traits are the 16 personality factors found on Cattell's (1949) Sixteen Personality Factors Questionnaire (16 PF scale). Because the 16 PF is a personality inventory in a questionnaire format, each of the 16 traits, of course, is obtained through Q media. The seven additional factors that make up the total of 23 normal traits were originally identified only through L data, although some of them, particularly J (Zeppia) and K (social uncon-cern), show up in the more sophisticated measures of Q data (Cattell, 1979–1980). Table 12.1 depicts the 23 primary source traits found in normal personality of both adults and children. Cattell made up unusual trait names, because he wanted peo-ple to see each of these traits without a predisposition to attach conventional meanings to them. He began his career with no bias regarding the number or name of traits and types, and he wished that others would also see traits from an unbiased point of view. In his words, he "forsook the 'mainstream' of existing concepts about personality types and traits, and started by factoring afresh the 'personality sphere' of total human behavior" (Cattell, 1990, p. 101).

As seen in Table 12.1, normal primary source traits in L and Q data are lettered from A through Q_7. (Traits identified through T media are numbered according to the Universal Index system, for example, U.I.1, U.I.2, U.I.3, etc.). Traits are lettered in descending order of magnitude. In other words, Factor A (Sizia/Affectia) is the largest factor, meaning that it emerges the most clearly from factor analyses and accounts for the largest amount of variance. The size of this factor agrees with clinical practice and with everyday observation, which suggests that an obvious dimension of personality is flatness of affect (Sizia) vs. proneness to affect (Affectia). Likewise, Factor B (Intelligence) is a substantial factor easily noted in the mea-surement of personality. Incidentally, Factor B represents the ability dimension of personality, whereas the other primary source traits are basically temperament traits. Because each succeeding factor becomes "fuzzier" or more difficult to extract, Factors N through Q_7 are termed traits of lesser variance (Cattell, 1979–1980). These latter factors are successively weaker and more difficult for the factor analyst to identify with certainty.

The 23 traits reveal a complete picture of normal personality, at least in terms of temperament traits. All measures of normal temperament, whether from Cattell's laboratory or from some other source, whether obtained from adult samples or from children, should match with one or more of these 23 primary traits. In other words, probably all the important personality traits have now been identified by Cattell and his associates. Cattell, in fact, stated some time ago that "the pioneer years of hewing out the major human personality structures are essentially over" (Cattell, 1974a, p. 86). Subsequent work has been aimed at identifying traits across the three media sources within each of the various age groups and across cultures, and at refining the precise psychological meaning of these 23 traits (Cattell, 1993).

Abnormal Traits

Cattell believes that pathological individuals possess the same traits as normal people, but, in addition, they exhibit certain abnormal traits. However, normal and abnormal traits overlap to some extent. For example, factors such as low ego strength and guilt proneness are strongly characteristic of neurotic and psychotic individuals, although they also appear among the 23 normal factors (Cattell, 1979–1980).

TABLE 12.1   Cattell's 23 Normal Primary Source Traits

FACTOR	LOW SCORE DESCRIPTION	HIGH SCORE DESCRIPTION
A	SIZIA Reserved, detached, critical, aloof	AFFECTIA Warmhearted, outgoing, easygoing, participating
B	LOW INTELLIGENCE[1] Low mental capacity, dull, quitting	HIGH INTELLIGENCE High mental capacity, bright, persevering
C	LOW EGO STRENGTH Affected by feelings, easily upset, changeable	HIGH EGO STRENGTH Emotionally stable, faces reality, calm
D	PHLEGMATIC TEMPERAMENT[2] Undemonstrative, deliberate, inactive, stodgy	EXCITABILITY Excitable, impatient, demanding, overactive, unrestrained
E	SUBMISSIVE Obedient, mild, easily led, docile, accommodating	DOMINANCE Assertive, aggressive, competitive, stubborn
F	DESURGENCY Sober, taciturn, serious	SURGENCY Enthusiastic, heedless, happy-go-lucky
G	LOW SUPEREGO STRENGTH Disregards rules and group moral standards, expedient	HIGH SUPEREGO STRENGTH Conscientious, persistent, moralistic, staid
H	THRECTIA Shy, timid, restrained, threat-sensitive	PARMIA Adventurous, "thick-skinned," socially bold
I	HARRIA Tough-minded, rejects illusions	PERMSIA Tender-minded, sensitive, dependent, overprotected
J	ZEPPIA[2] Zestful, liking group action	COASTHENIA Circumspect individualism, reflective, internally restrained
K	SOCIAL UNCONCERN[2] Socially untutored, unconcerned, boorish	SOCIAL-ROLE CONCERN Socially mature, alert, self-disciplined
L	ALAXIA Trusting, accepting conditions	PROTENSION Suspecting, jealous, dogmatic
M	PRAXERNIA Practical, has "down to earth" concerns	AUTIA Imaginative, bohemian, absent-minded
N	NAIVETE Forthright, unpretentious	SHREWDNESS Astute, worldly, polished, socially aware

[1] Factor B (INTELLIGENCE) is an ability trait rather than a temperament trait.
[2] One of the "seven missing factors," so termed because they were not identified by the original 16 PF.
SOURCE: R. B. Cattell, Personality and learning theory, Vol. 1. New York: Springer Publishing Company, 1979–1980, pp. 61–73. Copyright 1979 by Springer Publishing Company, Inc., New York 10012. Adapted by permission.

TABLE 12.1   *Cattell's 23 Normal Primary Source Traits (continued)*

FACTOR	LOW SCORE DESCRIPTION	HIGH SCORE DESCRIPTION
O	UNTROUBLED ADEQUACY Self-assured, placid, secure, complacent	GUILT PRONENESS Apprehensive, self-reproaching, insecure, troubled
P	CAUTIOUS INACTIVITY[2] Melancholy, cautious, takes no risks	SANGUINE CASUALNESS Sanguine, speculative, independent
Q_1	CONSERVATISM Disinclined to change, respects traditional values	RADICALISM Experimenting, analytic, free-thinking
Q_2	GROUP DEPENDENCY A "joiner," sound follower	SELF-SUFFICIENCY Self-sufficient, resourceful, prefers own decisions
Q_3	LOW SELF-SENTIMENT Uncontrolled, lax, follows own urges	HIGH SELF-SENTIMENT Controlled, exacting will power, socially precise, compulsive, follows self-image
Q_4	LOW ERGIC TENSION Relaxed, tranquil, unfrustrated, composed	HIGH ERGIC TENSION Tense, frustrated, driven, overwrought, fretful
Q_5	LACK OF SOCIAL CONCERN[2] Does not volunteer for social service, experiences no obligation, self-sufficient	GROUP DEDICATION WITH SENSED INADEQUACY Concerned with social good works, not doing enough, joins in social endeavors
Q_6	SELF-EFFACEMENT[2] Quiet, self-effacing	SOCIAL PANACHE Feels unfairly treated by society, self-expressive, makes abrupt antisocial remarks
Q_7	LACKS EXPLICIT SELF-EXPRESSION[2] Is not garrulous in conversation	EXPLICIT SELF-EXPRESSION Enjoys verbal-social expression, likes dramatic entertainment, follows fashionable ideas

Cattell (1973) hypothesizes two forms of pathology. The first is an *imbalance of normal function*. For example, Affectia (Factor A) carried to extreme would result in a manic-depressive disorder. The second form of abnormality is a separate and distinct disease process, characterized by traits not found among the 23 normal factors. The abnormal traits listed in Table 12.2 represent the second category, that is, *pathological traits as separate factors*. The first seven, symbolized by the letter D, represent depressive traits. The last five (Pa, Pp, Sc, As, Ps) are not only more serious clinically, but, as factors, they are also more readily identified than the depressive traits.

Cattell isolated these 12 factors using primarily Q data obtained from items on the Minnesota Multiphasic Personality Inventory (MMPI) (Hathaway & McKinley,

TABLE 12.2   *Cattell's 12 Abnormal Primary Source Traits*

FACTOR	LOW SCORE DESCRIPTION	HIGH SCORE DESCRIPTION
D_1	LOW HYPOCHONDRIASIS Is happy, mind works well, does not find ill health frightening	HIGH HYPOCHONDRIASIS Shows overconcern with bodily functions, health, or disabilities
D_2	ZESTFULNESS Is contented about life and surroundings, has no death wishes	SUICIDAL DISGUST Is disgusted with life, harbors thoughts or acts of self-destruction
D_3	LOW BROODING DISCONTENT Avoids dangerous and adventurous undertakings, has little need for excitement	HIGH BROODING DISCONTENT Seeks excitement, is restless, takes risks, tries new things
D_4	LOW ANXIOUS DEPRESSION Is calm in emergency, confident about surroundings, poised	HIGH ANXIOUS DEPRESSION Has disturbing dreams, is clumsy in handling things, tense, easily upset
D_5	HIGH ENERGY EUPHORIA Shows enthusiasm for work, is energetic, sleeps soundly	LOW ENERGY DEPRESSION Has feelings of weariness, worries, lacks energy to cope
D_6	LOW GUILT AND RESENTMENT Is not troubled by guilt feelings, can sleep no matter what is left undone	HIGH GUILT AND RESENTMENT Has feelings of guilt, blames self for everything that goes wrong, is critical of self
D_7	LOW BORED DEPRESSION Is relaxed, considerate, cheerful with people	HIGH BORED DEPRESSION Avoids contact and involvement with people, seeks isolation, shows discomfort with people
Pa	LOW PARANOIA Is trusting, not bothered by jealousy or envy	HIGH PARANOIA Believes is being persecuted, poisoned, controlled, spied on, mistreated
Pp	LOW PSYCHOPATHIC DEVIATION Avoids engagement in illegal acts or breaking rules, sensitive	HIGH PSYCHOPATHIC DEVIATION Has complacent attitude toward own and others' antisocial behavior, is not hurt by criticism, likes crowds
Sc	LOW SCHIZOPHRENIA Makes realistic appraisals of self and others, shows emotional harmony and absence of regressive behavior	HIGH SCHIZOPHRENIA Hears voices or sounds without apparent source outside self, retreats from reality, has uncontrolled and sudden impulses
As	LOW PSYCHASTHENIA Is not bothered by unwelcome thoughts and ideas or compulsive habits	HIGH PSYCHASTHENIA Suffers insistent, repetitive ideas and impulses to perform certain acts
Ps	LOW GENERAL PSYCHOSIS Considers self as good, dependable, and smart as most others	HIGH GENERAL PSYCHOSIS Has feelings of inferiority and unworthiness, timid, loses head easily

SOURCE: *The Manual for the Clinical Analysis Questionnaire (CAQ). Copyright by the Institute for Personality and Ability Testing, Inc., 1975. All rights reserved. Reproduction by permission of the copyright owner.*

1951). In addition, he has used textbook descriptions of abnormal behavior, and he and his associates have written new items as their work continued. Subjects from whom measures were obtained included samples from both normal and abnormal populations. Interestingly, when used with normal subjects, factor analysis of these "abnormal" items revealed the same normal traits found with nonpathological items. Alongside these 23 traits, though, were the 12 pathological factors. This lends some support to the hypothesis that abnormal people are, first of all, people like everyone else, but with some additional traits that happen to be pathological (Cattell, 1979–1980).

Second-Stratum Traits

Because Cattell assumed an intercorrelation among the primary source traits, he was able to factor analyze the results of the original factor analysis and determine which of the first-order traits tend to cluster together. His results have consistently identified eight second-stratum traits and tentatively isolated at least seven more. Because these last seven still need more cross-validation, we will be concerned here only with the more firmly established original eight second-stratum factors and the primary factors that contribute most heavily to their makeup. Second-

According to Cattell, abnormal people are much like everyone else, but with some additional, pathological traits.

TABLE 12.3 *Cattell's Second-Stratum Source Traits*

FACTOR	NAME	PRIMARY FACTORS		DESCRIPTIVE LABEL
QI	EXVIA (Extraversion)	A F H Q_2—	Affectia Surgency Parmia Group Dependency	Sociable Enthusiastic Adventurous Dependent
QII	ANXIETY	C— H— L O Q_3— Q_4	Low Ego Strength Threctia Protension Guilt Proneness Low Self-Sentiment High Ergic Tension	Easily upset Shy, Timid Suspicious Apprehensive Uncontrolled Tense
QIII	CORTERIA (Cortical Alertness)	A— I— M	Sizia Harria Praxernia	Unsociable Insensitive Practical
QIV	INDEPENDENCE	E F H L	Dominance Surgency Parmia Protension	Dominant Enthusiastic Adventurous Suspicious
QV	DISCREETNESS	A N	Affectia Shrewdness	Sociable Astute, Socially aware
QVI	SUBJECTIVITY	M Q_1	Autia Radicalism	Unconcerned Radical
QVII	INTELLIGENCE	B	Intelligence	Intelligent
QVIII	GOOD UPBRINGING	E— F— G Q_3	Submissive Desurgency High Superego Strength High Self-Sentiment	Obedient, Docile Taciturn Emotionally stable Controlled

SOURCE: *This table is based on the mean pattern loadings from 14 studies summarized in R. B. Cattell,* Personality and learning theory, *Vol. 1. New York: Springer Publishing Company, 1979–1980, p. 80. Copyright 1979 by Springer Publishing Company, Inc., New York 10012. Adapted by permission.*

stratum factors are assigned roman numerals and the Q preface signifies Q data (questionnaire).

In interpreting Table 12.3, the reader should note that four primary factors contribute to second-stratum Factor QI (Exvia). Primary Factors A, F, and H are positively correlated with QI, whereas Primary Factor Q_2 (group dependency) is negatively correlated with it. Also, realize that Exvia (extraversion) has an opposite pole called Invia (introversion). Again, second-stratum source traits are numbered in descending order of magnitude, so that QI (Exvia/Invia) and QII (Anxiety) are the strongest and most readily identified of these factors. This is consistent with other personality theorists such as Jung who, using clinical methods, identified extraversion and introversion as basic types, and with Freud, Sullivan, and others who noted the importance of anxiety in shaping different personalities. Likewise, Eysenck, employing a different factor analytic technique, has recognized the importance of extraversion/introversion plus an anxiety factor he terms "neuroticism."

Measurement of Traits

To measure normal traits Cattell (1949) developed several forms of the 16 PF: the Pre-School Personality Questionnaire (PSPQ) for ages 4–6; the Early School Personality Questionnaire (ESPQ) for ages 6–8; the Child Personality Questionnaire (CPQ) for ages 8–12; and the High School Personality Questionnaire (HSPQ) for ages 12–18. These questionnaires ask subjects to select from one of two alternatives such as, "Can you spell as well as other children or do most children spell better?" and "Would you rather play with your toys or with friends?"

In addition, Delhees and Cattell (1971) have constructed the Clinical Analysis Questionnaire (CAQ), an instrument designed to assess the 12 abnormal traits along with the 16 normal personality traits and nine second-order factors. Scores are reported in terms of *stens*, that is, a 10-unit scale ranging from low scores of 1 to high scores of 10. The profile for Holly, our 24-year-old case study, is seen in Figure 12.2. Second-order factors were not scored. One can see how Holly's high scores on radicalism and self-sufficiency coupled with low scores on conformity, shrewdness, and self-discipline might lead to trouble with any supervisor who demands conformity and submissiveness.

Dynamic Traits

Besides temperament, Cattell recognizes motivation traits that underlie the *dynamics of personality*. The general personality traits discussed above include ability (Factor B, Intelligence), and some generalized dynamic traits (Cattell, 1979–1980). However, they are largely temperament traits. We turn now to a more specific discussion of motivation; that is, the dynamics of personality, which includes *attitudes*, *ergs*, and *sems*.

Attitudes

The cornerstone of Cattell's dynamic traits is the concept of **attitude**. An attitude is not an opinion for or against something, but a concept with a much more basic definition. It is a specific course of action, or desire to act, in response to a given situation (Cattell & Child, 1975). For example, let us consider a college student, Monica, whose desire to study French with a particular classmate would be an attitude. Like all attitudes, hers includes a particular stimulus or situation, an interest (intensity level of the desire), the response, and an object. In this example it makes no difference whether or not Monica actually studies with the classmate. The attitude is present in either case and serves as a motive for behavior.

Cattell assumes that motivation is complex and that a network of motives, or **dynamic lattice**, is involved with nearly any attitude. A variety of motives, not all of which are conscious, would doubtless enter into the above example. Monica may desire to do well in French in order to maintain her reputation as a good student; she may wish to spend time with a potential sexual partner; or she may be lonely and simply desire the company of another person. In addition to this network of motives, a **subsidiation chain** underlies nearly all motivation. This simply means that some motives are subsidiary to others; that is, they are directed toward subgoals that must be reached in order to attain the next goal. Assuming motivation to be conscious (which is not always so), a subsidiation chain could be revealed

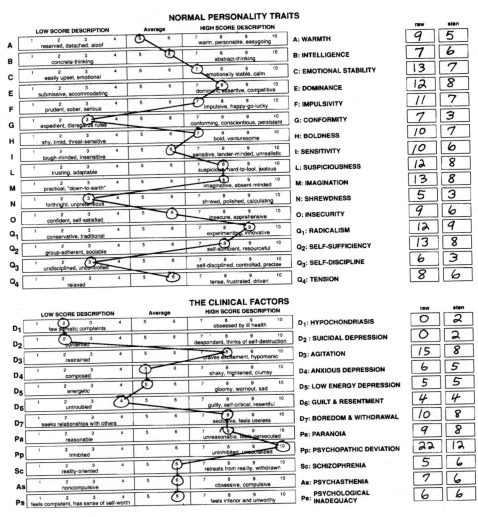

Figure 12.2   *Profile for a 24-Year-Old Female on the Clinical Analysis Questionnaire (CAQ)*

by asking the person a series of "Why" questions. In our example with Monica, the first question would be "Why do you want to study French with Glenn?" Answer: To pass French. "Why?" To graduate from college. "Why?" To get a job. "Why?" To be able to eat. At this point, an innate drive (hunger) is reached and no further questions are needed. Each motive in the chain is subsidiary to the next and all eventually lead to the innate drive for food.

Ergs

Innate drives or motives are called **ergs** (Cattell, 1983). The term *erg* refers to the energy inherent in primary or unlearned drives such as sex, hunger, curiosity, anger, and other motives, most of which are not limited to humans, but also are found in the primates and other higher mammals. In identifying dynamic traits, Cattell began with no preconceived biases as to their nature or their number. Unlike other personality theorists such as Freud (Chapter 2), he did not presuppose the existence of basic primary drives or instincts. Rather, he started with a heterogeneous array of objective test items (T data), administered them to children and adults in different cultures, factor analyzed the results, and thereby mapped out human motivation mathematically rather than logically (Cattell, 1983).

As a consequence of this approach, Cattell has extracted with a high level of confidence some 10 ergs, most of which are also found in the other mammals. Cattell (1979–1980) saw this as a reason to believe that these dynamic traits are not acquired through enculturation. In fact, he suggested that ergic factors are the human equivalents of animal instinctual patterns. The presently mapped human ergic goals and their corresponding emotions are shown in Table 12.4. The first 10 have been consistently identified as independent factors; the next four are of uncertain independence; and the final two are even more questionable as factors.

Sems

The third component in Cattell's theory of motivation are **sems**, which are learned or acquired dynamic traits. Sems receive their energy from the ergs and give some organization and stability to the attitudes. Originally, Cattell called these acquired traits **sentiments**, but he later termed them *sems*, an acronym for "socially shaped ergic manifolds." Sems are socially acquired and, ordinarily, satisfy several ergs at the same time. We have seen that an attitude is an action, or desire to act, in response to a particular situation, and that attitudes ordinarily can be traced to primary, innate drives called ergs. The intermediate goals between attitudes and ergs are the sems. In the earlier example of our student, Monica, and her desire to study French with a classmate, we saw that her strong wish to study represented her attitude and that her ultimate goal of food was an erg. The network of subgoals bridging the span between attitude and erg is comprised of various sems (see Figure 12.3). For example, Monica's wish to maintain her reputation as a diligent student is part of her self-sentiment and her motivation to study French with a friend

TABLE 12.4   *List of Experimentally Presently Mapped Human Ergs*

GOAL TITLE	EMOTION	STATUS OF EVIDENCE
Food-seeking	Hunger	
Mating	Sex	
Gregariousness	Loneliness	
Parental protectiveness	Pity	
Exploration	Curiosity	
Escape to security	Fear	Consistently identified
Self-assertion	Pride	
Narcissistic sex	Sensuousness	
Pugnacity	Anger	
Acquisitiveness	Greed	
Appeal	Despair	
Rest-seeking	Sleepiness	
Constructiveness	Creativity	Uncertain independence
Self-abasement	Humility	
Disgust	Disgust	
Laughter	Amusement	Questionable factors

SOURCE: R. B. *Cattell and* P. *Kline* (1977). The scientific analysis of personality and motivation. *Orlando, FL: Academic Press, p.* 181. *Copyright* 1977 *by Academic Press. Used by permission of Academic Press and R. B. Cattell.*

connects directly with the loneliness erg. This example shows that several sems can be subsidiated in one erg. For example, self and superego are both connected to pride. With the complexity of human motivation, it is also quite likely that several ergs will be involved with one sem. For example, the family and home sem may relate to the ergs of sex and loneliness.

Because sems are learned, they may be either unique or common traits. Unique factors, remember, are peculiar to the individual and are determined through the P correlational technique. Common traits are those found in many people and emerge through factor analyses of correlations obtained through the R technique. Although unique motivational traits are important in psychotherapy or vocational guidance where the psychologist is working with one person, they do not have a separate factor analytical existence. In other words, the dynamic factors that are extracted through the use of the P technique should be the same as those obtained through the R technique (Cattell & Cross, 1952).

Because sems are culturally acquired, their number differs with different cultures and among various age groups. Cattell has thus far identified some 27 sems.

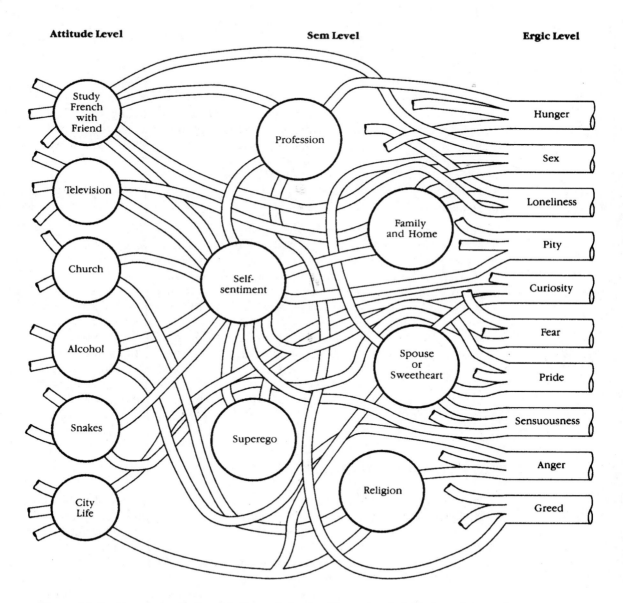

Figure 12.3 *Fragments of a Person's Dynamic Lattice, Illustrating Subsidiation Chains and Their Component Attitudes, Sems, and Ergs*

The strongest mathematically and most important clinically are those shown in Figure 12.3, namely profession, family and home, spouse or sweetheart, self-sentiment, superego, and religion. The *self-sentiment* has some special importance because of its crucial position in integrating other sems. The self-sentiment is the psychometric equivalent of the clinically derived term of self-concept. However, it is no different from the other sems in quality and origin. Like the others, it is peculiarly human and learned through one's culture.

Each of the semic subgoals has a pattern of attitudes that correlate (positively or negatively) to it. For example, three attitudes that load heavily on the Religious Factor are a desire to feel in touch with God, a wish to maintain or increase standards of organized religion, and an interest in seeking and heeding advice from one's parents. Attitudes that contribute to the self-sentiment include the desire to attain control of impulses and mental processes, to maintain self-respect, to excel in one's career, and to maintain a good reputation (Cattell & Child, 1975).

The Dynamic Lattice

The interrelationships among the dynamic traits of an individual can be expressed pictorially by the dynamic lattice (see Figure 12.3), which consists of a complex network of attitudes, ergs, and sems underlying a person's motivational structure. To understand the dynamic lattice shown in Figure 12.3, begin with the ergs—the innate human drives—on the right side of the diagram. Each erg affects one or more of the sems (depicted in large circles in the center). Recall that sems are learned dynamic traits that can satisfy one or more ergs. Notice that the profession sem is subsidiary to, that is, receives its basic energy from both hunger and greed. The small circles at the left of the diagram represent attitudes, that is, a person's tendency to action in a particular situation. Monica's attitude toward studying French with Glenn is energized directly by the sex erg, indirectly by hunger, through the profession sem, and also indirectly by pride, through the self-sentiment.

THE DYNAMIC CALCULUS

In the broad sense of the word, Cattell is a behaviorist; that is, his ultimate aim is to understand and predict behavior. Traits of temperament, ability, and motivation are measured not in terms of properties owned by an individual but rather in terms of behavior. How can behavior be predicted most accurately? Cattell's response is to employ the **dynamic calculus**, a complex procedure for determining the strength and direction of attitudes.

In the dynamic calculus, ergs and sems are considered to be the roots of all motivation, and they enter into the **behavioral equation,** which allows one to predict the behavior of a given individual (Cattell & Child, 1975). Cattell's early work of identifying various source traits, as well as the different ergs and sems (sentiments), simply provided the structure of personality. As Cattell (1982, p. 14) put it, "This unitary trait structure research yields a description of the pieces on the chess board, but not of the rules of the game."

The dynamic calculus provides those rules. It allows for the prediction of strength of attitudes and is sufficiently practical to enable the clinician, for example, to recommend equally satisfying but less destructive and fatiguing ways of behaving. It also permits the specific calculation of such previously amorphous concepts as conflict, repression, and decision making. Through precise mathematical means, the investigator can determine the exact weights attached to the various ergs and sems, and then fit these weights into the behavioral formulas, thereby yielding an accurate prediction of people's attitudes, that is, their specific course of action or desire to act (Cattell, 1982, 1985).

THE HERITABILITY OF TRAITS

Cattell has long been interested in behavior genetics and the heritability of the various source traits such as intelligence, ego strength, and superego strength. Using factor analytic methods and a sample of over 3000 related and unrelated subjects, Cattell and his associates have provided tentative answers to such questions as: Is intelligence acquired or inherited? How much of ego strength and superego strength are due to heredity and how much to environmental factors?

Estimates of heritability (H) of the various source traits have been provided by Cattell and his colleagues. Heritability (H) of a trait is the ratio of the genetically determined variance to the total variance so that an H of .60 for intelligence, for example, would mean that 60 percent of the total variance of intelligence is accounted for by genetic factors. Variance refers to the extent to which scores spread out over the entire scale. If everyone in a sample obtained the same score, then variance for those scores would be zero. If people do not all score the same, the difference must be due to something—heredity, environment, or an interaction of the two. Cattell's H is simply an estimate of the extent to which the variance of a given trait is due to heredity. The statistical technique used to obtain an H is Multiple Abstract Variance Analysis, or MAVA (Cattell, 1979–1980, 1983).

Cattell feels that MAVA is superior to the older twin methods, which simply compared differences among identical twins, fraternal twins, and siblings. Multiple Abstract Variance Analysis has the advantage, among other things, of being sensitive to differences in the environment for identical twins as compared to fraternal twins. It also allows analysis within families as well as between families. The technique has the capacity to measure genetic, environmental, and total variances for pairs of children (or other people) in the following family constellations: (1) identical twins reared together; (2) fraternal twins reared together; (3) siblings reared together; (4) half siblings reared together; (5) unrelated children reared together; (6) siblings reared apart; (7) unrelated children (adopted) reared apart; and so on. In addition, identical twins reared apart could also be included, but due to their relative scarcity (MAVA only utilizes large sample sizes), this constellation has not been included by Cattell.

Cattell and his associates have published several studies that have used some or all of a total sample of more than 3000 boys aged 12 to 18. All must be of the same sex because identical twins are necessarily of the same sex. Most of the 2973 unrelated boys living apart were from the original norm group for the American edition of the High School Personality Questionnaire (HSPQ), a form of the 16 PF.

In one study, Cattell, Schuerger, and Kline (1982) investigated the heritability of three primary source traits: Ego Strength (Factor C), Superego Strength (Factor G), and Self-sentiment (Factor Q_3). These three factors, sometimes called the "controlling triumvirate," were chosen because of their substantial interest to clinicians. The researchers administered a 10-hour battery of tests to 94 identical twins reared together, 124 fraternal twins reared together, 470 brothers reared together, and 2973 unrelated children reared apart. This latter category was considered as a general population group. Using the MAVA method, the authors found, as one might expect, that very little of the variance for superego strength (Factor G) was accounted for by heredity. For the general population the H was .05, which indicates that superego is mostly a function of education or environment. For ego strength (Factor C) and self-sentiment (Factor Q_3), however, the H values were considerably higher. For the general population, heritability of ego strength was about .40, whereas the within-family H was a little lower, between .30 and .40. For self-sentiment, the heritability for the general population was even higher, .63, an interesting finding in view of Cattell's assumption that sentiments are culturally acquired. However, in looking at the H values for within- and between-families, the authors found that self-sentiment has a higher heritability for between-families (.65) than for within-families (.46). This suggests that brothers have a similar exposure to cultural influences within the family, at least as far as self-sentiment (self-concept) is concerned.

Cattell (1979–1980) has averaged results from earlier studies and has compiled estimates of H for 18 primary- and 13 second-stratum source traits. Interestingly, the H for both Sizia/Affectia and Exvia/Invia is estimated at 50 percent. Sizia/Affectia is a basic primary source trait that describes people in terms of reserved and detached vs. outgoing and warmhearted. Exvia/invia is a second stratum source trait roughly equivalent to Jung's concept of extraversion/introversion. For both these strong traits, Cattell estimated that approximately half the variance is accounted for by heritability factors and about half by the environment.

Before looking at the controversial issue of the heritability of intelligence, we should understand that Cattell differentiates between fluid and crystallized intelligence. *Fluid intelligence* is that which enables one to adapt to new kinds of material regardless of previous experiences with it. *Crystallized intelligence*, on the other hand, is that which depends on previous learnings to solve present problems. Primary Factor B is considered as crystallized intelligence, and Cattell estimates that it has a heritability value of 60 percent. For fluid intelligence, a second-stratum trait, the estimate is .65 (Cattell, 1979–1980). These relatively high heritability values suggest that intelligence is probably due more to heredity than to environment.

EYSENCK'S FACTOR THEORY

Hans Eysenck's approach to theory building differs from Cattell's in several respects. First, he is more likely to use the *hypothetico-deductive* method of theorizing *before* factor analyzing data. Second, he has only three basic *types*, rather than 35 traits. Third, Eysenck uses factor analysis as only one means of answering important questions on personality theory. In an interview with Richard Evans he said,

> I think probably of all the factor analysts you may know, I'm the one who thinks least of it. I regard it as a useful adjunct, a technique that was invaluable under certain circumstances, but one which we must leave behind as soon as possible in order to get a proper causal type of understanding of the factors and to know just what they mean. (Evans, 1976, p. 259)

Eysenck, then, is a generalist, not merely a factor analyst. His range of interests is broad; his willingness to step into a controversy is legendary. He has been a gadfly to the conscience of psychology since he first entered its ranks. He upset many psychoanalysts and other therapists in the early 1950s with his contention that no evidence exists to suggest that psychotherapy is more effective than spontaneous remission. In other words, those people who receive no therapy are just as likely to get better as are those who undergo expensive, painful, prolonged psychotherapy with expertly trained psychoanalysts and psychologists (Eysenck, 1952a). Eysenck is not afraid to take an unpopular stand, as witnessed by his defense of Arthur Jensen and his contention that IQ cannot be significantly increased by well-intentioned social programs, but is largely genetically determined. Eysenck's book *The IQ Argument* (1971) was so controversial that elements in the United States "threatened booksellers with arson if they dared to stock the book; well-known 'liberal' newspapers refused to review it; and the outcome was that it was largely impossible in the land of free speech to discover the existence of the book or to buy it" (Eysenck, 1980a, p. 175).

In England he was "attacked and beaten up by some left-wing hooligans" while preparing to deliver a speech on a separate topic (Eysenck, 1980a, p. 175). Eysenck's enemies and critics, however, do not only come from the political left; his battles with the fascist right go back even further.

BIOGRAPHY OF HANS J. EYSENCK

Hans Jurgen Eysenck was born in Berlin, Germany, on March 4, 1916, the child of a theatrical family. His mother was Ruth Werner, a starlet at the time of Hans's birth, who later became a German silent film star under the stage name of Helga Molander. His father, Anton Eduard Eysenck, was a comedian, singer, and actor. When Hans was two, his mother and father divorced and he went to live with his maternal grandmother, who had also been in the theater, but whose promising career in opera was cut short by a crippling fall (Eysenck, 1982). Although his grandmother was a devout Catholic, neither parent was religious, and Hans grew up without any formal religious commitment (Gibson, 1981).

He also grew up with little parental discipline and few strict controls over his behavior. Neither parent seemed interested in curtailing his actions, and his grandmother had a quite permissive attitude toward him. This benign neglect is exemplified by two incidents. In the first, his father had bought Hans a bicycle and had promised to teach him to ride. "He took me to the top of a hill, told me that I had to sit on the saddle and pump the pedals and make the wheels go round. He then went off to release some balloons . . . leaving me to learn how to ride all by myself" Eysenck (1990c, p. 12). In the second incident, an adolescent Eysenck told his grandmother that he was going to buy some cigarettes, expecting her to forbid it. However, his grandmother simply said: " 'If you like it, do it by all means' " (Eysenck, 1990c, p. 14). According to Eysenck, environmental experiences, such as these two, have little to do with personality development. To him, genetic factors have a greater impact on subsequent behavior than do experiences. Thus, his permissive upbringing neither helped nor hindered him in becoming a famous scientist.

Even as a schoolboy, Eysenck was not afraid to take an unpopular stand, often challenging his teachers, especially those with militaristic leanings. He was skeptical of much of what they taught and was not always reluctant to embarrass them with his superior knowledge. In his autobiography he described himself as "a sanctimonious prig . . . who didn't suffer fools (or even ordinarily bright people) gladly" (Eysenck, 1990c, p. 31).

Eysenck suffered the deprivation of many post-World War I Germans who were faced with astronomical inflation, mass unemployment, and near starvation, and his future appeared no brighter after Hitler came to power. As a condition of studying physics at the University of Berlin, he was told that he would have to join the Nazi secret police, an idea he found so repugnant that he decided to leave Germany.

This encounter with the fascist right and his later battles with the radical left suggested to him that the trait of tough-mindedness or authoritarianism was equally prevalent in both extremes of the political spectrum. He later found some scientific support for this hypothesis in a study which demonstrated that, although communists were radical and fascists were conservative on one dimension of personality, on the tough-minded vs. tender-minded dimension, both groups were more authoritarian, rigid, and intolerant of ambiguity (tough-minded) than a control group (Eysenck, 1954; Eysenck & Coulter, 1972).

As a consequence of Nazi tyranny, Eysenck, at age 18, left Germany and eventually settled in England, where he tried to enroll in the University of London. He was an avid reader, interested in both the arts and the sciences, but his first choice of curriculum was physics. However, a chance event altered the flow of his life and, consequently, the course of the history of psychology. In order to be accepted at the university he was required to pass an entrance examination, which he took after a year's study at a commercial college. After passing the exam, he confidently enrolled in the University of London intending to major in physics. However, he was told that he had taken the wrong subjects in his exam and therefore was not eligible to pursue a course in physics. Rather than waiting another year to take the right subjects, he inquired if there were not some scientific subject that he was qualified to pursue. When told he could always take psychology, he asked, "What on earth is psychology?" (Eysenck, 1982, p. 290).

The University of London's psychology department was basically pro-Freudian, but it was also psychometrically oriented, with Charles Spearman having just left and with Cyril Burt still presiding. Eysenck received a bachelor's degree in 1938, about the same time he married Margaret Davies, a Canadian woman with a degree in mathematics. In 1940 he was awarded a Ph.D. from the University of London, but by this time England and most of Europe were at war.

As a German national, he was considered an enemy alien and not allowed to enter the Royal Air Force (his first choice) or any other branch of the military. Instead, with no training as a psychiatrist or as a clinical psychologist, he went to work at the Mill Hill Emergency Hospital, treating patients who were suffering from a variety of psychological symptoms, including anxiety, depression, and hysteria. Eysenck, however, was not comfortable with most of the traditional clinical diagnostic categories. Using factor analysis, he found that two major personality factors—neuroticism and extraversion/introversion—could account for all the traditional diagnostic groups. These early theoretical ideas led to the publication of his first book, *Dimensions of Personality* (Eysenck, 1947). After the war he became director of the Psychology Department at Maudsley Hospital and later became a Reader in Psychology at the University of London.

In 1949 Eysenck traveled to North America to examine the clinical psychology programs in the United States and Canada with the idea of setting up a clinical psychology profession in Great Britain. He obtained a visiting professorship at the University of Pennsylvania for the year 1949–1950, but he spent much of that year traveling throughout the United States and Canada looking over clinical psychology programs, which he found to be totally unscientific (Eysenck, 1980a, 1990c).

Eysenck and his wife had been growing steadily apart, and his marriage was not improved when his traveling companion to Philadelphia was Sybil Rostal, a beautiful quantitative psychologist and the daughter of a famous violinist. On returning to England, Hans obtained a divorce from his first wife, and on October 30, 1950, he married Sybil. Hans and Sybil Eysenck have coauthored several publications, and their marriage has produced three sons and a daughter. Eysenck's son from his first marriage, Michael, is a widely published author of psychology articles and books.

After returning from North America, Eysenck established a clinical psychology department at the University of London and in 1955 became professor of psychology. While in the United States he had begun *The Structure of Human Personality* (1952b), in which he argued for the efficacy of factor analysis as the best method of representing the known facts of human personality.

Eysenck surpasses even Cattell for volume of published works. Along with more than 700 journal articles or book chapters, he has published 75 books, several of which have titles with popular appeal such as *Uses and Abuses of Psychology* (1953); *Sense and Nonsense in Psychology* (1956); *Fact and Fiction in Psychology* (1965); *Psychology Is about People* (1972b); *You and Neurosis* (1977b); *Sex, Violence and the Media* (with D. K. B. Nias, 1978); *The Causes and Effects of Smoking* (1980b); and *Smoking, Personality, and Stress* (1991d).

In 1983 Eysenck retired as professor of psychology at the Institute of Psychiatry, University of London, and as senior psychiatrist at the Maudsley and Bethlehem Royal hospitals. He is currently Professor Emeritus at the University of London, but he remains active on a variety of projects, especially on behavioral interventions in cancer and heart disease (to be discussed later). He also remains active with tennis, his favorite hobby and a sport he played with great skill as a younger man.

The range of Eysenck's interests is revealed by the variety of publications he has authored or co-authored in the last few years. In 1990 he wrote *Decline and Fall of the Freudian Empire* (Eysenck, 1990b), in which he challenged the validity of *everything* Freud wrote. In addition, he has been involved in projects comparing intelligence and reaction time of Chinese and British children (Chan, Eysenck, & Lynn, 1991; Lynn, Chan, & Eysenck, 1991); raising IQs through vitamin and mineral supplements (Eysenck, 1991); comparing personality characteristics in England and Russia (Hanin, Eysenck, Eysenck, & Barrett, 1991); studying the effects of behavior therapy on boxers and soccer players (Grossarth-Maticek, Eysenck, Rieder, & Rakic, 1990); and investigating Machiavellianism as a component in psychoticism and extraversion (Allsopp, Eysenck, & Eysenck, 1991).

MEASUREMENT OF PERSONALITY

Three people—Cyril Burt, Charles Spearman, and Ivan Pavlov—have had the greatest influence on Eysenck's theory of personality. Burt, his professor, and Spearman, whose lectures he attended, showed him that personality could best be investigated psychometrically. Pavlov, whom he never knew personally, taught him that there is a biological basis for personality structure (Cohen, 1977). Thus, Eysenck's theory has strong psychometric and biological components.

Criteria for Identifying Factors

Eysenck (1977b) contended that psychometric sophistication alone is not sufficient to measure the structure of human personality, and that types arrived at through factor analytic methods are sterile and meaningless unless they have been shown to possess a biological existence. In fact, he listed four criteria for the identification of a factor. First, *psychometric evidence* for the factor's existence must be established. A corollary to this criterion is that the factor must be reliable and replicable. Other investigators, from separate laboratories, must also be able to find the factor. A second criterion is that the factor must also possess *heritability* and must fit an established genetic model. This criterion eliminates learned characteristics, such as the ability to mimic the voices of well-known people or a religious or political belief. Third, the factor must *make sense from a theoretical view.* Eysenck employs the deductive method of investigation, beginning with a theory and then gathering data that are logically consistent with that theory. The final criterion for the existence of a factor is that it must *possess social relevance;* that is, it must be demonstrated that mathematically derived factors have a relationship (not necessarily causal) with such socially relevant variables as drug addiction, accident proneness, outstanding performance in sports, psychotic behavior, criminality, and so on.

Hierarchy of Measures

Eysenck (1947, 1990a) has long recognized a four-level hierarchy of behavior organization. At the lowest level are *specific acts or cognitions,* individual behaviors or thoughts that may or may not be characteristic of the person. A student finishing a reading assignment would be an example of a specific response. At the second level are the *habitual acts or cognitions,* that is, responses that recur under similar conditions. For example, if a student frequently keeps at an assignment until it is finished, then this behavior becomes a habitual response. As opposed to specific responses, habitual responses must be reasonably reliable or consistent.

Several related habitual responses form a *trait*—the third level of behavior. Eysenck (1981, p. 3) defined traits as "important semi-permanent personality disposition." For example, students would have the trait of persistence if they habitually complete class assignments, and keep working at other endeavors until they are finished. Although traits can be identified intuitively, trait and factor theorists rely on a more systematic approach, namely factor analysis. Trait-level behaviors are extracted through factor analysis of habit-level responses just as habitual responses are mathematically extracted through factor analysis of specific responses. Traits, then, are "defined in terms of significant intercorrelations between different habitual behaviors" (Eysenck, 1990a, p. 244). Cattell ordinarily works with factors at this third (trait) level of organization, which largely accounts for the fact that he has identified far more personality factors than Eysenck (see box—"What Dimensions Underlie Personality?").

In contrast to Cattell, Eysenck has concentrated on the fourth level, that of **types** or superfactors. A type is made up of several interrelated traits. For example, persistence may be related to inferiority, poor emotional adjustment, social shyness, and several other traits, with the entire cluster forming the *introverted type*. These four levels of behavior organization are shown in Figure 12.4. Remember that Eysenck's structure of personality rests on the more generalized type-level factors, whereas Cattell's theory is based largely on trait-level factors (Eysenck & Eysenck, 1979).

What Dimensions Underlie Personality?

What basic dimensions underlie personality? If Cattell and Eysenck are both measuring human personality and using precise mathematical procedures, why do they produce such divergent results? Before we answer this question, let's consider an analogy.

Cattell and Eysenck can be compared to two cartographers who set out to map the earth. One cartographer may decide to chart the entire globe, every mountain, river, hill, and stream. This mapmaker would be like Cattell, who assigned himself the task of measuring the entire sphere of human personality. The second cartographer may decide to measure more obvious features of the earth—the continents and the oceans. This mapmaker would be analogous to Eysenck, who has looked at the more global features of personality. In addition, the tools of the cartographers might differ, just as Cattell and Eysenck used different factor analytic techniques. Cattell's inductive method can be compared to a mapmaker who uses a variety of surveying instruments, with no preconceived notion of what he is going to find. On the other hand, Eysenck's deductive method would be more like a cartographer who takes aerial photos of preselected locations and then interprets these pictures from a predetermined view. With these vastly different approaches, we would expect differences in what the two explorers find.

Thus, the work of Cattell and Eysenck has produced different results because each man has mapped different parts of the sphere of human personality. Moreover, Cattell and Eysenck have arrived at a different number of factors because they are working at different levels of factoring. Therefore, Cattell's 35 traits cannot be directly compared with Eysenck's three types, because traits are at the third level of the hierarchical structure, and types are at the fourth level. Nevertheless, one might still inquire into the number and nature of primary dimensions that underlie human personality.

During the early 1960s, two studies strongly suggested that five and only five dimensions explain nearly all human traits. Tupes and Christal (1961) conducted one of the earliest investigations into the number of basic dimensions by reanalyzing eight studies that had used Cattell's 35 scales or revisions of them. They found "five relatively strong and recurrent factors and nothing more of any consequence" (Tupes & Christal, 1961, p. 14). They labeled these factors (I) Surgency, (II) Agreeableness, (III) Dependability, (IV) Emotional Stability, and (V) Culture. Two years later Warren Norman (1963), using peer nominations and four samples of male students at the University of Michigan, extracted nearly identical factors. Norman's five factors, which subsequently have been called

TYPES

Eysenck has extracted three general types or superfactors—**extraversion** (E), **neuroticism** (N), and **psychoticism** (P). Neuroticism and psychoticism are not limited to pathological individuals, although disturbed people score high on scales measuring these two factors. Eysenck regards all three types as part of normal personality structure. All three types are bipolar, with extraversion being on one end of Factor E and introversion occupying the opposite pole. Similarly, neuroticism is opposed to stability, whereas psychoticism is opposed to the superego function.

the "Big Five," included: (I) *Extroversion* (talkative, adventurous, sociable, frank, assertive) vs. *Surgency* (quiet, shy, unsociable, reserved, withdrawn); (II) *Agreeableness* (good-natured, sympathetic, kind, warm, gentle); (III) *Conscientiousness* (responsible, orderly, thorough); (IV) *Emotional Stability* (relaxed, not neurotic, stable, calm); and (V) *Culture* (intellectual, cultured, open, imaginative). These descriptive labels bear a strong resemblance to terms used to describe Cattell's second-stratum source traits (see Table 12.3) and Eysenck's three superfactors (see Figure 12.5).

Since then evidence for Norman's Big Five has been found in a variety of studies. Perhaps the most comprehensive of these studies has been Lewis Goldberg's (1990) work involving three separate investigations, all of which supported the notion of five and only five basic dimensions of personality. In the Netherlands, Willem K. Hofstee and his associates (Brokken, 1978; de Raad, Mulder, Kloosterman, & Hofstee, 1988; Hofstee, de Raad, & Goldberg, 1992) have consistently found that factor analyses of Dutch-language adjectives yield five dimensions, each easily identifiable as the Big Five. Oliver John and his associates (John, Goldberg, & Angleitner, 1984) reported on a study in which German-American bilingual subjects provided personality descriptions in both German and English. Results from this ongoing project suggest high cross-language correlations between German and English versions of the Big Five dimensions.

In another study Noller, Law, and Comrey (1987) administered the 16PF, the Eysenck Personality Inventory, and the Comrey Personality Scales (Comrey, 1970) to a sample of Australian undergraduate students, factor analyzed the results, and found a group of five factors very similar to Norman's Big Five. In addition, Church and Katigbak (1989) asked Filipino college students to describe individuals who *have* or *do not have* good psychological health and personality functioning. Subjects used both English and Tagalog personality descriptors. Factor analyses revealed five broad personality dimensions that strongly resembled the Big Five. In the United States, Peabody and Goldberg (1989) also uncovered personality structures similar to Norman's Big Five, and, similar to most investigations, they found that Surgency, Agreeableness, and Conscientiousness were stronger than Emotional Stability and Culture. Moreover, Peabody and Goldberg introduced simple verbal labels for the Big Five. For Surgency, they suggested Power; for Agreeableness, Love; for Conscientiousness, Work; for Emotional Stability, Affect; and for Culture, Intellect. What dimensions underlie personality in a variety of cultures? In everyday English terms, we suggest that the answer is Power, Love, Work, Affect, and Intellect.

Type:

Traits:

Habits:

Specific Behaviors:

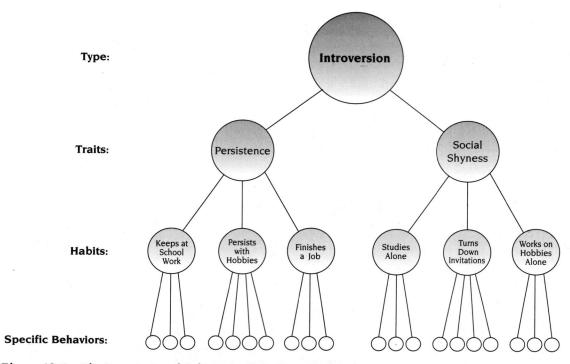

Figure 12.4   *The Organization of Behavior into Specific Actions, Habitual Responses, Traits, and Types. Besides Persistence and Social Shyness, other traits such as Inferiority, Low Activity, and Serious-Mindedness contribute to Introversion.*

The bipolarity of Eysenck's factors does not imply that most people are on one end or the other of the three main poles. Each type is unimodally, rather than bimodally, distributed. Extraversion, for example, is fairly normally distributed in much the same fashion as intelligence or height. Most people are near the center of a bell-shaped distribution, which means that Eysenck (1976a) does not believe that people can be neatly divided into mutually exclusive types. Despite important differences between Cattell and Eysenck at the trait level, considerable agreement exists between them at the type level (Royce & Powell, 1983). Eysenck's E (Extraversion), for example, appears to be comparable to Cattell's QI (Exvia/Invia); and his N (Neuroticism) may be the same factor as Cattell's QII (Anxiety).

Extraversion

In Chapter 5 we saw that Jung conceptualized two broad personality types called "extraversion" and "introversion." We also noted some differences between his definitions and the prevailing notion of these two terms. Jung saw extraverted people as having an objective or nonpersonalized view of the world, whereas introverts have essentially a subjective or individualized way of looking at things. Eysenck's concepts of extraversion and introversion are closer to the popular usage. Extraverted types are characterized primarily by sociability and impulsiveness, but also by jocularity, liveliness, quick-wittedness, optimism, and other traits indicative of people who are rewarded for their association with others (Eysenck & Eysenck, 1969). Our case study, Holly, is somewhat more extraverted than introverted. She enjoys high-risk activities such as mountain climbing and sky diving. In addition, she is willing to gamble her health against the pleasures of smoking, drinking, and using marijuana.

Introverts are characterized by traits opposite those of extraverts. They can be described as quiet, passive, unsociable, careful, reserved, thoughtful, pessimistic, peaceful, sober, and controlled (Eysenck, Nias, & Cox, 1982). According to Eysenck (1982), however, the principal differences between extraversion and introversion are not behavioral, but rather biological and genetic in nature.

Eysenck (1968, 1990a) believes that the primary cause of differences between extraverts and introverts is one of *cortical arousal level*, a physiological condition that is largely inherited rather than learned. Because extraverts have a lower level of cortical arousal than introverts, they have higher sensory thresholds and, thus, lesser reactions to sensory stimulation. Introverts, conversely, are characterized by a higher level of arousal and, as a result of a lower sensory threshold, they experience greater reactions to sensory stimulation. To maintain an optimal level of stimulation, therefore, introverts with their congenitally low sensory threshold must seek to avoid situations that will cause too much excitement. Hence, introverts should be expected to shun such activities as wild social events, downhill skiing,

Extraverts enjoy exciting and stimulating activities.

sky diving, competitive sports, leading a fraternity or sorority, or playing practical jokes.

On the other hand, because extraverts have a habitually low level of cortical arousal, they need a high level of sensory stimulation to maintain an optimal level of stimulation. Therefore, extraverts should participate more often in exciting and stimulating activities. Taking only one example, Eysenck (1976b) hypothesized that extraverts, as opposed to introverts, will engage in sexual intercourse earlier, more frequently, with more different partners, in more different positions, with a greater variety of sexual behaviors, and will indulge in longer precoital love play. Because extraverts have a lower level of cortical arousal, however, they become more quickly accustomed to strong stimuli (sexual or otherwise) and respond less and less to the same stimuli, whereas introverts are less likely to become bored and uninterested in routine activities carried on with the same people.

Neuroticism

The second type extracted by Eysenck is neuroticism/stability (N). Like extraversion/introversion, Factor N has a strong hereditary component. Eysenck (1967) reported several studies that have found evidence of a genetic basis for such neurotic traits as anxiety, hysteria, and obsessive-compulsive disorders. In addition, he has found a much greater agreement among identical twins than among fraternals on a number of antisocial and asocial behaviors such as adult crime, childhood behavior disorders, homosexuality, and alcoholism (Eysenck, 1974).

How can neurotics be described? Because neuroticism can be combined with different points on the extraversion scale, no single syndrome can define neurotic behavior. Eysenck's factor analytic technique assumes the independence of types, which means that the neuroticism scale is at right angles (signifying zero correlation) to the extraversion scale. Thus several people can all score high on the N scale, yet display quite different symptoms, depending on their degree of introversion or extraversion. Figure 12.5 shows the extraversion/introversion pole with zero correlation with the neuroticism/stability pole. Consider subjects A, B, and C, all equal on the neuroticism scale, but representing three distinct points on the extraversion scale. Subject A, an introverted neurotic, is characterized by anxiety, depression, phobias, and obsessive-compulsive symptoms; subject B is neither introverted nor extraverted and is likely to be characterized by hysteria (a neurotic disorder associated with emotional instability), suggestibility, and somatic symptoms; subject C, an extraverted neurotic, will probably manifest psychopathic qualities such as criminality and delinquent tendencies (Eysenck, 1967). Consider, also, subjects A, D, and E—all equally introverted, but with three different levels of emotional stability. Subject A is the introverted neurotic described above; B is equally introverted, but is neither severely neurotic nor emotionally stable; and E is both extremely introverted and psychologically healthy.

Figure 12.6 shows only five subjects, all of whom have at least one extreme score. Most other people, of course, would score near the mean on both scales. As

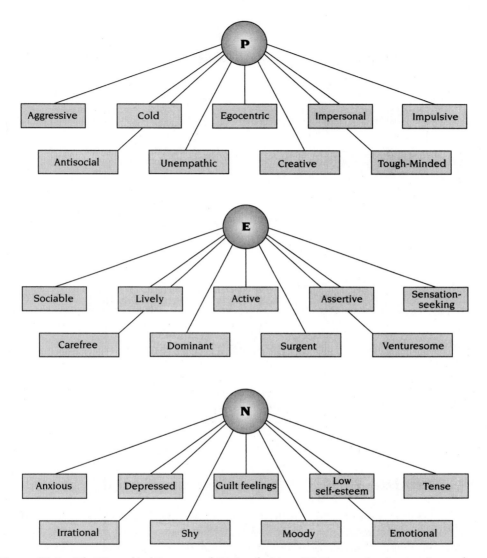

Figure 12.5 *The Hierarchical Structure of* (P) *Psychoticism,* (E) *Extraversion-Introversion, and* (N) *Neuroticism*

scores move toward the outer limits of the diagram, they become increasingly less and less frequent, just as scores toward the outer limits of a bell-shaped curve are less frequent than those near the mid-point.

Eysenck has developed two widely used personality inventories that measure E and N. The first, the Maudsley Personality Inventory, or MPI (Eysenck, 1959), appeared to yield some correlation between E and N. For this reason, Eysenck

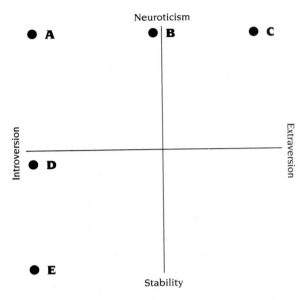

Figure 12.6   *Two-Dimensional Scheme Depicting Several Extreme Points on Eysenck's E and N Scales*

began work on another test, the Eysenck Personality Inventory, or EPI (Eysenck & Eysenck, 1964), which is an improved version of the MPI. This later inventory measures extraversion (E) and neuroticism (N) independently and also contains a lie (L) scale to detect faking.

Psychoticism

Eysenck's original theory of personality was based on only two types—extraversion and neuroticism. After several years of alluding to psychoticism (P) as an independent personality type, he finally elevated it to a position equal to E and N (Eysenck & Eysenck, 1976). This is reminiscent of Freud elevating aggression to an equal place with sex. In both cases a long-held theory received a substantial addition, and in both cases colleagues and followers were slow to accept the change (Broadbent, 1981).

The psychoticism/superego dimension is independent of both E and N. Figure 12.7 shows the three factors at right angles with one another. (Because three-dimensional space cannot be faithfully produced on a two-dimensional plane, the reader is asked to look at Figure 12.7 as if the solid lines represent the corner of a room where two walls meet the floor. Each line can then be seen as perpendicular to the other two.) Eysenck's view of personality, therefore, allows each person to be mea-

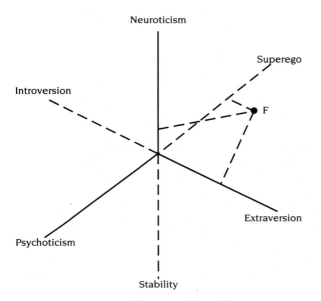

Figure 12.7 *Three-Dimensional Scheme Depicting One Individual's Scores on Each of Eysenck's Major Dimensions of Personality*

sured on three independent factors and resultant scores to be plotted in space having three coordinates. Subject F in Figure 12.7, for example, is very high on superego, somewhat high on extraversion, and near the midpoint on the neuroticism/stability scale.

High P scorers are egocentric, cold, nonconforming, aggressive, impulsive, hostile, suspicious, and antisocial. Low P scorers (in the direction of superego function) tend to be empathic, caring, cooperative, and highly socialized (Eysenck, Nias, & Cox, 1982). In addition, high P scorers tend to be male and low scorers female. Not as much research has been conducted on the psychoticism scales as on the two older ones, but Fulker (1981) reported some evidence for a high heritability of psychoticism as well as extraversion and neuroticism.

Psychoticism, like extraversion and neuroticism, has a strong genetic component, with about three-fourths of the variance of all three factors accounted for by heredity and about one-fourth by environmental factors. Eysenck (1990a) summarized much of the evidence for a strong biological component in personality. First, nearly identical factors have been found among people in various parts of the world, "from Uganda and Nigeria to Japan and mainland China, from the capitalist countries of the West and the American continent to Eastern-bloc countries such as the Soviet Union, Hungary, Czechoslovakia, Bulgaria, and Yugoslavia" (Eysenck, 1990a, pp. 245–246). Second, Eysenck cited evidence that individuals tend to maintain their position on the three dimensions of personality. And third, studies of twins suggest a higher concordance between identical twins than between same-gender fraternal twins reared together, suggesting that genetic factors play a dominant part in determining individual differences in personality.

 CONCEPT OF HUMANITY

How do trait and factor theorists view humanity? Cattell and Eysenck are not concerned with traditional themes such as *determinism vs. free choice, optimism vs. pessimism,* and *teleological vs. causal* influences. In fact, their theories do not even lend themselves to speculation of these topics. What, then, can we say concerning their view of humanity?

First, we know that Cattell and Eysenck see humans as being different from other animals. From a psychometric view, people can be differentiated from other beings on the basis of their ability to report data about themselves. Animal data can be collected by life records (L data) and by objective measurement of performance (T data). However, only humans are capable of answering questions about themselves (Q data). From this fact, it can be inferred that Cattell and Eysenck believe that humans possess not only *consciousness,* but self-consciousness as well. People are also able to evaluate their performance and to render reasonably reliable reports concerning their attitudes, temperament, needs, interests, and behaviors.

Second, both Cattell and Eysenck, place heavy emphasis on *genetic factors* of personality. Eysenck insists that the traits of extraversion, neuroticism, and psychoticism all have strong hereditary components, but he does not dismiss social factors altogether. Instead, he says that humans are biosocial organisms whose behaviors are "determined equally by biological factors such as hunger, thirst, sexual appetite, etc., and by social constraints enforced by the government . . . or by public approval and disapproval" (Eysenck, 1990c, p. 64). Nevertheless, on the dimension of *biological vs. social* influences, trait and factor theories strongly favor biology as a determinant of personality.

On the dimension of *individual differences vs. similarities,* trait and factor theories lean toward individual differences. Factor analysis rests on the premise of differences among individuals and thus variability in their scores. If scores on individuals did not differ, correlations would be impossible and factor analysis unthinkable. Even though common factors are ordinarily derived from factor analysis, trait theorists still place heavy emphasis on individual differences. Eysenck (1981, p. xi), for instance, stated that "people are above all else *individuals.*" Common traits do not require that similarities be emphasized. Individual differences can be accentuated by plotting one person's scores on each of several traits. In addition, Cattell has pioneered the use of the P technique, which begins with a large pool of scores obtained from a single individual and results in the identification of individual traits. Thus, trait theorists are more concerned with individual differences than with similarities among people.

Related Research

During the past decade, much research has been reported testing Eysenck's speculations on the complex interaction among genetic factors, stress, personality, and behaviors such as smoking in the development of lung cancer and coronary heart disease (CHD). Eysenck (1984) has argued that cancer has many causes, and that no single factor is both *sufficient* and *necessary* to cause the disease. With his model, stress, smoking, personality type, and heredity are *cofactors* in the development of lung cancer and heart disease, and the presence of two or more of these factors will have a **synergistic** effect on that disease. A synergistic effect results when the combined effects of two risk factors is equal to more than the sum of their individual risks.

Recent research by Eysenck and his associates has suggested that personality type is a much better predictor of death from cancer than is cigarette smoking. In addition, Eysenck (1991d) has argued that cognitive behavioral therapy can mold personality types in ways that prevent both cancer and coronary heart disease.

Eysenck's (1987, 1988a, 1991a, 1991c, 1991d) claims are based on research findings of Yugoslav physician and psychologist Ronald Grossarth-Maticek. During the 1960s, Grossarth-Maticek began to find a marked relationship between such personality traits as hopelessness and helplessness and death from cancer. He also noted that angry, aggressive, hostile people are more likely to die from coronary heart disease than are people who do not have these characteristics.

Grossarth-Maticek's early findings were so astounding that he was accused of falsifying data. His research fell on hard times financially when the Cancer Society and other possible sources of funds rebuffed his requests. Earlier, Eysenck had teamed with a Scottish oncologist, David M. Kissen, to demonstrate that low neuroticism scores, which were indicative of suppressed emotions, predicted cancer, and that high scores, which were indicative of expressed emotions, predicted an absence of cancer (Kissen & Eysenck, 1962). After Kissen died, Eysenck looked for another physician who would allow him to test cancer patients. However, "through lack of interest on the part of the establishment," he had to give up his pursuit (Eysenck, 1991c, p. 298). Twenty years later Eysenck read about Grossarth-Maticek's work, went to see him, and, in 1980, agreed to become chairman of Grossarth-Maticek's project. With Eysenck's knowledge of behavior therapy and personality types, and with research grants from R. J. Reynolds and Phillip Morris, two large companies with interests in cigarette production, the research took on a new dimension (Eysenck, 1990c).

Using a short questionnaire and a long personal interview, about 90 percent of Grossarth-Maticek's subjects in Heidelberg, Germany, and in Crevenka, Yugoslavia, could be placed into one of four personality groups. *Type* I includes those people who want to get close to others and who have a helpless/hopeless reaction to stress. These people also have a rational, nonemotional reaction to life events and do not readily express strong feelings, such as fear or anger. Eysenck refers to these people as "cancer prone." He believes that Type I people would score high on his neuroticism (N) scale (personal communication, November 17, 1987).

Type II persons are easily frustrated by other people and by events, and they blame others for their distress and unhappiness. They typically react to frustration with anger, aggression, and emotional arousal. Eysenck calls these people "coronary heart disease prone."

Type III people are ambivalent, shifting from the typical reaction of Type I individuals to the typical reaction of Type IIs, and then back again.

Type IV people are characterized by personal autonomy, regarding their own autonomy and that of others as important conditions for personal wellbeing and happiness.

In the original study in Yugoslavia, 1353 subjects were recruited by selecting the oldest person in every second household in a town of 4000 people. Most of the subjects were between 59 and 65 years old. Ten years later the researchers measured the incidences of death from cancer and cardiovascular disease (heart disease and stroke) for each of the four personality types. Astonishingly, more than 45 percent of the people with a Type I personality had died of cancer, but only 5 percent of Type II people had died as the result of cancer. For cardiovascular disease, the proportions were reversed. About 30 percent of Type II people had died of cardiovascular disease, while less than 10 percent of the people with a Type I personality had died of this disease.

Interestingly, Type III individuals—those who shifted between a hopeless/helpless approach and an aggressive/hostile one—were not likely to have died from either cancer or heart disease after 10 years. Only 5 percent had died from cancer and 10 percent from cardiovascular disease. The incidence of death from cancer and cardiovascular disease among Type IV people was less than 5 percent for both diseases combined (see Figure 12.8).

Eysenck (1991c, 1991d) reported on a 1982–1986 follow-up of the Yugoslav subjects and found a very similar pattern of deaths. During this five-year follow-up, more than 20 percent of Type I subjects (cancer prone) had died of cancer, but less than 5 percent had died from cardiovascular disease. For Type II subjects (coronary heart disease prone) the ratio was reversed; more than 15 percent had died of cardiovascular disease, but less than 1 percent had died of cancer.

Grossarth-Maticek, Eysenck, and Vetter (1988) replicated the Yugoslav study in Heidelberg, Germany, using somewhat younger subjects. Because the people were younger, death rates (especially from cancer) were lower. However, the results were quite consistent with those found in Yugoslavia. In Heidelberg, the researchers studied both a group of normal subjects as well as a group of subjects nominated by friends and relatives as being "highly stressed." Once again, cancer was overwhelmingly the leading cause of death among Type I

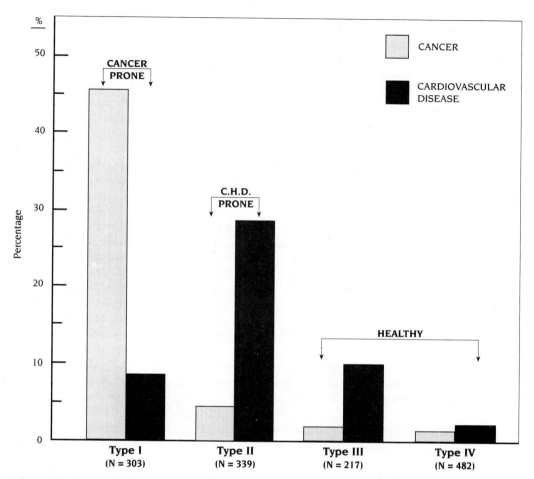

Figure 12.8 *Deaths from Cancer and Cardiovascular Disease, by Personality Type (Yugoslav Study)*

people, whereas heart disease was much more likely to be the cause of death for people with Type II personalities. The results were even more pronounced in the stressed group.

If Eysenck's complex model of cofactors in disease is valid, then changing risk factors for cancer and cardiovascular disease should lower mortality rates for these two leading causes of death. Before looking at research on prevention, let's consider the synergistic effects of the various cofactors. Eysenck, Grossarth-Maticek, and Everitt (1991) demonstrated that personality type, stress, cigarette smoking, and genetic predisposition have more than an additive effect on cancer and heart disease: They have a synergistic effect. Eysenck et al. argued that no single factor (such as smoking) leads to mortality, but that the combination of factors greatly exceeds the sum of individual risks. Therefore, prevention interventions should be aimed at people who combine several risks, for instance, smoking, high stress, and either Type I or Type II personality. Getting people to simply stop smoking, Eysenck (1991d) contended, will have little effect on death rates for lung cancer or cardiovascular disease. But quitting smoking, reducing stress, and changing one's reaction to emotion can have an important prophylactic effect.

Grossarth-Maticek and Eysenck (1991) have used a type of behavior therapy called "creative novation behavior therapy" to train cancer-prone individuals and coronary heart disease subjects to reduce their risks of death from these diseases. Creative novation behavior therapy makes use of different techniques of coping with stress, including Wolpe's (1973) method of desensitization, but mostly it emphasizes the importance of personal autonomy in dealing with life's stresses. The term "novation" suggests that patients are to learn new types of behaviors, ones that are different from the hopeless/helpless, emotion-repressing reactions of cancer-prone patients and the angry, hostile, and aggressive reactions of the coronary-prone patients. The term "creative" suggests that patients are "encouraged to develop these novel behaviours creatively through self-observation and experience of [their] actions" (Grossarth-Maticek & Eysenck, 1991, p. 2).

Eysenck (1987, 1991d) has reported the results of behavioral interventions designed to teach Type I subjects to express their emotions more readily. In this study 100 subjects from the Heidelberg stressed group were randomly divided into a control and a therapy group. The 50 people in the therapy group received individual behavior therapy designed to *change their behavior* from that typical of Type I individuals to that more characteristic of Type IV (the healthy type). In 20 to 30 hourly sessions, the therapist (Grossarth-Maticek) encouraged patients to behave more autonomously, express emotions more freely, and cope with stress more effectively. People in the control group received no therapy.

A 13-year follow-up traced all 100 subjects, living or dead. Of the 50 people in the control group, only 19 were still living; 16 had died of cancer and 15 from other causes. Of the 50 people who had received therapy, 45 were still living; none had died of cancer, and five had died from other causes. These results strongly suggest that creative novation behavior therapy can reshape the personality of cancer-prone individuals and thereby prolong their life.

Behavior therapy appears to be equally effective with people prone to coronary heart disease. Drawing from the same Heidelberg pool of subjects, Eysenck and Grossarth-Maticek (1991) randomly assigned 92 Type II subjects to either a control group or to a therapy group. The 13-year follow-up revealed that only 17 of 46 subjects in the control group were still living; 16 had died of coronary heart disease and 13 had died of other causes. In contrast, 37 of 46 subjects in the therapy group were still living; 3 had died of heart disease, and 6 had died of other causes. Again, these results suggest a strong protective effect of creative novation behavior therapy.

Would any psychotherapeutic intervention be equally effective? Eysenck and Grossarth-Maticek (1991) addressed this question by looking at the records of patients who had received psychoanalysis. Interestingly, they found that psychoanalysis may do more harm than good, and that people who continue in psychoanalytic treatment for more than two years do worst of all. Examining more closely the potentially lethal effects of psychoanalysis, Eysenck and Grossarth-Maticek asked patients who had received psychoanalytic treatment if they believed that their therapy was aimed at increasing or decreasing their autonomy. They found that patients who saw psychoanalysis as increasing their personal autonomy were more likely to survive those who judged their treatment as decreasing autonomy.

In summary, Eysenck et al. (1991, p. 321) stated that "personality and stress exert a powerful effect on a person's likelihood of dying of cancer and CHD, and interact strongly with more widely studied risk factors, such as smoking." More importantly, behavior therapy may help prevent cancer and cardiovascular disease if it can train people prone to these diseases to become more autonomous, to manage stress, and to learn more appropriate ways of expressing emotion.

CRITIQUE OF TRAIT AND FACTOR THEORIES

The trait and factor theories of Cattell and Eysenck are examples of a strictly empirical approach to personality investigation. Both theories were built by collecting as much data as possible on a large number of people, intercorrelating the scores, factor analyzing correlation matrices, and applying appropriate psychological significance to the resultant factors. Psychometrics, rather than clinical judgment, is the cornerstone of trait and factor theories. The approach is scientifically sound; the results, though promising, are nevertheless disappointing. Hypothetically, if two factor analysts set out to measure the same entity (human personality), they should report the same findings just as two chemists should each find the same chemical elements when conducting an analysis of a single compound. However, Cattell has set out trying to measure the entire sphere of human personality, whereas Eysenck has limited himself to only a small area of personality. Therefore, Cattell and Eysenck do not arrive at the same destination after setting out on their journeys to discover the structure of personality.

Nevertheless, we should not dismiss trait and factor theories simply because they have not yet produced a single description of human personality. Like other theories, those of Cattell and Eysenck must be judged by five criteria of a useful theory

First, do trait and factor theories *generate research*? On this criterion the theories of Cattell and Eysenck must be rated high. Cattell, especially, has built his theory inductively, without reliance on a preconceived notion of what personality ought to be. This highly empirical procedure may appear to be atheoretical, but it is actually a sound method of building a theory. In this manner, theory and observation never become estranged. Factor analytic methods not only create hypotheses, they are capable of testing them as well. Cattell and Eysenck have each constructed several personality inventories that have generated a prodigious amount of research. Although many of these investigations are not direct tests of the theory on which the inventories are based, trait and factor theories have generated an impressive amount of research.

Second, do trait and factor theories *organize knowledge*? On this criterion they receive a very high rating. Anything that is truly known about personality should be reducible to some quantity. Anything that can be quantified can be measured, and anything that can be measured can be factor analyzed. The extracted factors then provide a convenient and accurate description of personality in terms of traits. These traits, in turn, can present a framework for organizing many disparate observations about human personality. Traits possess a high level of versatility. They can be viewed as highly specific factors, not much broader than a habit, or they can be clustered to form generalized dispositions or types; they can be seen as individual traits (peculiar to one person) or as common traits (shared by many); and they can be viewed as unitary (unrelated to other traits). In addition, people can be seen in terms of normal or pathological traits and also in terms of learned or inherited traits. Trait and factor theories, then, have the power to give meaning to much of what is known about personality.

A third criterion of a useful theory is the power to *guide the actions of practitioners*. On this criterion, trait and factor theories receive mixed reviews. In general, they provide a comprehensive and structured taxonomy or classification. A taxonomy, though impotent in generating testable hypotheses, is a necessary condition for theory and for science. The classification system provided by trait theorists, particularly Cattell, serves as a useful guide to the researcher and the theory builder, but it is less useful to psychotherapists, teachers, and parents who look toward a sound theoretical system to answer many of their everyday questions.

Are trait and factor theories *internally consistent*? Again, the rating must be equivocal. Each theory alone is a model of consistency, but the two theories taken together are somewhat inconsistent. This presents a problem, especially because factor analysis is a precise mathematical procedure, and because factor theories are heavily empirical.

The final criterion of a useful theory is *parsimony*. Ideally, trait and factor theories should receive an excellent rating on this standard, because factor analysis is predicated on the idea of the fewest number of explanatory factors possible. In other words, the very purpose of factor analysis is to reduce a large number of variables to as few as possible. This is the essence of parsimony. Eysenck, with only three factors, certainly has epitomized parsimony. Cattell, on the other hand, has not only extracted many more factors but has also applied neologistic labels to most of them, thus rendering his language troublesome for the uninitiated.

Chapter Summary

A summary of the assumptions underlying trait and factor theories has been provided by Eysenck (1981, p. 3), who believes that eight statements have now been firmly established and are acceptable not only to him, but also to Cattell.

1. Individuals differ with respect to their location on important semi-permanent personality dispositions, known as "traits."
2. Personality traits can be identified by means of correlational (factor analytical) studies.
3. Personality traits are importantly determined by hereditary factors.
4. Personality traits are measurable by means of questionnaire data.
5. The interactive influence of traits and situations produces transient internal conditions, known as "states."
6. Personality states are measurable by means of questionnaire data.
7. Traits and states are intervening variables or mediating variables that are useful in explaining individual differences in behavior to the extent that they are incorporated into an appropriate theoretical framework.
8. The relationship between traits or states and behavior is typically indirect, being affected or "moderated" by the interactions that exist among traits, states, and other salient factors.

Cattell's theory of personality is psychometrically rather than clinically based. He began with no preconceived ideas on the structure of human personality; proceeded inductively to gather quantified information from life reports (L data), self-reports (Q data), and objective test performance (T data); obtained intercorrelations of scores; and then extracted *primary factors* from the correlation matrices. These factors emerged as psychologically meaningful traits within three modalities of personality—*temperament, ability,* and *motivation.*

In all, Cattell identified 35 *first-order personality traits*—23 within the realm of normal personality, plus 12 pathological traits. These factors are themselves intercorrelated, thus allowing for further factoring and the extraction of at least 15 *second-stratum factors.* These primary and secondary factors are called "general personality traits," but they are largely traits of temperament.

Cattell has also been able to classify ability and motivation traits. Motivation (*dynamic traits*) is divided into innate drives (or *ergs*) and culturally acquired motives called sentiments, or *sems.* Both are part of the *dynamic lattice,* which also includes the more fundamental concept of *attitudes.* After more than 50 years of work, Cattell, who set out to explore the entire sphere of human personality, has succeeded in mapping a comprehensive taxonomy of personality structure and suggesting possible means of predicting behavior.

In contrast, Eysenck has had more modest goals. Relying more on a *hypothetio-deductive approach*, he has extracted only three bipolar factors—extraversion/introversion, neuroticism/stability, and psychoticism/superego.

Extraversion is characterized by sociability and impulsiveness—-

introversion by passivity and thoughtfulness; *neuroticism* by anxiety and compulsivity—*stability* by their absence; *psychoticism* by antisocial behavior—*superego* by empathy and cooperation.

Both Cattell and Eysenck place heavy emphasis on *biological components of personality.*

Suggested Readings

CATTELL, R. B. (1974). An autobiography. In G. Lindzey (Ed.), A *history of psychology in autobiography* (Vol. 6) (pp. 59–100). Englewood Cliffs, NJ: Prentice-Hall.
Although this autobiography is several years old, it provides an interesting account of Cattell's early life in England, his settling in the United States, and his lengthy search for various components of personality.

CATTELL, R. B. (1983). *Structured personality-learning theory: A wholistic multivariate research approach.* New York: Praeger.
Although sections of this book, with their complicated mathematical formulas, are difficult to comprehend, Cattell offers much to the interested reader.

CATTELL, R. B. (1990). Advances in Cattellian personality theory. In L. A. Pervin (Ed.), *Handbook of personality: Theory and research* (pp. 101–110). New York: Guilford Press.
With this chapter Cattell provides a brief update of his theory and research, including a description of the dynamic calculus, and a guide for future research.

EYSENCK, H. J. (1982). Personality. In H. J. Eysenck, *Personality, genetics, and behavior: Selected papers* (pp. 49–109). New York: Praeger.
A selection of six papers on personality including a brief discussion of the three superfactors—extraversion, neuroticism, and psychoticism.

EYSENCK, H. J. (1990). *Rebel with a cause: The autobiography of H. J. Eysenck.* London: W. H. Allen.
Although literary expression is not one of Eysenck's principal strengths, this autobiography is consistently informative, interesting, and witty. Eysenck writes of his relationship with Cyril Burt and Ronald Grossarth-Maticek, among many others.

Psychology of the Individual

Chapter Thirteen

OVERVIEW
BIOGRAPHY OF GORDON ALLPORT
ALLPORT'S APPROACH
    Open System
    Eclecticism
PERSONALITY DEFINED
STRUCTURE OF PERSONALITY
    Personal Dispositions
    Proprium
BOX: MR. CLEAN MEETS DR. FREUD
GROWTH OF PERSONALITY
    The Developing Person
    Cultural Influences
    Motivation
    The Healthy Personality
THE STUDY OF THE INDIVIDUAL
    Morphogenic Science
    Letters from Jenny
CONCEPT OF HUMANITY
RELATED RESEARCH
CRITIQUE OF ALLPORT
CHAPTER SUMMARY
SUGGESTED READINGS

ALLPORT

As she lay in her bed in a home for aged women, Jenny was unable to sleep. The lights from a saloon across the street, the pain from a recent broken foot, the constant worry about money, and the doubts about the honesty of the nurses caring for her all made her restless. Suddenly, she felt a hand on her neck and back. Terrified with fright, she struck out at her intruder, hitting her on the breast and head and calling her an assortment of foul names. Jenny was sure that the nurse was trying to steal her money. People at the "home" couldn't be trusted. They were a bunch of hypocrites, liars, and double dealers.

The next morning Jenny apologized to the nurse whom she had attacked. When the nurse explained that she was only trying to see if Jenny was warm enough, Jenny didn't believe her. In fact, she trusted almost no one. She detested the other residents and turned her face to the wall when meeting them in the corridor. She was suspicious of the staff, accusing them of opening her mail, inadequately feeding her, and trying to steal her money. Jenny's animosity was especially virulent against women, but men were not spared her wrath either.

Jenny was nearly 70 years old and had less than a year to live. Except for the pleasure she received from reading great literature, visiting art museums, and viewing beautiful sunsets, her life now had few pleasant moments.

Jenny was the oldest in a family of seven children that included five sisters and a brother. When she was 18, her father died, so Jenny was forced to quit school and go to work to help support her family. After her brother and sisters became self-supporting, Jenny, who had always been considered rebellious, married a divorced man. This further alienated her from her conservatively religious family.

After only two years of marriage her husband died, and her son Ross was born a month later. The next 17 years were somewhat contented ones for Jenny. Her world revolved around her son, and she worked hard to ensure that he had everything he wanted. She told Ross that, aside from art, the world was a miserable place, and that it was her duty to sacrifice for him because she was responsible for his existence.

When Ross moved away to attend college, Jenny continued to scrimp in order to pay all his bills. As Ross began to become interested in women, his idyllic relationship with his mother came to an end. The two quarreled often and bitterly over his women friends. Jenny referred to each of them as prostitutes or whores, including the woman Ross married. With that marriage, Jenny and Ross became temporarily estranged.

At about that same time, Jenny began to correspond with Ross's former college roommate, Glenn, and his wife Isabel. During the next 11 and a half years Jenny wrote a series of 301 letters to the young couple in which she revealed much about both her life and her personality. The early letters showed that she was deeply concerned with money, death, and Ross. She felt that Ross was ungrateful and that he had abandoned her for another woman, and a prostitute at that. She continued her bitterness toward him until he and his wife were divorced. She then moved to the apartment next to Ross and, for a short time, Jenny was happy. But soon Ross was seeing other women and Jenny inevitably found something wrong with each. Her letters to Glenn and Isabel were filled with animosity for Ross, a suspicious and cynical attitude toward others, and a morbid yet dramatic approach to life.

Three years into the correspondence, Ross suddenly died. Now Jenny's letters expressed a somewhat more favorable attitude toward him. Now she did not have to share him with anyone. Now he was safe—no more prostitutes.

For the next eight years, Jenny continued writing to Glenn and Isabel, and they usually answered her. However, they served mostly as neutral listeners and not as advisors or confidantes. Jenny continued to be overly concerned with death and money. She increasingly blamed others for her misery and intensified her suspicions and hostility toward her caregivers. After Jenny died, Isabel commented that, in the end, Jenny was "the same only more so."

OVERVIEW

Later in this chapter we will learn more about Jenny. Her letters represent the kind of personal documents used by Gordon W. Allport to support his ideas that personality should be studied from the individual's point of view. Allport insisted that the study of the person must take into consideration the uniqueness of every individual. This concern for individuality makes Allport himself rather unique among personality theorists, most of whom look for general laws based on common elements among people. In contrast, Allport advocated the study of the individual.

Allport was concerned with uniqueness and individuality because he firmly believed that the psychology of personality must occupy an intermediate position between universal laws and generalities on the one hand, and the anarchy of complete individuality on the other. He leaned far in the direction of individuality in order to balance existing theories, which he believed were overly inclined toward a generalized concept of humanity.

As a reaction to psychoanalysis and learning theory, Allport's psychology of the individual attempted to swing the pendulum back to a middle position—a position that even he might have found more satisfying than the completely individualistic one he sometimes advocated. His intention was to supplement rather than supplant the findings of psychoanalysis, stimulus–response theories, operant conditioning, and social psychology.

Allport was eclectic in his acceptance of certain observations cited by these older schools, but he feared that they might hide the individual essence of personality. He believed that only by using the findings of psychoanalysis, learning theory, and social psychology, in conjunction with the findings and procedures of his individual psychology, could the psychology of personality strike a happy middle ground. Many of his writings therefore are controversial and overstated, but that was his intention. He once wrote, "I know in my bones that my opponents are partly right" (Allport, 1968, p. 405).

BIOGRAPHY OF GORDON ALLPORT

Gordon W. Allport was born on November 11, 1897, in Montezuma, Indiana, the youngest of four sons. His father, a country doctor, and his mother, a former schoolteacher, moved their family to the Cleveland, Ohio, area, where Gordon received his first 12 years of schooling.

The youngest child by five years, Allport developed an early interest in philosophical and religious questions and more facility for words than for games. Although he graduated second in his high school class of 100, he did not consider himself an inspired scholar (Allport, 1967).

In the fall of 1915, Allport entered Harvard, following in the footsteps of his older brother, Floyd, who had graduated two years earlier and was at that time a graduate assistant in psychology. His enrollment at Harvard marked the beginning of a 50-year association with that university, which was interrupted only briefly on several occasions. He received his bachelor's degree in 1919 with a major in philosophy and economics. However, he was still uncertain about a future career. He had taken undergraduate courses in psychology and social ethics, and both disciplines had made a lasting impression on him. When he received an opportunity to teach in Turkey, he saw it as a chance to find out whether or not he would enjoy teaching. He spent the academic year 1919–1920 in Europe teaching English and sociology at Robert College in Istanbul.

Allport returned to Harvard in 1920 with a fellowship for graduate study but not before an interesting meeting with Sigmund Freud. With a certain audacity, the 22-year-old Allport wrote to Freud announcing his intention to visit Vienna and offered the father of psychoanalysis an opportunity to meet with him. The encounter was significant to Allport, who, not knowing what to talk about, told Freud about seeing a small boy on the train that same day who had displayed a dirt phobia, constantly complaining to his mother about the filthy conditions on the train. After Allport completed the story, Freud looked at him and said, "And was that little boy you?"

This single response was to have great meaning for Allport. Although not an anti-Freudian, he was later to evolve a personality theory that was almost diametrically opposed to psychoanalysis concerning the importance of unconscious motivation. Whereas Freud assumed an underlying unconscious meaning to such stories, Allport was inclined to accept self-reports at face value. This simple anecdote reveals a basic dichotomy between Allport and Freud in their approach to the scientific study of behavior.

Back at Harvard, Allport quickly finished his work, receiving a Ph.D. in psychology in 1922 at age 24. The following two years he spent in Europe studying under the great German psychologists Max Wertheimer, Wolfgang Kohler, William Stern, Heinz Werner, and others in Berlin and Hamburg. The latter half of his European experience was spent in Cambridge, England, where he had a chance to absorb what he had learned in Germany.

In 1924 he returned again to Harvard to teach, among other classes, a new course in the psychology of personality. After two years he took a position at Dartmouth College, but four years later he returned to Harvard, where he remained until his death. He died on October 9, 1967, of lung cancer.

In 1925 Allport married Ada Lufkin Gould, whom he had met when both were graduate students in psychology, and who later became a clinical psychologist. Their son Robert became a pediatrician, thus sandwiching Allport between two generations of physicians, a fact that seemed to have pleased him in no small measure (Allport, 1967). Allport's awards and honors have been many. His popularity among his students and his student's students contributed to a colloquium series at the Berkeley campus of the University of California in 1987 celebrating the 50th anniversary of the publication of *Personality: A Psychological Interpretation* (Allport, 1937).

In 1939, Allport was elected president of the American Psychological Association (APA). In 1963 he received the Gold Medal Award of the APA; in 1964 he was awarded the Distinguished Scientific Contribution Award of the APA, and in 1966 he was honored as the first Richard Clarke Cabot Professor of Social Ethics at Harvard. However, he received his most prized honor in 1963 when 55 of his former Ph.D. students presented him with two volumes of their own writings dedicated to him "in appreciation of his respect for their individuality" (Allport, 1967, p. 24).

ALLPORT'S APPROACH

Allport criticized older theories of personality for losing sight of the normal, psychologically healthy individual. Most people, he believed, are motivated by present drives rather than past events. They are aware of what they are doing and have some understanding of why they are doing it. They not only seek to reduce tensions but to establish new ones as well. They have the potential to learn new patterns of behavior and to grow during any period of their lives.

In his approach to personality, Allport adopted an *open system* and was *eclectic* in his construction of a personality theory.

Open System

In advocating an **open system** in the study of personality, Allport was suggesting that any theory of personality must take into consideration the fact that people not only react to their environment but also shape their environment and cause it to react to them. Personality is a growing system, allowing new elements constantly to enter into and change the person.

Allport (1960) believed that many theories of personality are not based on an open system, but rather on a partially closed one, which does not adequately allow for possibilities of growth. Psychoanalysis and the various learning theories are basically homeostatic and view humanity as a quasiclosed system. These theories can also be called *reactive theories* because they treat human personality as basically reactive; that is, they see people being motivated primarily by needs to reduce tension and to return to a state of equilibrium.

A truly open system of personality must allow for **proactive behavior**, meaning that it must view people as being capable of consciously acting upon their environment in new and innovative ways that permit them to grow toward psychological health. Also an open system must meet four criteria, the first two of which also apply to partially closed systems:

1. "There is intake and output of both matter and energy" (Allport, 1960, p. 303). Any system, whether machine, animal, or human, meets this criterion. In fact, this is the basic definition of a system.

2. "There is achievement and maintenance of steady (homeostatic) states, so that intrusion of outer energy will not seriously disrupt internal form and order" (Allport, 1960, p. 303). Theories based on reduction of tensions, satisfaction of needs, and other homeostatic concepts meet this criterion, but they usually do not go beyond this point. (An exception is Maslow's theory, [see Chapter 15], which is based on satisfaction of needs, but it nevertheless allows for psychological growth.) Theories that meet only the first two criteria regard the person as an essentially static animal, constantly driven by internal or external forces to seek a state of equilibrium.

   No theory of personality is based on a completely closed system. Openness is a matter of degree. Allport believed that most theories of personality meet these first two criteria. However, those that satisfy only these two are quasiclosed or merely partially open. Allport, of course, advocated a completely open system in personality theory, one that meets the third and fourth criteria as well as the first two.

3. "There is generally an increase of order over time, owing to an increase in complexity and differentiation of parts" (Allport, 1960, p. 303). An open system of personality must meet this third criterion; that is, it must allow

for fundamental change and growth within the organism. Allport's theory repeatedly emphasizes the point that people not only attempt to reduce tension, but they also, at times, actually *seek* tension and enjoy its maintenance. Other theories that postulate growth, notably those of Jung (Chapter 5), Maslow (Chapter 15), and Rogers (Chapter 16), also meet this key criterion.

4. "There is more than mere intake and output of matter and energy; there is extensive transactional commerce with the environment" (Allport, 1960, p. 303). This criterion points toward the importance of culture or society and insists that the person and the environment comprise one mutually interactive system. Field theories, which insist that people cannot be viewed apart from their surroundings, meet this fourth criterion.

Allport suggested that controversies in personality theory arise from two basic opposing views: the *homeostatic position* espoused by Freud, Skinner, and others; and the *growth theories* advocated by Maslow, Rogers, and others. The homeostatic theorists emphasize the first two criteria of an open system, the growth theorists stress the latter two, especially the third criterion. Although Allport advocated an open system, he emphasized that any adequate theory of personality must be able to incorporate the explanation of *reactive theories*, while at the same time it must make allowances for *proactive theories* that stress change and growth. In other words, a complete personality theory must meet all four criteria of an open system. Allport, therefore, argued for a psychology that, on the one hand, studies behavioral patterns and general laws (the subject matter of traditional psychology) and, on the other, growth and individuality.

Eclecticism

Because an adequate theory of personality must explain proactive as well as reactive behavior, it must be sufficiently broad in scope and procedure to encompass the growing, evolving person on the one hand, and the static, adjustive person on the other. Thus Allport advocated an **eclectic** approach to theory building. He argued against particularism, or theories that emphasize a single approach, and he went on to warn theorists not to "forget what you have decided to neglect" (Allport, 1968, p. 23). In other words, no theory is completely comprehensive, and one should always realize that much of human nature is not included in any single theory.

Allport accepted the contributions of Freud, Cattell, Skinner, and others, but he believed that these theorists were unable to explain the growing, changing personality. The growth theories of Maslow, Rogers, and Allport himself add to the earlier foundation formed by psychoanalysis and learning theory, but none is complete by itself. Allport (1968), therefore, favored eclecticism over particularism because it is less restrictive and offers more hope in understanding the complete and unique person. Broader theories, even when they do not generate specific testable hypotheses, are preferable to narrow ones, because they organize known facts from all kinds of research as well as from intuition.

PERSONALITY DEFINED

Few psychologists have been as painstaking and exhaustive as Allport in defining terms. His pursuit of a definition of personality is a classic. He traced the etymology of the word *persona* back to early Greek roots, including the Old Latin and Etruscan meanings. As we saw in Chapter 1, the word personality probably comes from **persona**, which refers to the theatrical mask used in ancient Greek drama during the first and second centuries before Christ. After tracing the history of the term, Allport spelled out 49 definitions of personality as used in theology, philosophy, law, sociology, and psychology. He then offered a 50th definition, which in 1937 was *"the dynamic organization within the individual of those psychophysical systems that determine his unique adjustments to his environment* (Allport, 1937, p. 48).

By 1961 he had changed the last phrase to read *"that determine his characteristic behavior and thought"* (Allport, 1961, p. 28). The change was significant and reflected Allport's penchant for accuracy. By 1961 he realized that the phrase "adjustments to his environment" could imply that people merely adapt to their environment. In his later definition Allport conveys the idea that behavior is *expressive* as well as adaptive. People not only adjust to their environment, but also reflect on it and interact with it in such a way as to cause their environment to adjust to them.

Allport chose each phrase of his definition carefully so that each word conveys precisely what he wanted to say. The term *dynamic organization* implies an integration or interrelatedness of the various aspects of personality. Personality is organized and patterned. However, the organization is always subject to change, hence the qualifier "dynamic." Personality is not a static organization; it is constantly growing or changing.

The term *psychophysical* emphasizes the importance of both the psychological and the physical aspects of personality.

Allport (1960, p. 302) defined the word *system* as a "complex of elements in mutual interaction." Traits, for example, are systems. So too are habits and sentiments. System implies activity, either as potentiality or as action itself.

Another word in the definition that implies action is *determine*, which implies that "personality is something and does something" (Allport, 1961, p. 29). In other words, personality is not merely the mask we wear; nor is it simply behavior. It refers to the person behind the façade, the organism behind the action.

By *characteristic* Allport wished to imply individual or unique. The word "character" originally meant a marking or engraving, terms that give flavor to what Allport meant by "characteristic." All persons stamp their unique mark or engraving on their personality, and their characteristic behavior and thought set them apart from all other people. Characteristics are marked with a unique engraving, a stamp, or marking that no one else can duplicate.

The words *behavior and thought* simply refer to anything the person does. They are omnibus terms meant to include internal behaviors (thoughts) as well as external behaviors such as words and actions.

Allport's comprehensive definition of personality suggests that human beings are both product and process; people have some organized structure while, at the same time, they possess the capability of change. Pattern co-exists with growth, order with diversification.

Personality is everything, both physical and psychological; it includes both overt behaviors and covert thoughts; it not only *is* something, but it *does* something. Personality is both substance and change; both product and process; both structure and growth.

STRUCTURE OF PERSONALITY

The structure of personality refers to its basic units or building blocks. To Freud the basic units are instincts; to Cattell and Eysenck they are *traits*. To Allport, the most important structures are those that permit the description of the person in terms of individual characteristics. Thus, the two basic units of personality are *personal dispositions* and the *proprium*.

Personal Dispositions

In a conversation with Richard Evans (1976), Allport rejected the label of trait psychologist because he believed that the term *trait* implies a general characteristic held in common by several people. Allport was careful to distinguish between *common traits* and individual traits, or *personal dispositions* (PDs). **Common traits** are those aspects of human personality that lend themselves to interindividual comparisons. They provide the means by which the characteristics of people within a given culture can be compared. Whereas common traits are important for studies that make comparisons among people, personal dispositions are of even greater importance because they permit researchers to study a single individual.

Allport used the term personal dispositions (PDs) rather than individual traits because it is more descriptive and less likely to be confused with common traits. He defined a **personal disposition** as "a generalized neuropsychic structure (peculiar to the individual), with the capacity to render many stimuli functionally equivalent, and to initiate and guide consistent (equivalent) forms of adaptive and stylistic behavior" (Allport, 1961, p. 373). The most important distinction between a personal disposition and a common trait is indicated by the parenthetical phrase "peculiar to the individual." Personal dispositions are individual; common traits are shared by several people.

To identify personal dispositions, Allport and Odbert (1936) counted approximately 18,000 personally descriptive words in the 1925 edition of *Webster's New International Dictionary*, about a fourth of which described personality characteristics.

Some of these terms, usually referred to as *traits,* described relatively stable characteristics such as sociable or introverted; others, usually referred to as *states,* described temporary characteristics such as happy or angry; others described evaluative characteristics such as unpleasant or wonderful; and still others referred to physical characteristics such as tall or obese.

How many personal dispositions does one person have? This question cannot be answered without reference to the degree of dominance the PD has in the individual's life. If we count those personal dispositions that are central to a person, then each person probably has 10 or fewer. However, if all tendencies or dispositions are included, then each person may have hundreds of PDs.

Levels of Personal Dispositions

Allport placed personal dispositions on a continuum from those that are most central to those that are of only peripheral importance to a person.

CARDINAL TRAITS.   Some people possess an eminent trait or ruling passion so outstanding that it dominates their lives. Allport (1961) called these personal dispositions **cardinal traits**. They are so obvious that they cannot be hidden; nearly every action in a person's life revolves around this one cardinal disposition. Most people do not have a cardinal trait, but those few people who do are often known by that single characteristic.

Allport identified several historical people and fictional characters who possessed a disposition so outstanding that they have become associated with that trait name. Some examples of these traits include quixotic, narcissistic, sadistic, a Don Juan, and so forth. Because personal dispositions are individual and not shared with any other person, only Don Quixote was truly quixotic; only Narcissus was completely narcissistic; only the Marquis de Sade possessed the cardinal disposition of sadism. When these names are used to describe characteristics in others, they then become common traits.

CENTRAL TRAITS.   Few people have cardinal dispositions, but everyone has several central traits. These central personal dispositions include the five to ten most outstanding characteristics around which a person's life focuses. Allport (1961) described central dispositions as those that would be listed in an accurate letter of recommendation written by someone who knew the person quite well.

We began this chapter with the story of Jenny, a woman with strong love/hate feelings for her son Ross. Through Jenny's letters to Ross's friends, we find that she possessed seven or eight central traits that characterized the last 12 years of her life, if not her entire life. She was aggressive, suspicious, possessive, aesthetic, sentimental, morbid, dramatic, and self-centered. These central dispositions were sufficiently powerful so that she was described in terms similar to these both by Isabel, who knew her well, and by independent researchers, who studied her letters (Allport, 1965).

Similarly, most people who knew Gordon Allport described him as reserved, prim, and orderly (see Mary H. Hall's 1968 interview with A. H. Maslow). Allport's reputation as "Mr. Clean Personality" (Elms, 1972) has raised interesting questions about his single encounter with Sigmund Freud (see box—"Mr. Clean Meets Dr. Freud").

SECONDARY TRAITS. Less conspicuous but far greater in number than central traits are the **secondary traits** or dispositions. Everyone has many secondary dispositions. These are traits that are not central to the personality, yet they occur with some regularity and are responsible for much of one's specific behaviors.

The three levels of personal dispositions or traits are, of course, arbitrary points on a continuous scale from most appropriate to least appropriate. Cardinal dispositions, which are exceedingly prominent in a person, shade into central dispositions, which are less dominating, but which nevertheless mark the person as unique. Central PDs, which guide much of a person's adaptive and stylistic behavior, blend into secondary dispositions, which are less descriptive of that individual. We cannot say, however, that one person's secondary dispositions are less intense than another person's central PDs. Interperson comparisons are inappropriate to personal dispositions, and any attempt to make such comparison transforms the personal dispositions into common traits (Allport, 1961).

Motivational and Stylistic Traits

All personal dispositions are dynamic in the sense that they have motivational power. Nevertheless, some are much more strongly felt than others, and Allport called these intensely experienced PDs *motivational traits*. These strongly felt traits receive their motivation from basic needs and drives. Allport referred to personal dispositions that are less intensely experienced as *stylistic traits*, even though these traits possess some motivational power. Stylistic traits *guide* action, whereas motivational traits *initiate* action. An example of a stylistic PD might be impeccable personal appearance. People are motivated to dress because of a basic need to stay warm, but the manner in which they attire themselves is determined by their stylistic personal dispositions (Allport, 1961).

No sharp line exists between motivational and stylistic personal dispositions, because all PDs have some motivational power. Although some traits are clearly stylistic, others are obviously based on a strongly felt need and are thus motivational. Politeness, for example, is a stylistic trait, whereas eating is more motivational. How people eat (their style) depends at least partially on how hungry they are, but it also depends on the strength of their stylistic dispositions. A usually polite but hungry person may forego manners while eating alone, but if the politeness trait is strong enough and if others are present, then that person may eat with etiquette and courtesy, despite being famished.

Whether motivational or stylistic, some personal dispositions are close to the core of personality, whereas others are more on the periphery. Those that are at the center of personality are experienced by the person as being an important part of self. They are the ones an individual refers to in such terms as, "That is me," or "This is mine." All characteristics that are "peculiarly mine" belong to *proprium* (Allport, 1955).

Proprium

Allport used the term **proprium** to refer to those behaviors and characteristics that we regard as warm, central, and important in our lives. The proprium is not the whole personality, because many characteristics and behaviors of a person are not warm and central; rather they exist on the periphery of personality. These non-propriate behaviors include (1) basic drives and needs that are ordinarily met and satisfied without much trouble; (2) tribal customs such as saying "hello" to people, wearing clothes, and driving on the right side of the road; and (3) habitual behaviors,

Mr. Clean Meets Dr. Freud

Although he was not an anti-Freudian, Allport advocated views on the importance of unconscious motivation that were directly opposite to those of Freud. According to Allport, mentally disturbed people may frequently be driven by unconscious strivings, but most adults are aware of their reasons for acting. We need not go below surface behavior to detect the meaning of other people's actions.

In his autobiography, Allport (1967) reported that his single meeting with Freud in Vienna convinced him that psychoanalysis was mistaken in its penchant for looking beneath the surface for some unconscious motive. During this meeting with Freud, when Allport could not think of anything to say, he related the story of a young boy on the train whom he had seen earlier that same day. The boy, about four years old, had displayed an obvious dirt phobia, and Allport claimed that he chose this particular incident in order to get Freud's reaction to a dirt phobia in a child so young. He was quite flabbergasted, however, when Freud "fixed his kindly therapeutic eyes upon [him] and said, 'And was that little boy you?' " (Allport, 1967, p. 8).

Allport told this story many times as an illustration of the silliness of psychoanalytic procedures. How could Freud have been so blind as to overlook the obvious? Why read hidden meaning into a story that was selected more or less at random? Freud obviously was accustomed to looking for underlying significance in even the most innocent and innocuous statements. Allport thought that Freud had misunderstood his manifest motivation in telling the story, and he was amused by Freud's misunderstanding. But was Freud really on the wrong track?

Some psychoanalytically oriented writers have taken Allport to task for his naivete. M. D. Faber (1970, p. 61), writing in *The Psychoanalytic Review*, contended that "Allport missed and misinterpreted the significance of the entire incident." Faber believed that Freud, indeed, made exactly the correct interpretation in suggesting that the little boy was, in fact, Gordon Allport. He suggested that Allport chose that particular story because of his preconception that Freud liked to hear "dirty" stories. Allport was "naughty" in presuming to call on Freud and he showed his naughtiness by "pulling a dirty trick" on Freud. Freud immediately saw that it was such as smoking and brushing one's teeth, that are performed automatically and that are not crucial to the person's sense of self.

As the warm center of personality, the proprium includes those aspects of a person that are regarded as important to a sense of self-identity and self-enhancement (Allport, 1955). The proprium includes a person's values, as well as that part of the conscience that is personal and consistent with one's adult beliefs. A generalized conscience (one shared by most people within a given culture) may be only peripheral to a person's sense of personhood and thus outside that person's proprium.

GROWTH OF PERSONALITY

Allport's theory of personality rests on a dual system of motivation. People are driven by both the need *to adjust* to their environment *and* by the tendency *to grow*

Allport who was dirty, and his own question was an attempt to put the conversation on an honest level. Furthermore, Faber contended, Allport unconsciously knew before he arrived at Freud's house that Freud would be psychoanalyzing him and, after the incident, he unconsciously knew that Freud had seen through him.

Alan Elms (1972), in a later article in the same publication, added to Faber's interpretation of the incident. He looked to Allport's childhood for clues concerning his motivation in telling Freud about the clean little boy. In his autobiography, Allport (1967, p. 4) wrote that his early life "was marked by plain Protestant piety." His father was a physician who, lacking adequate outside facilities, turned the Allport household into a miniature hospital. Both patients and nurses occupied the home, and a clean, sterile atmosphere prevailed. With this background, Elms asserted, Allport was preoccupied with cleanliness and, in fact, was later known as "Mr. Clean Personality." Elms believed that Freud immediately saw through Allport's "pathological" concern with dirt. Allport admitted that he felt guilty when Freud asked if the little boy was him, and he therefore contrived to change the subject. Elms saw Allport's em-

barrassment as evidence that Allport knew unconsciously that Freud was right.

How convincing is such evidence? Are people ordinarily aware of the reasons for their actions, as Allport contended, or are they motivated by hidden forces beneath their consciousness? Can such incidents as Allport's meeting with Freud be taken at face value or must one look for sinister intentions behind these stories? Was Freud really so perceptive that he could immediately see Allport's true intentions, as Faber and Elms claimed?

Perhaps we need not adopt either the psychoanalytic or the Allport view of this incident. Quite possibly, Allport's choice of the clean little boy story was not entirely random but a reflection of his personality and his early training in cleanliness. But at the same time, we need not imbue Freud with superhuman powers of perception. After all, Freud *asked* if the little boy was Allport; he did not state it as a fact. In other words, he was guessing that his young visitor was intentionally disguising himself, a strategy not uncommon in psychotherapeutic patients. Allport was *not* the little boy, but the selection of that particular incident may not have been an entirely chance event.

or to become more and more self-actualized. Adjustment needs and growth needs exist side by side within the same person, and any adequate theory of personality, Allport said, must take into consideration the fact that people are both reactive and proactive.

The Developing Person

Allport (1961) believed that the sense of self evolves from birth to adulthood in seven overlapping and cumulative stages. At birth, Allport contended, infants do not have a personality because they possess no characteristic modes of behavior and thought. Thus they have only potential personality, one based on genetic endowment. Unlike most psychologists, Allport believed that the first year of life is the *least* important one.

The first three or four years of life comprise the three earliest aspects of self-hood—the bodily sense, self-identity, and ego-esteem. The first aspect of selfhood to evolve is the *bodily sense* (Allport, 1961). Throughout our lives our bodies provide us with a reference for self-awareness. If I scrape my arm, I know that the blood and the pain are "peculiarly mine." They belong to no other person and give me a bodily sense of self.

A second early aspect of the developing proprium is the sense of continuing *self-identity* (Allport, 1961). This feeling of who I am includes my thoughts and actions as well as my memory of them and the acceptance of them as mine. At first, the sense of self-identity is weak, and children may accept imaginary characteristics as their own. Their self-identity is closely bound to their social surroundings, especially the family: "This is my house" or "That tricycle is mine." The words "I," "me," and "mine" dominate the vocabulary of young children.

The third aspect of early self is ego-enhancement or *self-esteem* (Allport, 1961). Self-esteem, which can be both positive and negative, is that property of the proprium that involves pride, selfishness, narcissism, and other behaviors and sentiments related to exaltation of the ego.

From ages four to six, children are extremely egocentric. While their bodily sense, self-identity, and self-esteem continue to grow during this period, a fourth and fifth stage of the proprium begin to emerge. The fourth is the *extension of self* and the fifth is the *self-image*. Children broaden their sense of self to include possessions (clothes, toys, and pets), as well as mother, father, sisters, and brothers. Self-image refers to one's view of present abilities, status, and roles and also to one's aspirations or future goals. It consists largely of the child's image of self as a "good" or "bad" person—in Freudian terms, one's ego-ideal and conscience (Allport, 1961).

The years from six to twelve are important because school extends a child's life beyond the family. During this period of reality testing, challenges by classmates and teachers modify the child's self-identity, self-esteem, and self-image. The sixth stage, the *rational-self*, which develops during these early school years, is capable of rationalization and denials, but it is also capable of reasoning correctly and finding solutions to the problems of living. The rational-self is responsible for formal and

An infant's developing selfhood includes a growing sense of "me" and "not me."

reflective thought and reconciling inner needs with demands of the external world (Allport, 1961).

Adolescence brings about a seventh and final aspect of the self as object, namely **propriate strivings**. At this level a person emerges as a truly unique individual with a clearly defined sense of personhood and a well-developed proprium, which unifies the other six aspects of self. Propriate strivings also lead to some consistency in actions and thoughts and allow the person to set goals that maintain tension rather than merely reduce it (Allport, 1961).

Propriate strivings are those that are close to the person; that is, they are experienced as "peculiarly mine." They rely on memory of past experiences, but they also include thoughts of the future in the form of realistic planning and intention. The problems of selecting a mate and choosing a career can be successfully pursued only through propriate strivings, although some people stumble into choosing a spouse or a job without any sense of purpose. When people drift into decisions, their striving is called "opportunistic," because it is not part of the proprium and exists only on the periphery of personality (Allport, 1961). In a real sense, the goals of propriate strivings are not attainable because people constantly seek to maintain tension and to strive for goals they may never reach (Allport, 1955).

In addition to these seven stages, Allport (1961) identified an eighth aspect of self called the *self as knower*, or the subjective self. However, only the first seven aspects of self belong to the proprium. The self as knower is the "I" that is aware of the objective "me." When I think of my self, I can think only of my objective self; that is, my physical self, my reputation, my self-image, and so on. But who is the "I" doing the thinking? This is also my self, but it is the self as knower and cannot be part of my proprium.

Personality and proprium are not synonymous, because personality includes many habits, emotions, traits, tribal customs, opportunistic strivings, adjustment patterns, and chance factors that are not warm and central to the person. Some skills such as typing or driving a car may be propriate in the beginning, but later they lose their central importance and become opportunistic. Others, such as language, are not ordinarily propriate, but when denied to a person or when accomplished only through great difficulty, they can become part of the proprium.

Cultural Influences

The growth of personality always takes place within a cultural setting, but Allport placed only moderate emphasis on cultural and social factors. He recognized the importance of environmental influences in helping to shape personality, but, unlike his brother, Floyd, he cannot be called a social psychologist. Rather, he sought a balance between those theories that emphasize individual development and those that stress the importance of society. Allport (1955) believed that culture is important, but he insisted that personality has some life of its own. On the one hand, a person can change while society remains relatively stable, but, on the other hand, an individual will often maintain a consistent personality even in the face of great social upheaval. Culture can influence our language, our morals, our values, our fashions, and so forth, but how each of us reacts to cultural forces depends on our unique personality and our basic motivation.

Motivation

Allport (1961) contended that an adequate theory of motivation must consider that peripheral motives and propriate strivings are not of the same kind. Peripheral motives are those that *reduce a need*, whereas propriate strivings seek to *maintain tension and disequilibrium*. Adult behavior is both reactive and proactive, and an adequate theory of motivation must be able to explain both. Allport claimed that theories of unchanging motives are incomplete because they are limited to an explanation of reactive behavior. The mature person, however, is not motivated merely to seek pleasure and reduce pain but to acquire new systems of motivation that are functionally independent from their original motives.

Functional Autonomy

The concept of **functional autonomy** represents Allport's most distinctive and, at the same time, most controversial postulate. It is Allport's (1961) explanation for the myriad human motives that seemingly are not accounted for by hedonistic or drive-reduction principles. Functional autonomy represents a theory of changing rather than unchanging motives and is the capstone of Allport's ideas on motivation.

In general, the concept of functional autonomy holds that some, but not all, human motives are functionally independent from the original motive responsible for the behavior. If a motive is functionally autonomous it is the explanation for behavior, and we need not look beyond it for hidden or primary causes. In other words, if hoarding money is a functionally autonomous motive, then the miser's behavior is *not* traceable to anal needs or to childhood experiences with reward and punishment. Rather, the miser simply *likes* money, and this is the only explanation necessary. This idea that much of our behavior is based on present interests and on conscious preferences is in harmony with the commonsense belief of many people who hold that people do things simply because they like to do them.

Functional autonomy is a reaction to what Allport called theories of unchanging motives, namely Freud's pleasure principle and the drive-reduction hypothesis of stimulus–response psychology. Allport held that both theories are concerned with *historical facts* rather than *functional facts*. He believed that adult motives are built primarily on conscious, self-sustaining, contemporary systems. Functional autonomy represents his attempt to explain these conscious, self-sustaining contemporary motivations.

Admitting that some motivations are unconscious and others are the result of drive reduction, Allport contended that, because some behavior is functionally autonomous, theories of unchanging motives are inadequate. He listed four requirements of an adequate theory of motivation. Functional autonomy, of course, meets each criterion.

1. An adequate theory of motivation *"will acknowledge the contemporaneity of motives."* In other words, "Whatever moves must move us now" (Allport, 1961, p. 220). The past per se is unimportant. The history of an individual is significant only when it has a present effect on motivation.

2. *"It will be a pluralistic theory—allowing for motives of many types"* (Allport, 1961, p. 221). On this point, Allport was critical of Freud and his two-instinct theory, Adler and the single striving for success, and all theories that emphasize self-actualization as the ultimate motive. Allport was emphatically opposed to reducing all human motivation to one master drive. He contended that adults' motives are basically different from those of children and that the motivations of neurotic individuals are not the same as those of normal people. In addition, some motivations are conscious, others unconscious; some are transient, others recurring; some are peripheral, others propriate; and some are tension-reducing, others tension-maintaining. Motives that appear to be different really are different, not only in form but also in substance.

3. *"It will ascribe dynamic force to the cognitive processes—e.g., to planning and intention"* (Allport, 1961, p. 222). Allport argued that most people are busy living their lives into the future, but that many psychological theories are "busy tracing these lives backward into the past. And while it seems to each of us that we are spontaneously *active*, many psychologists are telling us that we are only *reactive*" (Allport, 1961, p. 206). Although intention is involved in all motivation, this third requirement refers more generally to

long-range intention. A young woman declines an offer to see a movie because she *prefers* to study anatomy. This preference is consistent with her *purpose* of making good grades at college and relates to her *plans* of being admitted to medical school, which is necessary in order for her to fulfill her *intention* of being a doctor. The lives of healthy adults are future-oriented, involving preferences, purposes, plans, and intentions. These, of course, are not always completely rational processes, as when we allow our anger to dominate our plans and intentions.

4. An adequate theory of motivation is one that *"will allow for the concrete uniqueness of motives"* (Allport, 1961, p. 225). A concrete unique motive is different from an abstract generalized one, the latter being based on a pre-existent theory rather than the actual motivation of a real person. An example of a concrete unique motive would be Duane, who is interested in improving his bowling game. His motive is concrete, and his manner of seeking improvement is unique to him. Some theories of motivation may ascribe Duane's behavior to an aggressive need, others to an inhibited sexual drive, and still others to a secondary drive learned on the basis a primary drive. Allport would simply say that Duane wants to improve his bowling game because he wants to improve his bowling game. This is Duane's unique concrete, and functionally autonomous motive.

In summary, a functionally autonomous motive is one that is contemporary, self-sustaining, growing out of an earlier motive, but functionally independent of it. Allport (1961, p. 229) defined functional autonomy as *"any acquired system of motivation in which the tensions involved are not of the same kind as the antecedent tensions from which the acquired system developed."* In other words, what begins as one motive may grow into a new one that is historically continuous with the original but functionally autonomous from it. For example, a person may originally plant a garden to satisfy a hunger drive but eventually become interested in gardening for its own sake.

Allport (1961) recognized two levels of functional autonomy—perseverative and propriate.

PERSEVERATIVE FUNCTIONAL AUTONOMY.   The more elementary of the two is **perseverative functional autonomy**. Allport borrowed this term from the word *perseveration*, which is the tendency of an impression to leave an influence on subsequent experience. Perseverative functional autonomy is found in animals as well as humans and is based on simple neurological principles. An example of perseverative functional autonomy would be a rat that has learned to run a maze in order to be fed but then continues to run the maze even after it has become satiated. Why does it continue to run? Allport would say that the rat runs the maze just for the fun of it.

Allport (1961) listed other examples of perseverative functional autonomy that involve human rather than animal motivation. The first is an addiction to alcohol, tobacco, or other drugs when there is no physiological hunger for them. Alcoholics continue to drink although their current motivation is functionally independent from their original motive.

Another example concerns uncompleted tasks. A problem once started, but then interrupted, will perseverate, creating a new tension to finish the task. This new tension is different from the initial motivation. For example, college students are offered 10 cents for every piece of a 500-piece jigsaw puzzle they successfully put together. Assume that these students do not have a pre-existing interest in solving jigsaw puzzles and that their original motivation is solely for the money. Also assume that their monetary reward is limited to $45.00, so that after they have completed 450 pieces they will no longer be paid. Will these students finish the remaining 50 pieces in the absence of monetary reward? If they do, then a new tension has been created, and their motive to complete the task is functionally autonomous from the original motive of getting paid.

PROPRIATE FUNCTIONAL AUTONOMY.   The master system of motivation that confers unity on personality is **propriate functional autonomy**, which refers to those self-sustaining motives that are related to the proprium. Jigsaw puzzles and alcohol are seldom regarded as "peculiarly mine." They are not part of the proprium, but exist only on the periphery of personality. On the other hand, occupation, hobbies, and interests are closer to the core of personality, and many of our motivations concerning them become functionally autonomous. For example, a woman may originally take a job because she needs money. At first, the work is uninteresting, perhaps even distasteful. As the years pass, however, she develops a consuming passion for the job itself, spending some vacation time at work and, perhaps, even developing a hobby that is closely related to her occupation.

CRITERION FOR FUNCTIONAL AUTONOMY.   In general, *a present motive is functionally autonomous to the extent that it seeks new goals*, meaning that the behavior will continue even as the motivation for it changes. For example, children first learning to walk are perhaps motivated by some maturational drive, but later they may walk to increase mobility or to build self-confidence. Similarly, scientists may be dedicated to searching for answers to difficult problems. Their satisfaction comes more from the search than from the solution, and their method of searching may vary as the problem changes. As one problem is solved, scientists search for another area of inquiry even though the new field may be somewhat different from the previous one. New tensions are established that are separate and autonomous from the antecedent ones. Each new finding leads to higher levels of aspiration and to the establishment of new goals.

LIMITATIONS OF FUNCTIONAL AUTONOMY.   Functional autonomy is not an explanation for all human motivation. Allport (1961) listed several processes that are not functionally autonomous. These include (1) biological drives, such as eating, breathing, and sleeping; (2) motives directly linked to the reduction of basic drives; (3) reflex actions such as an eye blink; (4) constitutional equipment, namely physique, intelligence, and temperament; (5) habits in the process of being formed; (6) patterns

A person might begin jogging to lose weight but continue because running is enjoyable. The motive for continuing to run is then functionally autonomous from the motive for beginning to run.

of behavior that require primary reinforcement; (7) nonproductive behaviors, such as compulsions, fixations, and regressions; and (8) sublimations that can be tied to childhood sexual desires.

Not all pathological symptoms, however, lie beyond the range of functional autonomy. Some serve a contemporary life-style and are presently independent of an earlier trauma that may have instigated the pathology. Many symptoms, however, are traceable to childhood experiences and, therefore, are not functionally autonomous. Compulsions may seem similar to perseverative functional autonomy, but they are not self-sustaining and can be eliminated through behavior modification or some other method of therapy. In contrast, functionally autonomous symptoms cannot be extinguished through psychotherapy and do not change as the self-concept changes.

Conscious and Unconscious Motivation

More than any other personality theorist, Allport emphasized the importance of conscious motivation; healthy adults are generally aware of what they are doing and their reasons for doing it.

However, Allport (1961) did not ignore the existence or even the importance of unconscious processes. He recognized the fact that some motivation is driven by hidden impulses and sublimated drives. He believed, for example, that most symptomatic behaviors are automatic repetitions, usually self-defeating, and motivated by unconscious tendencies. They often originate in childhood and retain a childish flavor into adult years.

For the healthy individual, however, consciousness is in control of behavior. Allport insisted that normal behavior is functionally autonomous and is motivated by conscious processes that are not only separate from unconscious motivation, but have their own ignition and spark. In summary, psychologically healthy adults are motivated principally by conscious thoughts, with unconscious processes playing only a minor role in their behavior.

The Healthy Personality

Allport saw a dichotomy between the psychologically healthy or mature personality and the one who is unhealthy or neurotic. Because healthy individuals are motivated by conscious processes, they are more flexible and autonomous than the unhealthy who remain dominated by unconscious motives that spring from childhood experiences. Mature people are also characterized by activity, security, and freedom of choice. Ordinarily they have experienced a relatively trauma-free childhood, even though their later years may be tempered by conflict and suffering. Healthy individuals are not without foibles and idiosyncrasies. In fact, individuality and uniqueness would be expected. Age is not a requisite for maturity, although healthy persons seem to become even more healthy as they get older.

What are the requirements for psychological health? Allport (1961) identified six criteria for the mature personality. The number is somewhat arbitrary, yet the list is descriptive of the healthy personality as seen by Allport.

The first criterion of psychological health is an *extension of the sense of self*. Mature people continually seek to identify with and participate in events outside themselves. They are not self-centered but are able to become involved in problems and activities that are not centered on themselves. They develop a nonegotistical interest in work, play, and recreation. Social interest, family, and spiritual life are important to them. Eventually, these outside activities become part of the proprium. Allport (1961 p. 285) summed up this first criterion by saying: "Everyone has self-love, but only self-extension is the earmark of maturity."

Second, mature personalities are characterized by a *"warm relating of self to others"* (Allport, 1961, p. 285). They have the capacity to love others in an intimate and compassionate manner. Warm relating, of course, is dependent on the ability to extend the sense of self. Only by looking beyond themselves can mature people love others nonpossessively and unselfishly. Psychologically healthy individuals treat other people with respect, and they realize that the needs, desires, and hopes of others are not completely foreign to their own. In addition, they have a healthy sexual attitude and do not exploit others for personal gratification.

A third criterion is *emotional security* or *self-acceptance*. Mature individuals accept themselves for what they are, and they possess what Allport (1961) called *emotional*

Sometimes people are motivated to seek tension, not merely reduce it.

poise. These psychologically healthy people are not overly upset when things do not go as planned or when they are simply "having a bad day." They do not dwell on minor irritations, and they recognize that frustrations and inconveniences are a part of living.

Healthy people also possess a *realistic perception*. They do not live in a fantasy world or bend reality to fit their own wishes. They are problem-oriented rather than self-centered, in touch with the world as most others see it, and capable of supporting themselves economically (Allport, 1961).

A fifth criterion is *insight and humor*. Mature people know themselves and, therefore, have no need to attribute their own sins and weaknesses to others. They also have a nonhostile sense of humor, which gives them the capacity to laugh at themselves rather than relying on sexual or aggressive themes to elicit laughter from others. Allport (1961) believed that insight and humor are closely related and may be aspects of the same thing, namely self-objectification. Healthy individuals see themselves objectively. They are able to perceive the incongruities and absurdities in life and have no need to pretend or to put on airs.

The final criterion of maturity is *a unifying philosophy of life*. Healthy people have a clear view of the purpose of life. Without this, their insight would be empty and barren and their humor would be trivial and cynical. The unifying philosophy of life may or may not be religious, but Allport (1954, 1963), on a personal level, seemed to have felt that a mature religious orientation is a crucial ingredient in lives of most mature individuals. Although many churchgoing people have an immature religious philosophy and narrow racial and ethnic prejudices, a mark of maturity is often a strong religious motivation. Allport was never far from a consideration of religion and published six lectures on the subject under the title *The Individual and His Religion* (Allport, 1950). The person with a mature religious attitude and a unifying philosophy of life has a well-developed conscience and, quite likely, a strong desire to serve others.

THE STUDY OF THE INDIVIDUAL

Because psychology has historically dealt with general laws and characteristics that people have in common, Allport repeatedly advocated the development and use of research methods that study the individual. To balance the predominant normative or group approach, he suggested that psychologists employ methods that study the motivational and stylistic behaviors of the single case.

Morphogenic Science

Early in his writings, Allport distinguished between two scientific approaches: the **nomothetic**, which seeks general laws; and the **idiographic**, which refers to that which is peculiar to the single case. Because the term *idiographic* was so often misused, misunderstood, and misspelled (being confused with "ideographic," or the representation of ideas by graphic symbols), Allport (1968) abandoned the term in his later writings and spoke of **morphogenic procedures**. While *idiographic* and morphogenic pertain to the individual, the first term does not suggest structure or pattern. In contrast, morphogenic refers to patterned properties of the whole organism and allows for intraperson comparisons. The pattern or structure of one's traits are important. For example, Jim may be intelligent, introverted, and strongly motivated by achievement needs, but the unique manner in which his intelligence is related to his introversion and his needs for achievement form a structured pattern. These individual patterns are the subject matter of morphogenic science.

What are the methods of morphogenic psychology? Allport (1962) listed many, some completely morphogenic, some partly so. Examples of wholly morphogenic, first-person methods are verbatim recordings, including interviews, dreams, and confessions; diaries and letters; personalized questionnaires and self-anchoring scales; and expressive and projective documents, including literary works, art forms, automatic writings, doodles, handshakes, voice patterns, body gestures, handwriting, gait, and autobiographies. When Allport met Hans Eysenck, the famous British factor analyst and believer in nomothetic science (Chapter 12), he told Eysenck that one day he would write his autobiography. Eventually, Eysenck (1990c) did indeed publish an autobiography in which he admitted that Allport was right; that is, that morphogenic methods such as one's description of one's own life and work can have validity.

Semimorphogenic approaches include self-rating scales, such as the adjective checklist; standardized tests using ipsative scores in which people are compared to themselves rather than a norm group; the Allport-Vernon-Lindzey *Study of Values* (1960); and the Q-sort technique of Stephenson (1953), which we discuss in Chapter 16.

Consistent with common sense, but contrary to many psychologists, Allport was willing to accept at face value the self-disclosure statements of most subjects. A psychologist who wishes to learn the personal dynamics of people, need simply ask them what they think of themselves. Answers to direct questions should be accepted as valid unless subjects are young children, psychotic, or extremely defensive. Allport (1962, p. 413) said that, "Too often we fail to consult the richest of all sources of data, namely, the subject's own self-knowledge."

Letters from Jenny

We introduced this chapter with an unusually illuminating example of the morphogenic method, namely letters written by Jenny to her son's former roommate, Glenn, and his wife Isabel. These letters came into Allport's possession during the early 1940s and were later published as *Letters from Jenny* (Allport, 1965). For years these personal documents were subjected to close analysis and study by Allport and his students who sought to build the structure of a single personality by identifying central traits or dispositions.

The letters from Jenny Gove Masterson (a fictitious name) reveal the story of an older woman and her intense love/hate feelings toward her son Ross. Between March 1926 (when she was 58) and October 1937 (when she died), Jenny wrote a series of 301 letters to Glenn and Isabel. These letters represent an unusually rich source of morphogenic material for several reasons. First, all 301 letters were preserved by the recipients, which is itself an unusual occurrence. Second, Jenny was a gifted and interesting writer, avoiding everyday mundane matters while revealing her innermost thoughts in an open, un-self-conscious manner. Third, the content of the letters is not a reflection of a growing relationship between the writer and the recipients. Indeed, the relationship did not seem to change over the years. The young couple simply provided Jenny with a forum to pour forth her feelings toward life in general, and her son Ross in particular. A fourth serendipitous circumstance was the discovery of the letters by an erudite psychologist with a pre-existing, passionate interest in personal documents.

One of Allport's students, Alfred Baldwin (1942) developed a technique called *personal structure analysis*, which he used to analyze approximately one-third of the letters. The purpose of this technique was to analyze the structure of Jenny's personality from her letters. Baldwin used two strictly morphogenic procedures, frequency and contiguity, for gathering evidence. The first simply involves a notation of the frequency with which an item appears in the case material. For example, how often did Jenny mention Ross, or money, or herself? Contiguity refers to the proximity of two items in the letters. How often did the category "Ross—unfavorable" occur in close correspondence with "herself—self-sacrificing"? Freud and other psychoanalysts intuitively used this technique of contiguity to discover an association between two items in a subject's unconscious mind. Baldwin, however, refined it by determining statistically those correspondences that occur more frequently than could be expected by chance alone.

Using the personal structure analysis, Baldwin identified three clusters of categories in Jenny's letters. The first related to Ross, women, the past, and herself—self-sacrificing. The second dealt with Jenny's search for a job, and the third cluster revolved around her attitude toward money and death. The three clusters are independent of each other even though a single topic, such as money, may appear in all three clusters.

The reader will note that Baldwin's original clusters resembled those that might be found in factor analysis (see Chapter 12). Indeed, Jeffrey Paige (1966), another student of Allport, later published a factor analytic study of Jenny's letters. He extracted and identified a total of eight factors: aggression, possessiveness, affiliation, autonomy, familial acceptance, sexuality, sentience, and martyrdom.

Paige's study is interesting for two reasons. First, he identified eight factors, a number that corresponds very well with the number of central dispositions or traits—5 to 10—that Allport had earlier hypothesized would be found in most people. Second, the results are quite similar to those Allport (1965) found when he used a somewhat commonsense approach.

In Allport's (1965) study, 36 judges listed what they thought were Jenny's essential characteristics. They recorded 198 descriptive adjectives, many of which were synonymous and overlapping. Allport then grouped the terms into eight clusters: quarrelsome–suspicious; self-centered; independent–autonomous; dramatic–intense; aesthetic–artistic; aggressive; cynical–morbid; and sentimental.

Comparing this commonsense, clinical approach with Paige's factorial study, Allport (1966) presented the following parallel:

COMMONSENSE TRAITS (Allport)	FACTORIAL TRAITS (Paige)
Quarrelsome–suspicious Aggressive	Aggression
Self-centered (possessive)	Possessiveness
Sentimental	Need for affiliation Need for family acceptance
Independent–autonomous	Need for autonomy
Aesthetic–artistic	Sentience
Self-centered (self-pitying)	Martyrdom
(No parallel)	Sexuality
Cynical–morbid	(No parallel)
Dramatic–intense	("Overstate"—that is, the tendency to be dramatic and to overstate her concerns)

The close agreement between the clinical, commonsense approach and the factor analytic method does not prove the validity of either. It does, however, indicate the feasibility of morphogenic studies. Psychologists can analyze one person and and identify central dispositions with consistency even when they use two different procedures.

CONCEPT OF HUMANITY

Allport had a basically *optimistic* and hopeful view of life. He rejected the psychoanalytic and behavioral views of humanity as being too deterministic and too mechanistic. He believed that our fates and our traits are not determined by unconscious motives originating in early childhood but by conscious choices we make in the present. We are not simply automatons blindly reacting to the forces of reward and punishment. Instead, we are able to interact with our environment and make it reactive to us. This view is similar to that of Bandura (see Chapter 10), the social-cognitive theorist, who believes that cognition is at least partially responsible for shaping behavior.

Allport believed that people not only seek to reduce tensions but to establish new ones. Healthy individuals desire both change and challenge. They are active, purposive, flexible, and enjoy the new and the unexpected.

Because people have the potential to learn a variety of responses and traits in many situations, psychological growth can take place at any age. Personality is not established in early childhood, even though for some people infantile influences remain strong. Early childhood experiences are important only to the extent that they exist in the present. Although early security and love leave lasting marks, children need more than love: They need an opportunity to shape their own existence creatively, to resist conformity, and to be free, self-directed individuals.

Although society has some power to mold personality, Allport believed that it does not hold the answer to the nature of humanity. The factors shaping personality, Allport held, are not as important as personality itself. Heredity, environment, and the nature of the organism are important, but people are essentially proactive and free to follow the prevailing dictates of society or to chart their own life course.

People, however, are not completely free. Allport (1961) adopted a *limited-freedom* approach. He was often critical of the existential view that allows for absolute freedom, but he also opposed the psychoanalytic and behavioral views, which he regarded as denying free will. Allport's position was somewhere in the middle. Although free will exists, some people are more capable of making choices than are others. A healthy person has more freedom than a child or a severely disturbed adult. The intelligent, reflective person has more capacity for free choice than the nonreflective, mentally deficient one. Again, this stance is similar to the one adopted by Bandura (1986), who holds that people are partially free and that different individuals have different degrees of freedom.

Even though freedom is limited, Allport maintained that it can be expanded. The more self-insight a person develops, the greater that person's freedom of choice. The more objective a person becomes, that is, the more the blindfolds of self-concern and egotism are removed, the greater that person's degree of freedom. As serious compulsions and restrictive habits are overcome (as in successful psychotherapy or some other growth process), a person becomes more and more free to engage in spontaneous and flexible behavior.

Education and knowledge also expand the amount of freedom we have. The greater our knowledge of a particular area, the broader becomes our freedom in that area. To have a broad general education means that, to some extent, one has a wider choice of jobs, recreational activities, reading materials, and friends. Finally, our freedom can be expanded by our mode of choosing. If we stubbornly adhere to a familiar course of action simply because it is more comfortable, our freedom remains largely restricted. On the other hand, if we adopt an open-minded mode of solving problems, then we broaden our perspective and increase our alternatives, that is, we expand our freedom to choose (Allport, 1955).

Allport's view of humanity is more *teleological* than causal. Personality, to some extent, is influenced by past experiences, but the behaviors that make us human are those that are motivated by our expectations of the future. In other words, we are healthy individuals to the extent that we set and seek future purposes and aspirations. Those factors that make one person different from another are not so much the basic drives, but rather self-erected goals and intentions.

In summary, Allport held an optimistic view of humanity, maintaining that people have at least limited freedom. Human beings are goal-oriented, proactive, and motivated by a variety of forces, most of which are within their realm of awareness. Early childhood experiences are of relatively minor importance and are significant only to the extent that they exist in the present. Both differences and similarities among people are important, but *individual differences and uniqueness* receive far greater emphasis in Allport's psychology.

Related Research

More than any other personality theorist, Gordon Allport maintained a lifelong active interest in the scientific study of religion (Allport, 1950). On a personal level, Allport was a devout Episcopalian, and from 1938 to 1966 he offered a series of 33 meditations in Appleton Chapel, Harvard University (Allport, 1978).

Allport believed that a deep religious commitment was a mark of a mature individual. However, not all churchgoers have a mature religious orientation. Some, in fact, are highly prejudiced. Allport and J. Michael Ross (1967) looked at earlier studies that had found a **curvilinear relationship** between church attendance and various forms of prejudice. That is, many previous investigations had reported that some churchgoers were highly prejudiced, whereas others had very little prejudice.

In order to understand this curvilinear relationship, Allport and Ross (1967) developed a Religious Orientation Scale (ROS) to measure type of religious commitment. The scale assumes both an extrinsic and an intrinsic orientation toward religion. People with an *extrinsic orientation* have a utilitarian view of religion, that is, they see it as a means to an end. Theirs is a self-serving religion of comfort and social convention. Their beliefs are lightly held and easily reshaped when convenient. On the other hand, people with an *intrinsic orientation* live their religion and find their master motive in their religious faith. Rather than using religion for some end, they bring other needs into harmony with their religious values. They have an internalized creed and follow it fully.

With this distinction in mind, Allport and Ross (1967) developed two subscales for the ROS—one consisting of Extrinsic (E) items and the other of Intrinsic (I) items. Examples of Extrinsic items are, "What religion offers me most is comfort when sorrow and misfortune strike" and "One reason for my being a church member is that such membership helps to establish a person in the community" (Allport & Ross, 1967, p. 436). People who definitely disagree or tend to disagree with these type of statements are scored in the direction of an Intrinsic orientation. People who definitely agree or tend to agree with these items are scored in an Extrinsic direction. Examples of Intrinsic items are, "My religious beliefs are what really lie behind my whole approach to life" and "I try hard to carry my religion over into all my other dealings in life" (Allport & Ross, 1967, p. 436). A person who agrees with statements of this nature score high on the Intrinsic scale, whereas a person who disagrees with these statements scores high on the Extrinsic scale.

Although Allport originally thought that religious orientation would be a bipolar trait, he soon realized that not everyone could easily be fit into either the Extrinsic or the Intrinsic pole. Some people *endorsed both* the Extrinsic and the Intrinsic statements. These people formed a third group called *indiscriminately proreligious*, Others tended to *disagree with both* the Extrinsic and the Intrinsic items, and these people made up a fourth group called *indiscriminately antireligious* or nonreligious. All subjects in Allport and Ross's (1967) study, however, were churchgoers, so this fourth category does not include people who never attend church.

Allport and Ross (1967) found that high Extrinsic scorers were more prejudiced than high Intrinsic scorers, but that churchgoers who were indiscriminately proreligious were more prejudiced than either of these two groups. This last finding may account for the fact that previous studies had found a curvilinear relationship between church attendance and prejudice. Some churchgoers harbor a great deal of prejudice, but those who live their religion (Intrinsics) have very little prejudice.

Since its development, the Religious Orientation Scale has been refined (Hood, 1970) and employed in dozens of studies on religious commitment. Donahue (1985) reviewed many of these studies and analyzed their combined findings. He reported that the ROS is a generally useful measure of religious orientation. In conclusion, he stated, "Intrinsic religiousness serves as an excellent measure of religious commitment as distinct from religious belief, church membership, liberal-conservative theological orientation, and related measures" (Donahue, 1985, p. 415).

More recently, the Religious Orientation Scale has been found to relate to psychological health. For example, Bergin, Master, and Richards (1987) found that the Intrinsic scale was negatively related to anxiety and positively related to self-control and better personal functioning. The opposite relationships were noted for the Extrinsic scale. Also, Watson, Morris, and Hood (1990) found that people who score high on the Intrinsic scale are characterized by good mental health, whereas those who score high on the Extrinsic scale have many more personal problems. Interestingly, indiscriminately proreligious as well as antireligious people tend to have mixed mental health. These studies tend to support Allport's notion of differing types of religiousness and to obviate the argument that strongly religious people are generally neurotic. Some are, others are not, depending on their personal view of religion.

Allport, undoubtedly, would be pleased that in recent years psychology and religion have become less estranged. In its infancy psychology had an intimate relationship with both religion and philosophy, but later, during the behaviorist influence, religion ceased to be regarded an an important psychological variable. Gorsuch (1988) has traced psychologists' interest in religion and found that, whereas the psychology of religion is still not well integrated within psychology in general, there has been a resurgence of research activity. Much of the activity is due to Allport's passionate interest in both psychology and religion (see Wulff [1991] for a review of research on the Religious Orientation Scale).

CRITIQUE OF ALLPORT

Allport's theory is based more on philosophical speculation and commonsense than on original scientific investigations. Unlike Bandura and Cattell, Allport did not conduct a vast number of investigations testing hypotheses drawn from his own theory. Nevertheless, he was quite familiar with much of the literature, and his theorizing never ventured too far beyond what was then known about human personality. Remember, it was not Allport's intention to construct a completely new theory of personality. He was eclectic, carefully borrowing from older theories those elements that were consistent with his conviction that most people are best thought of as conscious, forward-looking, tension-seeking individuals. To people who are offended by the deterministic theories of Freud and Skinner, Allport's view of humanity is philosophically refreshing. As with any other theory, however, it must be evaluated on a scientific basis.

The first consideration is whether or not Allport's approach is truly a theory of personality. It certainly deals with personality. In fact, Allport probably did more than any other psychologist to define personality and to categorize other definitions of the term. But did he have a *theory* in the sense of stating a set of related assumptions that generate testable hypotheses? On this criterion Allport's exhortations rate a qualified "Yes." It is a limited theory, offering explanations for a fairly narrow scope of personality, namely, certain kinds of motivation. The functionally autonomous motives of psychologically healthy adults are covered quite adequately by Allport's theory. But what of the motives of children and of psychotic and neurotic adults? What moves them and why? What about ordinarily healthy adults who uncharacteristically behave in a strange manner? What accounts for these inconsistencies? What explanation did Allport offer for the bizarre dreams, fantasies, and hallucinations of mature individuals? Unfortunately, his account of personality is not broad enough to adequately answer these questions.

Despite its limitations as a useful theory, Allport's approach to personality is both stimulating and enlightening. Anyone interested in building a theory of personality should first become familiar with Allport's writings. Few other psychologists have made as much effort to place personality theory in perspective; few have been as careful in defining terms, in categorizing previous definitions, or in questioning what units should be employed in personality theory. The work of Allport has set a standard for clear thinking and precision that future theorists would do well to emulate.

Has the theory *generated research*? On this criterion Allport's theory receives a moderate rating. His Religious Orientation Scale and the Study of Values have led to multiple studies on the scientific study of religion and of values. In addition to these areas of inquiry, Allport's advocacy of morphogenic studies remains a steady influence on many current researchers. For example, Roy Baumeister (1990) continues to use autobiographical narratives in much of his research.

A useful theory provides an *organization for observations*. Does Allport's theory meet this criterion? Again, only for a narrow range of adult motives does the theory offer a meaningful organization for observations. Much of what is known about human personality cannot be easily integrated into Allport's theory. Specifically, behaviors motivated by unconscious forces as well as those that are stimulated by primary drives were not adequately explained by Allport. He recognized the existence of these kinds of motivations, but seemed content to allow the psychoanalytical and behavioral explanations to stand without further elaboration. This limitation, however, does not devastate Allport's theory. To accept the validity of other theoretical concepts is a legitimate approach to theory building. Nevertheless, Allport might have been more specific in identifying those elements of earlier theories that he accepted and those that he rejected.

As a *guide for the practitioner*, Allport's theory has moderate usefulness. It certainly serves as a beacon to the teacher and the therapist, illuminating the view of personality which suggests that people should be treated as individuals. The details, unfortunately, are left unspecified.

On the fourth and fifth criteria of a useful theory, Allport's psychology of the individual is highly rated on each. His precise language renders the theory both *internally consistent* and *parsimonious*.

Chapter Summary

Allport attempted to restore balance to the study of personality by emphasizing the uniqueness of the individual, a stance opposed to most of the existing approaches to personalty theory. He did not discount the insights from psychoanalysis and learning theory; he was *eclectic* in his acceptance of ideas from a variety of sources. Most of these earlier theories, however, were reactive, and he wished to advocate a *proactive* position, one that could meet the criteria he established for an *open system* approach to personality. Unlike many other theories which hold that people are primarily motivated to seek rewards or to reduce tension, Allport's psychology of the individual suggests that people desire *growth and change* and are motivated to *seek new tensions*, as well as to maintain the status quo and to reduce tensions.

Allport's emphasis on uniqueness led him to de-emphasize common traits and to espouse *individual traits* or *personal dispositions*. Three levels of personal dispositions are (1) cardinal traits, (2) central traits, and (3) secondary traits. Few people have a *cardinal trait*, that is, a personal disposition so outstanding that it cannot be hidden. Most of us have six to ten *central traits*, characteristics that would be used in an honest description of us by people who know us very well. Central traits blend into *secondary traits*, which are less reliable but far more numerous.

All individual traits are dynamic, but those that initiate actions are called *motivational*, whereas those that guide actions are called *stylistic*.

The *proprium* refers to those behaviors and personal dispositions that we regard as peculiarly our own. Not all personality belongs to the proprium, only those aspects that are warm, central, and important to our lives.

Childhood is relatively unimportant in Allport's theory. Ordinarily, not until adolescence do people develop a clearly defined sense of personhood and a well-developed proprium that leads them to be motivated by *propriate strivings*.

Probably Allport's most controversial concept is that of *functional autonomy*, which holds that the motivation for some behavior is functionally independent from the motives that were originally responsible for that behavior. *Perseverative functional autonomy* refers to those habits and behaviors that are not part of one's proprium; *propriate functional autonomy* includes all those self-sustaining motivations that are related to the proprium.

Allport believed that *psychologically healthy people* are motivated largely by conscious processes, have an extended sense of self, relate warmly to others, accept themselves for who they are, have a realistic perception of the world, and possess insight, humor, and a unifying philosophy of life.

Research methods that emphasize general laws, Allport insisted, must be balanced by morphogenic procedures that stress the study of the individual. Personal documents, such as the famous *Letters from Jenny* (Allport,

1965), provide insights into the whole of humanity by revealing outstanding characteristics of the single individual.

Allport's concept of humanity is optimistic and is welcomed by those who believe that commonsense has been abandoned by some of the earlier personality theorists. Throughout our lifetime, Allport insisted, we have some freedom to grow and to seek new challenges.

Allport's psychology of the individual receives high ratings for its internal consistency and parsimony, but, on its capacity to organize knowledge, its ability to generate research, and its usefulness to the practitioner, its ratings are somewhat lower.

Suggested Readings

ALLPORT, G. W. (1955). *Becoming: Basic considerations for a psychology of personality*. New Haven, CT:Yale University Press.
Allport's perceptive thinking and cogent writing are evidenced in this brief book that discusses a wide range of topics pertinent to personality.

ALLPORT, G. W. (1961). *Pattern and growth in personality*. New York: Holt, Rinehart and Winston.
A completely revised edition of Allport's classic 1937 book on personality, this volume once again focuses on the study of the individual. The book is essential to an understanding of Allport's conception of personality.

ALLPORT, G. W. (1965). *Letters from Jenny*. New York: Harcourt, Brace & World.
A fascinating account of Jenny, our case study, as seen through her eyes and from the view of others who knew her.

ALLPORT, G. W. (1967). An autobiography. In E. G. Boring & G. Lindzey (Eds.), A *history of psychology in autobiography* (Vol. 5). New York: Appleton-Century-Crofts.
Allport's interesting account of his life, including his encounter with Sigmund Freud.

PART FIVE

Humanistic/Existential

Theories

14 Kelly
Psychology of Personal Constructs

15 Maslow
Holistic-Dynamic Theory

16 Rogers
Person-Centered Theory

17 May
Existential Psychology

Psychology of Personal Constructs

OVERVIEW
BIOGRAPHY OF GEORGE KELLY
KELLY'S PHILOSOPHICAL POSITION
    Person as Scientist
    Scientist as Person
    Constructive Alternativism
PERSONAL CONSTRUCTS
    Basic Postulate
    Supporting Corollaries
APPLICATIONS OF PERSONAL CONSTRUCT THEORY
    Abnormal Development
    Psychotherapy
    The Rep Test
CONCEPT OF HUMANITY
RELATED RESEARCH
CRITIQUE OF KELLY
CHAPTER SUMMARY
SUGGESTED READINGS

Chapter
Fourteen

KELLY

*L*ike many other college students, Arlene works hard—not necessarily on school work, but on her job. Arlene works 30 to 40 hours a week at a convenience store and carries a full load of classwork as a political science major. Despite a hectic schedule that calls for driving to morning classes, then across town to her job, and then back to her apartment, Arlene has been able to keep up with her studies, her job, and an active social life—that is, until her 10-year-old car broke down.

Now she has been told by the garage mechanic that her repair bill will be almost as much as the car is worth. Arlene had planned to buy a new car after she graduated and has saved some money for that purchase. Should she buy a new car now? How about another used car? Should she have her old car fixed? What if it breaks down again? If she buys a new car, what kind should she get? What color? What brand? How much can she afford?

Does Arlene have other alternatives? Could she use public transportation? Depend on friends for a ride? Quit her job and find one closer to her apartment and school? Walk to work? Quit school and move back home with her parents? The number of possibilities goes on and on.

How did Arlene solve this problem? According to the personal construct theory of George Kelly, Arlene made her decision in much the same manner that a scientist makes decisions. She observed her environment, asked questions, anticipated answers, perceived relationships between events, hypothesized about possible solutions to her dilemma, asked more questions, and predicted potential outcomes. In addition, she attempted to control her environment and the behavior of others just as a psychologist tries to control behavior.

Many of the steps in Arlene's "scientific" process were not put into words. For example, she did not consciously think about walking the four miles to work, or about relying on friends for transportation. Yet each of these possibilities, on some level, was considered. Each was rejected just as a scientist might reject some hypotheses as being unworthy of experimental testing. On a more overt level, Arlene considered most of the other options. She looked at new car advertisements, visited several dealers, bargained over price, compared her bank account and current income against possible monthly payments, and then rejected that course of action. She repeated (replicated) that same procedure with reference to used cars. The resulting evidence supported the hypothesis that she would be able to afford a late-model Honda. When she found the car she liked, she tested it by driving it, then took it to a mechanic to cross-validate the word of the dealer and her own opinion. After reviewing all the evidence, Arlene purchased the car.

With the purchase Arlene's scientific quest did not stop. She continued to evaluate her decision. Was her evidence complete? Was it valid? Was a Honda the right choice? Before she bought the car she had no particular preference for a Honda, but having committed herself (in the form of a down payment and a promise to pay monthly notes), she became convinced that Hondas are superior to other cars of comparable price. In other words, like all other people (including "professional" scientists), her perceptions of reality were colored by her *personal constructs*, that is, her way of looking at, explaining, and interpreting events in her world.

OVERVIEW

Kelly's theory of personal constructs is like no other personality theory. It has been variously called a cognitive theory, a behavioral theory, an existential theory, and a phenomenological theory. Yet it is none of these. Perhaps the most appropriate term would be metatheory, or a theory about theories. According to Kelly, all people (including those who build personality theories) anticipate events by the meanings or interpretations they place on those events. These meanings or interpretations are called *constructs*. People exist in a real world, but their behavior is shaped by their gradually expanding interpretation or *construction* of that world. They construe the world in their own way, and every construction is open to revision or replacement. People are not victims of circumstances, because alternative constructions are always available. Kelly called this philosophical position *constructive alternativism*.

Constructive alternativism is implied by Kelly's theory of personal constructs, a theory he expressed in one basic postulate and 11 supporting corollaries. The basic postulate assumes that people are constantly active and that their activity is guided by the way they anticipate events.

BIOGRAPHY OF GEORGE KELLY

George Alexander Kelly was born April 28, 1905, on a farm near Perth, Kansas, a small town 35 miles south of Wichita. George was the only child of Theodore V. Kelly, an ordained Presbyterian minister and Elfleda M. Kelly, a former schoolteacher. By the time George was born, his father had given up the ministry in favor of becoming a Kansas farmer. Both parents were well-educated and both helped in the formal education of their son, a fortunate circumstance because George's schooling was rather erratic.

When Kelly was four, the family moved to eastern Colorado, where his father staked a claim on some of the last free land in that part of the country. While in Colorado, Kelly attended school only irregularly, seldom for more than a few weeks at a time (Thompson, 1968).

Lack of water drove the family back to Kansas, where George attended four different high schools in four years. At first he commuted to high school, but at age 13 he was sent to school in Wichita. From that time on, he mostly lived away from home. After graduation he spent three years at Friends University in Wichita and one year at Park College in Parkville, Missouri. Both schools had religious affiliations, which may account for the fact that many of Kelly's later writings are sprinkled with biblical references.

Kelly was a man of many and varied interests. His undergraduate degree was in physics and math, but he was also a member of the college debate team and, as such, became intensely concerned with social problems. This interest led him to the University of Kansas, where he received a master's degree with a major in educational sociology and a minor in labor relations and sociology.

During the next few years, Kelly moved several times and held a variety of positions. First, he went to Minneapolis, where he taught soap-box oratory at a special college for labor organizers, conducted classes in speech for the American Bankers Association, and taught government to an Americanization class for prospective citizens (Kelly, 1969a). In 1928, he moved to Sheldon, Iowa, where he taught at a junior college and coached drama. While there, he met his future wife, Gladys Thompson, an English teacher at the same school. After a year and a half, he moved back to Minnesota, where he taught a

summer session at the University of Minnesota. Next, he returned to Wichita to work for a few months as an aeronautical engineer. From there he went to the University of Edinburgh in Scotland as an exchange student, receiving an advanced professional degree in education.

At this point in his life, Kelly "had dabbled academically in education, sociology, economics, labor relations, biometrics, speech pathology, and anthropology, and had majored in psychology for a grand total of nine months" (Kelly, 1969a, p. 48). After returning from Edinburgh, however, he began in earnest to pursue a career in psychology. He enrolled at the State University of Iowa in 1930, and the following year completed a Ph.D. with a dissertation on common factors in speech and reading disabilities.

Once again Kelly returned to Kansas, beginning his academic career in 1931 at Fort Hays State College in Hays, Kansas, by teaching physiological psychology. With the dust bowl and the Great Depression, however, he soon became convinced that he should "pursue something more humanitarian than physiological psychology" (Kelly, 1969a, p. 48). Consequently, he decided to become a psychotherapist, counseling college and high school students in the Hays community. True to his psychology of personal constructs, Kelly (1969a) pointed out that *circumstances* did not dictate his decision, but rather his *interpretation* of events; that is, his own construction of reality altered his life course.

Everything around us "calls," if we choose to heed. Moreover, I have never been completely satisfied that becoming a psychologist was even a very good idea in the first place.... The only thing that seems clear about my career in psychology is that it was I who got myself into it and I who have pursued it. (Kelly, 1969a, p. 49)

Now a psychotherapist, Kelly obtained legislative support for a program of traveling psychological clinics in Kansas. He and his students traveled widely throughout the state, providing psychological services during those hard economic times. During this period he evolved his own approach to therapy, abandoning the Freudian techniques that he had previously used.

During World War II, Kelly joined the Navy as an aviation psychologist. After the war he taught at the University of Maryland for a year and then, in 1946, joined the faculty at Ohio State University as a professor and director of the Psychological Clinic. There he worked with Julian Rotter (see Chapter 11), who succeeded him as director of the clinic. Kelly had been gradually formulating his theory of personality, and in 1955 his most important work, The Psychology of Personal Constructs, was published in two volumes.

Many of his summers were spent as a visiting professor at such schools as the University of Chicago, the University of Nebraska, the University of Southern California, Northwestern, Brigham Young University, Stanford, and City College of New York. During those post-war years, Kelly became a major force in clinical psychology in the United States. He was president of both the Clinical and the Consulting Divisions of the American Psychological Association and was also head of the American Board of Examiners in Professional Psychology.

In 1965 he accepted a position at Brandeis University, where, for a brief time, he was a colleague of A. H. Maslow (see Chapter 15). Kelly died on March 6, 1967, before he could complete revisions of his theory of personal constructs.

Although Kelly's popularity with American psychologists has waned somewhat since his death, his ideas are widely known among psychologists in England. The late Donald Bannister was instrumental in spreading Kelly's theories throughout Britain (Bannister, 1970, 1975, 1977; Bannister & Fransella, 1966, 1971; Bannister & Mair, 1968), and Fay Fransella in London helped open the Center of Personal Construct Psychology, with a mission to train clinicians in the theory and practice of personal construct psychology. In addition, Nigel Beail (1985) has helped apply personal construct theory to clinical and educational settings, and other British psychologists have applied Kelly's ideas to industrial and organizational settings. In the United States, Alvin Landfield of the University of Nebraska has championed personal construct theory (Landfield, 1971; Landfield & Epting, 1987; Landfield & Leitner, 1980; Landfield, Stefan, & Dempsey, 1990).

Kelly's diverse life experiences, from the wheatfields of Kansas to some of the major universities of the world, from education to labor relations, from drama and debate to psychology, are consistent with his theory of personality, which emphasizes the possibility of interpreting events from many possible angles.

KELLY'S PHILOSOPHICAL POSITION

Is human behavior (such as Arlene's decision to buy a late-model used car) based on reality or on our perception of reality? George Kelly would say *both*. He did not accept Skinner's (see Chapter 9) position that behavior is shaped by the environment, that is, reality. On the other hand, he also rejected a strictly *phenomenological* approach (see Combs & Snygg, 1959), which holds that the only reality is what we perceive. Kelly (1955) believed that the universe is real, but that different people construe it in different ways. Thus, our **personal constructs**, or ways of interpreting and explaining events, hold the key to predicting our behavior.

Personal construct theory does not try to explain nature. Rather it is a theory of our *construction* of events, that is, our personal inquiry into our world. It is "a psychology of the human quest. It does not say what has or will be found, but proposes rather how we might go about looking for it" (Kelly, 1970, p. 1).

Person as Scientist

When her car broke down, Arlene (our case study) acted in much the same manner as a scientist does. She asked questions, formulated hypotheses, tested them, and drew conclusions. She attempted to predict future events ("If I buy a reliable car, I will be able to continue my job.") and to control them ("By purchasing this car I will be free to drive to work and earn enough money to stay in school."). In a similar manner, all of us, in our quest for meaning, make observations, construe relationships among events, formulate theories, generate hypotheses, test those that are plausible, and reach conclusions from our experiments. As with any scientist, our conclusions are not fixed or final. They are open to question and reconsideration. Kelly was hopeful that people individually, as well as humanity in general, would find better ways of restructuring their lives through imagination and foresight.

Scientist as Person

If people can be seen as scientists, then scientists can also be seen as people. Therefore, the pronouncements of scientists should be regarded with the same skepticism with which we view any behavior. Every scientific observation can be looked at from a different perspective. Every theory can be slightly tilted and viewed from a new angle. This means, of course, that Kelly's theory is not exempt from restructuring. Kelly (1969b) presented his theory as a set of half-truths and recognized the inaccuracy of its constructions. Like Carl Rogers (see Chapter 16), Kelly hoped that his theory would be overthrown and replaced by a better one. Indeed, Kelly, more than other personality theorist, formulated a theory that encourages its own demise. Just as all of us can use our imagination to see everyday events differently, personality theorists can use their ingenuity to construe better theories.

Constructive Alternativism

As already mentioned, Kelly began with the assumption that the universe really exists and that it functions as an integral unit, with all its parts interacting precisely with each other. Moreover, the universe is constantly changing so that something is happening all the time. Added to these basic assumptions is the notion that people's thoughts also really exist and that people strive to make sense out of their continuously changing world. Different people construe reality in different ways and the same person is capable of changing his or her view of the world.

In other words, people always have alternative ways of looking at things. Kelly (1965, p. 15) assumed *"that all of our present interpretations of the universe are subject to revision or replacement."* He referred to this assumption as **constructive alternativism** and summed up the notion with these words. "The events we face today are subject to as great a variety of constructions as our wits will enable us to contrive" (Kelly, 1970, p. 1). The philosophy of constructive alternativism assumes that the piece-by-piece accumulation of facts does not add up to truth, but rather that facts can be looked at from different perspectives. Kelly agreed with Adler (see Chapter 4) that our interpretation of events is more important than the events themselves. In contrast to Adler, however, Kelly stressed the notion that interpretations have meaning in the dimension of time, and what is valid at one time becomes false when construed differently at a later time. For example, when Freud (see Chapter 2) originally heard his patients' accounts of childhood seduction, he believed that early sexual experiences were responsible for later hysterical reactions. If Freud had continued to construe his patients' reports in this fashion, the entire history of psychoanalysis would have been quite different. But then, for a variety of reasons, Freud restructured his data and gave up his seduction hypothesis. Shortly thereafter, he tilted the picture a little and saw a very different view. With this new view, he concluded that these seduction reports were merely childhood fantasies. His alternative hypothesis was the Oedipus complex, a concept that permeates all of current psychoanalytic theory, and one that is 180 degrees removed from his original seduction theory. If we view Freud's observations from yet another angle, such as Erikson's perspective (see Chapter 3), then we might reach a still different conclusion.

Kelly believed that the *person*, not the facts, holds the key to an individual's future. Facts and events do not dictate conclusions, but rather they carry meanings for us to discover. We are all constantly faced with alternatives, which we can explore if we choose, but, in any case, we must assume responsibility for how we construe our worlds. We are victims neither of our history nor our present circumstances. That is not to say that we can make of our world whatever we wish. We are "limited by our feeble wits and our timid reliance upon what is familiar" (Kelly, 1970, p. 3). We do not always welcome new ideas. Like scientists in general and personality theorists in particular, we often find restructuring disturbing and thus hold on to ideas that are comfortable and theories that are well-established.

PERSONAL CONSTRUCTS

Kelly's philosophy assumes that our interpretation of a unified, ever-changing world constitutes our reality. "Man looks at his world through transparent patterns or templates which he creates and then attempts to fit over the realities of which the world is composed" (Kelly, 1955, pp. 8–9). Although these patterns or templates do not always fit accurately, they are the means by which we make sense out of the world. Kelly referred to these patterns as *personal constructs*:

> They are ways of construing the world. They are what enables man, and lower animals too, to chart a course of behavior, explicitly formulated or implicitly acted out, verbally expressed or utterly inarticulate, consistent with other courses of behavior or inconsistent with them, intellectually reasoned or vegetatively sensed. (Kelly, 1955, p.9)

A personal construct is our way of seeing how things (or people) are alike and yet different from other things (or people). For example, we may see how Betty and Jane are alike and how they are different from Carol. The comparison and the contrast must occur within the same context. For example, to say that Betty and Jane are attractive and Carol is religious would not constitute a personal construct, because attractiveness is one dimension and religiosity is another. A construct would be formed if we see that Betty and Jane are attractive and Carol is unattractive, or if we view Betty and Jane as irreligious and Carol as religious. Both the comparison and the contrast are essential.

Whether they are clearly perceived or dimly felt, personal constructs shape an individual's behavior. As an example, consider Arlene, our case study. After her old car broke down, her personal constructs molded her subsequent course of action, but not all constructs were clearly defined. For instance, she may have decided to buy a late-model Honda because she interpreted the dealer's friendliness and persuasiveness as meaning that the car was reliable. Arlene's personal constructs may be accurate or inaccurate, but, in either case, they are her means of predicting and controlling her environment.

Arlene tried to increase the accuracy of her predictions (that the car would provide reliable, economical, and comfortable transportation) by increasing her store of information. She researched her purchase, asked others' opinions, tested the car, and had it checked by a mechanic. In much the same manner, all of us attempt to validate our constructs. We look for better-fitting templates and thus try to improve our personal constructs. However, personal improvement is not inevitable, because the investment we make in our established constructs blocks the path of forward development. The world is constantly changing so that what is accurate at one time may not be accurate at another. The reliable blue bicycle Arlene rode during childhood should not mislead her to construe that all blue vehicles are reliable.

Kelly's basic theory is expressed in one fundamental postulate, or assumption, and elaborated by means of 11 supporting corollaries.

Basic Postulate

The fundamental postulate of personal construct theory is that *"a person's processes are psychologically channelized by the ways in which he [or she] anticipates events"* (Kelly, 1955, p. 46).

This statement assumes that our behaviors (thoughts and actions) are directed by the way we see the future. This postulate is not intended as an absolute statement of truth but is a tentative assumption open to question and scientific testing.

Kelly (1955, 1970) clarified this fundamental assumption by defining its key terms. First, the phrase *person's processes* refers to a living, changing, moving human being. Kelly was not concerned here with animals, with society, or with any part or function of the person. He did not recognize motives, needs, drives, or instincts as forces underlying motivation. Life itself accounts for our movement. "The person is not an object which is temporarily in a moving state but is himself a form of motion" (Kelly, 1955, p. 48).

Kelly chose the term *channelized* to suggest that people move with a direction through a network of pathways or channels. The network, however, is flexible, both facilitating and restricting one's range of action. In addition, the term avoids the implication that some sort of energy is being transformed into action. People are already in movement; they merely channelize or direct their processes toward some end or purpose.

The next key phrase is *ways of anticipating events*, which suggests that people guide their actions according to the ways they predict the future. Neither the past nor the future per se determine behavior. Rather, our present view of the future shapes our actions. Arlene did not buy a blue Honda because she had a blue bicycle when she was a child, although that fact may have helped her construe the present so that she anticipated that her Honda would be a reliable car in the future. "It is the future which tantalizes man, not the past. Always he reaches out to the future through the window of the present" (Kelly, 1955, p. 49).

Supporting Corollaries

To elaborate his theory of personal constructs, Kelly proposed 11 supporting corollaries, all of which can be inferred from his basic postulate.

Similarities among Events

No two events are exactly alike, yet we construe similar events so that they are perceived as being the same. One sunrise is never identical to another, but our construct *dawn* conveys our recognition of some similarity or some replication of events. Two dawns are never exactly alike, although they may be similar enough for us to construe them as the same event. Kelly (1955, 1970) referred to this similarity among events as the **construction corollary**.

The construction corollary states that *"a person anticipates events by construing their replications* (Kelly, 1955, p. 50). This corollary again points out that people are forward-looking; their behavior is molded by their anticipation of future events. It also emphasizes the notion that people construe or interpret future events according to recurrent themes or replications.

The construction corollary may seem little more than common sense. We see similarities among events and use a single concept to describe the common properties. Kelly, however, felt that it was necessary to include the obvious when building a theory.

Differences among People

Kelly's second corollary is equally obvious. *"Persons differ from each other in their construction of events"* (Kelly, 1955, p. 55). Kelly called this emphasis on individual differences the **individuality corollary**.

People have different experiences and construe things in different ways, so that even when two constructions appear the same, they are not identical to two different individuals. In addition, no two people put an experience together in exactly the same way. In other words, both the substance and the form of the construct are different. For example, a philosopher may subsume the construct *truth* under the rubric of eternal values; a lawyer may view truth as a relative concept, useful for a particular purpose; and a scientist may construe truth as an ever-elusive goal, something to be sought, but never attained. For the philosopher, the lawyer, and the scientist, *truth* has a different substance, a different meaning. Moreover, each person arrived at his or her particular construction in a different manner and thus give it a different form.

Even identical twins living in nearly identical environments do not construe events exactly the same. For example, part of Twin A's environment includes Twin B, an experience not shared by Twin B. In addition, each twin experiences a unique self as the central figure of life.

Although Kelly (1955) emphasized individual differences, he pointed out that experiences can be shared and that people can find a common ground for construing experiences. This allows people to communicate both verbally and nonverbally. However, due to individual differences, the communication is never perfect.

Relationships among Constructs

Kelly's third corollary, the **organization corollary**, emphasizes relationships among constructs and states that people *"characteristically evolve, for [their] convenience in anticipating events, a construction system embracing ordinal relationships between constructs"* (Kelly, 1955, p. 56).

The first two corollaries assume similarities among events and differences among people. The third emphasizes that different people organize similar events in a manner that minimizes incompatibilities and inconsistencies. We arrange our constructions so that we may move from one to another in an orderly fashion, which allows us to anticipate events in ways that transcend contradictions and avoid needless conflicts.

The organization corollary also assumes an ordinal relationship of constructs so that one construct may be subsumed under another. Figure 14.1 illustrates a hierarchy of constructs as they might apply to Arlene, our case study. In deciding a course of action after her car broke down, Arlene may have seen her situation in terms of dichotomous superordinate constructs such as good vs. bad. To Arlene, *independence* (of friends or parents) is good, whereas *dependence* is bad. However, her personal construct system would undoubtedly include a variety of constructs subsumed under good and bad. For example, Arlene would probably construe intelligence and health as good, and stupidity and illness as bad. Likewise, independence

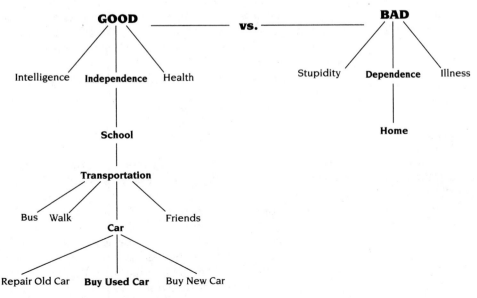

Figure 14.1   *Complexity of Relationships among Constructs*

and dependence have a multitude of subordinate constructs. But for Arlene, in this situation, continuation in school was construed as independence, whereas returning home meant dependence. In order to remain in school and continue her job, Arlene needed transportation. There are many means of transportation, but Arlene considered only four: riding a public bus, walking, relying on friends, or driving her own car. Subsumed under the construct of car were three subordinate constructs: repairing her old car, buying a new one, or purchasing a late-model used car. This example not only suggests that constructs have a complex ordinal relationship with each other but a dichotomous one as well.

Dichotomy of Constructs

Now we come to a corollary that is not so obvious. The **dichotomy corollary** states that *"a person's construction system is composed of a finite number of dichotomous constructs"* (Kelly, 1955, p. 59).

Kelly insisted that a construct is an either/or proposition—black or white, with no shades of gray. In nature things may not be either/or, but natural events have no meanings other than those attributed to them by an individual's personal construct system. In nature the color blue may have no opposite pole (except on a color chart), but people attribute contrasting qualities to blue, such as *light* blue vs. *dark* blue or *pretty* vs. *ugly*.

In order to form a construct, we must be able to see similarities between events, but we must also contrast those events with their opposite pole. Kelly (1955, p. 61) stated it this way: "In its minimum context a construct is a way in which at least two elements are similar and contrast with a third." As an example, let us return to Figure 14.1. How are *intelligence* and *independence* alike? Their common element has no meaning without contrasting it to an opposite. Intelligence and independence have no overlapping element when compared to purple or modern. By contrasting intelligence with stupidity and independence with dependence, we see how they are alike and how they can be organized under the construct "good" as opposed to "bad."

Choice between Dichotomies

If people construe events in dichotomized fashion, then it follows that they have some choice in following alternative courses of action. This is Kelly's **choice corollary**, paraphrased as follows: *People choose for themselves that alternative in a dichotomized construct through which they anticipate the greater possibility for extension and definition of future constructs.*

This corollary assumes much of what is stated in Kelly's basic postulate and in the preceding corollaries. People make choices on the basis of how they anticipate events, and those choices are between dichotomous alternatives. In addition, the choice corollary assumes that people choose those actions that are most likely to extend their future range of choices.

People choose between alternatives, based on their anticipation of future events.

Arlene's decision to buy a used car was based on a series of previous choices, each of which was between dichotomized alternatives and each of which broadened her range of future choices. First, she chose the *independence* of school over the *dependence* of going home to live with her parents. Next, buying a car offered more freedom than relying on friends or on bus schedules or walking (which she perceived as time consuming). Repairing her old car was *financially risky* compared to the greater *safety* of buying a used one. Purchasing a new car was too *expensive* compared to the relatively *inexpensive* used car. Each choice was between alternatives in a dichotomized construct, and with each Arlene anticipated the greater possibility for extending and defining future constructs.

Range of Convenience

Kelly's **range corollary** assumes that personal constructs are finite and not relevant to everything. "*A construct is convenient for the anticipation of a finite range of events only*" (Kelly, 1955, p. 68). In other words, a construct is limited to a particular *range of convenience.*

The construct *independence* was within Arlene's range of convenience when she was deciding to buy a car, but on other occasions independence would be outside those boundaries. Independence carries with it the notion of *dependence.* Arlene's freedom to remain in school, to continue her job, and to move quickly from place to place without relying on others—all fall within her independence/dependence range of convenience. However, Arlene's construct of independence excludes all irrelevancies such as up/down, light/dark, or wet/dry; that is, it is convenient only for a finite range of events.

The range corollary allowed Kelly to distinguish between a *concept* and a *construct*. A concept includes all elements having a common property, and it excludes those that do not have that property. The concept *tall* includes all those people and objects having extended height and excludes all other concepts, even those that are outside its range of convenience. Therefore, *fast* or *independent* or *dark* are all excluded from the concept *tall* because they do not have extended height. But such exclusions are both endless and needless. The idea of construct contrasts tall with short, thus limiting its range of convenience. "That which is outside the range of convenience of the construct is not considered part of the contrasting field but simply an area of irrelevancy" (Kelly, 1955, p. 69). Thus we see that dichotomies limit a construct's range of convenience.

Experience and Learning

Basic to personal construct theory is the anticipation of events. We look to the future and make guesses as to what will happen. Then, as events become revealed to us, we either validate our existing constructs or restructure them to match our experience. The restructuring of events allows us to learn from our experiences.

The **experience corollary** states: "A person's construction system varies as he [or she] successively construes the replications of events" (Kelly, 1955, p. 72). Kelly used the word "successively" to point out that we pay attention to only one thing at a time. "The events of one's construing march single file along the path of time" (Kelly, 1955, p. 73).

Experience consists of the successive construing of events. The events themselves do not constitute experience—it is the meaning we attach to them that changes our lives. To illustrate this point, let us return to Arlene and her personal construct, *independence*. When her old car (a high school graduation gift from her parents) broke down, Arlene decided to remain in school rather than to return to the security and dependent status of living at home. As Arlene subsequently encountered successive events, she had to make decisions without benefit of parental consultation, a task that forced her to restructure her notion of independence. Earlier she had construed independence as freedom from outside interference. After deciding to go into debt for a used car, she began to alter her meaning of independence to include responsibility and anxiety. The events themselves did not force a restructuring. Arlene could have become a spectator to the events surrounding her. Instead, her existing constructs were flexible enough to allow her to adapt to experience.

Adaptation to Experience

Arlene's flexibility illustrates Kelly's **modulation corollary**. "*The variation in a person's construction system is limited by the permeability of the constructs within whose range of* *convenience the variants lie"* (Kelly, 1955, p. 77). This corollary follows from and expands the experience corollary. It assumes that the extent to which we revise our constructs is related to the degree of **permeability** of our existing constructs. A construct is permeable if new elements can be added to it. Impermeable or concrete constructs do not admit new elements. If a man believes that women are inferior to men, then contradictory evidence will not find its way into his range of convenience. Instead, he will attribute the achievements of women to luck or unfair social advantage. A change in events means a change in constructs only if those constructs are permeable.

Arlene's personal construct of *independence vs. dependence* was sufficiently permeable to take in new elements. When, without parental consultation, she made the decision to buy a used car, the construct of *maturity vs. childishness* penetrated *independence vs. dependence* and added a new flavor to it. Previously the two constructs had been separated, and Arlene's notion of independence was limited to the idea of doing as she chose, while dependence was associated with parental domination. Now she construed independence as meaning mature responsibility and dependence as signifying a childish leaning on parents. In such a manner, we all modulate or adjust our personal constructs.

Incompatible Constructs

Although Kelly assumed an overall stability or consistency of a person's construction system, his **fragmentation corollary** allows for the incompatibility of specific elements. *"A person may successively employ a variety of constructive subsystems which are inferentially incompatible with each other"* (Kelly, 1955, p. 83).

At first it may seem as if personal constructs must be compatible, but if we look to our own behavior and thinking we can easily see some inconsistencies. In Chapter 11 we saw that Walter Mischel (a student of Kelly's) believed that behavior is usually more inconsistent than trait theorists would have us believe. Children are often patient in one situation, yet impatient in another. Similarly, a person may be brave while confronting a vicious dog, but cowardly when confronting a boss or teacher. Whereas Mischel tends to emphasize inconsistencies in behaviors, Kelly saw underlying stability in most of our actions. For example, a man might be protective of his wife, yet encourage her to be more independent. Protection and independence may be incompatible with each other on one level, but on a larger level both are subsumed under the construct of *love*. Thus, his actions to protect his wife and to encourage her to be more independent are consistent with a larger, superordinate construct.

Superordinate systems may also change, but those changes take place within a still larger system. In the above example, for instance, the man's love for his wife may gradually shift to hatred, but that change remains within a larger construct of *self-interest*. The previous love for his wife and the present hatred are both consistent with his view of self-interest. If incompatible constructs could not coexist, people would be locked into a fixed construct, which would make change nearly impossible.

Similarities among People

Recall that Kelly's second supporting corollary assumed that people are different from each other. Now we see that he also assumed similarities among people. His slightly revised **commonality corollary** reads: *"To the extent that one person employs a construction of experience which is similar to that employed by another, his [or her] processes are psychologically similar to those of the other person"* (Kelly, 1970, p. 20).

Two people need not experience the same event or even similar events in order for their processes to be psychologically similar; they must merely *construe* their experiences in a similar fashion. Because people actively construe events by asking questions, forming hypotheses, drawing conclusions, and then asking more questions, different people with widely different experiences may construe events in very similar ways. For example, two people might arrive at similar political views although they come from disparate backgrounds. One may have come from a wealthy family, having lived a life of leisure and contemplation, while the other may have survived a destitute childhood, struggling constantly for survival. Yet both adopt a liberal political view.

Although people of different backgrounds can have similar constructs, people with similar experiences are more likely to construe events along similar lines. Americans tend to construe *democracy* in a somewhat similar manner, and one that differs from the construction of democracy held by people in India.

Within a given social group, people may employ similar constructions, but it is always the individual, never society, that construes events. Moreover, no two people ever interpret experiences exactly the same. Americans may have a similar construction of *democracy*, but no two Americans see it in identical terms.

Social Processes

"People belong to the same cultural group, not merely because they behave alike, nor because they expect the same things of others, but especially because they construe their experience in the same way" (Kelly, 1955, p. 94).

The final supporting corollary, the **sociality corollary**, states: *"To the extent that one person construes the construction processes of another, he [or she] may play a role in a social process involving the other person"* (Kelly, 1955, p. 95).

We do not communicate with one another simply on the basis of common experiences or even similar construction; we communicate because we construe the constructions of each other. In our interpersonal relations, we not only observe the behavior of the other person, we also interpret what that behavior means to that person. When Arlene was negotiating with the used-car dealer, she was not only aware of his words and actions, but also their meanings. She realized that to him she was a potential buyer, someone who might provide him with a substantial commission. She construed his words as exaggerations and, at the same time, realized that he construed her indifference as an indication that she construed his motivations differently from her own.

In our interpersonal relationships, we observe not only the behavior of the other person, but we also interpret what that behavior means to that person.

All this seems rather complicated, but Kelly is simply suggesting that we are actively involved in interpersonal relations and realize that we are part of the other person's construction system.

Kelly also introduced the notion of **role** with his sociality corollary. A role refers to a pattern of behavior that results from a person's understanding of the constructs of others with whom that person is engaged in a task. For example, when Arlene was negotiating with the used-car dealer, she construed her role as that of a potential buyer because she understood that that was his expectation of her. At other times and with other people, she construes her role as student, employee, daughter, girlfriend, and so on.

Kelly construed roles from a psychological rather than a sociological perspective. One's role does not depend on one's place or position in a social setting but rather on how one interprets that role. Kelly also stressed the point that one's construction of a role need not be accurate in order for the person to play that role.

Arlene's roles as student, employee, and daughter would be considered *peripheral roles*. More central to her existence would be her core role. With our *core role* we define ourselves in terms of who we really are. It gives us a sense of identity and provides us with guidelines for everyday living.

APPLICATIONS OF PERSONAL CONSTRUCT THEORY

Like most personality theorists, Kelly evolved his theoretical formulations from his practice as a psychotherapist. He spent more than 20 years conducting therapy before he published *The Psychology of Personal Constructs* in 1955. In this section we look at his views of abnormal development, his approach to psychotherapy, and, finally, his Role Construct Repertory (Rep) Test.

Abnormal Development

In Kelly's view, psychologically healthy people validate their personal constructs against their experience with the real world. They are like competent scientists who test reasonable hypotheses, accept the results without denial or distortion, and then willingly alter their theories to match available data. Healthy individuals not only anticipate events but are also able to make satisfactory adjustments when things do not turn out as they expected.

Unhealthy people, on the other hand, stubbornly cling to outdated personal constructs, fearing validation of any new constructs that would upset their present, comfortable view of the world. They are similar to incompetent scientists who test unreasonable hypotheses, reject or distort legitimate results, and refuse to amend old theories that are no longer useful. Kelly (1955, p. 831) defined a disorder as *"any personal construction which is used repeatedly in spite of consistent invalidation."*

A person's construction system exists in the present—not the past or future. Psychological disorders, therefore, also exist in the present; they are caused neither by childhood experiences nor by future events. Because construction systems are *personal*, Kelly objects to traditional classifications of abnormalities. Labeling a person as a manic-depressive or a paranoid schizophrenic is likely to result in misconstruing the person's unique constructions.

Psychologically unhealthy people, like everyone else, possess a complex construction system. Their personal constructs, however, often fail the test of permeability in one of two ways: They may be either too impermeable, or they may be too flexible. In the first instance, new experiences do not penetrate the construction system so that the person fails to adjust to the real world. For example, an abused child may construe intimacy with parents as bad and solitude as good. Psychological disorders result when the child's construction system rigidly denies the value of any intimate relationship and clings to the notion that either withdrawal or attack is a preferred mode of solving interpersonal problems.

On the other hand, a construction system that is too loose or flexible leads to disorganization, an inconsistent pattern of behavior, and a transient set of values. Such an individual is too easily "shaken by the impact of unexpected minor daily events" (Kelly, 1955, p. 80).

Although Kelly did not use traditional labels in describing psychopathology, he did identify four common elements in most human disturbance: threat, fear, anxiety, and guilt.

Threat

Threat is experienced when people perceive that the stability of their basic constructs is likely to be shaken. Kelly (1955, p. 489) defined threat as *"the awareness of imminent comprehensive change in one's core structures."* We can be threatened by either people or events, and sometimes the two cannot be separated. For example, during psychotherapy clients often feel threat from the prospect of change, even change for the better. A therapist who is seen as the instigator of change is therefore viewed as threatening. Clients frequently resist change and construe their therapist's behavior in a negative fashion. Such resistance and "negative transference" are means of reducing threat and maintaining existing personal constructs.

Fear

By Kelly's definition, threat involves a *comprehensive* change in a person's core structures. **Fear**, on the other hand, is more *specific* and *incidental*. Kelly (1955) illustrated the difference between threat and fear with the following example. A man may drive his car dangerously as the result of anger or exuberance. These impulses become *threatening* when the man realizes that he may run over a child, be arrested for reckless driving, and end up as a criminal. In this case, a comprehensive portion of his personal constructs is threatened. However, if he is suddenly confronted with the probability of crashing his car, he will experience *fear*. Threat demands a comprehensive restructuring—fear an incidental one. Psychological disturbance results when either threat or fear persistently prevent a person from feeling secure.

Anxiety

Kelly (1955, p. 495) defined **anxiety** as *"the recognition that the events with which one is confronted lie outside the range of convenience of one's construct system."* We are likely to feel anxious when we are experiencing a new event. For example, when Arlene, our case study, was bargaining with the used-car dealer she was not sure what to do or say. She had never before negotiated over such a large amount of money, and therefore this experience was outside the range of her convenience. As a consequence, she felt anxiety, but it was a normal level of anxiety and did not result in incapacitation.

Pathological anxiety exists when incompatible constructs can no longer be tolerated and one's construction system breaks down. Recall that Kelly's fragmentation corollary assumes that people can evolve construction subsystems that are incompatible with one another. For example, when a person who has erected the rigid construction that all people are trustworthy is blatantly cheated by a colleague, that person may for a time tolerate the ambiguity of the two incompatible subsystems. However, when evidence of the untrustworthiness of others becomes overwhelming, the person's construct system may break down. The result is a relatively permanent and debilitating experience of anxiety.

Guilt

Kelly's sociality corollary assumes that people construe a core role that gives them a sense of identity within a social environment. When that core role is weakened or dissolved, they develop a feeling of guilt. Kelly (1970, p. 27) defined **guilt** as *"the sense of having lost one's core role structure."* In other words, people feel guilty when they behave in ways that are inconsistent with their sense of who they are.

People who have never developed a core role do not feel guilty. They may be anxious or confused, but, without a sense of personal identity, they do not experience guilt. For example, people without a conscience have no integral sense of self, no core role structure. Such people have no stable guidelines to violate and hence will not feel guilty regardless of their behavior.

Psychotherapy

Psychological distress exists whenever people have difficulty validating their personal constructs, anticipating future events, and controlling their present environment. When distress becomes unmanageable, they may seek outside help in the form of psychotherapy.

In Kelly's view, people should be free to choose those courses of action most consistent with their prediction of events. In therapy this means that clients, not the therapist, select the goal. Clients are active participants in the therapeutic process, and the therapist's role is to assist them to alter their construct systems in order to improve efficiency in making predictions.

As a technique for altering the clients' constructs, Kelly used a procedure called *fixed-role therapy*. The purpose of fixed-role therapy is to help clients change their outlook on life (personal constructs) by acting out a predetermined role, first within the relative security of the therapeutic setting and then in the environment beyond therapy where they enact the role continuously over a period of several weeks. Together with the therapist, clients work out a role, one that includes attitudes and behaviors not currently part of their core role. In writing the fixed-role sketch, the client and therapist are careful to include the construction systems of other people. How will the client's spouse or parents or boss or friends construe and react to this new role? Will their reactions help the client reconstrue events more productively?

This new role is then tried out in everyday life in much the same manner that a scientist tests a hypothesis—cautiously and objectively. In fact, the fixed-role sketch is typically written in the third person, with the actor assuming a new identity. The client is not trying to be another person but is merely playing the part of someone who is worth knowing. The role should not be taken too seriously; it is only an act, something that can be altered as evidence warrants.

Fixed-role therapy is not aimed at solving specific problems or "repairing" obsolete constructs. It is a creative process that allows clients to gradually discover previously hidden aspects of themselves. In the early stages, clients are introduced only to peripheral roles, but then, after they have had time to become comfortable with minor changes in personality structure, they try out new core roles, which permit more profound personality change (Kelly, 1955).

Prior to developing the fixed-role approach, Kelly (1969) stumbled on an unusual procedure that strongly resembles fixed-role therapy. After becoming uncomfortable with Freudian techniques, he decided to offer his clients "preposterous interpretations" for their complaints. Some were far-fetched Freudian interpretations, but, nevertheless, most clients accept these "explanations" and used them as guides to future action. For example, Kelly might tell a client that strict toilet training has caused him to construe his life in a dogmatically rigid fashion, but that he need not continue to see things in this way. To Kelly's surprise, many of his clients began to function better! The key to change was the same as with fixed-role therapy—clients must begin to interpret their lives from a different perspective and see themselves in a different role.

The Rep Test

Another procedure used by Kelly, both inside and outside therapy, was the *Role Construct Repertory (Rep) Test*. The purpose of the Rep Test is to discover ways in which people construe significant people in their lives.

With the Rep Test, a subject is given a Role Title List and asked to designate people who fit the role titles by writing their names on a card. For example, for "a teacher you liked" the subject must supply a particular name. The number of role titles can vary, but Kelly (1955) listed 24 on one version (see Table 14.1). Next, the subject is given three names from the list and asked to judge which two people are alike and yet different from the third. Recall that a construct requires both a similarity and a contrast, so that three is the minimum number for any construct. Say, for example, that a subject construes Number 1 ("A teacher you liked") and Number 6 ("Your mother") as similar and Number 9 ("Your sister nearest your age") as different. Then the subject is asked how mother and favorite teacher are alike and yet different from sister. The *reason* a person gives for the similarity and contrast constitutes the construct. If the subject gives a superficial response such as "They're both old and my sister is young," the examiner will say, "That's one way they are alike. Can you think of another?" The subject might then say, "My mother and my favorite teacher are both unselfish and my sister is very self-centered." The examiner records the construct and then asks the subject to sort three more cards. Not all combinations of sorts are elicited, and the examiner has some latitude in determining which combinations to use.

After a number of sorts are completed, the examiner transfers the information to a repertory grid (see Figure 14.2 for an example). In this particular grid, 19 role titles are listed along the horizontal axis and 22 personal constructs along the vertical axis. On Sort Number 1, this subject construed Persons 17 and 18 alike because they don't believe in God and Person 19 as being different because he or she is very religious. The subject also checked Persons 7, 10, and 12 because they are construed as similar to the two people in the emergent pole, that is, they too

TABLE 14.1   *Example of a List of Role Titles Used for the Rep Test*

1. A teacher you liked. (Or the teacher of a subject you liked.)
2. A teacher you disliked. (Or the teacher of a subject you disliked.)
3a. Your wife or present girl friend.
3b. (for women) Your husband or present boy friend.
4. An employer, supervisor, or officer under whom you worked or served and whom you found hard to get along with. (Or someone under whom you worked in a situation you did not like.)
5. An employer, supervisor, or officer under whom you worked or served and whom you liked. (Or someone under whom you worked in a situation you liked.)
6. Your mother. (Or the person who has played the part of a mother in your life.)
7. Your father. (Or the person who has played the part of a father in your life.)
8. Your brother nearest your age. (Or the person who has been most like a brother.)
9. Your sister nearest your age. (Or the person who has been most like a sister.)
10. A person with whom you have worked who was easy to get along with.
11. A person with whom you have worked who was hard to understand.
12. A neighbor with whom you get along well.
13. A neighbor whom you find hard to understand.
14. A boy you got along well with when you were in high school. (Or when you were 16.)
15. A girl you got along well with when you were in high school. (Or when you were 16.)
16. A boy you did not like when you were in high school. (Or when you were 16.)
17. A girl you did not like when you were in high school. (Or when you were 16.)
18. A person of your own sex whom you would enjoy having as a companion on a trip.
19. A person of your own sex whom you would dislike having as a companion on a trip.
20. A person with whom you have been closely associated recently who appears to dislike you.
21. The person whom you would most like to be of help to. (Or whom you feel most sorry for.)
22. The most intelligent person whom you know personally.
23. The most successful person whom you know personally.
24. The most interesting person whom you know personally.

SOURCE:: *The psychology of personal constructs* by G. A. Kelly, 1955 (pp. 221–222), New York: Norton. Copyright 1955 by W. W. Norton & Company. Used by permission.

do not believe in God. Similarly, the subject checks each row until the entire grid is completed.

There are several versions of the Rep Test and the repertory grid, but all are designed to assess personal constructs. A subject, for example, can see how her father and boss are alike or different; whether or not she identifies with her mother; how her boyfriend and father are alike; or how she construes members of the opposite sex. Also the test can be given early in therapy and then again at the end. Changes in personal constructs reveal the nature and degree of movement made during therapy.

Kelly and his colleagues have used the Rep Test in a variety of forms, and no set scoring rules apply. Reliability and validity of the instrument are not very high and its usefulness depends largely on the skill and experience of the examiner (Adams-Webber, 1970; Fransella & Bannister, 1977).

CONSTRUCTS

Elements (columns 1–19):
1 Self, 2 Mother, 3 Father, 4 Brother, 5 Sister, 6 Spouse, 7 Ex-flame, 8 Pal, 9 Ex-pal, 10 Rejecting Person, 11 Pitied Person, 12 Threatening Person, 13 Attractive Person, 14 Accepted Teacher, 15 Rejected Teacher, 16 Boss, 17 Successful Person, 18 Happy Person, 19 Ethical Person

SORT NO.	EMERGENT POLE	IMPLICIT POLE
1	Don't believe in God	Very religious
2	Same sort of education	Complete different education
3	Not athletic	Athletic
4	Both girls	A boy
5	Parents	Ideas different
6	Understand me better	Don't understand at all
7	Teach the right thing	Teach the wrong thing
8	Achieved a lot	Hasn't achieved a lot
9	Higher education	No education
10	Don't like other people	Like other people
11	More religious	Not religious
12	Believe in higher education	Not believing in too much education
13	More sociable	Not sociable
14	Both girls	Not girls
15	Both girls	Not girls
16	Both have high morals	Low morals
17	Think alike	Think differently
18	Same age	Different ages
19	Believe the same about me	Believe differently about me
20	Both friends	Not friends
21	More understanding	Less understanding
22	Both appreciate music	Don't understand music

Figure 14.2 *Example of a Repertory Grid* (From The psychology of personal constructs, by G. A. Kelly, 1955, p. 270, New York: Norton. Copyright 1955 by W. W. Norton & Company. Used by permission.)

CONCEPT OF HUMANITY

Kelly had an essentially *optimistic* view of human nature. He saw people as anticipating the future and living their lives in accordance with those anticipations. People are capable of changing their personal constructs at any time of life, but those changes are seldom easy. Kelly's modulation corollary suggests that constructs are permeable or resilient, meaning that new elements can be admitted. Not all people, however, have equally permeable constructs. Some accept new experiences and restructure their interpretations accordingly, whereas others possess concrete constructs that are very difficult to alter. Nevertheless, Kelly was quite optimistic in his belief that therapeutic experiences can help people live more productive lives.

On the dimension of *determinism vs. free choice*, Kelly's theory leans toward free choice. The environment, although it has a real existence, can never make us free; that is, no one can grant us freedom; no event can unloose our chains. Only within our own personal construct system are we free to make a choice (Kelly, 1980). We choose between alternatives within a construct system that we ourselves have built. We make those choices on the basis of our anticipation of events. But more than that, we choose those alternatives that appear to offer us the greater opportunity for further elaboration of our anticipatory system. Kelly (1980) referred to this as the **elaborative choice**, that is, in making present choices, we look ahead and pick the alternative that will increase our range of future choices.

Kelly adopted a *teleological* as opposed to a causal view of human personality. He repeatedly insisted that childhood events per se do not shape current personality. Our present construction of past experiences may have some influence on present behavior, but that influence is quite limited. Personality is much more likely to be guided by our present anticipation of future events. Kelly's fundamental postulate—the one on which all corollaries and assumptions stand—is that all human activity is directed by the way that we anticipate events (Kelly, 1955). There can be no question, then, that Kelly's theory is essentially teleological.

Kelly emphasized *conscious processes* more than unconscious ones. However, he did not stress conscious *motivation* because motivation plays no part in personal construct theory. Kelly speaks of levels of cognitive awareness. High levels of awareness refer to those psychological processes that are easily symbolized in words and can be accurately expressed to other people. Low-level processes are incompletely symbolized and are difficult or impossible to communicate.

There are several reasons why some processes are at low levels of awareness. First, some constructs are preverbal, because they were formed before a person acquired meaningful language, and hence they are not capable of being symbolized even to oneself. Second, some processes are at a low level of awareness because a person sees only similarities and fails to make meaningful contrasts. For example, a person may construe all people as trustworthy. However, the implicit pole of untrustworthiness is denied. Because the person's superordinate construction system is rigid, he or she fails to adopt a realistic construct of trustworthy/untrustworthy and tends to see the actions of others as completely trustworthy. Third, some subordinate constructs may remain at a low level of awareness as superordinate constructs are changing. In the above example, for instance, even after changing one's view to the notion that people are not trustworthy, the person may be reluctant to construe one particular individual as untrustworthy. This means that a subordinate construct has not yet caught up to a superordinate one. Finally, some events may lie outside our range of convenience, so that certain experiences do not become part of our construct system. For example, such automatic processes as heart beat, blood circulation, eye blink, and digestion are ordinarily outside our range of convenience, and we are usually not aware of them.

On the issue of *biological vs. social influences*, Kelly was inclined more toward the social, but his emphasis on social forces was not strong. His sociality corollary assumes that, to some extent, we are influenced by others and, in turn, have some impact on them. When we accurately construe the constructions of another person, we may play a role in a social process involving that other person. Kelly assumed that our interpretation of the construction systems of important other people (such as parents, spouse, and friends) may have some influence on our future constructions. Recall that in fixed-role therapy clients adopt the identity of a fictitious person and, by trying out that role in various social settings, they may come to experience some change in their personal constructs. However, the actions of others do not mold their behavior, rather their interpretation of events changes their behavior.

On the final dimension for a conception of humanity—*uniqueness vs. similarities*—Kelly emphasized the uniqueness of personality. This emphasis, however, was tempered by his commonality corollary, which assumes that people from the same sociocultural background tend to have had the same kinds of experience and therefore construe events similarly. Nevertheless, Kelly held that our individual interpretations of events are crucial and that no two persons ever have precisely the same personal constructs.

Related Research

Kelly's theory has sparked more clinical use than empirical research. Nevertheless, some recent publications have included research related to personal construct theory. The *International Journal of Personal Construct Psychology* regularly publishes research reports along with more applied articles. Also, books edited by Nigel Beail (1985) and Eric Button (1985b) both include chapters that report research on personal construct theory.

Fay Fransella and A. H. Crisp (1979) have studied weight-related personal constructs of groups of neurotic women, normal women, and women with **anorexia nervosa**. They reasoned that each of these groups of women would respond differently to such personal constructs as "me at my present weight" and "me at my ideal weight." To test their assumptions, they asked 12 anorexic women, 20 neurotic women without eating disorders, and 20 normal women to fill out a repertory grid consisting of the following elements: (a) four individuals who the subject construes as fitting role titles of an admired person, someone not liked, someone pitied, and someone in whose presence the subject feels anxious or uneasy; (b) four self-constructs, including "like me at my present weight," "like me if I were fat," "like me if I were much thinner," and "like I'd like to be;" and (c) two parental constructs, namely, "like my father in character" and "like my mother in character."

Fransella and Crisp found that anorexic patients saw their world differently from both neurotic or normal women, and that these differences could not be explained on the basis of age, social class, or level of mental health. Both the normal and the neurotic women construed being sexually attractive as very desirable, whereas the anorexics saw it as being less desirable. Both normals and neurotics construed a very close relationship between their ideal self and their ideal weight, but anorexic women reported no significant relationship on this factor, indicating that their ideal self was not dependent on achieving an ideal weight.

In 1985, Eric Button, a former student of Fransella, reported on a study of 20 anorexic patients in treatment. He asked these women patients to complete repertory grids on four occasions: (1) at first admission, (2) at discharge, (3) at a two-month follow-up, and (4) at an eight-month follow-up. Button (1985a, p. 155) began with the assumption that anorexic women "resist change because life is more meaningful than if they were to change to being normal in weight." One of Button's most interesting findings was that women who had "tight" or *impermeable* constructs at the beginning of treatment showed poor prognosis for treatment. Moreover, patients who showed good outcome began treatment with somewhat permeable constructs, "tightened" these constructs at the time of discharge, but then dramatically "loosened" them during both follow-up periods. This suggests that people with an inflexible view of themselves tend to resist change and are poor candidates for successful treatment in therapy.

In a more recent study, Smith, Stefan, Kavaleski, and Johnson (1991) used a version of Kelly's Rep Test called the Dependency Grid (Fransella & Bannister, 1977) to investigate the personal construct systems of psychiatric patients who were hospitalized repeatedly (recidivists). The purpose of this study was to view rehospitalization through the eyes of the patient rather than hospital personnel. "Capturing the patient's perspective while minimizing the bias of one's own framework is a major obstacle for research in this area" (Smith et al., 1991, p. 160).

Smith and her associates assumed that having few people on whom one can rely would be related to psychiatric disorders. But turning inappropriately to a large number of people might also be related to psychiatric problems. Therefore, Smith et al. hypothesized that, compared with first-admission patients and nonpsychiatric controls, recidivists would have the smallest resource network on whom they could draw for social support. Second, they hypothesized that first-admission patients would identify the largest number of people on whom they could rely in a crisis, even though many of these people would be unable or unwilling to offer such support. In contrast, nonpsychiatric controls would report the largest social network, but they would be more selective in identifying people on whom they could rely in a crisis.

Smith et al. administered a modified version of the Dependency Grid to a recidivist group, a first-admission group, and a control group comprised of people in training to become therapy aides. The Dependency Grid consisted of 17 role titles on one dimension and 22 situations on the other. Role titles included people such as self, mother, father, boss, friend, and so forth. Situations included vocation, opposite sex, finances, health, taken advantage of, and so forth. Subjects were requested to identify people who fulfilled requirements for each of the 17 role titles and then to think of a time when one of the 22 situations applied to them. Next, subjects were asked to identify those individuals to whom they could turn for help in a particular crisis.

Smith et al. found support for their main hypotheses. People who are repeatedly admitted to psychiatric hospitals construe their social network as being small; that is, they see themselves as having few people on whom they can rely in times of crises. The authors pointed out that direction of cause and effect is not known, meaning that having few friends may cause psychiatric disorders, being psychiatrically impaired may eliminate some friends, or some other factors may influence both recidivism and social network.

Second, Smith et al. found that first-admission psychiatric patients claimed that they could rely on a large portion of their social network, although that network was not as large as the one reported by the controls. In other words, these psychiatric patients' construction of their world was inappropriately optimistic with regard to the number of their acquaintances who might be interested in providing them with help. The nonpsychiatric control group reported the greatest number of social resources potentially available to them, but they were selective in choosing people on whom they would rely. This study is unique among recidivism studies because it relied on the perceptions of psychiatric patients (their personal constructs) to uncover factors that relate to their repeated hospitalization.

In summary, these and other studies that use various versions of the repertory grid technique illustrate clinical application for Kelly's theory of personal constructs.

CRITIQUE OF KELLY

Kelly's personal construct theory is like no other personality theory discussed in this book. I have included it with the humanistic theories, but it might just as easily be placed among the cognitive theorists. Indeed, Kelly has probably had more influence on cognitive theorists than on humanistic theorists. Rotter and Bandura have been indirectly influenced by him, and Mischel's theory has borrowed even more directly from Kelly's personal construct theory. Cantor and Zirkel (1990, pp. 137–138) believe that "Kelly and Rotter have influenced almost all of what has come to be known as 'cognitive personality theory,' but this influence is most clearly seen among those researchers [who] emphasize the role played by perception and mental transformations of experiences."

On the surface, Kelly seems to be remarkably open-minded. He repeatedly states that all theories, including his own, should be open to reconstruction. He insisted that events can always be construed differently, and that alternative ways of looking at things always exist. Contrary to this broadminded stance, however, is Kelly's lack of toleration for existing theories. As Holland (1970) pointed out, Kelly frequently attacked Freudian theory, behavior theories, cognitive theories, existentialism, and phenomenology. He seems to have been rather nonacceptant of these constructive alternatives.

Most of Kelly's professional career was spent working with relatively normal, intelligent college students. Understandably, his theory seems most applicable to these people. He made no attempt to elucidate early childhood experiences (as did Freud) or maturity and old age (as did Erikson). To him, people live solely in the present, with one eye always on the future. This view, while somewhat optimistic, fails to account for developmental and cultural influences on personality.

How does his theory rate on the five criteria of a useful theory? First, personal construct theory must be rated low on the amount of *research* it has rated. The Rep Test and the repertory grid have generated some research, especially in Great Britain, but these instruments are not used much by psychologists in the United States. Despite the relative parsimony of Kelly's basic postulate and 11 supporting corollaries, the theory does not easily lend itself to the formation of testable hypotheses. Therefore, little research is currently being conducted on specific hypotheses drawn from personal construct theory.

Second, does personal construct theory *organize knowledge* about human behavior? On this criterion, the theory must be rated very low. Kelly's avoidance of the problems of motivation, developmental influences, and cultural forces limits his theory's ability to give meaning to much of what is currently known about the complexity of personality.

The theory also falls short as a *guide to action*. Kelly's ideas on psychotherapy are rather innovative and suggest to the practitioner some interesting techniques. Playing the role of a fictitious person, someone the client would like to know, is indeed an unusual and practical approach to therapy. Kelly relied heavily on "common sense" in this therapeutic practice and what worked for him might not work for someone else. That would be quite acceptable to Kelly, however, because he viewed therapy as a scientific experiment. The therapist is like a scientist, using imagination to test a variety of hypotheses, that is, to try out new techniques and to explore alternate ways of looking at things. Nevertheless, Kelly's theory offers few specific suggestions to parents, therapists, researchers, and others who are trying to understand human behavior.

Fourth, is the theory *internally consistent*, with a set of operationally defined terms? On the first part of this question, personal construct theory rates very high. Kelly was exceptionally careful in choosing terms and concepts to explain his fundamental postulate and the 11 corollaries. His language, although frequently difficult, is both elegant and precise. *The Psychology of Personal Constructs* (Kelly, 1955) contains over 1200 pages, but the entire theory is pieced together like a finely woven fabric. Kelly always seems to have been aware of what he had already said and what he was going to say.

On the second half of this criterion, Kelly's theory falls short. Like most theorists discussed in this book, Kelly did not define his terms operationally. However, he was exemplary in writing comprehensive and exacting definitions of nearly all terms used in the basic postulate and supporting corollaries.

Finally, is the theory *parsimonious*? Despite the length of Kelly's two-volume book, the theory of personal constructs is exceptionally straightforward and economical. The basic theory is stated in one fundamental postulate and then elaborated by means of 11 corollaries. All other concepts and assumptions can be easily related to this relatively simple structure.

Chapter Summary

According to Kelly, our personality is shaped by our idiosyncratic interpretation of events. Although the outside world is real, it does not directly influence our behavior. Instead, our actions are guided by the way we anticipate events, and we anticipate events by our *personal constructs*, that is, the meanings or interpretations we place on our experience.

Kelly sees people as scientists, asking questions, testing hypotheses, formulating theories, asking additional questions, and making interpretations.

Basic to Kelly's theory is the idea of *constructive alternativism*, or the notion that our present interpretations are subject to change.

Kelly's theory can be summarized in his one fundamental postulate and 11 supporting corollaries. His *basic postulate* assumes that all our psychological processes are directed by the ways in which we anticipate events. The 11 corollaries derive from and elaborate the one fundamental postulate.

1. *Construction Corollary.* We anticipate future events according to our interpretations of recurrent themes.

2. *Individuality Corollary.* People have different experiences and, therefore, construe events in different ways.

3. *Organization Corollary.* We organize our personal constructs in a hierarchical system, with some constructs in a superordinate positions and others subordinate to them. This organization allows us to minimize incompatible constructs.

4. *Dichotomy Corollary.* All personal constructs are dichotomous, that is, we construe events in an either/or manner.

5. *Choice Corollary.* We choose the alternative in a dichotomized construct that we see as extending our range of future choices.

6. *Range Corollary.* Constructs are limited to a particular range of convenience, that is, they are not relevant to all situations.

7. *Experience Corollary.* We continually revise our personal constructs as the result of experience.

8. *Modulation Corollary.* Not all new experiences lead to a revision of personal constructs. To the extent that constructs are permeable they are subject to change through experience. Concrete or impermeable constructs resist modification regardless of our experience.

9. *Fragmentation Corollary.* Our behavior is sometimes inconsistent because our construct system can readily admit incompatible elements.

10. *Commonality Corollary.* To the extent that we have had experiences similar to others, our personal constructs tend

to be similar to the construction systems of those people.

11. *Sociality Corollary.* We are able to communicate with others because we can construe their constructions. We not only observe the behavior of others, but we also interpret what that behavior means to them.

The application of Kelly's theory can be divided into (1) *abnormal development,* (2) *psychotherapy,* and (3) *the Role Construct Repertory (Rep) Test.*

In Kelly's view, unhealthy people are like incompetent scientists who test unreasonable hypotheses and refuse to modify their constructs in the light of contradictory evidence. They persist in using personal constructs that have consistently failed the test of validation.

Kelly's psychotherapeutic approach relies heavily on the clients' ability to actively participate with the therapist in restructuring their construct systems and making them more efficient predictors of future events. *Fixed-role therapy* calls for clients to act out predetermined roles continuously for a couple of weeks. The clients' peripheral and core roles may gradually change as significant others begin reacting differently to them.

The purpose of the *Rep Test* is to discover ways in which people construe important people in their lives.

Kelly has an optimistic view of humanity and sees people as forward-looking and ultimately in charge of their lives.

Unfortunately, personal construct theory falls short on the most crucial standards for a useful theory. Aside from the Rep Test, it has generated very little research, and its ability to organize knowledge is limited by Kelly's avoidance of developmental issues and his rejection of such concepts as learning and motivation.

Suggested Readings

BUTTON, E. (1985). Personal construct theory: The concepts. In E. Button (Ed.), *Personal construct theory & mental health* (pp. 3–30), Cambridge, MA: Brookline Books.
    In this chapter Button presents an excellent summary of Kelly's personal construct theory, including fresh examples of the various corollaries and ways of looking at psychological disorders and mental health from the view of personal constructs.
KELLY, G. A. (1963). A *theory of personal constructs: The psychology of personal constructs.* New York: Norton.
    This small paperback contains the first three chapters of Kelly's The *Psychology of Personal Constructs* (1955). These three chapters present the essence of Kelly's theory—constructive alternativism, the basic theory, and the nature of personal constructs.
KELLY, G. A. (1969). The autobiography of a theory. In B. Maher (Ed.), *Clinical psychology and personality: The selected papers of George Kelly* (pp. 46–65). New York: Wiley.
    Perhaps the most interesting of all of Kelly's writings, this chapter combines personal glimpses with theoretical insights to produce the story of how personal construct theory came into being.

KELLY, G. A. (1970). A brief introduction to personal construct theory. In D. Bannister (Ed.), *Perspectives in personal construct theory* (pp. 1–29). London: Academic Press.
Written the year preceding Kelly's death, this chapter was originally intended as an introduction to a book Kelly never finished. It presents an updated but briefer version of his 1955 book.

LANDFIELD, A. W., & EPTING, F. R. (1987). *Personal construct psychology: Clinical and personality assessment.* New York: Human Sciences Press.
Although intended mainly for the clinician, this book can be easily understood by students interested in the practical applications of personal construct theory.

Chapter
Fifteen

Holistic-Dynamic Theory

OVERVIEW
BIOGRAPHY OF ABRAHAM H. MASLOW
MOTIVATION
    Hierarchy of Needs
    Aesthetic Needs
    Cognitive Needs
    Neurotic Needs
    General Discussion of Needs
SELF-ACTUALIZATION
    Values of Self-Actualizers
    Definition and Description
    Characteristics of Self-Actualizing People
    Love, Sex, and Self-Actualization
APPLICATIONS OF MASLOW'S THEORY
    Abnormal Development
    Psychotherapy
BOX: CAN YOU FAKE SELF-ACTUALIZATION?
PHILOSOPHY OF SCIENCE
RESEARCH METHODS
CONCEPT OF HUMANITY
RELATED RESEARCH
    Research on Hierarchy of Needs
    Research on the Peak Experience
CRITIQUE OF MASLOW
CHAPTER SUMMARY
SUGGESTED READINGS

MASLOW

When Julius was 39 years old, his wife died, leaving him with two small children and a large farm. For the next dozen years Julius devoted much time to his daughters while struggling to hold on to his farm during years of drought, grasshoppers, and low prices. Finally, after four consecutive years of losing money, he sold his farm and moved to town.

After a series of odd jobs, Julius, at age 58, found regular work with one of the local farmers. For another 20 years he drove a tractor, worked with cattle, fixed fences, repaired farm machinery, and performed dozens of other jobs required of a farm laborer.

Ten years after his younger daughter had left home, Julius married again. Unlike many older widowers, he was not driven into marriage by loneliness or the need to have someone look after him. He had always been very independent and quite capable of caring for himself. He and and his second wife, Anna, were married simply because they both wanted it.

Julius found pleasure in little things. He enjoyed his work on the farm and looked forward each morning to the day's activities. He worked long hours, six days a week during the spring and summer, but fewer hours the rest of the year. On Sunday, he often drove his pickup truck to the farm to look after his employer's land, cattle, and fences. He never considered charging for this consideration; he simply enjoyed farming and ranching. Julius also enjoyed growing his own vegetables and flowers, and he spent many hours in his garden, sometimes with Anna, sometimes alone. His appreciation for growth and change extended to his grandchildren, whom he saw only a few times a year. He was greatly fond of them and took a keen interest in their academic, social, and emotional development.

Julius was not well known by the people of his town. Except for church, he seldom attended social functions. His close friends were limited to his boss and his co-workers. The people who knew him well regarded him as no one special, simply a pleasant old man with a refreshing sense of humor and an optimistic attitude toward life. Abraham H. Maslow might have regarded him as *self-actualizing*, the ultimate level of healthy human functioning.

OVERVIEW

The concept of self-actualization and the name Abraham Maslow have been closely associated for many years. Although Maslow did not coin the term and is not the only personality theorist to use it, he has done more than any other psychologist to popularize the notion of self-actualization.

Maslow's theory of personality, however, goes far beyond a consideration of self-actualization. His **holistic-dynamic theory** holds that people are constantly being motivated by one need or another. Few of us ever reach self-actualization. Instead, we are motivated by lower-level needs such as hunger, safety, love, and self-esteem. In addition, other dimensions of needs, namely, cognitive and aesthetic, help shape our behavior. Moreover some of us are driven by neurotic needs to perpetuate the status quo rather than to move in the direction of psychological health or self-actualization.

Although often thought of as the father of the *Third Force in psychology* (the first force is psychoanalysis and its modifications; the second is behaviorism), Maslow (1971) did not regard himself as either anti-Freudian or anti-behavioristic. In fact, he perceived himself to be both a psychoanalyst and a behaviorist. He repudiated neither and saw much of value in both of these earlier theories. However, he held that both had a limited view of humanity. Neither psychoanalysis nor behaviorism deal adequately with the normal, healthy person such as Julius. Neither of the older theories give humans enough credit for reaching toward higher values and goals. Only relatively recently, Maslow believed, has psychology in particular and science in general paid much attention to people's higher nature. Maslow (1970) called this the "unnoticed revolution" and he found evidence for its existence in various scientific disciplines as well as in philosophy. Maslow believed that humans have a higher nature than was formerly thought, and he spent the last years of his life trying to discover what it is like to achieve the ultimate in psychological health.

BIOGRAPHY OF ABRAHAM H. MASLOW

Abraham Harold Maslow was born on April 1, 1908, in Brooklyn, New York. The oldest of seven children, he was not especially close to either parent but felt more affection toward his father, a Russian-Jewish immigrant from Kiev. Toward his mother he felt hatred and deep-seated animosity, not only during his childhood, but until the day she died just a couple of years before Maslow's own death. His mother was a very religious woman who often threatened young Abe with punishment from God, and from her Maslow learned to hate and mistrust religion. Although never a practicing Jew, he felt the sting of anti-Semitism from a young age onward. His feelings of persecution were not as intense as those of Freud, but, nevertheless, they were probably somewhat exaggerated (Hoffman, 1988). Throughout early childhood Maslow was extremely lonely, shy, and depressed. He felt ugly and inferior and later described himself as being neurotic during this time (Wilson, 1972).

Possibly as a defense against the anti-Semitic attitudes of his classmates, he turned to books and scholarly pursuits. He spent little time at home, preferring either the company of a maternal uncle who lived nearby or the confines of the public library, where he spent many hours reading on a variety of subjects.

During Abe's childhood the Maslow family gradually rose from the slums to lower-middle-class respectability. In later years his three younger brothers became financially independent as owners of the Maslow Cooperage Corporation.

Maslow's father wanted him to be a lawyer and, while attending the City College of New York, Maslow also enrolled in law school. However, he walked out of law classes one night leaving his books behind. Significantly, he felt that law dealt too much with evil people and was not sufficiently concerned with the good. His father, although initially disappointed, eventually accepted Abe's decision to quit law school (Hall, 1968).

Maslow was a mediocre student at CCNY, and after three semesters, he transferred to Cornell University. There, too, his scholastic work was poor. His introductory psychology professor was Edward B. Titchener, a renowned pioneer in psychology who taught all his classes in full academic robes. Titchener's "bloodless" approach to psychology left Maslow cold and indifferent (Hoffman, 1988).

After one semester Maslow returned to the City College of New York, partly to be nearer his first cousin, Bertha Goodman. He loved Bertha in a distant, bashful sort of way, having never touched her or expressed his feelings. Then, suddenly, a fortuitous event changed his life. While visiting his Aunt Pearl (Bertha's mother), his cousin, Anna (Bertha's older sister), shoved Abe toward Bertha, saying, "For the love of Pete, kiss her, will ya!" (Hoffman, 1988, p. 29). He did, and to his surprise Bertha did not fight back. She kissed him, and from that time his life became meaningful.

Abe and Bertha were married during Christmas recess, 1928, when he was 20 and she 19. Maslow's parents stubbornly resisted the marriage, fearing hereditary defects in any possible offspring. This resistance was ironic in light of the fact that Abe's parents themselves were first cousins and had had seven healthy children!

Maslow had earlier enrolled at the University of Wisconsin and, after their marriage, Bertha went west to join him. At Wisconsin, Maslow became interested in psychology and his grades showed a marked improvement. His life, by his own reckoning, began at this time (Hall, 1968).

As a student, Maslow was greatly influenced by two forces that, at first glance, seem far removed from the holistic and humanistic leanings that so strongly characterize his later works. The first of these was behaviorism. The influence of John B. Watson was strong on American campuses during the 1930s and Maslow became excited about the potential of behaviorism to remake the world. The second influence was Harry Harlow and his experiments with monkeys. Maslow not only worked in Harlow's laboratories, but made some important discoveries on dominance and sexual behavior among monkeys.

Although Maslow's later researches on self-actualizing people seem far removed from either behaviorism or experiments with monkeys, these two early experiences played an important role in the evolution of his thinking. For example, after studying the sexual behavior of monkeys, Maslow moved easily to the field of human sexuality and made important contributions to that area several years before Kinsey's (Kinsey, Pomeroy, & Martin, 1948) landmark research appeared. The destruction wrought by World War II moved him to devote his life to the study of the best in human beings, and his experiences gained from interviewing people on sexual behavior proved useful in interviewing healthy individuals.

After receiving a Ph.D. from Wisconsin in 1934, Maslow could not find an academic position due in part to the Great Depression and to anti-Semitic prejudice still strong on many American campuses in those years. Consequently, he continued to teach at Wisconsin for a short time and even enrolled in medical school there. However, medical school bored him, and he felt that, like law school, it reflected a dispassionate and negative view of people. Whenever Maslow became bored with something, he usually quit it, and medical school was no exception.

In 1935, he returned to New York to become E. L. Thorndike's research assistant at Teacher's College, Columbia University. Because Maslow scored 195 on Thorndike's intelligence test, Thorndike, demonstrating confidence in both Maslow and his own test, gave his assistant free reign to do as he wished. Maslow's fertile mind thrived in this situation, but after a year and a half of doing research on human sexuality, he left Columbia to join the faculty of Brooklyn College.

Living in New York during the 1930s and 1940s afforded Maslow an opportunity to come into contact with many of the European psychologists who had escaped Nazi rule. Among others he met Erich Fromm, Karen Horney, Max Wertheimer, and Kurt Goldstein. Maslow was influenced by each of these as well as by Alfred Adler, who was living in New York at that time. Adler held seminars in his home on Friday nights, and Maslow was a frequent visitor to these sessions, as was Julian Rotter (see Chapter 11). In a personal letter to Frank Goble, Maslow wrote:

> I think it's fair to say that I have had the best teachers, both formal and informal, of any person who ever lived, just because of being in New York City when the cream of European intellect was migrating away from Hitler. . . I learned from all of them. . . . So I could not be said to be a Goldsteinian nor a Frommian nor an Adlerian or whatever. I never accepted any of the invitations to join any of these parochial and

sectarian organizations. I learned from all of them and refused to close any doors. (Goble,1970, pp. 11-12)

While at Brooklyn College, Maslow underwent a partial psychoanalysis with Emil Oberholzer, a New York psychiatrist. Despite this and later psychoanalytic treatments, Maslow never lost his hatred for his mother and even refused to attend her funeral.

During the mid-1940s Maslow's health began to deteriorate. In 1946, at age 38, he suffered a strange illness that left him weak, faint, and "barely able to stand for more than a few minutes at a time" (Hoffman, 1988, p. 176). In 1947 he took a medical leave and, with Bertha and their two daughters, moved to Pleasanton, California, where, in name only, he was plant manager of a branch of the Maslow Cooperage Corporation. His light work schedule enabled him to read biographies and histories in a search for information on self-actualizing people. By 1949, his health had improved and he went back to teaching at Brooklyn College.

In 1951 Maslow took a position as chairman of the psychology department at the recently established Brandeis University in Waltham, Massachusetts. During his Brandeis years he began writing extensively in his journals, jotting down at irregular intervals his thoughts, opinions, feelings, social activities, important conversations, and concerns for his health (Maslow, 1979).

Despite achieving fame during the 1960s, Maslow was not happy with his work during this time. He became increasingly disenchanted with students and faculty at Brandeis. Some students rebelled against his teaching methods, demanding more experiential involvement and less of an intellectual and scientific approach. In addition, he suffered a severe but nonfatal heart attack in December of 1967. He then learned that his strange malady more than 20 years earlier had been an undiagnosed heart attack.

In poor health and disappointed with the academic atmosphere at Brandeis, Maslow accepted an offer to join the Saga Administrative Corporation in Menlo Park, California. He had no particular job there and was free to think and write as he wished. He enjoyed that freedom, but on June 8, 1970, while slowly jogging, he suddenly collapsed and died of a massive heart attack. He was 62.

Maslow received many honors during his lifetime, including his election to the presidency of the American Psychological Association for the year 1967–68. At the time of his death he was well known, not only within the profession of psychology, but among educated people generally, particularly in business management, marketing, theology, counseling, education, nursing, and other health-related fields.

Maslow's personal life was filled with pain, both physical and psychological. As an adolescent, he was terribly shy, unhappy, isolated, and self-rejecting. His love for Bertha made him miserable because he did not know how to act or what Bertha felt toward him. Those problems were solved by his marriage, but he continued to be painfully shy. He was terrified of public speaking and was past 50 before he was able to overcome some of his stage fright. He never overcame the intense hatred of his mother, and in 1969 he wrote in his journal these thoughts concerning her.

> What I had reacted against and totally hated and rejected was not only her physical appearance, but also her values and world view, her stinginess, her total selfishness, her lack of love for anyone else in the world, even her own husband and children . . . her assumption that anyone was wrong who disagreed with her, her lack of concern for her grandchildren, her lack of friends, her sloppiness and dirtiness, her lack of family feeling for her own parents and siblings. . . . I've always wondered where my Utopianism, ethical stress, humanism, stress on kindness, love, friendship, and all the rest came from. I knew certainly of the direct consequences of having no mother-love. But the whole thrust of my life-philosophy and all my research and theorizing also has its roots in a hatred for and revulsion against everything she stood for. (Maslow, 1979, p. 958)

Maslow's physical health was never robust, and he suffered from a series of ailments, including chronic fatigue, hypoglycemia, an arthritic hip, and chronic heart problems. His journals (Maslow, 1979) are sprinkled with references to ill health. In his last journal entry (May 7, 1970) one month before his death, he complained about people expecting him to be a courageous leader and spokesperson. He wrote: "I am not temperamentally 'courageous.' My courage is really an overcoming of all sorts of inhibitions, politeness, gentleness, timidities— and it always cost me a lot in fatigue, tension, apprehension, bad sleep" (Maslow, 1979, p. 1307).

MOTIVATION

Maslow's theory of personality rests on several basic assumptions regarding motivation. First, Maslow (1970) adopted a *holistic approach to motivation*, repeatedly pointing out that the whole person, not any single part or function, is motivated.

Second, *motivation is usually complex*, meaning that surface behavior is often an expression of a hidden, more basic need. Motivation is often more complex than it appears because an unconscious need underlies the behavior. One important way in which Maslow differed from Allport was in his emphasis on unconscious motivation. Whereas Allport might say that a person plays golf "just for the fun of it," Maslow would look beneath the surface for hidden and often complex reasons for playing.

A third assumption is that *people are continually motivated by one need or another*. A satisfied need ordinarily loses its motivational power and is thus replaced by another one. For example, so long as people's hunger needs are frustrated they will strive for food, but when they do have enough to eat they move on to other needs such as shelter and companionship.

Another assumption is that *all people everywhere are motivated by the same basic needs.* The manner in which people in different cultures obtain food, build shelter, express friendship, and so forth may vary widely, but the fundamental needs for food, safety, and friendship are common to the entire species.

A final assumption concerning motivation is that *needs can be arranged on a hierarchy* (Maslow, 1943, 1970).

Hierarchy of Needs

Maslow's hierarchy of needs concept assumes that basic or lower-level needs must be satisfied or at least relatively satisfied before higher-level needs become motivators. Needs can be arranged on a hierarchy or staircase, with each ascending step representing a higher need but one less basic to survival (see Figure 15.1). The hierarchy of needs is also referred to as the *theory of prepotent needs.* Lower-level needs have prepotency over higher-level needs, meaning that lower needs must be satisfied in order for people to strive for higher needs. For example, an artist at work in his studio may be satisfying higher-level needs such as esteem or self-actualization, but eventually he will become hungry and leave his work to find food (a lower-level need). Hunger, then, has prepotency over both esteem and self-actualization.

Maslow (1970) listed the following needs in order of their prepotency: physiological, safety, love and belongingness, esteem, and self-actualization.

Physiological Needs

The most basic needs of any person are *physiological,* including food, water, oxygen, maintenance of body temperature, and so on. Physiological needs are the most prepotent of all. Hungry people are motivated to eat, not to make friends or gain self-esteem. They do not see beyond food, and so long as this need remains unsatisfied, their primary motivation is to obtain something to eat. Perpetually hungry people come to believe that food is the ultimate goal, and they delude themselves with the belief that if only they could get enough to eat, they would be forever happy.

In affluent societies most people satisfy their hunger needs as a matter of course. They usually have enough to eat, so when they say they are hungry they are really speaking of appetites, not hunger. A truly hungry person will not be overly particular about taste, smell, temperature, or texture of the food.

Maslow (1970, p. 38) said: "It is quite true that man lives by bread alone—when there is no bread." When people do not have their physiological needs satisfied, they live primarily for those needs and strive constantly to satisfy them. Starving people become preoccupied with food and are willing to do nearly anything to obtain it (Keys, Brozek, Henschel, Mickelsen, & Taylor, 1950).

Physiological needs differ from other needs in at least two important respects. First, they are the only needs that can be completely satisfied or even overly satisfied. One can get enough to eat so that food completely loses its motivational

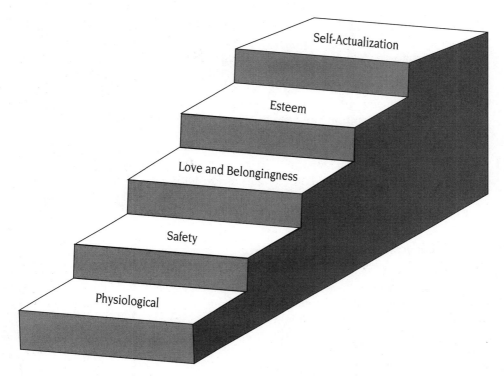

Figure 15.1 *Maslow's Hierarchy of Needs. One must reach self-actualization one step at a time.*

power. For someone who has just finished a large meal, the thought of more food can even have a nauseating effect. A second characteristic peculiar to physiological needs is their recurring nature. After we have eaten we will eventually become hungry again, we constantly need to replenish our water supply, and one breath of air must be followed by another. Other-level needs do not constantly recur. Once love and esteem needs are relatively met, they remain satisfied, but physiological needs continually reappear.

Safety Needs

When our physiological needs are satisfied or relatively well satisfied, then we become motivated by needs for *safety*, including physical security, stability, dependency, protection, and freedom from such threatening forces as illness, fear, anxiety, danger, and chaos. The need for law, order, and structure are also safety needs (Maslow, 1970).

Safety needs differ from physiological needs in that they cannot be overly satiated; we can never have too much safety. We can never be completely protected from meteorites, fires, floods, or the dangerous acts of others.

In societies not at war, most healthy adults satisfy their safety needs most of the time, thus making these needs relatively unimportant. Children, however, are more often motivated by safety needs because they live with such threats as darkness, animals, strangers, and punishments from parents. Neurotic adults also feel relatively unsafe because they retain irrational fears from childhood, which cause them to act as if they were afraid of parental punishment. They imagine their physical well-being to be threatened and therefore constrict themselves to the safe and the familiar. They spend far more energy than do healthy people trying to satisfy safety needs, and when they are not successful in their attempts, they suffer from what Maslow (1970) called **basic anxiety**.

For both healthy and unhealthy people, safety needs become activated during emergency situations such as natural disasters, injury, accidents, and war. At least during short periods of immediate danger, higher-level needs—love, esteem, and self-actualization—lose their potency and people become motivated primarily by safety needs.

Love and Belongingness Needs

For most of us, physiological and safety needs are fairly well satisfied and do not dominate our lives. *Love and belongingness needs*, however, are a different matter. Most of us get caught at this level and strive more or less constantly to be accepted and loved by other people (Maslow, 1970).

After we partially satisfy our physiological and safety needs, we become motivated by love and belongingness needs, such as the desire for friendship, the wish for a mate and children, the need to belong to a family, a club, a neighborhood, or a nation. Love and belongingness also include some aspects of sex and human contact, as well as the need to both give and receive love.

Motivation for love is ordinarily strongest when the need is partially denied. People who have never received love, who have never been kissed or cuddled, can go for long periods without these things and not panic. They take absence of love for granted and eventually devalue this need. Conversely, people who have had love and belongingness needs adequately satisfied from early years also will not panic when denied love. These people have confidence that they are accepted by those who are important to them, so if other people reject them, they do not feel devastated.

On the other hand, people who have tasted love only in small doses will be strongly motivated to seek satisfaction of love and belongingness needs. In other words, people who have received only a small amount of love have stronger needs for affection and acceptance than do people who have received either a healthy amount of love or none at all (Maslow, 1970).

Children need love in order to grow psychologically, and their attempts to satisfy this need are usually straightforward and direct. Adults, too, need love, but their attempts to attain it are sometimes cleverly disguised. They often engage in self-defeating behaviors, such as pretending to be aloof from other people or adopting a cynical, cold, and calloused manner in their interpersonal relationships. They may give the appearance of self-sufficiency and independence, but in reality they have a strong need to be accepted and loved by other people. Other adults whose

In addition to physiological and safety needs, children have love and belongingness needs.

love needs remain largely unsatisfied adopt more obvious ways of trying to satisfy them, but they undermine their own success by striving too hard. Their constant supplications for acceptance and affection leave others suspicious, unfriendly, and impenetrable.

If people have had love needs gratified from childhood, they gain a feeling of self-esteem, and they may even become self-actualizing adults who are no longer dependent upon the continual love and acceptance of other people. As self-actualizing adults, they maintain their feelings of self-esteem even when scorned, rejected, and dismissed by other people. In other words, esteem and self-actualization are no longer dependent upon the satisfaction of love and belonging needs; that is, they are now *functionally autonomous* from the lower-level needs that gave them birth (see Chapter 13 for Allport's discussion of functional autonomy).

Esteem Needs

To the extent that people satisfy their love and belongingness needs they are free to pursue *esteem needs*, such as self-respect, confidence, competence, and the esteem of others. Maslow (1970) identified two levels of esteem needs—reputation and self-esteem. Reputation is the perception of the prestige, recognition, or fame people have achieved in the eyes of others, whereas self-esteem is the person's own feelings of worth and confidence. Self-esteem is based on more than reputation or prestige; it reflects a "desire for strength, for achievement, for adequacy, for mastery and competence, for confidence in the face of the world, and for independence and freedom" (Maslow, 1970, p. 45). In other words, self-esteem is based on real competence and not merely on others' opinions.

Once people meet their esteem needs, they stand on the threshold of self-actualization, the highest need recognized by Maslow.

Self-Actualization Needs

When lower-level needs are satisfied, people proceed more or less automatically to the next level. However, once esteem needs are met, they do not always move to the level of *self-actualization*. Originally, Maslow assumed that self-actualization needs become potent whenever esteem needs have been met. However, during the 1960s he came to realize that many of the young students at Brandeis and other campuses around the country had all their basic needs gratified, including reputation and self-esteem, and yet they did not become self-actualizing (Frick, 1971, 1982; Maslow, 1967, 1971). Why some people step over the threshold from esteem to self-actualization and others do not is a matter of whether or not they embrace the B-*values* (B-values will be discussed later). People who hold in high respect such values as truth, beauty, justice, and the other B-values become self-actualizing after their esteem needs are met, whereas those who do not embrace these values are frustrated in their self-actualization needs even though they have satisfied each of their other basic needs.

Self-actualization is the desire for self-fulfillment, to realize all of one's potential, to become everything that one can, and to become creative in the full sense of the word (Maslow, 1970). People who have reached the level of self-actualization become fully human, satisfying needs that others merely glimpse or never view at all. They are natural in the same sense that animals and infants are natural; that is, they express their basic human needs and do not allow them to be suppressed by culture. (A more complete sketch of self-actualizing people will follow the present discussion of needs.)

The five needs comprising this hierarchy are **conative needs**, which Maslow often referred to as *basic needs*. However, he also identified other needs, *aesthetic* and *cognitive*, which are sometimes preconditions for satisfying basic needs but nevertheless operate on a separate dimension. In addition to these needs are the *neurotic needs*, which tend to oppose basic needs and block psychological health.

Aesthetic Needs

Unlike conative needs, **aesthetic needs** are not universal, but at least some people in every culture seem to be motivated by the need for beauty and aesthetically pleasing experiences (Maslow, 1967). Historically, humanity has produced art for art's sake from the days of the cave dweller down to the present time.

People with strong aesthetic needs desire beautiful and orderly surroundings, and, when these needs are not met, they become sick in the same way that they become sick when their conative needs are frustrated. People prefer beauty to ugliness, and they may even become physically and spiritually ill when forced to live in squalid, disorderly environments.

Because the various needs overlap, we cannot always identify the true bases of a particular need. For example, the needs for order and symmetry may be aesthetic needs, but they might also satisfy the conative need for safety. Then again, they could also satisfy cognitive needs, especially those involving mathematics and numbers (Maslow, 1970).

Cognitive Needs

In addition to conative and aesthetic needs, people also possess a desire to know, to solve mysteries, to understand, and to be curious (Maslow, 1970). These are the **cognitive needs** and, although they have an interdependence with conative needs, they belong to a different dimension. When cognitive needs are blocked, all other needs are threatened. Knowledge is necessary to satisfy each of the five conative needs. People can gratify their physiological needs by knowing how to secure food; safety needs by knowing how to build a shelter; love needs by knowing how to relate to people; esteem needs by attaining some knowledge and acquiring some level of self-confidence with that knowledge; and they can achieve self-actualization by fully using their cognitive potentials (although self-actualizing people need not have outstanding innate intellectual powers).

When people cannot satisfy their cognitive needs, they become pathological, just as they become sick when their conative and aesthetic needs are thwarted (Maslow, 1970). Ignorance, dishonesty, and secrecy all frustrate our need to know and therefore undermine our psychological health. We become sick, paranoid, and depressed when we are consistently lied to, denied knowledge, or deprived of curiosity. Our physical health may suffer when our work does not challenge our intellectual capacities, and we may become skeptical, disillusioned, and cynical when we do not hear the whole truth.

Besides having a synergistic relationship with conative needs, cognitive needs have a separate existence. The need to know is important in itself and is not always specifically related to the satisfaction of another need. Knowledge brings with it the desire to know more, to theorize, to test hypotheses, or to find out how something works just for the satisfaction of knowing (Maslow, 1968b).

Neurotic Needs

The satisfaction of conative, aesthetic, and cognitive needs is basic to one's physical and psychological health, and their frustration leads to some level of illness. On the other hand, a fourth category of needs, **neurotic needs**, results only in stagnation and pathology, whether or not they are satisfied (Maslow, 1970).

By definition, neurotic needs are nonproductive. They perpetuate an unhealthy style of life and have no value in the striving for self-actualization. Neurotic needs are usually reactive; that is, they serve as compensation for unsatisfied basic needs. People who do not satisfy their safety needs, for example, may develop a strong desire to hoard money or property. The hoarding drive is a neurotic need, worthless as a motivator toward health. Then again, when love and belongingness needs are not fulfilled, people may become overly aggressive and hostile toward others. Aggressive and hostile needs are also neurotic and play no positive role in one's movement toward self-actualization.

As we have seen, neurotic needs are distinguishable from basic needs in that their satisfaction does not foster health. As Maslow (1970, p. 274) said,

> Giving a neurotic power seeker all the power he wants does not make him less neurotic, nor is it possible to satiate his neurotic need for power. However much he is fed he still remains hungry (because he's really looking for something else). It makes little difference for ultimate health whether a neurotic need be gratified or frustrated.

General Discussion of Needs

Maslow (1970) estimated that the hypothetical average person has his or her needs satisfied to approximately these levels: physiological, 85%; safety, 70%; love and belongingness, 50%; esteem, 40%; and self-actualization, 10% percent. The more a lower-level need is satisfied, the greater the emergence of the next-level need. For example, if love needs are only 10% satisfied, esteem needs may not be active at all. But if love needs are 25% satisfied, esteem may emerge 5% as a need. If love is 75% satisfied, then esteem may emerge 50%, and so on. Needs, therefore, emerge gradually, and a person may be simultaneously motivated by needs from two or more levels. For example, a self-actualizing person may be the honorary guest at a dinner given by close friends in a peaceful restaurant. The act of eating gratifies a physiological need, but, at the same time, the guest of honor may be satisfying safety, love, esteem, and self-actualization needs.

Reversed Order of Needs

Even though needs are generally satisfied in the same order, occasionally they are reversed. For some people, the drive for creativity (a self-actualization need) may take precedence over safety and physiological needs. An enthusiastic artist may risk safety and health in order to complete an important work. For years, the late sculptor Korczak Ziolkowski endangered his health and abandoned companionship to work on carving a mountain in the Black Hills into a monument to Chief Crazy Horse.

Reversals, however, are usually more apparent than real, and some seemingly obvious deviations in the order of needs are not variations at all. If we understood the *unconscious motivation* underlying the behavior, we would recognize that the needs are not reversed.

Unconscious Motivation

Maslow believed that much of our surface behavior is really an expression of a more basic, often unconscious need. This can be observed at the level of love and belongingness needs, which some people try to satisfy by behaviors that are self-defeating but yet appear to be motivated by esteem or self-actualization needs. On the surface, these people may disdain social contact and pretend not to care whether or not others accept them. They may boast about their accomplishments and possessions in an apparent move to satisfy competence and prestige needs. In reality, however, they are attempting an indirect approach to get people to like them, albeit an unsuccessful and self-defeating one.

Unmotivated Behavior

Maslow believed that, even though all behaviors have a cause, some behaviors are not motivated. In other words, not all determinants are motives. Some behavior is not caused by needs, but by other factors such as conditioned reflexes, maturation, or drugs. Motivation is limited to the striving for the satisfaction of some need. Much of what Maslow (1970) called "expressive behavior" is unmotivated.

Expressive and Coping Behavior

Maslow (1970) distinguished between expressive behavior, which is often unmotivated, and coping behavior, which is always motivated and aimed at satisfying a need.

Expressive behavior is often an end in itself and serves no other purpose than to be. It is often unconscious and usually takes place naturally and with little effort. Also, expressive behavior is usually unlearned, spontaneous, and determined by forces within the person rather than the environment. It has no goals or aim but is merely the person's mode of expression. Expressive behavior includes such actions as slouching, looking stupid, being relaxed, showing anger, and expressing joy. Expressive behavior can continue even in the absence of reinforcement or reward. For example, a frown, a blush, or a twinkle of the eye are not ordinarily specifically reinforced. Expressive behaviors also include one's gait, gestures, voice, and smile (even when alone). A person, for example, may express a methodical, compulsive personality simply because she is what she is and not because of any need to do so. Other examples of expression include art, play, enjoyment, appreciation, wonder, awe, and excitement.

On the other hand, *coping behavior* is usually conscious, effortful, learned, and determined by the external environment. It involves the individual's attempts to cope with the environment, to secure food and shelter, to make friends, and to receive acceptance, appreciation, and prestige from others. Coping behavior serves some aim or goal (although not always conscious or known to the person), and it is always motivated by some deficit need (Maslow, 1970).

Deprivation of Needs

Lack of satisfaction of any of the basic needs leads to some kind of pathology. Deprivation of physiological needs results in fatigue, loss of energy, malnutrition, obsession with sex, and so on. Threat to safety leads to fear, insecurity, and dread. When love needs go unfulfilled, a person becomes defensive, overly aggressive, or socially shy. Lack of esteem also results in the illnesses of self-doubt, self-depreciation, and lack of confidence. Deprivation of self-actualization needs likewise leads to pathology, or more accurately, **metapathology**. Maslow (1967) defined metapathology as the absence of values, lack of fulfillment, and the loss of meaning in life.

If deprived needs cause us to become ill, then satisfied needs move us toward physical and psychological health. In fact, Maslow (1967) considered the satisfaction of needs to be the definition of health. Traditionally, many philosophers and even psychologists have held the opposite view, believing that health and happiness come from the renunciation of basic needs. For example, some religious leaders have advocated fasting and other forms of self-sacrifice as a means of self-control and spiritual growth. Maslow, however, insisted that self-actualization (the essence of psychological health) is characterized by the full enjoyment of food, sex, and other sensuous pleasures.

Instinctoid Nature of Needs

Maslow (1970) rejected the classical instinct theories of Freud and William McDougall (1933), but he also refused to accept the newer, anti-instinct concepts of the behaviorists. Instead, he proposed a middle position, which hypothesizes that some human needs are innately determined even though they can be modified by learning. These are called **instinctoid needs**.

One criterion for separating instinctoid from noninstinctoid needs is the level of pathology upon being frustrated. The thwarting of instinctoid needs produces pathology; the frustration of other needs does not. For example, when people are denied sufficient love, they become sick and are blocked from achieving psychological health. Likewise, when people are frustrated in satisfying their physiological, safety, esteem, and self-actualization needs, they become sick. Therefore, these needs are instinctoid. On the other hand, the need to comb one's hair or to speak one's native tongue are learned, and their frustration does not ordinarily produce illness. If people would become psychologically ill as the result of not being able to comb their hair or to speak their native language, then the frustrated need is actually a basic instinctoid need, perhaps love and belongingness or possibly esteem.

A second criterion for distinguishing between the two types of needs is that instinctoid needs are persistent and their satisfaction leads to psychological health, whereas noninstinctoid needs are usually temporary and their satisfaction is not a prerequisite for health.

Instinctoid needs are basic and not the result of secondary reinforcement. Moreover, instinctoid behavior is species-specific, and, therefore, animal instincts cannot be used as a model for their study. On the other hand, not all instinctoid needs are unchangeable. Some can be molded, inhibited, or altered by environmental influences. Because many instinctoid needs (for example, love) are weaker than cultural forces (for example, aggression in the form of crime or war), Maslow (1970, p. 82) insisted that society should "protect the weak, subtle, and tender instinctoid needs if they are not to be overwhelmed by the tougher, more powerful culture." Stated another way, even though instinctoid needs are basic, unlearned drives, they can be changed and even destroyed by the more powerful forces of civilization. Hence, society would be well advised to seek ways in which its members can receive satisfaction not only for physiological and safety needs but for love, esteem, and self-actualization needs as well.

Comparison of Higher and Lower Needs

Important similarities and differences exist between higher-level needs (love, esteem, and self-actualization) and lower-level needs (physiological and safety). Higher needs are similar to lower ones in that they are instinctoid. Maslow (1970) insisted that love, esteem, and self-actualization are just as biological as thirst, sex, and hunger.

Differences between higher needs and lower ones are those of degree and not of kind. First, higher-level needs are later on the phylogenetic or evolutionary scale. For instance, only humans (a relatively recent species) have the need for self-actualization. Also, higher needs appear later during the course of individual development; lower-level needs must be cared for in infants and children before higher-level needs become operative.

Second, higher-level needs produce more happiness and more peak experiences (although satisfaction of lower-level needs may produce a degree of pleasure). Hedonistic pleasure, however, is usually temporary and not comparable to the quality of happiness produced by the satisfaction of higher needs. Also, the satisfaction of higher-level needs is more subjectively desirable to those people who have experienced both higher- and lower-level needs. In other words, a person who has reached the level of self-actualization would have no motivation to return to a lower stage of development (Maslow, 1970).

SELF-ACTUALIZATION

Maslow's devotion to the study of health rather than illness is most clearly visible in his research on self-actualizing people. His ideas on self-actualization began soon after he received his Ph.D., when he became puzzled as to why two of his teachers in New York City, Ruth Benedict and Max Wertheimer, were so different from average people. His love and admiration for each of these two unusual people led him to take notes describing fundamental characteristics of each. Soon it became clear to him that, although the two were different from each other, a single pattern seemed to characterize their lives. He began to look for others who fit this pattern and found many. To Maslow, these people represented the highest level of human development, and he called that level "self-actualization," a term borrowed from Kurt Goldstein, another New York mentor who was then at Columbia University.

Values of Self-Actualizers

Maslow (1971) held that self-actualizing people are motivated by the "external verities" or what he called **B-values**. These "Being" values are indicators of psychological health and are opposed to deficiency needs, which motivate nonself-actualizers. B-values are not needs in the same sense as food, shelter, or companionship. They are called "metaneeds," meaning that they are the ultimate or highest level of needs. Maslow distinguished between ordinary need motivation and the motives of self-actualizing people, which he called **metamotivation**.

Metamotivation is characterized by expressive rather than coping behavior and is associated with the B-values. It differentiates self-actualizing people from those who are not. In other words, metamotivation was Maslow's tentative answer to the problem of why some people, who have their lower needs satisfied, are capable of giving and receiving love, and hence possess a great amount of confidence and self-esteem, and yet fail to pass over the threshold to self-actualization. The lives of these people are meaningless and lacking in B-values. Only people who live among the B-values are self-actualizing, and they alone are capable of metamotivation.

Maslow identified 14 B-values, but the exact number is not important, because ultimately all become one, or at least all are highly correlated. The values of self-actualizing people include *truth, goodness, beauty, wholeness or the transcendence of dichotomies, aliveness, uniqueness, perfection, completion, justice and order, simplicity, richness or totality, effortlessness, playfulness and humor,* and *self-sufficiency or autonomy* (see Figure 15.2).

These values distinguish self-actualizing people from those whose psychological growth is stunted after they reach esteem needs. Maslow (1971) hypothesized that when metaneeds are not met, we experience illness, an existential sickness. We all have a holistic tendency to move toward completeness or totality, and when this movement is thwarted, we suffer feelings of inadequacy, disintegration, and unfulfillment. Absence of the B-values leads to pathology just as surely as lack of food results in malnutrition. When denied the truth, we suffer from paranoia; when we live in ugly surroundings, we become physically ill; without justice and order we experience fear and anxiety; without playfulness and humor we become stale, rigid, and somber. Deprivation of any of the B-values results in *metapathology,* or the lack of a meaningful philosophy of life.

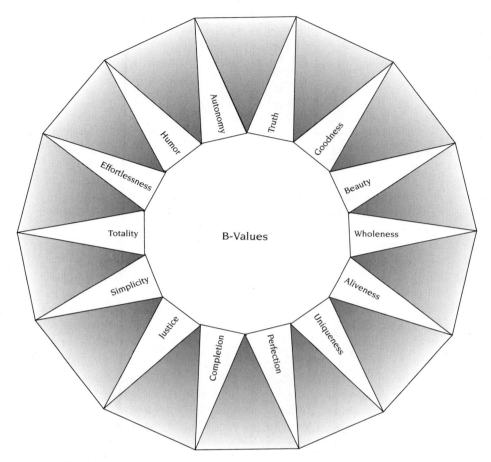

Figure 15.2   *Maslow's B-Values: A Single Jewel with Many Facets*

Definition and Description

Using research methods described later, Maslow (1970) identified a self-actu-alizing *syndrome* while studying healthy people. These individuals, to a greater or lesser extent, possessed characteristics consistent with that syndrome, so that eventually a pattern of self-actualization emerged. Maslow (1970, p. 150) defined self-actualization as the "full use and exploitation of talents, capacities, potenti-alities, etc."

In identifying self-actualizing people Maslow used both negative and positive criteria. First, *these people must be free from psychopathology.* They must not be neurotic or psychotic or have a tendency toward these psychological disturbances. This is an important negative criterion because some neurotic and psychotic individuals have some things in common with self-actualizing people, namely such character-istics as a heightened sense of reality, mystical experiences, creativity, and detach-ment from other people. When any of Maslow's subjects showed definite signs of psychopathology (excepting some psychosomatic illnesses), they were eliminated from the list of possible self-actualizing people.

Second, *self-actualizing people have progressed through the hierarchy of needs*, and, there-fore, they live above the subsistence level of existence and have no ever-present threat to their safety. But more importantly, they must also have experienced love and have a well-rooted sense of self-worth and esteem. Because they have had their lower-level needs satisfied, self-actualizing people are better able to tolerate the frustration of these needs. Even when hungry, self-actualizing people do not panic when food is not immediately available. They do not have the desperate need for money or security often found in people operating at the level of physiological and safety needs. Because they feel loved, they have no neurotic need to have everyone love them. They can tolerate rejection, and their esteem remains intact even in the face of criticism and scorn. They are capable of loving a wider variety of people than are nonself-actualizing persons, but they do not feel an obligation to love everyone they meet.

The third criterion for self-actualization is the *full realization of one's needs to grow, to develop, and to increasingly become what one is capable of becoming*. This, in essence, is Maslow's definition of self-actualization. However, in order to fully utilize their capacities, self-actualizing people must embrace the B-values.

Julius, the farm laborer we introduced in our case study, seems to have met these criteria. He was free from psychopathology, had his lower-level needs rela-tively well satisfied, and was motivated to use his talents and potentialities. In many ways he was childlike (but not childish). He was unpretentious, spontaneous, cre-ative, and naive. He enjoyed work for its own sake, taking a keen interest in the various farm activities and performing many jobs with no expectation of pay. He approached work as if it were a game, something enjoyable for its own sake. As we will soon see, Julius had other characteristics of self-actualizing people.

Characteristics of Self-Actualizing People

Most people identified by Maslow as being self-actualizing were private indi-viduals, not widely known to the general public. However, he did study some his-torical and several then-living public persons whom he regarded as self-actualizing. These included Thomas Jefferson, Abraham Lincoln (in his later years), Albert Einstein, Jane Addams, William James, Albert Schweitzer, Aldous Huxley, Benedict de Spinoza, and Eleanor Roosevelt, our case study in Chapter 3.

What characteristics do these and other self-actualizing people tend to have in common? In his 1970 publication, *Motivation and Personality*, Maslow listed 15 ten-tative qualities that characterize these people to at least some degree.

More Efficient Perception of Reality

Self-actualizing people can more easily detect phoniness in others. They can discriminate between the genuine and the fake not only in people but also in literature, art, and music. They are not fooled by façades and can see both positive and negative underlying traits in others, which are not readily apparent to most people. They perceive ultimate values more clearly than nonself-actualizing people and are less prejudiced and less likely to see the world as they wish it to be.

Also, self-actualizing people are less afraid and more comfortable with the unknown. They not only have a greater tolerance of ambiguity, they actively seek it and feel comfortable with problems and puzzles that have no definite right or wrong solution. They welcome doubt, uncertainty, indefiniteness, and uncharted paths, a quality that makes self-actualizing people particularly well suited to be philosophers, explorers, or scientists.

Julius was not a philosopher, an explorer, or a scientist; he had worked on a farm his entire life. Yet, in many ways, he possessed an efficient perception of reality. He had a knack for seeing solutions to the problems of construction and repair frequently faced by farmers. Although not gifted as a mechanic or a carpenter, he could see better than others how parts could be successfully fit together. Also, he would usually be the first to realize that some problems had no solutions, and he did not allow his perception to be clouded by wishful thinking.

Acceptance of Self, Others, and Nature

Self-actualizing people can accept themselves the way they are. They lack defensiveness, phoniness, and self-defeating guilt; have good, hearty, animal appetites for food, sleep, and sex; are not overly critical of their own shortcomings; and are not burdened by undue anxiety or shame. In similar fashion, they are accepting of others. They have no compelling need to instruct, inform, or convert. They can tolerate weaknesses in others and are not threatened by their strengths. They accept nature, including human nature, as it is and do not expect perfection in either themselves or in others. They realize that people suffer, grow old, and die.

While other farm people complained about the weather being too hot, too cold, too dry, and occasionally too wet, Julius always accepted weather conditions, knowing that he could not change them. He also accepted his own mortality. As an old man in his late seventies, he frequently said, "Well, this will probably be my last winter." He would make this comment without intending to draw out sympathy or protest; it was simply a matter-of-fact, realistic statement.

Spontaneity, Simplicity, and Naturalness

Self-actualizing people are spontaneous, simple, and natural. They are unconventional but not compulsively so; they are highly ethical but may appear unethical or nonconforming. They usually behave conventionally, either because the issue is not of great importance or out of deference to others. But when the situation warrants it, they can be unconventional and uncompromising even at the price of ostracism and censure. The similarity between self-actualizing people and children and animals is in their spontaneous and natural behavior. They ordinarily live simple lives in the sense that they have no need to erect a complex veneer designed to deceive the world.

Julius was completely unpretentious. He was not afraid or ashamed to express his joy and awe toward a beautiful sunrise or sunset.

Problem-Centered

A fourth characteristic of self-actualizing people is their interest in problems outside themselves. Neurotics and, to a lesser extent, average people, are self-centered, tending to see all the world's problems in relation to themselves. Self-actualizing people, however, are task-oriented and concerned with problems outside themselves. This interest allows them to develop a mission in life, a purpose for living that spreads beyond self-aggrandizement. Their occupation is not merely a means to earning a living but a vocation, a calling, an end in itself. As noted earlier, Julius frequently used his own time and transportation to look after cattle and crops that he did not own.

Self-actualizing people extend their frame of reference far beyond self. They are concerned with eternal problems and adopt a solid philosophical and ethical basis for handling these problems. They are unconcerned with the trivial and the petty. Their realistic perception enables them to clearly distinguish between the important and the unimportant issues in life.

The Need for Privacy

Self-actualizing people have a quality of detachment that allows them to be alone without being lonely. Unlike neurotics, who often have difficulty with interpersonal relations but must be surrounded by others, healthy individuals feel relaxed and comfortable when they are either with people or alone. They enjoy solitude and privacy and have no desperate need for others, having already satisfied their love and belongingness needs.

Unfortunately, this quality of detachment is not always understood or accepted by others. Self-actualizing people may be seen as aloof or uninterested, but, in fact, their disinterest is limited to minor matters. They have a global concern for the welfare of others without becoming entangled in minute and insignificant problems. Because they spend little energy attempting to impress others or trying to gain love and acceptance, they have more ability to make responsible choices. They are self-movers, resisting society's attempts to make them adhere to convention.

Being alone was never a problem for Julius. He often spent up to 14 hours a day driving a tractor, isolated from the rest of the world and listening to nothing but the roar of the engine. But when the occasion called for him to work cooperatively with others, he always enjoyed that also.

Autonomy

A related characteristic is autonomy or the ability to be independent of culture and environment. Self-actualizing people depend on themselves for growth even though at some time in the past they had to have received love and security from others. No one is born autonomous, and therefore no one is completely independent of people. Autonomy can be achieved only through satisfactory relations with others. However, the confidence that one is loved and accepted for what one is, without conditions or qualifications, can be a powerful force in contributing to feelings of self-worth. Once that confidence is attained, a person no longer depends on others for self-esteem. Self-actualizing people have that confidence and therefore a large measure of autonomy that allows them to be not only unperturbed by criticism but also unmoved by flattery. This independence also gives them an inner peace and serenity not enjoyed by those who live for the approval of others.

When his first wife died, Julius had no desperate need to immediately remarry. He had loved his wife and enjoyed her companionship, but he was also quite capable of living without her. After his daughters married and left his home, he lived alone for six years without being lonely. Then, he married his friend, Anna, not because he was incapable of caring for himself but simply because he wanted to.

Continued Freshness of Appreciation

Maslow (1970, p. 163) said that "self-actualizing people have the wonderful capacity to appreciate again and again, freshly and naïvely, the basic goods of life, with awe, pleasure, wonder, and even ecstasy." The most intense of these feelings comes only occasionally, but they are experienced most often by self-actualizers who are constantly aware of their good fortune, health, friends, and political freedom. Unlike others who take their blessings for granted, healthy individuals see with a fresh vision such everyday phenomena as flowers, food, and friends. They have an appreciation of their possessions and do not waste time complaining about a boring, uninteresting existence.

The Peak Experience

As Maslow's study of self-actualizers continued, he made the unexpected discovery that many of his subjects had had experiences that were mystical in nature and that somehow gave them a feeling of transcendence. Originally, he thought that these so-called "peak experiences" were far more common among actualizers than among nonself-actualizers. Later, however, Maslow (1971, p. 175) stated that "most people, or almost all people, have peak experiences, or ecstasies."

Peak experiences are not spiritual or supernatural, although they are religious in their core (Maslow, 1964). Also, they are not all of equal intensity; some are only mildly sensed, others moderately felt, and some are quite intensely experienced. In their mild form these peak experiences probably occur in everyone, although they are seldom noticed. For example, long-distance runners often report a sort of tran-scendence, a loss of self, or a feeling of being separated from their body. Sometimes during periods of intense pleasure or satisfaction people will experience mystical or peak experiences. Viewing a sunset or some other grandeur of nature may pre-cipitate a peak experience, but these experiences cannot be brought on by an act of the will; often they occur at unexpected, quite ordinary moments (Maslow, 1970).

What is it like to have a peak experience? Maslow (1964) described several guidelines that may help answer this question. First, although peak experiences have a religious core, they are not supernatural events. They are quite natural and are part of our human makeup. Second, people having a peak experience see the whole universe as unified or all in one piece, and they see clearly their place in that universe. Also, during this mystical time, peakers feel both more humble and more powerful at the same time. They feel passive, receptive, more desirous of listening, and more capable of hearing. Simultaneously, they feel more responsible for their activities and perceptions, more active, and more self-determined. Peakers experi-ence a loss of fear, anxiety, and conflict and become more loving, accepting, and spontaneous. Although peakers often report such emotions as awe, wonder, rap-ture, ecstasy, reverence, humility, and surrender, they are not likely to want to get something practical from the experience. They often experience a disorientation in time and space, a loss of self-consciousness, an unselfish attitude, and an ability to transcend everyday polarities.

The peak experience is unmotivated, nonstriving, and nonwishing, and during such an experience a person experiences no needs, wants, or deficiencies. In addi-tion, Maslow (1964, p. 63) says, "the peak experience is seen only as beautiful, good, desirable, worthwhile, etc., and is never experienced as evil or undesirable." Maslow also believed that the peak experience often has a lasting effect on a per-son's life.

Julius apparently was a "nonpeaker" and seemed to have had no comprehen-sion of what was meant by the term "peak experience."

Gemeinschaftsgefühl

Self-actualizing people possess **Gemeinschaftsgefühl**, Adler's term for social interest, community feeling, or a sense of oneness with all humanity. Maslow found that his healthy subjects had a kind of caring attitude toward other people. Although they often feel like aliens in a foreign land, self-actualizers nevertheless identify with all other people and have a genuine interest in helping others—strangers as well as friends.

Profound Interpersonal Relations

Related to *Gemeinschaftsgefühl* is a special quality of interpersonal relations that involves deep and profound feelings for individuals. Self-actualizers have a nurtur-ant feeling toward people in general, but their close friendships are limited to only a few. They have no desperate need to be friends with everyone, but the few important interpersonal relationships they do have are quite deep and intense. They tend to choose other very healthy people as friends and avoid intimate interpersonal relationships with dependent or neurotic people, although their social interest allows them to have a special feeling of empathy for these less healthy persons.

We have seen that self-actualizers are often misunderstood and sometimes despised by others. On the other hand, many are greatly loved and attract a large group of admirers and even worshipers, especially if they have made a notable contribution to their business or professional fields. Those healthy people studied by Maslow (1970) felt uneasy and embarrassed by this veneration, preferring instead relationships that were mutual rather than one-sided.

The Democratic Character Structure

Maslow found that all his subjects possessed democratic values. They could be friendly and considerate with other people regardless of class, color, age, or sex, and, in fact, they seemed to be quite unaware of superficial differences among people.

Each of the three previous characteristics described Julius, at least to some extent. He seemed to have had genuine feelings of empathy for people he saw on television who were starving or who had lost their homes to wars or natural disasters. He had few close friends among the townsfolk, but he enjoyed the love of his wife, daughters, and grandchildren. He made no distinction among people based on social class, gender, or skin color. His employer was a friend, not a superior; his grandchildren were individuals, not inferiors.

Discrimination between Means and Ends

Self-actualizing people have a clear sense of right and wrong conduct and have little conflict about basic values. They set their sights on ends rather than means and have an unusual ability to distinguish between the two. What other people consider to be a means (for example, eating or exercise), self-actualizing people often see as an end in itself. They enjoy doing something for its own sake and not just because it is a means to some other end.

Philosophical Sense of Humor

Another distinguishing characteristic of self-actualizing people is their philosophical, nonhostile sense of humor. Most of what passes for humor or comedy is basically hostile, sexual, or scatological. The laugh is usually at someone else's expense. Healthy people see little humor in put-down jokes. They may poke fun at themselves, but not masochistically so. They make fewer tries at humor than others, but their attempts serve a purpose beyond making people laugh. They amuse, inform, point out ambiguities, provoke a smile rather than a guffaw.

The humor of a self-actualizing person is intrinsic to the situation rather than contrived; it is spontaneous rather than planned. Because it is situation-dependent, it usually cannot be repeated. For those who look for examples of a philosophical sense of humor, disappointment is inevitable. A retelling of the incident almost invariably loses its original quality of amusement. One must "be there" to appreciate it.

Julius had a marvelous sense of humor. One example shows the nonsexual, nonaggressive nature of his humor. After he and his fellow workers had looked long and hard for a particular wrench, Julius, upon finding it, held it aloft and quietly remarked. "Let's use this one until we can find the other one." The statement elicited no roaring laughter, but it was genuinely funny.

Creativeness

All self-actualizing subjects studied by Maslow (1970) were creative in some sense of the word. In fact, Maslow suggested that creativity and self-actualization may be one and the same. However, not all self-actualizers are talented or creative in the arts, but all are creative in their own way. They have a keen perception of truth, beauty, and reality—ingredients that form the foundation of true creativity.

Self-actualizing people need not be poets or artists to be creative. In speaking of his mother-in-law (who was also his aunt), Maslow (1968a), vividly pointed out that creativity can come from almost anywhere. He said that, whereas his self-actualizing mother-in-law had no special talents as a writer or artist, she was truly creative in preparing homemade soup. Maslow remarked that first-rate soup was more creative than second-rate poetry!

In a similar, unspectacular manner Julius was creative. His solutions to problems were often innovative and refreshingly simple.

Resistance to Enculturation

A final characteristic identified by Maslow was resistance to enculturation. Self-actualizing people have a detachment from their surroundings and are able to transcend a particular culture. They are neither antisocial nor consciously nonconforming. Rather, they are autonomous, following their own standards of conduct and not blindly obeying the rules of others.

Self-actualizing people do not waste energy fighting against insignificant customs and regulations of society. Such folkways as dress, hairstyle, and traffic laws are relatively arbitrary and unimportant, and self-actualizing people do not make a conspicuous show of defying these conventions. Because they accept conventional style and dress, they are not too different in appearance from anyone else. However, on important matters they can become strongly aroused to seek social change and to resist society's attempts to enculturate them. Self-actualizing people do not merely have different social mores, but, Maslow (1970, p. 174) hypothesized, they are "less enculturated, less flattened out, less molded."

Although not necessarily artistic, self-actualizers are creative in their own ways.

For this reason, these healthy people are more individualized and less homogenized than others. They are not all alike. In fact, the term "self-actualization" means to become everything that one can become, to actualize or fulfill all of one's potential. When people can accomplish this, they become unique, more heterogeneous, and less shaped by a given culture (Maslow, 1970).

This last characteristic does not seem to apply to Julius. His personal standards of conduct were congruent with those of his society, and he had no history of fighting for social change.

Love, Sex, and Self-Actualization

Before people can become self-actualizing, they must satisfy their love and belongingness needs. It follows then that self-actualizing people are capable of both giving and receiving love and are no longer motivated by the kind of deficiency love **(D-love)** that characterizes people motivated by lower-level needs. Self-actualizing people are capable of **B-love**, which is love for the essence or "Being" of the other. B-love is mutually felt and shared and not motivated by a deficiency or incompleteness within the lover. In fact, it is unmotivated, expressive behavior. Self-actualizing people do not love because they expect something in return. They simply love and are loved. Their love is never harmful. It is the kind of love that allows lovers to be relaxed, open, and nonsecretive (Maslow, 1970).

Because self-actualizers are capable of a deeper level of love, Maslow (1970) believed that sex between two B-lovers often becomes a kind of mystical experience. Although they are lusty people, fully enjoying sex, food, and other sensuous pleasures, self-actualizers are not dominated by sex. They can more easily tolerate the absence of sex (as well as other basic needs), because they have no deficiency need for it. Sexual activity between B-lovers is not always a heightened emotional experience; sometimes it is taken quite lightly in the spirit of playfulness and humor. But this is to be expected, because playfulness and humor are B-values, and, like the other B-values, they characterize all aspects of a self-actualizer's life, including sexual relationships.

APPLICATIONS OF MASLOW'S THEORY

Although Maslow was primarily interested in the psychologically healthy person, his theory can be applied to the study of the abnormal personality and to the process of psychotherapy. In addition, Maslow's philosophy of science and his research methods are integral to an understanding of how he arrived at his concept of self-actualization.

Abnormal Development

According to Maslow (1970), everyone is born with a will toward health, a tendency to grow toward self-actualization. Failure of personal growth results in neuroses and abnormal development. Strictly considered, anything less than self-actualization is abnormal. That which is usually considered "normal" in psychology is

Can You Fake Self-Actualization?

Now that you have some information about the characteristics of self-actualizing people, would it be possible for you to fake self-actualization? Because authenticity or naturalness is one of the characteristics of self-actualizing people, and because authenticity cannot be faked, the answer would appear to be "no."

Faking self-actualization would, of course, present other difficulties as well. First, one would need to have love and belongingness needs satisfied. If people do not like you, and if you do not like people, it would be extremely difficult for you to maintain any pretense of love or affection.

Another problem in simulating self-actualization involves the question, "What should I do; that is, how should I behave?"

Although Maslow reported 15 general characteristics of self-actualizing people, he did not tell us much about how they specifically behaved. Because self-actualization means to actualize one's true self, it follows that different self-actualizers would behave in different ways. In fact, one might argue that greater individual behavioral differences would emerge among self-actualizers than among other people. For these reasons, then, it is safe to say that self-actualization per se cannot be faked.

A somewhat different but related question is: Can one fake the right answers on standardized instruments designed to measure self-actualization? The most widely used of these instruments is the **Personal Orientation Inventory** (Shostrom, 1974), merely descriptive of the majority. The average person falls short of full human potential and is thus "abnormal." The normal human condition is health; the usual condition is somewhat less.

If the normal human condition is self-actualization, what prevents people from reaching this level? Growth toward normal healthy personality is blocked by an absence of basic need gratification. If people cannot provide for food and shelter, they cannot reach their full potential for psychological growth. Many people, however, have their physiological and safety needs relatively satisfied, and yet they remain blocked at the level of love and belongingness needs. They find it difficult to give and receive love and to develop feelings of belongingness because, as children, they did not experience healthy parental love. Even when people satisfy their love needs and gain self-esteem, they do not automatically reach self-actualization (Maslow, 1970).

One abnormal syndrome that often blocks people's growth toward self-actualization is the **Jonah complex**, or the fear of being one's best. The Jonah complex is characterized by attempts to run away from one's destiny just as the biblical Jonah tried to escape from his fate. The Jonah complex, which is found in nearly everyone, represents a fear of success, a fear of being one's best, and a feeling of awesomeness in the presence of beauty and perfection (Maslow, 1971).

Why do people run away from greatness and self-fulfillment? Maslow (1971) offered the following rationale. First, the human body is simply not strong enough to endure the ecstasy of fulfillment for any length of time, just as peak experiences

and research indicates that the POI is extremely resistant to faking—unless one is familiar with Maslow's description of a self-actualizing person. In the POI Manual, Shostrom (1974) cited several studies in which subjects were asked to "fake good" or "make a favorable impression" in filling out the inventory. When subjects followed these instructions, they generally scored lower (in the direction away from self-actualization) than they did when responding honestly to the statements.

This, indeed, is an interesting finding. Why should subjects lower their scores when trying to look good? The answer lies in Maslow's concept of self-actualization. Statements that might be true for self-actualizers are not necessarily socially desirable and do not always conform to cultural standards. For example, the item "I must strive for perfection in everything I undertake" might seem like a desirable goal to someone trying to simulate self-actualization, but an actualizer probably would not feel the necessity to constantly strive for perfection. Because one of the characteristics of self-actualizing people is resistance to enculturation, it should not be surprising that attempts by naive subjects to make a good impression usually result in failure.

Interestingly, Maslow himself seemed not to have faked the POI when he was asked to take it. Despite the fact that he helped in the construction of the POI, Maslow's own scores were only in the direction of self-actualization and not nearly as high as the scores of people who were definitely self-actualized (Shostrom, 1974).

and sexual orgasms would be overly taxing if they lasted too long. Therefore, the intense emotion that accompanies perfection and fulfillment carries with it a shattering sensation such as "this is too much," or "I can't stand it anymore."

A second explanation for the evasion of growth is the necessity of humility. Maslow (1971) reasoned that most of us have a private ambition to be great, to write a great novel, to be a movie star, to become a world-famous scientist, and so on. However, when we compare ourselves with those who have accomplished greatness we are appalled by our own arrogance. "Who am I to think I could do as well as this great person?" As a defense against this grandiosity or "sinful pride," we lower our aspirations, feel stupid and humble, and adopt the self-defeating approach of running away from the realization of our full potentials.

Although the Jonah complex stands out most sharply in neurotic people, nearly all of us have some timidity toward seeking perfection and greatness. We allow false humility to stifle creativity, and thus we prevent ourselves from becoming self-actualizing.

Psychotherapy

Maslow's (1970) approach to psychotherapy followed from his hierarchy of needs theory. Because physiological and safety needs are prepotent, they must be met before the needs for love, self-confidence, and self-actualization can become activated. It follows, then, that a starving person will not ordinarily be motivated to seek psychotherapy but rather to obtain nourishment.

Most people who come for therapy have difficulty satisfying love and belongingness needs. Therefore, psychotherapy is largely an interpersonal process. Through a warm, loving interpersonal relationship with the therapist, the client gains satisfaction of love and belongingness needs and thereby acquires feelings of confidence and self-worth. A healthy interpersonal relationship between client and therapist is therefore the best psychological medicine. This accepting relationship gives clients a feeling of being worthy of love and facilitates their ability to establish other healthy relationships outside of therapy.

To Maslow (1970), the aim of therapy would be to free clients from their dependency on others so that their natural impulse toward growth and self-actualization could become active. Psychotherapy cannot be value-free but must take into consideration the fact that everyone has an inherent tendency to move toward a better, more enriching condition, namely self-actualization.

PHILOSOPHY OF SCIENCE

Traditional science, Maslow (1966) contended, has been too limited to properly study human personality. It does not help us to understand people because its philosophy has been value-free and its methodology has been sterile and nonemotional. Maslow argued for a different philosophy of science, a humanistic, holistic approach that is not value-free and that has scientists who *care* about the subjects they investigate.

Maslow agreed with Allport (see Chapter 13) that psychological science should stress the importance of individual procedures as opposed to the study of groups. Subjective reports should be favored over rigidly objective ones, and people should be allowed to tell about themselves in a holistic fashion instead of the more orthodox approach that studies people in bits and pieces. Traditional psychology has dealt with sensations, intelligence, attitudes, stimuli, reflexes, test scores, and hypothetical constructs from an external point of view. It has not concerned itself much with the whole person as seen from that person's subjective view.

Maslow was critical of scientists who have **"desacralized"** science; that is, removed the emotion, joy, wonder, awe, and rapture from their study in order to purify and objectify it. Orthodox science has no ritual or ceremony. Maslow believed that scientists should put values, emotion, and ritual back into their work and be creative in their pursuit of knowledge. They must be willing to **"resacralize"** science or to instill it with human values, emotion, and ritual. Astronomers must not only study the stars, they must be awestruck by them; psychologists must not only study human personality, they must do so with enjoyment, excitement, wonder, and affection.

Maslow (1966) argued for a **Taoistic attitude** for psychology, one that would be noninterfering, passive, and receptive. This new psychology would abolish prediction and control as the major goals of science and replace them with sheer fascination and the desire to release people from controls so that they can grow and become less predictable. The proper response to mystery, Maslow (1966) said, is not analysis but awe.

The new scientific psychologists must themselves be healthy people, able to tolerate ambiguity and uncertainty. They must be intuitive, nonrational, insightful, and courageous enough to ask the right questions. They must also be willing to flounder, to be imprecise, to question their own procedures, and to take on the important problems of psychology. Maslow (1966) contended that there is no need to do well that which is not worth doing. Rather, it is better to do poorly that which is important.

RESEARCH METHODS

In his study of self-actualizing people and peak experiences, Maslow employed research methods consistent with his philosophy of science. He began intuitively, often "skating on thin ice," then attempted to verify his hunches using idiographic and subjective methods. He often left to others the technical work of gathering evidence. His personal preference was to "scout out ahead," leaving one area when he grew tired of it and going on to explore new ones (Hall, 1968).

Maslow's (1970) approach to studying self-actualizing people was to begin by selecting from among friends, acquaintances, and public and historical persons those people who appeared to him to be healthy, strong, creative, saintly, and wise. In addition, he attempted to study 3000 college students, but found only one who was definitely self-actualizing. He later searched for relatively self-actualizing people, arbitrarily defined as the healthiest 1 percent of Brandeis University students.

After selecting his original subjects on the basis of somewhat arbitrary and unscientific definitions, Maslow carefully studied these people in order to establish a *syndrome for psychological health*. Next, he refined the original definition and then reselected the subjects, retaining some, eliminating others, and adding new ones. Then he repeated the entire procedure with the second group, making some changes in the definition and criteria of self-actualization. Maslow continued this cyclical process to a third or fourth selection group or until he was satisfied that he had refined a vague unscientific concept into a precise operational definition and that his study of self-actualization was indeed scientific.

Maslow's methods of investigation, however, are subject to severe criticism. In his study of self-actualizing people, he selected subjects from among personal acquaintances, friends, and public and historical persons. Therefore, most of his subjects were from the middle and upper classes, highly intelligent, and well-educated.

In addition, Maslow has left unanswered several important questions concerning self-actualization. First, is self-actualization limited to highly intelligent individuals? Are feeble-minded people capable of full use of their capacities and talents? Maslow, in an interview with Willard Frick (1971), said that he did not know what self-actualization means in feeble-minded people.

A second question not fully answered involves the possibility of intentionally striving toward self-actualization. Can people consciously and willfully move themselves in the direction of high-level motivation? In the same interview, Maslow alluded to certain people who consciously set metamotivation as a goal, but added that "they're doing it stupidly and inefficiently and incapably and they want it *now*" (Frick, 1971, p. 36).

Another question concerns replication, a critical ingredient in scientific methodology. Because Maslow failed to give us an operational definition of self-actualization and a full description of his sampling procedures, researchers cannot be certain that they are repeating Maslow's original study or that they are identifying the same syndrome of self-actualization. In addition, Daniels (1982) has criticized Maslow for not comparing his group of self-actualizers with a control group and for his failure to renounce earlier formulations of self-actualization as he continued to expand and reshape the concept.

CONCEPT OF HUMANITY

In Maslow's view, people have a natural tendency to move toward self-actualization, and the basic needs that motivate them are precisely those that ultimately result in positive growth and health. Human nature is structured in such a happy way that our activated needs are exactly what we desire most.

For example, children first want food, then protection, love, praise, and finally self-fulfillment.

Although Maslow was generally optimistic and hopeful, he recognized that people are capable of great evil and destruction. Evil, however, stems from the frustration or thwarting of basic needs, not from the essential nature of people. When basic needs are not met, people may steal, cheat, lie, or kill. Although Maslow believed that human perfection is not possible, he insisted that certain individuals are capable of far greater growth and improvement than is generally supposed. Society, too, can be improved although not perfected. Growth, both individually and culturally, is slow and painful, but it seems to be part of our evolutionary history. Maslow (1970, p. 70) insisted on the ultimate improvability of humans, but he also realized that "most men are doomed to wish for what they do not have." In other words, although all people have the potential for self-actualization, most will live out their lives struggling for food, safety, or love. Most societies, Maslow believed, emphasize these lower-level needs and and base their educational and political systems on an invalid concept of humanity.

Truth, love, beauty, and so on are instinctoid and are just as basic to our nature as hunger, sex, and aggression. All people have the potential to strive toward self-actualization just as they have the motivation to seek food and protection. Because Maslow held that basic needs are structured the same for everyone, but that people satisfy these needs at their own rate, his holistic-dynamic theory of personality places moderate emphasis on the dimension of *uniqueness vs. similarities*.

From both a historical and an individual point of view, humans are an evolutionary animal. We are in the process of becoming more and more fully human; that is, we are more motivated by metaneeds. High-level needs exist, at least as potentiality, in everyone. Because people aim toward self-actualization, Maslow's view can be considered *teleological and purposive*.

Because Maslow's view of humanity is comprehensive, it is difficult to classify on such dimensions as determinism vs. free choice, optimism vs. pessimism, conscious vs. unconscious, or biological vs. social determinants of personality. In general, the behavior of people motivated by physiological and safety needs is *determined by outside forces*, whereas the behavior of self-actualizing people is *motivated by internal forces*.

As noted earlier, Maslow was basically *optimistic*, but he was also realistic enough to recognize that most people never achieve self-actualization, and their lives are not as fulfilling as they might have been under different circumstances.

On the dimension of *consciousness vs. unconscious*, Maslow held that self-actualizing people are ordinarily more aware than others of what they are doing and why. However, motivation is so complex that people may be driven by several needs at the same time, and even healthy people are not always fully aware of all the reasons underlying their behavior.

As for *biological vs. social influences*, Maslow would have insisted that this is a false dichotomy. Individuals are shaped by both biology *and* society, and the two cannot be separated. Inadequate genetic endowment does not condemn a person to an unfulfilled life, just as a poor social environment does not preclude growth. When people achieve self-actualization, they experience a wonderful synergy among the biological, social, and spiritual aspects of their lives. Self-actualizers receive more physical enjoyment from the sensuous pleasures; they experience deeper and richer interpersonal relationships; and they receive pleasure from spiritual qualities such as beauty, truth, goodness, justice, and perfection.

Related Research

Maslow's theory has generated substantial research, much of it outside the field of psychology. Education, marketing, management, mass communication, nursing, and other disciplines frequently include research related to Maslow's concepts of needs and self-actualization. This review presents a sample of the psychology literature related to Maslow's hierarchy of needs and his concept of the peak experience.

Research on Hierarchy of Needs
For many years Maslow's hierarchy of needs concept has generated both interest and research, but this section looks at only two such studies. In 1983, Lester, Hvezda, Sullivan, and Plourde developed the Need Satisfaction Inventory to measure the degree to which the average person satisfies Maslow's five basic needs, but they did not publish this scale until 1990 (see Lester, 1990). The scale consists of 50 items, 10 for each of the 5 needs of the hierarchy. Sample items include: "In general, my health is good" (Physiological); "I think the world is a pretty safe place these days" (Safety); "I am involved in a significant love relationship with another" (Love and Belongingness); "I feel respected by my peers" (Esteem); and "My life has meaning" (Self-actualization). Some items were phrased negatively to avoid response bias.

Lester (1990) administered the Need Satisfaction Inventory along with the Eysenck Personality Inventory (see Chapter 12) to college students and then correlated scores for each of the five need levels with each other and with each of the three Eysenck personality factors, namely Psychoticism, Extraversion, and Neuroticism. Lester found strong negative correlations between each of Malsow's needs and Neuroticism, indicating that students who were satisfied in their basic needs tended to score low on the Neuroticism scale of the Eysenck Personality Inventory. On the other hand, high Extraversion scores were significantly related to satisfaction of love and belongingness, esteem, and self-actualization needs. This study generally supports Maslow's notion that deprivation of basic needs is related to pathology, that is, to neuroticism.

Williams and Page (1989) also found support for Maslow's hypothesis that positive psychological health is related to basic need gratification. Because most college students in the United States have physiological needs fairly well satisfied, and very few are motivated by self-actualization needs, Williams and Page devised a scale that measured the three middle needs in Maslow's hierarchy. The result was the Maslowian Assessment Survey (MAS) designed to assess safety, belonging, and esteem needs, as well as four subscales for each of these three need levels. The subscales included (1) need gratification, or the extent to which the need is satisfied; (2) need importance, or whether or not the need is motivating a person; (3) need salience, or the extent to which a person is preoccupied with a class of needs; and (4) self-concept, or how the subject is like the prototypic person at each level of needs.

Following Maslow, Williams and Page hypothesized that satisfied needs would lose their importance, become less salient, and be negatively related to self-concept. They administered the MAS to 612 college students and found correlations among its various scales and subscales. Consistent with Maslow's theory, they found that once people pass through a particular need level, they become less preoccupied with that need, see it as less important in their lives, and no longer see themselves as being similar to the prototypic person who is trying to satisfy that need. They also found that gratification of needs was negatively related to both depression, as measured by the Beck Depression Inventory (Beck, 1967) and neuroticism, as measured by the Eysenck Personality Inventory.

In summary, both Lester (1990) and Williams and Page (1989) found support for some of Maslow's more obvious hypotheses, namely that unsatisfied needs relate to psychopathology and also to active concern with that need.

Research on the Peak Experience

The notion of the peak experience, however, is not so obvious, and since Maslow's original description, several investigators have tested his assumptions about this experience. Some of these researchers have been critical, some supportive. Blanchard (1969) claimed that the peak experience is not always pleasant and good, and that Maslow contaminated his results by asking his subjects for their "most wonderful experiences." Blanchard suggested that the peak experience is neither good nor bad but rather the presence of creative possibility. However, Panzarella (1980) found evidence that supported Maslow's notion that a peak experience will have a lasting effect on a person's life. In this study musically and artistically oriented people claimed that a peak experience not only permanently changed their life, but it deepened their appreciation of music and art. At the same time, they described these mystical moments as providing a sense of renewal and as producing an urge to be more creative.

Athletes sometimes report intense peak experiences while participating in sports. Ravizza (1977) found that during these experiences athletes felt no fear, were totally immersed in the activity, experienced a temporary loss of ego, felt a unity with the experience and with the universe, and experienced a disorientation of time and space. Because the moment was experienced as perfect, they felt passive, saw their activity as effortless, and described it in terms of awe, wonder, and ecstasy. However, contrary to Maslow, these athletes did not see the experience as pivotal in their lives and generally gave it a narrower focus of attention than that described by Maslow.

Gordon (1985) provided a description of peak experiences during times of near-perfect communication with another human being. He asked first- and second-year college men and women to reveal their peak moments in communication, a time when they felt completely understood by another person and were able to completely understand that person. He then factor analyzed the results and found six major factors that explained most of these reports. The most dominant factor was Loving Acceptance, followed in order of strength by Openminded Insight, Spontaneity, Pleasant Fear, Absorption, and Self-Detachment. However, men and women were not equal on these dimensions: Women rated their peak communication experience higher than men on Loving Acceptance and Spontaneity, suggesting that these two qualities are a more important part of personal communication for women than for men.

Yeagle, Privette, and Dunham (1989) assumed that all people can report a peak experience and that the peak experiences of diverse groups of people would be quite similar. To test this assumption, they obtained information on peak experiences from 29 exhibiting artists and 123 university students enrolled in social science courses. The two groups differed on more than artistic interests. The professional artists were significantly older, better educated, and more evenly distributed between men and women. In addition, the college students and the artists differed with respect to the events that triggered their peak experiences. For example, students were more likely to report that some interpersonal experience immediately precipitated their peak experience, whereas artists identified a creative activity or a beautiful sight as the trigger. Despite these differences, exhibiting artists and college social science students reported peak experiences that were remarkably similar. For both groups the experience was marked by intensity, personal value, absorption, and personal expression, many of the same characteristics Maslow had used to describe peak experiences of self-actualizing persons.

Many researchers agree with Blanchard (1969) that the peak experience may be defined in terms of either positive or negative affect. Studying both kinds of intense personal experiences, Wilson and Spencer (1990) found that positive and negative experiences were similar in the effects they had on later life. In the first part of their study, Wilson and Spencer asked students in sociology classes and their acquaintances to describe their most intense positive and negative drug- and non-drug-induced experiences. In this first survey, only nondrug experiences were included. Subjects described their most intense positive experience and their most intense negative experience in much the same language, except of course that the affect was different. With both types of experience, subjects were likely to report alterations in consciousness as measured by changes in quality of perception, awareness of bodily sensations, awareness of a new reality, and felt changes in personality. In addition, subjects saw positive and negative experiences as equally likely to prompt changes in their life. However, Wilson and Spencer found that positive experiences frequently have a mystical or religious interpretation, whereas negative experiences seldom do.

In the second part of this study, Wilson and Spencer compared the most positive and negative experiences of these same subjects with those of 31 members of a yoga ashram. They used both drug- and non-drug-induced experiences of the non-ashram subjects but did not ask yogas for their drug-induced experiences. Wilson and Spencer found that all three types of intense experience (drug-induced, non-drug-induced, and yoga) were similar, except that drug-induced and yoga experiences were more likely to produce altered states of consciousness. Although many of the ashram respondents described their most intense experience in terms very similar to Maslow's ideal-type peak experience, few of the non-ashram subjects reported such experiences. Wilson and Spencer (1990, p. 572) concluded that "while some people may experience selected elements of the true peak, very few people come close to approximating the ideal-type described by Maslow." They also suggested that these intense positive and negative experiences very seldom initiate self-actualizing changes, but that negative experiences are just as potentially therapeutic as positive ones.

CRITIQUE OF MASLOW

A useful theory of personality must generate relevant research, organize what is known about a particular discipline, serve as a guide to action, have internal consistency, and be parsimonious. How does Maslow's theory rate on these five criteria?

First, on its ability to *generate research*, Maslow's personality theory has been quite fruitful. Tenets of the theory suggest an almost unlimited number of testable hypotheses. A large body of research exists on Maslow's hierarchy of needs concept, and self-actualization remains one of the most frequently studied topics in psychology, with hundreds of articles published yearly on this topic. In addition, some investigators have become interested in studying the peak experience, one characteristic of self-actualizing people.

Second, Maslow's hierarchy of needs framework gives his theory excellent flexibility to *organize what is known about human behavior*. Maslow's theory is also quite consistent with common sense. For example, common sense suggests that a person must have enough to eat before being motivated by other matters. Starving people care little about political philosophy. Their primary motivation is to obtain food, not to sympathize with one political philosophy or another. Similarly, people living under threat to their physical well-being will be motivated mostly to secure safety, and people who have physiological and safety needs relatively satisfied will strive to be accepted and to establish a love relationship.

Does Maslow's theory serve as *a guide to the practitioner*? On this criterion, the theory is rated as highly useful. Psychotherapists adhering to Maslow's theory know that if clients believe that their safety needs are threatened, then they must provide a safe and secure environment for those clients. Once clients have satisfied physiological and safety needs, the therapist can work to provide them with feelings of love and belongingness. Likewise, personnel managers in business and industry can use Maslow's theory to motivate workers. The theory suggests that increases in pay cannot satisfy any needs beyond the physiological and safety levels. Because physiological and safety needs are already largely gratified by the average worker in the United States, wage increases per se will not permanently increase worker morale and productivity. Pay raises can satisfy higher-level needs only when workers see them as recognition for a job well done. McGregor (1960) has suggested that workers will produce more when their esteem and self-actualization needs are activated. This means that managers should allow workers more responsibility and freedom, tap into their ingenuity and creativity in solving problems, and encourage them to use their intelligence and imagination on the job. Maslow's theory suggests many techniques for motivating workers on the level of esteem and self-actualization.

Is the theory *internally consistent*? Unfortunately, Maslow's arcane and often unclear language makes important parts of his theory ambiguous and inconsistent. Apart from the problem of idiosyncratic language, however, Maslow's theory ranks high on the criterion of internal consistency. The hierarchy of needs concept follows a logical progression, and Maslow hypothesized that the order of needs is the same for everyone, although he does not overlook the possibility of certain reversals. Aside from some deficiencies in his scientific methods, Maslow's theory has a consistency and precision that give it popular appeal.

Is Maslow's theory *parsimonious*, or does it contain superfluous fabricated concepts and models? At first glance the theory seems quite simplistic. A hierarchy of needs model with only five steps gives the theory a deceptive appearance of simplicity. A full understanding of Maslow's total theory, however, suggests a far more complex model. Overall, the theory receives a moderate rating on parsimony.

Chapter Summary

Maslow's holistic-dynamic theory of personality is largely a theory of human motivation. It assumes that (1) the *whole person* is motivated, (2) *motivation is complex* and often *unconscious*, (3) people are *continually motivated* by one need or another, and (4) the *same basic needs apply to all people*.

Maslow recognized four major dimensions to needs: (1) the *conative needs*; 2) *cognitive needs*, including knowledge; (3) *aesthetic needs*, including love of beauty and order; and (4) *neurotic needs*, which produce neuroses whether or not they are satisfied.

The conative needs can be arranged on a *hierarchy*, meaning that one need must be relatively satisfied before the next one can become active. The most basic needs are *physiological*, including food, water, oxygen, and so forth. After physiological needs are satisfied, people are motivated to seek *safety*. When safety needs are relatively satisfied, *love and belongingness* needs become motivators. To the extent that people satisfy their needs for love, they acquire self-esteem. When *esteem* needs are adequately met, people will either remain on that level or cross the threshold to *self-actualization*.

Occasionally, needs on the hierarchy can be *reversed*, but ordinarily people from all cultures proceed in the same order through the hierarchy. *Unconscious motivation* frequently blurs one's view of the true need underlying a particular behavior.

Maslow believed that all behavior has a cause but not all behavior is motivated. *Coping behavior*, which stems from basic needs, is motivated, whereas expressive behavior frequently is not. *Expressive behavior* has no goal; it is simply our way of expressing ourselves.

Conative needs, including self-actualization, are *instinctoid*; that is, their deprivation leads to pathology. The frustration of self-actualization needs results in *metapathology*.

Self-actualizing people are motivated by the B-*values*. In fact, acceptance of B-values (truth, beauty, humor, and so forth) is the criterion that separates self-actualizing people from those who are merely healthy but mired at the level of self-esteem.

In addition, self-actualizers are characterized by: (1) a more efficient perception of reality; (2) acceptance of self, others, and nature; (3) spontaneity, simplicity, and naturalness; (4) a problem-centered approach to life; (5) the need for privacy; (6) autonomy; (7) freshness of appreciation; (8) peak experiences; (9) social interest; (10) profound interpersonal relations; (11) a democratic attitude; (12) the ability to discriminate means from ends; (13) a philosophical sense of humor; (14) creativeness; and (15) resistance to enculturation.

In addition, self-actualizers are capable of B-*love*, or love for the essence of another. Maslow also hypothesized that sex between two self-actualizers is both more mystical and more pleasurable than sex between non-actualizers.

Abnormal development arises when people are frustrated in any of their basic needs, but especially love and belongingness. The *Jonah complex* is the fear of being or doing one's best. *Psychotherapy* to rectify abnormal development should be directed at the need level currently being thwarted.

In his *philosophy of science*, Maslow argued for a *Taoistic attitude*, one that is noninterfering, passive, receptive, and subjective. The subject matter of psychology must be viewed with joy, wonder, awe, and affection. Maslow's own *research methods* followed a Taoistic approach, but he was less than careful in reporting his procedures.

Nevertheless, Maslow's holistic-dynamic theory is quite useful in generating research, organizing knowledge, and serving as a guide to the practitioner. Maslow's language is not always clear, but his theory is rated adequate on both internal consistency and parsimony.

Suggested Readings _____

FRICK, W. B. (1971). Interview with Dr. Abraham Maslow. In W. B. Frick, *Humanistic psychology: Interviews with Maslow, Murphy and Rogers* (pp. 18–49). Columbus, OH: Merrill.
During the last years of his life Maslow granted many interviews. This one with Willard Frick is stimulating, comprehensive, and well-organized.

HOFFMAN, E. (1988). *The right to be human*: A *biography of Abraham Maslow*. Los Angeles: Tarcher.

Hoffman interviewed dozens of Maslow's family members, friends, and associates to write this fascinating biography. The result is a very readable, informative, and comprehensive book.

MASLOW, A. H. (1964). *Religions, values, and peak-experiences*. Columbus: Ohio State University Press.

In this brief book, Maslow discusses the differences between personalized and institutionalized religious experiences and also describes the religious aspects of the peak experience.

MASLOW, A. H. (1970). *Motivation and personality* (2d ed.). New York: Harper & Row.

Maslow's basic theories of motivation and self-actualization are presented. This book should be required reading for anyone interested in Maslow's holistic-dynamic theory.

MASLOW, A. H. (1971). *The farther reaches of human nature*. New York: Viking Press.

Published after his death, this work is an extension of Maslow's (1968b) *Toward a Psychology of Being*. Among other topics, Maslow discusses B-values, metamotivation, creativeness, and peak experiences.

Person-Centered Theory

OVERVIEW
BIOGRAPHY OF CARL ROGERS
PERSON-CENTERED THEORY
Basic Assumptions
The Self
Awareness
Needs
Conditions of Worth
Psychological Stagnation
PSYCHOTHERAPY
Conditions
Process
Outcomes
THE PERSON OF TOMORROW
Characteristics
Implications
BOX: THE ROGERS/SKINNER DEBATE
PHILOSOPHY OF SCIENCE
CONCEPT OF HUMANITY
RELATED RESEARCH
Chicago Studies
Later Research on the Growth-Facilitative Conditions
The Case of Mrs. Oak
CRITIQUE OF ROGERS
CHAPTER SUMMARY
SUGGESTED READINGS

ROGERS

*M*rs. Oak was miserable. Filled with self-doubts, despair, and hostility, she quarreled endlessly with her husband, and the arguments seemed to be about nothing. Although she romanticized the sexual aspects of her marital relationship, she did not enjoy the sex act and had some confusion over her sexual identity. She had not worked outside the home since her marriage, and, as a consequence, she felt extremely dependent upon her husband.

In addition to troubles with her husband, Mrs. Oak was also deeply disturbed over her relationship with her teenage daughter, blaming herself for her daughter's recent serious illness. In fact, she had a strong sense of duty toward others, but she did little to make her own life more fulfilling. She was a dependent, passive person who felt rejected both at home and in social groups. Lonely, unhappy, and without friends, she harbored deep resentment toward others, especially women. Although lacking in feelings of self-worth and self-confidence, she had high aspirations and hoped for some great personal accomplishments. Her daydreams of achieving glory occupied her time and prevented her from dealing realistically with daily problems. Actually, she had almost no self-generated goals but allowed others or "society" to determine her responsibilities. She resented these outside forces, not realizing that they were mostly of her own creation.

In her late thirties, feeling unattractive, guilty, frustrated, and generally miserable, Mrs. Oak decided to seek psychotherapy. Consequently, she entered the Counseling Center at the University of Chicago, received help, and in turn, helped Carl Rogers better understand the process of personality change that seems to take place during *client-centered therapy*.

OVERVIEW

The process of growth experienced by Mrs. Oak and dozens of other people as a result of client-centered psychotherapy was studied in depth by a research team at the University of Chicago, and these studies helped lay the foundation for Rogers's *person-centered theory of personality*. Later in this chapter, we will look again at Mrs. Oak and chart her progress toward becoming what Rogers called "a fully functioning person."

Although he is best known as the founder of client-centered therapy, Rogers also developed a theory of personality that grew out of his experiences as a practicing psychotherapist. Unlike Freud, who was primarily a theorist and secondarily a therapist, Rogers was a consummate therapist but only a reluctant theorist (Rogers, 1959). He was more concerned with helping people than with discovering why they behaved as they did. He was more likely to ask, "How can I help this other person grow and develop?" than he was to ponder the question, "What caused this person to develop in this manner?"

Even though he formulated a rigorous, internally consistent theory of personality, Rogers did not feel comfortable with the notion of theory. His personal preference was to be a helper of people and not a constructor of theories. To him, theories seemed to make things too cold and external, and he worried that his theory might imply a measure of finality.

During the 1950s, at a midpoint in his career, Rogers was invited to write what was then called the "client-centered" theory of personality, and his original statement is found in Volume 3 of Sigmund Koch's *Psychology: A Study of a Science* (see Rogers, 1959). Even at that time, Rogers realized that 10 or 20 years hence his theories would be different, but, unfortunately, throughout the intervening years he never systematically reformulated his theory of personality. Although many of his subsequent experiences altered some of those earlier ideas, his final theory of personality rests on that original foundation, which he spelled out in the Koch series.

BIOGRAPHY OF CARL ROGERS

Carl Ransom Rogers was born on January 8, 1902, in Oak Park, Illinois, the fourth of six children born to Walter and Julia Cushing Rogers. Carl was closer to his mother than to his father, who, during the early years, was often away from home working as a civil engineer. Walter Rogers eventually became a successful businessman, so Carl was truly a product of middle-class, midwestern America. Walter and Julia Rogers were both devoutly religious, and Carl became interested in the bible, reading from it and other books even as a preschool child.

As a child in Oak Park, Rogers attended school with Ernest Hemingway, who was two years older, and the children of Frank Lloyd Wright, the great American architect.

Carl was an excellent student, but he was also a dreamer who loved adventure books. Although he was from a large family, he was a loner and quite unsocial at school. Being a sensitive boy, he was easily hurt by the teasing he received from his classmates and siblings.

At the beginning of his high school years, Carl moved with his family to a farm 25 miles west of Chicago. His father was not a farmer but by this time was running a successful construction company. Carl's parents hoped the move to the farm would provide a more wholesome and religious atmosphere for their children. The house was more of a mansion than a farmhouse, having eight bedrooms, five baths, a tile roof, and a tennis court. In this environment young Carl developed a passionate interest in nature and adopted a scientific attitude toward farming, taking detailed notes of his observations of both plants and animals. This scientific attitude was to remain with him for a lifetime, and his early interest in plants became a satisfying hobby in his later years.

Rogers had intended to become a farmer, and after he graduated from high school in 1919, he entered the University of Wisconsin with agriculture as his major. During his freshman year at the university he made the first close friendships outside his family. That year also marked the beginning of a more intense interest in religion and a lessening of his desire to become a farmer.

By his third year at Wisconsin, he was deeply involved with religious activities on campus and spent six months during his junior year traveling to China to attend a student religious conference. This trip made a lasting impression on Rogers. The interaction with other young religious leaders changed him into a more liberal thinker and moved him toward independence from his parents' religious views. These experiences with his fellow leaders also gave him more self-confidence in social relationships. Unfortunately, he paid a price for these rapid personal changes—he returned from the journey with an ulcer. Subsequently, he spent a year recuperating by working on the farm and also at a local lumberyard. After returning to Wisconsin, he joined a fraternity, displayed more self-confidence, and, in general, was a changed student from his pre-China days.

As an adolescent, Rogers was nearly as shy around girls as was Abraham Maslow (see Chapter 15), and this shyness had greatly restricted his experiences with women and girls. When he originally entered Wisconsin he had only enough courage to ask out a young lady whom he had known in elementary school in Oak Park. This young lady was Helen Elliott, whom Carl married in 1924. Carl and Helen had two children—David, born in 1926, and Natalie, born in 1928.

After their marriage Carl and Helen traveled to New York, where Carl entered the Union Theological Seminary with the intention of becoming a minister. While at the seminary, Rogers enrolled in several psychology and education courses at neighboring Columbia University. He was influenced by the progressive education movement of John Dewey, which was then strong at Teachers College, Columbia. Gradually, he became disenchanted with the doctrinaire attitude of religious work. Even though Union Theological Seminary was quite liberal, Rogers decided that he did not wish to express a fixed set of beliefs but desired more freedom to explore new ideas. Finally, in the fall of 1926, he crossed the street to attend Teachers College on a full-time basis with a major in clinical and educational psychology. From that point on, he never returned to formal religion. His life would now take a new direction—toward psychology and education.

In 1927 Rogers served as a Fellow at the new Institute for Child Guidance in New York City and continued to work there while completing his doctoral degree. At the institute he gained an elementary knowledge of Freudian psychoanalysis, but he was not much influenced by it, even though he tried it out in his practice. He also attended a lecture by Alfred Adler, who shocked Rogers and the other staff members with his contention that an elaborate case history was unnecessary for psychotherapy.

Rogers received a Ph.D. from Columbia in 1931 after having already moved to Rochester, New York, to work with the Rochester Society for the Prevention of Cruelty to Children. During this early phase of his professional career, he was strongly influenced by the practice—but not the theory—of Otto Rank, who had been of of Freud's closest associates. Rogers was mostly unconcerned with theoretical formulations, but he gradually developed his own techniques for treating problem children. Because he was isolated from the academic world and from mainstream psychology, he was not aware that his practice of psychotherapy was either unique or novel.

Rogers spent 12 years at Rochester working at a job that might easily have isolated him from a successful academic career. He had harbored a desire to teach in a university after a rewarding teaching experience during the summer of 1935 at Teachers College and after having taught courses in sociology at the University of Rochester. During this period he wrote his first book, *The Clinical Treatment of the Problem Child* (1939), the publication of which led to a teaching offer from Ohio State University. Despite his fondness for

teaching, he might have turned down the offer if his wife had not urged him to accept and if Ohio State had not agreed to start him at the top, with the academic rank of full professor. In 1940, at the age of 38, Rogers moved to Columbus to begin a new career.

Pressed by his graduate students at Ohio State, Rogers gradually conceptualized his own ideas on psychotherapy, not intending them to be unique and certainly not controversial. These ideas were put forth in *Counseling and Psychotherapy*, published in 1942. In this book, which was a reaction to the older approaches to therapy, Rogers minimized the causes of disturbances and the identification and labeling of disorders. Instead, he emphasized the importance of growth within the patient (called by Rogers the "client").

In 1944, as part of the war effort, Rogers took a leave from Ohio State to move back to New York as Director of Counseling Services for the United Services Organization. After one year he took a position at the University of Chicago, where he established a counseling center and was allowed more freedom to do research on the process and outcome of psychotherapy. The years 1945 to 1957 at Chicago were the most productive and creative of his career. His therapy evolved from one that emphasized methodology, or what in the early 1940s was called the "nondirective" technique, to one in which the sole emphasis was on the client/therapist relationship. Always the scientist, Rogers, along with his students and colleagues, produced the most original and sophisticated research on the process and effectiveness of psychotherapy published to that date. Mrs. Oak, our case study, was one of the subjects of that research.

Wanting to expand his research and his ideas to psychiatry, Rogers accepted a position at the University of Wisconsin in 1957. However, he was disappointed with his stay at Wisconsin because he was unable to unite the professions of psychiatry and psychology, and because he felt that some members of his own research staff had engaged in dishonest and unethical behavior (Kirschenbaum, 1979). Nevertheless, he did have an opportunity to influence both psychiatry and psychology and also to work with both normal and psychotic clients as opposed to the largely neurotic subjects he encountered at Chicago and Ohio State.

Disappointed with his job at Wisconsin, Rogers moved to California in 1964, where he joined the Western Behavioral Sciences Institute (WBSI) and became increasingly interested in encounter groups. He also became interested in expanding the "person-centered" approach to education and to larger social issues, including politics and international affairs (Heppner, Rogers, & Lee, 1984; Rogers, 1982b).

He resigned from WBSI when he felt it was becoming less democratic and, along with about 75 others from the institute, formed the Center for Studies of the Person. He continued to work with encounter groups but extended his person-centered methods to education (including the training of physicians) and to international politics. During the last years of his life he led workshops in such countries as Hungary, Brazil, South Africa, and the former Soviet Union (Gendlin, 1988). He died on February 4, 1987, following surgery for a broken hip.

The personal life of Carl Rogers was characterized by change and openness to experience. As a youth he was a shy loner with an active fantasy life, which he later believed probably would have been diagnosed as "schizoid" (Rogers, 1980, p. 30). A socially inept youngster, Rogers grew to become a leading proponent of the notion that the interpersonal relationship between two individuals is a powerful ingredient that cultivates psychological growth within both persons. The transition, however, was not easy. He abandoned the formalized religion of his parents, gradually shaping a humanistic, and then an existential, philosophy that he hoped would bridge the gap between Eastern and Western thought.

Rogers received many honors during his long professional life. He was the first president of the American Association for Applied Psychology and helped bring that organization and the American Psychological Association (APA) back together. He served as president of APA for the year 1946–1947 and served as first president of the American Academy of Psychotherapists. In 1956 he was co-winner, along with Kenneth Spence and Wolfgang Kohler, of the first Distinguished Scientific Contribution Award presented by APA. This award was especially satisfying to Rogers because it highlighted his skill as a researcher, and demonstrated to others that he was more than just a psychotherapist.

Rogers originally saw little need for a theory of personality. But under pressure from others and also to satisfy an inner need to be able to explain the phenomena he was observing, he evolved his own theory, which was first tentatively expressed in his APA Presidential address (Rogers, 1947). His theory was more fully espoused in *Client-Centered Therapy* (1951) and was expressed in even greater detail in the Koch series (Rogers, 1959). However, Rogers always insisted that the theory should remain tentative, and it is with this thought that one should approach a discussion of Rogerian personality theory.

PERSON-CENTERED THEORY

The therapy and theory of Rogers underwent several changes in name, but no substantive changes in philosophy occurred from the early years, when the therapy was known as "nondirective," until the final years, when the theory was called "person-centered." During the intervening years, his approach was variously termed client-centered, student-centered, group-centered, and person-to-person (Frick, 1971; Rogers & Stevens, 1967). In the present text, the label **client-centered** is used in reference to *therapy*, whereas the more inclusive term **person-centered** refers to Rogerian personality *theory*.

Person-centered theory is a holistic theory and, like other holistic theories, it can be outlined and divided only arbitrarily. Each assumption is interrelated with every other concept and cannot be considered apart from the whole of the theory. Rogers, however, was able to state many of the assumptions of his theory in an if–then framework. A general example would be: *if* certain conditions exist, *then* a process will occur; *if* this process occurs, *then* certain outcomes can be expected. A more specific example is found in therapy: *If* the therapist possesses unconditional positive regard (a concept to be discussed in the section on therapy), *then* therapeutic change will occur; *if* therapeutic change occurs, *then* the client will experience more self-acceptance, greater trust of self, and so on. Person-centered theory is one of very few personality theories stated in such a precise fashion (see Rogers, 1959).

Basic Assumptions

What are the basic assumptions of person-centered theory? Rogers postulated two broad assumptions—the formative tendency and the actualizing tendency.

Formative Tendency

Rogers (1978, 1980) believed that there is a tendency for all matter, both organic and inorganic, to evolve from simpler to more complex forms. For the entire universe, a creative process, rather than a disintegrative one, is in operation. Rogers called this the **formative tendency** and pointed to many examples from nature. For instance, complex galaxies of stars form from a less well-organized mass; crystals such as snowflakes emerge from formless vapor; complex organisms develop from single cells; and human consciousness evolves from a primitive unconsciousness to a highly organized awareness.

Actualizing Tendency

An interrelated and more pertinent assumption is the **actualizing tendency**, the tendency within all human beings to move toward completion or fulfillment of potentials (Rogers, 1980). Individuals have within themselves the creative power to solve problems, to alter their self-concepts, and to become increasingly self-directed. The source of psychological growth and maturity resides within the individual and is not found in outside forces. Individuals perceive their experiences as reality, and they know their reality better than anyone else. They do not need to be directed, controlled, exhorted, or manipulated in order to spur them toward actualization.

Although we have a variety of needs and behave in many different ways, all our behavior is relative to this single actualizing tendency. Because we operate as one complete organism, actualization involves our whole person—physiological and intellectual, rational and emotional, conscious and unconscious. The need to satisfy our hunger drive, to express deep emotions when they are felt, and to accept ourselves, are all examples of the single motive of actualization.

If we all possess the same actualization tendency, why are we not all completely actualized? The answer is that certain *conditions* must exist in order for us to be able to activate our capacities for growth. Specifically, we must be involved in a relationship with a partner who is *genuine* or *authentic*, and who demonstrates *unconditional acceptance* and *empathy* toward us. These three characteristics (genuineness, unconditional acceptance, and empathy) will be more fully discussed below in the section on therapy, but we must emphasize here that our partner's possession of these three qualities does not *cause* us to move toward constructive personal change. It does, however, permit us to actualize our own tendency toward self-fulfillment. In fact, Rogers (1961) contended that when these three conditions are present in a relationship, psychological growth will invariably occur. For this reason, Rogers regarded genuineness, acceptance, and empathy as *necessary* and *sufficient* conditions for growth.

The Self

The self begins to emerge early in infancy when a portion of experience becomes personalized and differentiated in *awareness* as "I" or "me" experiences. Infants gradually become aware of their own identity as they begin to learn what tastes good and what tastes bad, what feels pleasant and what does not. They then begin to evaluate experiences as positive or negative, using as a criterion the actualizing tendency. Because nourishment is a requirement for actualization, infants value food and devalue hunger. They also value sleep, fresh air, physical contact, and health because each of these is needed for actualization (Rogers, 1959).

Once the self structure is established, the tendency to actualize the self begins to evolve. **Self-actualization** is a subsystem of the actualization tendency and is therefore not synonymous with it. The *actualization tendency* refers to organismic experiences of the individual, that is, to the whole person—conscious and unconscious, physiological and cognitive. On the other hand, *self-actualization* is the tendency to actualize the self as *perceived in awareness*. When the organism and the perceived self are in harmony, the two tendencies are identical; but when an incongruence exists between what one truly is and one's self-perception, then a discrepancy between the two actualization tendencies is created, which results in conflict and inner tension (Rogers, 1959).

Rogers postulated that the self has two subsystems, *the self-concept* and the *ideal self.*

The Self-Concept

The **self-concept** includes all those aspects of one's being and one's experiences that are perceived in awareness (though not always accurately) by the individual. The self-concept is not identical with the organismic self. Portions of the organismic self may be beyond our awareness or simply not owned by us. My stomach is part of my organismic self, but unless it malfunctions and causes concern, it is not likely to be part of my self-concept. Similarly, I can disown certain

Incongruence between the ideal self and the perceived self can result in conflict and unhappiness.

aspects of my self, for example, experiences of dishonesty, when they are not consistent with my self-concept.

Thus, once we form our self-concept, we find change and significant learnings quite difficult. Experiences that are inconsistent with our self-concept usually are either denied or accepted only in distorted forms (Rogers, 1959). Take, for example, a man who sees himself as a faithful husband who could not possibly be attracted to any woman other than his wife. If, on an organismic level, he experiences sexual feelings for another woman, he will either deny the feelings to his awareness or reshape them, possibly by projecting them onto the woman.

An established self-concept does not make change impossible, merely difficult. Change most readily occurs in an atmosphere of acceptance by others, which allows a person to reduce anxiety and threat and to take ownership of previously rejected experiences.

The Ideal Self

The second subsystem of the self is the **ideal self**, defined as our view of our self as we would like to be. The ideal self contains all those attributes, usually positive, that we aspire to possess. Operationally, both the self-concept and the ideal self can be measured by such psychometric devices as the Q-*sort technique* (an instrument that will be more fully discussed later). A wide gap between the ideal self and the self-concept indicates **incongruence** and unhealthy personality. Psychologically healthy individuals perceive little discrepancy between their self-concept and what they ideally would like to be.

Awareness

Without awareness the self-concept and the ideal self would not exist. Rogers (1959, p. 198) defined *awareness* as "the symbolic representation (not necessarily in verbal symbols) of some portion of our experience." He used the term synonymously with both consciousness and symbolization.

Levels of Awareness

Rogers (1959) recognized three levels of symbolization or awareness. First, some events are experienced below the threshold of awareness and are either *ignored* or *denied*. Ignored experiences can be illustrated by a woman walking down a busy street, an activity that presents many potential stimuli, particularly of sight and sound. Because she cannot attend to all of them, many remain *ignored*. An example of *denied* experience might be seen in a mother who never wanted children, but out of guilt she becomes oversolicitous to them. Her anger and resentment toward her children may be hidden to her for years, never reaching consciousness but yet remaining a part of her experience and coloring her conscious behavior toward them. Rogers (1959) also used the term *subceived* to refer to experiences that are perceived but yet not accepted into awareness. **Subception** refers to the process of perceiving stimuli without an awareness of the perception, and includes experiences that are denied.

Second, Rogers (1959) hypothesized that some experiences are *accurately symbolized* and freely admitted to the self-structure. Such experiences are both non-threatening and consistent with the existing self-concept. For example, if a pianist, who has full confidence in his piano-playing ability, is told by a friend that his playing is excellent, he may hear these words, accurately symbolize them, and freely admit them to his self-concept.

A third level of awareness involves experiences that are perceived in a *distorted* form. When our experience is not consistent with our view of self, we reshape or distort the experience so that it can be assimilated into our existing self-concept. If the gifted pianist from the above example were to be told by a distrusted competitor that his playing was excellent, he might react very differently than he did when he heard the same words from a trusted friend. He may hear the remarks but distort their meaning because he feels threatened. "Why is this person trying to flatter me? This doesn't make sense." His experiences are inaccurately symbolized in awareness and therefore can be distorted so that they conform to an existing self-concept that, in part, says, "I am a person who does not trust my piano-playing competitors, especially those who are trying to trick me."

Denial of Positive Experiences

From the preceding example, we can see that it is not only the negative or derogatory experiences that are distorted or denied to awareness; many people have difficulty accepting genuine compliments and positive feedback, even when deserved. A student who feels inadequate but yet makes a superior grade, might say to herself, "I know this grade should be evidence of my scholastic ability, but somehow I just don't feel that way. This class was the easiest one on campus. The other students just didn't try. My teacher did not know what she was doing." Compliments, even those genuinely dispensed, seldom have a positive influence on the self-concept of the recipient (Rogers, 1961). They may be distorted because the person distrusts the giver or they may be denied because the recipient does not feel deserving of them; in all cases, a compliment from another also implies the right of that person to criticize or condemn, and thus the compliment carries an implied threat.

Needs

As we have seen, Rogers believed that people possess an inherent tendency to move toward actualization. Experiences that are seen as either maintaining or enhancing that movement are positively valued; those that are not are negatively valued. The basic needs of all of us, therefore, are *maintenance* and *enhancement*.

Maintenance

The need for **maintenance** of our organismic self involves the satisfaction of basic needs such as food, air, and safety, but it also includes the tendency to resist change and to seek the status quo. The conservative nature of maintenance needs finds expression in our desire to protect our current, comfortable self-concept. We fight against new ideas; we distort experiences that do not quite fit; we find change painful and growth frightening.

Enhancement

Even though we have a strong desire to maintain the status quo, we are still willing to learn and to change. This need to become more, to develop, and to achieve growth is called **enhancement**.

The need for enhancing the self is manifested in our willingness to learn things that are not immediately rewarding. Other than enhancement, what motivation does a child have in learning to walk? Crawling can satisfy the need for mobility, whereas walking is associated with falling and with pain. Rogers's position is that we are willing to face threat and pain because of a biologically based tendency for the organism to fulfill its basic nature.

Enhancement needs are expressed in a variety of forms, including curiosity, playfulness, self-exploration, maturation, and friendship. Even food and sex are usually expressions of the organism's need to enhance itself. Both might also be maintenance needs, particularly when they are largely unsatisfied. However, for most people, the pursuit of food and sex is conducted in ways that enhance the self-concept.

Positive Regard

As the awareness of self emerges, the infant begins to develop a need to be loved, liked, or accepted by another person, a need Rogers (1959) referred to as **positive regard**. The need for positive regard is found in all human beings and remains a strong and persistent motivator throughout our lives. We value those experiences that satisfy our needs for positive regard. Unfortunately, the positive regard we receive from a significant other may be more powerful than the reward we receive by meeting our organismic needs. For example, a child who, on an organismic level is afraid of a large dog, may hear his father say, "Show me how brave you are. Go ahead and touch the dog." The child may then deny or distort his fear in order to receive the praise (positive regard) from his father.

Self-Regard

After the self emerges, we begin to develop the need for **self-regard** as the result of our experiences with the satisfaction or frustration of our need for positive regard. In the above example, when the child receives praise from his father for courageous behavior, he may acquire positive self-regard for being brave, and negative self-regard for acting cowardly. If the child generally dislikes himself, then he will develop feelings of negative self-regard. But if he likes himself independently of others' attitudes toward him, then he will continue to have positive self-regard. Positive self-regard is similar to Maslow's concept of self-esteem and includes feelings of self-confidence and self-worth.

How do we acquire positive self-regard? Originally, the need is dependent upon the perception that others, especially significant others, care for, prize, or value us. If we perceive that we are liked or loved by others, then our need to receive positive regard is at least partially satisfied. Positive regard is a prerequisite for self-regard, but once positive self-regard is established it becomes independent of the continual need to be loved (Rogers, 1959). This conception is quite similar to Maslow's notion that we must satisfy our love and belongingness needs before self-esteem needs can become active, but once we begin to feel confident and worthy, we no longer require a replenishing supply of love and approval from others.

The source of positive self-regard, then, lies in the positive regard we receive from others, but once established, it is autonomous and self-perpetuating. As Rogers (1959, p. 224) stated it, the person then "becomes in a sense his own significant social other."

Conditions of Worth

Instead of unconditional acceptance, most of us receive **conditions of worth**; that is, we feel that we are loved and accepted only if we meet the other person's expectations and approval. "A condition of worth arises when the positive regard of a significant other is conditional, when the individual feels that in some respects he is prized and in others not" (Rogers, 1959, p. 209).

Although maintenance and enhancement are basic needs, conditions of worth can also become a criterion by which we accept or reject our experiences. We gradually assimilate into our self-structure the attitudes we perceive others as expressing toward us, and eventually we come to evaluate our experiences on this basis.

As the self begins to evolve during early childhood, we learn to attach worth and value to those experiences that we see as meeting the approval of our parents and significant others. If we perceive that our behavior is disapproved, we feel rejected. But our feelings of rejection are not limited to that specific behavior—they permeate our entire person because we feel that *we* are rejected. Eventually, we come to believe those reflected appraisals of others that are consistent with our view of self. We ignore our own primary sensory and visceral perceptions and gradually become less acquainted with our real or organismic self.

Acceptance by others is so important that when it is not forthcoming, we desperately seek it, even at the expense of our own enhancement. From early childhood forward, most of us, to some extent, learn to disregard our own organismic valuations and, instead, look beyond ourselves for direction and guidance. To the degree that we introject the values of others, that is, accept conditions of worth, we tend to be incongruent or out of balance. Other people's values can be assimilated only in distorted fashion or at the risk of creating disequilibrium and conflict within the self (Rogers, 1959).

Inner conflict and incongruence, then, are due to the disparity between one's own values, which are formed from direct organismic experience, and the more or less distorted values that one has introjected from others. External evaluations, either positive or negative, do not foster psychological health, but rather prevent us from being completely open to our own experiences. For example, we may reject experiences that feel pleasant on an organismic level because we believe that other people do not approve of them. When our own experiences are distrusted, we distort our awareness of them, thus solidifying the discrepancy between our organismic evaluation and the values we have introjected from others. As a result we may become psychologically maladjusted (Rogers, 1959).

Psychological Stagnation

To understand Rogers's view of abnormal development, we should remember that the organism and the self are two separate entities that may or may not be congruent with one another. We should also recall that actualization refers to the organism's tendency to move toward fulfillment, whereas self-actualization is the desire of the perceived self to reach fulfillment. These two tendencies are sometimes at variance with one another.

Incongruence

Psychological disequilibrium begins when we fail to recognize our organismic experiences as self-experiences; that is, when we do not accurately symbolize organismic experiences into awareness because they appear to be inconsistent with our emerging self-concept. This *incongruence* between our self-concept and our organismic experience is the source of psychological maladjustment. Conditions of worth that we received during early childhood lead to a somewhat false self-concept, one based on distortions and denials. The self-concept that emerges includes subceived perceptions that are not in harmony with our organismic experiences, and this incongruence between self and experience leads to discrepant and seemingly inconsistent behaviors. Sometimes we behave in ways that maintain or enhance our actualizing tendency, and, at other times, we may behave in a manner designed to maintain or enhance a self-concept founded on other people's expectations and evaluations of us.

The greater the incongruence between our perceived self (self-concept) and our organismic experience, the more vulnerable we are. Rogers (1959) believed that people are **vulnerable** when they are unaware of the discrepancy between their self and their experience. Lacking awareness of their incongruence, vulnerable people often behave in ways that are incomprehensible not only to others but also to themselves. For example, a person may say, "I don't know why I say such childish things to my boss. I know she must think I'm an idiot. I don't want to do it, but every time I open my mouth I say something stupid." The person fails to understand her own behavior because she is completely unaware of the incongruence between her organismic self and her perceived self.

Anxiety and Threat

If vulnerability exists when we have no awareness of the incongruence within our self, then anxiety and threat are experienced as we become more and more aware of such an incongruence. When we become dimly aware, or subceive, that the discrepancy between our organismic experience and our self-concept may become conscious, we feel anxious. Rogers (1959, p. 204) defined **anxiety** as "a state of uneasiness or tension whose cause is unknown." As we become even more aware of the incongruence between our organismic experience and our perception of self, our anxiety begins to evolve into **threat**, that is, an awareness that our self is no longer whole or congruent. Although anxiety and threat represent steps toward psychological health, they are not pleasant or comfortable feelings, because they signal to us that our organismic experience is inconsistent with our self-concept (Rogers, 1959).

Defensiveness

In order to prevent this inconsistency from occurring, we react in a defensive manner. **Defensiveness** is the protection of the self-concept against anxiety and threat by the denial or distortion of experiences inconsistent with it (Rogers, 1959). Because the self-concept consists of many self-descriptive statements, it is a many-faceted phenomenon. When one of our experiences is inconsistent with one part of our self-concept, we will behave in a defensive manner in order to protect our self-concept's current structure.

The two chief defenses are *distortion* and *denial*. With **distortion**, we misinterpret an experience in order to fit it into some aspect of our self-concept. We perceive the experience in awareness, but we fail to understand its true meaning. With **denial**, we refuse to perceive an experience in awareness, or at least we keep some aspect of it from reaching symbolization. Denial is not as common as distortion because most experiences can be twisted or reshaped to fit the current self-concept. According to Rogers (1959), both distortion and denial serve the same purpose—they keep our perception of our organismic experiences consistent with our self-concept.

Distortion and denial lead to absolutistic and rigid behaviors, such as rationalization (giving reasonable-sounding but invalid explanations for our behavior), compensation (making up for feelings of inadequacy by pretending to be somebody other than what we truly are), paranoia, delusions, hallucinations, and a multitude of other "neurotic" or "psychotic" behaviors.

Behavior can become disorganized or even psychotic when one's defenses fail to operate properly.

Disorganization

Defensiveness is characteristic of so-called normal and neurotic individuals. When people's defenses fail to operate properly, their behavior becomes disorganized or psychotic. But why would defenses fail to function?

To answer this question, we must trace the course of disorganized behavior, which has the same origins as both normal defensive and neurotic behaviors, namely discrepancy between our organismic experience and our view of self. In normal and neurotic cases, denial and distortion prevent us from recognizing this discrepancy. In contrast, people who engage in disorganized behavior have a large degree of incongruence between their perceived self and their organismic experience. This discrepancy is either too obvious to be denied or distorted or it occurs so suddenly that it becomes overwhelming and is experienced as a threat to the self-structure. Because people are forced into an awareness of this inconsistency, their previously unified self-structure becomes broken. The resulting disorganization can occur suddenly, or it can take place gradually over a long period of time. Ironically, people are particularly vulnerable to disorganization during therapy, especially if a therapist accurately interprets their actions and also insists that they face the experience prematurely (Rogers, 1959).

In a state of disorganization, people sometimes behave consistently with their organismic experience, and, at other times, they act in accordance with their shattered self-concept. An example of the first case is a previously prudish and proper woman who suddenly begins to use language explicitly sexual and scatological. The second case can be illustrated by a man who, because his self-concept is no longer a gestalt or unified whole, begins to behave in a confused, inconsistent, and totally unpredictable manner. In both cases behavior is still consistent with the self-concept, but the self-concept has been broken and thus the behavior appears bizarre and confusing.

Although Rogers was even more tentative than usual when he first put forth his views of disorganized behavior in 1959, he made no important revisions in this portion of his theory. He never wavered in his disdain for using diagnostic labels to describe people. Traditional classifications such as hypochondrias, paranoid schizophrenia, homosexuality, or bipolar disorder have never been part of the vocabulary of person-centered theory. In fact, Rogers always remained uncomfortable with the terms neurotic and psychotic, preferring instead to speak of defensive and disorganized behaviors, terms that more accurately convey the idea that psychological maladjustment is on a continuum from the slightest discrepancy between self and experience to the most incongruent.

PSYCHOTHERAPY

Client-centered therapy is deceptively simple in statement but decidedly difficult in practice. Briefly, the client-centered approach holds that in order for vulnerable or anxious people to grow psychologically, they must simply come into contact with a therapist who is congruent and whom they perceive as providing an atmosphere of unconditional acceptance and accurate empathy—but therein lies the difficulty. The counselor qualities of congruence, unconditional positive regard, and empathic understanding are not easily obtainable.

The client-centered counseling approach can be stated in an if–then fashion. If the *conditions* of therapist congruence, empathic listening, and unconditional positive regard are present in a client/counselor relationship, then the *process* of therapy will transpire. If the process of therapy takes place, then certain predictable *outcomes* can be noted. Rogerian therapy, therefore, can be viewed in terms of conditions, process, and outcomes.

Conditions

Rogers (1959) postulated that in order for therapeutic growth to take place, the following conditions are necessary and sufficient. First, an anxious or vulnerable client must come into contact with a congruent therapist who also possesses empathy and unconditional positive regard for that client. Second, the client must perceive these characteristics in the therapist. Third, contact between client and therapist must be of some duration.

The significance of the Rogerian hypothesis is revolutionary. With nearly any psychotherapy, the first and third conditions are present; that is, the client or patient is motivated by some sort of tension to seek help, and the relationship between the client and the therapist will last for some period of time.

Effective client-centered therapy requires a congruent counselor who feels empathy and unconditional positive regard for the client.

Client-centered therapy is unique in its insistence that the conditions of *counselor congruence, unconditional positive regard,* and *empathic listening* are both necessary and sufficient (Rogers, 1957).

Even though all three conditions are necessary for psychological growth, Rogers (1980) believed that congruence is more basic than either unconditional positive regard or empathic listening. Congruence is a general quality possessed by the therapist, whereas the other two conditions are specific feelings or attitudes that the therapist has for an individual client.

Counselor Congruence

The first necessary and sufficient condition for therapeutic change is a congruent therapist. **Congruence** exists when a person's organismic experiences are matched by an awareness of them and by an ability and willingness to openly express these feelings (Rogers, 1980). To be congruent means to be real or genuine, to be whole or integrated, to be what one truly is. A congruent counselor is not simply a kind and friendly person but rather a complete human being with feelings of joy, anger, frustration, confusion, and so on. When these feelings are experienced, they are neither denied nor distorted but flow easily into awareness and are freely expressed. A congruent therapist, therefore, is not passive, not aloof, and not "non-directive" (Rogers, 1980).

Congruent therapists are not static. Like most other people, they are constantly exposed to new organismic experiences, but, unlike most people, they accept these experiences into awareness, which contributes to their psychological growth. They wear no mask, do not attempt to fake a pleasant façade, and avoid any pretense of friendliness and affection when these are not truly felt. Also, they do not fake anger, toughness, or ignorance, nor do they cover up feelings of joy, elation, or happiness. In addition, they are able to match feelings with awareness and both of these with honest expression.

Because congruence involves feelings, awareness, and expression, incongruence can arise from either of two points. First, there can be a breakdown between feelings and awareness. A person may be feeling angry, and the anger may be obvious to others, but the angry person is unaware of the feeling. ("I'm not angry. How dare you say I'm angry!") The second source of incongruence is a discrepancy between awareness of an experience and the ability or willingness to express it to another. ("I know I'm feeling bored by what is being said, but I don't dare verbalize my disinterest, because my client will think that I am not a good therapist.") Rogers (1961) stated that therapists will be more effective if they communicate genuine feelings, even when those feelings are negative or threatening. To do otherwise would be dishonest, and clients will detect (although not necessarily consciously) any significant indicators of incongruence.

Although congruence is a necessary ingredient in successful therapy, Rogers (1980) did not believe that it is essential that a therapist be congruent in all relationships outside the therapeutic process. One can be less than perfect and yet become an effective psychotherapist. Also, a therapist need not be absolutely congruent in order to facilitate some growth within a client. As with empathic listening and unconditional positive regard, different degrees of congruence exist. The more the client perceives each of these qualities as characterizing the therapist, the more successful will be the therapeutic process.

Unconditional Positive Regard

Positive regard is the need to be liked, prized, or accepted by another person. When this need exists without any conditions or qualifications, **unconditional positive regard** occurs (Rogers, 1980). Therapists have unconditional positive regard when they are "experiencing a warm, positive and accepting attitude toward what *is* the client" (Rogers, 1961, p. 62). The attitude is without possessiveness, without evaluations, and without reservations.

A therapist with unconditional positive regard toward a client will show a nonpossessive warmth and acceptance, not an effusive, effervescent persona. To have nonpossessive warmth means to care about another without smothering or owning that person. It includes the attitude "Because I care about you, I can permit you to be autonomous and independent of my evaluations and restrictions. You are a separate person with your own feelings and opinions regarding what is right or wrong. The fact that I care for you does not mean that I must guide you in making choices, but that I can allow you to be yourself and to decide what is best for you." This kind of permissive attitude earned for Rogers the undeserved reputation of being passive or nondirective in therapy, but, as seen above, a client-centered therapist must be actively involved in a relationship with the client.

Therapists with unconditional positive regard do not evaluate a client, nor do they accept one action and reject another. External evaluation, whether positive or negative, is always restricting and leads to client defensiveness rather than growth. "My therapist thinks I'm so brilliant. However, I don't feel very smart so I'm having a hard time fitting together her evaluation of me and my own feelings about myself." When a client-centered therapist experiences unconditional positive regard for a client, no conditions of worth exist and no evaluations are made.

Unconditional positive regard means that therapists accept their clients without any restrictions or reservations. Regardless of clients' behavior, therapists continue to prize the person. Although therapists may value some client behaviors more than others, their positive regard remains constant and unwavering, whether a client is frightened, obnoxious, angry, or loving (Rogers, 1959).

Although unconditional positive regard is a somewhat awkward term, all three words are important. "Regard" means that there is a close relationship and that the therapist sees the client as an important person; "positive" indicates that the direction of the relationship is toward warm and caring feelings; and "unconditional" suggests that the positive regard is no longer dependent on specific client behaviors and does not have to be continually earned.

Empathic Listening

The third necessary and sufficient condition of psychological growth is **empathic listening**. Empathy exists when therapists accurately sense the feelings of their clients and are able to communicate these perceptions so that the clients know that another person has entered their world of feelings without prejudice, projection, or evaluation. To Rogers (1980, p. 142) empathy "means temporarily living in the other's life, moving about in it delicately without making judgments." Empathy does not involve interpreting clients' meanings or uncovering their unconscious feelings, procedures that would entail an external frame of reference and threat to clients. In contrast, empathy suggests that the therapist sees things from the client's point of view and that the client feels safe and unthreatened.

Client-centered therapists do not take empathy for granted; they check the accuracy of their sensings by trying them out on the client. "You seem to be telling me that you feel a great deal of resentment toward your father." Valid empathic understanding is often followed by an exclamation from the client along these lines: "Yes, that's it exactly! I really do feel resentful."

Empathic listening is a powerful tool, which, along with genuineness and caring, facilitates personal growth within the client. What, precisely, is the role of empathy in psychological change? How does an empathic therapist help a client move toward wholeness and psychological health? Rogers's (1980, p. 156) own words provide the best answer to these questions.

> When persons are perceptively understood, they find themselves coming in closer touch with a wider range of their experiencing. This gives them an expanded referent to which they can turn for guidance in understanding themselves and directing their behavior. If the empathy has been accurate and deep, they may also be able to unblock a flow of experiencing and permit it to run its uninhibited course.

Empathy is effective because it enables clients to listen to themselves and, in effect, become their own therapists.

Empathy should not be confused with sympathy. The latter term suggests a feeling *for* the client, whereas empathy connotes a feeling *with* another. Sympathy is never therapeutic, because it stems from external evaluation and usually leads to clients feeling sorry for themselves. Self-pity is a deleterious attitude that weakens the self-concept and creates disequilibrium within the self-structure. Also empathy does not mean that a therapist has the same feelings as the client. A therapist does not feel anger, frustration, confusion, resentment, or sexual attraction at the same time a client experiences them. Rather, a therapist is experiencing the depth of the client's feeling, while permitting the client to be a separate person. A therapist has an emotional as well as a cognitive reaction to a client's feelings, but *the feelings belong to the client*, not the therapist. A therapist does not take ownership of the client's experiences but is able to convey to the client an understanding of what it means to be the client at that particular moment (Rogers, 1961).

Process

If the conditions of therapist congruence, unconditional positive regard, and empathy are present, then the process of therapeutic change will be set in motion. Although each person seeking psychotherapy is unique, Rogers (1959) believed that a certain lawfulness characterizes the process of therapy.

The process of constructive personality change can be placed on a continuum from most defensive to most integrated. Rogers (1961) has arbitrarily divided this continuum into seven stages.

Stage One is characterized by an unwillingness to communicate anything about oneself. People at this stage ordinarily do not seek help, but, if for some reason they come to therapy, they are extremely rigid and resistant to change. They do not recognize any problems and refuse to own any personal feelings or emotions.

In *Stage Two* clients become slightly less rigid. They discuss external events and other people, but they still disown or fail to recognize their own feelings. However, they may talk about personal feelings as if such feelings were objective phenomena.

As clients enter into *Stage Three*, they can more freely talk about self, although still as an object. "I'm doing the best I can at work, but my boss still doesn't like me." Clients talk about feelings and emotions in the past or future tense and avoid present feelings. They refuse to accept their emotions, keep personal feelings at a distance from the here-and-now situation, only vaguely perceive that they can make personal choices, and deny individual responsibility for most of their decisions.

Clients in *Stage Four* begin to talk of deep feelings but not ones presently felt. "I was really burned up when my teacher accused me of cheating." When clients do express present feelings, they are usually surprised by this expression. They deny or distort experiences, although they may have some dim recognition that they are capable of feeling emotions in the present. They begin to question some values that have been introjected from others, and they start to see the incongruence between their perceived self and their organismic experience. They accept more freedom and responsibility than they did in Stage Three and begin to tentatively allow themselves to become involved in a relationship with the therapist.

By the time clients reach *Stage Five*, they have begun to experience significant change and growth. They can express feelings in the present, although they have not yet accurately symbolized those feelings. They are beginning to rely on an internal locus of evaluation for their feelings and to make fresh and new discoveries about themselves. They also experience a greater differentiation of feelings and develop more appreciation for nuances among them. In addition, they begin to make their own decisions and to accept responsibility for their choices.

Stage Six is characterized by dramatic growth, with people at this stage moving irreversibly closer to becoming fully functioning or self-actualizing individuals. They freely allow into awareness those experiences that they had previously denied or distorted. They become more congruent and are able to match their present experiences with awareness and with open expression. They no longer evaluate their own behavior from an external viewpoint but rely on their organismic self as the criterion for evaluating experiences. They begin to develop unconditional self-regard, which means that they have a feeling of genuine caring and affection for the person they are becoming.

An interesting concomitant to this stage is a physiological loosening. These people experience their whole organismic self, as their muscles relax, tears flow, circulation improves, and physical symptoms disappear.

In many ways Stage Six signals an end to therapy. Indeed, if therapy were to be terminated at this point, clients would still progress to the next level.

Stage Seven can occur outside the therapeutic encounter, because growth at Stage Six seems to be irreversible. Clients who reach Stage Seven become fully functioning "persons of tomorrow" (a concept more fully explained later). They are able to generalize their in-therapy experiences to their world beyond therapy. They possess the confidence to be themselves at all times, to own and to feel deeply the totality of their experiences, and to live those experiences in the present. Their organismic self, now unified with the self-concept, becomes the locus for evaluating their experiences. People at Stage Seven receive pleasure in knowing that these evaluations are fluid and that change and growth will continue. In addition, they

Persons of tomorrow are confident in themselves and comfortable with change.

become congruent, possess unconditional self-regard, and are able to be loving and empathic toward others.

Now that we have described the dynamics of therapeutic change, we must look at the theoretical formulations evoked to explain this process. Rogers's (1980) explanation follows this line of reasoning. When persons come to experience themselves as prized and unconditionally accepted, they realize, perhaps for the first time, that they are lovable. The example of the therapist enables them to prize and accept themselves, to have unconditional positive self-regard. As clients perceive that they are emphatically understood, they are freed to listen to themselves more accurately, to have empathy for their own feelings. As a consequence, when persons come to prize themselves and to accurately understand themselves, their perceived self becomes more congruent with their organismic experiences. They now possess the same three therapeutic characteristics as any effective helper and, in effect, they become their own therapists.

Outcomes

If the process of therapeutic change is set in motion, then certain observable outcomes can be expected. Rogers (1959) elaborated these predictable outcomes with enough precision to allow for research on the effectiveness of psychotherapy.

The most basic outcome of successful client-centered therapy is a congruent client who is less defensive and more open to experience. Each of the remaining outcomes is a logical extension of this basic one.

As a result of being more congruent and less defensive, clients have a clearer picture of themselves and a more realistic view of the world. They are better able to assimilate experiences into the self on the symbolic level; they are more effective in solving problems; and they have a higher level of positive self-regard.

Being realistic, they have a more accurate view of their potentials, which permits them to narrow the previously wide gap between their self-ideal and their real self. Typically, this gap is narrowed because both the ideal self and the true self show some movement. Clients, because they are more realistic, lower their expectations of what they should be or would like to be, and, because they have an increase in positive self-regard, they raise their view of what they really are.

Because their ideal self and their real self are more congruent, clients experience less physiological and psychological tension, are less vulnerable to threat, and have less anxiety. They are less likely to look to others for direction and less likely to use others' opinions and values as the criteria for evaluating their own experiences. Instead, they become more self-directed and more likely to perceive that the locus of evaluation resides within themselves. They no longer feel compelled to please other people and to meet external expectations. They feel sufficiently safe to take ownership of an increasing number of their experiences and comfortable enough with themselves to lessen the need for denial and distortion.

Their relationships with others are also changed. They become more accepting of others, make fewer demands, and simply allow others to be themselves. Because they have less need to distort reality, they have less desire to force others to meet their expectations. They are also perceived by others as being more mature, more likable, and more socialized. Their genuineness, positive self-regard, and empathic understanding are extended beyond therapy, and they become better able to participate in other growth-facilitating relations (Rogers, 1959, 1961).

THE PERSON OF TOMORROW

The interest shown by Rogers in the psychologically healthy individual is rivaled only by that of Maslow (see Chapter 15). Whereas Maslow was primarily a researcher and more intensely dedicated to the study of the self-actualizing person, Rogers was first of all a psychotherapist more concerned with formulating a theory of the fully functioning person that would be a logical extension of his general theory. In 1951 Rogers first briefly put forward his "characteristics of the altered personality," then he enlarged on the concept of the "fully functioning person" in an unpublished paper (Rogers, 1953). In 1959 his theory of the healthy personality was expounded in the Koch series, and he returned to this topic frequently during the early 1960s (Rogers, 1961, 1962, 1963). Somewhat later he described both the world of tomorrow and "the person of tomorrow" (Rogers, 1980).

Characteristics

If the three necessary and sufficient therapeutic conditions of congruence, unconditional positive regard, and empathy are optimal, what kind of theoretically possible person would emerge? Rogers (1961, 1980) listed five characteristics.

First, persons of tomorrow would be in a *constant state of change*. They would not be end products, but emerging, evolving individuals. They would have self-structures that are fluid and flexible, and they would be comfortable with change and confident that the present, for all its richness of feeling, is not the final goal. They would realize that they have not "arrived" and that life will continue to open before them, bringing new and unexpected experiences and an accompanying change in the self-structure.

Second, persons of tomorrow would be *open to their experiences*, accurately symbolizing them in awareness rather than denying or distorting them. This simple statement is pregnant with meaning. For people who are open to experience, all stimuli, whether stemming from within the organism or from the external environment, are freely received by the self. Fully functioning people can openly accept their experiences, which allows their self-structure to be in a continual state of change and growth. For the average person, this might be a rather frightening situation, because it signifies that outside events cannot be completely controlled.

A related characteristic of persons of tomorrow is a *freshness of attitude and approach*. Because these people are open to their experiences, they are in a constant state of fluidity and change. What they experience in each moment is new and unique, something never before experienced by their evolving self. They see each experience with a new freshness, and they appreciate fully the present moment. Their experience may not be pleasant or even welcome, but they openly live it in the here and now.

Rogers (1961) referred to this tendency to live in the moment as **existential living**. This freshness of attitude and approach to each new situation becomes possible as the need for defensiveness declines. Persons of tomorrow would permit even undesirable and repugnant experiences to be symbolized in consciousness, because they have no need to deceive themselves and no reason to impress others. They are young in mind and spirit, with no preconceptions about how the world should be. They discover what an experience means to them by living that experience without the prejudice of prior expectations. They do not live by "shoulds" and "oughts" but by what is. They are unique and creative in their search for new means of adapting new solutions to problems and new ways of being.

A fourth characteristic of psychologically healthy people is a *trust in their organismic selves*. Persons of tomorrow do not depend on others for guidance because they realize that their own experiences are the best criteria for making choices; they do what feels right for them because they trust their own inner feelings more than the pontifications of parents or the rigid rules of society. However, they perceive clearly the rights and feelings of other people, which they take into consideration when making decisions.

Unlike most people who have a cloudy view of themselves and whose memories and expectations are colored by wishful thinking, persons of tomorrow would assimilate experiences without denial and distortion. Thus, their own perceptions would be their most reliable guide to action. The meanings they have discovered in their own experiences, although not infallible, would be more trustworthy than the values or opinions of any other person. Nevertheless, they would value other people and seek harmonious relationships with them.

Finally, persons of tomorrow would remain confident of their own ability to experience *harmonious relations with others*. They would feel no need to be liked or loved by everyone, because they already know that they are unconditionally prized and accepted by someone. They would seek intimacy with another person who is probably equally healthy, and such a relationship itself would contribute to the continual growth of each partner.

Persons of tomorrow would be authentic in their relations with others. They would be what they appear to be, without deceit or fraud, without defenses and façades, without hypocrisy and sham. They would care about others, but in a nonjudgmental manner. They would seek meaning beyond themselves and would yearn for the spiritual life and inner peace (Rogers, 1980).

Implications

Rogers believed that when people experience the necessary conditions for growth they become more and more fully functioning and eventually emerge as

The Rogers/Skinner Debate

One of the most famous debates in the history of American psychology took place during the mid-1950s and early 1960s between Carl Rogers and B. F. Skinner. Philosophical differences between Rogers and Skinner led to three face-to-face confrontations between them concerning the problem of freedom and control.

The initial confrontation was the most famous and took place during the 1956 convention of the American Psychological Association, where Rogers had just received the Distinguished Scientific Contribution Award. Skinner was already one of the best-known psychologists in the country, so the debate created much interest and excitement among those attending the convention and among those reading the account of it later that year in *Science* (Rogers & Skinner, 1956).

The two men were worthy adversaries. Each held firm opinions, possessed an easy command of the language, and had a good sense of humor. The symposium, titled "Some Issues Concerning the Control of Human Behavior," followed the style of a formal debate, with Skinner first presenting the behaviorist's side of the controversy, then Rogers reading his paper and reacting to Skinner's presentation, and finally Skinner giving his rebuttal to Rogers's remarks.

Two less publicized meetings followed. The first was in December of 1960 and was persons of tomorrow. What implications does this hypothesis have for the individual and for society? Rogers (1961, 1972, 1980) listed at least four.

Persons of tomorrow become *more integrated*, more whole, more "all one piece" (Rogers, 1962). They no longer have an artificial boundary between their consciousness and their unconsciousness, because they are able to accurately symbolize all their experiences in awareness; they clearly see the difference between what is and what should be, because they use their organismic feelings as criteria for evaluating their experiences; they bridge the gap between their real self and their ideal self, because they have no need for self-importance and taking pleasure in simply being themselves; they present no façades to other people, because they have confidence in who they are and can openly express whatever feelings they are experiencing (Rogers, 1962).

Second, psychologically healthy people are *more adaptable* and, thus, from an evolutionary viewpoint, they are more likely to survive—hence the title "persons of tomorrow." They are not conformists and do not adjust to a static environment. They realize that conformity and adjustment to a fixed condition have little long-term survival value. Persons of tomorrow can afford to be adaptable because they feel comfortable with change. They live in harmony with other people and balance their contributions to society with the satisfaction of their own needs.

A third implication of Rogers's description of persons of tomorrow is the *basic trustworthiness of human nature*. Psychologically healthy people will not harm others merely for personal gain, because they care about others and are ready to help when needed, even though "they are suspicious of the professional 'helpers'" (Rogers, 1980, p. 351). They experience anger, but they can be trusted not to strike out

sponsored by the American Academy of Arts and Sciences; the second took place in June of 1962 on the Duluth campus of the University of Minnesota.

In general, Skinner, during these meetings and in *Beyond Freedom and Dignity* (1971), argued that people are always controlled, whether they realize it or not. Because we are controlled mostly by haphazard contingencies that have no grand design or plan, we often have the illusion that we are free. Although we struggle for freedom, we do so in order to avoid or escape from punitive conditions within the environment, not because we have an inherent free will.

Rogers recognized the validity of much of Skinner's argument, conceding that much of human behavior is controlled by heredi-tary and environmental forces. He contended, however, that people retain some measure of freedom, some degree of subjective choice, and some capacity to be self-directed. The portion of human behavior that is controlled, predictable, and lawful comes under the aegis of science, whereas the major values and choices that people make are outside science's realm. Because science can be a powerful tool in shaping human behavior, Rogers argued, the issue of control is of grave concern to everyone. He worried about such questions as: "Who will control?" "Who will be controlled?" "What type of control will be used?" and, perhaps, most important, "For what purpose will control be exercised?" (Rogers, 1968; Rogers & Skinner, 1956).

unreasonably against others when they are angry. They feel aggression, but they can channel it in appropriate directions (Rogers, 1961).

Finally, because persons of tomorrow are open to all their experiences, they enjoy a *greater richness in life* than do other people. They neither distort internal stimuli nor buffer their emotions. Consequently they feel more deeply than others. They are able to experience both negative and positive emotions to the fullest extent. They vividly feel anger, pain, and sorrow, but they are also capable of intense joy, elation, pleasure, and love. They live in the present and thus participate more richly in the ongoing moment. The near complete confidence they have in themselves allows them to enjoy lives that are "enriching, exciting, rewarding, challenging, meaningful" (Rogers, 1961, p. 32).

Rogers (1961, p. 32) summed up the implications of fully functioning living with these words:

> This process of healthy living is not, I am convinced, a life for the fainthearted. It involves the stretching and growing of becoming more and more one's potentials. It involves the courage to be. It means launching oneself fully into the stream of life. Yet the deeply exciting thing about human beings is that when the individual is inwardly free, he chooses this process of becoming. (Rogers, 1962, p. 32)

PHILOSOPHY OF SCIENCE

According to Rogers (1968), science begins and ends with the subjective experience. Scientists must have many of the characteristics of the person of tomorrow. They must be inclined to look within, to be in tune with internal feelings and values, to be intuitive and creative, to be open to experiences, to be able to change, to have a fresh outlook, and to possess a solid trust in themselves.

In addition, scientists should be completely involved in the phenomena being studied. They must not view those phenomena too objectively, as detached outsiders. Rogers (1968) believed that people who conduct research on psychotherapy, for example, must first have had long careers as therapists. Scientists must care about and care for newly born ideas and nurture them lovingly through their fragile infancy.

Science begins when an intuitive scientist starts to perceive patterns among phenomena. At first, these dimly seen relationships may be too vague to be communicated to others, but they are nourished by a caring scientist until eventually they can be formulated into testable hypotheses. These hypotheses, then, are the consequence of the open-minded personal experiences of the scientist and not the result of pre-existing stereotypical thought. The scientist formulates hypotheses not to fit existing tools of measurement, but in accordance with the phenomena being investigated.

At this point methodology enters the picture. Although the creativity of a scientist may yield innovative methods of research, these procedures themselves must be rigorously controlled, empirical, and objective. Precise methods prevent the scientist from self-deception and from intentionally or unintentionally manipulating the observations. But this precision should not be confused with science. It is only the *methods* of science that are precise and objective.

The scientist then communicates the findings of scientific methodology to others, but the communication itself is subjective. The people receiving the communication bring their own degrees of open-mindedness or defensiveness into this process. They have varying levels of readiness to receive the findings, depending on the prevailing climate of scientific thought and the personal subjective experiences of each individual.

Consistent with his philosophy of science, Rogers did not permit methodology to dictate the nature of his research. In his investigations of the outcomes of client-centered psychotherapy, he allowed the problem to take precedence over methodology and measurement. He did not formulate hypotheses simply because the tools for testing them were readily available. Instead, he began by sensing vague impressions from clinical experience and gradually forming these into testable hypotheses. It was only then that he dealt with the task of finding or inventing instruments by which these hypotheses could be tested.

CONCEPT OF HUMANITY

Rogers evolved a basically positive and *optimistic* view of humanity. He believed that people are essentially forward-moving and, under proper conditions, will grow toward self-actualization. People are basically trustworthy, socialized, and constructive. They ordinarily know what is best for themselves and will strive for completion provided they are prized and understood by another healthy individual.

This tendency toward growth and self-actualization has a biological basis. Just as plants and animals have in their basic nature some tendency toward growth and fulfillment, so, too, do human beings. All organisms actualize themselves, but only humans can become self-actualizing. Humans are different from plants and animals primarily because they have self-awareness. To the extent that we have awareness, we are able to make free choices and to play an active role in forming our personalities. Other organisms do not possess this power. Rogers, then, is rated high on the dimension of *free choice*.

Rogers's person-centered theory is also rated high on *teleology* because it holds that people strive with purpose toward goals that they freely set for themselves. Again, under proper therapeutic conditions, people consciously desire to become more fully functioning, more open to their experiences, and more accepting of self and others.

Rogers placed more emphasis on individual differences and *uniqueness* than on similarities. If plants have individual potential for growth, people have even greater uniqueness and individuality. Within a nurturant environment, people can grow in their own fashion toward being more fully functioning. Although common elements can be extracted from an analytical study of this process, people themselves are becoming more unique and more completely themselves as this process continues.

Although Rogers did not deny the importance of unconscious processes, his primary emphasis was on the ability of people to *consciously* choose their own course of action. Fully functioning people are ordinarily aware of what they are doing and have some understanding of their reasons for doing it.

On the dimension of *biological vs. social influences*, Rogers favored the latter. Psychological growth is not automatic. In order to move toward actualization, one must experience empathic understanding and unconditional positive regard from another person who is genuine or congruent. Rogers firmly held that, although much of our behavior is determined by heredity and environment, we have within us the capacity to choose and to become self-directed. Not only do we possess the ability to choose, but under nurturant conditions "choice always seems to be in the direction of greater socialization, improved relationships with others" (Rogers, 1982a, p. 8).

People are not by nature ego-centered, socially dangerous, or evil (Rogers, 1982a, p. 8), but neither do they possess an innate morality. Rogers did not claim that, if left alone, people would be righteous, virtuous, or honorable. However, in an atmosphere without threat, people are free to become what they potentially can be. This is neither good nor bad, because these terms imply some standard of evaluation. No evaluation in terms of morality applies to the nature of humanity. People simply have the potential for growth, the need for growth, and the desire for growth. By nature they will strive for completion even under unfavorable conditions, but under poor conditions they do not realize their full potential for psychological health. However, under the most nurturant and favorable conditions, people will become more self-aware, trustworthy, congruent, and self-directed. They will become psychologically adjusted, rational, realistic, and will move toward becoming the persons of tomorrow.

Related Research

Much of the research on the effectiveness of client-centered therapy has been done by Rogers and his colleagues, first at the University of Chicago (Rogers & Dymond, 1954) and then with schizophrenic patients at the University of Wisconsin (Rogers, Gendlin, Kiesler, & Truax, 1967). His elaborate, well-designed research is unparalleled by other practicing therapists, many of whom assume the effectiveness of their therapy without benefit of scientific evidence. Rogers, on the other hand, was a researcher as well as a theorist and therapist. He designed research to test the validity of his early theoretical hunches, and, as the results of this testing tended to confirm his assumptions, he became encouraged to set forth his first tentative theory of personality (Rogers, 1959).

In this section we look at Rogers's famous Chicago studies, more recent research on client-centered theory, and then return to the case of Mrs. Oak.

Chicago Studies

Scientifically, the years Rogers spent at the University of Chicago were his most productive, even though throughout his entire career he was fervently devoted to science and its findings. During his Wisconsin period he was deeply involved with a major study of psychotherapy with schizophrenics (Rogers et al., 1967), and in California he continued to conduct research on the person-centered approach to teaching and learning (Rogers, 1974, 1983). However, his research at the Counseling Center at Chicago best exemplifies his scientific work (Rogers & Dymond, 1954).

The purpose of the Chicago studies was to investigate both the process and the outcomes of client-centered therapy. The therapists were of a "journeyman" level. They included Rogers and other faculty members, but graduate students also served as therapists. Although they ranged widely in experience and ability, all were basically client-centered in approach (Rogers, 1955, 1961; Rogers & Dymond, 1954).

Hypotheses

Research at the Counseling Center was built around the basic client-centered hypothesis, which states that all persons have within themselves the capacity, either active or latent, for self-understanding as well as the capacity and tendency to move in the direction of self-actualization and maturity. This tendency will become realized provided the therapist creates the proper psychological atmosphere (Rogers, 1954).

More specifically, Rogers hypothesized that during therapy clients would assimilate into their self-concepts feelings and experiences previously denied to awareness; the discrepancy between real self and ideal self would lessen as a concomitant of therapy; the observed behavior of clients would become more socialized and mature as a result of therapy; during and after therapy clients would become both more self-accepting and more accepting of others. These hypotheses, in turn, became the foundation for several more specific hypotheses, which were operationally stated and then tested.

Selection of Instruments

Because the hypotheses of the study dictated that subtle subjective personality changes be measured in an objective fashion, the selection of measurement instruments was difficult. To assess change from an external viewpoint, the researchers used the Thematic Apperception Test (TAT), the Self-Other Attitude Scale (S-O Scale), and the Willoughby Emotional Maturity Scale (E-M Scale). The TAT, a projective personality test developed by Henry Murray (1938), was used to test hypotheses that called for a standard clinical diagnosis; the S-O Scale, an instrument compiled at the Counseling Center from several earlier sources, measures antidemocratic trends and ethnocentrism; the E-M Scale was used to compare descriptions of clients' behavior and emotional maturity as seen by two close friends and by the clients themselves.

To measure change from the client's point of view (a procedure quite consistent with client-centered theory) the Research Group relied on the then-new **Q-sort** technique developed by William Stephenson of the University of Chicago (Stephenson, 1953). The Q-sort technique begins with a universe of 100 self-referent statements printed on 3 × 5 cards, which subjects are requested to sort into nine piles from "most like me" to "least like me." Some of the items were judged by an independent group of clinicians to describe the well-adjusted person, some the poorly-adjusted person, and for others the clinicians could not agree. Examples of these self-referent items include: "I express my emotions freely"; "My personality is attractive to the opposite sex"; "I put on a false front"; "I really am disturbed"; and "I am a submissive person" (Dymond, 1954a). Researchers asked the subjects to sort the cards into piles of 1, 4, 11, 21, 26, 21, 11, 4, and 1. The resulting distribution approximates a normal curve and allows statisticians to analyze the data by correlational and factor analytic means. At various points throughout the study, subjects were requested to sort the cards to describe the self, the ideal self, and the ordinary person.

Subjects and Procedure

Subjects for the study were 18 men and 11 women who had sought therapy at the Counseling Center at the University of Chicago. They ranged in age from 21 to 40 with a mean of 27. More than half were university students, whereas the others were from the surrounding community. These subjects, called the experimental or *therapy group*, were randomly selected from the population of adult clientele at the Counseling Center. They were, however, stratified for sex and student/nonstudent status. All subjects in the experimental group received at least six therapeutic interviews and each session was electronically recorded and transcribed, a procedure Rogers had pioneered as early as 1938, and one that typically required approximately 700 hours of data gathering per subject (Grummon, 1954).

The researchers used two different methods of control. First, they asked half the people in the therapy group to wait 60 days before they would receive therapy. These subjects, known as the own-control or *wait group*, were required to wait before receiving therapy in order to determine if motivation to change rather than the therapy itself might cause people to get better. The other half of the therapy group, called the *no-wait group*, received therapy immediately.

The second control consisted of a separate group of "normals" who had volunteered to serve as subjects for "research on personality." This group was matched with the therapy group on sex, student/nonstudent status, and approximate socioeconomic level. Researchers needed this control group to determine the effects of such variables as passage of time, knowledge that one is part of an experiment (the placebo effect), and the impact of repeated testing. The 23 subjects in this *control group* were divided into a *wait group* and a *nonwait group*, which corresponded to the wait and nonwait therapy groups. Researchers tested both the therapy wait group and the control wait group four times: at the beginning of the 60-day wait period, prior to therapy, immediately after therapy, and after a 6- to 12-month follow-up period. They administered the nonwait

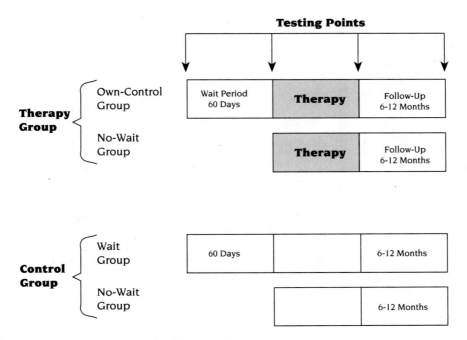

Figure 16.1 *Design of the Chicago Study*

groups the same tests on the same occasions, except, of course, prior to the wait period. The follow-up period was used as a check for the permanence of any change that might take place during therapy. The overall design of the study is shown in Figure 16.1.

Findings

As hypothesized, the therapy group showed less discrepancy between self and self-ideal after therapy than before. Prior to counseling the correlation between self and self-ideal was −0.01, indicating an almost total lack of relationship. After therapy the correlation was 0.34, demonstrating a significant (but still modest) degree of congruence between self and self-ideal. At the end of the follow-up period, subjects had retained most of their gains, as indicated by a positive correlation of 0.31.

In contrast, the control group showed almost no change from the initial testing until the final follow-up. The corresponding correlations between self and self-ideal for the control group were 0.58 and 0.59, thus indicating a higher level of congruence at both the beginning and the end of the study. The higher correlations were expected, because these were normal subjects who were not seeking therapy but merely volunteering for a research study.

The researchers also hypothesized that the real self of the therapy group would change more than the ideal self. Although the gap between the real and the ideal self narrowed because the ideal self became more "realistic" and the real self became healthier, the greater change took place in the real self, thereby supporting the hypothesis (Butler & Haigh, 1954).

The real self also changed more than the clients' perception of the ordinary person, meaning that, although clients showed little change in their notion of what the average person was like, they manifested marked change in their perceptions of self. This finding suggests that intellectual insight does not result in psychological growth (Rudikoff, 1954).

Using the TAT as a criterion for change, the researchers found that the therapy group, which prior to therapy was more disturbed than the control group, showed marked improvement at the posttherapy point and also at the end of the follow-up period. The control group made no corresponding gains. This is an important finding because the TAT is based on theoretical grounds nearly 180 degrees removed from Rogerian theory (Dymond, 1954b).

To test the hypothesis that clients in therapy would change their attitudes toward others, the researchers used the S-O Scale, which was designed to measure prejudicial and authoritarian attitudes toward others. Because the researchers found no significant changes in the experimental group from pretherapy to posttherapy to follow-up and also no significant differences between the therapy group and the control group in authoritarian attitudes, they were forced to conclude that clients receiving client-centered therapy do *not* demonstrate a greater acceptance of and respect for others (Gordon & Cartwright, 1954).

Does therapy bring about noticeable changes in clients' behavior as perceived by close friends? All subjects, in both the therapy and the control groups, were asked to supply the experimenters with names of two intimate friends who would be in a position to judge overt behavioral changes. Researchers used letters to contact these friends, who did not know the true nature of the study. Subjects and friends alike filled out the Willoughby E-M Scale, rating the subject for emotional maturity in several everyday situations.

The friends reported no significant behavioral changes in the clients from the pretherapy period to posttherapy. However, this global rating of no change was due to a counterbalancing effect. Clients judged by their therapists as being most improved received higher posttherapy maturity scores from their friends, while those rated as least improved received lower scores from their friends. Interestingly, before therapy, clients typically rated themselves less mature than their friends rated them, but as therapy progressed, they began to rate themselves higher and, therefore, more in agreement with their friends' ratings. Subjects in the control group showed no changes throughout the study in emotional maturity as judged by friends (Rogers & Dymond, 1954).

Summary of Results

The Chicago studies continue to be some of the best-designed investigations of the outcomes of psychotherapy. The studies demonstrated that people receiving client-centered therapy, in general, show some growth or improvement. However, improvement fell short of the optimum. The therapy group began treatment as less healthy than the control group, then showed growth during therapy and retained most of it throughout the follow-up period. However, they never attained the level of psychological health demonstrated by those in the control group.

Looking at these outcomes another way, the typical person receiving client-centered therapy probably never approaches Stage Seven, hypothesized by Rogers and discussed above. A more realistic expectation might be for the client to advance to Stage Three or Four. Client-centered therapy is effective, but it does not result in the fully functioning person.

Later Research on the Growth-Facilitative Conditions

Since Rogers and Dymond's (1954) report, other investigators have looked at the outcomes of client-centered therapy. Charles Truax and Robert Carkhuff (1967) slightly changed Rogers's necessary and sufficient conditions to (1) accurate empathy, (2) nonpossessive warmth, and (3) counselor genuineness. Next, they developed scales to measure these conditions and then conducted more than a dozen studies, using several different therapeutic orientations, different levels of therapist experience, and a wide variety of clients in both group and individual therapy. They also used a variety of dependent variables, including grade point average (for college students), Q-sort ratings, and standardized personality inventories.

In support of Rogers, Truax and Carkhuff found that accurate empathy, nonpossessive warmth, and genuineness were related to positive change over a wide range of therapies. But they also found that other conditions, such as time limits and frequency of sessions, were likewise related to successful outcome. They therefore concluded that "the therapeutic triad may or may not be 'necessary' but it is clearly not 'sufficient'" (Truax & Carkhuff, 1967, p. 114).

During the past decade, Duncan Cramer in Great Britain has investigated the therapeutic qualities of Rogers's facilitative conditions in interpersonal relationships outside of therapy. Typically, Cramer administers the Rosenberg (1965) Self-Esteem Scale and the revised Relationship Inventory (Barrett-Lennard, 1964) to a group of college women and men to determine the relationship between Rogers's facilitative conditions and self-esteem. The Barrett-Lennard (1962, 1964) Relationship Inventory was developed to assess client's perceptions of therapist's congruence, unconditional positive regard, and empathy, but it divides unconditional positive regard into two separate components, namely level of regard and unconditionality of regard. Thus, the revised Relationship Inventory measures four facilitative conditions, but it is not limited to clients' perception of their therapist—it can be used to describe any relationship. The four scales contain 16 items each. Examples include: "She/he cares for me" (level of regard); "Her/his feelings toward me don't depend on how I feel toward him/her" (unconditionality of regard); "She/he almost always knows exactly what I mean" (empathy); and "She/he is comfortable and at ease in our relationship" (congruence). Cramer employs the revised Relationship Inventory to assess college students' perception of various close relationships.

In one study, for example, Cramer (1985) used the Rosenberg Self-Esteem Scale as a measure of psychological health and the revised Relationship Inventory as an assessment of Rogerian facilitative conditions. Rather than requiring subjects to use a therapist as the target person, Cramer asked subjects for their descriptions of a close friend. He found significant positive correlations for female students between their level of self-esteem and all four facilitative conditions, suggesting that women perceive their close friends as being congruent and as providing unconditional positive regard and empathy. For men the correlations were positive, but, because the sample size was small, they were significant only for level of regard and for the combination of all four facilitative conditions.

Because he tested few men in his 1985 study, Cramer (1987) conducted a similar investigation using a larger sample size. Besides including more men, he also used a statistical analysis that allowed him to determine which of four facilitative conditions was most directly related to self-esteem, and he also tested the hypothesis that advice from a close friend would be negatively related to self-esteem. In this study Cramer asked 232 women and 87 men to describe their relationship with their closest friend. He also constructed a 16-item scale for measuring the importance of advice received from a friend and incorporated this scale into the Relationship Inventory. Again, he used the Rosenberg Self-Esteem Scale as a measure of self-esteem and psychological health.

Cramer (1987) found significant positive correlations between self-esteem and all four facilitative variables for women, and between self-esteem and level of regard, congruence, and empathy for men. Thus, the only condition that did not attain significance was unconditionality of regard for male students. The correlations, however, were only low to moderate, and when the influence of level of regard was controlled for, the correlations between the three remaining facilitative conditions and self-esteem failed to reach significance. This finding tends to support Rogers's hypothesis that all three conditions are necessary; that is, the therapist must be perceived as exhibiting all of the conditions, not just one or two.

Contrary to Rogers, however, Cramer could find no negative correlation between self-esteem and providing advice. In fact, he found that both female and male students saw their closest friend as giving them advice, and that friends who provide advice are the ones who are seen as exhibiting positive regard, unconditionality of regard, empathy, and congruence.

In 1988, Cramer conducted a similar study, except that he introduced the element of time; that is, he asked college students to respond to the Self-Esteem Scale and the Barrett-Lennard Relationship Inventory near the beginning of the school year and then again 15 weeks later. He obtained complete data from 35 women and 27 men. For the first testing, self-esteem was related only to level of regard, perhaps because students did not yet know one another well, or because they named friends from whom they were separated. For the second testing session, however, Cramer found significant and positive correlations between self-esteem and level of regard, empathy, congruence, and total score. Thus, unconditionality of regard had the weakest relationship with self-esteem.

Cramer (1989) expanded his study once more—this time to include parents as well as close friends. He asked 163 female and 31 male subjects, 16 to 18 years old, to fill out the Self-Esteem Scale and the revised Relationship Inventory, which targeted their mother, father, closest friend of the same sex, and closest friend of the opposite sex. Again, he found positive relationships between self-esteem and the facilitative conditions, but, more importantly, he found no differences in the size of the correlations for the four facilitative conditions among any of the four relationships, which suggests that young people with positive self-esteem tend to have growth-producing relationships with more than one person.

Next, Cramer (1990) determined the correlations among self-esteem, disclosure of personal problems, and the facilitative conditions of unconditional acceptance, empathy, and congruence. He administered the Rosenberg Self-Esteem Scale and the revised Barrett-Lennard Relationship Inventory along with an index of disclosure of personal problems to 104 young women and 19 young men and asked them to target four different relationships—a casual friend, the closest friend of the same sex, the closest friend of the opposite sex, and a romantic partner. Cramer found that self-esteem was most closely associated with the facilitative conditions in the romantic partner. Interestingly, the second highest correlations were found for self-esteem and the facilitative qualities in the casual friend. In addition, Cramer found that disclosure of personal problems was positively related to the facilitative conditions, meaning that people were willing to reveal important aspects of themselves to friends whom they perceived as being congruent and as possessing empathy and unconditional positive regard.

These studies suggest that Rogers's "necessary and sufficient" conditions are related to self-esteem and psychological health, but they do not prove that congruence, unconditional positive regard, and empathy *cause* people to move toward becoming fully functioning. More experimental research is clearly needed in both therapeutic and everyday relationships before Rogers's basic hypotheses can be demonstrated.

The Case of Mrs. Oak

Rogers's philosophy of science was broad enough to include **quasi-experimental designs**, such as the one used in the Chicago studies, as well as case studies, such as Mrs. Oak, the woman we met at the beginning of this chapter (Rogers, 1954a).

When Mrs. Oak (a fictitious name) sought help at the University of Chicago Counseling Center, she was frustrated, miserable, and generally unhappy. A housewife in her late thirties, she complained of an antagonistic relationship with her husband and of guilt over her adolescent daughter's psychosomatic illness. During the early stages of therapy, she talked mostly of other people. When she did speak about herself, it was as if she were an object, someone who was burdened with problems and who wanted to find the causes of her unhappiness. She had unrealistically high aspirations and a strong need to be perfect in nearly everything she did. At this time she felt unattractive, rebellious, useless, and deeply conflicted over her sexual identity. Her therapist saw her as shy, almost nondescript, and nearly incoherent. She expressed herself in "jumbled analogies, half-sentences, and incomplete thoughts" (Rogers, 1954a, p. 164). As therapy progressed, Mrs. Oak became less problem-oriented, better able to express herself, and more self-confident.

Once she realized that the therapist *cared* for her, she began to experience herself in a more positive way. "She gradually became aware of the fact that, though she had searched in every corner of herself, there was nothing fundamentally bad but, rather, at heart she was positive and sound" (Rogers, 1954a, p. 263).

At the end of 40 counseling interviews, Mrs. Oak had experienced considerable change in her self-concept. She saw herself as being more self-sufficient, more integrated or whole, and less threatened by people. She was still in conflict over her sexuality and continued to be somewhat pessimistic and depressed. Nevertheless, she was confident that she would continue to make progress even in the absence of further psychotherapy.

However, Mrs. Oak did receive more psychotherapy. Seven months after therapy, she returned for follow-up testing and at that time decided to resume counseling in order to clear up a few things. Subsequently, she received eight additional therapy sessions.

When therapy was over, Mrs. Oak had divorced her husband, taken a job, and improved her relationship with her daughter. She was no longer striving to be perfect but was content to relax and enjoy life.

Many months before this case study was completed, Rogers (1951, p. 195) had written a theoretical statement that predicted the changes that took place within Mrs. Oak during the process of therapy:

> Thus therapy produces a change in personality organization and structure, and a change in behavior, both of which are relatively permanent. It is not necessarily a reorganization which will serve for a lifetime. It may still deny to awareness certain aspects of experience, may still exhibit certain patterns of defensive behavior. There is little likelihood that any therapy is in this sense complete. Under new stresses of a certain sort, the client may find it necessary to seek further therapy, to achieve further reorganization of self. But whether there be one or more series of therapeutic interviews, the essential outcome is a more broadly based structure of self, an inclusion of a greater proportion of experience as part of self, and a more comfortable and realistic adjustment to life.

CRITIQUE OF ROGERS

How well does Rogerian theory satisfy the five criteria of a useful theory? The first criterion of a useful theory is the ability to *generate research* and testable hypotheses. Although Rogerian theory has generated much research in the realm of psychotherapy and classroom learning (see Rogers, 1983), it has been only moderately productive outside these two areas and thus receives only an average rating on its ability to spark research activity within the general field of personality.

Does Rogerian theory *organize knowledge* into a meaningful framework? Although much of the research generated by the theory has been limited to interpersonal relations, the theory nevertheless can be extended to a relatively wide range of human personality. Rogers's interests went beyond the consulting room and included group dynamics, classroom learning, social problems, and international relations. Thus person-centered theory receives a high rating on its ability to explain what is currently known about human behavior.

How does person-centered theory serve as a *guide for the solution of practical problems*? For the psychotherapist, the answer is unequivocal. To bring about personality change, the therapist must possess congruence and be able to demonstrate empathic understanding and unconditional positive regard for the client. Rogers suggested that these three conditions are both necessary and sufficient to effect growth in any interpersonal relationship, including those outside of therapy.

The fourth criterion of a useful theory is *internal consistency* and a set of operational definitions. Person-centered theory must receive a very high rating for its consistency and its carefully worked-out operational definitions. Future theory builders can learn a valuable lesson from Rogers's pioneering work in constructing a theory of personality.

Finally, is Rogerian theory *parsimonious* and free from cumbersome concepts and difficult language? The theory itself is unusually clear and economical, but some of the language seems needlessly awkward and vague. Concepts such as "unconditional positive regard," "organismic experiencing," "becoming," "symbolization," and "fully functioning" are too broad and imprecise to have any scientific meaning. This is a small criticism, however, in comparison with the overall tightness and parsimony of person-centered theory.

Chapter Summary

Person-centered theory of personality grew out of Rogers's experiences as a client-centered therapist, and is an expression of his fundamental belief that, under proper conditions, people will move inevitably toward psychological growth and fulfillment. This assumption follows from a more general notion that all matter, both organic and inorganic, tends to evolve from simple to more complex forms. Rogers called this the *formative tendency.*

Somewhat more specific is the *actualizing tendency*, or people's movement toward completion or fulfillment. During early infancy a person begins to evolve a self-system, which eventually includes a *self-concept* (perceived self). At that point the person seeks *self-actualization*, or fulfillment of the self as perceived. *Incongruence* develops when the organismic (real) self and the perceived self do not match. In order to bring the organismic self and the perceived self together, people distort or deny certain aspects of their experience.

Rogers postulated that we are guided by two basic needs— *maintenance* and *enhancement* of our perceived selves. In addition, we need positive regard, first from others, then from ourselves. Conditions of worth and external evaluation prevent us from experiencing unconditional positive regard and may lead to psychological maladjustment.

Maladjusted people are characterized by incongruence between self and experience; *vulnerability*, or an unawareness of their incongruence; and *anxiety*, *threat*, and *defensiveness*. When their defenses of *denial* and *distortion* are insufficient to block out incongruence, they become *disorganized.*

Rogerian therapy can be stated quite simply. If clients receive certain *conditions*, then they will undergo the *process* of therapy, which will have certain predictable *outcomes.* The three necessary and sufficient therapeutic *conditions* are (1) *counselor congruence*, (2) *empathic listening*, and (3) *unconditional positive regard.*

The *process* of therapeutic personality change ranges from extreme defensiveness, or unwillingness to talk about self, to the final stage in which clients are their own therapists and are able to continue psychological growth outside the therapeutic setting.

The basic *outcomes* of client-centered counseling are congruent clients who are open to experiences and who have no need to be defensive. They approach Rogers's concept of a *fully functioning person*, or *person of tomorrow*. They are characterized by (1) a constant state of change, (2) an increasing openness to experience, (3) a fresh attitude and approach toward life, (4) trust in self, and (5) harmonious relations with others.

Rogers's view of humanity was basically positive and optimistic, because it holds that through proper conditions people will move toward becoming more open to their experiences and more self-actualizing.

Suggested Readings

EVANS, R. I. (1981). *Dialogue with Carl Rogers.* New York: Praeger.
   Evans's book contains not only his lively discussion with Rogers but also the Rogers/ Skinner debate, a tribute to Rogers by Richard Farson, Rogers's 1973 address to the APA, and one of Rogers's latest papers on "the emerging person."

KIRSCHENBAUM, H. (1979). *On becoming Carl Rogers.* New York: Delacorte Press.

   The best and most complete source for biographical information on Rogers, Kirschenbaum's book adopts a highly favorable attitude toward the father of client-centered therapy and person-centered theory.

KIRSCHENBAUM, H., & HENDERSON, V. L. (Eds.). (1989). *The Carl Rogers reader.* Boston: Houghton Mifflin.

   In this single volume, Kirschenbaum and Henderson have managed to include nearly all of Rogers's most important writings, including his 1959 chapter, "A Theory of Therapy, Personality, and Interpersonal Relationships, As Developed in the Client-Centered Framework."

ROGERS, C. R. (1959). A theory of therapy, personality, and interpersonal relationships, as developed in the client-centered framework. In S. Koch (Ed.), *Psychology: A study of a science* (Vol. 3) (pp. 184-246). New York: McGraw-Hill.

   Although this chapter is included in the Kirschenbaum and Henderson (1989) book of readings, it is important enough to recommend again in the event that the Kirschenbaum and Henderson book is not available. Rogers remained disappointed that this frequently referenced chapter was not more widely read.

ROGERS, C. R. (1961). *On becoming a person: A therapist's view of psychotherapy.* Boston: Houghton-Mifflin.

   Rogers's most popular book, this volume is actually a collection of papers written during the previous decade.

ROGERS, C. R. (1980). *A way of being.* Boston: Houghton-Mifflin.

   Reflecting changes that occurred in his life and work during the decade of the 1970s, this book presents Rogers's most recent thoughts.

THORNE, B. (1992). *Carl Rogers.* London: Sage.

   In this brief book, Thorne presents an overview of Rogers's life, his theoretical contributions, and his views on psychotherapy. Thorne also includes a critique of Rogers and a summary of his contributions to the creation of a person-centered society.

Existential Psychology

OVERVIEW
BIOGRAPHY OF ROLLO MAY
BACKGROUND OF EXISTENTIALISM
    What Is Existentialism?
    Basic Concepts
ANXIETY
    Normal Anxiety
    Neurotic Anxiety
GUILT
INTENTIONALITY
CARE, LOVE, AND WILL
    Union of Love and Will
    Forms of Love
FREEDOM AND DESTINY
    Freedom Defined
    Forms of Freedom
    Destiny Defined
    Philip's Destiny
THE POWER OF MYTH
PSYCHOPATHOLOGY
PSYCHOTHERAPY
CONCEPT OF HUMANITY
RELATED RESEARCH
CRITIQUE OF MAY
CHAPTER SUMMARY
SUGGESTED READINGS

Chapter
Seventeen

M A Y

Photo credit: Jill Krementz

*T*wice married, twice divorced, Philip was struggling through yet another relationship. A successful architect in his mid-fifties, Philip could offer Nicole both love and financial security.

Six months after Philip met Nicole, a writer in her mid-forties, the two spent an idyllic summer together at his retreat. Nicole's two small sons were with their father and Philip's three children were by then young adults who could care for themselves. At the beginning of the summer Nicole talked about the possibility of marriage, but Philip replied that he was against it, citing his two previous unsuccessful marriages as his reason. Aside from this brief disagreement, the time they spent together that summer was completely pleasurable. Their intellectual discussions were gratifying to Philip and their lovemaking was the most satisfying he had ever experienced, often bordering on ecstasy. In addition to the intellectual and sexual stimulation, both Philip and Nicole were able to work productively—he on his architectural designs, she on her writing.

At the end of this romantic summer, Nicole returned home alone to put her children in school. The day after she arrived home, Philip telephoned her, but somehow her voice seemed strange. The next morning he called again and got the feeling that someone else was with Nicole. That afternoon he called several more times but kept getting a busy signal. When he finally got through, he asked her if someone had, indeed, been with her that morning. Without hesitation, Nicole reported that Craig, an old friend from her college days, had been staying with her and that she had fallen in love with him. Moreover, she planned to marry Craig at the end of the month and move to another part of the country.

Philip was devastated. He felt betrayed and abandoned. He lost weight, resumed smoking, and suffered from insomnia. When he saw Nicole again, he expressed his anger at her "crazy" plan. This outburst of rage was rare for Philip. He seldom showed anger, perhaps for fear of losing the one he loved. To complicate matters, Nicole said she still loved Philip and continued to see him whenever Craig was not available. Eventually, Nicole lost her infatuation for Craig and told Philip that, as he well knew, she could never leave him. This surprised Philip because he knew no such thing. Nevertheless, he accepted her statement because he needed to be desired by Nicole.

About a year later, Philip learned that Nicole had had another affair, but before he could confront her and break off their relationship, he had to leave for a five-day business trip. By the time he returned he was able to reason that, perhaps, he could accept Nicole's right to sleep with other men. Also, Nicole convinced him that the other man didn't mean anything to her and that she loved only Philip.

A little later, Nicole had a third affair, one which she made sure Philip would discover. Once again, Philip was filled with anger and jealousy. But once again, Nicole reassured him that the man meant nothing to her.

On one level Philip wished to accept Nicole's behavior, but on another he felt betrayed by her affairs. Yet, he did not seem to be able to leave her and to search for some other woman to love. He was paralyzed—unable to change his relationship with Nicole, but also unable to break it off. At this point in Philip's life, he sought therapy from Dr. Rollo May.

OVERVIEW

Shortly after World War II a new psychology—existential psychology—began to spread from Europe to the United States. Existential psychology is rooted in the philosophy of Søren Kierkegaard, Friedrich Nietzsche, Martin Heidegger, Jean-Paul Sartre, and other European writers. The first existential psychologists were also Europeans, and these included Ludwig Binswanger, Medard Boss, Victor Frankl, and others.

For the past 40 years the foremost spokesperson for existential psychology in the United States has been Rollo May. During his years as a psychotherapist, May evolved a new way of looking at human beings. His approach is not based on any controlled scientific research, but rather on clinical experience. He sees people as living in the world of present experiences and ultimately being responsible for what they become. May's penetrating insights and profound analyses of the human condition have made him a popular writer among lay people and professional psychologists.

Many people, May believes, lack the courage to face their destiny, and in the process of fleeing from it they give up much of their freedom. Having negated their freedom, they likewise run away from their responsibility. Not being willing to make choices, they lose sight of who they are and develop a sense of insignificance and alienation. Healthy people, on the other hand, challenge their destiny, cherish their freedom, and live authentically with other people and with themselves. They recognize the inevitability of death and have the courage to live life in the present.

BIOGRAPHY OF ROLLO MAY

Rollo Reese May was born April 21, 1909, in Ada, Ohio, the first son of the six children born to Earl Tittle May and Matie Boughton May. Neither parent was very well educated and May's early intellectual climate was virtually nonexistent. In fact, when his older sister had a psychotic breakdown some years later, May's father attributed it to too much education (Bilmes, 1978)!

At an early age, May moved with his family to Marine City, Michigan, where he spent most of his childhood. As a child Rollo was not particularly close to either of his parents, who frequently argued with each other and eventually separated. May's father was a YMCA secretary who moved frequently during Rollo's youth. His mother, according to May's description, was a "bitch-kitty on wheels," and he attributed his own two failed marriages to her unpredictable behavior and to his older sister's psychotic episode (Rabinowitz, Good, & Cozad, 1989, p. 437).

During his childhood, May found solitude and relief from family strife by playing on the shores of the St. Clair River. The river became his friend, a serene place to swim during the summer and to ice skate during the winter. He claimed to have learned more from the river than from the school he attended in Marine City (Rabinowitz et al., 1989). As a youth he acquired an interest in art and literature, interests that never left him. He attended college at Michigan State, where he majored in English. However, he was asked to leave school soon after he became editor of a radical student magazine. May then transferred to Oberlin College in Ohio, from which he received a bachelor's degree in 1930.

For the next three years, May followed a course very similar to the one traveled by Erik Erikson (see Chapter 3) some 10 years earlier. He roamed throughout eastern and southern Europe as an artist painting pictures and studying native art (Harris, 1969). Actually, the nominal purpose for May's trip was to tutor English at Anatolia College, in Saloniki, Greece. This job provided him time to work as an itinerant artist in Turkey, Poland, Austria, and other countries. However, by his second year, May was beginning to become lonely. As a consequence, he poured himself into his work as a teacher, but the harder he worked the less effective he became.

> Finally in the spring of that second year I had what is called, euphemistically, a nervous breakdown. Which meant simply that the rules, principles, values, by which I used to work and live simply did not suffice anymore. I got so completely fatigued that I had to go to bed for two weeks to get enough energy to continue my teaching. I had learned enough psychology at college to know that these symptoms meant that something was wrong with my whole way of life. I had to find some new goals and purposes for my living and to relinquish my moralistic, somewhat rigid way of existence. (May, 1985, p. 8)

From that point on, May began to listen to his inner voice, the one that spoke to him of beauty. "It seems it had taken a collapse of my whole former way of life for this voice to make itself heard" (May, 1985, p. 13).

A second experience in Europe also left a lasting impression on him, namely his attendance at Alfred Adler's summer seminars at a resort in the mountains above Vienna. May greatly admired Adler and learned much about human behavior and about himself during that time (Rabinowitz et al., 1989).

After May returned to the United States in 1933, he enrolled at Union

Theological Seminary in New York, the same seminary Carl Rogers had attended 10 years earlier. Unlike Rogers, however, May did not enter the seminary in order to become a minister but rather to ask the ultimate questions concerning the nature of human beings (Harris, 1969). While at the Union Theological Seminary, he met the renowned existential theologian and philosopher Paul Tillich, then a recent refugee from Germany and a faculty member at the seminary. May learned much of his philosophy from Tillich, and the two men remained friends for over 30 years.

Although May had not gone to seminary to be a preacher, he was ordained as a Congregational minister in 1938 after receiving a Master of Divinity degree. He then served as a pastor for two years, but, finding parish work meaningless, he quit in order to pursue his interest in psychology. He studied psychoanalysis at the William Alanson White Institute of Psychiatry, Psychoanalysis, and Psychology while working as a counselor to male students at City College of New York. At about this time he met Harry Stack Sullivan (see Chapter 6), president and co-founder of the William Alanson White Institute. May was impressed with Sullivan's notion that the therapist is a participant observer and that therapy is a human adventure capable of enhancing the life of both patient and therapist. He also met and was influenced by Erich Fromm (see Chapter 7), who at that time was a faculty member at the William Alanson White Institute.

In 1946, May opened his own private practice and two years later joined the faculty of the William Alanson White Institute. In 1949, at the relatively advanced age of 40, he earned the first Ph.D. in clinical psychology awarded by Columbia University. He continued to serve as assistant professor of psychiatry at the William Alanson White Institute until 1974.

Prior to receiving his doctorate, May underwent the most profound experience of his life. While still in his early thirties, he contracted tuberculosis and spent three years at the Saranac Sanitarium in upstate New York. At that time no medication for the disease was available, and for a year and a half May did not know whether he would live or die. He felt helpless and had little to do except wait for the monthly X-ray that would tell whether the cavity in his lung was getting larger or smaller (May, 1972).

At that point, he began to develop some insight into the nature of his illness. He realized that the disease was taking advantage of his helpless and passive attitude. He saw that the patients around him who accepted their illness were the very ones who tended to die, whereas those who fought against their condition tended to survive. "Not until I developed some 'fight,' some sense of personal responsibility for the fact that it was *I* who had the tuberculosis, an assertion of my own will to live, did I make lasting progress" (May, 1972, p. 14).

As May learned to listen to his body he discovered that healing is an active, not a passive, process. The person who is sick, be it physiologically or psychologically, must be an active participant in the therapeutic process. May realized this truth for himself as he recovered from tuberculosis, but it was only later that he was able to see that his psychotherapy patients also had to fight against their disturbance in order to get better (May, 1972).

During his illness and recovery, May was writing a book on anxiety. To better understand the subject, he read both Freud and Søren Kierkegaard, the great Danish existential philosopher and theologian. He admired Freud, but he was more deeply moved by Kierkegaard's view of anxiety as a struggle against *nonbeing*: that is, loss of consciousness (May, 1969a).

After May recovered from his illness, he wrote his dissertation on the subject of anxiety and the next year published it under the title *The Meaning of Anxiety* (May, 1950). Three years later he wrote *Man's Search for Himself* (May, 1953), the book that gained for him some recognition, not only in professional circles, but among other educated people as well. In 1958 he collaborated with Ernest Angel and Henri Ellenberger to publish *Existence: A New Dimension in Psychiatry and Psychology*. This book introduced American psychotherapists to the concepts of existential therapy and continued the popularity of the existential movement. May's best-known work, *Love and Will* (1969c), became a national best-seller and won the 1970 Ralph Waldo Emerson Award for humane scholarship. In 1971, the American Psychological Association awarded him for distinguished contribution to the science and profession of clinical psychology, and in 1972, the New York Society of Clinical Psychologists presented him with the Dr. Martin Luther King, Jr.,

Award for his book, *Power and Innocence* (1972).

May has been a visiting professor at both Harvard and Princeton and has lectured at such institutions as Yale, Dartmouth, Columbia, Vassar, Oberlin, and the New School for Social Research. In addition, he has been an adjunct professor at New York University, chairman for the Council for the Association of Existential Psychology and Psychiatry, president of the New York Psychological Association, and a member of the Board of Trustees of the American Foundation for Mental Health. May, who is twice married, twice divorced, has twin daughters and a son from his first marriage. He has lived in Tiburon, California, since 1975.

Through his books, articles, and lectures, May has become the best-known American representative of the existential movement. Nevertheless, he has spoken out against the tendency of some existentialists to slip into an antiscientific or even anti-intellectual posture (May, 1962). He has been critical of any attempt to dilute existential psychology into a painless method of reaching self-fulfillment. People can aspire to psychological health only through coming to grips with the unconscious core of their existence. Although he is philosophically aligned with Carl Rogers (see Chapter 16), May takes issue with what he sees as Rogers's naïve view that evil is a cultural phenomenon. To May (1982), human beings are both good and evil, prompting them to create cultures that are both good and evil.

BACKGROUND OF EXISTENTIALISM

Modern existential psychology has it roots in the writings of Søren Kierkegaard (1813–1855), Danish philosopher and theologian. Kierkegaard was concerned with the increasing trend in modern societies toward the dehumanization of people. He opposed any attempt to see people merely as objects, but, at the same time, he opposed the view that subjective perceptions are one's only reality. Instead, Kierkegaard was concerned with *both* the experiencing person and the person's experience. He wished to understand people as they exist in the world as thinking, active, and willing beings. As May (1967, p. 67) put it, "Kierkegaard sought to overcome the dichotomy of reason and emotion by turning men's attentions to the reality of the immediate experience which underlies both subjectivity and objectivity."

Kierkegaard, like later existentialists, emphasized a balance between *freedom* and *responsibility*. People acquire freedom of action through expanding their self-awareness and then by assuming responsibility for their actions. The acquisition of freedom and responsibility, however, is achieved only at the expense of anxiety. As people realize that, ultimately, they are in charge of their own destiny, they experience the burden of freedom and the pain of responsibility.

Kierkegaard's views had little effect on philosophical thought during his comparatively short lifetime (he died at age 42), but the work of two German philosophers, Friedrich Nietzsche (1844–1900) and Martin Heidegger (1899–1976), helped carry existential philosophy into the 20th century. Heidegger especially exerted considerable influence on two Swiss psychiatrists, Ludwig Binswanger and Medard Boss. Binswanger and Boss, along with Karl Jaspers, Victor Frankl, and others, adapted the philosophy of existentialism to the practice of psychotherapy.

Existentialism has also permeated modern literature through the work of the French writer Jean-Paul Sartre and the French-Algerian novelist Albert Camus; religion through the writings of Martin Buber, Paul Tillich, and others; and the world of art through the work of Cezanne, Matisse, and Picasso, whose paintings break through the boundaries of realism and demonstrate a freedom of being rather than the freedom of doing (May, 1981).

After World II, European existentialism in its various forms spread to the United States and became even more diversified as it was taken up by an assorted collection of writers, artists, dissidents, college professors and students, playwrights, clergy, and others. The variety of interpretations threatened the existence of existentialism as a meaningful entity. In more recent years, however, existentialism has lost some of its popularity and, paradoxically, has strengthened its position as an alternate means of understanding humanity.

What Is Existentialism?

Although philosophers and psychologists still interpret existentialism in a variety of ways, some common elements are found among most existential thinkers. First, *existence* takes precedence over *essence*. Existence means to emerge or to become; essence implies a static immutable substance. Existence suggests process; essence refers to a product. Existence is associated with growth and change; essence signifies stagnation and finality. Western civilization, and particularly Western science, has traditionally valued essence over existence. It has sought to understand the essential composition of things, including humans. Existentialists, on the other hand, affirm that people's essence is their power to continually redefine themselves through the choices they make.

Second, existentialism opposes the split between subject and object. May (1958b, p. 11) defined existentialism as *"the endeavor to understand man by cutting below the cleavage between subject and object."* As we have seen, Kierkegaard opposed those who saw the person only as a subjective, thinking being. May (1969a, p. 6) quotes Kierkegaard as saying, "Truth exists for the individual only as he himself produces it in action." In other words, people find the truth by living honest and authentic lives and not by armchair contemplation. On the other hand, Kierkegaard also criticized those who wished to make people into machines or objects. Each individual is a unique being and must not be viewed as a mere cog in the machinery of an industrialized society.

Third, people search for some meaning to their lives. They ask (though not always consciously) the important questions concerning their being. Who am I? Is life worth living? Does it have a meaning? How can I realize my humanity?

Fourth, existentialists hold that ultimately each of us is responsible for who we are and what we become. We cannot blame parents, teachers, employers, God, or circumstances. As Sartre (1957, p. 15) said, "Man is nothing else but what he makes of himself. Such is the first principle of existentialism." Although we may associate with others in productive and healthy relationships, in the end, we are each alone. We can choose to become what we can be, or we can choose to avoid commitment and choice, but, ultimately, it is our choice.

Fifth, existentialists are basically antitheoretical. To them, theories further dehumanize people and render them as objects. As we saw in Chapter 1, theories are constructed, in part, to explain phenomena. Existentialists are generally opposed to this. Authentic experience takes precedence over artificial explanations. When experiences are molded into some pre-existing theoretical model, they lose their authenticity and become divorced from the individual who experienced them.

Basic Concepts

Before proceeding to Rollo May's view of humanity, we will pause to look at two basic concepts of existentialism, namely, being-in-the-world and nonbeing.

Being-in-the-World

Existentialists adopt a phenomenological approach to understanding humanity. To them, we exist in a world that can be best understood from our own perspective. When scientists study people from an external frame of reference, they violate both the subjects and their existential world. The basic unity of person and environment is expressed in the German word **Dasein**, meaning to exist there. Hence, *Dasein* literally means to exist in the world and is generally written as **being-in-the-world**. The hyphens in this term imply a oneness of subject and object, of person and world.

Many people suffer from anxiety and despair brought on by their alienation from themselves and/or from their world. They either have no clear image of themselves, or they feel isolated from a world that seems distant and foreign. They have no sense of *Dasein*, no unity of self and world. As people strive to gain power over nature, they lose touch with their relationship to the natural world. As they come to rely on the products of the industrial revolution, they become more alienated from the stars, the soil, and the sea. Alienation from the world includes being out of touch with one's own body as well. Recall that Rollo May began his recovery from tuberculosis only after realizing that it was he who had the illness.

This feeling of isolation and alienation of self from the world is suffered not only by pathologically disturbed individuals but also by most individuals in modern societies. Alienation is the illness of our time, and it manifests itself in three areas: (1) separation from nature, (2) lack of meaningful interpersonal relations, and (3) alienation from one's authentic self. Thus, three simultaneous aspects or modes of the world characterize people in their being-in-the-world. The first of these is **Umwelt**, or the environment around us. The second is **Mitwelt** (literally, "the with world"), which refers to our relations with other people. Third is **Eigenwelt** or our relationship with our self.

Umwelt is the world of objects and things and would exist even if people had no awareness. It is the world of nature and natural law and includes our biological drives, such as hunger and sleep, and such natural phenomena as birth and death. We cannot escape *Umwelt*; we must learn to live in the world around us and to adjust to changes within this world. Freud's theory, with its emphasis on biology and instincts, deals mostly with *Umwelt*.

But we do not live only in *Umwelt*. We also live in the world with people: that is, *Mitwelt*. We must relate to people as people, not as things. If we treat people as objects, then we are living solely in *Umwelt*. The difference between *Umwelt* and *Mitwelt* can be seen by contrasting sex with love. If I use another as an instrument for sexual gratification, then *Umwelt* dominates my life in relation to that person. However, love demands that I make a commitment to the other person. If I love someone, then I respect that person's being-in-the-world; I don't try to mold or change that person. If I relate to a person with love, then I am living in *Mitwelt*. Not every *Mitwelt* relationship necessitates love. The essential criterion is that the *Dasein* of the other person is respected. The theories of Sullivan and Rogers, with their emphasis on interpersonal relations, deal mostly with *Mitwelt*.

Eigenwelt refers to our relationship with our self. It is a world not usually explored by other personality theorists. To live in *Eigenwelt* means to be aware of our self as a human being and to grasp who we are as we relate to the world of things and to the world of people. What does this sunset mean to me? How is this other person a part of my life? What characteristics of mine allow me to love this person? How do I perceive this experience?

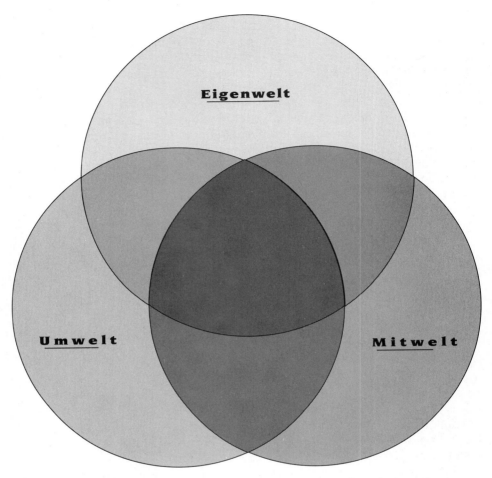

Figure 17.1   *Healthy people live simultaneously in Umwelt, Mitwelt, and Eigenwelt.*

Healthy people live in *Umwelt*, *Mitwelt*, and *Eigenwelt* simultaneously (see Figure 17.1). They adapt to the natural world, relate to others as humans, and have a keen awareness of what all these experiences mean to them (May, 1958a).

Nonbeing

Being-in-the-world necessitates an awareness of self as a living, emerging being. This awareness, in turn, leads to the dread of not being: that is, **nonbeing** or **nothingness**. May (1958a, pp. 47–48) writes that

to grasp what it means to exist, one needs to grasp the fact that he might not exist, that he treads at every moment on the sharp edge of possible annihilation and can never escape the fact that death will arrive at some unknown moment in the future.

The dread of nonbeing can take the form of isolation and alienation.

Death is not the only avenue of nonbeing, but it is the most obvious one. Life becomes more vital, more meaningful when we confront the possibility of our death. May (1958, p. 49) views death as "the one fact of my life which is not relative but absolute, and my awareness of this gives my existence and what I do each hour an absolute quality."

When nonbeing is not courageously confronted through contemplation of death, it manifests itself in a variety of other forms, including addiction to alcohol or other drugs, promiscuous sexual activity, and other compulsive behaviors. Nonbeing is also expressed by a blind conformity to society's expectations and by a generalized hostility that pervades our relations to others.

The fear of death or nonbeing often provokes us to live defensively and to receive less from life than if we would confront the issue of our nonexistence. As May (1991, p. 202) said, "we are afraid of nonbeing and so we shrivel up our being." We flee from making active choices, that is, choices based on a consideration of who we are and what we want. We may try to avoid the dread of nonbeing by dimming our self-awareness and denying our individuality, but such choices leave us with feelings of despair and emptiness. Thus, we escape the dread of nonbeing at the expense of a constricted existence. A healthier alternative is to face the inevitability of death and to realize that nonbeing is an inseparable part of being.

ANXIETY

The failure to confront death serves as a temporary escape from the anxiety or dread of nonbeing. But the escape cannot be permanent. Death is the one absolute of life that sooner or later everyone must face. We experience **anxiety** when we become aware that our existence or some value identified with it might be destroyed. May (1958a, p. 50) defined anxiety as "the subjective state of the individual's becoming aware that his existence can be destroyed, that he can become 'nothing.'" At another time he defined anxiety as a threat to some important value. Anxiety, May (1967, p. 72) said, is *"the apprehension cued off by a threat to some value which the individual holds essential to his existence as a self."*

Anxiety, then, can spring either from an awareness of our nonbeing or from a threat to some value essential to our existence. It exists when we confront the issue of fulfilling our potentialities (May, 1958a). This confrontation can lead to stagnation and decay, but it can also result in growth and change.

The acquisition of freedom inevitably leads to anxiety. Freedom cannot exist without anxiety, nor can anxiety exist without an awareness of the possibility of freedom. May (1981, p. 185) quotes Kierkegaard as saying that "anxiety is the dizziness of freedom." Anxiety, like dizziness, can be either pleasurable or painful, constructive or destructive. It can give us energy and zest, but it can also paralyze and panic us. Moreover, anxiety can be either normal or neurotic.

Normal Anxiety

We live in an age of anxiety. No one can escape its effects. To grow and to change one's values means to experience constructive or normal anxiety. May (1967, p. 80) defined **normal anxiety** as that "which is proportionate to the threat, does not involve repression, and can be confronted constructively on the conscious level."

As we grow from infancy to old age, our values change and with each step normal anxiety is experienced. "All growth consists of the anxiety-creating surrender of past values" (May, 1967, p. 80). Normal anxiety is also experienced during those creative moments when an artist, a scientist, or a philosopher suddenly achieves an insight that leads to a recognition that one's life, and perhaps the lives of countless others, will be permanently changed. For example, scientists who witnessed the first atomic bomb tests in Alamogordo, New Mexico, experienced normal anxiety with the realization that from that moment forward, everything had been changed (May, 1981).

Neurotic Anxiety

Normal anxiety, the type experienced during periods of growth or of threat to one's values, is experienced by everyone. It can be constructive provided it remains proportionate to the threat. But anxiety can become neurotic or sick. May (1967, p. 80) defined **neurotic anxiety** as "a reaction which is disproportionate to the threat, involves repression and other forms of intrapsychic conflict, and is managed by various kinds of blocking-off of activity and awareness."

Whereas normal anxiety is felt whenever values are threatened, neurotic anxiety is experienced whenever values become transformed into dogma. To be absolutely right in our beliefs provides us with temporary security, but it is security "bought at the price of surrendering [our] opportunity for fresh learning and new growth" (May, 1967, p. 80).

Philip, the case study introduced at the beginning of this chapter, suffered from neurotic anxiety. Like others who experience neurotic anxiety, Philip behaved in a nonproductive, self-defeating manner. Although he was deeply hurt by Nicole's unpredictable and "crazy" behavior, he became paralyzed with inaction and could not break off their relationship. Nicole's actions seemed to engender in Philip a sense of duty toward her. Because she obviously needed him, he felt obligated to take care of her.

Philip's attachment to unpredictable and "crazy" women began in early child-hood. During the first two years of his life, his world was inhabited primarily by just two other people—his mother and a sister two years older than him. His mother was a borderline schizophrenic whose behavior toward Philip alternated between tenderness and cruelty. His sister was definitely schizophrenic, and later spent some time in a mental hospital.

> Thus, Philip endured his first years in the world learning to deal with two exceed-ingly unpredictable women. Indeed, he must have had inescapably imprinted on him that he needed not only to rescue women, but that one of his functions in life was to stick by them, especially when they acted their craziest. Life, then, for Philip would understandably not be free, but rather would require that he be continuously on guard or on duty. (May, 1981, p. 30)

We will return to Philip later in this chapter, but at this point his story can be used to illustrate how neurotic anxiety blocks growth and productive action. Philip could find no new way of behaving toward Nicole. His approach seemed to be a recapitulation of childhood behaviors toward his mother and sister.

GUILT

We have said that anxiety arises when we are faced with the problem of fulfilling our potentialities. **Guilt** arises when we deny our potentialities, fail to accurately perceive the needs of our fellow humans, or remain oblivious to our dependence on the natural world (May, 1958a). Just as May uses the term anxiety to refer to large issues dealing with our being-in-the-world, so, too, does he employ the concept of guilt. In this sense, both anxiety and guilt are **ontological**; that is, they refer to the nature of being and not to feelings arising from specific situations or transgressions.

In all, May (1958a) recognized three forms of ontological guilt, each corresponding to the three modes of being-in-the-world, U*mwelt*, M*itwelt*, and E*igenwelt*. To understand the first form of guilt (that corresponding to U*mwelt*), we should recall that ontological guilt need not stem from our own actions or failures to act; it can arise from a lack of awareness of our being-in-the-world. As civilization advances technologically and scientifically, we become further and further removed from nature, that is, from U*mwelt*. This alienation leads to a form of ontological guilt that is especially prevalent in "advanced" societies where people live in heated or cooled dwellings, use motorized means of transportation, and consume food gathered and prepared by others. Our undiscerning reliance on other people for these and other needs contributes to our first form of ontological guilt. Because this type of guilt is a result of our separation from nature, May (1958a) also referred to it as *separation guilt*, a concept similar to Fromm's notion of the human dilemma (see Chapter 7).

The second form of guilt stems from our inability to perceive accurately the world of others (M*itwelt*). We can see other people only through our own eyes and can never perfectly judge their needs. Thus, we do violence to their true identity. Because we cannot unerringly anticipate the needs of others, we feel inadequate in our relations with them. This then leads to a pervasive condition of guilt, one experienced by all of us to some extent. May (1958a, p. 54) said that "this is not a question of moral failure . . . it is an inescapable result of the fact that each of us is a separate individuality and has no choice but to look at the world through [our] own eyes."

The third form of ontological guilt is associated with our denial of our own potentialities or with our failure to fulfill them. In other words, it is grounded in our relationship with self (E*igenwelt*). Again, this form of guilt is universal, because none of us can completely fulfill all our potentials. This third type of guilt is reminiscent of Maslow's concept of the *Jonah complex*, or the fear of being one's best (see Chapter 15).

Like anxiety, ontological guilt can have either a positive or a negative effect on personality. We can use it to develop a healthy sense of humility, to improve our relations with others, and to creatively use our potentialities. However, when we refuse to accept ontological guilt it becomes neurotic or morbid. Neurotic guilt, like neurotic anxiety, then leads to nonproductive or neurotic symptoms such as sexual impotency, depression, cruelty to others, or inability to make a choice.

INTENTIONALITY

The ability to make a choice implies some underlying structure upon which that choice is made. The structure that gives meaning to our experience and allows us to make decisions about the future is called **intentionality** (May, 1969c). Without intentionality we could neither choose nor act upon our choice. Action implies intentionality, just as intentionality implies action. The two are inseparable: "The act is in the intention, and the intention in the act" (May, 1969c, p. 242).

May uses the term intentionality to bridge the gap between subject and object. Intentionality is "the structure of meaning which makes it possible for us, subjects that we are, to see and understand the outside world, objective that it is. In intentionality, the dichotomy between subject and object is partially overcome" (May, 1969c, p. 225).

To illustrate how intentionality partially bridges the gap between subject and object, May (1969c) used a simple example of a man (the subject) seated at his desk observing a piece of paper (the object). The man can write on the paper, fold it into a paper airplane for his grandson, or sketch a picture on it. In all three instances the subject and object are identical, but the man's actions depend on his intentions and on the meaning he gives to his experience. That meaning is a function of both himself (subject) and his environment (object).

Intentionality is not always conscious. It "goes below levels of immediate awareness, and includes spontaneous, bodily elements and other dimensions which are usually called 'unconscious' " (May, 1969c, p. 234). Unconscious intentionality can be illustrated with our case study, Philip, who felt a duty to take care of Nicole despite her unpredictable and "crazy" behavior. Philip did not see that his actions were in some way connected to his early experiences with his unpredictable mother and his "crazy" sister. He was trapped in his unconscious belief that unpredictable and "crazy" women must be cared for, and this intentionality made it impossible for him to discover new ways of relating to Nicole.

CARE, LOVE, AND WILL

Philip had a history of taking care of others, especially women. He had given Nicole a "job" with his company that permitted her to work at home and earn enough money to live on. In addition, after she ended her affair with Craig and gave up her "crazy" plan to move across country, Philip gave her several thousand dollars. He previously had felt a duty to take care of his two wives and, before that, his mother and sister.

In spite of Philip's pattern of taking care of women, he never really learned to care for them. To care for someone means to recognize that person as a fellow human being, to identify with that person's pain or joy, guilt or pity. Care is an active process, the opposite of apathy. "Care is a state in which something does *matter*" (May, 1969c, p. 289).

Care is not the same as love, but it is the source of love. To love means to care, to recognize the essential humanity of the other person, to have an active regard for that person's development. May (1953, p. 206) defined love as a "delight in the presence of the other person and an affirming of his value and development as much as one's own." Without care there can be no love—only empty sentimentality or transient sexual arousal.

Care is also the source of will. May (1969c, p. 218) defined **will** as "the capacity to organize one's self so that movement in a certain direction or toward a certain goal may take place." May distinguished between will and wish, the latter simply meaning *"the imaginative playing with the possibility* of some act or state occurring" (May, 1969c, p. 218). More forcefully he stated:

"Will" requires self-consciousness; "wish" does not. "Will" implies some possibility of either/or choice; "wish" does not. "Wish" gives the warmth, the content, the imagination, the child's play, the freshness, and the richness to will." "Will" gives the self-direction, the maturity to "wish." "Will" protects "wish," permits it to continue without running risks which are too great. (May, 1969c, p. 218)

Union of Love and Will

Modern society, May (1969c) claims, is suffering from an unhealthy division of love and will. Love has become associated with sensual love or sex, whereas will has come to mean a dogged determination or will power. Neither concept captures the true meaning of these two terms. When love is seen as sex, it becomes temporary and lacking in commitment; there is no will, but only wish. When will is seen as will power, it becomes self-serving and lacking in passion; there is no care, but only manipulation.

Love and will "are not united by automatic biological growth but must be part of our conscious development" (May, 1969c, p. 283). In fact, there are biological reasons why love and will are separated. When we first come into the world, we are at one with the universe (Umwelt), our mother (Mitwelt), and ourself (Eigenwelt). "Our needs are met without self-conscious effort on our part, as, biologically, in the early condition of nursing at the mother's breast. This is the first freedom, the first 'yes'" (May, 1969c, p. 284).

Then, when will begins to develop, it manifests itself as opposition, the first "no." The blissful existence of early infancy is now opposed by the emerging willfulness of late infancy. The "no" should not be seen as a statement against the parents, but rather a positive assertion of self. Unfortunately, parents often interpret the "no" negatively and therefore stifle the child's self-assertion. As a result, children learn to disassociate will from the blissful love they had previously enjoyed.

Our task, says May, is to unite love and will. This is not easy, but it is possible. Neither blissful love nor self-serving will have a role in the uniting of love and will. For the mature person, both love and will mean a reaching out toward another person. Both involve care, both necessitate choice, both imply action, and both require responsibility (May, 1969c, 1990c).

Forms of Love

Love is obviously more than sex, but sex is one form of love. May (1969c) identifies four kinds of love in Western tradition—sex, eros, philia, and agape.

Sex

Sex is a biological function that can be satisfied through sexual intercourse or some other release of sexual tension. Although it has become cheapened in modern Western societies, "it still remains the power of procreation, the drive which perpetuates the race, the source at once of the human being's most intense pleasure and his most pervasive anxiety" (May, 1969c, p. 38).

May (1969c) believes that in ancient times sex was taken for granted, just as eating and sleeping were taken for granted. In modern times sex has become a problem. First, during the Victorian period, Western societies generally denied sexual feelings, and sex was not a topic of conversation in polite company. Then, in the 1920s, people reacted against this sexual suppression and sex suddenly came into the open. Since that time our preoccupation with sex has caused it to become trivialized. As May (1969c) pointed out, we went from a period when having sex was fraught with guilt and anxiety to a time when not having it brought about guilt and anxiety.

Eros

In our society sex is frequently confused with eros. Sex is a physiological need that seeks gratification through the release of tension. **Eros** is a psychological desire that seeks procreation or creation through an enduring union with a loved one. In comparing eros to sex, May (1969c, p. 74) wrote:

> Eros, on the other hand, takes wings from human imagination and is forever transcending all techniques, giving the laugh to all the "how to" books by gaily swinging into orbit above our mechanical rules, making love rather than manipulating organs.

Eros is built on care and tenderness. It longs to establish an enduring union with the other person, such that both partners experience delight and passion and both are broadened and deepened by the experience. Eros is the kind of love that draws two people together to form a lasting relationship, for example, in marriage. Because the human species could not survive without desire for a lasting union, eros can be regarded as the salvation of sex.

Philia

Eros, the salvation of sex, is built on the foundation of **philia**, that is, an intimate nonsexual friendship between two people. Philia cannot be rushed; it takes time to grow, to develop, to sink its roots, for example, the slowly evolving love between siblings or between lifelong friends. "Philia does not require that we do anything for the beloved except accept him, be with him, and enjoy him. It is friendship in the simplest, most direct terms" (May, 1969a, p. 31).

In Chapter 6 we saw that Harry Stack Sullivan placed great importance on pre-adolescence, that developmental epoch characterized by the need for a chum, someone who is more or less like oneself. According to Sullivan, chumship or philia is a necessary requisite for healthy erotic relationships during early and late adolescence. May, who was influenced by Sullivan at the William Alanson White Institute, agrees that philia makes eros possible. The gradual, relaxed development of true friendship is a prerequisite for the enduring union of two people.

Agape

Just as eros depends on philia, so philia needs agape. May (1969c, p. 319) defines **agape** as "esteem for the other, the concern for the other's welfare beyond any gain that one can get out of it; disinterested love, typically, the love of God for man."

Agape is altruistic love. It is a kind of spiritual love that carries with it the risk of playing God. It does not depend on any behaviors or characteristics of the other person. In this sense, it is undeserved and unconditional.

Healthy, adult relationships, May believes, blend all four forms of love. They are based on sexual satisfaction, a desire for an enduring union, genuine friendship,

Agape is altruistic love that requires nothing in return.

and an unselfish concern for the welfare of the other person. Such authentic love, unfortunately, is quite difficult. It requires self-affirmation and the assertion of oneself. "At the same time it requires tenderness, affirmation of the other, relaxing of competition as much as possible, self-abnegation at times in the interests of the loved one, and the age-old virtues of mercy and forgiveness" (May, 1981, p. 147).

FREEDOM AND DESTINY

We have seen that a blend of the four forms of love requires both self-assertion and an affirmation of the other person. It also requires an assertion of one's *freedom* and a confrontation with one's *destiny*. Healthy individuals are able both to assume their freedom and to face their destiny.

Freedom Defined

In an early definition May (1967, p. 175) said that "freedom is the individual's capacity to *know that he is the determined one.*" The word "determined" in this definition is synonymous with what May (1981) would later call *destiny*. Freedom, then, comes from an understanding of our destiny: an understanding that death is a possibility at any moment, that we are male or female, that we have inherent weaknesses, that early childhood experiences dispose us toward certain patterns of behavior.

Freedom is the possibility of changing, although we may not know what those changes might be. Freedom "entails being able *to harbor different possibilities in one's mind even though it is not clear at the moment which way one must act*" (May, 1981, pp. 10–11). This condition often leads to increases in anxiety, but it is normal anxiety, the kind that healthy people welcome and are able to manage.

Forms of Freedom

May (1981) recognized two forms of freedom—freedom of doing and freedom of being. The first he called existential freedom; the latter, essential freedom.

Existential Freedom

Existential freedom, May insists, should not be identified with existential philosophy or existential psychology. It is the freedom of action—the freedom of doing. Most middle-class, adult Americans enjoy large measures of existential freedom. They are free to travel across state lines, to choose their associates, to vote for their representatives in government, and so on. On a more trivial scale, they are free to push their shopping carts through a supermarket and select from among thousands of items. Existential freedom, then, is the freedom to act on the choices that one makes.

Essential Freedom

Freedom of action, however, does not ensure freedom of being. At times, in fact, it seems that existential freedom makes **essential freedom** more difficult. May (1981) cites several examples of prisoners and inmates in concentration camps who speak enthusiastically of their "inner freedom." Perhaps solitary confinement or the denial of liberty allows people to face their destiny and to gain their freedom of being. May (1981, p. 60) framed this question in these words: "Do we get to essential freedom only when our everyday existence is interrupted?"

May's answer is: "No." One need not be imprisoned to attain essential freedom; that is, freedom of being. Destiny itself is our prison—our concentration camp that allows us to be less concerned with freedom of doing and more concerned with essential freedom.

> Does not the engaging of our destiny—which is the design of our life—hedge us about with the confinement, the sobriety, indeed, often the cruelty, which forces us to look beyond the limits of day-to-day action? Is not the inescapable fact of death . . . the concentration camp of us all? Is not the fact that life is a joy and a bondage at the same time enough to drive us to consider the deeper aspect of being? (May, 1981, p. 61)

Destiny Defined

May (1981, p. 89) defined destiny "as the pattern of limits and talents that constitutes the 'givens' in life." Destiny is *"the design of the universe speaking through the design of each one of us"* (May, 1981, p. 90). Our ultimate destiny is death, but on a lesser scale our destiny includes other biological properties such as intelligence, gender, size and strength, and genetic predisposition toward certain illnesses. In addition, psychological and cultural factors contribute to our destiny.

Destiny does not mean preordained or foredoomed. It is our destination, our terminus, our goal. Within the boundaries of our destiny we have the power to choose, and this freedom allows us to confront and challenge our destiny. It does not, however, permit any change we wish. We cannot be successful at any job, conquer any illness, enjoy a fulfilling relationship with any person. "Our destiny cannot be cancelled out; we cannot erase it or substitute anything else for it. But we can choose how we shall respond, how we shall live out our talents which confront us" (May, 1981, p. 89).

May suggests that freedom and destiny, like love–hate, life–death, are not antithetical but rather a normal paradox of life. "The paradox is that freedom owes its vitality to destiny, and destiny owes its significance to freedom" (May, 1981, p. 17). Freedom and destiny are thus inexorably intertwined; one cannot exist without the other. Freedom without destiny is license. Ironically, license leads to anarchy and the ultimate destruction of freedom. Without destiny, then, we have no freedom, but without freedom our destiny is meaningless.

Destiny is our "concentration camp" that, paradoxically, defines our essential freedom.

Freedom and destiny give birth to each other. As we challenge our destiny, we gain freedom, and as we achieve freedom, we push at the boundaries of destiny.

Philip's Destiny

When Philip, our case study, first walked into Rollo May's office, he was paralyzed with inaction because he refused to accept his destiny. He saw no connection between his adult pattern of relating to women and the strategy that, as an infant, he had adopted in order to survive in an unpredictable and "crazy" world. His destiny was not fixed by those early experiences. Philip, like other people, had the freedom to change his destiny, but first he had to recognize his biological, social, and psychological limitations, and then he had to possess the courage to make choices within those limitations. Philip lacked both the understanding and the courage to confront his destiny. Up to the point of seeking therapy, he had tried to compensate for his destiny, to consciously deny it. "He had been searching for someone who would make up for his having been born into an unwelcoming world consisting of a disturbed mother and a schizophrenic sister, a destiny that he did not in the slightest choose" (May, 1981, p. 88). Philip's denial of his destiny "only contributed to resentment, a longing and yearning that he could not understand" (May, 1981, p. 89).

Philip's inability or unwillingness to face his destiny robbed him of personal freedom and kept him tied to his mother. He treated his wives and Nicole in the same way that earlier had proven successful with his mother and sister. He could not dare express his anger to women, but, instead, he adopted a charming though somewhat possessive and protective attitude toward them. May (1981, p. 89) insisted that "the freedom of each of us is in proportion to the degree with which we confront and live in relation to our destiny." After several weeks of psychotherapy Philip was able to stop blaming his mother for not doing what he thought she should have done. When he began to see the positive things she *did* do, he began to change his attitude toward her. The objective facts of his childhood had not changed, but his subjective perceptions had. As Philip came to terms with his destiny, he began to be able to express his anger, to feel less trapped in his relationship with Nicole, and to become more aware of his possibilities. In other words, he gained his freedom of being.

THE POWER OF MYTH

May has long been concerned with the powerful effects of **myths** on individuals and cultures—a concern that culminated in his book, *The Cry for Myth* (1991). May contends that the people of Western civilization have an urgent need for myths at this time. Lacking myths to believe in, they turn to religious cults, drug addiction, and popular culture in a vain effort to find meaning in their lives. Myths are not falsehoods; rather, they are conscious and unconscious belief systems that provide explanations for personal and social problems. May (1991, p. 15) says that "myths are like the beams in a house; not exposed to outside view, they are the structure which holds the house together so people can live in it."

From earliest times and in diverse civilizations, people have found meaning in their lives by the myths they share with others in their culture. May, however, is more interested in contemporary American myths (or their lack) than in ancient or Eastern mythology. Myths are the stories that unify a society; "they are essential to the process of keeping our souls alive and bringing us new meaning in a difficult and often meaningless world" (May, 1991, p. 20).

May believes that people communicate with one another on two levels. The first is rationalistic language, and on this level truth takes precedence over the people who are communicating. The second is through myths, and on this level the total human experience is more important than the empirical accuracy of the communication. We use myths and symbols to transcend the immediate concrete situation, to expand self-awareness, and to search for identity.

May (1990a, 1991) holds that the Oedipus story is a powerful myth in our culture because it contains elements of existential crises common to us all. These crises include birth, separation or exile from parents and home, sexual union with one parent and hostility toward the other, the assertion of independence and the search for identity, and finally death. The Oedipus myth has meaning for us because it deals with all these crises. Like Oedipus, we are removed from our mother and father and are driven by the need to know who we are. Our struggle for self-identity, however, is not easy, and it may even result in tragedy as it did for Oedipus when he insisted on knowing the truth about his origins. After being told that he had killed his father and married his mother, Oedipus put out his eyes, depriving himself of the ability to see, that is, to be aware, to be conscious.

The Oedipus myth holds meaning for us even today because it deals with existential crises common to us all.

But the Oedipus narration does not end with denial of consciousness. At this point in Sophocles's trilogy, Oedipus once again is exiled, an experience May sees as symbolic of our own isolation and ostracism. As an old man, Oedipus is seen contemplating his tragic suffering and accepting responsibility for killing his father and marrying his mother. His late life meditations bring him peace and understanding and the ability to accept death with grace. The central themes of Oedipus's life—birth, exile and separation, identity, incest and patricide, repression of guilt, and finally, conscious meditation and death—touch us all and make this myth a potentially powerful healing force in our lives.

May's concept of myths is comparable to Jung's idea of a collective unconscious in that myths are archetypal patterns in the human experience; they are avenues to universal images that lie beyond our individual experience. And like archetypes, myths can contribute to our psychological growth if we will embrace them and allow them to open up for us a new reality. On the other hand, if we deny our universal myths or see only their regressive functions, we risk alienation, apathy, and emptiness—the principal ingredients of psychopathology.

PSYCHOPATHOLOGY

According to May, apathy and emptiness—not anxiety and guilt—are the malaise of our time. When people deny their destiny or abandon their myths, they lose their purpose for being, they become directionless. Without some goal or destination people become sick and engage in a variety of self-defeating and self-destructive behaviors. "The human being cannot live in a condition of emptiness for very long: if he is not growing toward something, he does not merely stagnate; the pent-up potentialities turn into morbidity and despair, and eventually into destructive activities" (May, 1953, p. 24).

Many people in modern Western societies feel alienated from the world (U*mwelt*); from others (M*itwelt*); and especially from themselves (E*igenwelt*). They experience a sense of helplessness to prevent natural disasters, to reverse industrialization, or to make contact with another human being. They feel insignificant in a world that increasingly dehumanizes the individual. This sense of insignificance leads to *apathy* and to a state of diminished consciousness (May, 1967).

May sees psychopathology as lack of communicativeness. It is the "inability to participate in the feelings and thoughts of others or to share oneself with others" (May, 1981, p. 21). Psychologically disturbed individuals deny their destiny and, in the process, lose their freedom. They erect a variety of neurotic symptoms, not to regain their freedom but to renounce it. Symptoms narrow the person's phenomenological world to the size that makes coping easier. The compulsive person adopts a rigid routine, thereby making new choices unnecessary.

Symptoms may be temporary, as when stress produces a headache, or they may be relatively permanent and stem from early childhood experiences. Philip's psychopathology was tied to his early environment with a disturbed mother and a schizophrenic sister. These experiences did not *cause* his pathology in the sense that they alone produced it. However, they did set up Philip to learn to adjust to his world by containing his anger, by developing a sense of apathy, and by trying to be a "good little boy." Neurotic symptoms, therefore, do not represent a failure of adjustment, but rather a proper and necessary adjustment by which one's *Dasein* can be preserved. Philip's behavior toward his two wives and Nicole represents a denial of his freedom and a self-defeating attempt to escape from his destiny.

PSYCHOTHERAPY

Unlike Freud, Adler, Rogers, and other clinically oriented personality theorists, May has not established a school of psychotherapy that has yielded avid followers and identifiable techniques. He has, however, written extensively on the subject.

As noted above, May does not regard anxiety and guilt as the primary ingredients in psychopathology and, consistent with this view, he does not believe that the goal of therapy should be their alleviation. In fact, he does not think that psychotherapy should be aimed at curing patients of a particular disorder, or eliminating a specific problem. Instead, he suggests that the purpose of therapy is to make people more human, to help them expand and develop their consciousness so that they will be in a better position to make choices (Hall, 1967). These choices, then, lead to the simultaneous growth of freedom and responsibility.

May (1981, pp. 19–20) states that *"the purpose of psychotherapy is to set people free. . . .* I believe that the therapist's function should be to help people become free to be aware of and to experience their possibilities." May (1990c) believes that therapists who concentrate on a patient's symptoms are missing the more important picture. Neurotic symptoms are simply ways of running away from freedom and an indication that patients' inner possibilities are not being used. When patients become more free, more human, their neurotic symptoms usually disappear; their neurotic anxiety gives way to normal anxiety; and their neurotic guilt is replaced by normal guilt. But these are secondary gains and not the central purpose of therapy. May insists that psychotherapy must be concerned with helping people experience their existence, and that "any cure of symptoms which will last must be a by-product of that" (May, 1967, p. 86).

How does a therapist help patients become free, responsible human beings? May does not offer many specific directions for therapists to follow. Existential therapists have no special set of techniques or methods that can be applied to all patients. Instead, they have only themselves, their own humanity to offer. They must establish a one-to-one relationship (*Mitwelt*) that enables patients to become more aware of themselves and to live more fully in their own world (*Eigenwelt*). This may mean challenging patients to confront their destiny, to experience despair, anxiety, and guilt. But it also means establishing an I–thou encounter where both therapist and patient are viewed as subjects rather than objects. "In this encounter I have to be able, to some extent, to experience what the patient in experiencing. My job as a therapist is to be open to his world" (May, 1967, p. 108).

May (1991) has also described therapy as partly religion, partly science, and partly friendship. The friendship, however, is not an ordinary social relationship; rather it calls for the therapist to be confronting and to challenge the patient. May believes that the relationship itself is therapeutic, and its transforming effects are independent of anything therapists might say or any theoretical orientation they might have.

Our task is to be guide, friend, and interpreter to persons on their journeys through their private hells and purgatories. Specifically our task is to help patients get to the point where they can decide whether they wish to remain victims . . . or whether they choose to leave this victim-state and venture through purgatory with the hope of achieving some sense of paradise. Our patients often, toward the end, are understandably frightened by the possibility of freely deciding for themselves whether to take their chances by completing the quest they have bravely begun. (May, 1991, p. 165)

Philosophically, May holds many of the same beliefs as Carl Rogers (see Chapter 16). Basic to both approaches is the notion of therapy as a human encounter; that is, an I–thou relationship with the potential to facilitate growth within both therapist and patient (May, 1990b). In practice, however, May is much more likely to ask questions, to delve into a patient's early childhood, and to suggest possible meanings of present behavior. For example, he explained to Philip that his relationship with Nicole was an attempt to hold on to his mother. Rogers would reject such a technique because it emanates from an external (that is, the therapist's) frame of reference. May, however, believes that these kinds of interpretations can be an effective means of confronting patients with information that they have been hiding from themselves.

Another technique May used with Philip was the suggestion that he hold a fantasy conversation with his dead mother. In this conversation Philip spoke for both himself and his mother. When talking for his mother, he was able for the first time to empathize with her, to see himself from her point of view. Speaking for his mother, he said that she was very proud of him and that he had always been her favorite child. Then talking for himself, he told his mother that he appreciated her courage and recalled an incident when her courage saved his eyesight. When Philip finished the fantasy conversation he said, "'I never in a thousand years would have imagined *that* would come out'" (May, 1981, p. 39).

May also asked Philip to bring a photo of himself when he was a little boy. Philip then had a fantasy conversation with "Little Philip." As the conversation ensued, "Little Philip" explained that he had triumphed over the problem that had most troubled grown Philip, namely, the fear of abandonment. "Little Philip" became Philip's friendly companion and helped him overcome his loneliness and allay his jealousy of Nicole.

At the end of therapy Philip did not become a new person, but he did become more conscious of a part of himself that had been there all the time. An awareness of new possibilities allowed him to move in the direction of personal freedom. For Philip, the end of therapy was the beginning of "the uniting of himself with that early self that he had had to lock up in a dungeon in order to survive when life was not happy but threatening" (May, 1981, p. 41).

CONCEPT OF HUMANITY

Like Erik Erikson (see Chapter 3), May has offered a new way of looking at things. His view of humanity is both broader and deeper than those of most other personality theorists. He sees people as complex beings, capable of both tremendous good and immense evil.

According to May, people have become estranged from the natural world, from other people, and, most of all, from themselves. The threat of nuclear war has turned impotence into anxiety, *"anxiety into regression and apathy, these in turn into hostility, and the hostility into an alienation of man from man"* (May, 1967, p. 32).

As people become more alienated from other people and from themselves, they surrender portions of their consciousness. They become less aware of themselves as a subject, that is, the person who is aware of the experiencing self. As the subjective self becomes obscured, people lose some of their capacity to make choices. This progression, however, is not inevitable. May believes that people, within the confines of their destiny, have the ability to make free choices. Each choice pushes back the boundaries of determinism and permits new choices. People generally have much more potential for freedom than they realize. However, free choice does not come without anxiety. Choice demands the courage to confront one's destiny, to look within and to recognize the evil as well as the good.

Choice also implies action. Without action, choice is merely a wish, an idle desire. With action comes responsibility. Freedom and responsibility are always commensurable. A person cannot have more freedom than responsibility, nor can one be shackled with more responsibility than freedom. Healthy individuals welcome both freedom and responsibility, but they realize that choice is often painful, anxiety-provoking, and difficult.

May believes that many people have surrendered some of their ability to choose, but that capitulation itself, he insists, is a choice. Ultimately, each of us is responsible for the choices we make, and those choices define us as unique human beings. May, therefore, must be rated high on the dimension of *free choice*.

Is May *optimistic* or *pessimistic*? Although he sometimes paints a rather gloomy picture of humanity, May is not pessimistic. He sees the present age as merely a plateau in humanity's quest for new symbols and new myths that will vitalize the species with renewed spirit.

Although May recognizes the potential impact of childhood experiences on adult personality, he clearly favors *teleology* over causality. In a comment on Clement Reeves's (1977) book, May stated: "I believe in a teleological approach—that each person, by virtue of his being a person, has certain potentialities that he is required, by life itself, to live out" (May 1977b, pp. 303–304). Each of us has a particular destiny that we must discover and challenge or else risk alienation and neurosis.

May assumes a moderate stance on the issue of *conscious* vs. *unconscious* forces in personality development. By their nature, people have enormous capacity for self-awareness, but often that capacity remains fallow. People sometimes lack the courage to face their destiny or to recognize the evil that exists within their culture as well as within themselves. Consciousness and choices are interrelated. As people make more free choices, they gain more insight into who they are; that is, they develop a greater sense of being. This sharpened sense of being, in turn, facilitates the ability to make further choices. Awareness of self and capacity for free choice are hallmarks of psychological health.

May also takes an intermediate position on *social* vs. *biological* influences. Society contributes to personality principally through interpersonal relationships. Our relations with other people can have either a freeing or an enslaving effect. Sick relationships, such as those Philip experienced with his mother and sister, can stifle personal growth and leave us with an inability to participate in a healthy encounter with another person. Without the capacity to relate to people as people, life becomes meaningless, and we develop a sense of alienation not only from others but from ourselves as well. Biology also contributes to personality. Biological factors such as gender, physical size, predisposition to illnesses, and ultimately death itself shape a person's destiny. Everyone must live within the confines of destiny, even though those confines can be expanded.

On the dimension of *uniqueness* vs. *similarities*, May's view of humanity leans toward uniqueness. Each of us is responsible for shaping our own personality within the limits imposed by destiny. No two of us make the same sequence of choices and no two develop identical ways of looking at things. May's emphasis on phenomenology implies individual perceptions and therefore unique personalities.

Related Research

Humanistically oriented theorists such as Allport, Maslow, Rogers, and Kelly advocate an approach to psychological science that emphasizes individual procedures (idiographic) rather than those based on general laws (nomothetic). They also suggest that human agency (free will or volition of the subjects) exerts some influence on behavior. Rollo May agrees that modern science is too rationalistic, too objective, and that a new science is needed in order to grasp the total, living person. People must be seen as subjects, not merely objects. The *Dasein* or being-in-the-world of the observer has an influence on the reactions of the people being observed, an influence that is often overlooked by traditional psychology. Both the observer and the observed are changed by their encounter with each other.

Recently, George S. Howard and his associates at the University of Notre Dame have extensively studied the effects of human agency (free will, volition, or self-determination) on a variety of dependent variables such as eating peanuts (Howard & Conway, 1986), snacking on carrot and celery sticks (Lazarick, Fishbein, Loiello, & Howard, 1988), and alcohol and milk consumption (Howard, Curtin, & Johnson, 1991). Howard believes that humans are not free to behave in any manner they please, but neither are their actions completely determined by environmental forces or by internal factors, such as hunger or thirst. "Thus, although each person may be the captain of his or her own ship (agency), the ship is subject to all the nonagentic natural processes (like wind and currents) that influence any ship's course" (Howard & Myers, 1990).

A study by Howard and Myers (1990) gives a flavor of the research conducted on self-determination or agency. This study, however, was somewhat unique in that it compared the effectiveness of three distinct methodological perspectives. The first perspective was a nonagentic (environmentally controlled) and nomothetic (general or universal) approach typical of most psychology studies; the second was a nonagentic, idiographic (unique) analysis that considered subjects' choices; and the third perspective was an agentic one in which subjects' own volition served as the independent variable. In the volition intervention phase of the study, subjects told themselves to "try to exercise" on some days or to "try not to exercise" on other days. The experimenters selected exercise because it is a behavior that seemingly can be controlled both by external factors, such as the weather, school and social obligations, and daily schedule (nonagentic factors), and by a person's desire to exercise (an agentic factor).

In a complex analysis of the three methodological approaches, Howard and Myers found that idiographic variables (those chosen by the subjects) were better predictors of how much exercise a person would do than nomothetic variables (chosen by the experimenters). But more important to the humanistic perspective, the agentic approach in which subjects told themselves to try to exercise on some days and to try not to exercise on other days demonstrated that volition or self-determination can be an accurate predictor of behavior.

Although this and other studies by Howard and his associates were not specifically conducted to test hypotheses from May's theory, they are philosophically consistent with the existential emphasis on the uniqueness of the individual and on the impact of a person's ability to choose.

CRITIQUE OF MAY

Existentialism in general and May's psychology in particular have been criticized as being anti-intellectual and antitheoretical. May acknowledges the claim that his views do not conform to the traditional concept of theory, but he staunchly defends his psychology against the charge of being anti-intellectual or antiscientific. He points to the sterility of conventional scientific methods and their inability to unlock the ontological character of willing, caring, and acting human beings.

May holds that a new scientific psychology must recognize such human characteristics as uniqueness, personal freedom, destiny, phenomenological experiences, and especially our capacity to relate to ourselves as both object and subject. A new science of humans must also include ethics. "The actions of living, self-aware human beings are never automatic, but involve some weighing of consequences, some potentiality for good or ill" (May, 1967, p. 199).

May concludes his position on a new psychology with these words:

> The outlines of a science of man we suggest will deal with man as the symbol-maker, the reasoner, the historical mammal who can participate in his community and who possesses the potentiality of freedom and ethical action. The pursuit of this science will take no less rigorous thought and wholehearted discipline than the pursuit of experimental and natural science at their best, but it will place the scientific enterprise in a broader context. Perhaps it will again be possible to study man scientifically and still see him whole. (May, 1967, p. 199)

Until this new science acquires greater maturity, we must evaluate May's views by the same criteria used for each of the other personality theorists.

Have May's ideas *generated scientific research*? May has not formulated his views in a theoretical structure, and a paucity of hypotheses are suggested by his writings. Some current research, such as that being conducted by George Howard and discussed above, relate generally to existential psychology, but it does not specifically flow from May's theory. On this first criterion of a useful theory, therefore, May's existential psychology receives a very low score.

Second, does May's philosophically oriented psychology help *organize what is currently known about human nature*? On this criterion May would receive a high rating. Compared to most theorists discussed in this book, May has more closely followed Allport's dictum, "Do not forget what you have decided to neglect" (Allport, 1968, p. 23). May has not forgotten that he has excluded discourses on developmental stages, basic motivational forces, and other factors that tend to segment the human experience. Yet May's philosophical writings have reached deep into the far recesses of the human experience and have explored aspects of humanity not examined by other personality theorists. His popularity is due in part to his ability to touch individual readers, to connect with their humanity. May's use of certain concepts are at times inconsistent and confusing, yet his ideas affect people in ways that other theorists do not.

As a *practical guide to action*, May's theory is quite weak. Although he possesses a keen understanding of human personality, May's writings are more philosophical than scientific. In fact, he has no objection to being called a philosopher and frequently refers to himself as a philosopher-therapist.

On the criterion of *internal consistency*, May's existential psychology, again, falls short. He offers a variety of definitions for such concepts as anxiety, guilt, intentionality, will, and destiny. Unfortunately, none of these terms is ever operationally defined. This imprecise terminology has contributed to the lack of research on May's ideas.

The final criterion of a useful theory is *parsimony*, and on this standard May's psychology receives a moderate rating. His writings, at times, are cumbersome and awkward, but, to his credit, he deals with complex issues and does not attempt to oversimplify human personality.

Chapter Summary

During the past 45 years existential psychology, which began in Europe, has secured a hold in the United States. Rooted in the philosophy of Kierkegaard, Nietzsche, Sartre, and others, existential psychology holds that people are largely responsible for their own personalities. Existence is given priority over essence; growth and change are seen as being more important than stable and fixed characteristics; and process receives preference over product.

At the vanguard of existential psychology in the United States is

Rollo May, a philosophically oriented psychologist who came to existentialism from a background of art and psychotherapy. May, like other existentialists, believes that (1) existence precedes essence, meaning that what people *do* is more important than what they *are*; (2) people are both subjective and objective; that is, they are thinking as well as acting beings; (3) people are motivated to search for answers to important questions regarding the meaning of life; (4) *freedom* and *responsibility* are always balanced; that is, a person cannot have one without the other; and (5) fixed personality theories tend to dehumanize people and turn them into objects or things to be observed.

Existentialists generally take a *phenomenological* approach to understanding humanity, insisting that people can best be studied from their own point of view. The unity of people and their phenomenological world is expressed by the term *Dasein*, or being-in-the-world.

There are three modes of being-in-the-world: U*mwelt*, our relationship with the world of objects or things; *Mitwelt*, our world with people; and E*igenwelt*, our relationship with ourself. Healthy people live in all three worlds simultaneously.

If people are aware of their being-in-the-world, then they are also aware of the possibility of *nonbeing* or nothingness. Life becomes more meaningful when we confront the inevitability of death or nonbeing.

The awareness of nonbeing contributes to the experience of *anxiety*, but anxiety is also increased when people realize that they are free to choose and have responsibility for their actions. N*ormal anxiety* is experienced by everyone. It is proportionate to the threat and can be managed constructively on a conscious level. N*eurotic anxiety* is disportionate to the threat, involves repression, and is handled in a self-defeating manner.

Just as anxiety is a normal aspect of the human condition, so too is *guilt*. People experience guilt as a result of their (1) separation from the natural world; (2) inability to judge the needs of others; and (3) denial of their own potentials.

Intentionality is the underlying structure that gives meaning to experience and allows people to make decisions about the future. Intentionality implies action, not merely idle wishing.

Both *love* and *will* involve *care*, both necessitate choice, and both require responsibility. Love means taking delight in the presence of the other person and affirming that person's value as much as one's own; will calls for a conscious commitment to action. May identifies four aspects of love: (1) *sex*, which is a physiological function; (2) *eros*, which seeks an enduring union with a loved one; (3) *philia*, or nonsexual friendship between two people; and (4) *agape*, or an altruistic love that demands nothing in return.

May holds that freedom comes from one's confrontation with *destiny* and with an understanding that death or nonbeing is a possibility at any moment. Many people have *freedom of action*, but a deeper, more rare kind of freedom is *freedom of being*. People can be free within themselves even though they may be physically imprisoned. May also believes that a breakdown in our cultural myths has contributed to social upheaval and personal feelings of alienation.

Although May has been a psychotherapist for many years, he has not written extensively on techniques or methods of existential therapy. Because psychopathology is the result of alienation from nature, others, and self, May asserts that the purpose of therapy is to help people expand their consciousness so that they can make free choices and be at one with nature, other people, and self.

In his concept of humanity, May places high emphasis on uniqueness, free choice, and teleology. Existential psychology receives high marks for its ability to organize that which is known about human personality, but it falls short as a scientific theory, having little heuristic value either in generating research or in guiding the practitioner.

Suggested Readings

HALL, M. H. (1967, September). An interview with "Mr. Humanist": Rollo May. *Psychology Today*, pp. 25–29, 72–73.
Although this article is more than 25 years old, it reflects many ideas that are appropriate today
MAY, R. (1958). The origins and significance of the existential movement in psychology. In R. May, E. Angel, & H. F. Ellenberger (Eds.), *Existence: A new dimension in psychiatry and psychology* (pp. 3–36). New York: Basic Books.
With this chapter, May introduced existential psychology to many American readers. The philosophical background, rationale, and terminology of existential psychology are presented.
MAY, R. (1969). The emergence of existential psychology. In R. May (Ed.), *Existential psychology* (2d ed.) (pp. 1–48). New York: Random House.
Another introductory chapter in which May discusses the meaning of existentialism and the implications of existential psychology for science and psychotherapy.
MAY, R. (1969). *Love and will*. New York: Norton.
May's most popular book, this volume discusses the failure of modern culture to understand the meaning of love and will. Included are chapters on intentionality and care.
MAY, R. (1991). *The cry for myth*. New York: Norton.
In this book May argues for the importance of durable myths and discusses their therapeutic impact on people's lives.

PART SIX

Conclusions

A Final Word

CONCEPTS OF HUMANITY SUMMARIZED
EVALUATION OF PERSONALITY THEORIES
THEORISTS OF PERSONALITY
FUTURE DIRECTIONS

Chapter Eighteen

*I*n the years since Freud began seriously formulating the first modern theory of personality, the world has seen unprecedented change. When Breuer and Freud published *Studies in Hysteria* in 1895, Henry Ford had not yet mass-produced the automobile, the Wright brothers had not flown at Kitty Hawk, Marconi had not yet built the wireless radio, and bleeding was a treatment sometimes still used in medicine.

What progress has personality theory made in the intervening decades? Obviously the advances have not been as dramatic as those in technology. Some observers may believe that few if any major advances have been made since Freud's elaborate and fascinating description of human personality.

From a scientific view, however, considerable progress has been made. Consider, for example, the work of Bandura, currently the most active theory builder discussed in these pages. Bandura's cautious mixture of research and theoretical speculation serves as a model for correct theory building. Although his theory may lack the breadth and the colorful appeal of Freud's psychoanalysis, it is, nevertheless, several steps in front as a rigorous scientific theory. If personality theory is to serve as a tool for explaining, predicting, and controlling human behavior, it must be modeled more on the pattern of current theorists rather than on the highly speculative formulations of the original triumvirate, namely, Freud, Adler, and Jung.

CONCEPTS OF HUMANITY SUMMARIZED

In the opening chapter, we pictured Sigmund Freud as a young Viennese neurologist contemplating the nature of human nature, something philosophers had done for thousands of years. However, Freud added two important ingredients to the speculations of philosophers—controlled observations and testable hypotheses. This mix eventually led to the field of psychology called personality theory. In the more than 100 years since Freud's early contemplations, many other observers of personality have contributed their ideas and their research to this field, and in the previous 16 chapters we discussed 23 different theories constructed by these people.

Return once more to the young Dr. Freud and his thinking about human personality. In Chapter 1, we listed several questions that Freud eventually considered, either explicitly or implicitly. What motivates people? Do people strive toward some goal or is behavior without purpose? What accounts for similarities and differences among people? What makes people act in predictable or unpredictable ways? Do dreams have a meaning? What unconscious forces underlie human behavior? What are the causes of mental disturbances? Is personality determined more by hereditary and biological forces or by environmental and social factors? What is the nature of human nature? Some of these questions have endured to the present time and currently spark both debate and research. Others, such as the meaning of dreams, no longer hold a central place in personality theory.

We have formulated the more durable questions into six broad and somewhat overlapping dimensions and then rated the various personality theorists on each of these dimensions. These basic questions reflect the theorists' philosophical stance as well as their scientific perspectives.

The first dimension for a concept of humanity concerns the theorist's belief that behavior is determined either by forces outside the individual or by the individual's ability to freely choose. Interestingly, two theories that have little else in common—Freud's psychoanalysis and Skinner's behavioral analysis—are the only ones rated very high on determinism, that is, very low on free choice (see Table 18.1). Humanistically oriented theorists, including Allport and Kelly, are all rated high on the free choice dimension.

The second dimension involves an optimistic view of humanity versus a pessimistic one. Some people—philosophers, novelists, playwrights, and personality theorists—see human existence as a hopeless and perpetual struggle against powerful internal or external forces. Others see people as having the capacity to conquer these forces and to live satisfying and fulfilling lives. The most optimistic of our personality theorists have been Adler and Rogers, whereas Freud was probably the most pessimistic.

The third dimension of a concept of humanity is causality versus teleology. Theorists rated high on causality emphasize past experiences as critical determinants of present behavior, whereas those high on teleology believe that present expectations of future goals shape our behavior. Freud and Skinner are both rated very high on causality, because both believed that our past determines our present. For Freud, early childhood experiences, many of which have been repressed, greatly influence personality. For Skinner, our previous experiences with reinforcement and, to a lesser extent, punishment, along with genetics and culture, shape present behavior. Adler's goal-oriented theory and Kelly's personal construct theory receive the highest ratings on teleology, because both theorists saw personality as being molded by a person's beliefs concerning the future.

A fourth question concerns the role of conscious vs. unconscious forces in shaping personality. All personality theorists believe that some of our behaviors and the motives behind them can be unconscious. Even Allport, who placed the highest emphasis on consciousness, believed that psychologically disturbed individuals are at least partly motivated by forces beyond their awareness. In addition to Allport, the cognitive theorists (Bandura, Rotter, and Mischel), and the humanistic/existential theorists (except May) all emphasize conscious motivation over unconscious drives. Freud, of course, is rated very high on unconscious determi-

TABLE 18.1   *Summary of Major Personality Theorists' Concepts of Humanity*

	FREE CHOICE	OPTIMISTISM	CAUSALITY	UNCONSCIOUS INFLUENCES	SOCIAL INFLUENCES	UNIQUENESS
Freud	VL	L	VH	VH	VL	M
Erikson	M	H	H	M	H	H
Adler	H	VH	VL	H	H	H
Jung	M	M	H	VH	L	L
Sullivan	M	M	M	H	VH	L
Horney	H	H	M	M	H	L
Fromm	M	M	L	M	VH	M
Klein	L	M	H	H	H	L
Dollard & Miller	L	M	H	H	H	H
Skinner	VL	M	VH	VH	H	H
Bandura	M	M	M	L	VH	H
Rotter	H	M	L	L	VH	M
Mischel	H	M	L	L	VH	H
Cattell/Eysenck	NA	NA	NA	M	VL	H
Allport	H	H	L	VL	M	VH
Kelly	H	H	VL	L	M	H
Maslow	H	H	L	M	M	H
Rogers	H	VH	L	L	H	H
May	H	M	L	M	M	H

VH = *Very High*   H = *High*   M = *Moderate*   L = *Low*   VL = *Very Low*   NA = *Not Applicable*

nants, as is Jung with his concept of the collective unconscious. Not quite so obvious is the very high rating that Skinner receives on unconscious influences. Skinner believed that people seldom have any conscious knowledge of the complex of genetic, cultural, and environmental contingencies responsible for their behaviors.

The fifth dimension concerns biological factors (largely heredity) and social factors (that is, environmental influences). This is no longer an issue of nature *versus* nurture; all personality theorists recognize that personality results form an interaction of hereditary and environmental factors. The question now is one of emphasis. We have rated Freud very high on biology (very low on social influences), but Eysenck and perhaps Cattell put even greater weight on genetic influences. Theorists on the social end of this dimension include Sullivan, Fromm, Bandura, Rotter, and Mischel.

And finally, can personality best be conceptualized in terms of unique patterns of behavior or in terms of similar elements among people? Although Adler, the learning and cognitive theorists, and the humanistic/existential theorists all placed high emphasis on uniqueness among people, none could rival Allport for dedication to individuality.

These six dimensions relate to philosophical positions more than to scientific issues. Pervin (1990b) has listed 10 largely scientific issues that have endured throughout the history of personality study. Many of these issues are the same or similar to our six philosophical dimensions, underscoring personality theory's debt to both philosophical speculation and scientific observations.

Pervin's first enduring issue is the definition of personality. Not all theorists have been concerned with defining personality, but all have worked around at least an implicit definition. Second, personality has an important relationship with and is deeply embedded within general psychology. Such has not always been true. Introductory psychology textbooks of 40 and 50 years ago seldom contained a chapter devoted to "theories of personality." Now all do. Personality also has an established relationship with other subspecialties within psychology, such as clinical, developmental, and social. Pervin's third issue is the view of science within psychology and personality. Although people who have studied personality did not always use the same scientific tools as those of other psychologists, Pervin advocates methods of science that both personality psychologists and other psychologists can employ.

Pervin's fourth issue concerns the basic nature of people. Are people naturally good, evil, or neither? This is a philosophical issue that, perhaps, can never be settled by science. Fifth, is personality best studied from a nomothetic perspective that emphasizes universal laws and procedures or from an idiographic view that considers the single individual? Pervin correctly pointed out that Allport, Freud, and Skinner all favored idiographic research. The sixth issue regards the problem of person versus situation. This, too, is no longer an either/or issue, because all people who study personality see behavior as flowing from an interaction of person and situation. As Pervin (1990a, p. 14) said, "although we are all pretty much interactionists at this point, there remains considerable disagreement about *what* in the person interacts *how* with *what* in the situation."

Perhaps the oldest issue of all is nature versus nurture, a question we discussed above and one that involves heredity and environment, as well as biology and sociology.

Pervin calls his eighth issue the time dimension, by which he means past influences versus future expectations. Only present factors can motivate us, but, as we have seen, personality theorists differ greatly on whether present factors are shaped by people's past experiences or by their anticipation of future events. Ninth is persistence and change in personality. Does personality persist throughout the years, or do people grow psychologically and change their basic personality? Finally, Pervin addresses the issue of conscious versus unconscious processes, a dimension we have already discussed. Because these issues have endured for at least some number of years, we might expect that most will continue to be important problems in the years to come.

EVALUATION OF PERSONALITY THEORIES

In the first chapter, I defined scientific theory as a set of related assumptions from which, by logical deductive reasoning, testable hypotheses can be drawn. Chapters 2 to 17 examined in some detail a number of theories of personality and evaluated each theory on the basis of five criteria of a useful theory. Table 18.2 presents a summary of my evaluation of these theories.

First, how well do current personality theories generate research? Although much of current psychological research is without theoretical focus, a significant portion has been stimulated by attempts to test hypotheses drawn from established theories, including those within the scope of personality. Freud's theory alone has generated thousands of research studies and continues to stimulate dozens of important studies each year. A weakness of Freud's theory, as well as other philosophically based theories, is a lack of verifiability. Although these theories have heuristic value in generating research, results of that research can usually be explained in other ways and thus do not specifically support the parent theory.

Nevertheless, most personality theories, especially those of Adler, Skinner, Bandura, Mischel, Cattell, and Maslow have been exceptionally productive of research. Moreover, Rotter's notion of locus of control continues to be a popular topic in the psychological literature as does his interpersonal trust scale. In addition, Allport's Religious Orientation Scale, Jung's concept of personality types, Rogers's facilitative conditions, and Kelly's Rep test are all currently producing some research. Taken as a totality, personality theory has sparked a substantial amount of research and is largely responsible for much of what is now known about human behavior.

Second, how well do personality theories organize knowledge? Most findings from psychological research can be explained by one or more of these theories. Human behavior, from the most mundane to the most fanciful, from the simplest to the most complex, from the most altruistic to the most sadistic, from the most healthy to the most psychotic, can be explained by at least one, but usually most, of these theories. Not all explanations, of course, would be the same, and some may be quite unsatisfactory to some readers. This situation is understandable, because readers have their own personal preference and can reject explanations not compatible with their philosophical orientation.

Explanation is precisely what personality theories do best. Personality theories are considerably more useful and accurate in explaining behavior than they are in predicting or controlling behavior. Encouragingly, the more recently developed the-

TABLE 18.2   *Ratings of Personality Theorists on Criteria of a Useful Theory*

	GENERATE RESEARCH	ORGANIZE KNOWLEDGE	GUIDE ACTION	INTERNALLY CONSISTENT	PARSIMONIOUS
Freud	VH	M	M	L	M
Erikson	M	H	M	H	M
Adler	H	H	H	L	M
Jung	M	H	L	L	L
Sullivan	L	M	M	M	L
Horney	VL	L	L	L	L
Fromm	VL	H	L	L	L
Klein	L	L	H	H	L
Dollard & Miller	H	H	H	H	M
Skinner	VH	M	VH	VH	H
Bandura	VH	VH	H	VH	VH
Rotter	H	H	M	H	H
Mischel	M	M	M	H	H
Cattell/Eysenck	H	H	M	M	H
Allport	M	L	M	H	H
Kelly	L	VL	L	VH	VH
Maslow	VH	VH	H	M	M
Rogers	H	H	M	VH	VH
May	VL	H	VL	L	M

VH = *Very High*   H = *High*   M = *Moderate*   L = *Low*   VL = *Very Low*

ories are becoming more sophisticated at predicting human behavior, and they are also more effective at suggesting the means to control it. The earlier theories, especially those of Freud and Adler, are extremely useful in explaining what is already known about human behavior, but they are less proficient at predicting it. Although Freud's psychoanalysis can accommodate nearly anything human, I gave it only a moderate rating on its ability to organize knowledge, because it often offers the same explanation for contradictory findings and contradictory explanations for the same finding. However, I gave Adler's theory a high rating on this criterion because nearly all behavior can be seen as either useless or useful attempts to gain superiority or success. The only two theories with very high ratings on their usefulness in organizing knowledge are those of Bandura and Maslow. Bandura's concept of reciprocal determinism explains much of our behaviors, including those stemming from chance events. Maslow's theory is able to organize most of behavior in terms of the hierarchy of needs concept and to offer an explanation for a wide range of human activity.

The third criterion for evaluating personality theory is the extent to which it serves as a guide for the practitioner. The majority of our theories receive at least a moderate rating on this criterion. However, this rating presupposes that the practitioner, be it a psychotherapist, plant manager, parent, politician, or teacher, has extensive knowledge of at least one theory. However, without that knowledge the theory has no value as a practical tool, and, even with that knowledge, the practitioner will sometimes face problems for which contemporary personality theory offers no ready-made solutions. Despite these shortcomings, knowledge of the various personality theories serves as a practical guide for those who must understand, explain, control, or predict human behavior. Table 18.2 reveals that Skinner's behavioral analysis receives a very high rating as a guide to the practitioner, and that the theories of Adler, Klein, Dollard and Miller, Bandura, and Maslow all receive a high rating.

This third criterion of a useful theory is sometimes overlooked by those who believe that theory and practice are necessarily antithetical and that theory exists only in some abstract realm far removed from practical concerns. For the person making daily decisions about human behavior, knowledge of one or more personality theories can eliminate endless floundering and serve as a practical guide to action.

The fourth criterion of a useful theory is internal consistency. In general, older theories are less internally consistent than later ones, partly because they employ terminology that is difficult to operationally define. Later personality theorists, such as Bandura and Mischel, have been more precise in defining terms in ways that suggest testable hypotheses. Several other theories, including those of Erikson, Klein, Dollard and Miller, Skinner, Rotter, Allport, Kelly, and Rogers receive a high or very high rating on internal consistency.

Finally, are current personality theories parsimonious? A review of Table 18.2 reveals that no theory is rated very low on this criterion, despite the tremendous diversity and complexity of human personality. Several, however, are probably needlessly cumbersome, notably those of Jung, Sullivan, Horney, Fromm, and Klein. All of these theorists introduced terms or concepts that have detracted from their theory's simplicity.

The ratings in Table 18.2, of course, are not chiseled in stone. They merely represent my judgment of where each theory falls on the five criteria of a useful theory. Also, the table is but a synopsis of the ratings. A more detailed discussion is found in the "Critique" section of the 16 preceding chapters. Notice also that these personality theories receive the highest marks on their ability to organize knowledge and to explain what is known about human behavior. Only Horney, Klein, Allport, and Kelly fail to receive at least a "Moderate" rating on this criterion. In summary, useful theories are practical. Not only do they explain data and offer guidance to the researcher, but they also help the clinician, teacher, parent, and administrator make decisions that involve human behavior.

THEORISTS OF PERSONALITY

In the present volume, I have devoted a little more space to the lives of the theorists than is typically found in personality textbooks. One reason for this is my hypothesis that personality differences among the theorists account, at least in part, for differences among their theories. Differences in birth order, family size, religious and socioeconomic backgrounds, closeness to mother or father, training, and education, in part, account for differences in the manner in which these theorists view the world and also their concepts of humanity.

On the other hand, these theorists have also been similar in some respects. For example, each of these persons has been motivated to construct and publish a personal view of human personality. Not every observer of human behavior is so disposed. What other characteristics do these theorists have in common? Without indulging in too much groundless speculation, I can say that all of them have possessed superior intelligence, nearly all have been highly creative, and most have had outstanding literary skills. Several of the theorists have been unusually romantic, almost to the point of sentimentality. Many were lonely, at least at one time or another during their lives. Freud remained somewhat distrustful of outsiders throughout his life; Jung retreated into extreme isolation during his late 30s; Klein had difficulties with many of her colleagues and waged a bitter and endless war with her own daughter; Eysenck was not close to either parent, and was literally a man without a country for some time; Maslow was painfully shy during his youth; Rogers, who like Maslow came from a large family, spent most of his childhood and adolescence as a loner; and Sullivan, an only child, had difficulties with interpersonal relationships during most of his life. Another characteristic shared by most of these theorists is the fervent belief that they were scientists and were making observations and constructing theories within the framework of science.

FUTURE DIRECTIONS

Perhaps the only accurate statement one can make about the future is this: "No accurate statements can be made about the future." Nevertheless, I will venture a few guesses about the future direction of personality theory, guesses that do not require prophetic vision, because most of these forecasts simply call for extending current trends.

First, recent years have seen a shift away from practicing clinicians formulating grand, all-encompassing theories based largely on their therapeutic experiences. This was the procedure followed by many early theorists—Freud, Erikson, Adler, Jung, Sullivan, Horney, Fromm, Klein, and Kelly. Personality theories are now being built piece by piece on the foundation of empirical research, and it appears that this trend will continue. These newer theories are less inclusive, less speculative, and less philosophical than those that emanated from the consulting rooms and libraries of the above-mentioned theorists.

These smaller, lower-level theories are being developed by academic, research-oriented psychologists studying one variable at a time and developing a limited model to explain that variable. Being less philosophical, these theories will be less concerned with such topics as causality versus teleology. They will avoid postulating a single master motive, such as self-actualization or striving for success. Conscious versus unconscious motivation and human agency versus determinism will be matters for empirical research, not personal opinion. Hard data will replace philosophical speculation as the cornerstone of future personality theories.

Although these newer theories may be less global than the older ones, they nevertheless will borrow data from a variety of related fields. Pervin (1990b) pointed out that progress in the study of personality is currently closely tied to developments in other fields of psychology. He went on to predict that progress in other disciplines, such as biopsychology, neuropsychology, computer science, sociology, and anthropology may facilitate developments in personality theory, provided personality theorists keep up with progress in these other fields and do not allow such progress to destroy the identity of personality study.

Another trend in personality theory is the greater reliance on team effort rather than on the work of a single person. The vast research on which future theories will be constructed can only be conducted by a well-coordinated group effort. Carl Rogers initiated this procedure nearly 50 years ago by relying on graduate students and colleagues for assistance in conducting research on client-centered psychotherapy. Albert Bandura has refined this approach, but has been much more empirical. Bandura is building a social-cognitive theory in small increments as he gathers data from studies carried out by him and his colleagues.

No single individual will be able to conduct enough research to support an adequate theory of personality. At the very least, a lifetime of solid empirical research by one person would be needed before a theory could begin to have firm underpinnings. For one person to come up with insightful, comprehensive, consistent, and researchable ideas concerning the nature of human personality is one thing; but for that same person to single-handedly conduct research, compile data, and publish results covering the full range of personality would seem to be impossible. Only a cooperative team approach can provide sufficient data for even a moderately comprehensive theory of personality.

GLOSSARY

A

accusation Adlerian safeguarding tendency whereby one protects magnified feelings of self-esteem by blaming others for one's own failures.

acrophobia An intense fear of high places.

active imagination Technique used by Jung to uncover collective unconscious material. Subjects are asked to concentrate on an image until a series of fantasies are produced.

activity (Adler) Degree of activity is the level of energy or interest with which one moves toward finding solutions to life's problems.

actualizing tendency (Rogers) Tendency within all people to move toward completion or fulfillment of potentials.

adolescence (Erikson) An important psychosocial stage when ego identity should be formed. Adolescence is characterized by puberty and the crisis of identity vs. identity confusion.

adulthood (Erikson) The ages from about 31 to 60 that are characterized by the psychosexual mode of procreativity and the crisis of generativity vs. stagnation.

aesthetic needs (Maslow) Needs for art, music, beauty, and the like. Although they may be related to the basic conative needs, aesthetic needs are a separate dimension.

agape Altruistic love.

aggression (Adler) Safeguarding tendencies that may include depreciation or accusation of others, as well as self-accusation, all designed to protect exaggerated feelings of personal superiority by striking out against other people.

aggression (Freud) One of two primary instincts or drives that motivate people. Aggression is the outward manifestation of the death instinct and is at least a partial explanation for wars, personal hostility, sadism, masochism, and murder.

amnesia The inability to recall past experiences. May be due to physical or psychological trauma.

anal character Freudian term for a person characterized by compulsive neatness, stubbornness, and miserliness.

anal phase (Freud) Sometimes called the anal-sadistic phase, this second stage of the infantile period is characterized by a child's attempts to gain pleasure from the excretory function and by such related behaviors as destroying or losing objects, stubbornness, neatness, and miserliness. Corresponds roughly to the second year of life.

anal triad (Freud) The three traits of compulsive neatness, stubbornness, and miserliness that characterize the anal character.

anal-urethral-muscular Erikson's term for the young child's psychosexual mode of adapting.

Analytical psychology Theory of personality and approach to psychotherapy founded by Carl Jung.

anima Jungian archetype that represents the feminine component in the personality of males and originates from men's inherited experiences with women.

animus Jungian archetype that represents the masculine component in the personality of females and originates from women's inherited experiences with men.

anorexia nervosa Eating disorder characterized by intentional starvation, distorted body image, excessive amounts of energy, and an intense fear of gaining weight.

anxiety A felt, affective, unpleasant state accompanied by the physical sensation of uneasiness.

anxiety (Kelly) The recognition that the events with which one is confronted lie outside the range of convenience of one's construct system.

anxiety (May) The experience of the threat of imminent nonbeing.

apathy (Sullivan) Dynamism that reduces tensions of needs through the adoption of an indifferent attitude.

approach-avoidance conflict (Dollard & Miller) Conflict arising whenever the same stimulus carries both a positive and a negative value.

approach gradient (see **gradient of approach**)

archetypes Jung's concept that refers to the contents of the collective unconscious. Archetypes, also called primordial images or collective symbols, represent psychic patterns of inherited behavior and are thus distinguished from instincts, which are physical impulses toward action. Typical archetypes are the anima, animus, and shadow.

attention (Bandura) First of four processes that govern modeling, attention refers to the active perception of others' behavior.

attitude (Cattell) A motivational trait that refers to a specific course of action in response to a given situation. In Cattell's definition, an attitude includes a particular situation, interest, response, and object.

attitude (Jung) A predisposition to act or react in a characteristic manner, that is, in either an introverted or an extraverted direction.

authoritarianism (Fromm) The tendency to give up one's independence and to unite with another person or persons in order to gain strength. Takes the form of masochism or sadism.

autism Pathological condition characterized by the tendency to perceive the world in terms of one's own personality rather than in terms of reality. Withdrawal from real life through daydreams, bizarre fantasies, and private language.

autistic language (Sullivan) Private or parataxic language, which makes little or no sense to other people.

autoeroticism Self-gratification. In Freudian theory, infants are seen as exclusively autoerotic because their interest in pleasure is limited to themselves.

aversive stimulus A painful or undesired stimulus that, when associated with a response, decreases the tendency of that response to be repeated in similar situations.

avoidance-avoidance conflict (Dollard & Miller) Conflict arising whenever a person is trapped midway between two negative stimuli of equal value.

avoidance gradient (see **gradient of avoidance**)

axiology That realm of philosophy dealing with the nature of values.

B

B-love (Maslow) Love between self-actualizing people and characterized by the love for the *being* of the other.

B-values (Maslow) The values of self-actualizing people, including beauty, truth, goodness, justice, wholeness, and the like.

basic anxiety (Fromm) The feeling of being alone and isolated, separated from the natural world.

basic anxiety (Horney) Feelings of isolation and helplessness in a potentially hostile world.

basic anxiety (Maslow) Anxiety arising from inability to satisfy physiological and safety needs.

basic conflict (Horney) The incompatible tendency to move toward, against, and away from people.

basic strength The ego quality that emerges from the conflict between antithetical elements in Erikson's stages of development.

behavior potential (Rotter) The possibility of a particular response occurring at a given time and place as calculated in relation to the reinforcement of that response.

behavioral equation Cattell's basic formula for representing and predicting behavior.

behaviorism A "school" of psychology that limits its subject matter to observable behavior. John B. Watson is usually credited with being the founder of behaviorism, with B. F. Skinner its most notable proponent.

being-in-the-world (see **Dasein**)

biophilia (May) Love of life.

bipolar factors Factors with two poles, that is, factors scaled from a minus point to a positive point, with zero representing the midpoint.

C

cardinal traits (Allport) (see **disposition, cardinal**)

care (Erikson) A commitment to take care of the people and things that one has learned to care for.

castration anxiety (Freud) (see **castration complex**)

castration complex (Freud) Condition that accompanies the Oedipus complex, but takes different forms in the two sexes. In boys it takes the form of *castration anxiety*, or fear of having one's penis removed, and is responsible for shattering the Oedipus complex. In girls it takes the form of *penis envy*, or the desire to have a penis, and it precedes and instigates the Oedipus complex.

causality An explanation of behavior in terms of past experiences.

central traits (Allport) (see **disposition, central**)

chance encounters (Bandura) An unintended meeting of persons unfamiliar to each other.

character (Fromm) Relatively permanent acquired qualities through which people relate themselves to others and to the world.

choice corollary Kelly's assumption that people choose the alternative in a dichotomized construct that they perceive as extending their range of future choices.

client-centered therapy Approach to psychotherapy originated by Rogers, which is based on respect for the person's capacity to grow within a nurturant climate.

cognitive needs (Maslow) Needs for knowledge and understanding; related to basic or conative needs, yet operate on a different dimension.

collective unconscious Jung's idea of an inherited unconscious, which is responsible for many of our behaviors, ideas, and dream images. The collective unconscious lies beyond our personal experiences and originates with repeated experiences of our ancestors.

common traits (Allport) (see **trait, common**)

commonality corollary (Kelly) The personal constructs of people with similar experiences tend to be similar.

competencies (Mischel) People's cognitive and behavioral construction of what they can and cannot do, based on their observations of the world, themselves, and others.

complex (Jung) An emotionally toned conglomeration of ideas, which comprise the contents of the personal unconscious. Jung originally used the Word Association Test to uncover complexes.

compulsion The irresistible repetition of an act.

conative Pertaining to willful, purposive striving.

conditioned reinforcer (Skinner) Environmental event that is not by nature satisfying but becomes so because it is associated with unlearned or unconditioned reinforcers such as food, sex, and the like.

conditions of worth (Rogers) Restrictions or qualifications attached to one person's regard for another.

conformity (Fromm) Means of escaping from isolation and aloneness by giving up one's self and becoming whatever others desire.

congruence (Rogers) The matching of organismic experiences with awareness and with the ability to express those experiences. One of three "necessary and sufficient" therapeutic conditions.

conscience (Freud) The part of the superego that results from experience with punishment and that, therefore, tells a person what is wrong or improper conduct.

conscious (Freud) Those mental elements in awareness at any given time.

conscious (Jung) Mental images that are sensed by the ego and that play a relatively minor role in Jungian theory.

consensual validation (Sullivan) The agreement of two or more people on the meaning of experiences, especially language.

consistency paradox Mischel's term for the observation that clinical intuition and the perceptions of laypeople suggest that behavior is consistent, whereas research finds that it is not.

constructing obstacles (Adler) Safeguarding tendency in which people create a barrier to their own success, thus allowing them to protect their self-esteem by either using the barrier as an excuse for failure or by overcoming it.

construction corollary Kelly's assumption that people anticipate events according to their interpretations of recurrent themes.

constructive alternativism Kelly's view that events can be looked at (construed) from a different (alternative) perspective.

continuous schedule (Skinner) The reinforcement of an organism for every correct trial; opposed to the intermittent schedule in which only certain selected responses are reinforced.

conversion hysteria Neurotic reaction characterized by the transformation of repressed psychological conflicts into overt physical symptoms.

core pathology (Erikson) A psychosocial disorder at any of the eight stages of development that results from too little basic strength.

correlation coefficient A mathematical index used to measure the direction and magnitude of the relationship between two variables.

cosmology That realm of philosophy dealing with the nature of causation.

countertransference Strong undeserved feelings the therapist develops toward the patient during the course of treatment. These feelings can be either positive or negative and are considered by most writers to be a hindrance to successful psychotherapy.

cue (Dollard & Miller) Any stimulus distinctive enough to guide responses but not strong enough to serve as a drive.

cue-producing responses (Dollard & Miller) A series of responses, each of which produces cues that, in turn, lead to additional responses.

curvilinear A relationship between two variables in which scores on the first variable increase with increases of scores on the second, but only to a certain point where they then begin to decrease.

D

D-love (Maslow) Deficiency love or affection (attachment) based on the lover's specific deficiency and the loved one's ability to satisfy that deficit.

Dasein An existential term meaning a sense of self as a free and responsible person whose existence is embedded in the world of things, of people, and of self-awareness.

death instinct (Freud) One of two primary drives or impulses, the death instinct is also known as Thanatos or aggression.

deductive method Approach to factor analytical theories of personality that gathers data on the basis of previously determined hypotheses or theories. Reasoning from the general to the particular.

defense mechanisms (Freud) Techniques such as repression, reaction formation, sublimation, and the like, whereby the ego defends itself against the pain of anxiety.

defensiveness (Rogers) Protection of the self-concept against anxiety and threat by denial and distortion of experiences inconsistent with it.

degree of activity (Adler) (see **activity**)

delay of gratification Refers to the observation that some people some of the time will prefer more valued delayed rewards over lesser valued immediate ones.

denial (Rogers) The blocking of an experience or some aspect of an experience from awareness because it is inconsistent with the self-concept.

dependent variable A variable within an experimental design whose value is hypothesized to change as a result of changes in the independent variable.

depreciation Adlerian safeguarding tendency whereby another's achievements are undervalued and one's own are overvalued.

depressive position (Klein) Feelings of anxiety over losing a loved object coupled with a sense of guilt for wanting to destroy that object.

desacralization (Maslow) The process of removing respect, joy, awe, and rapture from an experience, which then purifies or objectifies that experience.

destructiveness (Fromm) Method of escaping from freedom by eliminating people or objects, thus restoring feelings of power.

dichotomy corollary Kelly's assumption that people construe events in an either/or (dichotomous) manner.

differential R (dR technique) Correlational procedure pioneered by Cattell, which correlates scores of a large number of people on many tests obtained at two different occasions. The dR technique measures consistency of the scores.

disengagement of behavior (Bandura) Just-ification of otherwise reprehensible behavior through one of four techniques: (1) redefinition of behavior; (2) distortion of the effects of behavior; (3) denial of responsibility; or (4) dehumanization or blaming the victim.

disengagement of internal standards (Bandura) The displacement or diffusion of responsibility for the injurious effects of one's actions.

disposition, cardinal (Allport) Personal traits so dominant in an individual's life that they cannot be hidden. Most people do not have a cardinal disposition.

disposition, central (Allport) The five to ten personal traits around which a person's life focuses.

disposition, secondary (Allport) The least characteristic and reliable of the personal traits that still appear with some regularity in an individual's life.

dissociation (Sullivan) The process of separating unwanted impulses, desires, and needs from the self-system.

distortion (Rogers) Misinterpretation of an experience so that it is seen as fitting into some aspect of the self-concept.

double approach–avoidance conflict (Dollard & Miller) Conflict arising whenever a person is trapped midway between two stimuli, each of which has both a negative and a positive value.

drive (Dollard & Miller) Any stimulus strong enough to impel action.

dynamic calculus Cattell's complex procedure for determining the strength and direction of attitudes. The dynamic calculus includes the more specific behavioral equation, which permits the specific prediction of behavior.

dynamic lattice Cattell's term for a network of motives that includes attitudes, sems, and ergs.

dynamics of personality Refers to motivation or those units that drive people to respond.

dynamisms (Sullivan) Relatively consistent patterns of action that characterize the person throughout a lifetime. Similar to traits or habit patterns.

dystonic Erikson's term for the negative element in each pair of opposites that characterizes the eight stages of development.

E

earliest recollections Technique proposed by Adler to understand the pattern or theme that runs throughout a person's style of life.

early childhood (Erikson) The second stage of psychosocial development, characterized by the anal-urethral-muscular psychosexual mode and by the crisis of autonomy vs. shame and doubt.

eclecticism Approach that allows selection of usable elements from different theories or approaches and combines them in a consistent and unified manner.

ego (Freud) The province of the mind that refers to the "I" or those experiences that are owned (not necessarily consciously) by the person. As the only region of the mind in contact with the real world, the ego is said to serve the reality principle.

ego (Jung) The center of consciousness. In Jungian psychology the ego is of lesser importance than the more inclusive self and is limited to consciousness.

ego-ideal (Freud) The part of the superego that results from experiences with reward and that, therefore, teach a person what is right or proper conduct.

eidetic personifications (Sullivan) Imaginary traits attributed to real or imaginary people in order to protect one's self-esteem.

Eigenwelt An existentialist term meaning the world of one's relationship to self. One of three simultaneous modes of being-in-the-world.

elaborative choice (Kelly) Making choices that will increase a person's range of future choices.

empathic listening (Rogers) The accurate sensing of the feelings of another and the communication of these perceptions. One of three "necessary and sufficient" therapeutic conditions.

empathy (Sullivan) An indefinite process through which anxiety is transferred from one person to another, for example, from mother to infant.

empirical Based on experience, systematic observation, and experiment rather than on logical reasoning or philosophical speculation.

empirical law of effect (Rotter) Behaviors that move people in the direction of their goals are more likely to be reinforced.

encoding strategies (Mischel) People's ways of transforming stimulus inputs into information about themselves, other people, and the world.

energy transformations (Sullivan) Overt or covert actions designed to satisfy needs or reduce anxiety.

enhancement needs (Rogers) The need to develop, to grow, and to achieve.

entropy The principle stating that when objects of differing temperatures meet, heat flows from the hotter to the colder, bringing about an equalization of temperature. Jung emphasized that tension is generated by the meeting of opposites.

epigenetic principle Erikson's term meaning that one component grows out of another in its proper time and sequence.

epistemology That branch of philosophy which deals with the nature of knowledge.

equivalence The principle of equivalence states that when a given quantity of energy is expended in the performance of an activity, an equal amount of energy will appear elsewhere. Jung emphasized that psychic energy is not destroyed but merely displaced.

ergs Energy inherent in primary or innate drives or motives. In Cattell's theory, ergs are contrasted to sentiments or sems, which are learned motives.

erogenous zones Organs of the body that are especially sensitive to the reception of pleasure. In Freudian theory, the three principal erogenous zones are the mouth, anus, and genitals.

eros The desire for an enduring union with a loved one.

essential freedom (May) The freedom of being or the freedom of the conscious mind. Essential freedom cannot be limited by chains or bars.

excuses Adlerian safeguarding tendencies whereby the person, through the use of reasonable sounding justifications, becomes convinced of the reality of self-erected obstacles.

existential freedom (May) The freedom of doing one's will. Existential freedom can be limited by chains or bars.

existential living Rogers' term indicating a tendency to live in the moment.

existential needs (Fromm) Peculiarly human needs aimed at moving people toward a reunification with the natural world. Fromm listed relatedness, transcendence, rootedness, a sense of identity, and a frame of orientation as existential or human needs.

expectancy The subjective probability held by a person that any specific reinforcement or set of reinforcements will occur in a given situation.

experience corollary Kelly's view that people continually revise their personal constructs as the result of experience.

exploitative orientation (Fromm) Refers to people who take from others, either by force or cunning.

external evaluation (Rogers) Conditions of worth placed on a person, which may then serve as a criterion for evaluating one's own conduct. Conditions of worth block growth and interfere with one's becoming fully functioning.

external reinforcement (Rotter) The positive or negative value of any reinforcing event, as seen from the view of societal or cultural values.

extinction The tendency of a previously acquired response to become progressively weakened upon nonreinforcement.

extraversion (E) (Eysenck) One of three types of superfactors, identified by Eysenck, and consisting of two opposite poles—extraversion and introversion. *Extraverts* are characterized behaviorally by sociability and impulsiveness and physiologically by a low level of cortical arousal. *Introverts*, by contrast, are characterized by unsociability and caution and by a high level of cortical arousal.

extraversion (Jung) An attitude or type marked by the turning outward of psychic energy so that a person is oriented toward the objective world.

F

factor A unit of personality derived through factor analysis. However, the term is sometimes used more generally to include any underlying aspect of personality.

factor analysis A mathematical procedure for reducing a large number of variables to a few. Used by Cattell and Eysenck to identify personality traits.

factor loadings The amount of correlation that a score contributes to a given factor.

fear (Kelly) A specific threat to one's personal constructs.

feeling (Jung) A rational function that tells us the value of something. The feeling function can be either extraverted (directed toward the objective world) or introverted (directed toward the subjective world).

fiction (Adler) A belief or expectation of the future, which serves to motivate present behavior. The truthfulness of a fictional idea is immaterial since the person acts as if the idea were true.

fixation A defense mechanism that arises when psychic energy is blocked at one stage of development, thus making change or psychological growth difficult.

fixation (Fromm) The nonproductive form of rootedness marked by a reluctance to grow beyond the security provided by one's mother.

fixed-interval (Skinner) Intermittent reinforcement schedule whereby the organism is reinforced for its first response following a designated period of time (for example, FI 10 means that the animal is reinforced for its initial response after 10 minutes have elapsed since its previous reinforcement).

fixed-ratio (Skinner) Reinforcement schedule in which the organism is reinforced intermittently according to a specified number of responses it makes (for example, FR 7 means that the organism is reinforced for every seventh response).

formative tendency (Rogers) Tendency in all matter to evolve from simpler to more complex forms.

fortuitous events (Bandura) Environmental events that are unexpected and unintended.

fragmentation corollary Kelly's assumption that behavior is sometimes inconsistent because one's construct systems can admit incompatible elements.

frame of orientation (Fromm) The need for humans to develop a unifying philosophy or consistent way of looking at things.

free association Technique used in Freudian psychotherapy in which the therapist instructs the patient to verbalize every thought that comes to mind, no matter how irrelevant or repugnant it may appear.

freedom of movement (Rotter) The mean expectancy of being reinforced for performing all those behaviors that are directed toward the satisfaction of some general need.

frustration-aggression hypothesis Dollard and Miller's original contention that frustration inevitably leads to aggression and that aggression is always produced by frustration. Later amended to read that frustration may lead to a variety of responses, aggression being one of them.

fully functioning person (Rogers) (see **person of tomorrow**)

functional autonomy (Allport) The tendency for some motives to become independent from the original motive responsible for the behavior.

G

Gemeinschaftsgefühl (see **social interest**)

generalization The transfer of the effects of one learning situation to another.

generalized expectancy (Rotter) Expectation based on similar past experiences that a given behavior will be reinforced.

generalized reinforcer (Skinner) A conditioned reinforcer that has been associated with several primary reinforcers. Money, for example, is a generalized reinforcer because it is associated with food, shelter, and other primary reinforcers.

genital-locomotor Erikson's term for the preschool child's psychosexual mode of adapting.

genital stage (Freud) Period of life beginning with puberty and continuing through adulthood and marked by full sexual identity.

genital stage (Klein) Comparable to Freud's phallic stage, that is, the time around three to five when the Oedipus complex reaches its culmination.

genitality (Erikson) The psychosexual mode of young adulthood characterized by mutual trust and a sharing of sexual satisfactions.

gradient of approach (Dollard & Miller) The tendency to approach a goal becomes stronger as a person nears the goal.

gradient of avoidance (Dollard & Miller)   The tendency to avoid a feared stimulus becomes stronger as a person nears it. The gradient of avoidance is steeper (progressively stronger) than the gradient of approach.

gradient of reinforcement (Dollard & Miller)   Refers to the sequence of responses leading to the final reinforced one. Each response in the sequence is progressively strengthened by reinforcement.

great mother   Jungian archetype of the opposing forces of fertility and destruction.

guilt (Kelly)   The sense of having lost one's core role structure.

guilt (May)   An ontological characteristic of human existence arising from our separation from the natural world (*Umwelt*), from other people (*Mitwelt*), or from our self (*Eigenwelt*).

H

hero   A Jungian archetype representing the myth of the godlike man who conquers or vanquishes evil, usually in the form of a monster, dragon, or serpent.

hesitating (Adler)   Safeguarding tendency characterized by vacillation or procrastination designed to provide a person with the excuse "It's too late now."

heuristic   Pertaining to a method or theory that leads to the discovery of new information.

hierarchy of needs   Maslow's concept that needs are ordered in such a manner that those on a lower level must be satisfied before higher-level needs become activated.

hoarding characters (Fromm)   People who seek to save and not let go of material possessions, feelings, or ideas.

holistic-dynamic theory   Maslow's theory of personality, which stresses both the unity of the organism and the motivational aspects of personality.

humanistic psychoanalysis   Fromm's theory of personality that combines the basics of both psychoanalysis and humanistic psychology.

humanistic psychology   Ill-defined term referring to those theories and systems of psychology that, in general, emphasize the power of the individual to make conscious rational decisions and that stress the primacy of humans to other beings.

hypochondriasis   Exaggerated attention to and anxiety about one's health.

hypothesis   An assumption or educated guess that can be scientifically tested.

hysteria (Freud)   A mental disorder marked by the conversion of repressed psychical elements into somatic symptoms such as impotency, paralysis, or blindness, when no physiological bases for these symptoms exist.

I

id (Freud)   The region of personality that is alien to the ego because it includes experiences that have never been owned by the person. The id is the home base for all the instincts, and its sole function is to seek pleasure regardless of consequences.

ideal self (Rogers)   One's view of self as one would like to be.

idealistic principle (Freud)   Refers to the demands of the superego that the ego oppose the pleasure-seeking id and instigate, instead, behaviors consistent with the child's perception of parental standards.

idealization   Adlerian safeguarding tendency whereby the individual, in order to maintain exaggerated feelings of inferiority, sets up an ideal model so that any real person, by comparison, will inevitably fall short and thus be depreciated.

idealized self-image (Horney)   An attempt to solve basic conflicts by adopting a belief in one's godlike qualities.

identity crisis   Erickson's term for a crucial period or turning point in the life cycle that may result in either more or less ego strength. Identity crises can be found in those Eriksonian stages that follow the development of identity, ordinarily during adolescence.

idiographic Approach to the study of personality, which is based on the single case.

incestuous symbiosis (Fromm) Extreme dependence on a mother or mother substitute.

incongruence (Rogers) The perception of discrepancies between organismic self, self-concept, and ideal self.

independent variable A variable that is manipulated by the experimenter in order to assess its possible effects on behavior, that is, on the dependent variable.

Individual Psychology Theory of personality and approach to psychotherapy founded by Alfred Adler.

individuality corollary Kelly's assumption that people have different experiences and therefore construe events in different ways.

individuation Jung's term for the process of becoming a whole person, that is, an individual with a high level of psychic development.

inductive method Approach to factor analytic theories of personality that gathers data with no preconceived hypotheses or theory in mind. Reasoning from the particular to the general.

infancy (Erikson) The first stage of psychosocial development—one marked by the oral-sensory mode and by the crisis of basic trust vs. basic mistrust.

infantile stage (Freud) First four or five years of life characterized by autoerotic or pleasure-seeking behavior and consisting of the oral, anal, and phallic substages.

inferiority complex (Adler) Exaggerated or abnormally strong feelings of inferiority, which usually interfere with socially useful solutions to life's problems.

instinct (Freud) From the German *Trieb*, meaning drive or impulse, this term refers to an internal stimulus that impels action or thought. The two primary instincts are sex and aggression.

instinct (Jung) An unconscious physical impulse toward action. Instincts are the physical counterpart of archetypes.

instinctoid needs (Maslow) Needs that are innately determined but that can be modified through learning. The frustration of instinctoid needs leads to various types of pathology.

intentionality (May) The underlying structure that gives meaning to our experience.

interactionist One who believes that behavior results from an interaction of environmental variables and person variables, including cognition.

intermittent schedule (Skinner) The reinforcement of an organism on only certain selected occurrences of a response. Opposed to a continuous schedule in which the organism is reinforced for every correct trial. The four most common intermittent schedules are: fixed-ratio, variable-ratio, fixed-interval, and variable-interval.

internal reinforcement (Rotter) The individual's perception of the positive or negative value of any reinforcing event.

internalization (object relations theory) A process in which the person takes in (introjects) aspects of the external world and then organizes those introjections in a psychologically meaningful way.

internalized object relationships (Kernberg) Basic structural units in any personality organization, consisting of an self-image, an object-image, and an affect.

interpersonal trust (Rotter) A generalized expectancy held by a person that other people can be relied on to keep their word. The Interpersonal Trust Scale attempts to measure degree of interpersonal trust.

intimacy (Erikson) The ability to fuse one's identity with that of another person without fear of losing it. The syntonic element of young adulthood.

intimacy (Sullivan) Conjunctive dynamism marked by a close personal relationship with another person who is more or less of equal status.

introjection (Klein) The symbolic taking of external objects, such as the mother's breast, into one's own body.

introversion (Eysenck) (see **extraversion, Eysenck**)

introversion (Jung) An attitude or type characterized by the turning inward of psychic energy with an orientation toward the subjective.

intuition (Jung)   An irrational function that involves perception of elementary data that are beyond our awareness. Intuitive people "know" something without understanding how they know.

ipsative   Refers to a method of measurement that uses the person's own behavior or scores as a standard of reference; opposed to the normative method, which compares a person's scores to those obtained by a norm group.

irrational functions (Jung)   Methods of dealing with the world without evaluation or thinking. Sensing and intuiting are the two irrational functions.

isolation (Erikson)   The inability to share true intimacy or to take chances with one's identity. The dystonic element of young adulthood.

isolation (Freud)   A defense mechanism; also a type of repression, whereby the ego attempts to isolate an experience by establishing a period of blacked-out affect immediately following that experience.

J

Jonah complex   The fear of being one's best.

L

L data   Cattell's term for life record or information collected on a person by objective observation.

latency (Erikson)   The psychosexual mode of the school age child. A period of little sexual development.

latency stage (Freud)   The time between infancy and puberty when psychosexual growth is at a standstill.

latent dream content (Freud)   The underlying, unconscious meaning of a dream. Freud held that the latent content, which can only be revealed through dream interpretation, was more important than the surface or manifest content.

libido (Freud)   Psychic energy of the life instinct; sexual drive or energy.

life instinct (Freud)   One of two primary drives or impulses, the life instinct is also called Eros or sex.

locus of control (Rotter)   Refers to the belief people have that their attempts to reach a goal are within their control (internal locus of control) or primarily due to powerful events such as fate, chance, or other people (external locus of control). Locus of control is measured by the Internal–External Control Scale.

love (Fromm)   A union with another person in which a person retains separateness and integrity of self.

love (May)   To delight in the presence of the other person and to affirm that person's value and development as much as one's own.

lust (Sullivan)   Isolating dynamism in which one person has an impersonal sexual interest in another.

M

maintenance needs (Rogers)   Those basic needs that protect the status quo. They may be either physiological (for example, food) or interpersonal (for example, the need to maintain the current self-concept).

malevolence   Sullivan's term for those destructive behavior patterns dominated by the attitude that people are evil and harmful and that the world is a bad place to live.

malignant aggression (Fromm)   The destruction of life for reasons other than survival.

mandala (Jung)   Symbol representing the striving for unity and completion. It is often seen as a circle within a square or a square within a circle.

manifest dream content (Freud)   The surface or conscious level of a dream. Freud believed that the manifest level of a dream has no deep psychological significance and that the unconscious or latent level holds the key to the dream's true meaning.

marketing characters (Fromm)   People who see themselves as commodities, with their personal value dependent on their ability to sell themselves.

masculine protest   Adler's term for the neurotic and erroneous belief held by some men and women that men are superior to women.

masochism   A condition characterized by the reception of sexual pleasure from suffering pain and humiliation inflicted either by self or by others.

maturity (Freud)   The final psychosexual stage following infancy, latency, and the genital period. Hypothetically, maturity would be characterized by a strong ego in control of the id and the superego and by an ever-expanding realm of consciousness.

mean   The arithmetic average score in a distribution.

mechanisms of defense (Freud)   (see **defense mechanisms**)

mediation   The cognitive or mental process ensuing between the physical stimulus and the subsequent response.

metamotivation (Maslow)   The motives of self-actualizing people, including especially the B-values.

metapathology (Maslow)   Illness characterized by absence of values, lack of fulfillment, and loss of meaning that results from deprivation of self-actualization needs.

metaphysics   That branch of philosophy dealing with the nature of reality.

metavalues (Maslow)   (see **B-values**)

minimal goal level (Rotter)   Lowest possible reinforcement accepted as positive.

Mitwelt   An existentialist term meaning the world of one's relationship to other people. One of three simultaneous modes of being-in-the-world.

mode   The most frequent score in a distribution.

modeling (Bandura)   One of two basic sources of learning, modeling involves the observation of others and thus learning from their actions. More than simple imitation, modeling entails the addition and subtraction of specific acts and the observation of consequences of others' behavior.

modulation corollary (Kelly)   To the degree that personal constructs are permeable (resilient), they are subject to change through experience.

moral hypochondriasis (Fromm)   Preoccupation with guilt about things one has done wrong.

morphogenic   Allport's concept of science, which deals with idiographic or individual methods of data gathering.

motor production (Bandura)   Third of four processes that affect modeling, motor production involves the conversion of cognitive representations into appropriate actions.

moving against people   One of Horney's neurotic trends in which neurotics protect themselves against the hostility of others by adopting an aggressive strategy.

moving away from others   One of Horney's neurotic trends in which neurotics protect themselves against feelings of isolation by adopting a detached attitude.

moving backward (Adler)   Safeguarding inflated feelings of superiority by reverting to a more secure period of life.

moving toward people   One of Horney's neurotic trends in which neurotics develop a need for others as a protection against feelings of helplessness.

myth (May)   Belief system that provides explanations for personal and social problems.

N

narcism (Cattell)   An erg or innate drive to be interested in one's own body and appearance (see also **narcissism**).

narcissism   Love of self or the attainment of erotic pleasure from viewing one's own body.

necrophilia   Love of death.

need potential (Rotter)   Refers to the possible occurrence of a set of functionally related behaviors directed toward the satisfaction of the same goal or a similar set of goals.

need value (Rotter)   The degree to which a person prefers one set of reinforcements to another.

negative reinforcement   The removal of any aversive stimulus that, when removed from a situation, increases the probability that a given behavior will occur.

negative transference   Strong, hostile, and undeserved feelings the patient develops toward the analyst during the course of treatment.

neurasthenia   Neurotic condition characterized by excessive fatigue, chronic aches and pains, and low motivational level.

neurosis   Somewhat dated term signifying mild personality disorders, as opposed to the more severe psychotic reactions. Neuroses are generally characterized by one or more of the following: anxiety, hysteria, phobias, obsessive–compulsive reactions, depression, chronic fatigue, and hypochondriacal reactions.

neurotic anxiety (May)   A reaction that is disproportionate to the threat and that leads to repression and defensive behaviors.

neurotic claims (Horney)   Unrealistic demands and expectations of neurotics to be entitled to special privilege.

neurotic needs (Horney)   Original 10 defenses against basic anxiety.

neurotic needs (Maslow)   Nonproductive needs that are opposed to the basic needs and that block psychological health whether or not they are satisfied.

neurotic pride (Horney)   A false pride based on one's idealized image of self.

neurotic search for glory   Horney's concept for the comprehensive drive toward actualizing the ideal self.

neurotic trends   Horney's term for the three basic attitudes toward self and others—moving toward people, moving against people, and moving away from people; a revision of her original list of 10 neurotic needs.

neuroticism (N) (Eysenck)   One of three types or superfactors identified by Eysenck. Neuroticism is a bipolar factor consisting of neuroticism at one pole and stability at the other. High scores on N may indicate anxiety, hysteria, obsessive-compulsive disorders, or criminality.

nomothetic   An approach to the study of personality that is based on general laws or principles.

nonbeing   The awareness of the possibility of one's not being through death or loss of awareness.

normal anxiety (May)   The experience of threat that accompanies growth or change in one's values.

normal autism (Mahler)   The stage in an infant's development when all its needs are satisfied automatically, that is, without the infant having to deal with the external world.

normal symbiosis (Mahler)   The second developmental stage marked by a dual unity of infant and mother.

nothingness   (see **nonbeing**)

O

object   Psychoanalytic term referring to the person or part of a person that can satisfy an instinct or drive.

object relations theory   Refers to the work of Melanie Klein and others who have extended Freudian psychoanalysis with their emphasis on early relations to parents (objects) that influence later interpersonal relationships.

obsession   A persistent or recurrent idea, usually involving an urge toward some action.

Oedipus complex   Term used by Freud to indicate the situation in which the child of either sex develops feelings of love and/or hostility for the parent. In the simple male Oedipus complex, the boy has incestuous feelings of love for the mother and hostility toward the father. The simple female Oedipus complex exists when the girl feels hostility for the mother and sexual love for the father.

old age (Erikson)   The eighth and final stage of the life cycle, marked by the psychosocial crisis of integrity vs. despair and the basic strength of wisdom.

old wise man   Jungian archetype of wisdom and meaning.

ontology   That branch of philosophy dealing with the nature of being.

open system (Allport)   Any approach to personality that takes into consideration the observation that people are not only reactive to their environment but also act upon the environment and are capable of causing the environment to react to them. An open system permits growth and change within the individual that is independent of environmental determinants.

operant conditioning (Skinner)   A type of learning in which reinforcement, which is contingent upon the occurrence of a particular response, increases the probability that the same response will occur again.

operant discrimination (Skinner)   As a consequence of an organism's reinforcement history, it learns to respond to some elements in the environment but not to others. Operant discrimination does not exist within the organism but is a function of environmental variables and the organism's previous history of reinforcement.

operant extinction (Skinner)   The loss of an operantly conditioned response due to the systematic withholding of reinforcement.

operational definition   A definition of a concept in terms of specific operations to be carried out.

oral phase (Freud)   The earliest stage of the infantile period, the oral phase is characterized by attempts to gain pleasure through the activity of the mouth, especially sucking, eating, and biting; corresponds roughly to the first 12–18 months of life.

oral-sensory   Erikson's term for the infant's first psychosexual mode of adapting.

organ dialect (Adler)   The expression of a person's underlying intentions or style of life through a diseased or dysfunctional bodily organ.

organismic   Referring to that approach to psychological theories which emphasizes the notion that the entire organism develops in a unified manner.

organismic self (Rogers)   A more general term than self-concept, the organismic self refers to the entire person, including those aspects of existence beyond awareness.

organization corollary   Kelly's notion that people arrange their personal constructs in a hierarchical system.

P

P technique   Correlational procedure pioneered by Cattell that utilizes variables or scores taken from one person obtained on many different occasions.

paranoia   Mental disorder characterized by unrealistic feelings of persecution, grandiosity, and a suspicious attitude toward others.

paranoid-schizoid position (Klein)   A tendency of the infant to see the world as having the same destructive and omnipotent qualities that it possesses.

parapraxes   Freudian slips such as slips of the tongue or pen, misreading, incorrect hearing, temporary forgetting of names and intentions, and the misplacing of objects.

parataxic (Sullivan)   Referring to a mode of cognition characterized by attribution of cause and effect when none is present; private language not consensually validated (that is, not able to be accurately communicated to others).

parataxic distortion (Sullivan)   The process of seeing a cause and effect relationship between two events in close proximity when there is no such relationship.

parsimony   Criterion of a useful theory, which states that when two theories are equal on other criteria, the simpler one is preferred.

peak experience (Maslow)   An intense, mystical experience often characteristic of self-actualizing people, but not limited to them.

penis envy (Freud)   (see **castration complex**)

perceptual-conscious (Freud)   The system that perceives external stimuli through sight, sound, taste, and so on and that communicates them to the conscious system.

perseverative functional autonomy (Allport)   Functionally independent motives that are not part of the proprium; includes addictions, the tendency to finish uncompleted tasks, and other acquired motives.

person of tomorrow (Rogers)   The psychologically healthy individual in the process of evolving into all that he or she can become.

person-centered theory   The theory of personality founded by Carl Rogers as an outgrowth of his client-centered psychotherapy.

persona   Jungian archetype that represents the side of personality that one shows to the rest of the world. Also, the mask worn by ancient Roman actors in the Greek theater, and thus the root of the word "personality."

personal constructs (Kelly)   A person's way of interpreting, explaining, and predicting events.

personal disposition (Allport)   A relatively permanent neuropsychic structure peculiar to the individual, which has the capacity to render different stimuli functionally equivalent and to initiate and guide personalized forms of behavior.

Personal Orientation Inventory (POI)   Test designed by E. L. Shostrom to measure Maslow's concept of self-actualizing tendencies in people.

personal unconscious   Jung's term for those repressed experiences that pertain exclusively to one particular individual; opposed to the collective unconscious, which pertains to unconscious experiences that originate with repeated experiences of our ancestors.

personality   A global concept referring to all those relatively permanent traits, dispositions, or characteristics within the individual, which give some degree of consistency to that person's behavior.

personifications (Sullivan)   Images a person has of self or others, such as "good-mother," "bad-mother," "good-me," and "bad-me."

phallic phase (Freud)   The third and latest stage of the infantile period, the phallic phase is characterized by the Oedipus complex. Although anatomical differences between the sexes are responsible for important differences in the male and female Oedipal periods, Freud used the term phallic phase to signify both male and female development.

phenomenology   A philosophical position emphasizing that behavior is caused by one's perceptions rather than by external reality.

philia   Brotherly or sisterly love. Friendship.

philosophy   Love of wisdom.

placebo effect   Changes in behavior or functioning brought about by one's beliefs or expectations.

play age (Erikson)   The third stage of psychosocial development, encompassing the time from about ages 3 to 5 and characterized by the genital-locomotor psychosexual mode and the crisis of initiative vs. guilt.

play construction   Erikson's projective technique for assessing personality dynamics in children through the use of toys.

pleasure principle (Freud)   The motivation of the id to seek immediate reduction of tension through the gratification of instinctual drives.

positions (Klein)   Ways in which an infant organizes its experience in order to deal with its basic conflict of love and hate. The two positions are the paranoid-schizoid position and the depressive position.

positive freedom (Fromm)   Spontaneous activity of the whole, integrated personality, positive freedom signals a reunification with others and with the world.

positive regard (Rogers)   The need to be loved, liked, or accepted by another.

positive reinforcer   Any stimulus that, when added to a situation, increases the probability that a given behavior will occur.

preconscious (Freud)   Those mental elements that are currently not in awareness, but that can become conscious with varying degrees of difficulty.

primary narcissism (Freud)   The infant's investment of libido in its own ego; self-love or autoerotic behavior of the infant (see **narcissism**).

primary process (Freud)   Refers to the id, which houses the primary motivators of behavior called instincts.

primary traits   First-order traits extracted through factor analysis of more specific behaviors.

principle of entropy (Jung)   (see **entropy**)

principle of equivalence (Jung)   (see **equivalence**)

proactive (Allport)   Concept that presupposes that people are capable of consciously acting upon their environment in new and innovative ways, which then feed new elements into the system and stimulate psychological growth.

procreativity (Erikson)   The drive to have children and to care for them.

progression (Jung)   The forward flow of psychic energy; involves the extraverted attitude and movement toward adaptation to the external world.

projection   A defense mechanism whereby the ego reduces anxiety by attributing an unwanted impulse to another person.

projective identification (Klein)   A psychic defense mechanism in which infants split off parts of themselves, project them onto another object, and then introject them in a distorted form.

projective techniques Various methods used to discover conscious or unconscious motivations and attitudes through the analysis of responses to unstructured or ambiguous stimuli. The Rorschach (inkblot) test is, perhaps, the best-known projective instrument, but Freud's technique of free association, Adler's early recollections, and Jung's active imagination are other examples.

propriate functional autonomy (Allport) The concept of a master system of motivation that confers unity on personality by relating self-sustaining motives to the proprium.

propriate strivings (Allport) Motivation toward goals that are consistent with an established proprium and that are uniquely one's own.

proprium (Allport) All those characteristics that people see as peculiarly their own and that are regarded as warm, central, and important.

prototaxic Primitive, presymbolic, undifferentiated mode of experience that cannot be communicated to others.

psychoanalysis Theory of personality, approach to psychotherapy, and method of investigation founded by Freud.

psychoanalytical social theory Horney's theory of personality that emphasizes cultural influence in shaping both normal and neurotic development.

psychodynamic Loosely defined term usually referring to those psychological theories that heavily emphasize unconscious motivation. The theories of Freud, Erikson, Adler, Jung, Sullivan, Horney, and Klein are usually considered to be psychodynamic.

psychoid unconscious Jung's term for those elements in the unconscious that are not capable of becoming conscious.

psychological situation (Rotter) That part of the external and internal world to which an individual is responding.

psychology The scientific study of human behavior; the discipline that includes the study of personality.

psychoneuroimmunology A multidisciplinary field that focuses on the interactions among behavior, the nervous system, the endocrine system, and the immune system.

psychoneurosis (see **neurosis**)

psychopathology General term referring to various levels and types of mental disturbances or behavior disorders, including neuroses, psychoses, and psychosomatic ailments.

psychoses Severe personality disorders, as opposed to the more mild neurotic reactions. Psychoses interfere seriously with the usual functions of life and include both organic brain disorders and functional (learned) conditions.

psychoticism (P) (Eysenck) One of three superfactors or types identified by Eysenck. Psychoticism is a bipolar factor consisting of psychoticism at one pole and superego function at the other. High P scores indicate hostility, self-centeredness, suspicion, and nonconformity.

punishment The presentation of an aversive stimulus or the removal of a positive one. Punishment sometimes, but not always, weakens a response.

Q

Q data Cattell's term for questionnaire information or self-report data.

Q sort Inventory technique originated by William Stephenson in which the subject is asked to sort a series of self-referent statements into several piles, the size of which approximates a normal curve.

quasi-experimental designs Scientific studies in which the values of the independent variable are not manipulated but are selected by the experimenter after the groups have naturally divided themselves.

quaternity (Jung) An archetype symbolized by figures with four equal sides or four elements.

R

radical behaviorism Skinner's view that psychology as a science can only advance when psychologists stop attributing behavior to hypothetical constructs and begin writing and talking strictly in terms of observable behavior.

range corollary Kelly's assumption that personal constructs are limited to a finite range of convenience.

rational functions (Jung) Methods of dealing with the world that involve thinking and feeling (valuing).

reaction formation A defense mechanism in which a person represses one impulse and adopts the exact opposite form of behavior, which ordinarily is exaggerated and ostentatious.

reactive (Allport) Referring to those theories that view people as being motivated by tension reduction and by the desire to return to a state of equilibrium.

reality principle (Freud) The motivation of the ego, to realistically arbitrate the conflicting demands of the id, the superego, and the external world.

receptive orientation (Fromm) Trait of people who relate to the world through receiving love, knowledge, and material possessions.

reciprocal determinism (Bandura) Scheme that includes environment, behavior, and person as mutually interacting to determine personal conduct.

regression (Freud) A defense mechanism whereby a person returns to an earlier stage in order to protect the ego against anxiety.

regression (Jung) The backward flow of psychic energy. Regression involves the introverted attitude and movement toward adaptation to the internal world.

reinforcement (Dollard & Miller) Any event that strengthens the connection between a cue and a response, thereby increasing the tendency for a response to be repeated.

reinforcement (Skinner) Any condition within the environment that strengthens a behavior (see also **negative reinforcement** and **positive reinforcer**).

reinforcement–reinforcement sequences Rotter's term indicating that the value of a reinforcement is a function of one's expectation that this reinforcement will lead to future reinforcements.

reinforcement value (Rotter) The preference a person attaches to any reinforcement when the probabilities are equal for the occurrence of a number of different reinforcements.

relatedness (Fromm) The need for union with another person or persons. Expressed through submission, power, or love.

reliability The extent to which a test or other measuring instrument yields consistent results.

repetition compulsion (Freud) The tendency of an instinct, especially the death instinct, to repeat or recreate an earlier condition, particularly one that was frightening or anxiety-arousing.

repression (Freud) The forcing of unwanted, anxiety-laden experiences into the unconscious in order to defend a person against the pain of that anxiety.

resacralization (Maslow) The process of returning respect, joy, awe, and rapture to an experience in order to make that experience more subjective and personal.

resistance Category of unconscious responses by patients designed to block therapeutic progress.

respondent conditioning Often called *classical conditioning* and sometimes *Pavlovian conditioning*. In respondent conditioning a neutral (conditioned) stimulus is paired with, that is, immediately precedes, an unconditioned stimulus a number of times until it is capable of bringing about a previously unconditioned response, now called the conditioned response.

respondent extinction The loss of any behavior acquired through respondent conditioning. Respondent extinction takes place when the conditioned stimulus is presented several times in the absence of the unconditioned stimulus.

response (Dollard & Miller) Behavior that occurs as a reaction to drives and cues.

response consequences (Bandura) One of two basic sources of learning. Response consequences involve the observation of the effects of a response.

retention (Bandura) Second of four steps that affect modeling. Retention refers to the symbolic representation in memory of a response pattern observed in another person.

role (Kelly)   A pattern of behavior that results from people's understanding of the constructs of others with whom they are engaged in some task.

role repudiation (Erikson)   The inability to synthesize different self-images and values into a workable identity.

rootedness (Fromm)   The human need to establish roots, that is, to find a home again in the world.

S

sadism   A condition in which a person receives sexual pleasure by inflicting pain or humiliation on another person.

sadistic–anal phase (Freud)   (see **anal phase**)

safeguarding tendencies (Adler)   Protective mechanisms such as aggression, withdrawal, and so on that maintain exaggerated feelings of superiority.

schizophrenia   Psychotic disorder characterized by fundamental disturbances in perception of reality, severe apathy, and loss of affect.

science   A branch of study concerned with observation and classification of data and with the verification of general laws through the testing of hypotheses.

school age (Erikson)   The fourth stage of psychosocial development, school age covers the period from about six to 12 or 13 and is characterized by psychosexual latency and the psychosocial crisis of industry vs. inferiority.

secondary narcissism (Freud)   Self-love or auto-erotic behavior in an adolescent (see **narcissism**).

secondary process (Freud)   Refers to the ego, which chronologically is the second region of the mind (after the id or primary process). Secondary process thinking is in contact with reality.

secondary reinforcement   Learned reinforcement. If a previously ineffective event—for example, money—increases the likelihood that learning will take place, then that event is a secondary reinforcer.

secondary traits (Allport)   (see **disposition, secondary**)

security operations (Sullivan)   Behaviors aimed at reducing interpersonal tension.

selective activation   Refers to Bandura's belief that self-regulatory influences are not automatic but rather operate only if they are activated.

selective inattention (Sullivan)   The control of focal awareness, which involves a refusal to see those things that one does not wish to see.

self (Jung)   The most comprehensive of all archetypes, the self includes the whole of personality, although it is mostly unconscious. The self is often symbolized by the mandala motif.

self-accusation   Adlerian safeguarding tendency whereby a person aggresses indirectly against others through self-torture and guilt.

self-actualization (Maslow)   The highest level of human motivation in which people fully develop all of their psychological capacities.

self-actualization (Rogers)   A subsystem of the actualizing tendency. The tendency to actualize the self as perceived.

self-concept   Those aspects of one's experiences that are perceived by the individual.

self-efficacy (Bandura)   People's expectation that they are capable of performing those behaviors that will produce desired outcomes in any particular situation.

self-hatred (Horney)   The powerful tendency for neurotics to despise the real self.

selfobjects (Kohut)   Parents or other significant adults in a child's life who eventually become incorporated into the child's sense of self.

self-realization (Jung)   The highest possible level of psychic maturation, it necessitates a balance between conscious and unconscious, ego and self, masculine and feminine, and introversion and extraversion. All four functions (thinking, feeling, sensing, and intuiting) would be fully developed by self-realized people.

self-regard (Rogers)   The need to accept, like, or love oneself.

self-regulatory system (Mischel)   The control of one's own behavior through self-imposed goals and self-produced consequences.

self system (Bandura)   Cognitive structure of personality that provides reference for perceiving, evaluating, and regulating behavior.

self-system (Sullivan)   Complex of dynamisms that protect a person from anxiety and maintain interpersonal security.

sems (Cattell)   Learned dynamic traits or sentiments.

sensation (Jung)   An irrational function that receives physical stimuli and transmits them to perceptual consciousness. People may rely on either extraverted sensing (outside perceptions) or on introverted sensing (internal perceptions).

sense of identity (Fromm)   The distinctively human need to develop a feeling of "I."

sentiments   Learned dynamic traits. In Cattell's theory, sentiments are contrasted to ergs, which refer to energy inherent in innate drives. Also called *sems*.

separation-individuation (Mahler)   The third major stage of development marked by the child's becoming an individual, separate from its mother; spans the period from 4 or 5 months to about 30 to 36 months.

shadow   Jungian archetype representing the inferior or dark side of personality.

shaping   Conditioning a response by first rewarding gross approximations of the behavior, then closer approximations, and finally the desired behavior itself.

social interest (Adler)   Translation of the German *Gemeinschaftsgefühl*, meaning a community feeling or a sense of feeling at one with all human beings.

sociality corollary   Kelly's notion that people can communicate with others because they are able to construe their constructions.

solicitude   Adlerian safeguarding tendency whereby the individual depreciates another and receives an inflated feeling of superiority by acting as if other people are incapable of caring for themselves.

somnolent detachment (Sullivan)   Dynamism that protects a person from increasingly strong and painful effects of severe anxiety.

splitting   According to object relations theory, a psychic defense mechanism in which the child subjectively separates incompatible aspects of an object.

standing still (Adler)   Safeguarding tendency characterized by lack of action as a means of avoiding failure.

states   Temporary conditions within an individual such as anger, stress, sexual arousal, or fear; opposed to traits that are more permanent.

stereotypes (Sullivan)   Imaginary traits attributed to a group of people.

stimulus generalization   (see **generalization**)

structure of personality   The basic units or building blocks of personality.

style of life (Adler)   A person's individuality that expresses itself in any circumstance or environment; the "flavor" of a person's life.

subception (Rogers)   The process of perceiving stimuli without an awareness of the perception.

sublimation   A defense mechanism that involves the repression of the genital aim of Eros and its substitution by a cultural or social aim.

subsidiation chain   Cattell's term for the complex of subgoals underlying motivation. A subsidiation chain generally traces motivation to some innate drive.

successive approximations   Procedure used to shape an organism's actions by rewarding behaviors as they become closer and closer to the target behavior.

superego (Freud)   As the moral or ethical processes of personality, the superego has two subsystems—the conscience, which tells us what is wrong, and the ego-ideal, which tells us what is right.

superiority complex (Adler)   Exaggerated and unrealistic feelings of personal superiority as an overcompensation for unusually strong feelings of inferiority.

suppression   The blocking or inhibiting of an activity by either a conscious act of the will or by an outside agent, such as parents or other authority figures. It differs from repression, which is the unconscious blocking of anxiety-producing experiences.

syndrome   A group of concurrent symptoms or characteristics.

synergistic effect   The combined effect of two or more factors that equals more than their additive effects.

synergy The combined effectiveness of two or more actions.

syntaxic (Sullivan) Consensually validated experiences that represent the highest level of cognition and that can be accurately communicated to others, usually through language.

syntonic Erikson's term for the positive element in each pair of opposites that characterize his eight stages of development.

systematic desensitization A behavior therapy technique used to inhibit or extinguish phobias and fears through the use of relaxation.

T

T data Cattell's term for test scores or objective information obtained from observation of performance.

Taoistic attitude (Maslow) Noninterfering, passive, receptive attitude that includes awe and wonder toward that which is observed.

taxonomy A system of classification of data according to their natural relationships.

teleology An explanation of behavior in terms of future goals or purposes.

temperament An inherited tendency to act or react in a given manner.

tenderness (Sullivan) Tension within the mothering one that is aroused by the manifest needs of the infant. The child feels tenderness as the need to receive care.

tension (Sullivan) The potentiality for action, which may or may not be experienced in awareness.

theory A set of related assumptions from which, by logical deductive reasoning, testable hypotheses can be drawn.

thinking (Jung) A rational function that tells us the meaning of an image that originates either from the external world (extraverted) or from the internal world (introverted).

third force Somewhat vague term referring to those approaches to psychology that have reacted against the older psychodynamic and behavioristic theories. The third force is usually thought to include humanistic, existential, and phenomenological theories.

threat (Kelly) The anticipation of danger to the stability of one's personal constructs.

threat (Rogers) Results from the perception of an experience that is inconsistent with one's organismic self.

trait A relatively permanent disposition of an individual, which is inferred from behavior. Cattell, Eysenck, and Allport each have slightly different definitions of traits.

trait, common (Allport) Relatively permanent neuropsychic structure with the capacity to render disparate stimuli functionally equivalent and to initiate and guide action.

transcendence (Fromm) The need for humans to rise above their passive animal existence through either creating or destroying life.

transference Strong, undeserved feelings the patient develops toward the analyst during the course of treatment. These feelings may be either sexual or hostile, but they stem from the patient's earlier experiences with parents.

transformation Psychotherapeutic approach used by Jung in which the therapist is transformed into a healthy individual who can aid the patient in establishing a philosophy of life.

types (factor theorists) A cluster of primary traits. Eysenck recognized three general types— extraversion (E), neuroticism (N), and psychoticism (P).

types (Jung) Classification of people based on the two-dimensional scheme of attitudes and functions. The two attitudes of extraversion and introversion and the four functions of thinking, feeling, sensing, and intuiting combine to produce eight possible types.

tyranny of the should (Horney) A key element in the neurotic search for glory, it includes an unconscious and unrelenting drive for perfection.

U

Umwelt An existentialist term meaning the world of things or objects. One of three simultaneous modes of being-in-the-world.

unconditional positive regard (Rogers)   The need to be accepted and prized by another without any restrictions or qualifications. One of three "necessary and sufficient" therapeutic conditions.

unconscious (Freud)   All those mental elements of which a person is unaware. Two levels of the unconscious are the unconscious proper and the preconscious. Unconscious ideas can become conscious only through great resistance and difficulty.

undoing (Freud)   A defense mechanism which is a type of repression whereby the ego attempts to do away with unpleasant experiences and their consequences by spending energy on compulsive ceremonial activities.

unipolar factors   Factors with only one pole, that is, those scaled from zero to some large amount, as opposed to bipolar factors that are scaled from a minus point, through zero, to a positive point.

V

validity   The extent to which a test or other measuring instrument measures what it is supposed to measure; accuracy.

variable-interval (Skinner)   Intermittent reinforcement schedule in which the organism is reinforced after a lapse of random and varied periods of time (for example, VI 10 means that the animal is reinforced for its first response following random-length intervals that average 10 minutes).

variable-ratio (Skinner)   Intermittent reinforcement schedule in which the organism is reinforced for every *nth* response on the average (for example, VR 50 means that the animal is reinforced on the average of one time for every 50 responses).

variance   A measure of the extent to which individual scores differ from one another.

verifiability   The ability of a theory to be either confirmed or disconfirmed through research evidence.

vicarious experience   Learning by observing the consequences of others' behavior.

voyeurism   The reception of sexual pleasure from viewing certain objects, persons, or activities.

vulnerability (Rogers)   A condition that exists when people are unaware of the discrepancy between their organismic selves and their experiences. Vulnerable people often behave in ways incomprehensible to themselves and to others.

W

will (May)   A conscious commitment to action.

withdrawal (Adler)   Safeguarding one's exaggerated sense of superiority by establishing a distance between oneself and one's problems.

Y

young adulthood (Erikson)   The age from about 18 to 30 when a person gains mature genitality and experiences the crisis of intimacy vs. isolation.

REFERENCES

Adams-Webber, J. R. (1970). An analysis of the discriminant validity of several repertory grid indices. *British Journal of Psychology, 60,* 83–90.

Adler, A. (1907/1917). *Study of organ inferiority and its psychical compensation.* New York: Nervous and Mental Disease Publishing Co.

Adler, A. (1925/1968). *The practice and theory of Individual Psychology.* Totowa, NJ: Littlefield Adams.

Adler, A. (1927). *Understanding human nature.* New York: Greenberg.

Adler, A. (1929/1964). *Problems of neurosis.* New York: Harper Torchbooks.

Adler, A. (1929/1969). *The science of living.* New York: Anchor Books.

Adler, A. (1930). Individual Psychology. In C. Murchinson (Ed.), *Psychologies of 1930.* Worcester, MA: Clark University Press.

Adler, A. (1931). *What life should mean to you.* New York: Capricorn Books.

Adler, A. (1956). *The Individual Psychology of Alfred Adler: A systematic presentation in selections from his writings.* H. L. Ansbacher & R. R. Ansbacher (Eds.). New York: Basic Books.

Adler, A. (1964). *Superiority and social interest: A collection of later writings.* H. L. Ansbacher & R. R. Ansbacher (Eds.). New York: Norton.

Allers, C. T., White, J., & Hornbuckle, D. (1990). Early recollections: Detecting depression in the elderly. *Individual Psychology, 46,* 61–66.

Allport, G. W. (1937). *Personality: A psychological interpretation.* New York: Henry Holt.

Allport, G. W. (1942). *The use of personal documents in psychological science.* New York: Social Science Research Council, Bulletin 49.

Allport, G. W. (1950). *The individual and his religion.* New York: Macmillan.

Allport, G. W. (1954). *The nature of prejudice.* Reading, MA: Addison Wesley.

Allport, G. W. (1955). *Becoming: Basic considerations for a psychology of personality.* New Haven, CT: Yale University Press.

Allport, G. W. (1960). The open system in personality theory. *Journal of Abnormal and Social Psychology, 61,* 301–310.

Allport, G. W. (1961). *Pattern and growth in personality.* New York: Holt, Rinehart and Winston.

Allport, G. W. (1962). The general and the unique in psychological science. *Journal of Personality, 30,* 405–422.

Allport, G. W. (1963). Behavioral science, religion and mental health. *Journal of Religion and Health, 2,* 187–197.

Allport, G. W. (1965). *Letters from Jenny.* New York: Harcourt, Brace & World.

Allport, G. W. (1966). Traits revisited. *American Psychologist, 21,* 1–10.

Allport, G. W. (1967). An autobiography. In E. G. Boring & G. Lindzey (Eds.), *A history of psychology in autobiography.* Vol. 5 (pp. 1–27). New York: Appleton-Century-Crofts.

Allport, G. W. (1968). *The person in psychology.* Boston: Beacon Press.

Allport, G. W. (1978). *Waiting for the Lord: 33 meditations on God and man.* New York: Macmillan.

Allport, G. W., & Odbert, H. S. (1936). Trait-names: A psycho-lexical study. *Psychological Monographs, 47,* 1–171.

Allport, G. W., & Ross, J. M. (1967). Personal religious orientation and prejudice. *Journal of Personality and Social Psychology, 5,* 432–443.

Allport, G. W., Vernon, P. E., & Lindzey, G. (1960). *A study of values.* Boston: Houghton Mifflin.

Allsopp, J., Eysenck, H. J., & Eysenck, S. B. (1991). Machiavellianism as a component in psychoticism and extraversion. *Personality and Individual Differences, 12,* 29–41.

Alpher, V. S. (1991). Assessment of ego functioning in multiple personality disorder. *Journal of Personality Assessment, 56,* 373–387.

American Psychiatric Association. (1987). *Diagnostic and statistical manual of mental disorders* (3rd edition-revised) (DSM-III-R). Washington, DC: Author.

Ansbacher, H. L. (1985). The significance of Alfred Adler for the concept of narcissism. *American Journal of Psychiatry, 142,* 203–207.

Apostal, R. A. (1991). College students' career interests and sensing-intuition personality. *Journal of College Student Development, 32,* 4–7.

Bachofen, J. J. (1861/1967). *Myth, religion, and mother right: Selected writings of Johann Jacob Bachofen* (R. Manheim, Trans.). Princeton, NJ: Princeton University Press.

Baldwin, A. F. (1942). Personal structure analysis: A statistical method for investigating the single personality. *Journal of Abnormal and Social Psychology, 37,* 163–183.

Balmary, M. (1979/1982). *Psychoanalyzing psychoanalysis: Freud and the hidden fault of the father.* Baltimore: Johns Hopkins University Press.

Bandura, A. (1977a). Self-efficacy: Toward a unifying theory of behavior change. *Psychological Review, 84,* 191–215.

Bandura, A. (1977b). *Social learning theory.* Englewood Cliffs, NJ: Prentice-Hall.

Bandura, A. (1978a). On paradigms and recycled ideologies. *Cognitive Therapy and Research, 2,* 79–103.

Bandura, A. (1978b). The self system in reciprocal determinism. *American Psychologist, 33,* 344–358.

Bandura, A. (1979). Self-referent mechanisms in social learning theory. *American Psychologist, 34,* 439–441.

Bandura, A. (1981). Self-referent thought: A developmental analysis of self-efficacy. In J. H. Flavell & L. D. Ross (Eds.), *Cognitive social development: Frontiers and possible futures.* New York: Cambridge University Press.

Bandura, A. (1982a, July). Model of causality in social learning theory. Paper presented at the meeting of the Japanese Psychological Association, Kyoto.

Bandura, A. (1982b). The psychology of chance encounters and life paths. *American Psychologist, 37,* 747–755.

Bandura, A. (1982c). Self-efficacy mechanisms in human agency. *American Psychologist, 37,* 122–147.

Bandura, A. (1983). Self-efficacy determinants of anticipated fears and calamities. *Journal of Personality and Social Psychology, 45,* 464–469.

Bandura, A. (1984). Recycling misconceptions of perceived self-efficacy. *Cognitive Therapy and Research, 8,* 231–255.

Bandura, A. (1986). *Social foundations of thought and action: A social cognitive theory.* Englewood Cliffs, NJ: Prentice-Hall.

Bandura, A. (1988a, August). Human agency in social cognitive theory. Paper presented at the XXIV International Congress of Psychology, Sydney, Australia.

Bandura, A. (1988b). Self-regulation of motivation and action through goal systems. In V. Hamilton, G. H. Bower, & N. H. Fryda (Eds.), *Cognitive perspectives on emotion and motivation.* Dordrecht: Kluwer: Academic Publishers.

Bandura, A. (1988c). Social cognitive theory. In R. Vasta (Ed.), *Annals of child development* (Vol. 6). Greenwich, CT: JAI Press.

Bandura, A. (1989). Human agency in social cognitive theory. *American Psychologist, 44,* 1175–1184.

Bandura, A. (1991a). Social cognitive theory of moral thought and action. In W. M. Kurtiness & J. L. Gewirtz (Eds.), *Handbook of moral behavior and development: Vol. 1. Theory* (pp. 45–103). Hillsdale, NJ: Erlbaum.

Bandura, A. (1991b). Social cognitive theory of self-regulation. *Organizational Behavior and Human Decision Processes, 50,* 248–287.

Bandura, A., & Adams, N. E. (1977). Analysis of self-efficacy theory of behavioral change. *Cognitive Therapy and Research, 1,* 287–310.

Bandura, A., Adams, N. E., Hardy, A. B., & Howells, G. N. (1980). Tests of the generality of self-efficacy theory. *Cognitive Therapy and Research, 4,* 39–66.

Bandura, A., Blanchard, E. B., & Ritter, B. (1969). The relative efficacy of desensitization and modeling approaches for inducing behavioral, affective, and attitudinal changes. *Journal of Personality and Social Psychology, 13,* 173–199.

Bandura, A., & Cervone, D. (1983). Self-evaluative

and self-efficacy mechanisms governing the motivational effects of goal systems. *Journal of Personality and Social Psychology, 45*, 1017–1028.

Bandura, A., & Jourden, F. J. (1991). Self-regulatory mechanisms governing the impact of social comparison on complex decision making. *Journal of Personality and Social Psychology, 60*, 941–951.

Bandura, A., & Mischel, W. (1965). Modification of self-imposed delay of reward through exposure to live and symbolic models. *Journal of Personality and Social Psychology, 2*, 698–705.

Bandura, A., Ross, D., & Ross, S. A. (1963). Imitation of film-mediated aggressive models. *Journal of Abnormal and Social Psychology, 66*, 3–11.

Bandura, A., & Walters, R. H. (1959). *Adolescent aggression.* New York: Ronald Press.

Bannister, D. (1970). *Perspectives in personal construct theory.* London: Academic Press.

Bannister, D. (Ed.). (1975). *Issues and approaches in the psychological therapies.* London: Wiley.

Bannister, D. (1977). *New perspectives in personal construct theory.* London: Academic Press.

Bannister, D., & Fransella, F. (1966). A grid test of schizophrenic thought disorder. *British Journal of Social and Clinical Psychology, 5*, 95–102.

Bannister, D., & Fransella, F. (1971). *Inquiring man: The theory of personal constructs.* Harmondsworth, England: Penguin Books.

Bannister, D., & Mair, J. M. M. (1968). *The evaluation of personal constructs.* London: Academic Press.

Barrett-Lennard, G. T. (1962). Dimensions of therapist response as causal factors in therapeutic change. *Psychological Monographs: General and Applied, 76* (43, Whole No. 562).

Barrett-Lennard, G. T. (1964). *The Relationship Inventory. Forms OS-M-64 and MO-M-64 plus MO-F-64.* Unpublished manuscript, University of New England.

Baumeister, R. F. (1990). Victim and perpetrator accounts of interpersonal conflict: Autobiographical narratives about anger. *Journal of Personality and Social Psychology, 59*, 994–1005.

Beail, N. (Ed.). (1985). *Repertory Grid technique and personal constructs: Applications in clinical & educational settings.* Cambridge, MA: Brookline.

Beck, A. T. (1967). *Depression: Clinical, experimental and theoretical aspects.* New York: Harper & Row.

Bell, M. D., Billington, R., & Becker, B. (1986). A scale for the assessment of object relationships: Reliability, validity, and factorial invariance. *Journal of Clinical Psychology, 42*, 733–741.

Benjamin, L. S. (1974). Structural analysis of social behavior. *Psychological Review, 81*, 392–425.

Benson, H. (1975). *The relaxation response.* New York: Morrow.

Bergin, A. E., Masters, K. S., & Richards, P. S. (1987). Religiousness and mental health reconsidered: A study of an intrinsically religious sample. *Journal of Counseling Psychology, 34*, 197–204.

Berkowitz, L. (1958). Expression and reduction of hostility. *Psychological Bulletin, 55*, 257–283.

Berkowitz, L. (1962). *Aggression: A social psychological analysis.* New York: McGraw-Hill.

Berkowitz, L. (1969). The frustration-aggression hypothesis revisited. In L. Berkowitz (Ed.), *Roots of aggression: A re-examination of the frustration-aggression hypothesis.* New York: Atherton.

Berkowitz, L. (1978). Whatever happened to the frustration-aggression hypothesis? *American Behavioral Scientist, 21*, 691–708.

Bettelheim, B. (1982, March 1). Freud and the soul. *The New Yorker*, pp. 52–93.

Bettelheim, B. (1983). *Freud and man's soul.* New York: Knopf.

Bilmes, M. (1978). Rollo May. In R. S. Valle & M. King (Eds.), *Existential-phenomenological alternatives for psychology* (pp. 290–294). New York: Oxford University Press.

Bilsker, D., & Marcia, J. E. (1991). Adaptive regression and ego identity. *Journal of Adolescence, 14*, 75–84.

Bilsker, D., Schiedel, D., & Marcia, J. E. (1988). Sex differences in identity status. *Sex Roles, 18*, 231–236.

Black, R. (1940). *Eleanor Roosevelt: A biography.* New York: Duell, Sloan and Pearce.

Blanchard, W. H. (1969). Psychodynamic aspects of the peak experience. *Psychoanalytic Review, 46*, 87–112.

Block, J. H., & Block, J. (1969). *The California Child Q-Set*. Unpublished manuscript, Department of Psychology, University of California at Berkeley.

Bottome, P. (1939). *Alfred Adler: Apostle of freedom*. London: Faber & Faber.

Breuer, J., & Freud, S. (1895/1955). *Studies on hysteria*. In J. Strachey (Ed. and Trans.), *The standard edition of the complete psychological works of Sigmund Freud* (Vol. 2). London: Hogarth Press.

Brokken, F. B. (1978). *The language of personality*. Meppel, The Netherlands: Krips.

Brome, V. (1978). *Jung*. New York: Atheneum.

Brown, I., Jr., & Inouye, D. K. (1978). Learned helplessness through modeling: The role of perceived similarity in competence. *Journal of Personality and Social Psychology, 36*, 900–908.

Bruhn, A. R. (1989). *The early memories procedure manual*. Bethesda, MD: Psychline Press.

Bruhn, A. R. (1990). *Earliest childhood memories: Vol. 1. Theory and application to clinical practice*. New York: Praeger.

Burston, D. (1991). *The legacy of Erich Fromm*. Cambridge, MA: Harvard University Press.

Buss, A. H. (1961). *The psychology of aggression*. New York: Wiley.

Buchanan, L. P., Kern, R., & Bell-Dumas, J. (1991). Comparison of content in created versus actual early recollections. *Individual Psychology, 47*, 348–355.

Busick, B. S. (1989). "Living with cancer": A transpersonal course. *Hospice Journal, 5*, 67–78.

Butler, J. M., & Haigh, G. V. (1954). Changes in the relation between self-concepts and ideal concepts consequent upon client-centered counseling. In C. R. Rogers & R. F. Dymond (Eds.), *Psychotherapy and personality change: Co-ordinated research studies in the client-centered approach* (pp. 55–75). Chicago: University of Chicago Press.

Button, E. (1985a). Eating disorders: A quest for control. In E. Button (Ed.), *Personal construct theory & mental health: Theory, research and practice* (pp. 153–168). Cambridge, MA: Brookline.

Button, E. (Ed.). (1985b). *Personal construct theory & mental health: Theory, research and practice*. Cambridge, MA: Brookline.

Byck, R. (Ed.). (1974). *Cocaine papers by Sigmund Freud*. New York: Meridian.

Cantor, N., & Zirkel, S. (1990). Personality, cognition, and purposive behavior. In L. A. Pervin (Ed.), *Handbook of personality: Theory and research* (pp. 135–164). New York: Guilford Press.

Caper, R. (1988). *Immaterial facts: Freud's discovery of psychic reality and Klein's development of his work*. Northvale, NJ: Aronson

Carlson, R. (1980). Studies of Jungian typology: II, Representation of the personal world. *Journal of Personality and Social Psychology, 38*, 801–810.

Carroll, W. R., & Bandura, A. (1982). The role of visual monitoring in observational learning of action patterns: Making the observable observable. *Journal of Motor Behavior, 14*, 153–167.

Carroll, W. R., & Bandura, A. (1985). Role of timing of visual monitoring and motor rehearsal in observational learning of action patterns. *Journal of Motor Behavior, 17*, 269–281.

Cashdan, S. (1988). *Object relations therapy: Using the relationship*. New York: Norton.

Cattell, R. B. (1949). *Manual for Forms A and B: Sixteen Personality Factors Questionnaire*. Champaign, IL: IPAT.

Cattell, R. B. (1950). *Personality: A systematic, theoretical and factual study*. New York: McGraw-Hill.

Cattell, R. B. (1957). *Personality and motivation structure and measurement*. Yonkers-on-Hudson, NY: World Book.

Cattell, R. B. (1971). *Abilities: Their structure, growth, and action*. Boston: Houghton Mifflin.

Cattell, R. B. (1972a). *A new morality from science: Beyondism*. New York: Pergamon Press.

Cattell, R. B. (1972b). The 16 PF and basic personality structure: A reply to Eysenck. *Journal of Behavioral Science, 1*, 169–187.

Cattell, R. B. (1974a). An autobiography. In G. Lindzey (Ed.), *A history of psychology in autobiography* (Vol. 6). Englewood Cliffs, NJ: Prentice-Hall.

Cattell, R. B. (1974b). Travels in psychological hyperspace. In T. S. Krawiec (Ed.), *The Psychologists* (Vol. 2). New York: Oxford University Press.

Cattell, R. B. (1979–1980). *Personality and learning theory: Vol. 1. The structure of personality in its* environment: Vol. 2. A systems theory of maturation and structure learning: Vol. 3. New York: Springer.

Cattell, R. B. (1983). Structured personality—learning theory: A wholistic multivariate research approach. New York: Praeger.

Cattell, R. B. (1985). Human motivation and the dynamic calculus. New York: Praeger.

Cattell, R. B. (1987). Psychotherapy by structured learning theory. New York: Springer.

Cattell, R. B. (1990). Advances in Cattellian personality theory. In L. A. Pervin (Ed.), Handbook of personality: Theory and research (pp. 100–101). New York: Guilford Press.

Cattell, R. B. (1993). Planning basic clinical research. In C. E. Walker (Ed.), The history of clinical psychology in autobiography: Vol. 2 (pp. 101–111). Pacific Grove, CA: Brooks/Cole.

Cattell, R. B., & Cross, P. (1952). Comparison of the ergic and self-sentiment structures found in dynamic traits by R and P techniques. Journal of Personality, 21, 250–270.

Cattell, R. B., Ebert, H. W., & Tatsuoka, M. M. (1970). Handbook for the sixteen personality factor questionnaire. Champaign, IL: IPAT.

Cattell, R. B., & Kline, P. (1977). The scientific analysis of personality and motivation. New York: Academic Press.

Cattell, R. B., Schuerger, J. M., & Klein, T. W. (1982). Heritabilities of ego strength (Factor C), superego strength (Factor G), and self-sentiment (Factor Q_3) by multiple abstract variance analysis. Journal of Clinical Psychology, 38, 769–779.

Cattell, R. B., & Warburton, E. W. (1967). Objective personality and motivation tests. Urbana, IL: University of Illinois Press.

Chambliss, C. A., & Murray, E. J. (1979). Cognitive procedures for smoking reduction: Symptom attribution versus efficacy attribution. Cognitive Therapy and Research, 3, 91–95.

Chan, J. W., Eysenck, H. J., & Lynn, R. (1991). Reaction times and intelligence among Hong Kong children. Perceptual and Motor Skills, 72, 427–433.

Chaplin, M. P., & Orlofsky, J. L. (1991). Personality characteristics of male alcoholics as revealed through their early recollections. Individual Psychology, 47, 356–371.

Chapman, A. H. (1976). Harry Stack Sullivan: His life and his work. New York: Putnam.

Chodorow, N. J. (1989). Feminism and psychoanalytic theory. New Haven, CT: Yale University Press.

Church, A. T., & Katigbak, M. S. (1989). Internal, external, and self-report structure of personality in a non-Western culture: An investigation of cross-language and cross-cultural generalizability. Journal of Personality and Social Psychology, 57, 857–872.

Clark, R. W. (1980). Freud: The man and the cause. New York: Random House.

Cohen, D. (1977). Psychologists on psychology. New York: Taplinger.

Coles, R. (1970). Erik H. Erikson: The growth of his work. Boston: Little, Brown.

Combs, A. W., & Snygg, D. (1959). Individual behavior: A perceptual approach to behavior. New York: Harper & Row.

Comrey, A. L. (1970). Manual for the Comrey Personality Scales. San Diego, CA: Educational and Industrial Testing.

Coram, G. J., & Shields, D. J. (1987). Early recollections of criminal justice majors and nonmajors. Psychological Reports, 60, 1287–1290.

Cramer, D. (1985). Psychological adjustment and the facilitative nature of close personal relationships. British Journal of Medical Psychology, 58, 165–168.

Cramer, D. (1987). Self-esteem, advice-giving, and the facilitative nature of close personal relationships. Person-Centered Review, 2, 99–110.

Cramer, D. (1988). Self-esteem and facilitative close relationships: A cross-lagged panel correlation analysis. British Journal of Social Psychology, 27, 115–126.

Cramer, D. (1989). Self-esteem and the facilitativeness of parents and close friends. Person-Centered Review, 4, 61–76.

Cramer, D. (1990). Disclosure of personal problems, self-esteem, and the facilitativeness of friends and lovers. British Journal of Guidance and Counseling, 18, 186–196.

Crandall, J. E. (1975). A scale for social interest. *Journal of Individual Psychology, 31*, 187–195.

Crandall, J. E. (1981). *Theory and measurement of social interest: Empirical tests of Alfred Adler's concept.* New York: Columbia University Press.

Crandall, J. E. (1984). Social interest as a moderator of life stress. *Journal of Personality and Social Psychology, 47*, 164–174.

Crandall, J. E., & Lehman, R. E. (1987). Relationship of stressful life events to social interest, locus of control and psychological adjustment. *Journal of Consulting and Clinical Psychology, 45*, 1208.

Crandall, J. E., & Putnam, E. L. (1980). Relations between measures of social interest and psychological well-being. *Journal of Individual Psychology, 36*, 156–168.

Croake, J. W. (1975). An Adlerian view of life style. *Journal of Clinical Psychology, 31*, 513–518.

Daniels, M. (1982). The development of the concept of self-actualization in the writings of Abraham Maslow. *Current Psychological Reviews, 2*, 61–76.

Delhees, K. H., & Cattell, R. B. (1971). *Manual for the Clinical Analysis Questionnaire* (CAQ). Champaign, IL: IPAT.

de Raad, B., Mulder, E., Kloosterman, K., & Hofstee, W. K. (1988). Personality-descriptive verbs. *European Journal of Personality, 2*, 81–96.

Dollard, J., Doob, L. W., Miller, N. E., Mowrer, O. H., & Sears, R. R. (1939). *Frustration and aggression.* New Haven, CT: Yale University Press.

Dollard, J., & Miller, N. E. (1950). *Personality and psychotherapy: An analysis in terms of learning, thinking, and culture.* New York: Knopf.

Donahue, M. J. (1985). Intrinsic and extrinsic religiousness: Review and meta-analysis. *Journal of Personality and Social Psychology, 48*, 400–419.

Dymond, R. F. (1954a). Adjustment changes over therapy from self-sorts. In C. R. Rogers & R. F. Dymond (Eds.), *Psychotherapy and personality change: Co-ordinated research studies in the client-centered approach* (pp. 76–84). Chicago: University of Chicago Press.

Dymond, R. F. (1954b). Adjustment changes over therapy from Thematic Apperception Test ratings. In C. R. Rogers & R. F. Dymond (Eds.), *Psychotherapy and personality change: Co-ordinated research studies in the client-centered approach* (pp. 109–120). Chicago: University of Chicago Press.

Ellenberger, H. F. (1970). *The discovery of the unconscious.* New York: Basic Books.

Elms, A. C. (1972). Allport, Freud, and the clean little boy. *The Psychoanalytic Review, 59*, 627–632.

Elms, A. C. (1981). Skinner's dark year and *Walden Two. American Psychologist, 36*, 470–479.

Epstein, S. (1979). The stability of behavior. I. On predicting most of the people most of the time. *Journal of Personality and Social Psychology, 37*, 1097–1126.

Epstein, S. (1980). The stability of behavior. II. Implications for psychological research. *American Psychologist, 35*, 790–806.

Erikson, E. H. (1950). *Childhood and society.* New York: Norton.

Erikson, E. H. (1958). *Young man Luther: A study in psychoanalysis and history.* New York: Norton.

Erikson, E. H. (1963). *Childhood and society.* (2d ed.). New York: Norton.

Erikson, E. H. (1968). *Identity: Youth and crisis.* New York: Norton.

Erikson, E. H. (1969). *Gandhi's truth: On the origins of militant nonviolence.* New York: Norton.

Erikson, E. H. (1974). *Dimensions of a new identity: The 1973 Jefferson Lectures in the Humanities.* New York: Norton.

Erikson, E. H. (1975). *Life history and the historical moment.* New York: Norton.

Erikson, E. H. (1977). *Toys and reasons: Stages in the ritualization of experience.* New York: Norton.

Erikson, E. H. (1979). Reflections on Dr. Borg's life cycle. In D. D. Van Tassel (Ed.), *Aging, death, and the completion of being* (pp. 29–67). Philadelphia: University of Pennsylvania Press.

Erikson, E. H. (1980). *Identity and the life cycle.* New York: Norton.

Erikson, E. H. (1982). *The life cycle completed: A review.* New York: Norton.

Erikson, E. H. (1987). Problems of infancy and early childhood. In S. Schlien (Ed.), *A way of looking at* things: Selected papers from 1930 to 1980: Erik H. Erikson (pp. 547–568). New York: Norton.

Erikson, E. H. (1989). Elements of psychoanalytic theory of psychosocial development. In S. I. Greenspan, & G. H. Pollock (Eds.), The course of life, Vol. 1: Infancy (pp. 15–83). Madison, CT: International Universities Press.

Erikson, E. H., Erikson, J. M., & Kivnick, H. Q. (1986). Vital involvement in old age. New York: Norton.

Erikson, J. M. (1988). Wisdom and the senses: The way of creativity. New York: Norton.

Evans, R. I. (1966). Dialogue with Erich Fromm. New York: Harper & Row.

Evans, R. I. (1967). Dialogue with Erik Erikson. New York: Harper & Row.

Evans, R. I. (1976). The making of psychology: Discussion with creative contributors. New York: Knopf.

Evans, R. I (1981). Dialogue with Carl Rogers. New York: Praeger.

Evans, R. I. (1989). Albert Bandura: The man and his ideas—A dialogue. New York: Praeger.

Eysenck, H. J. (1947). Dimensions of personality. London: Routledge & Kegan Paul.

Eysenck, H. J. (1952a). The effects of psychotherapy: An evaluation. Journal of Consulting Psychology, 16, 319–324.

Eysenck, H. J. (1952b). The structure of human personality. London: Methuen.

Eysenck, H. J. (1953). Uses and abuses of psychology. Baltimore: Penguin.

Eysenck, H. J. (1954). The psychology of politics. London: Routledge & Kegan Paul.

Eysenck, H. J. (1956). Sense and nonsense in psychology. London: Penguin.

Eysenck, H. J. (1959). Manual for the Maudsley Personality Inventory. London: University of London Press.

Eysenck, H. J. (1964). Crime and personality. Boston: Houghton Mifflin.

Eysenck, H. J. (1965). Fact and fiction in psychology. London: Penguin.

Eysenck, H. J. (1967). The biological basis of personality. Springfield, IL: Charles C Thomas.

Eysenck, H. J. (1971). The IQ argument. New York: The Library Press. (British edition: Race, intelligence and education. London: Maurice Temple Smith, 1971).

Eysenck, H. J. (1972a). Primaries or second-order factors: A critical consideration of Cattell's 16 PF Battery. British Journal of Social and Clinical Psychology, 11, 265–269.

Eysenck, H. J. (1972b). Psychology is about people. London: Allen Lane.

Eysenck, H. J. (1976a). Genetic factors in personality development. In A. R. Kaplan (Ed.), Human behavior genetics. Springfield, IL: Charles C Thomas.

Eysenck, H. J. (1976b). Sex and personality. Austin: University of Texas Press.

Eysenck, H. J. (1977). You and neurosis. London: Temple Smith.

Eysenck, H. J. (1980). An autobiography. In G. Lindzey (Ed.), A history of psychology in autobiography (Vol. 7). San Francisco: Freeman.

Eysenck, H. J. (Ed.). (1981). A model for personality. New York: Springer.

Eysenck, H. J. (1982). Personality, genetics and behavior: Selected papers. New York: Praeger.

Eysenck, H. J. (1984). Lung cancer and the stress-personality inventory. In C. L. Cooper (Ed.), Psychosocial stress and cancer. Chichester, England: Wiley.

Eysenck, H. J. (1987, November). Personality, stress and cancer: Prediction and prophylaxis. Paper presented at the meeting of the Louisiana Psychological Association, New Orleans.

Eysenck, H. J. (1988a, December). Health's character. Psychology Today, pp. 28–35.

Eysenck, H. J. (1988b). Skinner, Skinnerism, and the Skinnerian in psychology. Special Issue: Stress counseling. Counseling Psychology Quarterly, 1, 299–301.

Eysenck, H. J. (1990a). Biological dimensions of personality. In L. A. Pervin (Ed.), Handbook of personality: Theory and research (pp. 244–276). New York: Guilford Press.

Eysenck, H. J. (1990b). Decline and fall of the Freudian empire. Washington, DC: Scott-Townsend.

Eysenck, H. J. (1990c). Rebel with a cause: The autobiography of H. J. Eysenck. London: W. H. Allen.

Eysenck, H. J. (1991a). Personality as a risk factor in coronary heart disease. *European Journal of Personality, 5*, 81–92.

Eysenck, H. J. (1991b). Raising I. Q. through vitamin and mineral supplementation: An introduction. *Personality and Individual Differences, 12*, 329–333.

Eysenck, H. J. (1991c). Reply to criticisms of the Grossarth-Maticek studies. *Psychological Inquiry, 2*, 97–323.

Eysenck, H. J. (1991d). *Smoking, personality and stress: Psychosocial factors in the prevention of cancer and coronary heart disease.* New York: Springer-Verlag.

Eysenck, H. J., & Coulter, T. (1972). The personality and attitudes of working class British Communists and Fascists. *Journal of Social Psychology, 87*, 59–73.

Eysenck, H. J., & Eysenck, S. B. G. (1964). *Manual of the Eysenck Personality Inventory.* London: University of London Press.

Eysenck, H. J., & Eysenck, S. B. G. (1969). *Personality structure and measurement.* San Diego: R. R. Knapp.

Eysenck, H. J., & Eysenck, S. B. G. (1976). *Psychoticism as a dimension of personality.* London: Hodder & Stoughton.

Eysenck, H. J., & Grossarth-Maticek, R. (1991). Creative novation behaviour therapy as a prophylactic treatment for cancer and coronary heart disease: Part II—Effects of treatment. *Behaviour Research Therapy, 29*, 17–31.

Eysenck, H. J., Grossarth-Maticek, R., & Everitt, B. (1991). Personality, stress, smoking, and genetic predisposition as synergistic risk factors for cancer and coronary heart disease. *Integrative Physiological and Behavioral Science, 26*, 309–322.

Eysenck, H. J., & Nias, D. K. B. (1978). *Sex, violence and the media.* New York: Harper & Row.

Eysenck, H. J., Nias, D. K. B., & Cox, D. N. (1982). Sport and personality. *Advances in Behavior Research and Therapy, 4*, 1–56.

Faber, M. D. (1970). Allport's visit with Freud. *The Psychoanalytic Review, 57*, 60–64.

Fakouri, M. E., & Hafner, J. L. (1984). Early recollections of first-borns. *Journal of Clinical Psychology, 40*, 209–213.

Fakouri, M. E., Hartung, J. R., & Hafner, J. L. (1985). Early recollections of neurotic depressive patients. *Psychological Reports, 57*, 783–786.

Federn, E. (1988). Psychoanalysis—The fate of a science in exile. In E. Timms & N. Segal (Eds.), *Freud in exile: Psychoanalysis and its vicissitudes* (pp. 156–162). New Haven, CT: Yale University Press.

Fern, T. L. (1991). Identifying the gifted child humorists. *Roeper Review, 14*, 30–34.

Ferster, C. B., & Skinner, B. F. (1957). *Schedules of reinforcement.* New York: Appleton-Century-Crofts.

Fransella, F., & Bannister, D. (1977). *A manual for repertory grid technique.* London: Academic Press.

Fransella, F., & Crisp, A. H. (1979). Comparisons of weight concepts in groups of neurotic, normal and anorexic females. *British Journal of Psychiatry, 134*, 79–86.

Freud, A. (1946). *The ego and the mechanisms of defense.* New York: International Universities Press.

Freud, S. (1896/1962). The aetiology of hysteria. In J. Strachey (Ed. and Trans.), *The standard edition of the complete psychological works of Sigmund Freud* (Vol. 3). London: Hogarth Press.

Freud, S. (1900/1953). *The interpretation of dreams.* In *Standard edition* (Vols. 4 & 5).

Freud, S. (1901/1953). On dreams. In *Standard edition* (Vol. 5).

Freud, S. (1901/1960). *Psychopathology of everyday life.* In *Standard edition* (Vol. 6).

Freud, S. (1905/1953a). Fragment of an analysis of a case of hysteria. In *Standard edition* (Vol. 7).

Freud, S. (1905/1953b). On psychotherapy. In *Standard edition* (Vol. 7).

Freud, S. (1905/1953c). Three essays on the theory of sexuality. In *Standard edition* (Vol. 7).

Freud, S. (1905/1960). *Jokes and their relation to the unconscious.* In *Standard edition* (Vol. 8).

Freud, S. (1909/1955). Analysis of a phobia in a five-year-old boy. In *Standard edition* (Vol. 10).

Freud, S. (1910/1957). Leonardo da Vinci and a memory of his childhood. In *Standard edition* (Vol. 11).

Freud, S. (1911/1958). Formulations on the two principles of mental functioning. In *Standard edition* (Vol. 12).

Freud, S. (1913/1953). *Totem and taboo*. In *Standard edition* (Vol. 13).

Freud, S. (1914/1953). The Moses of Michelangelo. In *Standard edition* (Vol. 13).

Freud, S. (1914/1957). On narcissism: An introduction. In *Standard edition* (Vol. 14).

Freud, S. (1915/1957a). Instincts and their vicissitudes. In *Standard edition* (Vol. 14).

Freud, S. (1915/1957b). The unconscious. In *Standard edition* (Vol. 14).

Freud, S. (1917/1955a). A difficulty in the path psycho-analysis. In *Standard edition* (Vol. 17).

Freud, S. (1917/1955b). On transformations of instinct as exemplified in anal erotism. In *Standard edition* (Vol. 17).

Freud, S. (1917/1963). *Introductory lectures on psychoanalysis*. In *Standard edition* (Vol. 15 & 16).

Freud, S. (1920/1955a). *Beyond the pleasure principle*. In *Standard edition* (Vol. 18).

Freud, S. (1920/1955b). The psychogenesis of a case of homosexuality in a woman. In *Standard edition* (Vol. 18).

Freud, S. (1922/1955). Some neurotic mechanisms in jealousy, paranoia and homosexuality. In *Standard edition* (Vol. 18).

Freud, S. (1923/1961a). *The ego and the id*. In *Standard edition* (Vol. 19).

Freud, S. (1923/1961b). The infantile genital organization: An interpolation into the theory of sexuality. In *Standard edition* (Vol. 19).

Freud, S. (1924/1961). The dissolution of the Oedipus complex. In *Standard edition* (Vol. 19).

Freud, S. (1925/1959). An autobiographical study. In *Standard edition* (Vol. 20).

Freud, S. (1925/1961). Some psychical consequences of the anatomical distinction between the sexes. In *Standard edition* (Vol. 19).

Freud, S. (1926/1959a). *Inhibitions, symptoms and anxiety*. In *Standard edition* (Vol. 20).

Freud, S. (1926/1959b). *The question of lay analysis*. In *Standard edition* (Vol. 20).

Freud, S. (1931/1961). Female sexuality. In *Standard edition* (Vol. 21).

Freud, S. (1933/1964). *New introductory lectures on psychoanalysis*. In *Standard edition* (Vol. 22).

Freud, S. (1940/1964). *An outline of psychoanalysis*. In *Standard edition* (Vol. 23).

Freud, S. (1950/1966). Project for a scientific psychology. In *Standard edition* (Vol. 1).

Freud, S. (1960). *Letters of Sigmund Freud* (E. L. Freud, Ed.; T. Stern & J. Stern, Trans.). New York: Basic Books.

Freud, S. (1985). *The complete letters of Sigmund Freud to Wilhelm Fliess, 1887–1904* (J. M. Masson, Ed. and Trans.). Cambridge, MA: Harvard University Press.

Freud, S., & Bullitt, W. C. (1967). *Thomas Woodrow Wilson: A psychological study*. Boston: Houghton Mifflin.

Frick, W. B. (1971). *Humanistic psychology: Interviews with Maslow, Murphy, and Rogers*. Columbus, OH: Merrill.

Frick, W. B. (1982). Conceptual foundations of self-actualization: A contribution to motivation theory. *Journal of Humanistic Psychology, 22*, 33–52.

Fromm, E. (1941). *Escape from freedom*. New York: Holt, Rinehart and Winston.

Fromm, E. (1947). *Man for himself: An inquiry into the psychology of ethics*. New York: Holt, Rinehart and Winston.

Fromm, E. (1950). *Psychoanalysis and religion*. New Haven, CT: Yale University Press.

Fromm, E. (1951). *The forgotten language: An introduction to the understanding of dreams, fairy tales and myths*. New York: Rinehart.

Fromm, E. (1955). *The sane society*. New York: Holt, Rinehart and Winston.

Fromm, E. (1956). *The art of loving*. New York: Harper & Brothers.

Fromm, E. (1959). *Sigmund Freud's mission*. New York: Harper & Brothers.

Fromm, E. (1961). *Marx's concept of man*. New York: Ungar.

Fromm, E. (1962). *Beyond the chains of illusion*. New York: Simon and Schuster.

Fromm, E. (1963). *The dogma of Christ and other essays on religion, psychology, and culture*. New York: Holt, Rinehart and Winston.

Fromm, E. (1964). *The heart of man*. New York: Harper & Row.

Fromm, E. (1973). *The anatomy of human destructiveness*. New York: Holt, Rinehart and Winston.

Fromm, E. (1976). *To have or be*. New York: Harper & Row.

Fromm, E. (1981). *On disobedience and other essays*. New York: Seabury Press.

Fromm, E. (1986). *For the love of life* (H. J. Schultz, Ed.; R. Kimber & R. Kimber, Trans.). New York: Free Press. (Original works published 1972, 1974, 1975, 1983).

Fromm, E., & Maccoby, M. (1970). *Social character in a Mexican village*. Englewood Cliffs, NJ: Prentice-Hall.

Fulker, D. W. (1981). The genetic and environmental architecture of psychoticism, extraversion and neuroticism. In H. J. Eysenck (Ed.), *A model for personality*. New York: Springer.

Funk, R. (1982). *Erich Fromm; The courage to be human*. New York: Continuum.

Furtmuller, C. (1964). Alfred Adler: A biographical essay. In H. L. Ansbacher & R. R. Ansbacher (Eds.), *Superiority and social interest: A collection of later writings*. Evanston, IL: Northwestern University Press.

Gallop, J. (1982). *The daughter's seduction: Feminism and psychoanalysis*. Ithaca, NY: Cornell University Press.

Garner, D. M., Olmstead, M. P., & Polivy, J. (1983). Development and validation of a multidimensional eating disorder inventory for anorexia nervosa and bulimia. *International Journal of Eating Disorder, 2*, 15–34.

Gay, P. (1988). *Freud: A life for our time*. New York: Norton.

Gendlin, E. T. (1988). Carl Rogers (1902–1987). *American Psychologist, 43*, 127–128.

Gibson, H. B. (1981). *Hans Eysenck: The man and his work*. London: Peter Owen.

Gilgen, A. R. (1982). *American psychology since World War II: A profile of the discipline*. Westport, CT: Greenwood.

Goble, F. G. (1970). *The third force: The psychology of Abraham Maslow*. New York: Grossman.

Goldberg, L. R. (1990). An alternative "description of personality": The Big-Five factor structure. *Journal of Personality and Social Psychology, 59*, 1216–1229.

Gordon, R. D. (1985). Dimensions of peak communication experiences: An exploratory study. *Psychological Reports, 57*, 824–826.

Gordon, T., & Cartwright, D. (1954). The effects of psychotherapy upon certain attitudes toward others. In C. R. Rogers & R. F. Dymond (Eds.), *Psychotherapy and personality change: Co-ordinated research studies in the client-centered approach* (pp. 167–195). Chicago: University of Chicago Press.

Gorsuch, R. L. (1988). Psychology of religion. *Annual Review of Psychology, 39*, 201–221.

Greever, K. B., Tseng, M. S., & Friedland, B. U. (1973). Development of the Social Interest Index. *Journal of Consulting and Clinical Psychology, 41*, 454–458.

Greever, K. B., Tseng, M. S., & Friedland, B. U. (1974). Measuring change in social interest in community college freshmen. *Individual Psychologist, 11*, 4–6.

Gross, A. M., Sanders, S., Smith, C., & Samson, G. (1990). Increasing compliance with orthodontic treatment. *Child & Family Behavior Therapy, 12*, 13–23.

Grossarth-Maticek, R., & Eysenck, H. J. (1991). Creative novation behaviour therapy as a prophylactic treatment for cancer and coronary heart disease: Part I—Description of treatment. *Behaviour Research and Therapy, 29*, 1–16.

Grossarth-Maticek, R., Eysenck, H. J., Rieder, H., & Rakic, L. (1990). The effects of behaviour therapy. Special Issue: Sport and leisure: Therapeutic aspects. *International Journal of Sport Psychology, 21*, 237–255.

Grossarth-Maticek, R., Eysenck, H. J., & Vetter, H. (1988). Personality type, smoking habit and their interaction as predictors of cancer and coronary heart disease. *Personality and Individual Differences, 9*, 479–495.

Grosskurth, P. (1986). *Melanie Klein: Her world and her work*. New York: Knopf.

Grummon, D. L. (1954). Design, procedures, and subjects for the first block. In C. R. Rogers & R. F. Dymond (Eds.), *Psychotherapy and personality change: Co-ordinated research studies in the client-centered approach* (pp. 35–52). Chicago: University of Chicago Press.

Gurtman, M. B. (1992). Trust, distrust, and interpersonal problems: A circumplex analysis. *Journal of Personality and Social Psychology, 62,* 989–1002.

Hafner, J. L., Fakouri, M. E., & Chesney, S. M. (1988). Early recollections of alcoholic women. *Journal of Clinical Psychology, 44,* 302–306.

Hall, E. (1983, June). A conversation with Erik Erikson. *Psychology Today,* pp. 22–30.

Hall, M. H. (1967, September). An interview with "Mr. Humanist": Rollo May. *Psychology Today,* pp. 25–29, 72–73.

Hall, M. H. (1968, July). A conversation with Abraham Maslow. *Psychology Today,* pp. 35–37; 54–57.

Hamachek, D. E. (1988). Evaluating self-concept and ego development within Erikson's psychosocial framework: A formulation. *Journal of Counseling and Development, 66,* 354–360.

Hanin, Y., Eysenck, S. B., Eysenck, H. J., & Barrett, P. (1991). A cross-cultural study of personality: Russia and England. *Personality and Individual Differences, 12,* 265–271.

Harris, T. G. (1969, August). The devil and Rollo May. *Psychology Today,* pp. 13–16.

Hartmann, H. (1939/1958). *Ego psychology and the problem of adaptation.* (D. Rapaport, Trans.). New York: International Universities Press.

Hartshorne, H., & May, M. A. (1928). *Studies in the nature of character: Vol. 1. Studies in deceit.* New York: Macmillan.

Hathaway, S. R., & McKinley, J. C. (1951). *The Minnesota Multiphasic Personality Inventory Manual* (Revised). New York: The Psychological Corp.

Hausdorff, D. (1972). *Erich Fromm.* New York: Twayne.

Heesacker, R. S., & Neimeyer, G. J. (1990). Assessing object relations and social cognitive correlates of eating disorders. *Journal of Counseling Psychology, 37,* 419–426.

Henry, W. P., Schacht, T. E., & Strupp, H. H. (1990). Patient and therapist introject, interpersonal process, and differential psychotherapy out-come. *Journal of Consulting and Clinical Psychology, 58,* 768–774.

Heppner, P. L., Rogers, M. E., & Lee, L. A. (1984). Carl Rogers: Reflections on his life. *Journal of Counseling and Development, 63,* 14–20.

Higgins, S. T., Delaney, D. D., Budney, A. J., Bickel, W. K., Hughes, J. R., Foerg, F., & Fenwick, J. W. (1991). A behavioral approach to achieving initial cocaine abstinence. *American Journal of Psychiatry, 148,* 1218–1224.

Hoffman, E. (1988). *The right to be human: A biography of Abraham Maslow.* Los Angeles: Tarcher.

Hofstee, W. K. B., de Raad, B., & Goldberg, L. R. (1992). Integration of the Big Five and circumplex approaches to trait structure. *Journal of Personality and Social Psychology, 61,* 146–163.

Holder, A. (1988). Reservations about the *Standard Edition.* In E. Timms & N. Segal (Eds.), *Freud in exile: Psychoanalysis and its vicissitudes* (pp. 210–214). New Haven, CT: Yale University Press.

Holland, N. (1986). Not so Little Hans: Identity and aging. In K. Woodward & M. M. Schwartz (Eds.), *Memory and desire: Aging—literature—psychoanalysis* (pp. 51–75). Bloomington: Indiana University Press.

Holland, R. (1970). George Kelly: Constructive innocent and reluctant existentialist. In D. Bannister (Ed.), *Perspectives in personal construct theory.* London: Academic Press.

Holt, R. R. (1989). *Freud reappraised: A fresh look at psychoanalytic theory.* New York: Guilford Press.

Hood, R. W., Jr. (1970). Religious orientations and the report of religious experiences. *Journal for the Scientific Study of Religion, 9,* 285–291.

Horney, K. (1917/1968). The technique of psychoanalytic therapy. *American Journal of Psychoanalysis, 28,* 3–12.

Horney, K. (1937). *The neurotic personality of our time.* New York: Norton.

Horney, K. (1939). *New ways in psychoanalysis.* New York: Norton.

Horney, K. (1942). *Self-analysis.* New York: Norton.

Horney, K. (1945). *Our inner conflicts: A constructive theory of neurosis.* New York: Norton.

Horney, K. (1950). *Neurosis and human growth: The*

struggle toward self-realization. New York: Norton.

Horney, K. (1967). The neurotic need for love. In H. Kelman (Ed.), *Feminine psychology* (pp. 245–258). New York: Norton.

Horney, K. (1987). *Final lectures*. D. H. Ingram (Ed.). New York: Norton.

Horowitz, L. M., Locke, K. D., Morse, M. B., Waikar, S. V., Dryer, D. C., Tarnow, E., & Ghannam, J. (1991). Self-derogations and interpersonal theory. *Journal of Personality and Social Psychology, 61,* 68–79.

Horowitz, L. M., Rosenberg, S. E., Baer, B. A., Ureño, G., & Villaseñor, V. S. (1988). Inventory of Interpersonal Problems: Psychometric properties and clinical applications. *Journal of Consulting and Clinical Psychology, 56,* 885–892.

Howard, G. S., & Conway, C. G. (1986). Can there be an empirical science of volutional action? *American Psychologist, 41,* 1241–1251.

Howard, G. S., Curtin, T. D., & Johnson, A. J. (1991). Point estimation techniques in psychological research: Studies on the role of meaning in self-determined action. *Journal of Counseling Psychology, 38,* 219–226.

Howard, G. S., & Myers, P. R. (1990). Predicting human behavior: Comparing idiographic, nomothetic, and agentic methodologies. *Journal of Counseling Psychology, 37,* 227–233.

Hughes, J. M. (1989). *Reshaping the psychoanalytic domain: The work of Melanie Klein, W. R. D. Fairbairn, and D. W. Winnicott.* Berkeley, CA: University of California Press.

Irigaray, L. (1986). This sex which is not one. In H. Cixous & C. Clement (Eds.), *The newly born woman.* Minneapolis: University of Minnesota Press.

Isbister, J. N. (1985). *Freud: An introduction to his life and work.* Cambridge, England: Polity Press.

Jacka, B. (1991). Personality variables and attitudes toward dream experiences. *Journal of Psychology, 125,* 27–31.

Jacobi, J. (1973). *The psychology of C. G. Jung: An introduction with illustrations.* New Haven, CT: Yale University Press.

Jacobs, M. (1992). *Sigmund Freud.* London: Sage.

Jacobson, E. (1938). *Progressive relaxation: A physiological and clinical investigation of muscle states and the significance in psychology and medical practice* (2d ed.). Chicago: University of Chicago Press.

Janeway, E. (1971). *Man's world, woman's place.* New York: Morrow.

Jankowicz, A. D. (1987). Whatever became of George Kelly? Applications and implications. *American Psychologist, 42,* 481–487.

John, O. P., Goldberg, L. R., & Angleitner, A. (1984). Better than the alphabet: Taxonomies of personality-descriptive terms in English, Dutch, and German. In H. Bonarius, G. van Heck, & N. Smid (Ed.), *Personality psychology in Europe: Theoretical and empirical developments* (pp. 83–100). Berwyn, PA: Swets North America.

Johnson, R. C. (1980). Summing up. [A review of Raymond B. Cattell's *Personality and Learning Theory. Vol. 1: The Structure of Personality in Its Environment.*] *Contemporary Psychology, 25,* 299–300.

Jones, E. (1953, 1955, 1957). *The life and work of Sigmund Freud* (Vols. 1–3). New York: Basic Books.

Jung, C. G. (1916/1953). The structure of the unconscious. In H. Read, M. Fordham, & G. Adler (Eds.), R. F. C. Hull (Trans.), *The collected works of C. G. Jung* (Vol. 7). New York: Pantheon Books.

Jung, C. G. (1916/1960). General aspects of dream psychology. In *Collected works* (Vol. 8).

Jung, C. G. (1921/1971). Psychological types. In *Collected works* (Vol. 6).

Jung, C. G. (1928/1960). On psychic energy. In *Collected works* (Vol. 8).

Jung, C. G. (1931/1954a). The aims of psychotherapy. In *Collected works* (Vol. 16).

Jung, C. G. (1931/1954b). Problems of modern psychotherapy. In *Collected works* (Vol. 16).

Jung, C. G. (1931/1960a). The stages of life. In *Collected works* (Vol. 8).

Jung, C. G. (1931/1960b). *The structure of the psyche.* In *Collected works* (Vol. 8).

Jung, C. G. (1934/1954a). The development of personality. In *Collected works* (Vol. 17).

Jung, C. G. (1934/1954b). The practical use of dream-analysis. In *Collected works* (Vol. 16).

Jung, C. G. (1934/1960). The soul and death. In *Collected works* (Vol. 8).

Jung, C. G. (1935/1968). The Tavistock lectures. In *Collected works* (Vol. 18).

Jung, C. G. (1937/1959). The concept of the collective unconscious. In *Collected works* (Vol. 9, pt. 1).

Jung, C. G. (1939/1959). Conscious, unconscious, and individuation. In *Collected works* (Vol. 9, pt. 1).

Jung, C. G. (1943/1953). *The psychology of the unconscious.* In *Collected works* (Vol. 7).

Jung, C. G. (1945/1953). *The relations between ego and the unconscious.* In *Collected works* (Vol. 7).

Jung, C. G. (1946/1964). The fight with the shadow. In *Collected works* (Vol. 10).

Jung, C. G. (1948/1960a). Instinct and the unconscious. In *Collected works* (Vol. 8).

Jung, C. G. (1948/1960b). On the nature of dreams. In *Collected works* (Vol. 8).

Jung, C. G. (1950/1959). Concerning rebirth. In *Collected works* (Vol. 9, pt. 1).

Jung, C. G. (1951/1959a). *Aion: Researches into the phenomenology of the self.* In *Collected works* (Vol. 9, pt. 2).

Jung, C. G. (1951/1959b). The psychology of the child archetype. In *Collected works* (Vol. 9, pt. 1).

Jung, C. G. (1952/1956). *Symbols of transformation.* In *Collected works* (Vol. 5).

Jung, C. G. (1952/1968). *Psychology and alchemy* (2d ed.). In *Collected works* (Vol. 12).

Jung, C. G. (1954/1959a). *Archetypes and the collective unconscious.* In *Collected works* (Vol. 9, pt. 1).

Jung, C. G. (1954/1959b). Concerning the archetypes, with special reference to the anima concept. In *Collected works* (Vol. 9, pt. 1).

Jung, C. G. (1954/1959c). Psychological aspects of the mother archetype. In *Collected works* (Vol. 9, pt. 1).

Jung, C. G. (1961). *Memories, dreams, reflections.* (A. Jaffé, Ed.). New York: Random House.

Jung, C. G. (1964). *Man and his symbols.* Garden City, NY: Doubleday.

Jung, C. G. (1979). *Word and image.* (A. Jaffé, Ed.). Princeton, NJ: Princeton University Press.

Jung, C. G., & Riklin, F. (1904/1973). The associations of normal subjects. In *Collected works* (Vol. 2).

Kean, R. C., Mehlhoff, C., & Sorensen, R. (1988). Using the Myers-Briggs Type Indicator to assess student needs. *Clothing and Textiles Journal, 6,* 37–42.

Kelly, G. A. (1955). *The psychology of personal constructs* (Vols. 1 and 2). New York: Norton.

Kelly, G. A. (1963). *A theory of personality: The psychology of personal constructs.* New York: Norton.

Kelly, G. A. (1969a). The autobiography of a theory. In B. Maher (Ed.), *Clinical psychology and personality: The selected papers of George Kelly.* New York: Wiley.

Kelly, G. A. (1969b). Man's construction of his alternatives. In B. Maher (Ed.), *Clinical psychology and personality: The selected papers of George Kelly.* New York: Wiley.

Kelly, G. A. (1970). A brief introduction to personal construct theory. In D. Bannister (Ed.), *Perspectives in personal construct theory.* London: Academic Press. Also in J. C. Mancuso (Ed.), *Readings for a cognitive theory of personality.* New York: Holt, Rinehart and Winston.

Kelly, G. A. (1980). A psychology of the optimal man. In A. W. Landfield & L. M. Leitner (Eds.), *Personal construct psychology: Psychotherapy and personality.* New York: Wiley.

Kernberg, O. F. (1975). *Borderline conditions and pathological narcissism.* New York: Aronson.

Kernberg, O. F. (1976). *Object-relations theory and clinical psychoanalysis.* New York: Aronson.

Kernberg, O. F. (1984). *Severe personality disorders: Psychotherapeutic strategies.* New Haven, CT: Yale University Press.

Kernberg, O. F. (1986). Structural derivatives of object relationships. In P. Buckley (Ed.); *Essential papers on object relations* (pp. 350–384). New York: New York University Press.

Keys, A., Brozek, J., Henschel, A., Mickelsen, O., & Taylor, H. L. (1950). The biology of human starvation (Vols. 1 and 2). Minneapolis: University of Minnesota Press.

Kihlstrom, J. F. (1987). The cognitive unconscious. *Science, 237,* 1445–1452.

Kihlstrom, J. F. (1990). The psychological unconscious. In L. A. Pervin (Ed.), *Handbook of person-*

ality: Theory and research (pp. 445–464). New York: Guilford Press.

King, P. (1991). Conclusions. In P. King & R. Steiner (Eds.), *The Freud-Klein controversies 1941–1945* (pp. 920–931). London: Tavistock/Routledge.

King, P., & Steiner, R. (Eds.). (1991). *The Freud-Klein controversies 1941–1945.* London: Tavistock/Routledge.

Kinsey, A. C., Pomeroy, W., & Martin, C. (1948). *Sexual behavior in the human male.* Philadelphia: Saunders.

Kirschenbaum, H. (1979). *On becoming Carl Rogers.* New York: Delacorte Press.

Kirschenbaum, H., & Henderson, V. L. (Eds.). (1989). *The Carl Rogers reader.* Boston: Houghton Mifflin.

Kissen, D. M., & Eysenck, H. J. (1962). Personality and male lung cancer patients. *Journal of Psychosomatic Research, 6,* 123–137.

Klein, M. (1930). The importance of symbol-formation in the development of the ego. In M. Klein (1964). *Contributions to psycho-analysis, 1921–1945* (pp. 236–250). New York: McGraw-Hill.

Klein, M. (1932). *The Psycho-analysis of children.* London: Hogarth Press.

Klein, M. (1933). The early development of conscience in the child. In M. Klein (1964). *Contributions to psycho-analysis, 1921–1945* (pp. 267–277). New York: McGraw-Hill.

Klein, M. (1935). A contribution to the psychogenesis of manic-depressive states. In J. Mitchell (Ed.), *The selected Melanie Klein* (pp. 145–166). New York: Free Press.

Klein, M. (1940). Mourning and its relation to manic-depressive states. In M. Klein (1964). *Contributions to psycho-analysis, 1921–1945* (pp. 311–338). New York: McGraw-Hill.

Klein, M. (1943). Memorandum on her technique by Melanie Klein. In P. King & R. Steiner (Eds.) (1991). *The Freud-Klein controversies 1941– 945* (pp. 635–638). London: Tavistock/Routledge.

Klein, M. (1945). The Oedipus complex in the light of early anxieties. In M. Klein (1984). *Love, guilt and reparation and other works, 1921–1945* (pp. 370–419). New York: Macmillan.

Klein, M. (1946). Notes on some schizoid mechanism. In M. Klein (1975). *Envy and gratitude and other works, 1946–1963* (pp. 1–24). New York: Delta Books.

Klein, M. (1948). *Contributions to psycho-analysis, 1921–45.* London: Hogarth.

Klein, M. (1952). *Envy and gratitude.* London: Tavistock.

Klein, M. (1955). The psycho-analytic play technique: Its history and significance. In J. Mitchell (Ed.) (1986). *The selected Melanie Klein* (pp. 35–54). New York: Free Press.

Klein, M. (1959). Our adult world and its roots in infancy. In M. Klein (1984). *Envy and gratitude and other works, 1946–1963* (pp. 247–263). New York: Macmillan.

Klein, M. (1991). The emotional life and ego-development of the infant with special reference to the depressive position. In P. King & R. Steiner (Eds.), *The Freud-Klein controversies 1941–1945* (pp. 552–577). London: Tavistock/Routledge.

Klerman, G. L. (1989a). Evaluating the efficacy of psychotherapy for depression: The USA experience. *European Archives of Psychiatry and Neurological Science, 238,* 240–246.

Klerman, G. L. (1989b). The interpersonal model. In J. J. Mann (Ed.), *Models of depressive disorders: Psychological, biological, and genetic perspectives* (pp. 45–77). New York: Plenum Press.

Klerman, G. L., & Weissman, M. M. (1991). Interpersonal psychotherapy: Research program and future prospects. In L. E. Beutler & M. Crago (Eds.), *Psychotherapy research: An international review of programmatic studies* (pp. 33–40). Washington, DC: American Psychological Association.

Klerman, G. L., Weissman, M. M., Rounsaville, B. J., & Chevron, E. S. (1984). *Interpersonal psychotherapy of depression.* New York: Basic Books.

Kline, P. (1984). *Psychology and Freudian theory: An introduction.* London: Methuen.

Knapp, G. P. (1989). *The art of living: Erich Fromm's life and works.* New York: Peter Lang.

Kohut, H. (1971). *The analysis of the self: A systematic approach to the treatment of narcissistic personality disorders*. New York: International Universities Press.

Kohut, H. (1977). *The restoration of the self*. New York: International Universities Press.

Kohut, H. (1987). *The Kohut Seminars on self psychology and psychotherapy with adolescents and young adults*. M. Elson (Ed.). New York: Norton.

Korn, J. M., Davis, R., & Davis, S. F. (1991). Historians' and chairpersons' judgments of eminence among psychologists. *American Psychologist, 46,* 789–792.

Kowaz, A. M., & Marcia, J. E. (1991). Development and validation of a measure of Eriksonian industry. *Journal of Personality and Social Psychology, 60,* 390–397.

Kurzweil, E. (1989). *The Freudians: A comparative perspective*. New Haven, CT: Yale University Press.

Landis, B., & Tauber, E. S. (1971). Erich Fromm: Some biographical notes. In B. Landis & E. S. Tauber (Eds.). *In the name of life: Essays in honor of Erich Fromm*. New York: Holt, Rinehart and Winston.

Landfield, A. W. (1971). *Personal construct systems in psychotherapy*. Chicago: Rand-McNally.

Landfield, A. W., & Epting, F. R. (1987). *Personal construct psychology: Clinical and personality assessment*. New York: Human Sciences Press.

Landfield, A. W., & Leitner, L. M. (Eds.). (1980). *Personal construct psychology: Psychotherapy and personality*. New York: Wiley.

Landfield, A. W., Stefan, R., & Dempsey, D. (1990). Single and multiple self implications for change grids: Studies of consistency. *International Construct Psychology, 3,* 423–436.

Last, J. M. (1983). *Comprehensive early memory scoring system manual*. Unpublished manuscript.

Last, J., & Bruhn, A. R. (1983). The psychodiagnostic value of children's early memories. *Journal of Personality Assessment, 47,* 597–603.

Lazarick, D. L., Fishbein, S. S., Loiello, M. A., & Howard, G. S. (1988). Practical investigations of volition. *Journal of Counseling Psychology, 35,* 15–26.

Lerman, H. (1986). *A mote in Freud's eye: From psychoanalysis to the psychology of women*. New York: Springer.

Lester, D. (1990). Maslow's hierarchy of needs and personality. *Personality and Individual Differences, 11,* 1187–1188.

Lester, D., Hvezda, J., Sullivan, S., & Plourde, R. (1983). Maslow's hierarchy of needs and psychology health. *Journal of General Psychology, 109,* 83–85.

Levy, N., & Ridley, S. E. (1987). Stability of Jungian personality types within a college population over a decade. *Psychological Reports, 60,* 419–422.

Lonky, E., Kaus, C. R., & Roodin, P. A. (1984). Life experience and mode of coping: Relation to moral judgment in adulthood. *Developmental Psychology, 20,* 1159–1167.

Lynn, R., Chan, J. W., & Eysenck, H. J. (1991). Reaction times and intelligence in Chinese and British children. *Perceptual and Motor Skills, 72,* 443–452.

Lyon, D., & Greenberg, J. (1991). Evidence of codependency in women with an alcoholic parent: Helping out Mr. Wrong. *Journal of Personality and Social Psychology, 61,* 435–439.

Mahler, M. S. (1952). On child psychosis and schizophrenia: Autistic and symbiotic infantile psychoses. *Psychoanalytic Study of the Child, 7,* 286–305.

Mahler, M. S. (1967). On human symbiosis and the vicissitudes of individuation. *Journal of the American Psychoanalytic Association, 15,* 740–762.

Mahler, M. S. (1972). On the first three subphases of the separation-individuation process. *International Journal of Psycho-Analysis, 53,* 333–338.

Mahler, M. S., Pine, F., & Bergman, A. (1975). *The psychological birth of the human infant*. New York: Basic Books.

Manaster, G. J., & Perryman, T. B. (1974). Early recollections and occupational-choice. *Journal of Individual Psychology, 30,* 232–237.

Manaster, G. J., & Perryman, T. B. (1979). Manaster-Perryman manifest content early recollection scoring manual. In H. Olson (Ed.)., *Early recollections: Their use in diagnosis and psychotherapy* (pp. 347–350). Springfield, IL: Charles C Thomas.

Marcia, J. E. (1966). Development and validation of ego-identity status. *Journal of Personality and Social Psychology, 3,* 551–558.

Marcia, J. E. (1976). Identity six years after: A follow-up study. *Journal of Youth and Adolescence, 5,* 145–160.

Marcia, J. E. (1980). Identity in adolescence. In J. Adelson (Ed.), *Handbook of adolescent psychology* (pp. 159–187). New York: Wiley.

Marcia, J. E. (1987). The identity status approach to the study of ego identity development. In T. Honess & K. Yardley (Eds.), *Self and identity: Perspectives across the lifespan* (pp. 161–171). Boston: Routledge & Kegan Paul.

Marshall, G. N. (1991). A multidimensional analysis of internal health locus of control beliefs: Separating the wheat from the chaff? *Journal of Personality and Social Psychology, 61,* 483–491.

Maslow, A. H. (1941). Deprivation, thirst, and frustration. *Psychological Review, 48,* 364–366.

Maslow, A. H. (1943). A theory of human motivation. *Psychological Review, 50,* 370–396.

Maslow, A. H. (1950). Self-actualizing people: A *study of psychological.* New York: Grune & Stratton.

Maslow, A. H. (1964). *Religions, values, and peak-experiences.* Columbus: Ohio State University Press.

Maslow, A. H. (1966). *The psychology of science.* New York: Harper & Row.

Maslow, A. H. (1967). A theory of metamotivation: The biological rooting of the value-life. *Journal of Humanistic Psychology, 7*(2), 93–127.

Maslow, A. H. (1968a). *Self-actualization* (Film). Santa Ana, CA: Psychological Films.

Maslow, A. H. (1968b). *Toward a psychology of being* (2d ed.). New York: Van Nostrand.

Maslow, A. H. (1970). *Motivation and personality* (2d ed.). New York: Harper & Row.

Maslow, A. H. (1971). *The farther reaches of human nature.* New York: Viking.

Maslow, A. H. (1979). *The Journals of* A. H. Maslow (2 vols.). R. J. Lowry (Ed.). Monterey, CA: Brooks/Cole.

Masson, J. M. (1984). *The assault on truth: Freud's suppression of the seduction theory.* New York: Farrar, Straus and Giroux.

May, R. (1950). *The meaning of anxiety.* New York: Ronald Press.

May, R. (1953). *Man's search for himself.* New York: Norton.

May, R. (1958a). Contributions of existential psychotherapy. In R. May, E. Angel, & H. F. Ellenberger (Eds.), *Existence: A new dimension in psychiatry and psychology.* New York: Basic Books.

May, R. (1958b). The origins and significance of the existential movement in psychology. In R. May, E. Angel, & H. F. Ellenberger (Eds.), *Existence: A new dimension in psychiatry and psychology.* New York: Basic Books.

May, R. (1962). Dangers in the relation of existentialism to psychotherapy. In. H. M. Ruitenbeek (Ed.), *Psychoanalysis and existential philosophy.* New York: Dutton.

May, R. (1967). *Psychology and the human dilemma.* Princeton, NJ: Van Nostrand.

May, R. (1969a). The emergence of existential psychology. In R. May (Ed.), *Existential psychology* (2d ed.). New York: Random House.

May, R. (1969b). Existential bases of psychotherapy. In R. May (Ed.), *Existential psychology* (2d ed.). New York: Random House.

May, R. (1969c). *Love and will.* New York: Norton.

May, R. (1972). *Power and innocence: A search for the sources of violence.* New York: Norton.

May, R. (1977a). *The meaning of anxiety* (Rev. Ed.). New York: Norton.

May, R. (1977b). Reflections and commentary by Rollo May. In C. Reeves, *The psychology of Rollo May* (pp. 295–309). San Francisco: Jossey-Bass.

May, R. (1981). *Freedom and destiny.* New York: Norton.

May, R. (1982). The problem of evil: An open letter to Carl Rogers. *Journal of Humanistic Psychology, 22*(3), 10–21.

May, R. (1985). *My quest for beauty.* San Francisco: Saybrook.

May, R. (1990a). The meaning of the Oedipus myth. *Review of Existential Psychology and Psychiatry:* 1986–87. Special Issue, *20,* 169–177.

May, R. (1990b). On the phenomenological bases of therapy. *Review of Existential Psychology and Psychiatry:* 1986–87. Special Issue, *20,* 49–61.

May, R. (1990c). Will, decision and responsibility.

Review of Existential Psychology and Psychiatry: 1986. Special Issue, *20,* 269–278.

May, R. (1991). *The cry for myth.* New York: Norton.

May, R., Angel, E., & Ellenberger, H. F. (Eds.). (1958). *Existence: A new dimension in psychiatry and psychology.* New York: Basic Books.

McAdams, D. P., & de St. Aubin, E. (1992). A theory of generativity and its assessment through self-report, behavioral acts, and narrative themes in autobiography. *Journal of Personality and Social Psychology, 62,* 1003–1015.

McCaulley, M. H. (1990). The Myers-Briggs Type Indicator: A measure for individuals and groups. *Measurement and Evaluation in Counseling and Development, 22,* 181–195.

McCrae, R. R., & Costa, P. T. (1989). Reinterpreting the Myers-Briggs Type Indicator from the perspective of the five-factor model of personality. *Journal of Personality, 57,* 17–40.

McDougall, W. (1933). *The energies of men.* New York: Scribner's.

McGregor, D. (1960). *The human side of enterprise.* New York: McGraw-Hill.

McGuire, W. (Ed.). (1974). *The Freud/Jung letters: The correspondence between Sigmund Freud and C. G. Jung.* Princeton, NJ: Princeton University Press.

Menninger, K. (1942). *Love against hate.* New York: Harcourt, Brace & World.

Messer, S. B., & Warren, S. (1990). Personality change and psychotherapy. In L. A. Pervin (Ed.), *Handbook of personality: Theory and research* (pp. 371–398). New York: Guilford Press.

Miller, N. E. (1941). The frustration-aggression hypothesis. *Psychological Review, 48,* 337–342.

Miller, N. E. (1944). Experimental studies of conflict behavior. In J. McV. Hunt (Ed.), *Personality and behavior disorders* (Vol. 1). New York: Ronald Press.

Miller, N. E. (1951). Learnable drives and rewards. In S. S. Stevens (Ed.), *Handbook of experimental psychology.* New York: Wiley.

Miller, N. E. (1959). Liberalization of basic S-R concepts: Extensions to conflict behavior, motivation and social learning. In S. Koch (Ed.), *Psy-chology: A study of science* (Vol. 2). New York: McGraw-Hill.

Miller, N. E. (1982). John Dollard (1900–1980): Obituary. *American Psychologist, 37,* 587–588.

Miller, N. E. (1983). Behavioral medicine: Symbiosis between laboratory and clinic. *Annual Review of Psychology, 34,* 1–31.

Miller, N. E. (1984a). *Bridges between laboratory and clinic.* New York: Praeger.

Miller, N. E. (1984b). Learning: Some facts and needed research relevant to maintaining health. In J. D. Matarazzo, S. M. Weiss, J. A. Herd, N. E. Miller, & S. M. Weiss (Eds.), *Behavioral health: A handbook of health enhancement and disease prevention* (pp. 199–208). New York: Wiley.

Miller, N. E., & Dollard, J. (1941). *Social learning and imitation.* New Haven, CT: Yale University Press.

Mills, J. K. (1991). Control orientation as a personality dimension among alcoholic and obese adult men undergoing addictions treatment. *Journal of Psychology, 125,* 537–542.

Mischel, H. N., & Mischel W. (Eds.). (1973). *Readings in personality.* New York: Holt, Rinehart and Winston.

Mischel, W. (1958). Preference for delayed reinforcement: An experimental study of cultural observation. *Journal of Abnormal and Social Psychology, 56,* 57–61.

Mischel, W. (1961a). Delay of gratification, need for achievement, and acquiesce in another culture. *Journal of Abnormal and Social Psychology, 62,* 543–552.

Mischel, W. (1961b). Preference for delayed reinforcement and social responsibility. *Journal of Abnormal and Social Psychology, 62,* 1–7.

Mischel, W. (1965). Predicting success of Peace Corps volunteers in Nigeria. *Journal of Personality and Social Psychology, 1,* 510–517.

Mischel, W. (1968). *Personality and assessment.* New York: Wiley.

Mischel, W. (1971). *Introduction to personality.* New York: Holt, Rinehart and Winston.

Mischel, W. (1973). Toward a cognitive social learning reconceptualization of personality. *Psychological Review, 80,* 252–283.

Mischel, W. (1976). Introduction to personality (2d ed.). New York: Holt, Rinehart and Winston.

Mischel, W. (1977). The interaction of person and situation. In D. Magnusson & N. S. Endler (Eds.), Personality at the crossroads: Current issues in interactional psychology. Hillsdale, NJ: Erlbaum.

Mischel, W. (1979). On the interface of cognition and personality: Beyond the person-situation debate. American Psychologist, 34, 740–754.

Mischel, W. (1981a). Introduction to personality (3d ed.). New York: Holt, Rinehart and Winston.

Mischel, W. (1981b). Personality and cognition: Something borrowed something new? In N. Cantor & J. F. Kihlstrom (Eds.), Personality, cognition, and social interaction. Hillsdale, NJ: Erlbaum.

Mischel, W. (1986). Introduction to personality: A new look (4th ed.). New York: Holt, Rinehart and Winston.

Mischel, W. (1990). Personality dispositions revisited and revised: A view after three decades. In L. A. Pervin (Ed.), Handbook of personality: Theory and research (pp. 111–134). New York: Guilford Press.

Mischel, W. (1993). Introduction to personality (5th ed.). Fort Worth: Harcourt Brace Jovanovich.

Mischel, W., & Baker, N. (1975). Cognitive appraisals and transformations in delay behavior. Journal of Personality and Social Psychology, 31, 254–261.

Mischel, W., & Ebbesen, E. B. (1970). Attention in delay of gratification. Journal of Personality and Social Psychology, 16, 329–337.

Mischel, W., Ebbesen, E. B., & Zeiss, A. R. (1972). Cognitive and attentional mechanisms in delay of gratification. Journal of Personality and Social Psychology, 21, 204–218.

Mischel, W., & Metzner, R. (1962). Preference for delayed reward as a function of age, intelligence, and length of delay interval. Journal of Abnormal and Social Psychology, 64, 425–431.

Mischel, W., & Mischel, H. N. (1976). A cognitive social learning approach to morality and self-regulation. In T. Lickona (Ed.), Moral development and behavior: Theory, research, and social issues. New York: Holt, Rinehart and Winston.

Mischel, W., & Mischel, H. N. (1983). Development of children's knowledge of self-control strategies. Child Development, 54, 603–619.

Mischel, W., & Moore, B. (1973). Effects of attention to symbolically presented rewards upon self-control. Journal of Personality and Social Psychology, 28, 172–179.

Mischel, W., & Peake, P. K. (1982). Beyond déja vu in the search for cross-situational consistency. Psychological Review, 89, 730–755.

Mischel, W., Shoda, Y., & Peake, P. K. (1988). The nature of adolescent competencies predicted by preschool delay of gratification. Journal of Personality and Social Psychology, 54, 687–696.

Mischel, W., Shoda, Y., & Rodriguez, M. L. (1989). Delay of gratification in children. Science, 244, 933–938.

Mischel, W., & Staub, E. (1965). Effects of expectancy on working and waiting for larger rewards. Journal of Personality and Social Psychology, 2, 625–633.

Moreau, D., Mufson, L., Weissman, M. M., & Klerman, G. L. (1991). Interpersonal psychotherapy for adolescent depression: Description of modification and preliminary application. Journal of the American Academy of Child and Adolescent Psychiatry, 38, 642–651.

Mosak, H. H. (1958). Early recollections as a projective technique. Journal of Projective Techniques, 22, 302–311.

Mozdzierz, G. J., & Semyck, R. W. (1980). The social interest index: A study of construct validity. Journal of Clinical Psychology, 36, 417–422.

Murray, H. A. (1938). Explorations in personality. New York: Oxford University Press.

Murray, J. B. (1990). Review of research on the Myers-Briggs Type Indicator. Perceptual and Motor Skills, 70, 1187–1202.

Murray, L. (1991). Intersubjectivity, object relations theory, and empirical evidence from mother-infant interactions. Special Issue: The effects of relationships on relationships. Infant Mental Health Journal, 12, 219–232.

Myers, I. B. (1962). Myers-Briggs Type Indicator Manual. Palo Alto, CA: Consulting Psychologists Press.

Myers, I. B., & McCaulley, M. H. (1985). *Manual: A guide to the development and use of the Myers-Briggs Type Indicator.* Palo Alto, CA: Consulting Psychologists Press.

Nolan, L. L., & Patterson, S. J. (1990). The active audience: Personality type as an indicator of TV program preference. *Journal of Social Behavior and Personality, 5,* 697–710.

Noller, P., Law, H., Comrey, A. L. (1987). Cattell, Comrey, and Eysenck personality compared: More evidence for the five robust factors? *Journal of Personality and Social Psychology, 53,* 775–782.

Norman, W. T. (1963). Toward an adequate taxonomy of personality attributes. Replicated factor structure in peer nomination personality ratings. *Journal of Abnormal and Social Psychology, 66,* 574–583.

O'Connell, A. N. (1990). Karen Horney (1885–1952). In A. N. O'Connell & N. F. Russo (Eds.), *Women in psychology: A bio-bibliographic sourcebook* (pp. 185–196). New York: Greenwood Press.

Ogden, T. H. (1990). *The matrix of the mind: Object relations and the psychoanalytic dialogue.* Northvale, NJ: Aronson.

Olds, J., & Milner, P. (1954). Positive reinforcement produced by electrical stimulation of the septal area and other regions of the rat brain. *Journal of Comparative and Physiological Psychology, 47,* 419–427.

Orlofsky, J. L., Marcia, J. E., & Lesser, I. M. (1973). Ego identity status and the intimacy versus isolation crisis of young adulthood. *Journal of Personality and Social Psychology, 27,* 211–219.

Ozer, E. M., & Bandura, A. (1990). Mechanisms governing empowerment effects: A self-efficacy analysis. *Journal of Personality and Social Psychology, 58,* 472–486

Paige, J. M. (1966). Letters from Jenny: An approach to the clinical analysis of personality structure by computer. In P. J. Stone (Ed.), *The general enquirer: A computer approach to content analysis.* Cambridge, MA: M.I.T. Press.

Panzarella, R. (1980). The phenomenology of aesthetic peak experiences. *Journal of Humanistic Psychology, 20*(1), 69–85.

Peabody, D., & Goldberg, L. R. (1989). Some determinants of factor structures from personality-trait descriptors. *Journal of Personality and Social Psychology, 57,* 552–567.

Perry, H. S. (1982). *Psychiatrist of America: The life of Harry Stack Sullivan.* Cambridge, MA: The Belknap Press.

Pervin, L. A. (1990a). A brief history of modern personality theory. In L. A. Pervin (Ed.), *Handbook of personality: Theory and research* (pp. 3–18). New York: Guilford.

Pervin, L. A. (1990b). Personality theory and research: Prospects for the future. In L. A. Pervin (Ed.), *Handbook of personality: Theory and research* (pp. 723–727). New York: Guilford.

Pines, M. (1978, September). Invisible playmates. *Psychology Today,* pp. 38–42, 106.

Popper, K. R. (1963). *Conjectures and refutations: The growth of scientific knowledge.* New York: Harper & Row.

Prager, K. (1986). Identity development, age, and college experience in women. *Journal of Genetic Psychology, 147,* 31–36.

Quinn, S. (1987). *A mind of her own: The life of Karen Horney.* New York: Summit Books.

Rabinowitz, F. E., Good, G., & Cozad, L. (1989). Rollo May: A man of meaning and myth. *Journal of Counseling and Development, 67,* 436–441.

Rattner, J. (1983). *Alfred Adler* (H. Zohn, Trans.). New York: Frederick Ungar. (Original work published 1983).

Ravizza, K. (1977). Peak experiences in sport. *Journal of Humanistic Psychology, 17*(4), 35–40.

Reeves, C. (1977). *The psychology of Rollo May.* San Francisco: Jossey-Bass.

Rest, J. R. (1979). *Revised manual for the Defining Issues Test.* Minneapolis: Minnesota Moral Research Projects.

Roazen, P. (1976). *Erik H. Erikson: The power and limits of a vision.* New York: Free Press.

Rogers, C. R. (1939). *The clinical treatment of the problem child.* Boston: Houghton Mifflin.

Rogers, C. R. (1942). *Counseling and psychotherapy: Newer concepts in practice.* Boston: Houghton Mifflin.

Rogers, C. R. (1947). Some observations on the organization of personality. *American Psychologist, 2,* 358–368.

Rogers, C. R. (1951). *Client-centered therapy: Its current practice, implications, and theory.* Boston: Houghton Mifflin.

Rogers, C. R. (1953). A *concept of the fully functioning person.* Unpublished manuscript, University of Chicago Counseling Center, Chicago.

Rogers, C. R. (1954a). The case of Mrs. Oak: A research analysis. In C. R. Rogers & R. F. Dymond (Eds.), *Psychotherapy and personality change: Co-ordinated research studies in the client-centered approach* (pp. 259–348). . Chicago: University of Chicago Press.

Rogers, C. R. (1954b). Introduction. In C. R. Rogers & R. F. Dymond (Eds.), *Psychotherapy and personality change: Co-ordinated research studies in the client-centered approach* (pp. 3–11). Chicago: University of Chicago Press.

Rogers, C. R. (1955). Personality change in psychotherapy. *The International Journal of Social Psychiatry, 1,* 31–41.

Rogers, C. R. (1957). The necessary and sufficient conditions of therapeutic personality change. *Journal of Consulting Psychology, 21,* 95–103.

Rogers, C. R. (1959). A theory of therapy, personality, and interpersonal relationships, as developed in the client-centered framework. In S. Koch (Ed.), *Psychology: A study of a science* (Vol. 3). New York: McGraw-Hill.

Rogers, C. R. (1961). *On becoming a person: A therapist's view of psychotherapy.* Boston: Houghton Mifflin.

Rogers, C. R. (1962). Toward becoming a fully functioning person. In A. W. Combs (Ed.), *Perceiving, behaving, becoming: Yearbook* (pp. 21–33). Washington, DC: Association for Supervision and Curriculum Development.

Rogers, C. R. (1963). The concept of the fully functioning person. *Psychotherapy: Theory, Research, and Practice, 1*(1), 17–26.

Rogers, C. R. (1968). Some thoughts regarding the current presuppositions of the behavioral sciences. In W. R. Coulson & C. R. Rogers (Eds.), *Man and the science of man.* Columbus, OH: Merrill.

Rogers, C. R. (1978). The formative tendency. *Journal of Humanistic Psychology, 18*(1), 23–26.

Rogers, C. R. (1980). A *way of being.* Boston: Houghton Mifflin.

Rogers, C. R. (1982a). Notes on Rollo May. *Journal of Humanistic Psychology, 22*(3), 8–9.

Rogers, C. R. (1982b). A psychologist looks at nuclear war: Its threat; its possible prevention. *Journal of Humanistic Psychology, 22*(4), 9–20.

Rogers, C. R. (1983). *Freedom to learn for the 80's.* Columbus, OH: Merrill.

Rogers, C. R. (1989). *The Carl Rogers reader.* H. Kirschenbaum & V. L. Henderson (Eds.). Boston: Houghton Mifflin.

Rogers, C. R., & Dymond, R. F. (Eds.). (1954). *Psychotherapy and personality change: Co-ordinated research studies in the client-centered approach.* Chicago: University of Chicago Press.

Rogers, C. R., Gendlin, E., Kiesler, D., & Truax, C. (1967). *The therapeutic relationship and its impact: A study of psychotherapy with schizophrenics.* Madison, WI: University of Wisconsin Press.

Rogers, C. R., & Skinner, B. F. (1956). Some issues concerning the control of human behavior. *Science, 124,* 1057–1066.

Rogers, C. R., & Stevens, B. (1967). *Person to person: The problem of being human: A new trend in psychology.* Lafayette, CA: Real People Press.

Rosen, D. H., Smith, S. M., Huston, H. L., & Gonzalez, G. (1991). Empirical study of associations between symbols and their meaning: Evidence of collective unconscious (archetypal) memory. *Journal of Analytical Psychology, 36,* 211–228.

Rosenberg, M. (1965). *Society and the adolescent self-image.* Princeton, NJ: Princeton University Press.

Rosenthal, T. L., & Bandura, A. (1978). Psychological modeling: Theory and practice. In S. L. Garfield & A. E. Bergin (Eds.), *Handbook of psychotherapy and behavior change: An empirical analysis.* New York: Wiley.

Ross, C. A., Heber, S., Norton, G. R., & Anderson, G. (1989). Differences between multiple personality disorder and diagnostic groups on structured interview. *Journal of Nervous and Mental Disease, 177,* 489–491.

Rotter, J. B. (1954). *Social learning and clinical psychology*. Englewood Cliffs, NJ: Prentice-Hall.

Rotter, J. B. (1964). *Clinical psychology*. Englewood Cliffs, NJ: Prentice-Hall.

Rotter, J. B. (1966). Generalized expectancies for internal versus external control of reinforcement. *Psychological Monographs, 80* (Whole No. 609).

Rotter, J. B. (1967). A new scale for the measurement of interpersonal trust. *Journal of Personality, 35,* 651–665.

Rotter, J. B. (1970). Some implications of a social learning theory for the practice of psychotherapy. In D. J. Levis (Ed.), *Learning approaches to therapeutic behavior change*. Chicago: Aldine.

Rotter, J. B. (1971). Generalized expectancies for interpersonal trust. *American Psychologist, 26,* 443–452.

Rotter, J. B. (1975). Some problems and misconceptions related to the construct of internal vs. external control of reinforcement. *Journal of Consulting and Clinical Psychology, 43,* 56–67.

Rotter, J. B. (1978). Generalized expectancies for problem solving and psychotherapy. *Cognitive Therapy and Research, 2,* 1–10.

Rotter, J. B. (1980). Interpersonal trust, trustworthiness, and gullibility. *American Psychologist, 35,* 1–7.

Rotter, J. B. (1982). *The development and applications of social learning theory: Selected papers*. New York: Praeger.

Rotter, J. B. (1993). Expectancies. In C. E. Walker (Ed.), *The history of clinical psychology in autobiography*: Vol. 2 (pp. 273–284). Pacific Grove, CA: Brooks/Cole.

Rotter, J. B., Chance, J. E., & Phares, E. J. (1972). *Applications of a social learning theory of personality*. New York: Holt, Rinehart and Winston.

Rotter, J. B., & Hochreich, D. J. (1975). *Personality*. Glenview, IL: Scott, Foresman.

Royce, J. R., & Powell, A. (1983). *Theory of personality and individual differences: Factors, systems and processes*. Englewood Cliffs, NJ: Prentice-Hall.

Rubins, J. L. (1978). *Karen Horney: Gentle rebel of psychoanalysis*. New York: Dial Press.

Rudikoff, E. C. (1954). A comparative study of the changes in the concepts of the self, the ordinary person, and the ideal in eight cases. In C. R. Rogers & R. F. Dymond (Eds.), *Psychotherapy and personality change: Co-ordinated research studies in the client-centered approach* (pp. 85–98). Chicago: University of Chicago Press.

Sartre, J. P. (1957). *Existentialism and human emotions*. New York: Wisdom Library.

Savill, G. E., & Eckstein, D. G. (1987). Changes in early recollections as a function of mental status. *Individual Psychology, 43,* 3–17.

Sayers, J. (1991). *Mothers of psychoanalysis: Helene Deutsch, Karen Horney, Anna Freud, Melanie Klein*. New York: Norton.

Schlein, S. (Ed.) (1987). *A way of looking at things: Selected papers of Erik Erikson*. New York: Norton.

Schur, M. (1972). *Freud: Living and dying*. New York: International Universities Press.

Segal, H. (1979). *Melanie Klein*. New York: Viking Press.

Sheffield, F. D. (1966a). A drive theory of reinforcement. In R. N. Haber (Ed.), *Current research in motivation*. New York: Holt, Rinehart and Winston.

Sheffield, F. D. (1966b). New evidence on the drive-induction theory of reinforcement. In R. N. Haber (Ed.), *Current research in motivation*. New York: Holt, Rinehart and Winston.

Shelburne, W. A. (1988). *Mythos and logos in the thought of Carl Jung: The theory of the collective unconscious in scientific perspective*. Albany: State University of New York Press.

Shoda, Y., Mischel, W., & Peake, P. K. (1990). Predicting adolescent cognitive and self-regulatory competencies from preschool delay of gratification: Identifying diagnostic conditions. *Developmental Psychology, 26,* 978–986.

Shostrom, E. (1974). *Manual for the Personal Orientation Inventory*. San Diego: Educational and Industrial Testing Service.

Sicher, L. ((1991). *The collected works of Lydia Sicher: An Adlerian perspective*. A. K. Davidson (Ed.). Ft. Bragg, CA: QED Press.

Silverman, L. H. (1983). The subliminal psychodynamic activation method: Overview and comprehensive listing of studies. In J. Masling (Ed.), *Empirical studies of psychoanalytic theories* (pp. 69–100). Hillsdale, NJ: Erlbaum.

Silverman, L. H., & Weinberger, J. (1985). Mommy and I are one: Implications for psychotherapy. *American Psychologist, 40,* 1296–1308.

Skinner, B. F. (1938). *The behavior of organisms: An experimental analysis.* Englewood Cliffs, NJ: Prentice-Hall.

Skinner, B. F. (1945). The operational analysis of psychological terms. *Psychological Review, 52,* 270–277; 291–294.

Skinner, B. F. (1948b). *Walden two.* New York: Macmillan.

Skinner, B. F. (1953). *Science and human behavior.* New York: Macmillan.

Skinner, B. F. (1967). An autobiography. In E. G. Boring & G. Lindzey (Eds.), *A history of psychology in autobiography* (Vol. 5). New York: Appleton-Century-Crofts.

Skinner, B. F. (1969). *Contingencies of reinforcement: A theoretical analysis.* New York: Appleton-Century-Crofts.

Skinner, B. F. (1971). *Beyond freedom and dignity.* New York: Knopf.

Skinner, B. F. (1974). *About behaviorism.* New York: Knopf.

Skinner, B. F. (1976). *Particulars of my life.* New York: Knopf.

Skinner, B. F. (1978). *Reflections on behaviorism and society.* Englewood Cliffs, NJ: Prentice-Hall.

Skinner, B. F. (1979). *The shaping of a behaviorist.* New York: Knopf.

Skinner, B. F. (1983). *A matter of consequences.* New York: Knopf.

Skinner, B. F. (1987a). *Upon further reflection.* Englewood Cliffs, NJ: Prentice-Hall.

Skinner, B. F. (1987b). Whatever happened to psychology as the science of behavior? *American Psychologist, 42,* 780–786.

Skinner, B. F. (1988). The operant side of behavior therapy. *Journal of Behavior Therapy and Experimental Psychiatry, 19,* 171–179.

Skinner, B. F. (1989). The origins of cognitive thought. *American Psychologist, 44,* 13–18.

Skinner, B. F. (1990a). Can psychology be a science of the mind? *American Psychologist, 45,* 1206–1210.

Skinner, B. F. (1990b). To know the future. *Behavior Analyst, 13,* 103–106.

Skinner, B. F., & Vaughan, M. E. (1983). *Enjoy old age: A program for self-management.* New York: Norton.

Smith, J. E., Stefan, C., Kovaleski, M., & Johnson, G. (1991). Recidivism and dependency in a psychiatric population: An investigation with Kelly's dependency grid. *International Journal of Personal Construct Psychology, 4,* 157–173.

Sobel, D. (1980, March 19). Erich Fromm. *The New York Times.* p. B11.

Stanford, R, G. (1987). The out-of-body experience as an imaginal journey: The developmental perspective. *Journal of Parapsychology, 51,* 137–155.

Statton, J. E., & Wilborn, B. (1991). Adlerian counseling and the early recollections of children. *Individual Psychology, 47,* 338–347.

Steele, R. S., & Kelley, T. J. (1976). Eysenck Personality Questionnaire and Jungian Myers-Briggs Type Indicator correlations of extraversion-introversion. *Journal of Consulting and Clinical Psychology, 44,* 690–691.

Steinberg, A. (1958). *Mrs. R: The life of Eleanor Roosevelt.* New York: Putnam.

Steiner, R. (1985). Some thoughts about tradition and change arising from an examination of the British Psycho-Analytical Society's controversial discussions (1943–1944). *International Review of Psycho-Analysis, 12,* 27–71.

Stephenson, W. (1953). *The study of behavior: Q-technique and its methodology.* Chicago: University of Chicago Press.

Stevens, A. (1990). *On Jung.* London: Routledge.

Strickland, B. R. (1989). Internal-external control expectancies: From contingency to creativity. *American Psychologist, 44,* 1–12.

Sullivan, H. S. (1953a). *Conceptions of modern psychiatry.* New York: Norton.

Sullivan, H. S. (1953b). *The interpersonal theory of psychiatry.* New York: Norton.

Sullivan, H. S. (1954). *The psychiatric interview.* New York: Norton.

Sullivan, H. S. (1956). *Clinical studies in psychiatry.* New York: Norton.

Sullivan, H. S. (1962). *Schizophrenia as a human process.* New York: Norton.

Sullivan, H. S. (1964). *The fusion of psychiatry and social science.* New York: Norton.

Sullivan, H. S. (1972). *Personal psychopathology.* New York: Norton.

Sulloway, F. J. (1979). *Freud, biologist of the mind: Beyond the psychoanalytical legend.* New York: Basic Books.

Suzuki, D. T., Fromm, E., & DeMartino, R. (1960). *Zen Buddhism and psychoanalysis.* New York: Grove Press.

Thompson, G. G. (1968). George A. Kelly (1905–1967). *Journal of General Psychology, 79,* 19–24.

Thorn, F. C. (1975). The life style analysis. *Journal of Clinical Psychology, 31,* 236–240.

Thorne, B. (1992). *Carl Rogers.* London: Sage.

Thorton, P. I., Igleheart, H. C., & Silverman, L. H. (1987). Subliminal stimulation of symbiotic fantasies as an aid in the treatment of drug abusers. *International Journal of the Addictions, 22,* 751–765.

Truax, C. B., & Carkhuff, R. R. (1967). *Toward effective counseling and psychotherapy.* Chicago: Aldine.

Tupes, E. C., & Christal, R. E. (1961). Recurrent personality factors based on trait ratings. (Technical Report No. ASD-TR-61-97). Lackland, TX: U.S. Air Force.

Vaihinger, H. (1911/1925). *The philosophy of "as if."* New York: Harcourt, Brace & Co.

Vitz, P. C. (1988). *Sigmund Freud's Christian unconscious.* New York: Guilford Press.

Wallston, B. S., Wallston, K. A., Kaplan, G. D., & Maides, S. A. (1976). Development and validation of the Health Locus of Control (HLC) Scale. *Journal of Consulting and Clinical Psychology, 44,* 580–585.

Wallston, K. A., Wallston, B. S., & DeVellis, R. F. (1978). Development of the Multidimensional Health Locus of Control (MHLC) Scales. *Health Education Monographs, 6,* 161–170.

Watson, P. J., Morris, R. J., & Hood, R. W. (1990). Extrinsic Scale factors: Correlations and construction of religious orientation types. *Journal of Psychology and Christianity, 9,* 35–46.

Weinberger, J., & Silverman, L. H. (1990). Testability and empirical verification of psychoanalytic dynamic propositions through subliminal psychodynamic activation. *Psychoanalytic Psychology, 7,* 299–339.

Westen, D. (1990a). Psychoanalytic approaches to personality. In L. A. Pervin (Ed.), *Handbook of personality: Theory and research* (pp. 21–65). New York: Guilford Press.

Westen, D. (1990b). Towards a revised theory of borderline object relations: Contributions of empirical research. *International Journal of Psycho-Analysis, 71,* 661–693.

Westen, D., Klepser, J., Ruffins, S. A., Silverman, M., Lifton, N., & Boekamp, J. (1991). Object relations in childhood and adolescence: The development of working representations. *Journal of Consulting and Clinical Psychology, 59,* 400–409.

Westen, D., Lohr, N., Silk, K. R., Gold, L., & Kerber, K. (1990). Object relations and social cognition in borderlines, major depressives, and normals: A Thematic Apperception Test analysis. *Psychological Assessment, 2,* 355–364.

Westen, D., Ludolph, P., Block, M. J., Wixom, J., & Wiss, F. C. (1990). Developmental history and object relations in psychiatrically disturbed adolescent girls. *American Journal of Psychiatry, 147,* 1061–1068.

Westen, D., Ludolph, P., Misle, B., Ruffins, S., & Block, J. (1990). Physical and sexual abuse in female adolescents with borderline personality disorder. *American Journal of Orthopsychiatry, 60,* 55–66.

Wheeler, M. S., Kern, R. M., & Curlett, W. L. (1982). *Wheeler-Kern-Curlette life style personality inventory.* Unpublished manuscript.

Wheeler, M. S., Kern, R. M., & Curlette, W. L. (1986). Factor analytic scales designed to measure Adlerian life style themes. *Individual Psychology, 42,* 1–16.

Wheeler, M. S., Kern, R. M., & Curlett, W. L. (1991). Life-style can be measured. *Individual Psychology, 47,* 229–239.

Wheelright, J. B., Wheelwright, J. A., & Buehler, J. A. (1974). *Jungian Type Survey Manual*. San Francisco: Society of Jungian Analysts of Northern California.

Wiedenfeld, S. A., O'Leary, A., Bandura, A., Brown, S., Levine, S., & Raska, K. (1990). Impact of perceived self-efficacy in coping with stressors on components of the immune system. *Journal of Personality of Social Psychology, 59*, 1082–1094.

Wiggins, J. S. (1982). Circumplex models of interpersonal behavior in clinical psychology. In P. C. Kendall & J. N. Butcher (Eds.), *Handbook of research methods in clinical psychology* (pp. 183–221). New York: Wiley.

Williams, D. E., & Page, M. M. (1989). A multi-dimensional measure of Maslow's hierarchy of needs. *Journal of Research in Personality, 23*, 192–213.

Wilson, C. (1972). *New pathways in psychology: Maslow and the post-Freudian revolution*. New York: Taplinger.

Wilson, S. R., & Spencer, R. C. (1990). Intense personal experiences: Subjective effects, interpretations, and after-effects. *Journal of Clinical Psychology, 46*, 565–573.

Winson, J. (1985). *Brain and psyche: The biology of the unconscious*. Garden City, NY: Anchor Press/Doubleday.

Woehlke, P. A., & Piper, R. B. (1980). Factorial validity of the Jungian Type Survey. *Educational and Psychological Measurement, 40*, 1051–1058.

Wolpe, J. (1973). *The practice of behavior therapy*. New York: Pergamon Press.

Wright, J. C., & Mischel, W. (1987). A conditional approach to disposition constructs: The local predictability of social behavior. *Journal of Personality and Social Psychology, 53*, 1159–1177.

Wright, J. C., & Mischel, W. (1988). Conditional hedges and the intuitive psychology of traits. *Journal of Personality and Social Psychology, 55*, 454–469.

Wulff, D. M. (1991). *Psychology of religion: Classic and contemporary views*. New York: Wiley.

Yeagle, E. H., Privette, G., & Dunham, F. Y. (1989). Highest happiness: An analysis of artists' peak experience. *Psychological Reports, 65*, 523–530.

Youniss, J. (1980). *Parents and peers in social development: A Sullivan-Piaget perspective*. Chicago: University of Chicago Press.

Zarski, J. J., Sweeney, T. J., & Barcikowski, R. S. (1977). Counseling effectiveness as a function of counselor social interest. *Journal of Counseling Psychology, 24*, 1–5.

Zarski, J. J., West, J. D., & Bubenzer, D. L. (1982). Social interest, running, and life adjustment. *Personnel and Guidance Journal, 61*, 146–149.

Zuroff, D. (1986). Was Gordon Allport a trait theorist? *Journal of Personality and Social Psychology, 51*, 993–1000.

Name Index

Abraham, K., 59, 242, 295
Abrahamsen, K., 79
Achilles, 171
Adams, N. E., 409, 420
Adams-Webber, J. R., 580
Addams, J., 610
Adler, Alexandria, 124
Adler, Alfred., 5, 17, 30, 79, 94,
    118–155, 175, 187, 191, 233,
    244, 258, 277, 380, 400, 406,
    426, 433, 539, 565, 595, 637,
    678, 698, 712, 715, 716, 717,
    718, 720
Adler, K., 124
Adler, R. E., 124
Adler, S., 121, 123
Allers, C. T., 151
Allport, A. L., 527
Allport, F., 526, 538
Allport, G., 5, 6, 321, 338–339,
    364, 400, 426, 454, 477, 481,
    483, 523–554, 597, 601, 621,
    702, 704, 713, 715, 716, 718,
    719
Allport, R., 527
Allsopp, J., 502
Alpher, V. S., 315
Amos, 261
Anderson, G., 233
Andreas-Salomé, L., 58, 59
Angel, E., 680, 706
Angleitner, A., 505
Ansbacher, H. L., 131, 153, 155
Ansbacher, R. R., 153, 155
Apostal, R., 195

Bachofen, J. J., 263, 267
Baer, B. A., 464
Baker, N., 466–467
Baldwin, A., 546, 547

Balmary, M., 32, 58, 72
Bandura, A., 5, 9, 72, 323, 310–
    429, 452, 454, 456, 459, 464,
    465, 468, 548, 551, 585, 712,
    713, 715, 716, 718, 720
Bandura, C., 394
Bandura, M., 394
Bandura, V. V., 394, 398
Bannister, D., 563, 580, 584, 589
Barcikowski, R. S., 152
Barnes, C. (see Rotter, C. B.)
Barrett, P., 502
Barrett-Lennard, G. T., 667–669
Baumeister, R. F., 552
Beall, N., 563, 583
Beck, A. T., 232, 625
Becker, B., 314
Beethoven, L., 128
Bell, M. D., 314
Bell-Dumas, J., 150, 151
Bellinger, C., 204
Benedict, R., 79, 607
Benson, H., 331
Bergin, A. E., 551
Bergman, A., 307
Berkowitz, L., 338
Bernays, Martha (see Freud, M.
    B.)
Bernays, Minna, 59
Bettelheim, B., 71, 74–75
Billington, R., 314
Bilsker, D., 112
Binswanger, L., 677, 681
Black, R., 99
Blanchard, E. B., 420
Blanchard, W. H., 625
Bleuler, E., 160
Block, J., 314
Blos, P., 80
Blue, Y. (see Skinner, Y. B.)

Boekamp, J., 314
Bonaparte, M., 58, 59
Bonaparte, N. (see Napoleon)
Boring, E. G., 554
Boss, M., 677, 681
Bottome, P., 121
Breuer, J., 27, 28, 190,
    712
Brokken, F., B., 505
Brome, V., 161, 162
Brown, I., 409
Brown, S., 425–426
Brozek, J., 598
Bruhn, A. R., 151
Bubenzer, D. L., 152
Buber, M., 681
Buchanan, L. P., 150, 151
Buddha, 172
Buehler, J., 194
Bullitt, W., 106
Burston, D., 288
Burt, C., 501, 502, 520
Busick, B. S., 197
Buss, A. H., 338
Butler, J. M., 666
Button, E., 583–584,
    588
Byck, R., 27

Caesar, J., 380
Camus, A., 681
Cantor, N., 585
Caper, R., 316
Carkhuff, R. R., 667
Carlson, R., 194
Carroll, W. R., 414
Cartwright, D., 666
Cashdan, S., 313
Cattell, A. S., 479, 481
Cattell, M. R., 479

Cattell, R. B., 5, 9, 17, 452, 474–
    499, 502, 503, 504–505, 506,
    517–520, 529, 551, 715, 716
Cervone, D., 411
Cezanne, P., 681
Chambliss, C. A., 409
Chan, J. W., 502
Chance, J. E., 434, 437, 442–443,
    452
Chaplin, M. P., 151
Chapman, A. H., 204, 236
Charcot, J. M., 27, 28
Chesney, J. M., 151
Chevron, E. S., 233
Child, D., 491, 496
Chodorow, N., 58
Christal, R. E., 504
Church, A. T., 505
Clark, R. W., 31
Cohen, D., 502
Coles, R., 79, 116
Combs, A. W., 564
Comrey, A. L., 505
Conway, C. G., 702
Copernicus, N., 68
Coram, G. J., 151
Costa, P. T., 194
Coulter, T., 500
Cox, D. N., 507, 511
Cozad, L., 678
Cramer, D., 667–669
Crandall, J. E., 152
Crazy Horse, 604
Crisp, A. H., 583
Croake, J. W., 136
Cross, P., 494
Curlett, W. L., 152

Da Vinci, L., 106
Daniels, M., 622
Danielsen, B., 242
Danielsen, C. R., 242
Dart, R., 399
Darwin, C., 68
Davidson, A. K., 155
Davies, M. (see Eysenck, M. D.)
Davis, R., 386
Davis, S. F., 386
Delhees, K. H., 491
Demonsthenes, 128
Dempsey, D., 563
de Raad, B., 505
de Sade, 532
de Spinoza, B., 610
de St. Aubin, E., 112–113

Deutsch, H., 58
Devellis, R. F., 463
Dewey, J., 636
Dieterich, A., 166
Dollard, J., 5, 105, 262, 293–294,
    316–342, 349, 394, 412, 718
Donahue, M. J., 550–551
Duncan, King, 48
Dunham, F. Y., 626
Dymond, R. F., 662, 663, 664, 666

Ebbesen, E. B., 457, 465
Eckstein, D. J., 137, 151
Einstein, A., 610
Eissler, K., 75
Eitingon, M., 59
Elijah, 173
Ellenberger, H., 26, 27, 29, 30,
    31, 75, 122, 123, 155, 159, 680,
    706
Elliott, H. (see Rogers, H. E.)
Ellis, A., 124
Elms, A. C., 351, 352, 533, 535
Elson, M., 311
Epstein, R. (see Adler, R. E.)
Epting, F. R., 563, 589
Ericsson, L., 81
Erikson, E. H., 5, 76–116, 121,
    158, 207, 233, 244, 258, 310,
    565, 585, 678, 700, 718, 720
Erikson, J. M., 80–81, 102, 103,
    116
Erikson, K., 81
Evans, R. I., 83, 84, 85, 88, 89,
    261, 418, 422, 429, 499, 531,
    672
Everitt, B., 515
Eysenck, A. E., 499
Eysenck, H. J., 5, 17, 72, 195, 385,
    399, 477, 479, 491, 499–520,
    545, 715, 719
Eysenck, Michael, 502
Eysenck, Margaret D., 501
Eysenck, S. B. G., 501–502, 504,
    507, 510

Faber, M. D., 534, 535
Fairbairn, W. R. D., 315–316
Fakouri, M. E., 151
Farson, R., 672
Federn, E., 71
Ferenczi, S., 30, 59, 206, 295
Fern, T. L., 233
Ferster, C. B., 362
Fishbein, S. S., 702

Fliess, W., 29, 32, 59, 72
Ford, H., 712
Frankl, V., 677, 681
Fransella, F., 563, 580, 583, 584
Freeman, A. (see Fromm, A. F.)
Freud, Amalie N., 26, 59
Freud, Anna., 28, 33, 46, 58, 79,
    80, 82, 83, 296, 312
Freud, E., 26
Freud, Jacob, 26, 27, 29, 33
Freud, John, 26
Freud, M. B., 27, 30, 58
Freud, Pauline, 26
Freud, Phillip, 26
Freud, S., 4, 5, 11, 12, 13, 14, 16,
    17, 22–75, 81, 82, 83, 84, 87,
    91, 92, 93, 95, 105, 106, 109,
    110, 113, 114, 115, 116, 121,
    122, 123, 124, 127, 131, 137,
    141, 143, 144, 147, 152, 153,
    158, 161, 162, 163, 164, 166,
    167, 168, 175, 182, 186, 187,
    188–189, 191, 206, 207, 231,
    233, 242, 243, 244–245, 258,
    259, 260, 261, 262, 263, 267,
    272, 275, 277, 284, 285, 288,
    292–293, 298, 303–307, 309–
    310, 312, 313, 316, 317, 318,
    319, 326, 327, 334, 336, 338,
    339, 340, 341, 343, 349, 372,
    380, 385, 400, 406, 426, 433,
    452, 453, 491, 493, 501, 502,
    510, 526–527, 529, 533, 534–
    535, 536, 539, 551, 554, 565,
    585, 593, 606, 635, 637, 680,
    683, 698, 712, 713, 715, 716,
    717, 720
Frick, W., 602, 622, 629, 639
Friedland, B. U., 152
Fromm, A. F., 263
Fromm, E., 5, 206, 241–242, 243,
    244, 260–288, 317, 426, 595,
    679, 688, 715, 718, 720
Fromm, H. G., 263
Fromm, N., 260
Fromm, R., 260
Fromm-Reichman, F., 206, 243,
    262
Frost, R., 350
Fulker, D. W., 511
Furtmuller, C., 122

Gallop, J., 58
Gandhi, M., 105, 106–108, 110,
    459

Garner, D. M., 315
Gay, P., 4, 29, 31, 58, 59, 75
Gendlin, E. T., 638, 662
Gibson, H. B., 500
Glover, E., 296
Goble, F., 595–596
Goethe, J. W., 124, 159
Gold, L., 314
Goldberg, L. R., 505
Goldstein, K., 595, 608
Gonzalez, G., 195–196
Good, G., 678
Goodman, A., 594
Goodman, B. (see Maslow, B. G.)
Goodman, P., 594, 616
Gordon, R. D., 626
Gordon, T., 666
Gorky, M., 105
Gorsuch, R. L., 551
Gould, A. L. (see Allport, A. L.)
Graf, H., 292–293, 299, 303, 305,
    319, 322, 327, 334, 335
Graf, M., 292–293
Greenberg, J., 282–283
Greenspan, S. I., 116
Greever, K. B., 152
Gross, A. M., 385
Grossarth-Maticek, R., 502, 513–
    517, 520
Grosskurth, P., 294, 295, 343
Grummon, D. L., 664
Gurland, H. (see Fromm, H. G.)
Gurtman, M. B., 464

Hafner, J. L., 151
Haigh, G. V., 666
Hall, E., 89, 102, 116
Hall, M. H., 533, 594, 621, 699,
    706
Hamachek, D. E., 113
Hanin, Y., 502
Hardy, A. B., 409
Harlow, H., 595
Harris, T. G., 678, 679
Hartmann, H., 83, 318
Hartshorne, H., 455
Hartung, J. R., 151
Hathaway, S. R., 487
Hausdorff, D., 261
Heber, S., 233
Heesacker, R. S., 315
Heidegger, M., 677, 681
Hemingway, E., 635
Henderson, V. L., 673
Henry, W. P., 232

Henschel, A., 598
Heppner, P. L., 638
Herd, J. A., 342
Higgins, S. T., 384–385
Hitler, A., 105, 276, 278, 279–281,
    285, 500, 595
Hochreich, D. J., 434, 435–437,
    440, 441–444, 449
Hoffman, E., 593, 594, 596, 630
Hofstee, W. K., 505
Holder, A., 71
Holland, N., 293
Holland, R., 585
Holt, R. R., 71
Homburger, E. (see Erikson, E.
    H.)
Homburger, T., 79, 80
Hood, R. W., 550, 551
Hornbuckle, D., 151
Horney, K. D., 5, 81, 124, 206,
    240–260, 262, 275, 277, 281–
    288, 294, 295, 317, 426, 595,
    718, 719, 720
Horney, O., 242–243
Horowitz, L. M., 232, 464
Hosea, 261
Howard, G. S., 702–703, 704
Howells, G. N., 409
Hughes, J. M., 296, 313
Hull, C., 317, 395
Huston, H. L., 195–196
Huxley, A., 610
Hvezda, J., 624

Igleheart, H. C., 70
Inouye, D. K., 409
Inscoe, J., 207
Irigaray, L., 58
Isaiah, 261
Isbister, J. N., 31, 75

Jacka, B., 195
Jacobi, J., 199
Jacobs, M., 75
Jacobson, E., 331
Jaffe, A., 199
James, W., 610
Janet, P., 160
Janeway, E., 109
Jasper, K., 681
Jefferson, T., 610
Jensen, A., 499
Jesus, 172, 285, 380
John, O., 505
Johnson, G., 584–585

Jones, E., 26, 29, 31, 59, 124, 295,
    297
Jourden, F. J., 423–424
Juan, D., 225, 532
Jung, C. G., 5, 17, 30, 34, 59, 79,
    124, 147, 153, 156–199, 231,
    244, 340, 426, 491, 506, 529,
    697, 712, 716, 718, 719, 720
Jung, E. P., 159–160, 177
Jung, E. R., 160, 162
Jung, P., 159–160

Kahane, M., 30
Kaplan, G. D., 463
Kaska, K., 425–426
Katigbak, M. S., 505
Kaus, C. R., 283–284
Kavaleski, M., 584–585
Kean, R. C., 195
Kelley, T. J., 194–195
Kelly, E. M., 561
Kelly, G. A., 5, 434, 453–454,
    559–589, 701, 713, 716, 718,
    719, 720
Kelly, G. T., 562
Kelly, T. V., 561
Kelman, H., 288
Keniston, K., 116
Kerber, K., 314
Kern, R. M., 150, 151, 152
Kernberg, O., 5, 296–297, 306,
    309–311, 312, 313, 343
Keys, A., 598
Kierkegaard, S., 677, 680, 681,
    682, 686, 704
Kiesler, D., 662
King, P., 296, 342
Kinsey, A. C., 33, 595
Kissen, D. M., 513
Kirschenbaum, H., 638, 673
Kivnick, H. Q., 81, 102, 103
Klein, A., 294–295
Klein, E., 295
Klein, H., 295, 296
Klein, Melanie, 5, 58, 293–306,
    307, 309, 310, 312, 313, 315–
    316, 340–341, 343, 718, 719,
    720
Klein, Melitta (see Schmideberg,
    M. K.)
Klein, T. W., 498
Klepser, J., 314
Klerman, G. L., 233
Kline, P., 71, 482, 494
Kloosterman, K., 505

Knapp, G. P., 262, 288
Koch, S., 635, 639, 656, 643, 646
Kohler, W., 527, 638
Kohut, H., 5, 297, 306, 311–313, 343
Koller, C., 27
Korn, J. M., 386
Kowaz, A. M., 111
Krause, L., 260–261
Kurzwell, E., 30

Landfield, A., 563, 589
Landis, B., 261, 263
Lasswell, H., 206
Last, J., 151
Lazarick, D. L., 702
Lee, L. A., 638
Lehman, R. E., 152
Leitner, L. M., 563
Lerman, H., 33, 72
Lesser, I. M., 111
Lester, D., 624, 625
Levine, S., 425–426
Levy, N., 195
Lewin, K., 81
Lifton, N., 314
Lincoln, A., 459, 610
Lindzey, G., 554
Lohr, N., 314
Loiello, M. A., 702
Lonky, E., 283–284
Ludolph, P., 314
Luther, M., 105, 106, 110
Lynn, R., 502
Lyon, D., 282–283

Macbeth, 171
Macbeth, Lady, 48
Maccoby, M., 278–279
Maher, B., 588
Mahler, M., 5, 296–297, 306–309, 310, 312, 316
Maides, S. A., 463
Mair, J. M. M., 563
Malcolm, J., 75
Manaster, G., 150
Marconi, G., 712
Matisse, H., 681
Marcia, J., 111, 112, 113
Martin, C., 595
Marx, K., 242, 262, 263, 267, 285
Marshall, G. N., 464
Maslow, A. H., 5, 78, 124, 288, 338, 383, 398–399, 426, 478, 528, 529, 533, 563, 590–630,

636, 645, 656, 688, 702, 716, 718, 719
Maslow, B. G., 399, 594, 596
Mason, M., 317
Masson, J. M., 33, 59, 72, 75
Master, K. S., 551
Matarazzo, J. D., 342
May, E. T., 677
May, M. A., 455
May, M. B., 677
May, R. R., 5, 124, 674–706, 713
McAdams, D. P., 112–113
McCain, G., 18
McCaulley, M. H., 194, 195
McClelland, D., 454
McCrae, R. R., 194
McDougall, W., 606
McGregor, D., 628
McGuire, W., 30, 31, 161
McKinley, J. C., 487
Mead, G. H., 206
Mead, M., 81, 243
Mehlhoff, R. C., 195
Menninger, K., 338, 433
Messer, S. B., 12
Metzner, R., 465
Meyer, A., 206
Michelangelo, 50
Mickelsen, O., 598
Mill, J. S., 31
Miller, N., 5, 293–294, 316–343, 349, 394, 412, 718
Mills, J. K., 464
Milner, P., 339
Mindess, H., 388
Mischel, H. N., 454
Mischel, T., 453
Mischel, W., 5, 9, 434, 452–470, 573, 585, 713, 715, 716, 718
Misle, B., 314
Mithras, 166
Molander, H. (see Werner, R.)
Moore, B., 457, 465
Moreau, D., 233
Morris, R. J., 551
Mosak, H. H., 137
Mower, O. H., 317
Mozdzierz, G. J., 152
Mufson, L., 233
Mulder, E., 505
Murray, E. J., 409
Murray, H., 81, 454, 663
Murray, J. B., 195
Murray, L., 314
Myers, I. B., 194, 195

Myers, P. R., 702

Napoleon, 54
Narcissus, 532
Neimeyer, G. J., 315
Nias, D. K. B., 502, 507, 511
Nietzsche, F., 677, 681, 704
Nerlov, H. (see Mischel, H. N.)
Nolan, L. L., 195
Noller, P., 505
Norman, W., 504–505
Norton, G. R., 233

Oberholzer, E., 596
O'Connell, A. N., 288
Odbert, H. S., 483, 531
Oedipus, King of Thebes, 55, 696–697
Ogden, T. H., 299
Olds, J., 339
O'Leary, A., 425–426
Olmstead, M. P., 315
Orgler, H., 155
Orlofsky, J. L., 111
Ozer, E. M., 425

Page, M. M., 624–625
Paige, J., 547
Panzarella, R., 625
Park, R. E., 206
Pasteur, L., 382
Patterson, S. J., 195
Pavlov, I., 351, 354, 502
Peake, P. K., 467
Perry, H. S., 205, 206, 207, 236
Perryman, T., 150
Pervin, L. A., 470, 520, 715–716, 720
Phares, E. J., 434, 437, 442–443, 452, 470
Piaget, J., 236
Picasso, P., 681
Pine, F., 307
Pines, M., 233
Piper, R. B., 194
Plourde, R., 624
Polivy, J., 315
Pollock, G. H., 116
Pomeroy, W., 595
Popper, K., 72
Powell, A., 506
Prager, K., 111
Preiswerk, E. (see Jung, E. P.)
Preiswerk, H., 159
Preiswerk, S., 159

Privette, G., 626
Putman, E. L., 152

Quinn, S., 242, 243, 263, 288
Quixote, D., 532

Rabinowitz, F. E., 678
Rakic, L., 502
Rank, O., 59, 637
Rattner, J., 121, 124, 155
Rauschenbach, E. (*see* Jung, E. R.)
Ravizza, K., 625
Reeses, C., 701
Reichman, F. (*see* Fromm-
  Reichman, F.)
Reitler, R., 30
Reizes, E., 294
Reizes, L. D., 294
Reizes, M., 294
Rest, J. R., 283
Richards, P. S., 551
Ridley, S. E., 195
Rieder, H., 502
Riklin, F., 187
Ritter, B., 420
Riviere, J., 58, 59
Roazen, P., 80, 116
Rodriguez, M. L., 467, 470
Rogers, C. R., 5, 9, 13, 71, 124,
  288, 383, 411, 434, 529, 585,
  632–673, 679, 680, 683, 698,
  700, 702, 713, 716, 718, 719,
  720
Rogers, D., 636
Rogers, H. E., 636, 637
Rogers, J. C., 635, 610
Rogers, M. (*see* Cattell, M. R.)
Rogers, M. E., 638
Rogers, N., 636
Rogers, W., 635
Roodin, P. A., 283–284
Roosevelt, A. E., 78–79, 93, 95,
  98, 99, 101, 103, 610
Roosevelt, F. D., 78–79, 98, 99,
  101, 103
Roosevelt, T., 79
Rosen, D. H., 195–196
Rosenberg, M., 667
Rosenberg, S. E., 464
Rosenthal, T. L., 419
Ross, C. A., 233
Ross, D., 418
Ross, J. M., 549
Ross, S. A., 418
Rostal, S. (*see* Eysenck, S. B. G.)

Rotter, C. B., 433
Rotter, Jean, 434
Rotter, Julian, B., 5, 17, 124, 395,
  433–452, 453–454, 464, 467–
  471, 563, 585, 595, 713, 715,
  716, 718
Rotter, R., 434
Rounsaville, B. J., 233
Royce, J. R., 506
Rubins, J. L., 242, 288
Rudikoff, E. C., 666
Ruffins, S. A., 314
Russell, B., 351
Russo, N. F., 288

Sachs, H., 59, 262, 317
Salome, 173
Samson, G., 385
Sanders, S., 385
Sapir, E., 206
Sartre, J. P., 677, 681, 682, 704
Savill, G. E., 137, 151
Sayers, J., 294
Schacht, T. E., 232
Schiedel, D., 112
Schlein, S., 82
Schmideberg, M. K., 295, 296
Schmideberg, W., 296
Schuerger, J. M., 498
Schuettler, A. (*see* Cattell, A. S.)
Schur, M., 29
Schweitzer, A., 610
Sears, R., 317, 394
Segal, E. M., 18
Segal, H., 294
Segal, J., 343
Semyck, R. W., 152
Serson, J. (*see* Erickson, J. M.)
Shakespeare, W., 48, 124
Sheffield, F. D., 339
Shelburne, W. A., 199
Shields, D. J., 151
Shoda, Y., 467, 470
Shostrom, E., 618–619
Sicher, L., 155
Siegfried, 168
Silberstein, E., 31
Silk, K. R., 314
Silverman, L. H., 70
Silverman, M., 314
Skinner, B. F., 5, 8, 15, 340, 346–
  388, 393, 395–396, 400, 412,
  415, 421, 426, 427, 433, 434,
  437, 441, 479, 529, 551, 564,

658–659, 713, 714, 715, 716,
  718
Skinner, D., 351, 352
Skinner, E. J., 348, 350, 369
Skinner, G. M. B., 349
Skinner, J., 351
Skinner, W., 349–350
Skinner, Y. B., 351
Smith, C., 385
Smith, J. E., 584–585
Smith, S. M., 195–196
Snygg, D., 564
Sobel, D., 263
Sophocles, 55
Sorensen, R., 195
Souvestre, M., 78, 98
Spearman, C., 478, 501, 502
Spence, K., 638
Spencer, R. C., 626–627
Stanford, R. G., 233
Stanovich, K. E., 18
Statton, J. E., 137, 151
Staub, E., 460–461, 462
St. Clair, M., 343
Steele, R. S., 194–195
Stefan, C., 584–585
Stefan, R., 563
Steinberg, A., 93
Steiner, R., 296, 297, 342
Stekel, W., 30
Stephenson, W., 546, 664
Stevens, B., 638
Stern, W., 527
Stevens, A., 199
Strachey, J., 65, 71, 75
Strickland, B. R., 468
Strupp, H. H., 232
Sullivan, E. S., 203–204
Sullivan, H. S., 5, 81, 124, 200–
  236, 243, 260, 262, 275, 277,
  298, 317, 379, 380, 400, 426,
  491, 678, 683, 692, 715, 718,
  719, 720
Sullivan, J. I., 207
Sullivan, S., 624
Sullivan, T., 203–204
Sulloway, F., 28, 31, 75
Swales, P., 75
Sweeney, T. J., 152
Suzuki, D. T., 236

Tauber, E. S., 261, 263
Taylor, H. L., 598
Thomas, W. I., 206
Thompson, C., 206, 262

Thompson, G. G., 562
Thorndike, E. L., 478, 595
Thorne, B., 673
Thorne, F. C., 152
Thorton, P. I., 70
Tillich, P., 679, 681
Titchener, E. B., 594
Truax, C. B., 662, 667
Tseng, M. S., 152
Tupes, E. C., 504

Ureño, G., 464

Vaihinger, H., 127
Varns, V. (see Bandura, V. V.)
Vaughan, M. E., 375
Vetter, H., 514
Villaseñor, V. S., 464
Vitz, P. C., 26, 31, 72

Walker, C. E., 471
Wallston, B. S., 463–464
Wallston, K. A., 463–464
Walters, R. H., 394

Warburton, E. W., 482
Warren, S., 12
Watson, J. B., 350, 594
Watson, P. J., 551
Weinberger, J., 70
Weiss, Sharlene, M., 342
Weiss, Stephen, M., 342
Weissman, M. M., 233
Werner, H., 527
Werner, R., 499
Wertheimer, M., 243, 527, 595, 607
West, J. D., 152
Westen, D., 37, 72, 314
Wheeler, M. S., 152
Wheelwright, J. A., 194
Wheelwright, J. B., 194
White, A., 304
White, C. T., 151
White, W. A., 205, 206
Wiedenfeld, S. A., 425–426
Wiggins, J. S., 464
Wilborn, B., 137, 151
Williams, D. E., 624–625

Winnicott, D. W., 315–316
Wilson, C., 594
Wilson, S. R., 626–627
Wilson, W., 106
Winson, J., 69–70
Wiss, F. C., 314
Woehlke, P. A., 194
Wolpe, J., 419, 516
Wright, J. C., 461
Wright, F., 635
Wright, O., 712
Wright, W., 712
Wulff, D. M., 551
Yeagle, E. H., 626
York, A., 405
Youniss, J., 236

Zarski, J. J., 152
Zeiss, A. R., 457, 465
Ziolkowski, K., 604
Zirkel, S., 585
Zohn, H., 155

Subject Index

Abnormal Behavior
    Adler's concept of, 139–145
    Bandura's concept of, 416–418
    Dollard and Miller's concept
        of, 334–336
    Freud's concept of, 65
    Fromm's concept of, 274–277
    Kelly's concept of, 576–578,
        588
    Maslow's concept of, 618–620
    May's concept of, 698
    Rogers's concept of, 646–649,
        672
    Rotter's concept of, 448–449
    Skinner's concept of, 377–380
    Sullivan's concept of, 227, 228
Accusation, 142–143
    self, 142–143
Active imagination, 189–190,
        199
Actualizing tendency, 640, 641,
        672
Adolesence (Erikson's stage of),
        95–98, 115
Adulthood (Erikson's stage of),
        100–101, 115
Adulthood (Sullivan's stage of),
        227, 235
Affection, 245, 247, 258, 442
    as a coping strategy, 247
    need for, 245, 258, 442
Agape, 692–693, 705
Aggression, 44, 132, 142–143,
        251, 258, 417–418
    malignant, 266
    neurotic need for, 251, 258
Aids, physical, 376
Air Crib (see Baby-tender)
Alcoholics Anonymous, 384
Anal character, 24–25, 47, 53

Anal phase of development, 53–
        54, 89, 304
Anal triad, 53
Anal-urethral-muscular mode,
        89, 90, 114–115
Analytical psychology (Jung),
        156–199
Anima, 158, 168–169, 171, 198
Animus, 169, 171, 198
Anna O., case of, 28–29
Anorexia nervosa, 583–584
Anxiety, 44–51, 74, 209–210, 217,
        218–229, 235, 577, 647,
        672, 683, 686–688
    basic, 241, 246–247, 250, 269,
        286, 600
    castration, 55, 305
    defined, 45, 209, 247, 577, 647,
        686
    dreams and, 63–64
    moral, 45
    neurotic, 45, 687, 705
    normal, 686, 705
    ontological, 688
    realistic, 45
    Rogers's view of, 647, 672
    self-system and, 212–214
    Sullivan's definition of, 209–
        210
    threat and, 647, 672
Apathy, 219
Approach-avoidance conflicts,
        330–331, 342
Approach, gradient of, 328–329
Archetypes, 165–174, 171, 172,
        195, 197, 198, 697
Archetypal Symbol Inventory,
        195–196
Arousal, physiological, 410–411,
        466

Assimilation, 274
Association for the Advancement
        of Psychoanalysis, 244,
        262
Attention, observational learning
        and, 413
Attitudes, 176–177, 180, 199,
        473–474, 495
Attribution of performance, 402
Austen Riggs Treatment Center,
        81
Autonomy vs. shame and doubt,
        89, 90, 115
Authoritarianism, 270, 287
Autism, normal, 307
Autistic language, 219
Avoidance-avoidance conflicts,
        322, 342
    double, 333–334, 342
Avoidance, gradient of, 328
Awareness, 642–643
    defined, 642
    levels of, 642–643
Axiology, 8

B-love, 617, 629
B-values, 602, 610, 617, 629, 630
Baby-tender, 352
Barrett-Lennard Relationship
        Inventory, 667–669
Basic anxiety (see Anxiety, basic)
Basic conflict (see Conflict, basic)
Basic mistrust, 85, 88, 89, 114
Basic Postulate (Kelly's), 567,
        587
Basic prediction formula
        (Rotter's), 439–440, 469
Basic strength, 85, 114
Basic trust, 85, 88, 89, 114

Beck Depression Inventory, 232, 625
Behavior
    abnormal (see Abnormal behavior)
    complex, 369–373
    control of, 373–377
    coping, 339, 605–606, 629
    disengagement of, 404–406
    disorganized, 648–649
    dysfunctional, 416–418, 428
    elicited, 355
    emitted, 355
    expressive, 605–606, 629
    inappropriate, 377–380
    interpretation of, 354, 387
    maladaptive, 448–449
    prediction of, 435–448, 469
    proactive, 528
    reflexive, 354
    restrained, excessively, 379
    social, 372–373
    unconscious, 371–372
    unmotivated, 605, 629
    verbal, 366
    vigorous, excessively, 378
Behavior therapy, 513, 516–517
Behavioral potential, 435–436
Behavioral analysis (Skinner), 346–388, 713
Behavioral equation, 496
Behavioral health, 384
Behavioral production
    observational learning and, 414
Behaviorism, 595
    radical, 348–388,
    scientific, 353–365
Being-in-the-world, 682–684, 702, 705
Bell Object Relations Inventory, 314–315
Berlin Psychoanalytic Institute, 262
Big Bad Wolf, 301
Biography
    Adler's, 121–124
    Allport's, 526–527
    Bandura's, 393–394
    Cattell's, 477–479
    Dollard's, 317–318
    Erikson's, 79–82
    Eysenck's, 499–502
    Freud's, 26–31
    Fromm's, 260–263

    Horney's, 242–244
    Jung's, 159–162
    Kelly's, 561–564
    Klein's, 294–296
    Kernberg's, 309
    Kohut's, 311
    Mahler's, 306
    Maslow's, 593–597
    May's, 677–680
    Miller's, 318
    Mischel's, 453–454
    Rogers's, 635–639
    Rotter's, 433–434
    Skinner's, 349–353
    Sullivan's, 203–207
Biophilia, 273, 274, 287
Birth order, 145–147, 148, 154
Birth, psychological, 307
Body ego, 83

Cancer
    personality and, 513–517
Capitalism, rise of, 242, 267, 281
Cardiovascular disease
    personality and, 513–517
Care, 101, 115, 689
    love, will and, 689–693
Castration anxiety, 55
Castration complex, 55
Catharsis, 27
Causality, 15, 17, 127, 175, 187
    vs. teleology, 15, 17, 127, 175, 714
Center for the Study of the Person, 638
Center of Personal Construct Psychology, 563
Chance encounters, 393–394, 398–400, 427
Character, 271
Character Orientations (Fromm), 271–274, 287
    nonproductive, 272–273, 287
        exploitative, 272, 287
        hoarding, 272–273, 287
        marketing, 273, 278, 287
        receptive, 272, 287
    productive, 273–274, 287
Chicago Psychoanalytic Institute, 262, 311
Chicago studies, 663–667
Childhood, 182–183, 199, 219–221, 235, 245–246
    early, 89–91

Child Personality Questionnaire (CPQ), 491
Choice corollary, 570–571, 587
Choice elaborative, 582
Client-centered therapy, 634, 639, 649–667, 672
    effectiveness of, 663–667
Clinical Analysis Questionnaire (CAQ), 491, 492
Cocaine, 27, 384, 385
Codependency, 250
Cognition, 396–397
    levels of, 215–217
Cognitive mediation, 420
Cognitive social learning theory (Mischel), 452–470
Collective symbols (see Archetypes)
Collective unconscious, 34, 159, 162, 164–174, 197, 198, 381, 697
    phylogenetic endowment and, 34
Comfort, need for, 442
Commonality corollary, 574, 587–588
Compensation for feelings of inferiority, 133–134
Competence, 93, 94–95, 115
Competencies, 456, 459, 469
Competition, 222, 224, 245
Complexes, 164
Compliance to medical treatment, 385
Comprehensive Early Memory Scoring System, 151
Compromise, 222, 224
Compulsion, 48, 49, 91, 115
Compulsion, repetition, 62
Concept of Humanity, 16, 17
    Adler's, 149–150
    Allport's, 548–549
    Bandura's, 420–423
    Cattell's, 512
    dimensions for a, 15–16
    Dollard and Miller's, 337–338
    Erikson's, 109–110
    Eysenck's, 512
    Freud's, 67–69
    Fromm's, 281–282
    Horney's, 281–282
    Jung's, 193–194
    Kelly's, 581–583
    Maslow's, 622–624
    May's, 700–701

Mischel's, 462–463
Rogers's, 661–662
Rotter's, 462–463
Skinner's, 381–383
Sullivan's, 230–231
summary of, 712–716
Condensation in dreams, 62–63
Conditioning operant, 354–365,
    373–374, 387
    respondent, 354–355, 361
Conflict, 327–334, 335, 342
    types of, 329–334, 342
Conflict, basic, 250, 252, 259
Conflicts, intrapsychic, 253–258,
    286
Conformity, 270–271, 287
Congruence, 650–651, 656, 672
Conscience, 40, 126–127
Conscious, 31, 73, 163, 171
    perceptual, 35
    vs. unconscious, 15, 17, 714
Consciousness, 31, 35–37
Consistency paradox, 455–461,
    469
Constructing obstacles, 144
Construction corollary, 568, 587
Constructive alternativism, 561,
    565–566, 587
Contingency management, 384–
    385
Contingencies, describing, 374
Cooperation, 222, 223–224
Core pathology, 89
Correlation coefficient, 18, 480
Cosmology, 8, 353
Countercontrol, 367, 373, 379,
    421
Countertransference, 106, 192,
    277
Creative novation behavior
    therapy, 515–516
Creative power, 125, 132, 134,
    138–39, 140, 149, 153,
    154
Creativity, 371, 616, 629
Crevenka Yugoslavia Project,
    513–517
Cues, 294, 321–322, 341–342
Curvilinear relationship, 549–550

D-love, 617
Dasein, 682–684, 698, 702, 705 (see
    also Being-in-the-world)
Death, 42, 298, 685

Decay, syndrome of, 276, 279,
    280–281, 287
Defense mechanisms, 39, 46–51,
    74, 300–302, 303, 380
    disengagement of internal
        control and, 406
    psychic, 300–302
    safeguarding tendencies and,
        141
Defensiveness, 647, 672
Defining Issues Test, 283
Denial, 647, 672
Dependency Grid, 584
Dependency, need for, 442
Depreciation, 142
Depressive position, 300
Depressive reactions, 416–417
Deprivation, 374
Desensitization, systematic, 419
Destiny, 693–696, 705
    defined, 694–695
    freedom and, 693–696
Destructive instinct, 44
Destructiveness, 270, 287
Detailed inquiry stage
    (psychotherapy), 229
Determinism
    meaning of, 398
    vs. free choice, 15, 17, 714
Development, stages of
    Allport's concept of, 536–538
    Erikson's concept of, 85–105
    Freud's concept of, 51–61, 74
    Jung's concept of, 182–185
    Mahler's concept of, 307–309
    Sullivan's concept of, 207,
        218–227
Dichotomy corollary, 570, 587
Differential R (dR) technique,
    481–482
Discrimination, operant, 357
Disdain, 103
Disengagement of internal
    control, 404–406, 428
    blame the victims, 406
    defense mechanisms and, 406
    diffusion of responsibility, 405
    displacement of responsibility,
        405
    disregard of consequences,
        405
    distortion of consequences,
        406
    redefinition of behavior, 404–
        405

Disorganization, 648–649, 672
Displacement, in dreams, 62–63
Dissociation, 213, 226
Distortion, 647, 672
Dominance, need for, 441
Dramatizations, 220
Dreams, 33, 160, 165–166, 168,
    170, 195
    Adler's view of, 147–148
    anxiety, 63–64
    Freud's view of, 62–65, 66, 74
    Fromm's view of, 277
    Horney's view of, 259–260
    Jung's early childhood, 165–
        166
    Jung's view of, 187–189, 199
    latent content, 62
    manifest content, 62
    Skinner's view of, 372
    Sullivan's view of, 230
Drive-induction theory, 339
Drive-reduction hypothesis, 338–
    339
Drives, 42–44, 292, 320–321, 341,
    368 (see also Instinct;
    Motivation)
    compulsive, 248–253
    defined, 320
    innate (primary), 320–321
    learned (secondary), 321
    mediated, 325
Dr. Martin Luther King, Jr.
    Award, 680
Drugs, 376–378
Dynamic calculus, 496–497,
    519
Dynamic lattice, 492, 495, 496,
    519
Dynamisms, 208, 210–214, 217,
    220

Early adolescence, 224–226, 235
Early childhood (Erikson's stage
    of), 89–91, 114–115
Early memories (see Early
    recollections)
Early recollections, 136–137, 147,
    150–151, 154
Early School Personality
    Questionnaire (ESPQ),
    491
Eating Disorder Inventory, 315
Eating disorders, 315
Eclecticism, 529–530

Ego, 37, 38, 39–40, 41, 73, 82–85, 115, 137, 163, 171, 303, 341
  higher mental processes and, 324
Ego-ideal, 40, 83
Ego identity, 83, 94, 95, 111–112, 310
Eidetic personifications, 215
Eidetic playmates (see Imaginary playmates)
Eigenwelt, 683–684, 688, 690, 698, 699, 705
Electra complex, 56 (see also Oedipus complex, female)
Emotions, 368–369
Empathic listening, 650, 652–653, 672 (see also Empathy)
Empathy, 209, 218, 300, 650, 652–653, 672
Empirical law of effective, 435
Enactive attainments, 408
Encoding strategies, 457, 459, 469
Energy transformations, 208, 210, 217
Entropy, principle of, 174–175, 198
Epigenetic principle, 84–85, 115
Epistemology, 8
Equivalence, principle of, 174–175, 198
Ergs, 493, 494, 495, 496, 497, 519
Erogenous zones, 42, 51–59
Eros, 42, 691, 705
Escape from social control, 376, 377
Escape, mechanisms of (Fromm), 269–271, 287
Esteem needs, 601–602, 619, 628
Ethics, 703
Euphemistic labels, 405
Euphoria, 210
Evolution, cultural, 366–367, 387 (See also Natural selection)
Evaluation, standards of, 403
Exclusivity, 99
Excuses, 142
Existential Coping interview, 283–284
Existential dichotomies (Fromm), 264

Existential living, 657
Existential needs, 264–269
Existential Psychology (May), 674–706
Existentialism, 677, 681–702, 704–706
  background of, 681
  defined, 681–682
Expectancies, 436–437, 457–458, 459, 469
  generalized, 436–437, 440–448, 469
  low, eliminating, 450–452
  specific, 436–437
Experience corollary, 572, 587
Experiences, vicarious, 409, 428
External control of reinforcement, 445–446, 468, 469 (see also Internal control of reinforcement)
Extinction, 364–365
  operant, 364
  respondent, 364
Extraversion, 176, 177–180, 199, 501, 505, 506–508, 509, 510, 511, 520 (see also Introversion)
Eysenck Personality Inventory, 195, 505, 510, 624, 625

Factor analysis, 477, 479–480, 547–548
Factor loadings, 480
Factor Theory (Eysenck), 477, 479, 499–520
Factors, 477, 479–480, 503, 519
Fantasies, 297–298
Fear, 577
Feeling, 178–179, 180, 181, 199
  extraverted, 178–179
  introverted, 179
Feminine position, 395
Feminine psychology
  .Adler's view of, 144–145
  Erikson's view of, 108–109
  Freud's view of, 58–59
  Horney's view of, 258–259
  Klein's view of, 305–306
Fictionalism, 127–128
Fictions, 127
Fidelity, 93, 97–98, 115
Fixation, 47, 143, 267
Fixed-role therapy, 578–579, 582, 588

Foresight, 325
Formal inception stage (psychotherapy), 228
Formative tendency, 639–640, 672
Fortuitous events, 393, 398–400, 427
Fragmentation corollary, 553, 577, 587
Free association, 27, 66, 74, 147, 259
Free choice, determinism, vs., 15, 17, 714
Free will, 702–703
Freedom, 269, 693–696, 705
  burden of, 269–271
  defined, 693
  destiny and, 693–696
  essential, 693–694
  existential, 693
  forms of, 693–694
  positive, 270, 287
Freedom of action, 693
Freedom of being, 694
Freedom of movement, 440, 443, 444, 449, 450, 451, 469
Freudian slips, 65, 74
Frustration, aggression and, 338–339
Fully functioning person, 634, 656 (see also Person of tomorrow)
Functional autonomy, 321, 364, 538–542, 601
  criteria for, 539–540
  definition of, 540, 541
  learned drives and, 321
  limitations of, 541–542
  perseverative, 540–541, 553
  propriate, 541, 553
Functions, 176, 177–181, 199
  inferior, 180–181
  irrational, 181
  rational, 181
  secondary, 180–181
  superior, 180–181

Gemeinschaftsgefühl (see Social interest)
General Mills Inc., 359
General prediction formula, 444–445, 479
Generalization, 419, 440, 451
  stimulus, 357

Generalized expectancies, 440–448, 469
Generalized sensuality, 102, 115
Generativity, 112
Generativity vs. stagnation, 100–101, 115
Genital-locomotor mode, 91–92, 115
Genital stage of development, 51, 61–62, 95, 304–305
Genitality, 98, 115
Goals, 132–133, 461, 541
  changing, 449–450
  final, 132–133, 154
Goethe prize, 31
Gratification, delay of, 452, 457, 463, 465–467, 468, 469
Great mother, 169–170, 198
Growth, syndrome of, 276, 277
Guilt, 558, 687–688, 705
  ontological, 688

Hallucinations, 166
Health Locus of Control Scale, 463–464
Health psychology, 384
Heart disease (see Cardiovascular disease)
Heidelberg Project, 513–517
Heir conditioner (see Baby-tender)
Hero, 170–171, 198
Hesitating, 143–144
Hierarchy of needs, 598–602, 628
High School Personality Questionnaire (HSPQ), 491, 498
Holistic-Dynamic Theory (Maslow), 590–630
Hope, 88–89, 114
Hostility, 245
Human agency, 702–703
Human dilemma (Fromm), 264, 688
Human needs (Fromm), 264–269, 287
Humanity, concept of, 13, 14–15, 18, 712–716
  Adler's, 149–50
  Allport's, 548–549
  Bandura's, 420–423
  Cattell's, 512
  Dollard and Miller's, 337–338
  Erikson's, 109–110
  Eysenck's, 512

Freud's, 67–69
Fromm's, 281–282
Horney's, 281–282
Jung's, 193–194
Kelly's, 581–583
Klein's, 313
May's, 700–702
Maslow's, 622–624
Mischel's, 462–463
Rogers's, 661–662
Rotter's, 462–463
Skinner's, 381–383
Sullivan's, 230–231
Humanistic Psychoanalysis (Fromm), 260–282
Humor, 544, 615–616, 629
Hypnosis, 27
Hypochondrias, 275
  moral, 275
Hypothesis, 9, 11–12
Hypothesis testing, 14
Hysteria, 4, 27–28
  male, 27–28

Id, 37–39, 41, 73, 82–83, 303
Idealistic principle, 40 (see also Superego)
Idealized self-image, 253–256, 259, 286
Identification, 54, 310
Identity, 86, 95–98, 111–112, 114, 254
  achievement, 111
  confusion, 96
  diffusion, 111
  foreclosure, 111
  moratorium, 111
  sense of, 254, 267–268, 269, 287, 307
  status, 111–112
Identity crisis, 79, 86, 96, 115, 351
Identity status interview, 111
Identity vs. identity confusion, 95, 96, 115
Idiographic approach, 545–548, 702, 715
Imaginary playmates, 204, 220–221, 233, 235
Images (see Archetypes)
Imperial Society of Physicians of Vienna, 28
Incestuous symbiosis, 275–277, 280, 281 (see also

Symbiotic relationships)
Incongruence, 642, 646–647, 672
Independence, need for, 442
Individual Psychology (Adler), 118–155
Individual corollary, 568–569, 587
Individuation, 163, 185–186, 191, 199
Industry vs. inferiority, 93, 94, 115
Inertia, 94
Infancy, 51–59, 87–89, 114, 218–219, 235
Infancy
  Erikson's stage of, 87–89, 114
  Sullivan's stage of, 218–219, 235
Infantile sexuality, 51–59
Infantile stage of development
  Freud's concept of, 51–59
Initiative vs. guilt, 92, 115
Inner states, 367–369
Instinct, 42–44, 165
  aggression, 44
  death, 42, 298
  destructive, 44
  life, 42, 298
  sexual, 42–44
Institute for Personality and Ability Testing (IPAT), 478
Institute for Psychoanalysis, 243
Institute for Research on Morality and Adjustment, 479
Integrity vs. despair, 102, 115
Intelligence, 497, 498
  crystallized, 498
  fluid, 498
Intention, 369, 539–540
Intentionality, 688–689, 705
Interactionist position, 434, 456–461
Internal control of reinforcement, 445–446, 468, 469 (see also External control of reinforcement)
Internal–External Control Scale, 446, 464, 469
Internalizations, 302–306
Internalized object relationships, 309

International Institute of Social Research, 262
International Psychoanalytic Association, 30, 122, 160, 161
Interpersonal circumplex, 464
Interpersonal theory (Sullivan), 200–236
Interpersonal Trust Scale, 446–448, 464, 469
Intimacy, 98, 204, 211–212, 217, 221, 223–224, 226, 235
Intimacy vs. isolation, 98–99, 115
Intrapsychic conflict (see Conflicts, intrapsychic)
Introjection, 297, 298, 301, 303, 310
Introversion, 176, 177–180, 199, 501, 506–508, 509, 510, 511, 520 (see also Extraversion)
Intuition, 179–189, 181, 199
    extraverted, 180
    introverted, 180
Inventory of Interpersonal Problems, 464
Isolation, 48–49, 99, 245, 251

Jenny, case of, 524–525, 532, 546–548, 554
Jonah complex, 619–620, 629, 688
Judgmental processes, 401–402
Jungian Type Survey, 194
Juvenile era, 221–223, 235

Kamikaze pigeons, 352, 359
Karen Horney Clinic, 244
Karen Horney Psychoanalytic Institute, 244

L data, 482–485, 519
Language, autistic, 219
Late adolescence, 226, 235
Latency stage of development, 51, 60, 93, 115
Law of the low doorway, 138–139
Learning, 319–324, 411–416, 428, 433–469
    enactive, 414–416, 428
    fundamentals of, 319–324
    modeling, 412–413, 419, 428, 444
    observational, 393, 412–414, 428

Libido, 42
Life instinct, 42
Life style (see Style of life)
Life Style Analysis, The, 152
Life Style Personality Inventory, 152
Little Hans, case of, 292–293, 295, 298, 299, 303, 305, 318–319, 322, 334, 335
Locus of control, 716 (see also External control of reinforcement; Internal control of reinforcement)
Love, 43, 99, 115, 223, 227, 265–266, 271, 273, 442
    aim-inhibited, 42–43
    care, will, and, 689–693
    Erikson's definition of, 99
    Freud's concept of, 43
    Fromm's definition of, 265
    May's definition of, 689
    productive, 273, 274
    Sullivan's definition of, 223
    forms of, 690–693
Love and belongingness needs, 442, 600–601, 628, 645
Loyola Generativity Scale, 112
Lust, 212, 217, 223, 224–226, 235

Male hysteria (see Hysteria)
Malevolence, 210, 211, 220, 221, 224
Malignant aggression (see Aggression, malignant)
Manaster-Perryman Manifest Content Early Recollection Scoring Manual, 150, 151
Mandala, 171–173
Masculine protest, 132, 144–145, 258
Maslow Cooperage Corporation, 594, 596
Maslowian Assessment Survey, 625
Masochism, 43, 44, 270, 380
Mastery-modeling programs, 425
Masturbation, suppression of, 54
Matriarchal societies, 263, 267
Maturity stage of development, 51, 61
Maudsley Personality Inventory, 509

Mechanisms of defense (see Defense mechanisms)
Mechanisms of escape (see Escape, mechanisms of)
Mental processes, higher, 322, 324–327, 370–371
Metamotivation, 608, 630
Metaneeds, 608
Metapathology, 606, 629
Metaphysics, 8
Metatheory, 561
Middle life, 183–184
Minnesota Multiphasic Personality Inventory (MMPI), 487
Misery, 335
Missiles, pigeon-guided, 353, 359
Mithras, Persian god of light, 166
Mitwelt, 683–684, 688, 690, 698, 699, 705
Modeling, 419 (see also Learning, modeling; Learning, observational)
Modulation corollary, 572–573, 581, 587
Montessori education, 80
Moral hypochondrias, 275
Moral justification, 404–405
Moralistic principle, 40, 74
Morphogenic methods, 545–548, 553–554
Mother complex, 170
Mother fixation, 275
Motivation, 42–46, 132–136, 248–253, 319–321, 414, 415, 535–545, 597–607, 628
    Allport on, 535–545, 553
    Bandura on, 414
    Cattell on, 491–496
    Maslow on, 597–607, 628–629
    conscious, 542–543
    observational learning and, 414
    unconscious, 369, 542–543, 605, 629
Moving against people, 241, 249, 252
Moving away from people, 241, 249, 251–252
Moving backward, 143
Moving toward people, 241, 249–250

Mr. Clean Personality, 533, 534–535
Mrs. Oak, case of, 634, 638, 662, 669–670
Multidimensional Health Locus of Control Scales, 463–464
Multiple Abstract Variance Analysis (MAVA), 497–498
Myers–Briggs Type Indicator, 194–195, 197
Mythological images (see Archetypes)
Myths, 230, 696–698, 706

Narcissism, 43, 131, 275, 288, 280–281, 287
   malignant, 275, 280–281, 287
   primary, 41
   secondary, 41
Narcotics Anonymous, 384
Natural selection, 365–366, 387
Necrophilia, 274, 276, 280, 287
Need components, 442–444
Need potential, 442–443, 444, 469
Need Satisfaction Inventory, 624
Need value, 443–444, 449, 469
Needs, 208–209, 217, 441–444, 597–607, 643–645
   achievement, 249
   admiration, 249
   aesthetic, 602–603, 628
   affection, 245, 248, 442
   basic, 602
   belongingness, 600–601, 628
   categories of, 441–444
   cognitive, 603, 628
   conative (striving), 598–602, 628, 629
   dominance, 441
   deprivation of, 606
   enhancement, 643, 644, 645, 672
   esteem, 601–602, 628
   exploitation, 249
   general, 208
   hierarchy of, 598–602, 624–625
   independence, 249, 442
   instinctoid, 606–607, 629
   interpersonal, 208
   love, 442, 600–601, 628
   maintenance, 663, 644, 645, 672

   Maslow on, 597–607
   neurotic, 248–249, 252, 286, 603–604, 629
   physiological, 598–599, 628
   perfection, 254
   physical comfort, 442
   power, 248
   prepotency of, 598
   protection-dependency, 442
   recognition, 249, 441
   regard, 644, 672
   reputation, 601–602
   reversed order of, 604–605, 629
   Rogers on, 643–645, 672
   Rotter on, 441–445
   safety, 599–600, 628
   self-actualization, 602, 628
   self-esteem, 601–602, 645
   self-regard, 644–645, 672
   self-sufficiency, 249
   Sullivan on, 208–209, 217
   zonal, 208
Neurotic ambition, 254
Neurotic claims, 255, 275
Neurotic needs (see Needs, neurotic)
Neurotic pride, 255–256
Neurotic search for glory, 254–255, 259
Neurotic trends (see Trends, neurotic)
Neuroticism, 501, 505, 508–510, 511, 513, 514, 520
New School for Social Research, 243
New York Psychoanalytic Institute, 243
Nomothetic approach, 545, 702, 715
Nonbeing, 684–686, 705
   death and, 685
Nothingness, 684–686, 705 (see also Nonbeing)

Objects, 43, 44, 45, 297, 298
Object relations theory, 293–316
   Kernberg's view of, 309–311
   Klein's view of, 293–306
   Kohut's view of, 311–313
   Mahler's view of, 306–309
Observation(s), 12
   media of, 482–483
   theory and, 12

Observational learning, 393, 412–414, 428
Obsessions, 48, 49
Oedipus complex, 30, 54–59, 60, 91–93, 94, 95, 258, 261, 293, 298, 302, 303, 304–306, 341, 381, 565
   male, 54–56, 57, 305
   female, 30, 56–59, 305–306
Oedipus myth, 696–698
Old age (Erikson's stage of), 101–104, 115
Old age (Jung's stage of), 184–185
Old wise man, 170, 198
One-genus hypothesis, 230
Ontology, 8, 688
Open system, 528–529
Operational definitions, 13
Oral phase of development, 51–52, 87, 304
Oral-receptive period, 52
Oral-sadistic period, 52
Oral-sensory mode, 88
Organ dialect, 126
Organ inferiorities, 128
Organ jargon, 126
Organizational corollary, 569–570, 587
Orientation, frame of, 268, 269, 287

P technique, 481–482, 494
Palliative comparisons, 405
Paranoia, 35, 50
Paranoid-schizoid position, 299–300
Parapraxes, 65
Parataxic distortions, 229
Parataxic experiences, 215, 216, 217, 219, 226
Parsimony, theory and, 14, 17
Participant observer, 228
Passive resistance, 107, 377
Pavlovian conditioning, 354
Peace Corps, 454, 455
Peak experiences, 607, 613–614, 625–627, 629, 630
Penis envy, 56, 57, 258
Perceptual conscious system, 35
Performance attribution, 402
Person variables, 456–459
Persona, 6, 17, 167, 198, 530
Person as scientist, 564

Person-centered theory (Rogers), 632–673
Personal construct theory, 558–589
Personal constructs, 564, 566–575, 587
  permeability of, 573, 587
Personal dispositions, 455, 461, 531–534, 553 (see also Traits)
  cardinal, 532, 533, 553
  central, 532–533, 553
  a conditional view of, 461
  defined, 531
  levels of, 532–533, 553
  secondary, 533, 553
Personal Orientation Inventory (POI), 618–619
Personal standards, 401
Personal structure analysis, 546–547
Personal superiority, 134
Personal unconscious, 163–164, 171, 198
Personality, 5–7, 530–531
  cultural influences on, 538
  definition of, 5–7, 715–716
    Allport's, 6, 530–531
    Cattell's, 483
    Sullivan's, 207
  dimensions of, 504–505
  dynamics of, 42–46
  growth of, 535–545, 553
  healthy (Allport's concept of), 543–545
  measurement of, 502–504
  structure of, 531–535
  theorists of, 719
  unity of, 125–127
Personality inventories, 16
Personality theories
  Adler's, 118–155
    critique of, 152–153
  Allport's, 523–554
    critique of, 551–552
  Bandura's, 310–429
    critique of 426–427
  Cattell's, 474–499, 517–520
    critique of, 517–518
  Dollard and Miller's, 293–294, 317–342
    critique of, 339–340
  Erikson's, 76–116
    critique, 113–114
  Eysenck's, 499–520

  critique of, 517–518
  Freud's, 22–75
    critique of, 71–73
  Fromm's, 260–288
    critique of, 284–285
  Jung's, 155–199
    critique of, 196–198
  Horney's of, 240–260, 281–288
    critique of, 284–285
  Kelly's, 558–589
    critique of, 585–586
  Klein's, 293–306
    critique of, 315–316
  Kernberg's, 309–311
  Kohut's, 311–313
  Mahler's, 306–309
  Maslow's, 590–630
    critique of, 627–628
  May's, 674–706
    critique of, 703–704
  Mischel's, 433, 452–470
    critique of, 467–469
  Rogers's, 632–673
    critique of, 671
  Rotter's, 433–452, 464, 457–471
    critique of, 467–468
  Skinner's, 346–386
    critique of, 385, 387
  Sullivan's, 200–236
    critique of, 233–234
Personifications, 214–215
  bad mother, 214, 219, 302
  eidetic, 215, 220
  good mother, 214, 219, 302
  me, 214–215, 220
  not-me, 215
Persons of tomorrow, 656–660, 672
  characteristics of, 657–658
  implications for society, 658–660, 672
Pessimism vs. optimism, 15, 17, 714
Phallic phase of development, 54–59, 91, 304
Phantasies (see Fantasies)
Phenomenological approach, 564
Philia, 691–692, 705
Philip, case of, 676–677, 687, 689, 695–696, 698, 700
Phillip Morris Company, 513
Philosophical position,
  Kelly's, 564–566
  Maslow's, 620–621

Philosophy, 8
Phobias, 292, 293, 417, 451
Phylogenetic endowment, 34, 55, 166–167
  collective unconscious and, 34
Physical comfort, need for, 442
Physical deficiencies, exaggerated, 140
Physiological needs, 598–599, 628
Placebo effect, 664
Play age (Erikson's stage of), 91–93, 115
Play construction 108–109
Play therapy, 312
Pleasure principle, 38, 73–74 (see also Id)
Positions, 298–300
  depressive, 300
  paranoid-schizoid, 299–300
Possession, 247
Post-Freudian theory (Erikson), 76–116
Power, 247
Preadolescence, 223–224, 235, 692
Preconscious, 35, 36, 73, 164
Preoccupations, 220
Pre-School Personality Questionnaire (PSPQ), 491
Prestige, 247
Primary process, 39 (see also Id)
Primordial images (see Archetypes)
Private intelligence, 139
Procreativity, 100, 115
Progression, 175–176, 185, 198
Project for scientific psychology (Freud's), 29
Project Pigeon, 359
Projection, 49–50, 297, 301, 303
Projective identification, 302
Propriate strivings, 537, 553
Proprium, 534–535, 536, 537–538, 553
Protection, need for, 442
Prototaxic experiences, 216, 217
Pseudospecies, 84, 101
Psychoanalysis, 9, 22–75, 161, 244–245, 258, 285, 295, 309, 317, 385, 517, 528, 637, 713 (see also Psychoanalytic personality theory)

Psychoanalytic learning theory
        (Dollard and Miller),
        293–294, 317–342
Psychoanalytic personality
        theory, 22–75, 244–245,
        258, 297
Psychoanalytic social theory,
        238–288
    Fromm's concept of, 241, 242,
        260–282
    Horney's concept of, 241–260
Psychobiography (see
        psychohistory)
Psychohistory, 106–108, 279–281
Psychology of the individual
        (Allport), 523–554
Psychological situation, 438–439,
        469
Psychological stagnation, 646–
        649, 672
Psychology of personal
        constructs (Kelly), 558,
        589
Psychoneuroimmunology, 426
Psychopathology, 51 (see also
        Abnormal behavior)
Psychosis, 67
Psychotherapy
    Adler and, 148–149
    Bandura and, 418–420
    Dollard and Miller and, 336
    Freud and, 65–67
    Fromm and, 277
    Horney and, 259–260
    Jung and, 190–193
    Kelly and, 578–579
    Klein and, 312
    Maslow and, 620
    May and, 698–700, 706
    Rogers and, 649–667, 672
    Rotter and, 449–452
    Skinner and, 380–381
    Sullivan and, 228–230
Psychoticism, 505, 510–512, 520
Puberty, 95
Punishment, 360–361, 373, 387,
        418
    effects of, 360–361
    reinforcement and, 361
Purpose, 92, 115, 369

Q data, 482–485, 489, 519
Q-sort technique (see Q
        technique)
Q technique, 546, 642, 664, 667

R. J. Reynolds Company, 513
R technique, 481, 494
Radical behaviorism, 348–388,
        393, 427, 433
Ralph Waldo Emerson Award,
        680
Range corollary, 571–572, 587
Rapid eye movement (REM)
        sleep, 69–70
Rational-emotive therapy, 124
Reaction formation, 35, 44, 47,
        372
Reality, blocking out, 379
Reality principle, 39, 74 (see also
        Ego)
Reasoning, 325–326
Rebirth, 170
Recidivism, 584
Reciprocal determinism, 395–
        400, 427
    differential contributions, 397
Recognition, need for, 442
Reconnaissance stage
        (Psychotherapy), 228
Regression, 48, 143, 175–176,
        185, 198
Reinforcement, 294, 322–324,
        342, 354, 356, 358–360,
        387, 393, 415–416, 445–
        446
    defined, 322, 358, 435
    drive-induction theory of, 339
    drives and, 323–324
    external, 438
    gradient of, 323
    internal, 438
    negative, 358–360, 373, 387,
        418, 437
    positive, 358, 373, 387, 417,
        437
    primary, 361
    schedules of, 355, 362–364,
        387
        continuous, 362
        fixed-interval, 364, 387
        fixed-ratio, 362, 387
        intermittent, 355, 362–364,
        387
        variable-interval, 363, 387
        variable-ratio, 363–364, 387
    secondary, 323
Reinforcement-reinforcement
        sequences, 438
Reinforcement value, 437–438,
        469

Reinforcers, 354, 387
    conditioned, 361
    generalized, 361–362
    negative, 358–359, 387
    positive, 357, 358, 387
Rejectivity, 101
Relatedness, 264–266, 268, 269,
        287
Relationship Inventory (see
        Barrett-Lennard
        Relationship Inventory)
Relaxation,
    meditative, 331
    progressive, 331
Reliability, 16
Religion, Allport, on, 545, 549–
        551
Religious Orientation Scale
        (ROS), 550–551, 552,
        716
Representation, observational
        learning and, 413–414
Repression, 33–34, 39, 46–47, 74,
        334, 335
    unconscious and, 334
Reputation, as an esteem need,
        601–602
Research, 11–12, 16–17, 720
    Adler and, 136–137, 150–151,
        152
    Allport and, 549–551
    Bandura and, 418, 423–426
    Cattell and, 481–483, 517–518
    Dollard and Miller and, 338–
        339
    Erikson and, 108–109, 111–113
    Eysenck and, 513–517
    Freud and, 69–71
    Fromm and, 278–279, 283–284
    Horney and, 282–283
    Jung and, 184–196, 197
    Kelly and, 583–585
    Klein and, 313–315
    Maslow and, 621–622, 624–627
    May and, 702–703
    Mischel and, 457, 460–461,
        465–467
    Rogers and, 662–670
    Rotter and, 463–464
    Skinner and, 383–385
    Sullivan and, 232–233
Resistance to therapy, 67
Reponses, 294, 342
    conditioned, 354
    cue-producing, 325, 342

Reponses, (cont.)
   elicited, 355
   emitted, 355
   habitual, 503, 506
Restraint, physical, 374, 376
Revolt against social control, 377
Rogers/Skinner Debate, 658–659
Role, 575, 579–581, 588
   core, 575, 579–581, 588
   peripheral, 575, 588
Role Construct Repertory (REP)
      Test, 676, 577–581, 584,
      586, 588, 716
Role repudiation, 97
Rootedness, 266–267, 268, 269,
      287
Rorschach Inkblot Test, 278, 394,
      482
Rosenberg Self-Esteem Scale,
      667–669
Rotter Incomplete Sentences
      Blank, 434

Sadism, 43–44, 270
Sadistic-anal phase of
      development, 53–54 (see
      also Anal phase of
      development)
Safeguarding tendencies, 141–
      144, 380, 406
   defense mechanisms and, 141
   disengagement of internal
      control and, 406
Safety needs, 599–600, 628
Saga Administration
      Corporation, 596
Satiation, 374, 376
Satyagrapha, 107
Schizophrenia, Sullivan and, 205,
      227
School age (Erikson's stage of),
      93–95, 115
Science, 8, 354, 620–621, 629,
      660–661
   desacralized, 621
   morphogeneic, 545–548
   resacralized, 621
   philosophy of, 354, 620–621,
      629, 660–661
Scientist as person, 564–565
Secondary process, 39 (see also
      Ego)
Second-stratum traits, 489–491,
      419
Security operations, 213, 224
Seduction theory (Freud), 32–33

Selective inattention, 213–214,
      226, 379, 380
Selective activation, 403–404
Self, 171–174, 198, 536–538, 543,
      640–642, 672
   acceptance, 543
   as knower, 537
   as objective, 537
   extension of, 536
   ideal, 642, 672
   identity, 536
   image, 536, 537
   rational, 536–537
   Rogers on, 640–641, 672
   Skinner on, 367–368
Self-absorption, 101
Self-actualization, 78, 592, 593,
      606, 607–618, 629, 641
   defined, 609–610
   description of, 609–610
   faking, 618–619
   love and, 617–618
   sex and, 617–618
   values and, 608
Self-actualization needs, 602,
      628
Self-actualizing people, 595, 608
   characteristics of, 610–617,
      629
   description of, 609–610
   love, sex and, 617–618
   values of, 608
Self-awareness, 367–368, 536–
      538
Self-concept, 641–642, 672
Self-control of behavior, 375–
      377, 388
Self-defense training, 425
Self-deprivation, 376
Self-dynamism, 220
Self-efficacy, 406–411, 420, 423–
      426, 428
   defined, 407
   enactive attainments and, 408
   outcome expectations and,
      407
   predictor of behavior, 411
   sources of, 407–411
Self-esteem, 601–602, 605
Self-Esteem Scale, 667–669
Self-hatred, 256–258, 259, 286
Self-knowledge, defective, 380–
      381
Self-observation, 401
Self-Other Attitude Scale (S-O
      Scale), 663, 666

Self-reaction, 402
Self-realization, 167, 171, 185–
      186, 191, 199, 253, 259,
      281
Self-regard, 644–645, 672
Self-regulation, 401–406, 423–
      424, 428, 459, 470
   external factors in, 403–406
Self-sentiment, 496, 498
Self-system
   Bandura, 400–411, 427
   Sullivan, 212–214, 220, 227
Selfhood, 536–538
   bodily sense, 536
   ego-enhancement, 536
   extension of, 536
   rational, 536–537
   self-identity, 536
   self-image, 536, 537
   self as object, 537
Selfobjects, 311
Sems, 493–496, 497, 519
Sensation, 179, 180, 181, 199
   extraverted, 179
   introverted, 179
Sentiments, 493 (see also Sems)
Separation-individualization,
      307–308
Sex, 690, 691, 705
   as a form of love, 690, 691,
      705
Sexual instinct, 42–44
Shadow, 162, 167–168, 198
Shaping, 355–357
Siegfried, 168
Sixteen Personality Factors
      Questionnaire (16 PF
      scale), 484, 491, 498
Sleep, 69–70, 230
   REM, 69–70
Snow White and the Seven
      Dwarfs, 301
Social character, 278–279
Social cognitive theory
      (Bandura), 310–429
Social control of behavior, 373–
      375
Social interest, 125, 129–132,
      134, 135, 148, 154, 191,
      543, 614
   criterion of human values,
      131–132
   development of, 127–130
   necessity of, 131
   underdeveloped, 139
Social Interest Index, 152

Social learning theory (Rotter), 433–452, 467–471
Social training, 326–327
Sociality corollary, 574–575, 578, 588
Socialization, 274
Society for Free Psychoanalysis, 123
Society for Individual Psychology, 123, 433
Society of Multivariate Experimental Psychology, 479
Somnolent detachment, 219
South German Institute for Psychoanalysis, 262
Speculation, theory and, 8–9
Splitting, 301–302, 303, 310
Stability vs. neuroticism, 508–510, 520
Stages of development
    Allport's concept of, 536–538
    Erikson's concept of, 85–105
    Freud's concept of, 51–61, 74
    Jung's concept of, 182–185
    Mahler's concept of, 307–309
    Sullivan's concept of, 218–227
Stagnation, 101
Standards of evaluation, 403
Standing still, 143
States, 482
    inner, 367–369
Stimulus
    aversive, 358–360, 376, 380, 387
    changing, 376
    conditioned, 364
    unconditioned, 364
Strong–Campbell Interest Inventory, 195
Structural Analysis of Social Behavior, 232
Study of Values, 546, 552
Stupidity, 335–336
Style of life, 125, 136–138, 140–141, 154
    pampered, 140–141
    neglected, 141
Subception, 642–643
Subjective perceptions (Adler), 125, 127–128, 154
Sublimation, 50
Subliminal perception, 70–71, 154
Submissiveness, as a coping strategy, 247

Subsidiation chain, 492–493, 495
Success, striving for, 125, 132–136, 154, 400
Successive approximations, 356
Sun-phallus, 166
Superego, 37, 38, 40–42, 73, 303–304, 341, 510
Superego vs. psychoticism, 505, 510–512, 520
Superfactors (see Types)
Superiority, striving for, 125, 132–136, 154
Supporting corollaries (Kelly's), 568–575
Symbiosis, normal, 307
Symbiotic relationships, 275–276
Synergistic effect, 513, 515–516
Syntaxic experiences, 213, 217, 218, 219, 220, 226

T data, 482–483, 519
Taoistic attitude, 621, 629
Taxonomy, theory and, 9
Teleology, 15, 17, 127, 175, 187
    causality vs. 15, 17, 127, 175
Tenderness, 208, 219
Tensions, 208–210, 217
Termination stage (psychotherapy), 229
Thematic Apperception Test (TAT), 278, 314, 663, 666
Theory, 7–14, 17
    defined, 9–10, 716
    evaluation of, 716–719
    future directions, 719–720
    as a guide to action, 13
    hypothesis and, 9, 11
    internal consistency, 13–14
    observations and, 10
    parsimony and, 14
    personality, 4
    proactive, 529
    as an organizer of data, 12–13
    reactive, 529
    research and, 11–12
    seduction (Freud's), 32–33
    speculation and, 8–9
    taxonomy and, 9
    usefulness of, 10–14
    value of, 10–16
    verifiability of, 11–12, 69
    what it is not, 7–9
Therapy, 418–420 (see also Psychotherapy)
Thinking, 178, 180, 181, 199

    extraverted, 178
    introverted, 178
Third force in psychology, 593
Threat, 577, 647, 672
Toilet training, 53
Training, social, 326–327
Trait and factor theories, 474–520
Trait and theory (Cattell), 474–499, 517–520
Traits, 400, 453, 477, 480–498, 531–535, 553 (see also Personal dispositions)
    ability, 483, 519
    abnormal, 485–489
    bipolar, 480, 486
    cardinal, 532, 533, 553
    central, 532–533, 553
    common, 481, 531, 553
    defined, 482, 503
    heritability of, 497–498
    measurement of, 491
    motivational (dynamic), 483, 491–496, 519, 533–534, 553
    normal, 484–485
    primary, 484–489, 519
    secondary, 533, 553
    second-stratum, 489–491, 519
    source, 483–496, 497
    stylistic, 533–534, 553
    surface, 483
    temperament, 483–491
    unipolar, 480
    unique, 481, 511
Transformation, 191
Transcendence, 266, 268, 269, 287
Transference, 66–67, 106, 191, 277
Trends, neurotic, 249–253, 270, 286
Types, 177–181, 504–512
Tyranny of the should, 254

Umwelt, 683–684, 688, 690, 698, 705
Uncanny emotion, 215, 227
Undoing, 48–49
Unity of personality (Adler), 125–127
Unconditional acceptance, 640 (see also Unconditional positive regard)
Unconditional positive regard, 650, 651–652, 672

Unconscious, 15, 17, 31, 32–35, 36, 73, 126–127, 163–174, 334
  repression and, 33–34, 334
  vs. conscious, 15, 17
Unity of personality, 125–127
Universal Index system, 485

Validity, 17
Values, subjective, 458–459
Verbal persuasion, 409–410, 428
Verifiability of a theory, 11–12, 69, 152
Vicarious experiences, 409, 428
Vienna Imperial Society of Physicians, 27, 28
Vienna Psychoanalytic Institute, 81, 318
Vienna Psychoanalytic Society, 30, 121, 122, 123

Vindictive triumph, drive toward, 254
Vulnerability, 646–647, 672

Walden Two, Skinner, 352, 378–379
Weaning, 52
Wednesday Psychological Society, 30, 292
Western Behavioral Sciences Institute (WBSI), 638
Will, 89, 90–91, 115, 689–693
  care, love and, 689–693
  union with love, 690
Will to power, 132
William Alanson White Institute of Psychiatry, Psychoanalysis and Psychology, 206, 263, 679, 692

Willoughby Emotional Maturity Scale (E-M Scale), 663, 666
Wisdom, 103, 115
Withdrawal, 89, 143–144, 247
  as a coping strategy, 247
Word association test, 147, 160, 186–187, 199
Worth, conditions of, 645–646, 672

Yale Institute of Human Relations, 81, 105, 317, 318, 394
Yang, 172–173, 176
Yin, 172–173, 176
Young adulthood (Erikson's stage of), 98–99, 115
Youth, 183

Zen Buddhism, 263
Zodiac group, 206, 243

PHOTO CREDITS

CHAPTER 1
Page 7: © Elizabeth Crews.

CHAPTER 2
Page 23: Historical Pictures/Stock Montage
Page 28: A.W. Freud et al., from a print supplied by the Freud Museum, London
Page 52: © Erika Stone/Peter Arnold, Inc.
Page 66: Edmund Englman.

CHAPTER 3
Page 77: Historical Pictures/Stock Montage
Page 97: © Spencer Grant/The Picture Cube
Page 103: © James R. Holland/Stock, Boston
Page 107: The Bettman Archive.

CHAPTER 4
Page 119: Historical Pictures/Stock Montage
Page 130: © Michael Weisbrot/Stock, Boston
Page 146: © J. Berndt/Stock, Boston.

CHAPTER 5
Page 157: The Bettmann Archive
Page 192: Hugo Charteris/Princeton University Press. Photo courtesy of William McGuire.

CHAPTER 6
Page 201: courtesy of the W.A. White Institute
Page 212: © Bill Price/Photo Researchers
Page 221: © Paul S. Conklin/Monkmeyer Press
Page 225: © Richard Hutchings/Photo Edit.

CHAPTER 7
Page 239: courtesy Renate Horney
Page 239: UPI/Bettmann
Page 252: © Bob Krueger/Photo Researchers
Page 257: © Joel Gordon
Page 265: UPI/Bettmann Newsphotos
Page 279: UPI/Bettmann Newsphotos.

CHAPTER 8
Page 291 (top): Wellcome Institute Library, London
Page 291 (lower left): Manuscripts and Archives, Yale University Library
Page 291 (lower right): © AP/Wide World Photos
Page 306: from the Archives of the American Psychiatric Association
Page 309: New York Hospital–Cornell Medical Center, Westchester Division
Page 310: Institute for Psychoanalysis.

CHAPTER 9
Page 347: Culver Pictures
Page 357: © Jean-Claude Lejeune/Stock, Boston
Page 363: © Inge Morath/Magnum
Page 370: © Barbara Alper/Stock, Boston
Page 375: © Danny Lyon/Magnum.

CHAPTER 10
Page 391: Albert Bandura
Page 408: © Robin Forbes/The Image Bank
Page 410: © Elizabeth Crews/Stock, Boston
Page 413: © Elizabeth Crews/Stock, Boston.

CHAPTER 11
Page 431 (left): University of Connecticut Office of Public Information
Page 431 (right): © Samuel Teicher
Page 439: © Sam Zarember/The Image Bank
Page 447: © Leo Mason/The Image Bank
Page 459: © Roswell Angier/Stock, Boston.

CHAPTER 12
Page 475 (left): photograph courtesy of University Archives, University of Illinois at Urbana Champaign
Page 475 (right): © Topham/The Image Works
Page 489: © Deborah Kahn Kalas/Stock, Boston
Page 507: © Bill Ross/Woofin Camp.

CHAPTER 13
Page 523: courtesy of the Harvard University News Office
Page 537: © Erika Stone/Peter Arnold, Inc.
Page 542: © KK Group/The Image Bank
Page 544: © Karee Galloway.

CHAPTER 14
Page 559: courtesy of Brandeis University Photography Department
Page 571: © Carey Wolinsky/Stock, Boston
Page 575: © Joel Gordon.

CHAPTER 15
Page 591: The Bettmann Archive
Page 601: © Elizabeth Crews/Stock, Boston
Page 617: © John Maher/Stock, Boston.

CHAPTER 16
Page 633: Center for Studies of the Person, La Jolla, California
Page 641: © George White
Page 648: © Alfred Gescheidt/The Image Bank
Page 650: © Rhoda Sidney/PhotoEdit
Page 655: © Jean-Claude Lejeune/Stock, Boston.

CHAPTER 17
Page 675: © Jill Krementz
Page 685: © Alfred Gescheidt/The Image Bank
Page 692: UPI Bettmann
Page 695: © Arthur Tress/Photo Researchers
Page 697: Historical Pictures/Stock Montage.

ACKNOWLEDGMENTS OF PERMISSION

Figures 3.1, 3.2, & 3.3, Reprinted from *The Life Cycle Completed, a review* by Erik H. Erikson, by permission of W. W. Norton & Company, Inc. Copyright © 1982 by Rikan Enterprises, Ltd.

Figures 8.1, 8.2, 8.3, 8.4, & 8.5, Adapted from *Personality and Psychotherapy* by J. Dollard and N. Miller. Copyright © 1950 by J. Dollard and M. Miller. Reprinted by permission of McGraw-Hill, Inc.

Figures 10.1 & 10.2, Adapted from Albert Bandura, *Social Foundations of Thought and Action: A Social Cognitive Theory*, © 1986, pp. 24, 376. Reprinted by permission of Prentice Hall, Englewood Cliffs, New Jersey.

Table 12.1 Adapted from *Personality and Learning Theory*: Vol. 1 by R. B. Cattell. Copyright © 1979 by R. B. Cattell. Used by permission of Springer Publishing Company, Inc., New York 10012.

Table 12.2, From *The Manual for the Clinical Analysis Questionnaire* (CAQ). Copyright © 1975 by the Institute for Personality and Ability Testing, Inc. All rights reserved. Reproduced by permission of the copyright owner.

Table 12.3, Adapted from *Personality and Learning Theory*: Vol. 1 by R. B. Cattell. Copyright © 1979 by R. B. Cattell. Used by permission of Springer Publishing Company, Inc., New York 10012.

Figure 12.2, Adapted from the CAQ Individual Record Folder. Copyright © 1980 by the Institute for Personality and Ability Testing, Inc. All rights reserved. Reproduced by permission.

Table 12.4, From *The Scientific Analysis and Motivation* by R. B. Cattell and P. Cline. Copyright © 1977 by R. B. Cattell and P. Cline. Reprinted by permission of Academic Press.

Figure 12.5, From *Handbook of Personality: Theory and Research* by H. J. Eysenck, edited by L. A. Pervin. Copyright © 1990 by L. A. Pervin. Reprinted by permission of Guilford Press.

Figure 12.8, From *Personality, Stress, and Cancer: Predication and Prophylaxis* (Paper presented at the meeting of the Louisiana Psychological Association) by Dr. Hans J. Eysenck. Reprinted by permission.

Figure 14.2, From *The Psychology of Personal Constructs*, by G. A. Kelly, by permission of W. W. Norton & Company, Inc. Copyright © 1955 by G. A. Kelly.

Figure 16.1, From *Psychotherapy and Personality Change* by C. R. Rogers and R. F. Dymond. Copyright © 1954 by C. R. Rogers and R. F. Dymond. Reprinted by permission of The University of Chicago Press.

CHAPTER 9

B. F. Skinner

Human behavior is shaped by natural selection and cultural practices but mostly by one's personal history of operant conditioning. Both positive reinforcement (presentation of a reward) and negative reinforcement (removal of an unpleasant stimulus) strengthen behavior, and the effects of both are much more predictable than the effects of punishment.

CHAPTER 10

Albert Bandura

Human functioning is a product of the mutual interaction of behavior, environment (including chance encounters and fortuitous events), and personal factors (including self-efficacy and other cognitions). Humans use language to transform experiences into consistent patterns of behavior called the self system. Through observation, people can learn without performing an action.

CHAPTER 11

Julian Rotter

People's behavior in specific situations is estimated by the basic prediction formula and is a function of the expectations of reinforcements and the strength of needs satisfied by those reinforcements. People also have generalized expectancies (such as locus of control and interpersonal trust) that determine their behavior in more general situations.

CHAPTER 13

Gordon Allport

An open system allows for growth and change while emphasizing the notion that people are motivated both to reduce tension and to seek new tensions. Personal dispositions are individualized traits, unique to each individual, that both motivate and guide behavior. Some motives are functionally autonomous, independent of the motivations upon which they were originally formed.

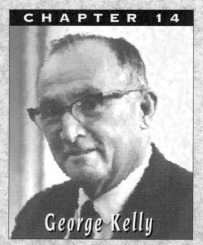

CHAPTER 14

George Kelly

Like scientists, people ask questions about their world, test hypotheses, formulate theories, ask additional questions, and then make interpretations. Constructive determinism suggests that present interpretations are subject to change. Kelly's basic postulate assumes that all psychological processes are directed by the ways in which people anticipate events.

CHAPTER 15

Abraham Maslow

Motivation is unified, continuous, complex, and often unconscious. Moreover, people in different cultures follow the same hierarchy of needs (physiological, safety, love and belongingness, esteem, and self-actualization). A tiny percentage of people reach self-actualization, are motivated by metaneeds, embrace the B-values, and are capable of B-love.